MILESTONE DOCUMENTS IN AMERICAN HISTORY

Exploring the Primary Sources
That Shaped America

MILESTONE DOCUMENTS
IN AMERICAN HISTORY

Exploring the Primary Sources
That Shaped America

Volume 3: 1888 – 1955

Paul Finkelman
Editor in Chief

Bruce A. Lesh
Consulting Editor

Schlager Group

Schlager Group Inc.
2501 Oak Lawn Avenue, Suite 440
Dallas, Tex. 75219
USA

You can find Schlager Group on the World Wide Web at
http://www.schlagergroup.com
http://www.milestonedocuments.com
Text and cover design by Patricia Moritz

Printed in the United States of America

10 9 8 7 6 5 4 3 2

ISBN: 978-0-9797758-0-2

This book is printed on acid-free paper.

CONTENTS

VOLUME 1: 1763–1823

VOLUME 2: 1824–1887

VOLUME 3: 1888–1955

VOLUME 4: 1956–2003

MILESTONE DOCUMENTS IN AMERICAN HISTORY

Exploring the Primary Sources
That Shaped America

Congress of the United States of America;

At the First Session,

Begun and held at the City of Washington on Monday, the second day of December, one thousand eight hundred and eighty-nine.

AN ACT

To protect trade and commerce against unlawful restraints and monopolies.

Be it enacted by the Senate and House of Representatives of the United States of America in Congress assembled,

Sec. 1. Every contract, combination in the form of trust or otherwise, or conspiracy, in restraint of trade or commerce among the several States, or with foreign nations, is hereby declared to be illegal. Every person who shall make any such contract or engage in any such combination or conspiracy, shall be deemed guilty of a misdemeanor, and, on conviction thereof, shall be punished by fine not exceeding five thousand dollars, or by imprisonment not exceeding one year, or by both said punishments, in the discretion of the court.

Sec. 2. Every person who shall monopolize, or attempt to monopolize, or combine or conspire with any other person or persons, to monopolize any part of the trade or commerce among the several States, or with foreign nations, shall be deemed guilty of a misdemeanor, and, on conviction thereof, shall be punished by fine not exceeding five thousand dollars, or by imprisonment not exceeding one year, or by both said punishments, in the discretion of the court.

Sec. 3. Every contract, combination in form of trust or otherwise, or conspiracy, in restraint of trade or commerce in any Territory of the United States or of the District of Columbia, or in restraint of trade or commerce between any such Territory and another, or between any such Territory or Territories and any State or States or the District of Columbia, or with foreign nations, or between the District of Columbia and any State or States or foreign nations, is hereby declared illegal. Every person who shall make any such contract or engage in any such combination or conspiracy, shall be deemed guilty of a misdemeanor, and, on conviction thereof, shall be punished by fine not exceeding five thousand dollars, or by imprisonment not exceeding one year, or by both said punishments, in the discretion of the court.

Sec. 4. The several circuit courts of the United States are hereby

The Sherman Antitrust Act (National Archives and Records Administration)

SHERMAN ANTITRUST ACT

"Every contract ... in restraint of trade or commerce ... is hereby declared to be illegal."

Overview

The oldest of America's antitrust laws, the Sherman Antitrust Act was signed into law on July 2, 1890, by President Benjamin Harrison. The Sherman Antitrust Act was the first action taken by the federal government to place limits on business monopolies and cartels and to prevent restraints on trade, such as price fixing. Violations of the act were treated as misdemeanors. The Sherman Antitrust Act, written by the Republican senator John Sherman of Ohio, vested government attorneys and courts with both the authority and the responsibility to seek out and investigate suspected violators of the terms specified in the act. The original intention of the Sherman Antitrust Act was to protect consumers from big businesses that were using unscrupulous means to raise prices artificially, such as intentionally producing too few goods to meet consumer demand and thereby driving up the products' value and price. As one of the Sherman Antitrust Act's supporters, the Massachusetts senator George Hoar explained that if a business received its market share because it produced the best product or provided the best service, then the business was not in violation of the Sherman Antitrust Act. Then Illinois representative William Mason, another advocate of the Sherman Antitrust Act, declared that even though trusts had resulted in lower prices in some cases, the act "would not right the wrong done to people of this country by the trusts which have destroyed legitimate competition and driven honest men from legitimate business enterprise" (*Congressional Record*, vol. 21, p. 4100).

While the Sherman Antitrust Act passed in 1890 in the Senate with a vote of 51 to 1 and in the House with a vote of 242 to 0, the act was not seriously enforced until President Theodore Roosevelt took office and used the act to break up the Northern Securities Company, a large railroad trust formed by John D. Rockefeller and J. P. Morgan, among others. President William Howard Taft also utilized the Sherman Antitrust Act to divide the American Tobacco Company, the merger of several large tobacco manufacturers. Perhaps the best-known case is that of Standard Oil. In 1911 the U.S. Department of Justice sued the company under the Sherman Antitrust Act, dividing the company into thirty-four separate companies.

Context

Beginning in 1865 events began to coalesce into a set of circumstances that provided a foundation for unprecedented growth in business and industrialization, allowing for the rise of big business and an increasing gap between the extremely wealthy and the very poor.

First, the end of the American Civil War (1861–1865) ushered in unparalleled changes in virtually every aspect of American life. In the South, Reconstruction—the period immediately following the end of the Civil War from 1865 to 1877—saw an influx of northern businessmen and industrialization into the defeated Confederacy. This influx brought new technologies, improved transportation methods, and northern businessmen who were hoping to make their fortune in a traditionally agrarian and now impoverished region. With the war over and the country united again, the nation concentrated on rebuilding itself based on an industrial global economy rather than an agrarian one.

The period between 1865 and 1900 is also termed the Second Industrial Revolution. This period marks the emergence of the great global industrial powers, including Great Britain, Germany, and the United States. Advances were seen in steam power, steel industries, petroleum, chemical industries, and communication as well as electricity and the internal combustion engine. In addition, improvements in the manufacturing of goods led to mass production and the assembly line. The steel industry alone grew from producing about seventy tons in 1870 to over 4 million tons in just twenty years. These businesses were truly global. For instance, improvements in transportation meant that businesses could get their goods to more places more quickly. The steam engine and better railways meant that businesses were no longer dependent on access to ports and waterways to ship goods. Just the use of refrigerated railcars meant a boon for the meatpacking industry.

All of these advances in mechanization and production led to the rise of big business. As 1900 approached, banking, meatpacking, oil, railroads, steel, and manufacturing were all

Time Line

1873

■ **May 9**
The Vienna Stock Exchange collapses.

■ **September 18**
Jay Cooke and Company, a Philadelphia banking firm, goes bankrupt, setting off the Panic of 1873, which leads to the rise of business monopolies.

1887

■ **February 4**
President Grover Cleveland signs the Interstate Commerce Act and creates the Interstate Commerce Commission to regulate businesses, especially railroads.

1890

■ **February 27**
The Sherman Antitrust Act, which had been introduced to the Senate the previous December, goes before the Committee of the Whole.

■ **March 18**
The Senate Finance Committee makes changes to the antitrust bill.

■ **April 8**
The Sherman Antitrust Act is passed in the Senate.

■ **July 2**
The Sherman Antitrust Act is signed by President Benjamin Harrison.

■ **September 25**
A lawsuit is brought against the Jellico Mountain Coal Company, among others, in the hope of preventing a number of coal-mining companies from fixing prices and controlling coal production in Tennessee and Kentucky. The company is found to be in violation of the Sherman Antitrust Act.

1894

■ **May 11**
The Pullman strike begins; the Sherman Antitrust Act is used against the American Railway Union, and the president of the union, Eugene V. Debs, is imprisoned for contempt of court.

dominated by a few huge corporations run by corporate giants like John D. Rockefeller, Cornelius Vanderbilt, J. P. Morgan, and Andrew Carnegie. These "robber barons," men who dominated their industries, lived lives of extreme privilege and wealth. In 1861, when the Civil War began, the United States was home to approximately four hundred millionaires, but by 1892 that number had risen to over four thousand. Rockefeller's Standard Oil Company alone was worth over $600 million. As the wealthy became even more rich and their displays of opulence and waste even more extravagant, they came under more and more scrutiny and criticism. The overt displays of wealth and conspicuous consumption led the writer Mark Twain to refer to the period as the "Gilded Age."

One of the most outspoken groups of critics was the muckrakers. These journalists and writers sought to uncover waste, crime, corruption, and abuse in the private and public sectors. One of the most famous novels of the time was Upton Sinclair's *Jungle* (1906). In the book, Sinclair uses an immigrant family to show the level of poverty and terrible working and living conditions of the working class, most of whom lived in crowded, dirty tenements and worked from dawn until dusk in dangerous and dirty conditions for very little pay.

With this extreme wealth and luxury juxtaposed against extreme poverty and hopelessness, the time was ripe for reform. The era saw a whole host of reformers, such as Jane Addams, winner of the Nobel Peace Prize, who opened the Hull House to help immigrants improve their lives in city slums; even the robber baron and ruthless businessman Andrew Carnegie donated millions of dollars to charities, hospitals, libraries, and schools. The federal government also sought to initiate reform with such legislation as the Interstate Commerce Act, the McKinley Tariff, the Pendleton Act, and the Sherman Antitrust Act.

About the Author

Senator John Sherman, known as the "Ohio Icicle," was born in Lancaster, Ohio, on May 10, 1823, to Charles and Mary Sherman; Sherman's older brother William Tecumseh Sherman became a general during the Civil War. After working for a time on canal projects with an engineering company, Sherman studied law with his brother Charles and passed the Ohio bar exam when he was twenty-one years old. Graduating from law school in 1844, Sherman then went into practice with his brother.

During the 1840s Sherman began to develop an interest in politics. In 1848 he was appointed as a delegate and secretary to the Whig National Convention. This same year he married Margaret Sarah Stewart. In 1854 Sherman was elected to the U.S. House of Representatives. Serving on the House's Ways and Means Committee from 1859 to 1861, he firmly believed that the federal government should reduce its spending. Sherman was reelected to the House in 1860, and the Ohio legislature then elected him as one of the state's senators, replacing Senator Salmon P. Chase, who had resigned to become secretary of the treasury. During the Civil War, Sherman was instrumental in passing the

Legal Tender Act of 1862, allowing the government to issue paper money to pay its debts. He also sponsored the National Bank Act in 1863, giving the government the same rights as privately held banks. Sherman also supported the gold standard, a currency backed by gold rather than silver, and helped to build up the nation's reserve of gold.

In 1877 President Rutherford B. Hayes appointed Sherman secretary of the treasury. When his term expired in March 1881, Sherman was reelected to the Senate. Although he was ultimately unsuccessful, Sherman made three campaigns as the Republican candidate for president in the elections of 1880, 1884, and 1888. Sherman was never elected president, but he retained his seat in the Senate. It was during this time that he drafted what became the Sherman Antitrust Act, a measure allowing the federal government to break up any businesses that held monopolies and limited competition. President Benjamin Harrison signed the act into law in 1890. Sherman left the Senate in 1897 when President William McKinley appointed him secretary of state. Sherman resigned the position in April 1898 after Congress declared war against Spain. Once he resigned as secretary of state, Sherman essentially retired from public life. He died in Washington, D.C., on October 22, 1900.

Explanation and Analysis of the Document

Section 1 of the Sherman Antitrust Act declares that any contract, such as a trust or a conspiracy, designed to place restraints on trade or commerce with states or foreign nations is illegal. The section goes on to proclaim that any person in violation of the Sherman Antitrust Act will be deemed guilty of a misdemeanor, punishable by up to one year in jail, a fine not to exceed $5,000, or both.

Section 2 mirrors Section 1 and indicates that any monopoly designed to restrain trade or commerce is considered illegal. Any person who monopolizes, attempts to monopolize, or conspires to monopolize trade or commerce among the states or with foreign nations is also guilty of a misdemeanor, punishable by up to a year in jail, a fine not to exceed $5,000, or both.

Section 3 builds on the two previous sections of the act by specifying that any trust or restraint of trade within any territory of the United States or the District of Columbia, or between U.S. territories, states, foreign nations, and the District of Columbia in any combination is illegal and is punishable by up to a year in jail, a fine not to exceed $5,000, or both.

Section 4 outlines the enforcement procedures of the act. In this section, circuit courts are given jurisdiction over Sherman Antitrust Act violations. Further, U.S. district attorneys, under the oversight of the attorney general, are charged with beginning proceedings to address violations by issuing a petition outlining the violation or violations. Once the company in question has been notified that a petition has been issued against it, a hearing is held to determine the case. Once a petition is pending, the court can place temporary restraining orders or other limits on the company until the case has been heard and decided.

Time Line

1895

■ **January 21**
The Supreme Court decides *United States v. E. C. Knight Co.*, 156 U.S. 1.

1903

■ **February 11**
Congress passes an act to speed up hearings and cases brought forth under the Sherman Antitrust Act.

■ **February 25**
Congress appropriates $500,000 to the attorney general to hire employees who would handle Sherman Antitrust Act cases.

1911

■ **May 15**
The Supreme Court upholds a lower court's decision to force Standard Oil to separate into thirty-four different companies.

1914

■ **September 26**
The Federal Trade Commission is established to prevent unfair business practices.

■ **October 15**
President Woodrow Wilson signs the Clayton Antitrust Act, which more clearly defines and strengthens the Sherman Antitrust Act.

Section 5 authorizes the court to subpoena anyone for an antitrust case and require the individual to appear before the court regardless of whether the person resides in the hearing court's district. It is the duty of the individual's district marshal to serve the subpoena.

Section 6 calls for any property owned by a trust and being transported from one state to another state or a foreign nation to be surrendered to the federal government. The actual forfeiture or seizure of any such property is to follow the laws pertaining to any property imported illegally into the United States.

Section 7 allows for any person whose business or property has been injured or damaged by a person or company engaging in any act outlawed by the Sherman Antitrust Act to sue the violator in any circuit court in the district where the defendant lives or is located. The section goes on to state that if the defendant is found guilty, then the plaintiff will be awarded three times the damages he sustained as well as all court and attorney fees.

Section 8 defines the use of the terms person and persons within the text of the act to include corporations and

Senator John Sherman of Ohio (Library of Congress)

associations existing under the laws of the United States, territories, individual states, or foreign countries.

Audience

As a governmental act, the Sherman Antitrust Act was written for the American people as a whole. Groups with a specific interest in the act, however, would be the three branches of government, especially the judicial branch, which is charged with enforcing the Sherman Antitrust Act, as well as all those involved in business. For instance, the Sherman Antitrust Act put all businesses, especially big businesses, on notice that they would no longer be allowed to monopolize a market and that free and unrestrained competition was not only encouraged but indeed protected under the law.

Impact

Although it was passed in 1890, the Sherman Antitrust Act was not seriously enforced until 1901. Ironically, the only successfully prosecution of the Sherman Antitrust Act during the nineteenth century was not against big business but against labor unions during the Pullman strike of 1894. The government argued that by striking, the railroad workers were placing a restraint on trade and commerce, resulting in a direct violation of the Sherman Antitrust Act.

Then, just a year later, in *United States v. E. C. Knight Co.*, which is known as the Sugar Trust Case, the Supreme Court essentially weakened the Sherman Antitrust Act by ruling that the American Sugar Refining Company was not in violation of the Sherman Antitrust Act. Even though the company held 98 percent of the sugar-refining industry in the United States, the Supreme Court ruled that manufacturing, such as refining, was a local activity and therefore was not subject to the interstate commerce regulations of the Sherman Antitrust Act. This ruling ultimately meant that any legal action against manufacturing had to take place at the state level rather than at the federal level.

The Sherman Antitrust Act was finally used against big business during the administrations of President Theodore Roosevelt (1901–1909) and President William Howard Taft (1909–1913). Between the two presidents, 135 cases were won against big business, including Northern Securities Company, Standard Oil, U.S. Steel, and American Tobacco. By the end of Taft's term in office, big business was severely weakened. In 1914 the Clayton Antitrust Act was passed with the hope of remedying weaknesses in the Sherman Antitrust Act. For instance, the Clayton Antitrust Act prohibits using antitrust legislation against unions.

Today antitrust legislation remains controversial. More recently, both Microsoft and Walt Disney have been sued under the Sherman Antitrust Act. For example, in 1999 the courts decided that Microsoft's hold on computer operating systems did constitute a monopoly. In particular, the bundling of Microsoft's Web browser, Internet Explorer, with the operating system restricted the market for other Web browsers. Microsoft was ordered to break into two units, one that produces the operating system and another that produces everything else. Microsoft appealed the case.

Related Documents

Sherman, John. *Selected Speeches and Reports on Finance and Taxation, from 1869 to 1878.* New York: D. Appleton, 1879. This book contains many of Sherman's speeches and reports from his time on the House Ways and Means Committee and the Senate Finance Committee.

———. *John Sherman's Recollections of Forty Years in the House, Senate and Cabinet: An Autobiography.* Chicago: Werner, 1895. This work details Sherman's fifty-year political career from 1848 to 1898 as well as his childhood and family history.

Sherman, William T. *The Sherman Letters: Correspondence between General and Senator Sherman from 1837 to 1891,* ed. Rachel Sherman Thorndike. New York: Charles Scribner's Sons, 1894. This work consists of the complete correspondence between Senator John Sherman and his brother General William Tecumseh Sherman.

Standard Oil Co. of New Jersey v. United States, 221 U.S. 1 (1910). Decided in May 1911, the Standard Oil case is one of the first major cases under the Sherman Antitrust Act.

> "*Every contract, combination in the form of trust or otherwise, or conspiracy, in restraint of trade or commerce among the several States, or with foreign nations, is hereby declared to be illegal.*"

(Section 1)

> "*Every person who shall monopolize, or attempt to monopolize, or combine or conspire with any other person or persons, to monopolize any part of the trade or commerce among the several States, or with foreign nations, shall be deemed guilty of a misdemeanor, and, on conviction thereof, shall be punished by fine not exceeding five thousand dollars, or by imprisonment not exceeding one year, or by both said punishments, in the discretion of the court.*"

(Section 2)

> "*Any person who shall be injured in his business or property by any other person or corporation by reason of anything forbidden or declared to be unlawful by this act, may sue therefore in any circuit court of the United States in the district in which the defendant resides or is found ... and shall recover three fold the damages by him sustained, and the costs of suit, including a reasonable attorney's fee.*"

(Section 7)

Bibliography

■ Articles

Bention, J. H. "The Sherman or Anti-Trust Act." *Yale Law Journal* 18, no. 5 (March 1909): 311–327.

Binder, John J. "The Sherman Antitrust Act and the Railroad Cartels." *Journal of Law Economics* 31, no. 2 (October 1988): 443–468.

Evans, Harold. "The Supreme Court and the Sherman Anti-Trust Act." *University of Pennsylvania Law Review and American Law Register* 59, no. 2 (November 1910): 61–76.

Graglia, Lino A. "One Hundred Years of Antitrust." *Public Interest* 104 (Summer 1991): 50–66.

Grandy, Christopher. "Original Intent and the Sherman Antitrust Act: A Re-examination of the Consumer-Welfare Hypothesis." *Journal of Economic History* 53, no. 2 (June 1993): 359–376.

Hazlett, Thomas W. "The Legislative History of the Sherman Act Re-examined." *Economic Inquiry* 30, no. 2 (April 1992): 263–275.

Libecap, Gary D. "The Rise of the Chicago Packers and the Origins of Meat Inspection and Antitrust." *Economic Inquiry* 30, no. 2 (April 1992): 242–262.

Mayhew, Anne. "How American Economists Came to Love the Sherman Antitrust Act." *History of Political Economy* 30, Supplement (1998): 179–201.

Posner, Richard A. "A Statistical Study of Antitrust Enforcement." *Journal of Law and Economics* 13, no. 2 (October 1970): 365–419.

Stigler, George J. "The Origin of the Sherman Act." *Journal of Legal Studies* 14, no. 1 (January 1985): 1–12.

Tozzi, John. "The Pulse on Google's Antitrust Claim." *Business Week Online* (June 11, 2007): 7. Available online. URL: http://

www.businessweek.com/technology/content/jun2007/tc20070611_083974.htm?. Accessed on January 12, 2008.

■ Books

Berman, Edward. *Labor and the Sherman Act*. New York: Harper & Brothers Publishers, 1930.

Congressional Record, 51st Cong., 1st sess., June 20, 1890. Vol. 21, p. 4100.

Burton, Theodore E. *John Sherman*. Boston: Houghton Mifflin, 1906.

Hadlick, Paul E. *Criminal Prosecutions under the Sherman Anti-Trust Act*. Washington, D.C.: Ransdell, 1939.

Kerr, Winfield Scott. *John Sherman, His Life and Public Services*. Boston: Sherman, French & Company, 1908.

Letwin, William. *Law and Economic Policy in America: The Evolution of the Sherman Antitrust Act*. New York: Random House, 1965.

Singer, Eugene M. *Antitrust Economics: Selected Legal Cases and Economic Models*. Englewood Cliffs, N.J.: Prentice-Hall, 1968.

Sullivan, E. Thomas, ed. *The Political Economy of the Sherman Act: The First One Hundred Years*. New York: Oxford University Press, 1991.

Taft, William H. *The Anti-trust Act and the Supreme Court*. New York: Harper & Brothers, 1914.

U.S. Department of Justice. *The Sherman Antitrust Act and Its Enforcement*. Durham, N.C.: Duke University Press, 1940.

Walker, Albert H. *History of the Sherman Law of the United States of America*. New York: Equity Press, 1910.

■ Web Sites

Edwards, Rebecca. "Trusts and Monopolies." Vassar College Web site.
http://projects.vassar.edu/1896/trusts.html. Accessed on October 14, 2007.

"John Sherman." Ohio History Central Web site.
http://www.ohiohistorycentral.org/entry.php?rec=338. Accessed on October 14, 2007.

—By Lisa A. Ennis

1. Compare and contrast the Sherman Antitrust Act of 1890 and the Interstate Commerce Act of 1887. How is the Sherman Act broader and stronger in scope?

2. Compare and contrast the Sherman Antitrust Act and the Clayton Antitrust Act. How does the Clayton Antitrust Act strengthen the former act? Was the Clayton Act necessary? Why or why not?

3. The Sherman Antitrust Act was enacted in 1890 to combat the rise of monopolies by big business. Is it still relevant today? Does it need to be repealed? Why or why not?

4. Discuss the recent antitrust issues with Microsoft and Walt Disney. Do you believe that these corporations are in violation of the Sherman Antitrust Act? Why or why not?

5. Examine the Pullman Strike of 1894. Was the government correct to use the Sherman Antitrust Act to end the strike? Why or why not?

Glossary

Attorney-General	an appointed office and the main legal adviser of the federal government
circuit court	a court that serves one or more states in its jurisdiction
condemned	acquired for public use without having paid compensation to the owner
contract	a written agreement between two or more people
damages	the money or award paid after a successful decision in a civil case
district attorneys	local public officials who represent the government as prosecutors in criminal cases
misdemeanor	a crime, but one less serious than a felony
monopolies	market situations in which one group has control of the supply of a good or a service and new groups are prevented from entering the market
restrain	to limit, impede, or keep under control
subpoenas	legal orders to appear at a certain place at a certain time to provide testimony on a certain topic
trust	a corporate monopoly in which firms are consolidated to gain control of a particular industry

SHERMAN ANTITRUST ACT

Fifty-first Congress of the United States of America, At the First Session,

Begun and held at the City of Washington on Monday, the second day of December, one thousand eight hundred and eighty-nine.

◆ An Act to Protect Trade and Commerce against Unlawful Restraints and Monopolies

Be it enacted by the Senate and House of Representatives of the United States of America in Congress assembled,

Sec. 1. Every contract, combination in the form of trust or otherwise, or conspiracy, in restraint of trade or commerce among the several States, or with foreign nations, is hereby declared to be illegal. Every person who shall make any such contract or engage in any such combination or conspiracy, shall be deemed guilty of a misdemeanor, and, on conviction thereof, shall be punished by fine not exceeding five thousand dollars, or by imprisonment not exceeding one year, or by both said punishments, at the discretion of the court.

Sec. 2. Every person who shall monopolize, or attempt to monopolize, or combine or conspire with any other person or persons, to monopolize any part of the trade or commerce among the several States, or with foreign nations, shall be deemed guilty of a misdemeanor, and, on conviction thereof, shall be punished by fine not exceeding five thousand dollars, or by imprisonment not exceeding one year, or by both said punishments, in the discretion of the court.

Sec. 3. Every contract, combination in form of trust or otherwise, or conspiracy, in restraint of trade or commerce in any Territory of the United States or of the District of Columbia, or in restraint of trade or commerce between any such Territory and another, or between any such Territory or Territories and any State or States or the District of Columbia, or with foreign nations, or between the District of Columbia and any State or States or foreign nations, is hereby declared illegal. Every person who shall make any such contract or engage in any such combination or conspiracy, shall be deemed guilty of a misdemeanor, and, on conviction thereof, shall be punished by fine not exceeding five thousand dollars, or by imprisonment not exceeding one year, or by both said punishments, in the discretion of the court.

Sec. 4. The several circuit courts of the United States are hereby invested with jurisdiction to prevent and restrain violations of this act; and it shall be the duty of the several district attorneys of the United States, in their respective districts, under the direction of the Attorney-General, to institute proceedings in equity to prevent and restrain such violations. Such proceedings may be by way of petition setting forth the case and praying that such violation shall be enjoined or otherwise prohibited. When the parties complained of shall have been duly notified of such petition the court shall proceed, as soon as may be, to the hearing and determination of the case; and pending such petition and before final decree, the court may at any time make such temporary restraining order or prohibition as shall be deemed just in the premises.

Sec. 5. Whenever it shall appear to the court before which any proceeding under section four of this act may be pending, that the ends of justice require that other parties should be brought before the court, the court may cause them to be summoned, whether they reside in the district in which the court is held or not; and subpoenas to that end may be served in any district by the marshal thereof.

Sec. 6. Any property owned under any contract or by any combination, or pursuant to any conspiracy (and being the subject thereof) mentioned in section one of this act, and being in the course of transportation from one State to another, or to a foreign country, shall be- forfeited to the United States, and may be seized and condemned by like proceedings as those provided by law for the forfeiture, seizure, and condemnation of property imported into the United States contrary to law.

Sec. 7. Any person who shall be injured in his business or property by any other person or corporation by reason of anything forbidden or declared to be unlawful by this act, may sue therefor in any circuit court of the United States in the district in which the defendant resides or is found, without respect to the amount in controversy, and shall recover three fold the damages by him sustained, and the costs of suit, including a reasonable attorney's fee.

Sec. 8. That the word "person," or "persons," wherever used in this act shall be deemed to include corporations and associations existing under or authorized by the laws of either the United States, the laws of any of the Territories, the laws of any State, or the laws of any foreign country.

Approved, July 2, 1890.

w Washington   Board measure

l-

DRESS BY BOOKER T. WASHINGTON, PRINCIPAL

RMAL AND INDUSTRIAL INSTITUTE, TUSKEGEE, ALABAMA,

AT OPENING OF ATLANTA EXPOSITION,

Sept. 18th, 1895.

Gentlemen of the Board of Directors and Citizens:

of the population of the South is of the Negro

rprise seeking the material, civil or moral welfare

n can disregard this element of our population and

est success. I but convey to you, Mr. President and

sentiment of the masses of my race, when I say that

the value and manhodd of the American Negro been

and generously recognized, than by the managers of

nt Exposition at every stage of its progress. It is

which will do more to cement the friendship of the

any occurrence since the dawn of our freedom.

this, but the opportunity here afforded will awaken

era of industrial progress. Ignorant and inexper-

not strange that in the first years of our new life

he top instead of the bottom, that a seat in Congress

Legislature was more sought t an real-estate or indus-

that the political convention, or stump speaking had

ons that starting a dairy farm or truck-garden.

Booker T. Washington's Speech at the Atlanta Exposition (Library of Congress)

Booker T. Washington's Atlanta Exposition Address

"In all things that are purely social we can be as separate as the fingers, yet one as the hand in all things essential to mutual progress."

Overview

Late on an unseasonably hot mid-September afternoon in 1895, Booker T. Washington delivered a short speech to a standing-room-only crowd packed into the auditorium in Atlanta's Exposition Park during the opening ceremonies of the Cotton States and International Exposition. The address, which ran a little over ten minutes, propelled the previously unknown principal of Tuskegee Institute, a small black college in rural Alabama, into the national spotlight. By almost any measure, it (along with Martin Luther King, Jr.'s, 1963 "I Have a Dream" Speech) was one of the most important speeches presented by an African American. The immediate response, both in Atlanta and across the country, was overwhelmingly positive, but over time both Washington and his address have been sharply criticized, especially by other African American intellectuals and leaders. These critics termed the Atlanta address the "Atlanta Compromise" and made Washington a symbol of accommodation and acquiescence to southern racism, segregation, and the political disenfranchisement of African Americans. Throughout much of the twentieth century Washington and his famous (or infamous) address were a defining element in the African American political debate.

The assessment of Washington's Atlanta Exposition Address is clouded by the problem that Washington's actual words are less known than the responses and the analysis of those words by Washington's allies and especially by his opponents. As soon as the news of Washington's triumph at Atlanta spread across the country, friends and foes began to dissect his words and to interpret various phrases or images that he utilized. As a result, the speech itself quickly faded from memory, while discrete segments of the speech became permanently imbedded in American racial discourse, both within the African American community and among white Americans. The original context of the address, as well as its complex and nuanced arguments, gave way to the overly simplified and largely inaccurate view that Washington had surrendered the rights that African Americans had won during the Civil War and Reconstruction. By the time of Washington's death twenty years later,

African American leadership was divided into Bookerite (pro-Washington) and anti-Bookerite factions, and Washington's opponents increasingly dominated the debate.

Context

The 1890s were a difficult decade for African Americans. Many of the gains they had achieved both in securing their political and civil rights and in attaining a measure of physical security gave way to an assault on their rights as citizens and on their personal safety. During Reconstruction three constitutional amendments (the Thirteenth, Fourteenth, and Fifteenth Amendments) and the Civil Rights Acts of 1866 and 1875 had secured African American freedom and equal rights. The military occupation of the former Confederate States and federal legislation like the Civil Rights Act of 1871 (also known as the Ku Klux Klan Act) greatly diminished organized violence against blacks and their white political allies. In the late 1870s and 1880s these gains began to unravel. In the aftermath of the disputed presidential election of 1876, the last federal troops were withdrawn from the South. In 1883 the Supreme Court ruled in the Civil Rights Cases that the Fourteenth Amendment did not protect against discrimination by individuals or businesses, and three years later, for the first time in U.S. history, more blacks than whites were the victims of lynching.

In the 1890s racial conditions in the United States continued to deteriorate. In *Plessy v. Ferguson* (163 U.S. 537 [1896]), the Supreme Court legitimized state-sponsored segregation as long as "separate but equal" facilities were provided for blacks, and in 1898 the Court ruled that literacy tests and other similar methods of restricting the right to vote did not violate the Fifteenth Amendment. The 1890s witnessed more lynchings of blacks than any other decade in U.S. history. As the decade came to an end, race riots broke out in Wilmington, North Carolina (1898); New Orleans, Louisiana (1900); and New York (1900) as violence against blacks escalated. African Americans struggled to respond to this new wave of discrimination and violence without much success. The federal government, on which African Americans had depended during Reconstruction,

Time Line

1856
■ **April 5**
Booker T. Washington is born into slavery on the farm of James Burroughs near Hale's Ford in the foothills of the Blue Ridge Mountains in Franklin County, Virginia.

1865
■ **August**
Freed by the defeat of the South in the Civil War, Washington and his family move to Malden, West Virginia.

1872
■ **October 5**
Washington leaves home and enrolls in Hampton Institute.

1881
■ **July 4**
Washington opens the Tuskegee Institute in Tuskegee, Alabama, modeling the school's curriculum on that of the Hampton Institute.

1895
■ **February 20**
Frederick Douglass, the most prominent African American leader of his generation, dies in Washington, D.C.

■ **September 18**
Washington delivers his Atlanta Exposition Address during the opening ceremonies of the Cotton States and International Exposition.

1896
■ **May 18**
In *Plessy v. Ferguson*, the Supreme Court rules that a Louisiana law segregating passengers on railroads is legal because it provides "separate but equal" facilities; this ruling validates a number of laws that segregate African Americans.

1898
■ **April 25**
In *Williams v. State of Mississippi*, the Supreme Court rules that a Mississippi law allowing poll taxes and literacy tests to be used as voter qualifications is legal, legitimizing the tactics used by southern states to deny African Americans the right to vote.

---

was no longer a reliable ally. The Democrats had regained control of southern state governments in the 1870s and won the presidency in 1884 and again in 1892. The Republican Party's commitment to civil rights also had waned. Frederick Douglass, who led the struggle against slavery and was an outspoken advocate of equal rights, died in February 1895, depriving African Americans of their best-known and most effective leader at this very crucial time.

Against this background Atlanta businessmen conceived of an international exposition, a small-scale world's fair, which would highlight the emergence of a "New South," promote the city and the entire region as a progressive area, and attract new business and investment capital. They hoped to capture some of the positive press coverage and economic benefits that Chicago had received with the 1893 Columbian Exposition. In the spring of 1894 Washington and several other African Americans were asked to join a delegation of prominent southerners to lobby Congress for an appropriation to support the Atlanta Exposition. Congress appropriated the funding, and as planning for the event proceeded, Washington was consulted again on the issue of the "Negro" exhibits. At some point, and after some controversy, exposition officials decided to involve African Americans in the opening ceremonies. On August 23, 1895, about three weeks before opening day, organizers of the exposition asked Washington to represent African Americans at this event.

The decision to involve African Americans so prominently in the exposition was interesting. Two years earlier black leaders had been unhappy with the way they were treated at the World's Columbian Exposition in Chicago. Their exhibits were segregated in Negro buildings, and blacks felt that as both exhibitors at and visitors to the fair, they had faced broken promises and discrimination. Consequently, a number of African American leaders were reluctant to support the Negro exhibits at this much smaller provincial event. Washington, however, cooperated with the organizers and urged others to do likewise, even though blacks had to fund their own exhibits and these exhibits would be housed in a separate building. Appreciation of Washington's assistance with Congress and his support of the event brought him to the podium on opening day.

About the Author

Booker Taliaferro Washington was born on a farm near Hale's Ford in the foothills of the Blue Ridge Mountains in Franklin County, Virginia. While his exact birth date is not clear, most authorities place it on April 5, 1856. Washington spent the first eight years of his childhood as a slave. Following emancipation he moved with his mother, brother, and sister to join his stepfather, who had found employment in the saltworks in Malden, West Virginia. Emancipation did not significantly raise the economic well-being of the family. The young Washington alternated between working in the saltworks and attending school. In 1867 his situation improved dramatically when he took a job in the home of General Lewis Ruffner, one of Malden's wealthiest citizens, serving as houseboy and companion for Viola Ruffner, the general's New England wife. Washington later credited Mrs. Ruffner for much of his early education and especially with preparing him for college.

At age sixteen Washington left home to further his education at Hampton Institute, which allowed impoverished black students to work at the school to pay the costs of their education. Three years later he graduated as one of its top students. After a short stint as a schoolteacher in Malden, he returned to Hampton to teach and to acquire additional education. During his time as a student and then as a teacher at Hampton, Washington became a protégé of General Samuel C. Armstrong and a student of Armstrong's theory of industrial education. In May 1881 the board of a recently authorized Alabama state normal school for black students asked Armstrong to recommend a white educator to serve as its principal. Armstrong recommended his prize student. After hesitation and with reluctance, the board accepted Washington to head the school.

When Washington arrived in Tuskegee, he discovered that the school existed only on paper—he literally had to find land, build buildings, and recruit faculty. It is to Washington's credit that in spite of his youth and inexperience, he mastered the political, administrative, and financial skills he needed to create a black institution in the inhospitable hills of northern Alabama. By the early 1890s Tuskegee had become a success, and Washington was beginning to address the broader political and economic issues that confronted African Americans.

The Atlanta Exposition Address transformed Washington from a southern educator to the most influential and powerful African American in the United States. He consulted with presidents and corporate leaders, and headed a political machine that dispersed funds from white philanthropists and political patronage throughout the black community. In the early twentieth century opposition to Washington's leadership increased, especially that organized around Du Bois. The founding of the NAACP in 1910 and Du Bois's prominent role in that organization deflected some white support from Washington. During the last years of Washington's life the African American leadership was increasingly divided into pro-Washington and pro–Du Bois/NAACP camps. Nevertheless, at the time of his death in November 1915, Washington was still the most widely known and respected African American leader in the United States.

Explanation and Analysis of the Document

Washington's Atlanta Exposition Address was presented in the auditorium on the exposition grounds. The auditorium was packed, mostly with whites, but there was also a segregated Negro section. Washington was one of two blacks seated on the stage, but he was the only one to speak. The speech itself was brief. In written form it is eleven paragraphs; Washington delivered it in about ten minutes.

Time Line

1901

■ **March**
Washington publishes his best-known autobiography, *Up from Slavery.*

■ **July 16**
Controversy arises after Washington dines at the White House while consulting President Theodore Roosevelt about political appointments in the South.

1903

■ **April 18**
W. E. B. Du Bois begins his criticism of Washington's leadership with the publication of the essay "Of Mr. Booker T. Washington and Others" in his book *The Souls of Black Folk.*

1905

■ **July 10**
Twenty-nine African Americans, including Du Bois, meet in Fort Erie, Ontario, to create a civil rights organization. The resulting Niagara Movement directly challenges Washington's leadership and policies.

1910

■ **May 14**
The biracial National Negro Conference officially gives birth to the National Association for the Advancement of Colored People (NAACP), the oldest civil rights organization in the United States.

1915

■ **November 14**
Washington dies at home in Tuskegee.

In the first paragraph Washington notes the significance of the occasion. First, he emphasizes the significance of African Americans to the South—"One-third of the population of the South is of the Negro race"—and observes that no enterprise for the development of the South that ignores that element of the population will "reach the highest success." In this sentence, Washington introduces the major theme of his address: that the destinies and well-being of African American southerners and white southerners are inextricably linked. He returns to this theme again and again. Washington concludes this paragraph by praising the leaders of the exposition for recognizing the "value and manhood of the American Negro" throughout the plan-

Booker T. Washington (Library of Congress)

ning and staging of the event. This statement is often viewed as obsequious; however, the role afforded African Americans, from the lobbying efforts, the planning of the black exhibits, and Washington's participation in the opening ceremonies, contrasted considerably with the World's Columbian Exposition of 1893 as well as other previous expositions.

The second paragraph contains the type of language that most irritated Washington's critics. After the rather serious opening, Washington feeds negative racial stereotypes when he essentially apologizes for the ignorance and inexperience that led newly emancipated blacks to make unwise choices, seeking political office rather than land or industrial skills and prizing political activity over entrepreneurship. Critics cite this paragraph as evidence that Washington acquiesced to white efforts to deprive blacks of their political rights. In truth, Washington consistently opposed both publically and privately the disenfranchisement of southern blacks. However, Washington did feel that blacks should place greater emphasis on their economic betterment.

The third paragraph centers on one of Washington's best-known homilies. This is the story of the ship lost at sea, its crew dying of thirst and sending out a desperate cry for water, only to be told, "Cast down your bucket where you are." Washington uses this story to admonish the blacks in his audience to "cast down your bucket where you are," that is, to remain in the South rather than attempt to better their condition in a "foreign land." Washington con-

sistently advised African Americans not to follow the Exodusters west, join the trickle to northern cities that twenty years later became the black migration, or follow those who advocated emigration to a black-governed country, such as Haiti or Liberia. As discrimination and racial violence intensified, many considered Washington's advice to be misguided, binding blacks to a new slavery. Washington, however, argued that African Americans must work with their white neighbors—but without surrendering their dignity: "Cast down your bucket where you are'—cast it down in making friends *in every manly way* of all the people of all races by whom we are surrounded" (emphasis added).

The next paragraph continues this argument. Still addressing the African Americans in the audience, Washington continues: "Cast it down in agriculture, mechanics, in commerce, in domestic service, and in the professions." Here Washington is laying out his economic agenda. While he is usually cited for promoting only low-skilled, working-class, and agricultural labor for blacks, here he is quite specific—his list of occupations includes commerce and the professions. Washington acknowledges that initially, lacking skills, capital, and education, most blacks will survive by the labor "of [their] hands," and he warns blacks not to denigrate the dignity and importance of this type of work. He also warns blacks not to sacrifice the habits of thrift and the accumulation of property and real wealth by conspicuous consumption and the superficial trappings of opulence. He notes that "there is as much dignity in tilling a field as in writing a poem," not to criticize poets but to recognize the importance of farmers. Finally, he warns blacks not to let discrimination and injustice blind them to the opportunities that surround them. In other words, if they focus only on their victimization, they will not succeed.

In paragraph 5, Washington shifts his focus to the white portion of his audience. Very carefully he lays out what white southerners must do, always recognizing that if he pushes too hard or too far he will fail and that failure would jeopardize Tuskegee and possibly his own safety. He begins with the very gentle phrase, "were I permitted I would repeat what I say to my own race"; then he tells white southerners to "'Cast down your bucket where you are.' Cast it down among the eight millions of Negroes whose habits you know, whose fidelity and love you have tested in days when to have proved treacherous meant the ruin of your firesides." Washington is telling white southerners to employ African Americans, not the immigrants who are pouring into the country from southern and eastern Europe; his reference to "strikes and labour wars" refers to the turmoil of recent clashes between unions and factory owners, such as the Homestead Strike (1892) among steelworkers and the Pullman Strike (1894) of factory workers. In his reference to black fidelity and love being tested, he is referring to the Civil War and reminding whites that at the time they were most vulnerable, with most men off at war, blacks did not strike down the families they left behind. In discussing the contributions of blacks to the development of the South, Washington refers to both tilling the fields and building the cities, and for the future he depicts blacks buying land, making waste areas blossom, and running factories. Throughout this section Washington softens his message with references to the African American people as law-abiding, unresentful, loyal, and faithful, and he reminds his audience that blacks have nursed whites' children, cared for their aged, and mourned their dead.

Washington concludes paragraph 5 with his most famous statement: "In all things that are purely social we can be as separate as the fingers, yet one as the hand in all things essential to mutual progress." This sentence is at the heart of the criticism of Washington and the Atlanta Exposition Address. Looked at out of context, it seems to acquiesce to "separate but equal" segregation. However, the sentence was spoken in a context that leaves the meaning less clear. Immediately preceding it, Washington spoke of blacks "interlacing our industrial, commercial, civil, and religious life with yours in a way that shall make the interests of both races one," picking up the theme introduced in the first paragraph that the destinies of black and white southerners are intertwined.

In the very short sixth paragraph, Washington continues to discuss the connectedness of blacks and whites, observing that the security of both races requires the "highest intelligence and development of all" and urging whites to invest in the advancement of African Americans for the betterment of all.

In paragraph 7, Washington breaks the narrative and quotes from the poem "At Port Royal," written by the abolitionist poet John Greenleaf Whittier in 1862 to celebrate the November 1861 Union victory over the South and the occupation of the Port Royal area on the Georgia and South Carolina coasts. This battle was significant because the Union army liberated a number of slaves. It was one of the earliest steps towards emancipation. Quoting the most celebrated abolitionist poet to a largely white audience in Atlanta was very daring of Washington. Washington's message is one of oppressor and oppressed, bound together, confronting one fate. It is very likely that most whites in the audience knew the poem.

For those in the audience who might not know the poem or understand its message, Washington repeats it in very clear, unambiguous language in paragraph 8. Either blacks and whites cooperate for the betterment of the South, or blacks will work against whites and retard progress; either blacks will constitute one-third of the South's "intelligence and progress" and one-third of its "business and industrial prosperity," or "we shall prove a veritable body of death, stagnating, depressing, retarding every effort to advance the body politic." Washington threatens white southerners with economic and social catastrophe unless they are willing to work with blacks and allow blacks to share appropriately in southern progress and development.

After stating this grim warning, Washington turns to humor to defuse the tension. He begins paragraph 9 with a reference that caters to the white stereotype of blacks as petty thieves—much to the dismay of his critics. The rest of the paragraph is conciliatory. Washington describes the advances and accomplishments that African Americans had

made in the thirty years since emancipation and the assistance from southern states and northern philanthropists that made this progress possible.

Paragraph 10 consists of three often-quoted sentences. In the first Washington asserts that "agitation of questions of social equality is the extremest folly" but that progress toward equality will result from "severe and constant struggle" rather than from "artificial forcing." Here again Washington is ambiguous, on the one hand denouncing agitation and on the other advocating prolonged struggle. The difference may lie in the term *social equality*, which some scholars suggest southerners equated with intermarriage. The second sentence reflects Washington's conviction that economic prosperity would erase racial prejudice. Washington ends this paragraph by asserting that at the current time, it is more important that blacks achieve the right to work in a factory than to buy a seat in the opera house. Again Washington expresses his belief that in the short term, economic priority should be the highest priority for African Americans. His critics accused him of again accepting segregation.

In the final paragraph, Washington ends where he began, praising the organizers of the exhibition and observing the tremendous progress blacks and whites have made, the former starting as slaves with nothing and the latter coming out of a war in which they lost everything. He again links the destiny of the two races and adds a religious component. It is God who has laid before the South the task of creating a just society, free of "sectional differences and racial animosities and suspicions." If whites, with the support of blacks, resolve this problem, they will bring into the South a "new heaven and a new earth," a reference drawn from Revelation 21:1. Left unspoken is the alternative described in Revelation 21:8 and known to most listeners. The failure to create a just society (a new heaven and a new earth) will be a fate shared by all southerners—the "lake which burneth with fire and brimstone: which is the second death."

Audience

The initial audience that Washington addressed was a few thousand southerners gathered in Atlanta for the opening of the exposition. Louis Harlan, Washington's principal biographer, describes the auditorium as "packed with humanity from bottom to top"; outside were "thousands more … unable to get in" (Harlan, 1972, p. 215). Still, this was a relatively small but important audience. The majority were white southerners, a very difficult audience for Washington to face. In 1895 few white southerners would have tolerated being lectured to by a black man. Washington had to make his points both gently and diplomatically without surrendering his dignity or his convictions. Also present in audience were black southerners, fewer in number, attracted to the auditorium by the unusual opportunity to see a black man address an audience of prominent whites. Washington could also expect that his words, at least in part, would be reported throughout the black community.

"'Cast down your bucket where you are.' Cast it down among the eight millions of Negroes whose habits you know, whose fidelity and love you have tested in days when to have proved treacherous meant the ruin of your firesides."

(Paragraph 5)

"In all things that are purely social we can be as separate as the fingers, yet one as the hand in all things essential to mutual progress."

(Paragraph 5)

"We shall contribute one-third to the business and industrial prosperity of the South, or we shall prove a veritable body of death, stagnating, depressing, retarding every effort to advance the body politic."

(Paragraph 8)

"The wisest among my race understand that the agitation of questions of social equality is the extremest folly, and that progress in the enjoyment of all the privileges that will come to us must be the result of severe and constant struggle rather than of artificial forcing."

(Paragraph 10)

"No race that has anything to contribute to the markets of the world is long in any degree ostracized."

(Paragraph 10)

"The opportunity to earn a dollar in a factory just now is worth infinitely more than the opportunity to spend a dollar in an opera-house."

(Paragraph 10)

What Washington did not anticipate was the much larger national audience that his speech would reach. Within in a few days his Atlanta Exposition Address was reported in whole or in part in newspapers across the country. Washington would quickly become the most widely known African American in the country, and passages from his speech would become fixed in popular culture and American memory.

Impact

The immediate response to the speech was phenomenal. In the auditorium the audience burst into thunderous applause the moment Washington finished speaking; the former governor of Georgia, who had presided over the proceedings, rushed forward to congratulate Washington.

Newspapers around the country reported the address and reprinted the speech. Perhaps none did so as effusively as Joseph Pulitzer's *New York World*, with headlines announcing that "A Negro Moses Spoke for a Race." The reporter described Washington facing the crowd with the sun in his eyes, his "whole face lit up with the fire of prophecy.… It electrified the audience, and the response was as if it had come from the throat of a whirlwind" (Harlan, 1972–1989, vol. 4, pp. 3–15). Within days, letters and telegrams poured in praising Washington and his speech, anointing Washington as the successor to the recently deceased Frederick Douglass and comparing the speech to Lincoln's Gettysburg Address. One who sent his congratulations was Du Bois, who telegraphed, "Let me heartily congratulate you on your phenomenal success in Atlanta—it was a word fitly spoken" (Harlan, 1972–1989, vol. 4, p. 26), and followed it up with a letter to the *New York Age*, praising the Atlanta speech as a basis for a real settlement of the racial problems in the South. There was also some opposition, especially among northern blacks. The *Washington Bee* published a very critical editorial depicting the speech as a surrender to whites. Others rejected the comparison of Washington to Douglass, while still others cringed at Washington's use of stereotyped images of blacks as a source of humor. On the whole, however, public comment, black and white, was very favorable. The real criticism would come later.

The Atlanta Exposition Address made Washington a national figure and the most influential and powerful African American in the United States. In 1898 President William McKinley visited Tuskegee, affirming Washington's new prominence, and in 1901 Washington dined with President Roosevelt in the White House. Less publicly but even more significantly, President McKinley, President Roosevelt, and President William Taft regularly consulted with Washington on issues of significance to African Americans and on their appointments of both blacks and many white southerners to federal positions. Washington, in turn, developed a powerful political machine with allies among most prominent black Republicans and many black newspaper editors. Parallel to his expanding political power, Washington established close contacts among many of the most powerful white business leaders. In the process, he expanded his already effective fund-raising operation for Tuskegee into an economic machine that effectively controlled the distribution of white philanthropy into the black community.

History, however, has not been kind to Washington or his Atlanta address. By 1910 Du Bois and most northern black intellectuals either viewed the Atlanta speech as a surrender to white racism or blamed Washington and the policies enunciated in Atlanta for the deterioration of African American rights and the rise in racial violence. Within the black community this negative view persisted throughout most of the twentieth century. Finally, the Atlanta address, accurately or inaccurately, has become a symbol of a dichotomy in African American political thought—the division between those advocating a nonconfrontational economic and community-building approach to America's racial problems and those who push a more militant program of integration and immediate civil and political rights.

Related Documents

"South's New Epoch." *New York World*, September 19, 1895. University of Illinois Press Web site. http://www.historycooperative.org/btw/Vol.4/html/3.html. Accessed on October 17, 2007. This article is a lengthy newspaper account of the opening ceremonies of the Atlanta Exposition by a reporter who was on the scene.

Washington, Booker T. *An Autobiography: The Story of My Life and Work*. Chicago: J. L. Nichols, 1900. This is Washington's first autobiography. While it is largely ghostwritten and poorly done, it contains much information about his life and career up to 1900.

———. *Up from Slavery: An Autobiography*. New York: Doubleday, 1901. This is Washington's major autobiography. He was actively involved in writing this book, and it presents his perspective on his early life and career, including the Atlanta Exposition Address.

Bibliography

■ Books

Brundage, W. Fitzhugh, ed. *Booker T. Washington and Black Progress: Up from Slavery 100 Years Later*. Gainesville: University of Florida Press, 2003.

Harlan, Louis R. *Booker T. Washington: The Making of a Black Leader, 1856–1901*. New York: Oxford University Press, 1972.

———. *Booker T. Washington: The Wizard of Tuskegee, 1901–1915*. New York: Oxford University Press, 1983.

———, et al., eds. *The Booker T. Washington Papers*. 14 vols. Urbana: University of Illinois Press, 1972–1989.

Meier, August. *Negro Thought in America, 1880–1915: Racial Ideologies in the Age of Booker T. Washington*. Ann Arbor: University of Michigan Press, 1968.

Moore, Jacqueline H. *Booker T. Washington, W. E. B. Du Bois, and the Struggle for Racial Uplift*. Wilmington, Del.: Scholarly Resources, 2003.

West, Michael Rudolph. *The Education of Booker T. Washington: American Democracy and the Idea of Race Relations*. New York: Columbia University Press, 2006.

Wolters, Raymond. *Du Bois and His Rivals*. Columbia: University of Missouri Press, 2002.

■ Web Sites

"The Booker T. Washington Papers." University of Illinois Press Web site.

http://www.historycooperative.org/btw/info.html. Accessed on
October 17, 2007.

"Booker T. Washington National Monument, Virginia." National
Park Service Web site.
http://www.nps.gov/bowa/index.htm. Accessed on October 17,
2007.

—By Cary D. Wintz

Questions for Further Study

1. Critics of Washington and his Atlanta Exposition Address have accused him of betraying African Americans by giving in to southern perceptions of the racial inferiority of African Americans and accepting segregation and the loss of the African American political rights and the right to vote. To what extent is this criticism valid? To what extent is it not valid?

2. What rights does Washington assert for African Americans in the Atlanta address? How do these rights differ from those championed by the organizers of the Niagara Movement in their 1905 Declaration of Principles?

3. Washington delivered this speech in Atlanta, Georgia, in 1895. How did the location of the speech affect what Washington said? How might the speech have been different had Washington delivered it in New York rather than Atlanta?

4. One theme that Washington develops in this speech is the concept that the destinies of black southerners and white southerners are intertwined. How does Washington argue this point? What is the significance of this argument? Explain whether this argument is an effective basis for resolving racial problems in the South.

Glossary

animosities	hostilities; bitter anger
body politic	the people as a whole in a state or a nation
bowels	the deep interior or the depths of something
exposition	a public exhibition or fair
fidelity	faithfulness to one's duties and obligations; loyalty
letters	literature
mandates	authoritative demands or requirements
ostracized	systematically excluded or discriminated against
philanthropists	persons who contribute to the betterment of others, usually by charitable donations of money
sectional	related to one part or state of a country over another

BOOKER T. WASHINGTON'S ATLANTA EXPOSITION ADDRESS

Mr. President and Gentlemen of the Board of Directors and Citizens:

One-third of the population of the South is of the Negro race. No enterprise seeking the material, civil, or moral welfare of this section can disregard this element of our population and reach the highest success. I but convey to you, Mr. President and Directors, the sentiment of the masses of my race when I say that in no way have the value and manhood of the American Negro been more fittingly and generously recognized than by the managers of this magnificent Exposition at every stage of its progress. It is a recognition that will do more to cement the friendship of the two races than any occurrence since the dawn of our freedom.

Not only this, but the opportunity here afforded will awaken among us a new era of industrial progress. Ignorant and inexperienced, it is not strange that in the first years of our new life we began at the top instead of at the bottom; that a seat in Congress or the state legislature was more sought than real estate or industrial skill; that the political convention or stump speaking had more attractions than starting a dairy farm or truck garden.

A ship lost at sea for many days suddenly sighted a friendly vessel. From the mast of the unfortunate vessel was seen a signal, "Water, water; we die of thirst!" The answer from the friendly vessel at once came back, "Cast down your bucket where you are." A second time the signal, "Water, water; send us water!" ran up from the distressed vessel, and was answered, "Cast down your bucket where you are." And a third and fourth signal for water was answered, "Cast down your bucket where you are." The captain of the distressed vessel, at last heeding the injunction, cast down his bucket, and it came up full of fresh, sparkling water from the mouth of the Amazon River. To those of my race who depend on bettering their condition in a foreign land or who underestimate the importance of cultivating friendly

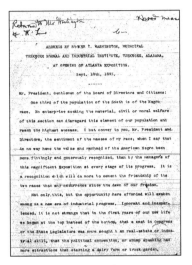

relations with the Southern white man, who is their next-door neighbor, I would say: "Cast down your bucket where you are"—cast it down in making friends in every manly way of the people of all races by whom we are surrounded.

Cast it down in agriculture, mechanics, in commerce, in domestic service, and in the professions. And in this connection it is well to bear in mind that whatever other sins the South may be called to bear, when it comes to business, pure and simple, it is in the South that the Negro is given a man's chance in the commercial world, and in nothing is this Exposition more eloquent than in emphasizing this chance. Our greatest danger is that in the great leap from slavery to freedom we may overlook the fact that the masses of us are to live by the productions of our hands, and fail to keep in mind that we shall prosper in proportion as we learn to dignify and glorify common labour, and put brains and skill into the common occupations of life; shall prosper in proportion as we learn to draw the line between the superficial and the substantial, the ornamental gewgaws of life and the useful. No race can prosper till it learns that there is as much dignity in tilling a field as in writing a poem. It is at the bottom of life we must begin, and not at the top. Nor should we permit our grievances to overshadow our opportunities.

To those of the white race who look to the incoming of those of foreign birth and strange tongue and habits for the prosperity of the South, were I permitted I would repeat what I say to my own race, "Cast down your bucket where you are." Cast it down among the eight millions of Negroes whose habits you know, whose fidelity and love you have tested in days when to have proved treacherous meant the ruin of your firesides. Cast down your bucket among these people who have, without strikes and labour wars, tilled your fields, cleared your forests, builded your railroads and cities, and brought forth treasures from the bowels of the earth, and helped make possible this magnificent representation of the progress of the South. Casting down your bucket among my people, helping and encouraging them as you are doing on these grounds, and to education of head, hand, and heart, you will find that they will buy your surplus land, make blossom the waste places in your fields, and run your factories. While doing this, you can be sure in the future, as in the past, that you and your families will be surrounded by the most patient, faithful, law-abiding, and unresentful people that the world has seen. As we have proved our loyalty to you in the past, in nursing your children, watching by the sick-bed of your mothers and fathers, and often following them with tear-dimmed eyes to their graves, so in the future, in our humble way, we shall stand by you with a devotion that no foreigner can approach, ready to lay down our lives, if need be, in defense of yours, interlacing our industrial, commercial, civil, and religious life with yours in a way that shall make the interests of both races one. In all things that are purely social we can be as separate as the fingers, yet one as the hand in all things essential to mutual progress.

There is no defense or security for any of us except in the highest intelligence and development of all. If anywhere there are efforts tending to curtail the fullest growth of the Negro, let these efforts be turned into stimulating, encouraging, and making him the most useful and intelligent citizen. Effort or means so invested will pay a thousand per cent interest. These efforts will be twice blessed—blessing him that gives and him that takes. There is no escape through law of man or God from the inevitable:

The laws of changeless justice bind Oppressor with oppressed;

And close as sin and suffering joined We march to fate abreast…

Nearly sixteen millions of hands will aid you in pulling the load upward, or they will pull against you the load downward. We shall constitute one-third and more of the ignorance and crime of the South, or one-third [of] its intelligence and progress; we shall contribute one-third to the business and industrial prosperity of the South, or we shall prove a veritable body of death, stagnating, depressing, retarding every effort to advance the body politic.

Gentlemen of the Exposition, as we present to you our humble effort at an exhibition of our progress, you must not expect overmuch. Starting thirty years ago with ownership here and there in a few quilts and pumpkins and chickens (gathered from miscellaneous sources), remember the path that has led from these to the inventions and production of agricultural implements, buggies, steam-engines, newspapers, books, statuary, carving, paintings, the management of drug stores and banks, has not been trodden without contact with thorns and thistles. While we take pride in what we exhibit as a result of our independent efforts, we do not for a moment forget that our part in this exhibition would fall far short of your expectations but for the constant help that has come to our educational life, not only from the Southern states, but especially from Northern philanthropists, who have made their gifts a constant stream of blessing and encouragement.

The wisest among my race understand that the agitation of questions of social equality is the extremest folly, and that progress in the enjoyment of all the privileges that will come to us must be the result of severe and constant struggle rather than of artificial forcing. No race that has anything to contribute to the markets of the world is long in any degree ostracized. It is important and right that all privileges of the law be ours, but it is vastly more important that we be prepared for the exercise of these privileges. The opportunity to earn a dollar in a factory just now is worth infinitely more than the opportunity to spend a dollar in an opera-house.

In conclusion, may I repeat that nothing in thirty years has given us more hope and encouragement, and drawn us so near to you of the white race, as this opportunity offered by the Exposition; and here bending, as it were, over the altar that represents the results of the struggles of your race and mine, both starting practically empty-handed three decades ago, I pledge that in your effort to work out the great and intricate problem which God has laid at the doors of the South, you shall have at all times the patient, sympathetic help of my race; only let this he constantly in mind, that, while from representations in these buildings of the product of field, of forest, of mine, of factory, letters, and art, much good will come, yet far above and beyond material benefits will be that higher good, that, let us pray God, will come, in a blotting out of sectional differences and racial animosities and suspicions, in a determination to administer absolute justice, in a willing obedience among all classes to the mandates of law. This, coupled with our material prosperity, will bring into our beloved South a new heaven and a new earth.

Supreme Court of the United States,

No. 210 , October Term, 1895.

Homer Adolph Plessy
Plaintiff in Error,

vs.

J. H. Ferguson, Judge of Section "A" Criminal District Court for the Parish of Orleans.

In Error to the Supreme Court of the State of Louisiana

This cause came on to be heard on the transcript of the record from the Supreme Court of the State of Louisiana, and was argued by counsel.

On consideration whereof, It is now here ordered and adjudged by this Court that the judgment of the said Supreme Court, in this cause, be, and the same is hereby, Affirmed with costs.

Per Mr. Justice Brown,
May 18, 1896.

Dissenting:
Mr. Justice Harlan

Plessy v. Ferguson (National Archives and Records Administration)

PLESSY V. FERGUSON

"If one race be inferior to the other socially, the constitution of the United States cannot put them upon the same plane."

Overview

Plessy v. Ferguson, argued on April 13, 1896, and decided on May 18, 1896, is probably best known for giving the United States the separate but equal doctrine. The case probably ranks close to *Dred Scott v. Sandford* (1857) as one of the most influential and thoroughly repudiated cases the Supreme Court has ever decided. The majority opinion was written by Justice Henry Billings Brown of Massachusetts, and it gained the assent of six additional justices. That opinion provided a legal imprimatur to segregation and the Jim Crow system of laws that flourished from the late nineteenth century through much of the twentieth century. *Plessy* held that notwithstanding the Reconstruction amendments (the Thirteenth, Fourteenth, and Fifteenth Amendments), which were passed in the wake of the Civil War to grant equal citizenship to African Americans and promised the equal protection of the laws to all persons, the United States Constitution allowed states to segregate their black and white citizens when traveling on intrastate railroads. The separate but equal doctrine was applied to more than just railroads and supported segregation until it was largely repudiated, though not explicitly overruled, in *Brown v. Board of Education of Topeka* (1954).

Justice John Marshall Harlan of Kentucky wrote the sole dissent in *Plessy*, which provided much of the rhetorical support for the twentieth-century civil rights movement. Justice Harlan argued that the Reconstruction amendments' guarantees of equality were so incompatible with segregation that segregation was unconstitutional. Justice David Brewer did not participate in the case.

Context

Although the Civil War ended just over thirty years before *Plessy v. Ferguson* was decided, the case was yet a result of the lingering conflict that existed after the war. During the decade following the Civil War, known as the Reconstruction era, America was a place of great change with respect to race relations. During the five years follow-

ing the end of the war, the Thirteenth, Fourteenth, and Fifteenth Amendments (collectively known as the Civil War or Reconstruction amendments) were passed. The Thirteenth Amendment outlawed slavery. The Fourteenth Amendment was passed after it became clear that the Thirteenth Amendment could not guarantee that individual states would grant the full equality that many had believed would result from the end of slavery. The Fifteenth Amendment, which stated that voting rights could not be abridged based on race, color, or previous condition of servitude, was ratified to guarantee political equality for African American men. Taken together, these amendments were designed to make African Americans (former slaves and free blacks) full and equal participants in American society. In addition, Congress passed a number of laws designed to protect the newly won civil rights of black citizens and allow the full enjoyment of equal citizenship. For example, Congress passed the Civil Rights Act of 1875, which required that black citizens be provided the same access to public accommodations, such as railroads, theaters, and inns, as white citizens.

Although race relations were hardly smooth after the Civil War, Congress made clear that equality under the law was to be the order of the day. However, the presidential election of 1876 changed the course of the country. Rutherford Hayes and Samuel Tilden ran a very close election that had to be decided in the House of Representatives. In exchange for support to become president, Hayes agreed to end the Reconstruction era in the South and withdraw the remaining federal troops there. The withdrawal of troops signaled the psychological end to Reconstruction and the coming of a Jim Crow society based on racial separation and racial caste.

Louisiana's story tracks that of the South, though New Orleans had always enjoyed more racial mixing than other parts of the South. For example, just after the end of the Civil War, Louisiana enacted its Black Code. However, in 1868 Louisiana ratified a state constitution that provided equal rights to African Americans. Around this time, Louisiana also desegregated its schools. As with the rest of the South, however, the end of Reconstruction triggered the arrival of Jim Crow laws. Both Louisiana and New Orleans slid toward state-mandated segregation.

Time Line

1875

■ **March 1**
The Civil Rights Act of 1875 is passed, barring racial discrimination in public accommodations, including public conveyances.

1877

■ The Compromise of 1877 allows Rutherford B. Hayes to become president on the condition that Hayes remove remaining federal troops from the South.

1880s

■ Some southern states begin to require segregated railroad cars.

1883

■ **October 16**
The Supreme Court decides that the Civil Rights Cases deeming the Civil Rights Act of 1875 unconstitutional are outside congressional scope of power.

1890s

■ Some southern states revise constitutions in large part to disenfranchise African Americans and limit other civil rights.

1890

■ The Supreme Court decides *Louisville, New Orleans & Texas Railway Co. v. Mississippi*, which denies interstate commerce–based challenge to Mississippi's Separate Car Act.

■ **July 10**
Louisiana passes the Separate Car Act, which Plessy eventually challenges.

1892

■ **June 7**
Homer Plessy is arrested after boarding a train and refusing to sit in the car assigned for colored people.

1893

■ The Panic of 1893 triggers an economic depression in the United States.

The segregationists consolidated power through the 1870s and the 1880s. In the 1880s many southern states began to pass laws requiring the segregation of railroad cars. In 1890 Louisiana joined those states in passing the Separate Car Act of 1890. As a result of the legislation, a number of African Americans created the Citizens' Committee to Test the Constitutionality of the Separate Car Act to challenge the law and to attempt to protect the gains won for African Americans during the Reconstruction era. Homer Plessy's case was a test case designed specifically to challenge the Separate Car Act and the coming of the Jim Crow laws. The case had the potential to either stem the tide of racial separatism or drive a nail in the coffin of racial equality and reconciliation.

About the Author

Justice Henry Billings Brown wrote the majority opinion in *Plessy v. Ferguson*. Brown was born on March 2, 1836, in South Lee, Massachusetts. After graduating from Yale College, he studied law at Yale Law School and Harvard Law School. He served as a U.S. deputy marshal, assistant U.S. attorney, and federal judge of the Eastern District of Michigan for fifteen years before being confirmed to the U.S. Supreme Court in 1890. He retired from the Court in 1906 and died on September 4, 1913.

Justice John Marshall Harlan wrote the sole dissenting opinion in *Plessy v. Ferguson*. Harlan was born on June 1, 1833, in Boyle County, Kentucky. After graduating from Centre College, he studied law at Transylvania University. Although he was a former slaveholder, Harlan fought for the Union Army in the Civil War. Harlan opposed abolition before the war and full equality for blacks just after the war. However, in the wake of the Civil War, Harlan joined the Republican Party and reversed his view of slavery and many racial equality issues. Harlan was confirmed to the Court on November 29, 1877. In addition to the *Plessy* dissent, he dissented in the Civil Rights Cases (1883), arguing that the Civil Rights Act of 1875 was constitutional and should have been held to legally require equal public accommodations for those of all races. Harlan served on the Court until his death on October 14, 1911.

Explanation and Analysis of the Document

◆ Statement of the Case

The case begins with a recitation of the facts of the case and its legal posture. On June 7, 1892, Plessy, the defendant also known as the plaintiff in error, paid for a first-class train ticket on the East Louisiana Railway headed from New Orleans to Covington, Louisiana, and sat down in an empty seat in the railroad car reserved for whites. He was "of seven-eighths Caucasian and one-eighth African blood" and had such a light complexion that one could not tell that he had any African ancestry. However, Plessy had already decided to challenge the law before boarding the train. Thus, after sitting down, Plessy informed the conductor that he was of mixed blood. He was told he had to move to the section for nonwhites or get off the train. Plessy was "forcibly ejected from said coach" and taken to jail after he refused to move.

Plessy was charged with violating an act of the Louisiana legislature commonly known as the Separate Car Act of 1890. In response to the charge, Plessy asserted that the act violated the U.S. Constitution. The Louisiana trial court disagreed and, according to the statement of the case as noted in the *Plessy* decision, stated that unless "the judge of the said court be enjoined by a writ of prohibition from further proceeding in such case, the court will proceed to fine and sentence petitioner to imprisonment." Plessy sought a writ of prohibition that would stop the court from enforcing the act. The Louisiana Supreme Court determined that the Separate Car Act was constitutional and denied the writ of prohibition. Consequently, Plessy "prayed for a writ of error from this court" and the case came to the United States Supreme Court.

◆ Majority Opinion of Justice Henry Billings Brown

Brown's opinion for the Court follows the recitation of facts. It begins by noting that the key issue is "the constitutionality of an act of the general assembly of the state of Louisiana, passed in 1890, providing for separate railway carriages for the white and colored races." The opinion then describes the content of the statute. The first section of the statute requires that railway companies other than street railroads provide "equal but separate accommodations for the white, and colored races," either by providing separate train cars or by erecting partitions in a single rail-car that separates the races. The second section of the statute requires that the companies segregate their passengers by race. Train conductors and other company employees were required to assign passengers to respective accommodations by race. Passengers who refused to go to their assigned accommodations and train employees who intentionally assigned passengers to the wrong accommodations were liable for a fine of $25 or up to twenty days in jail. A railway company could refuse to carry a passenger who refused to sit in his or her assigned car, and no damages would arise based on the refusal. The third section of the act provides penalties for employees of the railway company who refuse to comply with the act, but it excepts "nurses attending children of the other race." According to Brown, the fourth section of the act is immaterial.

The opinion repeats facts from the statement of the case: that Plessy was of seven-eighths Caucasian and one-eighth African blood, that one could not tell that he was part African by looking at him, that he sat down in a vacant seat in the coach assigned for whites, that he did not move when he was told to move, that he was removed from the train, and that he was taken to the parish jail. Brown notes that Plessy claims that the Separate Car Act is unconstitutional under both the Thirteenth and Fourteenth Amendments. Brown quickly addresses the Thirteenth Amendment claim and then spends the rest of the opinion addressing the Fourteenth Amendment claim.

Time Line

1895

■ **September 18**
Booker T. Washington gives his Atlanta Exposition Address, arguing for accommodation to segregation and urging focus on economic self-determination rather than on integration.

1896

■ **May 18**
Plessy v. Ferguson is decided.

1897

■ **January 11**
Plessy pleads guilty to violating the Separate Car Act and pays a $25 fine.

1898

■ Louisiana holds a constitutional convention that effectively disenfranchises its African American citizens.

1909

■ **February 12**
The National Association for the Advancement of Colored People is formed.

Brown explains that the Thirteenth Amendment addresses slavery and like conditions such as "Mexican peonage or the Chinese coolie trade." In addition, the amendment applies to attempts to place people into involuntary servitude or to place badges of slavery on former slaves. However, says Brown, the Thirteenth Amendment is not applicable to this case. The statute at issue makes a distinction between the races based on color but does not seek to "destroy the legal equality of the two races, or re-establish a state of involuntary servitude." Brown notes that in cases like this one where a law allows or requires discrimination, if any amendment will apply, it will be the Fourteenth, not the Thirteenth. This is because the Fourteenth Amendment was passed to address race-based distinctions that some believed effectively devalued the freedom given by the Thirteenth Amendment.

Brown begins his explanation of the applicability of the Fourteenth Amendment with an elucidation of its scope and limitations. He notes that the purpose of the amendment is "to establish the citizenship of the negro, to given definitions of citizenship of the United States and of the states, and to protect from the hostile legislation of the states the privileges and immunities of citizens of the United States, as distinguished from those of citizens of the states." Simply, the amendment provides equality of the races before the law. Equality before the law is not necessarily inconsistent with making race-based distinctions or even segregating the races, however. Brown notes that school segregation was allowed even in jurisdictions that scrupulously provided equal political rights between the races, citing Justice Lemuel Shaw's opinion in the 1849 case *Roberts v. City of Boston*. Although that case was decided before the Civil War and the passage of the Fourteenth Amendment and could not be deemed binding on any construction of the Fourteenth Amendment, Brown's point appears to be that there is a distinction between requiring equality before the law and requiring what he believes constituted social equality. In making his point, Brown previews an argument, which he would use later in the opinion, that enforced separation of the races does not suggest the inferiority of either race.

Brown argues that the Fourteenth Amendment is a limitation on states when political or civil equality is at stake, rather than a mandate to allow Congress to grant positive rights to support notions of equality. For example, the Fourteenth Amendment requires that blacks and whites be treated equally when civil rights such as the ability to serve on a jury are at issue. Conversely, when social equality issues are at stake, such as conditions of travel, the Fourteenth Amendment leaves those matters to the states to regulate so long as no other constitutional provisions are violated. For example, when Louisiana sought to regulate racial aspects of how passengers were to be treated when traveling through the state in interstate travel, it would have been able to do so had the law not been related to interstate commerce, the regulation of which is left to Congress under the Constitution. That the Fourteenth Amendment generally leaves state prerogatives to regulate intact was made clear when the Court passed on the Civil Rights Act of 1875 in the Civil Rights Cases. There, the Court indicated that the Fourteenth Amendment does not give Congress the power to pass legislation that provides positive rights in areas of state prerogative such as the public accommodation of the races with respect to private businesses. Simply, the Fourteenth Amendment does not provide positive rights; it merely limits the kind of legislation states can pass.

Brown then directly addresses the constitutionality of the Separate Car Act. Although the act forced segregation, Brown finds that it does not harm the rights of African Americans because it "neither abridges the privileges or immunities of the colored man, deprives him of his property without due process of law, nor denies him the equal protection of the laws, within the meaning of the fourteenth amendment." The act had the potential to harm the rights of whites, however. If, as Plessy argues in the claim, the reputation of being a white person in a mixed-race community is like property, the act may have gone too far in protecting a conductor who improperly assigns whites to the black car and therefore damages the property value of the white person. Brown notes that this problem is of no moment to Plessy's claim, because a black man like Plessy loses no property value in his reputation by being improperly categorized as a white person.

In response to the argument that allowing racial separation opens the door to allowing the state to create other arbi-

trary distinctions based on race, Brown answers that the exercise of the state's police power itself has to be reasonable. The question is whether the Separate Car Act is reasonable based on "the established usages, customs, and traditions of the people, and with a view to the promotion of their comfort, and the preservation of the public peace and good order." Based on that standard, it is unclear that the segregation here is any worse than school segregation that, according to Brown, most courts appear to agree is constitutional.

After determining that the act is constitutional, Brown attempts to explain why the rule itself treats the races equally. He reprises his argument that forced segregation does not suggest the inferiority of either race and states that any inferiority that black citizens may feel comes from the spin blacks give to the act and not from the act itself. Indeed, he suggests that if a majority-black legislature had passed the act, whites would not feel inferior to blacks. Oddly, Brown then explains that voluntary mingling between the races is acceptable, but forced mingling by the state is not required. Given that the statute at issue stops voluntary mingling, Brown's argument is somewhat nonsensical. Brown ends the argument by suggesting that formal civil and political equality is as far as the Constitution does and can go. If the races are social unequals, the Constitution cannot remedy that situation. Brown ends his opinion by noting that it is unclear how much African blood makes one black for purposes of segregation statutes, but he leaves that issue to the individual states to decide.

◆ Dissenting Opinion of Justice John Marshall Harlan

Harlan begins by highlighting a few of the statute's salient points. He notes that the statute requires strict separation of the races with the exception of a nurse caring for a child of a different race. Indeed, a personal attendant could not attend to the needs of her employer if the attendant and employer were of different races unless the attendant wished to be held criminally liable. However, he notes, regardless of the fairness of the statute, the question for the Court is whether the statute's explicit regulation based on race is constitutional.

Harlan provides the general structure of his argument. The civil rights of all citizens are to be protected equally. Consequently, there is no reason for the government to consider the race of any person when regulating civil rights. When a government considers race when legislating regarding civil rights, not only does it improperly provide civil rights, it also improperly affects the liberty of all United States residents.

Harlan then indicates the purpose of the Reconstruction amendments The Reconstruction amendments provide a broad protection for the rights of all citizens. The Thirteenth Amendment abolishes slavery, "prevents the imposition of any burdens or disabilities that constitute badges of slavery or servitude," and "decreed universal civil freedom in this country." But the Thirteenth Amendment was not strong enough to fully protect the rights of former slaves. Consequently, the Fourteenth Amendment was ratified to ensure that the freedom provided by the Thirteenth

GEORGE SHIRAS, JR.

HORACE GRAY.

STEPHEN J. FIELD.

RUFUS W. PECKHAM.

CHIEF JUSTICE FULLER.

DAVID J. BREWER.

EDWARD D. WHITE.

HENRY B. BROWN.

JOHN M. HARLAN.

JUSTICES OF THE
United States Supreme Court.

Copyright 1896 by M.G.Steel.

A view of the Supreme Court justices in 1896 (Library of Congress)

Amendment could be fully exercised. By explicitly making African Americans citizens and by stopping states from regulating rights based on race, the Fourteenth Amendment "added greatly to the dignity and glory of American citizenship, and to the security of personal liberty." In combination, the Thirteenth and Fourteenth Amendments were supposed to guarantee that "all the civil rights that pertain to freedom and citizenship" would be protected. The Fifteenth Amendment, which states that the right to vote is not provided on the basis of race, color, or previous condition of servitude, was added to guarantee that all citizens could participate "in the political control of his country." As a group, the Reconstruction amendments were designed to guarantee that African Americans enjoyed the same rights as whites in the eyes of the law.

The Reconstruction amendments were meant to ensure that blacks and former slaves were to be equal with whites and would enjoy the same rights. Even though the Fourteenth Amendment does not give positive rights, it does stop state governments from treating blacks badly merely because of their skin color. Indeed, the Supreme Court has made clear that with respect to civil and political rights, "all citizens are equal before the law." In concrete terms, this means that blacks cannot, for example, be kept from serving on juries. Harlan notes that the Supreme Court had decided so in *Strauder v. West Virginia* (1880).

Harlan then begins his attack on the majority's opinion by noting that the statute is clearly designed to keep blacks away from whites and that anyone who claims otherwise is lacking in candor. Then, rather than focusing directly on the equality issue, he suggests that the statute imperils liberty interests. That is, if people of different races want to sit together on a train, they are not allowed to do so under the statute without breaking the law.

Harlan next suggests that allowing the law to stand could lead to ludicrous results, such as requiring that blacks use one side of the street and whites use the other side or requiring that blacks use one side of the courtroom and whites use the other side. Harlan's suggestion that blacks and whites might be segregated in the jury box is particularly biting, given that the Court had made clear in prior cases that blacks had a right to serve on integrated juries. How an integrated jury in a segregated jury box might work is anyone's guess.

Harlan then challenges the majority's notion that reasonableness is a ground on which to determine the constitutionality of a statute. He suggests that reasonableness is an issue for the legislature when passing a law. Constitutionality is an issue for the Court when reviewing legislation. It may be acceptable to consider reasonableness when determining how a statute will be interpreted consistent with legislative intent, but it is not acceptable to consider it when determining whether the legislature is allowed to pass a certain statute under the Constitution.

Harlan next begins a discussion that, through the years, would overtake the majority opinion in significance. First, he asserts that the Constitution is color-blind. Harlan, making his point in terms that are harsh to twenty-first-

century ears, notes that the white race is dominant in America and that it likely would continue to be so. However, he states that the dominance of the white race does not mean that there is a caste system in America. Indeed, he argues that notwithstanding the relative position of the races, individuals must be treated as equals under the law. He states that the most powerful has no greater rights than the least powerful has and that the Court does a disservice when it claims otherwise. Harlan suggests, in fact, that the Court's vision is so troubling and antithetical to equality that the *Plessy* decision would become as nettlesome as the *Dred Scott* decision.

The effect of the *Plessy* decision, so suggests Harlan, would be to encourage some to create a caste system that would be antithetical to the Reconstruction amendments. The decision is likely to cause great harm, given that blacks and whites need to learn to live together. Harlan suggests that laws like Louisiana's, which imply that blacks are "so inferior and degraded that they cannot be allowed to sit in public coaches occupied by white citizens," would elicit discord, distrust, and hate between the races.

Harlan then attacks the notion that the case is about social equality. The statute at issue relates to allowing people to sit in the same train car. Social equality is no more relevant to that issue than it is to the issue of having citizens of different races share the same street, share the same ballot box, or stand together at a political assembly. Indeed, Harlan notes, it is odd that one would raise the social equality issue in this context, given that the Chinese are considered so different from Americans that they are not allowed to become citizens. Although the Chinese cannot become citizens, they are allowed to ride in the same car as whites. Given that blacks are supposed to have equal rights as citizens, that they have fought in wars to preserve the Union, and that they have the right to share political control of the country, it is odd that they would not be allowed to share the same railway car with whites. In fact, Harlan argues, "the arbitrary separation of citizens, on the basis of race, while they are on a public highway, is a badge of servitude wholly inconsistent with the civil freedom and the equality before the law established by the constitution. It cannot be justified upon any legal grounds."

Harlan suggests that any harm that might come from having blacks and whites share railcars pales in comparison to the problems that will arise from denying civil rights by separating the races. If separation is appropriate, it is unclear why separation would not be appropriate when blacks are exercising rights that the Court agrees they must be allowed to exercise. He again suggests that, under the reasoning of *Plessy*, there would be nothing unconstitutional in a state forcing jury boxes to be partitioned on the basis of race.

As he moves toward the conclusion of the dissent, Harlan argues that the cases that Brown cites to support segregation are from a bygone, pre–Civil War era during which inequality and slavery ruled. Given the mind-set of those who passed the laws and the absence of the Reconstruction amendments, such cases are inapplicable to this situation and should be ignored. The question is not how to think

"We consider the underlying fallacy of the plaintiff's argument to consist in the assumption that the enforced separation of the two races stamps the colored race with a badge of inferiority. If this be so, it is not by reason of anything found in the act, but solely because the colored race chooses to put that construction upon it."

(Justice Henry Billings Brown, Majority Opinion)

"The argument also assumes that social prejudices may be overcome by legislation, and that equal rights cannot be secured to the negro except by an enforced commingling of the two races. We cannot accept that proposition. If the two races are to meet upon terms of social equality, it must be the result of natural affinities, a mutual appreciation of each other's merits, and a voluntary consent of individuals."

(Justice Henry Billings Brown, Majority Opinion)

"If the civil and political rights of both races be equal, one cannot be inferior to the other civilly or politically. If one race be inferior to the other socially, the constitution of the United States cannot put them upon the same plane."

(Justice Henry Billings Brown, Majority Opinion)

"The white race deems itself to be the dominant race in this country. And so it is, in prestige, in achievements, in education, in wealth, and in power. So, I doubt not, it will continue to be for all time.... But in view of the constitution, in the eye of the law, there is in this country no superior, dominant, ruling class of citizens.... Our constitution is color-blind, and neither knows nor tolerates classes among citizens."

(Justice John Marshall Harlan, Dissenting Opinion)

"In my opinion, the judgment this day rendered will, in time, prove to be quite as pernicious as the decision made by this tribunal in the Dred Scott Case."

(Justice John Marshall Harlan, Dissenting Opinion)

about rights in an era of admitted inequality, but what to do in an era when free blacks and former slaves are citizens and must be provided equal rights.

Harlan finishes by arguing that the law at issue is an affront to the liberty of all citizens and is inconsistent with the Constitution. He notes that if similar laws were passed by states and localities, trouble would ensue. Lastly, he indicates that if the right to provide rights unequally to citizens is allowed, black citizens who are full members in society would be placed "in a condition of legal inferiority." For the aforementioned reasons, Harlan notes, he is required to dissent.

Audience

Although the *Plessy* opinion was of particular use to Congress and the state legislatures that were beginning to impose the Jim Crow laws, the intended audience for the case was the country as a whole. Given that this was a decision of the Supreme Court, it is unclear that it should be taken as a call to action. Rather, it can be taken as an exposition on the meaning of the United States Constitution that might have the effect of emboldening state legislatures or cowing Congress but probably not as a case that was intended to have that effect.

Impact

The effect of *Plessy v. Ferguson* on the first half of the twentieth century cannot be overstated. Although the *Plessy* Court was not the first Court to provide a cramped reading of the Fourteenth Amendment, the context in which the reading occurred was important. Before *Plessy*, the Supreme Court decided that the Reconstruction amendments could not be used to allow Congress to provide many positive rights to African Americans, notwithstanding the enforcement power provided to Congress in Section 5 of the amendment. However, *Plessy* limited the use of the Reconstruction amendments by the courts to block state legislation that provided unequal rights to African Americans. Given the Fourteenth Amendment's equal protection clause, the blocking function was arguably the narrowest and most essential function the Reconstruction amendments could have had. Without the Reconstruction amendments being broadly available to stop attempts to limit participation of African Americans in as much of American life as possible, the proponents of Jim Crow laws had a largely open field. *Plessy* simply helped extend and legitimize the Jim Crow era, during which blacks would lose many of the gains made in the South since the end of the Civil War. It allowed for years of poor treatment of blacks at the hands of state legislatures rather than merely at the hands of private actors.

The separate but equal doctrine was the *Plessy* Court's lasting legacy. The doctrine was simple and effective. It provided segregationists with a simple tool and a constitu-

tional imprimatur to regulate out of existence many rights thought to be protected by the Fourteenth Amendment. That doctrine provided constitutional protection to those who sought to limit the equality of African Americans. Segregationists were not simply allowed to make black citizens somewhat invisible through segregation; they were also emboldened to push the envelope of disenfranchisement and inequality as far as possible, knowing that the Supreme Court likely would not act to protect the equality of African Americans. Indeed, a number of southern states, including Louisiana, reworked their constitutions in the late nineteenth century to implicitly or explicitly take rights away from African Americans. Although some of these attempts predated *Plessy*, the results of some of those actions were effectively immunized by *Plessy*. *Plessy* simply made a caste system legally enforceable under a Constitution that guaranteed due process and equal protection.

Plessy was not a radical decision that took the country in a shockingly new direction. However, it did confirm a type of legislation that had been of questionable constitutionality in light of the Fourteenth Amendment. At the time of its passage, *Plessy* was not overly controversial to any of the justices save Harlan and possibly Brewer, who took no part in the decision. Indeed, the decision was not a widely cited constitutional case at its time or for a number of ensuing decades. Until the notion of separate but equal was challenged through cases brought by the National Association for the Advancement of Colored People and others, *Plessy* was standard constitutional law fare.

Over time, the majority opinion in *Plessy* fell out of favor, though many held on to the notion that separate but equal was a reasonable goal. The doctrine was the touchstone for segregationists for years. Segregationists, however, tended to adhere to the separate part of the doctrine but not the equal part. The claims of separate but equal facilities rang hollow when various groups documented the separate and unequal conditions that tended to exist in the South. The arguments eventually became too strong for the doctrine to resist. The doctrine was discarded in a string of Supreme Court cases throughout the middle part of the twentieth century, including *Brown v. Board of Education of Topeka*.

The eventual discarding of the majority opinion means that Harlan's dissent is far more well known and arguably more important than the majority opinion is today. The dissent not only predicted the racial discord that would follow *Plessy*; it also gave us the notion of a color-blind Constitution. The phrase *color-blind Constitution* was a slogan used to argue for an end to segregation and other racist laws. However, it has been used recently by some to argue that affirmative action and other race-conscious laws and remedies are inconsistent with constitutional doctrine. That battle continues to rage and is unlikely to be resolved any time soon.

Related Documents

Brown v. Board of Education, 347 U.S. 483 (1954). This is the case that determined that the separate but equal doctrine could not be applied to public schools. This case is most closely associated with the repudiation of *Plessy v. Ferguson*.

Civil Rights Cases, 109 U.S. 3 (1883). This set of five cases helped usher in the Jim Crow era by limiting the methods Congress could use to ensure equal rights. The case specifically deemed unconstitutional the Civil Rights Act of 1875 and its provisions regarding equal public accommodations for African Americans with respect to railroads, theaters, and hotels.

"Louisiana Constitution of 1898." In *Constitution of the State of Louisiana: Adopted in Convention at the City of New Orleans, May 12, 1898*. New Orleans, La.: H. J. Hearsey, 1898. This constitution was Louisiana's first constitution after *Plessy*. It was a thinly veiled attempt to disenfranchise blacks and guarantee the voting rights of most whites. It included the notorious grandfather clause, which allowed the sons and grandsons of those who could vote on January 1, 1867, to register to vote. This provision helped provide the ballot to whites who were otherwise ineligible to vote based on the provisions placed in the constitution to stop blacks from voting, such as the need to be able to read and write.

Bibliography

■ Books

Fireside, Harvey. *Separate and Unequal: Homer Plessy and the Supreme Court Decision That Legalized Racism*. New York: Carroll & Graf, 2004.

Klarman, Michael J. *From Jim Crow to Civil Rights: The Supreme Court and the Struggle for Racial Equality*. New York: Oxford University Press, 2004.

Lofgren, Charles A. *The Plessy Case: A Legal-Historical Interpretation*. New York: Oxford University Press, 1987.

Medley, Keith Weldon. *We as Freemen: Plessy v. Ferguson*. Gretna, La.: Pelican, 2003.

Meyer, Howard N. *The Amendment That Refused to Die: Equality and Justice Deferred, A History of the Fourteenth Amendment*. Lanham, Md.: Madison Books, 2000.

Patrick, John J. *The Young Oxford Companion to the Supreme Court of the United States*. New York: Oxford University Press, 1998.

Woodward, C. Vann. "The Case of the Louisiana Traveler." In *Quarrels That Have Shaped the Constitution* ed. John A. Garraty. New York: Harper & Row, 1987.

■ Web Sites

"*Plessy v. Ferguson*." Landmark Supreme Court Cases Web site. http://www.landmarkcases.org/plessy/home.html. Accessed on October 2, 2007.

—By Henry L. Chambers, Jr.

Questions for Further Study

1. Compare the majority opinions in *Plessy v. Ferguson* and *Dred Scott v. Sandford*. Many claim that both were riddled with factual and logical errors. However, taking the facts as the authors of the majority opinions claimed them to be, were either, both, or neither consistent with the Constitution as it was then written?

2. Compare *Plessy v. Ferguson* with *Brown v. Board of Education of Topeka*. Is the key distinction between them that the *Brown* Court took the harms of segregation seriously while the *Plessy* Court did not, or are there other distinctions that explain why the cases were decided so differently? How could each opinion have garnered such large majorities of the Court's justices? How could both cases be consistent with the Constitution?

3. Did *Plessy v. Ferguson* effectively gut the Reconstruction amendments in general or the Fourteenth Amendment in particular?

4. Should the legacy of Jim Crow laws be placed at Justice Brown's feet, as he was the writer of the *Plessy v. Ferguson* majority opinion?

5. What would a world governed by Harlan's dissent in *Plessy v. Ferguson* have looked like twenty years after the case was decided?

averring	asserting
chattel	property
coolie	manual laborer, usually of Chinese descent, who was brought to United States to help build railroads (now considered a racial slur)
damages	monies paid for harm caused
defendant in error	the party that is defending the lower court's ruling
demurrer	contention by the defendant that although the facts put forward by the plaintiff may be true, they do not entitle the plaintiff to prevail in the lawsuit.
due process	the appropriate procedures that are necessary to affect a person's right to life, liberty, or property
eminent domain	the right of a jurisdiction to take property for a public purpose if adequate compensation is paid
equal protection of the laws	the requirement that all persons be provided the same rights under the law and be granted equal treatment by the laws
immunity	exemption
information	a substitute for a grand jury indictment issued directly by a prosecutor
intermarriage	interracial marriage
liability	responsibility for causing harm
naturalized	made a citizen without being born a citizen
parish	in some regions, a political subdivision or county
peonage	a style of forced labor generally associated with Mexico
petitioner	the party filing for relief in court
plaintiff in error	the party that has appealed a lower court's ruling
prayed	asked
respondent	party defending against a suit
writ of error	an order of an appellate court requesting the records of a lower court so the appellate court can examine the record for mistakes that may affect the lower court's judgment
writ of prohibition	an order from a court directing a lower court to refrain from prosecuting a case

PLESSY V. FERGUSON

May 18, 1896.

This was a petition for writs of prohibition and certiorari originally filed in the supreme court of the state by Plessy, the plaintiff in error, against the Hon. John H. Ferguson, judge of the criminal district court for the parish of Orleans, and setting forth, in substance, the following facts:

That petitioner was a citizen of the United States and a resident of the state of Louisiana, of mixed descent, in the proportion of seven-eighths Caucasian and one-eighth African blood; that the mixture of colored blood was not discernible in him, and that he was entitled to every recognition, right, privilege, and immunity secured to the citizens of the United States of the white race by its constitution and laws; that on June 7, 1892, he engaged and paid for a first-class passage on the East Louisiana Railway, from New Orleans to Covington, in the same state, and thereupon entered a passenger train, and took possession of a vacant seat in a coach where passengers of the white race were accommodated; that such railroad company was incorporated by the laws of Louisiana as a common carrier, and was not authorized to distinguish between citizens according to their race, but, notwithstanding this, petitioner was required by the conductor, under penalty of ejection from said train and imprisonment, to vacate said coach, and occupy another seat, in a coach assigned by said company for persons not of the white race, and for no other reason than that petitioner was of the colored race; that, upon petitioner's refusal to comply with such order, he was, with the aid of a police officer, forcibly ejected from said coach, and hurried off to, and imprisoned in, the parish jail of New Orleans, and there held to answer a charge made by such officer to the effect that he was guilty of having criminally violated an act of the general assembly of the state, approved July 10, 1890, in such case made and provided.

The petitioner was subsequently brought before the recorder of the city for preliminary examination,

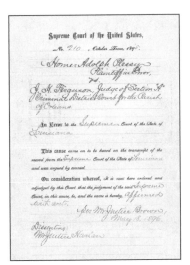

and committed for trial to the criminal district court for the parish of Orleans, where an information was filed against him in the matter above set forth, for a violation of the above act, which act the petitioner affirmed to be null and void, because in conflict with the constitution of the United States; that petitioner interposed a plea to such information, based upon the unconstitutionality of the act of the general assembly, to which the district attorney, on behalf of the state, filed a demurrer; that, upon issue being joined upon such demurrer and plea, the court sustained the demurrer, overruled the plea, and ordered petitioner to plead over to the facts set forth in the information, and that, unless the judge of the said court be enjoined by a writ of prohibition from further proceeding in such case, the court will proceed to fine and sentence petitioner to imprisonment, and thus deprive him of his constitutional rights set forth in his said plea, notwithstanding the unconstitutionality of the act under which he was being prosecuted; that no appeal lay from such sentence, and petitioner was without relief or remedy except by writs of prohibition and certiorari. Copies of the information and other proceedings in the criminal district court were annexed to the petition as an exhibit.

Upon the filing of this petition, an order was issued upon the respondent to show cause why a writ of prohibition should not issue, and be made perpetual, and a further order that the record of the proceedings had in the criminal cause be certified and transmitted to the supreme court.

To this order the respondent made answer, transmitting a certified copy of the proceedings, asserting the constitutionality of the law, and averring that, instead of pleading or admitting that he belonged to the colored race, the said Plessy declined and refused, either by pleading or otherwise, to admit that he was in any sense or in any proportion a colored man.

The case coming on for hearing before the supreme court, that court was of opinion that the law under which the prosecution was had was constitutional and denied the relief prayed for by the petitioner (Ex parte Plessy, 45 La. Ann. 80, 11 South. 948); whereupon petitioner prayed for a writ of error from this court, which was allowed by the chief justice of the supreme court of Louisiana.

Mr. Justice Harlan dissenting.

A. W. Tourgee and S. F. Phillips, for plaintiff in error.

Alex. Porter Morse, for defendant in error.

◆ Mr. Justice Brown, after Stating the Facts in the Foregoing Language, Delivered the Opinion of the Court.

This case turns upon the constitutionality of an act of the general assembly of the state of Louisiana, passed in 1890, providing for separate railway carriages for the white and colored races. Acts 1890, No. 111, p. 152.

The first section of the statute enacts "that all railway companies carrying passengers in their coaches in this state, shall provide equal but separate accommodations for the white, and colored races, by providing two or more passenger coaches for each passenger train, or by dividing the passenger coaches by a partition so as to secure separate accommodations: provided, that this section shall not be construed to apply to street railroads. No person or persons shall be permitted to occupy seats in coaches, other than the ones assigned to them, on account of the race they belong to."

By the second section it was enacted "that the officers of such passenger trains shall have power and are hereby required to assign each passenger to the coach or compartment used for the race to which such passenger belongs; any passenger insisting on going into a coach or compartment to which by race he does not belong, shall be liable to a fine of twenty-five dollars, or in lieu thereof to imprisonment for a period of not more than twenty days in the parish prison, and any officer of any railroad insisting on assigning a passenger to a coach or compartment other than the one set aside for the race to which said passenger belongs, shall be liable to a fine of twenty-five dollars, or in lieu thereof to imprisonment for a period of not more than twenty days in the parish prison; and should any passenger refuse to occupy the coach or compartment to which he or she is assigned by the officer of such railway, said officer shall have power to refuse to carry such passenger on his train, and for such refusal neither he nor the railway company which he represents shall be liable for damages in any of the courts of this state."

The third section provides penalties for the refusal or neglect of the officers, directors, conductors, and employees of railway companies to comply with the act, with a proviso that "nothing in this act shall be construed as applying to nurses attending children of the other race." The fourth section is immaterial.

The information filed in the criminal district court charged, in substance, that Plessy, being a passenger between two stations within the state of Louisiana, was assigned by officers of the company to the coach used for the race to which he belonged, but he insisted upon going into a coach used by the race to which he did not belong. Neither in the information nor plea was his particular race or color averred.

The petition for the writ of prohibition averred that petitioner was seven-eights Caucasian and one-eighth African blood; that the mixture of colored blood was not discernible in him; and that he was entitled to every right, privilege, and immunity secured to citizens of the United States of the white race; and that, upon such theory, he took possession of a vacant seat in a coach where passengers of the white race were accommodated, and was ordered by the conductor to vacate said coach, and take a seat in another, assigned to persons of the colored race, and, having refused to comply with such demand, he was forcibly ejected, with the aid of a police officer, and imprisoned in the parish jail to answer a charge of having violated the above act.

The constitutionality of this act is attacked upon the ground that it conflicts both with the thirteenth amendment of the constitution, abolishing slavery, and the fourteenth amendment, which prohibits certain restrictive legislation on the part of the states.

1. That it does not conflict with the thirteenth amendment, which abolished slavery and involuntary servitude, except a punishment for crime, is too clear for argument. Slavery implies involuntary servitude, a state of bondage; the ownership of mankind as a chattel, or, at least, the control of the labor and services of one man for the benefit of another, and the absence of a legal right to the disposal of his own person, property, and services. This amendment was said in the Slaughter-House Cases, 16 Wall. 36, to have been intended primarily to abolish slavery, as it had been previously known in this country, and that it equally forbade Mexican peonage or the Chinese coolie trade, when they amounted to slavery or involuntary servitude, and that the use of the word "servitude" was intended to prohibit the use of all forms of involuntary slavery, of whatever class or name. It was intimated, however, in that case, that this amendment was regarded by the statesmen of that day as insufficient to protect the colored race from certain laws which had been enacted in the Southern states, imposing upon the colored race onerous disabilities and burdens, and curtailing their rights in the pursuit of life, liberty, and property to such an extent that their freedom was of little value; and that the fourteenth amendment was devised to meet this exigency.

So, too, in the Civil Rights Cases, 109 U.S. 3, 3 Sup. Ct. 18, it was said that the act of a mere individual, the owner of an inn, a public conveyance or place of amusement, refusing accommodations to colored people, cannot be justly regarded as imposing any badge of slavery or servitude upon the applicant, but only as involving an ordinary civil injury, properly cognizable by the laws of the state, and presumably subject to redress by those laws until the contrary appears. "It would be running the slavery question into the ground," said Mr. Justice Bradley, "to make it apply to every act of discrimination which a person may see fit to make as to the guests he will entertain, or as to the people he will take into his coach or cab or car, or admit to his concert or theater, or deal with in other matters of intercourse or business."

A statute which implies merely a legal distinction between the white and colored races—a distinction which is founded in the color of the two races, and which must always exist so long as white men are distinguished from the other race by color—has no tendency to destroy the legal equality of the two races, or re-establish a state of involuntary servitude. Indeed, we do not understand that the thirteenth amendment is strenuously relied upon by the plaintiff in error in this connection.

2. By the fourteenth amendment, all persons born or naturalized in the United States, and subject to the jurisdiction thereof, are made citizens of the United States and of the state wherein they reside; and the states are forbidden from making or enforcing any law which shall abridge the privileges or immunities of citizens of the United States, or shall deprive any person of life, liberty, or property without due process of law, or deny to any person within their jurisdiction the equal protection of the laws.

The proper construction of this amendment was first called to the attention of this court in the Slaughter-House Cases, 16 Wall. 36, which involved, however, not a question of race, but one of exclusive privileges. The case did not call for any expression of opinion as to the exact rights it was intended to secure to the colored race, but it was said generally that its main purpose was to establish the citizenship of the negro, to give definitions of citizenship of the United States and of the states, and to protect from the hostile legislation of the states the privileges and immunities of citizens of the United States, as distinguished from those of citizens of the states. The object of the amendment was undoubtedly to enforce the absolute equality of the two races before the law, but, in the nature of things, it could not have been intended to abolish distinctions based upon color, or to enforce social, as distinguished from political, equality, or a commingling of the two races upon terms unsatisfactory to either. Laws permitting, and even requiring, their separation, in places where they are liable to be brought into contact, do not necessarily imply the inferiority of either race to the other, and have been generally, if not universally, recognized as within the competency of the state legislatures in the exercise of their police power. The most common instance of this is connected with the establishment of separate schools for white and colored children, which have been held to be a valid exercise of the legislative power even by courts of states where the political rights of the colored race have been longest and most earnestly enforced.

One of the earliest of these cases is that of *Roberts v. City of Boston*, 5 Cush. 198, in which the supreme judicial court of Massachusetts held that the general school committee of Boston had power to make provision for the instruction of colored children in separate schools established exclusively for them, and to prohibit their attendance upon the other schools. "The great principle," said Chief Justice Shaw, "advanced by the learned and eloquent advocate for the plaintiff [Mr. Charles Sumner], is that, by the constitution and laws of Massachusetts, all persons, without distinction of age or sex, birth or color, origin or condition, are equal before the law.... But, when this great principle comes to be applied to the actual and various conditions of persons in society, it will not warrant the assertion that men and women are legally clothed with the same civil and political powers, and that children and adults are legally to have the same functions and be subject to the same treatment; but only that the rights of all, as they are settled and regulated by law, are equally entitled to the paternal consideration and protection of the law for their maintenance and security." It was held that the powers of the committee extended to the establishment of separate schools for children of different ages, sexes and colors, and that they might also establish special schools for poor and neglected children, who have become too old to attend the primary school, and yet have not acquired the rudiments of learning, to enable them to enter the ordinary schools. Similar laws have been enacted by congress under its general power of legislation over the District of Columbia (sections 281–283, 310, 319, Rev. St. D. C.), as well as by the legislatures of many of the states, and have been generally, if not uniformly, sustained by the courts. *State v. McCann*, 21 Ohio St. 210; *Lehew v. Brummell* (Mo. Sup.) 15 S. W. 765; *Ward v. Flood*, 48 Cal. 36; *Bertonneau v. Directors of City Schools*, 3 Woods, 177, Fed. Cas. No. 1,361; *People v. Gallagher*, 93 N. Y. 438; *Cory v. Carter*, 48 Ind. 337; *Dawson v. Lee*, 83 Ky. 49.

Laws forbidding the intermarriage of the two races may be said in a technical sense to interfere with the freedom of contract, and yet have been universally recognized as within the police power of the state. *State v. Gibson*, 36 Ind. 389.

The distinction between laws interfering with the political equality of the negro and those requiring the separation of the two races in schools, theaters, and railway carriages has been frequently drawn by this court. Thus, in *Strauder v. West Virginia*, 100 U.S. 303, it was held that a law of West Virginia limiting to white male persons 21 years of age, and citizens of the state, the right to sit upon juries, was a discrimination which implied a legal inferiority in civil society, which lessened the security of the right of the colored race, and was a step towards reducing them to a condition of servility. Indeed, the right of a colored man that, in the selection of jurors to pass upon his life, liberty, and property, there shall be no exclusion of his race, and no discrimination against them because of color, has been asserted in a number of cases. *Virginia v. Rivers*, 100 U.S. 313; *Neal v. Delaware*, 103 U.S. 370; *Bush v. Com.*, 107 U.S. 110, 1 Sup. Ct. 625; *Gibson v. Mississippi*, 162 U.S. 565, 16 Sup. Ct. 904. So, where the laws of a particular locality or the charter of a particular railway corporation has provided that no person shall be excluded from the cars on account of color, we have held that this meant that persons of color should travel in the same car as white ones, and that the enactment was not satisfied by the company providing cars assigned exclusively to people of color, though they were as good as those which they assigned exclusively to white persons. *Railroad Co. v. Brown*, 17 Wall. 445.

Upon the other hand, where a statute of Louisiana required those engaged in the transportation of passengers among the states to give to all persons traveling within that state, upon vessels employed in that business, equal rights and privileges in all parts of the vessel, without distinction on account of race or color, and subjected to an action for damages the owner of such a vessel who excluded colored passengers on account of their color from the cabin set aside by him for the use of whites, it was held to be, so far as it applied to interstate commerce, unconstitutional and void. *Hall v. De Cuir*, 95 U.S. 485. The court in this case, however, expressly disclaimed that it had anything whatever to do with the statute as a regulation of internal commerce, or affecting anything else than commerce among the states.

In the Civil Rights Cases, 109 U.S. 3, 3 Sup. Ct. 18, it was held that an act of congress entitling all persons within the jurisdiction of the United States to the full and equal enjoyment of the accommodations, advantages, facilities, and privileges of inns, public conveyances, on land or water, theaters, and other places of public amusement, and made applicable to citizens of every race and color, regardless of any previous condition of servitude, was unconstitutional and void, upon the ground that the fourteenth amendment was prohibitory upon the states only, and the legislation authorized to be adopted by congress for enforcing it was not direct legislation on matters respecting which the states were prohibited from making or enforcing certain laws, or doing certain acts, but was corrective legislation, such as might be necessary or proper for counter-acting and redressing the effect of such laws or acts. In delivering the opinion of the court, Mr. Justice Bradley observed that the fourteenth amendment "does not invest congress with power to legislate upon subjects that are within the domain of state legislation, but to provide modes of relief against state legislation or state action of the kind referred to. It does not authorize congress to create a code of municipal law for the regulation of private rights, but to provide modes of redress against the operation of state laws, and the action of state officers, executive or judicial, when these are subversive of the fundamental rights specified in the amendment. Positive rights and privileges are undoubtedly secured by the fourteenth amendment; but they are secured by way of prohibition against state laws and state proceedings affecting those rights and privileges, and by power given to congress to legislate for the purpose of carrying such prohibition into effect; and such legislation must necessarily be predicated upon such supposed state laws or state proceedings, and be directed to the correction of their operation and effect."

Much nearer, and, indeed, almost directly in point, is the case of the Louisville, *N. O. & T. Ry. Co. v. State*, 133 U.S. 587, 10 Sup. Ct. 348, wherein the railway company was indicted for a violation of a statute of Mississippi, enacting that all railroads carrying passengers should provide equal, but separate, accommodations for the white and colored races, by providing two or more passenger cars for each passenger train, or by dividing the passenger cars by a partition, so as to secure separate accommodations. The case was presented in a different aspect from the one under consideration, inasmuch as it was an indictment against the railway company for failing to provide the separate accommodations, but the question considered was the constitutionality of the law. In that case, the supreme court of Mississippi (66 Miss. 662, 6 South. 203) had held that the statute applied solely to commerce within the state, and, that being the construction of the state statute by its highest court, was accepted as conclusive. "If it be a matter," said the court (page 591, 133 U. S., and page 348, 10 Sup. Ct.), "respecting commerce wholly within a state, and not interfering with commerce between the states, then, obviously, there is no violation of the commerce clause of the federal constitution. … No question arises under this section as to the power of the state to separate in different compartments interstate passengers, or affect, in any manner, the privileges and rights of such passengers. All that we can consider is whether the state has the power to require that railroad trains within her limits shall have separate accommodations for the two races. That affecting only commerce within the state is no invasion of the power given to congress by the commerce clause."

A like course of reasoning applies to the case under consideration, since the supreme court of Louisiana, in the case of *State v. Judge*, 44 La. Ann. 770, 11 South. 74, held that the statute in question did not apply to interstate passengers, but was confined in its application to passengers traveling exclusively within the borders of the state. The case was decided largely upon the authority of Louisville, *N. O. & T. Ry. Co. v. State*, 66 Miss. 662, 6 South, 203, and affirmed by this court in 133 U.S. 587, 10 Sup. Ct. 348. In the present case no question of interference with interstate commerce can possibly arise, since the East Louisiana Railway appears to have been purely a local line, with both its termini within the state of Louisiana. Similar statutes for the separation of the two races upon public conveyances were held to be constitutional in *Railroad v. Miles*, 55 Pa. St. 209; *Day v. Owen* 5 Mich. 520; *Railway Co. v.*

Williams, 55 Ill. 185; *Railroad Co. v. Wells*, 85 Tenn. 613; 4 S. W. 5; *Railroad Co. v. Benson*, 85 Tenn. 627, 4 S. W. 5; The Sue, 22 Fed. 843; *Logwood v. Railroad Co.*, 23 Fed. 318; *McGuinn v. Forbes*, 37 Fed. 639; *People v. King* (N. Y. App.) 18 N. E. 245; *Houck v. Railway Co.*, 38 Fed. 226; *Heard v. Railroad Co.*, 3 Inter St. Commerce Com. R. 111, 1 Inter St. Commerce Com. R. 428.

While we think the enforced separation of the races, as applied to the internal commerce of the state, neither abridges the privileges or immunities of the colored man, deprives him of his property without due process of law, nor denies him the equal protection of the laws, within the meaning of the fourteenth amendment, we are not prepared to say that the conductor, in assigning passengers to the coaches according to their race, does not act at his peril, or that the provision of the second section of the act that denies to the passenger compensation in damages for a refusal to receive him into the coach in which he properly belongs is a valid exercise of the legislative power. Indeed, we understand it to be conceded by the state's attorney that such part of the act as exempts from liability the railway company and its officers is unconstitutional. The power to assign to a particular coach obviously implies the power to determine to which race the passenger belongs, as well as the power to determine who, under the laws of the particular state, is to be deemed a white, and who a colored, person. This question, though indicated in the brief of the plaintiff in error, does not properly arise upon the record in this case, since the only issue made is as to the unconstitutionality of the act, so far as it requires the railway to provide separate accommodations, and the conductor to assign passengers according to their race.

It is claimed by the plaintiff in error that, in an mixed community, the reputation of belonging to the dominant race, in this instance the white race, is "property," in the same sense that a right of action or of inheritance is property. Conceding this to be so, for the purposes of this case, we are unable to see how this statute deprives him of, or in any way affects his right to, such property. If he be a white man, and assigned to a colored coach, he may have his action for damages against the company for being deprived of his so-called "property." Upon the other hand, if he be a colored man, and be so assigned, he has been deprived of no property, since he is not lawfully entitled to the reputation of being a white man.

In this connection, it is also suggested by the learned counsel for the plaintiff in error that the same argument that will justify the state legislature in requiring railways to provide separate accommodations for the two races will also authorize them to require separate cars to be provided for people whose hair is of a certain color, or who are aliens, or who belong to certain nationalities, or to enact laws requiring colored people to walk upon one side of the street, and white people upon the other, or requiring white men's houses to be painted white, and colored men's black, or their vehicles or business signs to be of different colors, upon the theory that one side of the street is as good as the other, or that a house or vehicle of one color is as good as one of another color. The reply to all this is that every exercise of the police power must be reasonable, and extend only to such laws as are enacted in good faith for the promotion of the public good, and not for the annoyance or oppression of a particular class. Thus, in *Yick Wo v. Hopkins*, 118 U.S. 356, 6 Sup. Ct. 1064, it was held by this court that a municipal ordinance of the city of San Francisco, to regulate the carrying on of public laundries within the limits of the municipality, violated the provisions of the constitution of the United States, if it conferred upon the municipal authorities arbitrary power, at their own will, and without regard to discretion, in the legal sense of the term, to give or withhold consent as to persons or places, without regard to the competency of the persons applying or the propriety of the places selected for the carrying on of the business. It was held to be a covert attempt on the part of the municipality to make an arbitrary and unjust discrimination against the Chinese race. While this was the case of a municipal ordinance, a like principle has been held to apply to acts of a state legislature passed in the exercise of the police power. *Railroad Co. v. Husen*, 95 U.S. 465; *Louisville & N. R. Co. v. Kentucky*, 161 U.S. 677, 16 Sup. Ct. 714, and cases cited on page 700, 161 U. S., and page 714, 16 Sup. Ct.; *Daggett v. Hudson*, 43 Ohio St. 548, 3 N. E. 538; *Capen v. Foster*, 12 Pick. 485; *State v. Baker*, 38 Wis. 71; *Monroe v. Collins*, 17 Ohio St. 665; *Hulseman v. Rems*, 41 Pa. St. 396; *Osman v. Riley*, 15 Cal. 48.

So far, then, as a conflict with the fourteenth amendment is concerned, the case reduces itself to the question whether the statute of Louisiana is a reasonable regulation, and with respect to this there must necessarily be a large discretion on the part of the legislature. In determining the question of reasonableness, it is at liberty to act with reference to the established usages, customs, and traditions of the people, and with a view to the promotion of their comfort, and the preservation of the public peace and good order. Gauged by this standard, we cannot say that a law which authorizes or even requires the separation of the two races in public conveyances is unreasonable, or more obnoxious to the fourteenth amendment than the acts of congress requiring separate schools for colored children in the District of Columbia, the constitutionality of which does not seem to have been questioned, or the corresponding acts of state legislatures.

We consider the underlying fallacy of the plaintiff's argument to consist in the assumption that the enforced separation of the two races stamps the colored race with a badge of inferiority. If this be so, it is not by reason of anything found in the act, but solely because the colored race chooses to put that construction upon it. The argument necessarily assumes that if, as has been more than once the case, and is not unlikely to be so again, the colored race should become the dominant power in the state legislature, and should enact a law in precisely similar terms, it would thereby relegate the white race to an inferior position. We imagine that the white race, at least, would not acquiesce in this assumption. The argument also assumes that social prejudices may be overcome by legislation, and that equal rights cannot be secured to the negro except by an enforced commingling of the two races. We cannot accept this proposition. If the two races are to meet upon terms of social equality, it must be the result of natural affinities, a mutual appreciation of each other's merits, and a voluntary consent of individuals. As was said by the court of appeals of New York in *People v. Gallagher*, 93 N. Y. 438, 448: "This end can neither be accomplished nor promoted by laws which conflict with the general sentiment of the community upon whom they are designed to operate. When the government, therefore, has secured to each of its citizens equal rights before the law, and equal opportunities for improvement and progress, it has accomplished the end for which it was organized, and performed all of the functions respecting social advantages with which it is endowed." Legislation is powerless to eradicate racial instincts, or to abolish distinctions based upon physical differences, and the attempt to do so can only result in accentuating the difficulties of the present situation. If the civil and political rights of both races be equal, one cannot be inferior to the other civilly or politically. If one race be inferior to the other socially, the constitution of the United States cannot put them upon the same plane.

It is true that the question of the proportion of colored blood necessary to constitute a colored person, as distinguished from a white person, is one upon which there is a difference of opinion in the different states; some holding that any visible admixture of black blood stamps the person as belonging to the colored race (*State v. Chavers*, 5 Jones [N. C.] 1); others, that it depends upon the preponderance of blood (*Gray v. State*, 4 Ohio, 354; *Monroe v. Collins*, 17 Ohio St. 665); and still others, that the predominance of white blood must only be in the proportion of three-fourths (*People v. Dean*, 14 Mich. 406; *Jones v. Com.*, 80 Va. 544). But these are questions to be determined under the laws of each state, and are not properly put in issue in this case. Under the allegations of his petition, it may undoubtedly become a question of importance whether, under the laws of Louisiana, the petitioner belongs to the white or colored race.

The judgment of the court below is therefore affirmed.

Mr. Justice BREWER did not hear the argument or participate in the decision of this case.

◆ Mr. Justice Harlan Dissenting.

By the Louisiana statute the validity of which is here involved, all railway companies (other than street-railroad companies) carry passengers in that state are required to have separate but equal accommodations for white and colored persons, "by providing two or more passenger coaches for each passenger train, or by dividing the passenger coaches by a partition so as to secure separate accommodations." Under this statute, no colored person is permitted to occupy a seat in a coach assigned to white persons; nor any white person to occupy a seat in a coach assigned to colored persons. The managers of the railroad are not allowed to exercise any discretion in the premises, but are required to assign each passenger to some coach or compartment set apart for the exclusive use of is race. If a passenger insists upon going into a coach or compartment not set apart for persons of his race, he is subject to be fined, or to be imprisoned in the parish jail. Penalties are prescribed for the refusal or neglect of the officers, directors, conductors, and employees of railroad companies to comply with the provisions of the act.

Only "nurses attending children of the other race" are excepted from the operation of the statute. No exception is made of colored attendants traveling with adults. A white man is not permitted to have his colored servant with him in the same coach, even if his condition of health requires the constant personal assistance of such servant. If a colored maid insists upon riding in the same coach with a white woman whom she has been employed to serve, and who may need her personal attention while traveling, she is subject to be fined or imprisoned for such an exhibition of zeal in the discharge of duty.

While there may be in Louisiana persons of different races who are not citizens of the United States, the words in the act "white and colored races" necessarily include all citizens of the United States of both races residing in that state. So that we have before us a state enactment that compels, under penalties, the separation of the two races in railroad passenger coaches, and makes it a crime for a citizen of either race to enter a coach that has been assigned to citizens of the other race.

Thus, the state regulates the use of a public highway by citizens of the United States solely upon the basis of race.

However apparent the injustice of such legislation may be, we have only to consider whether it is consistent with the constitution of the United States.

That a railroad is a public highway, and that the corporation which owns or operates it is in the exercise of public functions, is not, at this day, to be disputed. Mr. Justice Nelson, speaking for this court in *New Jersey Steam Nav. Co. v. Merchants' Bank*, 6 How. 344, 382, said that a common carrier was in the exercise "of a sort of public office, and has public duties to perform, from which he should not be permitted to exonerate himself without the assent of the parties concerned." Mr. Justice Strong, delivering the judgment of this court in *Olcott v. Supervisors*, 16 Wall. 678, 694, said: "That railroads, though constructed by private corporations, and owned by them, are public highways, has been the doctrine of nearly all the courts ever since such conveniences for passage and transportation have had any existence. Very early the question arose whether a state's right of eminent domain could be exercised by a private corporation created for the purpose of constructing a railroad. Clearly, it could not, unless taking land for such a purpose by such an agency is taking land for public use. The right of eminent domain nowhere justifies taking property for a private use. Yet it is a doctrine universally accepted that a state legislature may authorize a private corporation to take land for the construction of such a road, making compensation to the owner. What else does this doctrine mean if not that building a railroad, though it be built by a private corporation, is an act done for a public use?"

So, in *Township of Pine Grove v. Talcott*, 19 Wall. 666, 676: "Though the corporation [a railroad company] was private, its work was public, as much so as if it were to be constructed by the state." So, in *Inhabitants of Worcester v. Western R. Corp.*, 4 Metc. (Mass.) 564: "The establishment of that great thoroughfare is regarded as a public work, established by public authority, intended for the public use and benefit, the use of which is secured to the whole community, and constitutes, therefore, like a canal, turnpike, or highway, a public easement." "It is true that the real and personal property, necessary to the establishment and management of the railroad, is vested in the corporation; but it is in trust for the public."

In respect of civil rghts, common to all citizens, the constitution of the United States does not, I think, permit any public authority to know the race of those entitled to be protected in the enjoyment of such rights. Every true man has pride of race, and under appropriate circumstances, when the rights of others, his equals before the law, are not to be affected, it is his privilege to express such pride and to take such action based upon it as to him seems proper. But I deny that any legislative body or judicial tribunal may have regard to the race of citizens when the civil rights of those citizens are involved. Indeed, such legislation as that here in question is inconsistent not only with that equality of rights which pertains to citizenship, national and state, but with the personal liberty enjoyed by every one within the United States.

The thirteenth amendment does not permit the withholding or the deprivation of any right necessarily inhering in freedom. It not only struck down the institution of slavery as previously existing in the United States, but it prevents the imposition of any burdens or disabilities that constitute badges of slavery or servitude. It decreed universal civil freedom in this country. This court has so adjudged. But, that amendment having been found inadequate to the protection of the rights of those who had been in slavery, it was followed by the fourteenth amendment, which added greatly to the dignity and glory of American citizenship, and to the security of personal liberty, by declaring that "all persons born or naturalized in the United States, and subject to the jurisdiction thereof, are citizens of the United States and of the state wherein they reside," and that "no state shall make or enforce any law which shall abridge the privileges or immunities of citizens of the United States; nor shall any state deprive any person of life, liberty or property without due process of law, nor deny to any person within its jurisdiction the equal protection of the laws." These two amendments, if enforced according to their true intent and meaning, will protect all the civil rights that pertain to freedom and citizenship. Finally, and to the end that no citizen should be denied, on account of his race, the privilege of participating in the political control of his country, it was declared by the fifteenth amendment that "the right of citizens of the United States to vote shall not be denied or abridged by the United States or by any state on account of race, color or previous condition of servitude."

These notable additions to the fundamental law were welcomed by the friends of liberty throughout the world. They removed the race line from our governmental systems. They had, as this court has said, a common purpose, namely, to secure "to a race recently emancipated, a race that through many generations have been held in slavery, all the civil rights that the superior race enjoy." They declared, in legal effect, this court has further said, "that the law in the states shall be the same for the black as for the white; that all persons, whether colored or white, shall stand equal before the laws of the states; and in regard to the colored race, for whose protection the amendment was primarily designed, that no discrimination shall be made against them by law because of their color." We also said: "The words of the amendment, it is true, are prohibitory, but they contain a necessary implication of a positive immunity or right, most valuable to the colored race, the right to exemption from unfriendly legislation against them distinctively as colored; exemption from legal discriminations, implying inferiority in civil society, lessening the security of their enjoyment of the rights which others enjoy; and discriminations which are steps towards reducing them to the condition of a subject race." It was, consequently, adjudged that a state law that excluded citizens of the colored race from juries, because of their race, however well qualified in other respects to dischar e the duties of jurymen, was repugnant to the fourteenth amendment. *Strauder v. West Virginia*, 100 U.S. 303, 306, 307 S.; *Virginia v. Rives*, Id. 313; Ex parte Virginia, Id. 339; *Neal v. Delaware*, 103 U.S. 370, 386; *Bush v. Com.*, 107 U.S. 110, 116, 1 S. Sup. Ct. 625. At the present term, referring to the previous adjudications, this court declared that "underlying all of those decisions is the principle that the constitution of the United States, in its present form, forbids, so far as civil and political rights are concerned, discrimination by the general government or the states against any citizen because of his race. All citizens are equal before the law." *Gibson v. State*, 162 U.S. 565, 16 Sup. Ct. 904.

The decisions referred to show the scope of the recent amendments of the constitution. They also show that it is not within the power of a state to prohibit colored citizens, because of their race, from participating as jurors in the administration of justice.

It was said in argument that the statute of Louisiana does not discriminate against either race, but prescribes a rule applicable alike to white and colored citizens. But this argument does not meet the difficulty. Every one knows that the statute in question had its origin in the purpose, not so much to exclude white persons from railroad cars occupied by blacks, as to exclude colored people from coaches occupied by or assigned to white persons. Railroad corporations of Louisiana did not make discrimination among whites in the matter of commodation for travelers. The thing to accomplish was, under the guise of giving equal accommodation for whites and blacks, to compel the latter to keep to themselves while traveling in railroad passenger coaches. No one would be so wanting in candor as to assert the contrary. The fundamental objection, therefore, to the statute, is that it interferes with the personal freedom of citizens. "Personal liberty," it has been well said, "consists in the power of locomotion, of changing situation, or removing one's person to whatsoever places one's own inclination may direct, without imprisonment or restraint, unless by due course of law." 1 Bl. Comm. 134. If a white man and a black man choose to occupy the same public conveyance on a public highway, it is their right to do so; and no government, proceeding alone on grounds of race, can prevent it without infringing the personal liberty of each.

It is one thing for railroad carriers to furnish, or to be required by law to furnish, equal accommodations for all whom they are under a legal duty to carry. It is quite another thing for government to forbid citizens of the white and black races from traveling in the same public conveyance, and to punish officers of railroad companies for permitting persons of the two races to occupy the same passenger coach. If a state can prescribe, as a rule of civil conduct, that whites and blacks shall not travel as passengers in the same railroad coach, why may it not so regulate the use of the streets of its cities and towns as to compel white citizens to keep on one side of a street, and black citizens to keep on the other? Why may it not, upon like grounds, punish whites and blacks who ride together in street cars or in open vehicles on a public road or

street? Why may it not require sheriffs to assign whites to one side of a court room, and blacks to the other? And why may it not also prohibit the commingling of the two races in the galleries of legislative halls or in public assemblages convened for the consideration of the political questions of the day? Further, if this statute of Louisiana is consistent with the personal liberty of citizens, why may not the state require the separation in railroad coaches of native and naturalized citizens of the United States, or of Protestants and Roman Catholics?

The answer given at the argument to these questions was that regulations of the kind they suggest would be unreasonable, and could not, therefore, stand before the law. Is it meant that the determination of questions of legislative power depends upon the inquiry whether the statute whose validity is questioned is, in the judgment of the courts, a reasonable one, taking all the circumstances into consideration? A statute may be unreasonable merely because a sound public policy forbade its enactment. But I do not understand that the courts have anything to do with the policy or expediency of legislation. A statute may be valid, and yet, upon grounds of public policy, may well be characterized as unreasonable. Mr. Sedgwick correctly states the rule when he says that, the legislative intention being clearly ascertained, "the courts have no other duty to perform than to execute the legislative will, without any regard to their views as to the wisdom or justice of the particular enactment." Sedg. St. & Const. Law, 324. There is a dangerous tendency in these latter days to enlarge the functions of the courts, by means of judicial interference with the will of the people as expressed by the legislature. Our institutions have the distinguishing characteristic that the three departments of government are co-ordinate and separate. Each much keep within the limits defined by the constitution. And the courts best discharge their duty by executing the will of the law-making power, constitutionally expressed, leaving the results of legislation to be dealt with by the people through their representatives. Statutes must always have a reasonable construction. Sometimes they are to be construed strictly, sometimes literally, in order to carry out the legislative will. But, however construed, the intent of the legislature is to be respected if the particular statute in question is valid, although the courts, looking at the public interests, may conceive the statute to be both unreasonable and impolitic. If the power exists to enact a statute, that ends the matter so far as the courts are concerned. The adjudged cases in which statutes have been held to be void, because unreasonable, are those in which the means employed by the legislature were not at all germane to the end to which the legislature was competent.

The white race deems itself to be the dominant race in this country. And so it is, in prestige, in achievements, in education, in wealth, and in power. So, I doubt not, it will continue to be for all time, if it remains true to its great heritage, and holds fast to the principles of constitutional liberty. But in view of the constitution, in the eye of the law, there is in this country no superior, dominant, ruling class of citizens. There is no caste here. Our constitution is color-blind, and neither knows nor tolerates classes among citizens. In respect of civil rights, all citizens are equal before the law. The humblest is the peer of the most powerful. The law regards man as man, and takes no account of his surroundings or of his color when his civil rights as guarantied by the supreme law of the land are involved. It is therefore to be regretted that this high tribunal, the final expositor of the fundamental law of the land, has reached the conclusion that it is competent for a state to regulate the enjoyment by citizens of their civil rights solely upon the basis of race.

In my opinion, the judgment this day rendered will, in time, prove to be quite as pernicious as the decision made by this tribunal in the Dred Scott Case.

It was adjudged in that case that the descendants of Africans who were imported into this country, and sold as slaves, were not included nor intended to be included under the word "citizens" in the constitution, and could not claim any of the rights and privileges which that instrument provided for and secured to citizens of the United States; that, at time of the adoption of the constitution, they were "considered as a subordinate and inferior class of beings, who had been subjugated by the dominant race, and, whether emancipated or not, yet remained subject to their authority, and had no rights or privileges but such as those who held the power and the government might choose to grant them." 17 How. 393, 404. The recent amendments of the constitution, it was supposed, had eradicated these principles from our institutions. But it seems that we have yet, in some of the states, a dominant race—a superior class of citizens—which assumes to regulate the enjoyment of civil rights, common to all citizens, upon the basis of race. The present decision, it may well be apprehended, will not only stimulate aggressions, more or less brutal and irritating, upon the admitted rights of colored citizens, but will encourage the

belief that it is possible, by means of state enactments, to defeat the beneficent purposes which the people of the United States had in view when they adopted the recent amendments of the constitution, by one of which the blacks of this country were made citizens of the United States and of the states in which they respectively reside, and whose privileges and immunities, as citizens, the states are forbidden to abridge. Sixty millions of whites are in no danger from the presence here of eight millions of blacks. The destinies of the two races, in this country, are indissolubly linked together, and the interests of both require that the common government of all shall not permit the seeds of race hate to be planted under the sanction of law. What can more certainly arouse race hate, what more certainly create and perpetuate a feeling of distrust between these races, than state enactments which, in fact, proceed on the ground that colored citizens are so inferior and degraded that they cannot be allowed to sit in public coaches occupied by white citizens? That, as all will admit, is the real meaning of such legislation as was enacted in Louisiana.

The sure guaranty of the peace and security of each race is the clear, distinct, unconditional recognition by our governments, national and state, of every right that inheres in civil freedom, and of the equality before the law of all citizens of the United States, without regard to race. State enactments regulating the enjoyment of civil rights upon the basis of race, and cunningly devised to defeat legitimate results of the war, under the pretense of recognizing equality of rights, can have no other result than to render permanent peace impossible, and to keep alive a conflict of races, the continuance of which must do harm to all concerned. This question is not met by the suggestion that social equality cannot exist between the white and black races in this country. That argument, if it can be properly regarded as one, is scarcely worthy of consideration; for social equality no more exists between two races when traveling in a passenger coach or a public highway than when members of the same races sit by each other in a street car or in the jury box, or stand or sit with each other in a political assembly, or when they use in common the streets of a city or town, or when they are in the same room for the purpose of having their names placed on the registry of voters, or when they approach the ballot box in order to exercise the high privilege of voting.

There is a race so different from our own that we do not permit those belonging to it to become citizens of the United States. Persons belonging to it are, with few exceptions, absolutely excluded from our country. I allude to the Chinese race. But, by the statute in question, a Chinaman can ride in the same passenger coach with white citizens of the United States, while citizens of the black race in Louisiana, many of whom, perhaps, risked their lives for the preservation of the Union, who are entitled, by law, to participate in the political control of the state and nation, who are not excluded, by law or by reason of their race, from public stations of any kind, and who have all the legal rights that belong to white citizens, are yet declared to be criminals, liable to imprisonment, if they ride in a public coach occupied by citizens of the white race. It is scarcely just to say that a colored citizen should not object to occupying a public coach assigned to his own race. He does not object, nor, perhaps, would he object to separate coaches for his race if his rights under the law were recognized. But he does object, and he ought never to cease objecting, that citizens of the white and black races can be adjudged criminals because they sit, or claim the right to sit, in the same public coach on a public highway. The arbitrary separation of citizens, on the basis of race, while they are on a public highway, is a badge of servitude wholly inconsistent with the civil freedom and the equality before the law established by the constitution. It cannot be justified upon any legal grounds.

If evils will result from the commingling of the two races upon public highways established for the benefit of all, they will be infinitely less than those that will surely come from state legislation regulating the enjoyment of civil rights upon the basis of race. We boast of the freedom enjoyed by our people above all other peoples. But it is difficult to reconcile that boast with a state of the law which, practically, puts the brand of servitude and degradation upon a large class of our fellow citizens, our equals before the law. The thin disguise of "equal" accommodations for passengers in railroad coaches will not mislead any one, nor atone for the wrong this day done.

The result of the whole matter is that while this court has frequently adjudged, and at the present term has recognized the doctrine, that a state cannot, consistently with the constitution of the United States, prevent white and black citizens, having the required qualifications for jury service, from sitting in the same jury box, it is now solemnly held that a state may prohibit white and black citizens from sitting in the same passenger coach on a public highway, or may require that they be separated by a "par-

tition" when in the same passenger coach. May it not now be reasonably expected that astute men of the dominant race, who affect to be disturbed at the possibility that the integrity of the white race may be corrupted, or that its supremacy will be imperiled, by contact on public highways with black people, will endeavor to procure statutes requiring white and black jurors to be separated in the jury box by a "partition," and that, upon retiring from the court room to consult as to their verdict, such partition, if it be a movable one, shall be taken to their consultation room, and set up in such way as to prevent black jurors from coming too close to their brother jurors of the white race. If the "partition" used in the court room happens to be stationary, provision could be made for screens with openings through which jurors of the two races could confer as to their verdict without coming into personal contact with each other. I cannot see but that, according to the principles this day announced, such state legislation, although conceived in hostility to, and enacted for the purpose of humiliating, citizens of the United States of a particular race, would be held to be consistent with the constitution.

I do not deem it necessary to review the decisions of state courts to which reference was made in argument. Some, and the most important, of them, are wholly inapplicable, because rendered prior to the adoption of the last amendments of the constitution, when colored people had very few rights which the dominant race felt obliged to respect. Others were made at a time when public opinion, in many localities, was dominated by the institution of slavery; when it would not have been safe to do justice to the black man; and when, so far as the rights of blacks were concerned, race prejudice was, practically, the supreme law of the land. Those decisions cannot be guides in the era introduced by the recent amendments of the supreme law, which established universal civil freedom, gave citizenship to all born or naturalized in the United States, and residing ere, obliterated the race line from our systems of governments, national and state, and placed our free institutions upon the broad and sure foundation of the equality of all men before the law.

I am of opinion that the state of Louisiana is inconsistent with the personal liberty of citizens, white and black, in that state, and hostile to both the spirit and letter of the constitution of the United States. If laws of like character should be enacted in the several states of the Union, the effect would be in the highest degree mischievous. Slavery, as an institution tolerated by law, would, it is true, have disappeared from our country; but there would remain a power in the states, by sinister legislation, to interfere with the full enjoyment of the blessings of freedom, to regulate civil rights, common to all citizens, upon the basis of race, and to place in a condition of legal inferiority a large body of American citizens, now constituting a part of the political community, called the "People of the United States," for whom, and by whom through representatives, our government is administered. Such a system is inconsistent with the guaranty given by the constitution to each state of a republican form of government, and may be stricken down by congressional action, or by the courts in the discharge of their solemn duty to maintain the supreme law of the land, anything in the constitution or laws of any state to the contrary notwithstanding.

For the reason stated, I am constrained to withhold my assent from the opinion and judgment of the majority.

William Jennings Bryan (Library of Congress)

WILLIAM JENNINGS BRYAN'S "CROSS OF GOLD" SPEECH

"You shall not crucify mankind upon a cross of gold."

Overview

On July 8, 1896, at the Democratic National Convention in Chicago, William Jennings Bryan gave one of the most memorable political addresses in American history. Dubbed the "Cross of Gold" Speech because of its vivid image of crucifying humankind upon a golden cross, the oration propelled Bryan to the Democratic nomination for president of the United States. In the speech, Bryan articulated the feelings of Americans from the South and West who felt that the currency system and its effects had injured their financial and cultural interests. These sections saw a more flexible monetary system and some degree of inflation as a cure for the economic ills that afflicted farmers, miners, and industrial workers. Bryan captured their grievances and gave them eloquent expression in his "Cross of Gold" Speech.

To understand why Bryan's speech had the impact it did requires some knowledge of the state of the American economy and political system in 1896. Bryan's remarks, which he had given in earlier speeches, spoke to the specific discontent of Democratic leaders and their constituents. His words resonated because they summed up the feelings of alienation from the political system and from the emerging industrial society that so many Americans felt in that summer of a presidential election.

Context

The events that led to Bryan's oration grew out of the history of the Democratic Party during the 1890s. In 1892 the party had elected Grover Cleveland to a second term as president. After just a few weeks in office, Cleveland faced an economic crisis. The Panic of 1893 (depressions were called "panics" at the time) occurred, with bank failures, mass unemployment, and the bankruptcies of many businesses. This downturn exposed fault lines within the Democratic ranks. Cleveland and eastern party members believed that the solution lay in allegiance to the "gold standard," meaning that the government should issue dol-

lars based on the amount of gold bullion the nation held in its treasury. Because the world supply of gold was limited, the amount of dollars and credit in circulation would be restricted as well. Only in that way, Cleveland argued, could the nation regain its economic health.

Democrats in the West and South, however, countered that the problem lay elsewhere. These agricultural regions faced declining prices for staple crops such as wheat and cotton, which they produced. Farmers in these areas also had debts for land and equipment that they found more difficult to pay. As a result, these agrarians argued that the government should put more money into circulation, thereby raising prices and making debts easier to pay. They proposed to accomplish these ends through what was then known as "free silver," a shorthand phrase for the free and unlimited coinage of silver into money at a fixed ratio with gold.

Silver had been part of the American financial system until 1873, when the U.S. Treasury moved to an exclusively gold basis. People who supported the use of silver called this change the "Crime of 1873." Economics dictated the shift to gold: The market price of silver had fallen because of extensive mining, and the government would have lost money by producing silver dollars. More important, the lesser value of silver dollars would have caused the hoarding of gold dollars because of the higher value of the gold-backed currency. There would also have been problems with inflation.

Despite these arguments, advocates of silver saw that metal as the answer to the nation's financial woes. The People's Party, which had run well in elections in the South and West in 1892, made free silver one of its key planks. Democrats in those regions shared these convictions and wanted their party to abandon the hard-money, gold-standard views of President Cleveland. These differences were papered over during the 1892 campaign. When the Panic of 1893 hit, however, the Democrats fractured over which course to take in dealing with the hard times.

President Cleveland decided that a single piece of legislation had brought on the depression. In 1890 Congress had enacted the Sherman Silver Purchase Act, which mandated that the government purchase 4.5 million ounces of silver each month. Cleveland charged that this measure unsettled business confidence because of the subsidy it provided to silver miners, and, in turn, undermined confi-

1893

■ **August 7**
Special session of Congress is called to repeal Sherman Silver Purchase Act.

■ **August 16**
William Jennings Bryan speaks out against repeal of the Sherman Act.

1894

■ **December 22**
Bryan attacks Grover Cleveland's policies in a House of Representatives speech.

1895

■ **March 5**
Bryan and fellow Democrats, calling themselves "Silver Democrats," appeal for wider use of silver.

1896

■ **June 18**
William McKinley is nominated for president by the Republicans; he runs on a gold-standard platform.

■ **July 7**
Democratic National Convention opens in Chicago.

■ **July 8**
Bryan gives "Cross of Gold" Speech.

■ **July 9**
Bryan is nominated for president.

■ **July 22**
People's Party endorses Bryan's nomination.

■ **November 3**
William McKinley defeats Bryan in presidential contest with 271 electoral votes to 176 for Bryan.

1900

■ **November 6**
Bryan loses presidential election to McKinley a second time.

1908

■ **November 3**
Bryan loses third race for presidency to William Howard Taft.

1925

■ **July 26**
Bryan dies.

---

dence in the gold standard. Cleveland called Congress to a special session in August 1893 to repeal the Sherman law.

The ensuing debate revealed the deep divisions among the Democrats. Among the leaders of the opposition to the president's policy was a thirty-three-year-old Nebraska congressman, William Jennings Bryan. Bryan joined other Democrats from the South and West in denouncing what Cleveland wanted to do. His speech on August 16, 1893, won wide acclaim. With the help of the Republicans, however, the president succeeded in repealing the Sherman Act. The outcome left the Democratic Party in disarray.

The party's troubles worsened during 1894. Congress and Cleveland continued their disagreements while economic discontent mounted throughout the country. Unemployed workers marched toward Washington, D.C., to record their protests against the lack of work and opportunity. Jacob S. Coxey was the most famous of these protestors, leading his "Coxey's Army" to the nation's capital. In Chicago a strike against the Pullman Palace Car Company, a maker of railroad sleeper cars, grew into a nationwide walkout that the Cleveland administration broke by using federal troops. Popular unhappiness with the Democrats mounted as the 1894 congressional elections neared.

At the polls in 1894, voters rejected Democratic candidates. In the largest transfer of congressional strength up to that time, Republicans gained 113 seats in the House of Representatives and made smaller gains in the Senate. The Cleveland administration had been greatly reduced. Now, free-silver Democrats resolved to control the nomination of a presidential candidate in 1896.

In an age that valued skill as an orator, Bryan was a talented public speaker. He had a clear, musical voice that could be heard at the back of a hall—an important quality in the age before the use of amplification and microphones. Moreover, he had the capacity to articulate the ideas of his constituents in pleasing tones that carried conviction and sincerity. Bryan knew that if he could have a chance to address an audience of pro-silver Democrats, he could make a speech that would energize the crowd. During 1895 and 1896, he tested lines in his standard speeches to his fellow Democrats, perfecting the argument that he would advance in Chicago.

Because of his youth, Bryan knew that he had to proceed with caution in seeking the nomination in 1896. He adopted a strategy of becoming the second choice of many delegates at the convention. When the front-runners faltered, as he was sure they would, Bryan would make his move. The two leading candidates, Richard Parks Bland of Missouri and Horace Boies of Iowa, did not inspire much enthusiasm among faithful Democrats. Bryan planned to have himself become the party's top choice as the ballots at the convention went forward.

Bryan sought an opportunity to make the speech of his life. The debate over the issue of silver in the party's platform provided the chance he was seeking. Bryan arranged to speak last on the program and persuaded the other free-silver orator, Benjamin R. Tillman of South Carolina, to go first in making the case for silver. There would be three pro-gold speakers: David B. Hill of New York, William F.

THE SACRILEGIOUS CANDIDATE.

No man who drags into the dust the most sacred symbols of the Christian world is fit to be president of the United States.

This cartoon from 1896 portrays William Jennings Bryan as an anarchist threat to religion. (Library of Congress)

Vilas of Wisconsin, and William E. Russell of Massachusetts. When the debate started, Tillman went first. His speech, which attacked the northern Democratic delegates and went on too long, fell flat. The three gold-standard advocates then made their critical comments; the crowd, most of whom supported silver, listened patiently but without enthusiasm. Bryan then gave his speech.

About the Author

William Jennings Bryan was just thirty-six years old when he delivered the "Cross of Gold" Speech at the 1896 Democratic National Convention. He was born in Salem, Illinois, on March 19, 1860. During the late 1880s, after attending Whipple Academy and Illinois College, Bryan studied law and moved to Nebraska. He soon plunged into Democratic politics. Elected to Congress in 1890, he served two terms in the House before seeking a Senate seat in 1894. That campaign failed, and Bryan turned his attention to the Democratic presidential nomination in 1896.

Bryan lost the 1896 general election to William McKinley, and he lost again to McKinley in 1900 and to William Howard Taft in 1908. In 1925 he played a key role in the famed Scopes Monkey Trial in Tennessee, in which he argued that the teaching of evolution should be banned in public schools. He died in Dayton, Tennessee, on July 26, 1925, just five days after the Scopes trial ended.

Explanation and Analysis of the Document

In the first paragraph, Bryan begins humbly with a disclaimer about his ability to measure up to "the distinguished gentlemen to whom you have listened" and notes that "this is not a contest between persons." He then asserts that "the humblest citizen in all the land, when clad in the armor of a righteous cause, is stronger than all the hosts of error."

By the third paragraph, Bryan moves into the heart of his oration. He alludes to the fervor with which the followers of Peter the Hermit (1050–1115) joined in the First Crusade. This was a common image in the Gilded Age and Progressive Era to convey a sense of determination and fervor. Bryan says that the debate over free silver has been divisive and intense but argues that the advocates of silver have prevailed. In the fourth paragraph, Bryan assures the former Massachusetts governor William Russell and the gold delegates that they have disturbed the business interests of the West as much as the silver men have caused dismay in the East.

In the sixth paragraph, Bryan reaches a key point in his speech. He says that the workers, farmers, and miners of the West are businessmen in the same sense that corporate officers, lawyers, and merchants in the East bear that title. Bryan's comments address sectional divisions and demonstrate that he is speaking for those who did as much labor as traditional business figures did in the East.

Bryan then advances the claims of those westerners who deserve better treatment from the rest of the country. He galvanizes the crowd when he says at the end of these comments in paragraph 7: "We have petitioned, and [our] petitions have been scorned; we have entreated, and our entreaties have been disregarded; we have begged, and they have mocked when our calamity came. We beg no longer; we entreat no more; we petition no more. We defy them."

Critics of Bryan likened his appeal to that of Maximilien Robespierre, the radical Jacobin of the French Revolution who was likewise preaching social revolution. In answering this charge from the former Wisconsin senator William F. Vilas, a major figure among Cleveland Democrats, Bryan associates himself with the aspirations of President Andrew Jackson, who, Bryan notes, resisted "the encroachments of organized wealth" in his fight against the Second Bank of the United States during the 1830s.

In paragraph 9, Bryan answers some of his critics within the Democratic Party. The Democratic platform endorsed an income tax that the Supreme Court the year before had ruled unconstitutional. The major source of government revenue in 1896 came from a tariff that assessed taxes on imports. Bryan wanted to overturn the tariff policy and shift the burden of taxes to those with higher incomes.

When Bryan in the tenth paragraph talks about "national bank currency," he is referring to the form of money that then existed—namely, notes, based on gold deposits, which were issued by national banks and circulated as legal tender. Bryan, along with many other party members in 1896, was not satisfied with this system, believing that the national government should issue the currency based on both gold and silver. In his remarks, Bryan refers to Senator Thomas Hart Benton (1782–1858) of Missouri, a Jacksonian politician of the mid-nineteenth century. Bryan includes another allusion to Jackson's conflict with the Second Bank of the United States. Bryan looks back to the history of Rome with a reference to the Cataline conspiracy of 62 BCE that the famous orator Cicero helped to thwart.

The Democrats had come out against life tenure in the civil service. Since the judiciary stayed in office until retirement or death, the idea had come under attack on that ground. Bryan's tenth paragraph responds to these allegations.

In discussing paragraph 12, Bryan reassures his opponents that the adoption of free silver would not undermine existing contracts that specified payment in gold. At the same time, he includes a reminder about the "Crime of 1873" and what that measure did to affect debtors.

Paragraph 13 brings Bryan into the substance of his argument for free silver. The gold supporters argued that the silver policy could not bring the white metal into a financial parity with gold within a year. The market price of silver was low at this time, and raising it to a ratio of sixteen to one (which was what Bryan favored) would have required large subsidies from the treasury. Bryan brushes that argument aside. One of the devices that moderate thinkers on both sides of the issue advanced was the concept of an international agreement to use silver more widely. This was dubbed "international bimetallism." The large flaw in that proposal was the opposition of Great Britain, the leading champion of gold, to any such endeavor.

The Republicans and the gold-supporting Democrats wanted to base the campaign on the tariff issue. Bryan would have none of that, and in paragraph 14 he utters one of the phrases most identified with this speech: "If protection has slain its thousands, the gold standard has slain its tens of thousands." (Bryan here makes a biblical reference to the first book of Samuel, which says that "Saul hath slain his thousands, and David his ten thousands.")

Bryan mocks William McKinley and the Republicans for their stand on the gold standard in his fifteenth paragraph. He contends that the political position has deteriorated since the Republican convention nominated McKinley on the gold standard and a promise to seek an international agreement on silver. The Republicans inserted that language at the behest of McKinley to placate silver supporters in the West. Since Republicans often compared McKinley, who was not a tall man, to the small-sized French dictator Napoléon I, Bryan has fun with the topic. McKinley faces his electoral Waterloo and will, like the French leader, end up in exile in the political equivalent of the remote Atlantic Ocean island of Saint Helena.

This alleged plunge in Republican fortunes, Bryan argues in his sixteenth paragraph, has occurred because McKinley and his party have become associated with the gold standard and the readiness to place American monetary affairs in the hands of other countries through an international bimetallic agreement.

In paragraph 17, Bryan further ridicules the idea of international bimetallism and accuses his opponents of being willing to abandon the gold standard even as they say that he is doing the same thing. He cites American history for his contention that the nation had never adopted an out-and-out gold standard. He adds that "the common people" had not come out for gold—only "the holders of the fixed investments."

John G. Carlisle, who is mentioned in the eighteenth paragraph, was Grover Cleveland's secretary of the treasury in 1896. When he was a member of the House of Representatives in 1878, Carlisle had made a pro-silver speech. Bryan uses Carlisle's words about "the idle holders of capital" and "the struggling masses" to ask where the Democrats would stand. He maintains that the party's sympathies "are on the side of the struggling masses who have ever been the foundation of the Democratic party." (Note how, in Bryan's last two sentences, he alludes to what has been called the "trickle down" theory often associated with the Republican Party and the contrasting approach identified with the Democrats.)

The nineteenth paragraph is brief, but it contains the core of Bryan's argument in the speech:

You come to us and tell us that the great cities are in favor of the gold standard; we reply that the great cities rest upon our broad and fertile prairies. Burn down your cities and leave our farms and your cities will spring up again as if by magic; but destroy our farms and the grass will grow in the streets of every city in the country.

Those sentences are some of the best expressions of the agrarian values that underlay the Democratic Party in 1896.

Bryan is now moving toward his conclusion. In paragraph 20, he reiterates the point that free silver could be implemented "without waiting for the aid or consent of any other nation on earth." He predicts victory across the country, and then he evokes the spirit of the American Revolution: "It is the issue of 1776 all over again." In 1896, as during the time of the battle against the British, the voters would display their political independence. The Democrats would institute bimetallism on their own without asking permission of England or other countries. If the fight was to be made over the gold standard itself, however, Bryan would welcome that as well.

As he prepared to utter his final words, Bryan turned to gestures he had practiced before. "Having behind us the producing masses of this nation and the world," he says, "we will answer their demand for a gold standard by saying to them: You shall not press down upon the brow of labor this crown of thorns; you shall not crucify mankind upon a cross of gold." When he referred to "this crown of thorns," Bryan pressed his hands down on his forehead. When he ended with the words "crucify mankind upon a cross of gold," he spread his arms to make a cross of his own.

Audience

Bryan had two audiences in mind when he gave his speech. The first, of course, comprised the delegates inside the convention hall. His goal was to sway the gathering to select him as presidential candidate during the next day's balloting. In that, he was brilliantly successful. The delegates and the galleries, filled with proponents of free silver, responded with intense enthusiasm and spontaneous demonstrations of support for Bryan and his remarks. There was immediate talk in the hall that the Nebraskan should be named the Democratic nominee.

To succeed as the presidential candidate, Bryan needed to get his message out to the nation at large. The proceedings of the convention received intense press coverage. Bryan's speech immediately gathered public attention and made him a national figure. Newspapers reprinted in full the text of his remarks, and the oration was also published as a pamphlet. For Democrats and Populists in agrarian areas, Bryan became an articulate advocate in the summer of 1896 and remained so the rest of his life.

Impact

Once Bryan finished speaking, some enthusiastic Democrats wanted to have the convention start voting right

"*The humblest citizen in all the land, when clad in the armor of a righteous cause, is stronger than all the hosts of error.*"

(Paragraph 1)

"*We beg no longer; we entreat no more; we petition no more. We defy them.*"

(Paragraph 7)

"*You come to us and tell us that the great cities are in favor of the gold standard; we reply that the great cities rest upon our broad and fertile prairies. Burn down your cities and leave our farms and your cities will spring up again as if by magic; but destroy our farms and the grass will grow in the streets of every city in the country.*"

(Paragraph 19)

"*You shall not press down upon the brow of labor this crown of thorns; you shall not crucify mankind upon a cross of gold.*"

(Paragraph 20)

away for its candidate. Bryan's opponents resisted and said that the balloting should occur on schedule. Bryan agreed; he told friends that if the support for him did not last overnight, it would not endure until November. Bryan and his aides needed time to gather the delegates' votes and to plot their strategy.

The voting for the nominee came on July 9, the evening of the day after Bryan's now-famous speech. It took five ballots for Bryan to emerge as the choice of the Democrats. Bryan took the lead on the fourth ballot and then, midway through the fifth ballot, passed the two-thirds needed for victory. Bryan was nominated unanimously. He selected a Maine Democrat named Arthur Sewall as his running mate in an effort to balance the ticket and appeal to the Northeast, where Bryan was weakest. Sewall was also a businessman for free silver, a rare combination in 1896. The Democrats achieved a ticket but at the cost of defections among the gold-supporting Democrats who resisted Bryan and the allure of free silver.

The campaign that followed saw Bryan make intense efforts to win the White House. He gained the support of the People's Party for his candidacy, although the Populists nominated a different vice president to run with him. Bryan went out on the stump to take his case to the Amer-

ican people. The Democrats lacked the money of the well-funded Republicans. The major newspapers were opposed to Bryan and denied him full coverage in their columns. To get his message out to the electorate, Bryan crisscrossed the country, making hundreds of speeches during the fall campaign season. In the aftermath of the "Cross of Gold" Speech (as it was quickly named), Bryan even seemed to have taken the lead from McKinley and the Republicans.

As the campaign entered the fall, however, the Republicans rebounded. They had raised more than $3 million for their war chest, money that they used to pour out pamphlets and other literature attacking Bryan's reliance on free silver. McKinley stayed at his home in Canton, Ohio, but Republicans brought an estimated 750,000 people there to hear the candidate's daily remarks. The McKinley campaign argued that inflation, which was at the heart of Bryan's appeal, would hurt workers on a fixed income. Tariff protection, they said, was a more effective answer to hard times. By October, Bryan's momentum had stalled, and the election had turned toward McKinley.

The results on election day confirmed that judgment. McKinley won 271 electoral votes to 176 for Bryan. In the popular vote, the Republican gained a 600,000-vote majority over Bryan, the largest such margin in a quarter of a century. Bryan carried the South and West; McKinley won significantly in the Northeast and Midwest. Bryan conceded that the "first battle," as he called it, had not gone for the Democrats. He promised to make a renewed effort in 1900, and there was already talk among Democrats of another Bryan nomination.

The "Cross of Gold" Speech had propelled Bryan to the Democratic nomination, though it did not take him to the White House. The oration established Bryan as a major force in American politics, a position he occupied for the next thirty years until his death in 1925. His dramatic speech was soon recognized as one of the classic events of American political oratory. More than a century after it was delivered, it remains one of the rare speeches given at the right moment to make the speaker a national figure.

Related Documents

Bryan, William Jennings. *The First Battle*. Chicago: W. B. Conkey Co., 1898. This work is Bryan's memoir of the 1896 campaign and includes an account of his speech.

Morison, Elting E., et al., eds. *Letters of Theodore Roosevelt*. 8 vols. Cambridge, Mass.: Harvard University Press, 1951–1954. The first volume provides Theodore Roosevelt's letters during the summer and fall of 1896 as he reacted to Bryan's candidacy.

Smith, Joseph P., ed. *McKinley's Speeches in September*. Canton, Ohio: Repository Press, 1896. McKinley's speeches from his front porch illustrate how the Republicans countered Bryan's appeal.

Bibliography

■ Books

Coletta, Paolo E. *William Jennings Bryan*, Vol. 1: *Political Evangelist, 1860–1908*. Lincoln: University of Nebraska Press, 1964.

Jones, Stanley L. *The Presidential Election of 1896*. Madison: University of Wisconsin Press, 1964.

Kazin, Michael. *A Godly Hero: The Life of William Jennings Bryan*. New York: Knopf, 2006.

Koenig, Louis W. *Bryan: A Political Biography of William Jennings Bryan*. New York: Putnam, 1971.

Morgan, H. Wayne. *William McKinley and His America*, rev. ed. Kent, Ohio: Kent State University Press, 2003.

Williams, R. Hal. *Years of Decision: American Politics in the 1890s*. Prospect Heights, Ill.: Waveland Press, 1993.

Witcover, Jules. *Party of the People: A History of the Democrats*. New York: Random House, 2003.

■ Web Sites

"Cross of Gold." The American Experience, "America: 1900" Web site.
http://www.pbs.org/wgbh/amex/1900/filmmore/reference/primary/crossofgold.html. Accessed on February 12, 2008.

—By Lewis L. Gould

1. How did the circumstances of the Democratic National Convention and the debate at Chicago about the gold standard work to Bryan's advantage as a potential nominee? What had he done to ensure that his address had maximum political impact?

2. What was Bryan's view of American society in 1896? Did he argue that there were serious class and regional divisions? What was his interpretation of the role of farmers and rural residents in the life of the nation?

3. What place did Bryan envision for the federal government in the operation of the monetary system? How did he distinguish himself from his opponents?

4. What was Bryan's opinion on the merits of international bimetallism as a solution to the crisis between silver and gold?

5. In what ways did Bryan attempt to identify the Democrats who favored free silver with the broad currents of American history?

6. Why did Bryan's speech have the effect that it did on the delegates in Chicago?

Glossary

bimetallism	the use of gold and silver as the standards of value, within a fixed ratio to each other
counsel	attorney
encroachments	trespasses or transgressions
entreaties	pleas; requests
free coinage	the system by which the government coins either silver or gold into money at no charge or at cost.
instructions	in a political convention, binding orders to a delegation to vote for a candidate or platform plank
magnates	important business leaders
presumptuous	too bold or forward
protection	the policy of encouraging industry through customs duties on imported goods

WILLIAM JENNINGS BRYAN'S "CROSS OF GOLD" SPEECH

Mr. Chairman and Gentlemen of the convention: I would be presumptuous, indeed, to present myself against the distinguished gentlemen to whom you have listened if this was a mere measuring of abilities; but this is not a contest between persons. The humblest citizen in all the land, when clad in the armor of a righteous cause, is stronger than all the hosts of error. I come to speak to you in defense of a cause as holy as the cause of liberty, the cause of humanity.

When this debate is concluded a motion will be made to lay upon the table the resolution offered in commendation of the administration and also the resolution offered in condemnation of the administration. We object to bringing this question down to the level of persons. The individual is but an atom; he is born, he acts, he dies; but principles are eternal; and this has been a contest over a principle.

Never before in the history of this country has there been witnessed such a contest as that through which we have just passed. Never before in the history of American politics has a great issue been fought out, as this issue has been, by the voters of a great party. On the fourth of March, 1895, a few Democrats, most of them Members of Congress, issued an address to the Democrats of the nation, asserting that the money question was the paramount issue of the hour; declaring that a majority of the Democratic party had the right to control the action of the party on this paramount issue; and concluding with the request that the believers in the free coinage of silver in the Democratic party should organize, take charge of and control the policy of the Democratic party. Three months later, at Memphis, an organization was perfected, and the silver Democrats went forth openly and courageously proclaiming their belief, and declaring that, if successful, they would crystallize into a platform the declaration which they had made. Then began the conflict. With a zeal approaching the zeal which inspired the crusaders who followed Peter the Hermit, our silver Democrats went forth from victory unto victory until they are now assembled, not to discuss, not to debate, but to enter up the judgment already rendered by the plain people of this country. In this contest brother has been arrayed against brother, father against son. The warmest ties of love, acquaintance and association have been disregarded; old leaders have been cast aside when they have refused to give expression to the sentiments of those whom they would lead, and now leaders have sprung up to give direction to this cause of truth. Thus has the contest been waged, and we have assembled here under as binding and solemn instructions as were ever imposed upon representatives of the people.

We do not come as individuals. As individuals we might have been glad to compliment the gentleman from New York, but we know that the people for whom we speak would never be willing to put him in a position where he could thwart the will of the Democratic party. I say it was not a question of persons; it was a question of principle, and it is not with gladness, my friends, that we find ourselves brought into conflict with those who are now arrayed on the other side.

The gentleman who preceded me spoke of the State of Massachusetts; let me assure him that not one present in all this convention entertains the least hostility to the people of the State of Massachusetts, but we stand here representing people who are the equals before the law of the greatest citizens in the State of Massachusetts. When you come before us and tell us that we are about to disturb your business interests, we reply that you have disturbed our business interests by course.

We say to you that you have made the definition of a business man too limited in its application. The man who is employed for wages is as much a business man as his employer; the attorney in a country town is as much a business man as the corporation counsel in a great metropolis; the merchant at the crossroads store is as much a business man as the merchant of New York; the farmer who goes forth in the morning and toils all day—who begins in the spring and toils all summer—and who by the application of brain and muscle to the natural resources of the country creates wealth, is as much a business man as the man who goes upon the board of trade and bets upon the price of grain; the miners who go down a thousand feet into the earth, or climb two thousand feet upon the cliffs, and bring forth from their hiding-places the precious metals to be poured in the channels of trade, are as much business men as the few financial magnates who, in a back room, corner the money of the world. We come to speak for this broader class of business men.

Ah, my friends, we say not one word against those who live upon the Atlantic coast, but the hardy pioneers who have braved all the dangers of the wilderness, who have made the desert to blossom as the rose—the pioneers away out there, who rear their children near to Nature's heart, where they can mingle their voices with the voices of the birds—out there where they have erected schoolhouses for the education of their young, churches where they praise their Creator, and cemeteries where rest the ashes of their dead—these people, as we say, are as deserving of the consideration of our party as any people in this country. It is for these that we speak. We do not come as aggressors. Our war is not a war of conquest; we are fighting in the defense of our homes, our families, and posterity. We have petitioned, and out (sic) petitions have been scorned; we have entreated, and our entreaties have been disregarded; we have begged, and they have mocked when our calamity came. We beg no longer; we entreat no more; we petition no more. We defy them.

The gentleman from Wisconsin has said that he fears a Robespierre. My friends, in this land of the free you need not fear a tyrant that will spring up from among the people. What we need is an Andrew Jackson to stand, as Jackson stood, against the encroachments of organized wealth.

They tell us that this platform was made to catch votes. We reply to them that changing conditions make new issues; that the principles upon which democracy rests are as everlasting as the hills, but that they must be applied to new conditions as they arise. Conditions have arisen, and we are here to meet those conditions. They tell us that the income tax ought not to be brought in here; that it is a new

idea. They criticize us for our criticism of the Supreme Court of the United States. My friends, we have not criticized; we have simply called attention to what you already know. If you want criticisms, read the dissenting opinions of the court. There you will find criticisms. They say that we passed an unconstitutional law; we deny it. The income-tax law was not unconstitutional when it went before the Supreme Court for the first time; it did not become unconstitutional until one of the judges changed his mind, and we cannot be expected to know when a judge will change his mind. The income tax is just. It simply intends to put the burdens of government justly upon the backs of the people. I am in favor of an income tax. When I find a man who is not willing to bear his share of the burdens of the government which protects him, I find a man who is unworthy to enjoy the blessings of a government like ours.

They say that we are opposing national bank currency; it is true. If you will read what Thomas Benton said, you will find he said that, in searching history, he could find but one parallel to Andrew Jackson; that was Cicero, who destroyed the conspiracy of Catiline and saved Rome. Benton said that Cicero only did for Rome what Jackson did for us when he destroyed the bank conspiracy and saved America. We say in our platform that we believe that the right to coin and issue money is a function of government. We believe it. We believe that it is a part of sovereignty, and can no more with safety be delegated to private individuals than we could afford to delegate private individuals the power to make penal statues or levy taxes. Mr. Jefferson, who was once regarded as good Democratic authority, seemed to have differed in opinion from the gentleman who has addressed us on the part of the minority. Those who are opposed to this proposition tell us that the issue of paper money is a function of the bank, and that the Government ought to go out of the banking business. I stand with Jefferson rather than with them, and tell them, as he did, that the issue of money is a function of government, and that banks ought to go out of the governing business.

They complain about the plank which declares against life tenure in office. They have tried to strain it to mean that which it does not mean. What we oppose by that plank is the life tenure which is being built up in Washington, and which excludes from participation in official benefits the humbler members of society.

Let me call your attention to two or three important things. The gentleman from New York says that he will propose an amendment to the platform providing that the proposed change in our monetary system shall not affect contracts already made. Let me remind you that there is no intention of affecting those contracts which according to present laws are made payable in god, but if he means to say that we cannot change our monetary system without protecting those who have loaned money before the change was made, I desire to ask him where, in law or in morals, he can find justification for not protecting the debtors when the act of 1873 was passed, if he now insists that we must protect the creditors.

He says he will also propose an amendment which will provide for the suspension of free coinage if we fail to maintain the parity within a year. We reply that when we advocate a policy which we believe will be successful, we are not compelled to raise a doubt as to our own sincerity by suggesting what we shall do if we fail. I ask him, if he would apply his logic to us, why he doesn't apply himself. He says he wants this country to try to secure an international agreement. Why does he not tell us what he is going to do if he fails to secure an international agreement? There is more reason for him to do that than there is for us to provide against the failure to maintain the parity. Our opponents have tried for twenty years to secure an international agreement, and those are waiting for it most patiently who do not want it at all.

And now, my friends, let me come to the paramount issue. If they ask us why it is that we say more on the money question than we say upon the tariff question, I reply that, if protection has slain its thousands, the gold standard has slain its tens of thousands. If they ask us why we do not embody in our platform all the things that we believe in, we reply that when we have restored the money of the Constitution all other necessary reforms will be possible; but that until this is done there is no other reform that can be accomplished.

Why is it that within three months such a change has come over the country? Three months ago, when it was confidently asserted that those who believe in the gold standard would frame our platform and nominate our candidates, even the advocates of the gold standard did not think that we could elect a president. And they had good reason for their doubt, because there is scarcely a State here today asking for the gold standard which is not in the absolute control of the Republican party. But note the change. Mr. McKinley was nominated as St. Louis upon a platform which declared for the maintenance of the gold standard until it can be changed into bimetallism by international agreement. Mr. McKinley was the most popular man among the Republicans, and three months ago everybody in the Republican party prophesied his election. How is it today? Why, the man who was once pleased to think that he looked like Napolean—that man shudders today when he remembers that he was nominated on the anniversary of the battle of Waterloo. Not only that, as he listens, he can hear with ever-increasing distinctness the sound of the waves as they beat upon the lonely shores of St. Helena.

Why this change? Ah, my friends, is not the reason for change evident to anyone who will look at the matter? No private character, however pure, no personal popularity, however great, can protect form the avenging wrath of an indignant people a man who will declare that he is in favor of fastening the gold standard upon this country or who is willing to surrender the right of self-government and place the legislative control of our affairs in the hands of foreign potentates and powers.

We go forth confident that we shall win. Why? Because upon the paramount issue of this campaign there is not a spot of ground upon which the enemy will dare to challenge battle. If they tell us that the gold standard is a good thing, we shall point to their platform and tell them that their platform pledges the party to get rid of the gold standard and substitute bimetallism. If the gold standard is a good thing, why try to get rid of it? I call your attention to the fact that some of the very people who are in this convention today and who tell us that we ought to declare in favor of international bimetallism—thereby declaring that the gold standard is wrong and that the principle of bimetallism is better—these very people four months ago were open and avowed advocates of the gold standard, and were then telling us that we could not legislate two metals together, even with the aid of all the world. If the gold standard is a good thing, we ought to declare it in favor of its retention and not in favor of abandoning it; and if the gold standard is a bad thing why should we wait until other nations are willing to help us to let go? Here is the line of battle, and we care not upon which issue they force the fight; we are prepared to meet them on either issue or on both. If they tell us that the gold standard is the standard of civilization, we reply to them that this, the most enlightened of all the nations of the earth, has never declared for a gold standard and that both the great parties this year are declaring against it. If the gold standard is the standard of civilization, why, my friends, should we not have it? If they come to meet us on that issue we can present the history of our nation. More than that; we can tell them that they will search the pages of history in vain to find a single instance where the holders of fixed investments have declared for a gold standard, but not where the masses have.

Mr. Carlisle said in 1878 that this was a struggle between "the idle holders of capital" and "the struggling masses, who produce the wealth and pay the taxes of the country," and my friends, the question we are to decide is: Upon which side will the Democratic party fight: upon the side of the "idle holders of idle capital" or upon the side of "the struggling masses?" That is the question which the party must answer first, and then it must be answered by each individual hereafter. The sympathies of the Democratic party, as shown by the platform, are on the side of the struggling masses who have ever been the foundation of the Democratic party. There are two ideas of government. There are those who believe that, if you will only legislate to make the well-to-do prosperous, their prosperity will leak through on those below. The Democratic idea, however, has been that if you legislate to make the masses prosperous, their prosperity will find its way up through every class which rests upon them.

You come to us and tell us that the great cities are in favor of the gold standard; we reply that the great cities rest upon our broad and fertile prairies. Burn down your cities and leave our farms and your cities will spring up again as if by magic; but destroy our farms and the grass will grow in the streets of every city in the country.

My friends, we declare that this nation is able to legislate for its own people on every question, without waiting for the aid or consent of any other nation on earth; and upon that issue we expect to carry every state of New York by saying that, when they are confronted with the proposition, they will declare that this nation is not able to attend to its own business. It is the issue of 1776 over again. Our ancestors, when but three millions in number, had the courage to declare their political independence of every other nation; shall we, their descendants, when we have grown to seventy millions, declare that we are less independent than our forefathers? No, my friends, that will never be the verdict of our people. Therefore, we care not upon what lines the battle is fought. If they say bimetallism is good, but that we cannot have it until other nations help us, we reply that, instead of having a gold standard because England has, we will restore bimetallism, and then let England have bimetallism because the United States has it. If they dare to come out in the open field and defend the gold standard as a good thing, we will fight the to the uttermost. Having behind us the producing masses of this nation and the world, supported by the commercial interests, the laboring interests, and the toilers everywhere, we will answer their demand for a gold standard by saying to them: You shall not press down upon the brow of labor this crown of thorns; you shall not crucify mankind upon a cross of gold.

President William McKinley (Library of Congress)

WILLIAM MCKINLEY'S MESSAGE TO CONGRESS ABOUT CUBAN INTERVENTION

"I speak not of forcible annexation, for that can not be thought of."

Overview

During the spring of 1898, the tensions between the United States and Spain over the island of Cuba brought the two nations to the brink of war. The outbreak of the Cuban Revolution in 1895 and Spanish attempts to suppress the uprising had led to demands in the United States for intervention to stop the fighting. For several years, the quarrel between Washington and Madrid intensified. On February 15, 1898, the battleship *Maine* exploded in Havana Harbor, killing more than 260 crew members. The tragedy intensified calls for American action against Spain. By late March 1898 negotiations were at an impasse. Convinced that he had to intervene, President William McKinley sent a message to Congress asking for the authority to end the war in Cuba. He hoped to avoid a conflict involving the United States, but the Spanish declared that an American intrusion into the fighting would produce a wider war. McKinley's Message to Congress about Cuba became a decisive step in the process that led to the war with Spain.

Context

The central importance of McKinley's message rests on its role in bringing on the war with Spain in April 1898. That conflict has been one of the most controversial foreign-policy events in American history, because it resulted in an empire in Asia and dominance in the Caribbean. Every phase of the process that led to the war has thus been analyzed in detail. To understand why McKinley's words have become so crucial, therefore, a brief review of the tension with Spain over Cuba is in order.

The United States had long been interested in the future of Cuba during the nineteenth century as the residents of the island chafed under Spanish colonial rule. The problem became acute in 1895 when Cuban rebels initiated an uprising against Madrid. Soon violence raged across the island with a consequent impact on American investments. Efforts to provide arms to rebels from outside Cuba involved the U.S. Navy in Cuban waters. Throughout the United States, citizens read of the fighting in their newspapers and clamored for an end to the cruel and bloody struggle going on ninety miles from the mainland. Some activist politicians believed that the rebellion offered a rationale for annexing Cuba to the United States.

The major issue that divided Madrid and Washington emerged from the outbreak of the uprising. Spain believed that Cuba was part of its larger nation, that it was the last possession of the once-proud Spanish Empire. Americans, on the other hand, identified with the cause of the rebels in Cuba and wanted to see them achieve their independence from Spain. These two goals could not easily be reconciled. In the United States, sensational newspapers, known as the "yellow press" because of a cartoon character called "The Yellow Kid," advocated a more aggressive posture toward Madrid and Cuba.

The administration of President Grover Cleveland did not sympathize with the rebels' cause. The White House indicated to Spain that it would have to suppress the uprising at some point in the future. There were no deadlines for that political goal, and Cleveland made it clear that Washington would not interfere with Spanish actions. That policy was not very popular within the United States, where partisans of Cuba regarded the administration as pro-Spanish.

The presidential election of 1896 brought William McKinley into office. From the outset of his term, he made it clear that his administration would take a different stance from Cleveland's. Spain must bring the rebellion to an end, by force if possible but preferably through negotiations with the rebels. Any settlement of the conflict would have to be acceptable to the leaders of the rebellion. Since Spain would never grant independence to Cuba through such a process, the actual chances for a peaceful resolution between Washington and Madrid were very small as the McKinley administration began in 1897.

For the first year of the new presidency, the two sides explored their contrasting positions on Cuba. McKinley insisted that in pacifying the rebellion, the Spanish should not use inhumane methods to achieve their ends. The Spanish made some concessions to placate Washington, but the fundamental differences remained at the start of 1898. McKinley's strategy of intensifying diplomatic pres-

Time Line

1895

■ **February 24**
Cuban revolution against Spanish rule begins.

1896

■ **November 3**
William McKinley is elected president.

1897

■ **March 4**
McKinley is inaugurated as president.

■ **December 6**
In his annual message, McKinley says that Spain must pursue reforms looking toward peace in Cuba.

1898

■ **January 12**
Pro-Spanish military in Cuba riots against a program from Spain to give Cubans autonomy.

■ **February 9**
Letter of Spanish minister Dupuy de Lôme is published, which attacks McKinley and indicates that Spain is stalling for time.

■ **February 15**
The battleship *Maine* explodes in Havana Harbor.

■ **March 24**
McKinley receives a report blaming an external cause for the explosion of the *Maine*.

■ **March 29**
The United States proposes negotiations over the fate of Cuba to the Spanish.

■ **March 31**
Spain rejects American proposals.

■ **April 9**
Spain proposes suspension of hostilities but rejects Cuban independence.

■ **April 11**
McKinley submits Message to Congress about Cuba.

■ **April 20**
McKinley signs joint resolution.

■ **April 21**
Spain breaks diplomatic relations.

---

sure on Spain to persuade them to yield on Cuba was not working. The first three months of the new year produced an intensification of the crisis. Spain had granted Cuba some degree of autonomy in its domestic affairs in late 1897. Pro-Spanish crowds rioted in Havana against these changes in mid-January. Then, in early February, the Cuban rebels released a letter they had intercepted from the Spanish minister in Washington, Enrique Dupuy de Lôme. In it, he criticized McKinley as "weak and a bidder for the admiration of the crowd" (http://www.ourdocuments. gov/doc.php?doc=53&page=transcript). More important, he also indicated that the Spanish were stalling for time in the hope that American opinion might shift in their direction.

The battleship *Maine* had been sent to Havana in January on a goodwill mission. On February 15 it exploded, killing its 265 men. A wave of outrage swept the United States amid charges that the Spanish were responsible for the event. Modern research indicates that an internal explosion was the cause, but that was not known at the time. The disaster produced a naval inquiry about the cause of the explosion. If that panel reported that Spain was responsible, President McKinley would face great pressure from Congress to intervene in Cuba. His strategy of pressuring Spain to agree to a negotiated withdrawal from Cuba would then meet its most difficult test.

On March 19 the president learned that the naval panel was going to blame an external cause for the loss of the *Maine*. The president warned Madrid that a crisis was coming. At the end of the month the United States asked Madrid if it would accept an armistice and negotiations with the insurgent forces. The end of that process, though Washington did not say so, was independence for Cuba. By March 31 Spain gave its answer. It would not negotiate. The president prepared to send a message to Congress asking for the authority to intervene on April 6. Over the next five days, efforts went forward to avert war. Spain offered to cease hostilities, a move that did not involve official recognition of the rebellion. How long this military pause would last would be up to the Spanish commander in Cuba. There were other minor concessions, but on the essential point, future independence for Cuba, the Spanish were unwavering. Their final answer was negative. At that point, McKinley submitted his message to Congress.

About the Author

William McKinley was born in 1843. After service in the Civil War, he became a politician in Ohio and was elected to Congress in 1875. During the next fourteen years, he was identified with the protective tariff as a key part of his party's ideology. Defeated for reelection in 1890, he won the governorship of Ohio in 1891 and was reelected in 1893. His popularity among Republicans made him a front-runner for his party's presidential nomination in 1896. He defeated the democratic candidate, William Jennings Bryan, in the race for the White House. McKinley guided the United States to victory in the war with Spain. He advocated acquisition of the Philippine Islands. Following the success in the Spanish-American War, McKinley won reelection to a second term in another race against Bryan in 1900. He was shot by an assassin on September 6, 1901, in Buffalo, New York, and died on September 14.

McKinley was the first modern president. He improved relations with the press, worked well with Congress, and broadened the authority of the office. He acted as his own secretary of state and kept the reins of power in his own hands. His goal was to persuade Spain to withdraw from Cuba without a war. He insisted, however, that any resolution of the conflict be acceptable to the Cuban rebels. That meant that there was little room for compromise between Madrid and Washington. By April 1898, McKinley's efforts at inducing Spain to accept Cuban independence had clearly failed. Nonetheless, as his message would demonstrate, he was still hoping that diplomatic pressure from the United States might prevent bloodshed.

Explanation and Analysis of the Document

In the first two paragraphs, McKinley invokes the Constitution as his reason for reporting to Congress on the Cuban crisis with his recommendations about what needed to be done. He adds that the issue of what to do in Cuba has an "intimate connection" to the United States. Therefore, the president must decide how dealing with Cuba accords with the precepts of traditional American foreign policy.

McKinley notes in the third paragraph that the Cuban Revolution is part of a process of unrest and revolt on the island that has been going on for fifty years, with disturbing effects on commerce. More important for the president, the Spanish have engaged in "the exercise of cruel, barbarous, and uncivilized practices of warfare" that have "shocked the sensibilities and offended the humane sympathies of our people."

Paragraphs 4 through 6 outline what had happened in Cuba following the start of the revolution in February 1895. McKinley comments that the uprising and the effort to suppress it have produced a conflict in which "a dependent people striving to be free have been opposed by the power of the sovereign state." The president outlines the effects on Cuba and the United States. The agitation over Cuba has sparked a "perilous unrest among our own citizens" and called into question the principle of "the avoidance of all foreign entanglements."

In the seventh paragraph, McKinley describes the Cleveland administration's policies regarding Cuba. He indicates that the goal was "an honorable adjustment of the contest between Spain and her revolted colony, on the basis of some effective scheme of self-government for Cuba under the flag and sovereignty of Spain." The sticking point was Spain's refusal to negotiate unless the insurgents accepted Madrid's terms and submitted to Spanish rule.

In the ninth paragraph the president explains what his administration has done since March 1897. The Spanish

www.milestonedocuments.com

Time Line

1898

■ **April 24**
Spain declares war.

■ **April 25**
The United States declares war on Spain.

■ **May 1**
Admiral Dewey defeats Spanish fleet in Manila Bay.

■ **July 1**
The United States is victorious in battles of El Caney and San Juan Hill in Cuba.

■ **July 3**
Spanish fleet off Cuba is destroyed.

■ **July 17**
Cuban garrison surrenders.

■ **August 12**
Hostilities are terminated, and peace negotiations begin.

■ **December 10**
The Treaty of Paris is signed to end war; United States gains Philippine Islands.

1899

■ **February 6**
The treaty is ratified.

policy to which he refers is called "reconcentration." To dry up support for the rebellion, Cubans were relocated to camps where Spanish troops could control them. In his diplomatic messages, McKinley had urged the Spanish to seek a peaceful settlement acceptable to the rebels. The change of government in Spain in mid-1897 offered another chance for a resolution of the crisis.

As he states in the tenth paragraph, McKinley believed that neither side in Cuba could achieve a complete victory. The two parties would fight until both were exhausted, as had happened in the 1870s in "the truce of Zanjon." That outcome was unacceptable to "the civilized world" and especially to the United States. The president's narrative in the eleventh paragraph moves ahead to March 27, when he submitted proposals to Madrid hoping for an armistice and peace negotiations with McKinley as the mediator. The United States, as McKinley notes in the twelfth paragraph, also sought an end to the reconcentration policy and the sending of relief supplies to Cuba from America.

According to the thirteenth paragraph of McKinley's message, the Spanish reply came back on March 31 ("ultimo" in this context meaning "the preceding month"), and it represented a rejection of McKinley's initiative. First, the Cuban parliament would have to be considered, with the central government in Madrid having the final word. The

Spanish would stop hostilities if the insurgents asked for a cessation. The president notes that the length of such a pause in the fighting would be up to the Spanish military commander on the ground.

In the fourteenth paragraph, McKinley mentions how the negotiations between the American minister to Spain (General Stewart Woodford) and the government in Madrid have been conducted. From these conversations, McKinley knew that the Spanish would allow the Cuban parliament to reach a settlement with the rebels under the conditions that Madrid specified. As the president observes in the next brief paragraph, "with this last overture in the direction of immediate peace, and its disappointing reception by Spain, the Executive is brought to the end of his effort." What then should the United States do? In the sixteenth paragraph McKinley explores the United States' options in dealing with Cuba based on what he had told Congress in December 1897. At that time, he had rejected annexation of Cuba as "criminal aggression." Instead, McKinley outlines four alternatives in the ensuing paragraphs—to recognize the rebels as belligerents, to recognize Cuban independence, to encourage "a rational compromise" between the two parties, and, finally, to intervene in favor of one side or the other.

In paragraphs 17 through 20, McKinley presents the United States' options. Recognizing the Cubans as belligerents would bring on war with Spain but would leave the United States unable to intervene effectively. He does not favor recognition of the Cuban belligerents or a statement in favor of Cuban independence. In the latter case, as he notes in paragraph 20, the designation of "any particular government in Cuba might subject us to embarrassing conditions of international obligation toward the organization so recognized." The United States could do that at some later date, as he indicates in paragraph 21.

Having disposed of these alternatives, McKinley then says that the United States can intervene either as a neutral or the ally of the Cuban rebels. Despite the president's language in paragraph 22 about becoming "the active ally of the one party or the other," no one in the United States would have thought of intervening on the side of Spain. In paragraph 24, McKinley comes down on the side of acting "as a neutral to stop the war, according to the large dictates of humanity." In the next six paragraphs, McKinley lays out the reasons that would justify American intervention in Cuba. He cites the "cause of humanity" because of the bloodshed on the island. "It is specially our duty, for it is right at our door." In paragraph 27, he points out that the obligations the United States has toward the people of Cuba make it necessary to step in to provide legal protection that the Spanish cannot afford them. In paragraph 28, he alludes to the destruction of American property in Cuba.

Paragraph 29 provides the main ground for McKinley's argument to Congress for intervention. "The present condition of affairs in Cuba is a constant menace to our peace, and entails upon this Government an enormous expense." In paragraphs 30–32, the president discusses the sinking of the *Maine* and the conclusion of the navy's court of inquiry that an external explosion caused the disaster. Note that McKinley does not blame Spain for the event, but he does say that Madrid could not assure the safety of the vessel in Havana Harbor. In paragraph 33, McKinley concludes that Spain cannot repress the rebellion and that "the enforced pacification of Cuba" is the only option. Then he comes to his conclusion about the situation. "In the name of humanity, in the name of civilization, in behalf of endangered American interests which give us the right and the duty to speak and to act, the war in Cuba must stop."

McKinley then turns to what he would like Congress to do. Rather than asking directly for war with Spain, he seeks authorization to end hostilities between the Spanish and the Cubans, to secure a stable government on the island "capable of maintaining order and observing its international obligations" as well as providing peace and security, and to use the American military toward these ends. After mentioning the need to provide relief supplies in paragraph 35, the president asks Congress for action. In paragraph 36, he refers to Spain's offer to proclaim "a suspension of hostilities, the duration and details of which have not yet been communicated to me." The final paragraph leaves open the possibility that this last-minute move might help the situation. McKinley does not discuss the conditions of this pause in the fighting, even though Congress and the White House knew this was important. The Spanish action did not recognize the belligerency of the Cuban rebels, the Spanish commander would determine how long the suspension lasted, and in essence to Washington it seemed that once again Spain was stalling for time.

Audience

McKinley had not given Congress a war message. He left open the chance for further talks with Madrid. The way in which the president framed the issue of Cuban belligerency and its future independence ensured that Congress would talk about these matters for several days. McKinley's request was for large discretionary power to employ the military forces short of going to war. He was asserting his supremacy in the conduct of foreign policy and his role as commander in chief.

The message of April 11, 1898, was composed first to impart to members of Congress what the president wanted them to do about Cuba. Beyond that audience, the document sought to convey the White House's reasoning about the next steps in Cuba. Unlike modern messages of great importance from presidents that are usually delivered orally, McKinley's words would be read by clerks and printed in newspapers. The tradition was that presidents did not address Congress in person. While McKinley was a clear and direct writer, his message does not strive for literary effect and does not resonate with the lawmakers or the public in that respect. Because of the belief that the United States had no reason for war with Spain in 1898, many commentators have accused McKinley of poor reasoning and overlooking the concessions that Spain had supposedly made.

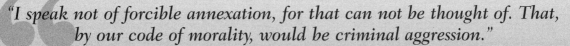

> *"I speak not of forcible annexation, for that can not be thought of. That, by our code of morality, would be criminal aggression."*
>
> (Paragraph 25)

> *"When it shall appear hereafter that there is within the island a government capable of performing the duties and discharging the functions of a separate nation, and having, as a matter of fact, the proper forms and attributes of nationality, such a government can be promptly and readily recognized and the relations and interests of the United States with such nation adjusted."*
>
> (Paragraph 34)

> *"In the name of humanity, in the name of civilization, in behalf of endangered American interests which give us the right and the duty to speak and to act, the war in Cuba must stop."*
>
> (Paragraph 50)

McKinley was not writing for the ages but rather to win the support of a restive and even rebellious Congress. The president still hoped that Spain might yield at the last minute, so the message could not be too warlike or it might leave Madrid with no option but war.

Impact

McKinley's Message to Congress did not satisfy members of either house who were eager for war with Spain. They believed that McKinley should have sought a declaration of war. Democrats who favored war were critical. Public opinion, however, was more favorable to the administration. The measured tone of the message and the moderation of McKinley's language buttressed his prestige at a decisive moment. The president had also set the terms of the debate that would lead to war with Spain in the ensuing weeks.

In the House, the Democrats offered a resolution that would have recognized the Cuban republic. The Republican majority voted that idea down. The lawmakers then endorsed the president's policy by a vote of 325 to 19. The road was more difficult in the Senate, however. Backers of Cuban independence offered an amendment to a draft resolution that would have recognized the Cuban republic as the legitimate government of the island. The amendment was adopted. A second amendment, introduced by Henry M. Teller of Colorado, disavowed an intention of annexing Cuba after the projected fighting had ended. The Senate resolution contained both of these amendments.

McKinley exercised his influence with the Republicans on Capitol Hill to obtain the defeat of the resolution recognizing Cuban independence. He could live with the Teller amendment. The president signed the resolution on April 20, and Spain immediately broke diplomatic relations. The United States imposed a naval blockade on April 22, and Spain declared war two days later. McKinley asked Congress for a declaration of war on April 25, and Congress compiled with a resolution that said war had existed since April 21. The fighting between the United States and Spain soon began.

McKinley's Message to Congress about Cuba remains one of the most controversial actions of his presidency. Although modern scholars no longer believe that the president submitted a war message, criticism of McKinley's language has focused on whether a peaceful settlement of the differences with Spain could have been achieved. A close examination of the situation between the two countries in April 1898 indicates the implausibility of such an outcome. But because the war with Spain led to the acquisition of the Philippine Islands and an American overseas empire, the prospect that such results could have been avoided heightens the significance of what McKinley wrote.

Related Documents

Spanish Diplomatic Correspondence and Documents, 1896–1900, Presented to the Cortes by the Minister of State. Washington, D.C.: Government Printing Office, 1905. This collection of Spanish diplomatic documents, translated and published by the United States, government is essential for understanding the point of view of Spain toward the Cuban issue.

U.S. Department of State. *Papers Relating to the Foreign Relations of the United States, 1898.* Washington, D.C.: Government Printing Office, 1899. An indispensable collection of diplomatic documents outlining the development of American foreign policy up to the submission of McKinley's message.

Bibliography

■ Books

Gould, Lewis L. *The Presidency of William McKinley.* Lawrence: University Press of Kansas, 1980.

Hoganson, Kristen. *Fighting for American Manhood: How Gender Politics Provoked the Spanish-American and Philippine-American Wars.* New Haven, Conn: Yale University Press, 1998.

LaFeber, Walter. *The New Empire; An Interpretation of American Expansion, 1860–1898.* Ithaca, N.Y.: Cornell University Press, 1963.

Leech, Margaret. *In the Days of McKinley* New York: Harper & Bros., 1959.

Offner, John L. *An Unwanted War: The Diplomacy of the United States and Spain, 1895–1898.* Chapel Hill: University of North Carolina Press, 1992.

May, Ernest R. *Imperial Democracy: The Emergence of America as a Great Power.* New York: Harcourt, Brace and World, 1961.

Morgan, H. Wayne. *William McKinley and His America*, rev. ed. Kent, Ohio: Kent State University Press, 2003.

Perez, Louis A., Jr. *The War of 1898: The United States and Cuba in History and Historiography.* Chapel Hill: University of North Carolina Press, 1998.

■ Web Sites

"The World of 1898: The Spanish-American War." Hispanic Division of the Library of Congress Web site.
   http://www.loc.gov/rr/hispanic/1898/chronology.html. Accessed on July 13, 2007.

"Transcript of De Lôme Letter (1898)." National Archives "Our Documents" Web site.
   http://www.ourdocuments.gov/doc.php?doc=53&page=transcript. Accessed on January 31, 2008.

"William McKinley War Message." Vincent Ferraro, Cogito, Ergo I.R. Web site.
   http://www.mtholyoke.edu/acad/intrel/mkinly2.htm. Accessed on July 13, 2007.

—By Lewis L. Gould

1. What were the differences over Cuba between Spain and the United States in April 1898 as President McKinley outlined them? Why did the United States have a right and a duty to be concerned about the revolution in Cuba? What traditions in American foreign policy might have shaped the attitudes of the McKinley administration and the people of the United States?

2. What are the major criticisms that the president makes of the tactics of the Spanish military in trying to put down the Cuban revolution? What does he mean by "cruel, barbarous, and uncivilized practices of warfare"? What have been the adverse effects of the situation in Cuba on the United States?

3. How has the McKinley administration endeavored to obtain a diplomatic solution to the problems of Cuba? What was the nature of the proposal that McKinley made on March 27, 1898, and how did the Spanish respond? How far did Spain go in meeting the demands that Washington had set? Why did the president regard the Spanish answer as "disappointing"?

4. What were the options for the United States in light of the Spanish answer to the American initiative? What effect would come if the United States recognized the Cubans as belligerents or endorsed independence for Cuba? What would have been the Spanish reaction to such moves? What are the merits of McKinley's argument against such a course? Why might the American government have doubted the capacity of the rebels to make an independent Cuban nation work? What did Americans think at the end of the nineteenth century about the abilities of the peoples of Latin America to govern themselves? How did racial attitudes influence these judgments?

5. What was McKinley asking the Congress to do? In what ways was he seeking to enhance presidential power? Is it surprising that some pro-war members of Congress reacted in a negative way to what McKinley proposed to do about Cuba? How has the process of taking the United States into wars or armed conflicts overseas changed since April 1898?

beget	to bring into being
belligerents	persons or nations at war
engross	occupy wholly
enjoin	order, enforce
equanimity	calmness
forbearance	restraint, patience
incumbent	resting on as an obligation or duty
insurrection	revolt or rebellion
lucrative	profitable
maxim	statement of general truth
onerous	burdensome
pacification	producing peace, sometimes through military action
precept	commandment or direction
reconcentration	process of moving the Cuban population into fortified areas
sanguinary	bloody
subjugation	state of being conquered
ultimo	old fashioned way of saying in the last month

WILLIAM McKINLEY'S MESSAGE TO CONGRESS ABOUT CUBAN INTERVENTION

To the Congress of the United States:

Obedient to that precept of the Constitution which commands the President to give from time to time to the congress information of the state of Union and to recommend to their consideration such measures as he shall judge necessary and expedient, it becomes my duty now to address your body with regard to the grave crisis that has arisen in the relations of the United States to Spain by reason of the warfare that for more than three years has raged in the neighboring island of Cuba.

I do so because of the intimate connection of the Cuban question with the state of our own Union and the grave relation the course which it is now incumbent upon the nation to adopt must needs bear to the traditional policy of our Government if it is to accord with the precepts laid down by the founders of the Republic and religiously observed by succeeding Administrations to the present day.

The present revolution is but the successor of other similar insurrections which have occurred in Cuba against the dominion of Spain, extending over a period of nearly half a century, each of which, during its progress, has subjected the United States to great effort and expense in enforcing its neutrality laws, caused enormous losses to American trade and commerce caused irritation, annoyance, and disturbance among our citizens, and by the exercise of cruel, barbarous, and uncivilized practices of warfare, shocked the sensibilities and offended the humane sympathies of our people.

Since the present revolution began in February, 1895, this country has seen the fertile domain at our threshold ravaged by fire and sword in the course of a struggle unequaled in the history of the island and rarely paralleled as to the numbers of the combatants and the bitterness of the contest by any revolution of modern times where dependent people striving to be free have been opposed by the power of the sovereign state.

Our people have beheld a once prosperous community reduced to comparative want, its lucrative commerce virtually paralyzed, its exceptional productiveness diminished, its fields laid waste, its mills in ruins, and its people perishing by tens of thousands from hunger and destitution. We have found ourselves constrained, in the observance of that strict neutrality which our laws enjoin, and which the law of nations commands, to police our own waters and watch our own seaports in prevention of any unlawful act in aid of the Cubans.

Our trade has suffered; the capital invested by our citizens in Cuba has been largely lost, and the temper and forbearance of our people have been so sorely tried as to beget a perilous unrest among our own citizens which has inevitably found its expression from time to time in the National Legislature, so that issues wholly external to our own body politic engross attention and stand in the way of the close devotion to domestic advancement that becomes a self-contained commonwealth whose primal maxim has been the avoidance of all foreign entanglements. All this must need awaken, and has, indeed, aroused the utmost concern on the part of this Government, as well during my predecessor's term as in my own.

In April, 1896, the evils from which our company suffered through the Cuban war became so onerous that my predecessor made an effort to bring about a peace through the mediation of this Government in any way that might tend to an honorable adjustment of the contest between Spain and her revolted colony, on the basis of some effective scheme of self-government of Cuba under the flag and sovereignty of Spain. It failed through the refusal of the Spanish Government then in power to consider any form of mediation or, indeed, any plan of settlement which did not begin with the actual submission of the insurgents to the mother country, and the only on such term as Spain herself might see fit to grant. The war continued unabated.

The resistance of the insurgents was in no wise diminished.

The efforts of Spain were increased, both by the dispatch of fresh levies to Cuba and by the addition to the horrors of the strife of a new and inhuman phase happily unprecedented in the modern history of civilized Christian peoples. The policy of devastation and concentration, inaugurated by the Captain-General's bando of October 21, 1896, in the Province of Pinar del Rio was thence extended to embrace all of the island to which the power of the Spanish arms was able to reach by occupation or by military operations. The peasantry, including all dwelling in the open agricultural interior, were driven into the garrison towns or isolated places held by the troops.

The raising and movement of provisions of all kinds were interdicted. The fields ware laid waste, dwellings unroofed and fired, mills destroyed, and, in short, everything that could desolate the land and render it unfit for human habitation or support was commanded by one or the other of the contending parties and executed by all the powers at their disposal.

By the time the present administration took office a year ago, reconcentration—so called—had been made effective over the better part of the four central and western provinces, Santa Clara, Matanzas, Havana, Pinar del Rio.

The agricultural population to the estimated number of 300,000 or more was herded within the towns and their immediate vicinage, deprived of the means of support, rendered destitute of shelter, left poorly clad, and exposed to the most unsanitary conditions. As the scarcity of food increased with the devastation of the depopulated areas of production, destitution and want became misery and starvation. Month by month the death rate increased in an alarming ration. By March, 1897, according to conservative estimates from official Spanish sources, the mortality among the reconcentrados from starvation and the diseases thereto incident exceeded 50 per centum of their total number.

No practical relief was accorded to the destitute. The overburdened towns, already suffering from the general dearth, could give no aid. So called "zones of cultivation" established within the immediate areas of effective military control about the cities and fortified camps proved illusory as a remedy for the suffering. The unfortunates, being for the most part women and children, with aged and helpless men, enfeebled by disease and hunger, could not have tilled the soil without tools, seed, or shelter for their own support or for the supply of the cities. Reconcentration, adopted avowedly as a ware measure in order to cut off the resources of the insurgents, worked its predestined result. As I said in my message of last December, it was not civilized warfare; it was extermination. The only peace it could beget was that of the wilderness and the grave.

Meanwhile the military situation in the island had undergone a noticeable change. The extraordinary activity that characterized the second year of the war, when the insurgents invaded even the thitherto unharmed fields of Pinar del Rio and carried havoc and destruction up to the walls of the city of Havana itself, had relapsed into a dogged struggle in the central and eastern provinces. The Spanish arms regained a measure of control in Pinar del Rio and parts of Havana, but, under the existing conditions of the rural country, without immediate improvement of their productive situation. Even thus partially restricted, the revolutionists held their own, and their conquest and submission, put forward by Spain as the essential and sole basis of peace, seemed as far distant as at the outset.

In this state of affairs my Administration found itself confronted with the grave problem of its duty. My message of last December reviewed the situation and narrated the steps taken with a view to relieving its acuteness and opening the way to some form of honorable settlement. The assassination of the Prime Minister, Canovas, led to a change of government in Spain. The former administration, pledged to subjugation without concession, gave place to that of a more liberal party, committed long in advance to a policy of reform, involving the wider principle of home rule for Cuba and Puerto Rico.

The overtures of this Government, made through its new envoy, General Woodford, and looking to an immediate and effective amelioration of the condition of the island, although not accepted to the extent of the condition of the island, although not accepted to the extent of admitted mediation in any shape, were met by assurances that home rule, in advanced phase, would be forthwith offered to Cuba, without waiting for the war to end, and that more humane methods should thenceforth prevail in the conduct of hostilities. Coincidentally with these declarations, the new Government of Spain continued and completed the policy already begun by its predecessor, of testifying friendly regard for this nation by releasing American citizens held under one charge or another connected with the insurrection, so that by the end of November not a single person entitled in any way to our national protection remained in a Spanish prison.

While these negotiations were in progress the increasing destitution of the unfortunate reconcentrados and alarming mortality among them claimed earnest attention. The success which had attended the limited measure of relief extended to the suffering American citizens among them by the judicious expenditure through the consular agencies of the money appropriated expressly for their succor by the joint resolution approved May 24, 1897, prompted the humane extension of a similar scheme of aid to the great body of sufferers. A suggestion to this end was acquiesced in by the Spanish authorities. On the 24th of December last I caused to be issued an appeal to the American people, inviting contributions in money or in kind for the succor of the starving sufferers in Cuba, following this on the 8th of January by a similar public announcement of the formation of a central Cuban relief committee, with headquarters in New York City, composed of three members representing the American National Red Cross and the religious and business elements of the community.

The efforts of that committee have been untiring and have accomplished much. Arrangements for free transportation to Cuba have greatly aided the charitable work. The president of the American Red Cross and representative of other contributory organizations have generously visited Cuba and cooperated with the consul-general and the local authorities to make effective distribution of the relief collected through the efforts of the central committee. Nearly $200,000 in money and supplies has already reached the sufferers and more is forthcoming. The supplies are admitted duty free, and transportation to the interior has been arranged so that the relief, at first necessarily confined to Havana and the larger cities, is now extended through most if not all of the towns where suffering exists.

Thousands of lives have already been saved. The necessity for change in the condition of the reconcentrados is recognized by the Spanish Government. Within a few days past the orders of General Weyler have been revoked; the reconcentrados, it is said, are to be permitted to return to their homes and aided to resume the self-supporting pursuits of peace. Public works have been ordered to give them employment, and a sum of $600,000 has been appropriated for their relief.

The war in Cuba is of such a nature that short of subjugation or extermination a final military victory for either side seems impracticable. The alternative lies in the physical exhaustion of the one or the other party, or perhaps of both—a condition which in effect ended the ten year's war by the truce of Zanjon. The prospect of such a protraction and conclusion of the present strife is a contingency hardly to be contemplated with equanimity by the civilized world, and least of all by the United States, affected and injured as we are, deeply and intimately, by its very existence.

Realizing this, it appeared to be my duty, in a spirit of true friendliness, no less to Spain than the Cubans who have so much to lose by the prolongation of the struggle, to seek to bring about an immediate termination of the war. To this end I submitted, on the 27th ultimo, as a result of much representation and correspondence, through the United States minister at Madrid, propositions to the Spanish Government looking to an armistice until October 1 for the negotiation of peace with the good offices of the President.

In addition, I asked the immediate revocation of the order of reconcentration, so as to permit the people to return to their farms and the needy to be relieved with provisions and supplies from the United States, cooperating with the Spanish authorities, so as to afford full relief.

The reply of the Spanish cabinet was received on the night of the 31st ultimo. It offered, as the means to bring about peace in Cuba, to confide the preparation thereof to the insular parliament, inasmuch as the concurrence of that body would be necessary to reach a final result, it being, however, understood that the powers reserved by the constitution to the central Government are not lessened or diminished. As the Cuban parliament does not meet until the 4th of May next, the Spanish Government would not object, for its part, to accept at one a suspension of hostilities if asked for by the insurgents from the general in chief, to whom it would pertain, in such case, to determine the duration and conditions of the armistice.

The propositions submitted by General Woodford and the reply of the Spanish Government were both in the form or brief memoranda, the texts of which are before me, and are substantially in the language above given. The function of the Cuban parliament in the matter of "preparing" peace and the manner of its doing so are not expressed in the Spanish memorandum; but from General Woodford's explanatory reports of preliminary discussions preceding the final conference it is understood that the Spanish Government stands ready to give the insular congress full powers to settle the terms of peace with the insurgents—whether by direct negotiation or indirectly by means of legislation does not appear.

With this last overture in the direction of immediate peace, and its disappointing reception by Spain, the Executive is brought to the end of his effort.

In my annual message of December last I said:

Of the untried measures there remained only: Recognition of the insurgents as belligerents; recognition of the independence of Cuba; neutral intervention to end the war by imposing a national a rational compromise between the contestants, and intervention in favor of one or the other party. I speak not of forcible annexation, for that can not be thought of. That, by our code of morality, would be criminal aggression.

Thereupon I reviewed these alternatives, in the light of President Grant's measured words, uttered in 1875, when after seven years of sanguinary, destructive, and cruel hostilities in Cuba he reached the conclusion that the recognition of the independence of Cuba was impracticable and indefensible, and that the recognition of belligerence was not warranted by the facts according to the tests of public law. I commented especially upon the latter aspect of the question, pointing out the inconveniences and positive dangers of a recognition of belligerence which, while adding to the already onerous burdens of neutrality within our own jurisdiction, could not in any way extend our influence or effective offices in the territory of hostilities.

Nothing has since occurred to change my view in this regard, and I recognize as fully now as then that the issuance of a proclamation of neutrality, by which process the so-called recognition of belligerents is published, could, of itself and unattended by other action, accomplish nothing toward the one end for which we labor—the instant pacification of Cuba and cessation of the misery that afflicts the island.

Turning to the question of recognizing at this time the independence of the present insurgent government in Cuba, we find safe precedents in our history from an early day. They are well summed up in President Jackson's message to Congress, December 21, 1836, on the subject of the recognition of the independence of Texas. He said:

In all the contest that have arisen out of the revolution of France, out of the disputes relating to the Crowns of Portugal and Spain, out of the separation of the American possessions of both from the European Governments, and out of the numerous and constantly occurring struggles for dominion in Spanish America, so wisely consistent with our just principles has been the action of our Government, that we have, under the most critical circumstances, avoided all censure, and encountered no other evil than the produced by a transient estrangement of good will in those against whom we have been by force of evidence compelled to decide.

It has thus made known to the world that the uniform policy and practice of the United States is to avoid all interference in disputes which merely relate to the internal government of other nations, and eventually to recognize the authority of the prevailing party without reference to our particular interests and views or to the merits of the original controversy.

… But on this, as on every other trying occasion, safety is to be found in a rigid adherence to principle.

In the contest between Spain and the revolted colonies we stood aloof, and waited not only until the ability of the new States to protect themselves was fully established, but until the danger of their being again subjugated had entirely passed away. Then, and not until then, were they recognized.

Such was our course in regard to Mexico herself.… It is true that with defeated, the chief of the Republic himself captured, and all present power to control the newly organized government of Texas annihilated within its confines; but, on the other hand, there is, in appearance, at least, an immense disparity of physical force on the side of Texas. The Mexican Republic, under another executive, is rallying its forces under a new lender and menacing a fresh invasion to recover its lost dominion.

Upon the issue of this threatened invasion the independence of Texas may be considered as suspended; and were there nothing peculiar in the relative situation of the United States and Texas, our acknowledgment of its independence at such a crisis could scarcely be regarded as consistent with the prudent reserve with which we have hitherto held ourselves bound to treat all similar questions.

Thereupon Andrew Jackson proceeded to consider the risk that there might be imputed to the United States motives of selfish interest in view of the former claim on our part to the territory of Texas, and of the avowed purpose of the Texas in seeking recognition of independence as an incident to the incorporation of Texas into the Union, concluding thus:

> Prudence, therefore, seems to dictate that we should still stand aloof and maintain our present attitude, if not until Mexico itself or one of the great foreign powers shall recognize the independence of the new government, at least until the lapse of time or the course of events shall have proved beyond cavil or dispute the ability of the people of that country to maintain their separate sovereignty and to uphold the government constituted by them. Neither of the contending parties can justly complain of this course. By pursuing it we are but carrying out the long-established policy of our Government, a policy which has secured to us respect and influence abroad and inspired confidence at home.

These are the words of the resolute and patriotic Jackson. They are evidence that the United States, in addition to the test imposed by public law as the condition of the recognition of independence by a neutral state (to wit, that the revolted state shall "constitute in fact a body politic, having a government in substance as well as in name, possessed of the elements of stability," and forming de facto, "if left to itself, a state among the nations, reasonably capable of discharging the duties of a state"), has imposed for its own governance in dealing with cases like these the further condition that recognition of independent statehood is not due to a revolted dependency until the danger of its being again subjugated by the parent state has entirely passed away.

This extreme test was, in fact, applied in the case of Texas. The Congress to whom President Jackson referred the question as one "probably leading to war," and therefore a proper subject for "a previous understanding with that body by whom war can alone be declared and by whom all the provisions for sustaining its perils must be furnished," left the matter of the recognition of Texas to the discretion of the Executive, providing merely for the sending of a diplomatic agent when the President should be satisfied that the Republic of Texas had become "an independent State." It was so recognized by President Van Buren,

who commissioned a charge d'affaires March 7, 1837, after Mexico had abandoned an attempt to reconquer the Texan territory, and when there was at the time no bona fide contest going on between the insurgent province and its former Sovereign.

I said in my message of December last, "It is to be seriously considered whether the Cuban insurrection possesses beyond dispute the attributes of statehood which alone can demand the recognition of belligerency in its favor." The same requirement must certainly be no less seriously considered when the graver issue of recognizing independence is in question, for no less positive test can be applied to the greater act than to the lesser; while, on the other hand, the influences and consequences of the struggle upon the internal policy of the recognizing State, which form important factors when the recognition of belligerency is concerned, are secondary, if not rightly eliminable, factors when the real question is whether the community claiming recognition is or is not independent beyond peradventure.

Nor from the standpoint of expediency do I think it would be wise or prudent for this Government to recognize at the present time the independence of the so-called Cuban Republic. Such recognition is not necessary in order to enable the United States to intervene and pacify the island. To commit this country now to the recognition of any particular government in Cuba might subject us to embarrassing conditions of international obligation toward the organization so recognized. In case of intervention our conduct would be subject to the approval or disapproval of such government. We would be required to submit to its direction and to assume to it the mere relation of a friendly ally.

When it shall appear hereafter that there is within the island a government capable of performing the duties and discharging the functions of a separate nation, and having, as a matter of fact, the proper forms and attributes of nationality, such government can be promptly and readily recognized and the relations and interests of the United States with such nation adjusted.

There remain the alternative forms of intervention to end the war, either as an impartial neutral by imposing a rational compromise between the contestants, or as the active ally of the one party or the other.

As to the first it is not to be forgotten that during the last few months the relations of the United States has virtually been one of friendly intervention in many ways, each not of itself conclusive, but all tending to the exertion of a potential influence toward an ultimate pacific result, just and honorable to all interests concerned. The spirit of all our acts hitherto has been an earnest, unselfish desire for peace and prosperity in Cuba, untarnished by differences between us and Spain, and unstained by the blood of American citizens.

The forcible intervention of the United States as a neutral to stop the war, according to the large dictates of humanity and following many historical precedents where neighboring States have interfered to check the hopeless sacrifices of life by internecine conflicts beyond their borders, is justifiable on rational grounds. It involves, however, hostile constraint upon both the parties to the contest as well to enforce a truce as to guide the eventual settlement.

The grounds for such intervention may be briefly summarized as, follows:

First. In the cause of humanity and to put an end to the barbarities, bloodshed, starvation, and horrible miseries now existing there, and which the parties to the conflict are either unable or unwilling to stop or mitigate. It is no answer to say this is all in another country, belonging to another nation, and is therefore none of our business. It is specially our duty, for it is right at our door.

Second. We owe it to our citizens in Cuba to afford them that protection and indemnity for life and property which no government there can or will afford, and to that end to terminate the conditions that deprive them of legal protection.

Third. The right to intervene may be justified by the very serious injury to the commerce, trade, and business of our people, and by the wanton destruction of property and devastation of the island.

Fourth, and which is of the utmost importance. The present condition of affairs in Cuba is a constant menace to our peace, and entails upon this Government an enormous expense. With such a conflict waged for years in an island so near us and with which our people have such trade and business relations; when the lives and liberty of our citizens are in constant danger and their property destroyed and themselves ruined; where our trading vessels are liable to seizure and are seized at our very door by war ships of a foreign nation, the expeditions of filibustering that we are powerless to prevent altogether, and the irritating questions and entanglements thus arising—all these and others that I need not mention, with the resulting strained relations, are constant menace to our peace, and compel us to keep on a semiwar footing with a nation with which we are at peace.

These elements of danger and disorder already pointed out have been strikingly illustrated by a tragic event which has deeply and justly moved the American people. I have already transmitted to Congress the report of the naval court of inquiry on the destruction of the battle ship Maine in the harbor of Havana during the night of the 15th of February. The destruction of that noble vessel has filled the national heart with inexpressible horror. Two hundred and fifty-eight brave sailors and marines and two officers of our Navy, reposing in the fancied security of a friendly harbor, have been hurled to death, grief and want brought to their homes, and sorrow to the nation.

The naval court of inquiry, which it is needless to say, commands the unqualified confidence of the Government, was unanimous in its conclusion that the destruction of the Maine was caused by an exterior explosion, that of a submarine mine. It did not assume to place the responsibility. That remains to be fixed.

In any event the destruction of the Maine, by whatever exterior cause, is a patent and impressive proof of a state of things in Cuba that is intolerable. That condition is thus shown to be such that the Spanish Government can not assure safety and security to a vessel of the American Navy in the harbor of Havana on a mission of peace, and rightfully there.

Further referring in this connection to recent diplomatic correspondence, a dispatch from our minister to Spain, of the 36th ultimo, contained the statement that the Spanish minister for foreign affairs assured him positively that the Spain will do all that the highest honor and justice require in the matter of the Maine. The reply above referred to of the 31st ultimo also contained an expression of the readiness of Spain to submit to an arbitration all the differences which can arise in this matter, which is subsequently explained by the note of the Spanish minister at Washington of the 10th instant, as follows:

> As to the question of fact which springs from the diversity of views between the reports of the American and Spanish boards, Spain proposes that the facts be ascertained by an impartial investigation by experts, whose decision Spain accepts in advance.

To this I have made no reply.

President Grant, in 1875, after discussing the phases of the contest as it then appeared, and its hopeless and apparent indefinite prolongation, said:

In such event, I am of opinion that other nations will be compelled to assume the responsibility which devolves upon them, and to seriously consider the only remaining measures possible—mediation and intervention. Owing, perhaps, to the large expanse of water separating the island from the Peninsula, … the contending parties appear to have within themselves no depository of common confidence, to suggest wisdom when passion and excitement have their away, and to assume the part of peacemaker.

In this view in the earlier days of the contest the good offices of the United States as a mediator were tendered in good faith, without any selfish purpose, in the interest of humanity and in sincere friendship for both parties, but were at the time declined by Spain, with the declaration, nevertheless, that at a future time they would be indispensable. No intimation has been received that in the opinion of Spain that time has been reached. And yet the strife continues with all its dread horrors and all its injuries to the interests of the United States and of other nations.

Each party seems quite capable of working great injury and damage to the other, as well as to all the relations and interests dependent on the existence of peace in the island; but they seem incapable of reaching any adjustment, and both have thus far failed of achieving any success whereby one party shall possess and control the island to the exclusion of the other. Under these circumstances, the agency of others, either by mediation or intervention, seems to be the only alternative which must sooner or later be invoked for the termination of the strife.

In the last annual message of my immediate predecessor, during the pending struggle, it was said:

when the inability of Spain to deal successfully with the insurrection has become manifest, and it is demonstrated that her sovereignty is extinct in Cuba for all purposes of its rightful existence, and when a hopeless struggle for its reestablishment has degenerated into a strife which means nothing more then the useless sacrifice of human life and the utter destruc-

tion of the very subject-matter of the conflict, a situation will be presented in which our obligations to the sovereignty of Spain will be superseded by higher obligations, which we can hardly hesitate to recognize and discharge.

In my annual message to Congress, December last, speaking to this question, I said:

The near future will demonstrate whether the indispensable condition of a righteous peace, just alike to the Cubans and to Spain, as well as equitable to all our interests so intimately involved in the welfare of Cuba, is likely to be attained. If not, the exigency of further and other action by the United States will remain to be taken. When the time comes that action will be determined in the line of indisputable right and duty. It will be faced, without misgiving or hesitancy, in the light of the obligation this Government over to itself, to the people who have confided to it the protection of their interests and honor, and to humanity.

Sure of the right, keeping free from all offense ourselves, actuated only by upright and patriotic considerations, moved neither by passion nor selfishness, the Government will continue its watchful care over the rights and property of American citizens and will abate none of its efforts to bring about by peaceful agencies a peace which shall be honorable and enduring. If it shall hereafter appear to be a duty imposed by our obligations to ourselves, to civilization and humanity to intervene with force, it shall be without fault on our part only because the necessity for such action will be so clear as to command the support and approval of the civilized world.

The long trail has proved that the object for which Spain has waged the war can not be attained. The fire of insurrection may flame or may smolder with varying seasons, but it has not been and it is plain that it can not be extinguished by present methods. The only hope of relief and repose from a condition which can no longer be endured is the enforced pacification of Cuba. In the name of humanity, in the name of civilization, in behalf of endangered American interests which gives us the right and the duty to speak and to act, the war in Cuba must stop.

In view of these facts and of these considerations, I ask the Congress to authorize and empower the President to take measure to secure a full and final termination of hostilities between the Government of Spain and the people of Cuba, and to secure in the island the establishment of a stable government, capable of maintaining order and observing its international obligations, insuring peace and tranquility and the security of its citizens as well as our own, and to use the military and naval forces of the United States as may be necessary for these purposes.

And in the interest of humanity and to aid in preserving the lives of the starving people of the island I recommend that the distribution of food and supplies be continued, and that an appropriation be made out of the public Treasury to supplement the charity of our citizens.

The issue is now with the Congress. It is a solemn responsibility. I have exhausted every effort to relieve the intolerable condition of affairs which is at our doors. Prepared to execute every obligation imposed upon me by the Constitution and the law, I await your action.

Yesterday, and since the preparation of the foregoing message, official information was received by me that the latest decree of the Queen Regent of Spain directs General Blanco, in order to prepare and facilitate peace, to proclaim a suspension of hostilities, the duration and details of which have not yet been communicated to me.

This fact with every other pertinent consideration will, I am sure, have your just and careful attention in the solemn deliberations upon which you are about to enter. If this measure attains a successful result, then our aspirations as a Christian, peace-loving people will be realized. If it fails, it will be only another justification for our contemplated action.

William McKinley

Executive Mansion, April 11, 1898.

John Marshall Harlan (Library of Congress)

"A false step at this time might be fatal to the development of what Chief Justice Marshall called the American Empire."

Overview

In *Downes v. Bidwell* the U.S. Supreme Court established that the United States was not just a nation of states and temporary territories; it was a nation of states and potentially permanent territories. Although the United States had always possessed territories, they were assumed to be transitional phases for areas under U.S. sovereignty. They were to be administered from the nation's capital until they had reached sufficient population size and had written constitutions establishing republican government, following the blueprint of the 1787 Northwest Ordinance. Congress could then annex U.S. territories as new states into the Union, which it ultimately did for thirty-one of the fifty states.

Justice Edward White's concurring opinion in *Downes v. Bidwell*, however, introduced a novel doctrine that distinguished between the United States' "incorporated" territories, those of continental North America as well as, later, Hawaii and Alaska, and its new, not-to-be-incorporated territories of Puerto Rico, the Philippines, and Guam. The United States acquired all three of those territories from Spain in the 1898 Treaty of Paris. The United States would also add American Samoa in 1899 in a tripartite arrangement with Great Britain and Germany and would annex the U.S. Virgin Islands in 1917 and the Northern Mariana Islands in 1976. Under Justice White's incorporation doctrine, the island territories could remain indefinitely outside of the American polity without needing to be on the road to statehood.

The decisions in *Downes v. Bidwell* and the other Insular Cases deeply divided the Court. Justice White's concurring opinion in *Downes* attracted the support of only three other votes on the Court; Justice Horace Gray, one of the three, agreed with the "substance" of Justice White's argument but wrote a separate concurring opinion. Chief Justice Melville Fuller assigned the Court's opinion to Justice Henry Billings Brown. But no other justice joined Brown's opinion, such that Fuller's dissent, fully joined by three other justices, actually attracted the highest number of justices. (Justice John Marshall Harlan also wrote a separate dissenting opinion.) The ruling in *Downes v. Bidwell* addressed only the constitutionality of the Organic Act of

1900, also called the Foraker Act, which established a government in Puerto Rico and imposed a tariff on trade between Puerto Rico and the mainland United States. Dozens of subsequent cases would be heard before the Supreme Court would articulate which constitutional provisions applied to the United States' new island territories—and before the incorporation doctrine first presented in *Downes v. Bidwell* would become entrenched.

In fact, at the start of the twenty-first century U.S. territories were still officially unincorporated territories. Thus, the inhabitants of Puerto Rico, Guam, the U.S. Virgin Islands, and the Northern Marianas were all considered U.S. citizens (with American Samoans being U.S. nationals), but none had votes in U.S. presidential elections, none had U.S. senators, and none had full-voting members in the U.S. House of Representatives. The Northern Marianas and American Samoa remained without any delegates at all representing them in Congress. Furthermore, not all rights and guarantees of the U.S. Constitution applied in full in these territories, while U.S. federal statutes still variably applied. The political limbo legitimated in *Downes v. Bidwell* remained.

Context

The United States seized control of Cuba and Puerto Rico during the Spanish-American War of 1898, acquiring the Philippines and Guam afterward in the peace settlement with Spain. Three days after that war ended, the United States annexed Hawaii through a joint congressional resolution, the Newlands Resolution. Expansionists in the administrations of William McKinley and Theodore Roosevelt and in the Republican Party sought to annex these islands for their strategic value as naval stations and coaling stations. The new bases in the Pacific Ocean and the Caribbean Sea would allow the U.S. Navy to protect American trade with the Far East and to guard the entrance to the planned isthmian canal connecting the Atlantic and Pacific oceans. American politicians, government officials, political writers, and others wished for the United States to emulate the other great world powers—Great Britain, France, Germany, and others—through the establishment

1898

■ **February 15**
Sinking of the USS *Maine* occurs in Havana harbor.

■ **April 19**
U.S. Congress passes the Teller Amendment, which holds that Cuba will not be annexed by the United States.

■ **April 25**
U.S. Congress declares state of war with Spain.

■ **July 6**
Hawaii is annexed by a congressional joint resolution.

■ **July 26**
President McKinley imposes tariffs on goods shipped from Puerto Rico or the Philippines to the mainland United States as well as vice versa.

1899

■ **February 6**
The U.S. Senate ratifies the Treaty of Paris, settling the terms of peace after the Spanish-American War.

1900

■ **April**
Congress passes the Foraker Act, which taxes trade between Puerto Rico and the several states.

1901

■ **January 14**
In *Neely v. Henkel*, Supreme Court unanimously recognizes Cuba as a foreign country.

■ **May 27**
The U.S. Supreme Court issues its decisions in *Downes v. Bidwell* and six other Insular Cases: *De Lima v. Bidwell*, *Goetze v. United States*, *Crossman v. United States*, *Dooley v. United States* (182 U.S. 222, known as *Dooley I*), *Armstrong v. United States*, and *Huus v. New York and Porto Rico Steamship Co.*

■ **September 14**
President McKinley dies from assassination; Theodore Roosevelt, the vice president, becomes the U.S. president.

---

of colonies and overseas empires. At the same time, the business allies of the McKinley and Roosevelt administrations were very aware of the economic potential, in sugar production especially, of the newly annexed islands.

Even if most Americans agreed that these islands should come under U.S. sovereignty, few wanted hundreds of thousands of Puerto Ricans and millions of Filipinos to become fellow citizens, equals in the American polity. In fact, just eight days after the signing of the 1898 Treaty of Paris, the Senate passed a resolution not to incorporate Filipinos as U.S. citizens and not to annex the Philippines. Just before the Spanish-American War, Congress had passed the Teller Amendment, which prohibited the United States from annexing Cuba. After the war, Congress passed the Platt Amendment, which guaranteed Cuba's independence under the conditions, among others, that the United States could intervene militarily in Cuba if need be and that the U.S. Navy could lease Guantánamo Bay and other naval bases. The Platt Amendment later became a part of the new Cuban constitution.

When Congress passed the Foraker Act in 1900, a tariff on trade between Puerto Rico and the mainland states was included; funds collected from the tariff were to be used for the administration of Puerto Rico, given the island's low tax base. The tariff, set at 15 percent of the existing Dingley Act tariff rates, was challenged by lawyers from Coudert Brothers, the international law firm that represented Samuel B. Downes & Co. and other trading firms, as a violation of the Constitution's uniformity clause, which stipulates that "all Duties, Imposts, and Excises" must "be uniform throughout the United States."

The attorneys for Downes & Co. argued that the duties imposed by the U.S. government on the oranges shipped from Puerto Rico to New York were unconstitutional, since the Constitution applied to the U.S. territories *ex proprio vigore*—through its own force. Furthermore, they contended, if the Constitution applied throughout the states and territories of the United States, as Chief Justice Roger B. Taney had argued in *Dred Scott v. Sandford*, then the uniformity clause should indeed apply to the new island territories. Chief Justice Fuller and Justices Harlan, David Brewer, and Rufus Peckham agreed with this position.

Attorneys for the McKinley administration and for the War Department, which administered the new U.S. territories, as well as many legal scholars and others held an opposing position: that the United States was composed solely of the several states. According to this view, Congress—the body representative of the people of the states—had to explicitly extend the Constitution to the U.S. territories for it to apply. From this perspective, the tariff contained in the Foraker Act was constitutional, since neither the Treaty of Paris nor Congress had explicitly determined that the U.S. Constitution was to apply to Puerto Rico or to any other U.S. island territories and since Congress had legitimately enacted a tariff on trade to and from Puerto Rico. This was Justice Brown's view as well; in fact, Brown was to draft the lead opinion in all but two of the cases decided in May and December 1901.

The Harvard government professor Abbott Lawrence Lowell (later the university's president) and a handful of other political writers voiced yet a third view on the application of the Constitution to the territories: that the United States consisted of the states and two different kinds of territories—those that a treaty or act of Congress had incorporated into the Union and those that had not been incorporated. In this view, in contrast to the view that the Constitution had to be explicitly extended, the Constitution nonetheless applied to the unincorporated territories because of Congress's authority under the territory clause. This was the view taken by Justices White; George Shiras, Jr.; Joseph McKenna; and, to a lesser degree, Gray.

About the Author

Henry Billings Brown, who wrote the lead opinion in *Downes v. Bidwell* and six other Insular Cases decided on May 27, 1901, grew up in South Lee, Massachusetts, in an upper-middle-class, Puritan, and Republican household. Brown attended Yale, Yale Law School, and Harvard Law School. He then moved west to Detroit, where he was appointed deputy U.S. marshal for Detroit and became an expert in admiralty law. Later, as district judge for the Eastern District of Michigan, Brown became renowned nationally for his mastery of admiralty law. President Benjamin Harrison appointed Brown to the Supreme Court in 1891, following Justice Samuel Miller's death.

Brown, who is best known for his lead opinion in *Plessy v. Ferguson* (1896), did not believe that the Constitution applied to Puerto Rico, the Philippines, or any other territory belonging to the United States in the absence of Congress's expressed extension of the Constitution. Brown was the swing judge for six of the seven Insular Cases decided in May 1901 and for the two cases of December 1901—all of which were decided by 5–4 margins. Whereas Brown upheld the constitutionality of the tariff in question, along with Justice White and the other justices in the *Downes* and *Dooley II* majorities, Brown joined Chief Justice Fuller and the *Downes* dissenters in the other Insular Cases of 1901.

Edward Douglass White, who wrote the concurring opinion in *Downes*, was born in 1845 near Thibodaux, Louisiana, to a former governor of Louisiana and sugar-plantation owner. White left college at the age of sixteen to serve in the Confederate army and returned to New Orleans after the Civil War. After studying law at what is now Tulane University, White became a leading lawyer in New Orleans and Louisiana and a successful Democratic politician. He was later appointed as a U.S. senator from Louisiana, serving for three years. In that period, he worked to uphold the gold standard, the interests of southern states, and other policies of the administration of Grover Cleveland. In 1894 President Cleveland chose White for the U.S. Supreme Court, acknowledging White's credentials as a conservative Democrat. White was later appointed chief justice of the United States in 1910—the first associate justice ever to be appointed chief justice—

Time Line

1901

■ **December 2**
Supreme Court decides two additional Insular Cases: *Dooley v. United States* (183 U.S. 151, known as *Dooley II*) and *Fourteen Diamond Rings v. United States.*

1902

■ **May 20**
Establishment of the Cuban republic, marking the end of U.S. occupation.

1903

■ **February 16**
The Roosevelt administration leases Guantánamo Bay from Cuba.

■ **June 1**
Hawaii v. Mankichi is decided.

■ **November 3**
Panama declares its independence from Colombia.

1904

■ **May 4**
United States begins construction on the Panama Canal.

■ **May 31**
Dorr v. United States is decided.

1905

■ **April 10**
Rasmussen v. United States is decided.

1922

■ **April 10**
Balzac v. Porto Rico is decided.

serving in that capacity until 1921. White argued that territories could be either fully included under the Constitution or subject to only some constitutional provisions, depending on the conditions specified by treaty or congressional legislation. He held that territories could even be divested by the United States, if Congress so chose.

Melville Weston Fuller, the author of one of the dissenting opinions in *Downes v. Bidwell*, grew up in an upper-class Maine family as the son of a lawyer and state politician. Fuller attended Bowdoin College and Harvard Law School. He left law school before graduating to work in his uncle's private practice, but at the age of twenty-three he left for Chicago. There, he became a successful Democratic politician, a member of the state legislature, and, at length, a leader of the Democrats in the Illinois

House of Representatives. After the Civil War, he became a prominent corporate lawyer and real estate investor. When Chief Justice Morrison Waite died, President Cleveland turned to Fuller to replace him; Fuller served as chief justice from 1888 to 1910. The Fuller Court is known for its conservative and pro-business rulings, such as its decisions in *Plessy v. Ferguson*, *Lochner v. New York*, *United States v. E. C. Knight Co.* (the Sugar Trust Case), and *In Re Debs*. Fuller himself is known for his antiregulatory and laissez-faire positions, per his opinions in *Pollock v. Farmers' Loan and Trust Co.* (the Income Tax Case), the Sugar Trust Case, and *Champion v. Ames* (the Lottery Case, in which he dissented). Fuller's antipathy toward government interference in commerce led him to oppose the majority opinion in *Downes*.

Explanation and Analysis of the Document

Justice Brown accepts the argument made by the War Department's Division of Insular Affairs, the U.S. solicitor general John K. Richards, and the U.S. attorney general John Griggs that Puerto Ricans should be considered subject to the complete sovereignty of the U.S. government. Specifically, Brown asserts that Puerto Ricans have no legal rights except those contained in the treaty with Spain. Since the U.S. government has full authority over its territories, the U.S. Constitution applies only when Congress extends its provisions. In Brown's view, Chief Justice Taney's argument in the *Dred Scott* case does not apply either. Taney's argument held that the Constitution applied throughout the U.S. territories (and states) dictum, but the Supreme Court had effectively overturned Taney's decision in the Mormon Church Case (*Late Corporation of the Church of Jesus Christ of Latter-Day Saints v. United States*, 1890), which held that the United States consisted of the states, and the states alone. Brown concedes that territorial residents are entitled to the "natural rights" of religious freedom, property, contract, free speech, and equal protection under the laws, among other rights. However, they are not entitled to the "rights of citizenship, to suffrage, and to the particular methods of procedure pointed out in the Constitution." These were "political rights" that Congress had to deliberately apply to territorial inhabitants.

Notwithstanding the fact that the leading lawyers of the McKinley administration also argued that the United States was composed only of the states, no other justices joined Brown's lead opinion. Instead, Justices Shiras and McKenna sided with Justice White, who argues in his opinion that the Constitution *does* apply to the U.S. territories. Still, he argues, the only constitutional provisions that apply are those that Congress itself decides to grant, given Congress's plenary authority under the territory clause. Since neither the Treaty of Paris nor the Foraker Act—nor any other legislation—explicitly incorporated the new territories of Puerto Rico and the Philippines into the United States, these were to be considered unincorporated territories, which Congress could govern as it chose. That is, in

White's opinion, the new island territories are not a part of the United States for the purposes of the tariff.

Chief Justice Fuller agrees with the plaintiff's lawyers, holding that taxes, imposts, and duties have to be uniform throughout the United States, whether in the states themselves, the District of Columbia, or "territory west of the Missouri." The chief justice argues in his dissent that the Constitution should apply wherever the United States exerts its sovereignty and that neither acts of Congress nor treaties with foreign nations could be in violation of the Constitution. The Constitution, in turn, could not be changed without a duly ratified amendment. Joining Fuller in his dissenting opinion were Justices Rufus Wheeler Peckham, the author of the "substantive due process" doctrine; David Brewer, an economic libertarian and the nephew of the former justice Stephen Field; and John Marshall Harlan, the "Great Dissenter" and grandfather of the later Supreme Court justice of the same name. Harlan also wrote a more pointed dissent responding to Justice Brown's and Justice White's opinions.

The other Insular Cases decided on May 27, 1901—*De Lima v. Bidwell*, *Goetze v. United States*, *Crossman v. United States*, *Dooley v. United States I*, and *Armstrong v. United States*—differed from *Downes v. Bidwell* insofar as the Supreme Court was in these other cases addressing the constitutionality of the Foraker Act in the period *before* it went into effect. These other cases were heard both before and after the ratification of the 1898 Treaty of Paris. During this earlier period, before Congress had enacted the tariff on island trade, the Court ruled that the island territories (including Hawaii) were a part of the United States for the purposes of the uniformity clause. This holding applied not just with respect to the tariffs paid on goods imported from the new territories into the states (*De Lima v. Bidwell* and *Goetze v. United States*) but also in cases where goods were taxed upon being imported into Puerto Rico from the states (*Armstrong v. United States* and *Dooley v. United States*).

In two cases from the first set of Insular Cases the Court delayed its decisions until December 1901. In *Fourteen Diamond Rings v. United States*, known as the Philippine Case, the Supreme Court established that the rulings with respect to Puerto Rico also held for the Philippines—even though government lawyers argued otherwise because of the continuation of military conflict in the Philippines. Justice Brown was again the swing judge, and in the case of diamonds being brought into Chicago by a returning serviceman, he argued that they were exempt from U.S. customs duties. In *Dooley v. United States II*, however, the Court ruled as it did in *Downes* (although with respect to goods being imported into Puerto Rico from the states, the Court ruled as in *Dooley I* and *Armstrong*). Furthermore, the prohibitions in the Constitution on imposing taxes on exports from the United States (the export clause) and on granting preferences among ports of the United States (the preference clause) were held not to restrict Congress's authority to set territorial policies under the territory clause. Again, since neither Puerto Rico nor the Philippines had been made a part of the United States for the purposes of the Constitution's provisions relating to taxes and commerce, the tariff was thus deemed constitutional. In this case, the chief justice dissented vigorously once more on the ground that the tariff was unconstitutional: If the tariffs did not violate the export clause in imposing taxes on foreign trade, he argued, then they necessarily violated the uniformity clause's mandate that trade be uniform throughout the United States.

The decisions in *Downes v. Bidwell* and the other Insular Cases of 1901 rested on fragile ground. Eight of these cases were decided by one-vote margins, such that each could be overturned by the death or retirement of a single Supreme Court justice. Furthermore, the Court had yet to address non-tariff issues apart from extradition (considered in *Neely v. Henkel*, a case that involved a crime committed in Cuba) and admirality law (touched upon in *Huus v. New York*, a case that concerned "coastwise shipping" rules). The Court ruled unanimously in both cases: Neely could be extradited even though Cuba was a foreign country, and Puerto Rico was part of the United States for the purposes of U.S. shipping regulations.

In the post-1901 Insular Cases, the Court clarified its positions regarding which constitutional provisions applied to the island territories. In the 1903 decision in *Hawaii v. Mankichi*, Justice Brown—joined by Justices Oliver Wendell Holmes, Jr., and William R. Day, the new appointees—held that the Hawaiian Supreme Court was not bound by the constitutional guarantees of a jury trial or of indictment by a grand jury in cases of felony. Justices White and McKenna concurred with this opinion, though on different grounds; White argued that since Hawaii had not been incorporated into the Union, neither the Fifth nor the Sixth Amendments applied. Chief Justice Fuller and Justices Harlan, Brewer, and Peckham dissented.

A case decided a year later, *Dorr v. United States*, permanently tipped the balance on the Court in favor of the incorporation doctrine and against the Constitution applying *ex proprio vigore*. Therein, Justice Day's lead opinion held that the defendant, Fred Dorr, was not guaranteed a jury trial and indictment by a grand jury. Since the Philippines were not incorporated, per Justice White's opinion in *Downes v. Bidwell*, Congress could "make laws for such territories, and subject [them] to such constitutional restrictions" as it thought suitable (195 U.S. 38 [1904]). In this particular case, now, Justices Peckham and Brewer and Chief Justice Fuller concurred with Day's opinion (Day was joined by Justices White, Brown, McKenna, and Holmes), for the reason that Day's opinion took pains to distinguish the application of the Constitution to criminal law from its application to the regulation of commerce. The result was an 8–1 decision in favor of the U.S. and Philippine governments. Less than a year later, in *Rasmussen v. United States*, the Court explicitly and almost unanimously endorsed the incorporation doctrine: Justice White's lead opinion was based solely on the incorporation doctrine and was joined not only by his ally McKenna but also by the two recent appointees, Holmes and Day, along with three of the four dissenters in the Insular Cases of 1901 and in *Hawaii v. Mankichi*—Chief Justice Fuller, Brewer, and Peckham. Brown and Harlan wrote separate concurring opinions.

Supreme Court Justice Edward Douglass White wrote a concurring opinion in Downes v. Bidwell. (Library of Congress)

The Supreme Court used the incorporation doctrine to deny territorial citizens the right to jury trial and other guarantees of the Fifth and Sixth Amendments. In *Hawaii v. Mankichi, Dorr v. United States, Balzac v. Porto Rico* (the last of the Insular Cases), and other cases, the Court denied territorial citizens the right to a jury trial by peers; rejected their right to grand jury indictment in felony cases; refused the right of the accused to protection against self-incrimination; disallowed defendants the right to "speedy and public trial" (*Hawaii v. Mankichi*, 190 U.S. 197 [1903]); and did not protect the right of the accused "to be confronted with witnesses against him" (*Dowdell v. United States*, 221 U.S. 325 [1911]). As a general rule, the Supreme Court upheld the right of the territorial governments, created by the U.S. Congress, to prosecute crimes—political crimes in particular—by the terms of their own laws and by those of the U.S. Congress. In contrast, the Court ruled in Insular Cases concerning issues of commerce and property that territories and their citizens were indeed to be protected under the U.S. Constitution. The uniformity clause, due process in the taking of property (the takings clause), and other commercial rights were protected in the territories unless Congress explicitly legislated otherwise.

The incorporation doctrine enabled the United States to divest itself of unincorporated territories, as it would do with the Philippines in 1946. The U.S. assistant attorney general, the U.S. solicitor general, the Philippine governor-general William Howard Taft, the president of the University of Chicago, and other legal experts agreed that the new island territories could be held in trust by the United States and then eventually divested if in the United States' best interest. That is, unlike states, unincorporated territories could be removed from the United States. As Justice White wrote in *Downes v. Bidwell*, a country conquered and occupied by the United States could be held "for an indefinite period" and then, as Congress wished, "either released or retained because it was apt for incorporation into the United States." If a territory was "unfit" to be a part of the United States, White stated, the United States could "terminate" its occupation.

The incorporation doctrine left important issues unsettled. One is that the doctrine by no means makes clear how territories are to be incorporated. In his concurring opinion in *Downes*, Justice White quoted from the 1898 Treaty of Paris to point out that the treaty did not contain the term *incorporation*, in contrast to the text of Article III of the 1803 treaty that annexed the Louisiana Territory and to that of the 1848 Treaty of Guadalupe Hidalgo, which annexed the northern portion of Mexico, the "Mexican Cession," constituting the southwestern United States. On the other hand, the language adding Alaska in 1867 also lacked reference to incorporation, yet the Court nevertheless decided that Alaska was an incorporated territory. A distinction between organized territories and unorganized governments also failed to decide matters, as incorporated territories could be organized (Hawaii) or unorganized (Alaska), and unincorporated territories, too, could be either organized (Puerto Rico) or unorganized (Guam).

Also left unresolved by the incorporation doctrine is the constitutional principle upon which territories can be kept as "unincorporated" territories. Chief Justice Taft's opinion in the capstone case *Balzac v. Porto Rico* (258 U.S. 298 [1922]) rests on a hazy results-oriented argument: that "locality" determines whether the Constitution applies or not. Even though neither Puerto Rico nor Alaska were annexed with explicit language of incorporation, the opinion holds, "Alaska was a very different case … an enormous territory, very sparsely settled, and offering opportunity and settlement by American citizens." The right to jury trial could not be granted, Taft quoted from *Dorr v. United States*, "no matter the needs or capacities of the people." For Taft and other Americans of the period, Puerto Rico, like the Philippines and other island territories, was one of a handful of "distant ocean communities of different origin and language from those of our continental people." In the multicultural and ethnically diverse United States of the twenty-first century, however, Taft's argument would seem to lose its force.

Audience

Downes v. Bidwell was, like other Supreme Court rulings, written for other judges, members of Congress, government officials, lawyers, and future members of the U.S. Supreme Court. Distinguishing the opinions in *Downes v. Bidwell*,

however, is the sweep of American history and the scale of the issue—the political identity of the United States—discussed by the several justices. Indeed, politicians, judges, journalists, lawyers, and members of the public closely followed the decisions in *Downes v. Bidwell* and the other Insular Cases of 1901, since the Court's decisions were to greatly affect the nature of the nation that the United States would be—ethnically and racially (as to which peoples were "American"), economically (as to whether tariff laws and other economic policies applied to the territories), politically (as to which branch of government was to determine the political status of territories), and, not least, strategically (as to whether the United States could have sovereignty over areas that did not come under all of the protections of the Constitution).

Impact

President McKinley, the members of his cabinet, Republican Party leaders, and many others in politics, law, and journalism celebrated the decision of May 27, 1901, in *Downes v. Bidwell* as a victory for the government and an endorsement of the McKinley administration's "insular policy." Others saw the decision as endorsing colonialism and contrary to the Constitution. Some thought that the ruling might become "the *Dred Scott* of Imperialism" (Richard Warren Barkley to John Marshall Harlan, May 28, 1901; qtd. in Yarbrough, p. 197).

The decisions in *Downes v. Bidwell* and the other early cases caused tremendous outcry, made newspaper headlines throughout the country and overseas—in many newspapers, for days on end—and were the subject of numerous editorial cartoons. Observers were prompted to call *Downes* the most important case since *Dred Scott v. Sandford* (1856). After the attention given to the Insular Cases of May and December 1901, however, politicians, the press, and legal and academic journals paid less attention to the Insular Cases of 1903, 1904, 1905, and subsequent years. It was clear that the United States would keep its new island possessions, and it also became clear from the difficult and costly insurrection in the Philippines that the United States was not going to annex new territories. In fact, the administrations of Roosevelt, Taft, and their successors declined to further add territories, despite the opportunities to do so in Santo Domingo (now the Dominican Republic) and other places in the Caribbean and in Central America. These U.S. presidents and their advisers realized that the United States could more easily exercise power informally—through the offices of friendly governments, with trade and investment, via cooperating international institutions, and by the occasional, timely use of force—instead of ruling directly over people and areas remote from continental North America.

Related Documents

Balzac v. Porto Rico, 258 U.S. 298 (1922). Chief Justice William Howard Taft ruled for a unanimous Supreme Court that Puerto

"A false step at this time might be fatal to the development of what Chief Justice Marshall called the American Empire."

(Justice Henry Billings Brown, Majority Opinion)

"In an international sense Porto Rico [sic] was not a foreign country, since it was subject to the sovereignty of and was owned by the United States, [but] it was foreign to the United States in a domestic sense, because the island had not been incorporated into the United States, but was merely appurtenant thereto as a possession."

(Justice Edward Douglass White, Concurring Opinion)

"The contention seems to be that, if an organized and settled province of another sovereignty is acquired by the United States, Congress has the power to keep it, like a disembodied shade, in an intermediate state of ambiguous existence for an indefinite period."

(Chief Justice Melville Fuller, Dissenting Opinion)

"The idea that this country may acquire territories anywhere upon the earth, by conquest or treaty, and hold them as mere colonies or provinces—the people inhabiting them to enjoy only such rights as Congress chooses to accord to them—is wholly inconsistent with the spirit and genius, as well as with the words, of the Constitution."

(Justice John Marshall Harlan, Dissenting Opinion)

"The Constitution follows the flag—but doesn't quite catch up with it."

(Secretary of War Elihu Root, qtd. in Kerr, pp. 40–41)

"No matther whether th' Constitution follows th' flag or not, th' Supreme Coort follows th' iliction returns."

(Finley Peter Dunne's fictitious Irishman Martin Dooley, commenting on the Court's decision in *Downes v. Bidwell;* Dunne, p. 26)

Ricans, despite their official status as U.S. citizens as of 1917, were not entitled to the protections of the Fifth and Sixth Amendments. The plaintiff was thus not entitled to a jury trial for his indictment of libel.

Dorr v. United States, 195 U.S. 138 (1904). *Dorr v. United States*, a libel case, marks a turning point in the history of the Insular Cases. Chief Justice Fuller, Justice Brewer, and Justice Peckham for the first time concurred with the 8–1 majority, which held that the U.S. Constitution's procedural rights of trial by jury were not among those rights protected for territorial residents, given that the Philippines were not incorporated. Justice John Marshall Harlan was left as the only "anti-imperial" judge on the Court.

Hawaii v. Mankichi, 190 U.S. 197 (1903). This case marked the first time that the Court had to grapple with the application of the Constitution to the territories with respect to criminal cases, rather than questions of commerce or the tariff. The two new justices on the bench, William R. Day and Oliver Wendell Holmes, both joined Justice Henry B. Brown's lead opinion in the 5–4 decision—in which Justice Edward D. White and Justice Joseph McKenna concurred—that held that the defendant, Mankichi, could be denied the rights to a jury trial and to indictment by a grand jury in cases of felony, despite the fact that Hawaii was now a territory of the United States.

Rassmussen v. United States, 197 U.S. 516 (1905). This case marks the triumph of Justice White's Incorporation Doctrine. White wrote the lead opinion for a unanimous Supreme Court—Justices Brown and Harlan concurred—and relied exclusively on the incorporation doctrine in his opinion for the seven-justice majority, explaining why Alaska was incorporated and why the plaintiff was entitled to a jury trial.

"Theodore Roosevelt's Corollary to the Monroe Doctrine (1905)." National Archives "Our Documents" Web site. http://www.ourdocuments.gov/doc.php?flash=true&doc=56. Accessed on January 28, 2008. The Monroe Doctrine was intended to keep European powers out of the Western Hemisphere; President Roosevelt went further to claim that the United States had a responsibility of its own to intervene in the affairs of Latin American states in cases of "chronic wrongdoing" or ineffectiveness. Furthermore, according to Roosevelt, the United States could decide when and where such cases existed.

"Transcript of Platt Amendment (1903)." National Archives "Our Documents" Web site. http://www.ourdocuments.gov/doc.php?doc=55&page=transcript. Accessed on January 28, 2008. The Platt Amendment, which became part of the Cuban constitution, specified the relationship between the United States and Cuba. The amendment granted the U.S. government "the right to intervene for the preservation of Cuban independence" and "the maintenance of a government adequate for the protection of life, property, and individual liberty."

"William McKinley War Message." Encyclopaedia Britannica Profiles the American Presidency Web site. http://www.britannica.com/presidents/article-9116941. Accessed on January 28, 2008. In this message President McKinley explains to Congress the justifications for going to war against Spain, given that Cubans had been fighting against Spain since 1895 and that U.S. newspapers had been calling for war since the sinking of the USS *Maine* in February 1898.

Bibliography

■ Articles

Burnett, Christina Duffy. "*Untied* States: American Expansion and Territorial Deannexation." *University of Chicago Law Review* 72, no. 3 (2005): 797–880.

LaFeber, Walter. "The 'Lion in the Path': The U.S. Emergence as a World Power." *Political Science Quarterly* 101, no. 5 (1986): 705–718.

■ Books

Burnett, Christina Duffy, and Burke Marshall, eds. *Foreign in a Domestic Sense: Puerto Rico, American Expansion, and the Constitution*. Durham: Duke University Press, 2001.

Dunne, Finley Peter. *Mr. Dooley's Opinions*. New York: R. H. Russell, 1901.

Fiss, Owen M. *Troubled Beginnings of the Modern State, 1888–1910*. Vol. 8: *History of the Supreme Court of the United States*. New York: Macmillan, 1993.

Foner, Philip S. *The Spanish-Cuban-American War and the Birth of American Imperialism, 1895–1902*. 2 vols. New York: Monthly Review Press, 1972.

Francisco, Luzviminda Bartolome, and Jonathan Shepard Fast. *Conspiracy for Empire: Big Business, Corruption, and the Politics of Imperialism in America, 1876–1907*. Quezon City, Philippines: Foundation for Nationalist Studies, 1985.

Howe, Albert H. *The Insular Cases, Comprising the Records, Briefs, and Arguments of Counsel in the Insular Cases of the October Term, 1900, in the Supreme Court of the United States, Including the Appendixes Thereto*. Washington, D.C.: Government Printing Office, 1901.

Kerr, James Edward. *The Insular Cases: The Role of the Judiciary in American Expansionism*. Port Washington, N.Y.: Kennikat Press, 1982.

Lawson, Gary, and Guy Seidman. *The Constitution of Empire: Territorial Expansion and American Legal History*. New Haven, Conn.: Yale University Press, 2004.

Pérez, Louis A. *Cuba between Empires, 1878–1902*. Pittsburgh: University of Pittsburgh Press, 1982.

———. *Cuba and the United States: Ties of Singular Intimacy*. Athens: University of Georgia Press, 1990.

Rivera Ramos, Efrén. *The Legal Construction of Identity: The Judicial and Social Legacy of American Colonialism in Puerto Rico*. Washington, D.C.: American Psychological Association, 2001.

Rosselló, Pedro. *The Unfinished Business of American Democracy*. San Juan, Puerto Rico: Public Policy Institute, Ana G. Méndez University System, 2005.

Sparrow, Bartholomew H. *The Insular Cases and the Emergence of American Empire*. Lawrence: University Press of Kansas, 2006.

Yarbrough, Tinsley E. *Judicial Enigma: The First Justice Harlan*. New York: Oxford University Press, 1995.

■ Web Sites

"The Insular Cases." Island Law Web site.

http://macmeekin.com/Library/Insular%20Cases.htm. Accessed
on January 28, 2008.

"'Insular Cases' Made Puerto Rican Status Unclear, Panel Says."
University of Virginia School of Law Web site.
   http://www.law.virginia.edu/html/news/2007_spr/insular.htm.
   Accessed on January 28, 2008.

—By Bartholomew H. Sparrow

Questions for Further Study

1. *Downes v. Bidwell*, along with the other decisions in the 1901 Insular Cases, was immensely controversial and has often been compared to the Taney Court's decision in *Dred Scott v. Sandford*. Do the differences in the two cases matter with respect to which U.S. territories were at issue and which constitutional provisions were in question? What appears to be the critical difference between the two rulings?

2. As of 2008, the United States remained in possession of five unincorporated island territories. Which arguments made by Justice Brown, Justice White, or Chief Justice Fuller, if any, apply to the modern status of the U.S. territories? Do the altered strategic place of the United States in the world and the nation's increasing ethnic and cultural diversity bear relevance here?

3. In the later Insular Cases, the Court appeared to make a general distinction between cases involving criminal proceedings (in which it supported territorial governments in their prosecutions and did not uphold constitutionally guaranteed rights and liberties) and issues of commerce (in which the Court generally upheld constitutional provisions relating to trade, the takings clause, and other economic liberties). Did this distinction make sense? In view of the North American Free Trade Association and globalization, does the distinction make sense in the modern era?

4. The "incorporation" of territories in the American polity and Justice White's incorporation doctrine preceded the more famous use of the term *incorporation* by the U.S. Supreme Court in twentieth-century decisions to extend the Bill of Rights to the states under the authority of the Fourteenth Amendment. Compare and contrast these two uses of *incorporation*. To what extent are they analogous? To what extent are they both relevant today?

admiralty jurisdiction	jurisdiction pertaining to shipping, navigation, coastal waters, and other maritime issues
appurtenant	annexed to a more important thing; a property considered incident to the principal property
Church of Jesus Christ of L. D. S. v. United States	1890 case (properly, *Late Corporation of the Church of Jesus Christ of Latter-Day Saints, et al. v. United States*) in which the Supreme Court upheld Congress's plenary power to regulate the territories of the United States, in this case with respect to the forfeiture of Mormon Church property
Loughborough v. Blake	1820 Supreme Court case in which Chief Justice John Marshall held that Congress could not impose a direct tax on the District of Columbia, since Washington, D.C., was part of the United States for the purpose of the uniformity clause, as were the states and western territories
plenary	full; complete; entire
tariff	a tax on trade
territorial clause	Article IV, Section 3, Clause 2, of the U.S. Constitution, which reads, "Congress shall have Power to dispose of and make all needful Rules and Regulations respecting the Territory or other Property belonging to the United States"
uniformity clause	Article I, Section 8, Clause 1, of the U.S. Constitution, which reads, "all Duties, Imposts and Excises shall be uniform throughout the United States"

DOWNES V. BIDWELL

This was an action begun in the circuit court by Downes, doing business under the firm name of S. B. Downes & Co., against the collector of the port of New York, to recover back duties to the amount of $659.35 exacted and paid under protest upon certain oranges consigned to the plaintiff at New York, and brought thither from the port of San Juan in the island of Porto Rico during the month of November, 1900, after the passage of the act temporarily providing a civil government and revenues for the island of Porto Rico, known as the Foraker act.

The district attorney demurred to the complaint for the want of jurisdiction in the court, and for insufficiency of its averments. The demurrer was sustained, and the complaint dismissed. Whereupon plaintiff sued out this writ of error.

Messrs. Frederic R. Coudert, Jr., and Paul Fuller for plaintiff in error.

Solicitor General Richards and Attorney General Griggs for defendant in error.

◆ Statement by Mr. Justice Brown

This case involves the question whether merchandise brought into the port of New York from Porto Rico since the passage of the Foraker act is exempt from duty, notwithstanding the 3d section of that act which requires the payment of "15 per centum of the duties which are required to be levied, collected, and paid upon like articles of merchandise imported from foreign countries."

1. The exception to the jurisdiction of the court is not well taken. By Rev. Stat. 629, subd. 4, the circuit courts are vested with jurisdiction "of all suits at law or in equity arising under any act providing for revenue from imports or tonnage," irrespective of the amount involved. This section should be construed in connection with 643, which provides for the removal from state courts to circuit courts of the United States of suits against revenue officers "on account of any act done under color of his office, or of any such [revenue] law, or on account of any right, title, or authority claimed by such officer or other person under any such law." Both these sections are taken from the act of March 2, 1833 (4 Stat. at L. 632, chap. 57) commonly known as the force bill, and are evidently intended to include all actions against customs officers acting under color of their office. While, as we have held in *De Lima v. Bidwell*, 181 U. S.—, ante, 743, 21 Sup. Ct. Rep. 743, Actions against the collector to recover back duties assessed upon non-importable property are not "customs cases" in the sense of the administrative act, they are, nevertheless, actions arising under an act to provide for a revenue from imports, in the sense of 629, since they are for acts done by a collector under color of his office. This subdivision of 629 was not repealed by the jurisdictional act of 1875, or the subsequent act of August 13, 1888, since these acts were "not intended to interfere with the prior statutes conferring jurisdiction upon the circuit or district courts in special cases and over particular subjects." *United States v. Mooney*, 116 U.S. 104, 107, 29 S. L. ed. 550, 552, 6 Sup. Ct. Rep. 304, 306. See also *Merchants' Ins. Co. v. Ritchie*, 5 Wall. 541, 18 L. ed. 540; *Philadelphia v. The Collector*, 5 Wall. 720, sub nom. *Philadelphia v. Diehl*, 18 L. ed. 614; *Hornthall v. The Collector*, 9 Wall. 560, sub nom. *Hornthall v. Keary*, 19 L. ed. 560 As the case "involves the construction or application of the Constitution," as well as the constitutionality of a law of the United States, the writ of error was properly sued out from this court.

2. In the case of *De Lima v. Bidwell* just decided, 181 U. S.—, ante, 743, 21 Sup. Ct. Rep. 743, we held that, upon the ratification of the treaty of peace with Spain, Porto Rico ceased to be a foreign country, and became a territory of the United States, and that duties were no longer collectible upon merchandise brought from that island. We are now asked to

hold that it became a part of the United States within that provision of the Constitution which declares that "all duties, imposts, and excises shall be uniform throughout the United States." Art. 1, 8. If Porto Rico be a part of the United States, the Foraker act imposing duties upon its products is unconstitutional, not only by reason of a violation of the uniformity clause, but because by 9 "vessels bound to or from one state" cannot "be obliged to enter, clear, or pay duties in another."

The case also involves the broader question whether the revenue clauses of the Constitution extend of their own force to our newly acquired territories. The Constitution itself does not answer the question. Its solution must be found in the nature of the government created by that instrument, in the opinion of its contemporaries, in the practical construction put upon it by Congress, and in the decisions of this court.

The Federal government was created in 1777 by the union of thirteen colonies of Great Britain in "certain articles of confederation and perpetual union," the first one of which declared that "the stile of this confederacy shall be the United States of America." Each member of the confederacy was denominated a state. Provision was made for the representation of each state by not less than two nor more than seven delegates; but no mention was made of territories or other lands, except in article 11, which authorized the admission of Canada, upon its "acceding to this confederation," and of other colonies if such admission were agreed to by nine states. At this time several states made claims to large tracts of land in the unsettled west, which they were at first indisposed to relinquish. Disputes over these lands became so acrid as nearly to defeat the confederacy, before it was fairly put in operation. Several of the states refused to ratify the articles, because the convention had taken no steps to settle the titles to these lands upon principles of equity and sound policy; but all of them, through fear of being accused of disloyalty, finally yielded their claims, though Maryland held out until 1781. Most of these states in the meantime having ceded their interests in these lands, the confederate Congress, in 1787, created the first territorial government northwest of the Ohio river, provided for local self-government, a bill of rights, a representation in Congress by a delegate, who should have a seat "with a right of debating, but not of voting," and for the ultimate formation of states therefrom, and their admission into the Union on an equal footing with the original states.

The confederacy, owing to well-known historical reasons, having proven a failure, a new Constitution was formed in 1787 by "the people of the United States" "for the United States of America," as its preamble declares. All legislative powers were vested in a Congress consisting of representatives from the several states, but no provision was made for the admission of delegates from the territories, and no mention was made of territories as separate portions of the Union, except that Congress was empowered "to dispose of and make all needful rules and regulations respecting the territory or other property belonging to the United States." At this time all of the states had ceded their unappropriated lands except North Carolina and Georgia. It was thought by Chief Justice Taney in the Dred Scott Case, 19 How. 393, 436, 15 L. ed. 691, 713, that the sole object of the territorial clause was "to transfer to the new government the property then held in common by the states, and to give to that government power to apply it to the objects for which it had been destined by mutual agreement among the states before their league was dissolved;" that the power "to make needful rules and regulations" was not intended to give the powers of sovereignty, or to authorize the establishment of territorial governments—in short, that these words were used in a proprietary, and not in a political, sense. But, as we observed in *De Lima v. Bidwell*, the power to establish territorial governments has been too long exercised by Congress and acquiesced in by this court to be deemed an unsettled question. Indeed, in the Dred Scott Case it was admitted to be the inevitable consequence of the right to acquire territory.

It is sufficient to observe in relation to these three fundamental instruments, that it can nowhere be inferred that the territories were considered a part of the United States. The Constitution was created by the people of the United States, as a union of states, to be governed solely by representatives of the states; and even the provision relied upon here, that all duties, imposts, and excises shall be uniform "throughout the United States," is explained by subsequent provisions of the Constitution, that "no tax or duty shall be laid on articles exported from any state," and "no preference shall be given by any regulation of commerce or revenue to the ports of one state over those of another; nor shall vessels bound to or from one state be obliged to enter, clear, or pay duties in another." In short, the Constitution deals with states, their people, and their representatives.

The 13th Amendment to the Constitution, prohibiting slavery and involuntary servitude "within the

United States, or in any place subject to their jurisdiction," is also significant as showing that there may be places within the jurisdiction of the United States that are no part of the Union. To say that the phraseology of this amendment was due to the fact that it was intended to prohibit slavery in the seceded states, under a possible interpretation that those states were no longer a part of the Union, is to confess the very point in issue, since it involves an admission that, if these states were not a part of the Union, they were still subject to the jurisdiction of the United States.

Upon the other hand, the 14th Amendment, upon the subject of citizenship, declares only that "all persons born or naturalized in the United States, and subject to the jurisdiction thereof, are citizens of the United States, and of the state wherein they reside." Here there is a limitation to persons born or naturalized in the United States, which is not extended to persons born in any place "subject to their jurisdiction."

The question of the legal relations between the states and the newly acquired territories first became the subject of public discussion in connection with the purchase of Louisiana in 1803. This purchase arose primarily from the fixed policy of Spain to exclude all foreign commerce from the Mississippi. This restriction became intolerable to the large number of immigrants who were leaving the eastern states to settle in the fertile valley of that river and its tributaries. After several futile attempts to secure the free navigation of that river by treaty, advantage was taken of the exhaustion of Spain in her war with France, and a provision inserted in the treaty of October 27, 1795, by which the Mississippi river was opened to the commerce of the United States. 8 Stat. at L. 138, 140, art. 4. In October, 1800, by the secret treaty of San Ildefonso, Spain retroceded to France the territory of Louisiana. This treaty created such a ferment in this country that James Monroe was sent as minister extraordinary with discretionary powers to co-operate with Livingston, then minister to France, in the purchase of New Orleans, for which Congress appropriated $2,000,000. To the surprise of the negotiators, Bonaparte invited them to make an offer for the whole of Louisiana at a price finally fixed at $15,000,000. It is well known that Mr. Jefferson entertained grave doubts as to his power to make the purchase, or, rather, as to his right to annex the territory and make it part of the United States, and had instructed Mr. Livingston to make no agreement to that effect in the treaty, as he believed it could not be legally done. Owing to a new war

between England and France being upon the point of breaking out, there was need for haste in the negotiations, and Mr. Livingston took the responsibility of disobeying his instructions, and, probably owing to the insistence of Bonaparte, consented to the 3d article of the treaty, which provided that "the inhabitants of the ceded territory shall be incorporated in the Union of the United States, and admitted as soon as possible, according to the principles of the Federal Constitution, to the enjoyment of all the rights, advantages, and immunities of citizens of the United States; and in the meantime they shall be maintained and protected in the free enjoyment of their liberty, property, and the religion which they profess." [8 Stat. at L. 202.] This evidently committed the government to the ultimate, but not to the immediate, admission of Louisiana as a state, and postponed its incorporation into the Union to the pleasure of Congress. In regard to this, Mr. Jefferson, in a letter to Senator Breckinridge of Kentucky, of August 12, 1803, used the following language: "This treaty must, of course, be laid before both Houses, because both have important functions to exercise respecting it. They, I presume, will see their duty to their country in ratifying and paying for it, so as to secure a good which would otherwise probably be never again in their power. But I suppose they must then appeal to the nation for an additional article to the Constitution approving and confirming an act which the nation had not previously authorized. The Constitution has made no provision for holding foreign territory, still less for incorporating foreign nations into our Union. The Executive, in seizing the fugitive occurrence which so much advances the good of our country, have done an act beyond the Constitution."

To cover the questions raised by this purchase Mr. Jefferson prepared two amendments to the Constitution, the first of which declared that "the province of Louisiana is incorporated with the United States and made part thereof;" and the second of which was couched in a little different language, viz.: "Louisiana, as ceded by France to the United States, is made a part of the United States. Its white inhabitants shall be citizens, and stand, as to their rights and obligations, on the same footing as other citizens in analogous situations." But by the time Congress assembled, October 17, 1803, either the argument of his friends or the pressing necessity of the situation seems to have dispelled his doubts regarding his power under the Constitution, since in his message to Congress he referred the whole matter to that body, saying that "with the wisdom of Congress it will rest to take those ulterior measures which may be necessary for the immediate occupation and temporary government of the country; for its incorporation into the Union." Jefferson's Writings, vol. 8, p. 269.

The raising of money to provide for the purchase of this territory, and the act providing a civil government, gave rise to an animated debate in Congress, in which two questions were prominently presented: First, whether the provision for the ultimate incorporation of Louisiana into the Union was constitutional; and, second, whether the 7th article of the treaty admitting the ships of Spain and France for the next twelve years "into the ports of New Orleans, and in all other legal ports of entry within the ceded territory, in the same manner as the ships of the United States coming directly from France or Spain, or any of their colonies, without being subject to any other or greater duty on merchandise or other or greater tonnage than that paid by the citizens of the United States" [8 Stat. at L. 204], was an unlawful discrimination in favor of those ports and an infringement upon art. 1, 9, of the Constitution, that "no preference shall be given by any regulation of commerce or revenue to the ports of one state over those of another." This article of the treaty contained the further stipulation that "during the space of time above mentioned to other nation shall have a right to the same privileges in the ports of the ceded territory; ... and it is well understood that the object of the above article is to favor the manufactures, commerce, freight, and navigation of France and Spain."

It is unnecessary to enter into the details of this debate. The arguments of individual legislators are no proper subject for judicial comment. They are so often influenced by personal or political considerations, or by the assumed necessities of the situation, that they can hardly be considered even as the deliberate views of the persons who make them, much less as dictating the construction to be put upon the Constitution by the courts. *United States v. Union P. R. Co.* 91 U.S. 72, 79, 23 S. L. ed, 224, 228. Suffice it to say that the administration party took the ground that, under the constitutional power to make treaties, there was ample power to acquire territory, and to hold and govern it under laws to be passed by Congress; and that as Louisiana was incorporated into the Union as a territory, and not as a state, a stipulation for citizenship became necessary; that as a state they would not have needed a stipulation for the safety of their liberty, property, and religion, but as territory this stipulation would govern and restrain

the undefined powers of Congress to "make rules and regulations" for territories. The Federalists admitted the power of Congress to acquire and hold territory, but denied its power to incorporate it into the Union under the Constitution as it then stood.

They also attacked the 7th article of the treaty, discriminating in favor of French and Spanish ships, as a distinct violation of the Constitution against preference being given to the ports of one state over those of another. The administration party, through Mr. Elliott of Vermont, replied to this that "the states, as such, were equal and intended to preserve that equality; and the provision of the Constitution alluded to was calculated to prevent Congress from making any odious discrimination or distinctions between particular states. It was not contemplated that this provision would have application to colonial or territorial acquisitions." Said Mr. Nicholson of Maryland, speaking for the administration: "It [Louisiana] is in the nature of a colony whose commerce may be regulated without any reference to the Constitution. Had it been the island of Cuba which was ceded to us, under a similar condition of admitting French and Spanish vessels for a limited time into Havana, could it possibly have been contended that this would be giving a preference to the ports of one state over those of another, or that the uniformity of duties, imposts, and excises throughout the United States would have been destroyed? And because Louisiana lies adjacent to our own territory is it to be viewed in a different light?"

As a sequence to this debate two bills were passed, one October 31, 1803 (2 Stat. at L. 245, chap. 1), authorizing the President to take possession of the territory and to continue the existing government, and the other November 10, 1803 (2 Stat. at L. 245, chap. 2), making provision for the payment of the purchase price. These acts continued in force until March 26, 1804, when a new act was passed providing for a temporary government (2 Stat. at L. 283, chap. 38), and vesting all legislative powers in a governor and legislative council, to be appointed by the President. These statutes may be taken as expressing the views of Congress, first, that territory may be lawfully acquired by treaty, with a provision for its ultimate incorporation into the Union; and, second, that a discrimination in favor of certain foreign vessels trading with the ports of a newly acquired territory is no violation of that clause of the Constitution (art. 1, 9) that declares that no preference shall be given to the ports of one state over those of another. It is evident that the constitutionality of this discrimination can only be supported upon the theory that ports of territories are not ports of state within the meaning of the Constitution. The same construction was adhered to in the treaty with Spain for the purchase of Florida (8 Stat. at L. 252) the 6th article of which provided that the inhabitants should "be incorporated into the Union of the United States, as soon as may be consistent with the principles of the Federal Constitution;" and the 15th article of which agreed that Spanish vessels coming directly from Spanish ports and laden with productions of Spanish growth or manufacture should be admitted, for the term of twelve years, to the ports of Pensacola and St. Augustine "without paying other or higher duties on their cargoes, or of tonnage, than will be paid by the vessels of the United States," and that "during the said term no other nation shall enjoy the same privileges within the ceded territories."

So, too, in the act annexing the Republic of Hawaii, there was a provision continuing in effect the customs relations of the Hawaiian islands with the United States and other countries, the effect of which was to compel the collection in those islands of a duty upon certain articles, whether coming from the United States or other countries, much greater than the duty provided by the general tariff law then in force. This was a discrimination against the Hawaiian ports wholly inconsistent with the revenue clauses of the Constitution, if such clauses were there operative.

The very treaty with Spain under discussion in this case contains similar discriminative provisions, which are apparently irreconcilable with the Constitution, if that instrument be held to extend to these islands immediately upon their cession to the United States. By article 4 the United States agree, for the term of ten years from the date of the exchange of the ratifications of the present treaty, to admit Spanish ships and merchandise to the ports of the Philippine islands on the same terms as ships and merchandise of the United States—a privilege not extending to any other ports. It was a clear breach of the uniformity clause in question, and a manifest excess of authority on the part of the commissioners, if ports of the Philippine islands be ports of the United States.

So, too, by article 13, "Spanish scientific, literary, and artistic works … shall be continued to be admitted free of duty in such territories for the period of ten years, to be reckoned from the date of the exchange of the ratifications of this treaty." This is also a clear discrimination in favor of Spanish literary productions into particular ports.

Notwithstanding these provisions for the incorporation of territories into the Union, Congress, not only in organizing the territory of Louisiana by act of March 26, 1804, but all other territories carved out of this vast inheritance, has assumed that the Constitution did not extend to them of its own force, and has in each case made special provision, either that their legislatures shall pass no law inconsistent with the Constitution of the United States, or that the Constitution or laws of the United States shall be the supreme law of such territories. Finally, in Rev. Stat. 1891, a general provision was enacted that "the Constitution and all laws of the United States which are not locally inapplicable shall have the same force and effect within all the organized territories, and in every territory hereafter organized, as elsewhere within the United States."

So, too, on March 6, 1820 (3 Stat. at L. 545, chap. 22), in an act authorizing the people of Missouri to form a state government, after a heated debate, Congress declared that in the territory of Louisiana north of 36°30' slavery should be forever prohibited. It is true that, for reasons which have become historical, this act was declared to be unconstitutional in *Scott v. Sandford*, 19 How. 393, 15 L. ed. 691, but it is none the less a distinct annunciation by Congress of power over property in the territories, which it obviously did not possess in the several states.

The researches of counsel have collated a large number of other instances in which Congress has in its enactments recognized the fact that provisions intended for the states did not embrace the territories, unless specially mentioned. These are found in the laws prohibiting the slave trade with "the United States or territories thereof;" or equipping ships "in any port or place within the jurisdiction of the United States;" in the internal revenue laws, in the early ones of which no provision was made for the collection of taxes in the territory not included within the boundaries of the existing states, and others of which extended them expressly to the territories, or "within the exterior boundaries of the United States;" and in the acts extending the internal revenue laws to the territories of Alaska and Oklahoma. It would prolong this opinion unnecessarily to set forth the provisions of these acts in detail. It is sufficient to say that Congress has or has not applied the revenue laws to the territories, as the circumstances of each case seemed to require, and has specifically legislated for the territories whenever it was its intention to execute laws beyond the limits of the states. Indeed, whatever may have been the fluctuations of opinion in other bodies (and even this court has not been exempt from them), Congress has been consistent in recognizing the difference between the states and territories under the Constitution.

The decisions of this court upon this subject have not been altogether harmonious. Some of them are based upon the theory that the Constitution does not apply to the territories without legislation. Other cases, arising from territories where such legislation has been had, contain language which would justify the inference that such legislation was unnecessary, and that the Constitution took effect immediately upon the cession of the territory to the United States. It may be remarked, upon the threshold of an analysis of these cases, that too much weight must not be given to general expressions found in several opinions that the power of Congress over territories is complete and supreme, because these words may be interpreted as meaning only supreme under the Constitution; her, upon the other hand, to general statements that the Constitution covers the territories as well as the states, since in such cases it will be found that acts of Congress had already extended the Constitution to such territories, and that thereby it subordinated, not only its own acts, but those of the territorial legislatures, to what had become the supreme law of the land. "It is a maxim not to be disregarded that general expressions, in every opinion, are to be taken in connection with the case in which those expressions are used. If they go beyond the case, they may be respected, but ought not to control the judgment in a subsequent suit when the very point is presented for decision. The reason of this maxim is obvious. The question actually before the court is investigated with care, and considered in its full extent. Other principles which may serve to illustrate it are considered in their relation to the case decided, but their possible bearing on all other cases is seldom completely investigated." *Cohen v. Virginia*, 6 Wheat. 264, 399, 5 L. ed. 257, 290.

The earliest case is that of *Hepburn v. Ellzey*, 2 Cranch, 445, 2 L. ed. 332, in which this court held that, under that clause of the Constitution limiting the jurisdiction of the courts of the United States to controversies between citizens of different states, a citizen of the District of Columbia could not maintain an action in the circuit court of the United States. It was argued that the word "state." in that connection, was used simply to denote a distinct political society. "But," said the Chief Justice, "as the act of Congress obviously used the word 'state' in reference to that term as used in the Constitution, it

becomes necessary to inquire whether Columbia is a state in the sense of that instrument. The result of that examination is a conviction that the members of the American confederacy only are the states contemplated in the Constitution, ... and excludes from the term the signification attached to it by writers on the law of nations." This case was followed in *Barney v. Baltimore*, 6 Wall. 280, 18 L. ed. 825, and quite recently in *Hooe v. Jamieson*, 166 U.S. 395, 41 L. ed. 1049, 17 Sup. Ct. Rep. 596. The same rule was applied to citizens of territories in *New Orleans v. Winter*, 1 Wheat. 91, 4 L. ed. 44, in which an attempt was made to distinguish a territory from the District of Columbia. But it was said that "neither of them is a state in the sense in which that term is used in the Constitution." In *Scott v. Jones*, 5 How. 343, 12 L. ed. 181, and in *Miners' Bank v. Iowa* ex rel. District Prosecuting Attorney, 12 How. 1, 13 L. ed. 867, it was held that under the judiciary act, permitting writs of error to the supreme court of a state in cases where the validity of a state statute is drawn in question, an act of a territorial legislature was not within the contemplation of Congress.

Loughborough v. Blake, 5 Wheat. 317, 5 L. ed. 98, was an action of trespass or, as appears by the original record, replevin, brought in the circuit court for the District of Columbia to try the right of Congress to impose a direct tax for general purposes on that District. 3 Stat. at L. 216, chap. 60. It was insisted that Congress could act in a double capacity: in one as legislating for the states; in the other as a local legislature for the District of Columbia. In the latter character, it was admitted that the power of levying direct taxes might be exercised, but for District purposes only, as a state legislature might tax for state purposes; but that it could not legislate for the District under art. 1, 8, giving to Congress the power "to lay and collect taxes, imposts, and excises," which "shall be uniform throughout the United States," inasmuch as the District was no part of the United States. It was held that the grant of this power was a general one without limitation as to place, and consequently extended to all places over which the government extends; and that it extended to the District of Columbia as a constituent part of the United States. The fact that art. 1, 2, declares that "representatives and direct taxes shall be apportioned among the several states ... according to their respective numbers" furnished a standard by which taxes were apportioned, but not to exempt any part of the country from their operation. "The words used do not mean that direct taxes shall be imposed on states only which are represented, or shall be apportioned to representatives; but that direct taxation, in its application to states, shall be apportioned to numbers." That art. 1, 9, 4, declaring that direct taxes shall be laid in proportion to the census, was applicable to the District of Columbia, "and will enable Congress to apportion on it its just and equal share of the burden, with the same accuracy as on the respective states. If the tax be laid in this proportion, it is within the very words of the restriction. It is a tax in proportion to the census or enumeration referred to." It was further held that the words of the 9th section did not "in terms require that the system of direct taxation, when resorted to, shall be extended to the territories, as the words of the 2d section require that it shall be extended to all the states. They therefore may, without violence, be understood to give a rule when the territories shall be taxed, without imposing the necessity of taxing them."

There could be no doubt as to the correctness of this conclusion, so far, at least, as it applied to the District of Columbia. This District had been a part of the states of Maryland and Virginia. It had been subject to the Constitution, and was a part of the United States. The Constitution had attached to it irrevocably. There are steps which can never be taken backward. The tie that bound the states of Maryland and Virginia to the Constitution could not be dissolved, without at least the consent of the Federal and state governments to a formal separation. The mere cession of the District of Columbia to the Federal government relinquished the authority of the states, but it did not take it out of the United States or from under the aegis of the Constitution. Neither party had ever consented to that construction of the cession. If, before the District was set off, Congress had passed an unconstitutional act affecting its inhabitants, it would have been void. If done after the District was created, it would have been equally void; in other words, Congress could not do indirectly, by carving out the District, what it could not do directly. The District still remained a part of the United States, protected by the Constitution. Indeed, it would have been a fanciful construction to hold that territory which had been once a part of the United States ceased to be such by being ceded directly to the Federal government.

In delivering the opinion, however, the Chief Justice made certain observations which have occasioned some embarrassment in other cases. "The power," said he, "to lay and collect duties, imposts, and excises may be exercised, and must be exercised, throughout the United States. Does this term designate the whole, or any particular portion of the American empire? Certainly this question can admit but of one answer. It is the name given to our great Republic which is composed of states and territories. The District of Columbia, or the territory west of the Missouri, is not less within the United States than Maryland or Pennsylvania; and it is not less necessary, on the principles of our Constitution, that uniformity in the imposition of imposts, duties, and excises should be observed in the one than in the other. Since, then, the power to lay and collect taxes, which includes direct taxes, is obviously coextensive with the power to lay and collect duties, imposts, and excises, and since the latter extends throughout the United States, it follows that the power to impose direct taxes also extends throughout the United States." So far as applicable to the District of Columbia, these observations are entirely sound. So far as they apply to the territories, they were not called for by the exigencies of the case.

In line with *Loughborough v. Blake* is the case of *Callan v. Wilson*, 127 U.S. 540, 32 L. ed. 223, 8 Sup. Ct. Rep. 1301, in which the provisions of the Constitution relating to trial by jury were held to be in force in the District of Columbia. Upon the other hand, in *De Geofroy v. Riggs* 133 U.S. 258, 33 L. ed. 642, 10 Sup. Ct. Rep. 295, the District of Columbia, as a political community, was held to be one of "the states of the Union" within the meaning of that term as used in a consular convention of February 23, 1853, with France. The 7th article of that convention provided that in all the states of the Union whose existing laws permitted it Frenchmen should enjoy the right of holding, disposing of, and inheriting property in the same manner as citizens of the United States; and as to the states of the Union by whose existing laws aliens were not permitted to hold real estate the President engaged to recommend to them the passage of such laws as might be necessary for the purpose of conferring this right. The court was of opinion that if these terms, "states of the Union," were held to exclude the District of Columbia and the territories, our government would be placed in the inconsistent position of stipulating that French citizens should enjoy the right of holding, disposing of, and inheriting property in like manner as citizens of the United States, in states whose laws permitted it, and engaging that the President should recommend the passage of laws conferring that right in states whose laws did not permit aliens to hold real estate, while at the same time refusing to citizens of France holding property in the District of Columbia and in some of the territories, where the power of the United States is in that respect unlimited, a like release from the disabilities of alienage, "thus discriminating against them in favor of citizens of France holding property in states having similar legislation. No plausible motive can be assigned for such discrimination. A right which the government of the United States apparently desires that citizens of France should enjoy in all the states it would hardly refuse to them in the district embracing its capital, or in any of its own territorial dependencies."

This case may be considered as establishing the principle that, in dealing with foreign sovereignties, the term "United States" has a broader meaning than when used in the Constitution, and includes all territories subject to the jurisdiction of the Federal government, wherever located. In its treaties and conventions with foreign nations this government is a unit. This is so, not because the territories comprised a part of the government established by the people of the states in their Constitution, but because the Federal government is the only authorized organ of the territories, as well as of the states, in their foreign relations. By art. 1, 10, of the Constitution, "no state shall enter into any treaty, alliance, or confederation, … [or] enter into any agreement or compact with another state, or with a foreign power." It would be absurd to hold that the territories, which are much less independent than the states, and are under the direct control and tutelage of the general government, possess a power in this particular which is thus expressly forbidden to the states.

It may be added in this connection, that to put at rest all doubts regarding the applicability of the Constitution to the District of Columbia, Congress by the act of February 21, 1871 (16 Stat. at L. 419, 426, chap. 62, 34), specifically extended the Constitution and laws of the United States to this District.

The case of *American Ins. Co. v. 356 Bales of Cotton*, 1 Pet. 511, 7 L. ed. 242, originated in a libel filed in the district court for South Carolina, for the possession of 356 bales of cotton which had been wrecked on the coast of Florida, abandoned to the insurance companies, and subsequently brought to Charleston. Canter claimed the cotton as bona fide purchaser at a marshal's sale at Key West, by virtue of a decree of a territorial court consisting of a notary and five jurors, proceeding under an act of the governor and legislative council of Florida. The case turned upon the question whether the sale by that court was effectual to divest the interest of the

underwriters. The district judge pronounced the proceedings a nullity, and rendered a decree from which both parties appealed to the circuit court. The circuit court reversed the decree of the district court upon the ground that the proceedings of the court at Key West were legal, and transferred the property to Canter, the alleged purchaser.

The opinion of the circuit court was delivered by Mr. Justice Johnson, of the Supreme Court, and is published in full in a note in Peters's Reports. It was argued that the Constitution vested the admiralty jurisdiction exclusively in the general government; that the legislature of Florida had exercised an illegal power in organizing this court, and that its decrees were void. On the other hand, it was insisted that this was a court of separate and distinct jurisdiction from the courts of the United States, and as such its acts were not to be reviewed in a foreign tribunal, such as was the court of South Carolina; "that the district of Florida was no part of the United States, but only an acquisition or dependency, and as such the Constitution per se had no binding effect in or over it." "It becomes," said the court "indispensable to the solution of these difficulties that we should conceive a just idea of the relation in which Florida stands to the United States…. And, first, it is obvious that there is a material distinction between the territory now under consideration and that which is acquired from the aborigines (whether by purchase or conquest) within the acknowledged limits of the United States, as also that which is acquired by the establishment of a disputed line. As to both these there can be no question that the sovereignty of the state or territory within which it lies, and of the United States, immediately attached, producing a complete subjection to all the laws and institutions of the two governments, local and general, unless modified by treaty. The question now to be considered relates to territories previously subject to the acknowledged jurisdiction of another sovereign, such as was Florida to the Crown of Spain. And on this subject we have the most explicit proof that the understanding of our public functionaries is that the government and laws of the United States do not extend to such territory by the mere act of cession. For in the act of Congress of March 30, 1822, 9, we have an enumeration of the acts of Congress which are to be held in force in the territory; and in the 10th section an enumeration, in the nature of a bill of rights, of privileges and immunities which could not be denied to the inhabitants of the territory if they came under the Constitution by the mere act of cession…. These states, this territory, and future states to be admitted into the Union are the sole objects of the Constitution; there is no express provision whatever made in the Constitution for the acquisition or government of territories beyond those limits." He further held that the right of acquiring territory was altogether incidental to the treaty-making power; that their government was left to Congress; that the territory of Florida did "not stand in the relation of a state to the United States;" that the acts establishing a territorial government were the Constitution of Florida; that while, under these acts, the territorial legislature could enact nothing inconsistent with what Congress had made inherent and permanent in the territorial government, it had not done so in organizing the court at Key West.

From the decree of the circuit court the underwriters appealed to this court, and the question was argued whether the circuit court was correct in drawing a distinction between territories existing at the date of the Constitution and territories subsequently acquired. The main contention of the appellants was that the superior courts of Florida had been vested by Congress with exclusive jurisdiction in all admiralty and maritime cases; that salvage was such a case, and therefore any law of Florida giving jurisdiction in salvage cases to any other court was unconstitutional. On behalf of the purchaser it was argued that the Constitution and laws of the United States were not per se in force in Florida, nor the inhabitants citizens of the United States; that the Constitution was established by the people of the United States for the United States; that if the Constitution were in force in Florida it was unnecessary to pass an act extending the laws of the United States to Florida. "What is Florida?" said Mr. Webster. "It is no part of the United States. How can it be? How is it represented? Do the laws of the United States reach Florida? Not unless by particular provisions."

The opinion of Mr. Chief Justice Marshall in this case should be read in connection with art. 3, 1 and 2, of the Constitution, vesting "the judicial power of the United States" in "one Supreme Court and in such inferior courts as the Congress may from time to time ordain and establish. The judges both of the Supreme and inferior courts shall hold their offices during good behavior," etc. He held that the court "should take into view the relation in which Florida stands to the United States;" that territory ceded by treaty "becomes a part of the nation to which it is annexed, either on the terms stipulated in the treaty of cession, or on such as its new master shall

impose." That Florida, upon the conclusion of the treaty, became a territory of the United States and subject to the power of Congress under the territorial clause of the Constitution. The acts providing a territorial government for Florida were examined in detail. He held that the judicial clause of the Constitution, above quoted, did not apply to Florida; that the judges of the superior courts of Florida held their office for four years; that "these courts are not, then, constitutional courts in which the judicial power conferred by the Constitution on the general government can be deposited;" that "they are legislative courts, created in virtue of the general right of sovereignty which exists in the government," or in virtue of the territorial clause of the Constitution; that the jurisdiction with which they are invested is not a part of judicial power of the Constitution, but is conferred by Congress in the exercise of those general powers which that body possesses over the territories of the United States; and that in legislating for them Congress exercises the combined powers of the general and of a state government. The act of the territorial legislature creating the court in question was held not to be "inconsistent with the laws and Constitution of the United States," and the decree of the circuit court was affirmed.

As the only judicial power vested in Congress is to create courts whose judges shall hold their offices during good behavior, it necessarily follows that, if Congress authorizes the creation of courts and the appointment of judges for a limited time, it must act independently of the Constitution and upon territory which is not part of the United States within the meaning of the Constitution. In delivering his opinion in this case Mr. Chief Justice Marshall made no reference whatever to the prior case of *Loughborough v. Blake*, 5 Wheat. 317, 5 L. ed. 98, in which he had intimated that the territories were part of the United States. But if they be a part of the United States, it is difficult to see how Congress could create courts in such territories, except under the judicial clause of the Constitution. The power to make needful rules and regulations would certainly not authorize anything inconsistent with the Constitution if it applied to the territories. Certainly no such court could be created within a state, except under the restrictions of the judicial clause. It is sufficient to say that this case has ever since been accepted as authority for the proposition that the judicial clause of the Constitution has no application to courts created in the territories, and that with respect to them Congress has a power wholly unrestricted by it. We must assume as a logical inference from this case that the other powers vested in Congress by the Constitution have no application to these territories, or that the judicial clause is exceptional in that particular.

This case was followed in *Benner v. Porter*, 9 How. 235, 13 L. ed. 119, in which it was held that the jurisdiction of these territorial courts ceased upon the admission of Florida into the Union, Mr. Justice Nelson remarking of them (p. 242, L. ed. p. 122), that "they are not organized under the Constitution, nor subject to its complex distribution of the powers of government, as the organic law; but are the creations, exclusively, of the legislative department, and subject to its supervision and control. Whether or not there are provisions in that instrument which extend to and act upon these territorial governments, it is not now material to examine. We are speaking here of those provisions that refer particularly to the distinction between Federal and state jurisdiction ... (p. 244, L. ed. p. 123). Neither were they organized by Congress under the Constitution, as they were invested with powers and jurisdiction which that body were incapable of conferring upon a court within the limits of a state." To the same effect are *Clinton v. Englebrecht*, 13 Wall. 434, 20 L. ed. 659; *Good v. Martin*, 95 U.S. 90, 98, 24 S. L. ed. 341, 344; and *McAllister v. United States*, 141 U.S. 174, 35 L. ed. 693, 11 Sup. Ct. Rep. 949.

That the power over the territories is vested in Congress without limitation, and that this power has been considered the foundation upon which the territorial governments rest, was also asserted by Chief Justice Marshall in *M'Culloch v. Maryland*, 4 Wheat. 316, 422, 4 L. ed. 579, 605, and in *United States v. Gratiot*, 14 Pet. 526, 10 L. ed. 573. So, too, in *Church of Jesus Christ of L. D. S. v. United States*, 136 U.S. 1, 34 L. ed. 478, 10 Sup. Ct. Rep. 792, in holding that Congress had power to repeal the charter of the church, Mr. Justice Bradley used the following forceful language: "The power of Congress over the territories of the United States is general and plenary, arising from and incidental to the right to acquire the territory itself, and from the power given by the Constitution to make all needful rules and regulations respecting the territory or other property belonging to the United States. It would be absurd to hold that the United States has power to acquire territory, and no power to govern it when acquired. The power to acquire territory, other than the territory northwest of the Ohio river (which belonged to the United States at the adoption of the Constitution), is derived from the treaty-making power and the power to declare and

carry on war. The incidents of these powers are those of national sovereignty and belong to all independent governments. The power to make acquisitions of territory by conquest, by treaty, and by cession is an incident of national sovereignty. The territory of Louisiana, when acquired from France, and the territories west of the Rocky mountains, when acquired from Mexico, became the absolute property and domain of the United States, subject to such conditions as the government, in its diplomatic negotiations, had seen fit to accept relating to the rights of the people then inhabiting those territories. Having rightfully acquired said territories, the United States government was the only one which could impose laws upon them, and its sovereignty over them was complete.... Doubtless Congress, in legislating for the territories, would be subject to those fundamental limitations in favor of personal rights which are formulated in the Constitution and its amendments, but those limitations would exist rather by inference and the general spirit of the Constitution, from which Congress derives all its powers, than by any express and direct application of its provisions." See also, to the same effect *First Nat. Bank v. Yankton County*, 101 U.S. 129, 25 L. ed. 1046; *Murphy v. Ramsey*, 114 U.S. 15, 29 L. ed. 47, 5 Sup. Ct. Rep. 747.

In *Webster v. Reid*, 11 How. 437, 13 L. ed. 761, it was held that a law of the territory of Iowa, which prohibited the trial by jury of certain actions at law founded on contract to recover payment for services, was void; but the case is of little value as bearing upon the question of the extension of the Constitution to that territory, inasmuch as the organic law of the territory of Iowa, by express provision and by reference, extended the laws of the United States, including the ordinance of 1787 (which provided expressly for jury trials), so far as they were applicable; and the case was put upon this ground. 5 Stat. at L. 235, 239, chap. 96, 12.

In *Reynolds v. United States*, 98 U.S. 145, 25 L. ed. 244, a law of the territory of Utah, providing for grand juries of fifteen persons, was held to be constitutional, though Rev. Stat. 808, required that a grand jury impaneled before any circuit or district court of the United States shall consist of not less than sixteen nor more than twenty-three persons. Section 808 was held to apply only to the circuit and district courts. The territorial courts were free to act in obedience to their own laws.

In Ross's Case, 140 U.S. 453, sub nom. *Ross v. McIntyre*, 35 L. ed. 581, 11 Sup. Ct. Rep. 897, petitioner had been convicted by the American consular tribunal in Japan, of a murder committed upon an American vessel in the harbor of Yokohama, and sentenced to death. There was no indictment by a grand jury, and no trial by a petit jury. This court affirmed the conviction, holding that the Constitution had no application, since it was ordained and established "for the United States of America," and not for countries outside of their limits. "The guaranties it affords against accusation of capital or infamous crimes, except by indictment or presentment by a grand jury, and for an impartial trial by a jury when thus accused, apply only to citizens and others within the United States, or who are brought there for trial for alleged offenses committed elsewhere, and not to residents or temporary sojourners abroad."

In *Springville v. Thomas*, 166 U.S. 707, 41 L. ed. 1172, 17 Sup. Ct. Rep. 717, it was held that a verdict returned by less than the whole number of jurors was invalid because in contravention of the 7th Amendment to the Constitution and the act of Congress of April 7, 1874 (18 Stat. at L. 27, chap. 80), which provide "that no party has been or shall be deprived of the right of trial by jury in cases cognizable at common law." It was also intimated that Congress "could not impart the power to change the constitutional rule," which was obviously true with respect to Utah, since the organic act of that territory (9 Stat. at L. 458, chap. 51, 17) had expressly extended to it the Constitution and laws of the United States. As we have already held, that provision, once made, could not be withdrawn. If the Constitution could be withdrawn directly, it could be nullified indirectly by acts passed inconsistent with it. The Constitution would thus cease to exist as such, and become of no greater authority than an ordinary act of Congress. In *American Pub. Co. v. Fisher*, 166 U.S. 464, 41 L. ed. 1079, 17 Sup. Ct. Rep. 618, a similar law providing for majority verdicts was put upon the express ground above stated, that the organic act of Utah extended the Constitution over that territory. These rulings were repeated in *Thompson v. Utah*, 170 U.S. 343, 42 L. ed. 1061, 18 Sup. Ct. Rep. 620, and applied to felonies committed before the territory became a state, although the state Constitution continued the same provision.

Eliminating, then, from the opinions of this court all expressions unnecessary to the disposition of the particular case, and gleaning therefrom the exact point decided in each, the following propositions may be considered as established:

1. That the District of Columbia and the territories are not states within the judicial clause of the Constitution giving jurisdiction in cases between citizens of different states;

2. That territories are not states within the meaning of Rev. Stat. 709, permitting writs of error from this court in cases where the validity of a state statute is drawn in question;

3. That the District of Columbia and the territories are states as that word is used in treaties with foreign powers, with respect to the ownership, disposition, and inheritance of property;

4. That the territories are not within the clause of the Constitution providing for the creation of a supreme court and such inferior courts as Congress may see fit to establish;

5. That the Constitution does not apply to foreign countries or to trials therein conducted, and that Congress may lawfully provide for such trials before consular tribunals, without the intervention of a grand or petit jury;

6. That where the Constitution has been once formally extended by Congress to territories, neither Congress nor the territorial legislature can enact laws inconsistent therewith.

The case of *Dred Scott v. Sandford*, 19 How. 393, 15 L. ed. 691, remains to be considered. This was an action of trespass vi et armis brought in the circuit court for the district of Missouri by Scott, alleging himself to be a citizen of Missouri, against Sandford, a citizen of New York. Defendant pleaded to the jurisdiction that Scott was not a citizen of the state of Missouri, because a negro of African descent, whose ancestors were imported as negro slaves. Plaintiff demurred to this plea and the demurrer was sustained; whereupon, by stipulation of counsel and with leave of the court, defendant pleaded in bar the general issue, and specially that the plaintiff was a slave and the lawful property of defendant, and, as such, he had a right to restrain him. The wife and children of the plaintiff were also involved in the suit.

The facts in brief were that plaintiff had been a slave belonging to Dr. Emerson, a surgeon in the army; that in 1834 Emerson took the plaintiff from the state of Missouri to Rock Island, Illinois, and subsequently to Fort Snelling, Minnesota (then known as Upper Louisiana), and held him there until 1838. Scott married his wife there, of whom the children were subsequently born. In 1838 they returned to Missouri.

Two questions were presented by the record: First, whether the circuit court had jurisdiction; and, second, if it had jurisdiction, was the judgment erroneous or not? With regard to the first question, the court stated that it was its duty "to decide whether the facts stated in the plea are or are not sufficient to show that the plaintiff is not entitled to sue as a citizen in a court of the United States," and that the question was whether "a negro whose ancestors were imported into this country and sold as slaves became a member of the political community formed and brought into existence by the Constitution of the United States, and as such became entitled to all the rights and privileges and immunities guaranteed by that instrument to the citizen, one of which rights is the privilege of suing in a court of the United States." It was held that he was not, and was not included under the word "citizens" in the Constitution, and therefore could claim "none of the rights and privileges which that instrument provides for and secures to citizens of the United States;" that it did not follow, because he had all the rights and privileges of a citizen of a state, he must be a citizen of the United States; that no state could by any law of its own "introduce a new member into the political community created by the Constitution;" that the African race was not intended to be included, and formed no part of the people who framed and adopted the Declaration of Independence. The question of the status of negroes in England and the several states was considered at great length by the Chief Justice, and the conclusion reached that Scott was not a citizen of Missouri, and that the circuit court had no jurisdiction of the case.

This was sufficient to dispose of the case without reference to the question of slavery; but, as the plaintiff insisted upon his title to freedom and citizenship by the fact that he and his wife, though born slaves, were taken by their owner and kept four years in Illinois and Minnesota, they thereby became and upon their return to Missouri became citizens of that state, the Chief Justice proceeded to discuss the question whether Scott was still a slave. As the court had decided against his citizenship upon the plea in abatement, it was insisted that further decision upon the question of his freedom or slavery was extrajudicial and mere obiter dicta. But the Chief Justice held that the correction of one error in the court below did not deprive the appellate court of the power of examining further into the record and correcting any other material error which may have been committed; that the error of an inferior court in actually pronouncing judgment for one of the parties, in a case in which it had no jurisdiction, can be looked into or corrected by this court, even though it had decided a similar question presented in the pleadings.

Proceeding to decide the case upon the merits, he held that the territorial clause of the Constitution was confined to the territory which belonged to the United States at the time the Constitution was adopted, and did not apply to territory subsequently acquired from a foreign government.

In further examining the question as to what provision of the Constitution authorizes the Federal government to acquire territory outside of the original limits of the United States, and what powers it may exercise therein over the person or property of a citizen of the United States, he made use of the following expressions, upon which great reliance is placed by the plaintiff in this case (p. 446, L. ed. p. 718): "There is certainly no power given by the Constitution to the Federal government to establish or maintain colonies bordering on the United States or at a distance, to be ruled and governed at its own pleasure; ... and if a new state is admitted, it needs no further legislation by Congress, because the Constitution itself defines the relative rights and powers and duties of the state, and the citizens of the state, and the Federal government. But no power is given to acquire a territory to be held and governed permanently in that character."

He further held that citizens who migrate to a territory cannot be ruled as mere colonists, and that, while Congress had the power of legislating over territories until states were formed from them, it could not deprive a citizen of his property merely because he brought it into a particular territory of the United States, and that this doctrine applied to slaves as well as to other property. Hence, it followed that the act of Congress which prohibited a citizen from holding and owning slaves in territories north of 36°30' (known as the Missouri Compromise) was unconstitutional and void, and the fact that Scott was carried into such territory, referring to what is now known as Minnesota, did not entitle him to his freedom.

He further held that whether he was made free by being taken into the free state of Illinois and being kept there two years depended upon the laws of Missouri, and not those of Illinois, and that by the decisions of the highest court of that state his status as a slave continued, notwithstanding his residence of two years in Illinois.

It must be admitted that this case is a strong authority in favor of the plaintiff, and if the opinion of the Chief Justice be taken at its full value it is decisive in his favor. We are not, however, bound to overlook the fact, that, before the Chief Justice gave utterance to his opinion upon the merits, he had already disposed of the case adversely to the plaintiff upon the question of jurisdiction, and that, in view of the excited political condition of the country at the time, it is unfortunate that he felt compelled to discuss the question upon the merits, particularly so in view of the fact that it involved a ruling that an act of Congress which had been acquiesced in for thirty years was declared unconstitutional. It would appear from the opinion of Mr. Justice Wayne that the real reason for discussing these constitutional questions was that "there had become such a difference of opinion" about them "that the peace and harmony of the country required the settlement of them by judicial decision." p. 455, L. ed. p. 721. The attempt was not successful. It is sufficient to say that the country did not acquiesce in the opinion, and that the Civil War, which shortly thereafter followed, produced such changes in judicial, as well as public, sentiment as to seriously impair the authority of this case.

While there is much in the opinion of the Chief Justice which tends to prove that he thought all the provisions of the Constitution extended of their own force to the territories west of the Mississippi, the question actually decided is readily distinguishable from the one involved in the cause under consideration. The power to prohibit slavery in the territories is so different from the power to impose duties upon territorial products, and depends upon such different provisions of the Constitution, that they can scarcely be considered as analogous, unless we assume broadly that every clause of the Constitution attaches to the territories as well as to the states—a claim quite inconsistent with the position of the court in the Canter Case. If the assumption be true that slaves are indistinguishable from other property, the inference from the Dred Scott Case is irresistible that Congress had no power to prohibit their introduction into a territory. It would scarcely be insisted that Congress could with one hand invite settlers to locate in the territories of the United States, and with the other deny them the right to take their property and belongings with them. The two are so inseparable from each other that one could scarcely be granted and the other withheld without an exercise of arbitrary power inconsistent with the underlying principles of a free government. It might indeed be claimed with great plausibility that such a law would amount to a deprivation of property within the 14th Amendment. The difficulty with the Dred Scott Case was that the court refused to make a distinction between property in general and a wholly exceptional class of property. Mr. Benton tersely stated the dis-

tinction by saying that the Virginian might carry his slaves into the territories, but he could not carry with him the Virginian law which made him a slave.

In his history of the Dred Scott Case, Mr. Benton states that the doctrine that the Constitution extended to territories as well as to states first made its appearance in the Senate in the session of 1848–1849, by an attempt to amend a bill giving territorial government to California, New Mexico, and Utah (itself "hitched on" to a general appropriation bill), by adding the words "that the Constitution of the United States and all and singular the several acts of Congress (describing them) be and the same hereby are extended and given full force and efficacy in said territories." Says Mr. Benton: "The novelty and strangeness of this proposition called up Mr. Webster, who repulsed as an absurdity and as an impossibility the scheme of extending the Constitution to the territories, declaring that instrument to have been made for states, not territories; that Congress governed the territories independently of the Constitution and incompatibly with it; that no part of it went to a territory but what Congress chose to send; that it could not act of itself anywhere, not even in the states for which it was made, and that it required an act of Congress to put it in operation before it had effect anywhere Mr. Clay was of the same opinion and added: 'Now, really, I must say the idea that eo Instanti upon the consummation of the treaty, the Constitution of the United States spread itself over the acquired territory and carried along with it the institution of slavery is so irreconcilable with my comprehension, or any reason I possess, that I hardly know how to meet it.' Upon the other hand, Mr. Calhoun boldly avowed his intent to carry slavery into them under the wing of the Constitution, and denounced as enemies of the south all who opposed it."

The amendment was rejected by the House, and a contest brought on which threatened the loss of the general appropriation bill in which this amendment was incorporated, and the Senate finally receded from its amendment. "Such," said Mr. Benton, "were the portentous circumstances under which this new doctrine first revealed itself in the American Senate, and then as needing legislative sanction requiring an act of Congress to carry the Constitution into the territories and to give it force and efficacy there." Of the Dred Scott Case he says: "I conclude this introductory note with recurring to the great fundamental error of the court (father of all the political errors), that of assuming the extension of the Constitution to the territories. I call it assuming, for it seems to be a naked assumption without a reason to support it, or a leg to stand upon, condemned by the Constitution itself and the whole history of its formation and administration. Who were the parties to it? The states alone. Their delegates framed it in the Federal convention; their citizens adopted it in the state conventions. The Northwest Territory was then in existence and it had been for three years; yet it had no voice either in the framing or adopting of the instrument, no delegate at Philadelphia, no submission of it to their will for adoption. The preamble shows it made by states. Territories are not alluded to in it."

Finally, in summing up the results of the decisions holding the invalidity of the Missouri Compromise and the self-extension of the Constitution to the territories, he declares "that the decisions conflict with the uniform action of all the departments of the Federal government from its foundation to the present time, and cannot be received as rules governing Congress and the people without reversing that action, and admitting the political supremacy of the court, and accepting an altered Constitution from its hands and taking a new and portentous point of departure in the working of the government."

To sustain the judgment in the case under consideration, it by no means becomes necessary to show that none of the articles of the Constitution apply to the island of Porto Rico. There is a clear distinction between such prohibitions as go to the very root of the power of Congress to act at all, irrespective of time of place, and such as are operative only "throughout the United States" or among the several states.

Thus, when the Constitution declares that "no bill of attainder or ex post facto law shall be passed," and that "no title of nobility shall be granted by the United States," it goes to the competency of Congress to pass a bill of that description. Perhaps the same remark may apply to the 1st Amendment, that "Congress shall make no law respecting an establishment of religion, or prohibiting the free exercise thereof; or abridging the freedom of speech, or of the press; or the right of the people to peacefully assemble and to petition the government for a redress of grievances." We do not wish, however, to be understood as expressing an opinion how far the bill of rights contained in the first eight amendments is of general and how far of local application.

Upon the other hand, when the Constitution declares that all duties shall be uniform "throughout the United States," it becomes necessary to inquire whether there be any territory over which Congress has jurisdiction which is not a part of the "United States," by which term we understand the states whose people united to form the Constitution, and such as have since been admitted to the Union upon an equality with them. Not only did the people in adopting the 13th Amendment thus recognize a distinction between the United States and "any place subject to their jurisdiction," but Congress itself, in the act of March 27, 1804 (2 Stat. at L. 298, chap. 56), providing for the proof of public records, applied the provisions of the act, not only to "every court and office within the United States," but to the "courts and offices of the respective territories of the United States and countries subject to the jurisdiction of the United States," as to the courts and offices of the several states. This classification, adopted by the Eighth Congress, is carried into the Revised Statutes as follows:

"Sec. 905. The acts of the legislature of any state or territory, or of any country subject to the jurisdiction of the United States, shall be authenticated," etc.

"Sec. 906. All records and exemplifications of books which may be kept in any public office of and state or territory, or of any country subject to the jurisdiction of the United States," etc.

Unless these words are to be rejected as meaningless, we must treat them as a recognition by Congress of the fact that there may be territories subject to the jurisdiction of the United States, which are not of the United States.

In determining the meaning of the words of article 1, section 8, "uniform throughout the United States," we are bound to consider, not only the provisions forbidding preference being given to the ports of one state over those of another (to which attention has already been called), but the other clauses declaring that no tax or duty shall be laid on articles exported from any state, and that no state shall, without the consent of Congress, lay any imposts or duties upon imports or exports, nor any duty on tonnage. The object of all of these was to protect the states which united in forming the Constitution from discriminations by Congress, which would operate unfairly or injuriously upon some states and not equally upon others. The opinion of Mr. Justice White in *Knowlton v. Moore*, 178 U.S. 41, 44 L. ed. 969, 20 Sup. Ct. Rep. 747, contains an elaborate historical review of the proceedings in the convention, which resulted in the adoption of these different clauses and their arrangement, and he there comes to the conclusion (p. 105, L. ed. p. 995, Sup. Ct. Rep. p. 772) that "although the provision as to preference between ports and that regarding uniformity of duties, imposts, and excises were one in purpose, one in their adoption," they were originally placed together, and "became separated only in arranging the Constitution for the purpose of style." Thus construed together, the purpose is irresistible that the words "throughout the United States" are indistinguishable from the words "among or between the several states," and that these prohibitions were intended to apply only to commerce between ports of the several states as they then existed or should thereafter be admitted to the Union.

Indeed, the practical interpretation put by Congress upon the Constitution has been long continued and uniform to the effect that the Constitution is applicable to territories acquired by purchase or conquest, only when and so far as Congress shall so direct. Notwithstanding its duty to "guarantee to every state in this Union a republican form of government" (art. 4, 4), by which we understand, according to the definition of Webster, "a government in which the supreme power resides in the whole body of the people, and is exercised by representatives elected by them," Congress did not hesitate, in the original organization of the territories of Louisiana, Florida, the Northwest Territory, and its subdivisions of Ohio, Indiana, Michigan, Illinois, and Wisconsin and still more recently in the case of Alaska, to establish a form of government bearing a much greater analogy to a British Crown colony than a republican state of America, and to vest the legislative power either in a governor and council, or a governor and judges, to be appointed by the President. It was not until they had attained a certain population that power was given them to organize a legislature by vote of the people. In all these cases, as well as in territories subsequently organized west of the Mississippi, Congress thought it necessary either to extend to Constitution and laws of the United States over them, or to declare that the inhabitants should be entitled to enjoy the right of trial by jury, of bail, and of the privilege of the writ of habeas corpus, as well as other privileges of the bill of rights.

We are also of opinion that the power to acquire territory by treaty implies, not only the power to govern such territory, but to prescribe upon what terms the United States will receive its inhabitants, and what their status shall be in what Chief Justice Marshall termed the "American empire." There seems to be no middle ground between this position and the doctrine that if their inhabitants do not become, immediately upon annexation, citizens of the United States, their children thereafter born, whether savages or civilized, are such, and entitled to all the rights, privileges and immunities of citizens. If such be their status, the consequences will be extremely serious. Indeed, it is doubtful if Congress would ever assent to the annexation of territory upon the condition that its inhabitants, however foreign they may be to our habits, traditions, and modes of life, shall become at once citizens of the United States. In all its treaties hitherto the treaty-making power has made special provision for this subject; in the cases of Louisiana and Florida, by stipulating that "the inhabitants shall be incorporated into the Union of the United States and admitted as soon as possible … to the enjoyment of all the rights, advantages, and immunities of citizens of the United States;" in the case of Mexico, that they should "be incorporated into the Union, and be admitted at the proper time (to be judged of by the Congress of the United States) to the enjoyment of all the rights of citizens of the United States;" in the case of Alaska, that the inhabitants who remained three years, "with the exception of uncivilized native tribes, shall be admitted to the enjoyment of all the rights," etc; and in the case of Porto Rico and the Philippines, "that the civil rights and political status of the native inhabitants … shall be determined by Congress." In all these cases there is an implied denial of the right of the inhabitants to American citizenship until Congress by further action shall signify its assent thereto.

Grave apprehensions of danger are felt by many eminent men—a fear lest an unrestrained possession of power on the part of Congress may lead to unjust and oppressive legislation in which the natural rights of territories, or their inhabitants, may be engulfed in a centralized despotism. These fears, however, find no justification in the action of Congress in the past century, nor in the conduct of the British Parliament towards its outlying possessions since the American Revolution. Indeed, in the only instance in which this court has declared an act of Congress unconstitutional as trespassing upon the rights of territories (the Missouri Compromise), such action was dictated by motives of humanity and justice, and so far commanded popular approval as to be embodied in the 13th Amendment to the Constitution. There are certain principles of natural justice inherent in the Anglo-Saxon character, which need no expression in constitutions or statutes to give them effect or to secure dependencies against legislation manifestly hostile to their real interests. Even in the Foraker act itself, the constitutionality of which is so vigorously assailed, power was given to the legislative assembly of Porto Rico to repeal the very tariff in question in this case, a power it has not seen fit to exercise. The words of Chief Justice Marshall in *Gibbons v. Ogden*, 9 Wheat. 1, 6 L. ed. 23, with respect to the power of Congress to regulate commerce, are pertinent in this connection: "This power," said he, "like all others vested in Congress, is complete in itself, may be exercised to its utmost extent, and acknowledges no limitations other than are prescribed in the Constitution.... The wisdom and discretion of Congress, their identity with the people, and the influence which their constituents possess at elections, are in this, as in many other instances—as that, for example, of declaring war—the sole restraints on which they have relied to secure them from its abuse. They are the restraints on which the people must often rely solely in all representative governments."

So too, in *Johnson v. M'Intosh*, 8 Wheat. 543, 583, 5 L. ed. 681, 691, it was said by him:

"The title by conquest is acquired and maintained by force. The conqueror prescribes its limits. Humanity, however, acting on public opinion, has established, as a general rule, that the conquered shall not be wantonly oppressed, and that their condition shall remain as eligible as is compatible with the objects of the conquest. Most usually they are incorporated with the victorious nation and become subjects or citizens of the government with which they are connected. The new and old members of the society mingle with each other; the distinction between them is gradually lost, and they make one people. Where this incorporation is practicable humanity demands, and a wise policy requires, that the rights of the conquered to property should remain unimpaired; that the new subjects should be governed as equitably as the old; and that confidence in their security should gradually banish the painful sense of being separated from their ancient connections and united by force to strangers.

"When the conquest is complete, and the conquered inhabitants can be blended with the conquerors, or safely governed as a distinct people, public opinion, which not even the con-

queror can disregard, imposes these restraints upon him; and he cannot neglect them without injury to his fame and hazard to his power."

The following remarks of Mr. Justice White in the case of *Knowlton v. Moore*, 178 U.S. 109, 44 L. ed. 996, 20 Sup. Ct. Rep. 774, in which the court upheld the progressive features of the legacy tax, are also pertinent:

"The grave consequences which it is asserted must arise in the future if the right to levy a progressive tax be recognized involves in its ultimate aspect the mere assertion that free and representative government is a failure, and that the grossest abuses of power are foreshadowed unless the courts usurp a purely legislative function. If a case should ever arise where an arbitrary and confiscatory exaction is imposed, bearing the guise of a progressive or any other form of tax, it will be time enough to consider whether the judicial power can afford a remedy by applying inherent and fundamental principles for the protection of the individual, even though there be no express authority in the Constitution to do so."

It is obvious that in the annexation of outlying and distant possessions grave questions will arise from differences of race, habits, laws, and customs of the people, and from differences of soil, climate, and production, which may require action on the part of Congress that would be quite unnecessary in the annexation of contiguous territory inhabited only by people of the same race, or by scattered bodies of native Indians.

We suggest, without intending to decide, that there may be a distinction between certain natural rights enforced in the Constitution by prohibitions against interference with them, and what may be termed artificial or remedial rights which are peculiar to our own system of jurisprudence. Of the former class are the rights to one's own religious opinions and to a public expression of them, or, as sometimes said, to worship God according to the dictates of one's own conscience; the right to personal liberty and individual property; to freedom of speech and of the press; to free access to courts of justice, to due process of law, and to an equal protection of the laws; to immunities from unreasonable searches and seizures, as well as cruel and unusual punishments; and to such other immunities as are indispensable to a free government. Of the latter class are the rights to citizenship, to suffrage (*Minor v. Happersett*, 21 Wall. 162, 22 L. ed. 627), and to the particular methods of procedure pointed out in the Constitution, which are peculiar to Anglo-Saxon jurisprudence, and some of which have already been held by the states to be unnecessary to the proper protection of individuals.

Whatever may be finally decided by the American people as to the status of these islands and their inhabitants—whether they shall be introduced into the sisterhood of states or be permitted to form independent governments—it does not follow that in the meantime, a waiting that decision, the people are in the matter of personal rights unprotected by the provisions of our Constitution and subject to the merely arbitrary control of Congress. Even if regarded as aliens, they are entitled under the principles of the Constitution to be protected in life, liberty, and property. This has been frequently held by this court in respect to the Chinese, even when aliens, not possessed of the political rights of citizens of the United States. *Yick Wo v. Hopkins*, 118 U.S. 356, 30 L. ed. 220, 6 Sup. Ct. Rep. 1064; *Fong Yue Ting v. United States*, 149 U.S. 698, 37 L. ed. 905, 13 Sup. Ct. Rep. 1016; *Lem Moon Sing*, 158 U.S. 538, 547, 39 S. L. ed. 1082, 1085, 15 Sup. Ct. Rep. 962; *Wong Wing v. United States*, 163 U.S. 228, 41 L. ed. 140, 16 Sup. Ct. Rep. 977. We do not desire, however, to anticipate the difficulties which would naturally arise in this connection, but merely to disclaim any intention to hold that the inhabitants of these territories are subject to an unrestrained power on the part of Congress to deal with them upon the theory that they have no rights which it is bound to respect.

Large powers must necessarily be entrusted to Congress in dealing with these problems, and we are bound to assume that they will be judiciously exercised. That these powers may be abused is possible. But the same may be said of its powers under the Constitution as well as outside of it. Human wisdom has never devised a form of government so perfect that it may not be perverted to bad purposes. It is never conclusive to argue against the possession of certain powers from possible abuses of them. It is safe to say that if Congress should venture upon legislation manifestly dictated by selfish interests, it would receive quick rebuke at the hands of the people. Indeed, it is scarcely possible that Congress could do a greater injustice to these islands than would be involved in holding that it could not impose upon the states taxes and excises without extending the same taxes to them. Such requirement would bring them at once within our internal revenue system, including stamps, licenses, excises, and all the paraphernalia of that system, and apply it to territories which have had no experience of this kind, and where it would prove an intolerable burden.

This subject was carefully considered by the Senate committee in charge of the Foraker bill, which found, after an examination of the facts, that property in Porto Rico was already burdened with a private debt amounting probably to $30,000,000; that no system of property taxation was or ever had been in force in the island, and that it probably would require two years to inaugurate one and secure returns from it; that the revenues had always been chiefly raised by duties on imports and exports, and that our internal revenue laws, if applied in that island, would prove oppressive and ruinous to many people and interests; that to undertake to collect our heavy internal revenue tax, far heavier than Spain ever imposed upon their products and vocations, would be to invite violations of the law so innumerable as to make prosecutions impossible, and to almost certainly alienate and destroy the friendship and good will of that people for the United States.

In passing upon the questions involved in this and kindred cases, we ought not to overlook the fact that, while the Constitution was intended to establish a permanent form of government for the states which should elect to take advantage of its conditions, and continue for an indefinite future, the vast possibilities of that future could never have entered the minds of its framers. The states had but recently emerged from a war with one of the most powerful nations of Europe, were disheartened by the failure of the confederacy, and were doubtful as to the feasibility of a stronger union. Their territory was confined to a narrow strip of land on the Atlantic coast from Canada to Florida, with a somewhat indefinite claim to territory beyond the Alleghenies, where their sovereignty was disputed by tribes of hostile Indians supported, as was popularly believed, by the British, who had never formally delivered possession under the treaty of peace. The vast territory beyond the Mississippi, which formerly had been claimed by France, since 1762 had belonged to Spain, still a powerful nation and the owner of a great part of the Western Hemisphere. Under these circumstances it is little wonder that the question of annexing these territories was not made a subject of debate. The difficulties of bringing about a union of the states were so great, the objections to it seemed so formidable, that the whole thought of the convention centered upon surmounting these obstacles. The question of territories was dismissed with a single clause, apparently applicable only to the territories then existing, giving Congress the power to govern and dispose of them.

Had the acquisition of other territories been contemplated as a possibility, could it have been foreseen that, within little more than one hundred years, we were destined to acquire, not only the whole vast region between the Atlantic and Pacific Oceans, but the Russian possessions in America and distant islands in the Pacific, it is incredible that no provision should have been made for them, and the question whether the Constitution should or should not extend to them have been definitely settled. If it be once conceded that we are at liberty to acquire foreign territory, a presumption arises that our power with respect to such territories is the same power which other nations have been accustomed to exercise with respect to territories acquired by them. If, in limiting the power which Congress was to exercise within the United States, it was also intended to limit it with regard to such territories as the people of the United States should thereafter acquire, such limitations should have been expressed. Instead of that, we find the Constitution speaking only to states, except in the territorial clause, which is absolute in its terms, and suggestive of no limitations upon the power of Congress in dealing with them. The states could only delegate to Congress such powers as they themselves possessed, and as they had no power to acquire new territory they had none to delegate in that connection. The logical inference from this is that if Congress had power to acquire new territory, which is conceded, that power was not hampered by the constitutional provisions. If, upon the other hand, we assume that the territorial clause of the Constitution was not intended to be restricted to such territory as the United States then possessed, there is nothing in the Constitution to indicate that the power of Congress in dealing with them was intended to be restricted by any of the other provisions.

There is a provision that "new states may be admitted by the Congress into this Union." These words, of course, carry the Constitution with them, but nothing is said regarding the acquisition of new territories or the extension of the Constitution over them. The liberality of Congress in legislating the Constitution into all our contiguous territories has undoubtedly fostered the impression that it went there by its own force, but there is nothing in the Constitution itself, and little in the interpretation put upon it, to confirm that impression. There is not even an analogy to the provisions of an ordinary mortgage, for its attachment to after-acquired property, without which it covers only property existing at the date of the mortgage. In short, there is absolute silence upon the subject. The executive and legislative departments of the government have for more than a century interpreted this silence as precluding the idea that the Constitution attached to these territories as soon as acquired, and unless such interpretation be manifestly contrary to the letter or spirit of the Constitution, it should be followed by the judicial department. Cooley, Const. Lim. 81-85. *Burrow-Giles Lithographic Co. v. Sarony*, 111 U.S. 53, 57, 28 S. L. ed. 349, 351, 4 Sup. Ct. Rep. 279; *Marshall Field & Co. v. Clark*, 143 U.S. 649, 691, 36 S. L. ed. 294, 309, 12 Sup. Ct. Rep. 495.

Patriotic and intelligent men may differ widely as to the desirableness of this or that acquisition, but this is solely a political question. We can only consider this aspect of the case so far as to say that no construction of the Constitution should be adopted which would prevent Congress from considering each case upon its merits, unless the language of the instrument imperatively demand it. A false step at this time might be fatal to the development of what Chief Justice Marshall called the American empire. Choice in some cases, the natural gravitation of small bodies towards large ones in others, the result of a successful war in still others, may bring about conditions which would render the annexation of distant possessions desirable. If those possessions are inhabited by alien races, differing from us in religion, customs, laws, methods of taxation, and modes of thought, the administration of government and justice, according to Anglo-Saxon principles, may for a time be impossible; and the question at once arises whether large concessions ought not to be made for a time, that ultimately our own theories may be carried out, and the blessings of a free government under the Constitution extended to them. We decline to hold that there is anything in the Constitution to forbid such action.

We are therefore of opinion that the island of Porto Rico is a territory appurtenant and belonging to the United States, but not a part of the United States within the revenue clauses of the Constitution; that the Foraker act is constitutional, so far as it imposes duties upon imports from such island, and that the plaintiff cannot recover back the duties exacted in this case.

The judgment of the Circuit Court is therefore affirmed.

NIAGARA MOVEMENT DECLARATION OF PRINCIPLES

"Any discrimination based simply on race or color is barbarous, we care not how hallowed it be by custom, expediency or prejudice."

Overview

The Niagara Movement Declaration of Principles outlined a philosophy and political program designed to address racial inequality in the United States. It had its origin on July 11, 1905, when twenty-nine African American men began deliberations at the Erie Beach Hotel in Fort Erie, Ontario, just across the border from Buffalo and Niagara, New York. When they adjourned three days later, the Niagara Movement had been born. The Niagara Movement had a limited impact on race relations in the United States. Within five years it would cease to exist, and in the history of the struggle for equal rights it has long been overshadowed by the more successful, long-lived, biracial National Association for the Advancement of Colored People (NAACP). Nevertheless, the Niagara Movement was an important landmark in U.S. and African American history.

Several factors distinguish the movement. First, it was a purely African American effort to address discrimination and racial inequality. No whites were involved in its creation, organization, or operation. Second, it enunciated a clearly defined philosophy and political program, embodied in the Declaration of Principles that was drafted and approved at the 1905 meeting. While rephrased and modified somewhat, the sentiments and tone of the Declaration of Principles would outlive the Niagara Movement and help define the agenda of the NAACP and the civil rights movement of the 1950s and early 1960s. Finally, the gathering in Fort Erie pointedly excluded the most prominent African American leader of the day, Booker T. Washington, as well as anyone perceived to be allied with him. In addition to confronting American racism, the Niagara Movement and its Declaration of Principles were also a challenge to Booker T. Washington's leadership and his program for the advancement of African Americans.

Context

There is no question that the racial situation in the United States in the first decade of the twentieth century called out for a strong and assertive civil rights organization. Race relations in the country had deteriorated steadily since the end of Reconstruction following the Civil War. By the turn of the century the promise of equality incorporated in the Reconstruction amendments to the U.S. Constitution and the Civil Rights Acts of 1866 and 1875 had been undone by state action and by the U.S. Supreme Court. A series of state laws and local ordinances segregating blacks and whites received sanction in the Supreme Court, culminating with the *Plessy v. Ferguson* decision in 1896. In this case the Supreme Court legitimized "separate but equal facilities" and provided the legal basis for segregation for the next half-century. At the same time, southern states began to place limits on the right of African American to vote, using tactics such as the grandfather clause, white primaries, literacy tests, residency requirements, and poll taxes to prevent blacks from voting. In 1898 the Supreme Court upheld so-called race-neutral restrictions on black suffrage in *Williams v. Mississippi*. The effect was virtually to eliminate black voting in the states of the South. African Americans did not fare much better in the North, where segregation, if not disenfranchisement, grew increasingly common.

Accompanying segregation and disenfranchisement was a resurgence in racial violence. While the Reconstruction Ku Klux Klan had been effectively suppressed by the mid-1870s, the late nineteenth century and early twentieth century experienced an unprecedented wave of racially motivated lynchings and riots. During the first decade of the twentieth century, between fifty-seven and 105 African Americans were lynched by white mobs each year. Lynch mobs targeted blacks almost exclusively, and any pretense of legalism and due process vanished. Furthermore, blacks more and more became victims of the more generalized racial violence of race riots. Race riots during this period typically involved whites rioting against blacks. Some, such as the 1898 riot in Wilmington, North Carolina, were linked to political efforts to stir up racial hostility as part of a campaign to disenfranchise blacks; others, such as the New York race riot of 1900 and the Atlanta race riot of 1906, grew out of resentment of the presence of blacks. To the degree that the rage they unleashed had an objective, it was to destroy the black community and put blacks in "their place."

Time Line

1895

■ **February 20**
Frederick Douglass dies at his home in Washington, D.C.

■ **September 18**
Washington delivers his Atlanta Exposition Address during the opening ceremonies of the Cotton States and International Exposition, which in the eyes of most Americans elevates him to the leadership of the African American community.

1896

■ **May 18**
In *Plessy v. Ferguson*, the Supreme Court rules that a Louisiana law segregating passengers on railroads was legal because it provided "separate but equal" facilities; this became the legal basis for the segregation of African Americans.

1898

■ **April 25**
In *Williams v. State of Mississippi*, the Supreme Court rules that a Mississippi law that allowed poll taxes and literacy tests to be used as voter qualifications is legal, legitimizing the efforts of southern states to deny African Americans the right to vote.

■ **November 10**
A race riot erupts in Wilmington, North Carolina, following a local election, as Democrats force blacks and Republicans to resign from their elected offices. A confirmed fourteen blacks are killed, although estimated deaths were several times that many; a number of leading black citizens are banished from the town.

1900

■ **August 15**
New York City race riot. White mobs, with the support of police, attack blacks in the Tenderloin district of New York City. Scores of blacks are beaten, with many requiring hospitalization.

As the racial scene deteriorated, African Americans faced a transition in leadership. Frederick Douglass, who had symbolized the African American struggle against slavery and had been an outspoken advocate for equal rights in the post–Civil War period, died in 1895. That same year Booker T. Washington rose to national prominence with his speech at the Cotton States and International Exposition in Atlanta. The southern-based Washington focused on the economic development of African Americans as the surest road to equality, and while he opposed segregation and black disenfranchisement, he eschewed militant rhetoric and direct confrontation. Washington essentially believed that rational argument and an appeal to southerners' self-interest would defeat prejudice. As time passed and the racial situation worsened, many blacks, especially college-educated northerners, grew impatient with Washington's leadership. By the early twentieth century, such critics as the Boston newspaper editor William Monroe Trotter had become increasingly outspoken about Washington's failures. After 1903 W. E. B. Du Bois emerged as the most respected opponent of Washington and his Tuskegee political machine, the loose coalition of friends and allies through which Washington exercised his political influence on the African American community.

About the Author

Most people assume that W. E. B. Du Bois was the author of the Declaration of Principles. Actually the authorship is not that simple or clear. The final form of the document would be approved by the twenty-nine delegates at the Fort Erie meeting. The actual drafting of the declaration was a collaboration between Du Bois and William Monroe Trotter.

W. E. B. Du Bois was born February 23, 1868, in Great Barrington, Massachusetts, and raised by his mother in an environment characterized by varying degrees of poverty. In spite of this, Du Bois excelled in school and achieved one of the most impressive educations of his generation. He took bachelor degrees at Fisk and then Harvard, pursued graduate work at Harvard and the University of Berlin, and earned his Ph.D. in history from Harvard in 1895. He held faculty positions at Wilberforce University and then Atlanta University and spent a year working for the University of Pennsylvania on a study of blacks in Philadelphia. In 1903 he published *The Souls of Black Folk*, his third book and the one that propelled him to the forefront of African American intellectuals; shortly thereafter he emerged as the most respected critic of Booker T. Washington. In 1905 he made his first major foray into racial politics when he assumed a major role in the creation and operation of the Niagara Movement.

William Monroe Trotter was born on April 7, 1872, in Chillicothe, Ohio, but was raised in Boston among the city's black elite. He attended Harvard, where he met Du Bois. After graduating Phi Beta Kappa, he worked in insurance and real estate. In 1901 he cofounded and became editor of the *Guardian*, a Boston newspaper noted for its militant, uncompromising, and often intemperate support of African American civil rights and racial justice and for its criticism and attacks on Booker T. Washington. In July 1903 he was the principal organizer of the "Boston Riot" and was sentenced to thirty days in jail for provoking the incident. While Du Bois was the leading African American intellectual of his day, Trotter was the race's most outspoken polemicist.

Although they were of different temperaments, Du Bois and Trotter worked well together on the Declaration of Principles. The document combined Du Bois's more scholarly approach with Trotter's more polemical style. The partnership did not last long. The two clashed over leadership issues, especially the role that whites should play in the Niagara Movement. Trotter withdrew from the organization and founded the National Equal Rights League in 1908. Although he participated in the creation of the NAACP, he objected to the dominant roles whites played in the organization. He continued to agitate for racial equality and publish the *Guardian* until his death in 1934. Du Bois assumed a major role in the NAACP, especially as editor of the *Crisis* from its founding in 1910 until he returned to Atlanta University in 1934. Du Bois was the premier African American intellectual of the twentieth century, as well as a civil rights advocate and an advocate of pan-Africanism. He died in Ghana in 1963.

Explanation and Analysis of the Document

The Declaration of Principles was approved by the assembly of African American men who met July 11–13, 1905, in Fort Erie, Ontario. The document drafted by W. E. B. Du Bois and William Monroe Trotter contains eighteen short paragraphs, each raising and briefly addressing a specific issue. The style of the declaration is that of a list or an outline rather than an analytical discussion of the status of African Americans. The first seventeen paragraphs contain a manifesto of grievances and demands; the eighteenth is a list of duties. Together they summarize the issues confronting African Americans in the early twentieth century and define the purpose and agenda of the Niagara Movement.

◆ Progress

The first section of the declaration, "Progress," comments on the gathering of the Niagara Movement and congratulates African Americans on progress they had achieved in the preceding ten years. These ten years essentially covered the time period since the death of Frederick Douglass and the rise to power of Booker T. Washington, and the Niagarites viewed this as a period of failed leadership and a decline in the rights of African Americans. The progress cited—the increase in intelligence and in the acquisition of property, and the creation of successful institutions—omits reference to the political and civil rights of African Americans.

◆ Suffrage, Civil Liberty, and Economic Opportunity

The next three paragraphs address in sequence "Suffrage," "Civil Liberty," and "Economic Opportunity"—areas

Time Line

1901

■ **November 9**
The *Guardian* (Boston) debuts under the editorship of William Monroe Trotter. The paper quickly becomes recognized for its radical support for equal rights and its attacks, often personal in nature, on the leadership of Booker T. Washington.

1903

■ **April 18**
W. E. B. Du Bois emerges as a major African American leader with the publication of *The Souls of Black Folk*. In this book Du Bois initiates his criticism of Washington's leadership with the chapter "Of Mr. Booker T. Washington and Others."

■ **July 30**
Boston riot. William Monroe Trotter and his allies disrupt a Booker T. Washington speech at the Columbus Avenue AME Zion Church in Boston. In the ensuing melee Trotter and one of his associates are arrested for inciting a riot. The incident deepens the rift between Washington and Du Bois.

1905

■ **July 11**
Twenty-nine African Americans, including W. E. B. Du Bois, meet in Fort Erie, Ontario, for three days to organize the Niagara Movement. Their Declaration of Principles outlines a new civil rights agenda.

1906

■ **September 22–25**
Atlanta race riot erupts as white mobs attack blacks and black neighborhoods, resulting in the deaths of at least ten blacks and leaving scores injured.

1908

■ **August 14**
A race riot erupts in Springfield, Illinois, as a white mob attacks, beats, and lynches blacks and burns black residences. The violence lasts two days, leaving two blacks dead and forty black families homeless. Sporadic violence against blacks continues for several weeks.

1909

■ May 31
A biracial committee, dominated by white liberals, meets in New York City and establishes the Negro National Committee to address racial violence and civil rights. Du Bois plays a major role in this meeting and the new organization.

1910

■ May 12–14
The Negro National Committee meets again in New York and reorganizes itself as the National Association for the Advancement of Colored People. Du Bois is the only black on the board of directors and also assumes the paid position of director of publications and research

■ November
Du Bois publishes the inaugural issue of the *Crisis*, the NAACP's monthly journal. Du Bois will serve as editor of the *Crisis* for twenty-four years.

1915

■ November 14
Booker T. Washington dies at his home in Tuskegee, Alabama.

1916

■ August 24–26
Amenia Conference, hosted by the NAACP president Joel E. Spingarn, brings together fifty prominent white and African American civil rights leaders in an effort to heal the breach between the followers of the late Booker T. Washington and W. E. B. Du Bois.

in which African Americans faced clear and increasing discrimination. Here the declaration lists grievances for the first time and evokes protest as an appropriate response to these grievances. The declaration asserts the importance of manhood suffrage and then notes that black political rights have been curtailed and that blacks cannot afford to place their political fate in the hands of others. This argument did not address the specifics of the strategies used to disenfranchise blacks—literacy tests, the grandfather clause, or similar practices. Instead, it asserted that all men deserve the right to vote. This approach distinguished the Niagarites from Booker T. Washington, who supported suf-

frage and attacked disenfranchisement on the basis that it treated blacks differently than whites. The declaration sees universal manhood suffrage as a fundamental right of all men and calls on blacks to protest "empathically and continually" as long as their political rights are violated. This introduces a theme that runs through the declaration: that discrimination is a violation of the rights of African Americans and that the response to these violations must be agitation and protest (not negotiation and patience).

The declaration continues this argument in its examination of civil liberty. It defines civil liberty as civil rights—rights shared equally by all citizens. It broadens the concept to include the right to "equal treatment in places of public entertainment," that is, restaurants, theaters, hotels, and other places of public accommodation. Exclusion from such places must not be based on race or color but on the individual's behavior and demeanor. The declaration demands equal access not to residences or other private spaces but to places open to the public, the same places blacks finally achieved access to in the Civil Rights Act of 1964. Furthermore, to gain their civil rights, blacks must be willing to protest.

As it turns to economic opportunity, the Declaration of Principles directly confronts the heart of Washington's program for African American advancement. Washington believed that the acquisition of property and prosperity would earn blacks the respect of whites and equal rights and that this prosperity could most easily be achieved in the South. The declaration rejects this, noting that African Americans are denied equal economic opportunity in the South and that prejudice and inequity in the law in that region undermine black economic efforts. Specifically, it protests the spread of peonage that has returned blacks to virtual slavery in large areas of the rural South and the practice of discrimination in hiring, wages, and credit that has "crushed" black labor and small businesses.

◆ Education

Education was a key issue for the Niagara Movement. Most of the delegates who attended the gathering were from the college-educated black elite, the group that Du Bois termed the "Talented Tenth" (http://www.yale.edu/glc/archive/1148.htm), and the group that most Niagarites believed would provide the leadership for African American advancement. Generally this group denigrated Booker T. Washington and his Tuskegee Institute for their focus on job training and practical education. However, the section on education in the Declaration of Principles recognizes the need for all forms of education in the African American community. It focuses its complaints on the lack of equal access to education for blacks, especially in the South. Specifically, it calls for "common" schools (basically elementary schools) to be free and compulsory for all children, regardless of race. It also calls for blacks to have access to high schools, colleges and universities, and trade and technical schools, and it calls for the U.S. government to aid common-school education, especially in the South.

What is striking about the statement on education is that it does not call for the desegregation of education. It specifically asks for an increase in the number of public high schools in the South, where blacks rarely had access to them, and it requests white philanthropists to provide adequate endowments for black institutions of higher education. The focus is clearly on improving black access to educational facilities of all types and at all levels. The language of this section is also much more conciliatory; agitation is suggested only to pressure the U.S. government to provide aid to black common schools. To understand this, it is important to remember that public school systems did not appear in most southern states prior to the period of Reconstruction, and in 1905 schools throughout the South were very poorly funded. Educational facilities for African Americans received significantly less support than did those for white students.

◆ Courts, Public Opinion, and Health

The next three paragraphs address three seemingly unrelated topics. The statement on courts begins with a "demand" for fair and honest judges, the inclusion without discrimination of blacks on juries, and fair and equitable sentencing procedures. It then lists additional needed reforms ranging from social-service institutions such as orphanages and reformatories and an end to the convict-lease system. In contrast, the statement on health begins, "We plead for health—for an opportunity to live in decent houses and localities." There was a connection between the two issues, although it was somewhat tenuous. Bringing justice to the criminal justice system extended to providing a decent environment for orphans, dependent children, and children in the court system; health was extended to include a healthy environment, both physically and morally, in which to raise children. While these concerns were not always at the forefront of civil rights agitation, these issues, especially those that relate to child welfare, reflected the social agenda voiced by white progressive reformers in the early years of the century.

The paragraph on public opinion introduces a new concern, a perceived shift away from the ideals of democracy that were voiced in the eighteenth century by the Founding Fathers. The last sentence, with its reference to "all men … created free and equal" and "unalienable rights," echoes the language of the Declaration of Independence. The Niagara delegates were not ignorant of the slavery and racial prejudice that were central to the founding of the United States, but their alarm over the "retrogression" was justified. Racial violence was rampant; democracy seemed challenged by labor wars and fears of unrestricted immigration; and the arts, sciences, and social sciences embraced a new scientific racism that was based on the application of Charles Darwin's "survival of the fittest" to efforts to categorize and rank human races.

◆ Employers and Labor Unions

The declaration's earlier discussion of economic opportunity focuses completely on conditions in the South. Now it turns to economic opportunity in the North, especially the abuses blacks have suffered at the hands of racially prejudiced labor unions and the practice of white employers exploiting blacks by using them as strike breakers. This situation, and especially the restrictive behavior of white labor unions, characterized the African American experience with organized labor throughout much of the twentieth century. It ran counter to the belief of many progressives and socialists that class unity would defeat racial prejudice. The declaration denounces the practices of both employers and unions in strong terms and blames them for contributing to class warfare.

◆ Protest

Protest, along with agitation, were central tenets of the Niagara Movement's strategy for achieving racial justice, and both terms appear frequently in the Declaration of Principles. In contrast to Booker T. Washington's Atlanta Exposition Address, with its ambiguity on the effectiveness of agitation, the Declaration of Principles is crystal clear—protest and agitation are necessary tools to combat injustice. However, the language and tone in the section specifically discussing protest are exceptionally mild. The term *agitation* is not used, and the word *protest* is used only once. The argument is that blacks must not "allow the impression to remain" that they assented to inferiority, were "submissive" to oppression, or were "apologetic" when faced with insults, and the argument is worded to suggest that Washington was both apologetic and submissive. But there is little power or threat in this language beyond the assurance that although blacks may of necessity submit to oppression, they must continue to raise their voices in protest.

◆ Color-Line

Beginning with this paragraph the Declaration of Principles returns to the issue of discrimination and its impact on African Americans. "Color-Line" discusses legitimate and illegitimate discrimination. The former included discrimination based intelligence, immorality, and disease (for example, quarantining someone with a highly infectious disease to protect public health). In contrast, discrimination based on physical conditions such as place of birth (immigrants) and race was never justified. The color line—segregation and discrimination based on race or skin color or both—is described in harsh terms, as barbarous and as a relic of unreasoning human savagery. According to the Declaration of Principles, the fact that the color line is sanctioned by law, custom, or community standards does nothing to legitimize it or to diminish the evil and injustice that it manifests.

◆ "Jim Crow" Cars, Soldiers, and War Amendments

These three paragraphs briefly address three specific issues related to discrimination. "'Jim Crow' cars" refers to the segregation of African Americans on railroads. This issue had both practical and symbolic importance. Railroads were by far the chief means of intercity transportation at the beginning of the twentieth century. Policies that restricted black passengers to overcrowded, rowdy Jim Crow cars affected all black passengers, especially women and the black elite. Virtually every black who traveled through the South suffered this indignity. Du Bois himself had been victimized by this practice and sought Washington's help in an unsuccessful effort to seek redress from the Southern Railway Company. The issue of Jim Crow segregation on railroads was the subject of the *Plessy v. Ferguson* case; the Supreme Court ruling legitimizing separate-but-equal segregation provided the legal basis for segregation in schools, parks, public accommodations, and almost all areas of life. The Declaration of Principles condemns Jim Crow cars as effectively crucifying "wantonly our manhood, womanhood and self-respect."

"Soldiers" puts the Niagara Movement on record protesting the inequity experienced by African Americans serving in the armed forces. This issue took on additional meaning a year later as blacks reacted to the harsh treatment of the black soldiers following a racial clash with local civilians in the so-called Brownsville incident in Brownsville, Texas, and it was revived again during World War I as black troops suffered from systematic discrimination and mistreatment.

One of the most frustrating issues facing African Americans was that along with abolishing slavery, the three Civil War amendments wrote civil rights and voting rights into the U.S. Constitution. The Fourteenth Amendment guaranteed all citizens, including blacks, equal protection under the law and equal rights and privileges; the Fifteenth Amendment provided that no citizen could be denied the right to vote "on account of race, color, or previous condition of servitude." What the Declaration calls for is legislation from Congress to enforce these provisions.

◆ Oppression and the Church

In examining the broad issue of oppression, the Declaration presents a broad litany of crimes perpetrated on African Americans, from their kidnapping in Africa to their ravishment and degradation in America; as they have struggled to advance themselves, again and again they have encountered criticism, hindrance, and violence. In a thinly veiled attack on Booker T. Washington, the Niagarites also place blame on African American leadership for providing in the face of oppression only cowardice and apology, essentially leaving it to the oppressor to define the rights of the oppressed. Finally, in the brief paragraph "The Church," the Declaration charges churches and organized religion with acquiescence to racial oppression and condemns them as "wrong, unchristian and disgraceful."

◆ Agitation

Following this litany of grievances, the Declaration of Principles reaffirms its commitment to protest and agitation. The delegates vow to voice their grievances "loudly and insistently" and note that "manly agitation is the way to liberty." As in the section on "Protest," the language is clear but measured and temperate rather than threatening.

◆ Help and Duties

The Declaration of Principles concludes with a section recognizing with gratitude the valuable assistance that African Americans had received throughout their history from their white friends and allies. It then lists eight duties that it expects blacks to follow as they pursue their rights. These duties include civic responsibilities, such as the duty to vote, work, and obey the law, as well as personal obligations, such as the duty to be clean and orderly and to educate their children. These last two sections softened the impact of the declaration and were intended to assure whites that the Niagara Movement was neither revolutionary nor antiwhite. Ironically, the tone of these concluding paragraphs is more that of Booker T. Washington than W. E. B. Du Bois. The final sentence of the Declaration notes that the document, characterized as a "statement, complaint and prayer," is being submitted to the American people and to God.

Taken as a whole, the Declaration of Principles is both an interesting and a compelling document. It is a comprehensive list of issues, concepts, grievances, and statements about the conditions confronting blacks at the beginning of the last century. What is compelling is that this was the most successful effort to date to express all of this in one place and do so in language that was pointed and uncompromising yet restrained. At the same time, the declaration is interesting for what it did not say. By the standards of the twenty-first century it is not a particularly radical document. Although the Niagara Movement was an all-black organization, there is no hint of black nationalism or separatism in its Declaration of Principles. Rather, it serves as a restrained, moderate document outlining a program of desegregation, equal rights, and racial justice. It praises white friends and allies for their support, and it reminds blacks that they have the duty and responsibility to be hardworking and law-abiding citizens who embody the values and habits of middle-class America. Despite the anti–Booker T. Washington nature of the Niagara Movement and its members and Washington's open hostility to both the Niagara Movement and its Declaration of Principles, there is little in the document that the Tuskegean could take issue with.

Audience

The authors of the Declaration of Principles concluded by submitting the document to the American people. While this may have represented the wishes of the group assembled at Fort Erie, the actual audience was much more modest. The initial audience for the document was that group of twenty-nine men assembled at the inaugural meeting of the Niagara Movement. The secondary audience was the four hundred or so men and women who would join the Niagara Movement before its demise in 1909. Of course, the intended audience was much larger. It included the African American community, especially in the North, and the intention was that blacks from all parts of the United States would hear about and read the document and join the Niagara Movement. The document was also crafted for a white audience. The language and moderate tone, as well as the specific statement of appreciation to white friends and allies, was intended to attract financial and political

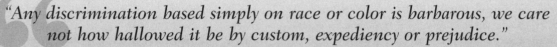

> "Any discrimination based simply on race or color is barbarous, we care not how hallowed it be by custom, expediency or prejudice."
>
> (Color-Line)

> "The Negro race in America stolen, ravished and degraded, struggling up through difficulties and oppression, needs sympathy and receives criticism; needs help and is given hindrance, needs protection and is given mob-violence, needs justice and is given charity, needs leadership and is given cowardice and apology, needs bread and is given a stone."
>
> (Oppression)

> "Of the above grievances we do not hesitate to complain, and to complain loudly and insistently. To ignore, overlook, or apologize for these wrongs is to prove ourselves unworthy of freedom."
>
> (Agitation)

support for the agenda or the movement and convince progressive whites that they offered a realistic and palatable alternative to the racial agenda of Booker T. Washington.

In the short term the audience was quite small, as press coverage of the Fort Erie meeting and the Declaration of Principles was limited. It is not clear how much coverage a small meeting of African Americans in Ontario would receive in the white press in ordinary circumstances, but in July 1905 a very effective campaign by the Tuskegee machine kept press coverage to a minimum. News of the Fort Erie events was kept out of most of the white press when a Washington ally went to the Buffalo Associated Press office and persuaded it not to forward the news of the Fort Erie meeting. There was some reporting in the African American press, especially in Atlanta and Washington, where there was widespread support for the Niagarites, and, of course, in Boston, where Trotter's *Guardian* pushed the story. But on the whole the black press remained loyal to Washington and withheld news of the meeting. Eventually the audience grew significantly. The Declaration of Principles and much of the agenda of the Niagara Movement were picked up by the NAACP and influenced its approach to civil rights.

Impact

Much like its audience, the impact of the Declaration of Principles grew over time. Initially, the influence of the

Niagara Movement and its Declaration of Principles was limited. Membership never exceeded about four hundred, and the dream of a vibrant organization with chapters nationwide was never realized. Feuding leadership and the failure to secure adequate funding doomed the organization, and membership and attendance at its annual meeting began to decline. The Niagara Movement shut down following its 1909 meeting. During its short life the declaration accomplished one thing: It defined the terms of the Du Bois–Washington debate. As the writer and civil rights activist James Weldon Johnson noted, the animosity between these two factions reached an intensity that is difficult to comprehend today.

The principal impact of the document followed the demise of the Niagara Movement, when it essentially set the agenda of the NAACP. The Declaration of Principle's focus on voting rights and discrimination and segregation were the focus of the NAACP for its first fifty years; protest and agitation were its tools. Perhaps the clearest example of this impact is the use of the declaration's statement on the Civil War amendments and its call for Congress to enforce the provisions of these amendments. This is exactly what the NAACP did, using the courts instead of Congress. In 1915 the NAACP scored one of its first major victories when it filed a brief in *Guinn v. United States*, the case in which the Supreme Court overturned Oklahoma's use of the grandfather clause to restrict black suffrage. In the 1930s the NAACP launched its legal assault on the continuing restrictions on black suffrage, provisions that kept blacks from serving on juries, and segregation, especially in public and higher education. Ultimately this campaign led to the reversal of *Plessy v. Ferguson* and separate-but-equal segregation. In the 1950s and 1960s the civil rights movement used the declaration strategy by successfully lobbying for a series of civil rights acts, finally enforcing provisions of the Fourteenth Amendment to attack segregation, and enacting the Voting Rights Act to enforce the Fifteenth Amendment.

Related Documents

"The Atlanta Exposition Address." National Park Service "Booker T. Washington National Monument" Web site. http://www.nps.gov/bowa/historyculture/atlanta1-1.htm. Accessed on February 4, 2008. To a large degree the Declaration of Principles was written as a response to Washington's approach to the advancement of African Americans and his leadership.

"Constitution of the United States." The U.S. Constitution Online Web site. http://www.usconstitution.net/const.html. Accessed on January 2, 2008. The Fourteenth and Fifteenth Amendments are two of the three "war amendments" referred to in the Declaration of Principles, and they provide the legal basis for most of the civil and political rights sought by the Niagara Movement.

Du Bois, W. E. B. "Address to the Nation." Wake Forest University Web site. http://www.wfu.edu/~zulick/341/niagara.html. Accessed on January 2, 2008. Du Bois expands on the Declarations of Principles at the second gathering of the Niagara Movement.

———. "Chapter 3: III. Of Mr. Booker T. Washington and Others." In *The Souls of Black Folk.* http://etext.virginia.edu/etcbin/toccer-new2?id=DubSoul.sgm&images=images/modeng&data=/texts/english/modeng/parsed&tag=public&part=3&division=div1. Accessed on January 2, 2008. In this 1903 critique of Booker T. Washington, Du Bois introduces several themes found in the Declaration of Principles.

Plessy v. Ferguson, 163 U.S. 537 (1896). This case provided the legal basis for segregation in the United States.

Bibliography

■ Books

Fox, Stephen R. *The Guardian of Boston: William Monroe Trotter.* New York: Atheneum, 1970.

Harlan, Louis R. *Booker T. Washington: The Wizard of Tuskegee, 1901–1915.* New York: Oxford University Press, 1983.

Lewis, David Levering. *W. E. B. Du Bois: Biography of a Race, 1868–1919.* New York: Henry Holt, 1993.

Marable, Manning. *W. E. B. Du Bois: Black Radical Democrat.* Boston: Twayne, 1986.

Meier, August. *Negro Thought in America, 1880–1915.* Ann Arbor: University of Michigan Press, 1968.

Moore, Jacqueline M. *Booker T. Washington, W. E. B. Du Bois, and the Struggle for Racial Uplift.* Wilmington, Del.: Scholarly Resources, 2003.

Rampersad, Arnold. *The Art and Imagination of W. E. B. Du Bois.* Cambridge, Mass.: Harvard University Press, 1976.

Rudwick, Elliott M. *W. E. B. Du Bois: Propagandist of the Negro Protest.* New York: Atheneum, 1969.

Wolters, Raymond. *Du Bois and His Rivals.* Columbia: University of Missouri Press, 2002.

■ Web Sites

Du Bois, W. E. B. "The Talented Tenth." In *The Negro Problem: A Series of Articles by Representative Negroes of To-day.* New York: J. Pott and Company, 1903. The Gilder Lehrman Center for the Study of Slavery, Resistance, and Abolition at Yale University.
    http://www.yale.edu/glc/archive/1148.htm. Accessed on February 5, 2008.

Manly, Howard. "Black History: The Niagara Movement." *Boston-Bay State Banner* Web site.
    http://www.baystatebanner.com/issues/2007/10/11/news/local10110711.htm#top. Accessed on January 2, 2008.

"The Niagara Movement." African American History of Western New York Web site.
    http://www.math.buffalo.edu/~sww/0history/hwny-niagara-movement.html. Accessed on January 2, 2008.

—By Cary D. Wintz

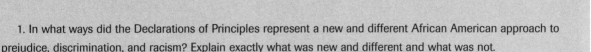

1. In what ways did the Declarations of Principles represent a new and different African American approach to prejudice, discrimination, and racism? Explain exactly what was new and different and what was not.

2. Was the Declaration of Principles a radical or a conservative document? Explain your answer both in the context of 1905 and in terms of concepts of radical, conservative, and civil rights today.

3. What is the difference between the Niagara Movement and the NAACP? Explain how the Declaration of Principles relates to each of these organizations.

4. The Declaration of Principles called upon Congress for the "enactment of appropriate legislation for securing the proper enforcement of those articles of freedom, the thirteenth, fourteenth and fifteenth amendments of the Constitution of the United States." In what sense were these three amendments "articles of freedom"? What freedoms did they guarantee? To what extent had they not been enforced? Since Congress had initially approved these amendments, why had they not been enforced?

5. "Agitation" and "protest" are recurring themes in the Declaration of Principles. What did the Niagara Movement mean by these terms? What did most Americans at the time think about African American agitation and protest? Explain how the Niagara Movement and later the NAACP utilized agitation and protest.

Abolitionist	a person who advocated the complete, immediate, and unconditional abolition of slavery, especially in the United States, prior to and during the Civil War
agitation	the persistent and sustained effort to create change or promote a cause through appeals, discussions, demonstrations, and other means
artisans	skilled craftsmen or workers
assents	agrees with; accepts, or admits as true
barbarous	uncivilized; savage; brutal; cruel
civil rights	rights guaranteed to all citizens by law or the Constitution regardless of such differences as race
common school	a free public elementary school
compulsory	required, usually by law or other authority
convict–lease system	a system of labor in which prisoners are leased to an employer by the court or the prison system
curtailment	the act of limiting or restricting; the act of taking away a right or privilege
deserts	that which is deserved; worthiness through good behavior
execration	vehement denunciation
hallowed	sacred; respected; venerated beyond question
iniquitous	unjust
"Jim Crow" car	a segregated railroad coach, usually of inferior quality, set aside for African Americans
orphanages	institutions that house and care for children who have no parents
peonage	a system of agricultural labor in which workers are bound to their job, often against their will, by economic debt or other means; virtual bondage
retrogression	a reversal in development of condition; moving backward or becoming worse
suffrage	the right to vote
upright	moral; honorable; fair and just
wantonly	cruelly; without mercy

NIAGARA MOVEMENT DECLARATION OF PRINCIPLES

Progress: The members of the conference, known as the Niagara Movement, assembled in annual meeting at Buffalo, July 11th, 12th and 13th, 1905, congratulate the Negro-Americans on certain undoubted evidences of progress in the last decade, particularly the increase of intelligence, the buying of property, the checking of crime, the uplift in home life, the advance in literature and art, and the demonstration of constructive and executive ability in the conduct of great religious, economic and educational institutions.

Suffrage: At the same time, we believe that this class of American citizens should protest emphatically and continually against the curtailment of their political rights. We believe in manhood suffrage; we believe that no man is so good, intelligent or wealthy as to be entrusted wholly with the welfare of his neighbor.

Civil Liberty: We believe also in protest against the curtailment of our civil rights. All American citizens have the right to equal treatment in places of public entertainment according to their behavior and deserts.

Economic Opportunity: We especially complain against the denial of equal opportunities to us in economic life; in the rural districts of the South this amounts to peonage and virtual slavery; all over the South it tends to crush labor and small business enterprises; and everywhere American prejudice, helped often by iniquitous laws, is making it more difficult for Negro-Americans to earn a decent living.

Education: Common school education should be free to all American children and compulsory. High school training should be adequately provided for all, and college training should be the monopoly of no class or race in any section of our common country. We believe that, in defense of our own institutions, the United States should aid common school education, particularly in the South, and we especially recommend concerted agitation to this end. We urge an increase in public high school facilities in the South, where the Negro-Americans are almost wholly without such provisions. We favor well-equipped trade and technical schools for the training of artisans, and the need of adequate and liberal endowment for a few institutions of higher education must be patent to sincere well-wishers of the race.

Courts: We demand upright judges in courts, juries selected without discrimination on account of color and the same measure of punishment and the same efforts at reformation for black as for white offenders. We need orphanages and farm schools for dependent children, juvenile reformatories fox delinquents, and the abolition of the dehumanizing convict-lease system.

Public Opinion: We note with alarm the evident retrogression in this land of sound public opinion on the subject of manhood rights, republican government and human brotherhood, arid we pray God that this nation will not degenerate into a mob of boasters and oppressors, but rather will return to the faith of the fathers, that all men were created free and equal, with certain unalienable rights.

Health: We plead for health—for an opportunity to live in decent houses and localities, for a chance to rear our children in physical and moral cleanliness.

Employers and Labor Unions: We hold up for public execration the conduct of two opposite classes of men: The practice among employers of importing ignorant Negro-American laborers in emergencies, and then affording them neither protection nor permanent employment; and the practice of labor unions in proscribing and boycotting and oppressing thousands of their fellow-toilers, simply because they are black. These methods have accentuated and will accentuate the war of labor and capital, and they are disgraceful to both sides.

Protest: We refuse to allow the impression to remain that the Negro-American assents to inferiority, is submissive under oppression and apologetic before insults. Through helplessness we may submit, but the voice of protest of ten million Americans must never cease to assail the ears of their fellows, so long as America is unjust.

Color-Line: Any discrimination based simply on race or color is barbarous, we care not how hallowed it be by custom, expediency or prejudice. Differences made on account of ignorance, immorality, or disease are legitimate methods of fighting evil, and against them we have no word of protest; but discriminations based simply and solely on physical peculiarities, place of birth, color of skin, are relics of that unreasoning human savagery of which the world is and ought to be thoroughly ashamed.

"Jim Crow" Cars: We protest against the "Jim Crow" car, since its effect is and must be to make us pay first-class fare for third-class accommodations, render us open to insults and discomfort and to crucify wantonly our manhood, womanhood and self-respect.

Soldiers: We regret that this nation has never seen fit adequately to reward the black soldiers who, in its five wars, have defended their country with their blood, and yet have been systematically denied the promotions which their abilities deserve. And we regard as unjust, the exclusion of black boys from the military and naval training schools.

War Amendments: We urge upon Congress the enactment of appropriate legislation for securing the proper enforcement of those articles of freedom, the thirteenth, fourteenth and fifteenth amendments of the Constitution of the United States.

Oppression: We repudiate the monstrous doctrine that the oppressor should be the sole authority as to the rights of the oppressed. The Negro race in America stolen, ravished and degraded, struggling up through difficulties and oppression, needs sympathy and receives criticism; needs help and is given hindrance, needs protection and is given mob-violence, needs justice and is given charity, needs leadership and is given cowardice and apology, needs bread and is given a stone. This nation will never stand justified before God until these things are changed.

The Church: Especially are we surprised and astonished at the recent attitude of the church of Christ—of an increase of a desire to bow to racial prejudice, to narrow the bounds of human brotherhood, and to segregate black men to some outer sanctuary. This is wrong, unchristian and disgraceful to the twentieth century civilization.

Agitation: Of the above grievances we do not hesitate to complain, and to complain loudly and insistently. To ignore, overlook, or apologize for these wrongs is to prove ourselves unworthy of freedom. Persistent manly agitation is the way to liberty, and toward this goal the Niagara Movement has started and asks the cooperation of all men of all races.

Help: At the same time we want to acknowledge with deep thankfulness the help of our fellowmen from the Abolitionist down to those who today still stand for equal opportunity and who have given and still give of their wealth and of their poverty for our advancement.

Duties: And while we are demanding, and ought to demand, and will continue to demand the rights enumerated above, God forbid that we should ever forget to urge corresponding duties upon our people:

The duty to vote.

The duty to respect the rights of others.

The duty to work.

The duty to obey the laws.

The duty to be clean and orderly.

The duty to send our children to school.

The duty to respect ourselves, even as we respect others.

This statement, complaint and prayer we submit to the American people, and Almighty God.

lously avoiding wrongdoing itself, to repel any wrong, and in exceptional cases to take action which in a more advanced stage of international relations would come under the head of the exercise of the international police. A great free people owes it to itself and to all mankind not to sink into helplessness before the powers of evil.

We are in every way endeavoring to help on, with cordial good will, every movement which will tend to bring us into more friendly relations with the rest of mankind. In pursuance of this policy I shall shortly lay before the Senate treaties of arbi-
Arbitration treaties. tration with all powers which are willing to enter into these treaties with us. It is not possible at this period of the world's development to agree to arbitrate all matters, but there are many matters of possible difference between us and other nations which can be thus arbitrated. Furthermore, at the request of the Interparliamentary Union, an eminent body composed of practical statesmen from all countries,
Second Hague conference. I have asked the Powers to join with this Government in a second Hague conference, at which it is hoped that the work already so happily begun at The Hague may be carried some steps further toward completion. This carries out the desire expressed by the first Hague conference itself.

It is not true that the United States feels any land hunger or entertains any projects as regards the other nations of the Western Hemisphere save such as are for their welfare. All that this country desires is to see the neighboring countries
Policy toward other nations of Western Hemisphere. stable, orderly, and prosperous. Any country whose people conduct themselves well can count upon our hearty friendship. If a nation shows that it knows how to act with reasonable efficiency and decency in social and political matters, if it keeps order and pays its obligations, it need fear no interference from the United States. Chronic wrongdoing, or an impotence which results in a general loosening of the ties of civilized society, may in America, as elsewhere, ultimately require intervention by some civilized nation, and in the Western Hemisphere the adherence of the United States to the Monroe Doctrine may force the United States, however reluctantly, in flagrant cases of such wrongdoing or impotence, to the exercise of an international police power. If every country washed by the Caribbean Sea would show the progress in stable and just civilization which with the aid of the Platt amendment Cuba has shown since our troops left the island, and which so many of the republics in both

President Theodore Roosevelt's Corollary to the Monroe Doctrine (National Archives and Records Administration)

ROOSEVELT COROLLARY TO THE MONROE DOCTRINE

1904

"All that this country desires is to see the neighboring countries stable, orderly, and prosperous."

Overview

On December 6, 1904, President Theodore Roosevelt submitted his annual message to the Congress of the United States. That document, now called the State of the Union address, was in written form. Since 1801, when Thomas Jefferson instituted the practice, presidents had transmitted their annual report about the issues facing the United States to lawmakers in writing. As was his custom, Roosevelt wrote at length about many national problems, from railroad regulation to conservation of natural resources. When it came to foreign policy, however, he wrote several long paragraphs about the relations between the United States and its neighbors in Latin America. In one key paragraph, the president modified the diplomatic policy that had come to be known as the Monroe Doctrine. Roosevelt asserted new American rights relative to other countries in the region and proclaimed a broad ability to set the rules for the Caribbean Sea and countries that surrounded it. What the president had done would come to be called the Roosevelt Corollary to the Monroe Doctrine.

Context

The Monroe Doctrine had first been enunciated by President James Monroe in his annual message to Congress in December 1823. The doctrine, the brainchild of his secretary of state, John Quincy Adams, set out several propositions governing American relations with European countries relative to the Western Hemisphere. North and South America, said Monroe, were not areas where European nations should look for further colonization. If they did so, the United States would take appropriate action (though they would have to depend on the fleet of Great Britain to make such moves stick). Over the rest of the nineteenth century, the Monroe Doctrine came up on occasion, as when the French set up a puppet regime in Mexico during the mid-1860s and in the Venezuelan crisis with Great Britain in 1895 and 1896, when the U.S. demanded that Britain submit its boundary dispute with Venezuela for arbitration.

By the early twentieth century, the Monroe Doctrine was a well-established precept of American foreign policy. When Roosevelt took over the presidency after the death of William McKinley in September 1901, the United States faced new challenges in Latin America that went beyond the limits of the Monroe Doctrine. For Roosevelt, the essential priorities, taken over from McKinley, were to build a canal across Central America and to make the Caribbean basin an area of clear United States dominance.

In the case of the canal, Roosevelt proceeded to do that through the process of first negotiating with Colombia for a canal across Panama, which was then part of the Colombian nation. When the government in Bogota declined to accept Roosevelt's terms in the treaty the two countries had negotiated, he encouraged a revolution in Panama that would see that country secede from Colombia. Once that was accomplished in late 1903, Roosevelt and his secretary of state, John Hay, worked out a treaty with the new Panamanian government that gave the United States the canal zone and the right to construct a canal.

The experience of working with the politicians in Colombia on this matter did not instill confidence in their ability as far as Roosevelt was concerned. Believing that the United States had the superior political system and culture, he looked down on the abilities and honesty of Latin American officials. Like so many in the United States, he believed that Americans were more intelligent, further advanced, and more responsible than their neighbors to the South. As a result, in Roosevelt's mind it was acceptable for the government to impose discipline and order on peoples who lacked those qualities on their own. Racism and ethnocentrism would play a large part in Roosevelt's approach to foreign relations during his presidency.

The president and his advisers also were aware of what they perceived to be a renewed threat from European nations to test the limits of the Monroe Doctrine. Latin American countries had borrowed funds from investors in Europe to finance economic development within their impoverished territories. When corruption, a lack of skill, or bad luck saw these investments go sour, Great Britain, Germany, and other powers asserted their right to compel the Latin American nations to pay their debts. On some occasions, these demands were backed up with gunboat

1823

■ **December 2**
President James Monroe announces the Monroe Doctrine in his annual message.

1895

■ **July 20**
Secretary of State Richard Olney asserts the Monroe Doctrine in the Venezuelan boundary dispute with Great Britain.

1901

■ **December 3**
Roosevelt writes in his annual message that the United States does not guarantee any country in the Americas "against punishment if it misconducts itself, provided that punishment does not take the form of the acquisition of territory by any non-American power" (http://www.miller center.virginia.edu/scripps/ digitalarchive/speeches/spe_ 1901_1203_roosevelt).

1902

■ **December**
Great Britain and Germany blockade Venezuela to collect debts owed to foreign powers.

1903

■ **October 17**
The United States declines the Belgian proposal to seize a customhouse in Santo Domingo, Dominican Republic, and govern the country through an international commission.

1904

■ **February 23**
In a private letter, Roosevelt disclaims any interest in annexing the Dominican Republic.

■ **May 17**
A Roosevelt letter to a Cuban Republic anniversary dinner sets out what would become the Roosevelt Corollary to the Monroe Doctrine.

■ **November 8**
Roosevelt is elected to a full term as president.

diplomacy and naval blockades. The presence of foreign vessels in the Caribbean for such purposes disturbed Roosevelt and the American military.

One nation that caused special concern was the Germany of Kaiser Wilhelm II. The U.S. government watched with unease the penetration of the Germans into the Caribbean, a process that began during the McKinley administration. German trade with the region was growing, and German settlers were making homes in South American nations. Was Berlin endeavoring to create a permanent presence in the region? The United States could not be sure of German intentions. These developments prompted American policy makers to consider what would happen if the Germans sought a naval base near the Caribbean. As a result, the United States and Great Britain drew closer together, and U.S. relations with Berlin grew less amicable.

An episode in 1902 underscored the American suspicion about the Germans and provided background for the Roosevelt statement in 1904. Germany had made extensive loans to the dictator of Venezuela, Cipriano Castro, reaching some seventy million marks. Castro did not pay any interest on these loans and in 1901 indicated that he did not plan to repay the money either. Great Britain went through a comparable experience with the Venezuelan ruler. The only feasible solution in the minds of Kaiser Wilhelm and his advisers was a blockade of Venezuela to collect the money that was owed.

This course raised questions for the U.S. government. The Germans told the Americans that they had no plans to establish permanent bases in Venezuela. They did concede, however, that they might have to occupy on a temporary basis some harbors in Venezuela where they could collect duties from foreign ships trading in those waters. Those assertions troubled Roosevelt, who worried that temporary occupations had a way of turning into more permanent arrangements. The Germans were reminded that a permanent base of any kind would be a violation of the Monroe Doctrine and traditional American foreign policy.

A year later, at the end of 1902, Great Britain, Germany, and Italy decided to blockade Castro's regime. The dictator rejected a European ultimatum, and the powers acted to compel him to give in. Faced with overwhelming power, Castro agreed to have the dispute submitted to international arbitration. Negotiations then broke down, and the European fleets remained in place. Shelling of Venezuelan installations took place in January 1903. Through all of these events, the United States kept its fleet on alert and ready to act if matters should get out of hand. For Roosevelt and the navy, there were some suggestions that the United States might not prevail in the event of a confrontation with Germany. The experience compelled Roosevelt to think about the Monroe Doctrine and his attitude toward protecting Latin American governments from the consequences of their own mistakes. He would later observe that his relations with Berlin and its attitude toward Latin America played a large part in shaping how he formulated the Roosevelt Corollary.

With the Panamanian and Venezuelan episodes in mind, Roosevelt took steps in the spring of 1904 to articulate the views that would find expression in his annual message. He asked his former secretary of war, Elihu Root, to read a letter at a dinner in May celebrating the second anniversary of the founding of the Cuban Republic following the war with Spain. In this document, Roosevelt said, "All we desire is to see all neighboring countries stable, orderly and prosperous." The president then went on to say, however, that "brutal wrongdoing, or an impotence which results in a general loosening of the ties of civilized society, may finally require intervention by some civilized nation, and in the western hemisphere the United States cannot ignore this duty." He added that all he and his country asked of his Latin American neighbors was that "they shall govern themselves well, and be prosperous and orderly" (Roosevelt to Root, May 20, 1904; qtd. in Roosevelt, 1951–1954, vol. 4, p. 801). Roosevelt put it with more candor in a letter to Root a month later. If the United States was saying "'hands off' to the powers of Europe, then sooner or later, we must keep order ourselves" (Roosevelt to Root, June 7, 1904; qtd. in Roosevelt, 1951–1954, vol. 4, pp. 821–822).

The nation that seemed to Roosevelt incapable of managing its own affairs at this time was the Dominican Republic. The government of that country had run up some $32 million in debts, most of them with European investors. By the opening months of 1904, reports reached Washington, D.C., that the Dominican economy was deteriorating. There were disclosures of apparent German interest in the area. The government of the island dispatched its foreign minister to request American aid. Roosevelt decided to be cautious in making a commitment. As he wrote in February 1904, "I want to do nothing but what a policeman has to do in Santo Domingo. As for annexing the island, I have about the same desire to annex it as a gorged boa constrictor might have to swallow a porcupine wrong-end-to" (Roosevelt to Joseph Bucklin Bishop, February 23, 1904; qtd. in Roosevelt, 1951–1954, vol. 4, p. 734).

With the impending election of 1904, Roosevelt concluded that his best strategy was to see what would happen in the Dominican crisis. As he did so, the financial condition of that country further worsened. Following his victory in the presidential election of November 1904, Roosevelt confronted complaints from European countries about the failure of the Dominican government to meet its claims. It was in this context that Roosevelt considered what to do in terms of asserting his view of the responsibilities of the governments in Latin America. The annual message, when he spoke to the whole nation and the world, seemed an ideal moment to set forth his ideas about the role of the United States relative to its neighbors.

About the Author

Theodore Roosevelt was forty-six in December 1904. He was born in New York City in 1858, and he entered politics in 1881 after graduation from Harvard University. During the next twenty years, he became one of the rising stars of the Republican Party. He served in the New York

Time Line	
1904	**■ December 6** Roosevelt enunciates the Roosevelt Corollary in the course of his annual message to Congress.
1905	**■ January 23** The United States and Dominican Republic agree to have the United States handle the foreign debt of the Dominican Republic. **■ February 7** The formal protocol is signed with Santo Domingo. **■ February 15** Roosevelt sends protocol to the United States Senate for its approval. **■ March 4** The Senate adjourns without acting on the treaty. **■ March 10** A Senate committee, in special session to act on the treaty, reports the document out with amendments; the treaty is not acted upon.
1907	**■ February 25** The Senate ratifies treaty-embodying protocol. **■ July 31** The United States withdraws from the Dominican Republic.

legislature, spent six years on the United States Civil Service Commission, and was a New York Police Commissioner in the mid-1890s. President William McKinley appointed him as assistant secretary of the navy in 1897, a post he held until the outbreak of the war with Spain in 1898. He raised a regiment called the "Rough Riders" and fought in Cuba at the battle of San Juan Hill. The Republicans nominated him for governor of New York in the fall of 1898, and he won a narrow victory. In 1900 the Republican National Convention selected him as McKinley's vice presidential candidate, and the ticket won the general election in November 1900. Following McKinley's assassination in 1901, Roosevelt assumed the presidency. He won the 1904 presidential election, serving until 1909. He died in 1919.

In foreign policy, Roosevelt operated from a number of well-defined ideas. He believed that power politics determined how a nation fared in the world. As a result, the United States must have a strong army and navy to defend itself. He quoted an African phrase that his country must

Theodore Roosevelt in a 1903 photograph (Library of Congress)

"speak softly and carry a big stick" (Roosevelt, 1904, p. 121). At the same time, he knew that American public opinion did not want overseas adventures. Despite his reputation for warlike rhetoric, Roosevelt was not reckless in seeking intervention abroad in the affairs of other nations.

As far as Latin America was concerned, however, Roosevelt believed that the United States had a responsibility to guide and tutor the unruly countries south of the border. Elements of racism entered his thinking on such issues. In his mind, peoples of Latin blood and temperament lacked the stability and sense of law and order that the Anglo-Saxons possessed. It was, therefore, the duty of civilized peoples to set a good example that Hispanic countries might follow. That the objects of his solicitude might resent his condescension never entered Roosevelt's thinking.

Believing, as he did, that the presidency offered him a platform for moral instruction, Roosevelt saw his annual message in 1904 as an excellent time to enunciate the principles of foreign policy that should govern American relations with Latin America. He framed several paragraphs that addressed the issues of national responsibility that the conduct of the Dominican Republic had raised. One paragraph, in particular, set forth the president's elaboration of the meaning of the Monroe Doctrine.

Explanation and Analysis of the Document

The heart of the Roosevelt Corollary occupies as a main subject a single paragraph in Roosevelt's annual message.

He begins in his first sentence by disclaiming "any land hunger" or other designs on the countries of the Western Hemisphere "save such as are for their welfare." The American goal is to see to it that "the neighboring countries" are "stable, orderly, and prosperous." The president then adds that any country "whose people conduct themselves well can count upon our hearty friendship." This type of language from the government was customary in approaching Latin American nations.

Roosevelt then sets up the problem that he hopes to resolve with his new approach to the Monroe Doctrine. For a nation that behaves "with reasonable efficiency and decency in social and political matters, if it keeps order and pays its obligations," the United States will not be a large element in its international relations. Then, Roosevelt comes to the core of his argument. He cites "chronic wrongdoing" and "an impotence which results in a general loosening of the ties of civilized society" as a cause for American concern. The Dominican Republic, of course, is on his mind, but he refers also to events with Colombia and Venezuela as examples of his argument.

In the remainder of this key sentence, Roosevelt notes that if the misbehavior he has mentioned necessitates intervention by some civilized nation, it might trigger the Monroe Doctrine and require the United States to exercise "an international police power." The civilized nations he alludes to are Great Britain, Italy, and Germany, which recently had used their naval power to compel Venezuela to pay its debts. Since the U.S. government is not pleased with the prospect of European countries wielding military force in the Western Hemisphere, the only alternative to Roosevelt's way of thinking is for the United States to compel correct policies through the application of diplomacy and, if necessary, force.

The president then cites the example of the island of Cuba, which had been liberated from Spanish rule during the war with Spain in 1898. Out of that process had come a new Cuban Republic, of which Americans during the Roosevelt era were very proud. To ensure that Cuba would not become the pawn of a European country, however, in 1901 the United States insisted that the new nation adhere to the terms of the Platt Amendment. That document, named after the Republican senator Orville H. Platt of Connecticut, was part of congressional action related to Cuba. The United States required that Cuba agree to the amendment's terms. The language included the right of the United States to intervene in Cuba to prevent dominance by a foreign power. The United States also received a perpetual lease on the naval base at Guantanamo Bay on the island. The Cuban Republic had regained its sovereignty but under terms that limited its autonomy to what the American government would accept. Roosevelt concludes in his address, "If every country washed by the Caribbean Sea would show the progress in stable and just civilization which with the aid of the Platt Amendment Cuba has shown since our troops left the island, and which so many of the republics in both Americas are constantly and brilliantly showing," there would be no need for the United States to intervene.

> "All that this country desires is to see the neighboring countries stable, orderly, and prosperous."

> "Chronic wrongdoing, or an impotence which results in a general loosening of the ties of civilized society, may in America, as elsewhere, ultimately require intervention by some civilized nation, and in the Western Hemisphere the adherence of the United States to the Monroe Doctrine may force the United States, however reluctantly, in flagrant cases of such wrongdoing or impotence, to the exercise of an international police power."

The president asserts that the United States and its southern neighbors have identical interests. If they follow the rules of civilized society, they have nothing to fear. Roosevelt promises in the next sentence that any intervention would be "only in the last resort" if the country in question "violated" American rights or "invited foreign aggression to the detriment of the entire body of American nations." The president, in closing his main discussion of affairs in Latin America, maintains that independence and international responsibility are inseparable. As he writes, "The right of such independence can not be separated from the responsibility of making good use of it."

In his next paragraph, Roosevelt discusses when the United States should be involved beyond its borders. He claims, "The cases in which we could interfere by force of arms as we interfered to put a stop to intolerable conditions in Cuba are necessarily very few." But it is in the national character for Americans to protest against atrocities that befall Jews in Russia or Armenians in the Ottoman Empire. The president then passes on to subjects relating to these problems.

Audience

The language in Roosevelt's annual message was aimed at two constituencies. First, he was preparing the American people for the potential need for further interventions in Latin America. His main targets, however, were the nations of the Western Hemisphere themselves and the European powers that might be tempted to establish a presence in the Caribbean. The Latin American countries resented American assertiveness but could do little at that time to resist the power of the United States in a direct way. At the same time, the European nations were mindful of the power of the navy of Great Britain, when combined with that of the United States, to exert power in the Caribbean. While Germany, in particular, chafed at the way in which Roosevelt wielded his

power over the next several years, there was little disposition in Berlin to provide a direct challenge to the United States. As long as American dominance of the region continued, the response in Europe and Latin America to the Roosevelt Corollary was one of grudging acquiescence.

Impact

The Roosevelt Corollary to the Monroe Doctrine, as it soon came to be known, was much discussed during 1905 as the president sought Senate approval of his arrangements with Santo Domingo. Since Democratic opposition persisted, Roosevelt elaborated on his views about the Monroe Doctrine in his annual message of December 5, 1905. "It must be understood," he wrote in that message, "that under no circumstances will the United States use the Monroe Doctrine as a cloak for territorial aggression." To further reassure his critics, the president added that any action to enforce the Roosevelt Corollary "will be taken at all only with extreme reluctance and when it has become evident that every other resource has been exhausted" (http://www.millercenter.virginia.edu/scripps/digitalarchive/speeches/spe_1905_1205_roosevelt). Despite these assurances of discretion in its use, the Roosevelt Corollary was implemented at various times by Roosevelt himself in the case of Cuba in 1906 and by Woodrow Wilson during his presidency in Nicaragua and Haiti. The public appetite for these adventures receded after World War I. By the late 1920s the Roosevelt Corollary seemed like a diplomatic relic, and President Calvin Coolidge repudiated it in 1928. Herbert Hoover and Franklin D. Roosevelt instituted the good neighbor policy, which no longer claimed the authority to have the United States supervise the political behavior of countries in the Western Hemisphere. Thus, the corollary came to be seen as an example of how the United States exercised its military and diplomatic supremacy at the turn of the twentieth century in a manner that a century later seemed unwise and inappropriate.

Related Documents

Roosevelt, Theodore. *Letters,* ed. Elting Elmore Morison. 8 vols. Cambridge, Mass.: Harvard University Press, 1951–1954. This eight-volume set includes the correspondence of Theodore Roosevelt as selected and edited by Morison.

U.S. Department of State. *Papers Relating the Foreign Relations of the United States, 1904.* Washington, D.C.: Government Printing Office, 1905. This source contains the text of Roosevelt's annual message and documents relating to the problems of the Dominican Republic that spurred Roosevelt to proclaim the Roosevelt Corollary.

Bibliography

■ Articles
Rippy, J. Fred. "The British Bondholders and the Roosevelt Corollary of the Monroe Doctrine." *Political Science Quarterly* 49 (June 1934): 195–206.

———. "Antecedents of the Roosevelt Corollary of the Monroe Doctrine." *Pacific Historical Review* 9 (September 1940): 267–279.

Vesser, Cyrus. "Inventing Dollar Diplomacy: The Gilded Age Origins of the Roosevelt Corollary to the Monroe Doctrine." *Diplomatic History* 27 (June 2003): 301–326.

■ Books
Beale, Howard K. *Theodore Roosevelt and the Rise of America to World Power.* Baltimore, Md.: Johns Hopkins University Press, 1959.

Brands, H. W. *T.R.: The Last Romantic.* New York: Basic Books, 1997.

Collin, Richard H. *Theodore Roosevelt's Caribbean: The Panama Canal, the Monroe Doctrine, and the Latin American Context.* Baton Rouge: Louisiana State University Press, 1990.

Dalton, Kathleen. *Theodore Roosevelt: A Strenuous Life.* New York: Alfred A. Knopf, 2002.

Gould, Lewis L. *The Presidency of Theodore Roosevelt.* Lawrence: University Press of Kansas, 1991.

Morris, Edmund. *Theodore Rex.* New York: Random House, 2001.

Munro, Dana G. *Intervention and Dollar Diplomacy in the Caribbean, 1900–1921.* Princeton, N.J.: Princeton University Press, 1964.

Roosevelt, Theodore. *Addresses and Presidential Addresses by Theodore Roosevelt, 1902–1904.* New York: G. P. Putnam's Sons, 1904.

Vesser, Cyrus. *A World Safe for Capitalism: Dollar Diplomacy and America's Rise to Global Power.* New York: Columbia University Press, 2002.

■ Web Sites
"Theodore Roosevelt Speeches: Fifth Annual Message (December 5, 1905)." Miller Center of Public Affairs Web site.
    http://www.millercenter.virginia.edu/scripps/digitalarchive/ speeches/spe_1905_1205_roosevelt. Accessed on February 11, 2008.

"Theodore Roosevelt Speeches: First Annual Message (December 3, 1901)." Miller Center of Public Affairs Web site.
    http://www.millercenter.virginia.edu/scripps/digitalarchive/ speeches/spe_1901_1203_roosevelt. Accessed on February 11, 2008.

—By Lewis L. Gould

Questions for Further Study

1. Roosevelt's enunciation of the corollary to the Monroe Doctrine arose from specific circumstances relating to American foreign policy during the early twentieth century. What were those events and how did they influence the president's thinking?

2. What assumptions about American values and principles in foreign policy did Roosevelt's statement reflect? Why were he and the nation he led in a position to instruct Latin American nations about how they should behave?

3. What recent experiences did Roosevelt refer to in making his case for the right of the United States to decide what civilized international behavior was? To which nations were his remarks directed?

4. What role might military power play in the execution of Roosevelt's new approach to Latin America?

5. Does Roosevelt's statement about American foreign policy a century ago have any contemporary echoes? To what degree did Roosevelt's comments embody enduring attitudes toward the role of his nation on the world stage?

Glossary

chronic	recurring often
detriment	damage or harm
flagrant	outrageous or notorious
impotence	in diplomacy, lacking in power or strength
land hunger	desire to expand national territory
Monroe Doctrine	a policy asserted by Monroe in 1823 that the United States would regard an expansion of European influence in the Western Hemisphere as an unfriendly act
obligations	responsibilities
Platt Amendment	an amendment adopted in 1901 that gave the United States a veto over the foreign policy of the Republic of Cuba
truism	obvious statement
wrongdoing	transgression

ROOSEVELT COROLLARY TO THE MONROE DOCTRINE

... It is not true that the United States feels any land hunger or entertains any projects as regards the other nations of the Western Hemisphere save such as are for their welfare. All that this country desires is to see the neighboring countries stable, orderly, and prosperous. Any country whose people conduct themselves well can count upon our hearty friendship. If a nation shows that it knows how to act with reasonable efficiency and decency in social and political matters, if it keeps order and pays its obligations, it need fear no interference from the United States. Chronic wrongdoing, or an impotence which results in a general loosening of the ties of civilized society, may in America, as elsewhere, ultimately require intervention by some civilized nation, and in the Western Hemisphere the adherence of the United States to the Monroe Doctrine may force the United States, however reluctantly, in flagrant cases of such wrongdoing or impotence, to the exercise of an international police power. If every country washed by the Caribbean Sea would show the progress in stable and just civilization which with the aid of the Platt Amendment Cuba has shown since our troops left the island, and which so many of the republics in both Americas are constantly and brilliantly showing, all question of interference by this Nation with their affairs would be at an end. Our interests and those of our southern neighbors are in reality identical. They have great natural riches, and if within their borders the reign of law and justice obtains, prosperity is sure to come to them. While they thus obey the primary laws of civilized society they may rest assured that they will be treated by us in a spirit of cordial and helpful sympathy. We would interfere with them only in the last resort, and then only if it became evident that their inability or unwillingness to do justice at home and abroad had violated the rights of the United States or had invited foreign aggression to the detriment of the entire body of American nations. It is a mere truism

to say that every nation, whether in America or anywhere else, which desires to maintain its freedom, its independence, must ultimately realize that the right of such independence can not be separated from the responsibility of making good use of it.

In asserting the Monroe Doctrine, in taking such steps as we have taken in regard to Cuba, Venezuela, and Panama, and in endeavoring to circumscribe the theater of war in the Far East, and to secure the open door in China, we have acted in our own interest as well as in the interest of humanity at large. There are, however, cases in which, while our own interests are not greatly involved, strong appeal is made to our sympathies. Ordinarily it is very much wiser and more useful for us to concern ourselves with striving for our own moral and material betterment here at home than to concern ourselves with trying to better the condition of things in other nations. We have plenty of sins of our own to war against, and under ordinary circumstances we can do more for the general uplifting of humanity by striving with heart and soul to put a stop to civic corruption, to brutal lawlessness and violent race prejudices here at home than by passing resolutions and wrongdoing elsewhere. Nevertheless there are occasional crimes committed on so vast a scale and of such peculiar horror as to make us doubt whether it is not our manifest duty to endeavor at least to show our disapproval of the deed and our sympathy with those who have suffered by it. The cases must be extreme in which such a course is justifiable. There must be no effort made to remove the mote from our brother's eye if we refuse to remove the beam from our own. But in extreme cases action may be justifiable and proper. What form the action shall take must depend upon the circumstances of the case; that is, upon the degree of the atrocity and upon our power to remedy it. The cases in which we could interfere by force of arms as we interfered to put a stop to intolerable conditions in Cuba are necessarily very few. Yet it is not to be expected that a people like ours, which in spite of certain very obvious shortcomings, nevertheless as a whole shows by its consistent practice its belief in the principles of civil and religious liberty and of orderly freedom, a people among whom even the worst crime, like the crime of lynching, is never more than sporadic, so that individuals and not classes are molested in their fundamental rights—it is inevitable that such a nation should desire eagerly to give expression to its horror on an occasion like that of the massacre of the Jews in Kishenef, or when it witnesses such systematic and long-extended cruelty and oppression as the cruelty and oppression of which the Armenians have been the victims, and which have won for them the indignant pity of the civilized world....

Justice David Josiah Brewer wrote the unanimous opinion in **Muller v. Oregon.** (Library of Congress)

"Her physical structure and a proper discharge of her maternal functions ... justify legislation to protect her from the greed as well as the passion of man."

Overview

In the late 1800s and early 1900s, political progressives pursued economic and political reforms. Many pushed hard to improve working conditions for men, women, and children laboring in shops and factories. The women's movement was pressing for the right to vote and the right to exercise autonomy in legal and economic affairs. In 1908, in *Muller v. Oregon*, the U.S. Supreme Court heard a case challenging a state law that regulated the employment of women. The Court's decision gave rise to many questions about the progressive agenda and how its goals might be best achieved.

The case arose when the owner of a laundry in Portland, Oregon, violated a state law limiting the number of hours a woman could work in his shop. The man challenged the constitutionality of this protective legislation; the direction the Supreme Court was taking in cases of this sort at the time portended a victory for the laundry owner. However, the Court, presented with a mountain of evidence demonstrating the danger to women workers of industrial practices left unregulated, unanimously upheld Oregon's law. This victory for progressives supporting worker protections thus came at a cost, as the Court's decision upholding protective legislation undermined women's rights.

Context

Rapid industrialization and increased urbanization in the United States in the late nineteenth century inspired reform campaigns associated with the progressive movement. In the early 1900s, progressives worked to secure the health of citizens, to address the plights of workers, and to win rights for women. While many tactics were employed and many roads taken, an especially successful, if often arduous, route lay in persuading legislatures to pass laws supporting the progressive agenda. Even after legislative victory, however, a formidable obstacle remained—the U.S. Supreme Court.

A conservative majority sat on the Court during the time of this progressive movement. When called on to deter-

mine the constitutionality of laws intended to alter social conditions and economic relations, this bloc of justices consistently struck down government regulation. The Court protected the private sector and enforced its own preferred system of economic relations, the laissez-faire doctrine. The prime case in which government regulation was defeated and individual economic liberty supported was *Lochner v. New York*, decided in 1905.

In *Lochner*, the Supreme Court considered New York's law restricting bakery employees to a sixty-hour workweek. The state argued that its law was a legitimate exercise of its police power, which included the authority to protect the health, safety, and welfare of its citizens. The Court thought otherwise, however, asserting that no reasonable foundation existed for the contention that the maximum-hours regulation was necessary or appropriate for the safeguarding of the health of the bakery employees or the public. The regulation was held to interfere with the right of individuals to contract in the labor market, which the Court identified as a liberty interest protected by the Fourteenth Amendment. The Court declared New York's law unconstitutional.

In cases that followed, the Court employed the principles put forth in *Lochner* to strike down state and federal legislation that regulated economic activity. Critics of these results argued that the Supreme Court was prioritizing abstract principles and was taking no account at all of the real-world conditions, social and economic, to which regulatory legislation was responding. The Court was failing, the critics contended, to consider the impact its decisions had on society. These arguments informed the supporters of government regulation who participated in the 1908 constitutional challenge to Oregon's law restricting the number of hours women could work in a laundry.

About the Author

The decision in *Muller v. Oregon* was unanimous, with Justice David J. Brewer writing the opinion for the Court. Born in 1837 in what is now the nation of Turkey to missionary parents, Brewer was a member of a family prominent in U.S. legal history. His uncle Stephen J. Field served

1903

■ **February 19**
Oregon legislature passes a law limiting to ten the number of hours a woman could work per day in a factory or laundry.

1905

■ **April 17**
U.S. Supreme Court announces its decision in *Lochner v. New York*, striking down a maximum-hours law for bakery employees in New York and stating that the right to contract is a liberty interest protected by the Fourteenth Amendment.

■ **September 4**
Emma Gotcher is forced by her employer to work more than ten hours at the Grand Laundry in Portland, Oregon, leading to conviction of and fine for the laundry owner who violated the 1903 law.

1906

■ **June 26**
Oregon Supreme Court affirms the conviction of the laundry owner in *State v. Muller*.

1908

■ **February 24**
Muller v. Oregon is decided by the U.S. Supreme Court.

1913

■ **February 25**
Oregon legislature passes a law limiting a workday in a factory to ten hours, with three additional hours to be paid at overtime wages.

1916

■ **June 5**
Louis Brandeis is sworn in as an associate justice of the Supreme Court.

1917

■ **April 9**
U.S. Supreme Court decides *Bunting v. Oregon*, upholding Oregon's 1913 law setting maximum work hours for factory workers.

1923

■ **April 9**
U.S. Supreme Court decides *Adkins v. Children's Hospital*, striking down a law that set a minimum wage for women workers.

on the Court from 1863 to 1897; Field's final years on the bench overlapped with Brewer's early years there. David Dudley Field, another uncle, was the driving force behind the development of the code of civil procedure, a major contribution to U.S. law. In 1890, President Benjamin Harrison appointed Brewer to the Supreme Court, where he served for 20 years. His votes consistently supported a free-market economy.

Louis D. Brandeis was not an author of the decision, but on behalf of the defendant he contributed the "Brandeis brief," for which the *Muller* case is known. Brandeis was a prominent attorney in Boston and was deeply involved in progressive and public-interest causes. When *Muller* was appealed to the Supreme Court, the National Consumers League, a pro-worker group advocating protective regulation, asked Brandeis to prepare a brief supporting Oregon's limit on working hours. Brandeis agreed on the condition that he would be the lead attorney for the Supreme Court appeal. Working closely with officials from the National Consumers League, Brandeis prepared the brief submitted to support Oregon's case. In its decision, the Court famously refers to the Brandeis brief. In 1916, President Woodrow Wilson appointed Brandeis to the Supreme Court; he served there until 1939.

Explanation and Analysis of the Document

The first party, Curt Muller, is the "plaintiff in error"; the Oregon Supreme Court decided against Muller, and in this case he appealed that decision to the U.S. Supreme Court. The second party is the State of Oregon, which convicted and fined Muller for violating the state law that set a limit on work hours. William D. Fenton, the lead attorney for Muller, was a member of a prominent Portland law firm. His regular clients included large corporate interests. For the State of Oregon, Louis Brandeis took charge of the case upon its appeal to the U.S. Supreme Court.

The Court begins by citing the Oregon law that Muller violated. An example of protective legislation, it is quite focused. It applies only to females and only to females working in particular places of employment. It sets maximum hours for any one day but does not restrict the number of days per week a woman might work. Moreover, this law does not limit the particular time during the day when a woman may work. Some protective laws, by contrast, set maximum working hours per week and prohibited women from working at nighttime.

The Court proceeds in paragraphs 2 and 3 to cite the enforcement mechanism contained in the law. This case arose from a complaint lodged by an employee of the Portland Grand Laundry, Emma Gotcher, who stated that her supervisor had forced her to work past the ten-hour daily limit. The laundry owner, Muller, was charged, found guilty by the circuit-court judge, and fined $10, the minimum penalty. Upon appeal, the Oregon Supreme Court upheld the conviction.

Much is implied by the Court in the first sentence of paragraph 4, which begins, "The single question." The issue in this case is whether Oregon's law is consistent with the U.S. Constitution, "so far as it affects the work of a female in a laundry." The Court signals that it will construct a holding that applies only to women workers engaged in a particular kind of labor. The ruling will not go beyond the facts of the case. In the next sentence, the Court, as is customary, accepts as authority the state supreme court's ruling that the law in question is consistent with the state's constitution. In the third sentence, the Court lists the arguments underlying the appeal by Muller. His "brief" consists of the written arguments prepared by his attorneys, setting out the facts and the legal issues as perceived by them in support of their side.

The Court lists three arguments brought by Muller, each grounded in the U.S. Constitution: First, Muller argues that Oregon's statute violates the Constitution by preventing persons (women working in laundries) who are sui juris (of age and of capacity to exercise their rights) from making their own contracts (deciding on their own how many hours in a day they wish to work). The right to contract, Muller argues, is protected by the Fourteenth Amendment. The text of the Fourteenth Amendment, quoted here, does not specifically mention a "right to contract," but the Court states that the amendment's due process clause included that right in 1905 in *Lochner v. New York*. (The "right to contract" established in *Lochner* is an example of a substantive due process right.)

Second, Muller argues that Oregon's statute violates the Fourteenth Amendment's equal protection clause: "No state shall … deny to any person within its jurisdiction the equal protection of the laws." The class of people treated differently by the state's legislation is women, in that it restricts their right to contract.

Third, Muller argues that "the statute is not a valid exercise of the police power" retained by the states under the Constitution, permitting them to protect the health, safety, morals, and general welfare of their citizens. *Lochner* set this standard: The state may use its police powers to restrict the right to contract, but the restriction must be fair, reasonable, and appropriate; it may not be unreasonable, unnecessary, or arbitrary. Muller argues that the legitimate goals of public health, safety, and welfare are not advanced by Oregon's restriction. The state's use of its police powers, Muller posits, is unconstitutional.

The Court proceeds to recognize that Oregon law establishes legal status for women equal to men's. Common law tradition merged a woman's legal status with her husband's, effectively making her a dependent in the eyes of the law. Statutes passed by Oregon in the late 1800s extended to women legal rights denied them under common law, including, as held by the state supreme court, the right to make binding contracts.

At issue in *Muller* was whether Oregon's law limiting daily work hours for a woman employed by a laundry was consistent with the U.S. Constitution; therefore, a woman's legal equality under Oregon law did not determine the decision in this case. (Even so, the state's supreme court, which recognized that a state law insured a woman's equal right to make a binding contract, had also ruled that the maximum-hours law for women under review in this case did not violate the state's constitution.)

Paragraph 6 contains the point upon which the case turned. In Oregon, the Court writes, women are equal to men regarding the right to contract, "putting to one side the elective franchise." (The state's woman suffrage proclamation would not be signed until 1912.) In *Lochner*, a law for maximum work hours applied to men was unconstitutional. Muller urges the Court to reach the same finding here. "But this," writes the Court, "assumes that the difference between the sexes does not justify a different rule respecting a restriction of the hours of labor." The direction the Court is taking is clear: Women in Oregon have an equal right to contract, but a state's police powers may apply different protections to women than to men.

In paragraph 7 the Court states that it will note "the course of legislation, as well as expressions of opinion from other than judicial sources." The nonjudicial information taken note of by the Court is abridged in the first footnote and famously includes over one hundred pages of "facts"—including laws passed in other jurisdictions protecting women employees and the opinions of government, medical, and social work experts who, based on their observations of modern industry, concluded that long hours of labor are dangerous for women.

This "very copious collection" of facts was compiled by Louis Brandeis, attorney for Oregon, and his collaborator, Josephine Goldmark, an official with the National Consumers League. That organization was lobbying hard around the nation for protective legislation advancing the cause of workers. The regulatory laws and expert opinions that Brandeis and Goldmark assembled and submitted as a brief, intending to overwhelm the Court with facts supporting a law protecting women workers, became known as the "Brandeis brief." It won acclaim as an early and auspicious demonstration of a realist style of argument bringing to bear on judicial reasoning the real-world causes and consequences of laws and of decisions made by courts.

In paragraph 8 the Court acknowledges and tries to explain its reliance on the nontraditional sources contained in the Brandeis brief, which "may not be, technically speaking, authorities." Here, the term *authorities* refers to the established sources relied on by the Court to arrive at decisions, a venerable example being precedent established in prior cases. Though technically not authorities, says the Court, the state laws and opinions contained in the Brandeis brief "are significant of a widespread belief" that a woman's physical structure and the functions she performs

Time Line

1937

■ March 29
U.S. Supreme Court decides *West Coast Hotel Co. v. Parrish*, upholding a minimum-wage law for women workers.

justify protective legislation that restricts "the conditions under which she should be permitted to toil." The Constitution places limits on legislative action "in unchanging form"; nevertheless, a "widespread and long continued belief"—here, regarding how a woman's physical nature affects her ability to work—may influence the extent to which a constitutional limitation is applied.

The Court next states the principles of *Lochner*: The right to contract is protected by the Fourteenth Amendment, but, consistent with the Constitution, a state may restrict that right, to an extent. The question begged is, of course, to what extent may that right be restricted? The answer, the Court asserts, can be found in three prior cases: *Allgeyer v. Louisiana* (1897), in which the Court struck down a state law prohibiting the purchase of insurance from companies outside the state because the law violated the Fourteenth Amendment rights of individuals; *Holden v. Hardy* (1898), in which the Court upheld a state law setting maximum work hours for coal miners owing to the dangers of exposure to coal dust; and *Lochner v. New York* (1905), in which the Court struck down a state law setting maximum work hours for bakery employees because the restriction was unreasonable and arbitrary.

In paragraphs 10 and 11 the Court states two findings that, as of 1908, added shape to the body of constitutional law then developing around the issues of right to contract and the government's power to regulate economic activity: Equal protection is not violated by Oregon's laws treating women differently than men, and women's physical nature and maternal functions permit states to restrict their right to contract in the way Oregon has done here. The Court surrounds these holdings with extensive commentary on the limitations placed on women by their physical nature and societal role.

Women, the Court states, have a particular physical structure, and they also perform maternal functions. Up to this point, nothing about Oregon's law or its application has been associated with "maternal functions." In fact, the generalization drawn by the Court ignores the truths that all women do not have the same "physical structure" and that not all women are mothers. Nonetheless, the opinion holds that these characteristics "place her at a disadvantage in the struggle for subsistence." The Court knows that, at this time in history, most women who work are paid low wages; but the law under review is not about pay—it is about maximum-hour regulations.

The Court sharpens its portrait of women by drawing comparisons to men. Women are held to be dependent on men, who are stronger. As such, courts have always made compensations for women. Although they have gained equal rights, their dispositions and habits of life keep them from asserting those rights. The opinion reads, "She is properly placed in a class by herself, and legislation designed for her protection may be sustained, even when like legislation is not necessary for men, and could not be sustained." The Court is rejecting Muller's second argument, that Oregon's maximum-hours law for women workers denies women the equal protection of the law. A woman may be singled out by legislation, the Court holds, for the sake of her own health and for the sake of the race, which depends on the "proper discharge of her maternal functions." The Court thus cements the connection it requires between the state's power to protect the health and safety of its citizens and its restriction on the number of hours women may work.

In paragraph 12 the Court notes for the second time that women are not able to vote in Oregon. Women's suffrage was a hotly debated issue throughout the country and would result four years later in the establishment of woman's right to vote in Oregon and a dozen years later in the Nineteenth Amendment to the U.S. Constitution, which nationalized suffrage for women. The Court states that its decision that Oregon may restrict working hours for women, even when a restriction on men would not stand, does not depend on Oregon's denial to women of the right to vote. "The reason runs deeper," the Court states, "and rests in the inherent difference between the two sexes."

In closing, the Court confirms that its decision in *Muller* is not to be extended past the facts of the case: Oregon's protective legislation does not violate the Constitution "so far as it respects the work of a female in a laundry." The decision in *Muller* does not challenge "in any respect" the decision in *Lochner*.

Audience

In the immediate audience were the two parties in the case. Oregon's law stands, along with Muller's conviction and fine. Progressives supporting protective regulations could take from this decision a victory for the present on the road to greater protection in the future. In their view, the decision to uphold Oregon's law protecting women who worked in laundries amounted to a wedge prying open possibilities for more comprehensive protective measures. One example among many such measures was a law passed by the Oregon legislature in 1913 setting maximum workday hours for all manufacturing employees (men and women) and providing for overtime pay when that maximum was exceeded.

At the same time, supporters of the right to contract in a free market where labor is exchanged for pay could take heart in the way the Court, in the decision's final paragraph, phrased its holding narrowly and endorsed *Lochner's* principles. After *Muller*, until 1937, the Court continued to strike down legislative measures protecting workers for unconstitutionally violating the right to contract, not every time but often.

Impact

The Court cabined, or kept narrow, its holding in *Muller*, but the long-term impacts of the decision were profound and far reaching. These effects traveled in two distinct directions. Along one path, *Muller* legitimated consid-

> "It may not be amiss, in the present case, before examining the constitutional question, to notice the course of legislation, as well as expressions of opinion from other than judicial sources. In the brief filed by Mr. Louis D. Brandeis for the defendant in error is a very copious collection of all these matters, an epitome of which is found in the margin."
>
> (Justice David Josiah Brewer, Majority Opinion)

> "Though limitations upon personal and contractual rights may be removed by legislation, there is that in her disposition and habits of life which will operate against a full assertion of those rights."
>
> (Justice David Josiah Brewer, Majority Opinion)

> "Even though all restrictions on political, personal, and contractual rights were taken away, and she stood, so far as statutes are concerned, upon an absolutely equal plane with him, it would still be true that she is so constituted that she will rest upon and look to him for protection; that her physical structure and a proper discharge of her maternal functions—having in view not merely her own health, but the well-being of the race—justify legislation to protect her from the greed as well as the passion of man."
>
> (Justice David Josiah Brewer, Majority Opinion)

eration by the Supreme Court of real-world conditions, as demonstrated in facts supplied by experts and scientists, when giving shape to the law. Along another path, *Muller* legitimated a view of women that supported sex discrimination, thus blocking or hindering the campaign for gender equality far into the twentieth century.

Predictably, the persuasive power of the Brandeis brief in *Muller* generated reliance on the same strategy in later cases. In state and federal courts alike, lawyers defending protective restrictions on economic activity compiled studies and statistics to bolster their cases. A high mark for sheer volume was achieved with the brief of over 1,000 pages prepared, again by Brandeis and Goldmark, to support a maximum-working-hours law for manufacturing employees, which was passed by the Oregon legislature in 1913 and promptly challenged in court. By 1917, when *Bunting v. Oregon* reached the Supreme Court, Brandeis had been appointed to a seat there. He recused himself from the case, which resulted in a 5–3 decision to uphold Oregon's restriction on the right to contract. Brandeis's selection to the Court signaled the respect given to the idea

that factual studies of real-world conditions merited consideration by courts. The approach has played a role in many cases since, including the landmark decision in *Brown v. Board of Education* (1954). There, the Court struck down separate-but-equal educational facilities for different racial groups, stating its reliance on "modern authority," including psychological and sociological studies (*Brown v. Board of Education*, 47 U.S. 483 [1954]).

In *Muller*, the Court justified Oregon's restriction on the right to contract by linking the state's protective regulation to cited characteristics of women workers emphasizing their relative weakness and their difference from men workers. Much of the Court's description of women in this vein was gratuitous. Observations on the weakness of women were iterated and then reiterated. A woman's "physical structure" and her "maternal functions," it was argued, justify the diminishing of her rights. The Court's view of women in the workplace did not arise solely from the Brandeis brief. The historian Nancy Woloch remarks, "Leaving the 'facts' of the Brandeis brief behind, [Justice] Brewer presented a timeless portrait of the 'dependent women'" (p.

38). One might easily imagine that the Brandeis brief supplied the Court (particularly Brewer, who wrote for the Court) with facts used to support opinions about women already held.

The decision in *Muller* marked an important step in the evolution of the law during the first four decades of the twentieth century regarding when government regulation may interfere with the right to contract. The case also stitched into the law a retro-view of women, as embodied in prior legal discourse, that equal rights advocates were fighting to change at the time the decision was announced. With respect to the decision in *Muller*, Kirp, Yudof, and Franks write, "This description of 'dependent' woman has its obvious antecedents in rationales for earlier common law paternalism. Women won their maximum-hours laws, but only because they could be described in a way which rendered such special treatment permissible, even laudable" (p. 38). Thus, the *Muller* decision and the Court's recognition of the Brandeis brief—victories for progressives campaigning for protective workplace measures—were at the same time defeats for progressives campaigning for women's equal rights. The view adopted in *Muller* that a particular characterization of women could form the basis for laws treating them unequally survived a long time. "For more than sixty years," writes political scientist Judith Baer, "courts upheld nearly all cases of sex discrimination, citing this case as binding precedent, following its lead in emphasizing permanent rather than temporary, physical rather than economic or social, aspects of women's condition" (pp. 66–67).

Related Documents

Brown v. Board of Education, 47 U.S. 483 (1954). The ruling in this case overturned that of *Plessy v. Ferguson* (1896; in which a "separate but equal" public school education had been established) by concluding that "separate educational facilities are inherently unequal."

Bunting v. Oregon, 243 U.S. 426 (1917). In this case, the Court upheld a maximum work hours law applied to manufacturing employees (women and men).

Lochner v. New York, 198 U.S. 45 (1905). This case established principles later cited by the Supreme Court in determining whether government regulations restricting the right to contract were constitutional.

West Coast Hotel Co. v. Parrish, 300 U.S. 379 (1937). Here, the Court upheld a minimum-wage law passed by the state of Washington and discarded the principles of *Lochner*.

"Women in Industry: Decision of the United States Supreme Court in Curt Muller *vs.* State of Oregon." Harvard University Library Web site. http://ocp.hul.harvard.edu/ww/outsidelink.html/http://nrs.harvard.edu/urn-3:HBS.BAKER:438596. Accessed on October 15, 2007. This site includes the *Muller* case's "Brandeis brief."

Bibliography

■ Articles

Erickson, Nancy S. "*Muller v. Oregon* Reconsidered: The Origins of a Sex-Based Doctrine of Liberty of Contract." *Labor History* 30, no. 2 (1989): 228–250.

Zimmerman, Joan G. "The Jurisprudence of Equality: The Women's Minimum Wage, the First Equal Rights Amendment, and *Adkins v. Children's Hospital*, 1905–1923." *Journal of American History* 78, no. 1 (1991): 188–225.

■ Books

Baer, Judith A. *The Chains of Protection: The Judicial Response to Women's Labor Legislation*. Westport, Conn.: Greenwood Press, 1978.

Kirp, David L., Mark G. Yudof, and Marlene Strong Franks. *Gender Justice*. Chicago: University of Chicago Press, 1986.

Mason, Alpheus Thomas. "The Case of the Overworked Laundress." In *Quarrels That Have Shaped the Constitution*, ed. John A. Garraty. New York: Harper & Row, 1964.

Rhode, Deborah L. *Justice and Gender: Sex Discrimination and the Law*. Cambridge, Mass.: Harvard University Press, 1989.

Sklar, Kathryn Kish. "Why Were Most Politically Active Women Opposed to the ERA in the 1920s?" In *Rights of Passage: The Past and Future of the ERA*, ed. Joan Hoff-Wilson. Bloomington: Indiana University Press, 1986.

Urofsky, Melvin I. *Louis D. Brandeis and the Progressive Tradition*. Boston: Little, Brown, 1981.

Woloch, Nancy. *Muller v. Oregon: A Brief History with Documents*. Boston: Bedford Books of St. Martin's Press, 1996.

■ Web Sites

"Muller v. Oregon (Supreme Court upholds maximum hour law), February 24, 1908." *Women Working, 1800–1930*, Harvard University Library Web site.

   http://ocp.hul.harvard.edu/ww/events_muller.html. Accessed on October 15, 2007.

—By Randy Wagner

1. In paragraph 9, the Court discusses how it is using legislation and opinions supplied in the Brandeis brief. These are not authorities typically relied on, and they do not address the case's constitutional question. Rather, they are "significant of a widespread belief" about a woman's structure and function. Untangle the rest of what the Court says in this paragraph and answer these questions: Is the Court relying on the facts presented in the Brandeis brief or on widespread belief derived from those facts? Is there a difference? Why?

2. Progressive organizations like the National Consumers League, whose official Josephine Goldmark played a key role in constructing the Brandeis brief, supported Oregon's 1903 law setting maximum workday hours for women in laundries and like establishments as a beginning step toward the larger goal of legislation protecting all workers in all industries. Use what the Court wrote to answer these questions: In what ways did the opinion in *Muller* support this agenda? In what ways did the opinion undermine this agenda? Overall, did the opinion support or undermine this agenda?

3. In paragraphs 11 and 12, the Court explains how Oregon's restriction on the right to contract legitimately relates to its power to protect the health, safety, and welfare of its citizens. Could the Court have written these passages in a way that would not have limited, or would have put fewer limits on, a woman's rights? Can you rewrite these passages to achieve those aims?

4. Consider *Muller v. Oregon* (upholding a maximum-hours law) in light of *Lochner v. New York* (striking down a maximum-hours law). Was the connection between a state's police powers and its regulation of workers better established in *Muller* than in *Lochner*? (Look especially at Justice John Marshall Harlan's dissent in *Lochner*.) Was the restriction placed on the right to contract by New York's law different than the restriction created by Oregon's law?

Glossary

feme sole	in the English-American common law tradition, an unmarried woman in charge of her separate estate and against whom legal obligations are enforceable; the term is of French origin
epitome	an abstract account of a longer text
sui juris	of age and capacity to take full possession of one's rights

MULLER V. OREGON

Messrs. William D. Fenton and Henry H. Gilfry for plaintiff in error.

Messrs. H. B. Adams, Louis Brandeis, John Manning, A. M. Crawford, and B. E. Haney for defendant in error.

◆ Mr. Justice Brewer Delivered the Opinion of the Court

On February 19, 1903, the legislature of the state of Oregon passed an act (Session Laws 1903, p. 148) the first section of which is in these words:

Sec. 1. That no female (shall) be employed in any mechanical establishment, or factory, or laundry in this state more than ten hours during any one day. The hours of work may be so arranged as to permit the employment of females at any time so that they shall not work more than ten hours during the twenty-four hours of any one day.

Sec. 3 made a violation of the provisions of the prior sections a misdemeanor subject to a fine of not less than $10 nor more than $25. On September 18, 1905, an information was filed in the circuit court of the state for the county of Multnomah, charging that the defendant "on the 4th day of September, A. D. 1905, in the county of Multnomah and state of Oregon, then and there being the owner of a laundry, known as the Grand Laundry, in the city of Portland, and the employer of females therein, did then and there unlawfully permit and suffer one Joe Haselbock, he, the said Joe Haselbock, then and there being an overseer, superintendent, and agent of said Curt Muller, in the said Grand Laundry, to require a female, to wit, one Mrs. E. Gotcher, to work more than ten hours in said laundry on said 4th day of September, A. D. 1905, contrary to the statutes in such cases made and provided, and against the peace and dignity of the state of Oregon."

A trial resulted in a verdict against the defendant, who was sentenced to pay a fine of $10. The supreme court of the state affirmed the conviction (48 Or. 252, 85 Pac. 855), whereupon the case was brought here on writ of error.

The single question is the constitutionality of the statute under which the defendant was convicted, so far as it affects the work of a female in a laundry. That it does not conflict with any provisions of the state Constitution is settled by the decision of the supreme court of the state. The contentions of the defendant, now plaintiff in error, are thus stated in his brief:

(1) Because the statute attempts to prevent persons sui juris from making their own contracts, and thus violates the provisions of the 14th Amendment, as follows:

No state shall make or enforce any law which shall abridge the privileges or immunities of citizens of the United States; nor shall any state deprive any person of life, liberty, or property, without due process of law; nor deny to any person within its jurisdiction the equal protection of the laws.

(2) Because the statute does not apply equally to all persons similarly situated, and is class legislation.

(3) The statute is not a valid exercise of the police power. The kinds of work prescribed are not unlawful, nor are they declared to be immoral or dangerous to the public health; nor can such a law be sustained on the ground that it is designed to protect women on account of their sex. There is no necessary or reasonable connection between the limitation prescribed by the act and the public health, safety, or welfare.

It is the law of Oregon that women, whether married or single, have equal contractual and personal rights with men. As said by Chief Justice Wolverton, in *First Nat. Bank v. Leonard*, 36 Or. 390, 396, 59 Pac. 873, 874, after a review of the various statutes of the state upon the subject:

We may therefore say with perfect confidence that, with these three sections upon the statute book, the wife can deal, not only with her separate property, acquired from whatever source, in the same manner as her husband can with property belonging to him, but that she may make contracts and incur liabilities, and the same may be enforced against her, the same as if she were a feme sole. There is now no residuum of civil disability resting upon her which is not recognized as existing against the husband. The current runs steadily and strongly in the direction of the emancipation of the wife, and the policy, as disclosed by all recent legislation upon the subject in this state, is to place her upon the same footing as if she were a feme sole, not only with respect to her separate property, but as it affects her right to make binding contracts; and the most natural corollary to the situation is that the remedies for the enforcement of liabilities incurred are made coextensive and coequal with such enlarged conditions.

It thus appears that, putting to one side the elective franchise, in the matter of personal and contractual rights they stand on the same plane as the other sex. Their rights in these respects can no more be infringed than the equal rights of their brothers. We held in *Lochner v. New York*, 198 U.S. 45, 49 L. ed. 937, 25 Sup. Ct. Rep. 539, that a law providing that no laborer shall be required or permitted to work in bakeries more than sixty hours in a week or ten hours in a day was not as to men a legitimate exercise of the police power of the state, but an unreasonable, unnecessary, and arbitrary interference with the right and liberty of the individual to contract in relation to his labor, and as such was in conflict with, and void under, the Federal Constitution. That decision is invoked by plaintiff in error as decisive of the question before us. But this assumes that the difference between the sexes does not justify a different rule respecting a restriction of the hours of labor.

In patent cases counsel are apt to open the argument with a discussion of the state of the art. It may not be amiss, in the present case, before examining the constitutional question, to notice the course of legislation, as well as expressions of opinion from other than judicial sources. In the brief filed by Mr. Louis D. Brandeis for the defendant in error is a very copious collection of all these matters, an epitome of which is found in the margin. While there have been but few decisions bearing directly upon the question, the following sustain the constitutionality of such leg-

islation: *Com. v. Hamilton Mfg. Co.* 120 Mass. 383; *Wenham v. State*, 65 Neb. 394, 400, 406, 58 L.R.A. 825, 91 N. W. 421; *State v. Buchanan*, 29 Wash. 602, 59 L. R. A. 342, 92 Am. St. Rep. 930, 70 Pac. 52; *Com. v. Beatty*, 15 Pa. Super. Ct. 5, 17; against them is the case of *Ritchie v. People*, 155 Ill. 98, 29 L.R. A. 79, 46 Am. St. Rep. 315, 40 N. E. 454.

The legislation and opinions referred to in the margin may not be, technically speaking, authorities, and in them is little or no discussion of the constitutional question presented to us for determination, yet they are significant of a widespread belief that woman's physical structure, and the functions she performs in consequence thereof, justify special legislation restricting or qualifying the conditions under which she should be permitted to toil. Constitutional questions, it is true, are not settled by even a consensus of present public opinion, for it is the peculiar value of a written constitution that it places in unchanging form limitations upon legislative action, and thus gives a permanence and stability to popular government which otherwise would be lacking. At the same time, when a question of fact is debated and debatable, and the extent to which a special constitutional limitation goes is affected by the truth in respect to that fact, a widespread and long continued belief concerning it is worthy of consideration. We take judicial cognizance of all matters of general knowledge.

It is undoubtedly true, as more than once declared by this court, that the general right to contract in relation to one's business is part of the liberty of the individual, protected by the 14th Amendment to the Federal Constitution; yet it is equally well settled that this liberty is not absolute and extending to all contracts, and that a state may, without conflicting with the provisions of the 14th Amendment, restrict in many respects the individual's power of contract. Without stopping to discuss at length the extent to which a state may act in this respect, we refer to the following cases in which the question has been considered: *Allgeyer v. Louisiana*, 165 U.S. 578, 41 L. ed. 832, 17 Sup. Ct. Rep. 427; *Holden v. Hardy*, 169 U.S. 366, 42 L. ed. 780, 18 Sup. Ct. Rep. 383; *Lochner v. New York*, supra.

That woman's physical structure and the performance of maternal functions place her at a disadvantage in the struggle for subsistence is obvious. This is especially true when the burdens of motherhood are upon her. Even when they are not, by abundant testimony of the medical fraternity continuance for a long time on her feet at work, repeating this from day to day, tends to injurious effects upon the body, and, as healthy mothers are essential to vigorous off-spring, the physical well-being of woman becomes an object of public interest and care in order to preserve the strength and vigor of the race.

Still again, history discloses the fact that woman has always been dependent upon man. He established his control at the outset by superior physical strength, may, without conflicting with the provisions and this control in various forms, with diminishing intensity, has continued to the present. As minors, thought not to the same extent, she has been looked upon in the courts as needing especial care that her rights may be preserved. Education was long denied her, and while now the doors of the schoolroom are opened and her opportunities for acquiring knowledge are great, yet even with that and the consequent increase of capacity for business affairs it is still true that in the struggle for subsistence she is not an equal competitor with her brother. Though limitations upon personal and contractual rights may be removed by legislation, there is that in her disposition and habits of life which will operate against a full assertion of those rights. She will still be where some legislation to protect her seems necessary to secure a real equality of right. Doubtless there are individual exceptions, and there are many respects in which she has an advantage over him; but looking at it from the viewpoint of the effort to maintain an independent position in life, she is not upon an equality. Differentiated by these matters from the other sex, she is properly placed in a class by herself, and legislation designed for her protection may be sustained, even when like legislation is not necessary for men, and could not be sustained. It is impossible to close one's eyes to the fact that she still looks to her brother and depends upon him. Even though all restrictions on political, personal, and contractual rights were taken away, and she stood, so far as

statutes are concerned, upon an absolutely equal plane with him, it would still be true that she is so constituted that she will rest upon and look to him for protection; that her physical structure and a proper discharge of her maternal functions—having in view not merely her own health, but the well-being of the race—justify legislation to protect her from the greed as well as the passion of man. The limitations which this statute places upon her contractual powers, upon her right to agree with her employer as to the time she shall labor, are not imposed solely for her benefit, but also largely for the benefit of all. Many words cannot make this plainer. The two sexes differ in structure of body, in the functions to be performed by each, in the amount of physical strength, in the capacity for long continued labor, particularly when done standing, the influence of vigorous health upon the future well-being of the race, the self-reliance which enables one to assert full rights, and in the capacity to maintain the struggle for subsistence. This difference justifies a difference in legislation, and upholds that which is designed to compensate for some of the burdens which rest upon her.

We have not referred in this discussion to the denial of the elective franchise in the state of Oregon, for while that may disclose a lack of political equality in all things with her brother, that is not of itself decisive. The reason runs deeper, and rests in the inherent difference between the two sexes, and in the different functions in life which they perform.

For these reasons, and without questioning in any respect the decision in *Lochner v. New York*, we are of the opinion that it cannot be adjudged that the act in question is in conflict with the Federal Constitution, so far as it respects the work of a female in a laundry, and the judgment of the Supreme Court of Oregon is affirmed.

Sixty-first Congress of the United States of America;

At the First Session,

Begun and held at the City of Washington on Monday, the fifteenth day of March, one thousand nine hundred and nine.

JOINT RESOLUTION

Proposing an amendment to the Constitution of the United States.

Resolved by the Senate and House of Representatives of the United States of America in Congress assembled (two-thirds of each House concurring therein), That the following article is proposed as an amendment to the Constitution of the United States, which, when ratified by the legislatures of three-fourths of the several States, shall be valid to all intents and purposes as a part of the Constitution:

"ARTICLE XVI. The Congress shall have power to lay and collect taxes on incomes, from whatever source derived, without apportionment among the several States, and without regard to any census or enumeration."

Speaker of the House of Representatives.

Vice-President of the United States and
President of the Senate.

Attest:

Clerk of the House of Representatives.

Charles G. Bennett
Secretary

By Henry H. Gilfry
Chief Clerk

The Sixteenth Amendment (National Archives and Records Administration)

SIXTEENTH AMENDMENT TO THE U.S. CONSTITUTION

1913

"The Congress shall have power to lay and collect taxes on incomes."

Overview

Written by Senator Norris Brown of Nebraska and Representative Cordell Hull of Tennessee, the Sixteenth Amendment to the U.S. Constitution, empowering the federal government to levy an income tax, was adopted in February 1913. After the Supreme Court declared the Wilson-Gorman Tariff Act unconstitutional in 1895, many felt that some sort of tax on income was necessary in order for government revenue to keep pace with the high cost of living. Nearly fifteen years passed before another income tax was proposed and accepted in Congress. Senator Brown, especially, wanted the income tax to be adopted as a constitutional amendment. Written in July 1909, the income tax amendment was not fully ratified by the required three-fourths majority of the states until February 1913. The amendment was signed into effect by Secretary of State Philander C. Knox on February 25, 1913. After the amendment was ratified, an income tax bill officially became law on October 3, 1913.

Context

The 1913 federal income tax amendment came about as a result of the 1895 court case *Pollock v. Farmers' Loan and Trust Co.* When the Civil War started in 1861, Congress initiated an income tax as a way to help pay for wartime expenses. Going into effect in 1862, this first income tax applied only to incomes over $800 and began at a flat rate of 3 percent; incomes greater than $10,000 were later taxed at 5 percent. Although it was proposed simply as a temporary emergency measure to raise money during the war, this tax remained in effect until 1872. In 1894 Congress instituted another income tax, the first established during peacetime, with the Wilson-Gorman Tariff Act. President Grover Cleveland refused to sign the document, but it was passed by both the House and Senate. A year later, Charles Pollock, a Farmers' Loan and Trust shareholder from Massachusetts, sued to prevent the Farmers' Loan and Trust Company from having to pay the tax. According to the Constitution, Congress was allowed to

institute a direct tax only if it was levied proportionally to the populations of each state. The Supreme Court determined that the Wilson-Gorman tax on income derived from property was a direct tax levied disproportionally and so declared the act unconstitutional.

Following the Supreme Court's ruling, many presidential candidates began to include the income tax on their platforms, and President Theodore Roosevelt advocated for a graduated income tax in 1906. President William Howard Taft, on the other hand, did not see the need for a constitutional amendment for federal income tax, although he did ultimately call a special session of Congress in March 1909 to discuss the issue of a new tariff bill. Democrats and progressive Republicans in the Senate proved resolute in their goal to add an income tax rider to the tariff reform bill. Senators Joseph Bailey and Albert Cummins joined forces in introducing a bill to tax income over $5,000.

Nonetheless, Senator Norris Brown of Nebraska was especially determined to draft a constitutional amendment for the income tax in the hope that such an amendment would result in a Constitution that could not be interpreted two ways. Brown teamed up with Representative Cordell Hull of Tennessee, a member of the House Ways and Means Committee, to draft the amendment. Hull modeled the new tax bill on the defunct 1894 law. After finally being passed in both the Senate and the House in July 1909, the amendment then needed to be approved by a three-fourths majority of the states.

Some people, including Governor Charles Evans Hughes of New York, opposed the amendment because of the inclusion of the phrase "from whatever source derived." To address this concern, Senator Norris Brown remarked, "I am sure I cannot see why, if we are making the taxing of incomes constitutional, we should not tax all incomes regardless of source. It is just as much income if it is derived from National, State, or Municipal securities as it is if derived from railway dividends, interest on corporation boards of any sort, industrial stock dividends, or the profits of ordinary mercantile business" (Ekirch, p. 178). Others in opposition did not want to cede money to the federal government when their own states might need the revenue. Industrialists, like John D. Rockefeller, opposed the tax out of the fear that "wealth must more and more pay the bills" (Ekirch, p. 178). On the

1861

■ **August 5**

Congress passes the Revenue Act of 1861, taxing personal incomes over $800 to help pay for expenses incurred during the Civil War; the bill goes into effect in July 1862 and is to be levied for three years beginning in July 1863.

1867

■ **March 2**

Congress amends the Revenue Act to include a fixed tax of 5 percent on all incomes over $10,000; the income tax is abolished in 1872.

1894

■ **August 27**

Wilson-Gorman Tariff Act is passed by the House and Senate, though it is not signed into law by President Grover Cleveland; this tariff reform bill also imposes a 2 percent direct tax on incomes over $4,000.

1895

■ **April 8**

In *Pollock v Farmers' Loan and Trust Co.*, the Supreme Court rules that general income taxes are unconstitutional since the Constitution stipulates that direct taxes are to be in proportion to each state's population; this decision essentially voids the Wilson-Gorman Tariff Act, in which the income tax was not apportioned according to the population.

1909

■ **March**

Democratic Senator Joseph W. Bailey of Texas introduces a bill to impose a 3 percent tax on the incomes of individuals and corporations, and Republican Senator Albert B. Cummins of Iowa proposes a graduated tax on individuals. Meanwhile, Senator Norris Brown of Nebraska argues for a constitutional amendment so that the Court could not strike down any such legislation.

■ **June**

President William Howard Taft proposes three new taxes to Congress, including a general income tax on all income over $3,000 without regard to state population.

other hand, many landowners from the more agricultural regions of the country were in favor of an income tax, fearing that Congress might instead enact a tax on property.

With the election of a new governor, New York ratified the amendment in 1910. The final state needed to ratify the amendment approved it in February 1913, almost four years after the amendment was introduced. With the three-fourths vote from the states to ratify the income tax amendment, Secretary of State Philander C. Knox signed the amendment into effect on February 25, 1913.

About the Author

Senator Norris Brown, a Republican from Nebraska, was born in Maquoketa, Iowa, on May 2, 1863. After finishing law school at the University of Iowa in 1883, he was admitted to the bar the following year. Brown practiced law in Iowa before moving to Nebraska in 1888. From 1892 to 1896 he was the attorney for Buffalo County, Nebraska. He practiced law in Nebraska for a number of years before serving as the state attorney general from 1904 to 1906. In 1906 Brown was elected to the U.S. Senate, where he would serve until 1913. In 1909, in response to several income tax proposals, Senator Brown introduced a bill that would add an amendment to the Constitution allowing for a federal income tax. After his first term, Brown failed to gain reelection for a second. Leaving Congress in 1913, he returned home to Nebraska, where he practiced law until 1942, when he retired and moved to Seattle, Washington. He remained there until his death on January 5, 1960.

Representative Cordell Hull was born in Pickett County, Tennessee, to William and Elizabeth Hull on October 2, 1871. Hull graduated from the Cumberland University School of Law in 1891. When he became old enough, he ran for the state legislature and was elected to the Tennessee House of Representatives from 1893 to 1897; he then left that office to serve in the Spanish-American War. When he returned, Hull was appointed a judge before being elected to the U.S. House of Representatives. He served on the Ways and Means Committee for eighteen of his twenty-two years in the House. In addition to helping draft the Sixteenth Amendment, Hull wrote the Revenue Act of 1916. Elected a U.S. senator in 1931, Hull resigned his position when President Franklin D. Roosevelt appointed him secretary of state in March 1933. In that office, Hull was a leading proponent of international trade agreements and low tariffs. He served as secretary of state until his retirement in December 1944 due to health problems. In 1945 Hull received the Nobel Peace Prize for his role in creating the United Nations. He continued to live in Washington, D.C., until his death on July 23, 1955.

Explanation and Analysis of the Document

One of the shortest constitutional amendments, the Sixteenth Amendment consists of just one sentence. The amendment may seem to have instituted the federal income tax; on the contrary, the text therein simply gives Congress the power to impose an income tax. The Sixteenth Amendment specifies that the tax does not have to be allotted according to a state's population, which the Constitution would otherwise require of such a direct tax. The amendment also specifies that income from any source, no matter where, would be subject to the tax.

Audience

Although it was directed at all citizens of the United States, the Sixteenth Amendment to the Constitution was perhaps most intended for the Supreme Court itself. After the Supreme Court ruled that the Wilson-Gorman Tariff Act was unconstitutional in 1895, some members of Congress were determined to provide an amendment to the Constitution that would allow for an income tax and could not be misinterpreted in any way.

Impact

One of the major impacts of the Sixteenth Amendment was that, with an income tax, America would no longer have to rely on tariffs to raise revenue. This fact would prove especially important since the country would enter World War I just a few years later. Indeed, upon America's entry into the war, the need for the income tax was immediately realized, for without it, the financing of the war would have been difficult. In fact, as the historians Baack and Ray contend, "No single element involved with the rapid assumption of economic power by the federal government was more important than the passage of the income tax, the means by which the increasing role of government was financed" (p. 607).

The 1913 tax marked the first time in American history that a tax had been applied so broadly to individuals and corporations alike. By 1916 two cases seeking the abolishment of the tax had made their way to the Supreme Court. In both *Brushaber v. Union Pacific Railroad Co.* and *Stanton v. Baltic Mining Co.*, wealthy stockholders attempted to convince the courts that their companies should not have to pay the tax.

The amendment allowing the federal government to impose an income tax also created more bureaucracy for the institution. Congress apportioned almost one million dollars for the collection of the taxes, and the newly formed Bureau of Internal Revenue—which would eventually be renamed the Internal Revenue Service—had thirty employees responsible for "handl[ing] the letters and telegrams asking about the tax" (Weisman, p. 282). By 1915, the Bureau of Internal Revenue employed more than 350 tax collectors.

Related Documents

Brown, Norris, and William Edgar Borah. "Shall the Income-Tax Amendment Be Ratified?" In *The Editorial Review*. Washington,

Time Line

1909

■ **June 16**
President Taft recommends that Congress pass a constitutional amendment to allow for the imposing of a federal income tax.

■ **July 12**
Congress passes the Sixteenth Amendment, as proposed by President Taft.

1913

■ **February 3**
Sixteenth Amendment to the U.S. Constitution is ratified.

■ **February 25**
Sixteenth Amendment goes into effect after being certified by Secretary of State Philander C. Knox.

■ **October 3**
Income tax law goes into effect, applying to all income, regardless of source, received after March 1 of that year; less than 1 percent of the population will be obligated to pay the tax.

1916

■ Original Sixteenth Amendment is revised to delete the word "lawful" in regards to income; as such, essentially all income, even that derived by illegal means, is taxable.

D.C.: Government Printing Office, 1910. Brown and Senator Borah of Idaho discuss their views of the proposed amendment.

Hull, Cordell. *The Federal Income Tax Law, Together with Synopsis of the Law.* New York: Guaranty Trust Company of New York, 1913. In this book, Hull reviews and summarizes the sixteenth amendment.

Seligman, Edwin R. A. "The Income-Tax Amendment." *Political Science Quarterly* 25, no. 2 (June 1910): 193–219. In this article, written just after New York governor Hughes expressed his disapproval of the proposed amendment, Seligman explains his own views on the subject. The work did much to promote the income tax.

———. "The Federal Income Tax." *Political Science Quarterly* 29, no. 1 (March 1914): 1–27. Seligman analyzes the proposed income tax amendment, discussing who is liable to the income tax and what is considered taxable income.

———. "The United States Federal Income Tax." *Economic Journal* 24, no. 93 (March 1914): 57–77. As with his other 1914 arti-

> "The Congress shall have power to lay and collect taxes on incomes, from whatever source derived, without apportionment among the several States, and without regard to any census or enumeration."

cle, Seligman analyzes the various components of the Sixteenth Amendment.

Shields, John Knight, Cordell Hull, and Thurlow M. Gordon. *The Income Tax: Opinions of Hon. John K. Shields, Hon. Cordell Hull, and Thurlow M. Gordon on the Proposed Income-Tax Provision of the Pending Tariff Bill*. Washington, D.C.: Government Printing Office, 1913. This work contains the men's thoughts and opinions on the income tax amendment.

Bibliography

■ Articles

Baack, Bennett D., and Edward John Ray. "Special Interests and the Adoption of the Income Tax in the United States." *Journal of Economic History* 45, no. 3 (September 1985): 607–625.

Blakey, Roy G. "The New Income Tax." *American Economic Review* 4, no. 1 (March 1914): 25–46.

Bowen, Howard R. "The Personal Income Tax and the Economy." *Annals of the American Academy of Political and Social Science* 266 (November 1949): 117–120.

Buenker, John D. "The Ratification of the Federal Income Tax Amendment." *Cato Journal* 1, no. 1 (Spring 1981): 183–223.

Ekirch, Arthur A., Jr. "The Sixteenth Amendment: The Historical Background." *Cato Journal* 1, no. 1 (Spring 1981): 161–182.

Herber, Bernard P. "Federal Income Tax Reform in the United States: How Did It Happen? What Did It Do? Where Do We Go from Here?" *American Journal of Economics and Sociology* 47, no. 4 (October 1988): 391–408.

Hill, Joseph A. "The Income Tax of 1913." *Quarterly Journal of Economics* 28, no. 1 (November 1913): 46–68.

Mehrotra, Ajay K. "'More Mighty Than the Waves of the Sea': Toilers, Tariffs, and the Income Tax Movement, 1880–1913." *Labor History* 45, no. 2 (May 2004): 165–198.

Seligman, Edwin R. A. "The Income Tax." *Political Science Quarterly* 9, no. 4 (December 1894): 610–648.

Smiley, Gene, and Richard H. Keehn. "Federal Personal Income Tax Policy in the 1920s." *Journal of Economic History* 55, no. 2 (June 1995): 285–303.

■ Books

Adams, Charles. *Those Dirty Rotten Taxes: The Tax Revolts That Built America*. New York: Free Press, 1998.

Blakey, Roy G., and Gladys C. Blakey. *The Federal Income Tax*. London: Longmans, Green, 1940.

Brownlee, W. Elliot. *Federal Taxation in America: A Short History*. Washington, D.C.: Woodrow Wilson Center Press, 1996.

Carson, Gerald. *The Golden Egg: The Personal Income Tax—Where It Came From, How It Grew*. Boston: Houghton Mifflin, 1977.

Conable, Jr., Barber B. *Congress and the Income Tax*. Norman: University of Oklahoma Press, 1989.

Garrison, John C. *The New Income Tax Scandal: How Congress Hijacked the Sixteenth Amendment*. Philadelphia: Xlibris, 2005.

Higgens-Evenson, R. Rudy. *The Price of Progress: Public Services, Taxation, and the American Corporate State, 1877 to 1929*. Baltimore: Johns Hopkins University Press, 2003.

Internal Revenue Service. *Income Taxes, 1862–1962: A History of the Internal Revenue Service*. Washington, D.C.: Government Printing Office, 1963.

Joseph, Richard J. *The Origins of the American Income Tax: The Revenue Act of 1894 and Its Aftermath*. Syracuse, N.Y.: Syracuse University Press, 2004.

Klein, Joseph J. *Federal Income Taxation*. New York: John Wiley & Sons, 1929.

Langenderfer, Harold Q. *The Federal Income Tax, 1861–1872*. New York: Arno Press, 1980.

Seligman, Edwin R. A. *The Income Tax: A Study of the History, Theory and Practice of Income Taxation at Home and Abroad*. New York: Macmillan, 1911.

Stanley, Robert. *Dimensions of Law in the Service of Order: Origins of the Federal Income Tax, 1861–1913.* New York: Oxford University Press, 1993.

Swisher, Carl Brent. *American Constitutional Development.* Boston: Houghton Mifflin, 1943.

Waltman, Jerold L. *Political Origins of the U.S. Income Tax.* Jackson: University Press of Mississippi, 1985.

Weisman, Steven R. *The Great Tax Wars: Lincoln to Wilson, the Fierce Battles over Money and Power That Transformed the Nation.* New York: Simon & Schuster, 2002.

Witte, John F. *The Politics and Development of the Federal Income Tax.* Madison: University of Wisconsin Press, 1985.

■ Web Sites

"History of the US Income Tax." Business Reference Services, Library of Congress "Business Reference Services" Web site.
  http://www.loc.gov/rr/business/hottopic/irs_history.html. Accessed on October 23, 2007.

"History of the U.S. Tax System." United States Department of the Treasury Web site.
  http://www.treas.gov/education/fact-sheets/taxes/ustax.shtml. Accessed on October 23, 2007.

"U.S. Constitution: Sixteenth Amendment." FindLaw Web site.
  http://caselaw.lp.findlaw.com/data/constitution/amendment16/. Accessed on October 23, 2007.

—By Nicole Mitchell

Questions for Further Study

1. Compare and contrast the 1861, 1894, and 1913 income tax acts. What are some similarities? What are some differences?

2. The tax historian Charles Adams wrote that "proponents of income tax in America were able to offer seventy years of British experience as strong proof that the tax would not destroy liberty and bring tyranny" (p. 152). Compare and contrast the American income tax system with the British income tax system.

3. Compare and contrast the careers, political views, and opinions of Senator Norris Brown and Representative Cordell Hull. What do they have in common? What are their differences?

4. The 1861 Revenue Act was supposed to remain in effect for only three years, yet it was not abolished until 1872. Why do you think this happened? What are some reasons why the income tax in question would have been imposed and allowed to stand?

5. The modern federal income tax has been in effect since 1913. Do you believe that the Sixteenth Amendment should be revised or reformed? Why or why not?

6. Enacted in 1894, the Wilson-Gorman Tariff Act was declared unconstitutional by the Supreme Court the following year. Do you agree with this decision? Why or why not?

Glossary

apportionment	the proportional distribution of the number of members of the U.S. House of Representatives on the basis of the population of each state
census	an official count of the population, with details as to age, sex, occupation, and so forth
enumeration	the act of determining the number of; counting or listing one by one
lay	to impose as a burden, duty, penalty, or the like

SIXTEENTH AMENDMENT TO THE U.S. CONSTITUTION

Sixty-first Congress of the United States of America, At the First Session,

Begun and held at the City of Washington on Monday, the fifteenth day of March, one thousand nine hundred and nine.

◆ Joint Resolution

Proposing an amendment to the Constitution of the United States.

Resolved by the Senate and House of Representatives of the United States of America in Congress assembled (two-thirds of each House concurring therein), That the following article is proposed as an amendment to the Constitution of the United States, which, when ratified by the legislature of three-fourths of the several States, shall be valid to all intents and purposes as a part of the Constitution:

"**ARTICLE XVI.** The Congress shall have power to lay and collect taxes on incomes, from whatever source derived, without apportionment among the several States, and without regard to any census or enumeration."

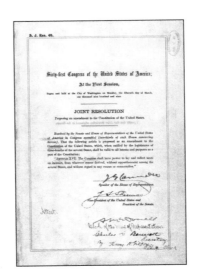

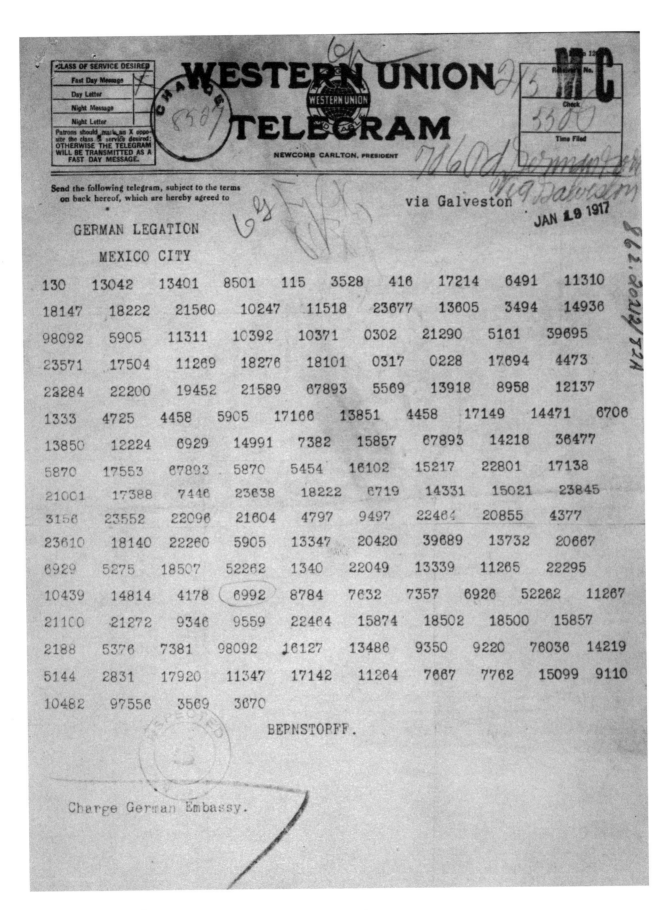

The Zimmermann Telegram (National Archives and Records Administration)

"An understanding on our part that Mexico is to reconquer the lost territory in Texas, New Mexico, and Arizona."

Overview

On January 19, 1917, Germany's foreign secretary, Arthur Zimmermann, cabled the German minister to Mexico. Zimmermann informed the minister that on February 1, Germany would begin unrestricted submarine warfare. The crux of the telegram, however, involved a proposal for a German-Mexican alliance. In the event of war between Germany and the United States, Germany and Mexico would make war and peace together. Germany would financially assist Mexico and, even more important, aid it in recovering Texas, New Mexico, and Arizona. A request was made to Japan, a member of the Allies, to join the Central powers. The British intercepted the cable and relayed it to the United States. Both inside the U.S. government and among the public, the cable was immediately denounced. It also gave momentum to those in the country arguing for entrance into World War I on the side of Britain and France and against Germany.

Context

In August 1914 all-out war erupted in Europe. Germany had long believed that it could not win a conflict in which it was forced to fight a war on two fronts. Hence, in 1905, Alfred von Schlieffen, German chief of the general staff, designed a plan by which France would be wiped clean before the Russians could mobilize successfully. To execute effectively what was called the "Schlieffen Plan," Germany invaded Belgium—a neutral state—on August 3. Although Belgium itself was soon overrun, within a day England had declared war on Germany on the ground that it had violated an international treaty made in 1839, in which the great powers had established Belgium as a new state and had guaranteed its neutrality. Because the German chief of staff Helmuth von Moltke weakened the left wing of his invading army, France was able to repulse his army in early September in a decisive battle on the Marne River. By October, French and British armies faced German armies along a line that extended across northern France and a small corner of Belgium. For close to four years the Ger-

mans were unable to recover the ground they had lost in September; the Allies, in turn, lacked the strength to force the invaders back into Germany.

On other fronts, there was less of a stalemate. By the end of 1914 the British and French had seized most of Germany's African colonies. The Japanese had taken the German position of Tsingtao on the coast of North China and a number of German islands in the South Pacific. In May 1916 a major naval engagement off Norway called the battle of Jutland resulted in major losses on both sides. The British, however, had the consolation of bottling up the German fleet for the rest of the conflict. In May 1915 Italy declared war on Germany's major ally, Austria-Hungary, but found itself continually defeated in the Isonzo River region north of Venice. By the end of 1916 the Central powers occupied Serbia and Romania. Furthermore, their armies had extended deeply into Russian Poland and the Ukraine.

Tremendous casualties were mounting. Between June and November 1916, Britain's offensive on France's Somme River resulted in four hundred thousand casualties, sixty thousand falling on one day alone. The ground gained was negligible. Almost simultaneously came the German assault at the French fortress of Verdun, a seven-month campaign that ended in September 1916. After a million casualties on both sides, Verdun still lay in French hands. Admittedly, in the summer of 1916 Russia had mounted impressive offensives. Still, even though the Central powers lost six hundred thousand men, the Russians had lost one million.

By this time the belligerents had extensive war aims. On January 12, 1917, the press reported the Allies' demands, which included the restoration of Belgium, Serbia, and Montenegro with indemnities for each; the German evacuation of France, Russia, and Romania with just reparation; the liberation of those Italians, Romanians, Slavs, and Czechoslovaks living under alien domination; the enfranchisement of populations subject to Turkish rule; and the expulsion of Turkey from Europe. Not mentioned were secret agreements dividing much of the Middle East into French and British spheres of influence; Italian annexation of South Tyrol, then a part of Austria-Hungary; and cession of the Turkish straits, including the city of Constantinople, to Russia.

1917

At a meeting at Pless Castle, Germany's highest military and civilian leaders decide to initiate unrestricted submarine warfare.

■ **January 19**
German Foreign Secretary Arthur Zimmermann cables Heinrich von Eckhardt, German minister in Mexico, to approach the Mexican chief of state Venustiano Carranza concerning the possibility of a German-Mexican military alliance against the United States.

■ **January 31**
Johann von Bernstorff, German ambassador to the United States, notifies Secretary of State Robert Lansing that Germany will resume unrestricted submarine warfare against all neutral and Allied shipping, effective February 1.

■ **February 3**
In an address to Congress, President Woodrow Wilson announces severance of diplomatic relations with Germany, a measure endorsed by the Senate on February 7 by a vote of 78 to 5.

■ **February 25**
Wilson learns of the Zimmermann Telegram.

■ **February 26**
Wilson asks Congress for authority to arm American merchantmen to deter German submarine attacks. On March 1, the House passes the bill 403 to 13, but in the Senate twelve senators filibuster the bill until the session ends on March 4.

■ **March 1**
The U.S. State Department releases news of the Zimmermann Telegram to the press.

■ **March 3**
Zimmermann freely admits writing the cable to Mexico.

German terms were equally imperialistic. In the east, they included the establishment of a puppet kingdom of Poland and German annexation of the Baltic provinces of Courland (later Latvia) and Lithuania. In the west, they involved "guarantees in Belgium," or the annexation of Liège and "corresponding areas"; the annexation of Luxembourg and the French territories of Briey and Longwy, both of which contained major iron deposits; strategic boundary adjustments in Alsace-Lorraine; and war indemnities (Link, 1965, p. 211). Overseas, Germany sought the return of most of its colonies. with the exception of some South Sea island chains. It also sought at least part of the Belgian Congo.

The historian Ross Gregory writes, "Each belligerent had come to measure its part in the war in terms of investment, and the longer the war lasted, the higher the cost and the less satisfactory an indecisive settlement. Each month of battle added to the difficulty of ending the stalemate" (p. 106). In an effort to break this deadlock, on January 31, 1917, Germany announced it was resuming unrestricted submarine warfare against all Allied and neutral shipping so as to starve out the British. By February, in light of increasing tension with the United States, it sent what has gone down in history as the "Zimmermann Telegram." In this cable, it sought an alliance with Mexico, promising it much of the land it had lost in the Mexican War of 1846–1848.

The concept behind the Zimmermann Telegram did not originate with German foreign secretary Arthur Zimmermann but with Hans Arthur von Kemnitz, a Latin American expert in the German foreign office. On November 3, 1916, Venustiano Carranza, ruler of Mexico who held the official title "First Chief," had offered submarine bases to the Germans. At the time, an American expedition, led by Brigadier General John J. Pershing and later known as the Punitive Expedition, was venturing deep into northern Mexico. Pershing sought to capture Francisco ("Pancho") Villa, a freebooting Mexican chieftain who had repeatedly raided Texas and New Mexico that spring. Although Germany declined Carranza's offer, von Kemnitz pushed the matter, finally persuading the foreign secretary, who cabled the proposal on January 19, 1917, to the German minister in Mexico, Heinrich von Eckhardt.

Early in the war, Britain had cracked the German diplomatic code. Hence, it quickly learned of the Zimmermann Telegram. The British delayed revealing the message to Walter Hines Page, American ambassador to London, until they were assured the Germans had no knowledge their ciphers had been cracked. It was not until February 25 that Frank L. Polk, acting secretary of state of the United States, learned of its existence. He immediately informed President Woodrow Wilson, who wanted to be sure the note was authentic and therefore delayed its release to the press for several days.

About the Author

Arthur Zimmermann was born on October 5, 1864, in Marggrabowa, East Prussia (now Olecko, Poland). After studying law at Königsberg, in 1893 he joined the German consular service, serving at Shanghai, Canton, and Tienstin in China before returning to Berlin in 1902 as legation counselor. Rising through the ranks as privy councillor and department director, he was appointed undersecretary of state in 1911. "A stout, ruddy, earthy bachelor," according to the historians Holger Herwig and Neil Heyman, "Zimmermann personified middle-class respectability and diligence" (p. 365).

On November 26, 1916, Zimmermann became foreign secretary. He was both the first commoner and the first diplomat from the consular service to hold such a high post. He received the appointment because of his endorsement of unrestricted submarine warfare, a policy pushed by Germany's leading military figures. His predecessor, Gottlieb von Jagow, called him a "fanatical U-boat warrior" who would always "swim with the stream and with those who shouted loudest" (Herwig and Heyman, p. 365). Surprisingly enough, American journalists considered Zimmermann a liberal, while Wilson's right-hand man, Colonel Edward M. House, thought of him as a friend. After the cable fiasco, Zimmermann became increasingly obscure, resigning his post on August 5, 1917. After several decades of retirement, he died in Berlin on June 7, 1940.

Explanation and Analysis of the Document

Zimmermann, writing on January 19, begins by noting that Germany would declare unrestricted submarine warfare on February 1. The decision had been made on January 9 at Pless Castle, headquarters of the eastern command. That meeting was chaired by Kaiser Wilhelm II, who had decided ahead of time that he was in favor of the move. Henning von Holtzendorff, who headed the German admiralty, predicted that England would be defeated in "six months at the most, in any case before an American had set foot on the mainland" (Link, 1965, p. 346). Field Marshal Paul von Hindenburg pointed to a forthcoming Allied offensive that would surpass the recent assault on the Somme. As it was crucial to block the arrival of fresh manpower and supplies to the enemy, he stressed that the measure must be implemented immediately. Until the last minute, Chancellor Theobald von Bethmann Hollweg voiced opposition, maintaining that an all-out campaign would lead to American intervention, which in turn would result in Germany's defeat.

The historian Arthur S. Link finds Germany committing one of the greatest blunders in history, for Wilson was devoting full attention to ending the war. In fact, Wilson envisioned a general peace conference with himself as mediator, personally tipping the scales for a just settlement. Conversely, Germany's decision makers saw themselves facing the choice of either continuing the suicidal trench warfare on their western front or starting full-scale U-boat warfare. By February 1 Germany could keep about twenty-five submarines in both western waters and in the Mediterranean, thereby giving it the power to levy an effective

blockade. A poor wheat harvest in the Americas added to German optimism.

After claiming that Germany would seek to keep America neutral, Zimmermann gets to the heart of the matter: a proposal for Germany to enter into a binding alliance with Mexico. Germany would not only offer "generous financial support" but also aid in regaining "the lost territory in Texas, New Mexico, and Arizona"—the areas Mexico had lost in its war with the United States (1846–1848). Zimmermann realized that American relations with Mexico had been extremely tense for a long time. On March 9, 1916, Pancho Villa burned the town of Columbus, New Mexico, killing nineteen inhabitants in the process. On March 18, Wilson ordered General Pershing south of the Rio Grande to capture the bandit leader. Within a month Mexican leaders suspected that Pershing intended to occupy northern Mexico permanently. One skirmish at Parral resulted in the death of forty Mexicans; another at Carrizal led to thirty Mexican fatalities and twenty-three American deaths. A Joint Mexican-American High Commission, meeting from September 6, 1916, through January 15, 1917, could not reach an agreement over the Carrizal matter. Sufficient time, however, had elapsed to diffuse the crisis.

Time Line

1917

■ **March 12**
The U.S. State Department announces that all American merchant vessels traveling through war zones will be armed, taking the position that under statute the president has such authority regardless of specific congressional authorization; the American steamer *Algonquin* is sunk without warning off the British Isles.

■ **March 18**
News reaches the United States that three American ships have been sunk: *City of Memphis* off the coast of Ireland; the *Illinois* in the English Channel near France; the *Vigilancia* off Britain's southwestern coast.

■ **March 29**
Zimmermann defends his cable to the Reichstag, claiming ignorance as to how the Americans intercepted the telegram.

■ **April 2**
Wilson delivers his war message. On April 4 the Senate votes in favor of his war resolution, 82 to 6, and on April 6 the House follows suit, 373 to 50.

"We make Mexico a proposal or alliance on the following basis: make war together, make peace together, generous financial support and an understanding on our part that Mexico is to reconquer the lost territory in Texas, New Mexico, and Arizona."

Each nation kept a wary eye on the other. In 1916 James W. Gerard, Wilson's ambassador to Berlin, warned that Germany contemplated fighting the United States through Mexico, while Robert Lansing warned the president that German submarines had secretly been visiting Mexican waters. All during the time of the Punitive Expedition, the secretary of state was receiving Secret Service reports of German intrigue in northern Mexico.

Zimmermann then asks Heinrich von Eckhardt, German minister in Mexico, to approach Mexico's de facto president, Venustiano Carranza, to invite Japan to participate in the Mexican-German alliance. To grant Zimmermann's wish, Japan would have to change course entirely, leaving the Allies to join the Central powers. One must ask to what degree Germany would recognize Japan's wartime conquests of its territory on the coast of China and in the South Seas. Certainly Japan would not join such an alliance without assurance of major compensation. The cable concludes with the optimistic prediction that the new U-boat warfare would defeat England within several months.

Audience

The telegram was written strictly for the German minister in Mexico, Heinrich von Eckhardt.

Impact

The note did not persuade Wilson to seek entry into the conflict, nor did it prompt him to ask Congress for authority to arm American merchant ships, as he had already made that decision. It did cause him to lose all faith in the German government, with the Germans therefore inadvertently making—in the words of the historian Arthur Link—"one of the most maladroit as well as monstrous blunders in modern diplomatic history" (Link, 1965, p. 346). Link describes the president as being shocked beyond measure to find that Germany had "been conniving to entice bankrupt and war-ravaged Mexico to attack the United States at the very time that he, Wilson, had been negotiating with the German leaders for peace and reconstruction of the international community!" (Link, 1965, p. 345). Since Decem-

ber 1916, Wilson had sought to have both sets of belligerents state their war aims, doing so in the hope of being able to mediate the conflict. Particularly horrifying was the fact that Zimmermann had used the U.S. Department of State's own cable, which had been given to Ambassador Johann von Bernstorff to expedite peace moves between the two countries. The German embassy had forwarded the message from Berlin to Mexico City via Washington.

On February 28 Wilson gave the Zimmermann note to the Associated Press, which published it the next day. Wilson did this for two reasons. First, he thought the public had the right to know of this German overture. Second, it helped him gain congressional support for his armed ship bill, though he believed this legislation would probably pass in some form anyhow. On February 28, the very day Wilson released the cable, Professor William Isaac Hull, part of a peace delegation meeting with the president, asked him to appeal to the German people directly. Wilson snapped, "Dr. Hull, if you knew what I know at this present moment ... you would not ask me to attempt further peaceful dealings with the Germans" (Link, 1965, p. 346).

Even the sinking of the *Lusitania*, much less the invasion of Belgium, did not carry the impact of the Zimmermann Telegram. Incredulity, outrage, fury—these were the dominant public reactions. As the historian Patrick Devlin notes, few Americans believed that a prosperous trade or travel on belligerent ships was worth entering such a bloody carnage. What the German foreign secretary did was to reinforce the claim that Germany actually menaced the United States "in language so crude as to be laughed at by the sophisticated but which the unsophisticated could understand. Moreover, he hit hard at the elements in America hitherto least affected by the war, those in the south for whom Mexico was not so far away and those by the Pacific where they were always afraid of infiltration by Japanese" (p. 655).

Little wonder that from every part of the land editors called for war. The powerful publisher William Randolph Hearst was very much in the minority by deeming the telegram a forgery, an argument also advanced by the German-American editor George Sylvester Viereck. According to Viereck, Zimmermann would never have used the word "please," would not have called the submarine campaign "ruthless," and would not have regarded it as necessary to preface his note with the word "confidential." He continued, "It is contrary to the German habit to divide the bearskin before they have caught the bear" (p. 139). Most of the German-language press, however, soon shared the indignation of the general populace. Furthermore, the foreign secretary undercut such defenders as Viereck when, on March 3, he blandly admitted authorship.

The Japanese embassy in Washington took pains to reaffirm its friendship for the United States, calling the cable "monstrous" and "outrageous." The Mexican foreign office had initially indicated some interest in Zimmermann's proposal, but Carranza told Eckhardt that its premature publication had made it impossible to implement. Japan reaffirmed its friendship with the United States because it feared that the United States might take seriously the Germany bid for an alliance with Japan and a positive Japanese response to that bid. There had been recent tension with Japan over Japanese immigrant penetration of California and Japan's notorious Twenty-One Demands on China, claiming special privileges in China.

Related Documents

Link, Arthur S. *The Papers of Woodrow Wilson.* 69 vols. Princeton, N.J.: Princeton University Press, 1966–1994. The result of a project unmatched in scope, this collection not only includes Wilson's own correspondence, speeches, and state papers but also documents by other leading diplomats and advisers.

Seymour, Charles, ed. *The Intimate Papers of Colonel House.* 4 vols. Boston: Houghton Mifflin, 1926–1928. Colonel House was by far Wilson's closest adviser. The documents were doctored at times by House's admiring editor and hence, if possible, need to be checked against reproductions in Link's edition of the Wilson papers. However, the Seymour edition remains a most valuable guide to this controversial and often enigmatic figure.

U.S. Department of State. *Papers Relating to the Foreign Relations of the United States.* Washington, D.C.: Government Printing Office. *The World War*, 9 vols., 1914–1919. *The Lansing Papers*, 2 vols., 1914–1920. *Foreign Relations* has long been the most crucial source for the study of American diplomacy. In these volumes are found relevant correspondence, notes, and memorandum organized by year.

Bibliography

■ Articles

Viereck, George Sylvester. "Some More Light on the Zimmermann Note." *American Weekly* 6 (April 14, 1917): 139.

■ Books

Ambrosius, Lloyd. *Wilsonian Statecraft: Theory and Practice of Liberal Internationalism during World War I.* Wilmington, Del.: Scholarly Resources, 1991.

Cecil, Lamar. *Wilhelm II.* 2 vols. Chapel Hill: University of North Carolina Press, 1989–1996.

Devlin, Patrick. *Too Proud to Fight: Woodrow Wilson's Neutrality.* New York: Oxford University Press, 1975.

Fischer, Fritz. *Germany's Aims in the First World War.* New York: W. W. Norton, 1967.

Gregory, Ross. *The Origins of American Intervention in the First World War.* New York: W. W. Norton, 1971.

Herwig, Holger H., and Neil M. Heyman. *Biographical Dictionary of World War I.* Westport, Conn.: Greenwood Press, 1982.

Link, Arthur S. *Wilson: Campaigns for Progressivism and Peace, 1916–1917.* Princeton, N.J.: Princeton University Press, 1965.

———. *Woodrow Wilson: Revolution, War, and Peace.* Wheeling, Ill.: Harlan Davidson, 1979.

May, Ernest R. *The World War and American Isolation, 1914–1917.* Cambridge, Mass.: Harvard University Press, 1959.

Tuchman, Barbara W. *The Zimmermann Telegram.* New York: Viking, 1958.

■ Web Sites

"Primary Documents." First World War.com Web site. http://www.firstworldwar.com/source. Accessed on August 28, 2007.

"The Zimmermann Telegram." Channel 4 "First World War" Web Site. http://www.channel4.com/history/microsites/F/firstworldwar/cont_cracking_3.html. Accessed on February 8, 2008.

—By Justus D. Doenecke

1. Would the United States have eventually entered the war if Germany had not sunk American ships and issued the Zimmermann Telegram? In other words, would the financial, commercial, and ideological ties with Britain and France have eventually resulted in U.S participation?

2. Given the gross imbalance in military strength between the United States and Mexico, how could Mexico have ever entertained such an alliance or even have offered the Germans submarine bases, as did Carranza in November 1916?

3. Why did Wilson not ask for a declaration of war once he learned of the cable? In his extensive war message of April 2, 1917, he devotes only one sentence to the Zimmermann Telegram.

4. At the time the Zimmermann Telegram was sent, Mexico was a government in name only, unable to exercise sovereignty of much of its territory. Germany could not even pierce the Allied defenses in France, much less cross the English Channel and invade Britain. How likely was it that Germany ever could have delivered on its commitment to help Mexico recover lost territory?

Glossary

President	the president of Mexico

Zimmermann Telegram

FROM 2nd from London # 5747.

We intend to begin on the first of February unrestricted submarine warfare. We shall endeavor in spite of this to keep the United States of America neutral. In the event of this not succeeding, we make Mexico a proposal or alliance on the following basis: make war together, make peace together, generous financial support and an understanding on our part that Mexico is to reconquer the lost territory in Texas, New Mexico, and Arizona. The settle-

ment in detail is left to you. You will inform the President of the above most secretly as soon as the outbreak of war with the United States of America is certain and add the suggestion that he should, on his own initiative, invite Japan to immediate adherence and at the same time mediate between Japan and ourselves. Please call the President's attention to the fact that the ruthless employment of our submarines now offers the prospect of compelling England in a few months to make peace.

Signed, ZIMMERMANN.

fol lit

8pt

~~ADDRESS.~~

GENTLEMEN OF THE CONGRESS:

I have called the Congress into extraordinary session because there are serious, very serious, choices of policy to be made, and made immediately, which it was neither right nor constitutionally permissible that I should assume the responsibility of making.

On the third of February last I officially laid before you the extraordinary announcement of the Imperial German Government that on and after the first day of February it was its purpose to put aside all restraints of law or of humanity and use its submarines to sink every vessel that sought to approach either the ports of Great Britain and Ireland or the western coasts of Europe or any of the ports controlled by the enemies of Germany within the Mediterranean. That had seemed to be the object of the German submarine warfare earlier in the war, but since April of last year the Imperial Government had somewhat restrained the commanders of its undersea craft in conformity with its promise then given to us that passenger boats should not be sunk and that due warning would be given to all other vessels which its submarines might seek to destroy, when no resistance was offered or escape attempted, and care taken that their crews were given at least a fair chance to save their lives in their open boats. The precautions taken were meagre and haphazard enough, as was proved in distressing instance after instance in the progress of the cruel and unmanly business, but a certain degree of restraint was observed. The new policy has swept every restriction aside. Vessels of every kind, whatever their flag, their character, their cargo, their destination, their errand, have been ruthlessly sent to the bottom without warning and without thought of help or mercy for those on board, the vessels of friendly neutrals along with those of belligerents. Even hospital ships and ships carrying relief to the sorely bereaved and stricken people of Belgium, though the latter were provided with safe conduct through the proscribed areas by the German Government itself and were distinguished by unmistakable marks of identity, have been sunk with the same reckless lack of compassion or of principle.

I was for a little while unable to believe that such things would in fact be done by any government that had hitherto subscribed to the

Woodrow Wilson's Joint Address to Congress (National Archives and Records Administration)

WOODROW WILSON: JOINT ADDRESS TO CONGRESS LEADING TO A DECLARATION OF WAR AGAINST GERMANY

"The world must be made safe for democracy."

Overview

One could argue that World War I formally began on July 28, 1914, when Austria-Hungary declared war on Serbia. Throughout the previous month, the European continent had experienced ever-increasing tension owing to the assassination of the Austrian archduke Francis Ferdinand by Serbian nationalists on June 28. Within days of the Austrian move, Germany had declared war on Russia and France, England had declared war on Germany, and Austria had declared war on Russia. By 1915 two major alliances were locked in deadly embrace: the Allies (the major powers being England, France, Russia, and Italy) and the Central powers (the major powers being Germany, Austria-Hungary, and the Ottoman Empire). On August 19, 1914, President Woodrow Wilson called upon Americans to be "impartial in thought as well as in action" (http://www.presidency.ucsb.edu/ws/index.php?pid=65382&st=&st1=), by which he meant that, regardless of their sentiments, they should keep the interests of the United States primary in their thinking.

For several years Wilson preserved his nation's neutrality and indeed sought to mediate the conflict. His task was made most difficult by German U-boat sinking of Allied ships carrying American passengers and goods and by a British blockade that involved seizures of American ships and goods, confiscation of American mail, and a blacklist of American firms doing business with the Central powers. On May 4, 1916, in what was known as the *Sussex* pledge (named after a passenger ferry that had been torpedoed by the Germans in the English Channel), Germany announced it would no longer sink Allied merchant ships without warning. Furthermore, in any such attack at sea, it would attempt to save human lives, unless the besieged ship sought to escape or offer resistance. At the same time, Germany said it would resume submarine warfare if the Allies refused to respect international law, which in effect meant that the Allies had to lift their blockade of food and raw materials bound for the Central powers.

Affairs remained in uneasy tension until February 1, 1917, when Germany announced that it was renewing unrestricted submarine assaults against all shipping—neutral as well as Allied. Germany's leadership acted on the assumption that by this action it could defeat England within several months, certainly before any American intervention could come to the rescue. By March 21 German U-boats had sunk five American merchant ships. On March 1 the U.S. State Department released the Zimmermann Telegram to the press; in this cable the German foreign secretary suggested to Mexico that they form a military alliance against the United States. After great introspection, particularly acute during the period March 12 to 20, Wilson opted on April 2 to ask Congress to recognize that a state of war existed between the United States and Germany.

Context

For several years Americans had soured on both sets of the belligerents. At first they designated Germany the prime culprit, for it was perceived as waging war in particularly ruthless fashion. Evidence included the devastation created by the German siege of the Belgian city of Louvain and the French city of Rheims, the U-boat sinking of such passenger ships as the *Lusitania* in May 1915, and efforts to sabotage American industrial plants supplying the Allies. Once tension with Germany ebbed thanks to the *Sussex* pledge of May 1916, tension with Britain increased. Britain had been successfully blocking much American trade with the Central powers within weeks after the war erupted. As the conflict continued year after year, the Allies ever expanded the list of contraband (that is, materials defined as directly supportive of an enemy's war effort), stopped merchant ships of neutral powers, hauled these craft into Allied ports, and confiscated any goods judged to be ultimately destined for its enemies. Other points of grievance included the ugly suppression of Ireland's Easter Rising of April 1916 (an attempt by rebellious Irish republicans to gain independence from Britain), a blacklist of American and Latin American firms with whom British subjects were forbidden to deal in any way, and mail seizures.

Most Americans did not adhere to the rigid neutralism exemplified by such figures as William Jennings Bryan, who resigned as secretary of state in June 1915 on the ground

1914

■ **August 4**
Britain declares war on Germany, thereby assuring that all the European powers were now at war.

■ **August 4**
Wilson proclaims American neutrality in the ongoing conflict.

1915

■ **February 4**
Germany declares a war zone around the British Isles; beginning on February 18 enemy merchant ships would be sunk on sight.

■ **February 10**
The U.S. State Department declares that it will hold Germany to strict accountability for the loss of American lives or vessels on the high seas.

■ **May 7**
A German submarine sinks British transatlantic passenger liner *Lusitania* off the Irish coast.

■ **September 1**
Germany pledges that nonresisting passenger ships would not be sunk without warning or provision made for the safety of the lives of noncombatants; this commitment was made after the United States protested the sinking of the *Arabic*, a British passenger ship downed off the Irish coast on August 19.

1916

■ **May 4**
In the wake of the *Sussex* incident, Germany pledges that U-boats will observe rules of visit and search before sinking nonresisting Allied merchant vessels; Germany warns, however, that submarine warfare might be resumed if the United States does not compel the British to lift its blockade of food and raw materials.

---

that the Wilson administration was too confrontational with the Germans. They also did not support the chauvinist posture of Theodore Roosevelt, who sought to defend American rights by force. Until the eve of American entry into the war, much of the public sought a middle ground, hoping to avoid war while preserving the nation's honor.

About the Author

Thomas Woodrow Wilson, the son of a Presbyterian minister, was born on December 28, 1856 in Staunton, Virginia. Wilson grew up in various southern cities and spent a year at Davidson College in Charlotte, North Carolina. He entered the College of New Jersey (named Princeton University in 1896) and graduated in 1879. He spent a year at the University of Virginia law school and was admitted to the Georgia bar, opening a law office in Atlanta. From 1883 to 1886 he studied political science at Johns Hopkins University and received a PhD. After teaching at Bryn Mawr College and Wesleyan University, he joined the Princeton faculty in 1890 and became its president in 1902. As an educator, he received national publicity for his efforts to modernize the curriculum and democratize student life. Wilson entered politics after falling afoul of powerful alumni and the graduate dean, Andrew Fleming West.

Wilson ran on the Democratic ticket and was elected governor of New Jersey in 1910. He again secured national visibility, this time as a political reformer attacking boss rule and corporate power. In 1912 he received the Democratic presidential nomination. Because of a split in Republican ranks between President William Howard Taft, running on the regular party ticket, and the former president Theodore Roosevelt, running as the Progressive Party candidate, Wilson swept into office, carrying both houses of Congress as well. His first term was marked by many domestic reforms, including the Underwood-Simmons Tariff, the Federal Reserve Act, the Federal Trade Commission Act, the Clayton Antitrust Act, the Federal Farm Loan Act, the Adamson Act (an eight-hour day for railroad workers), workman's compensation, and a child labor bill. Pursuing an active foreign policy, he sent troops to occupy Haiti in 1915 and the Dominican Republic in 1916. In an effort to depose Mexican dictator General Victoriano Huerta in 1915, he occupied Vera Cruz and a year later sent General John J. Pershing across the Mexican border to capture Mexican outlaw, Francisco ("Pancho") Villa.

Wilson was able to avoid direct American participation in World War I for over two and a half years, but he felt his hand forced in March 1917 by the sinking of three American ships. Once the United States entered the conflict, Wilson proved to be a most vigorous leader. Almost immediately, he fostered Selective Service, a measure that gave the president authorization to conscript men into military service, which resulted in the creation of an American Expeditionary Force that eventually totaled two million. He appointed a host of able, if occasionally controversial executives, among them the food administrator Herbert Hoover and the fuel administrator Harry Garfield. Others included Bernard Baruch as chairman of the War Industries Board, George Creel as chairman of the Committee on Public Information, and Treasury Secretary William Gibbs McAdoo as director general of the railroads.

Peacemaking proved more difficult. He delivered his own peace program on January 8, 1918, in an address to Congress. Here he propounded the Fourteen Points that would serve as his blueprint for a new, more democratic international order. Once the armistice of November 11, 1918, was signed, he traveled to Paris, there to bargain with such formidable national leaders as David Lloyd George of Britain, Georges Clemenceau of France, and Vittorio Orlando of Italy. The resulting Treaty of Versailles fell far short of Wilson's expectations, though he hoped that the newly created League of Nations, an integral part of the treaty, in time would alleviate major injustices. In this hope he was sorely disappointed, indeed devastated, for the Senate voted the treaty down in November 1919 and again in March 1920. In the meantime, exhausted by a national speaking tour to promote the League of Nations, he suffered a devastating stroke on October 2, 1919. Thereafter he was incapacitated, unable to devote significant time to the presidential office. On February 3, 1924, he died in Washington, D.C.

Explanation and Analysis of the Document

In paragraph 1 Wilson stresses that he is calling Congress into extraordinary session concerning a grave matter that needs immediate action. In paragraph 2 he notes his address to Congress on February 3, 1917, in which he announced that Germany has resumed unrestricted submarine warfare against both neutral and Allied shipping as of February 1. For the past nine months Germany had been most cautious. On April 26, 1916, because of the *Sussex* crisis, Ambassador Bernstorff learned from Berlin that the Imperial Government might be prepared to conduct all submarine operations according to the rules of cruiser warfare, and Germany made a formal pledge to this effect on May 4. That is, Germany would not sink passenger vessels and would give due warning to all other vessels that would not resist capture or attempt to escape. Between June 1 and September 24 German submarines had sunk 277 vessels of all nationalities. Sixty-six neutral vessels were included, fifteen of which were reportedly sunk without warning, and eighty-four lives were lost. Hence, while the Germans were avoiding attacks on passenger steamers, they were constantly violating the law of the seas with respect to other ships. In fact, during the week before the presidential election of November 1916, reports reached the State Department concerning the sinking of the following Allied ships: *Rowanmore*, *Marina*, *Rievaulx Abbey*, *Strathtay*, *Antwerpian*, and *Arabia*. All were sunk in accordance with the rules of cruiser warfare, but all had Americans onboard.

In announcing Germany's "new policy" of unrestricted submarine warfare on January 31, 1917, Wilson charges

Time Line

1917

■ **January 22**
Wilson delivers his "peace without victory" speech to the Senate ("Woodrow Wilson: Address to the Senate of the United States," http://www. presidency.ucsb.edu/ws/index. php?pid=65396&st=&st1=), in which he calls for naval disarmament, freedom of the seas, and the establishment of an international organization to guarantee an enduring world peace.

■ **January 31**
Johann von Bernstorff, German ambassador to the United States, notifies Secretary of State Robert Lansing that Germany will resume unrestricted submarine warfare against all neutral and Allied shipping effective February 1.

■ **February 3**
In an address to Congress, Wilson announces severance of diplomatic relations with Germany, a measure endorsed by the Senate on February 7 by a vote of 78 to 5.

■ **February 25**
A German submarine sinks the British passenger liner *Laconia* 150 miles off the Irish coast; two American lives are lost.

■ **February 26**
Wilson asks Congress for the authority to arm American merchantmen to deter German submarine attacks; on March 1 the House passes the bill 403 to 13, but in the Senate twelve senators filibuster the bill until the session ends on March 4.

■ **March 1**
The U.S. State Department releases news of the Zimmermann Telegram, written on January 19, to the press.

■ **March 12**
The U.S. State Department announces that all American merchant vessels traveling through war zones would be armed, taking the position that under statute the president has authority irrespective of specific congressional authorization; the American steamer the *Algonquin* is sunk off the British Isles without warning.

Time Line

1917

■ **April 2**
Wilson delivers his war message.

■ **June 14**
General John J. Pershing, commander of American Expeditionary Force, arrives in Paris.

■ **November 7**
The Bolshevik Revolution overturns the Russian provisional government.

1918

■ **January 8**
President Wilson presents his Fourteen Points to Congress.

■ **March 21**
Germans begin their spring offensive.

■ **June 6–July 1**
Americans fight their first sizable action at Belleau Wood.

■ **July 18–August 6**
The Allies undertake the Aisne-Marne offensive, marking the turning point of the war.

■ **November 11**
The armistice marks the cessation of hostilities.

1919

■ **January 18**
The Paris Peace Conference opens.

■ **June 28**
Germany signs Versailles Treaty.

of their limited space, submarines were unable to operate in this manner. They possessed thin hulls and were forced to sail at a slow speed; surfacing would expose them to being rammed by an enemy merchant or passenger ship. Their tight quarters would prevent them from picking up any survivors. Moreover, given the nature of such sea warfare, submarines would themselves be put in danger were they to take the time to discern enemy ships carrying contraband from those that did not. By the beginning of 1917 Wilson was not totally inflexible, recognizing Germany's right to attack armed ships or belligerent merchantmen while still sparing passenger ships.

He asserts, "Property can be paid for; the lives of peaceful and innocent people cannot be." Here he recognizes that the British had stopped American ships carrying goods bound for the Central powers, seizing and holding their cargoes. At the same time, he stresses that Germany had committed the more heinous offense of killing passengers and merchant seamen.

Paragraph 3 accuses Germany of waging "war against all nations," as American merchant ships were being sunk and "American lives taken." Wilson's definitive biographer, Arthur S. Link, finds that Wilson would have acquiesced had Germany limited its U-boat attacks to armed ships or belligerent merchantmen while sparing passenger ships and continuing cruiser-type operations against neutral merchantmen. In short, he would have accepted a violation of the *Sussex* pledge. What Wilson would not tolerate was the waging of naval warfare upon peaceful neutral shipping.

Although Wilson does not mention any craft by name, at the time of his address several vessels had been sunk. First was the *Housatonic*, hit on February 3 off the Isles of Scilly near the tip of southwestern Britain. The German U-boat gave warning, and no lives were lost. On February 12 the schooner *Lyman M. Law* was struck off the coast of Sardinia; however, warning was again given, and no lives were lost. By this time American commercial ships were fearful of venturing on the high sea; goods marked for export started piling up in warehouses.

On March 14 news reached the United States that a German U-boat, without warning, had sunk the *Algonquin*, an American steamer bound for London, sixty-five miles west of the British Isles. Although there was no loss of life and survivors were rescued after twenty-seven hours, the British historian Patrick Devlin writes, "It was not the most ruthless use of the submarine, but it was indubitably an overt act" (p. 663). Two days later, the *Vigilancia*, bound for Le Havre with a general cargo, was torpedoed without warning off Britain's southwest coast. Fifteen crewmembers were drowned while launching lifeboats, while the rest landed in the Isles of Scilly two days later, suffering greatly from exposure. On March 17 the *City of Memphis* was sunk off the coast of Ireland, though in this case the ship had been warned and there were no casualties. On March 18 the *Illinois* met with the same fate, being attacked off Alderney in the English Channel near France. There were no deaths; one crewmember was wounded. By now Wilson is convinced that Germany intends to destroy all commerce and

that Germany has "swept every restriction aside," ruthlessly sinking "vessels of every kind, whatever their flag, their character, their cargo, their destination, their errand." Even hospital ships and those sending relief supplies to occupied Belgium were not exempt. He expresses incredulity that such deeds would be performed by "any government that had hitherto subscribed to the humane practices of civilized nations" but finds himself forced to conclude that "German submarine warfare against commerce is a warfare against mankind."

Wilson then accuses Germany of violating international law. Here he is referring to the long-honored obligation of a warship to "visit and search"—that is, to board the neutral or enemy merchant ship and make provision for the safety of noncombatants before sinking any craft. Because

President Woodrow Wilson addressing Congress in 1917 (Library of Congress)

human life in the broad war zones. Still, in his war message, the chief executive endorses restraint and says, "We must put excited feeling away." The United States would not be motivated by revenge or sheer demonstration of physical might, but rather by "the vindication of the right, of human right, of which we are only a single champion."

In paragraph 4 Wilson explains why his policy of armed neutrality, proposed on February 26 and implemented on March 12, could not work. In letters to several people late in March, he had claimed that any defense of neutral rights must involve attacking submarines on sight, which is "practically to commit an act of war" (Link, 1965, p. 412). Now in his address to Congress, he notes that the Germans had intimated they would treat American armed merchantmen as pirates. Therefore, armed neutrality "is practically certain to draw us into the war without either the rights or the effectiveness of belligerents. There is one choice we cannot make, we are incapable of making: we will not choose the path of submission." At exactly this point Chief Justice Edward D. White led the assemblage in widespread applause. Continuing, Wilson contends that Germany's assault upon American lives and property so flagrantly denied American rights that only war could alleviate the situation. At stake are "the most sacred rights of our Nation and our people," for "the wrongs against which we now array ourselves are no common wrongs; they cut to the very roots of human life."

In paragraph 5 Wilson comes to the crux of the entire address. He calls upon Congress to recognize that a state of war already exists between the United States and Germany. Contrary to myth, Wilson is not asking Congress to declare war. His close adviser, Colonel Edward M. House, told the president several days previously that if Wilson left a declaration up to the Congress, he would simply create "acrimonious debate" (Seymour, p. 404). The chief executive asks that the nation be put immediately on a war footing. By the time Wilson spoke of America's duty to "bring the Government of the German Empire to terms and end the war," the entire chamber again burst into applause.

Paragraphs 6 to 8 develop the need for quick mobilization. Necessary steps include extending "the most liberal financial credit" to the Allies, fully equipping the navy, and adding 500,000 men to the army, preferably chosen through "universal liability to service." To prevent inflation, the war should be financed by taxes rather than through vast war loans. Wilson then moves to the need to supply the Allies with all needed materials. In paragraph 9 he outlines his war aims. After referring to his speeches of January 22, February 3, and February 26, 1917, he calls for vindicating "the principles of peace and justice in the life of the world as against selfish and autocratic power." He accuses "autocratic governments backed by organized force" of ignoring the will of their people in their efforts to "menace" the "peace and freedom" of the world's peoples. "Nations and their governments" must be held to the same "standards of conduct and responsibility" to which one holds individuals.

Wilson develops this notion in paragraph 10, where he denies that the German people were responsible for a conflict that, in reality, was "waged in the interests of dynasties or of little groups of ambitious men who were accustomed to use their fellow men as pawns and tools." Paragraph 11 centers on German espionage and sabotage efforts within the United States. Wilson speaks in general terms, though sufficient incidents had taken place to cause alarm. Unaccountable factory explosions had taken place, including a dozen in DuPont properties during 1916 alone. Two arms plants at Bridgeport, Connecticut; munitions works at the Bethlehem Steel plant at Newcastle, Pennsylvania; and a war materiel depot at Black Tom Island in New York Harbor were also hit. In April 1916 eight men were arrested in New Jersey on a charge of placing firebombs in the cargoes of ships sailing from American ports. The attempted assassination of the financier J. P. Morgan, Jr., whose firm negotiated major Allied loans, added to general public alarm. Such activities were impossible, Wilson claims in his war address, when a public demands full disclosure concerning the activities of its government.

In paragraph 12 Wilson calls for a "a steadfast concert for peace" manifested in a "partnership of democratic nations," though he expresses himself in extremely vague terms, such as "a league of honor, a partnership of opinion." On May 27, 1916, in a speech before the League to Enforce Peace, he had been far more concrete, endorsing a "universal association of the nations" to maintain the freedom of the seas and "to prevent any war begun either contrary to treaty covenants or without warning and full submission of the causes to the opinion of the world—a virtual guarantee of territorial integrity and political independence" (http://www.presidency.ucsb.edu/ws/index.php?pid=65391&st=&st1=).

The president then turns abruptly in paragraph 13 to the Russian Revolution of March 1917. Triggered by bread riots on February 24 in the Russian capital of Petrograd (the former Saint Petersburg), the rebellion toppled the whole czarist government in four days. A provisional government was formed that proclaimed civil liberties, announced a program of far-reaching social reforms, and sought to prosecute the war with renewed vigor. Wilson is delighted that he would not have to experience the embarrassment of having a despotic czarist regime as an ally. He claims that Russia had always been "democratic at heart, in all the vital habits of her thought, in all the intimate relationships of her people." The recently deposed Romanov government "was not in fact Russian in origin, character, or purpose." The president reveals himself as markedly ignorant of Russia's military weakness and widespread peace sentiment, factors that would trigger the Bolshevik Revolution in November 1917.

Paragraph 14 returns to the matter treated in paragraph 11, that of German espionage. Although Wilson mentions no names, he refers to "official agents of the Imperial Government." In December 1915 both the military attaché Captain Franz von Papen and the naval attaché Captain Karl Boy-Ed were deported on the ground that they were involved in espionage activities. Doctor Heinrich F. Albert, commercial attaché of the German embassy who directed German espionage in the United States, was also expelled from the United States once the American Secret Service, following him in July 1915 in Manhattan, snatched a briefcase full of incriminating data. The "intercepted note to the German Minister at Mexico City" obviously refers to the Zimmermann Telegram.

In paragraph 15 Wilson returns to the matter of American war aims, this time supplying more detail. He begins his presentation by claiming that the mere existence of Imperial Germany, a "natural foe to liberty," in itself threatened the world's democracies. In contrast, the United States would be fighting for "the ultimate peace of the world"; "the liberation of its peoples, the German peoples included"; and the "rights of nations great and small and the privilege of men everywhere to choose their way of life and of obedience." Upon the words "The world must be made safe for democracy," Senator John Sharp Williams of Mississippi began clapping, a move soon imitated by the entire chamber.

Paragraph 16 assures the world that the United States sought no spoils—to use Wilson's language, "no conquest," "no dominion," "no indemnities," and "no material compensation." Its only goal was to advance "the rights of mankind." Wilson then turns in paragraph 17 to the question of Austria-Hungary, Germany's leading ally. Because the Austrian government had not engaged in submarine warfare against Americans, he sought to postpone any declaration of war against it. At the same time, because Austria had endorsed the German U-boat effort, he could not receive Austria's ambassador-designate, Count Adam Tarnowski. He stresses again that the United States has been forced to enter the war, for "there are no other means of defending our rights."

In paragraph 18 Wilson affirms his friendship for the people of Germany, while making an implicit juxtaposition between people and rulers. He then moves to the sensitive matter of the German-American community, which in 1917 was a distinct entity carefully preserving its own identity. The 1910 census marked well over eight million people either born in Germany or possessing a German parent, a sum composing nearly 10 percent of America's total population. They were disproportionately located in such major northern cities as New York, Chicago, Cincinnati, Milwaukee, and St. Louis; read about five hundred German language newspapers; and were organized in such groups as the National German-American Alliance. The president calls upon his fellow Americans to extend their friendship to this group, most of whom were "as true and loyal Americans as if they had never known any other fealty or allegiance." Yet if "a lawless and malignant few" acted disloyally, they would face a "stern repression."

Paragraphs 19 and 20 show Wilson warning of the "many months of fiery trial and sacrifice" lying ahead. He then concludes on a lofty note, saying that American blood

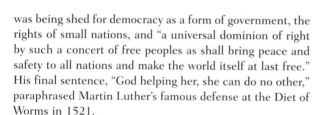

"Armed neutrality is ineffectual enough at best."

(Paragraph 4)

"The world must be made safe for democracy."

(Paragraph 15)

"It is a fearful thing to lead this great peaceful people into war."

(Paragraph 19)

"The right is more precious than peace."

(Paragraph 20)

"God helping her, she can do no other."

(Paragraph 20)

was being shed for democracy as a form of government, the rights of small nations, and "a universal dominion of right by such a concert of free peoples as shall bring peace and safety to all nations and make the world itself at last free." His final sentence, "God helping her, she can do no other," paraphrased Martin Luther's famous defense at the Diet of Worms in 1521.

Audience

Wilson's immediate audience was the members of Congress—both the Senate and the House—whose votes he needed to prosecute the war against Germany. Both houses were under Democratic Party control, so blatant partisanship could be minimized. At the same time, certain key party members were far more anti-interventionist than Wilson had ever been; among them were House majority leader Claude Kitchin of North Carolina; chairman of the powerful Senate Foreign Relations Committee, William J. Stone of Missouri; and Senator James K. Vardaman of Mississippi. The same was true for House minority leader James R. Mann of Illinois and certain Republicans of progressive leanings, such as Senators Robert M. La Follette of Wisconsin and George W. Norris of Nebraska. In March 1916 Wilson had to exercise all his political leverage to prevent Congress from passing a resolution introduced by Democratic Representative Jeff McLemore of Texas; it

requested the president to warn Americans not to travel on armed belligerent vessels. He had to exert similar pressure to block a similar resolution offered by Democratic Senator Thomas P. Gore of Oklahoma.

Wilson was also speaking to the American people and offering a rationale as to why the United States must enter the conflict. Admittedly, public opinion played a mostly negligible role in Wilson's own decision for war. Certainly, much of the urban press as well as many senators became belligerent once the Zimmermann cable became known, a sentiment reinforced on March 18 in the wake of the sinking of the three American ships on that day. But Arthur S. Link, Wilson's biographer, finds no "great, overwhelming, and irresistible national demand" to enter the conflict (1965, p. 411). Link argues that even as late as April 1, 1917, "the majority of people held firmly for peace" (1954, p. 275). Link continues in saying that popular belligerency, encouraged by Theodore Roosevelt's demand for immediate entry, was just beginning to burgeon as Wilson was making his own decision. Wilson hoped that his emphasis on what he called "the vindication of ... human right" as well as the altruistic nature of America's war aims would win over recalcitrant countrymen.

There was a third audience as well: world opinion. While he was obviously no longer endorsing a "peace without victory," he was putting the Allies on notice that the United States was fighting for "a universal dominion of right," not for territorial or commercial gain. He also wanted to absolve the German people, whom he portrayed as innocent of the warlike activities of their government. Similarly, he sought to stress that the new democratic Russia fully shared his goals of peace, justice, and freedom.

Impact

The speech met with strong congressional approval. The Republican Senator Henry Cabot Lodge of Massachusetts, who had long found Wilson far too conciliatory toward the Central powers, immediately told him, "Mr. President, you have expressed in the loftiest manner possible the sentiments of the American people" (Link, 1965, p. 426). Only La Follette stood motionless, chewing gum and bearing a sardonic smile on his face.

The press backed the president, with endorsement for a declaration of a state of war being vigorous and unanimous, according to the *Literary Digest*. Even German-American papers concurred; Link writes, "All public reactions indicated that the President had voiced the deepest thoughts and convictions and highest resolves of a united people" (1965, pp. 427–428). During the 1916 campaign Theodore Roosevelt had publicly claimed that Wilson had acted little better than a coward by failing to confront Germany head on; now the former president believed that Wilson's message would "rank in history among the great state papers" (*New York World*, p. 3).

Despite the warm reception for the speech itself, however, there was considerable dissent, particularly in German-American areas. In one such enclave—Sheboygan, Wisconsin—a referendum went 4,112 to 17 against a war resolution. In Manitowoc, Wisconsin, the vote was 1,460 to 15. On April 2, Socialists meeting in New York's Carnegie Hall booed upon hearing that Wilson had asked for a declaration of war.

At ten o'clock on the morning of April 4, a debate began in the Senate that lasted well into the night. Most members wanted to be on record in favor of the war resolution, which was introduced by Democratic Senator Thomas S. Martin of Virginia. The document argued that the German government had thrust a state of war upon the United States. Hence, the president was authorized "to employ the entire naval and military forces of the United States and the resources of the Government to carry on war against the Imperial German Government" (U.S. Congress, p. 200). There was some dissent. Republican Senator George Norris of Nebraska took a sharp swipe at the stress on maritime rights, claiming that the nation was "about to put the dollar sign upon the American flag" (qtd. in Link, 1965, p. 430). In a four-hour speech, La Follette accused Wilson of being unneutral and claimed that the vast majority of Americans opposed entering the conflict, at which point Democrat James A. Reed of Missouri accused the Nebraska senator of treason. Still, at exactly 11:11 PM, the motion passed 82 to 6.

Two days later, on April 6, it was the House's turn to vote on the same resolution. About one hundred members spoke on the matter. Majority leader Kitchin was one of twenty who voiced opposition. On April 4, which was Good Friday, the war resolution passed 383 to 50. Much opposition came from the Midwest, with, for example, all of Wisconsin's delegation being in the minority. Republican Jeanette Rankin of Montana, the first female congresswoman in American history, sobbed as she voted against the declaration. On April 6 Wilson signed the resolution, thereby leading his country into what was long called the Great War.

Related Documents

Page, Walter H. *The Life and Letters of Walter Hines Page*, 3 vols., ed. Burton J. Hendrick. Garden City, N.Y.: Doubleday, 1922–1926. Page, who served as American ambassador to Britain from 1913 to 1918, was such an extreme partisan of the Allied cause that the Wilson administration often ignored his advice. The reader nonetheless gets a good feel of the war as seen from London.

Roosevelt, Theodore. *The Letters of Theodore Roosevelt*, 8 vols., ed. Elting Morison and John Morton Blum. Cambridge, Mass.: Harvard University Press, 1951–1954. In his private correspondence, Roosevelt is even more vitriolic toward Wilson's foreign policy than he was in his speeches and articles.

Seymour, Charles, ed. *The Intimate Papers of Colonel House*, 4 vols. Boston: Houghton Mifflin, 1926. House was Wilson's closest adviser. At times the documents were doctored by House's admiring editor. Hence, when possible, they need to be checked against reproductions in Link's edition of the Wilson papers. The Seymour edition, however, remains a most valuable guide to this controversial and often enigmatic figure.

U.S. Department of State. *Papers Relating to the Foreign Relations of the United States*. Washington, D.C.: Government Printing Office. *The World War*, 9 vols., 1914–1919. *The Lansing Papers*, 2 vols., 1914–1920. *Foreign Relations* has been the most crucial source for the study of American diplomacy. Here are found relevant correspondence, notes, and memorandum organized by year.

Wilson, Woodrow. *The Papers of Woodrow Wilson*, 69 vols., ed. Arthur S. Link et al. Princeton, N.J.: Princeton University Press, 1966–1994. This collection includes not only Wilson's own correspondence, speeches, and state papers but also documents by other leading diplomats and advisers.

Bibliography

■ **Articles**
New York World, April 4, 1917.

■ **Books**
Ambrosius, Lloyd. *Wilsonian Statecraft: Theory and Practice of Liberal Internationalism during World War I*. Wilmington, Del.: Scholarly Resources, 1991.

von Bernstorff, Johann H. *My Three Years in America*. New York: Scribner, 1920.

Cooper, John Milton, Jr. *The Warrior and the Priest: Woodrow Wilson and Theodore Roosevelt*. Cambridge, Mass.: Belknap Press of Harvard University Press, 1983.

Devlin, Patrick. *Too Proud to Fight: Woodrow Wilson's Neutrality*. New York: Oxford University Press, 1975.

Gregory, Ross. *The Origins of American Intervention in the First World War*. New York: W. W. Norton, 1971.

Lansing, Robert. *War Memoirs of Robert Lansing, Secretary of State*. Indianapolis, Ind.: Bobbs-Merrill, 1935.

Link, Arthur S. *Woodrow Wilson and the Progressive Era, 1910–1917*. New York: Harper, 1954.

———. *Wilson*. Vol. 3: *The Struggle for Neutrality, 1914–1915*. Princeton, N.J.: Princeton University Press, 1960.

———. *Wilson*. Vol. 4: *Confusions and Crises, 1915–1916*. Princeton, N.J.: Princeton University Press, 1964.

———. *Wilson*. Vol. 5: *Campaigns for Progressivism and Peace, 1916–1917*. Princeton, N.J.: Princeton University Press, 1965.

———. *Woodrow Wilson: Revolution, War, and Peace*. Wheeling, Ill.: Harlan Davidson, 1979.

May, Ernest R. *The World War and American Isolation, 1914–1917*. Cambridge, Mass.: Harvard University Press, 1959.

Seymour, Charles. *American Neutrality, 1914–1917: Essays on the Causes of American Intervention in the World War*. New Haven, Conn.: Yale University Press, 1935.

Tansill, Charles C. *America Goes to War*. Boston: Little, Brown, 1938.

U.S. Congress. *Congressional Record*. 65th Cong., 1st sess., 1917. Vol. 55.

■ **Web Sites**

"Primary Documents—1914–17." First World War Web site.
   http://www.firstworldwar.com/source. Accessed on August 25, 2007.

"Woodrow Wilson (1856–1924)." Miller Center of Public Affairs at the University of Virginia "American President Online Reference Resource" Web site.
   http://www.millercenter.virginia.edu/academic/americanpresident/wilson. Accessed on August 25, 2007.

"Woodrow Wilson: Address Delivered at the First Annual Assemblage of the League to Enforce Peace." The American Presidency Project Web site.
   http://www.presidency.ucsb.edu/ws/index.php?pid=65391&st=&st1=. Accessed on February 11, 2008.

"Woodrow Wilson: Address to the Senate of the United States: 'A World League for Peace' (January 22, 1917)." The American Presidency Web site.
   http://www.presidency.ucsb.edu/ws/index.php?pid=65396&st=&st1=. Accessed on February 11, 2008.

Woodrow Wilson International Center for Scholars Web site.
   http://www.wilsoncenter.org. Accessed on August 25, 2007.

"Woodrow Wilson: Message on Neutrality (August 19, 1914)." The American Presidency Project Web site.
   http://www.presidency.ucsb.edu/ws/index.php?pid=65382&st=&st1=. Accessed on February 11, 2008.

—By Justus D. Doenecke

Questions for Further Study

1. Wilson thought the world was approaching an era "in which it will be insisted that the same standards of conduct and of responsibility for wrong done shall be observed among nations and their governments that are observed among the individual citizens of civilized states." Can any nation ever act according to such criteria?

2. Wilson juxtaposed Germany's rulers to "the German people" whom he said were ignorant of how their nation entered the conflict. Is this picture of the peace-loving nature of any public accurate, then or today?

3. Wilson implied that World War I was "provoked and waged in the interest of dynasties or of the little groups of ambitious men who were accustomed to use their fellow men as pawns and tools." Was this the reason for the outbreak of the conflict? Was he implying that the kaiser's regime alone prevented the triumph of international peace, order, and justice?

4. Wilson said, "A steadfast concert for peace can never be maintained except by a partnership of democratic nations." Can one assume that democracies always seek peace? Conversely, can one presume that nondemocratic states could never maintain such a peace?

5. Wilson claimed the United States was fighting for "a universal dominion of right by such a concert of free peoples as shall bring peace and safety to all nations and make the world itself at last free." Can such a goal ever possibly be attained? Can such a concert exist without the very alliance system the president spurned?

6. In the senatorial debate over the war resolution held on April 4, Republican Senator William E. Borah of Idaho remarked, "Suffice it to say now that there can, to my mind, be but one sufficient reason for committing this country to war, and that is the honor and security of our own people and our own Nation.… I join no crusade; I seek or accept no alliances" (U.S. Congress, p. 253). Should a nation ever fight for more abstract goals than those posited by Borah?

accredited	appointed as ambassador to foreign government
animus	hostility
autocracy	despotism; government by single person having unlimited power
belligerents	nations engaged in war
compensation	something given or received as an equivalent for a loss, service, or debt
credit	loan
cruisers	fast warships with a long cruising range, having less armor and firepower than a battleship
dominion	sovereignty; exercise of control
extirpate	root out
extraordinary	beyond the usual or commonplace; in this case, unscheduled
fealty	faithfulness; allegiance
forbearance	patience; restraint in the face of provocation
habitual	done constantly and repeatedly
increments	increases
liability	obligation
malignant	actively evil in nature
merchantmen	commercial ships
nullify	annul; make void
privateers	ships privately owned and manned but authorized by a government during wartime to attack and capture enemy vessels
proscribed	forbidden
punctilio	precise observance of formalities
right of dominion	the right to exclude other nations
throwing to the winds	recklessly casting aside or disregarding
vindicate	justify

Woodrow Wilson: Joint Address to Congress Leading to a Declaration of War against Germany

GENTLEMEN OF THE CONGRESS:

I have called the Congress into extraordinary session because there are serious, very serious, choices of policy to be made, and made immediately, which it was neither right nor constitutionally permissible that I should assume the responsibility of making.

On the third of February last I officially laid before you the extraordinary announcement of the Imperial German Government that on and after the first day of February it was its purpose

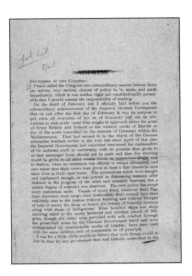

to put aside all restraints of law or of humanity and use its submarines to sink every vessel that sought to approach either the ports of Great Britain and Ireland or the western coasts of Europe or any of the ports controlled by the enemies of Germany within the Mediterranean. That had seemed to be the object of the German submarine warfare earlier in the war, but since April of last year the Imperial Government had somewhat restrained the commanders of its undersea craft in conformity with its promise then given to us that passenger boats should not be sunk and that due warning would be given to all other vessels which its submarines might seek to destroy when no resistance was offered or escape attempted, and care taken that their crews were given at least a fair chance to save their lives in their open boats. The precautions taken were meager and haphazard enough, as was proved in distressing instance after instance in the progress of the cruel and unmanly business, but a certain degree of restraint was observed. The new policy has swept every restriction aside. Vessels of every kind, whatever their flag, their character, their cargo, their destination, their errand, have been ruthlessly sent to the bottom: without warning and without thought of help or mercy for those on board, the vessels of friendly neutrals along with those of belligerents. Even hospital ships and ships carrying relief to the sorely bereaved and stricken people of Belgium, though the latter were provid-ed with safe conduct through the proscribed areas by the German Government itself and were distinguished by unmistakable marks of identity, have been sunk with the same reckless lack of compassion or of principle. I was for a little while unable to believe that such things would in fact be done by any government that had hitherto subscribed to the humane practices of civilized nations. International law had its origin in the attempt to set up some law which would be respected and observed upon the seas, where no nation had right of dominion and where lay the free highways of the world.... This minimum of right the German Government has swept aside under the plea of retaliation and necessity and because it had no weapons which it could use at sea except these which it is impossible to employ as it is employing them without throwing to the winds all scruples of humanity or of respect for the understandings that were supposed to underlie the intercourse of the world. I am not now thinking of the loss of property involved, immense and serious as that is, but only of the wanton and wholesale destruction of the lives of noncombatants, men, women, and children, engaged in pursuits which have always, even in the darkest periods of modern history, been deemed innocent and legitimate. Property can be paid for; the lives of peaceful and innocent people cannot be. The present German submarine warfare against commerce is a warfare against mankind.

It is a war against all nations. American ships have been sunk, American lives taken, in ways which it has stirred us very deeply to learn of, but the ships and people of other neutral and friendly nations have been sunk and overwhelmed in the waters in the same way. There has been no discrimination. The challenge is to all mankind. Each nation must decide for itself how it will meet it. The choice we make for ourselves must be made with a moderation of counsel and a temperateness of judgment befitting our character and our motives as a nation. We must put excited feeling away. Our motive will not be revenge or the victorious assertion of the physical might of the nation, but only the vindication of right, of human right, of which we are only a single champion.

When I addressed the Congress on the twenty-sixth of February last I thought that it would suffice to assert our neutral rights with arms, our right to use the seas against unlawful interference, our right to keep our people safe against unlawful violence. But armed neutrality, it now appears, is impracticable. Because submarines are in effect outlaws when used as the German submarines have been used against merchant shipping, it is impossible to defend ships against their attacks as the law of nations has assumed that merchantmen would defend themselves against privateers or cruisers, visible craft giving chase upon the open sea. It is common prudence in such circumstances, grim necessity indeed, to endeavor to destroy them before they have shown their own intention. They must be dealt with upon sight, if dealt with at all. The German Government denies the right of neutrals to use arms at all within the areas of the sea which it has proscribed, even in the defense of rights which no modern publicist has ever before questioned their right to defend. The intimation is conveyed that the armed guards which we have placed on our merchant ships will be treated as beyond the pale of law and subject to be dealt with as pirates would be. Armed neutrality is ineffectual enough at best; in such circumstances and in the face of such pretensions it is worse than ineffectual: it is likely only to produce what it was meant to prevent; it is practically certain to draw us into the war without either the rights or the effectiveness of belligerents. There is one choice we cannot make, we are incapable of making: we will not choose the path of submission and suffer the most sacred rights of our Nation and our people to be ignored or violated. The wrongs against which we now array ourselves are no common wrongs; they cut to the very roots of human life.

With a profound sense of the solemn and even tragical character of the step I am taking and of the grave responsibilities which it involves, but in unhesitating obedience to what I deem my constitutional duty, I advise that the Congress declare the recent course of the Imperial German Government to be in fact nothing less than war against the government and people of the United States; that it formally accept the status of belligerent which has thus been thrust upon it, and that it take immediate steps not only to put the country in a more thorough state of defense but also to exert all its power and employ all its resources to bring the Government of the German Empire to terms and end the war.

What this will involve is clear. It will involve the utmost practicable cooperation in counsel and action with the governments now at war with Germany, and, as incident to that, the extension to those governments of the most liberal financial credit, in order that our resources may so far as possible be added to theirs. It will involve the organization and mobilization of all the material resources of the country to supply the materials of war and serve the incidental needs of the Nation in the most abundant and yet the most economical and efficient way possible. It will involve the immediate full equipment of the navy in all respects but particularly in supplying it with the best means of dealing with the enemy's submarines. It will involve the immediate addition to the armed forces of the United States already provided for by law in case of war at least five hundred thousand men, who should, in my opinion, be chosen upon the principle of universal liability to service, and also the authorization of subsequent additional increments of equal force so soon as they may be needed and can be handled in training. It will involve also, of course, the granting of adequate credits to the Government, sustained, I hope, so far as they can equitably be sustained by the present generation, by well conceived taxation. I say sustained so far as may be equitable by taxation because it seems to me that it would be most unwise to base the credits which will now be necessary entirely on money borrowed. It is our duty, I most respectfully urge, to protect our people so far as we may against the very serious hardships and evils which would be likely to arise out of the inflation which would be produced by vast loans.

In carrying out the measures by which these things are to be accomplished we should keep constantly in mind the wisdom of interfering as little as possible in our own preparation and in the equipment of our own military forces with the duty—for it will be a very practical duty—of supplying the nations already at war with Germany with the materials which they can obtain only from us or by our assistance. They are in the field and we should help them in every way to be effective there.

I shall take the liberty of suggesting, through the several executive departments of the Government, for the consideration of your committees, measures for the accomplishment of the several objects I have mentioned. I hope that it will be your pleasure to deal with them as having been framed after very careful thought by the branch of the Government upon which the responsibility of conducting the war and safeguarding the Nation will most directly fall.

While we do these things, these deeply momentous things, let us be very clear, and make very clear to all the world what our motives and our objects are. My own thought has not been driven from its habitual and normal course by the unhappy events of the last two months, and I do not believe that the thought of the Nation has been altered or clouded by them. I have exactly the same things in mind now that I had in mind when I addressed the Senate on the twenty-second of January last, the same that I had in mind when I addressed the Congress on the third of February and on the twenty-sixth of February. Our object now, as then, is to vindicate the principles of peace and justice in the life of the world as against selfish and autocratic power and to set up amongst the really free and selfgoverned peoples of the world such a concert of purpose and of action as will henceforth insure the observance of those principles Neutrality is no longer feasible or desirable where the peace of the world is involved and the freedom of its peoples, and the menace to that peace and freedom lies in the existence of autocratic governments backed by organized force which is controlled wholly by their will, not by the will of their people. We have seen the last of neutrality in such circumstances. We are at the beginning of an age in which it will be insisted that the same standards of conduct and of responsibility for wrong done shall be observed among nations and their governments that are observed among the individual citizens of civilized states.

We have no quarrel with the German people. We have no feeling towards them but one of sympathy and friendship. It was not upon their impulse that their government acted in entering this war. It was not with their previous knowledge or approval. It was a war determined upon as wars used to be determined upon in the old, unhappy days when peoples were nowhere consulted by their rulers and wars were provoked and waged in the interest of dynasties or of little groups of ambitious men who were accustomed to use their fellow men as pawns and tools.

Selfgoverned nations do not fill their neighbor states with spies or set the course of intrigue to bring about some critical posture of affairs which will give them an opportunity to strike and make conquest. Such designs can be successfully worked out only under cover and where no one has the right to ask

questions. Cunningly contrived plans of deception or aggression, carried, it may be, from generation to generation, can be worked out and kept from the light only within the privacy of courts or behind the carefully guarded confidences of a narrow and privileged class. They are happily impossible where public opinion commands and insists upon full information concerning all the nation's affairs.

A steadfast concert for peace can never be maintained except by a partnership of democratic nations. No autocratic government could be trusted to keep faith within it or observe its covenants. It must be a league of honor, a partnership of opinion. Intrigue would eat its vitals away; the plottings of inner circles who could plan what they would and render account to no one would be a corruption seated at its very heart. Only free peonies can hold their purpose and their honor steady to a common end and prefer the interests of mankind to any narrow interest of their own.

Does not every American feel that assurance has been added to our hope for the future peace of the world by the wonderful and heartening things that have been happening within the last few weeks in Russia? Russia was known by those who knew it best to have been always in fact democratic at heart, in all the vital habits of her thought, in all the intimate relationships of her people that spoke their natural instinct, their habitual attitude towards life. The autocracy that crowned the summit of her political structure, long as it had stood and terrible as was the reality of its power, was not in fact Russian in origin, character, or purpose; and now it has been shaken off and the great, generous Russian people have been added in all their naive majesty and might to the forces that are fighting for freedom in the world, for justice, and for peace. Here is a fit partner for a League of Honor.

One of the things that has served to convince us that the Prussian, autocracy was not and could never be our friend is that from the very outset of the present war it has filled our unsuspecting communities and even our offices of government with spies and set criminal intrigues everywhere afoot against our national unity of counsel, our peace Within and without, our industries and our commerce. Indeed it is now evident that its spies were here even before the war began; and it is unhappily not a matter of conjecture but a fact proved in our courts of justice that the intrigues which have more than once come perilously near to disturbing the peace and dislocating the industries of the country have been carried on at the instigation, with the support, and even under the personal direction of official agents of the Imperial Government accredited to the Government of the United States. Even in checking these things and trying to extirpate them we have sought to put the most generous interpretation possible upon them because we knew that their source lay, not in any hostile feeling or purpose of the German people towards us (who were, no doubt, as ignorant of them as we ourselves were), but only in the selfish designs of a Government that did what it pleased and told its people nothing. But they have played their part in serving to convince us at last that that Government entertains no real friendship for us and means to act against our peace and security at its convenience. That it means to stir up enemies against us at our very doors the intercepted note to the German Minister at Mexico City is eloquent evidence.

We are accepting this challenge of hostile purpose because we know that in such a Government, following such methods, we can never have a friend; and that in the presence of its organized power, always lying in wait to accomplish we know not what purpose, there can be no assured security for the democratic Governments of the world. We are now about to accept gauge of battle with this natural foe to liberty and shall, if necessary, spend the whole force of the nation to check and nullify its pretensions and its power. We are glad, now that we see the facts with no veil of false pretense about them to fight thus for the ultimate peace of the world and for the liberation of its peoples, the German peoples included: for the rights of nations great and small and the privilege of men everywhere to choose their way of life and of obedience. The world must be made safe for democracy. Its peace must be planted upon the tested foundations of political liberty. We have no selfish ends to serve.

We desire no conquest, no dominion. We seek no indemnities for ourselves, no material compensation for the sacrifices we shall freely make. We are but one of the champions of the rights of mankind. We shall be satisfied when those rights have been made as secure as the faith and the freedom of nations can make them. Just because we fight without rancor and without selfish object, seeking nothing for ourselves but what we shall wish to share with all free peoples, we shall, I feel confident, conduct our operations as belligerents without passion and ourselves observe with proud punctilio the principles of right and of fair play we profess to be fighting for.

I have said nothing of the Governments allied with the Imperial Government of Germany because they have not made war upon us or challenged us to defend our right and our honor. The Austro-Hungarian Government has, indeed, avowed its unqualified endorsement and acceptance of the reckless and lawless submarine warfare adopted now without disguise by the Imperial German Government, and it has therefore not been possible for this Government to receive Count Tarnowski, the Ambassador recently accredited to this Government by the Imperial and Royal Government of Austria-Hungary; but that Government has not actually engaged in warfare against citizens of the United States on the seas, and I take the liberty, for the present at least, of postponing a discussion of our relations with the authorities at Vienna. We enter this war only where we are clearly forced into it because there are no other means of defending our rights.

It will be all the easier for us to conduct ourselves as belligerents in a high spirit of right and fairness because we act without animus, not in enmity towards a people or with the desire to bring any injury or disadvantage upon them, but only in armed opposition to an irresponsible government which has thrown aside all considerations of humanity and of right and is running amuck. We are, let me say again, the sincere friends of the German people, and shall desire nothing so much as the early reestablishment of intimate relations of mutual advantage between us, however hard it may be for them, for the time being, to believe that this is spoken from our hearts. We have borne with their present Government through all these bitter months because of that friendship, exercising a patience and forbearance which would otherwise have been impossible. We shall, happily, still have an opportunity to prove that friendship in our daily attitude and actions towards the millions of men and women of German birth and native sympathy who live amongst us and share our life, and we shall be proud to prove it towards all who are in fact loyal to their neighbors and to the Government in the hour of test. They are, most of them, as true and loyal Americans as if they had never known any other fealty or allegiance. They will be prompt to stand with us in rebuking and restraining the few who may be of a different mind and purpose. If there should be disloyalty, it will be dealt with with a firm hand of stern repression; but, if it lifts its head at all, it will lift it only here and there and without countenance except from a lawless and malignant few.

It is a distressing and oppressive duty, Gentlemen of the Congress, which I have performed in thus addressing you. There are, it may be many months of fiery trial and sacrifice ahead of us. It is a fearful thing to lead this great peaceful people into war, into the most terrible and disastrous of all wars, civilization itself seeming to be in the balance.

But the right is more precious than peace, and we shall fight for the things which we have always carried nearest our hearts; for democracy, for the right of those who submit to authority to have a voice in their own Governments, for the rights and liberties of small nations, for a universal dominion of right by such a concert of free peoples as shall bring peace and safety to all nations and make the world itself at last free. To such a task we can dedicate our Eves and our fortunes, every thing that we are and everything that we have, with the pride of those who know that the day has come when America is privileged to spend her blood and her might for the principles that gave her birth and happiness and the peace which she has treasured. God helping her, she can do no other.

frankness, a largeness of view, a generosity of spirit, and a universal human sympathy which must challenge the admiration of every friend of mankind; and they have refused to compound their ideals or desert others that they themselves may be safe. They call to us to say what it is that we desire, in what, if in anything, our purpose and our spirit differ from theirs; and I believe that the people of the United States would wish me to respond, with utter simplicity and frankness. Whether their present leaders believe it or not, it is our heartfelt desire and hope that some way may be opened whereby we may be privileged to assist the people of Russia to attain their utmost hope of liberty and ordered peace.

It will be our wish and purpose that the processes of peace, when they are begun, shall be absolutely open and that they shall involve and permit henceforth no secret understandings of any kind. The day of conquest and aggrandizement is gone by; so is also the day of secret covenants entered into in the interest of particular governments and likely at some unlooked-for moment to upset the peace of the world. It is this happy fact, now clear to the view of every public man whose thoughts do not still linger in an age that is dead and gone, which makes it possible for every nation whose purposes are consistent with justice and the peace of the world to avow now or at any other time the objects it has in view.

We entered this war because violations of right had occurred which touched us to the quick and made the life of our own people impossible unless they were corrected and the world secured once for all against their recurrence. What we demand in this war, therefore, is nothing peculiar to ourselves. It is that the world be made fit and safe to live in; and particularly that it be made safe for every peace-loving nation which, like our own, wishes to live its own life, determine its own institutions, be assured of justice and fair dealing by the other peoples of the world as against force and selfish aggression. All the peoples of the world are in effect partners in this interest, and for our own part we see very clearly that unless justice be done to others it will not be done to us. The programme of the world's peace, therefore, is our programme; and that programme, the only possible programme, as we see it, is this:

I. Open covenants of peace, openly arrived at, after which there shall be no private international understandings of any kind but diplomacy shall proceed always frankly and in the public view.

II. Absolute freedom of navigation upon the seas, outside territorial waters, alike in peace and in war, except as the seas may be closed in whole or in part by international action for the enforcement of international covenants.

Woodrow Wilson's Fourteen Points (National Archives and Records Administration)

WOODROW WILSON'S FOURTEEN POINTS

1918

"Unless justice be done to others it will not be done to us."

Overview

Following the assassination of Archduke Francis Ferdinand in the summer of 1914, Europe's major powers—linked into two rival alliances—mobilized their armed forces and plunged Europe into World War I. By the end of 1917, more than a million French soldiers lay dead. France's British, Russian, and Italian allies had suffered similar losses, as had their German, Austro-Hungarian, and Ottoman enemies. Still, after more than three years of war, none of these powers had publicly declared its war aims or had seriously sought a negotiated end to the war. This secrecy and determination to fight to the bitter end frustrated repeated American efforts to negotiate peace in 1916. After German submarines sank several U.S. merchant ships, President Woodrow Wilson persuaded Congress to declare war on Germany, and the United States joined the Allied coalition.

In asking Congress for a declaration of war against Germany, which he did on April 2, 1917, Wilson called for a war to make the world "safe for democracy" (http://www.ourdocuments.gov/doc.php?doc=61&page=transcript). This idealistic declaration set the United States apart from the other warring nations that fought for specific territorial goals, many of which they had outlined in secret treaties with one another. Wilson recognized that the United States would play an essential role in any Allied victory. He hoped to parlay the country's military importance into diplomatic leadership and to determine the foundations of the peace settlement and postwar international order. In an address to Congress on January 8, 1918, Wilson outlined fourteen points that he believed should be the basis of a peace agreement ending World War I. His Fourteen Points speech preempted the territorial claims of the United States' cobelligerents and successfully established his lofty goals as the starting point for peace negotiations. More than that, it marked a turning point in world politics. In Wilson's new international order, morality and law would replace self-interest; cooperation would replace conflict.

Context

The war remained deadlocked in bloody trench warfare when Wilson presented his Fourteen Points. Millions had died, and yet the frontlines had hardly moved in three years. These losses, rather than moving the warring nations to make peace, encouraged them to escalate their efforts and territorial demands so that the youths of their nations would not have died in vain. In 1915, for example, Allied leaders met in London and agreed that after victory France would receive Alsace-Lorraine and the Saar Valley, and the remaining German territory west of the Rhine would become an independent nation—a buffer. Italy would receive South Tyrol, Trieste, and other Austro-Hungarian territories. Russia would gain control of Constantinople and other Turkish territories, and other parts of the Ottoman Empire would go to Britain, France, Italy, and Greece. Germany's leaders, in turn, also hoped for substantial territorial gains, as did their Austrian and Turkish allies.

Peace movements, however, sprang up among the people in these nations and in the United States. These movements grew in size as the war continued, and their leaders presented varied suggestions for negotiating a peace settlement. Many of them also suggested creating an international organization tasked with preserving peace between nations and preventing war through collective action. Among the organizations was the League to Enforce Peace in the United States, which included former president William Howard Taft among its members, and the League of Nations Union in Great Britain.

In 1916 American efforts to negotiate peace led by both President Wilson and private citizens—including the automobile mogul Henry Ford and the noted reformer and activist Jane Addams—failed. That November, Wilson had won reelection with the slogan "He kept us out of war" (http://www.whitehouse.gov/history/presidents/ww28.html). Less than six months later, he led the nation into World War I. Yet Wilson remained suspicious of the British, French, and Italian allies and insisted that the United States remain an associated power rather than a full ally of its cobelligerents. This stance underlined Wilson's divergent war aims. Inspired by American progressives who had worked to clean up their cities, eliminate corruption, and

1914

■ **June 28**
Serbian-sponsored assassins murder the archduke Francis Ferdinand, the heir to the Austro-Hungarian throne, and his pregnant wife.

■ **July 28**
Austria-Hungary declares war on Serbia.

■ **August 1–4**
Germany declares war on Russia, France, and Belgium, and its troops invade Belgium.

■ **August 6**
Austria-Hungary declares war on Russia.

■ **September 5–10**
The German invasion of France is halted at the first battle of the Marne.

1915

■ **February 4**
Germany initiates a submarine blockade of Britain.

■ **May 7**
A German submarine sinks the passenger liner *Lusitania*, killing 1,198 crewmembers and passengers, including 128 Americans.

1916

■ **February 21– December 18**
German and French forces suffer roughly one million casualties at the battle of Verdun.

■ **March 24**
A German submarine attacks and damages the *Sussex*, a French passenger ship, and kills 50 people.

■ **May 4**
Germany, in response to American protests, issues the "*Sussex* Pledge," which states that its submarines will no longer attack passenger ships without warning.

■ **November 7**
Woodrow Wilson is reelected as president of the United States.

---

improve city services and society through collective action, Wilson hoped to remake the world and reform the international system. As he remarked in a speech to the Senate on January 22, 1917, he hoped for a "peace without victory"— a just peace that would allow the major powers to create institutions to preserve peace in the future (http://www.presidency.ucsb.edu/ws/index.php?pid=65396&st=&st1=).

About the Author

Woodrow Wilson, born on December 28, 1856, in Staunton, Virginia, grew up in a religious Presbyterian home. He attended Princeton University and graduated in 1879. After earning a law degree from the University of Virginia, he embarked on a brief legal practice but then returned to school, earning a doctoral degree in political science from Johns Hopkins University in 1886. A successful scholar, Wilson published several books, including *Congressional Government: A Study in American Politics* (1885) as well as the five-volume *History of the American People* (1902), a popular and well-regarded textbook. He taught political science at Bryn Mawr College, Wesleyan College, and Princeton University, where he served as president from 1902 to 1910. Having established a reputation as a reformer in higher education, Wilson was elected governor of New Jersey in 1910 and president of the United States in 1912. As president, Wilson established the Federal Reserve System to oversee the nation's banks and pushed a number of other progressive reforms through Congress, including the Clayton Antitrust Act, which strengthened business regulations, prohibited monopolies, and protected labor unions.

Wilson's progressive values influenced his approach to foreign policy. He refused to recognize the government of General Victoriano Huerta, who had come to power in Mexico through a violent coup, and supported Huerta's democratic opponents. After the outbreak of World War I in 1914, Wilson sought to negotiate a peaceful settlement and maintain American neutrality. He was reelected in 1916 on the slogan "He kept us out of war," but Germany's resumption of unrestricted submarine warfare in the opening months of 1917 forced Wilson to act. After German submarines sank several American merchant ships, Wilson asked Congress for a declaration of war, which Congress granted on April 6.

Confident of military victory, Wilson sought to establish the outlines of a peace settlement before the war ended, and he presented his Fourteen Points proposal, which won wide acclaim, on January 8, 1918. With the help of American troops, Allied armies turned back a German offensive and then pushed the German troops back. Germany, with its armies in retreat, appealed for peace and agreed to an armistice. In November 1918 Wilson joined other world leaders in Versailles, France, to negotiate the peace treaty. While he was forced to compromise on many of his Fourteen Points, the final treaty showed their influence and created the League of Nations. Unfortunately, the political tide had turned against Wilson during his six-month absence in France. Several prominent Republicans, who dominated the Senate after the 1918 election, opposed the treaty and U.S. membership in the League of Nations. Hoping to rally public support for the Treaty of Versailles, Wilson embarked on a nationwide speaking tour. His collapse following a speech in Pueblo, Colorado, and his subsequent stroke ended his vigorous fight for the treaty, which the Senate failed to ratify. Despite his fragile health, Wilson completed his term as president. He died three years after leaving office on February 3, 1924.

Explanation and Analysis of the Document

◆ Introduction

In his opening, Wilson seizes the moral high ground by reminding his listeners that, unlike the other warning nations, the United States is participating in the war not for selfish purposes such as acquiring new territory but rather to make the world "safe for every peace-loving nation." He establishes the United States as a moral example and implicitly challenges other nations to follow its example and to look beyond their own selfish interests. Wilson then declares that his intention is to change the international system. The old age, he declares, in which nations pursue their interests through force of arms is "dead and gone." So, too, is the network of competing alliances and secret treaties aimed at preserving a balance of power that had failed to prevent World War I. In their place Wilson offers a new system, one that would preserve peace and allow the prosperous development of all nations around the world. In this new world order, nations would treat each other with justice and as equals. The strong would not exploit the weak, and all nations would cooperate to punish aggressors and preserve peace. International opinion and the rule of law would replace alliances and national arsenals as the keys to international order, and nations would treat each other with respect and justice.

◆ Point-by-Point Analysis

Wilson then presents a point-by-point enumeration of the requirements for a peace settlement that would prevent future wars and promote international prosperity and stability. These principles, which he hopes would define the postwar international order, fall into three groups: (1) the evacuation of conquered territory, (2) territorial adjustments and the creation of new states to promote national sovereignty and self-determination, and (3) those proposals aimed at remaking the international system. Variations of those proposals in this last category had been suggested by others and embraced by liberal organizations in Europe and the United States, including the British Union of Democratic Control, the Woman's Peace Party, the League to Enforce the Peace in the United States, and the South German Social Democrats. Wilson had broached many of these ideas in previous foreign policy addresses and initiatives and had suggested the creation of a league of nations during his 1916 presidential campaign. Wilson considers

Time Line

1917

■ **February 1**
Germany announces unrestricted submarine warfare, meaning that all ships approaching Britain or France, regardless of nationality, will be attacked.

■ **February 3**
The United States severs diplomatic ties with Germany.

■ **March 1**
The Zimmermann Telegram is published in American newspapers.

■ **April 2**
Wilson asks Congress to declare on Germany a war that would "make the world safe for democracy." Congress passes the war resolution on April 6.

■ **June 26**
The first U.S. troops arrive in France.

■ **November 7**
The Bolshevik Revolution in Russia brings Communists to power.

1918

■ **January 8**
Wilson gives his Fourteen Points speech to the U.S. Congress.

■ **March 3**
Russia's new Communist government signs a peace agreement with Germany, the Treaty of Brest Litovsk, which cedes the Ukraine and Baltic states (Estonia, Latvia, and Lithuania) to Germany.

■ **October 3–4**
Germany and Austria-Hungary appeal for peace on the basis of Wilson's Fourteen Points.

■ **November 9**
Kaiser Wilhelm II abdicates his throne.

■ **November 11**
Germany, Britain, France, Italy, and the United States sign an armistice, ending the war.

1919

■ **June 28**
A peace agreement is signed at Versailles, France.

Time Line

1919

■ **September 25**
Wilson collapses following a
speech in Pueblo, Colorado,
ending his nationwide tour
promoting the Treaty of
Versailles and the League of
Nations.

1920

■ **March 19**
The U.S. Senate fails to ratify
the Treaty of Versailles.

the five points related to remaking the international system (Points I–IV and Point XIV), along with the evacuation of Belgian and Russian territory, essential to the peace. He considers the other territorial adjustments, most of which were suggested by a special committee he organized, important but open to negotiation. Wilson, who would expand on these ideas in later speeches, emphasizes that justice should govern the settlement of all issues.

◆ Points I and IV: Causes of War

The first and fourth of his Fourteen Points address what Wilson and many others considered primary causes of World War I: arms races between the major powers that provoked fear and distrust between rival nations and the secret treaties that had brought most of Europe's nations to war. In the twenty years before World War I, the world's major powers had invested increasing sums in new weapons, military technologies, and the infrastructure to support large military forces. The press routinely reported on this arms race, and arms—particularly battleships—became associated as much with status as with military power. Increasingly patriotic populations demanded that their governments match rival nations' new weapons with larger weapons of their own. The reduction of arms to the "lowest point consistent with domestic safety," Wilson notes in Point IV, would reduce tensions between nations and defuse this powder keg. It would also free industry and labor for peaceful production and trade, which would increase prosperity and further reduce tension.

As Europe's competing nations enlarged their national arsenals, they also sought allies in case war broke out. The assurance of support by secret allies helped lead to war. Austria-Hungary, certain of assistance from its German ally, remained intransigent and refused to negotiate a settlement with Serbia in 1914. Russia, with similar backing from France, also stood firm. Wilson believes that this secrecy and uncertainty helped produce war and argues in Point I that in the future all international treaties must be "open covenants"—that is, they must be announced and published so that everyone is aware of their details. Private negotiations are fine, but the final agreements must be made public.

◆ Points II and III: Free Trade

In Points II and III, Wilson proposes freedom of the seas and free trade. Both had long figured in American foreign policy. Demands for free trade helped provoke the American Revolution and then instigated conflicts between the new nation and France, the Barbary states, and Great Britain. The Monroe Doctrine (1823) opposed European colonialism so as to maintain free trade with the nations of Central and South America, while the Open Door letters circulated by U.S. Secretary of State John Hay in 1899 sought to establish free trade in China. During World War I both Britain's naval blockade of Germany and Germany's submarine campaign had interfered with American shipping and contributed to the American entry into the war.

Wilson sees freedom as a universal value and believes that free enterprise and free trade contribute to freedom and democracy in general. More than that, free trade would increase global prosperity. Nations that trade with one another would come to depend on one another, and this greater interdependence would reduce the chance of war. Nations, particularly democratic nations, bound by trade would not go to war with one another. They would solve disputes peacefully.

Wilson argues in Point II that economic blockades and boycotts would be an important tool for punishing aggressors and makes an exception for closing seas "by international action for the enforcement of international covenants." Otherwise, he advocates unfettered trade and the unrestricted use of the world's waterways. In Point XII he addresses the specific case of the Dardanelles, which the Ottoman government had periodically closed to shipping from particular nations, and demands that it be "opened as a free passage to the ships and commerce of all nations." Wilson implicitly means this to apply universally to all water passages, and he gives more weight to this in Points XI and XIII, in which he insists that Poland and Serbia receive outlets to the sea to foster economic development.

◆ Point V: Colonies

The desire for colonies had also contributed to the tense international climate that led to World War I. Germany was a relative latecomer to colonialism, and its leaders envied the large colonial empires of Britain and France. Any peace treaty would necessarily deal with the colonies of the defeated powers. In Point V, Wilson advocates "a free, open-minded, and absolutely impartial adjustment of all colonial claims" that would consider the "interests of the populations concerned," giving them "equal weight" to the "equitable claims" of the government desiring to acquire them. Demanding consideration of the opinions of colonial populations is unprecedented and anticipates the Treaty of Versailles's mandate system. in which nations receive colonies as mandates from the League of Nations, which would be tasked with supervising their rule and ensuring the preparation of colonial populations for self-government. While milder in expression than his other points, Point V shares their idealism and Wilson's hope for an international system centered on freedom, free trade, and national self-determination. While it would apply only to the colonies of Germany and the Ottoman Empire, Point V implicitly questions colonialism and advocates self-determination for all colonized peoples.

◆ Point VI: Russia

The question of Russia, which Wilson addresses in Point VI, would become more contentious. A revolution in March 1917 had established a weak democratic government in Russia, but its own internal divisions and efforts to continue the war against Germany fatally weakened it. In November 1917 Communists led by Lenin and his Bolshevik Party launched their own revolution and seized control of Russia. In December this new government concluded an armistice with Germany. Wilson hoped to keep Russia in the war, since her defeat would free German and Austrian troops to fight Italy and France.

Wilson assures Russia's new government of independence and the evacuation of its territory of German and other foreign troops, which includes some western soldiers sent to Russia to protect Allied arms shipments and prevent their falling into German or Communist hands. Wilson concludes that the "treatment accorded Russia by her sister nations in the months to come will be the acid test of their good will," and their willingness to abandon selfish aims and work for the common good. Wilson hopes that Russia will become the test case of his new international system. In this system, other nations—rather than pursuing their own interests and capitalizing on Russia's weakened state—would allow the Russian people to determine their own "political development and national policy." Events quickly outpaced Wilson's desires, however. In March 1918 the Bolsheviks, who had promised the Russian people "peace, land, and bread," signed the Treaty of Brest Litovsk, which ceded substantial territory to Germany in exchange for peace. Because Russia made separate peace with Germany and because most European leaders were suspicious of the Bolsheviks, Russia was not invited to the peace conference at Versailles.

◆ Point VII: Belgium

In Point VII, Wilson demands the evacuation of Belgium, most of which Germany had invaded and occupied as a route to invade France. Britain entered the war, in part, because it had pledged to defend Belgian neutrality, and all of the Allied nations advocated the restoration of Belgium. This is the only one of Wilson's points that was assured unanimous support among the war's victors.

◆ Points VIII and IX: French and Italian Territorial Demands

In Points VIII and IX, Wilson addresses the territorial demands of France and Italy, which are leading members of the Allied coalition. Wilson recognized that any peace settlement had to address their demands. France demanded the return of Alsace-Lorraine, seized by Germany following its victory in the Franco-Prussian War of 1870–1871, while Italy wanted to annex parts of the Austro-Hungarian Empire with large, ethnically Italian populations. Wilson

Woodrow Wilson in a 1916 photograph (Library of Congress)

saw justice in both these claims, and he certainly could not dismiss them out of hand. In his address, however, Wilson still seeks to accommodate the claims within his new international framework that privileges national self-determination. As with the lesser powers, which Wilson addresses in his next several points, the borders of the major powers could be adjusted to reflect the desires of local populations and national self-determination.

◆ Points X–XIII

In Points X–XIII, Wilson proposes substantial changes to the borders of Eastern Europe and the creation of several new states. He advocates sovereignty and independence for most of these ethnic minorities in this territory, while protecting the "autonomous development" of the Austrian, Hungarian, and Turkish peoples. Wilson demands independence and territorial integrity for Romania, Serbia, Montenegro, and unspecified other Balkan states and the reduction of the Ottoman Empire to areas of Turkish majority population. Wilson believes that this would defuse tensions among the many peoples of this region and prevent the exploitation of the weak by the strong.

Wilson elaborated on his intentions in later speeches, insisting that any territorial settlements be made for the benefits of their inhabitants and that they recognize their national aspirations whenever possible. He would later say that there must be equal justice for all peoples involved in the peace settlement, although he addressed most of his

> "*The day of conquest and aggrandizement is gone by.*"
>
> (Introduction)

> "*What we demand in this war, therefore, is nothing peculiar to ourselves. It is that the world be made fit and safe to live in; and particularly that it be made safe for every peace-loving nation which, like our own, wishes to live its own life, determine its own institutions, be assured of justice and fair dealing by the other peoples of the world as against force and selfish aggression.*"
>
> (Introduction)

> "*Unless justice be done to others it will not be done to us.*"
>
> (Introduction)

attention to the national aspirations of European minorities, saying little about the future of the diverse Arab population and other peoples of the Ottoman Empire.

The breakup of the Ottoman and Austro-Hungarian Empires in the last months of World War I allowed the peacemakers at Versailles to exceed Wilson's suggestions. These negotiators created a new Balkan state—Yugoslavia—centered on Serbia and Czechoslovakia, whose interim government in Paris Wilson had recognized before the war ended. Germany's defeat and Russia's internal turmoil prevented either nation from successfully opposing the creation of a Polish state with a corridor to the Baltic Sea carved through ethnically German territory.

◆ Point XIV: The League of Nations

Wilson saves his most important point for last. In Point XIV, Wilson calls for a general association of nations to maintain and enforce the peace. Wilson became a leading advocate for a league of nations in 1916 and believed that it was critical to maintaining world peace. The league would prevent special interests from overriding the common interests of the world, punish aggressors, and provide a forum for the peaceful settlement of international disputes. It would occupy the central place in Wilson's new world order, and it became a central part of the Treaty of Versailles, which created the League of Nations.

◆ Conclusion

Wilson sums up his philosophy in his conclusion and emphasizes that the Fourteen Points are not specifically aimed at Germany. This qualification and call for Germany

to embrace his ideas and a new international system based on "justice and law and fair dealing" could be considered a fifteenth point, similar to earlier assurances aimed at the Austrians and Turks. Wilson argues here that fair treatment of all nations, even the defeated, is an essential part of creating and maintaining peace.

Audience

Wilson hoped to remake the world; to do that, he aimed his address at several audiences throughout the world. Wilson, in fact, was the first national leader literally to address the world, thanks to new radio transmitters that relayed his address to Western Europe, South America, and Asia. He hoped to rally the American people to support both the war and his noble war aims. Wilson also hoped to persuade the governments and peoples of his nation's new allies to support his vision, particularly a league of nations, and to rescind their demands for a harsh peace, reparations, and the territorial acquisitions specified in the secret treaties that Russia's new Bolshevik government had recently revealed. Following the completion of a new radio transmitter in February, Wilson broadcast his address into enemy nations, where he hoped his generous terms and compelling vision would persuade the German and Austrian peoples to pressure their governments to make peace or even implement democratic reforms. The U.S. Committee on Public Information circulated more than sixty million copies of the Fourteen Points, some of which were dropped by Allied aircraft over German and Austrian troops.

Impact

Wilson's Fourteen Points won him acclaim around the globe. People from all walks of life welcomed Wilson's vision of an international system based on shared mutual interests and collective security. The Fourteen Points became the moral standard to which liberals and Socialists rallied. In the United States most progressive leaders embraced Wilson's ideas. Even Lenin, who later denounced Wilson's ideas as bourgeois and capitalist, responded positively and arranged the distribution of the Fourteen Points in Russia. Organizations advocating similar ideas, such as the League of Nations Society in Britain, grew dramatically after the speech. The German government, which initially rejected the Fourteen Points and imposed a harsh peace on Russia, appealed for peace on the basis of the Fourteen Points in October 1918 after suffering a succession of military defeats on the Western Front.

Still, most of the leaders of the warring nations opposed parts of the Fourteen Points. Many remained committed to reparations and a peace settlement that would leave Germany too weak to threaten world peace again. Others opposed Wilson's ideas about free trade, and many doubted that redrawing boundaries on the basis of nationality and self-determination was either desirable or possible. As the French premier Georges Clemenceau noted, "God gave us the Ten Commandments, and we broke them. Wilson gives us Fourteen Points. We shall see" (Bailey, p. 608). Wilson's speech set a standard almost impossible to meet, and Wilson compromised on much of his vision at the Versailles negotiations.

Related Documents

Borah, William E. *American Problems: A Selection of Speeches and Prophecies*, ed. Horace Green. 1924. Reprint. St. Clair Shores, Mich.: Scholarly Press, 1970. Borah, an ardent isolationist, emerged as one of the most outspoken and determined opponents of the League of Nations, and this collection includes several of his speeches supporting isolationism and denouncing Wilson, internationalism, and the League of Nations.

Link, Arthur S., ed. *The Papers of Woodrow Wilson.* 69 vols. Princeton, N.J.: Princeton University Press, 1966–1994. These sixty-nine volumes compiled by the Wilson biographer Arthur S. Link demonstrate Wilson's changing thought on foreign affairs and showcase the depth of his thought and insight. They are an unparalleled resource and include all of his important letters, speeches, and public papers as well as some press conferences and interviews.

Seymour, Charles, ed. *The Intimate Papers of Colonel House.* New York: Houghton Mifflin Company, 1926. Edward House was Wilson's primary foreign policy adviser, and his papers shed light on Wilson's efforts to arrange an equitable peace.

"The Versailles Treaty June 28, 1919." The Avalon Project at Yale Law School Web site. http://www.yale.edu/lawweb/avalon/imt/menu.htm. Accessed on February 11, 2008. Wilson spent six dif-

ficult months negotiating this treaty with fellow world leaders. Despite numerous compromises that distressed Wilson, the final document still showed the influence of Wilson's Fourteen Points. Note "The Covenant of the League of Nations," particularly Article 10, which calls for collective action to resist aggression. Other sections of the treaty address the territorial adjustments suggested in the Fourteen Points, such as the return of Alsace-Lorraine to France and the reestablishment of Poland.

Bibliography

■ Books

Ambrosius, Lloyd E. *Wilsonian Statecraft: Theory and Practice of Liberal Internationalism during World War I.* New York: Scholarly Resources, 1991.

Bailey, Thomas Andrew. *A Diplomatic History of the American People*, 7th ed. New York: Appleton-Century-Crofts, 1964.

Cooper, John M. *Breaking the Heart of the World: Woodrow Wilson and the Fight for the League of Nations.* New York: Cambridge University Press, 2001.

Ferrell, Robert H. *Woodrow Wilson and World War I, 1917–1921.* New York: Harper and Row, 1985.

Gardner, Lloyd. *Safe for Democracy: The Anglo-American Response to Revolution, 1913–1923.* New York: Oxford University Press, 1984.

Knock, Thomas J. *To End All Wars: Woodrow Wilson and the Quest for a New World Order.* New York: Oxford University Press, 1992.

Levin, Norman Gordon. *Woodrow Wilson and World Politics: America's Response to War and Revolution.* New York: Oxford University Press, 1968.

Link, Arthur S. *Woodrow Wilson: Revolution, War, and Peace.* Arlington Heights, Ill.: AHM Publishing, 1979.

■ Web Sites

"Primary Documents: Henry Cabot Lodge on the League of Nations, 12 August 1919." First World War.com Web site. http://www.firstworldwar.com/source/lodge_leagueofnations.htm. Accessed on September 28, 2007.

"Transcript of Joint Address to Congress Leading to a Declaration of War against Germany (1917)." National Archives "Our Documents" Web site. http://www.ourdocuments.gov/doc.php?doc=61&page=transcript. Accessed on February 11, 2008.

"Woodrow Wilson." The White House Web site. http://www.whitehouse.gov/history/presidents/ww28.html. Accessed on February 11, 2008.

"Woodrow Wilson: Address to the Senate of the United States: 'A World League for Peace' (January 22, 1917)." The American Presidency Web site.

http://www.presidency.ucsb.edu/ws/index.php?pid=65396&st=&st1=. Accessed on February 11, 2008.

The Woodrow Wilson Presidential Library Web site. http://www.woodrowwilson.org/. Accessed on September 28, 2007.

—By Stephen K. Stein

Questions for Further Study

1. Assess the territorial changes proposed in the Fourteen Points. What nations were likely to support these? What nations were likely to oppose them? What difficulties could be foreseen in their implementation?

2. Wilson emphasized the importance of free trade to a stable and peaceful world. Do you agree that the two are related? Are nations that trade together unlikely to go to war? Can you think of any exceptions to this idea?

3. Wilson believed that the League of Nations would preserve peace and provide a forum in which disputes, even disputes rooted in the Treaty of Versailles, would be settled peacefully. Why did the League of Nations fail?

4. Compare the Fourteen Points to Wilson's Joint Address to Congress Leading to a Declaration of War against Germany. What similarities do you see? What differences? In what ways had Wilson's war aims changed?

Glossary

aggrandizement	increase in the power, status, or wealth of
Alsace-Lorraine	French provinces lost to Germany in the Franco-Prussian War (1870–1871)
autonomous	independent
avow	declare openly
covenant	formal agreement
Dardanelles	the narrow strait in northwestern Turkey that controls the passage between the Black Sea and the Mediterranean Sea
pacific	peaceful
provocations	speeches or actions deliberately made to promote anger
rectifications	actions taken to make things right or correct
title	a claim to ownership (title to property)
unembarrassed	not hampered or impeded
unhampered	not hindered or impeded

WOODROW WILSON'S FOURTEEN POINTS

It will be our wish and purpose that the processes of peace, when they are begun, shall be absolutely open and that they shall involve and permit henceforth no secret understandings of any kind. The day of conquest and aggrandizement is gone by; so is also the day of secret covenants entered into in the interest of particular governments and likely at some unlooked-for moment to upset the peace of the world. It is this happy fact, now clear to the view of every public man whose thoughts do not still linger in an age that is dead and gone, which makes it possible for every nation whose purposes are consistent with justice and the peace of the world to avow nor or at any other time the objects it has in view.

We entered this war because violations of right had occurred which touched us to the quick and made the life of our own people impossible unless they were corrected and the world secure once for all against their recurrence. What we demand in this war, therefore, is nothing peculiar to ourselves. It is that the world be made fit and safe to live in; and particularly that it be made safe for every peace-loving nation which, like our own, wishes to live its own life, determine its own institutions, be assured of justice and fair dealing by the other peoples of the world as against force and selfish aggression. All the peoples of the world are in effect partners in this interest, and for our own part we see very clearly that unless justice be done to others it will not be done to us. The programme of the world's peace, therefore, is our programme; and that programme, the only possible programme, as we see it, is this:

I. Open covenants of peace, openly arrived at, after which there shall be no private international understandings of any kind but diplomacy shall proceed always frankly and in the public view.

II. Absolute freedom of navigation upon the seas, outside territorial waters, alike in peace and in war, except as the seas may be closed in whole or in part by international action for the enforcement of international covenants.

III. The removal, so far as possible, of all economic barriers and the establishment of an equality of trade conditions among all the nations consenting to the peace and associating themselves for its maintenance.

IV. Adequate guarantees given and taken that national armaments will be reduced to the lowest point consistent with domestic safety.

V. A free, open-minded, and absolutely impartial adjustment of all colonial claims, based upon a strict observance of the principle that in determining all such questions of sovereignty the interests of the populations concerned must have equal weight with the equitable claims of the government whose title is to be determined.

VI. The evacuation of all Russian territory and such a settlement of all questions affecting Russia as will secure the best and freest cooperation of the other nations of the world in obtaining for her an unhampered and unembarrassed opportunity for the independent determination of her own political development and national policy and assure her of a sincere welcome into the society of free nations under institutions of her own choosing; and, more than a welcome, assistance also of every kind that she may need and may herself desire. The treatment accorded Russia by her sister nations in the months to come will be the acid test of their good will, of their comprehension of her needs as distinguished from their own interests, and of their intelligent and unselfish sympathy.

VII. Belgium, the whole world will agree, must be evacuated and restored, without any attempt to limit the sovereignty which she enjoys in common with all other free nations. No other single act will serve as this will serve to restore confidence among the nations in the laws which they have themselves set and determined for the government of their relations with one another. Without this healing act the whole structure and validity of international law is forever impaired.

VIII. All French territory should be freed and the invaded portions restored, and the wrong done to France by Prussia in 1871 in the matter of Alsace-Lorraine, which has unsettled the peace of the world for nearly fifty years, should be righted, in order that peace may once more be made secure in the interest of all.

IX. A readjustment of the frontiers of Italy should be effected along clearly recognizable lines of nationality.

X. The peoples of Austria-Hungary, whose place among the nations we wish to see safeguarded and assured, should be accorded the freest opportunity to autonomous development.

XI. Rumania, Serbia, and Montenegro should be evacuated; occupied territories restored; Serbia accorded free and secure access to the sea; and the relations of the several Balkan states to one another determined by friendly counsel along historically established lines of allegiance and nationality; and international guarantees of the political and economic independence and territorial integrity of the several Balkan states should be entered into.

XII. The Turkish portion of the present Ottoman Empire should be assured a secure sovereignty, but the other nationalities which are now under Turkish rule should be assured an undoubted security of life and an absolutely unmolested opportunity of autonomous development, and the Dardanelles should be permanently opened as a free passage to the ships and commerce of all nations under international guarantees.

XIII. An independent Polish state should be erected which should include the territories inhabited by indisputably Polish populations, which should be assured a free and secure access to the sea, and whose political and economic independence and territorial integrity should be guaranteed by international covenant.

XIV. A general association of nations must be formed under specific covenants for the purpose of affording mutual guarantees of political independence and territorial integrity to great and small states alike.

In regard to these essential rectifications of wrong and assertions of right we feel ourselves to be intimate partners of all the governments and peoples associated together against the Imperialists. We cannot be separated in interest or divided in purpose. We stand together until the end.

For such arrangements and covenants we are willing to fight and to continue to fight until they are achieved; but only because we wish the right to prevail and desire a just and stable peace such as can be secured only by removing the chief provocations to war, which this programme does remove. We have no jealousy of German greatness, and there is nothing in this programme that impairs it. We grudge her no achievement or distinction of learning or of pacific enterprise such as have made her record very bright and very enviable. We do not wish to injure her or to block in any way her legitimate influence or power. We do not wish to fight her either with arms or with hostile arrangements of trade if she is willing to associate herself with us and the other peace-loving nations of the world in covenants of justice and law and fair dealing. We wish her only to accept a place of equality among the peoples of the world—the new world in which we now live—instead of a place of mastery.

Justice William R. Day wrote the majority opinion in **Hammer v. Dagenhart.** (Library of Congress)

HAMMER V. DAGENHART

"If there is any matter upon which civilized countries have agreed ... it is the evil of premature and excessive child labor."

Overview

In *Hammer v. Dagenhart*, also known as the Child Labor Case, the United States Supreme Court struck down the 1916 Keating-Owen Child Labor Act by the slimmest of margins. On its face, *Hammer* seemed an easy case given its subject matter, but the later discredited 5-to-4 decision demonstrated how resistant the Court under Chief Justice Edward Douglass White could be to the Progressive legislation of the day.

Roland Dagenhart, an employee at a cotton mill in Charlotte, North Carolina, sued his employer and W. C. Hammer, the U.S. attorney for the Western District of North Carolina, on behalf of himself and his minor sons, Reuben and John, who were also employed at the cotton mill. Dagenhart sought a reversal of Keating-Owen, a federal statute aimed at ending the exploitation of underage workers by prohibiting the sale through interstate commerce of goods made using child labor. The lower district court agreed with Dagenhart's argument that Keating-Owen interfered with his sons' right to work, and the Supreme Court upheld this ruling, declaring the statute an impermissible extension of federal commerce power. While the commerce clause—Article I, Section 8, Clause 3 of the Constitution—grants the federal government the right to regulate goods sold through interstate commerce, the Supreme Court in the *Hammer* case declared that while this power extends to goods that are inherently harmful, it cannot be used to control the process of their creation.

Context

The first two decades of the twentieth century in America were colored by initiatives spawned by the Progressive movement, a reformist agenda arising in reaction to the excesses of laissez-faire economics and social Darwinism that had dominated government policy since Reconstruction after the Civil War. The Fourteenth Amendment, ratified in 1868, originally had been intended to codify racial equality, but a series of reactionary Supreme Court decisions inter-preted the amendment's due process clause as a mechanism for restricting the governmental regulation of business activity, thereby promoting and protecting private enterprise.

The Progressive movement began as an unorganized response of middle-class consumers to the inequities of the Gilded Age, during which the few were vastly enriched at the expense of the many. In September 1891, however, after Vice President Theodore Roosevelt succeeded to the presidency following the assassination of William McKinley, the Progressives gained a champion. Roosevelt revived the dormant Sherman Antitrust Act of 1890 and sought to break up large-scale business combinations. Major trust-busting victories were achieved with cases such as *Northern Securities Co. v. United States* (1904) and *Swift & Co. v. United States* (1905). When Roosevelt was returned to office in 1904 with the largest popular majority of any previous presidential candidate, he pushed through other reforms, such as the Pure Food and Drug Act and the Hepburn Act (both passed in 1906). The Hepburn Act expanded the powers of the Interstate Commerce Commission, which regulated, among other things, railroad rates.

Roosevelt declined to run for another term, and in 1908 the Republicans nominated his handpicked successor, William Howard Taft. Taft handily beat the perennial Democratic candidate William Jennings Bryan, and he carried on with Roosevelt's reform agenda. Still, Taft failed to galvanize his party, and he alienated Progressives with his lukewarm response to congressional and tariff reform. In the 1910 off-year election the Democrats gained control of both houses of Congress, and Roosevelt returned to lead a coalition of Republican insurgents to form a third political party, the Progressives.

In 1912 Roosevelt and Taft, the Republican Party's nominee, essentially split the Republican vote, handing the presidency to the Democratic candidate Woodrow Wilson. Wilson, formerly governor of New Jersey, already had made a name for himself as a reformer, and with his New Freedom platform he now sought to break up trusts rather than simply controlling them. He moved quickly to reform the banking system and then ushered the Federal Trade Commission Act and the Clayton Antitrust Act through Congress. Progressive social justice issues, such as women's suffrage and child labor reform, remained on a back burn-

1868

■ **July 9**
Fourteenth Amendment is ratified.

1890

■ **July 2**
Sherman Antitrust Act, the first federal legislation to outlaw monopolistic business practices, becomes law.

1901

■ **September 14**
President William McKinley dies eight days after being shot; Theodore Roosevelt succeeds him, becoming the twenty-sixth president of the United States.

1904

■ **March 14**
U.S. Supreme Court decides *Northern Securities Co. v. United States*, breaking the railroad trust.

1905

■ **January 30**
U.S. Supreme Court decides *Swift & Co. v. United States*, disallowing price fixing in the meatpacking industry.

■ **March 4**
Theodore Roosevelt's second inauguration.

■ **April 17**
U.S. Supreme Court decides *Lochner v. New York*, overturning the state regulation of work hours and making substantive due process protection, in effect, a fundamental right of all "individuals," including business entities.

1906

■ **June 26**
The Hepburn Act is enacted, increasing the powers of the Interstate Commerce Commission.

■ **June 30**
The Pure Food and Drug Act becomes law.

1909

■ **March 4**
William Howard Taft is inaugurated as the twenty-seventh president of the United States.

er until the 1914 off-year election. Amid significant Republican electoral victories and strong indications that Teddy Roosevelt would once again be a candidate in 1916, Wilson pushed through Congress workers' compensation legislation and a farm loan bill that he had previously opposed. Most significantly, Wilson personally lobbied for the passage of a child labor bill, the 1916 Keating-Owen Child Labor Act, barring the interstate transportation of goods made using underage workers. The act marked the first time Congress had used its commerce power to regulate manufacturing.

About the Author

Born on April 17, 1849, in Ravenna, Ohio, William Rufus Day came from a long line of jurists. His great-grandfather served as chief justice of the state of Connecticut, his grandfather was a member of the Ohio Supreme Court, and his father was chief justice of the Ohio Supreme Court. William R. Day, as was the custom, read law in local law offices. He then attended the University of Michigan Law School for a year before taking and passing the Ohio bar exam.

Day set up a partnership in Canton, Ohio, which quickly became the city's most prominent law firm. He did not, however, confine his activities to legal practice; he pursued an interest in politics and befriended another local attorney with political ambitions, William McKinley. McKinley's career soared, taking him from the U.S. Congress to the Ohio governor's mansion and finally to the White House. Day, meanwhile, resigned an Ohio judgeship because of low pay and declined an appointment to the federal bench, citing poor health. But when his friend McKinley summoned him to Washington in 1897, Day acquiesced. He first served as assistant to Secretary of State John Sherman, and when Sherman was eased out of office in 1898, he took Sherman's place.

Day took command of the Department of State during the Spanish-American War, and he resigned his post there in 1899 to head the American delegation to the peace conference with Spain, where he negotiated the U.S. purchase of the Philippines. President McKinley rewarded him for this coup with an appointment that same year to the Sixth Circuit Court of Appeals. After McKinley's death in 1901, Day began marking his friend's birthday with an annual memorial service. During the January 1903 gathering, President Theodore Roosevelt made a premature announcement of his intention to appoint Day to the U.S. Supreme Court. Two months later Day was sworn in as an associate justice.

During the nearly two decades Day served on the Court, he acted primarily as a swing vote, manifesting attitudes that were alternately liberal and politically moderate. He endorsed the use of federal regulatory power embodied in the Sherman Antitrust Act, but in the opinion for which he is best remembered, *Hammer v. Dagenhart*, he declared the federal Child Labor Act unconstitutional because it violated the states' police powers. In the main, Day was over-shadowed by other figures with whom he shared the high bench, such as the towering intellectual Oliver Wendell Holmes, Jr., who wrote the powerful *Hammer* dissent that would later be used to overrule this decision.

Day retired from the Supreme Court on November 13, 1922. He served briefly as an umpire on the Mixed Claims Commission, which decided claims arising in the wake of World War I, before dying on Mackinac Island, Michigan, on July 9, 1923.

Explanation and Analysis of the Document

Justice Day, writing for the Supreme Court majority, opens with a brief rehearsal of the facts behind the case, including the decision of the United States District Court for the Western District of North Carolina. The district court has ruled in favor of the plaintiffs, declaring the Keating-Owen Child Labor Act unconstitutional and unenforceable. The case is now before the U.S. Supreme Court because the defendant, U.S. Attorney Hammer, has appealed the district court's judgment.

The case against the Child Labor Act rests on three arguments: 1) that it does not regulate interstate commerce or trade with a foreign country; 2) that it conflicts with the Tenth Amendment, which reserves to the states all powers not delegated to the federal government; and 3) that it conflicts with Fifth Amendment protections of due process. The question now before the Supreme Court concerns the federal government's constitutional right to regulate commerce between states: Does this power extend to prohibiting the sale of goods simply because they were produced in a factory that employs underage labor, possibly working too many hours per day, too many days per week, or after a certain hour? The federal government, for its part, cites the commerce clause of Article I of the Constitution as its authority for such control.

Seeking to define the government's commerce power, Day cites Chief Justice John Marshall's seminal opinion in *Gibbons v. Ogden* (22 U.S. 1 [1824]): "It is the power to regulate; that is, to prescribe the rule by which commerce is to be governed." For Justice Day, this definition does not include the power to prohibit the movement of "ordinary commodities" between states. He dismisses the cases cited by Hammer, which he declares rest upon the nature of the commodities in question: *Champion v. Ames* (1903) permitted Congress to outlaw the interstate transportation of lottery tickets; *Hipolite Egg Co. v. United States* (1911) upheld the Pure Food and Drug Act because it prevented the interstate transportation of contaminated foods and drugs; *Hoke v. United States* (1913) upheld the White-Slave Traffic Act (1910), also known as the Mann Act, because it prohibited the interstate transportation of women intended to work as prostitutes. In each of these cases, Day says, interstate transportation was necessary to accomplish the harmful effects associated with the respective products. Therefore, the only way to regulate or prevent the prolifer-

Time Line

1913

■ **March 4**
Woodrow Wilson is inaugurated as the twenty-eighth president of the United States.

1914

■ **September 26**
The Federal Trade Commission Act, promoting consumer protection, becomes law.

■ **October 15**
The Clayton Antitrust Act, expanding the Sherman Antitrust Act, becomes law.

1916

■ **September 1**
The Keating-Owen Child Labor Act, the first child labor bill, becomes law.

1918

■ **June 3**
The U.S. Supreme Court decides *Hammer v. Dagenhart*.

ation of gambling, tainted food and drugs, and prostitution was through the exertion of the federal government's commerce power.

The *Hammer* case, by way of contrast, concerns goods that are themselves harmless, Day asserts. The Child Labor Act attempts to outlaw the use of underage workers in the production of these goods, but by the time the products are ready for interstate transport, says Day, any harmful effect on the child laborers is long past. What is more, the act itself permits the interstate transport of the goods in question thirty days after they have been removed from the factory where they were made. The manufacture of goods does not constitute "commerce" and therefore cannot be controlled by the government's commerce power. The production of goods intended for transportation between states is, instead, subject to local control; if this were not so, all goods manufactured for interstate commerce would come under federal control, thereby usurping state authority in violation of the framers' intent when writing the commerce clause into the Constitution.

Justice Day next addresses Hammer's contention that allowing the interstate transport of goods made with child labor is, in effect, an endorsement of unfair competition because some states outlaw the use of underage workers while others do not. Lower-cost goods produced in states permitting child labor that are sold in states prohibiting the use of child labor have an inherent advantage over similar native commodities. However, Congress has no authority to prevent unfair competition. The constitutional grant of the commerce power was never intended to permit Congress to usurp individual states' power to control local trade and

This photo from 1916 shows messenger boys on strike in New York City (Library of Congress)

manufacturing. Such power is, in fact, reserved to the states by the Tenth Amendment, as the Supreme Court has held in numerous earlier decisions.

Justice Day concedes that limiting the use of child labor is a desired goal; indeed, every state of the Union has passed a law addressing this subject. Furthermore, while it might be desirable to standardize such laws, writes Day, it is not within the constitutionally "enumerated" powers of the federal government to mandate such uniformity among the states. States retain control of local government. Upholding the Child Labor Act would not be a recognition of the federal government's right to regulate interstate commerce but rather a sanction of federal invasion into state control of purely local matters. If Congress, by exercising its commerce power, were permitted to control matters entrusted to local authority, not only would the free flow of interstate commerce end, he writes, but also the country's very system of government, balancing the authority of the central government with states' rights, would be "practically destroyed." For all these reasons, Justice Day concludes that the ruling of the lower court must be upheld. As a result, the Keating-Owen Child Labor Act is found to be unconstitutional.

Justice Oliver Wendell Holmes, Jr., writing for a minority of four (including Joseph McKenna, Louis D. Brandeis, and John H. Clarke), penned a now-famous dissenting opinion. Holmes opens by rephrasing what is at issue in the case. For him, there is only one question: Does Congress have the power to prohibit the shipment in interstate or foreign commerce of goods manufactured less than thirty days prior to shipment using child labor, as defined by the Keating-Owen Child Labor Act? While granting that Congress does not have the authority to meddle with powers granted exclusively to the states, Holmes feels that no constitutional federal legislation should be struck down because of its indirect effects.

Holmes begins by stating that the statute in question is legitimate with regard to its immediate effects and could be considered unconstitutional only owing to some secondary consideration. For Holmes, the power to regulate interstate commerce includes the power to prohibit any part of that commerce Congress sees fit to prohibit. Unlike Justice Day, he sees decisions such as those in the Lottery Case (*Champion v. Ames*) as standing for the proposition that a law is not unconstitutional simply because it prohibits "certain transportation." Holmes is similarly firm in his belief that collateral effects on state police powers are no reason for striking down the Child Labor Act. Congress's commerce power will always trump any state's domestic controls:

I should have thought that that matter had been disposed of so fully as to leave no room for doubt. I should have thought that the most conspicuous decisions of this Court had made it clear that the power to regulate commerce and other constitutional powers could not be cut down or qualified by the fact that it might interfere with the carrying out of the domestic policy of any State.

Holmes goes on to cite numerous cases in which the Court has declined to inquire as to the intent or the effect of various statutes: a federal tax on margarine so onerous as to prevent the manufacture and sale of this commodity was upheld; another federal tax on state banks, obviously intended to drive them out of business, was similarly sustained in *Veazie Bank v. Fenno*, in which the Court declared, "The Judicial cannot prescribe to the Legislative Departments of the Government limitations upon the exercise of its acknowledged powers" (75 U.S. 533 [1869]). In numerous cases concerning the Sherman Antitrust Act, the Court repeatedly disregarded the argument that federal exercise of the commerce power interferes with state control of production. Finally, in *Hipolite Egg Co. v. United States*, the Court went so far as to say that "no trade can be carried on between the States to which it [the power of Congress to regulate commerce] does not extend" (220 U.S. 45 [1911]). It made no difference in these cases whether the harm Congress sought to prevent preceded or followed the transportation of inherently innocuous goods across state lines; if Congress believes that this transportation itself promotes social harm, Congress is within its rights to prohibit the goods from interstate commerce. In contrast to the majority holding that the Child Labor Act violates the Tenth Amendment's reservation to the states of unenumerated powers, Holmes cites with approval an earlier case, *Leisy v. Hardin*, in which the Court stated that "a subject matter which has been confided exclusively to Congress by the Constitution is not within the jurisdiction of the police power of the State unless placed there by congressional action" (135 U.S. 100 [1890]).

In what is perhaps the most famous passage in *Hammer*, Holmes writes that he cannot understand the majority's view that goods not themselves considered harmful should not be prohibited from interstate commerce. If there is anything that civilized countries can agree is evil, he asserts, it is not something like liquor, with which American society is preoccupied at the moment, but premature

"If Congress can thus regulate matters entrusted to local authority by prohibition of the movement of commodities in interstate commerce, all freedom of commerce will be at an end, and the power of the states over local matters may be eliminated, and thus our system of government be practically destroyed."

(Chief Justice Edward Douglass White, Majority Opinion)

"But if there is any matter upon which civilized countries have agreed—far more unanimously than they have with regard to intoxicants and some other matters over which this country is now emotionally aroused—it is the evil of premature and excessive child labor. I should have thought that if we were to introduce our own moral conceptions where is my opinion they do not belong, this was preeminently a case for upholding the exercise of all its powers by the United States."

(Justice Oliver Wendell Holmes, Jr., Dissenting Opinion)

"It is not for this Court to pronounce when prohibition is necessary to regulation if it ever may be necessary—to say that it is permissible as against strong drink but not as against the product of ruined lives. The Act does not meddle with anything belonging to the States. They may regulate their internal affairs and their domestic commerce as they like. But when they seek to send their products across the State line they are no longer within their rights."

(Justice Oliver Wendell Holmes, Jr., Dissenting Opinion)

"The national welfare as understood by Congress may require a different attitude within its sphere from that of some self-seeking State. It seems to me entirely constitutional for Congress to enforce its understanding by all the means at its command."

(Justice Oliver Wendell Holmes, Jr., Dissenting Opinion)

and prolonged child labor. If ever there were a case for upholding the exercise of federal power, this is it.

In the past, continues Holmes, the Court has declined to substitute its judgment for that of Congress in matters of public policy or morality. He adds that it is not appropriate for the Court now to say that while the federal prohibition of liquor is permissible, the congressional prohibition of practices that ruin lives is unacceptable. The Child Labor Act does not intrude on any state prerogatives. States may run their domestic affairs as they like, but as soon as they send their products across state lines, they have lost their right to control the products. Instead of being taxed on such goods, states must cede their right to control them to the federal government, whose responsibility it is to shape public policy for the nation as a whole. The welfare of the nation may not coincide with the aims of an individual state, and the Constitution empowers Congress to use "all the means at its command" to promote the greater good.

Audience

Like all U.S. Supreme Court cases, *Hammer* was intended for the nation as a whole. More specifically, however, it was meant to address members of the Progressive movement, whose efforts on behalf of social justice threatened to impede economic growth. Justice Holmes declared in his dissent to the most influential decision of the era, *Lochner v. New York*, that the Supreme Court's concern with protecting the right to formulate and implement business contracts was decided not on constitutional grounds but "upon an economic theory" (198 U.S. 45 ([1905]). Over the next three decades, conservative activists on the Court often held sway, favoring states' rights over federal governance and favoring business above all else. The reaction to progressive legislation was so powerful that in *Hammer* Justice Day was moved to declare that "if Congress can thus regulate matters entrusted to local authority ... all freedom of commerce will be at an end, and the power of the states over local matters may be eliminated, and thus our system of government be practically destroyed."

The Court that reached a 5-to-4 decision in *Hammer* was bitterly divided not only about policy issues but about the role of the Court itself. Both Day and Holmes were eager to avoid the label of judicial activist, responsible for substituting the Court's judgment for congressional acts. Whereas Day saw "the obligation to preserve inviolate the constitutional limitations upon the exercise of authority federal and state" as the Court's most important function, Holmes wrote, "I had thought that the propriety of the exercise of a power admitted to exist in some cases was for the consideration of Congress alone and that this Court always had disavowed the right to intrude its judgment upon questions of policy or morals." Both were nonetheless arguably activist jurists. Justice Day's point of view, a reaction to progressive reforms, prevailed for a time, only to be replaced by the more "restrained" approach advocated by Justice Holmes, who in dissent led the assault on laissez-faire economics and social Darwinism, the very philosophies that had provoked Progressivism.

Impact

The defeat of the Keating-Owen Child Labor Act in the Supreme Court prompted the passage of a second statute intended to protect child laborers through the exercise of Congress's taxing power. In *Bailey v. Drexel Furniture Co.* (1922), however, the Supreme Court also struck down the 1919 Child Labor Tax Act, declaring the 10 percent excise tax on the profits of companies employing children an unconstitutional penalty that usurped state authority. Two years later Congress adopted a constitutional amendment granting the federal government the power to regulate child labor. The amendment was never ratified and was eventually declared unnecessary after many states passed their own child labor laws. In 1938, however, Congress finally adopted a child labor law that passed constitutional muster: the Fair Labor Standards Act. The Supreme Court unanimously upheld this statute two years later in *United States v. Darby Lumber Co.* (1941), which also took the unusual step of specifically overruling a precedent, citing Justice Holmes's dissent in *Hammer* as the authority for this decision.

Hammer did not, however, remain dormant. Certain ambiguities in the Fair Labor Standards Act led to controversy over the applicability of the federal law to state workers. In *Maryland v. Wirtz* (1968) the Court nonetheless upheld the statute, declaring that the enforcement of its provisions on state workers did not violate state sovereignty. Just eight years later *Wirtz* was overturned in *National League of Cities v. Usury* (1976), in the process invoking *Hammer* to support the proposition that the Fair Labor Standards Act infringed upon "traditional aspects of state sovereignty."

Nine years later *National League of Cities* was itself overturned by *Garcia v. San Antonio Metropolitan Transit Authority* (1985), a 5-to-4 decision using the commerce clause to justify both the Fair Labor Standards Act and a powerful central government. The dissenters in *Garcia*, however, expressed their confidence that this case, too, would be overruled, returning power to the states. Although *United States v. Lopez* (1995) did not purport to overrule *Garcia*, it did endorse state autonomy by limiting congressional power to invoke the commerce clause when regulating matters having only a tangential relationship with interstate commerce. Profound questions remain concerning the Court's willingness to rein in the congressional assertion of its authority under the commerce clause, and the historical tension between centralized government and states' rights addressed in *Hammer* remains alive and well.

Related Documents

"Amendments to the Constitution of the United States of America." FindLaw Web site. http://caselaw.lp.findlaw.com/data/constitution/amendments.html. Accessed on December 30, 2007. The portion of the Fifth Amendment known as the due process clause provides that "no person shall be ... deprived of life, liberty, or property, without due process of law." The Tenth Amendment states that all powers not constitutionally granted to the federal government belong to the states or to the American people.

Bailey v. Drexel Furniture Co., 259 U.S. 20 (1922). In *Bailey*, also known as the Child Labor Tax Case, the Supreme Court struck down a tax law intended to regulate child labor on the ground that the Constitution sanctions only federal regulatory measures that have incidental effects on states' control of their internal affairs.

"Constitution of the United States of America." FindLaw Web site. http://caselaw.lp.findlaw.com/data/constitution/articles.html. Accessed on December 30, 2007. The commerce clause (Article I, Section 8, Clause 3) of the Constitution grants to Congress the authority to regulate commerce between states and with foreign powers and has been used to authorize all manner of federal legislation, affecting the balance of power between the federal government and the states.

"*Gibbons v. Ogden, 22 U.S. 1 (1824)*". U.S. Supreme Court Center Web site. http://supreme.justia.com/us/22/1/case.html. Accessed on February 5, 2008. With this case the Supreme Court granted control of all regulation of interstate commerce to Congress, overriding conflicting state laws.

"Keating-Owen Child Labor Act of 1916 (1916)." National Archives "Our Documents" Web site. http://www.ourdocuments.gov/doc.php?flash=true&doc=59. Accessed on December 30, 2007. Signed into law by President Woodrow Wilson, the Child Labor Act was intended to address the wrongs associated with the exploitation of child labor by prohibiting the sale across state lines of goods made by underage workers.

United States v. Darby, 312 U.S. 100 (1941). Referring to Justice Holmes's dissent in *Hammer v. Dagenhart*, this Supreme Court case overruled *Hammer* by upholding Congress's right under the commerce clause to regulate workers' wages and hours.

Bibliography

■ Books

Epstein, Lee. *Constitutional Law for a Changing America: Rights, Liberties, and Justice*, 6th ed. Washington, D.C.: CQ Press, 2007.

Kersch, Ken I. *Constructing Civil Liberties: Discontinuities in the Development of American Constitutional Law*. New York: Cambridge University Press, 2004.

Paddock, Lisa. *Facts about the Supreme Court of the United States.* New York: H. W. Wilson, 1996.

Schwartz, Bernard. *A History of the Supreme Court.* New York: Oxford University Press, 1993.

■ Web Sites

"*Hammer v. Dagenhart* (1918)." Landmark Supreme Court Cases Web site.

> http://www.landmarkcases.org/gibbons/hammer.html. Accessed on December 30, 2007.

"Hammer v. Dagenhart: Further Readings." *Great American Court Cases, vol. 18.* Law Library: American Law and Legal Information Web site.

> http://law.jrank.org/pages/13591/Hammer-v-Dagenhart.html. Accessed on December 30, 2007.

"Hipolite Egg Co. v. United States, 220 U.S. 45 (1911)." FindLaw Web site.

> http://caselaw.lp.findlaw.com/cgi-bin/getcase.pl?court=US&vol=220&invol=45. Accessed on February 5, 2008.

"Leisy v. Hardin 135 U.S. 100 (1890)." FindLaw Web site.

> http://caselaw.lp.findlaw.com/scripts/getcase.pl?court=US&vol=135&invol=100. Accessed on February 5, 2008.

"Lochner v. People of State Of New York, 198 U.S. 45 (1905)." FindLaw Web site.

> http://caselaw.lp.findlaw.com/scripts/getcase.pl?court=US&vol=198&invol=45. Accessed on February 5, 2008.

"Veazie Bank v. Fenno, 75 U.S. 533 (1869)." FindLaw Web site.

> http://caselaw.lp.findlaw.com/scripts/getcase.pl?navby=case&court=us&vol=75&invol=533. Accessed on February 5, 2008.

—By Lisa Paddock

Questions for Further Study

1. In *United States v. Darby* (1941) the Supreme Court overruled *Hammer v. Dagenhart*, citing Justice Holmes's dissent in the earlier case as authority. How does the *Darby* Court turn a dissenting opinion into a controlling one?

2. A legal doctrine known as the "dormant commerce clause" does not exist in the Constitution per se but has grown out of various Supreme Court justices' attempts to interpret the commerce clause. In effect, the dormant commerce clause holds that some aspects of commerce between the states or between states and foreign countries are subject to state regulation. How might modern Internet communications be governed by this version of the commerce clause?

3. In *Lochner v. New York* (1905) the Supreme Court elevated a legal concept rooted in the due process clause of the Fourteenth Amendment and known as "substantive due process"—essentially, the right of an individual to be free from arbitrary government intrusion—into an inalienable right. How does the due process clause of the Fourteenth Amendment differ from that of the Fifth Amendment, and how might substantive due process actually work against individual liberty?

Glossary

commerce clause	Article I, Section 8, Clause 3 of the Constitution provides that "Congress shall have the power … To Regulate Commerce with foreign Nations, and among the several States, and with the Indian Tribes"
enumerated powers	powers specifically granted in the Constitution to the various branches of federal government
jurisdiction	the power to hear and decide legal matters within a defined area of authority
police power	authority granted government, usually at the local level, to restrict individual rights in order to promote public welfare

HAMMER V. DAGENHART

A bill was filed in the United States District Court for the Western District of North Carolina by a father in his own behalf and as next friend of his two minor sons, one under the age of fourteen years and the other between the ages of fourteen and sixteen years, employees in a cotton mill at Charlotte, North Carolina, to enjoin the enforcement of the act of Congress intended to prevent interstate commerce in the products of child labor. Act Sept. 1, 1916, 39 Stat. 675, c. 432 (Comp. St. 1916, 8819a–8816f).

The District Court held the act unconstitutional and entered a decree enjoining its enforcement. This appeal brings the case here. The first section of the act is in the margin. Other sections of the act contain provisions for its enforcement and prescribe penalties for its violation.

The attack upon the act rests upon three propositions: First: It is not a regulation of interstate and foreign commerce; second: It contravenes the Tenth Amendment to the Constitution; third: It conflicts with the Fifth Amendment to the Constitution.

The controlling question for decision is: Is it within the authority of Congress in regulating commerce among the states to prohibit the transportation in interstate commerce of manufactured goods, the product of a factory in which, within thirty days prior to their removal therefrom, children under the age of fourteen have been employed or permitted to work, or children between the ages of fourteen and sixteen years have been employed or permitted to work more than eight hours in any day, or more than six days in any week, or after the hour of 7 o'clock p.m., or before the hour of 6 o'clock a.m.?

The power essential to the passage of this act, the government contends, is found in the commerce clause of the Constitution which authorizes Congress to regulate commerce with foreign nations and among the states.

In *Gibbons v. Ogdon*, 9 Wheat. 1, Chief Justice Marshall, speaking for this court, and defining the

extent and nature of the commerce power, said, "It is the power to regulate; that is, to prescribe the rule by which commerce is to be governed." In other words, the power is one to control the means by which commerce is carried on, which is directly the contrary of the assumed right to forbid commerce from moving and thus destroying it as to particular commodities. But it is insisted that adjudged cases in this court establish the doctrine that the power to regulate given to Congress incidentally includes the authority to prohibit the movement of ordinary commodities and therefore that the subject is not open for discussion. The cases demonstrate the contrary. They rest upon the character of the particular subjects dealt with and the fact that the scope of governmental authority, state or national, possessed over them is such that the authority to prohibit is as to them but the exertion of the power to regulate.

The first of these cases is *Champion v. Ames*, 188 U.S. 321, 23 Sup. Ct. 321, the so-called Lottery Case, in which it was held that Congress might pass a law having the effect to keep the channels of commerce free from use in the transportation of tickets used in the promotion of lottery schemes. In *Hipolite Egg Co. v. United States*, 220 U.S. 45, 31 Sup. Ct. 364, this court sustained the power of Congress to pass the Pure Food and Drug Act (Act June 30, 1906, c. 3915, 34 Stat. 768 [Comp. St. 1916, 8717–8728]), which prohibited the introduction into the states by means of interstate commerce of impure foods and drugs. In *Hoke v. United States*, 227 U.S. 308, 33 Sup. Ct. 281, 43 L. R. A. (N. S.) 906, Ann. Cas. 1913E, 905, this court sustained the constitutionality of the so-called "White Slave Traffic Act" (Act June 25, 1910, c. 395, 36 Stat. 825 [Comp. St. 1916, 8812–8819]), whereby the transportation of a woman in interstate commerce for the purpose of prostitution was forbidden. In that case we said, having reference to the authority of Congress, under the regulatory power, to protect the channels of interstate commerce:

If the facility of interstate transportation can be taken away from the demoralization of lotteries, the debasement of obscene literature, the contagion of diseased cattle or persons, the impurity of food and drugs, the like facility can be taken away from the systematic enticement to, and the enslavement in prostitution and debauchery of women, and, more insistently, of girls.

In *Caminetti v. United States*, 242 U.S. 470, 37 Sup. Ct. 1 2, L. R. A. 1917F, 502, Ann. Cas. 1917B, 1168, we held that Congress might prohibit the transportation of women in interstate commerce for the purposes of debauchery and kindred purposes. In *Clark Distilling Co. v. Western Maryland Railway Co.*, 242 U.S. 311, 37 Sup. Ct. 180, L. R. A. 1917B, 1218, Ann. Cas. 1917B, 845, the power of Congress over the transportation of intoxicating liquors was sustained. In the course of the opinion it was said:

The power conferred is to regulate, and the very terms of the grant would seem to repel the contention that only prohibition of movement in interstate commerce was embraced. And the cogency of this is manifest, since if the doctrine were applied to those manifold and important subjects of interstate commerce as to which Congress from the beginning has regulated, not prohibited, the existence of government under the Constitution would be no longer possible.

And concluding the discussion which sustained the authority of the Government to prohibit the transportation of liquor in interstate commerce, the court said:

… The exceptional nature of the subject here regulated is the basis upon which the exceptional power exerted must rest and affords no ground for any fear that such power may be constitutionally extended to things which it may not, consistently with the guaranties of the Constitution embrace.

In each of these instances the use of interstate transportation was necessary to the accomplishment of harmful results. In other words, although the power over interstate transportation was to regulate, that could only be accomplished by prohibiting the use of the facilities of interstate commerce to effect the evil intended.

This element is wanting in the present case. The thing intended to be accomplished by this statute is the denial of the facilities of interstate commerce to those manufacturers in the states who employ children within the prohibited ages. The act in its effect does not regulate transportation among the states, but aims to standardize the ages at which children may be employed in mining and manufacturing within the states. The goods shipped are of themselves harmless. The act permits them to be freely shipped after thirty days from the time of their removal from the factory. When offered for shipment, and before transportation begins, the labor of their production is over, and the mere fact that they were intended for interstate commerce transportation does not make their production subject to federal control under the commerce power.

Commerce "consists of intercourse and traffic … and includes the transportation of persons and property, as well as the purchase, sale and exchange of commodities." The making of goods and the mining of coal are not commerce, nor does the fact that these things are to be afterwards shipped, or used in interstate commerce, make their production a part thereof. *Delaware, Lackawanna & Western R. R. Co. v. Yurkonis*, 238 U.S. 439, 35 Sup. Ct. 902

Over interstate transportation, or its incidents, the regulatory power of Congress is ample, but the production of articles, intended for interstate commerce, is a matter of local regulation. "When the commerce begins is determined, not by the character of the commodity, nor by the intention of the owner to transfer it to another state for sale, nor by his preparation of it for transportation, but by its actual delivery to a common carrier for transportation, or the actual commencement of its transfer to another state." Mr. Justice Jackson in Re Greene (C. C.) 52 Fed. 113. This principle has been recognized often in this court. *Coe v. Errol*, 116 U.S. 517, 6 Sup. Ct. 475; *Bacon v. Illinois*, 227 U.S. 504, 33 Sup. Ct. 299, and cases cited. If it were otherwise, all manufacture intended for interstate shipment would be brought under federal control to the practical exclusion of the authority of the states, a result certainly not contemplated by the framers of the Constitution when they vested in Congress the authority to regulate commerce among the States. *Kidd v. Pearson*, 128 U.S. 1, 21, 9 S. Sup. Ct. 6.

It is further contended that the authority of Congress may be exerted to control interstate commerce in the shipment of child-made goods because of the effect of the circulation of such goods in other states where the evil of this class of labor has been recognized by local legislation, and the right to thus employ child labor has been more rigorously restrained than in the state of production. In other words, that the unfair competition, thus engendered, may be controlled by closing the channels of interstate commerce to manufacturers in those states where the local laws do not meet what Congress deems to be the more just standard of other states.

There is no power vested in Congress to require the states to exercise their police power so as to prevent possible unfair competition. Many causes may cooperate to give one state, by reason of local laws or conditions, an economic advantage over others. The commerce clause was not intended to give to Congress a general authority to equalize such conditions. In some of the states laws have been passed fixing minimum wages for women, in others the local law regulates the hours of labor of women in various employments. Business done in such states may be at an economic disadvantage when compared with states which have no such regulations; surely, this fact does not give Congress the power to deny transportation in interstate commerce to those who carry on business where the hours of labor and the rate of compensation for women have not been fixed by a standard in use in other states and approved by Congress.

The grant of power of Congress over the subject of interstate commerce was to enable it to regulate such commerce, and not to give it authority to control the states in their exercise of the police power over local trade and manufacture.

The grant of authority over a purely federal matter was not intended to destroy the local power always existing and carefully reserved to the states in the Tenth Amendment to the Constitution.

Police regulations relating to the internal trade and affairs of the states have been uniformly recognized as within such control. "This," said this court in *United States v. Dewitt*, 9 Wall. 41, 45, "has been so frequently declared by this court, results so obviously from the terms of the Constitution, and has been so fully explained and supported on former occasions, that we think it unnecessary to enter again upon the discussion." See *Keller v. United States*, 213 U.S. 138, 144, 145 S., 146, 29 Sup. Ct. 470, 16 Ann. Cas. 1066; Cooley's Constitutional Limitations (7th Ed.) p. 11.

In the judgment which established the broad power of Congress over interstate commerce, Chief Justice Marshall said (9 Wheat. 203):

They [inspection laws] act upon the subject, before it becomes an article of foreign commerce, or of commerce among the states, and prepare it for that purpose. They form a portion of that immense mass of legislation, which embraces everything within the territory of a state, not surrendered to the general government; all of which can be most advantageously exercised by the states themselves. Inspection laws, quarantine laws, health laws of every description, as well as laws for regulating the internal commerce of a state, and those which respect turnpike roads, ferries, etc., are component parts of this mass.

And in *Dartmouth College v. Woodward*, 4 Wheat. 518, the same great judge said:

That the framers of the Constitution did not intend to restrain the states in the regulation of their civil institutions, adopted for internal government, and that the instrument they have given us is not to be so construed may be admitted.

That there should be limitations upon the right to employ children in mines and factories in t e interest of their own and the public welfare, all will admit. That such employment is generally deemed to require regulation is shown by the fact that the brief of counsel states that every state in the Union has a law upon the subject, limiting the right to thus employ children. In North Carolina, the state wherein is located the factory in which the employment was had in the present case, no child under twelve years of age is permitted to work.

It may be desirable that such laws be uniform, but our federal government is one of enumerated powers; "this principle," declared Chief Justice Marshall in *McCulloch v. Maryland*, 4 Wheat. 316, "is universally admitted."

A statute must be judged by its natural and reasonable effect. *Collins v. New Hampshire*, 171 U.S. 30, 33, 34 S., 18 Sup. Ct. 768. The control by Congress over interstate commerce cannot authorize the exercise of authority not entrusted to it by the Constitution. Pipe Line Case, 234 U.S. 548, 560, 34 S. Sup. Ct. 956. The maintenance of the authority of the states over matters purely local is as essential to the preservation of our institutions as is the conservation of the supremacy of the federal power in all matters entrusted to the nation by the federal Constitution.

In interpreting the Constitution it must never be forgotten that the nation is made up of states to which are entrusted the powers of local government. And to them and to the people the powers not expressly delegated to the national government are reserved. *Lane County v. Oregon*, 7 Wall. 71, 76. The power of the states to regulate their purely internal affairs by such laws as seem wise to the local authority is inherent and has never been surrendered to the general government. *New York v. Miln*, 11 Pet. 102, 139; Slaughter House Cases, 16 Wall. 36, 63; *Kidd v. Pearson*, supra. To sustain this statute would not be in our judgment a recognition of the lawful exertion of congressional authority over interstate commerce, but would sanction an invasion by the federal power of the control of a matter purely local in its character, and over which no authority has been delegated to Congress in conferring the power to regulate commerce among the states.

We have neither authority nor disposition to question the motives of Congress in enacting this legislation. The purposes intended must be attained consistently with constitutional limitations and not by an invasion of the powers of the states. This court has no more important function than that which devolves upon it the obligation to preserve inviolate the constitutional limitations upon the exercise of authority federal and state to the end that each may continue to discharge, harmoniously with the other, the duties entrusted to it by the Constitution.

In our view the necessary effect of this act is, by means of a prohibition against the movement in interstate commerce of ordinary commercial commodities to regulate the hours of labor of children in factories and mines within the states, a purely state authority. Thus the act in a two-fold sense is repugnant to the Constitution. It not only transcends the authority delegated to Congress over commerce but also exerts a power as to a purely local matter to which the federal authority does not extend. The far reaching result of upholding the act cannot be more plainly indicated than by pointing out that if Congress can thus regulate matters entrusted to local authority by prohibition of the movement of commodities in interstate commerce, all freedom of commerce will be at an end, and the power of the states over local matters may be eliminated, and thus our system of government be practically destroyed. For these reasons we hold that this law exceeds the constitutional authority of Congress. It follows that the decree of the District Court must be

AFFIRMED.

Mr. Justice HOLMES, dissenting.

The single question in this case is whether Congress has power to prohibit the shipment in interstate or foreign commerce of any product of a cotton mill situated in the United States, in which within thirty days before the removal of the product children under fourteen have been employed, or children between fourteen and sixteen have been employed more than eight hours in a day, or more than six days in any week, or between seven in the evening and six in the morning. The objection urged against the power is that the States have exclusive control over their methods of production and that Congress cannot meddle with them, and taking the proposition in the sense of direct intermeddling I agree to it and suppose that no one denies it. But if an act is within the powers specifically conferred upon Congress, it seems to me that it is not made any less constitutional because of the indirect effects that it may have, however obvious it may be that it will have those effects, and that we are not at liberty upon such grounds to hold it void.

The first step in my argument is to make plain what no one is likely to dispute that the statute in question is within the power expressly given to Congress if considered only as to its immediate effects and that if invalid it is so only upon some collateral ground. The statute confines itself to prohibiting the carriage of certain goods in interstate or foreign commerce. Congress is given power to regulate such commerce in unqualified terms. It would not be argued today that the power to regulate does not include the power to prohibit. Regulation means the prohibition of something, and when interstate commerce is the matter to be regulated I cannot doubt that the regulation may prohibit any part of such commerce that Congress sees fit to forbid. At all events it is established by the Lottery Case and others that have followed it that a law is not beyond the regulative power of Congress merely because it prohibits certain transportation out and out. *Champion v. Ames*, 188 U.S. 321, 355, 359 S., 23 Sup. Ct. 321, et seq. So I repeat that this statute in its immediate operation is clearly within the Congress's constitutional power.

The question then is narrowed to whether the exercise of its otherwise constitutional power by Congress can be pronounced unconstitutional because of its possible reaction upon the conduct of the States in a matter upon which I have admitted that they are free from direct control. I should have thought that that matter had been disposed of so fully as to leave no room for doubt. I should have thought that the most conspicuous decisions of this Court had made it clear that the power to regulate commerce and other constitutional powers could not be cut down or qualified by the fact that it might interfere with the carrying out of the domestic policy of any State.

The manufacture of oleomargarine is as much a matter of State regulation as the manufacture of cotton cloth. Congress levied a tax upon the compound when colored so as to resemble butter that was so great as obviously to prohibit the manufacture and sale. In a very elaborate discussion the present Chief Justice excluded any inquiry into the purpose of an act which apart from that purpose was within the power of Congress. *McCray v. United States*, 195 U.S. 27, 24 Sup. Ct. 769, 1 Ann. Cas. 561. As to foreign commerce see *Weber v. Freed*, 239 U.S. 325, 329, 36 S. Sup. Ct. 131, Ann. Cas. 1916C, 317; *Brolan v. United States*, 236 U.S. 216, 217, 35 S. Sup. Ct. 285; *Buttfield v. Stranahan*, 192 U.S. 470, 24 Sup. Ct. 349. Fifty years ago a tax on state banks, the obvious purpose and actual effect of which was to drive them, or at least their circulation, out of existence, was sustained, although the result was one that Congress had no constitutional power to require. The Court made short work of the argument as to the purpose of the Act. "The Judicial cannot prescribe to the Legislative Departments of the Government limitations upon the exercise of its acknowledged powers." *Veazie Bank v. Fenno*, 8 Wall. 533. So it well might have been argued that the corporation tax was intended under the guise of a revenue measure to secure a control not otherwise belonging to Congress, but the tax was sustained, and the objection so far as noticed was disposed of by citing *McCray v. United States*; *Flint v. Stone Tracy Co.*, 220 U.S. 107, 31 Sup. Ct. 342, Ann. Cas. 1912B, 1312. And to come to cases upon interstate commerce notwithstanding *United States v. E. C. Knight Co.*, 156 U.S. 1, 15 Sup. Ct. 249, the Sherman Act (Act July 2, 1890, c. 647, 26 Stat. 209) has been made an instrument for the breaking up of combinations in restraint of trade and monopolies, using the power to regulate commerce as a foothold, but not proceeding because that commerce was the end actually in mind. The objection that the control of the States over production was interfered with was urged again and again but always in vain. *Standard Oil Co. v. United States*, 221 U.S. 1, 68, 69 S., 31 Sup. Ct. 502, 34 L. R. A. (N. S.) 834, Ann. Cas. 1912D, 734; *United States v. American Tobacco Co.*, 221 U.S. 106, 184, 31 S. Sup. Ct. 632; *Hoke v. United States*, 227

U.S. 308, 321, 322 S., 33 Sup. Ct. 281, 43 L. R. A. (N. S.) 906, Ann. Cas. 1913E, 905. See finally and especially *Seven Cases of Eckman's Alterative v. United States*, 239 U.S. 510, 514, 515 S., 36 Sup. Ct. 190, L. R. A. 1916D, 164.

The Pure Food and Drug Act which was sustained in *Hipolite Egg Co. v. United States*, 220 U.S. 45, 57, 31 S. Sup. Ct. 364, 367 (55 L. Ed. 364), with the intimation that "no trade can be carried on between the States to which it [the power of Congress to regulate commerce] does not extend," applies not merely to articles that the changing opinions of the time condemn as intrinsically harmful but to others innocent in themselves, simply on the ground that the order for them was induced by a preliminary fraud. *Weeks v. United States*, 245 U.S. 618, 38 Sup. Ct. 219, 62 L. Ed. It does not matter whether the supposed evil precedes or follows the transportation. It is enough that in the opinion of Congress the transportation encourages the evil. I may add that in the cases on the so-called White Slave Act it was established that the means adopted by Congress as convenient to the exercise of its power might have the character of police regulations. *Hoke v. United States*, 227 U.S. 308, 323, 33 S. Sup. Ct. 281, 43 L. R. A. (N. S.) 906, Ann. Cas. 1913E, 905; *Caminetti v. United States*, 242 U.S. 470, 492, 37 S. Sup. Ct. 192, L. R. A. 1917F, 502, Ann. Cas. 1917B, 1168. In *Clark Distilling Co. v. Western Maryland Ry. Co.*, 242 U.S. 311, 328, 37 S. Sup. Ct. 180, L. R. A. 1917B, 1218, Ann. Cas. 1917B, 845, *Leisy v. Hardin*, 135 U.S. 100, 108, 10 S. Sup. Ct. 681, is quoted with seeming approval to the effect that "a subject matter which has been confided exclusively to Congress by the Constitution is not within the jurisdiction of the police power of the State unless placed there by congressional action." I see no reason for that proposition not applying here.

The notion that prohibition is any less prohibition when applied to things now thought evil I do not understand. But if there is any matter upon which civilized countries have agreed—far more unanimously than they have with regard to intoxicants and some other matters over which this country is now emotionally aroused—it is the evil of premature and excessive child labor. I should have thought that if we were to introduce our own moral conceptions where is my opinion they do not belong, this was preeminently a case for upholding the exercise of all its powers by the United States.

But I had thought that the propriety of the exercise of a power admitted to exist in some cases was for the consideration of Congress alone and that this Court always had disavowed the right to intrude its judgment upon questions of policy or morals. It is not for this Court to pronounce when prohibition is necessary to regulation if it ever may be necessary—to say that it is permissible as against strong drink but not as against the product of ruined lives. The Act does not meddle with anything belonging to the States. They may regulate their internal affairs and their domestic commerce as they like. But when they seek to send their products across the State line they are no longer within their rights. If there were no Constitution and no Congress their power to cross the line would depend upon their neighbors. Under the Constitution such commerce belongs not to the States but to Congress to regulate. It may carry out its views of public policy whatever indirect effect they may have upon the activities of the States. Instead of being encountered by a prohibitive tariff at her boundaries the State encounters the public

policy of the United States which it is for Congress to express. The public policy of the United States is shaped with a view to the benefit of the nation as a whole. If, as has been the case within the memory of men still living, a State should take a different view of the propriety of sustaining a lottery from that which generally prevails, I cannot believe that the fact would require a different decision from that reached in *Champion v. Ames*. Yet in that case it would be said with quite as much force as in this that Congress was attempting to intermeddle with the State's domestic affairs. The national welfare as understood by Congress may require a different attitude within its sphere from that of some self-seeking State. It seems to me entirely constitutional for Congress to enforce its understanding by all the means at its command,

Mr. Justice McKENNA, Mr. Justice BRANDEIS, and Mr. Justice CLARKE concur in this opinion.

Sixty-sixth Congress of the United States of America;

At the First Session,

Begun and held at the City of Washington on Monday, the nineteenth day of May, one thousand nine hundred and nineteen.

JOINT RESOLUTION

Proposing an amendment to the Constitution extending the right of suffrage to women.

Resolved by the Senate and House of Representatives of the United States of America in Congress assembled (two-thirds of each House concurring therein), That the following article is proposed as an amendment to the Constitution, which shall be valid to all intents and purposes as part of the Constitution when ratified by the legislatures of three-fourths of the several States.

"ARTICLE —————.

"The right of citizens of the United States to vote shall not be denied or abridged by the United States or by any State on account of sex.

"Congress shall have power to enforce this article by appropriate legislation."

F. H. Gillett

Speaker of the House of Representatives.

Thos. R. Marshall

Vice President of the United States and
President of the Senate.

The Nineteenth Amendment (National Archives and Records Administration)

NINETEENTH AMENDMENT TO THE U.S. CONSTITUTION

"The right ... to vote shall not be denied ... on account of sex."

Overview

The struggle for women's suffrage was a long and protracted one that began in the 1840s and lasted nearly eighty years. The battle embraced a multitude of strategies and spanned two generations of leaders. It was not until the aftermath of World War I (1914–1918) that the long-anticipated passage of a constitutional amendment legalizing suffrage for women in the United States finally occurred. Its author, Susan B. Anthony, and its proponents had hoped the amendment would follow on the heels of the Fifteenth Amendment, providing for universal male suffrage in 1870. Their hope for a sixteenth amendment allowing women to vote was frustrated, however, and they had to settle for a fifty-year wait and the position as the Nineteenth Amendment to the Constitution. On June 4, 1919, forty-one years after its initial introduction, the United States Congress voted approval: the House of Representatives in a vote of 304 to 89 and the Senate in a vote of 56 to 25. The Sixty-sixth Congress proceeded to send the bill to the states for ratification. During the following fourteen months, thirty-six state legislatures voted in favor of the amendment, leading to its acceptance on August 18, 1920. As expected, the greatest support for the amendment derived from the Midwest and trans-Mississippi regions of the United States, with the states of the Northeast lagging behind only slightly. The strongest opposition came primarily from the South.

Anthony, the author of the amendment, did not live to see the passage or ratification of her proposal. Her death in 1906 followed a long career as a suffragist and general reformer. She wrote a women's suffrage amendment in 1878 and persuaded a sympathetic senator from California, Aaron Augustus Sargent, to introduce the measure in Congress that year. Although Congress failed to act on the resolution, it became a focal point for suffragist activity and public attention. Anthony's resolution, also known as the "Anthony Amendment," was reintroduced in every session of Congress with its wording unchanged until its passage forty-one years later, in 1919.

Final acceptance of the amendment can be attributed primarily to the plan introduced by Carrie Chapman Catt, president of the National American Woman Suffrage Association (NAWSA), at that organization's annual meeting in 1916 at Atlantic City, New Jersey. She called for cooperation across the suffragists' spectrum and the mobilization of state and local organizations for the cause. The plan also suggested the targeting of unsympathetic legislators at all levels. By 1918 she had secured the endorsement of President Woodrow Wilson. Although it required another eighteen months of diligence, the goal was accomplished, and women across the United States voted in the presidential election of 1920.

Context

The movement for women's suffrage in the United States can trace its beginnings to the eighteenth century and the period of the American Revolution. Women such as the playwright and historian Mercy Otis Warren; the writer and educational reformer Judith Sargent Murray; and Abigail Adams, the wife of President John Adams, questioned the traditional roles and limitations placed on American women. While Adams wrote to her husband advising him not to forget women at the same time that American male leaders were deliberating the rights of men, Murray contemplated the inequality of educational opportunities extended to male and female children. She argued, "How is the one exalted and the other depressed, by the contrary modes of education that are adopted! The one is taught to aspire, the other is early confined and limited" (qtd. in Flexner, p. 16). An Englishwoman, Mary Wollstonecraft, laid the theoretical bases and raised the fundamental questions pursued by American women's rights advocates for the next 120 years. The most fundamental and, at times, controversial tenet of her work *A Vindication of the Rights of Woman* was that the rights of men and of women were identical.

In the 1840s, during a period of more generalized reform efforts, the issue of women's rights emerged as a concerted cause. In the midst of earlier movements advocating reforms in education and prisons, abolition, and temperance, women began to question their status. Many outspoken advocates of reforms in education and for the

1848

■ **July 19–20**
Seneca Falls, New York, is the site of the first Women's Rights Convention, at which delegates endorse and sign the Declaration of Sentiments.

1866

■ **May 9–10**
The first organization aimed exclusively at the goal of universal suffrage, the American Equal Rights Association, is established by Elizabeth Cady Stanton and Susan B. Anthony in New York City.

1869

■ The American Equal Rights Association splits into the radical National Woman Suffrage Association, led by Stanton and Anthony, and the more conservative American Woman Suffrage Association, organized by Lucy Stone, Julia Ward Howe, and Henry Blackwell.

1872

■ **November 5**
Anthony and approximately 150 other women vote in the presidential election in Rochester, New York. They are arrested on November 22, Thanksgiving Day.

1878

■ **January 10**
A woman suffrage amendment, written by Anthony, is introduced to Congress by Senator Aaron Sargent of California. It is reintroduced with identical wording for the next forty-one years.

1890

■ **February**
The NWSA and the AWSA merge into the NAWSA under Stanton.

1912

■ **June**
The Bull Moose (Progressive) Party adopts woman suffrage as one of the planks in its party platform.

abolition of slavery, such as Sarah Grimké, Elizabeth Cady Stanton, and Anthony, found the suppression of their voices on the ground of their femininity frustrating and indicative of their larger problems. The exclusion of women from the World Anti-Slavery Conference in London in 1840 resulted in the direct comparison of slaves' and women's lack of freedoms. The Women's Rights Convention that met at Seneca Falls, New York, in July 1848 marks the official beginning of the women's rights movement in the United States. More than three hundred individuals, including Stanton, the Quaker social reformer Lucretia Coffin Mott, and the former slave and abolitionist Frederick Douglass, attended the conference, and at its conclusion sixty-eight women and thirty-two men signed the Declaration of Sentiments. Over the next decade the movement advocated not only for woman suffrage but also for more radical ideals, such as women's property rights, the abolition of a double standard in divorce laws, and the rights of women to testify and to sign contracts. The movement attracted supporters to the cause, most notably Anthony, who attended the annual convention in Syracuse in 1852. During the late 1850s and 1860s the movement's leaders and grassroots supporters channeled their efforts into Civil War work and the strident advocacy of abolition. They also conjectured that along with African Americans they would be legally recognized at the end of the struggle.

Although their hopes did not materialize, the training and experiences garnered during this period served them well during the decades that followed the war. In 1866 Stanton and Anthony established the American Equal Rights Association, an organization open to white and African American women whose aim was universal suffrage. The suffragists suffered a setback in 1868 when the states ratified the Fourteenth Amendment, which extended the protections of the Constitution to all citizens but defined a citizen as specifically male. Disputes over how to deal with crises created by the amendment's ratification and the proposed Fifteenth Amendment created a breach in the movement resulting in the establishment of two rival organizations. In 1869 Stanton and Anthony founded the National Woman Suffrage Association (NWSA) in New York. The more radical of two organizations, the NWSA limited its membership to women only and campaigned for a variety of women's social and economic issues in addition to suffrage. Its rival organization, the American Woman Suffrage Association (AWSA), was more conservative in nature. Its founders, Lucy Stone, Julia Ward Howe, and Henry Browne Blackwell, limited participation in national meetings to recognized delegates and its mission solely to suffrage. Its members believed that social and economic issues distracted their energies and alienated influential supporters. Rather than working for a national resolution, the group advocated a state-by-state approach to accomplishing its goal.

In 1878 Anthony wrote what would become known as the Anthony Amendment. Modeled on the recently ratified Fifteenth Amendment guaranteeing suffrage to all men regardless of race, this resolution would remove gender as a qualification for suffrage. Anthony and her colleagues in the NWSA persuaded a sympathetic senator from California, Aaron A. Sargent, to introduce it to Congress on January 10, 1878. Congress declined to act on the proposal, but its supporters continued to reintroduce it at every session of Congress until its eventual passage forty-one years later.

During that period the woman suffrage and rights movements underwent a multitude of changes and challenges. Perhaps most significant was the reconciliation of the NWSA and AWSA in 1890. Initiated in 1887 by members of the AWSA and negotiated by Alice Stone Blackwell (the daughter of Lucy Stone and Henry Browne Blackwell), their merger into the National American Woman Suffrage Association marked an important turning point in the movement. While the early leaders of both factions remained visible, younger women took up the standards and continued the fight. Anthony was among the last of the earlier generation and carefully cultivated her successors, Catt and Anna Howard Shaw. By 1910 all of the first generation had passed from the scene. Between 1890 and the passage of the Anthony Amendment by Congress in 1919 a variety of organizations joined the fight. The Woman's Christian Temperance Union had from its inception in 1878 supported woman suffrage as a tool for promoting temperance. The National Council of Jewish Women (1893), the National Association of Colored Women (1896), and the Women's Trade Union League (1903) broadened the movement's base of support and drew in women left at the fringes by the NAWSA, which tended to represent white, Protestant women of the middle and upper classes. The movement also had it opponents, including mainstream politicians, businessmen, liquor manufacturers, factions of the Catholic Church, and other women. The best-organized dissenting faction, the National Association Opposed to Woman Suffrage, emerged in 1911, led by Mrs. Arthur Dodge.

By the 1910s the question concerning woman suffrage became when and not if it would be achieved. In 1916 the NAWSA president, Catt, introduced her plan at the group's annual meeting in Atlantic City. She called on her membership to mobilize women at all levels of society, to curry support from all sources, and to target politicians whose positions were antithetical to the goal of woman suffrage. At the state level, a number of legislatures authorized partial or state suffrage. Another factor that worked in their favor was the growing anti-immigration sentiment across the nation. Ironically, many white, Protestant men of the middle and upper classes saw the suffragists and the allied causes as sympathetic to their interests and a way of balancing out the growing pool of naturalized immigrants joining the cadre of voters.

While the United States' entry into World War I temporarily dampened the suffragists' efforts as the majority of suffragists put their energies into war work, their patriotism and service ultimately had great benefits. Their efforts swayed many of their opponents to the cause. The most significant convert was President Woodrow Wilson, who voiced his support for the amendment in 1918.

It took an additional eighteen months to unseat some of the suffragists' staunchest opponents in Congress. The

Time Line

1913

■ **January 11**
Alice Paul and Lucy Burns establish the Congressional Union Party, later renamed the National Woman's Party, modeled after the British Women's Political and Social Union.

1914

■ National Federation of Women's Clubs, representing two million white and black women, adopts the suffrage campaign.

1916

■ **September**
Catt reveals her so-called winning plan to the NAWSA at their annual convention.

1919

■ **June 4**
Senate passes the Anthony Amendment by a vote of 56 to 25.

1920

■ **August 18**
Nineteenth Amendment is ratified.

1923

■ **March 24**
Alice Paul, president of National Women's Party, proposes the Equal Rights Amendment, contending that equality of rights could not be denied on the basis of sex.

Anthony Amendment passed through the House in May 1919 and was approved by the Senate on June 4 by a vote of fifty-six to thirty-two. Fourteen months later, on August 18, 1920, the state of Tennessee became the thirty-sixth state legislature to ratify the resolution, and the Nineteenth Amendment became law.

About the Author

Defining exactly who authored the Nineteenth Amendment is somewhat difficult. Susan B. Anthony is generally credited for its initial submission to Congress through her friend and sympathizer Aaron Sargent. After its first reading it became known as the Anthony Amendment in her honor. The amendment, itself, however, is a rewording of the earlier Fifteenth Amendment, which guaranteed universal male suffrage. Anthony, Stanton, and other leaders of the NWSA contributed to the cause.

Susan Brownell Anthony was born to Quaker parents, Daniel and Lucy, in Adams, Massachusetts, on February 15, 1820. Honoring the Quaker sensitivity for gender equality, her parents provided all of their children, male and female, an advanced education at a private Quaker boarding school in Philadelphia. There Anthony trained as a teacher and acquired her lifelong zeal for activism and reform. When Anthony's family relocated to Rochester, New York, in 1845, they continued to engage in a broad range of reform movements, including abolition, temperance, education, labor, and women's rights. Both of her parents and her sister Mary signed the Declaration of Sentiments at Seneca Falls in 1848. It was through this connection that Anthony met Elizabeth Cady Stanton and attended her first women's rights convention in Syracuse in 1852. Anthony became involved in work for women's rights through her engagement in the temperance movement. Active in the Daughters of Temperance, Anthony was refused the right to speak at a Sons of Temperance meeting in 1853, and the New York state legislature refused to recognize a petition limiting sale of alcohol circulated by Stanton and herself because most of the 28,000 signatures were by women.

Anthony, who never married, worked tirelessly for the suffragist movement for more than fifty years. During the 1850s Stanton, Anthony, and others allied themselves with the abolitionist movement and ultimately the Republican Party because they believed that their support would be rewarded by the extension of suffrage to women along with African American men. In the aftermath of the Civil War, frustrated and angered by their deliberate exclusion, they established the American Equal Rights Association in 1866 and an affiliated newspaper, the *Revolution*, in 1868. When the suffrage movement split in 1869, Anthony and Stanton established the NWSA to advocate not only suffrage but also broader social and economic reforms for women. Anthony and several others were arrested in Rochester in 1872 when they attempted to test the limits of the Fifteenth Amendment by voting in the presidential election. Although they successfully cast their ballots, they were later arrested, convicted, and fined. Anthony refused to pay the fine, hoping to take the case to the Supreme Court. Her plans were foiled by her lawyer, who paid the costs himself to keep Anthony out of jail.

In 1877, using the Fifteenth Amendment as model, she authored the Anthony Amendment, and Senator Sargent submitted it to Congress on January 10, 1878. Although both the House and the Senate refused to consider the action, Anthony saw its presentation at every session of Congress until her death in 1916. The tradition of the Anthony Amendment continued until its eventual passage in 1919.

Between 1878 and her death in 1906, Anthony continued to promote her cause. She participated in the reunion of the NWSA and the AWSA in 1890 and served as the NAWSA's second president (after Stanton) until 1900. She also broadened her horizons to establish the International Council of Women in 1888 and the International Woman Suffrage Council in 1904. To celebrate her eighty-sixth birthday, Anthony delivered the "Failure Is Impossible" speech, the title of which became the rallying cry of the woman suffrage movement. She returned to Rochester, New York, and on March 13, 1906, at her home, Anthony succumbed to congestive heart failure.

Explanation and Analysis of the Document

The document is divided into three parts: a preface, a definition of the desired goal, and the amendment itself. The amendment itself contains two sections.

The preface explains that the resolution is before the first session of the Sixty-Sixth Congress. (This count refers to the number of different Houses of Representatives elected since 1787.) The preface also includes the date, May 1919, and the location of the meeting, Washington, D.C.

The second portion of the document describes the resolution and the process of congressional approval and ratification by the states. The proposed amendment mandates a change in the U.S. Constitution to permit women to vote. It also indicates that in a joint session, both the House of Representatives and the Senate must approve by at least a two-thirds majority the resolution on the floor. It proceeds to state that the resolution becomes law when legislatures in "three-fourths" of the states (thirty-six) ratify it.

The final part of the document is the amendment itself. It states that gender does not constitute a basis for the denial of suffrage and thus defines women as citizens. It also affirms the right of the federal government to pass other legislation to enforce the suffrage provision.

Audience

This document had three separate but significant audiences: suffragists, politicians, and the general public. The first were its proponents; the second initially were in opposition. The public remained, in many ways, observers. All three responded in distinct ways to the document and shifted their attitudes over time.

The suffragists reacted to the amendment differently according to the period of time. Prior to the American Civil War, suffrage represented one of a number of significant women's rights issues. The leaders of the movement saw it as intertwined with married women's property rights, divorce standards, contract rights, and the right to bear witness in court. During Reconstruction and through the first decade of the 1900s, suffrage alone became their objective. Other issues faded into the background as a significant number of the suffragists became more conservative in their pursuits. In the years after World War I, however, the movement's leadership became increasingly convinced that suffrage alone was not sufficient.

The attitudes and reactions of politicians also changed, although less dramatically. Their relationship with the suffragists was a strained one. Male politicians had to be persuaded to grant rights and privileges to a group of individ-

"The right of the citizens of the United States to vote shall not be denied or abridged by the United States or by any State on account of sex."

(Section 1)

"Congress shall have power to enforce this article by appropriate legislation."

(Section 2)

uals who could not vote for them. Furthermore, politicians who supported woman suffrage ran the risk of alienating the more conservative of their constituencies. The majority came to support woman suffrage only as the suffragists themselves became more mainstream. President Wilson's decision to change his stance on suffrage after World War I is typical of this shift. Catt explained the relationship in an address to the NAWSA in 1920: "The only way to get things in this country, is from the inside of the political parties. More and more the parties have become the agencies through which powerful things have been accomplished. It is not a question of whether it is right for us but rather a realization of the fact. They are powerful" (http://www.fordham.edu/halsall/mod/1920womensvote.html).

For the general public the issue of woman suffrage was firmly tied to notions of traditional female interests. Those opposed to suffrage for women were convinced that voting would damage women's femininity. They feared that by transgressing beyond their traditional sphere in the social and cultural realms, women would cease to be nurturers and caretakers and lose the softer sides of their characters. Supporters suggested that rather than abandoning their social consciences, women would bring a more humanitarian character to political activities and concerns.

Impact

Despite the many predictions made concerning the effects of woman suffrage, the actual impact was relatively mild. While politicians now paid greater attention to women's issues, political activity and legislation did not become more feminine in nature, as both detractors and advocates had predicted. The welfare and social causes perceived as falling into women's spheres found only slightly more favor than they had prior to the passage of the Nineteenth Amendment. The suffragists also faced a difficult question: what was next.

After ratification, one particular transformation occurred rapidly. The NAWSA ceased to exist and reconstituted as the League of Women Voters. The avowed purpose of the

organization was to provide responsible leadership and information for women who were new to political activity. Among their challenges was to chart a path between allying with existing political parties and forming an independent political organization. Catt and others felt that the only way to accomplish their larger goals was to work through existing party structures. Other women, such as the social reformer Jane Addams, advocated policies of continued separate activity and independence. In the end, the league plotted a policy of nonpartisan activity aimed at keeping members informed and politicians honest in their approaches and promises to female voters.

Politicians at all levels reacted to their new female constituents cautiously. During the early 1920s local, state, and national legislators enacted laws favorable to women. Female lobbies and information campaigns had enough impact to affect legislative decisions. These concerned issues of maternity, length of the workday, and safety concerns. The predicted humanitarian transformation of politics caused by the infusion of feminine values, however, did not materialize, and by mid-decade their influence waned. The majority of women voted along lines that had more to do with their diverse socioeconomic statuses and their racial and ethnic backgrounds than any perceived nurturing instincts.

As American politics in general grew more conservative, women's rights advocates began to reconsider some issues deemed too radical only a decade earlier. Suffrage alone did not resolve the inequities still visited upon women; gender discrimination continued to exist. In 1923 Alice Paul of the National Woman's Party introduced the Equal Rights Amendment that would eventually bear her name. The Paul Amendment, or ERA, contended that equal rights could not be limited on the basis of gender. For Paul and those who were like-minded, the Nineteenth Amendment was merely the first step in the battle for equity.

Related Documents

Hooker, Isabella Beecher. "The Constitutional Rights of the Women of the United States: An Address before the International

Council of Women, Washington, D.C., March 30, 1888." Library of Congress "American Memory" Web site. http://memory.loc.gov/cgi-bin/query/r?ammem/naw:@field(DOCID+@lit(rbnawsan8333div0)). Accessed on January 15, 2008. This declaration outlines the principles and goals of American suffragists as they continued their campaign for a constitutional amendment authorizing suffrage for women.

"The Passage of the 19th Amendment, 1919–1920: Articles from *The New York Times*." Modern History Sourcebook Web site. http://www.fordham.edu/halsall/mod/1920womensvote.html. Accessed on January 15, 2008. These articles from the *New York Times* detail the struggle for the passage and ratification of the Nineteenth Amendment. They present a popular view of the events as they unfold.

Stanton, Elizabeth Cady. "Declaration of Sentiments." National Park Service Web site. http://www.nps.gov/wori/historyculture/declaration-of-sentiments.htm. Accessed on January 15, 2008. Penned by Elizabeth Cady Stanton with the aid of the McClintock family, the declaration launched the concerted campaign for women's rights and suffrage. One hundred of those attending the women's rights convention at Seneca Falls in 1848 signed the document.

———. "Solitude of Self." National Park Service Web site. http://www.nps.gov/wori/historyculture/solitude-of-self.htm. Accessed on January 15, 2008. Delivered before the Congressional Judiciary Committee in 1892, when Stanton was seventy-seven years old, this is generally considered one of Stanton's most eloquent orations. She addresses the fundamental equality of men and women.

Wollstonecraft, Mary. *A Vindication of the Rights of Woman*. University of Virginia Library Electronic Text Center Web site. http://etext.virginia.edu/toc/modeng/public/WolVind.html. Accessed on January 15, 2008. Published in England in 1790, Wollstonecraft's work was considered extraordinarily radical in that it advocated the basic equality of the sexes in all matters. Her work laid the foundation for women's rights movements in Europe and North America.

Bibliography

■ Books
Chafe, William H. *The Paradox of Change: American Women in the Twentieth Century*. New York: Oxford University Press, 1991.

Cott, Nancy F. *The Grounding of Modern Feminism*. New Haven, Conn.: Yale University Press, 1987.

Flexner, Eleanor. *Century of Struggle: The Woman's Rights Movement in the United States*. New York: Atheneum, 1972.

Kraditor, Aileen S. *The Ideas of the Woman Suffrage Movement, 1890–1920*. New York: Columbia University Press, 1965.

O'Neill, William L. *Everyone Was Brave: A History of Feminism in America*. Chicago: Quadrangle Books, 1971.

Woloch, Nancy. *Women and the American Experience*. New York: Alfred A. Knopf, 1984.

■ Web Sites
The Equal Rights Amendment Web site.
http://www.equalrightsamendment.org/. Accessed on January 15, 2008.

"The First Women's Rights Convention." National Park Service Web site.
http://www.nps.gov/wori/historyculture/the-first-womens-rights-convention.htm. Accessed on January 15, 2008.

"19th Amendment to the U.S. Constitution: Women's Right to Vote (1920)." National Archives "Our Documents" Web site.
http://www.ourdocuments.gov/doc.php?flash=true&doc=63. Accessed on January 15, 2008.

"Votes for Women: Selections from the National American Woman Suffrage Association Collection, 1848–1921." The Library of Congress American Memory Web site.
http://memory.loc.gov/ammem/naw/nawshome.html. Accessed on January 15, 2008.

"Women's Fight for the Vote: The Nineteenth Amendment." Exploring Constitutional Conflicts Web site.
http://www.law.umkc.edu/faculty/projects/ftrials/conlaw/nineteentham.htm. Accessed on January 15, 2008.

—By Martha Pallante

Questions for Further Study

1. Compare and contrast the Fifteenth and Nineteenth Amendments. How are the language and formats used in both alike, and how are they different?

2. What did the Nineteenth Amendment accomplish for the women's rights cause? What did it leave undone?

3. Why did activists such as Susan B. Anthony and Elizabeth Cady Stanton see woman suffrage as the most important cause of the women's rights movement?

4. Why were those engaged in suffragist activities primarily white, middle-class women?

5. Why are the arguments against woman suffrage less potent in the twentieth century than they were during the nineteenth century?

6. In your opinion, which is more radical: the Declaration of Sentiments (1848) or the Nineteenth Amendment?

7. What is the relationship of the Nineteenth Amendment to the Equal Rights Amendment proposed by Alice Paul in 1923? How is that relation similar and different to the one existing between the Fourteenth and Fifteenth Amendments?

Glossary

abridged	reduced or limited
account of sex	by reason of gender
Joint Resolution	resolution to both houses of Congress
ratified	approved or sanctioned, in this case by state legislatures
suffrage	right to vote

NINETEENTH AMENDMENT TO THE U.S. CONSTITUTION

Sixty-sixth Congress of the United States of America; At the First Session,

Begun and held at the City of Washington on Monday, the nineteenth day of May, one thousand nine hundred and nineteen.

◆ **Joint Resolution Proposing an Amendment to the Constitution Extending the Right of Suffrage to Women.**

Resolved by the Senate and House of Representatives of the United States of America in Congress assembled (two-thirds of each House concurring therein), That

the following article is proposed as an amendment to the Constitution, which shall be valid to all intents and purposes as part of the Constitution when ratified by the legislature of three-fourths of the several States.

ARTICLE ————.

"The right of citizens of the United States to vote shall not be denied or abridged by the United States or by any State on account of sex.

Congress shall have power to enforce this article by appropriate legislation."

Franklin D. Roosevelt (Library of Congress)

"The only thing we have to fear is fear itself."

Overview

When Franklin Delano Roosevelt delivered his First Inaugural Address on March 4, 1933, the United States was still in the midst of the Great Depression, which began after the stock market crash on what came to be known as Black Tuesday, October 29, 1929. The American economy hit rock bottom in the very month Roosevelt took his oath of office. In his First Inaugural Address, he treated this moment of history as unprecedented. Unlike his predecessor, Herbert Hoover, Roosevelt did not shy away from blaming the business community for incompetent and unethical practices that had led to economic disaster. While he emphasized that "the people of the United States have not failed," he regarded himself as the leader they elected to restore a sense of "discipline and direction."

Without outlining a specific program, Roosevelt signaled that the federal government would take a much more direct role in putting people to work and in managing the national economy. Roosevelt argued that only through major improvements on the domestic front could the United States hope to compete successfully in international markets. In effect, he declared a state of domestic emergency and called on Congress to grant him the broad executive powers required to deal with a crisis as great as war and as perilous as the invasion of a foreign foe.

Context

When Franklin Roosevelt took office, three Republicans—Warren G. Harding, Calvin Coolidge, and Herbert Hoover—had occupied the presidency for twelve years. Until 1929 these leaders had presided over a booming economy, characterized not only by the huge growth of corporations but also by the phenomenal success of individual investors in the stock market. The capitalist model of civilization seemed to promise wealth to everyone. It was a period also known as the Roaring Twenties, because many social restraints were abandoned. Flappers, women who wore short hair and skirts and seemed far more independ-

ent than earlier generations, became the subject of newspaper articles and stories. In general, men and women seemed attracted to unconventional modes of living, although much of the country remained conservative.

When the stock market crashed, this ebullient period ended. Millions lost their jobs, and many writers and intellectuals reconsidered their role in society. They wrote about the ruined economy and wondered whether capitalism itself might have failed. Some writers turned to communism and the ideal of a welfare state, in which the employment needs and health of citizens would become a government responsibility, as a solution to capitalism's inadequacies.

In his First Inaugural Address, Roosevelt was responding, therefore, to calls for government action. He was a traditional Democrat—not a Socialist or Communist—but his intention to invent large-scale government programs of relief and employment marked an unprecedented break with both the rhetoric and the policies of previous federal administrations. Rather than reassure Americans that traditional institutions were in good shape, Roosevelt believed that he had inherited a broken system that required radical repair. He spoke to a national sense of urgency, pledging immediate action and announcing, "The only thing we have to fear is fear itself."

About the Author

Franklin Delano Roosevelt was born on January 30, 1882, in Hyde Park, New York. The Roosevelts were a wealthy family and sent their son to the best private schools and universities (Groton, Harvard, and Columbia). Roosevelt became a member of the New York State Bar and practiced law in New York City for three years. Early on Roosevelt developed an interest in politics—stimulated, in part, by the career of his fifth cousin, Theodore Roosevelt, who in 1901, at age forty-two, became the youngest person to be elected president of the United States. In 1910 Franklin Roosevelt was elected to the New York State Senate, proving himself a zealous campaigner and an ambitious legislator.

Roosevelt's political connections led to his appointment as assistant secretary of the navy in Woodrow Wilson's

1929

■ **October 29**
The stock market crashes, a day known as Black Tuesday.

■ **November 13**
In all, $30 billion in the market value of listed stocks is wiped out.

1930

■ **December 11**
The Bank of the United States in New York City closes (the nation's largest bank failure), with some 400,000 depositors incurring losses.

1932

■ More than thirteen million are unemployed, and the stock market loses $75 billion in the market value of stocks.

■ **January 22**
The Reconstruction Finance Corporation is established, with $2 billion available for loans to failing banks and other financial institutions.

■ **February 27**
First Glass-Steagall Act, a credit expansion measure designed to counteract the hoarding of gold and currency that contributed to the Depression, is passed.

■ **July 21**
The Emergency Relief Act provides $300 million in loans to states for welfare.

■ **July 22**
The Federal Home Loan Bank Act creates twelve regional banks to discount home loans for building and loan associations, savings banks, and insurance companies.

■ **November 8**
Roosevelt is elected thirty-second president in a landslide, carrying forty-two states.

1933

■ **February 15**
Giuseppe Zangara fires six shots at president-elect Roosevelt, missing him but fatally wounding Mayor Anton Cermak of Chicago.

■ **March 4**
Roosevelt is inaugurated as president. He faces a banking crisis, with 5,504 banks shut down since the stock market crash.

administration (1913–1921). An able and hands-on administrator, Roosevelt modernized the navy and schooled himself in the workings of the federal government—an experience that would serve him especially well as a wartime president. Roosevelt's rapid rise in politics seemed to be halted when he contracted polio in 1921. Although his legs were paralyzed and he would never again walk, his physical stamina returned, and he courageously reentered public life. In 1929 he was elected governor of New York. Continuing the progressive agenda pursued by his predecessor, Al Smith, Roosevelt captured his party's nomination for president in 1932. As president, with the help of a large Democratic majority in Congress, Roosevelt passed a significant number of legislative acts aimed at economic recovery in both the agricultural and industrial sectors of the economy.

Although Roosevelt confronted a largely pacifist nation during the 1930s, his gradual and cunning support of Great Britain and its allies guided the nation toward a confrontation with Nazi Germany and imperial Japan that erupted in war after the Japanese attack on Pearl Harbor on December 6, 1941. Roosevelt's legacy as a war leader includes his vigorous prosecution of the war, steadfast support of his allies, and postwar plans for an international organization to facilitate cooperation in such areas as security, economic development, and human rights (which became the United Nations in 1945).

A controversial leader at home, Roosevelt's expansion of the federal government led to charges that he was turning the country into a socialist state. Others have viewed his legacy as a redemption of capitalism. Roosevelt broke the tradition of presidents serving no more than two terms. In 1944 he was elected to a fourth term, but he died of a cerebral hemorrhage on April 12, 1945.

Explanation and Analysis of the Document

When Franklin D. Roosevelt addressed the American people for the first time as their president, he believed that his primary task was to speak frankly and to calm public fears. Indeed, he believed that only through candor could he allay the pervasive public anxiety about the state of the nation. Although President Hoover's administration had taken certain measures to alleviate the suffering of the unemployed and to improve the business climate in the country, the public had been given assurances that there was nothing fundamentally wrong with America's institutions and that eventually the free marketplace would recover.

By the time Roosevelt took the oath of office, however, the Great Depression had already lasted three years. People were panicking and rushing to banks to withdraw their savings. Many states had declared bank closures to try to prevent the failure of yet more financial institutions. In his First Inaugural Address, Roosevelt makes the Great Depression a national problem—one that requires forceful executive leadership.

In his first three paragraphs, Roosevelt addresses the psychological state of the nation, declaring in the most famous phrase of his speech: "The only thing we have to fear is fear itself—nameless, unreasoning, unjustified terror which paralyzes needed efforts to convert retreat into advance." This phrase deliberately turns the Great Depression into a state of mind, not just an economic or social problem. Roosevelt's use of a military vocabulary (retreat and advance) suggests how much importance he placed on making Americans believe that they had the will to turn defeat into victory. Rather than lull the public into a sense of security, however, Roosevelt emphasizes that progress can only be made by facing the dire truth, which he relays in graphic language: "Values have shrunken to fantastic levels; taxes have risen; our ability to pay has fallen; government of all kinds is faced by serious curtailment of income; the means of exchange are frozen in the currents of trade; the withered leaves of industrial enterprise lie on every side; farmers find no markets for their produce; the savings of many years in thousands of families are gone." Through such statements, Roosevelt was communicating that this was no time for foolish optimism, especially when unemployment was the scourge of the nation.

Roosevelt does not hesitate to identify the causes of this massive unemployment. In his fourth paragraph, he notes that it was not an act of nature, not a "plague of locusts"—a phrase that prepares the way for his identification of who was responsible for so much suffering in a land that still had bountiful natural resources. He says, "The rulers of the exchange of mankind's goods have failed, through their own stubbornness and their own incompetence, have admitted their failure, and abdicated. Practices of the unscrupulous money changers stand indicted in the court of public opinion, rejected by the hearts and minds of men." Roosevelt blames the leaders of the business community, which is one reason why his fiercest critics accused him of attempting to destroy capitalism. The president's use of the phrase *money changers*, with its biblical connotations, suggests that the fault lay with the corrupt managers of the system, the "unscrupulous."

Roosevelt acknowledges that these "rulers of exchange" and "money changers" had attempted to right the system, but their actions were part of an "outworn tradition" that understands only self-seeking and profits. Having no vision of a just and equitable society (the standards implicit in Roosevelt's rejection of selfishness), these business leaders can only exhort people to have confidence in business as usual. As Roosevelt has noted, however, these false prophets had already lost the hearts and minds of the American people.

What is most striking in the first part of the address is Roosevelt's confidence that he has understood the public mood, which he cloaks in biblical terms in his sixth paragraph: "The money changers have fled from their high seats in the temple of our civilization. They have relinquished any claim to leadership. We may now restore that temple to the ancient truths. The measure of the restoration lies in the extent to which we apply social values more noble than mere monetary profit." Drawing on the New Testament account of Jesus throwing the money changers out of the temple, Roosevelt asserts that "we" will restore the temple (America) to

www.milestonedocuments.com

Time Line

1933	■ **March 19–June 16** The one hundred days during which Congress enacts many New Deal programs, including the Reforestation Relief Act, the Civilian Conservation Corps, the Federal Emergence Relief Act, the Agricultural Adjustment Act, the Tennessee Valley Authority, the Federal Securities Act, the National Employment Systems Act, and establishes the Public Works Administration and the National Recovery Administration.
1934– 1936	■ Congress continues to enact major New Deal legislation, such as the Farm Mortgage Refinancing Act, the Securities Exchange Act, the Emergency Relief Appropriation Act, the National Labor Relations Act, and the Social Security Act.
1938– 1939	■ The New Deal essentially comes to a close (very little major legislation is enacted) as Roosevelt and the nation begin to look toward events in Europe and the eruption of war.

its fundamental core values, which hold that money is not an end in itself; instead America is about the pursuit of creative endeavors and the thrill of achievement. These are moral, social, and community goals that have always united the country but that have now been deserted for "evanescent profits." The way out of the Great Depression, Roosevelt suggests, is by encouraging Americans to think of more than their well-being as individuals. By working on behalf of one another, Americans will benefit themselves.

Roosevelt's emphasis on happiness in paragraph 7 recalls the famous "pursuit of Happiness" phrase in the Declaration of Independence (http://www.ourdocuments.gov/doc.php?doc=2&page=transcript). It is an all-encompassing concept that far exceeds any notions of profit and worldly success. In other words, Roosevelt is making a direct appeal to moral, ethical, and spiritual values that he believes have been perverted by an unseemly haste to make money. "Our true destiny," the president emphasizes, "is not to be ministered unto." In other words, Roosevelt believes Americans should not expect benefits but will benefit from their care and concern for their fellow citizens. The idea that Americans have a "destiny" is a grand and uplifting conception of human existence that Roosevelt plays upon throughout his address.

Those in banking and business have been callous and dishonest, Roosevelt charges in paragraph 8, and have thought only of themselves and of safeguarding their positions. It is not surprising, therefore, that the public has lost confidence in the economic system. By focusing his attack directly on the country's commercial interests, Roosevelt shifts attention away from the idea that poverty and unemployment are a personal, individual responsibility. According to Roosevelt, it is not the working men and women who have let the country down, but the people who employ them, especially in the large corporations and businesses supported by financial institutions whose only concern is to maximize return on their investments and profits for shareholders.

Using phrases like the "sacredness of obligations" and "faithful protection," Roosevelt accuses big businesses of forfeiting the public's trust and of violating their responsibility for the peoples' welfare. Such religious phrases suggest that the commercial sector has sinned. In other words, instead of attributing the Great Depression to mere abuses of the system—as President Hoover did—Roosevelt tries to turn the country's recovery efforts into a crusade, a campaign against the evildoers. The key term for Roosevelt is "restoration." He is not advocating revolution but a return to the Founding Fathers' values and the fundamental tenets of the Judeo-Christian tradition.

Perhaps sensing that so far his words constitute merely an indictment of business as usual, in paragraph 9 Roosevelt speaks as the voice of the people, declaring that the nation wants "action now." And as part of that action, he announces in paragraph 10 his plans for the government to employ people immediately on projects developing the nation's "natural resources." Only the government, he implies, can mobilize an entire people now engaged in a challenge as great as the waging of war.

In one of his few specific proposals in this address, Roosevelt calls for better land use policies, although what he means by "redistribution" (paragraph 11) is perhaps left purposefully vague in order to forestall the notion that the government will nationalize land—that is, take it out of the hands of private ownership. (In fact, the Roosevelt administration later took an aggressive role in managing land when it established the Tennessee Valley Authority in May of 1933). Roosevelt mentions the tragedy of foreclosures on farms and small homes as an example of how individuals have been hurt by the banking system. He implies that if the values of agricultural goods can be raised and the transportation system improved, many of these human losses can be curtailed. Similarly, he says, relief efforts need to be coordinated so that the unemployed across the country can receive stable and consistent aid. Without doubt, Roosevelt is calling for an unprecedented role for the federal government, one in which it would take from the states the major responsibility of public welfare. To Roosevelt, this was the only way to ensure equal treatment for all citizens, because otherwise, relief payments in one state could be considerably higher or lower than in another.

In effect, then, when Roosevelt calls for government action, he is primarily proposing a much greater role for the federal government and for himself, which includes a series of measures aimed directly at the banking and financial sector. The stock market, for example, could no longer be allowed to function without some kind of federal government oversight. Two years after Roosevelt's address, the Securities and Exchange Commission would be established to monitor the buying and selling of stocks, bonds, and other securities.

To underline his determination to take immediate action, in paragraph 13 Roosevelt calls for a special session of Congress. This session would become the famous "100 days," in which the president sent Congress a flurry of bills proposing immediate relief for the unemployed, mortgage relief for farmers, and other measures aimed at directly supporting those who were not able to support themselves as well as funding regions of the country that needed economic development.

Other matters of concern—such as international trade and foreign policy—receive only a few paragraphs (14– 16) in this address because, as a practical matter, Roosevelt notes, they are secondary to the nation's need to put its own house in order. The president appeals to the pioneer spirit in Americans and to a sense of interdependence. The nation cannot thrive unless all regions of the country recognize their vital connection to one another.

Roosevelt's only specific comment on foreign policy is his announcement of his good neighbor policy (paragraph 16), which respects the rights of other countries and international agreements. While this terse statement seems to say little, it must be viewed in the context of U.S. interventions in Mexico, Central America, and parts of South America that Woodrow Wilson and other presidents sanctioned. While Roosevelt provides no specifics, his enunciation of the good neighbor principle certainly signals a change in foreign policy.

In the concluding paragraphs of his address, Roosevelt returns to the themes of interdependence and discipline, but with a difference. Whereas he began with an absolute conviction that he spoke for the public mood, he now introduces a note of modesty in paragraph 17 when he says, "If I read the temper of our people correctly, we now realize as we have never realized before our interdependence on each other." Progress, he says, depends on a sense of reciprocity, of Americans giving to and taking from each other.

The circular structure of Roosevelt's First Inaugural Address evokes the need not only to unify his thoughts but also to reiterate the assurances and pledges he has offered to Americans. He has called them to an awareness of national aspirations that go well beyond individual ambition and that, again, evoke both a spiritual and a militant mood: "The larger purposes will bind upon us all as a sacred obligation with a unity of duty hitherto evoked only in time of armed strife."

Roosevelt's own relish for the challenge ahead is obvious in his exclamation in paragraph 18: "With this pledge taken, I assume unhesitatingly the leadership of this great army of our people dedicated to a disciplined attack upon our common problems." Notice that in the phrase "great

An estimated crowd of 150,000 gathered to watch President Franklin D. Roosevelt deliver his First Inaugural Address. (AP Photo)

army of our people," he has made the national task of reconstruction and restoration into a metaphor. Indeed, programs like the Civilian Conservation Corps would be structured like a military organization with the discipline and camaraderie associated with a wartime footing.

Although Roosevelt has all along called for extraordinary measures to revive the nation, he now stresses the importance of the Constitution, which has been able to function in every crisis the United States has confronted. In effect, he emphasizes that however bold his measures may be, they will also conform to the law. As grave as the current crisis is, the president is reminding the country of other periods of emergency, noting in paragraph 19 that the Constitution has "met every stress of vast expansion of territory, of foreign wars, of bitter internal strife, of world relations."

Although Roosevelt anticipates that the traditional relationship between Congress and the executive will remain the same during his administration, he warns in paragraph 22 that should the crisis persist even after Congressional

action, he will not "evade the clear course of duty," meaning he will request from Congress "broad Executive power to wage a war against the emergency, as great as the power that would be given to me if we were in fact invaded by a foreign foe." The word *duty* is key, because it emphasizes that the president is not seizing control, or even advocating it, but rather responding to a situation so dire that he would be remiss if he did not exert unprecedented power. This assertion of power, however, is tempered by Roosevelt's acknowledgment that his authority stems from the trust of the people to whom he declares his devotion and courage (paragraph 24). "The people of the United States have not failed," he insists in paragraph 25, and democracy is as viable as ever.

In closing, Roosevelt stakes his warrant for action on the mandate the American people have given him for vigorous and direct action. Then he unites in one sentence what he expects from Americans and what they expect from him: "They have asked for discipline and direction under leader-

"The only thing we have to fear is fear itself."

(Paragraph 1)

"Where there is no vision the people perish."

(Paragraph 5)

"This Nation asks for action, and action now."

(Paragraph 9)

"I would dedicate this Nation to the policy of the good neighbor."

(Paragraph 6)

"The people of the United States have not failed."

(Paragraph 25)

ship." Returning to the humility that all American presidents have expressed in their public addresses, Roosevelt concludes not with his mandate but with his faith in a higher power: "In this dedication of a Nation we humbly ask the blessing of God. May He protect each and every one of us. May He guide me in the days to come." Using the first person singular and plural, Roosevelt makes his mission the American people's mission in the hope that the Creator's blessing sanctions both.

Audience

Roosevelt's audience in his First Inaugural Address was, of course, the American people, but his immediate listeners were some 150,000 people "spread over forty acres facing the Capitol," writes Jean Edward Smith (pp. 301–302). While Roosevelt lauded the spirit of the American people, he also targeted the business and banking sectors, excoriating corrupt commercial practices (including reckless speculation and unsound loans) that had led to massive unemployment and deep decreases in the country's productivity. Except for his one statement about his "good neighbor policy," Roosevelt did not address foreign powers. His audience was primarily national, not international. This was a time when Americans looked inward, so that the nation's relationships with the world seemed of secondary importance—as Roosevelt himself emphasized in his address.

Impact

As historian Kenneth S. Davis reports, Roosevelt's First Inaugural Address was received with great calm but also with "powerfully focused attention" (Davis, p. 29). Although his call to action stirred some listeners, others were disturbed because his words seemed "distressingly vague" (Davis, p. 30). Overall, however, the new president conveyed a spirit of courage and optimism. When he declared that he would not hesitate to call for broad executive power to combat the national crisis, he was greeted with a loud burst of applause. After Roosevelt asked for God's blessing, protection, and guidance, the audience fell silent and then erupted in cheers and applause.

Davis suggests that in the first thirty-six hours after his address, Roosevelt transformed the national mood, vanquishing the "gloomy compound of fear, anger, disgust, cynicism, and despair" (Davis, p. 34). Ted Morgan calls the national response "galvanic," though he notes that dissenters like Edmund Wilson scorned Roosevelt's boy scout enthusiasm while others, like the actress Lillian Gish, thought the new president's performance incandescent (Morgan, p. 375). Jean Edward Smith suggests that Roosevelt's words exceeded "even Lincoln's magnificent second inaugural in their immediate impact" (Smith, p. 302). "No one doubted a new era had come," Smith adds (Smith, p. 303). In the week after his First Inaugural Address, Roosevelt received a half million letters. Historian William E.

Leuchtenburg concludes that unlike Hoover, Roosevelt inspired in the public the image of an optimistic and forceful leader.

Roosevelt's ringing phrase, "we have nothing to fear but fear itself," has remained the signature statement of his first public speech as president. It typified his tendency to believe that in restoring Americans' confidence in themselves, he was also bringing the country back to a sense of its own greatness and ability to prosper.

Related Documents

"First Inaugural Address of Ronald Reagan." The Avalon Project at Yale University Web site. http://www.yale.edu/lawweb/avalon/presiden/inaug/reagan1.htm. Accessed on September 28, 2007. Ronald Reagan, a great admirer of Roosevelt, nevertheless grew to distrust the role of big government and sought ways to reform it.

"Inaugural Address of John F. Kennedy." The Avalon Project at Yale University Web site. http://www.yale.edu/lawweb/avalon/presiden/inaug/kennedy.htm. Accessed on September 28, 2007. John F. Kennedy's call for a "New Frontier" echoed Roosevelt's declaration that Americans deserved a New Deal, one that would inspire their sense of patriotism and willingness to work for the welfare of all Americans.

"Second Inaugural Address of Grover Cleveland." The Avalon Project at Yale University Web site. http://www.yale.edu/lawweb/avalon/presiden/inaug/cleve2.htm. Accessed on September 28, 2007. Like Roosevelt, Grover Cleveland faced a severe depression, which began in January 1893, and he had to decide on the proper role of the government in reforming the country's financial system.

"Second Inaugural Address of William J. Clinton; January 20, 1997." The Avalon Project at Yale University Web site. http://www.yale.edu/lawweb/avalon/presiden/inaug/clinton2.htm. Accessed on September 28, 2007. Bill Clinton sought to mediate between the Roosevelt and Reagan attitudes toward government by emphasizing—as both Roosevelt and Reagan did—the power of the people themselves to improve their lives and their nation.

Bibliography

■ Books

Black, Conrad. *Franklin Delano Roosevelt: Champion of Freedom.* New York: Public Affairs, 2005.

Burns, James MacGregor. *Roosevelt: The Lion and the Fox.* New York: Harcourt Brace, 1956.

Davis, Kenneth S. *FDR: The New Deal Years 1933–1937.* New York: Random House, 1986.

Freidel, Frank. *Franklin D. Roosevelt: A Rendezvous with Destiny.* Boston: Little, Brown, 1990.

Jenkins, Roy. *Franklin Delano Roosevelt.* New York: Henry Holt, 2003.

Leuchtenburg, William E. *Franklin D. Roosevelt and the New Deal 1932–1940.* New York: Harper & Row, 1963.

McJimsey, George. *The Presidency of Franklin Delano Roosevelt.* Lawrence: University of Kansas Press, 2000.

Morgan, Ted. *FDR: A Biography.* New York: Simon and Schuster, 1985.

Schlesinger, Arthur M., Jr. *The Age of Roosevelt.* Boston: Houghton Mifflin, 1957–1960.

Smith, Jean Edward. *FDR.* New York: Random House, 2007.

■ Web Sites

"Franklin D. Roosevelt." The White House Web site. http://www.whitehouse.gov/history/presidents/fr32.html. Accessed on September 25, 2007.

Franklin D. Roosevelt Presidential Library and Museum Web site. http://www.fdrlibrary.marist.edu/. Accessed on September 25, 2007.

"Transcript of Declaration of Independence (1776)." National Archives "Our Documents" Web site. http://www.ourdocuments.gov/doc.php?doc=2&page=transcript. Accessed on January 31, 2008.

—By Carl Rollyson

1. Compare and contrast President Grover Cleveland's second inaugural address (March 4, 1893) with Roosevelt's First Inaugural Address. Like Roosevelt, Cleveland is concerned about an economy in crisis, and like Roosevelt, Cleveland focuses on corruption in the business community and the need for government action: "To the extent that they can be reached and restrained by Federal power the General Government should relieve our citizens" from the actions of monopolistic business interests (http://www.yale.edu/lawweb/avalon/presiden/inaug/cleve2.htm). How does Cleveland's idea of government action differ from Roosevelt's?

2. Compare and contrast John F. Kennedy's First Inaugural Address (January 20, 1961) with Roosevelt's. In particular, compare Kennedy's famous statement "Ask not what your country can do for you—ask what you can do for your country" (http://www.yale.edu/lawweb/avalon/presiden/inaug/kennedy.htm) with Roosevelt's "We can not merely take but we must give as well; … if we are to go forward, we must move as a trained and loyal army willing to sacrifice for the good of a common discipline, because without such discipline no progress is made, no leadership becomes effective."

3. Compare and contrast the following remarks of Ronald Reagan in his first inaugural address (January 20, 1981) with Roosevelt's: "Now, so there will be no misunderstanding, it is not my intention to do away with government. It is, rather, to make it work—work with us, not over us; to stand by our side, not ride on our back. Government can and must provide opportunity, not smother it; foster productivity, not stifle it" (http://www.yale.edu/lawweb/avalon/presiden/inaug/reagan1.htm).

4. Compare and contrast the following remarks of Bill Clinton in his second inaugural address (January 20, 1997) with Roosevelt's First Inaugural Address: "And once again, we have resolved for our time a great debate over the role of government. Today we can declare: Government is not the problem, and government is not the solution. We, the American people, we are the solution" (http://www.yale.edu/lawweb/avalon/presiden/inaug/clinton2.htm).

Glossary

evanescent	illusory; tending to vanish
exhortations	expressions of encouragement
foreclosure	bank repossession of property that homeowners or businesses have bought with a mortgage
relief	during the Great Depression, a fixed number of payments to unemployed workers
strife	conflict
unscrupulous	lacking moral integrity
values	the price of goods and property

FRANKLIN D. ROOSEVELT'S FIRST INAUGURAL ADDRESS

I am certain that my fellow Americans expect that on my induction into the Presidency I will address them with a candor and a decision which the present situation of our Nation impels. This is preeminently the time to speak the truth, the whole truth, frankly and boldly. Nor need we shrink from honestly facing conditions in our country today. This great Nation will endure as it has endured, will revive and will prosper. So, first of all, let me assert my firm belief that the only thing we have to fear is fear itself— nameless, unreasoning, unjustified terror which paralyzes needed efforts to convert retreat into advance. In every dark hour of our national life a leadership of frankness and vigor has met with that understanding and support of the people themselves which is essential to victory. I am convinced that you will again give that support to leadership in these critical days.

In such a spirit on my part and on yours we face our common difficulties. They concern, thank God, only material things. Values have shrunken to fantastic levels; taxes have risen; our ability to pay has fallen; government of all kinds is faced by serious curtailment of income; the means of exchange are frozen in the currents of trade; the withered leaves of industrial enterprise lie on every side; farmers find no markets for their produce; the savings of many years in thousands of families are gone.

More important, a host of unemployed citizens face the grim problem of existence, and an equally great number toil with little return. Only a foolish optimist can deny the dark realities of the moment.

Yet our distress comes from no failure of substance. We are stricken by no plague of locusts. Compared with the perils which our forefathers conquered because they believed and were not afraid, we have still much to be thankful for. Nature still offers her bounty and human efforts have multiplied it. Plenty is at our doorstep, but a generous use of it languishes in the very sight of the supply. Primarily this is because the rulers of the exchange of mankind's goods have failed, through their own stubbornness and their own incompetence, have admitted their failure, and abdicated. Practices of the unscrupulous money changers stand indicted in the court of public opinion, rejected by the hearts and minds of men.

True they have tried, but their efforts have been cast in the pattern of an outworn tradition. Faced by failure of credit they have proposed only the lending of more money. Stripped of the lure of profit by which to induce our people to follow their false leadership, they have resorted to exhortations, pleading tearfully for restored confidence. They know only the rules of a generation of self-seekers. They have no vision, and when there is no vision the people perish.

The money changers have fled from their high seats in the temple of our civilization. We may now restore that temple to the ancient truths. The measure of the restoration lies in the extent to which we apply social values more noble than mere monetary profit.

Happiness lies not in the mere possession of money; it lies in the joy of achievement, in the thrill of creative effort. The joy and moral stimulation of work no longer must be forgotten in the mad chase of evanescent profits. These dark days will be worth all they cost us if they teach us that our true destiny is not to be ministered unto but to minister to ourselves and to our fellow men.

Recognition of the falsity of material wealth as the standard of success goes hand in hand with the abandonment of the false belief that public office and high political position are to be valued only by the standards of pride of place and personal profit; and there must be an end to a conduct in banking and in business which too often has given to a sacred trust the likeness of callous and selfish wrongdoing. Small wonder that confidence languishes, for it thrives only on honesty, on honor, on the sacredness of obligations, on faithful protection, on unselfish performance; without them it cannot live.

Restoration calls, however, not for changes in ethics alone. This Nation asks for action, and action now.

Our greatest primary task is to put people to work. This is no unsolvable problem if we face it wisely and courageously. It can be accomplished in part by direct recruiting by the Government itself, treating the task as we would treat the emergency of a war, but at the same time, through this employment, accomplishing greatly needed projects to stimulate and reorganize the use of our natural resources.

Hand in hand with this we must frankly recognize the overbalance of population in our industrial centers and, by engaging on a national scale in a redistribution, endeavor to provide a better use of the land for those best fitted for the land. The task can be helped by definite efforts to raise the values of agricultural products and with this the power to purchase the output of our cities. It can be helped by preventing realistically the tragedy of the growing loss through foreclosure of our small homes and our farms. It can be helped by insistence that the Federal, State, and local governments act forthwith on the demand that their cost be drastically reduced. It can be helped by the unifying of relief activities which today are often scattered, uneconomical, and unequal. It can be helped by national planning for and supervision of all forms of transportation and of communications and other utilities which have a definitely public character. There are many ways in which it can be helped, but it can never be helped merely by talking about it. We must act and act quickly.

Finally, in our progress toward a resumption of work we require two safeguards against a return of the evils of the old order; there must be a strict supervision of all banking and credits and investments; there must be an end to speculation with other people's money, and there must be provision for an adequate but sound currency.

There are the lines of attack. I shall presently urge upon a new Congress in special session detailed measures for their fulfillment, and I shall seek the immediate assistance of the several States.

Through this program of action we address ourselves to putting our own national house in order and making income balance outgo. Our international trade relations, though vastly important, are in point of time and necessity secondary to the establishment of a sound national economy. I favor as a practical policy the putting of first things first. I shall spare no effort to restore world trade by international economic readjustment, but the emergency at home cannot wait on that accomplishment.

The basic thought that guides these specific means of national recovery is not narrowly nationalistic. It is the insistence, as a first consideration, upon the interdependence of the various elements in all parts of the United States—a recognition of the old and permanently important manifestation of the American spirit of the pioneer. It is the way to recovery. It is the immediate way. It is the strongest assurance that the recovery will endure.

In the field of world policy I would dedicate this Nation to the policy of the good neighbor—the neighbor who resolutely respects himself and, because he does so, respects the rights of others— the neighbor who respects his obligations and respects the sanctity of his agreements in and with a world of neighbors.

If I read the temper of our people correctly, we now realize as we have never realized before our interdependence on each other; that we can not merely take but we must give as well; that if we are to go forward, we must move as a trained and loyal army willing to sacrifice for the good of a common discipline, because without such discipline no progress is made, no leadership becomes effective. We are, I know, ready and willing to submit our lives and property to such discipline, because it makes possible a leadership which aims at a larger good. This I propose to offer, pledging that the larger purposes will bind upon us all as a sacred obligation with a unity of duty hitherto evoked only in time of armed strife.

With this pledge taken, I assume unhesitatingly the leadership of this great army of our people dedicated to a disciplined attack upon our common problems.

Action in this image and to this end is feasible under the form of government which we have inherited from our ancestors. Our Constitution is so simple and practical that it is possible always to meet extraordinary needs by changes in emphasis and arrangement without loss of essential form. That is why our constitutional system has proved itself the most superbly enduring political mechanism the modern world has produced. It has met every stress of vast expansion of territory, of foreign wars, of bitter internal strife, of world relations.

It is to be hoped that the normal balance of executive and legislative authority may be wholly adequate to meet the unprecedented task before us. But it may be that an unprecedented demand and need for undelayed action may call for temporary departure from that normal balance of public procedure.

I am prepared under my constitutional duty to recommend the measures that a stricken nation in the midst of a stricken world may require. These measures, or such other measures as the Congress may build out of its experience and wisdom, I shall seek, within my constitutional authority, to bring to speedy adoption.

But in the event that the Congress shall fail to take one of these two courses, and in the event that the national emergency is still critical, I shall not evade the clear course of duty that will then confront me. I shall ask the Congress for the one remaining instrument to meet the crisis—broad Executive power to wage a war against the emergency, as great as the power that would be given to me if we were in fact invaded by a foreign foe.

For the trust reposed in me I will return the courage and the devotion that befit the time. I can do no less.

We face the arduous days that lie before us in the warm courage of the national unity; with the clear consciousness of seeking old and precious moral values; with the clean satisfaction that comes from the stem performance of duty by old and young alike. We aim at the assurance of a rounded and permanent national life.

We do not distrust the future of essential democracy. The people of the United States have not failed. In their need they have registered a mandate that they want direct, vigorous action. They have asked for discipline and direction under leadership. They have made me the present instrument of their wishes. In the spirit of the gift I take it.

In this dedication of a Nation we humbly ask the blessing of God. May He protect each and every one of us. May He guide me in the days to come.

(PUBLIC....No.....*17*.....73d CONGRESS)

Seventy-third Congress of the United States of America;
At the First Session,

Begun and held at the City of Washington on Thursday, the ninth
day of March, one thousand nine hundred and thirty-three.

AN ACT

To improve the navigability and to provide for the flood control
of the Tennessee River; to provide for reforestation and the proper
use of marginal lands in the Tennessee Valley; to provide for the
agricultural and industrial development of said valley; to provide for the national defense by the creation of a corporation for
the operation of Government properties at and near Muscle Shoals
in the State of Alabama, and for other purposes.

*Be it enacted by the Senate and House of Representatives of the
United States of America in Congress assembled,* That for the purpose of maintaining and operating the properties now owned by the
United States in the vicinity of Muscle Shoals, Alabama, in the
interest of the national defense and for agricultural and industrial
development, and to improve navigation in the Tennessee River and
to control the destructive flood waters in the Tennessee River and
Mississippi River Basins, there is hereby created a body corporate
by the name of the "Tennessee Valley Authority" (hereinafter
referred to as the "Corporation"). The board of directors first
appointed shall be deemed the incorporators, and the incorporation
shall be held to have been effected from the date of the first meeting
of the board. This Act may be cited as the "Tennessee Valley
Authority Act of 1933."

SEC. 2. (a) The board of directors of the Corporation (hereinafter referred to as the "board") shall be composed of three members, to be appointed by the President, by and with the advice and
consent of the Senate. In appointing the members of the board,
the President shall designate the chairman. All other officials,
agents, and employees shall be designated and selected by the board.

(b) The terms of office of the members first taking office after
the approval of this Act shall expire as designated by the President
at the time of nomination, one at the end of the third year, one at
the end of the sixth year, and one at the end of the ninth year,
after the date of approval of this Act. A successor to a member
of the board shall be appointed in the same manner as the original
members and shall have a term of office expiring nine years from
the date of the expiration of the term for which his predecessor was
appointed.

The Tennessee Valley Authority Act (National Archives and Records Administration)

TENNESSEE VALLEY AUTHORITY ACT

> *"There is hereby created a body corporate by the name of the 'Tennessee Valley Authority.'"*

Overview

On June 3, 1916, President Woodrow Wilson signed the National Defense Act, which called for the creation of a facility to produce nitrates for manufacturing munitions during the war and fertilizer during peacetime. The site selected, Muscle Shoals, was situated on the Tennessee River in northern Alabama. Construction began immediately on two plants and two hydroelectric dams to generate the power for the plants. Before construction was completed, however, the Great War ended, and public support for the project turned into suspicion of the government's intentions. Many feared the project would give the government a hold on public businesses, creating an environment where private businesses would be unable to compete. Thus, the plants and dams fell idle as politicians, businessmen, and the public fought over what to do with Muscle Shoals.

Two main camps emerged—those who believed that the government should lease the facility to private business for development and those who maintained that the government should not abandon the project but should continue it in the name of public good. Owing largely to the efforts and persistence of Nebraska's Senator George Norris, the government retained control of the Muscle Shoals project, making its development a cornerstone of Franklin D. Roosevelt's New Deal. By signing the Tennessee Valley Authority Act, Roosevelt created an independent public corporation, the Tennessee Valley Authority (TVA), charged with controlling the Tennessee River's floodwaters, improving the river's navigation, assisting area farmers, and creating cheap electric power, as well as the daunting task of improving the lives of the people living within the Tennessee River valley. The valley, consisting of nearly 41,000 square miles and portions of seven states, was home to almost three million of the poorest people in the United States—most living without electricity or indoor plumbing. Never before had the federal government attempted a public works program as broad and encompassing as the TVA.

Context

When the stock market crashed on October 29, 1929, the United States plummeted full force into the worldwide economic crisis of the Great Depression. In the United States approximately 25 percent of the workforce was without jobs, and for those with jobs, wages fell by as much as 43 percent. Factories, mills, and banks closed, and many farming families lost their farms and homes. People were desperate and took to the roads in search of employment. Little work was found, however, and "Hoovervilles"—shantytowns thrown together and named after President Hoover—sprang up all over the country. Hoover believed that the economic crisis would be short-lived and assured the American people that it would be over in sixty days. Hoover, a proponent of rugged individualism, did not believe the federal government should provide relief to the struggling public. The American people despised Hoover by the end of his term, and they were ready for a change.

Roosevelt promised the American people a "new deal," and he defeated Hoover in a landslide victory in the 1932 presidential election. Wasting no time, Roosevelt refused the traditional inaugural ball and parties and went right to work, calling Congress to a special session on his first day in office. Roosevelt focused on the "three Rs"—relief, recovery, and reform—and laid the groundwork for his New Deal. Dozens of executive orders were issued, major laws were passed, and agencies were formed, all with the goal of pulling America out of the Depression. Among these many agencies were groundbreaking programs like the Civilian Conservation Corps, Farm Credit Administration, National Industrial Recovery Act, Public Works Administration, and the TVA. Not without critics and challenges, the New Deal and Roosevelt received overwhelming support from the American people. World War II, however, brought about the end of the New Deal and the Great Depression.

About the Author

George William Norris, who sponsored the Tennessee Valley Authority Act in the Senate and who was the person

Time Line

1926

■ **January 5**
George Norris introduces Senate Joint Resolution 2147, a bill to expand the Muscle Shoals project and build more dams along the Tennessee River; no action is taken.

1927

■ **December 15**
Norris introduces Senate Joint Resolution 46, a bill calling for the completion of the second dam and the steam plant at the second nitrate plant for the manufacture and distribution of fertilizer and other purposes; the bill is passed in the House and Senate.

1928

■ **June**
President Calvin Coolidge pocket vetoes Senate Joint Resolution 46.

1929

■ **May 28**
Norris introduces Senate Joint Resolution 49, a bill calling for the creation of a corporation to operate government properties near Muscle Shoals; the bill is passed in both houses.

1931

■ **March 3**
Herbert Hoover vetoes the Senate Joint Resolution 49.

■ **December 9**
Norris introduces Senate Joint Resolution 15, which once again calls for the creation of a corporation to operate government properties near Muscle Shoals.

1933

■ **April 10**
President Franklin Roosevelt sends a letter to Congress calling for legislation to create the Tennessee Valley Authority.

■ **April 11**
Norris introduces Senate Joint Resolution 1272, a bill calling for efforts to provide flood control and other development and oversight of the Tennessee River and Muscle Shoals area.

■ **May 18**
The Tennessee Valley Authority Act, signed by President Roosevelt, creates the TVA.

most responsible for writing the act, was a senator from Nebraska, not the South. Norris, considered the "father of the Tennessee Valley Authority," was born in 1861 in York Township, Ohio, to a farming family. Although his father, Chauncey, had died when Norris was a child, his mother, Mary, ensured that Norris and his siblings received an education. He attended area public schools during the winter months and worked for neighboring farmers in the summers. He worked his way through Northern Indiana Normal School, earning a bachelor's degree and then a law degree. He graduated and was admitted to the bar in 1883 at the age of twenty-two.

After a short stint teaching, Norris settled in Nebraska in 1885. He married Pluma Lashley and began practicing law. In addition to building a successful law practice, he also served three terms as Furnas County's prosecuting attorney and gained a reputation for honesty and fairness. In 1895 Norris was elected judge for Nebraska's fourteenth judicial district, where he served until 1902. In 1901 Pluma died during childbirth, leaving Norris to care for their three daughters. Despite his loss and grief, Norris ran for and won a spot in the U.S. House of Representatives in 1902. He married Ellie Leonard in 1903 and spent the next ten years in the House of Representatives. In 1910 Norris participated in challenging the Speaker of the House's power to arbitrarily choose committee appointments, which resulted in a resolution that limited the Speaker's power. This strengthened Norris's reputation for integrity, and he was elected to the Senate in 1913, where he served until 1943.

Throughout his Senate career Norris was true to his beliefs. He was a supporter of Woodrow Wilson's progressive domestic policies, a vocal opponent of Wilson's foreign policies, and one of just six senators who voted against Wilson's war resolution. Although he was a Republican, Norris was often at odds with the Republican presidents of the 1920s. Norris continually pushed a progressive agenda that included farm relief, conservation, rural electricity, and improved working conditions for laborers. Roosevelt called Norris a "gentle knight of American progressive ideals" (http://www.senate.gov/artandhistory/history/minute/Death _of_a_Gentle_Knight.htm). Norris was not elected to a sixth term in the Senate. He died just two years later, on September 2, 1944.

Representative Joseph Lister Hill from Alabama worked with Norris and sponsored the Tennessee Valley Authority Act in the House. Hill was the son of a distinguished surgeon and was born in Montgomery, Alabama, on December 29, 1894. He received a law degree from the University of Alabama at just twenty years old. Hill practiced law until, in 1923, he was elected to the House, where he served for forty-six years. He was most well known for his landmark legislation in public health, including the Hill-Burton Act, also called the Hospital Survey and Construction Act of 1946. It is estimated that, at the time of his death, more than 9,200 medical facilities had been constructed or renovated because of the Hill-Burton Act.

Explanation and Analysis of the Document

The Tennessee Valley Authority Act, consisting of thirty sections, is a legal document that painstakingly outlines the creation of a new corporation, what it is to do, how it is to do it, and what it cannot do. This document represents one of the most ambitious and long-lasting experiments to come from Roosevelt's New Deal.

The first paragraph of Section 1 of the act opens with the act's definition, purpose, and goals. The document clearly outlines the desire to improve the navigability and control the flooding of the Tennessee River, reforest and replenish the land of the valley, develop the region both agriculturally and industrially, and create a corporation for the operation of government properties for national defense and other purposes. The second paragraph names the corporation the Tennessee Valley Authority and states that the corporation should be run by an appointed board of directors. This first section sets the lofty tone and goals of the act, while the rest of the document outlines how these specific tasks are to be accomplished.

The board of directors is the subject of the second section, which consists of eight parts. The first four parts describe the rules for forming the board. The TVA board is to consist of three members appointed by the president with the advice and consent of the Senate. The president also chooses a chairman from the three board members. Once the board is selected, they make all other appointments. The board members hold nine-year, renewable terms. If a board member leaves before the end of a term, then the new board member will finish the previous term; as long as there are two board members, the TVA can operate as normal while a search for a third is completed. The rest of the section describes the benefits and limitations placed on directors. To be a TVA director, one must be a United States citizen. The salary for the position is $10,000 a year, but board members are allowed to live on TVA property and will be reimbursed for any work-related business. Further, while in office, no board member is allowed to participate in any other work or have any financial or business interest in anything that is a competitor of the TVA. For instance, they cannot be involved with any fertilizer company or company that makes ingredients of fertilizer.

With the board in place, the act turns to the matter of employees in Section 3. Importantly, the TVA can appoint and hire without regard to civil service laws, meaning that they can quickly hire local people. The board is responsible for all aspects of hiring, including setting the pay rate, defining the duties, and developing a promotion system. The only restriction is that no one's salary can be more than the board members' salaries. Employee salaries are to be "not less than the prevailing rate of wages for work of a similar nature," and if a dispute arises about the prevailing rate, the board is to refer the issue to the secretary of labor. The jobs and pay from TVA work infused a much-needed economic boost to the extremely depressed area.

Section 4 deals with a number of issues arising when any new body is formed—adopting a corporate seal, creating and

Time Line

1935

■ **August 31**
An amendment to the Tennessee Valley Authority Act, authorizing the TVA to generate electricity at dams and creating a channel from Knoxville, Tennessee, to the mouth of the Tennessee River in Paducah, Kentucky, is signed by President Roosevelt.

1936

■ **February 17**
The Supreme Court rules that the TVA is constitutional and that the TVA can sell electricity produced at the Wilson Dam in *Ashwander v. Tennessee Valley Authority* (1936).

1938

■ **January 3**
In *Alabama Power Company v. Ickes* (1938) the Supreme Court decides that power companies have no grounds to challenge the constitutionality of federal loans and grants awarded to assist municipalities in creating distribution systems for electricity.

1939

■ **January 30**
In *Tennessee Electric Power Company v. Tennessee Valley Authority* (1939) the Supreme Court decides that power companies cannot restrain the TVA from selling power generated at any of its dams.

changing bylaws, making contracts, and appointing treasurers—but the core of this section involves property. In this section the board is given the power to acquire real estate to construct whatever it needs to carry out its charges. Ideally, the TVA would purchase the property from the owners, but in Section 4 the TVA is given the right to exercise eminent domain. The right of eminent domain means that the government, here the TVA, can condemn and seize any property deemed necessary to complete its task.

The largest section of the act, Section 5, deals with the production of nitrates. The first five parts focus on fertilizer to improve the land in the Tennessee Valley. Here the act calls for the TVA to arrange for the large-scale use of new fertilizers, develop county experiment stations and demonstration farms, develop methods for making fertilizer better and cheaper, and sell or donate the fertilizer. In the event of war or national emergencies, however, the facilities would switch from using nitrates to make fertilizer to using

George Norris of Nebraska sponsored the Tennessee Valley Authority Act in the Senate. (AP Photo)

nitrates to make explosives. Further, in part 1 of this section, the TVA is specifically charged with producing, distributing, and selling electrical power. However, nothing produced is to be sold outside the United States except to allies during wartime.

The next four sections are brief and cover a variety of operating procedures. For instance, Section 6 states that any appointment, hiring, or promotion must be based on merit and not on political test or qualification. Section 7 entrusts all current and future properties of the TVA to the board. Section 8 orders that the TVA must have a main office in the vicinity of Muscle Shoals and that the corporation is resident of northern Alabama. Since the Tennessee Valley crosses state lines, this means that in the event of a civil suit the TVA would be held to the laws of northern Alabama. According to Section 9, the board is required to file a detailed financial statement that includes the cost of power at each station and the number, names, salaries, and duties of employees making more than $1,500 a year.

The next four sections deal with the sale of electrical power. In Section 10 the board is authorized to sell surplus power to states, counties, municipalities, corporations, partnerships, and individuals. To do this, the board can enter contracts for not more than twenty years and must place priority on providing power to local citizens. Any contracts with private companies to resell power for profit can be terminated in five years with written notice. Further, the board is authorized to construct transmission lines to reach farmers and small towns without power. Section 11 restates a lot of Section 10 by placing an emphasis on providing power to farms and rural areas, but it adds that industry is a secondary consumer that should be used to ensure use and revenue to provide power to the people at the lowest possible rates. Section 12 deals exclusively with transmission lines. This section authorizes the TVA to construct, lease, purchase, or contract construction of transmission lines and to interconnect these lines with already established systems. In addition, the TVA is allowed to lease their lines, thereby generating revenue, as long as it does not interfere with TVA business. This section also allows for organizations that supply power to its residents to connect to the TVA's power lines as long as they adequately maintain the lines and sell the power without regard to the consumers' social class. Section 13 declares that a portion of the sales from certain power plants goes to either Alabama or Tennessee. For instance, 5 percent of gross proceeds from the Cove Creek Dam are paid to the state of Tennessee. These sections dramatically illustrate the importance placed on getting affordable electricity to the rural farmers and towns of the Tennessee Valley.

The dams themselves are the topic of the next three sections. First, Section 14 provides a process for determining the cost and value of the dams. Section 15 allows the TVA to sell fifty million dollars worth of bonds to construct future dams, steam plants, and other facilities. Section 16, acknowledging that the original dams and plants were completed, provides for the completion of the plants and dams near Muscle Shoals; Section 17 calls for the secretary of war or the secretary of the interior to construct a new dam located on the Clinch River in Tennessee. In order to empower the office that will build this new dam, Section 18 authorizes the use of eminent domain to secure a site as well as to enter contracts to relocate railroads, bridges, mills, ferries, and so forth. Section 19 gives the TVA access to the U.S. Patent Office for researching methods for the most efficient and economical way to produce fertilizer and hydroelectric power.

Since a primary function of the TVA is to generate nitrates for explosives in the event of war or national emergency, Section 20 authorizes the government to take possession of any TVA property to make munitions. This section, however, also allows those who had contracts for fertilizer or power to receive damages. With all that the TVA is authorized to do, Section 21 reminds it that all of the laws regarding larceny, embezzlement, and improper handling of government money apply to it. Further, defrauding the TVA will result in a fine of not more than $10,000 or imprisonment of not more than five years or both.

Sections 22 and 23 are the boldest of the sections of the Tennessee Valley Authority Act because within these two sections the TVA is charged with improving the lives of the people of the Tennessee River valley. For instance, section 22 of the act authorizes the president to order surveys and make plans to manage the extent, sequence, and nature of TVA development to ensure the area is developed for the best physical, economic, and social outcomes. As the work outlined in Section 22 develops, Section 23 authorizes the

"*That for the purpose of maintaining and operating the properties now owned by the United States in the vicinity of Muscle Shoals, Alabama, in the interest of the national defense and for agriculture and industrial development, and to improve navigation in the Tennessee River and to control the destructive flood waters in the Tennessee River and Mississippi River Basins, there is hereby created a body corporate by the name of the 'Tennessee Valley Authority.'*"

(Paragraph 2)

"*The board is hereby empowered and authorized to sell the surplus power not used in its operations, and for operation of locks and other works generated by it, to States, counties, municipalities, corporations, partnerships, or individuals.*"

(Section 10)

"*To aid further the proper use, conservation, and development of the natural resources of the Tennessee River drainage basin and of such adjoining territory as may be related to or materially affected by the development consequent to this Act, and to provide for the general welfare of the citizens of said areas.*"

(Section 22)

president to recommend legislation to Congress to ensure flood control, navigation of the Tennessee River, generation of power, proper use of land, reforestation, and boldly, "the economic and social well-being of the people living in said river basin."

The acquisition and disposition of property is a theme throughout the Tennessee Valley Authority Act, and in Section 24 the president is authorized to secure rights and buy titles as well as to lease facilities and land not currently being used by the TVA. The president is not authorized, however, to sell the land, since it may be needed later. Up to this point, eminent domain has only been mentioned, but in Section 25 the topic is covered in detail. The right of eminent domain means that the government can condemn and take possession of personal property for its own use; Section 25 carefully outlines the procedure for this process. The TVA will start proceedings in United States district court. The value of the property will then be determined by three court-appointed commissioners. These

commissioners will evaluate the property and interview witnesses to compile a report for the court. Once the report is filed, within twenty days either the TVA or the property owners can file exceptions, which would be heard by three federal judges who will then file their own valuation of the property. Then the TVA and property owners would have thirty days to appeal the judges' valuation to the circuit court of appeals, which would determine their own valuation of the property. When the valuation is not challenged or all challenges are exhausted, the property owners would receive the valuation of the property, and ownership would pass to the U.S. government. The section goes on to state that in the event the property owner is a minor, insane, incompetent, or dead their legal representative or guardian will act for them.

The finally five sections of the act are very brief and tie up loose ends. For instance, Section 26 states that any profit the TVA generates goes to the U.S. Treasury. Section 27 allocates the money for carrying out the provisions of

President Franklin D. Roosevelt is shown signing a law creating the Tennessee Valley Authority in this May 18, 1933 photo. (AP Photo)

the act, and Section 28 states that if anything is contradictory in the act, those parts are repealed. In Section 29 the right to alter, amend, or repeal the act is reserved. Finally, Section 30 declares that the sections of the act are separable, which means that if one part of the act is found to be unconstitutional, then only that part of the act would be thrown out, and the rest of the act would remain valid.

Audience

In general, all of the New Deal legislation was written for the American people. The specific audience for the text of these acts, however, is the three branches of government— executive, representative, and judicial—as well as those involved with administering the project. The Tennessee Valley Authority Act outlines, in very specific and legal language, the TVA's purposes and goals, what it is and is not allowed to do, and how it should be run. Another potential audience for the text is would-be challengers to the legality and constitutionality of the act. For instance, the last section of the act declares that if any section of the act is found unconstitutional, it does not negate the entire act.

Impact

The TVA's greatest impact was on the people of the Tennessee River valley. During the Great Depression, much of the rural South was already very poor, and those who had left the area to find work returned as the depression grew, creating even more strain on the depleted region. The vast majority of the valley's people lived without running water or electricity. They were hounded by disease and very low yearly income. One estimate says that over 30 percent of the people in the Tennessee River valley were infected with malaria, which peaked between 1932 and 1936 despite a

decline in the 1920s. Further, the land itself was suffering. The people of the Tennessee Valley were mostly subsistence farmers, had little understanding of crop rotation, and they farmed the land too hard for too long without allowing the soil to replenish itself. Timber had also been stripped from the land, which left the earth vulnerable to erosion and lowered crop yield even further. The Tennessee Valley Authority changed all this.

The TVA, designed to modernize the region, set out to teach farmers how to increase crops yields, to develop fertilizer, to reforest the land stripped of timber, to control forest fires, and to improve habitats for wildlife, including fish and other aquatics species. To control the floodwaters and generate more electricity, the TVA built more dams, which created jobs for local workers. In addition, the TVA funded more research than other organizations did in an effort to combat malaria. The biggest impact, however, came from the electricity generated by the TVA. Providing cheap electricity not only allowed the local people to have lights and modern appliances such as refrigerators for keeping food fresh but also made farming more productive and drew other industries to the area. For instance, a number of textiles mills were built in the area, which created jobs for local women.

By the end of World War II, one of the most economically depressed regions of the United States had been profoundly changed. Sixteen dams were constructed, acres of floodwater storage were created, and a 9-foot navigation channel was carved into the 650 miles of the Tennessee River from Knoxville, Tennessee, to Paducah, Kentucky, making the entire length of the river navigable. Kilowatt production increased by 127 percent, providing electricity to thousands of households. With readily available electricity and controlled floodwater, new towns and cities sprang up along the river, including Oak Ridge, Tennessee, which would play an important roll in the Manhattan Project (to develop the first nuclear weapon) and employ eighty thousand people during World War II. As technology, times, and presidential administrations changed, the Tennessee Valley Authority suffered inevitable ups and downs, but it remains one of the largest producers of electricity in the United States.

Related Documents

Federal Writers' Project. *These Are Our Lives: As Told by the People and Written by Members of the Federal Writers' Project of the Works Progress Administration in North Carolina, Tennessee, and Georgia.* Chapel Hill: University of North Carolina Press, 1939. This is one of many collections created by the Federal Writers' Project during the Great Depression. Consisting of interviews of biographies of actual residents of the rural South during the Depression, this and all the WPA collections are valuable resources for examining the culture and living conditions of the Tennessee Valley before the TVA.

Lilienthal, David E. *TVA: Democracy on the March.* New York: Harper and Brothers, 1944. One of the TVA's first directors, Lilienthal reports on the result of the TVA's efforts. He includes facts and figures and gives an inside view of the TVA.

Norris, George W. *Fighting Liberal: The Autobiography of George W. Norris.* New York: Macmillan, 1945. Norris writes, in his own words, about his personal and professional life, from growing up in Ohio to his farewell from the Senate. One chapter covers his views of the TVA.

Roosevelt, Franklin D. "White House Letter." Franklin D. Roosevelt Presidential Library and Museum Web site. http://www.fdrlibrary.marist.edu/odtvacon.html. Accessed on February 18, 2008. This White House letter was written by Franklin D. Roosevelt. It charges Congress with creating the TVA.

Bibliography

■ Articles

Berstein, Mark. "Arthur Ernest Morgan." *American History* 40, no. 4 (October 2005): 48, 50, 76.

Martin, Roscoe C. "The Tennessee Valley Authority: A Study of Federal Control." *Law and Contemporary Problems* 22, no. 3 (Summer 1957): 351–377.

Miller, Haskell M. "Marriage and Family in a Tennessee Valley Area." *Marriage and Family Living* 16, no. 3 (August 1954): 233–236.

O'Neill, Karen M. "Why the TVA Remains Unique: Interest Groups and the Defeat of the New Deal River Planning." *Rural Sociology* 67, no. 2 (June 2002): 163–182.

"The Tennessee Valley Authority Act." *The Yale Law Journal* 43, no. 5 (March 1934): 815–826.

Wengert, Norman. "The Land—TVA—and the Fertilizer Industry." *Land Economics* 25, no. 1 (February 1949): 11–21.

■ Books

Chandler, William U. *The Myth of the TVA: Conservation and Development in the Tennessee Valley, 1933–1983.* Cambridge, Mass.: Ballinger, 1984.

Duffus, R. L. *The Valley and Its People: A Portrait of the TVA.* New York: Alfred A. Knopf, 1944.

Hargrove, Erwin C. *Prisoners of Myth: The Leadership of the Tennessee Valley Authority, 1933–1990.* Princeton, N.J.: Princeton University Press, 1994.

Hubbard, Preston J. *Origins of the TVA: The Muscle Shoals Controversy, 1920–1932.* New York: W. W. Norton, 1968.

McCraw, Thomas K. *TVA and the Power Fight, 1933–1939.* Philadelphia: J. B. Lippincott, 1971.

Moore, John R. *The Economic Impact of TVA.* Knoxville, Tenn.: University of Tennessee Press, 1967.

Murchison, Kenneth M. *The Snail Darter Case: TVA Versus the Endangered Species.* Lawrence: University of Kansas Press, 2007.

Neal, Harry E. *The People's Giant: The Story of TVA.* New York: J. Messner, 1970.

Owen, Marguerite. *The Tennessee Valley Authority.* New York: Praeger, 1973.

■ Web Sites

"Death of a Gentle Knight." U.S. Senate "Art and History" Web site. http://www.senate.gov/artandhistory/history/minute/Death_of_a_Gentle_Knight.htm. Accessed on February 19, 2008.

"The Tennessee Valley Authority: Electricity for All." New Deal Network Web site. http://newdeal.feri.org/tva/index.htm. Accessed on September, 14, 2007.

Tennessee Valley Authority Web site. http://www.tva.gov/. Accessed on September, 14, 2007.

Wheeler, W. Bruce. "Tennessee Valley Authority." The Tennessee Encyclopedia of History and Culture Web site. http://tennesseeencyclopedia.net/imagegallery.php?EntryID=T072. Accessed on September, 14, 2007.

—By Lisa A. Ennis

1. During the expansion of the TVA and its efforts to control the river's floodwaters by creating floodwater storage areas, thousands of families were displaced and forced to move. Given the overall impact of the TVA on the region, was this a necessary evil? Why or why not?

2. Throughout its early history the TVA, as well as many other New Deal programs, faced numerous legal challenges from a variety of groups, including private businesses that claimed the government should not compete for customers with private business. The Supreme Court ruled that the Agricultural Adjustment Act and the National Industrial Recovery Act were unconstitutional but surprisingly ruled in favor of the TVA when it was challenged. What was different about the TVA? What gave the TVA the constitutionality that the other acts lacked?

3. In the first years of the TVA the three directors had vastly different views and ideas about how the TVA should be run. Their bickering cast a shadow on the TVA and resulted in Roosevelt firing one of them. Compare and contrast the three directors. Who do you think was right and why?

Glossary

Comptroller General	the director of the Government Accountability Office
eminent domain	the right of a government to take private property for public use
fixation of nitrogen	the process of converting inert nitrogen into a compound such as nitrate, which is used in fertilizer and explosives
hydroelectric power	electricity produced by dammed water to drive turbines and generators

TENNESSEE VALLEY AUTHORITY ACT

An Act to Improve the Navigability and to Provide for the Flood Control of the Tennessee River: To Provide for Reforestation and the Proper Use of Marginal Lands in the Tennessee Valley; to Provide for the Agricultural and Industrial Development of Said Valley; to Provide for the National Defense by the Creation of a Corporation for the Operation of Government Properties at and Near Muscle Shoals in the State of Alabama, and for Other Purposes May 18, 1933.

Be it enacted by the Senate and House of Representatives of the United States of America in Congress assembled, That for the purpose of maintaining and operating the properties now owned by the United States in the vicinity of Muscle Shoals, Alabama, in the interest of the national defense and for agriculture and industrial development, and to improve navigation in the Tennessee River and to control the destructive flood waters in the Tennessee River and Mississippi River Basins, there is hereby created a body corporate by the name of the "Tennessee Valley Authority" (hereinafter referred to as the "Corporation"). The board of directors first appointed shall be deemed the incorporators and the incorporation shall be held to have been effected from the date of the first meeting of the board. This Act may be cited as the "Tennessee Valley Authority Act of 1933."

Sec. 2. The board of directors of the Corporation (hereinafter referred to as the "board") shall be composed of three members, to be appointed by the President, by and with the advice and consent of the Senate. In appointing the members of the board, the President shall designate the chairman. All other officials, agents, and employees shall be designated and selected by the board.

(b) The terms of office of the members first taking office after the approval of this Act shall expire as designated by the President at the time of nomination, one at the end of the third year, one at the end

of the sixth year, and one at the end of the ninth year, after the date of approval of this Act. A successor to a member of the board shall be appointed in the same manner as the original members and shall have a term of office expiring nine years from the date of the expiration of the term for which his predecessor was appointed.

(c) Any member appointed to fill a vacancy in the board occurring prior to the expiration of the term for which his predecessor was appointed shall be appointed for the remainder of such term.

(d) Vacancies in the board so long as there shall be two members in office shall not impair the powers of the board to execute the functions of the Corporation, and two of the members in office shall constitute a quorum for the transaction of the business of the board.

(e) Each of the members of the board shall be a citizen of the United States, and shall receive a salary at the rate of $10,000 a year, to be paid by the Corporation as current expenses. Each member of the board, in addition to his salary, shall be permitted to occupy as his residence one of the dwelling houses owned by the Government in the vicinity of Muscle Shoals, Alabama, the same to be designated by the President of the United States. Members of the board shall be reimbursed by the Corporation for actual expenses (including traveling and subsistence expenses) incurred by them in the performance of the duties vested in the board by this Act. No member of said board shall, during his continuance in office, be engaged in other business, but each member shall devote himself to the work of the Corporation.

(f) No director shall have financial interest in any public-utility corporation engaged in the business of distributing and selling power to the public nor in any corporation engaged in the manufacture, selling, or distribution of fixed nitrogen or fertilizer, or any ingredients thereof, nor shall any member have any interest in any business that may be adversely affected by the success of the Corporation as a producer of concentrated fertilizers or as a producer of electric power.

(g) The board shall direct the exercise of all the powers of the Corporation.

(h) All members of the board shall be persons who profess a belief in the feasibility and wisdom of this Act.

Sec. 3. The Board shall without regard to the provisions of Civil Service laws applicable to officers and employees of the United States, appoint such managers, assistant managers, officers, employees, attorneys, and agents, as are necessary for the transaction of its business, fix their compensation, define their duties, require bonds of such of them as the board may designate, and provide a system of organization to fix responsibility and promote efficiency. Any appointee of the board may be removed in the discretion of the board. No regular officer or employee of the Corporation shall receive a salary in excess of that received by the members of the board.

All contracts to which the Corporation is a party and which require the employment of laborers and mechanics in the construction, alteration, maintenance or repair of buildings, dams, locks, or other projects shall contain a provision that not less than the prevailing rate of wages for work of a similar nature prevailing in the vicinity shall be paid to such laborers or mechanics.

In the event any dispute arises as to what are the prevailing rates of wages, the question shall be referred to the Secretary of Labor for determination, and his decision shall be final. In the determination of such prevailing rate or rates, due regard shall be given to those rates which have been secured through collective agreement by representatives of employers and employees.

Where such work as is described in the two preceding paragraphs is done directly by the Corporation the prevailing rate of wages shall be paid in the same manner as though such work had been let by contract.

Insofar as applicable, the benefits of the Act entitled "An Act to provide compensation for employees of the United States suffering injuries while in the performance of their duties, and for other purposes," approved September 7, 1916, as amended, shall extend to persons given employment under the provisions of this Act.

Sec. 4. Except as otherwise specifically provided in this Act, the Corporation—

(a) Shall have succession in its corporate name.

(b) May sue and be sued in its corporate name.

(c) May adopt and use a corporate seal, which shall be judicially noticed.

(d) May make contracts, as herein authorized.

(e) May adopt, amend, and repeal bylaws.

(f) May purchase or lease and hold such real and personal property as it deems necessary or convenient in the transaction of its business, and may dispose of any such personal property held by it.

The board shall select a treasurer and as many assistant treasurers as it deems proper, which treasurer and assistant treasurers shall give such bonds for the safe-keeping of the securities and moneys of the said Corporation as the board may require: Provided, That any member of said board may be removed from office at any time by a concurrent resolution of the Senate and the House of Representatives.

(g) Shall have such powers as may be necessary or appropriate for the exercise of the powers herein specifically conferred upon the Corporation.

(h) Shall have power in the name of the United States of America to exercise the right of eminent domain, and in the purchase of any real estate or the condemnation of real estate by condemnation proceedings, the title to such real estate shall be taken in the name of the United States of America, and thereupon all such real estate shall be entrusted to the Corporation as the agent of the United States to accomplish the purposes of this Act.

(i) Shall have power to acquire real estate for the construction of dams, reservoirs, transmission lines, power houses, and other structures, and navigation projects at any point along the Tennessee River, or any of its tributaries, and in the event that the owner or owners of such property shall fail and refuse to sell to the Corporation at a price deemed fair and reasonable by the board, then the Corporation may proceed to exercise the right of eminent domain, and to condemn all property that it deems necessary for carrying out the purposes of this Act, and all such condemnation proceedings shall be had pursuant to the provisions and requirements hereinafter specified, with reference to any and all condemnation proceedings.

(i) Shall have power to construct dams, reservoirs, power houses, power structures, transmission lines, navigation projects, and incidental works in the Tennessee River and its tributaries, and to unite the various power installations into one or more systems by transmission lines.

Sec. 5. The board is hereby authorized—

(a) To contract with commercial producers for the production of such fertilizers or fertilizer materials as may be needed in the Government's program of development and introduction in excess of that produced by Government plants. Such contracts may provide either for outright purchase of materials by the board or only for the payment of carrying charges on special materials manufactured at the board's request for its program.

(b) To arrange with farmers and farm organizations for large scale practical use of the new forms of fertilizers under conditions permitting an accurate measure of the economic return they produce.

(c) To cooperate with National, State, district, or county experimental stations or demonstration farms, for the use of new forms of fertilizer or fertilizer practices during the initial or experimental period of their introduction.

(d) The board in order to improve and cheapen the production of fertilizer is authorized to manufacture and sell fixed nitrogen, fertilizer, and fertilizer ingredients at Muscle Shoals by the employment of existing facilities, by modernizing existing plants, or by any other process or processes that in its judgment shall appear wise and profitable for the fixation of atmospheric nitrogen or the cheapening of the production of fertilizer.

(e) Under the authority of this Act the board may make donations or sales of the product of the plant or plants operated by it to be fairly and equitably distributed through the agency of county demonstration agents, agricultural colleges, or otherwise as the board may direct, for experimentation, education, and introduction of the use of such products in cooperation with practical farmers so as to obtain information as to the value, effect, and best methods of their use.

(f) The board is authorized to make alterations, modifications, or improvements in existing plants and facilities, and to construct new plants.

(g) In the event it is not used for the fixation of nitrogen for agricultural purposes or leased, then the board shall maintain in stand-by condition nitrate plant numbered 2, or its equivalent, for the fixation of atmospheric nitrogen, for the production of explosives in the event of war or a national emergency until the Congress shall by joint resolution release the board from this obligation, and if any part thereof be used by the board for the manufacture or phosphoric acid or potash, the balance of nitrate plant numbered 2 shall be kept in stand-by condition.

(h) To establish, maintain, and operate laboratories and experimental plants, and to undertake experiments for the purpose of enabling the Corporation to furnish nitrogen products for military purposes, and nitrogen and other fertilizer products for agricultural purposes in the most economical manner and at the highest standard of efficiency.

(i) To request the assistance and advice of any officer, agent, or employee of any executive department or of any independent office of the United States, to enable the Corporation the better to carry out its powers successfully, and as far as practicable shall utilize the services of such officers, agents, and employees, and the President shall, if in his opinion, the public interest, service, or economy so require, direct that such assistance, advice, and service be rendered to the Corporation, and any individual that may be by the President directed to render such assistance, advice, and service shall be thereafter subject to the orders, rules, and regulations of the board: Provided, That any invention or discovery made by virtue of and incidental to such service by an employee of the Government of the United States serving under this section, or by any employee of the Corporation, together with any patents which may be granted thereon, shall be the sole and exclusive property of the Corporation, which is hereby authorized to grant licenses thereunder as shall be authorized by the board: Provided further, That the board may pay to such inventor such sum from the income from sale of licenses as it may deem proper.

(j) Upon the requisition of the Secretary of War or the Secretary of the Navy to manufacture for and sell at cost to the United States explosives or their nitrogenous content.

(k) Upon the requisition of the Secretary of War the Corporation shall allot and deliver without charge to the War Department so much power as shall be necessary in the judgment of said Department for use in operation of all locks, lifts, or other facilities in aid of navigation.

(l) To produce, distribute, and sell electric power, as herein particularly specified.

(m) No products of the Corporation shall be sold for use outside of the United States, its Territories and possessions, except to the United States Government for the use of its Army and Navy, or to its allies in case of war.

(n) The President is authorized, within twelve months after the passage of this Act, to lease to any responsible farm organization or to any corporation organized by it nitrate plant number 2 and Waco Quarry, together with the railroad connecting said quarry with nitrate plant number 2, for a term not exceeding fifty years at a rental of not less than $1 per year, but such authority shall be subject to the express condition that the lessee shall use said property during the term of said lease exclusively for the manufacture of fertilizer and fertilizer ingredients to be used only in the manufacture of fertilizer by said lessee and sold for use as fertilizer. The said lessee shall covenant to keep said property in first-class condition, but the lessee shall be authorized to modernize said plant numbered 2 by the installation of such machinery as may be necessary, and is authorized to amortize the cost of said machinery and improvements over the term of said lease or any part thereof. Said lease shall also provide that the board shall sell to the lessee power for the operation of said plant at the same schedule of prices that it charges all other customers for power of the same class and quantity. Said lease shall also provide that if the said lessee does not desire to buy power of the publicly owned plant it shall have the right to purchase power for the operation of said plant of the Alabama Power Company or any other publicly or privately owned corporation engaged in the generation and sale of electrical power, and in such case the lease shall provide further that the said lessee shall have a free right of way to build a transmission line over Government property to said plant paying the actual expenses and damages, if any, incurred by the Corporation on account of such line. Said lease shall also provide that the said lessee shall covenant that during the term of said lease the said lessee shall not enter into any illegal monopoly, combination, or trust with any privately owned corporation engaged in the manufacture, production, and sale of fertilizer with the object or effect of increasing the price of fertilizer to the farmer.

Sec. 6. In the appointment of officials and the selection of employees for said Corporation, and in the promotion of any such employees or officials, no political test or qualification shall be permitted or given consideration, but all such appointments and promotions shall be given and made on the basis of merit and efficiency. Any member of said board who is found by the President of the United States to be guilty of a violation of this section shall be removed from office by the President of the United States, and any appointee of said board who is found by the board to be guilty of a violation of this section shall be removed from office by said board.

Sec. 7. In order to enable the Corporation to exercise the powers and duties vested in it by this Act—

(a) The exclusive use, possession, and control of the United States nitrate plants numbered 1 and 2, including steam plants, located, respectively, at Sheffield, Alabama, and Muscle Shoals, Alabama, together with all real estate and buildings connected therewith, all tools and machinery, equipment, accessories, and materials belonging thereto, and all laboratories and plants used as auxiliaries thereto; the fixed-nitrogen research laboratory, the Waco limestone quarry, in Alabama, and Dam Numbered 2, located at Muscle Shoals, its power house, and all hydroelectric and operating appurtenances (except the locks), and all machinery, lands, and buildings in connection therewith, and all appurtenances thereof, and all other property to be acquired by the Corporation in its own name or in the name of the United States of America, are hereby intrusted to the Corporation for the purposes of the Act.

(b) The President of the United States is authorized to provide for the transfer to the Corporation of the use, possession, and control of such other real or personal property of the United States as he may from time to time deem necessary and proper for the purposes of the Corporation as herein stated.

Sec. 8. (a) The Corporation shall maintain its principal office in the immediate vicinity of Muscle Shoals, Alabama. The Corporation shall be held to be an inhabitant and resident of the northern judicial district of Alabama within the meaning of the laws of the United States relating to the venue of civil suits.

(b) The Corporation shall at all times maintain complete and accurate books of accounts.

(c) Each member of the board, before entering upon the duties of his office, shall subscribe to an oath (or affirmation) to support the Constitution of the United States and to faithfully and impartially perform the duties imposed upon him by this Act.

Sec. 9. (a) The board shall file with the President and with the Congress, in December of each year, a financial statement and a complete report as to the business of the Corporation covering the preceding governmental fiscal year. This report shall include an itemized statement of the cost of power at each power station, the total number of employees and the names, salaries, and duties of those receiving compensation at the rate of more than $1,500 a year.

(b) The Comptroller General of the United States shall audit the transactions of the Corporation at such times as he shall determine, but not less frequently than once each governmental fiscal year, with personnel of his selection. In such connection he and his representatives shall have free and open access to all papers, books, records, files, accounts, plants, warehouses offices, and all other things, property and places belonging to or under the control of or used or employed by the Corporation, and shall be afforded full facilities for counting all cash and verifying transactions with and balance in depositaries. He shall make report of each such audit in quadruplicate, one copy for the President of the United States, one for the chairman of the board one for public inspection at the principal office of the Corporation, and the other to be retained by him for the uses of the Congress. The expenses for each such audit may be paid from moneys advanced therefor by the Corporation, or from any appropriation or appropriations for the General Accounting Office, and appropriations so used shall be reimbursed promptly by the Corporation as billed by the Comptroller General. All such audit expenses shall be charged to operating expenses of the Corporation. The Comptroller General shall make special report to the President of the United States and to the Congress of any transaction or condition found by him to be in conflict with the powers or duties intrusted to the Corporation by law.

Sec. 10. The board is hereby empowered and authorized to sell the surplus power not used in its operations, and for operation of locks and other works generated by it, to States, counties, municipalities, corporations, partnerships, or individuals, according to the policies hereinafter set forth—and to carry out said authority, the board is authorized to enter into contracts for such sale for a term not exceeding twenty years, and in the sale of such current by the board it shall give preference to States, counties, municipalities, and cooperative organizations of citizens or farmers, not organized or doing business for profit, but primarily for the purpose of supplying electricity to its own citizens or members: Provided, That all contracts made with private companies or individuals for the sale of power, which is to be resold for a profit, shall contain a provision authorizing the board to cancel said contract upon five years' notice in writing, if the board needs said power to supply the demands of States, counties, or municipalities. In order to promote and encourage the fullest possible use of electric light and power on farms within reasonable distance of any of its transmission lines the board in its discretion shall have power to construct transmission lines to farms and small villages that are not otherwise supplied with electricity at reasonable rates, and to make such rules and regulations governing such sale and distri-

bution of such electric power as in its judgment may be just and equitable: Provided further That the board is hereby authorized and directed to make studies, experiments, and determinations to promote the wider and better use of electric power for agricultural and domestic use, or for small or local industries, and it may cooperate with State governments, or their subdivisions or agencies with educational or research institutions, and with cooperatives or other organizations, in the application of electric power to the fuller and better balanced development of the resources of the region.

Sec. 11. It is hereby declared to be the policy of the Government so far as practical to distribute and sell the surplus power generated at Muscle Shoals equitably among the States, counties, and municipalities within transmission distance. This policy is further declared to be that the projects herein provided for shall be considered primarily as for the benefit of the people of the section as a whole and particularly the domestic and rural consumers to whom the power can economically be made available, and accordingly that sale to and use by industry shall be a secondary purpose, to be utilized principally to secure a sufficiently high load factor and revenue returns which will permit domestic and rural use at the lowest possible rates and in such manner as to encourage increased domestic and rural use of electricity. It is further hereby declared to be the policy of the Government to utilize the Muscle Shoals properties so far as may be necessary to improve, increase, and cheapen the production of fertilizer and fertilizer ingredients by carrying out the provisions of this Act.

Sec. 12. In order to place the board upon a fair basis for making such Contracts and for receiving bids for the sale of such power, it is hereby expressly authorized, either from appropriations made by Congress or from funds secured from the sale of such power, or from funds secured by the sale of bonds hereafter provided for, to construct, lease, purchase, or authorize the construction of transmission lines within transmission distance from the place where generated, and to interconnect with other systems. The board is also authorized to lease to any person, persons, or corporation the use of any transmission line owned by the Government and operated by the board, but no such lease shall be made that in any way interferes with the use of such transmission line by the board: Provided, That if any State, county, municipality, or other public or cooperative organization of citizens or farmers, not organized or doing business for profit, but primarily for the purpose of supplying electricity to its own citizens or members, or any two or more of such municipalities or organizations, shall construct or agree to construct and maintain a properly designed and built transmission line to the Government reservation upon which is located a Government generating plant, or to a main transmission line owned by the Government or leased by the board and under the control of the board, the board is hereby authorized and directed to contract with such State, county, municipality, or other organization, or two or more of them, for the sale of electricity for a term not exceeding thirty years; and in such case the board shall give to such State, county, municipality, or other organization ample time to fully comply with any local law now in existence or hereafter enacted providing for the necessary legal authority for such State, county, municipality, or other organization to contract with the board for such power: Provided further, That all contracts entered into between the Corporation and any municipality or other political subdivision or cooperative organization shall provide that the electric power shall be sold and distributed to the ultimate consumer without discrimination as between consumers of the same class, and such contract shall be voidable at the election of the board if a discriminatory rate, rebate, or other special concession is made or given to any consumer or user by the municipality or other political subdivision or cooperative organization: And provided further, That as to any surplus power not so sold as above provided to States, counties, municipalities, or other said organizations, before the board shall sell the same to any person or corporation engaged in the distribution and resale of electricity for profit, it shall require said person or corporation to agree that any resale of such electric power by said person or corporation shall be made to the ultimate consumer of such electric power at prices that shall not exceed a schedule fixed by the board from time to time as reasonable, just, and fair; and in case of any such sale, if an amount is charged the ultimate consumer which is in excess of the price so deemed to be just, reasonable, and fair by the board the contract for such sale between the board and such distributor of electricity shall be voidable at the election of the board: And provided further, That the board is hereby authorized to enter into contracts with other power systems for the mutual exchange of unused excess power upon suitable terms, for the conservation of stored water, and as an emergency or break-down relief.

Sec. 13. Five per centum of the gross proceeds received by the board for the sale of power generated at Dam Numbered 2, or from any other hydropower plant hereafter constructed in the State of Alabama, shall be paid to the State of Alabama; and 5 per centum of the gross proceeds from the sale of power generated at Cove Creek Dam, hereinafter provided for, or any other dam located in the State of Tennessee, shall be paid to the State of Tennessee. Upon the completion of said Cove Creek Dam the board shall ascertain how much additional power is thereby generated at Dam Numbered 2 and at any other dam hereafter constructed by the Government of the United States on the Tennessee River, in the State of Alabama, or in the State of Tennessee, and from the gross proceeds of the sale of such additional power two and a half per centum shall be paid to the State of Alabama and 2 and a half per centum to the State of Tennessee. These percentages shall apply to any other dam that may hereafter be constructed and controlled and operated by the board on the Tennessee River or any of its tributaries, the main purpose of which is to control flood waters and where the development of electric power is incidental to the operation of such flood-control dam. In ascertaining the gross proceeds from the sale of such power upon which a percentage is paid to the States of Alabama and Tennessee, the board shall not take into consideration the proceeds of any power sold or delivered to the Government of the United States, or any department or agency of the Government of the United States used in the operation of any locks on the Tennessee River or for any experimental purpose, or for the manufacture of fertilizer or any of the ingredients thereof, or for any other governmental purpose: Provided, That the percentages to be paid to the States of Alabama and Tennessee, as provided in this section, shall be subject to revision and change by the board, and any new percentages established by the board, when approved by the President, shall remain in effect until and unless again changed by the board with the approval of the President. No change of said percentages shall be made more often than once in five years, and no change shall be made without giving to the States of Alabama and Tennessee an opportunity to be heard.

Sec. 14. The board shall make a thorough investigation as to the present value of Dam Numbered 2, and the steam plants at nitrate plant numbered 1, and nitrate plant numbered 2, and as to the cost of Cove Creek Dam, for the purpose of ascertaining how much of the value or the cost of said properties shall be allocated and charged up to (1) flood control, (2) navigation, (3) fertilizer (4) national defense, and (5) the development of power. The findings thus made by the board, when approved by the President of the United States, shall be final, and such findings shall thereafter be used in all allocation of value for the purpose of keeping the book value of said properties. In a like manner, the cost and book value of any dams, steam plants, or other similar improvements hereafter constructed and turned over to said board for the purpose of control and management shall be ascertained and allocated.

Sec. 15. In the construction of any future dam, steam plant, or other facility, to be used in whole or in part for the generation or transmission of electric power the board is hereby authorized and empowered to issue on the credit of the United States and to sell serial bonds not exceeding $50,000,000 in amount, having a maturity not more than fifty years from the date of issue thereof, and bearing interest not exceeding 3-1/2 per centum per annum. Said bonds shall be issued and sold in amounts and prices approved by the Secretary of the Treasury, but all such bonds as may be so issued and sold shall have equal rank. None of said bonds shall be sold below par, and no fee, commission, or compensation whatever shall be paid to any person, firm, or corporation for handling, negotiating the sale, or selling the said bonds. All of such bonds so issued and sold shall have all the rights and privileges accorded by law to Panama Canal bonds, authorized by section 8 of the Act of June 28, 1902, chapter 1302, as amended by the Act of December 21, 1905 (ch. 3, sec. 1, 34 Stat. 5), as now compiled in section 743 of title 31 of the United States Code. All funds derived from the sale of such bonds shall be paid over to the Corporation.

Sec. 16. The board, whenever the President deems it advisable, is hereby empowered and directed to complete Dam Numbered 2 at Muscle Shoals Alabama, and the steam plant at nitrate plant numbered 2, in the vicinity of Muscle Shoals, by installing in Dam Numbered 2 the additional power units according to the plans and specifications of said dam, and the additional power unit in the steam plant at nitrate plant numbered 2.

Sec. 17. The Secretary of War, or the Secretary of the Interior, is hereby authorized to construct, either directly or by contract to the lowest responsible bidder, after due advertisement, a dam in and across Clinch River in the State of Tennessee, which has by long custom become known and designates as the Cove Creek Dam, together with a transmission line

from Muscle Shoals, according to the latest and most approved designs, including power house and hydroelectric installations and equipment for the generation of power, in order that the waters of the said Clinch River may be impounded and stored above said dam for the purpose of increasing and regulating the flow of the Clinch River and the Tennessee River below, so that the maximum amount of primary power may be developed at Dam Numbered 2 and at any and all other dams below the said Cove Creek Dam: Provided, however, That the President is hereby authorized by appropriate order to direct the employment by the Secretary of War, or by the Secretary of the Interior, of such engineer or engineers as he may designate, to perform such duties and obligations as he may deem proper, either in the drawing of plans and specifications for said dam, or to perform any other work in the building or construction of the same. The President may, by such order, place the control of the construction of said dam in the hands of such engineer or engineers taken from private life as he may desire: And provided further, That the President is hereby expressly authorized, without regard to the restriction or limitation of any other statute, to select attorneys and assistants for the purpose of making any investigation he may deem proper to ascertain whether, in the control and management of Dam Numbered 2, or any other dam or property owned by the Government in the Tennessee River Basin, or in the authorization of any improvement therein, there has been any undue or unfair advantage given to private persons, partnerships, or corporations, by any officials or employees of the Government, or whether in any such matters the Government has been injured or unjustly deprived of any of its rights.

Sec. 18. In order to enable and empower the Secretary of War, the Secretary of the Interior, or the board to carry out the authority hereby conferred, in the most economical and efficient manner, he or it is hereby authorized and empowered in the exercise of the powers of national defense in aid of navigation, and in the control of the flood waters of the Tennessee and Mississippi Rivers, constituting channels of interstate commerce, to exercise the right of eminent domain for all purposes of this Act, and to condemn all lands, easements, rights of way, and other area necessary in order to obtain a site for said Cove Creek Dam, and the flowage rights for the reservoir of water above said dam, and to negotiate and conclude contracts with States, counties, municipalities, and all State agencies and with railroads, railroad corporations, common carriers, and all public utility commissions and any other person, firm or corporation, for the relocation of railroad tracks, highways, highway bridges, mills, ferries, electric-light plants, and any and all other properties, enterprises, and projects whose removal may be necessary in order to carry out the provisions of this Act. When said Cove Creek Dam, transmission line, and power house shall have been completed, the possession, use, and control thereof shall be intrusted to the Corporation for use and operation in connection with the general Tennessee Valley project, and to promote flood control and navigation in the Tennessee River.

Sec. 19. The Corporation, as an instrumentality and agency of the Government of the United States for the purpose of executing its constitutional powers, shall have access to the Patent Office of the United States for the purpose of studying, ascertaining, and copying all methods, formulae, and scientific information (not including access to pending applications for patents) necessary to enable the Corporation to use and employ the most efficacious and economical process for the production of fixed nitrogen, or any essential ingredient of fertilizer, or any method of improving and cheapening the production of hydroelectric power, and any owner of a patent whose patent rights may have been thus in any way copied, used, infringed, or employed by the exercise of this authority by the Corporation shall have as the exclusive remedy a cause of action against the Corporation to be instituted and prosecuted on the equity side of the appropriate district court of the United States, for the recovery of reasonable compensation for such infringement. The Commissioner of Patents shall furnish to the Corporation, at its request and without payment of fees, copies of documents on file in his office: Provided, That the benefits of this section shall not apply to any art, machine, method of manufacture, or composition of matter, discovered or invented by such employee during the time of his employment or services with the Corporation or with the Government of the United States.

Sec. 20. The Government of the United States hereby reserves the right, in case of war or national emergency declared by Congress, to take possession of all or any part of the property described or referred to in this Act for the purpose of manufacturing explosives or for other war purposes; but, if this right is exercised by the Government, it shall pay the reasonable and fair damages that may be suffered by any party whose contract for the purchase of electric power or fixed nitrogen or fertilizer ingredients is hereby violated, after the amount of the damages has been fixed by the United States Court of Claims in proceedings instituted and conducted for that purpose under rules prescribed by the court.

Sec. 21. (a) All general penal statutes relating to the larceny, embezzlement, conversion, or to the improper handling, retention, use, or disposal of public moneys or property of the United States, shall apply to the moneys and property of the Corporation and to moneys and properties of the United States intrusted to the Corporation.

(b) Any person who, with intent to defraud the Corporation, or to deceive any director, officer, or employee of the Corporation or any officer or employee of the United States (1) makes any false entry in any book of the Corporation, or (2) makes any false report or statement for the Corporation, shall, upon conviction thereof, be fined not more than $10,000 or imprisoned not more than five years, or both.

(c) Any person who shall receive any compensation, rebate, or reward, or shall enter into any conspiracy, collusion, or agreement, express or implied, with intent to defraud the Corporation or wrongfully and unlawfully to defeat its purposes, shall, on conviction thereof, be fined not more than $5,000 or imprisoned not more than five years, or both.

Sec. 22. To aid further the proper use, conservation, and development of the natural resources of the Tennessee River drainage basin and of such adjoining territory as may be related to or materially affected by the development consequent to this Act, and to provide for the general welfare of the citizens of said areas, the President is hereby authorized, by such means or methods as he may deem proper within the limits of appropriations made therefor by Congress, to make such surveys of and general plans for said Tennessee basin and adjoining territory as may be useful to the Congress and to the several States in guiding and controlling the extent, sequence, and nature of development that may be equitably and economically advanced through the expenditure of public funds, or through the guidance or control of public authority, all for the general purpose of fostering an orderly and proper physical, economic, and social development of said areas; and the President is further authorized in making said surveys and plans to cooperate with the States affected thereby, or subdivisions or agencies of such States, or with cooperative or other organizations, and to make such studies, experiments, or demonstrations as may be necessary and suitable to that end.

Sec. 23. The President shall, from time to time, as the work provided for in the preceding section progresses, recommend to Congress such legislation as he deems proper to carry out the general purposes stated in said section, and for the especial purpose of bringing about in said Tennessee drainage basin and adjoining territory in conformity with said general purposes (1) the maximum amount of flood control; (2) the maximum development of said Tennessee River for navigation purposes; (3) the maximum generation of electric power consistent with flood control and navigation; (4) the proper use of marginal lands; (5) the proper method of reforestation of all lands in said drainage basin suitable for reforestation; and (6) the economic and social well-being of the people living in said river basin.

Sec. 24. For the purpose of securing any rights of flowage, or obtaining title to or possession of any property, real or personal, that may be necessary or may become necessary, in the carrying out of any of the provisions of this Act, the President of the United States for a period of three years from the date of the enactment of this Act, is hereby authorized to acquire title in the name of the United States to such rights or such property, and to provide for the payment for same by directing the board to contract to deliver power generated at any of the plants now owned or hereafter owned or constructed by the Government or by said Corporation, such future delivery of power to continue for a period not exceeding thirty years. Likewise, for one year after the enactment of this Act, the President is further authorized to sell or lease any parcel or part of any vacant real estate now owned by the Government in said Tennessee River Basin, to persons, firms, or corporations who shall contract to erect thereon factories or manufacturing establishments, and who shall contract to purchase of said Corporation electric power for the operation of any such factory or manufacturing establishment. No contract shall be made by the President for the sale of any of such real estate as may be necessary for present or future use on the part of the Government for any of the purposes of this Act. Any such contract made by the President of the United States shall be carried out by the board: Provided, That no such contract shall be made that will in any way abridge or take away the preference right to purchase power given in this Act to States, counties, municipalities, or farm organizations: Provided further, That no lease shall be for a term to exceed fifty years: Provided further, That any sale shall be on condition that said land shall be used for industrial purposes only.

Sec. 25. The Corporation may cause proceedings to be instituted for the acquisition by condemnation of any lands, easements, or rights of way which, in the opinion of the Corporation, are necessary to carry out the provisions of this Act. The proceedings shall be instituted in the United States district court for the district in which the land, easement, right of way, or other interest, or any part thereof, is located, and such court shall have full jurisdiction to divest the complete title to the property sought to be acquired out of all persons or claimants and vest the same in the United States in fee simple, and to enter a decree quieting the title thereto in the United States of America.

Upon the filing of a petition for condemnation and for the purpose of ascertaining the value of the property to be acquired, and assessing the compensation to be paid, the court shall appoint three commissioners who shall be disinterested persons and who shall take and subscribe an oath that they do not own any lands, or interest or easement in any lands, which it may be desirable for the United States to acquire in the furtherance of said project and such commissioners shall not be selected from the locality wherein the land sought to be condemned lies. Such commissioners shall receive a per diem of not to exceed $15 for their services, together with an additional amount of $5 per day for subsistence for time actually spent in performing their duties as commissioners.

It shall be the duty of such commissioners to examine into the value of the lands sought to be condemned, to conduct hearings and receive evidence, and generally to take such appropriate steps as may be proper for the determination of the value of the said lands sought to be condemned, and for such purpose the commissioners are authorized to administer oaths and subpoena witnesses, which said witnesses shall receive the same fees as are provided for witnesses in the Federal courts. The said commissioners shall thereupon file a report setting forth their conclusions as to the value of the said property sought to be condemned, making a separate award and valuation in the premises with respect to each separate parcel involved. Upon the filing of such award in court the clerk of said court shall give notice of the filing of such award to the parties to said proceeding, in manner and form as directed by the judge of said court.

Either or both parties may file exceptions to the award of said commissioners within twenty days from the date of the filing of said award in court.

Exceptions filed to such award shall be heard before three Federal district judges unless the parties, in writing, in person, or by their attorneys, stipulate that the exceptions may be heard before a lesser number of judges. On such hearing such judges shall pass de novo upon the proceedings had before the commissioners, may view the property, and may take additional evidence. Upon such hearings the said judges shall file their own award, fixing therein the value of the property sought to be condemned, regardless of the award previously made by the said commissioners.

At any time within thirty days from the filing of the decision of the district judges upon the hearing on exceptions to the award made by the commissioners, either party may appeal from such decision of the said judges to the circuit court of appeals, and the said circuit court of appeals shall upon the hearing on said appeal dispose of the same upon the record, without regard to the awards or findings theretofore made by the commissioners or the district judges, and such circuit court of appeals shall thereupon fix the value of the said property sought to be condemned.

Upon acceptance of an award by the owner of any property herein provided to be appropriated, and the payment of the money awarded or upon the failure of either party to file exceptions to the award of the commissioners within the time specified, or upon the award of the commissioners, and the payment of the money by the United States pursuant thereto, or the payment of the money awarded into the registry of the court by the Corporation, the title to said property and the right to the possession thereof shall pass to the United States, and the United States shall be entitled to a writ in the same proceeding to dispossess the former owner of said property, and all lessees, agents, and attorneys of such former owner, and to put the United States, by its corporate creature and agent, the Corporation, into possession of said property.

In the event of any property owned in Whole or in part by minors, or insane persons, or incompetent persons, or estates of deceased persons, then the legal representatives of such minors, insane persons, incompetent persons, or estates shall have power, by and with the consent and approval of the trial judge in whose court said matter is for determination, to consent to or reject the awards of the commissioners herein provided for, and in the event that there be no legal representatives, or that the legal representatives for such minors, insane persons, or incompetent persons shall fail or decline to act, then such trial judge may, upon motion, appoint a guardian ad litem to act for such minors, insane persons, or incompetent persons, and such guardian ad litem shall act to the full extent and to the same purpose and effect as his ward could act, if competent, and such guardian ad litem shall be deemed to have full power and authority to respond, to conduct, or to maintain any proceeding herein provided for affecting his said ward.

Sec. 26. The net proceeds derived by the board from the sale of power and any of the products manufactured by the Corporation, after deducting the cost of operation, maintenance, depreciation, amortization, and an amount deemed by the board as necessary to withhold as operating capital, or devoted by the board to new construction, shall be paid into the Treasury of the United States at the end of each calendar year.

Sec. 27. All appropriations necessary to carry out the provisions of this Act are hereby authorized.

Sec. 28. That all Acts or parts of Acts in conflict herewith are hereby repealed, so far as they affect the operations contemplated by this Act.

Sec. 29. The right to alter, amend, or repeal this Act is hereby expressly declared and reserved, but no such amendment or repeal shall operate to impair the obligation of any contract made by said Corporation under any power conferred in this Act.

Sec. 30. The sections of this Act are hereby declared to be separable, and in the event any one or more sections of this Act be held to be unconstitutional, the same shall not affect the validity of other sections of this Act.

Seventy-third Congress of the United States of America;

At the First Session,

Begun and held at the City of Washington on Thursday, the ninth
day of March, one thousand nine hundred and thirty-three.

AN ACT

To encourage national industrial recovery, to foster fair competition, and to provide for the construction of certain useful public
works, and for other purposes.

*Be it enacted by the Senate and House of Representatives of the
United States of America in Congress assembled,*

TITLE I—INDUSTRIAL RECOVERY

DECLARATION OF POLICY

SECTION 1. A national emergency productive of widespread unemployment and disorganization of industry, which burdens interstate
and foreign commerce, affects the public welfare, and undermines
the standards of living of the American people, is hereby declared
to exist. It is hereby declared to be the policy of Congress to remove
obstructions to the free flow of interstate and foreign commerce
which tend to diminish the amount thereof; and to provide for the
general welfare by promoting the organization of industry for the
purpose of cooperative action among trade groups, to induce and
maintain united action of labor and management under adequate
governmental sanctions and supervision, to eliminate unfair competitive practices, to promote the fullest possible utilization of the
present productive capacity of industries, to avoid undue restriction
of production (except as may be temporarily required), to increase
the consumption of industrial and agricultural products by increasing purchasing power, to reduce and relieve unemployment, to
improve standards of labor, and otherwise to rehabilitate industry
and to conserve natural resources.

ADMINISTRATIVE AGENCIES

SEC. 2. (a) To effectuate the policy of this title, the President is
hereby authorized to establish such agencies, to accept and utilize
such voluntary and uncompensated services, to appoint, without
regard to the provisions of the civil service laws, such officers and
employees, and to utilize such Federal officers and employees, and,
with the consent of the State, such State and local officers and employees, as he may find necessary, to prescribe their authorities,
duties, responsibilities, and tenure, and, without regard to the Classi-

The National Industrial Recovery Act (National Archives and Records Administration)

"A national emergency productive of widespread unemployment and disorganization of industry ... is hereby declared to exist."

Overview

On June 16, 1933, President Franklin D. Roosevelt, in response to the Great Depression, signed a bill that he saw as the linchpin of the New Deal program, the National Industrial Recovery Act (NIRA). This legislation was the boldest effort ever to coordinate the economy of the world's greatest industrial power. The NIRA was an omnibus bill, that is, one that addresses several diverse concerns, foremost among them the revival of business. It required any industry engaged in interstate commerce to draft a code that would be approved by the president. Each such code would limit production and thereby prevent cutthroat competition, the source of many business failures. The president was authorized to license businesses so as to police recalcitrant firms.

Labor, too, was intended to benefit. By acquiescing in corporate exemption from antitrust laws, labor would be granted the right to bargain collectively "through representatives of their own choosing." The bill's famous Section 7 (a) specifically outlawed the so-called yellow dog contract, by which a corporation could prohibit a prospective employee from joining a union. Also illegal was pressuring the employee to join a "company union" sponsored and controlled by management. The National Recovery Administration (NRA) codes would require minimum wages and humane working conditions, thereby preventing the continuation of sweatshop conditions.

The unemployed made up another group that would benefit from the new bill. A last-minute insertion allocated $3.3 billion for a massive works program, soon to be implemented by the Public Works Administration, or PWA. The consumer was not neglected, being aided by the general increase in purchasing power and by a specially created watchdog group, the Consumers Advisory Board.

Context

On October 29, 1929, a day known as "Black Tuesday," the Great Crash in the stock market triggered a panic on

Wall Street that, within months, led to general economic collapse. Practically any statistic one could cite—industrial production, retail sales, farm foreclosures, the gross national product—witnessed to three years of increasing misery. Private debts, contracted at higher price levels during the era of prosperity, threatened to break the nation's economy. Over half of home mortgages were in default. The United States had quickly become victim to a depression unparalleled in its history.

When President Roosevelt took the oath of office on March 4, 1933, as many as sixty million people, just about half the total population, lived in poverty. Possibly one-fourth of the labor force was unemployed, with the jobless rate averaging 35 percent in manufacturing industries and 75 percent in construction. Only a minority of Americans were still working full-time. Said Roosevelt in his inaugural address, "Our greatest primary task is to put people to work" (Doenecke, p. 179).

The NIRA was just one of a series of enactments passed by Congress in the late winter and spring of 1933 that were unprecedented in quantity and scope. Within three and a half months, Roosevelt sent fifteen messages to Congress and saw an equal number of major laws passed. The passage of eleven bills in the House took only forty hours of debate. As FDR assumed office, he noted, "There are about 350 plans here in Washington, public and private. I should say they are still coming in at the rate of 25 or 30 a day" (Doenecke, p. 26). Reporters, recalling Napoleon's mobilization of France in 1814, christened the period the "hundred days." As a result of this battery of legislation, bank deposits were insured, the currency was inflated, home owners received loans, alcoholic beverages could again be sold, and the railroad system was coordinated. Farmers received subsidies for cutting output. A new Civilian Conservation Corps enrolled a quarter of a million men, putting them to work planting trees, clearing brush, building dams, and fixing roads. Similarly Congress created the Tennessee Valley Authority, the greatest hydroelectric project in history, seeking to develop 640,000 square miles ranging from the Great Smoky Mountains to the rolling farms of Kentucky.

The NIRA itself was inadvertently triggered by the Democratic senator Hugo L. Black of Alabama, who in December 1932 introduced legislation aimed at creating

Time Line

1929

■ **October 29**
Black Tuesday on the New York Stock Exchange, with almost thirteen million shares exchanging hands.

1932

■ **November 8**
Franklin D. Roosevelt is elected president.

1933

■ **March 4**
Roosevelt delivers First Inaugural Address.

■ **May 17**
Roosevelt administration presents National Industrial Recovery Act to Congress.

■ **May 26**
House passes original NIRA bill after two days of debate.

■ **June 9**
Senate passes somewhat different NIRA bill.

■ **June 10**
House passes NIRA conference report.

■ **June 13**
Senate passes NIRA conference report.

■ **June 16**
Roosevelt signs the NIRA bill, which establishes the National Recovery Administration.

1934

■ **February 9**
Roosevelt appoints National Recovery Review Board, headed by the prominent attorney Clarence Darrow, to investigate NRA.

■ **May 21**
Darrow's first report finds code authorities acting as agents of monopoly.

■ **September 4**
Hugh Johnson resigns as NRA chief effective October 15.

■ **September 27**
Roosevelt appoints S. Clay Williams to head new National Industrial Recovery Board.

---

six million new jobs. The Black bill would have barred from interstate commerce any articles produced in factories or mines that employed workers for more than five days and thirty hours a week. In defending his proposal, the sponsor claimed that a shorter workweek would also raise declining labor standards and increase employee purchasing power. William Green, president of the American Federation of Labor (AFL), threatened a general strike of 2.5 million AFL members if Congress did not pass the bill.

On April 6, 1933, the Senate passed the measure by a vote of fifty-three to twenty, at which point President Roosevelt became most alarmed. FDR was repelled by the legislation's rigidity and feared that it might be unconstitutional. The real solution, maintained the chief executive, did not center on spreading out available jobs; it involved stimulating business confidence and creating new employment. Afraid that the Black bill could actually retard recovery, the new administration drew upon plans devised in 1931 by Henry I. Harriman, soon elected president of the U.S. Chamber of Commerce, and Gerald Swope, president of the General Electric Company. The Chamber had proposed a national advisory council of business leaders, which would be entrusted with controlling production, raising prices, and stabilizing wages. Similarly, Swope envisioned national planning through trade associations and a national economic council. When the Harriman-Swope proposals were first made, the then-incumbent president, Herbert Clark Hoover, found them sheer fascism. Certainly, Hoover believed, they would foster gigantic monopolies destructive of the entire American economic system.

Once the Senate passed the Black bill, two members of Roosevelt's "brain trust," a set of informal advisers who often exercised more influence than the president's cabinet, got immediately to work. They were the Columbia University professors Raymond Moley and Rexford Tugwell, who began meeting with Hugh S. Johnson, a flamboyant brigadier general whose knowledge of American industry was encyclopedic. The three men rapidly modified the Chamber's scheme to include substantial concessions to labor. Within twenty-four hours, Johnson had produced a draft bill that focused on industrial self-government. It was so terse that it was originally written on two large sheets of paper. Moley turned down the Johnson scheme on the ground that it gave the president dictatorial powers Roosevelt personally did not want. Johnson, now aided by the Chicago lawyer Donald Richberg, produced a new draft that included some public-works programs. Another group, led by the Democratic senator Robert F. Wagner of New York and assistant secretary of commerce John Dickinson, produced a different draft, one that stressed a more ambitious agenda of public works and guaranteed labor's right to collective bargaining. On May 10, Roosevelt insisted that the two proposals be merged, indeed that the framers "shut themselves up in a room" until this was done (Ohl, p. 100).

Just a week later Wagner introduced a bill incorporating both the Johnson-Richberg proposals and the Wagner-Dickinson ones. The House passed such a measure 325 to 76 on May 26 after two days of debate. On June 9, the Senate passed its own bill by a tally of fifty-eight to twenty-four. This bill, thanks to the Idaho Republican William E. Borah, banned "combinations in restraint of trade" (Hawley, 1966, p. 30) and included the proposal of the Wisconsin Republican Robert M. La Follette, Jr., to publish corporate and personal income-tax returns. Because the Senate's version differed in such particulars from that of the House, a conference committee was created. The conference report removed specific bans on such practices as price fixing and deprived La Follette's alteration of all meaning. On June 10, the House ratified the conference report, and three days later the Senate approved the measure by the surprisingly close vote of forty-six to thirty-nine. Roosevelt signed the legislation on June 16, 1933, promising that it would raise the purchasing power of labor and elevate labor standards. It was, he said, "the most important and far-reaching legislation ever enacted by the American Congress" (Bellush, p. 1). He immediately established the NRA, giving its head, General Hugh Samuel Johnson, the disarmingly modest title "administrator."

Labor leaders were most enthusiastic. The AFL's William Green deemed 7 (a) a "Magna Charta" for labor (Doenecke, p. 43). John L. Lewis, president of the United Mine Workers and an AFL vice president, put 7 (a) on a par with Lincoln's Emancipation Proclamation. A shrewd man, Lewis undoubtedly realized full well that Roosevelt was not yet a strong defender of unionization, but the United Mine Workers itself spearheaded its recruiting efforts with the slogan: "The President wants you to join the union" (Doenecke, p. 43). (Only if cornered would organizers grant that "the president" in mind was Lewis, not Roosevelt.)

Some were less enthralled. Old-time progressives, such as Senator Borah, saw monopoly receiving new protection. "Everyone who does not cooperate according to the agreement," he feared, "will be roped, branded, ears split, and made to run with the herd" (Doenecke, p. 43). The Democratic senator Huey P. Long of Louisiana spoke against the bill for two hours, denying that the legislation would create jobs: "There won't be any unemployment at all. They'll all be in jail for violating this infernal thing" (Bellush, p. 21). The more dignified National Association of Manufacturers found the NIRA tending to retard recovery, while the Socialist Party leader Norman Thomas saw the bill establishing "a capitalist syndicalism," "a scheme which is in essence fascist" (Doenecke, p. 43).

About the Author

As with much legislation, the NIRA obviously went through several hands. Raymond Moley, professor of government and public law at Columbia University, spearheaded the initial coordination of the bill. Originally a specialist in the field of criminal justice, he wrote major speeches for Roosevelt, in the course of which he coined the term "New Deal" and supplied much of the material of Roosevelt's First Inaugural Address. Moley strongly believed in government-business partnership and found national planning the only

Time Line

1935

■ **March 22**
Donald Richberg replaces Williams as head of the National Industrial Recovery Board.

■ **May 27**
Supreme Court ruling in *Schechter Poultry Corporation v. United States* dooms the NIRA.

alternative to wasteful competition. During the interregnum between Hoover and Roosevelt, his influence was felt so strongly that journalists would retitle a traditional Christian hymn to read "Moley, Moley, Moley, Lord God Almighty." By 1937, however, Moley had become a strong critic of the New Deal, indeed of all enlarged federal power, and found a forum for his views in *Newsweek* magazine.

Also influential was Donald Richberg, a Chicago-based reformer who had become prominent as a labor lawyer. Richberg had been the principal draftsman of the Railway Labor Act of 1926. He had also helped write the Norris-LaGuardia Act of 1932, which curbed the power of federal courts to ban certain union practices. A supporter of Roosevelt in 1932, he was recruited by Moley to aid Hugh Johnson in formulating the NIRA bill. Richberg helped draft both the industrial recovery and public-works sections. Like Moley, Richberg became increasingly conservative by the mid-1930s, spending his last decades attacking "labor union monopoly" (Vadney, p. 459).

One cannot ignore Rexford Guy Tugwell, a Columbia University economist whose specialty was agriculture. Even during the prosperous 1920s, Tugwell's writing focused on technological obsolescence, the folly of laissez-faire, overproduction among American farmers, and the growing inequities in the nation's economy. A firm believer in scientific management and social engineering, he wrote *The Industrial Discipline and the Governmental Arts* (1933), in which he claimed that a managed society was the only alternative to revolution. The federal government, he believed, must control prices, eliminate excessive competition, and allocate capital. Once, in a lighter mood, he scribbled a poem ending with, "I shall roll up my sleeves— make America over" (Schlesinger, 1957, p. 194). Tugwell soon served Roosevelt in a number of capacities, among them undersecretary of agriculture, director of the Resettlement Administration, and governor of Puerto Rico.

The bill was introduced by Democratic senator Robert Wagner of New York, who was primarily concerned with its labor provisions. Arriving from Germany as a child, Wagner was really a product of Manhattan's Upper East Side, an area packed with an immigrant and working-class population. He first sat in the New York legislature and then in the U.S. Senate. An urban Progressive despite his ties to the powerful Democratic machine called Tammany Hall, Wagner pushed reform legislation to such a degree that one

Rex Tugwell, left, and Raymond Moley, shown here in a 1938 photograph, were key figures in the drafting of the National Industrial Recovery Act. (AP Photo)

Roosevelt appointee later recalled, "The New Deal owed as much to Robert Wagner as to Franklin Roosevelt" (Huthmacher, p. 137). Because the National Association of Manufacturers sought to soften the guarantee of collective bargaining found in Section 7 (a) of the bill, Wagner once delivered an ultimatum to the drafters: "No 7(a), no bill" (Huthmacher, p. 147). While believing strongly in the public works and labor sections of the bill, Wagner did fear that new codes might encompass too many industries. Serving in the Senate until 1949, when he resigned for health reasons, Wagner was long a bulwark of reform legislation.

Most important of all was General Hugh Johnson, whose career was nothing if not colorful. "Old Ironpants," as he was called, had been, in turn, a writer of boys' adventure books, director of the World War I draft, an executive for a major farm implement firm, and economic adviser to financier Bernard Baruch. Indeed, the NRA was modeled in part after Baruch's War Industries Board of World War I. The historian Ellis Hawley writes, "Powerfully built, brusque in demeanor, and given to 'demonic activity,' he tried to project the image of a tough-minded troubleshooter cutting through the 'guff' to get things done" (1999, p. 83). As Hawley also notes, Johnson's career reflected the emergence of an American corporatism, which consigned social duties to business organizations and helped them to cooperate for public purposes. Johnson hoped that one could combine the virtues of free enterprise and national planning. Once he left the NRA, he grew increasingly critical of Roosevelt's leadership, voicing his views in a syndicated newspaper column until 1941, a year before his death.

Also involved in drafting the bill were John Dickinson, assistant secretary of commerce, who had been both a lawyer and an economist and had taught at such institutions as Princeton and the University of Pennsylvania;

Jerome Frank, solicitor to the Department of Agriculture; and Lewis Douglas, director of the budget, who had been a former state legislator and congressman from Arizona.

Explanation and Analysis of the Document

◆ An Act

The purpose of the bill is clearly stated: to revive the American economy, create a more equal economic playing field, and sponsor government construction projects.

◆ Title I—Industrial Recovery

In Section 1, the "Declaration of Policy," attention is immediately called to the existing economic crisis, particularly the all-pervading unemployment, and how the government planned to meet it. Crucial was the self-governing of industries, referred to as "promoting the organization of industry for the purpose of cooperative action among trade groups." Other goals were broad, ranging from the expansion of purchasing power to bettering labor conditions, from producing jobs to conserving natural resources. Ironically, in light of subsequent events, the bill claimed to avoid "undue restriction of production" and to remove "obstructions to the free flow of interstate … commerce."

Section 2 gives the president power to establish relevant agencies to accomplish the bill's objectives and to appoint their officers and staff. Henceforth, when the term *President* is used in the bill, it means the designated planning agencies and enforcement officers. In this case, the director of the newly formed National Recovery Administration would play the crucial role. All such powers would last only two years.

Section 3 presents the crux of the National Industrial Recovery Act, the codes that each industry was required to draft. It is clearly specified that such codes "are not designed to promote monopolies or to eliminate or oppress small enterprises," although such senators as Borah and the Republican Gerald P. Nye of North Dakota would soon challenge such claims. An effort is made to protect consumers, corporations, and employees by providing for hearings prior to the drafting of a code and, if necessary, specifying exceptions to its application. Once the president approved a code, however, its provisions would be designated the "standards of fair competition" for the relevant industry. Such codes had the power of law solidly behind them. Violators would be subject to proceedings initiated by the U.S. attorney general and prosecuted in district courts by district attorney generals. If an industry engaged in activities inimical to this legislation, the president might prescribe a code himself. Furthermore, foreign competition would not be allowed to undersell American products. If a foreign import threatened significantly to undercut a code by offering a lower price than its American counterpart, the U.S. Tariff Commission could ban any such items from entering the nation.

Sections 4–6 authorize the president to approve voluntary agreements concerning production activity. More important, at Johnson's insistence, the president has the power to grant and revoke licenses so as "to make effective a code of fair competition." Indeed, interstate shipments by unlicensed establishments were banned. Penalties were heavy, involving a fine of up to $500 per day of offense. A licensed firm might be exempted from antitrust laws for sixty days. All trade associations must file a statement describing any activities that lie under NIRA jurisdiction. To avoid favoritism of certain firms over others, the bill stipulates that such organizations must be truly representative of a particular industry. If necessary, the Federal Trade Commission, an agency established in 1914 to regulate business practices, could investigate possible offenses. Farmers and self-employed laborers received a waiver from NIRA provisions.

Section 7 (a) embodies the so-called Magna Charta of Labor, as it gave employees the right to form unions and bargain collectively, acting free from employer interference. Such activity had long been stifled by a variety of devices. Among them were puppet unions, established by a firm and called "company unions"; court injunctions, that is, court orders prohibiting certain union activities; and "yellow-dog contracts," agreements by which prospective employees pledged that, if hired, they would not join a union. Senator Bennett Champ Clark, a Missouri Democrat, had proposed an amendment that would have sanctioned company unions and might have negated the entire intent of 7 (a), but it met with AFL opposition and was defeated in the Senate. According to other provisions of Section 7, employees and employers could establish such labor standards as maximum hours and minimum wages by voluntary consent. Otherwise, the president would prescribe "a limited code of fair competition" that would stipulate such conditions.

Sections 8–10 first specify that the NIRA did not impinge upon the recently passed Agricultural Adjustment Act, a bill that subsidized farmers in return for a commitment to reduce their output. The law was specifically extended to the oil industry, with one provision requiring petroleum holding companies to make sure that the pipeline companies they controlled charged a fair rate. The president is authorized to carry out enabling regulations, a proviso somewhat similar to the "necessary and proper" clause of the U.S. Constitution (Article I, Section 8). The chief executive also possesses authority to cancel or modify any provisions in the new law.

◆ Title II—Public Works and Construction Projects

In Section 201, the NIRA created a public works program, soon to be named the Public Works Administration. Again the president was given wide discretionary powers in delegating his "functions and powers" to agency personnel. This agency, too, would be automatically terminated after two years. Roosevelt himself saw Title I, which focused on self-policing, as the basis for reforming the economy; Title II, with its stress on government projects, was simply a stopgap measure.

Sections 202–221 authorize a rich variety of public works: highways, roads, hospitals, slum clearance, flood control, federal buildings, and soil conservation. One sweeping provision calls for "construction, reconstruction, alteration, or repair" of low-cost housing. At the insistence of Johnson, the bill permitted the construction of naval vessels, an action that helped create an arms race with Japan. Other provisions center on coordination with various states and municipalities, the prohibition of convict labor, preferential hiring of servicemen with dependents, and details of financing, including capital stock and excess profits taxes. A thirty-hour week was designated for rank-and-file employees, though not for administrators. Wages should be sufficient for an employee to live "in decency and comfort." Section 203 (a) states the aim of this section: "With a view to increase employment quickly."

◆ Title III—Amendments to Emergency Relief and Construction Act and Miscellaneous Provisions

In Sections 301–303 some funding is provided by the Reconstruction Finance Corporation, an agency established originally in 1932 to advance money to banks, railroads, life insurance companies, and loan associations but which soon ventured out into loans to states and municipalities.

Audience

In the widest sense, the audience for the bill was the American public. Although few citizens would ever read the bill's provisions, it was assumed that they would be sufficiently familiar with the bill's contents to know that a new, all-encompassing government agency had been created, one that would restore prosperity to the nation.

As for those most likely to read the actual bill, some would be found in the administrative ranks of business and industry, for the legislation affected how many such people were required to conduct their enterprises. Labor organizers, too, would pay careful attention, for the bill provided for the right of collective bargaining and the establishment of labor standards. Giving the bill a particularly close reading would be government officials and attorneys, for they would have to be familiar with the technical language affecting the regulation of so many companies.

Impact

The NRA was launched with a tremendous amount of ballyhoo—parades, emblems, and mass rallies. For several months, its emblem, a blue eagle, was as familiar as Old Glory; indeed, it was so ubiquitous that it was even tattooed on men's biceps. Within several months after its creation, NRA codes were drafted in such major industries as textiles, shipbuilding, electricity, oil, steel, lumber, and coal. By May 1935, the NRA had approved codes for more than seven hundred occupations, among them, rabbit furriers, pretzel benders, milk evaporators, and producers of dog food. In total these codes filled eighteen volumes and thirteen thousand pages, a sum far greater than the volume

> "A national emergency productive of widespread unemployment and disorganization of industry ... is hereby declared to exist."
>
> (Section 1)

> "Employees shall have the right to organize and bargain collectively through representatives of their own choosing."
>
> (Section 7[a])

of all federal statues then in effect. All codes confirmed labor's right to organize and established scales specifying minimum wages and maximum hours. In return business received government approval for price fixing, production limits, and the banning of allegedly unfair competition—in essence, absolute self-government. Each code was administered by its own code authority, almost invariably staffed by the larger corporations in each industry. A massive bureaucracy of 4,500 NRA staffers issued eleven thousand administrative orders.

At first the effort appeared to be successful. As millions of employers pledged to abide by NRA labor standards, even more millions of customers vowed to support them. Hundreds of thousands of Americans were returning to work. Child labor was abolished in the textile industry—a particularly exploitative endeavor, where in 1933 fifteen thousand children, some as young as seven, toiled in the lint-laden air of southern mills.

Moreover, under Title II of the NIRA, a Public Works Administration was created, with $3.3 billion allocated in June 1933. The president hoped that the PWA would create massive employment almost immediately. Certainly the projects slated were rich and varied, some going beyond the concrete items specified in the NIRA bill. Waterworks for Spearfish, South Dakota; a sewer system for Poulsbo, Washington; more plumbing for Beech Grove, Indiana; more bathtubs for Arab, Alabama; a new home for lepers living in the Virgin Islands—all were PWA accomplishments. In the long run, the PWA could boast myriad highways, bridges, dams, canals, sewers, hospitals, and jails. Between 1933 and its demise in 1939, it helped construct 70 percent of the nation's new educational buildings; 65 percent of the courthouses, city halls, and sewage disposal plants; 35 percent of the hospitals and public health facilities; and 10 percent of all roads, bridges, and subways. Two aircraft carriers that played prominent roles in World War II, the *Yorktown* and *Enterprise*, were PWA projects. So was New York's Triborough Bridge, the Texas port of Brownsville, and the highway linking Key West to the Florida mainland. Still, if the PWA embodied an unprecedent-

ed program in public relief, it did little to accomplish its immediate aim: providing jobs for masses of the unemployed. In August 1933, two months after Congress passed the NIRA bill, the AFL index tallied the number of jobless at eleven million.

The agency's director, Harold Ickes, was so obsessed with the dangers of political intervention and the accompanying corruption that he was miserly in doling out the needed funds. Treasury Secretary Henry Morgenthau complained that Ickes "was so anxious to keep graft and politics out of the public works program that he practically spent money through a medicine dropper" (Doenecke, p. 68). Hence, the PWA did little to stimulate the economy. More than slightly paranoid, "Honest Harold," as he was called, encouraged employees to report on each other and even reprimanded them for extending their coffee breaks. A frustrated aide proclaimed, "He still has to learn that the Administrator of a $3 billion fund hasn't time to check every typewriter acquisition" (Doenecke, p. 68). Hence, close to a year after the NIRA was enacted, only $803 million of government funds had been spent on PWA projects. Only in 1935 did a new federal agency, the Works Progress Administration, and a new director, Harry Hopkins, begin to spend the massive sums Roosevelt desired. Several historians—Ellis W. Hawley and Bernard Bellush among them—have suggested that the more cautious Ickes would have been better as NRA administrator than Johnson, for he would never have insisted on codes for every enterprise. Conversely the more flamboyant Johnson, who was deeply disappointed not to head the public works program, would have spent massive sums quickly and generously.

Not everything was Ickes's fault. The entire process of executing a PWA project took much time, particularly when such projects as dams and battleships were involved. One had to sign loan agreements with the government, survey a project, advertise for bids, pick a contractor, order materials, and assemble work crews. It was not, in fact, Ickes's PWA that led to the NRA's downfall, but the industry codes that, from the beginning, lay at the core of this legislation. Despite the initial optimism fed by the incredible hoopla, many Americans were soon disillusioned. By the fall of 1933 the NRA was clearly in trouble. Codes were increasingly being violated. It soon became obvious that neither recovery nor reemployment was being achieved. Business hated the government edicts, bans on price raising, and section 7 (a). Labor found that fewer than 10 percent of the code authorities had labor representation. Big Steel and the automobile industries still adhered to the open shop. Consumers found that their input was minuscule. For the most part, the great majority of people still lacked spending money. When, in early October, Johnson launched a "Buy Now" program, an Illinois farmer snapped back, "With what?" (Doenecke, p. 55). More significantly, about eleven million workers remained unemployed. All this time Johnson was revealing himself as an incredibly inept administrator, whose bluster and bombast did little to hide his refusal to enforce the tough sanctions needed for the agency to work.

On February 19, 1934, Roosevelt, now on the defensive, created a National Review Board chaired by the famed criminal lawyer Clarence Darrow. Darrow held almost sixty hearings, listened to 113 witnesses, and considered about three thousand complaints. In three major reports, the Darrow board found that giant corporations dominated the code authority, in the process acting as agents of monopoly and bleeding small business, labor, and the public. On September 24, 1934, a besieged Hugh Johnson submitted a letter of resignation. Three days later, Roosevelt tried to revitalize the NRA by creating a new National Industrial Recovery Board chaired by S. Clay Williams, past president of R. J. Reynolds Tobacco Company. When, in late March 1935, Williams resigned as chairman of the NRA board, he was replaced by NRA general counsel Donald Richberg, whose pro-business leanings became increasingly pronounced.

Despite such administrative shuffles, however, the ineffective NRA limped along, a mere shadow of its former self, until the Supreme Court, in what could only be called an act of mercy killing, outlawed the entire enterprise in one of the most sweeping rulings in American jurisprudence. The decision was triggered by the Schechter brothers, wholesale poultry dealers who operated the two largest chicken jobbing plants in Brooklyn. According to NRA enforcers, their firm had violated a host of codes, among them the submission of false reports as to sales volume, working employees longer than the code allowed, paying less than code-designated wages, and tampering with rules concerning the method of customer purchases. In a unanimous decision delivered on May 27, 1935, nicknamed Black Monday, the Court not only upheld the Schechter brothers but also ruled that 557 NRA codes were no longer the law of the land. Chief Justice Charles Evans Hughes, speaking for the Court, ruled that "extraordinary conditions did not create or enlarge constitutional power." Congress, he declared, could not delegate legislative power to the president "to exercise an unfettered discretion to make whatever laws he thinks needed or advisable for the rehabilitation and expansion of trade or industry." In a concurring opinion Associate Justice Benjamin Cardozo said of the NRA codes, "This is delegation run riot. No such

plenitude of power is susceptible of transfer." If the NRA prevailed, "anything that Congress may do within the limits of the commerce clause for the betterment of business may be done by the President upon the recommendation of a trade association by calling it a code" (*Schechter Poultry Corporation v. United States,* 295 U.S. 495).

Roosevelt responded with bitterness, telling the press that the decision was the most momentous since that concerning Dred Scott. He protested that the United States had been "relegated to the horse-and-buggy definition of interstate commerce." According to the opinion, he claimed, the Court had ruled that manufacturing, mining, construction, and farming were no longer regarded as "directly" affecting interstate commerce. "Does this decision mean," he asked, "that the United States Government has no control over any national economic problem?" (Doenecke, pp. 111–112).

Today most historians would find that the NRA record was a mixed one at best. It gave jobs to two million relief workers, helped stop a highly destructive deflationary spiral, and improved business ethics. Maximum hours and minimum wages were established, trade unions were encouraged, and child labor and the sweatshop all but abolished. But the NRA failed in its major objective—to speed recovery—and its support of restricted production and price-fixing undoubtedly hindered it.

Related Documents

"A. L. A. Schechter Poultry Corporation v. United States 295 U.S. 495 (1935)." FindLaw Web site. http://caselaw.lp.findlaw.com/scripts/getcase.pl?court=US&vol=295&invol=495. Accessed on February 5, 2008. In this decision the Supreme Court killed the NRA.

Buhite, Russell D., and David W. Levy, eds. *FDR's Fireside Chats.* Norman: University of Oklahoma Press, 1992. Here, in a radio address delivered on July 23, 1933, Roosevelt praises the initial results of the recovery act.

Roosevelt, Franklin D. *The Public Papers and Addresses of Franklin D. Roosevelt,* 13 vols., ed. Samuel I. Rosenman. New York: Random House, 1938–1950. Vols. 2–4 contain Roosevelt's speeches, some of which underwent editing before publication.

———. *Complete Presidential Press Conferences of Franklin D. Roosevelt.* 25 vols. New York: De Capo Press, 1972–. Providing an excellent illustration of how Roosevelt dealt with his policies on and off the record, these press conferences are sometimes most valuable for the questions he dodged from hostile reporters.

Bibliography

■ **Books**

Bellush, Bernard. *The Failure of the NRA.* New York: W. W. Norton, 1975.

Bernstein, Irving. *Turbulent Years: A History of the American Worker, 1933–1941*. Boston: Houghton Mifflin, 1969.

Davis, Kenneth S. *FDR: The New Deal Years, 1933–1937: A History*. New York: Random House, 1986.

Doenecke, Justus D. *The New Deal*. Malabar, Fla.: Krieger, 2003.

Friedel, Frank. *Franklin D. Roosevelt*, Vol. 4: *Launching the New Deal*. Boston: Little, Brown, 1973.

Graham, Otis L., Jr., and Meghan Robinson Wander, eds. *Franklin D. Roosevelt, His Life and Times: An Encyclopedic View*. Boston: G. K. Hall, 1985.

Hawley, Ellis W. *The New Deal and the Problem of Monopoly: A Study in Economic Ambivalence*. Princeton, N.J.: Princeton University Press, 1966.

———. "Hugh Samuel Johnson." In *American National Biography*, vol. 12, eds. John A. Garraty and Mark C. Carnes. New York: Oxford University Press, 1999.

Himmelberg, Robert F. *The Origins of the National Recovery Administration*. New York: Fordham University Press, 1976.

Huthmacher, J. Joseph. *Senator Robert F. Wagner and the Rise of Urban Liberalism*. New York: Atheneum, 1968.

Irons, Peter H. *The New Deal Lawyers*. Princeton, N.J.: Princeton University Press, 1982.

Johnson, Hugh S. *The Blue Eagle from Egg to Earth*. Garden City, N.Y.: Doubleday, Doran, 1935.

Kennedy, David M. *Freedom from Fear: The American People in Depression and War, 1929–1945*. New York: Oxford University Press, 1999.

Leuchtenburg, William E. *Franklin D. Roosevelt and the New Deal, 1932–1940*. New York: Harper & Row, 1963.

Lyon, Leverett S. *The National Recovery Administration: An Analysis and Appraisal*. Washington, D.C.: Brookings Institution, 1935.

Moley, Raymond. *After Seven Years*. New York: Harper and Brothers, 1939.

———. *The First New Deal*. New York: Harcourt, Brace and World, 1966.

Ohl, John Kennedy. *Hugh S. Johnson and the New Deal*. DeKalb: Northern Illinois University Press, 1985.

Richberg, Donald. *My Hero: The Indiscreet Memoirs of an Eventful but Unheroic Life*. New York: Putnam, 1954.

Schlesinger, Arthur M., Jr., *The Age of Roosevelt*. Vol. 1: *The Crisis of the Old Order, 1919–1933*. Boston: Houghton Mifflin, 1957; Vol. 2: *The Coming of the New Deal*. Boston: Houghton Mifflin, 1959.

Tugwell, Rexford. *The Brains Trust*. New York: Viking, 1968.

Vadney, T. E. "Donald Randall Richberg." In *American National Biography*, vol. 18, eds. John A. Garraty and Mark C. Carnes. New York: Oxford University Press, 1999.

Weinstein, Michael M. *Recovery and Redistribution under the NIRA*. New York: North-Holland Publishing Company, 1980.

■ Web Sites

"Fireside Chats of Franklin Delano Roosevelt." Franklin D. Roosevelt Presidential Library and Museum Web site.
   http://www.fdrlibrary.marist.edu/firesi90.html. Accessed on December 27, 2007.

"Franklin Delano Roosevelt (1882–1945)." Miller Center of Public Affairs "American President: An Online Reference Source" Web site.
   http://www.millercenter.virginia.edu/academic/americanpresident/fdroosevelt. Accessed on December 27, 2007.

—By Justus D. Doenecke

Questions for Further Study

1. The Communist leader Robert Minor called the NRA emblem, the blue eagle, "a blue buzzard" for the workers, while the conservative Senator Thomas D. Schall found it "a Russian fish hook" (Doenecke, p. 53). Why would both conservatives and liberals be so vehement in their attacks on this legislation?

2. The framers of the NIRA assumed that business would use "self-regulation" in such a way as to protect the general welfare in a disinterested manner. Can one ever have such an expectation concerning any economic group in society? Moreover, can a class of informed and "objective" administrators ever orchestrate a massive economy into an integrated whole?

3. The NIRA was based on the assumption that full production and employment could be achieved by outlawing price competition and discouraging full production. Could one challenge such economic premises and, in fact, make the claim that in 1933 the United States needed new investment and a massive production increase? Was it overproduction that had caused the depression, and did salvation lie in creating scarcity?

4. The NIRA did not give the new NRA enabling power to determine desirable production goals for the entire economy, nor did it compel manufacturers to meet such goals. Can one achieve a planned economy without conferring such powers?

5. The historian Ellis W. Hawley claims the NRA would have worked better had it limited its operations to a few basic industries. Which industries might have been crucial?

Glossary

aggregate	the gathering together into a mass or sum so as to constitute a whole
assignee	one whose property rights or powers are transferred by another
bona fide	acting honestly and in good faith; without fraud, collusion, or participating in wrongdoing
bond	certificate of debt issued by a government or corporation guaranteeing payment of the original investment plus interest by a specified date
cash value	mean or going price
certificates of indebtedness	written contacts concerning the amount of debt specified
code	in the context of the NIRA, an agreement, drafted by a trade or industrial group, that had the force of law
collective bargaining	the process whereby workers organize as a group and negotiate with employers regarding hours, wages, working conditions, and benefits
compensatory rates	remuneration on the basis of equity
effectuate	bring about; cause to happen

eminent domain	the power of federal, state, and local governments to acquire private property by court action for public use
excess-profits tax	tax levied on profits that are beyond a business's normal profit
excise tax	tax imposed on the manufacture, sale, or use of certain goods (e.g., cigarette tax) or on an occupation or activity (e.g., license tax)
fair market value	price at which property would change hands between a willing buyer and willing seller, each having knowledge of all the relevant facts
feeder roads	minor roads joining a more prominent one
grade	slope or gradual inclination of a road or railroad
holding company	a company that owns part, majority, or all of other company's stock; it does not usually produce goods or services but exists solely by possessing shares of other companies
in lieu of	in place of
jurisdiction	right to interpret or apply the law
license	give permission, which can be revoked, to engage in a certain activity; proof of permission granted, usually in the form of a document
municipality	town, city, or local government entity as contrasted with a county, state, or national one
notes	certificates issued by a government or bank
penal bond	obligation to pay a designated sum given by an accused person or by another person if the accused fails to appear in court on a certain day
personal property	any movable or tangible thing subject to ownership and not classifiable as real property
premium	sum of money paid in addition to regular price of salary
prescribe	ordain; set down as a rule
proceedings in equity	the business conducted by a legal body that applies the principle of justice to supplement the law as applied to particular circumstances
real property	land property in contrast to personal property
retire	in a legal sense, to discharge or remove
sinking fund	a fund accumulated to pay off a public or corporation debt
surety	pledge given for the fulfillment of an undertaking; guarantee that an obligation will be met
surtax	additional tax imposed on something being taxed or on the primary tax itself
Treasury bills	a security that matures within a brief time from date of issue
trust funds	as applied to this legislation, funds held in trust by the government for use in carrying out certain purposes and programs
unobligated balances	unspent sums that had been previously allocated and which continue to be available for commitment in the future
vehicular	relating to motor transportation
vested	placed authority in the control of a certain office, person, or entity

NATIONAL INDUSTRIAL RECOVERY ACT

An act to encourage national industrial recovery, to foster fair competition, and to provide for the construction of certain useful public works, and for other purposes.

Be it enacted by the Senate and House of Representatives of the United States of America in Congress assembled

Title I—Industrial Recovery

◆ Declaration of Policy

SECTION 1. A national emergency productive of widespread unemployment and disorganization of industry, which burdens interstate and foreign commerce, affects the public welfare, and undermines the standards of living of the American people, is hereby declared to exist. It is hereby declared to be the policy of Congress to remove obstructions to the free flow of interstate and foreign commerce which tend to diminish the amount thereof; and to provide for the general welfare by promoting the organization of industry for the purpose of cooperative action among trade groups, to induce and maintain united action of labor and management under adequate governmental sanctions and supervision, to eliminate unfair competitive practices, to promote the fullest possible utilization of the present productive capacity of industries, to avoid undue restriction of production (except as may be temporarily required), to increase the consumption of Industrial and agricultural products by increasing purchasing power, to reduce and relieve unemployment, to improve standards of labor, and otherwise to rehabilitate industry and to conserve natural resources.

◆ Administrative Agencies

SEC. 2. (a) To effectuate the policy of this title, the President is hereby authorized to establish such agencies, to accept and utilize such voluntary and uncompensated services to appoint without regard to the provisions of the civil service laws, such officers

and employees, an to utilize such Federal officers and employees, and, with the consent of the State, such State and local officers and employees, as he may find necessary, to prescribe their authorities, duties, responsibilities, and tenure, and, without regard to the Classification Act of 1923, as amended, to fix the compensation of any officers and employees so appointed.

(b) The President may delegate any of his functions and powers under this title to such officers, agents, and employees as lie may designate or appoint, and may establish an industrial planning and research agency to aid in carrying out his functions under this title.

(c) This title shall cease to be in effect and any agencies established hereunder shall cease to exist at the expiration of two years after the date of enactment of this Act, or sooner if the President shall by proclamation or the Congress shall by joint resolution declare that the emergency recognized by section 1 has ended.

◆ Codes of Fair Competition

SEC. 3. (a) Upon the application to the President by one or more trade or industrial associations or groups the President may approve a code or codes of fair competition for the trade or industry or sub-division thereof, represented by the applicant or applicants, if the President finds (1) that such associations or groups impose no inequitable restrictions on admission to membership therein and are truly representative of such trades or industries or subdivisions thereof, and (2) that such code or codes are not designed to promote monopolies or to eliminate or oppress small enterprises and will not operate to discriminate against them, and will tend to effectuate the policy of this title: Provided, That such code or codes shall not permit monopolies or monopolistic practices: Provided further, That where such code or codes affect the services and welfare of persons engaged in other steps of the economic process, nothing in this section shall deprive such persons of the right to be heard prior to approval by the President of such code or codes. The President may, as a condition of his approval of any such code, impose such conditions (including requirements for the making of reports and the keeping of accounts) for the protection of consumers competitors, employees, and others, and in furtherance of the public interest, and may provide such exceptions to and exemptions from the provisions of such code, as the President in his discretion deems necessary to effectuate the policy herein declared.

(b) After the President shall have approved any such code, the provisions of such code shall be the standards of fair competition for such trade or industry or subdivision thereof. Any violation of such standards in any transaction in or affecting interstate or foreign commerce shall be deemed an unfair method of competition in commerce within the meaning of the Federal Trade Commission Act, as amended; but nothing in this title shall be construed to impair the powers of the Federal Trade Commission under such Act, as amended.

(c) The several district courts of the United States are hereby invested with jurisdiction to prevent and restrain violations of any code of fair competition approved under this title; and it shall be the duty of the several district attorneys of the United States, in their respective districts, under the direction of the Attorney General, to institute proceedings in equity to prevent and restrain such violations.

(d) Upon his own motion, or if complaint is made to the President that abuses inimical to the public interest and contrary to the policy herein declared are prevalent in any trade or industry or subdivision thereof, and if no code of fair competition therefor has theretofore been approved by the President, the President, after such public notice and hearing as he shall specify, may prescribe and approve a code of fair competition for such trade or industry or subdivision thereof, which shall have the same effect as a code of fair competition approved by the President under subsection (a) of this section.

(e) On his own motion, or if any labor organization, or any trade or industrial organization, association, or group, which has complied with the provisions of this title, shall make complaint to the President that any article or articles are being imported into the United States in substantial quantities or increasing ratio to domestic production of any competitive article or articles and on such terms or under such conditions as to render ineffective or seriously to endanger the maintenance of any code or agreement under this title, the President may cause an immediate investigation to be made by the United States Tariff Commission, which shall give precedence to investigations under this subsection, and if, after such investigation and such public notice and hearing as he shall specify, the President shall find the existence of such facts, he shall, in order to effectuate the policy of this title, direct that the article or articles concerned shall be permitted entry into the United States only upon such terms and conditions and subject to the payment of such fees and to such limitations in the total quantity which may be imported (in the course of any specified period or periods) as he shall find it necessary to prescribe in order that the entry thereof shall not render or tend to render ineffective any code or agreement made under this title. In order to enforce any limitations imposed on the total quantity of imports, in any specified period or periods, of any article or articles under this subsection, the President may forbid the importation of such article or articles unless the importer shall have first obtained from the Secretary of the Treasury a license pursuant to such regulations as the President may prescribe. Upon information of any action by the President under this subsection the Secretary of the Treasury shall, through the proper officers, permit entry of the article or articles specified only upon such terms and conditions and subject to such fees, to such limitations in the quantity which may be imported, and to such requirements of license, as the President shall have directed. The decision of the President as to facts shall be conclusive. Any condition or limitation of entry under this subsection shall continue in effect until the President shall find and inform the Secretary of the Treasury that the conditions which led to the imposition of such condition or limitation upon entry no longer exists.

(f) When a code of fair competition has been approved or prescribed by the President under this title, any violation of any provision thereof in any transaction in or affecting interstate, or foreign commerce shall be a misdemeanor and upon conviction thereof an offender shall be fined not more than $500 for each offense and each day such violation continues shall be deemed a separate offense.

◆ Agreements and Licenses

SEC. 4. (a) The President is authorized to enter into agreement with, and to approve voluntary agreements between and among, persons engaged in a trade or industry, labor organizations, and trade or industrial organizations, associations, or groups, relating to any trade or industry, if in his judgment such agreements will aid in effectuating the policy of this title with respect to transactions in or affecting interstate or foreign commerce, and will be consistent with the requirements of clause (2) of subsection (a) of section 3 for a code of fair competition.

(b) Whenever the President shall find that destructive wage or price cutting or other activities contrary to the policy of this title are being practiced in any trade or industry or any subdivision thereof, and, after such public notice and hearing as he shall specify, shall find it essential to license business enterprises in order to make effective a code of fair competition or an agreement under this title or otherwise to effectuate the policy of this title, and shall publicly so announce, no person shall, after a date fixed in such announcement, engage in or carry on any business, in or affecting interstate or foreign commerce, specified in such announcement, unless he shall have first obtained a license issued pursuant to such relations as the President shall prescribe. The President may suspend or revoke any such license, after due notice and opportunity for hearing, for violations of the terms or conditions thereof. Any order of the President suspending or revoking any such license shall be final if in accordance with law. Any person who, without such a license or in violation of any condition thereof, carries on any such business for which a license is so required, shall, upon conviction thereof, be fined not more than $500, or imprisoned not more than six months, or both, and each day such violation continues shall be deemed a separate offense. Notwithstanding the provisions of section 2 (c), this subsection shall cease to be in effect at the expiration of one year after the date of enactment of this Act or sooner if the President shall by proclamation or the Congress shall by joint resolution declare that the emergency recognized by section 1 has ended.

SEC. 5. While this title is in effect (or in the case of a license, while section 4 (a) is in effect) and for sixty days thereafter, any code, agreement, or license approved, prescribed, or issued and in effect under this title, and any action complying with the provisions thereof taken during such period, shall be exempt from the provisions of the antitrust laws of the United States.

Nothing in this Act, and no regulation thereunder, shall prevent an individual from pursuing the vocation of manual labor and selling or trading the products thereof; nor shall anything in this Act, or regulation thereunder, prevent anyone from marketing or trading the produce of his farm.

◆ **Limitations upon Application of Title**

SEC. 6. (a) No trade or industrial association or group shall be eligible to receive the benefit of the provisions of this title until it files with the President a statement containing such information relating to the activities of the association or group as the President shall by regulation prescribe.

(b) The President is authorized to prescribe rules and regulations designed to insure that any organization availing itself of the benefits of this title shall be truly representative of the trade or industry or subdivision thereof represented by such organization. Any organization violating any such rule or regulation shall cease to be entitled to the benefits of this title.

(c) Upon the request of the President, the Federal Trade Commission shall make such investigations as may be necessary to enable the President to carry out the provisions of this title, and for such purposes the Commission shall have all the powers vested in it with respect of investigations under the Federal Trade Commission Act, as amended.

SEC. 7. (a) Every code of fair competition, agreement, and license approved, prescribed, or issued under this title shall contain the following conditions: (1) That employees shall have the right to organize and bargain collectively through representatives of their own choosing, and shall be free from the interference restraint, or coercion of employers of labor, or their agents, in the designation of such representatives or in self-organization or in other concerted activities for the purpose of collective bargaining or other mutual aid or protection; (2) that no employee and no one seeking employment shall be required as a condition of employment to join any company union or to refrain from joining, organizing, or assisting a labor organization of his own choosing; and (3) that employers shall comply with the maximum hours of labor, minimum rates of pay, and other conditions of employment, approved or prescribed by the President.

(b) The President shall, so far as practicable, afford every opportunity to employers and employees in any trade or industry or subdivision thereof with respect to which the conditions referred to in clauses (1) and (2) of subsection (a) prevail, to establish by mutual agreement, the standards as to the maximum hours of labor, minimum rates of pay, and such other conditions of employment as may be necessary in such trade or industry or subdivision thereof to effectuate the policy of this title; and the standards established in such agreements, when approved by the President, shall have the same effect as a code of fair competition, approved by the President under subsection (a) of section 3.

(c) Where no such mutual agreement has been approved by the President he may investigate the labor practices, policies, wages, hours of labor, and conditions of employment in such trade or industry or subdivision thereof; and upon the basis of such investigations, and after such hearings as the President finds advisable, he is authorized to prescribe a limited code of fair competition fixing such maximum hours of labor, minimum rates of pay, and other conditions of employment in the trade or industry or subdivision thereof investigated as he finds to be necessary to effectuate the policy of this title, which shall have the same effect as a code of fair competition approved by the President under subsection (a) of section 3. The President may differentiate according to experience and skill of the employees affected and according to the locality of employment; but no attempt shall be made to introduce any classification according to the nature of the work involved which might tend to set a maximum as well as a minimum wage.

(d) As used in this title, the term "person" includes any individual, partnership, association, trust, or corporation; and the terms "interstate and foreign commerce" and "interstate or foreign commerce" include, except where otherwise indicated, trade or commerce among the several States and with foreign nations, or between the District of Columbia or any Territory of the United States and any State, Territory or foreign nation, or between any insular possessions or other places under the jurisdiction of the United States, or between any such possession or place and any State or Territory of the United States or the District of Columbia or any foreign nation, or within the District of Columbia or any Territory or any insular possession or other place under the jurisdiction of the United States.

◆ Application of Agricultural Adjustment Act

SEC. 8. (a) This title shall not be construed to repeal or modify any of the provisions of title I of the Act entitled "An Act to relieve the existing national economic emergency by increasing agricultural purchasing power, to raise revenue for extraordinary expenses incurred by reason of such emergency, to provide emergency relief with respect to agricultural

indebtedness, to provide for the orderly liquidation of joint-stock land banks, and for other purposes," approved May 12, 1933; and such title I of said Act approved May 12, 1933, may for all purposes be hereafter referred to as the "Agricultural Adjustment Act."

(b) The President may, in his discretion, in order to avoid conflicts in the administration of the Agricultural Adjustment Act and this title, delegate any of his functions and powers under this title with respect to trades, industries, or subdivisions thereof which are engaged in the handling of any agricultural commodity or product thereof, or of any competing commodity or product thereof, to the Secretary of Agriculture.

◆ Oil Regulation

SEC. 9. (a) The President is further authorized to initiate before the Interstate Commerce Commission proceedings necessary to prescribe regulations to control the operations of oil pipe lines and to fix reasonable, compensatory rates for the transportation of petroleum and its products by pipe lines, and the Interstate Commerce Commission shall grant preference to the hearings and determination of such cases.

(b) The President is authorized to institute proceedings to divorce from any holding company any pipeline company controlled by such holding company which pipeline company by unfair practices or by exorbitant rates in the transportation of petroleum or its products tends to create a monopoly.

(c) The President is authorized to prohibit the transportation in interstate and foreign commerce of petroleum and the products thereof produced or withdrawn from storage in excess of the amount permitted to be produced or withdrawn from storage by any State law or valid regulation or order prescribed thereunder, by any board, commission, officer, or other duly authorized agency of a State. Any violation of any order of the President issued under the provisions of this subsection shall be punishable by fine of not to exceed $1,000, or imprisonment for not to exceed six months, or both.

◆ Rules and Regulations

SEC. 10. (a) The President is authorized to prescribe such rules and regulations as may be necessary to carry out the purposes of this title, and fees for licenses and for filing codes of fair competition and agreements, and any violation of any such rule or regulation shall be punishable by fine of not to exceed $500, or imprisonment for not to exceed six months, or both.

(b) The President may from time to time cancel or modify any order, approval, license, rule, or regulation issued under this title; and each agreement, code of fair competition, or license approved, prescribed, or issued under this title shall contain an express provision to that effect.

Title II—Public Works and Construction Projects

◆ Federal Emergency Administration of Public Works

SECTION 201. (a) To effectuate the purposes of this title, the President is hereby authorized to create a Federal Emergency Administration of Public Works, all the powers of which; shall be exercised by a Federal Emergency Administrator of Public Works (hereafter referred to as the "Administrator"), and to establish such agencies, to accept and utilize such voluntary and uncompensated services, to appoint, without regard to the civil service laws, such officers and employees, and to utilize such Federal officers and employees, and, with the consent of the State, such State and local officers and employees as he may find necessary, to prescribe their authorities, duties, responsibilities, and tenure, and, without regard to the Classification Act of 1923, as amended, to fix the compensation of any officers and employees so appointed. The President may delegate any of his functions and powers under this title to such officers, agents, and employees as he may designate or appoint.

(b) The Administrator may, without regard to the civil service laws or the Classification Act of 1923, as amended, appoint and fix the compensation of such experts and such other officers and employees as are necessary to carry out the provisions of this title; and may make such expenditures (including expenditures for personal services and rent at the seat of government and elsewhere, for law books and books of reference, and for paper, printing and binding) as are necessary to carry out the provisions of this title.

(c) All such compensation, expenses, and allowances shall be paid out of funds made available by this Act.

(d) After the expiration of two years after the date of the enactment of this Act, or sooner if the President shall by proclamation or the Congress shall by joint resolution declare that the emergency recognized by section 1 has ended, the President shall not make any further loans or grants or enter upon any new construction under this title, and any agencies established hereunder shall cease to exist and any of their remaining functions shall be transferred to such departments of the Government as the President shall designate: Provided, That he may issue funds to a borrower under this title prior to January 23, 1939, under the terms of any agreement, or any commitment to bid upon or purchase bonds, entered into with such borrower prior to the date o termination, under this section, of the power of the President to make loans.

SEC. 202. The Administrator, under the direction of the President, shall prepare a comprehensive program of public works, which shall include among other things the following: (a) Construction, repair, and improvement of public highways and park ways, public buildings, and any publicly owned instrumentalities and facilities; (b) conservation and development of natural resources, including control, utilization, and purification of waters, prevention of soil or coastal erosion, development of water power, transmission of electrical energy, and construction of river and harbor improvements and flood control and also the construction of any river or drainage improvement required to perform or satisfy any obligation incurred by the United States through a treaty with a foreign Government heretofore ratified and to restore or develop for the use of any State or its citizens water taken from or denied to them by performance on the part of the United States of treaty obligations heretofore assumed: Provided, That no river or harbor improvements shall be carried out unless they shall have heretofore or hereafter been adopted by the Congress or are recommended by the Chief of Engineers of the United States Army; (c) any projects of the character heretofore constructed or carried on either directly by public authority or with public aid to serve the interests of the general public; (d) construction, reconstruction, alteration, or repair under public regulation or control of low-cost housing and slum-clearance projects; (e) any project (other than those included in the foregoing classes) of any character heretofore eligible for loans under sub-section (a) of section 201 of the Emergency Relief and Construction Act of 1932, as amended, and paragraph (3) of such subsection (a) shall for such purposes be held to include loans for the construction or completion of hospitals the operation of which is partly financed from public funds, and of reservoirs and pumping plants and for the construction of dry docks; and if in the opinion of the President it seems desirable, the construction of naval vessels within the terms and/or limits established by the London Naval Treaty of 1930 and of aircraft required therefor and construction of heavier-than-air aircraft and technical construction for the Army Air Corps and such Army housing projects as the President may approve, and provision of original equipment for the mechanization or motorization of such Army tactical units as he may designate: Provided, however, that in the event of an international agreement for the further limitation of armament to which the United States is signatory, the President is hereby authorized and empowered to suspend, in whole or in part, any such naval or military construction or mechanization and motorization of Army units: Provided further, That this title shall not be applicable to public works under the jurisdiction or control of the Architect of the Capitol or of any commission or committee for which such Architect is the contracting and/or executive officer.

SEC. 203. (a) With a view to increasing employment quickly (while reasonably securing any loans made by the United States) the president is authorized and empowered, through the Administrator or through such other agencies as he may designate or create, (1) to construct, finance, or aid in the construction or financing of any public works project included in the program prepared pursuant to section 202; (2) upon such terms as the President shall prescribe, to make grants to States, municipalities, or other public bodies for the construction, repair, or improvement of any such project, but no such grant shall be in excess of 30 per centum of the cost of the labor and materials employed upon such project; (3) to acquire by purchase, or by exercise of the power of eminent domain, any real or personal property in connection with the construction of any such project, and to sell any security acquired or any property so constructed or acquired or to lease any such property with or without the privilege of purchase: Provided, That all moneys received from any such sale or lease or the repayment of any loan shall be used to retire obligations issued pursuant to section 209 of this Act, in addition to any other moneys required to be used for such purpose; (4) to aid in the financing of such railroad maintenance and equipment as may be approved by the Interstate Commerce Commission as desirable for the improvement of transportation facilities; and (5) to advance, upon request of the Commission having jurisdiction of the project, the unappropriated balance of the sum authorized for carrying out the provisions of the Act entitled "An Act to provide for the construction and equipment of

an annex to the Library of Congress," approved June 13, 1930 (46 Stat. 583); such advance to be expended under the direction of such Commission and in accordance with such Act: Provided, That in deciding to extend any aid or grant hereunder to any State, county, or municipality the President may consider whether action is in process or in good faith assured therein reasonably designed to bring the ordinary current expenditures thereof within the prudently estimated revenues thereof. The provisions of this section and section 202 shall extend to public works in the several States, Hawaii, Alaska, the District of Columbia, Puerto Rico, the Canal Zone, and the Virgin Islands.

(b) All expenditures for authorized travel by officers and employees, including subsistence, required on account of any Federal public-works projects, shall be charged to the amounts allocated to such projects, notwithstanding any other provisions of law; and there is authorized to be employed such personal services in the District of Columbia and elsewhere as may be required to be engaged upon such work and to be in addition to employees otherwise provided for, the compensation of such additional personal services to be a charge against the funds made available for such construction work.

(c) In the acquisition of any land or site for the purposes of Federal public buildings and in the construction of such buildings provided for in this title, the provisions contained in sections 305 and 306 of the Emergency Relief and Construction Act of 1932, as amended shall apply.

(d) The President, in his discretion, and under such terms as he may prescribe, may extend any of the benefits of this title to any State, county, or municipality notwithstanding any constitutional or legal restriction or limitation on the right or power of such State, county, or municipality to borrow money or incur indebtedness.

SEC. 204. (a) For the purpose of providing for emergency construction of public highways and related projects, the President is authorized to make grants to the highway departments of the several States in an amount not less than $400,000,000, to be expended by such departments in accordance with the provisions of the Federal Highway Act, approved November 9, 1921, as amended and supplemented, except as provided in this title, as follows:

(1) For expenditure in emergency construction on the Federal aid highway system and extensions thereof into and through municipalities. The amount apportioned to any State under this paragraph may be

used to pay all or any part of the cost of surveys, plans, and of highway and bridge construction including the elimination of hazards to highway traffic, such as the separation of grades at crossing, the reconstruction of existing railroad grade crossing structures, the relocation of highways to eliminate railroad crossings the widening of narrow bridges and roadways, the building of footpaths, the replacement of unsafe bridges, the construction of routes to avoid congested areas, the construction of facilities to improve accessibility and the free flow of traffic, and the cost of any other construction that will provide safer traffic facilities or definitely eliminate existing hazards to pedestrian or vehicular traffic. No funds made available by this title shall be used for the acquisition of any land, right of way, or easement in connection with any railroad grade elimination project.

(2) For expenditure in emergency construction on secondary or feeder roads to be agreed upon by the State highway departments and the Secretary of Agriculture: Provided, That the State or responsible political subdivision shall provide for the proper maintenance of said roads. Such grants shall be available for payment of the full cost of surveys, plans, improvement, and construction of secondary or feeder roads, on which projects shall be submitted by the State highway department and approved by the Secretary of Agriculture.

(b) Any amount allocated by the President for grants under subsection (a) of this section shall be apportioned among the several States seven-eighths in accordance with the provisions of section 21 of the Federal Highway Act, approved November 9, 1921, as amended and supplemented (which Act is hereby further amended for the purposes of this title to include the District of Columbia), and one-eighth in the ratio which the population of each State bears to the total population of the United States, according to the latest decennial census and shall be available on July 1, 1933, and shall remain available until expended; but no part of the funds apportioned to any State need be matched by the State, and such funds may also be used in lieu of State funds to match unobligated balances of previous apportionments of regular Federal-aid appropriations.

(c) All contracts involving the expenditure of such grants shall contain provisions establishing minimum rates of wages, to be predetermined by the State highway department, which contractors shall pay to skilled and unskilled labor, and such minimum rates shall be stated in the invitation for bids and shall be included in proposals for bids for the work.

(d) In the expenditure of such amounts, the limitations in the Federal Highway Act, approved November 9, 1921, as amended and supplemented, upon highway construction, reconstruction, and bridges within municipalities and upon payments per mile which may be made from Federal funds, shall not apply.

(e) As used in this section the term "State" includes the Territory of Hawaii and the District of Columbia. The term "highway" as defined in the Federal Highway Act approved November 9, 1921 "as amended and supplemented," for the purposes of this section, shall be deemed to include such main parkways as may be designated by the State and approved by the Secretary of Agriculture as part of the Federal-aid highway system.

(f) Whenever, in connection with the construction of any highway project under this section or section 202 of this Act, it is necessary to acquire rights of way over or through any property or tracts of land owned and controlled by the Government of the United States, it shall be the duty of the proper official of the Government of the United States having control of such property or tracts of land with the approval of the President and the Attorney General of the United States, and without any expense whatsoever to the United States, to perform any acts and to execute any agreements necessary to grant the rights of way so required, but if at any time the land or the property the subject of the agreement shall cease to be used for the purposes of the highway, the title in and the jurisdiction over the land or property shall automatically revert to the Government of the United States and the agreement shall so provide.

(g) Hereafter in the administration of the Federal Highway Act, and Acts amendatory thereof or supplementary thereto, the first paragraph of section 9 of said Act shall not apply to publicly owned toll bridges or approaches thereto, operated by the highway department of any State, subject, however, to the condition that all tolls received from the operation of any such bridge, less the actual cost of operation and maintenance, shall be applied to the repayment of the cost of its construction or acquisition, and when the cost of its construction or acquisition shall have been repaid in full, such bridge thereafter shall be maintained and operated as a free bridge.

SEC. 205. (a) Not less than $50,000,000 of the amount made available by this Act shall be allotted for (A) national forest highways, (B) national forest roads, trails, bridges, and related projects, (C) national park roads and trails in national parks owned or authorized, (D) roads on Indian reservations, and (E) roads through public lands, to be expended in the same manner as provided in paragraph (2) of section 301 of the Emergency Relief and Construction Act of 1932, in the case of appropriations allocated for such purposes, respectively, in such section 301, to remain available until expended.

(b) The President may also allot funds made available by this Act for the construction, repair and improvement of public highways in Alaska, the Canal Zone, Puerto Rico, and the Virgin Islands.

SEC. 206. All contracts let for construction projects and all loans and grants pursuant to this title shall contain such provisions as are necessary to insure (1) that no convict labor shall be employed on any such project; (2) that (except in executive, administrative, and supervisory positions), so far as practicable and feasible., no individual directly employed on any such project shall be permitted to work more than thirty hours in anyone week; (3) that all employees shall be paid just and reasonable wages which shall be compensation sufficient to provide, for the hours of labor as limited, a standard of living in decency and comfort; (4) that in the employment of labor in connection with any such project, preference shall be given, where they are qualified, to ex-service men with dependents, and then in the following order: (A) To citizens of the United States and aliens who have declared their intention of becoming citizens, who are bona fide residents of the political subdivision and/or county in which the work is to be performed, and (B) to citizens of the United States and aliens who have declared their intention of becoming citizens, who are bona fide residents of the State Territory, or district in which the work is to be performed: Provided, That these preferences shall apply only where such labor is available and qualified to perform the work to which the employment relates; and (5) that the maximum of human labor shall be used in lieu of machinery wherever practicable and consistent with sound economy and public advantage.

SEC. 207. (a) For the purpose of expediting the actual construction of public works contemplated by this title and to provide a means of financial assistance to persons under contract with the United States to perform such construction, the President is authorized and empowered through the Administrator or through such other agencies as he may designate or create to approve any assignment executed by any such contractor, with the written consent of the surety or sureties upon the penal bond executed in connection with his contract, to any national or State bank, or his claim against the United States, or any part of such claim, under such contract; and any assignment so approved shall be valid for all purposes, notwithstanding the provisions of sections 3737 and 3477 of the Revised Statutes as amended.

(b) The funds received by a contractor under any advances made in consideration of any such assignment are hereby declared to be trust funds in the hands of such contractor to be first applied to the payment of claims of subcontractors, architects, engineers, surveyors, laborers, and material men in connection with the project, to the payment of premiums on the penal bond or bonds, and premiums accruing during the construction of such project on insurance policies taken in connection therewith. Any contractor and any officer, director or agent of any such contractor, who applies, or consents to the application of, such funds for any other purpose and fails to pay any claim or premium hereinbefore mentioned, shall be deemed guilty of a misdemeanor and shall be punished by a fine of not more than $1,000 or by imprisonment for not more than one year, or by both such fine and imprisonment.

(c) Nothing in this section shall be considered as imposing upon the assignee any obligation to see to the proper application of the funds advanced by the assignee in consideration of such assignment.

◆ Subsistence Homesteads

SEC. 208. To provide for aiding the redistribution of the overbalance of population in industrial centers $25,000,000 is hereby made available to the President, to be used by him through such agencies as he may establish and under such regulations as he may make, for making loans for and otherwise aiding in the purchase of subsistence homesteads. The moneys collected as repayment of said loans shall constitute a revolving fund to be administered as directed by the President for the purposes of this section.

◆ Rules and Regulations

SEC. 209. The President is authorized to prescribe such rules and regulations as may be necessary to carry out the purposes of this title, and any violation of any such rule or regulation shall be punishable by fine of not to exceed $500 or imprisonment not to exceed six months, or both.

◆ Issue of Securities and Sinking Fund

SEC. 210. (a) The Secretary of the Treasury is authorized to borrow, from time to time, under the Second Liberty Bond Act, as amended, such amounts as may be necessary to meet the expenditures authorized by this Act, or to refund any obligations previously issued under this section, and to issue therefor bonds, notes, certificates of indebtedness, or Treasury bills of the United States.

(b) For each fiscal year beginning with the fiscal year 1934 there is hereby appropriated, in addition to and as part of, the cumulative sinking fund provided by section 6 of the Victory Liberty Loan Act, as amended, out of any money in the Treasury not otherwise appropriated, for the purpose of such fund, an amount equal to 2 1/2 per centum of the aggregate amount of the expenditures made out of appropriations made or authorized under this Act as determined by the Secretary of the Treasury.

◆ Reemployment and Relief Taxes

SEC. 211. (a) Effective as of the day following the date of the enactment of this Act, section 617 (a) of the Revenue Act of 1932 is amended by striking out "1 cent" and inserting in lieu thereof "1 1/2 cents."

(b) Effective as of the day following the date of the enactment of this Act, section 617 (c) (2) of such: Act is amended by adding at the end thereof a new sentence to read as follows: "As used in this paragraph the term 'benzol' does not include benzol sold for use otherwise than as a fuel for the propulsion of motor vehicles, motor boats, or airplanes, and otherwise than in the manufacture or production of such fuel."

SEC. 212. Titles IV and V of the Revenue Act of 1932 are amended by striking out "1934" wherever appearing therein and by inserting in lieu thereof "1935." Section 761 of the Revenue Act of 1932 is further amended by striking out "and on July 1 1933" and inserting in lieu thereof "and on July 1, 1933, and on July 1, 1934."

SEC. 213. (a) There is hereby imposed upon the receipt of dividends (required to be included in the gross income of the recipient under the provisions of the Revenue Act of 1932) by any person other than a domestic corporation, an excise tax equal to 5 per centum of the amount thereof, such tax to be deducted and withheld from such dividends by the payor corporation. The tax imposed by this section shall not apply to dividends declared before the date of the enactment of this Act.

(b) Every corporation required to deduct and withhold any tax under this section shall, on or before the last day of the month following the payment of the dividend, make return thereof and pay the tax to the collector of the district in which its principal place of business is located, or, if it has no principal place of business in the United States, to the collector at Baltimore, Maryland.

(c) Every such corporation is hereby made liable for such tax and is hereby indemnified against the claims and demands of any person for the amount of any payment made in accordance with the provisions of this section.

(d) The provisions of sections 115, 771 to 774, inclusive, and 1111 of the Revenue Act of 1932 shall be applicable with respect to the tax imposed by this section.

(e) The taxes imposed by this section shall not apply to the dividends of any corporation enumerated in section 103 of the Revenue Act of 1932.

SEC. 214. Section 104 of the Revenue Act of 1932 is amended by striking out the words "the surtax" wherever occurring in such section and inserting in lieu thereof "any internal-revenue tax." The heading of such section is amended by striking out "surtaxes" and inserting in lieu thereof "internal-revenue taxes." Section 13 (c) of such Act is amended by striking out "surtax" and inserting in lieu thereof "internal-revenue tax."

SEC. 215. (a) For each year ending June 30 there is hereby imposed upon every domestic corporation with respect to carrying on or doing business for any part of such year an excise tax of $1 for each $1,000 of the adjusted declared value of its capital stock.

(b) For each year ending June 30 there is hereby imposed upon every foreign corporation with respect to carrying on or doing business in the United States for any part of such year an excise tax equivalent to $1 for each $1,000 of the adjusted declared value of capital employed in the transaction of its business in the United States.

(c) The taxes imposed by this section shall not apply:

(1) to any corporation enumerated in section 103 of the Revenue Act of 1932;

(2) to any insurance company subject to the tax imposed by section 201 or 204 of such Act;

(3) to any domestic corporation in respect of the year ending June 30, 1933, if it did not carry on or do business during a part of the period from the date of the enactment of this Act to June 30, 1933, both dates inclusive; or

(4) to any foreign corporation in respect of the year ending June 30, 1933, if it did not carry on or do business in the United States during apart of the period from the day of the enactment of this Act to June 30, 1933, both dates inclusive.

(d) Every corporation liable for tax under this section shall make a return under oath within one month after the close of the year with respect to which such tax is imposed to the collector for the district in which is located its principal place of business or, if it has no principal place of business in the United States, then to the collector at Baltimore, Maryland. Such return shall contain such information and be made in such manner as the Commissioner with the approval of the Secretary may by regulations prescribe. The tax shall, without assessment by the Commissioner or notice from the collector, be due and payable to the collector before the expiration of the period for filing the return. If the tax is not paid when due, there shall be added as part of the tax interest at the rate of 1 per centum a month from the time when the tax became due until paid. All provisions of law (including penalties) applicable in respect of the taxes imposed by section 600 of the Revenue Act of 1926 shall, in so far as not inconsistent with this section, be applicable in respect of the taxes imposed by this section. The Commissioner may extend the time for making the returns and paying the taxes imposed by this section, under such rules and regulations as he may prescribe with the approval of the Secretary, but no such extension shall be for more than sixty days.

(e) Returns required to be filed for the purpose of the tax imposed by this section shall be open to inspection in the same manner, to the same extent, and subject to the same provisions of law, including penalties, as returns made under title II of the Revenue Act of 1926.

(f) For the first year ending June 30 in respect of which a tax is imposed by this section upon any corporation, the adjusted declared value shall be the value, as declared by the corporation in its first return under this section (which declaration of value cannot be amended), as of the close of its last income-tax taxable year ending at or prior to the close of the year for which the tax is imposed by this section (or as of the date of organization in the case of a corporation having no income-tax taxable year ending at or prior to the close of the year for which the tax is imposed by this section). For any subsequent year ending June 30, the adjusted declared value in the case of a domestic corporation shall be the original declared value plus (1) the cash and fair market value of property paid in for stock or shares, (2) paid-in surplus and contributions to capital, and (3) earnings and profits, and minus (A) the value of property distributed in liquidation to shareholders,

(B) distributions of earnings and profits, and (C) deficits, whether operating or nonoperating; each adjustment being made for the period from the date as of which the original declared value was declared to the close of its last income-tax taxable year ending at or prior to the close of the year for which the tax is imposed by this section. For any subsequent year ending June 30, the adjusted declared value in the case of a foreign corporation shall be the original declared value adjusted, in accordance with regulations prescribed by the Commissioner with the approval of the Secretary, to reflect increases or decreases (for the period specified in the preceding sentence) in the capital employed in the transaction of its business in the United States.

(g) The terms used in this section shall have the same meaning as when used in the Revenue Act of 1932.

SEC. 216. (a) There is hereby imposed upon the net income of every corporation, for each income-tax taxable year ending after the close of the first year in respect of which it is taxable under section 215, an excess-profits tax equivalent to 5 per centum of such portion of its net income for such income-tax taxable year as is in excess of 12 1/2 per centum of the adjusted declared value of its capital stock (or in the case of a foreign corporation the adjusted declared value of capital employed in the transaction of its business in the United States) as of the close of the preceding income-tax taxable year (or as of the date of organization if it had no preceding income-tax taxable year) determined as provided in section 215. The terms used in this section shall have the same meaning as when used in the Revenue Act of 1932.

(b) The tax imposed by this section shall be assessed, collected, and paid in the same manner, and shall be subject to the same provisions of law (including penalties), as the taxes imposed by title I of the Revenue Act of 1932.

SEC. 217. (a) The President shall proclaim the date of:

(1) the close of the first fiscal year ending June 30 of any year after the year 1933, during which the total receipts of the United States (excluding public-debt receipts) exceed its total expenditures (excluding public-debt expenditures other than those chargeable against such receipts), or

(2) the repeal of the eighteenth amendment to the Constitution,

whichever is the earlier.

(b) Effective as of the 1st day of the calendar year following the date so proclaimed section 617 (a) of the Revenue Act of 1932, as amended, is amended by striking out "1 1/2 cents" and inserting in lieu thereof "1 cent."

(c) The tax on dividends imposed by section 213 shall not apply to any dividends declared on or after the 1st day of the calendar year following the date so proclaimed.

(d) The capital-stock tax imposed by section 215 shall not apply to any taxpayer in respect of any year beginning on or after the 1st day of July following the date so proclaimed.

(e) The excess-profits tax imposed by section 216 shall not apply to any taxpayer in respect of any taxable year after its taxable year during which the date so proclaimed occurs.

SEC. 218. (a) Effective as of January 1, 1933, sections 117, 23(i), 169, 187 and 205 of the Revenue Act of 1932 are repealed.

(b) Effective as of January 1,1933, section 23(r) (2) of the Revenue Act of 1932 is repealed.

(c) Effective as of January 1,1933, section 23(r) (3) of the Revenue Act of 1932 is amended by striking out all after the word "Territory" and inserting a period.

(d) Effective as of January 1,1933, section 182(a) of the Revenue Act of 1932 is amended by inserting at the end thereof a new sentence as follows: "No part of any loss disallowed to a partnership as a deduction by section 23(r) shall be allowed as a deduction to a member of such partnership in computing net income."

(e) Effective as of January 1, 1933, section 141 (c) of the Revenue Act of 1932 is amended by striking out "except that for the taxable years 1932 and 1933 there shall be added to the rate of tax prescribed by sections 13(a), 201(b), and 204(a), a rate of three fourths of 1 per centum" and inserting in lieu thereof the following: "except that for the taxable years 1932 and 1933 there shall be added to the rate of tax prescribe by sections 13 (a), 201 (b), and 204 (a), a rate of three fourths of 1 per centum and except that for the taxable years 1934 and 1935 there shall be added to the rate of tax prescribed by sections 13 (a), 201 (b), and 204 (a), a rate of 1 per centum."

(f) No interest shall be assessed or collected for any period prior to September 15, 1933, upon such portion of any amount determined as a deficiency in income taxes as is attributable solely to the amendments made to the Revenue Act of 1932 by this section.

(g) In cases where the effect of this section is to require for a taxable year ending prior to June 30, 1933, the making of an income tax return not other-wise required by law, the time for making the return and paying the tax shall be the same as if the return was for a fiscal-year ending June 30, 1933.

(h) Section 55 of the Revenue Act of 1932 is amended by inserting before the period at the end thereof a semicolon and the following: "and all returns made under this Act after the date of enactment of the National Industrial Recovery Act shall constitute public records and shall be open to public examination and inspection to such extent as shall be authorized in rules and regulations promulgated by the President."

SEC 219. Section 500 (a) (1) of the Revenue Act of 1926, as amended, is amended by striking out the period at the end of the second sentence thereof and inserting in lieu thereof a comma and the following: "except that no tax shall be imposed in the case of persons admitted free to any spoken play (not a mechanical reproduction), whether or not set to music or with musical parts or accompaniments, which is a consecutive narrative interpreted by a single set of characters, all necessary to the development of the plot, in two or more acts, the performance consuming more than 1 hour and 45 minutes of time."

◆ **Appropriation**

SEC. 220. For the purposes of this Act, there is hereby authorized to be appropriated, out of any money in the Treasury not otherwise appropriated, the sum of $3,300,000,000. The President is authorized to allocate so much of said sum, not in excess of $100,000,000, as he may determine to be necessary for expenditures in carrying out the Agricultural Adjustment Act and the purposes, powers, and functions heretofore and hereafter conferred upon the Farm Credit Administration.

SEC. 221. Section 7 of the Agricultural Adjustment Act, approved May 12, 1933, is amended by striking out all of its present terms and provisions and substituting therefor the following:

SEC. 7. The Secretary shall sell the cotton held by him at his discretion, but subject to the foregoing provisions: Provided, That he shall dispose of all cotton held by him by March 1, 1936: Provided further, That notwithstanding the provisions of section 6, the Secretary shall have authority to enter into option contracts with producers of cotton to sell to the producers such cotton held by him, in such amounts and at such prices and upon such terms and conditions as the Secretary may deem advisable, in combination with rental or benefit payments provided for in part 2 of this title.

"Notwithstanding any provisions of existing law, the Secretary of Agriculture may in the administration of the Agricultural Adjustment Act make public such information as he deems necessary in order to effectuate the purposes of such Act."

Title III—Amendments to Emergency Relief and Construction Act and Miscellaneous Provisions

SECTION 301. After the expiration of ten days after the date upon which the Administrator has qualified and taken office, (1) no application shall be approved by the Reconstruction Finance Corporation under the provisions of subsection (a) of section 201 of the Emergency Relief and Construction Act of 1932, as amended, and (2) the Administrator shall have access to all applications, files, and records of the Reconstruction Finance Corporation relating to loans and contracts and the administration of funds under such subsection: Provided, That the Reconstruction Finance Corporation may issue funds to a borrower under such subsection (a) prior to January 23, 1939, under the terms of any agreement or any commitment to bid upon or purchase bonds entered into with such borrower pursuant to an application approved prior to the date of termination, under this section, of the power of the Reconstruction Finance Corporation to approve applications.

◆ Decrease of Borrowing Power of Reconstruction Finance Corporation

SEC. 302. The amount of notes, debentures, bonds, or other such obligations which the Reconstruction Finance Corporation is authorized and empowered under section 9 of the Reconstruction Finance Corporation Act, as amended, to have outstanding at anyone time is decreased by $400,000,000.

◆ Separability Clause

SEC. 303. If any provision of this Act, or the application thereof to any person or circumstances, is held invalid, the remainder of the Act, and the application of such provision to other persons or circumstances, shall not be affected thereby.

◆ Short Title

SEC. 304. This Act may be cited as the "National Industrial Recovery Act."

(PUBLIC NO. *198*   74th CONGRESS)

Seventy-fourth Congress of the United States of America;

At the First Session,

Begun and held at the City of Washington on Thursday, the third
day of January, one thousand nine hundred and thirty-five.

AN ACT

To diminish the causes of labor disputes burdening or obstructing
interstate and foreign commerce, to create a National Labor
Relations Board, and for other purposes.

*Be it enacted by the Senate and House of Representatives of the
United States of America in Congress assembled,*

FINDINGS AND POLICY

SECTION 1. The denial by employers of the right of employees to
organize and the refusal by employers to accept the procedure of
collective bargaining lead to strikes and other forms of industrial
strife or unrest, which have the intent or the necessary effect of
burdening or obstructing commerce by (a) impairing the efficiency,
safety, or operation of the instrumentalities of commerce; (b) occurring in the current of commerce; (c) materially affecting, restraining,
or controlling the flow of raw materials or manufactured or processed
goods from or into the channels of commerce, or the prices of such
materials or goods in commerce; or (d) causing diminution of
employment and wages in such volume as substantially to impair or
disrupt the market for goods flowing from or into the channels
of commerce.

The inequality of bargaining power between employees who do
not possess full freedom of association or actual liberty of contract,
and employers who are organized in the corporate or other forms of
ownership association substantially burdens and affects the flow
of commerce, and tends to aggravate recurrent business depressions,
by depressing wage rates and the purchasing power of wage earners
in industry and by preventing the stabilization of competitive wage
rates and working conditions within and between industries.

Experience has proved that protection by law of the right of
employees to organize and bargain collectively safeguards commerce from injury, impairment, or interruption, and promotes the
flow of commerce by removing certain recognized sources of industrial strife and unrest, by encouraging practices fundamental to the
friendly adjustment of industrial disputes arising out of differences
as to wages, hours, or other working conditions, and by restoring
equality of bargaining power between employers and employees.

The National Labor Relations Act (National Archives and Records Administration)

"Employees shall have the right ...
to form, join, or assist labor organizations."

Overview

Guided at every stage by Senator Robert F. Wagner of New York, the National Labor Relations Act (NLRA) of 1935— also called the Wagner Act— sought to extend democracy in America to the workplace. By legal right enforced by the courts and government mechanisms, workers were now guaranteed the right to group together in organizations of their choice to bargain with employers on issues of wages and conditions, and employers were prevented from what were called "unfair practices" in resisting the right of workers to organize themselves. More important, wages and conditions improved dramatically as deals were struck between the representatives of the workers and their employers. Within a very few years, labor unions came to represent the majority of mass-production workers, where previously they had been all but nonexistent. Remarkably, the act's passage through Congress and into law provoked few contrary votes. At a stroke, industrial relations between workers and employers were transformed.

The Great Depression had triggered the most severe economic and political test of American democracy. By 1935 much of Franklin Roosevelt's New Deal had been put in place. Under the slogan "Relief, Recovery, Reform," Roosevelt sought to save American capitalism and American democracy. The NLRA was one of the two most radical pieces of legislation passed under President Franklin D. Roosevelt's New Deal (the other being the Social Security Act). While the New Deal had gone a long way to save American businesses from the worst effects of the depression and had made great strides to offer relief to the unemployed, effective action on behalf of those who still held jobs proved elusive. The vast majority of American workers, particularly those in agriculture and the mass production industries, were helpless in the face of their employers and the economic crisis.

While the NLRA is still in force today, it has been dramatically modified. Employer resistance to the legislation was constant from its beginning, though muted during World War II. Once the war was over, the political climate changed dramatically and led to the Taft-Hartley Act of 1947, a drastic reform of the NLRA. The decline of labor unions in America led to further modifications to the act, most notably in 1974.

Context

As the United States became an industrial nation, gigantic corporations came to dominate the economy. It became all too clear that individual workers had little bargaining power or leverage with their employers. As a consequence, for the bulk of America's workers, working lives were dangerous and unpredictable, more so than for workers in any other industrial country. Efforts by workers to combine into labor unions that might induce employers to negotiate over wages and conditions were, by the end of the 1920s, largely unsuccessful except among the most skilled workers.

The Great Depression of 1929–1941 provided a challenge to the United States unprecedented either before or since. By the time Franklin Roosevelt took the oath of office as president in March 1933, a quarter of America's workers were unemployed, and at least another quarter of workers were underemployed. As the Great Depression bit deeper, workers were unable to defend their livelihoods. They suffered wage cuts, deteriorating conditions of work, short time, layoffs, and unemployment. Industrial warfare broke out in 1933 and lasted until mass-production industries unionized beginning in 1937 and, that same year, the U.S. Supreme Court declared the NLRA constitutional in *NLRB v. Jones & Laughlin Steel Corp.*

Attempts to allow American workers some say in their working lives had some precedent in federal legislation but flew in the face of legal assumptions that placed the sanctity of private property ahead of the rights of the individual when it came to business and commercial activities. Beginning in the Progressive Era in a piecemeal way, a concept of industrial democracy and workers' rights in the workplace gained ground. New Deal reformers such as Senator Robert F. Wagner drew on Progressive ideas in putting together the program of the New Deal.

Time Line

1895–1904
- During the Great Merger Movement, gigantic corporations form that dominate industries and employ hundreds of thousands of workers each.

1914
- The Clayton Antitrust Act declares legal for the first time important labor union tools such as boycotts, peaceful strikes, and peaceful picketing.

1926
- The Railway Labor Act is passed to keep the railways working, protect the rights of employees to join unions, condemn antiunion discrimination by employers, and include a national administrative structure to enforce its provisions.

1932
- The Norris-LaGuardia Act gives freedom of association to workers to form labor unions if they wish without employer interference; bans the issuance of federal injunctions against strikes, picketing, and boycotts; and outlaws "yellow dog" contracts by which workers were forbidden to join unions as a condition of employment.

1933
- The National Industrial Recovery Act, Section 7 (a), part of the larger process of helping companies survive through agreed-upon industry codes of practice that stopped cutthroat competition during the depression, reaffirms the thrust of the Railway Labor Act and the Norris-LaGuardia Act by declaring it federal policy to endorse the right of workers to form unions free of employer interference and to bargain collectively with their bosses.

1934
- The Labor Disputes (Wagner) Bill, the first version of the NLRA, seeks to address the problems of enforcement of previous declarations of federal policy. The bill fails to pass in a busy election year.

About the Author

Although he was born in Germany, Robert F. Wagner (1877–1953) was a thorough New Yorker. He attended public schools in New York City, went to college there, attended New York Law School, and was admitted to the bar in 1900. Elected to the state assembly (1905–1908) and then to the state senate (1909–1918), where he became Democratic floor leader, he left to become a justice of the New York Supreme Court (1919–1926). His eminence in state political life was recognized when he was appointed chairman of the New York State Factory Investigating Commission, set up in the wake of the horrific Triangle Shirtwaist Factory fire in New York City in 1911—the largest industrial disaster in the history of the city of New York, causing the deaths of 148 garment workers. Winning a fight for the U.S. Senate in 1926, Wagner went on to become one of the most effective senators in U.S. history. He left his stamp on virtually every piece of major legislation passed under the New Deal. He introduced the National Industrial Recovery Act into the Senate in 1933, was the major sponsor of such relief agencies as the Civilian Conservation Corps and the Federal Emergency Relief Administration, introduced (unsuccessfully) two antilynching bills in 1934 and 1938, and steered passage of the NLRA. He was "the legislative instigator and tactician, and before Congress, the President, and the public he was its most ardent champion" (Huthmacher, p. 197).

Wagner was a product of the new urban America—pro-immigrant and pro-labor. From 1926 until his resignation in 1949 due to ill health, Wagner served four terms in the Senate. He became one of the most distinguished and accomplished senators in the history of the nation, dubbed by his biographer as the "Legislative Pilot of the New Deal" (Huthmacher, p. 137).

Explanation and Analysis of the Document

Two reasons for passage of the act are identified in the first section of the legislation. First is the problem of industrial unrest. The purpose of the act, as stated, is to provide a mechanism to lessen the causes of labor disputes. This was a matter of great public interest at the time, given the surge in industrial disputes that had taken place in the immediate past and that were continuing as the legislation was debated.

In putting forward the act, Wagner and his supporters were all too well aware that all the major pieces of New Deal legislation were under threat or had been declared unconstitutional by lower courts and even the U.S. Supreme Court. Thus they sought specifically to identify why the legislation was constitutional. It is for this reason that interstate and foreign commerce is cited as the justification for taking action through this legislation. Under Article 1, Section 8, of the U.S. Constitution, Congress is assigned the power "to regulate Commerce with foreign Nations, and among the several States." That Section 8 applied to matters of dispute between employers and workers had been a matter of considerable debate since the 1880s, and by 1935 there were established precedents to support both sides of the argument. In passing the NLRA, Congress was asserting its position on the issue and seeking a definitive answer to solve a serious national problem.

The second purpose of the act was to establish a National Labor Relations Board (NLRB). This was to be the major mechanism to reduce the causes of labor disputes. While a NLRB existed under the National Industrial Recovery Act and two earlier executive orders issued by President Roosevelt, it had no enforcement powers. Wagner's act laid out such powers for a new board.

◆ Findings and Policy

Section 1 lays out the assumptions and arguments underpinning the legislation. The first assumption is that collective bargaining—the process by which employers and representatives of their employees meet together to discuss matters of mutual concern in good faith—is the key to industrial harmony. A refusal by employers to allow employees to organize themselves into unions that can then bargain with the company on behalf of their workers is stated as the main cause of the high level of industrial strife in America. The pressing need for unions to represent workers in negotiating with employers is explained by reference to the inequality of power between individual employees, who do not have the right to organize themselves independent of the company (through freedom of association), and corporations, which are able to increase their own powerful position by membership in industry or larger business organizations such as the National Association of Manufacturers or United States Chamber of Commerce. The act seeks to redress the imbalance of power between workers and employers by setting out practices that would level the playing field, thus reducing the antagonistic state of industrial relations in America.

The reason this should be a matter for government legislation and not merely a private matter between workers and their bosses is also laid out in this section. In addition to the constitutional justification mentioned in the first sentence of the act and repeated in this section, an argument is made directly that inequality in bargaining power had a substantial negative effect on the economy as a whole. Indeed, it was blamed for making business depressions worse. With the Great Depression as a backdrop, this was a powerful argument to make. In keeping with much thinking behind the New Deal, the act offered a way to stabilize industry and improve economic performance generally. It sought to radically change the balance of power within the American economy. Its authors fully expected that by guaranteeing the right of workers to organize and to bargain collectively with employers, work conditions, wages, and hours would all be improved and lead to higher industry standards. With higher wages, there would be more money circulating in the economy, greater purchasing power, and therefore more economic stability.

Time Line

1935

■ In *Schechter Poultry Corp. v. United States*, also known as the Sick Chicken Case, the U.S. Supreme Court declares the National Industrial Recovery Act unconstitutional, throwing into question not only federal labor policy but also the entire approach to industrial recovery.

The NLRA replaces Section 7 (a) of the now-unconstitutional National Industrial Recovery Act and provides federal enforcement provisions protective of labor's right to organize without employer interference and to bargain collectively.

1936

■ The Walsh-Healey Act mandates federal contractors to pay prevailing union rates of pay to all their workers.

1937

■ In *NLRB v. Jones & Laughlin Steel Corp.* the U.S. Supreme Court, by a vote of five to four, rules the NLRA constitutional. It ends almost unanimous employer legal contempt for the NLRA and the rulings of the NLRB. Companies are now forced to participate and respect the law. Union membership and collective bargaining agreements shoot up in the aftermath of the decision.

1938

■ The Fair Labor Standards Act, the last piece of New Deal labor legislation, sets a national minimum wage, maximum hours of work, and child labor standards.

1939

■ The Smith Committee is set up by the Senate to investigate the NLRB for their alleged links with the Congress of Industrial Organizations and Communists. It works closely with the House Un-American Activities Committee.

1940

■ A new majority on the NLRB leads to replacement of staff and greater concern with employer rights, ending the radical, pro–Congress of Industrial Organizations phase of the board.

1947

■ The Taft-Hartley Act sharply amends the NLRA, providing for severe restrictions on unions, strengthening managerial prerogatives, and recasting the NLRB. It limits the right to strike, requires union officers to sign anti-Communist affidavits, and permits states to forbid standard forms of union security.

The section ends with an important declaration of policy. The United States would pursue its goal of eliminating important causes of obstruction to the free flow of commerce by encouraging collective bargaining and protecting the free exercise of labor unionization.

◆ Definitions

Section 2 of the act contains definitions of terms used in the rest of the legislative text. An "employer" is defined as anyone acting in the interests of an employer but specifically excludes government in the United States at whatever level or anyone covered by the Railway Labor Act or any labor union officer or agent except in their capacity as an employer. An "employee," beyond the obvious, includes anyone who ceases to be employed in connection with an ongoing labor dispute or any unfair labor practice if he or she has not obtained other roughly equivalent employment. Agriculture workers, domestic servants, and people employed by their families are not covered under the law.

A "labor organization" is defined as any organization of any kind that exists to deal with employers over workplace issues. That such an organization can be defined beyond merely labor unions is specified by the term "agency or employee representation committee or plan." Employee representation plans were company sponsored and relatively common in the mass-production industries of the 1920s. They continued into the 1930s, often declaring their independence by forming the basis of new labor union locals, especially in the upsurge in union membership that accompanied and followed passage of the National Industrial Recovery Act in 1933 and the NLRA itself in 1935. "Commerce," as used in the act, refers to interstate commerce, while "affecting commerce," always a negative term, is used to identify anything that tends to obstruct or burden interstate trade. A "labor dispute" is a disagreement about any of the terms of employment or concerning representation

of people in negotiating issues related to the terms of employment. Finally, the "National Labor Relations Board" refers to the body established by the NLRA, while "old board" means a body of the same name established by presidential order in 1934 but did not have the same powers.

◆ National Labor Relations Board

The NLRB was to consist of three members, two of whom would represent a quorum. In other words, if the third member of the board was absent or ill, had resigned, or had died, two members could exercise all the powers of the board. Members of the board were to serve terms of five years. They were to be appointed by the president but had to be confirmed by the Senate. The president had the power to name one of the members as chairman of the board and could remove board members after due process only for neglect of duty or wrongdoing while in office.

Other elements of Section 3 of the act stipulate that the NLRB should present a financial report to Congress and the president at the end of each financial year, specifying the cases heard, decisions rendered, details of all its employees, and a financial account. Salaries of board members are set in the wording of Section 4, as are parameters for hiring staff. To satisfy Frances Perkins, President Roosevelt's secretary of labor, who initially had been unenthusiastic about the proposed NLRA, the board is specifically denied authority to engage in conciliation or mediation activities or statistical work, services that remained under the Department of Labor. Everything from the old board was to be transferred to the new board, including employees, records, property, and papers. Section 5 states that the main office of the board is to be in Washington, D.C., though the board could meet anywhere else in the United States and exercise its powers. Section 6 gives authority to the board to make, amend, or revoke rules or regulations necessary to carry out the act.

◆ The Right to Organize into Labor Unions

One of the major reasons for introduction of the NLRA was that the labor protection portion of the National Industrial Recovery Act, Section 7 (a), had proved inadequate. In Section 7 of the NLRA, the wording states explicitly that employees have the right to organize themselves into unions, to have representatives of their own choosing for the purpose of bargaining collectively with their employers, and to pursue activities for their own protection and mutual aid.

◆ Unfair Labor Practices

Perhaps the most radical part of the NLRA lay in Section 8, which defines unfair labor practices. It was common practice for employers to resist the unionization efforts of their employees through a number of means, from outright dismissal to the use of spies and even private armies. In this act, the federal government interjects itself into relations between employees and employers to adjust the power relations between them. Employers are forbidden to interfere with the rights of workers to form or join a union and to exercise the functions of a union. Employers are also forbidden to interfere with or dominate the formation or administration of any labor organization. They are not allowed to discriminate against workers as labor union members in hiring or in holding a job. However, employers can make membership in a union duly certified as representing their employees a condition of employment. Employees who file charges or give testimony under the NLRA cannot be fired or discriminated against. Finally, it is deemed an unfair labor practice for employers to refuse to bargain collectively with the representatives of their employees chosen under the provisions of the act.

◆ Representatives and Elections

Section 9 of the act provides that representatives chosen by a majority of workers within a bargaining unit should be the exclusive representatives of those workers for the purposes of collective bargaining, provided that at any time any individual or group of employees has the right to present grievances to their employer. The NLRB itself has the right to define what constitutes a bargaining unit within a particular company or plant. It might be an entire company or a factory, or it might be subdivided into operative or craft units. Any disputes as to who are the true representatives of the employees can be investigated and determined by the board in a manner laid out under Section 10, by a secret ballot of the employees or through any other suitable method. The record of any board order resulting from such an investigation or any petition to the courts for enforcement or review of the order are to be included in the transcript of the entire record of the case. Whatever the courts subsequently decide is to be based on the contents of the NLRB transcript.

◆ Prevention of Unfair Labor Practices

Section 10 contains the real teeth of the legislation. It sets out the powers and procedures of the NLRB to prevent unfair labor practices. These powers are exclusive. In other words, in matters of unfair labor practices, no other code, law, or agreement can trump or outflank the jurisdiction of the NLRB.

When a charge of an unfair labor practice is brought, the NLRB or any agency or person acting in its behalf has the power to issue a formal complaint, stating the charges made. The complaint is then served upon the employer referred to in the charge. A notice of hearing at a time and place decided by the board within five days of the serving of the complaint is attached. The hearing takes place before the board or any member of it or an agent or agency nominated by the board. The person or employer complained of can file a response to the complaint and appear in person at the hearing if they so wish. The testimony given by them is then put into the record. If the board wishes, further testimony can be given and arguments heard at subsequent hearings. If at the end of the process the board believes that anyone named in the complaint has engaged in unfair labor practices, it issues a cease-and-desist order and takes action to put right the unfairness,

which can include reinstatement of employees. The board also can require periodic reports demonstrating the extent to which its order has been complied with. If after all its hearings and testimony the board decides that no unfair labor practice is proved, it states its findings and issues an order dismissing the complaint. The flexibility given to the board is reflected in the fact that it can modify the complaint at any time before it is served and modify or set aside a part or all of a finding or order before the transcript is filed in a court of law.

The NLRB does not, of course, have its own means to enforce its rulings. What made the NLRA so hated by business was the NLRB's power to have its orders taken up by the higher court system of the United States. Nothing is automatic, however. If an NLRB order is ignored, it has to certify and file a complete transcript of its proceedings with the court. The court will then take over jurisdiction in the case and endeavor to render judgment within ten days. It will serve notice on the person named in the NLRB order and can grant temporary relief or a restraining order until it determines whether the NLRB order should be enforced, modified, or set aside. The power of the courts is limited, however, as the purpose of the courts is to review how the NLRB conducted its proceedings and if its conclusions are sound in all respects. Thus, no new arguments can be considered by the courts unless there are extraordinary circumstances as to why they have not been made to the board. Similarly, all NLRB findings of fact have to be accepted by the courts. Additional evidence can be introduced only if it can be shown that there are reasonable grounds for the evidence not to be heard by the board during its hearings. The jurisdiction of the court is exclusive. Its judgment and decree are final except in the case of appeal to a higher court.

In addition to the power of the NLRB to petition the courts to enforce its orders, anyone aggrieved by a board order granting or denying relief sought for an alleged unfair labor practice can also petition the same courts of appeal for a review. The court will proceed in the same way as if the board had brought the matter before the court.

◆ Investigatory Powers

Section 11 of the NLRA lays out the investigatory powers of the NLRB. The board has the right to all relevant evidence in the case before it. It has the right to compel witnesses to appear and testify before the board and to produce evidence related to the investigation through the power of the subpoena. Board members or the board's designated agents can administer oaths, examine witnesses, and receive evidence. Refusal to obey a subpoena leads to an application by the board to the local district court, which has jurisdiction to order appearance before the board or the production of the required evidence. Failure to abide by such a court order will result in conviction for contempt of court. People cannot refuse to appear before the board or produce evidence on the ground that they would tend to incriminate themselves. Those who claim they would incriminate themselves if

"Employees shall have the right to self-organization, to form, join, or assist labor organizations, to bargain collectively through representatives of their own choosing, and to engage in concerted activities, for the purpose of collective bargaining or other mutual aid or protection."

(Section 7)

"The Board [National Labor Relations Board] is empowered, as hereinafter provided, to prevent any person from engaging in any unfair practice (listed in Section 8) affecting commerce. This power shall be exclusive, and shall not be affected by any other means of adjustment or prevention that has been or may be established by agreement, code, law, or otherwise."

(Section 10 [a])

"The Board shall have power to petition any circuit court of the United States ... wherein the unfair labor practice in question occurred or wherein such person resides or transacts business, for the enforcement of such order and for appropriate temporary relief or restraining order."

(Section 10 [e])

"Nothing in this Act shall be construed so as to interfere with or impede or diminish in any way the right to strike."

(Section 13)

they testified can be compelled to testify but cannot be prosecuted for anything revealed by the evidence or testimony, only for perjury committed in testifying. Acceptable means of serving complaints, orders, and other papers of the board are laid out, together with payments for witnesses making depositions and appearing before the board. Other government departments and agencies have to give the board all documentation relevant to any matter before the board upon the direction of the president. In Section 12, punishment for people interfering in any way with the board in the pursuit of its duties is specified to include fines and imprisonment.

◆ Limitations

In the final sections of the act, various limits are outlined. First, the right of workers to strike is specifically guaranteed by saying that nothing in the act should be interpreted to interfere with or diminish that right. Second, wherever provisions in previous acts of Congress might conflict with provisions of this act, the NLRA will prevail except in cases where the provisions of the NLRA cannot be validly enforced. Finally, if any part of the act or its provisions should be declared unconstitutional, the rest of the act should not be affected.

Audience

The NLRA was written first to win the votes of members of Congress. Its wider audience included President Franklin D. Roosevelt, the U.S. Supreme Court, the judicial system more generally, and the country at large. The language of the act was designed to satisfy legal standards so that the resulting law could be administered satisfactorily.

The NLRA was considered to be one of the most radical pieces of New Deal legislation. It transformed labor relations in the United States and signaled a profound change in the attitude of government to industrial relations. After an initial period of radical enforcement of the legislation that went hand in hand with aggressive unionization drives from the new Congress of Industrial Organizations and the American Federation of Labor, the NLRB moved to redress the balance of its rulings to take more account of the interests of business.

In addition, the NLRA solidified labor as a key component of the New Deal Democratic coalition. In the 1936 national elections, Democrats won by a landslide in large part because of the enthusiasm of workers. Initially, the NLRA had little impact on industrial relations, as employers virtually unanimously anticipated it would be declared unconstitutional by the Supreme Court (as had most of the important New Deal laws). Only after the Supreme Court ruled in *NLRB v. Jones & Laughlin Steel Corp.* in 1937 did the NLRB become fully effective. Opposition to the NLRB was led by the National Association of Manufacturers, the American Federation of Labor (AFL), and the American Communist Party.

The National Association of Manufacturers opposed the NLRA as a fundamental abridgement of its members' right to manage in any way they saw fit and particularly without any interference from government. The AFL opposed the NLRB after initially fighting for it because they saw the NLRB as favoring the new rival Congress of Industrial Organizations in competition for new members. It was particularly upset that the NLRB did not set bargaining units along traditional craft lines. The AFL also continued to cling to a notion of "voluntarism" that regarded industrial relations as a contest of strength between employers and unions in which government should play no part. Finally, the AFL leadership was militantly anti-Communist and was happy to join with groups like the National Association of Manufacturers in dubbing both the Congress of Industrial Organizations and NLRB "Communist-inspired." The 1939 investigation of the NLRB by the House Un-American Activities Committee was a good example of their cooperative efforts. The American Communist Party opposed the NLRA and NLRB as an insidious attempt to tame the class struggle through bureaucratic red tape and thus as an attempt to save American capitalism from revolutionary change. Even so, the NLRA served to encourage and assist the great labor upsurge of the 1930s and 1940s when labor union membership rose from 2.9 million in 1933 to 14.8 million in 1945.

The NLRA survives to this day as the major federal legislation governing industrial relations in the United States. Over the years, rulings of the NLRB have clarified and to some degree diluted the original, more radical purpose of the act. Two legislative initiatives have also modified the act: the Taft-Hartley Act of 1947 and the amendments of 1974. The 1974 amendments brought non-government-employed nurses back under the scope of the NLRA, something that had not happened since 1947.

Related Documents

Leiserson, William. *American Trade Union Democracy*. New York: Columbia University Press, 1959. A scholarly review of the development of "industrial democracy" from one who was at the heart of labor's partnership with government from the late 1920s through the 1950s.

McElvaine, Robert S. *Down and Out in the Great Depression: Letters from the "Forgotten Man"*. Chapel Hill: University of North Carolina Press, 1983. This volume offers views of the Great Depression from the stance of regular Americans who wrote in unprecedented numbers to President Roosevelt and his wife.

————. *The Depression and New Deal: A History in Documents*. New York: Oxford University Press, 2000. This collection contains documents regarding the major New Deal legislation and attitudes to them.

NLRB v. Jones & Laughlin Steel Corp. 301 U.S. 1 (1937). FindLaw Web site. http://caselaw.lp.findlaw.com/scripts/getcase.pl?navby=CASE&court=US&vol=301&page=1. Accessed on December 26, 2007. The U.S. Supreme Court ruling that defended the constitutionality of the NLRA.

Perkins, Frances. *The Roosevelt I Knew*. New York: Viking, 1946. Memoir of the recently deceased president by his secretary of labor.

Roosevelt, Eleanor. *This I Remember*. New York: Harper, 1949. Autobiography of Eleanor Roosevelt's life with Franklin Roosevelt.

Roosevelt, Franklin D. "Letter on the National Labor Relations Act." The American Presidency Project Web site. http://www.presidency.ucsb.edu/ws/index.php?pid=15652. Accessed on December 26, 2007. In this letter of June 10, 1938, Roosevelt informs Congressman Hatton W. Sumners that he has no intention of establishing a commission to study the NLRA.

U.S. Senate, Committee on Education and Labor Report. *Violations of Free Speech and Rights of Labor*. Washington, D.C.: Government Printing Office, 1939–1941. The famous La Follette Committee report investigating violations of the right of free speech and assembly and interference with the right of labor to organize and bargain collectively.

Bibliography

■ **Books**

Bernanke, Ben S. *Essays on the Great Depression*. Princeton, N.J.: Princeton University Press, 2000.

Dubofsky, Melvyn. *The State and Labor in Modern America*. Chapel Hill: University of North Carolina Press, 1994.

Edsforth, Ronald. *The New Deal: America's Response to the Great Depression*. Malden, Mass.: Blackwell, 2000.

Forbath, William E. *Law and the Shaping of the American Labor Movement*. Cambridge, Mass.: Harvard University Press, 1991.

Huthmacher, Joseph J. *Senator Robert F. Wagner and the Rise of Urban Liberalism*. New York: Atheneum, 1968.

Kennedy, David M. *Freedom from Fear: The American People in Depression and War, 1929–1945*. New York: Oxford University Press, 1999.

Klare, Karl E. "Judicial Deradicalization of the Wagner Act and the Origins of Modern Legal Consciousness, 1937–1941." In *The Great Depression and the New Deal*, vol. 7, ed. Melvyn Dubofsky and Stephen Burwood. New York: Garland, 1990.

Leuchtenburg, William E. *Franklin Roosevelt and the New Deal, 1932–1940*. New York, Harper & Row, 1963.

Shlaes, Amity. *The Forgotten Man: A New History of the Great Depression*. New York: HarperCollins, 2007.

Tomlins, Christopher L. *The State and the Unions: Labor Relations, Law, and the Organized Labor Movement in America, 1880–1960*. New York: Cambridge University Press, 1985.

———. "The New Deal, Collective Bargaining, and the Triumph of Industrial Pluralism." In *The Great Depression and the New Deal*, vol. 7, ed. Melvyn Dubofsky and Stephen Burwood. New York: Garland, 1990.

■ **Web Sites**

"1930s: National Labor Relations Act of 1935 ('The Wagner Act')." Charles University American Studies "Documents of American History II" Web site.
http://tucnak.fsv.cuni.cz/~calda/Documents/1930s/LaborRelationsAct_1935.html. Accessed on December 26, 2007.

National Labor Relations Board Web site.
http://www.nlrb.gov/. Accessed on December 26, 2007.

Wagner, Robert Ferdinand (1877–1953). Biographical Directory of the United States Congress.
http://bioguide.congress.gov/scripts/biodisplay.pl?index=W000021. Accessed on December 26, 2007.

—By Stephen Burwood

Questions for Further Study

1. The NLRA has been seen as one of the most radical pieces of legislation in American history. The Taft-Hartley Act, on the other hand, has been viewed by most liberals as a profoundly conservative reaction that gutted federal labor policy. Compare and contrast the two pieces of legislation to determine whether either view is fully justified.

2. The NLRA extended into law a view of industrial democracy developed by labor and its liberal allies over the previous thirty years. It was a view of rights and privileges that ran counter to the bulk of court rulings since the 1880s, in which the property rights of employers were considered paramount, corporations were considered to be individuals dealing in legal equality with their individual employees, and labor unions were considered to be coercive and illegitimate restraints on trade. How has this debate changed or remained the same in the twenty-first century?

3. The NLRA was passed to extend democracy to the workplace, to alter the relations of power between workers and their employers, and to eliminate what was seen as an abuse of power by employers through "unfair labor practices." How has the NLRA been altered in the years since 1935, and does it still fulfill these functions? In the twenty-first century, do you think it is still necessary or should employers have a free hand in the conduct of their own businesses?

adduce	to bring forward in evidence
affirmations	solemn declarations before a magistrate or judge, made without swearing an oath
aforesaid	said or mentioned previously
amendatory	serving to modify or correct
appropriations	monies authorized to be spent from the public treasury
certification	official license
certiorari	a legal writ that allows a superior court to review the record of a case in an inferior court
conciliation	the bringing together of opposed individuals or groups
construed	understood
contempt	willful disobedience or disrespect for the rules or orders of a court
contumacy	stubborn resistance to authority
diminution	reduction
disputants	people engaged in arguing a legal case or contract
docketed	listed for consideration by a court
forfeiture	loss as the result of being taken away by a legal ruling
grievances	official complaints of wrongdoing at work, usually brought by workers or unions against management
hereinabove	at a previous point in a document
jurisdiction	the region or area of authority of a court or other official body
malfeasance	wrongdoing
mediation	the process of reaching an agreement between opposed individuals or groups
pleadings	written statements setting out the cause of action or defense of a legal case
praying	requesting
proximate	near
pursuant	in accordance with
quorum	the minimum number required to be present to transact business or carry out an activity legally
receivers	people appointed by a court to administer the affairs of a bankrupt company or person
rescind	to repeal
severally	separately
subpena (subpoena)	a legal writ to summon a person or evidence before a court
therein	in that place or circumstance
thereupon	in consequence of
transacts	carries on negotiation to a settlement
trustees	people appointed to administer the affairs of a company

NATIONAL LABOR RELATIONS ACT

An act to diminish the causes of labor disputes burdening or obstructing interstate and foreign commerce, to create a National Labor Relations Board, and for other purposes.

Be it enacted by the Senate and House of Representatives of the United States of America in Congress assembled,

◆ Findings and Policy

Section 1. The denial by employers of the right of employees to organize and the refusal by employers to accept the procedure of collective bargaining lead to strikes and other forms of industrial strife or unrest, which have the intent or the necessary effect of burdening or obstructing commerce by (a) impairing the efficiency, safety, or operation of the instrumentalities of commerce; (b) occurring in the current of commerce; (c) materially affecting, restraining, or controlling the flow of raw materials or manufactured or processed goods from or into the channels of commerce, or the prices of such materials or goods in commerce; or (d) causing diminution of employment and wages in such volume as substantially to impair or disrupt the market for goods flowing from or into the channels of commerce.

The inequality of bargaining power between employees who do not possess full freedom of association or actual liberty of contract, and employers who are organized in the corporate or other forms of ownership association substantially burdens and affects the flow of commerce, and tends to aggravate recurrent business depressions, by depressing wage rates and the purchasing power of wage earners in industry and by preventing the stabilization of competitive wage rates and working conditions within and between industries.

Experience has proved that protection by law of the right of employees to organize and bargain collectively safeguards commerce from injury, impairment, or interruption, and promotes the flow of commerce by removing certain recognized sources of

industrial strife and unrest, by encouraging practices fundamental to the friendly adjustment of industrial disputes arising out of differences as to wages, hours, or other working conditions, and by restoring equality of bargaining power between employers and employees.

It is hereby declared to be the policy of the United States to eliminate the causes of certain substantial obstructions to the free flow of commerce and to mitigate and eliminate these obstructions when they have occurred by encouraging the practice and procedure of collective bargaining and by protecting the exercise by workers of full freedom of association, self-organization, and designation of representatives of their own choosing, for the purpose of negotiating the terms and conditions of their employment or their mutual aid or protection.

◆ Definitions

Sec. 2. When used in this Act—

(1) The term "person" includes one or more individuals, partnerships, associations, corporations, legal representatives, trustees, trustees in bankruptcy, or receivers.

(2) The term "employer" includes any person acting in the interest of an employer, directly or indirectly, but shall not include the United States, or any State or political subdivision thereof, or any person subject to the Railway Labor Act, as amended from time to time, or any labor organization (other than when acting as an employer), or anyone acting in the capacity of officer or agent of such labor organization.

(3) The term "employee" shall include any employee, and shall not be limited to the employees of a particular employer, unless the Act explicitly states otherwise, and shall include any individual whose work has ceased as a consequence of, or in connection with, any current labor dispute or because of any unfair labor practice, and who has not obtained any

other regular and substantially equivalent employment, but shall not include any individual employed as an agricultural laborer, or in the domestic service of any family or person at his home, or any individual employed by his parent or spouse.

(4) The term "representatives" includes any individual or labor organization.

(5) The term "labor organization" means any organization of any kind, or any agency or employee representation committee or plan, in which employees participate and which exists for the purpose, in whole or in part, of dealing with employers concerning grievances, labor disputes, wages, rates of pay, hours of employment, or conditions of work.

(6) The term "commerce" means trade, traffic, commerce, transportation, or communication among the several States, or between the District of Columbia or any Territory of the United States and any State or other Territory, or between any foreign country and any State, Territory, or the District of Columbia, or within the District of Columbia or any Territory, or between points in the same State but through any other State or any Territory or the District of Columbia or any foreign country.

(7) The term "affecting commerce" means in commerce, or burdening or obstructing commerce or the free flow of commerce, or having led or tending to lead to a labor dispute burdening or obstructing commerce or the free flow of commerce.

(8) The term "unfair labor practice" means any unfair labor practice listed in section 8.

(9) The term "labor dispute" includes any controversy concerning terms, tenure or conditions of employment, or concerning the association or representation of persons in negotiating, fixing, maintaining, changing, or seeking to arrange terms or conditions of employment, regardless of whether the disputants stand in the proximate relation of employer and employee.

(10) The term "National Labor Relations Board" means the National Labor Relations Board created by section 3 of this Act.

(11) The term "old Board" means the National Labor Relations Board established by Executive Order Numbered 6763 of the President on June 29, 1934, pursuant to Public Resolution Numbered 44, approved June 19, 1934 (48 Stat. 1183), and reestablished and continued by Executive Order Numbered 7074 of the President of June 15, 1935, pursuant to Title I of the National Industrial Recovery Act (48 Stat. 195) as amended and continued by Senate Joint Resolution 133 (1) approved June 14, 1935.

◆ National Labor Relations Board

Sec. 3. (a) There is hereby created a board, to be known as the "National Labor Relations Board" (hereinafter referred to as the "Board"), which shall be composed of three members, who shall be appointed by the President, by and with the advice and consent of the Senate. One of the original members shall be appointed for a term of one year, one for a term of three years, and one for a term of five years, but their successors shall be appointed for terms of five years each, except that any individual chosen to fill a vacancy shall be appointed only for the unexpired term of the member whom he shall succeed. The President shall designate one member to serve as chairman of the Board. Any member of the Board may be removed by the President, upon notice and hearing, for neglect of duty or malfeasance in office, but for no other cause.

(b) A vacancy in the Board shall not impair the right of the remaining members to exercise all the powers of the Board, and two members of the Board shall, at all times, constitute a quorum. The Board shall have an official seal which shall be judicially noticed.

(c) The Board shall at the close of each fiscal year make a report in writing to Congress and to the President stating in detail the cases it has heard, the decisions it has rendered, the names, salaries, and duties of all employees and officers in the employ or under the supervision of the Board, and an account of all moneys it has disbursed.

Sec. 4. (a) Each member of the Board shall receive a salary of $10,000 a year, shall be eligible for reappointment, and shall not engage in any other business, vocation, or employment. The Board shall appoint, without regard for the provisions of the civil-service laws but subject to the Classification Act of 1923, as amended, an executive secretary, and such attorneys, examiners, and regional directors, and shall appoint such other employees with regard to existing laws applicable to the employment and compensation of officers and employees of the United States, as it may from time to time find necessary for the proper performance of its duties and as may be from time to time appropriated for by Congress. The Board may establish or utilize such regional, local, or other agencies, and utilize such voluntary and uncompensated services, as may from time to time be needed. Attorneys appointed under this section may, at the direction of the Board, appear for and represent the Board in any case in court. Nothing in this Act shall be construed to authorize the

Board to appoint individuals for the purpose of conciliation or mediation (or for statistical work), where such service may be obtained from the Department of Labor.

(b) Upon the appointment of the three original members of the Board and the designation of its chairman, the old Board shall cease to exist. All employees of the old Board shall be transferred to and become employees of the Board with salaries under the Classification Act of 1923, as amended, without acquiring by such transfer a permanent or civil service status. All records, papers, and property of the old Board shall become records, papers, and property of the Board, and all unexpended funds and appropriations for the use and maintenance of the old Board shall become funds and appropriations available to be expended by the Board in the exercise of the powers, authority, and duties conferred on it by this Act.

(c) All of the expenses of the Board, including all necessary travelling and subsistence expenses outside the District of Columbia incurred by the members or employees of the Board under its orders, shall be allowed and paid on the presentation of itemized vouchers therefor approved by the Board or by any individual it designates for that purpose.

Sec. 5. The principal office of the Board shall be in the District of Columbia, but it may meet and exercise any or all of its powers at any other place. The Board may, by one or more of its members or by such agents or agencies as it may designate, prosecute any inquiry necessary to its functions in any part of the United States. A member who participates in such an inquiry shall not be disqualified from subsequently participating in a decision of the Board in the same case.

Sec. 6. (a) The Board shall have authority from time to time to make, amend, and rescind such rules and regulations as may be necessary to carry out the provisions of this Act. Such rules and regulations shall be effective upon publication in the manner which the Board shall prescribed.

◆ Rights of Employees

Sec. 7. Employees shall have the right to self-organization, to form, join, or assist labor organizations, to bargain collectively through representatives of their own choosing, and to engage in concerted activities, for the purpose of collective bargaining or other mutual aid or protection.

Sec. 8. It shall be an unfair labor practice for an employer—

(1) To interfere with, restrain, or coerce employees in the exercise of the rights guaranteed in section 7.

(2) To dominate or interfere with the formation or administration of any labor organization or contribute financial or other support to it: Provided, That subject to rules and regulations made and published by the Board pursuant to section 6(a), an employer shall not be prohibited from permitting employees to confer with him during working hours without loss of time or pay.

(3) By discrimination in regard to hire or tenure of employment or any term or condition of employment to encourage or discourage membership in any labor organization: Provided, That nothing in this Act, or in the National Industrial Recovery Act (U.S.C., Supp. VII, title 15, secs. 701-712), as amended from time to time, or in any code or agreement approved or prescribed thereunder, or in any other statute of the United States, shall preclude an employer from making an agreement with a labor organization (not established, maintained, or assisted by any action defined in this Act as an unfair labor practice) to require as a condition of employment membership therein, if such labor organization is the representative of the employees as provided in section 9(a), in the appropriate collective bargaining unit covered by such agreement when made.

(4) To discharge or otherwise discriminate against an employee because he has filed charges or given testimony under this Act.

(5) To refuse to bargain collectively with the representatives of his employees, subject to the provisions of Section 9(a).

◆ Representatives and Elections

Sec. 9. (a) Representatives designated or selected for the purposes of collective bargaining by the majority of the employees in a unit appropriate for such purposes, shall be the exclusive representatives of all the employees in such unit for the purposes of collective bargaining in respect to rates of pay, wages, hours of employment, or other conditions of employment: Provided, That any individual employee or a group of employees shall have the right at any time to present grievances to their employer.

(b) The Board shall decide in each case whether, in order to insure to employees the full benefit of their right to self-organization and to collective bargaining, and otherwise to effectuate the policies of this Act, the unit appropriate for the purposes of collective bargaining shall be the employer unit, craft unit, plant unit, or subdivision thereof.

(c) Whenever a question affecting commerce arises concerning the presentation of employees, the Board may investigate such controversy and certify to the parties, in writing, the name or names of the representatives that have been designated or selected. In any such investigation the Board shall provide for an appropriate hearing upon due notice, either in conjunction with a proceeding under section 10 or otherwise, and may take a secret ballot of employees, or utilize any other suitable method ascertain such representatives.

(d) Whenever an order of the Board made pursuant to section 10(c) is based in whole or in part upon facts certified following an investigation pursuant to subsection (c) of this section, and there is a petition for the enforcement or review of such order, such certification and the record of such investigation shall be included in the transcript of the entire record required to be filed under subsections 10(e) or 10(f), and thereupon the decree of the court enforcing, modifying, or setting aside in whole or in part the order of the Board shall be made and entered upon the pleadings, testimony, and proceedings set forth in such transcript.

◆ Prevention of Unfair Labor Practices

Sec. 10. (a) The Board is empowered, as hereinafter provided, to prevent any person from engaging in any unfair labor practice (listed in Section 8) affecting commerce. This power shall be exclusive, and shall not be affected by any other means of adjustment or prevention that has been or may be established by agreement, code, law, or otherwise.

(b) Whenever it is charged that any person has engaged in or is engaging in any such unfair labor practice, the Board, or any agent or agency designated by the Board for such purposes, shall have power to issue and cause to be served upon such person a complaint stating the charges in that respect, and containing a notice of hearing before the Board or a member thereof, or before a designated agent or agency, at a place therein fixed, not less than five days after the serving of said complaint. Any such complaint may be amended by the member, agent, or agency conducting the hearing or the Board in its discretion at any time prior to the issuance of an order based thereon. The person so complained of shall have the right to file an answer to the original or amended complaint and to appear in person or otherwise and give testimony at the place and time fixed in the complaint. In the discretion of the member, agent or agency conducting the hearing or the

Board, any other person may be allowed to intervene in the said proceeding and to prevent testimony. In any such proceeding in the rules of evidence prevailing in courts of law or equity shall not be controlling.

(c) The testimony taken by such member, agent or agency or the Board shall be reduced to writing and filed with the Board. Thereafter, in its discretion, the Board upon notice may take further testimony or hear argument. If upon all the testimony taken the Board shall be of the opinion that any person named in the complaint has engaged in or is engaging in any such unfair labor practice, then the Board shall state its findings of fact and shall issue and cause to be served on such person an order requiring such person to cease and desist from such unfair labor practice, and to take such affirmative action, including reinstatement of employees with or without back pay, as will effectuate the policies of this Act. Such order may further require such person to make reports from time to time showing the extent to which it has complied with the order. If upon all the testimony taken the Board shall be the opinion that no person named in the complaint has engaged in or is engaging in any such unfair labor practice, then the Board shall state its findings of fact and shall issue an order dismissing the said complaint.

(d) Until a transcript of the record in a case shall have been filed in a court, as hereinafter provided, the Board may at any time, upon reasonable notice and in such manner as it shall deem proper, modify or set aside, in whole or in part, any finding or order made or issued by it.

(e) The Board shall have power to petition any circuit court of appeals of the United States (including the Court of Appeals of the District of Columbia), or if all the circuit courts of appeals to which application may be made are in vacation, any district court of the United States (including the Supreme Court of the District of Columbia), within any circuit or district, respectively, wherein the unfair labor practice in question occurred or wherein such person resides or transacts business, for the enforcement of such order and for appropriate temporary relief or restraining order, and shall certify and file in the court a transcript of the entire record in the proceeding, including the pleadings and testimony upon which such order was entered and the findings and order of the Board. Upon such filing, the court shall cause notice thereof to be served upon such person, and thereupon shall have jurisdiction of the proceeding and of the question determined therein, and shall have power to grant such temporary relief or restraining order as it deems just and proper, and to make and enter upon the pleadings, testimony, and proceedings set forth in such transcript a decree enforcing, modifying, and enforcing as so modified, or setting aside in whole or in part the order of the Board. No objection that has not been urged the Board, its member, agent of agency, shall be considered by the court, unless the failure or neglect to urge such objection shall be excused because of extraordinary circumstances. The findings of the Board as to the facts, if supported by evidence, shall be conclusive. If either party shall apply to the court for leave to adduce additional evidence and shall show to the satisfaction of the court that such additional evidence is material and that there were reasonable grounds for the failure to adduce such evidence in the hearing before the Board, its member, agent, or agency, the court may order such additional evidence to be taken before the Board, its member, agent, or agency, and to be made a part of the transcript. The Board may modify its findings as to the facts, or make new findings, by reason of additional evidence so taken and filed, and it shall file such modified or new findings, which, if supported by evidence, shall be conclusive, and shall file its recommendations, if any, for the modification or setting aside of its original order. The jurisdiction of the court shall be exclusive and its judgment and decree shall be final, except that the same shall be subject to review by the appropriate circuit court of appeals if application was made to the district court as hereinabove provided, and by the Supreme Court of the United States upon write of certiorari or certification as provided in sections 239 and 240 of the Judicial Code, as amended (U.S.C., title 28, secs. 346 and 347).

(f) Any person aggrieved by a final order of the Board granting or denying in whole or in part the relief sought may obtain a review of such order in any circuit court of appeals of the United States in the circuit wherein the unfair labor practice in question was alleged to have been engaged in or wherein such person resides or transacts business, or in the Court of Appeals of the District of Columbia, by filing in such court written petition praying that the order of the Board be modified or set aside. A copy of such petition shall be forthwith served upon the Board, and thereupon the aggrieved party shall file in the court a transcript of the entire record in the proceeding, certified by the Board, including the pleading and testimony upon which the order complained of was entered and the findings and order of the Board. Upon such filing, the court shall proceed in

the same manner as in the case of an application by the Board under subsection (e), and shall have the same exclusive jurisdiction to grant to the Board such temporary relief or restraining order as it deems just and proper, and in like manner to make and enter a decree enforcing, modifying, and enforcing as so modified, or setting aside in whole or in part the order of the Board; and the findings of the Board as to the facts, if supported by evidence, shall in like manner be conclusive.

(g) The commencement of proceedings under subsection (e) or (f) of this section shall not, unless specifically ordered by the court, operate as a stay of the Board's order.

(h) When granting appropriate temporary relief or a restraining order, or making and entering a decree enforcing, modifying, and enforcing as so modified or setting aside in whole or in part an order of the Board, as provided in this section, the jurisdiction of courts sitting in equity shall not be limited by the Act entitled "An Act to amend the Judicial Code and to define and limit the jurisdiction of courts sitting in equity, and for other purposes", approved March 23, 1932 (U.S.C., Supp. VII, title 29, secs. 101-115).

(i) Petitions filed under this Act shall be heard expeditiously, and if possible within ten days after they have been docketed.

◆ Investigatory Powers

Sec. 11. For the purpose of all hearings and investigations, which, in the opinion of the Board, are necessary and proper for the exercise of the powers vested in it by section 9 and section 10—

(1) The Board, or its duly authorized agents or agencies, shall at all reasonable times have access to, for the purpose of examination, and the right to copy any evidence of any person being investigated or proceeded against that relates to any matter under investigation or in question. Any member of the Board shall have the power to issue subpoenas requiring the attendance and testimony of witnesses and the production of any evidence that relates to any matter under investigation or in question, before the Board, its member, agent, or agency conducting the hearing or investigation. Any member of the Board, or any agent or agency designated by the Board for such purposes, may administer oaths and affirmations, examine witnesses, and receive evidence. Such attendance of witnesses and the production of such evidence may be required from any place in the United States or any Territory or possession thereof, at any designated place of hearing.

(2) In case of contumacy or refusal to obey a subpoena issued to any person, any District Court of the United States or the United States courts of any Territory or possession, or the Supreme Court of the District of Columbia, within the jurisdiction of which the inquiry is carried on or within the jurisdiction of which said person guilty of contumacy or refusal to obey is found or resides or transacts business, upon application by the Board shall have jurisdiction to issue to such person an order requiring such person to appear before the Board, its member, agent, or agency, there to produce evidence if so ordered, or there to give testimony touching the matter under investigation or in question; and any failure to obey such order of the court may be punished by said court as a contempt thereof.

(3) No person shall be excused from attending and testifying or from producing books, records, correspondence, documents, or other evidence in obedience to the subpoena of the Board, on the ground that the testimony or evidence required of him may tend to incriminate him or subject him to a penalty or forfeiture; but no individual shall be prosecuted or subjected to any penalty or forfeiture for or on account of any transaction, matter, or thing concerning which he is compelled, after having claimed his privilege against self-incrimination, to testify or produce evidence, except that such individual so testifying shall not be exempt from prosecution and punishment for perjury committed in so testifying.

(4) Complaints, orders, and other process and papers of the Board, its member, agent, or agency, may be served either personally or by registered mail or by telegraph or by leaving a copy thereof at the principal office or place of business of the person required to be served. The verified return by the individual so serving the same setting forth the manner of such service shall be proof of the same, and the return post office receipt or telegraph receipt therefor when registered and mailed or telegraphed as aforesaid shall be proof of service of the same. Witnesses summoned before the Board, its member, agent, or agency, shall be paid the same fees and mileage that are paid witnesses in the courts of the United States, and witnesses whose depositions are taken and the persons taking the same shall severally be entitled to the same fees as are paid for like services in the courts of the United States.

(5) All process of any court to which application may be made under this Act may be served in the judicial district wherein the defendant or other person required to be served resides or may be found.

(6) The several departments and agencies of the Government, when directed by the President, shall furnish the Board, upon its request, all records, papers, and information in their possession relating to any matter before the Board.

Sec. 12. Any person who shall willfully resist, prevent, impede, or interfere with any member of the Board or any of its agents or agencies in the performance of duties pursuant to this Act shall be punished by a fine of not more than $5,000 or by imprisonment for not more than one year, or both.

◆ Limitations

Sec. 13. Nothing in this Act shall be construed so as to interfere with or impede or diminish in any way the right to strike.

Sec. 14. Wherever the application of the provisions of section 7 (a) of the National Industrial Act (U.S.C., Supp. VII, title 15, sec. 707 (a)), as amended from time to time, or of section 77 B, paragraphs (l) and (m) of the Act approved June 7, 1934, entitled "An Act to amend an Act entitled 'An Act to establish a uniform system of bankruptcy throughout the United States' approved July 1, 1898, and Acts amendatory thereof and supplementary thereto" (48 Stat. 922, pars. (l) and (m)), as amended from time to time, or of Public Resolution Numbered 44, approved June 19, 1934 (48 Stat. 1183), conflicts with the application of the provisions of this Act, this Act shall prevail: Provided, That in any situation where the provisions of this Act cannot be validly enforced, the provisions of such other Acts shall remain in full force and effect.

Sec. 15. If any provision of this Act, or the application of such provision to any person or circumstance, shall be held invalid, the remainder of this Act, or the application of such provision to persons or circumstances other than those as to which it is held invalid, shall not be affected thereby.

Sec. 16. This Act may be cited as the "National Labor Relations Act."

Seventy-fourth Congress of the United States of America;

At the First Session,

Begun and held at the City of Washington on Thursday, the third
day of January, one thousand nine hundred and thirty-five.

AN ACT

To provide for the general welfare by establishing a system of Federal
old-age benefits, and by enabling the several States to make more
adequate provision for aged persons, blind persons, dependent and
crippled children, maternal and child welfare, public health, and
the administration of their unemployment compensation laws; to
establish a Social Security Board; to raise revenue; and for other
purposes.

*Be it enacted by the Senate and House of Representatives of the
United States of America in Congress assembled,*

TITLE I—GRANTS TO STATES FOR OLD-AGE ASSISTANCE

APPROPRIATION

SECTION 1. For the purpose of enabling each State to furnish
financial assistance, as far as practicable under the conditions in such
State, to aged needy individuals, there is hereby authorized to be
appropriated for the fiscal year ending June 30, 1936, the sum of
$49,750,000, and there is hereby authorized to be appropriated for
each fiscal year thereafter a sum sufficient to carry out the purposes
of this title. The sums made available under this section shall be
used for making payments to States which have submitted, and had
approved by the Social Security Board established by Title VII
(hereinafter referred to as the "Board"), State plans for old-age
assistance.

STATE OLD-AGE ASSISTANCE PLANS

SEC. 2. (a) A State plan for old-age assistance must (1) provide
that it shall be in effect in all political subdivisions of the State, and,
if administered by them, be mandatory upon them; (2) provide for
financial participation by the State; (3) either provide for the establishment or designation of a single State agency to administer the
plan, or provide for the establishment or designation of a single State
agency to supervise the administration of the plan; (4) provide for
granting to any individual, whose claim for old-age assistance is
denied, an opportunity for a fair hearing before such State agency;
(5) provide such methods of administration (other than those relating to selection, tenure of office, and compensation of personnel) as

The Social Security Act (National Archives and Records Administration)

SOCIAL SECURITY ACT

"Every qualified individual ... shall be entitled to receive ... an old-age benefit."

Overview

The Great Depression plagued Americans following the stock market crash of 1929; by 1934 over 25 percent of the nation's workforce was unemployed. In a nation that equated poverty and idleness with personal moral failure, millions of formerly employed men lined up at soup kitchens; wandered the country looking for work; or stayed at home, scrounging for food. The elderly were particularly vulnerable; state aid was meager, and families often offered little to no support.

Facing a frustrated public, political challengers, and a Congress floating its own solutions, President Franklin Delano Roosevelt called for a national program for unemployment insurance and retirement income. The result, the Social Security Act of 1935, creates a unique system financed by employer and employee contributions instead of government payments. The Social Security Act provides the first public social safety net for Americans. Whereas old age or unemployment once guaranteed a life of poverty, Social Security affords a minimum level of income for unemployed and retired workers.

Context

By the early twentieth century, the United States was the only developed western country without a national system of social insurance. Many called for change when a 1911 fire at the Triangle Shirtwaist Factory killed 146 garment workers in New York City. Following the incident, Senator Franklin D. Roosevelt created the New York State Factory Investigating Commission to report on working conditions in the city; the commission's director was Frances Perkins, who later became President Roosevelt's secretary of labor, the country's first female cabinet member.

Unemployment was the gravest problem facing Roosevelt's administration, and many people proposed solutions. A few states—most notably Wisconsin—had their own unemployment insurance programs. Private pension plans, administered by employers, were few and often underfunded. Politicians and citizens proposed more radi-

cal solutions. Senator Huey Long, formerly governor of Louisiana, fueled a growing industry of "Share Our Wealth" clubs; according to his vision, every American family would receive an annual income of $5,000, and persons over the age of sixty would receive a pension. The California dentist Francis Townsend proposed that each person over sixty receive a government pension of $200 per month. After his concept was published in 1933, some 7,000 Townsend clubs sprang up across the country to support his plan. The novelist Upton Sinclair ran for governor of California in 1934 on a platform of ending poverty, including a $50-per-month pension to all needy people over age sixty. The National Union for Social Justice, led by Father Charles Coughlin, a radically anti-Communist priest, proposed a broad-based program of reforms. Finally, Democratic Senator Robert Wagner of New York and Democratic Representative David Lewis of Maryland introduced the Wagner-Lewis Bill in February of 1934, calling for national unemployment insurance.

As the chorus for change grew louder, Roosevelt initiated his own plan for addressing not only unemployment but the plight of the elderly as well. On June 29, 1934, he appointed the Committee on Economic Security (CES), consisting of Secretary of Labor Perkins, Secretary of the Treasury Henry Morgenthau, Attorney General Homer Cummings, Secretary of Agriculture Henry Wallace, and chief of the Federal Emergency Relief Administration Harry Hopkins to draft legislation. From the beginning, Roosevelt wanted to ensure that the old-age pension and unemployment assistance system would provide insurance, not a dole. He was equally committed to ensuring that every American would be protected throughout the duration of his or her lifetime. As a result of these mandates, the CES faced a number of daunting challenges, such as financing the program and ensuring that a federally administrated system of social insurance would hold up under Supreme Court scrutiny.

The result was the Social Security Act of 1935, a product of massive compromise and political wrangling. Unlike European social insurance programs, America's Social Security system is financed by both employer and employee contributions. The program consists of a purely federal retirement income component as well as a joint federal and

Time Line

1929

■ **October 29**
The stock market crashes on "Black Tuesday," ushering in the Great Depression.

1932

■ **November 8**
Franklin Roosevelt is elected to his first term as president.

1933

■ **May 12**
Congress authorizes $500 million in direct aid as part of Roosevelt's Federal Emergency Relief Agency program, providing first federal grants to states for unemployment assistance.

■ **September 30**
Francis Townsend publishes an article calling for flat-rate monthly pensions.

1934

■ **February**
The Wagner-Lewis Bill is presented to Congress.

■ **June 8**
Roosevelt issues a special message to Congress promising unemployment legislation.

■ **June 28**
Roosevelt gives a fireside chat on social insurance.

■ **June 29**
Roosevelt creates the Committee on Economic Security.

1935

■ **January 17**
The CES recommendations are presented to Congress.

■ **August 14**
Roosevelt signs the Social Security Act of 1935.

■ **August 26**
Senator Huey Long's filibuster kills funding for the Social Security Act.

1936

■ **February 13**
The first public assistance checks are mailed.

1937

■ **May 24**
The Supreme Court upholds the Social Security Act.

state system of unemployment insurance. Finally, the Social Security Act provides for direct federal aid (in the form of state grants) for public health services, assistance for the blind and disabled, and child welfare. Although criticized by those on the left and right, the Social Security Act redefines the nature of government, extending the role of the federal sector to provide citizens with a base level of economic stability.

About the Author

A number of key persons were involved in crafting the legislation. President Franklin D. Roosevelt (1882–1945) provided the impetus. He had been influenced by his older cousin, Theodore Roosevelt, the twenty-sixth president of the United States and a champion of Progressive causes. Elected to the New York state senate in 1910, Roosevelt began to develop his own sense of the role of government in society. As governor of New York, Roosevelt argued for social insurance as early as 1930. He believed that Social Security was one of the crowning accomplishments of his presidency.

Frances Perkins (1882–1965), Roosevelt's secretary of labor, served as chairperson of the CES. Perkins graduated from Mount Holyoke College and received a master's degree from Columbia University. She was executive secretary of the Consumer's League in New York City from 1910 to 1912, during which time she witnessed the Triangle Shirtwaist Factory fire. Perkins was Roosevelt's State Industrial Commissioner when he was governor of New York. In 1931 she traveled to the United Kingdom to research that country's old-age pension and unemployment insurance plans. Upon her return, she worked to persuade Roosevelt to pursue such plans and was thus instrumental in the development of Roosevelt's concept of Social Security.

Edwin Witte (1887–1960) is often referred to as "the father of the Social Security Act." He received his bachelor's degree and doctorate from the University of Wisconsin, where he studied with the economist John Commons, an early proponent of labor reforms. Witte was also influenced by the Wisconsin Progressive movement; Wisconsin was the first state to adopt an unemployment insurance plan. As executive director and research synthesizer for the CES, Witte drafted the committee's report and was instrumental in negotiating various modifications required to ensure that the Social Security Act would pass.

Explanation and Analysis of the Document

◆ Title I—Grants to States for Old-Age Assistance

A major issue of contention during congressional hearings was the respective federal and state roles in implementing the old-age assistance program. Some senators, primarily those from the South, argued that the bill gave too much power to the federal government. Jim Crow laws in the South allowed for segregation, and southern legislators did not want Washington to deny their states aid because of discriminatory practices. The final document reflects a weaker federal supervisory role as well as a clear sharing of financial responsibility between state and federal sectors.

Section 1 authorizes the federal government to make annual payments to states that have approved old-age assistance plans. These plans are for needy elderly individuals, hence the term *old-age assistance*. The more general Social Security retirement program for employees ("Federal Old-Age Benefits") is described in Title II.

◆ State Old-Age Assistance Plans

Section 2 lists the requirements for an approved state plan. Subsection (a)(1) prevents states from offering pension plans to only certain areas of the state, constituting political or racial discrimination in the program's application. Subsection (b) does not list conditions for eligibility (one of the complaints of the southern legislators), but rather lists three conditions that plans may *not* impose, related to age, residency, and citizenship.

◆ Payment to States

Section 3 addresses cost sharing between the federal and state governments in paying for public assistance. The federal government reimburses each state with a qualified plan for one-half of its direct payments in old-age assistance, with an additional 5 percent to defray administrative costs.

◆ Title II—Federal Old-Age Benefits

Old-Age Reserve Account. Section 201 establishes the Old-Age Reserve Account, the pool of funds available to pay to Social Security beneficiaries. The amount of the account is based on assumptions used to calculate the total amount of money needed to provide pension benefits for qualified Americans. These estimates were crucial, as the CES had to calculate how much it would need to collect in taxes. President Roosevelt was adamant that this portion of the program be self-funded.

Subsection (b) dictates that the account funds be invested solely in government bonds or in securities guaranteed by the U.S. government. The reserve account was a remarkably large amount of money to be held for any purpose. As the historian Edward D. Berkowitz notes, "The figure ($47 billion) represented eight times the amount of money then in circulation in the United States; nearly five times the amount of money in savings banks; enough money to buy all the farms in the United States, with $14 billion to spare" (Perkins, p. 281). Thus, it was critical that account funds remain in low-risk securities with high liquidity, such as U.S. Treasury bills and bonds. The Second Liberty Bond Act of 1917, referenced in (b)(2), gives the government authority to issue Treasury securities, guaranteed by the full faith and credit of the United States government.

Old-Age Benefit Payments. The CES argued at length over benefit payments. Should every qualified pensioner receive a lump sum, as had been proposed by Townsend? Or should benefits reflect the employee's wages, with higher wage earners receiving correspondingly higher benefits?

The committee reasoned that even though a level benefit would be easier to administer and in some ways more equitable, that would violate typical American attitudes about work. In the words of Frances Perkins, Americans believed that "a man who works hard, becomes highly skilled, and earns high wages 'deserves' more on retirement than one who had not become a skilled worker" (Kennedy, p. 267). Section 202, the result of the committee's deliberations, details the benefit calculation for Social Security retirement based on income. The benefit formula has changed many times since 1935. In this legislation, a person's total wages (up to the maximum of $45,000) were added together to calculate his or her retirement benefit. Today, Social Security retirement benefits are calculated based on average, not total, wages. The maximum wage base has been adjusted for inflation over the years.

Definitions. Eligibility for Social Security became a highly contested point of discussion among the committee members. Both President Roosevelt and the members of the CES envisioned a system that would cover all Americans—but the realities of financing such a system became all too clear. If the retirement benefits were financed by employee and employer contributions, how could the earliest retirees possibly contribute enough to fund their own looming retirements? The options were to charge this group extremely high tax rates, give them virtually no benefits, or delay the payment of benefits for many years. Roosevelt refused to consider any of these options and would not allow a future liability in the reserve account. If the first group of retirees received their full benefits, however, Social Security would be unable to meet its obligations by as early as 1965. The CES solved this dilemma by reducing the number of people eligible for Social Security and increasing the employment tax rate, thus ensuring benefits for the earliest retirees without jeopardizing the financial status of the entire system.

Treasury Secretary Henry Morgenthau proposed that the program exempt agricultural and domestic workers, and employees in organizations with fewer than ten workers. Despite intense opposition from Frances Perkins, the committee accepted these exemptions, which are reflected in Section 210. Other people not covered by this act are state and federal employees or those employed in the non-profit sector. Subsequent amendments to the Social Security Act of 1935 have removed most of these exemptions.

◆ Title III—Grants to States for Unemployment Compensation Administration

Title III describes the arrangement for financing unemployment insurance through federal matching grants to states with acceptable unemployment insurance plans. Section 303, subsection (a)(4) mentions the Unemployment Trust Fund, described in detail in Section 904. Although the tax-offset arrangement is more clearly discussed in Section 904, this section of Title III indicates that both the federal and state governments will pay funds into the Unemployment Trust Fund; it is not simply a federal grant.

President Franklin D. Roosevelt signs the Social Security Act on August 14, 1935. (AP Photo)

◆ Title IV—Grants to States for Aid to Dependent Children

Similarly to the old-age assistance plan, Title IV allows the federal government to provide financial aid to states with approved plans for helping dependent children. This was a particular problem during the Great Depression, as an increasing number of men abandoned their families when they could no longer find work.

◆ Title V—Grants to States for Maternal and Child Welfare

Part 1—Maternal and Child Health Services. In Edwin Witte's words, Title V is "a revival, increase, and extension of" (p. 165) the Sheppard-Towner Maternity and Infancy Protection Act of 1921, which funded nutritional advice and public health services for expectant mothers. Although it was discontinued in 1929 for political and financial reasons, a number of women's organizations strongly supported the act and successfully lobbied the committee to include what became Title V in the Social Security Act.

Section 502, subsection (a) allocates funds to states in terms of a lump sum ($20,000 per state) and proportional to the number of babies born in a given year. Those states with the highest birthrates (relative to the average for the country) receive the most aid. Unlike other programs, Maternal and Child Health Services fall under the management of the United States Children's Bureau, created in 1912 to foster child health and welfare.

Part 2—Services for Crippled Children. This section was added by the committee primarily because the members thought that Roosevelt, a victim of polio, would be interested in promoting state services in this area.

Part 3—Child Welfare Services. This part of the Social Security Act faced substantial Catholic opposition. Because initially federal funds would match money spent at the state and local level, Catholic representatives worried that federal grants to religious organizations involved in the care of children would violate the separation of church and state. This violation would constitute government meddling in the ways these religious charitable organizations were run.

After negotiations with key representatives from the Catholic community, the committee modified the original language of Title V, particularly Part 3. Parts 1, 2, and 3 did not require federal matching funds or state participation. All of the parts emphasize that services target rural populations; Catholic charities operated primarily in urban areas and so wanted federal aid to focus elsewhere.

Part 4—Vocational Rehabilitation. Section 531 was tacked onto the Social Security Act after Commissioner of Education John W. Studebaker requested that the legislation include an amendment calling for increased funding for vocational training for the disabled. The United States already had such a federal program, created by the National Vocational Rehabilitation Act of 1920, referred to in subsection (a).

◆ Title VI—Public Health Work

Members of the committee drafted this section of the Social Security Act to support the United States Public Health Service. Title VI was particularly popular with southern legislators, whose larger rural populations would benefit from expanded public health services. The medical community embraced increased funding because many doctors believed that it would divert attention from public health insurance. Roosevelt had initially asked the committee to develop plans for a national health care system. As soon as word of this got out to the medical community, physicians throughout the nation sent thousands of letters to Washington opposing any form of government-subsidized health insurance. Faced with such opposition, the Social Security Act did not address the concept of national health care.

◆ Title VII—Social Security Board Establishment

Title VII sets forth the requirements and duties of the Social Security Board. Section 701 prevents any one political party from monopolizing the board.

◆ Title VIII—Taxes with Respect to Employment

Title VIII details the ways in which employers and employees are taxed to collect funds for retirement benefits. Because Roosevelt envisioned a self-funded rather than a government-financed program, the committee considered various options, deciding on a combination of employee and employer contributions. Unemployment insurance would be funded by a payroll tax on employers based on a percentage of their payrolls; this tax would be offset by unemployment taxes paid to the state. Retirement benefits would be financed through contributions from employees as well as employers.

The major question was the tax rate for employers and employees. The original bill sets a rate on both employees and employers of 0.5 percent for five years, gradually increasing the rate to a maximum of 2.5 percent in 1957. However, this meant that the Social Security system would pay out more than it earned until 1957. Some estimated that the fund would develop a deficit by 1965, which would continue to build until 1980. The committee initially envisioned using funds from general tax revenues to make up the difference, but Roosevelt refused to entertain such an option. As a result, Treasury Secretary Morgenthau proposed higher tax rates. Sections 801 and 804 detail the schedule of employee and employer taxes respectively; the rate increases from 1 percent to 3 percent.

Section 803 refers to the Revenue Act of 1934, which modified the nation's income tax structure by increasing the tax rate on estates, corporations, and those with higher incomes.

In an era before computers, the administrative tasks associated with collecting and accounting for Social Security contributions were challenging. Section 802 designates the employer as the party responsible for deducting employee contributions. Section 808, subsection (a) lists a number of other methods for paying taxes; Section 809 discusses a system of stamps issued by post offices. The committee intentionally left the subject of administration open ended in the 1935 act so that the Social Security Board could study European social insurance systems.

Section 811 reiterates the categories of employees (and consequently employers) not covered by the act. One of the negative consequences of this section is that a vast majority of women and African American workers, who typically worked in the excluded jobs, initially were not covered by Social Security.

◆ Title IX—Tax on Employers of Eight or More

Title IX discusses the financing of unemployment benefits. Employers with fewer than eight employees are exempted. Section 901 indicates the tax schedule; the committee considered a system based on employer experience (record of unemployment claims), as used by Wisconsin, but instead agreed on a flat tax rate. Section 902 describes the tax offset, by which unemployment taxes paid to the state may be credited against this federal tax. Section 903 contains some worker protections: Workers do not have to take jobs that will involve strikebreaking, below-market wages, or prevention of unionization.

Unemployment Trust Fund. The language here is similar to that of Title II, Section 201, which describes the Old-Age Reserve Account. Accounting for unemployment contributions and disbursements, however, was more complex, as the act calls for a joint federal and state system of unemployment insurance rather than a single federal program. The committee debated whether to have segregated funds for each employer, or a single fund. Subsection (e) establishes a single fund with separate accounts for each state agency.

Definitions. Section 907 narrows the definitions of *employer*, in subsection (a), and *employee*, in subsection (c).

Allowance of Additional Credit and Conditions of Additional Credit Allowance. Sections 909 and 910 provide an additional tax credit for employment stabilization. The basic idea behind these two sections is that employers who build up substantial unemployment reserves (in other words, paying out fewer unemployment benefits than taxes taken in) should receive a tax credit over and above the one described in Section 902. The employers would receive this credit only if their state plan allowed them to reduce their contribution rate and if there is a verifiable record of employment stability at the facility or company. This provision rewards employers who retain employees yet maintains a safety net in the event the company suffers a setback.

◆ Title X—Grants to States for Aid to the Blind

Title X was a late addition to the Social Security Act. The CES did not specifically study programs for the blind, but several interest groups came forward during congressional committee hearings on the bill. The Senate Finance Committee proposed a blind pension program similar to the old-age pension plan. The advocate Helen Keller lobbied for allocating half the funds to other services, but the Senate committee viewed this as primarily benefiting social workers and retained Title X as a pension program.

Audience

The primary audience for the Social Security Act was Congress. Edwin Witte and the other authors of the document were well aware that the language used was crucial to pleasing both Democrats and Republicans in order to get the bill passed.

Another key audience for the act was the Supreme Court. The committee was not at all sure that the Social Security Act would pass muster with the Court and thus drafted the document to address concerns they believed the Court would have. For example, the committee put the Old-Age Retirement Account and the mechanism for collecting funds for that account into separate sections (Title II and Title VIII, respectively). This was intentional; they had doubts as to whether or not the Court would approve what was, in essence, a federal insurance scheme in which the government collected and paid out premiums. By distancing the taxes from the benefits, the drafters of the document attempted to assuage this potential argument from the Court.

The president was part of the audience as well as an author of the document. The committee had to remain true to Roosevelt's vision, while crafting legislation that would pass the scrutiny of Congress and the Court. The Social Security Act upholds Roosevelt's concept of social insurance financed through worker contributions, not solely through government expenditures. In order to create this balance, the committee had to compromise in other areas, such as worker eligibility. Nevertheless, the document reflects a uniquely American idea of social insurance.

Impact

Immediately after its passage, the Social Security Act became a campaign issue in the 1936 presidential election.

"An act to provide for the general welfare by establishing a system of Federal old-age benefits, and by enabling the several States to make more adequate provision for aged persons, blind persons, dependent and crippled children, maternal and child welfare, public health, and the administration of their unemployment compensation laws; to establish a Social Security Board; to raise revenue; and for other purposes."

(Paragraph 1)

"Every qualified individual (as defined in section 210) shall be entitled to receive, with respect to the period beginning on the date he attains the age of sixty-five, or on January 1, 1942, whichever is the later, and ending on the date of his death, an old-age benefit (payable as nearly as practicable in equal monthly installments)."

(Title II, Section 202 [a])

Although no taxes had been collected or benefits paid, opponents of the program sounded warnings of the consequences such taxes would have on the economy. The Republican presidential candidate Alf Landon used Social Security as a major component of his campaign. He proposed a repeal of the act, arguing that it encouraged deficit spending and government intrusion in people's lives. Landon referred to Social Security as "a fraud on the working-man" which was "unjust, unworkable, stupidly drafted and wastefully financed" (Altman, 103).

Social Security was attacked by the Left as well. Senator Huey Long, claiming that the Democrats had sold out to big business, conducted a filibuster on the floor of the Senate, blocking a vote on funding the Social Security Act in 1935. John W. Davis and Al Smith, two Democrats who had lost presidential bids, formed the American Liberty League in August 1934. Funded by William Randolph Hearst and the DuPont family, the Liberty League sought to defeat Roosevelt; league pamphlets referred to Social Security as "the end of democracy" (Altman, pp. 90–91).

Nevertheless, the program survived and has evolved over the years. The Social Security Act Amendments of 1939 address many early concerns. Benefits were calculated based on average income, not cumulative wages. Coverage was extended to dependent widows, spouses, and children. Following World War II, Social Security expanded dramatically, adding disability coverage; benefits for agricultural service, domestic service, and other previously excluded workers; and Medicare/Medicaid. Fueled by an expanding economy, Social Security benefits emphasized

aid to the less fortunate; private pension plans boomed in the postwar years, easing concerns of middle-class workers.

The Social Security situation changed in 1973. In the midst of the Watergate scandal, a sudden energy crisis, runaway inflation, and growing unemployment, Social Security faced its first deficit. Projections showed a long-term shortfall as the baby boomers (Americans born before 1964) began to retire and pull money out of the fund. Economists began to criticize Social Security as well, arguing for private-sector alternatives and the privatization of Social Security itself. In his February 2005 State of the Union address, President George W. Bush announced that Social Security was "headed toward bankruptcy" and called for major reforms, specifically individual accounts for each worker, in which the employee would make investment decisions. Although they were not enacted, these reforms represent a shift in attitude toward Social Security. Perhaps some Americans today have less faith in the program's ability to deliver, but Roosevelt's vision nevertheless remains a reality for the many Americans who, lacking private individual savings of their own, would be destitute without Social Security.

Related Documents

Agee, James. *Let Us Now Praise Famous Men*. Boston: Houghton Mifflin, 1941. Agee's portrait of southern sharecroppers' plight during the Depression is an excellent literary source for understanding the period.

Bennett, G. H. *Roosevelt's Peacetime Administrations, 1933–41: A Documentary History of the New Deal Years*. Manchester, U.K.: Manchester University Press, 2004. A collection of primary source documents from Roosevelt's presidency, including a sampling of comments by members of his administration.

Long, Huey P. *Every Man a King: The Autobiography of Huey P. Long*. New Orleans: National Book Company, 1933. One of Roosevelt's most strident political enemies offers a different perspective on the 1930s.

McElvaine, Robert S., ed. *Down and Out in the Great Depression: Letters from the "Forgotten Man"*. Chapel Hill: University of North Carolina Press, 1983. This collection of letters sent to the White House during the Depression gives a sense of the state of the nation during the 1930s.

Perkins, Frances. *The Roosevelt I Knew*. New York: Viking, 1946. Perkins offers her own insights into the Roosevelt administration, including the political negotiations involved with creating the Social Security Act as well as her own perspective regarding the creation of America's first social insurance program.

Bibliography

■ Books

Alter, Jonathan. *The Defining Moment: FDR's Hundred Days and the Triumph of Hope*. New York: Simon & Schuster, 2006.

Altman, Nancy J. *The Battle for Social Security: From FDR's Vision to Bush's Gamble*. Hoboken, N.J.: John Wiley & Sons, 2005.

Béland, Daniel. *Social Security: History and Politics from the New Deal to the Privatization Debate*. Lawrence: University Press of Kansas, 2005.

Davis, Kenneth. *FDR: The New Deal Years, 1933–1937*. New York: Random House, 1986.

Dawley, Alan. *Struggles for Justice: Social Responsibility and the Liberal State*. Cambridge, Mass.: Belknap Press of Harvard University Press, 1991.

Edsforth, Ronald. *The New Deal: America's Response to the Great Depression*. Oxford, U.K.: Blackwell Publishers, 2000.

Kennedy, David M. *Freedom from Fear: The American People in Depression and War, 1929–1945*. New York: Oxford University Press, 1999.

Leuchtenburg, William E. *Franklin Roosevelt and the New Deal: 1932–1940*. New York: Harper & Row, 1963.

———. *The FDR Years: On Roosevelt and His Legacy*. New York: Columbia University Press, 1995.

Myers-Lipton, Scott J., ed. *Social Solutions to Poverty: America's Struggle to Build a Just Society*. Boulder, Colo.: Paradigm Publishers, 2006.

Witte, Edwin E. *The Development of the Social Security Act: A Memorandum on the History of the Committee on Economic Security and Drafting and Legislative History of the Social Security Act*. Madison: University of Wisconsin Press, 1962.

■ Web Sites

Bush, George W. "State of the Union Address (February 2, 2005)." The White House Web site.
http://www.whitehouse.gov/news/releases/2005/02/20050202-11.html. Accessed on February 8, 2008.

The Franklin D. Roosevelt Presidential Library and Museum Web site.
http://www.fdrlibrary.marist.edu/index.html. Accessed on July 6, 2007.

"Social Security History." The Social Security Online Web site.
http://www.ssa.gov/history/history.html. Accessed on August 17, 2007.

—By Karen Linkletter

1. Have attitudes about retirement changed from what they were in 1935? Research changes in life expectancy, average retirement age, and other factors that might have an impact. Do we have different expectations with respect to lifestyle today?

2. Roosevelt was adamantly against a system that was "the dole." What would he think of Social Security today? Is the current system true to his vision, or is it something else? Would he modify it, or leave it as is?

3. What do you think will be the next modification to Social Security? Do you think private accounts will be created or that some other type of change will occur?

4. America has a long history of dealing with the conflict between federal and state power. Compare this act with the Constitution, paying special attention to the Tenth Amendment. Why do you think the Supreme Court upheld the Social Security Act?

5. How was unemployment described in American film during the Great Depression? How does it differ from our current view? Evaluate the Charlie Chaplin film *Modern Times* as a product of the 1930s.

Glossary

accrued	increased in value over time
actuarial	relating to statistical calculations for insurance purposes
allotments	shares given
appropriation	budgeted money set aside for a particular purpose
assignable	transferable, in terms of property rights or ownership, by an official act
attachment	legal seizure of people or property
audit	formal examination, correction, and endorsement of financial accounts
bona-fide	authentic
bond	certificate promising repayment of debt
certification	official documentation or evidence as proof of something, such as authenticity
community chest	fund raised by voluntary contributions for local charities and social welfare activities
domiciled	established with a place of residence
duly	properly and suitably
excise tax	tax paid for license, such as to engage in commercial activities
garnishment	a legal summons or warning concerning the taking of property or wages of a debtor to satisfy a debt
indemnified	protected against loss, damage, or liability

in loco parentis	having or taking on the responsibility of a parent when dealing with someone else's child
insolvency	condition of being unable to pay debts
instrumentality	a sub-branch of a department or agency
joint-stock companies	commercial enterprises whose capital is in shares that individual holders may transfer without the consent of the whole body
levy	impose or collect a tax under government authority
obligations	things owed, such as debts of the federal government
par	accepted or average value; the par value of a government security equals its value at issue.
premium	sum of money paid in addition to a normal price
redemption	ending of a financial obligation, such as the government's payment of loans to others in the form of Treasury bonds, notes, or bills
settlement	agreement out of court; payment of bill, debt, or claim
tables of mortality	tables listing life expectancy and death rate for various ages or occupations based on mortality statistics
tenure	appointment or period of appointment
tribunal	law court or judging body

SOCIAL SECURITY ACT

An act to provide for the general welfare by establishing a system of Federal old-age benefits, and by enabling the several States to make more adequate provision for aged persons, blind persons, dependent and crippled children, maternal and child welfare, public health, and the administration of their unemployment compensation laws; to establish a Social Security Board; to raise revenue; and for other purposes.

Be it enacted by the Senate and House of Representatives of the United States of America in Congress assembled,

Title I—Grants to States for Old-Age Assistance Appropriation

SECTION 1. For the purpose of enabling each State to furnish financial assistance, as far as practicable under the conditions in such State, to aged needy individuals, there is hereby authorized to be appropriated for the fiscal year ended June 30, 1936, the sum of $49,750,000, and there is hereby authorized to be appropriated for each fiscal year thereafter a sum sufficient to carry out the purposes of this title. The sums made available under this section shall be used for making payments to States which have submitted, and had approved by the Social Security Board established by Title VII (hereinafter referred to as the Board), State plans for old-age assistance.

◆ State Old-Age Assistance Plans

SEC. 2. (a) A State plan for old-age assistance must

(1) provide that it shall be in effect in all political subdivisions of the State, and, if administered by them, be mandatory upon them;

(2) provide for financial participation by the State;

(3) either provide for the establishment or designation of a single State agency to administer the plan, or provide for the establishment or designation of a single State agency to supervise the administration of the plan;

(4) provide for granting to any individual, whose claim for old-age assistance is denied, an opportunity for a fair hearing before such State agency;

(5) provide such methods of administration (other than those relating to selection, tenure of office, and compensation of personnel) as are found by the Board to be necessary for the efficient operation of the plan;

(6) provide that the State agency will make such reports, in such form and containing such information, as the Board may from time to time require, and comply with such provisions as the Board may from time to time find necessary to assure the correctness and verification of such reports; and

(7) provide that, if the State or any of its political subdivisions collects from the estate of any recipient of old-age assistance any amount with respect to old-age assistance furnished him under the plan, one-half of the net amount so collected shall be promptly paid to the United States. Any payment so made shall be deposited in the Treasury to the credit of the appropriation for the purposes of this title.

(b) The Board shall approve any plan which fulfills the conditions specified in subsection (a), except that it shall not approve any plan which imposes, as a condition of eligibility for old-age assistance under the plan—

(1) An age requirement of more than sixty-five years, except that the plan may impose, effective until January 1, 1940, an age requirement of as much as seventy years; or

(2) Any residence requirement which excludes any resident of the State who has resided therein five years during the nine years immediately preceding the application for old-age assistance and has resided therein continuously for one year immediately preceding the application; or (3) Any citizenship requirement which excludes any citizen of the United States.

Payment to States

SEC. 3. (a) From the sums appropriated therefor, the Secretary of the Treasury shall pay to each State which has an approved plan for old-age assistance, for each quarter, beginning with the quarter commencing July 1, 1935,

(1) an amount, which shall be used exclusively as old-age assistance, equal to one-half of the total of the sums expended during such quarter as old-age assistance under the State plan with respect to each individual who at the time of such expenditure is sixty-five years of age or older and is not an inmate of a public institution, not counting so much of such expenditure with respect to any individual for any month as exceeds $30, and

(2) 5 per centum of such amount, which shall be used for paying the costs of administering the State plan or for old-age assistance, or both, and for no other purpose: Provided, That the State plan, in order to be approved by the Board, need not provide for financial participation before July 1, 1937, by the State, in the case of any State which the Board, upon application by the State and after reasonable notice and opportunity for hearing to the State, finds is prevented by its constitution from providing such financial participation.

(b) The method of computing and paying such amounts shall be as follows:

(1) The Board shall, prior to the beginning of each quarter, estimate the amount to be paid to the State for such quarter under the provisions of clause (1) of subsection (a), such estimate to be based on

(A) a report filed by the State containing its estimate of the total sum to be expended in such quarter in accordance with the provisions of such clause, and stating the amount appropriated or made available by the State and its political subdivisions for such expenditures in such quarter, and if such amount is less than one-half of the total sum of such estimated expenditures, the source or sources from which the difference is expected to be derived,

(B) records showing the number of aged individuals in the State, and

(C) such other investigation as the Board may find necessary.

(2) The Board shall then certify to the Secretary of the Treasury the amount so estimated by the Board, reduced or increased, as the case may be, by any sum by which it finds that its estimate for any prior quarter was greater or less than the amount which should have been paid to the State under clause (1) of subsection (a) for such quarter, except to the extent that such sum has been applied to make the amount certified for any prior quarter greater or less than the amount estimated by the Board for such prior quarter.

(3) The Secretary of the Treasury shall thereupon, through the Division of Disbursement of the Treasury Department and prior to audit or settlement by the General Accounting Office, pay to the State, at the time or times fixed by the Board, the amount so certified, increased by 5 per centum.

Operation of State Plans

SEC. 4. In the case of any State plan for old-age assistance which has been approved by the Board, if the Board, after reasonable notice and opportunity for hearing to the State agency administering or supervising the administration of such plan, finds—

(1) that the plan has been so changed as to impose any age, residence, or citizenship requirement prohibited by section 2 (b), or that in the administration of the plan any such prohibited requirement is imposed, with the knowledge of such State agency, in a substantial number of cases; or

(2) that in the administration of the plan there is a failure to comply substantially with any provision required by section 2 (a) to be included in the plan; the Board shall notify such State agency that further payments will not be made to the State until the Board is satisfied that such prohibited requirement is no longer so imposed, and that there is no longer any such failure to comply. Until it is so satisfied it shall make no further certification to the Secretary of the Treasury with respect to such State.

Administration

SEC. 5. There is hereby authorized to be appropriated for the fiscal year ending June 30, 1936, the sum of $250,000, for all necessary expenses of the Board in administering the provisions of this title.

Definition

SEC. 6. When used in this title the term old age assistance means money payments to aged individuals.

Title II—Federal Old-Age Benefits Old-Age Reserve Account

Section 201. (a) There is hereby created an account in the Treasury of the United States to be known as the Old-Age Reserve Account hereinafter in this title called the Account. There is hereby authorized to be appropriated to the Account for each fiscal year, beginning with the fiscal year ending June 30, 1937, an amount sufficient as an annual premium to provide for the payments required under this title, such amount to be determined on a reserve basis in accordance with accepted actuarial principles, and based upon such tables of mortality as the Secretary of the Treasury shall from time to time adopt, and upon an interest rate of 3 per centum per annum compounded annually. The Secretary of the Treasury shall submit annually to the Bureau of the Budget an estimate of the appropriations to be made to the Account.

(b) It shall be the duty of the Secretary of the Treasury to invest such portion of the amounts credited to the Account as is not, in his judgment, required to meet current withdrawals. Such investment may be made only in interest-bearing obligations of the United States or in obligations guaranteed as to both principal and interest by the United States. For such purpose such obligations may be acquired

(1) on original issue at par, or

(2) by purchase of outstanding obligations at the market price. The purposes for which obligations of the United States may be issued under the Second Liberty Bond Act, as amended, are hereby extended to authorize the issuance at par of special obligations exclusively to the Account. Such special obligations shall bear interest at the rate of 3 per centum per annum. Obligations other than such special obligations may be acquired for the Account only on such terms as to provide an investment yield of not less than 3 per centum per annum.

(c) Any obligations acquired by the Account (except special obligations issued exclusively to the Account) may be sold at the market price, and such special obligations may be redeemed at par plus accrued interest.

(d) The interest on, and the proceeds from the sale or redemption of, any obligations held in the Account shall be credited to and form a part of the Account.

(e) All amounts credited to the Account shall be available for making payments required under this title.

(f) The Secretary of the Treasury shall include in his annual report the actuarial status of the Account.

◆ Old-Age Benefit Payments

SEC. 202. (a) Every qualified individual (as defined in section 210) shall be entitled to receive, with respect to the period beginning on the date he attains the age of sixty-five, or on January 1, 1942, whichever is the later, and ending on the date of his death, an old-age benefit (payable as nearly as practicable in equal monthly installments) as follows:

(1) If the total wages (as defined in section 210) determined by the Board to have been paid to him, with respect to employment (as defined in section 210) after December 31, 1936, and before he attained the age of sixty-five, were not more than $3,000, the old-age benefit shall be at a monthly rate of one-half of 1 per centum of such total wages;

(2) If such total wages were more than $3,000, the old-age benefit shall be at a monthly rate equal to the sum of the following:

(A) One-half of 1 per centum of $3,000; plus

(B) One-twelfth of 1 per centum of the amount by which such total wages exceeded $3,000 and did not exceed $45,000; plus

(C) One-twenty-fourth of 1 per centum of the amount by which such total wages exceeded $45,000.

(b) In no case shall the monthly rate computed under subsection (a) exceed $85.

(c) If the Board finds at any time that more or less than the correct amount has theretofore been paid to any individual under this section, then, under regulations made by the Board, proper adjustments shall be made in connection with subsequent payments under this section to the same individual.

(d) Whenever the Board finds that any qualified individual has received wages with respect to regular employment after he attained the age of sixty-five, the old-age benefit payable to such individual shall be reduced, for each calendar month in any part of which such regular employment occurred, by an amount equal to one month's benefit. Such reduction shall be made, under regulations prescribed by the Board, by deductions from one or more payments of old-age benefit to such individual.

◆ Payments upon Death

SEC. 203. (a) If any individual dies before attaining the age of sixty-five, there shall be paid to his estate an amount equal to 3 per centum of the total wages determined by the Board to have been paid to him, with respect to employment after December 31, 1936.

(b) If the Board finds that the correct amount of the old-age benefit payable to a qualified individual during his life under section 202 was less than 3 per centum of the total wages by which such old-age benefit was measurable, then there shall be paid to his estate a sum equal to the amount, if any, by which such 3 per centum exceeds the amount (whether more or less than the correct amount) paid to him during his life as old-age benefit.

(c) If the Board finds that the total amount paid to a qualified individual under an old-age benefit during his life was less than the correct amount to which he was entitled under section 202, and that the correct amount of such old-age benefit was 3 per centum or more of the total wages by which such old-age benefit was measurable, then there shall be paid to his estate a sum equal to the amount, if any, by which the correct amount of the old-age benefit exceeds the amount which was so paid to him during his life.

◆ Payments to Aged Individuals Not Qualified for Benefits

SEC. 204. (a) There shall be paid in a lump sum to any individual who, upon attaining the age of sixty-five, is not a qualified individual, an amount equal to 3 per centum of the total wages determined by the Board to have been paid to him, with respect to employment after December 31, 1936, and before he attained the age of sixty-five.

(b) After any individual becomes entitled to any payment under subsection (a), no other payment shall be made under this title in any manner measured by wages paid to him, except that any part of any payment under subsection (a) which is not paid to him before his death shall be paid to his estate.

◆ Amounts of $500 or Less Payable to Estates

SEC. 205. If any amount payable to an estate under section 203 or 204 is $500 or less, such amount may, under regulations prescribed by the Board, be paid to the persons found by the Board to be entitled thereto under the law of the State in which the deceased was domiciled, without the necessity of compliance with the requirements of law with respect to the administration of such estate.

◆ Overpayments during Life

SEC. 206. If the Board finds that the total amount paid to a qualified individual under an old-age benefit during his life was more than the correct amount to which he was entitled under section 202, and was 3 per centum or more of the total wages by which such old-age benefit was measurable, then upon his death there shall be repaid to the United States by his estate the amount, if any, by which such total amount paid to him during his life exceeds whichever of the following is the greater:

(1) Such 3 per centum, or

(2) the correct amount to which he was entitled under section 202.

◆ Method of Making Payments

SEC. 207. The Board shall from time to time certify to the Secretary of the Treasury the name and address of each person entitled to receive a payment under this title, the amount of such payment, and the time at which it should be made, and the Secretary of the Treasury through the Division of Disbursement of the Treasury Department, and prior to audit or settlement by the General Accounting Office, shall make payment in accordance with the certification by the Board.

◆ Assignment

SEC. 208. The right of any person to any future payment under this title shall not be transferable or assignable, at law or in equity, and none of the moneys paid or payable or rights existing under this title shall be subject to execution, levy, attachment, garnishment, or other legal process, or to the operation of any bankruptcy or insolvency law.

◆ Penalties

SEC. 209. Whoever in any application for any payment under this title makes any false statement as to any material fact, knowing such statement to be false, shall be fined not more than $1,000 or imprisoned for not more than one year, or both.

◆ Definitions

SEC. 210. When used in this title— (a) The term wages means all remuneration for employment, including the cash value of all remuneration paid in any medium other than cash; except that such term shall not include that part of the remuneration which, after remuneration equal to $3,000 has been paid to an individual by an employer with respect to employment during any calendar year, is paid to such employer with respect to employment during such calendar year.

(b) The term employment means any service, of whatever nature, performed within the United States by an employee for his employer, except—

(1) Agricultural labor;

(2) Domestic service in a private home;

(3) Casual labor not in the course of the employer's trade or business;

(4) Service performed as an officer or member of the crew of a vessel documented under the laws of the United States or of any foreign country;

(5) Service performed in the employ of the United States Government or of an instrumentality of the United States;

(6) Service performed in the employ of a State, a political subdivision thereof, or an instrumentality of one or more States or political subdivisions;

(7) Service performed in the employ of a corporation, community chest, fund, or foundation, organized and operated exclusively for religious, charitable, scientific, literary, or educational purposes, or for the prevention of cruelty to children or animals, no part of the net earnings of which inures to the benefit of any private shareholder or individual.

(c) The term qualified individual means any individual with respect to whom it appears to the satisfaction of the Board that—

(1) He is at least sixty-five years of age; and

(2) The total amount of wages paid to him, with respect to employment after December 31, 1936, and before he attained the age of sixty-five, was not less than $2,000; and

(3) Wages were paid to him, with respect to employment on some five days after December 31, 1936, and before he attained the age of sixty-five, each day being in a different calendar year.

Title III—Grants to States for Unemployment Compensation Administration Appropriation

SECTION 301. For the purpose of assisting the States in the administration of their unemployment compensation laws, there is hereby authorized to be appropriated, for the fiscal year ending June 30, 1936, the sum of $4,000,000, and for each fiscal year thereafter the sum of $49,000,000, to be used as hereinafter provided.

◆ Payments to States

SEC. 302. (a) The Board shall from time to time certify to the Secretary of the Treasury for payment to each State which has an unemployment compensation law approved by the Board under Title IX, such amounts as the Board determines to be necessary for the proper administration of such law during the fiscal year in which such payment is to be made. The Board's determination shall be based on

(1) the population of the State;

(2) an estimate of the number of persons covered by the State law and of the cost of proper administration of such law; and

(3) such other factors as the Board finds relevant. The Board shall not certify for payment under this section in any fiscal year a total amount in excess of the amount appropriated therefore for such fiscal year.

(b) Out of the sums appropriated therefor, the Secretary of the Treasury shall, upon receiving a certification under subsection

(a), pay, through the Division of Disbursement of the Treasury Department and prior to audit or settlement by the General Accounting Office, to the State agency charged with the administration of such law the amount so certified.

◆ Provisions of State Laws

SEC. 303. (a) The Board shall make no certification for payment to any State unless it finds that the law of such State, approved by the Board under Title IX, includes provisions for—

(1) Such methods of administration (other than those relating to selection, tenure of office, and compensation of personnel) as are found by the Board to be reasonably calculated to insure full payment of unemployment compensation when due; and

(2) Payment of unemployment compensation solely through public employment offices in the State or such other agencies as the Board may approve; and

(3) Opportunity for a fair hearing, before an impartial tribunal, for all individuals whose claims for unemployment compensation are denied; and

(4) The payment of all money received in the unemployment fund of such State, immediately upon such receipt, to the Secretary of the Treasury to the credit of the Unemployment Trust Fund established by section 904; and

(5) Expenditure of all money requisitioned by the State agency from the Unemployment Trust Fund, in the payment of unemployment compensation, exclusive of expenses of administration; and

(6) The making of such reports, in such form and containing such information, as the Board may from time to time require, and compliance with such provisions as the Board may from time to time find necessary to assure the correctness and verification of such reports; and

(7) Making available upon request to any agency of the United States charged with the administration of public works or assistance through public employment, the name, address, ordinary occupation, and employment status of each recipient of unemployment compensation, and a statement of such recipient's rights to further compensation under such law.

(b) Whenever the Board, after reasonable notice and opportunity for hearing to the State agency charged with the administration of the State law finds that in the administration of the law there is—

(1) a denial, in a substantial number of cases, of unemployment compensation to individuals entitled thereto under such law; or

(2) a failure to comply substantially with any provision specified in subsection (a); the Board shall notify such State agency that further payments will not be made to the State until the Board is satisfied that there is no longer any such denial or failure to comply. Until it is so satisfied it shall make no further certification to the Secretary of the Treasury with respect to such State.

Title IV—Grants to States for Aid to Dependent Children Appropriation

SECTION 401. For the purpose of enabling each State to furnish financial assistance, as far as practicable under the conditions in such State, to needy dependent children, there is hereby authorized to be appropriated for the fiscal year ending June 30, 1936, the sum of $24,750,000, and there is hereby authorized to be appropriated for each fiscal year thereafter a sum sufficient to carry out the purposes of this title. The sums made available under this section shall be used for making payments to States which have submitted, and had approved by the Board, State plans for aid to dependent children.

♦ State Plans for Aid to Dependent Children

SEC. 402. (a) A State plan for aid to dependent children must

(1) provide that it shall be in effect in all political subdivisions of the State, and, if administered by them, be mandatory upon them;

(2) provide for financial participation by the State;

(3) either provide for the establishment or designation of a single State agency to administer the plan, or provide for the establishment or designation of a single State agency to supervise the administration of the plan;

(4) provide for granting to any individual, whose claim with respect to aid to a dependent child is denied, an opportunity for a fair hearing before such State agency;

(5) provide such methods of administration (other than those relating to selection, tenure of office, and

compensation of personnel) as are found by the Board to be necessary for the efficient operation of the plan; and

(6) provide that the State agency will make such reports, in such form and containing such information, as the Board may from time to time require, and comply with such provisions as the Board may from time to time find necessary to assure the correctness and verification of such reports.

(b) The Board shall approve any plan which fulfills the conditions specified in subsection (a) except that it shall not approve any plan which imposes as a condition of eligibility for aid to dependent children, a residence requirement which denies aid with respect to any child residing in the State

(1) who has resided in the State for one year immediately preceding the application for such aid or

(2) who was born within the State within one year immediately preceding the application, if its mother has resided in the State for one year immediately preceding the birth.

♦ Payment to States

SEC. 403. (a) From the sums appropriated therefor, the Secretary of the Treasury shall pay to each State which has an approved plan for aid to dependent children, for each quarter, beginning with the quarter commencing July 1, 1935, an amount, which shall be used exclusively for carrying out the State plan, equal to one-third of the total of the sums expended during such quarter under such plan, not counting so much of such expenditure with respect to any dependent child for any month as exceeds $18, or if there is more than one dependent child in the same home, as exceeds $18 for any month with respect to one such dependent child and $12 for such month with respect to each of the other dependent children.

(b) The method of computing and paying such amounts shall be as follows:

(1) The Board shall, prior to the beginning of each quarter, estimate the amount to be paid to the State for such quarter under the provisions of subsection

(a), such estimate to be based on

(A) a report filed by the State containing its estimate of the total sum to be expended in such quarter in accordance with the provisions of such subsection and stating the amount appropriated or made available by the State and its political subdivisions for such expenditures in such quarter, and if such amount is less than two-thirds of the total sum of such estimated expenditures, the source or sources from which the difference is expected to be derived,

(B) records showing the number of dependent children in the State, and

(C) such other investigation as the Board may find necessary.

(2) The Board shall then certify to the Secretary of the Treasury the amount so estimated by the Board, reduced or increased, as the case may be, by any sum by which it finds that its estimate for any prior quarter was greater or less than the amount which should have been paid to the State for such quarter, except to the extent that such sum has been applied to make the amount certified for any prior quarter greater or less than the amount estimated by the Board for such prior quarter.

(3) The Secretary of the Treasury shall thereupon, through the Division of Disbursement of the Treasury Department and prior to audit or settlement by the General Accounting Office, pay to the State, at the time or times fixed by the Board, the amount so certified.

◆ **Operation of State Plans**

SEC. 404. In the case of any State plan for aid to dependent children which has been approved by the Board, if the Board, after reasonable notice and opportunity for hearing to the State agency administering or supervising the administration of such plan, finds—

(1) that the plan has been so changed as to impose any residence requirement prohibited by section 402 (b), or that in the administration of the plan any such prohibited requirement is imposed, with the knowledge of such State agency, in a substantial number of cases; or

(2) that in the administration of the plan there is a failure to comply substantially with any provision required by section 402 (a) to be included in the plan; the Board shall notify such State agency that further payments will not be made to the State until the Board is satisfied that such prohibited requirement is no longer so imposed, and that there is no longer any such failure to comply. Until it is so satisfied it shall make no further certification to the Secretary of the Treasury with respect to such State.

◆ **Administration**

SEC. 405. There is hereby authorized to be appropriated for the fiscal year ending June 30, 1936, the sum of $250,000 for all necessary expenses of the Board in administering the provisions of this title.

◆ **Definitions**

SEC. 406. When used in this title—

(a) The term dependent child means a child under the age of sixteen who has been deprived of parental support or care by reason of the death, continued absence from the home, or physical or mental incapacity of a parent, and who is living with his father, mother, grandfather, grandmother, brother, sister, stepfather, stepmother, stepbrother, stepsister, uncle, or aunt, in a place of residence maintained by one or more of such relatives as his or their own home;

(b) The term aid to dependent children means money payments with respect to a dependent child or dependent children.

Title V—Grants to States for Maternal and Child Welfare

◆ **Part 1—Maternal and Child Health Services**
Appropriation

SECTION 501. For the purpose of enabling each State to extend and improve, as far as practicable under the conditions in such State, services for promoting the health of mothers and children, especially in rural areas and in areas suffering from severe economic distress, there is hereby authorized to be appropriated for each fiscal year, beginning with the fiscal year ending June 30, 1936, the sum of $3,800,000. The sums made available under this section shall be used for making payments to States which have submitted, and had approved by the Chief of the Children's Bureau, State plans for such services.

Allotments to States

SEC. 502. (a) Out of the sums appropriated pursuant to section 501 for each fiscal year the Secretary of Labor shall allot to each State $20,000, and such part of $1,800,000 as he finds that the number of live births in such State bore to the total number of live births in the United States, in the latest calendar year for which the Bureau of the Census has available statistics.

(b) Out of the sums appropriated pursuant to section 501 for each fiscal year the Secretary of Labor shall allot to the States $980,000 (in addition to the allotments made under subsection (a)), according to the financial need of each State for assistance in carrying out its State plan, as determined by him after taking into consideration the number of live births in such State.

(c) The amount of any allotment to a State under subsection (a) for any fiscal year remaining unpaid to such State at the end of such fiscal year shall be available for payment to such State under section 504 until the end of the second succeeding fiscal year. No payment to a State under section 504 shall be made out of its allotment for any fiscal year until its allotment for the preceding fiscal year has been exhausted or has ceased to be available.

Approval of State Plans

SEC. 503. (a) A State plan for maternal and child-health services must (1) provide for financial participation by the State;

(2) provide for the administration of the plan by the State health agency or the supervision of the administration of the plan by the State health agency;

(3) provide such methods of administration (other than those relating to selection, tenure of office, and compensation of personnel) as are necessary for the efficient operation of the plan;

(4) provide that the State health agency will make such reports, in such form and containing such information, as the Secretary of Labor may from time to time require, and comply with such provisions as he may from time to time find necessary to assure the correctness and verification of such reports;

(5) provide for the extension and improvement of local maternal and child-health services administered by local child health units;

(6) provide for cooperation with medical, nursing, and welfare groups and organizations; and

(7) provide for the development of demonstration services in needy areas and among groups in special need.

(b) The Chief of the Children's Bureau shall approve any plan which fulfills the conditions specified in subsection (a) and shall thereupon notify the Secretary of Labor and the State health agency of his approval.

Payment to States

SEC. 504. (a) From the sums appropriate therefore and the allotments available under section 502 (a), the Secretary of the Treasury shall pay to each State which has an approved plan for maternal and child-health services, for each quarter beginning with the quarter commencing July 1935, an amount, which shall be used exclusively for carrying out the State plan, equal to one-half of the total sum expended during such quarter for carrying out such plan.

(b) The method of computing and paying such amounts shall be as follows:

(1) The Secretary of Labor shall, prior the beginning of each quarter, estimate the amount to be paid to the State for such quarter under the provisions of subsection (a), such estimate to be based on

(A) a report filed by the State containing its estimate of the total sum to be expended in such quarter in accordance with the provisions of such subsection and stating the amount appropriated or made available by the State and its political subdivisions for such expenditures in such quarter, and if such amount is less than one-half of the total sum of such estimated expenditures, the source or sources from which the difference is expected to be derived, and

(B) such investigation as he may find necessary.

(2) The Secretary of Labor shall then certify the amount so estimated by him to the Secretary of the Treasury, reduced or increased, as the case may be, by any sum by which the Secretary of Labor finds that his estimate for any prior quarter was greater or less than the amount, which should have been paid to the State for such quarter, except to the extent that such sum has been applied to make the amount certified for any prior quarter greater or less than the amount, estimated by the Secretary of Labor for such prior quarter.

(3) The Secretary of the Treasury shall thereupon, through the Division of Disbursement of the Treasury Department and prior to audit or settlement by the General Accounting Office, pay to the State, at the time or times fixed by the Secretary of Labor, the amount so certified.

(c) The Secretary of Labor shall from time to time certify to the Secretary of the Treasury the amounts to be paid to the States from the allotments available under section 502 (b), and the Secretary of the Treasury shall, through the Division of Disbursement of the Treasury Department and prior to audit or settlement by the General Accounting Office, make payments of such amounts from such allotments at the time or times specified by the Secretary of Labor.

Operation of State Plans

SEC. 505. In the case of any State plan for maternal and child-health services which has been approved by the Chief of the Children's Bureau, if the Secretary of Labor, after reasonable notice and opportunity for hearing to the State agency administering or supervising the administration of such plan, finds that in the administration of the plan there is a failure to comply substantially with any provision required by section 503 to be included in the plan, he shall notify such

State agency that further payments will not be made to the State until he is satisfied that there is no longer any such failure to comply. Until he is so satisfied he shall make no further certification to the Secretary of the Treasury with respect to such State.

◆ Part 2—Services for Crippled Children
Appropriation
SEC. 511. For the purpose of enabling each State to extend and improve (especially in rural areas and in areas suffering from severe economic distress), as far as practicable under the conditions in such State, services for locating crippled children and for providing medical, surgical, corrective, and other services and care, and facilities for diagnosis, hospitalization, and aftercare, for children who are crippled or who are suffering from conditions which lead to crippling, there is hereby authorized to be appropriated for each fiscal year beginning with the fiscal year ending June 30, 1936, the sum of $2,850,000. The sums made available under this section shall be used for making payments to States which have submitted, and had approved by the Chief of the Children's Bureau, State plans for such services.

Allotments to States
SEC. 512. (a) Out of the sums appropriated pursuant to section 511 for each fiscal year the Secretary of Labor shall allot to each State $20,000, and the remainder to the States according to the need of each State as determined by him after taking into consideration the number of crippled children in such State in need of the services referred to section 511 and the cost of furnishing such service to them

(b) The amount of any allotment to a State under subsection (a) for any fiscal year remaining unpaid to such State at the end of such fiscal year shall be available for payment to such State under section 514 until the end of the second succeeding fiscal year. No payment to a State under section 514 shall be made out of its allotment for any fiscal year until its allotment for the preceding fiscal year has been exhausted or has ceased to be available.

Approval of State Plans
SEC. 513. (a) A State plan for services for crippled children must

(1) provide for financial participation by the State;

(2) provide for the administration of the plan by a State agency or the supervision of the administration of the plan by a State agency;

(3) provide such methods of administration (other than those relating to selection, tenure of office, and compensation of personnel) as are necessary for the efficient operation of the plan;

(4) provide that the State agency will make such reports, in such form and containing such information, as the Secretary of Labor may from time to time require, and comply with such provisions as he may from time to time find necessary to assure the correctness and verification of such reports;

(5) provide for carrying out the purposes specified in section 511; and

(6) provide for cooperation with medical, health, nursing, and welfare groups and organizations and with any agency in such State charged with administering State laws providing for vocational rehabilitation of physically handicapped children.

(b) The Chief of the Children's Bureau shall approve any plan which fulfills the conditions specified in subsection (a) and shall thereupon notify the Secretary of Labor and the State agency of his approval.

Payment to States
SEC. 514. (a) From the sums appropriated therefore and the allotments available under section 512, the Secretary of the Treasury shall pay to each State which has an approved plan for services for crippled children, for each quarter, beginning the quarter commencing July 1, 1935, an amount which shall be used exclusively for carrying out the State plan, equal to one-half of the total sum expended during such quarter for carrying out such plan.

(b) The method of computing and paying such amounts shall be as follows:

(1) The Secretary of Labor shall, prior the beginning of each quarter, estimate the amount to be paid to the State for such quarter under the provisions of subsection (a), such estimate to be based on

(A) a report filed by the State containing its estimate of the total sum to be expended in such quarter in accordance with the provisions of such subsection and stating the amount appropriated or made available by the State and its political subdivisions for such expenditures in such quarter and if such amount is less than one-half of the total sum of such estimated expenditures the source or sources from which the difference is expected to be derived, and

(B) such investigation as he may find necessary.

(2) The Secretary of Labor shall then certify the amount so estimated by him to the Secretary of the Treasury, reduced or increased as the case may be, by any sum by which the Secretary of Labor finds that his estimate for any prior quarter was greater or less than the amount which should have been paid to the State

for such quarter, except to the extent that such sum has been applied to make the amount certified for any prior quarter greater or less than the amount estimated by the Secretary of Labor for such prior quarter.

(3) The Secretary of the Treasury shall thereupon, through the Division of Disbursement of the Treasury Department and prior to audit or settlement by the General Accounting Office, pay to the State, at the time or times fixed by the Secretary of Labor, the amount so certified.

Operation of State Plans

SEC. 515. In the case of any State plan for services for crippled children which has been approved by the Chief of the Children's Bureau, if the Secretary of Labor, after reasonable notice and opportunity for hearing to the State agency administering or supervising the administration of such plan finds that in the administration of the plan there a failure to comply substantially with any provision required by section 513 to be included in the plan, he shall notify such State agency that further payments will not be made to the State until he is satisfied that there is no longer any such failure to comply. Until he is so satisfied he shall make no further certification to the Secretary of the Treasury with respect to such State.

◆ Part 3—Child Welfare Services

SEC. 521. (a) For the purpose of enabling the United States, through the Children's Bureau, to cooperate with State public-welfare agencies establishing, extending, and strengthening, especially in predominantly rural areas, public-welfare services (hereinafter in this section referred to as child-welfare services) for the protection and care of homeless, dependent, and neglected children, and children in danger of becoming delinquent, there is hereby authorized to be appropriated for each fiscal year, beginning with the year ending June 30, 1936, the sum of $1,500,000. Such amount shall be allotted by the Secretary of Labor for use by cooperating State public-welfare agencies on the basis of plans developed jointly by the State agency and the Children's Bureau, to each State, $10,000, and the remainder to each State on the basis of such plans, not to exceed such part of the remainder as the rural population of such State bears to the total rural population of the United States. The amount so allotted shall be expended for payment of part of the cost of district, county or other local child-welfare services in areas predominantly rural, and for developing State services for the encouragement and assistance of adequate methods of community

child-welfare organization in areas predominantly rural and other areas of special need. The amount of any allotment to a State under this section for any fiscal year remaining unpaid to such State at the end of such fiscal year shall be available for payment to such State under this section until the end of the second succeeding fiscal year. No payment to a State under this section shall be made out of its allotment for any fiscal year until its allotment for the preceding fiscal year has been exhausted or has ceased to be available.

(b) From the sums appropriated therefore and the allotments available under subsection (a) the Secretary of Labor shall from time to time certify to the Secretary of the Treasury the amounts to be paid to the States, and the Secretary of the Treasury shall, through the Division of Disbursement of the Treasury Department and prior to audit or settlement by the General Accounting Office, make payments of such amounts from such allotments at the time or times specified by the Secretary of Labor.

◆ Part 4—Vocational Rehabilitation

SEC. 531. (a) In order to enable the United States to cooperate with the States and Hawaii in extending and strengthening their programs of vocational rehabilitation of the physically disabled, and to continue to carry out the provisions and purposes of the Act entitled An Act to provide for the promotion of vocational rehabilitation of persons disabled in industry or otherwise and their return to civil employment, approved June 2, 1920, as amended (U.S.C., title 29, ch. 4; U.S.C., Supp. VII title 29, secs. 31, 32, 34, 35, 37, 39, and 40), there is hereby authorized to be appropriated for the fiscal years ending June 30, 1936, and June 30, 1937, the sum of $841,000 for each such fiscal year in addition to the amount of the existing authorization, and for each fiscal year thereafter the sum of $1,938,000. Of the sums appropriated pursuant to such authorization for each fiscal year, $5,000 shall be apportioned to the Territory of Hawaii and the remainder shall be apportioned among the several States in the manner provided in such Act of June 2, 1920, as amended.

(b) For the administration of such Act of June 2, 1920, as amended, by the Federal agency authorized to administer it, there is hereby authorized to be appropriated for the fiscal years ending June 30, 1936, and June 30, 1937, the sum of $22,000 for each such fiscal year in addition to the amount of the existing authorization, and for each fiscal year thereafter the sum of $102,000.

Part 5—Administration

SEC. 541. (a) There is hereby authorized to be appropriated for the fiscal year ending June 30, 1936, the sum of $425,000, for all necessary expenses of the Children's Bureau in administering the provisions of this title, except section 531.

(b) The Children's Bureau shall make such studies and investigations as will promote the efficient administration of this title, except section 531.

(c) The Secretary of Labor shall include in his annual report to Congress a full account of the administration of this title, except section 531.

Title VI—Public Health Work Appropriation

SECTION 601. For the purpose of assisting States, counties, health districts, and other political subdivisions of the States in establishing and maintaining adequate public-health services, including the training of personnel for State and local health work, there is hereby authorized to be appropriated for each fiscal year, beginning with the fiscal year ending June 30, 1936, the sum of $8,000,000 to be used as hereinafter provided.

State And Local Public Health Services

SEC. 602. (a) The Surgeon General of the Public Health Service, with the approval of the Secretary of the Treasury, shall, at the beginning of each fiscal year, allot to the States the total of (1) the amount appropriated for such year pursuant to section 601; and (2) the amounts of the allotments under this section for the preceding fiscal year remaining unpaid to the States at the end of such fiscal year. The amounts of such allotments shall be determined on the basis of (1) the population; (2) the special health problems; and

(3) the financial needs; of the respective States. Upon making such allotments the Surgeon General of the Public Health Service shall certify the amounts thereof to the Secretary of the Treasury.

(b) The amount of an allotment to any State under subsection (a) for any fiscal year, remaining unpaid at the end of such fiscal year, shall be available for allotment to States under subsection (a) for the succeeding fiscal year, in addition to the amount appropriated for such year.

(c) Prior to the beginning of each quarter of the fiscal year, the Surgeon General of the Public Health Service shall, with the approval of the Secretary of the Treasury, determine in accordance with rules and regulations previously prescribed by such Surgeon General after consultation with a conference of the State and Territorial health authorities, the amount to be paid to each State for such quarter from the allotment to such State, and shall certify the amount so determined to the Secretary of the Treasury. Upon receipt of such certification, the Secretary of the Treasury shall, through the Division of Disbursement of the Treasury Department and prior to audit or settlement by the General Accounting Office, pay in accordance with such certification.

(d) The moneys so paid to any State shall be expended solely in carrying out the purposes specified in section 601, and in accordance with plans presented by the health authority of such State and approved by the Surgeon General of the Public Health Service.

Investigations

SEC. 603. (a) There is hereby authorized to be appropriated for each fiscal year, beginning with the fiscal year ending June 30, 1936, the sum of $2,000,000 for expenditure by the Public Health Service for investigation of disease and problems of sanitation (including the printing and binding of the findings of such investigations), and for the pay and allowances and traveling expenses of personnel of the Public Health Service, including commissioned officers, engaged in such investigations or detailed to cooperate with the health authorities of any State in carrying out the purposes specified in section 601: Provided, That no personnel of the Public Health Service shall be detailed to cooperate with the health authorities of any State except at the request of the proper authorities of such State.

(b) The personnel of the Public Health Service paid from any appropriation not made pursuant to subsection (a) may be detailed to assist in carrying out the purposes of this title. The appropriation from which they are paid shall be reimbursed from the appropriation made pursuant to subsection (a) to the extent of their salaries and allowances for services performed while so detailed.

(c) The Secretary of the Treasury shall include in his annual report to Congress a full account of the administration of this title.

Title VII—Social Security Board Establishment

SECTION 701. There is hereby established a Social Security Board (in this Act referred to as the

Board) to be composed of three members to be appointed by the President, by and with the advice and consent of the Senate. During his term of membership on the Board, no member shall engage in any other business, vocation, or employment. Not more than two of the members of the Board shall be members of the same political party. Each member shall receive a salary at the rate of $10,000 a year and shall hold office for a term of six years, except that

(1) any member appointed to fill a vacancy occurring prior to the expiration of the term for which his predecessor was appointed, shall be appointed for the remainder of such term; and

(2) the terms of office of the members first taking office after the date of the enactment of this Act shall expire, as designated by the President at the time of appointment, one at the end of two years, one at the end of four years, and one at the end of six years, after the date of the enactment of this Act. The President shall designate one of the members as the chairman of the Board.

◆ Duties of the Social Security Board

SEC. 702. The Board shall perform the duties imposed upon it by this Act and shall also have the duty of studying and making recommendations as to the most effective methods of providing economic security through social insurance, and as to legislation and matters of administrative policy concerning old-age pensions, unemployment compensation, accident compensation, and related subjects.

◆ Expenses of the Board

SEC. 703. The Board is authorized to appoint and fix the compensation of such officers and employees, and to make such expenditures, as may be necessary for carrying out its functions under this Act. Appointments of attorneys and experts may be made without regard to the civil-service laws.

◆ Reports

SEC. 704. The Board shall make a full report to Congress, at the beginning of each regular session, of the administration of the functions with which it is charged.

Title VIII—Taxes with Respect to Employment

◆ Income Tax on Employees

SECTION 801. In addition to other taxes, there shall be levied, collected, and paid upon the income of every individual a tax equal to the following percentages of the wages (as defined in section 811) received by him after December 31, 1936, with respect to employment (as defined in section 811) after such date:

(1) With respect to employment during the calendar years 1937, 1938, and 1939, the rate shall be 1 per centum.

(2) With respect to employment during the calendar years 1940, 1941, and 1942, the rate shall be 1 per centum.

(3) With respect to employment during the calendar years 1943, 1944, and 1945, the rate shall be 2 per centum.

(4) With respect to employment during the calendar years 1946, 1947, and 1948, the rate shall be 2 per centum.

(5) With respect to employment after December 31, 1948, the rate shall be 3 per centum.

◆ Deduction of Tax from Wages

SEC. 802. (a) The tax imposed by section 801 shall be collected by the employer of the taxpayer by deducting the amount of the tax from the wages as and when paid. Every employer required so to deduct the tax is hereby made liable for the payment of such tax, and is hereby indemnified against the claims and demands of any person for the amount of any such payment made by such employer.

(b) If more or less than the correct amount of tax imposed by section 801 is paid with respect to any wage payment, then, under regulations made under this title, proper adjustments, with respect both to the tax and the amount to be deducted, shall be made, without interest, in connection with subsequent wage payments to the same individual by the same employer.

◆ Deductibility from Income Tax

SEC. 803. For the purposes of the income tax imposed by Title I of the Revenue Act of 1934 or by any Act of Congress in substitution therefor, the tax imposed by section 801 shall not be allowed as a deduction to the taxpayer in computing his net income for the year in which such tax is deducted from his wages.

◆ Excise Tax on Employers

SEC. 804. In addition to other taxes, every employer shall pay an excise tax, with respect to having individuals in his employ, equal to the following percentages of the wages (as defined in section 811)

paid by him after December 31, 1936, with respect to employment (as defined in section 811) after such date:

(1) With respect to employment during the calendar years 1937, 1938, and 1939, the rate shall be 1 per centum.

(2) With respect to employment during the calendar years 1940, 1941, and 1942, the rate shall be 1 per centum.

(3) With respect to employment during the calendar years 1943, 1944, and 1945, the rate shall be 2 per centum.

(4) With respect to employment during the calendar years 1946, 1947, and 1948, the rate shall be 2 per centum.

(5) With respect to employment after December 31, 1948, the rate shall be 3 per centum.

◆ Adjustment of Employers Tax

SEC. 805. If more or less than the correct amount of tax imposed by section 804 is paid with respect to any wage payment, then, under regulations made under this title, proper adjustments with respect the tax shall be made, without interest, in connection with subsequent wage payments to the same individual by the same employer.

◆ Refunds and Deficiencies

SEC. 806. If more or less than the correct amount of tax imposed by section 801 or 804 is paid or deducted with respect to any wage payment and the overpayment or underpayment of tax cannot be adjusted under section 802 (b) or 805 the amount of the overpayment shall be refunded and the amount of the underpayment shall be collected in such manner and at such times (subject to the statutes of limitations properly applicable thereto) as may be prescribed by regulations made under this title.

◆ Collection and Payment of Taxes

SEC. 807. (a) The taxes imposed by this title shall be collected by the Bureau of Internal Revenue under the direction of the Secretary of the Treasury and shall be paid into the Treasury of the United States as internal-revenue collections. If the tax is not paid when due, there shall be added as part of the tax interest (except in the case of adjustments made in accordance with the provisions of sections 802 (b) and 805) at the rate of one-half of 1 per centum per month from the date the tax became due until paid.

(b) Such taxes shall be collected and paid in such manner, at such times, and under such conditions,

not inconsistent with this title (either by making and filing returns, or by stamps, coupons, tickets, books, or other reasonable devices or methods necessary or helpful in securing a complete and proper collection and payment of the tax or in securing proper identification of the taxpayer), as may be prescribed by the Commissioner of Internal Revenue, with the approval of the Secretary of the Treasury.

(c) All provisions of law, including penalties, applicable with respect to any tax imposed by section 600 or section 800 of the Revenue Act of 1926 and the provisions of section 607 of the Revenue Act of 1934, shall, insofar as applicable and not inconsistent with the provisions of this title, be applicable with respect to the taxes imposed by this title.

(d) In the payment of any tax under this title a fractional part of a cent shall be disregarded unless it amounts to one-half cent or more, in which case it shall be increased to 1 cent.

◆ Rules and Regulations

SEC. 808. The Commissioner of Internal Revenue, with the approval of the Secretary of the Treasury, shall make and publish rules and regulations for the enforcement of this title.

◆ Sale of Stamps by Postmasters

SEC. 809. The Commissioner of Internal Revenue shall furnish to the Postmaster General without prepayment a suitable quantity of stamps, coupons, tickets, books, or other devices prescribed by the Commissioner under section 807 for the collection or payment of any tax imposed by this title, to be distributed to, and kept on sale by, all post offices of the first and second classes, and such post offices of the third and fourth classes as

(1) are located in county seats, or

(2) are certified by the Secretary of the Treasury to the Postmaster General as necessary to the proper administration of this title. The Postmaster General may require each such postmaster to furnish bond in such increased amount as he may from time to time determine, and each such postmaster shall deposit the receipts from the sale of such stamps, coupons, tickets, books, or other devices, to the credit of, and render accounts to, the Postmaster General at such times and in such form as the Postmaster General may by regulations prescribe. The Postmaster General shall at least once a month transfer to the Treasury, as internal-revenue collections all receipts so deposited together with a statement of the additional expenditures in the District of Colum-

bia and elsewhere incurred by the Post Office Department in performing the duties imposed upon said Department by this Act, and the Secretary of the Treasury is hereby authorized and directed to advance from time to time to the credit of the Post Office Department from appropriations made for the collection of the taxes imposed by this title, such sums as may be required for such additional expenditures incurred by the Post Office Department.

◆ Penalties

SEC. 810. (a) Whoever buys, sells, offers for sale, uses, transfers, takes or gives in exchange, or pledges or gives in pledge, except as authorized in this title or in regulations made pursuant thereto, any stamp, coupon, ticket, book, or other device, prescribed by the Commissioner of Internal Revenue under section 807 for the collection or payment of any tax imposed by this title, shall be fined not more than $1,000 or imprisoned for not more than six months, or both.

(b) Whoever, with intent to defraud, alters, forges, makes, or counterfeits any stamp, coupon, ticket, book, or other device prescribed by the Commissioner of Internal Revenue under section 807 for the collection or payment of any tax imposed by this title, or uses, sells, lends, or has in his possession any such altered, forged, or counterfeited stamp, coupon, ticket, book, or other device, or makes, uses, sells, or has in his possession any material in imitation of the material used in the manufacture of such stamp, coupon, ticket, book, or other device, shall be fined not more than $5,000 or imprisoned not more than five years, or both.

◆ Definitions

SEC. 811. When used in this title— (a) The term wages means all remuneration for employment, including the cash value of all remuneration paid in any medium other than cash; except that such term shall not include that part of the remuneration which, after remuneration equal to $3,000 has been paid to an individual by an employer with respect to employment during any calendar year, is paid to such individual by such employer with respect to employment during such calendar year.

(b) The term employment means any service, of whatever nature, performed within the United States by an employee for his employer, except—

(1) Agricultural labor;

(2) Domestic service in a private home;

(3) Casual labor not in the course of the employer's trade or business;

(4) Service performed by an individual who has attained the age of sixty-five;

(5) Service performed as an officer or member of the crew of a vessel documented under the laws of the United States or of any foreign country;

(6) Service performed in the employ of the United States Government or of an instrumentality of the United States;

(7) Service performed in the employ of a State, a political subdivision thereof, or an instrumentality of one or more States or political subdivisions;

(8) Service performed in the employ of a corporation, community chest, fund, or foundation, organized and operated exclusively for religious, charitable, scientific, literary, or educational purposes, or for the prevention of cruelty to children or animals, no part of the net earnings of which inures to the benefit of any private shareholder or individual.

Title IX—Tax on Employers of Eight or More

◆ Imposition of Tax

SECTION 901. On and after January 1, 1936, every employer (as defined in section 907) shall pay for each calendar year an excise tax, with respect to having individuals in his employ, equal to the following percentages of the total wages (as defined in section 907) payable by him (regardless of the time of payment) with respect to employment (as defined in section 907) during such calendar year:

(1) With respect to employment during the calendar year 1936 the rate shall be 1 per centum;

(2) With respect to employment during the calendar year 1937 the rate shall be 2 per centum;

(3) With respect to employment after December 31, 1937, the rate shall be 3 per centum.

◆ Credit against Tax

SEC. 902. The taxpayer may credit against the tax imposed by section 901 the amount of contributions, with respect to employment during the taxable year, paid by him (before the date of filing of his return for the taxable year) into an unemployment fund under a State law. The total credit allowed to a taxpayer under this section for all contributions paid into unemployment funds with respect to employment during such taxable year shall not exceed 90 per centum of the tax against which it is credited, and credit shall be allowed only for contributions made under the laws of States certified for the taxable year as provided in section 903.

◆ Certification of State Laws

SEC. 903 (a) The Social Security Board shall approve any State law submitted to it, within thirty days of such submission, which it finds provides that—

(1) All compensation is to be paid through public employment offices in the State or such other agencies as the Board may approve;

(2) No compensation shall be payable with respect to any day of unemployment occurring within two years after the first day of the first period with respect to which contributions are required;

(3) All money received in the unemployment fund shall immediately upon such receipt be paid over to the Secretary of the Treasury to the credit of the Unemployment Trust Fund established by section 904;

(4) All money withdrawn from the Unemployment Trust Fund by the State agency shall be used solely in the payment of compensation, exclusive of expenses of administration;

(5) Compensation shall not be denied in such State to any otherwise eligible individual for refusing to accept new work under any of the following conditions:

(A) If the position offered is vacant due directly to a strike, lockout, or other labor dispute;

(B) if the wages, hours, or other conditions of the work offered are substantially less favorable to the individual than those prevailing for similar work in the locality;

(C) if as a condition of being employed the individual would be required to join a company union or to resign from or refrain from joining any bona-fide labor organization;

(6) All the rights, privileges, or immunities conferred by such law or by acts done pursuant thereto shall exist subject to the power of the legislature to amend or repeal such law at any time. The Board shall, upon approving such law, notify the Governor of the State of its approval.

(b) On December 31 in each taxable year the Board shall certify to the Secretary of the Treasury each State whose law it has previously approved, except that it shall not certify any State which, after reasonable notice and opportunity for hearing to the State agency, the Board finds has changed its law so that it no longer contains the provisions specified in subsection (a) or has with respect to such taxable year failed to comply substantially with any such provision.

(c) If, at any time during the taxable year, the Board has reason to believe that a State whose law it has previously approved, may not be certified under subsection (b), it shall promptly so notify the Governor of such State.

◆ Unemployment Trust Fund

SEC. 904. (a) There is hereby established in the Treasury of the United States a trust fund to be known as the Unemployment Trust Fund, hereinafter in this title called the Fund. The Secretary of the Treasury is authorized and directed to receive and hold in the Fund all moneys deposited therein by a State agency from a State unemployment fund. Such deposit may be made directly with the Secretary of the Treasury or with any Federal reserve bank or member bank of the Federal Reserve System designated by him for such purpose.

(b) It shall be the duty of the Secretary of the Treasury to invest such portion of the Fund as is not, in his judgment, required to meet current withdrawals. Such investment may be made only in interest-bearing obligations of the United States or in obligations guaranteed as to both principal and interest by the United States. For such purpose such obligations may be acquired

(1) on original issue at par, or

(2) by purchase of outstanding obligations at the market price. The purposes for which obligations of the United States may be issued under the Second Liberty Bond Act, as amended, are hereby extended to authorize the issuance at par of special obligations exclusively to the Fund. Such special obligations shall bear interest at a rate equal to the average rate of interest, computed as of the end of the calendar month next preceding the date of such issue, borne by all interest-bearing obligations of the United States then forming part of the public debt; except that where such average rate is not a multiple of one eighth of 1 per centum, the rate of interest of such special obligations shall be the multiple of one-eighth of 1 per centum next lower than such average rate. Obligations other than such special obligations may be acquired for the Fund only on such terms as to provide an investment yield not less than the yield which would be required in the case of special obligations if issued to the Fund upon the date of such acquisition.

(c) Any obligations acquired by the Fund (except special obligations issued exclusively to the Fund) may be sold at the market price, and such special obligations may be redeemed at par plus accrued interest.

(d) The interest on, and the proceeds from the sale or redemption of, any obligations held in the

Fund shall be credited to and form a part of the Fund.

(e) The Fund shall be invested as a single fund, but the Secretary of the Treasury shall maintain a separate book account for each State agency and shall credit quarterly on March 31, June 30, September 30, and December 31, of each year, to each account, on the basis of the average daily balance of such account, a proportionate part of the earnings of the Fund for the quarter ending on such date.

(f) The Secretary of the Treasury is authorized and directed to pay out of the Fund to any State agency such amount as it may duly requisition, not exceeding the amount standing to the account of such State agency at the time of such payment.

◆ Administration, Refunds, and Penalties

SEC. 905. (a) The tax imposed by this title shall be collected by the Bureau of Internal Revenue under the direction of the Secretary of the Treasury and shall be paid into the Treasury of the United States as internal-revenue collections. If the tax is not paid when due, there shall be added as part of the tax interest at the rate of one-half of 1 per centum per month from the date the tax became due until paid.

(b) Not later than January 31, next following the close of the taxable year, each employer shall make a return of the tax under this title for such taxable year. Each such return shall be made under oath, shall be filed with the collector of internal revenue for the district in which is located the principal place of business of the employer, or, if he has no principal place of business in the United States, then with the collector at Baltimore, Maryland, and shall contain such information and be made in such manner as the Commissioner of Internal Revenue, with the approval of the Secretary of the Treasury, may by regulations prescribe. All provisions of law (including penalties) applicable in respect of the taxes imposed by section 600 of the Revenue Act of 1926, shall, insofar as not inconsistent with this title, be applicable in respect of the tax imposed by this title. The Commissioner may extend the time for filing the return of the tax imposed by this title, under such rules and regulations as he may prescribe with the approval of the Secretary of the Treasury, but no such extension shall be for more than sixty days.

(c) Returns filed under this title shall be open to inspection in the same manner, to the same extent, and subject to the same provisions of law, including penalties, as returns made under Title II of the Revenue Act of 1926.

(d) The taxpayer may elect to pay the tax in four equal installments instead of in a single payment, in which case the first installment shall be paid not later than the last day prescribed for the filing of returns, the second installment shall be paid on or before the last day of the third month, the third installment on or before the last day of the sixth month, and the fourth installment on or before the last day of the ninth month, after such last day. If the tax or any installment thereof is not paid on or before the last day of the period fixed for its payment, the whole amount of the tax unpaid shall be paid upon notice and demand from the collector.

(e) At the request of the taxpayer the time for payment of the tax or any installment thereof may be extended under regulations prescribed by the Commissioner with the approval of the Secretary of the Treasury, for a period not to exceed six months from the last day of the period prescribed for the payment of the tax or any installment thereof. The amount of the tax in respect of which any extension is granted shall be paid (with interest at the rate of one-half of 1 per centum per month) on or before the date of the expiration of the period of the extension.

(f) In the payment of any tax under this title a fractional part of a cent shall be disregarded unless it amounts to one-half cent or more, in which case it shall be increased to 1 cent.

◆ Interstate Commerce

SEC. 906. No person required under a State law to make payments to an unemployment fund shall be relieved from compliance therewith on the ground that he is engaged in interstate commerce, or that the State law does not distinguish between employees engaged in interstate commerce and those engaged in intrastate commerce.

◆ Definitions

SEC. 907. When used in this title— (a) The term employer does not include any person unless on each of some twenty days during the taxable year, each day being in a different calendar week, the total number of individuals who were in his employ for some portion of the day (whether or not at the same moment of time) was eight or more.

(b) The term wages means all remuneration for employment, including the cash value of all remuneration paid in any medium other than cash.

(c) The term employment means any service, of whatever nature, performed within the United States by an employee for his employer, except—

(1) Agricultural labor;

(2) Domestic service in a private home;

(3) Service performed as an officer or member of a crew of a vessel on the navigable waters of the United States;

(4) Service performed by an individual in the employ of his son, daughter, or spouse, and service performed by a child under the age of twenty-one in the employ of his father or mother;

(5) Service performed in the employ of the United States Government or of an instrumentality of the United States;

(6) Service performed in the employ of a State, a political subdivision thereof, or an instrumentality of one or more States or political subdivisions;

(7) Service performed in the employ of a corporation, community chest, fund, or foundation, organized and operated exclusively for religious, charitable, scientific, literary, or educational purposes, or for the prevention of cruelty to children or animals, no part of the net earnings of which inures to the benefit of any private shareholder or individual.

(d) The term State agency means any State officer, board, or other authority, designated under a State law to administer the unemployment fund in such State.

(e) The term unemployment fund means a special fund, established under a State law and administered by a State agency, for the payment of compensation.

(f) The term contributions means payments required by a State law to be made by an employer into an unemployment fund, to the extent that such payments are made by him without any part thereof being deducted or deductible from the wages of individuals in his employ.

(g) The term compensation means cash benefits payable to individuals with respect to their unemployment.

◆ Rules and Regulations

SEC. 908. The Commissioner of Internal Revenue, with the approval of the Secretary of the Treasury, shall make and publish rules and regulations for the enforcement of this title, except sections 903, 904, and 910.

◆ Allowance of Additional Credit

SEC. 909. (a) In addition to the credit allowed under section 902, a taxpayer may, subject to the conditions imposed by section 910, credit against the tax imposed by section 901 for any taxable year after the taxable year 1937, an amount, with respect to each State law, equal to the amount, if any, by which the contributions, with respect to employment in such taxable year, actually paid by the taxpayer under such law before the date of filing his return for such taxable year, is exceeded by whichever of the following is the lesser— (1) The amount of contributions which he would have been required to pay under such law for such taxable year if he had been subject to the highest rate applicable from time to time throughout such year to any employer under such law; or (2) Two and seven-tenths per centum of the wages payable by him with respect to employment with respect to which contributions for such year were required under such law.

(b) If the amount of the contributions actually so paid by the taxpayer is less than the amount which he should have paid under the State law, the additional credit under subsection (a) shall be reduced proportionately.

(c) The total credits allowed to a taxpayer under this title shall not exceed 90 per centum of the tax against which such credits are taken.

◆ Conditions of Additional Credit Allowance

SEC. 910. (a) A taxpayer shall be allowed the additional credit under section 909, with respect to his contribution rate under a State law being lower, for any taxable year, than that of another employer subject to such law, only if the Board finds that under such law—

(1) Such lower rate, with respect to contributions to a pooled fund, is permitted on the basis of not less than three years of compensation experience;

(2) Such lower rate, with respect to contributions to a guaranteed employment account, is permitted only when his guaranty of employment was fulfilled in the preceding calendar year, and such guaranteed employment account amounts to not less than 7 per centum of the total wages payable by him, in accordance with such guaranty, with respect to employment in such State in the preceding calendar year;

(3) Such lower rate, with respect to contributions to a separate reserve account, is permitted only when

(A) compensation has been payable from such account throughout the preceding calendar year, and

(B) such account amounts to not less than five times the largest amount of compensation paid from such account within any one of the three preceding calendar years, and

(C) such account amounts to not less than 7 per centum of the total wages payable by him (plus the total wages payable by any other employers who may be contributing to such account) with respect to employment in such State in the preceding calendar year.

(b) Such additional credit shall be reduced, if any contributions under such law are made by such taxpayer at a lower rate under conditions not fulfilling the requirements of subsection (a), by the amount bearing the same ratio to such additional credit as the amount of contributions made at such lower rate bears to the total of his contributions paid for such year under such law.

(c) As used in this section—

(1) The term reserve account means a separate account in an unemployment fund, with respect to an employer or group of employers, from which compensation is payable only with respect to the unemployment of individuals who were in the employ of such employer, or of one of the employers comprising the group.

(2) The term pooled fund means an unemployment fund or any part thereof in which all contributions are mingled and undivided, and from which compensation is payable to all eligible individuals, except that to individuals last employed by employers with respect to whom reserve accounts are maintained by the State agency, it is payable only when such accounts are exhausted.

(3) The term guaranteed employment account means a separate account, in an unemployment fund, of contributions paid by an employer (or group of employers) who

(A) guarantees in advance thirty hours of wages for each of forty calendar weeks (or more, with one weekly hour deducted for each added week guaranteed) in twelve months, to all the individuals in his employ in one or more distinct establishments, except that any such individual's guaranty may commence after a probationary period (included within twelve or less consecutive calendar weeks), and

(B) gives security or assurance, satisfactory to the State agency, for the fulfillment of such guaranties, from which account compensation shall be payable with respect to the unemployment of any such individual whose guaranty is not fulfilled or renewed and who is otherwise eligible for compensation under the State law.

(4) The term year of compensation experience, as applied to an employer, means any calendar year throughout which compensation was payable with respect to any individual in his employ who became unemployed and was eligible for compensation.

Title X—Grants to States for Aid to the Blind
Appropriation

SECTION 1001. For the purpose of enabling each State to furnish financial assistance, as far as practicable under the conditions in such State, to needy individuals who are blind, there is hereby authorized to be appropriated for the fiscal year ending June 30, 1936, the sum of $3,000,000, and there is hereby authorized to be appropriated for each fiscal year thereafter a sum sufficient to carry out the purposes of this title. The sums made available under this section shall be used for making payments to States which have submitted, and had approved by the Social Security Board, State plans for aid to the blind.

◆ State Plans for Aid to the Blind
SEC. 1002. (a) A State plan for aid to the blind must

(1) provide that it shall be in effect in all political subdivisions of the State, and, if administered by them, be mandatory upon them;

(2) provide for financial participation by the State;

(3) either provide for the establishment or designation of a single State agency to administer the plan, or provide for the establishment or designation of a single State agency to supervise the administration of the plan;

(4) provide for granting to any individual, whose claim for aid is denied, an opportunity for a fair hearing before such State agency;

(5) provide such methods of administration (other than those relating to selection, tenure of office, and compensation of personnel) as are found by the Board to be necessary for the efficient operation of the plan;

(6) provide that the State agency will make such reports, in such form and containing such information, as the Board may from time to time require, and comply with such provisions as the Board may from time to time find necessary to assure the correctness and verification of such reports; and

(7) provide that no aid will be furnished any individual under the plan with respect to any period with respect to which he is receiving old-age assistance under the State plan approved under section 2 of this Act.

(b) The Board shall approve any plan which fulfills the conditions specified in subsection (a), except that it shall not approve any plan which imposes, as a condition of eligibility for aid to the blind under the plan—

(1) Any residence requirement which excludes any resident of the State who has resided therein five years during the nine years immediately preceding the application for aid and has resided therein continuously for one year immediately preceding the application or

(2) Any citizenship requirement which excludes any citizen of the United States.

◆ Payment to States

SEC. 1003. (a) From the sums appropriated therefor, the Secretary of the Treasury shall pay to each State which has an approved plan for aid to the blind, for each quarter, beginning with the quarter commencing July 1, 1935,

(1) an amount which shall be used exclusively as aid to the blind equal to one-half of the total of the sums expended during such quarter as aid to the blind under the State plan with respect to each individual who is blind and is not an inmate of a public institution not counting so much of such expenditure with respect to any individual for any month as exceeds $30, and

(2) 5 per centum of such amount, which shall be used for paying the costs of administering the State plan or for aid to the blind, or both, and for no other purpose.

(b) The method of computing and paying such amounts shall be as follows:

(1) The Board shall, prior to the beginning of each quarter, estimate the amount to be paid to the State for such quarter under provisions of clause (1) of subsection (a), such estimate to be based on

(A) a report filed by the State containing its estimate of the total sum to be expended in such quarter in accordance with the provisions of such clause, and stating the amount appropriated or made available by the State and its political subdivisions for such expenditures in such quarter, and if such amount is less than one-half of the total sum of such estimated expenditures, the source or sources from which the difference is expected to be derived,

(B) records showing the number of blind individuals in the State, and

(C) such other investigation as the Board may find necessary.

(2) The Board shall then certify to the Secretary of the Treasury the amount so estimated by the Board, reduced or increased, as the case may be, by any sum by which it finds that its estimate for any prior quarter was greater or less than the amount which should have been paid to the State under clause (1) of subsection (a) for such quarter, except to the extent that such sum has been applied to make the amount certified for any prior quarter greater or less than the amount estimated by the Board for such prior quarter.

(3) The Secretary of the Treasury shall thereupon, through the Division of Disbursement of the Treasury Department and prior to audit or settlement by the General Accounting Office, pay to the State, at the time or times fixed by the Board, the amount so certified, increased by 5 per centum.

◆ Operation of State Plans

SEC. 1004. In the case of any State plan for aid to the blind which has been approved by the Board, if the Board, after reasonable notice and opportunity for hearing to the State agency administering or supervising the administration of such a plan, finds—

(1) that the plan has been so changed as to impose any residence or citizenship requirement prohibited by section 1002 (b), or that in the administration of the plan any such prohibited requirement is imposed, with the knowledge of such State agency, in a substantial number of cases; or

(2) that in the administration of the plan there is a failure to comply substantially with any provision required by section 1002 (a) be included in the plan; the Board shall notify such State agency that further payments will not be made to the State until the Board is satisfied that such prohibited requirement is no longer so imposed, and that there is no longer any such failure to comply. Until it is satisfied it shall make no further certification to the Secretary of the Treasury with respect to such State.

◆ Administration

SEC. 1005. There is hereby authorized to be appropriated for the fiscal year ending June 30, 1936 the sum of $30,000, for all necessary expenses of the Board in administering the provisions of this title.

◆ Definition

SEC. 1006. When used in this title the term aid to the blind means money payments to blind individuals.

Title XI—General Provisions

◆ Definitions

SECTION 1101. (a) When used in this Act—

(1) The term State (except when used in section 531) includes Alaska, Hawaii, and the District of Columbia.

(2) The term United States when used in a geographical sense means the States, Alaska, Hawaii, and the District of Columbia.

(3) The term person means an individual, a trust or estate, a partnership, or a corporation.

(4) The term corporation includes associations, joint-stock companies, and insurance companies.

(5) The term shareholder includes a member in an association, joint-stock company, or insurance company.

(6) The term employee includes an officer of a corporation.

(b) The terms includes and including when used in a definition contained in this Act shall not be deemed to exclude other things otherwise within the meaning of the term defined.

(c) Whenever under this Act or any Act of Congress, or under the law of any State, an employer is required or permitted to deduct any amount from the remuneration of an employee and to pay the amount deducted to the United States, a State, or any political subdivision thereof, then for the purposes of this Act the amount so deducted shall be considered to have been paid to the employee at the time of such deduction.

(d) Nothing in this Act shall be construed as authorizing any Federal official, agent, or representative, in carrying out any of the provisions of this Act, to take charge of any child over the objection of either of the parents of such child, or of the person standing in loco parentis to such child.

◆ **Rules and Regulations**

SEC. 1102. The Secretary of the Treasury, the Secretary of Labor, and the Social Security Board respectively, shall make and publish such rules and regulations, not inconsistent with this Act, as may be necessary to the efficient administration of the functions with which each is charged under this Act.

◆ **Separability**

SEC. 1103. If any provision of this Act, or the application thereof to any person or circumstance is held invalid, the remainder of the Act, and the application of such provision to other persons or circumstances shall not be affected thereby.

◆ **Reservation of Power**

SEC. 1104. The right to alter, amend, or repeal any provision of this Act is hereby reserved to the Congress.

◆ **Short Title**

SEC. 1105. This Act may be cited as the Social Security Act.

or hate where the sole thought is the welfare of the United States
of America. No man can occupy the office of President without
realizing that he is President of all the people. And no man can
sit through four years such as these last four years without pouring out every ounce of his physical strength, his patience and intelligence for the fulfillment of that trust for the well-being
of all the people.

It is because I have sought to think in terms of the whole
Nation that I am confident that today, just as four years ago, the
people want more than promises.

Our vision for the future contains more than promises.

~~That~~ This is our answer to those who, silent about their own plans,
ask us to state our objectives. Of course we will continue to seek
~~in every way~~ to improve working conditions for the workers of
America -- to reduce hours over-long, to increase wages that spell
starvation, to end the labor of children, to wipe out sweatshops.
Of course we will continue every effort to end monopoly in business,
to support collective bargaining, to stop unfair competition, to

Franklin D. Roosevelt's Campaign Address at Madison Square Garden (National Archives and Records Administration)

FRANKLIN D. ROOSEVELT'S CAMPAIGN ADDRESS AT MADISON SQUARE GARDEN

"I should like to have it said of my first Administration that in it the forces of selfishness and of lust for power met their match."

Overview

President Franklin D. Roosevelt's October 31, 1936, campaign speech to a cheering audience in New York City's Madison Square Garden culminated an aggressive campaign in which the Democratic incumbent drew enormous enthusiastic crowds. The substantive issue in the campaign was whether to continue to go forward with the New Deal reforms, particularly those adopted as part of what scholars call the Second New Deal, or to turn away from these changes as radical and dangerous to the idea of limited government. Although unemployment remained high, the New Deal had stimulated a significant degree of recovery from the low point of the depression, provided relief and government employment to millions of Americans, and instituted substantial social and regulatory reforms, most important the establishment of Social Security and a labor relations system designed to assist workers in establishing unions and winning collective bargaining rights.

The president responds to criticisms coming from Republicans and employers, says that he welcomes the hatred of the rich, and promises to continue to serve both the interests of the American people as a whole and the unemployed, workers, farmers, and young people. Roosevelt responds with vehemence to a last-minute "paycheck" campaign by Republicans trying to convince workers that the payroll tax that would begin on January 1, 1937, was unfair, would rise substantially in the future, and would never be returned to them in benefits. Roosevelt points out that employers and employees paid equal amounts for the old-age-insurance Social Security program and that employers alone paid for the unemployment insurance compensation system also established by the Social Security Act. The election resulted in the biggest popular vote mandate in U.S. history and a widening of the already substantial Democratic margin in Congress.

Context

The devastation of the worst depression in U.S. history and the inadequate response to it of the Republican presi-

dent Herbert Hoover led to Roosevelt's 57.4 percent popular vote victory in 1932 and sizable Democratic majorities in Congress. The Roosevelt administration's provision of significant help to millions of Americans of all classes and the president's engaging personal style made him a popular president. However, the expansion of federal power to aid nonbusiness groups and a major strike wave in 1934 led to opposition from big-business interests and conservatives of both major parties in the American Liberty League. Roosevelt also faced opposition by panacea movements led by Louisiana's Senator Huey Long; Charles Coughlin, a Catholic priest from Michigan; and the California physician Francis Townsend. When the Democrats defied precedent by picking up seats in the 1934 congressional election, Roosevelt and the Democratic Congress moved further to the left, enacting a set of far-reaching Second New Deal measures in 1935. The Social Security Act established a federal social welfare system that provided unemployment compensation for workers, old-age pensions for the elderly, and assistance to the needy elderly, disabled persons, and dependent children. The National Labor Relations Act created a system of federal regulation of industrial relations in which workers received support in exercising their right to form unions and to engage in collective bargaining. Troubling to Roosevelt and his supporters, however, was a series of conservative Supreme Court decisions nullifying early New Deal legislation, but Roosevelt said little in public about the issue.

Public opinion polls at the beginning of 1936 indicated that the presidential election would be close. A third party composed of the three panacea movements was expected to aid Republicans by drawing votes from the Democrats for not going far enough. The Republicans nominated Governor Alf Landon of Kansas, a moderate-to-liberal figure who could appeal to independent voters. The Republicans also had most newspapers on their side and $14 million to spend compared with the Democrats' $9 million.

Roosevelt campaigned aggressively as a champion of workers, farmers, and the unemployed and effectively communicated his caring philosophy in person and on the radio. The Democrats ran a well-organized grassroots campaign, and the economy was on the upswing. Right-wing charges that Roosevelt was communistic fell flat. Republi-

1929

■ **August**
The Great Depression begins.

1932

■ **November 8**
Roosevelt is elected with 57.4 percent of the popular vote over incumbent Republican Herbert Hoover, and Democrats win large majorities in both houses of Congress.

1933

■ **March 4–June 16**
First one hundred days brings major series of reform legislation and establishes set of new "alphabet agencies": National Recovery Administration (NRA), Agricultural Adjustment Administration (AAA), Civilian Conservation Corps (CCC), Public Works Administration (PWA), Civil Works Administration (CWA), and the Tennessee Valley Authority (TVA).

1934

■ **Massive strike wave is** highlighted by San Francisco General Strike (which began on July 16 and lasted four days); the American Liberty League attacks Roosevelt.

■ **November 6**
Democrats gain new seats in congressional election.

1935

■ **May 27**
Schechter Poultry Co. v. United States. Supreme Court declares the National Industrial Recovery Act unconstitutional.

■ **July 5**
Roosevelt signs the National Labor Relations Act.

■ **August 14**
Roosevelt signs the Social Security Act.

1936

■ **June 1**
In *Morehead v. Tipaldo* the Supreme Court by 5-to-4 vote nullifies a New York law establishing minimum wage for women workers.

cans' ability to campaign as defenders of the Supreme Court was undermined by the highly unpopular *Morehead v. Tipaldo* (1936) decision nullifying a state minimum-wage law for women. Conservative Republicans resorted to attacking the Social Security Act, claiming that every worker would be required to wear a metal dog tag. As the campaign drew to a close, scientifically conducted polls indicated that Roosevelt would easily win.

Landon spoke at Madison Square Garden just two nights before Roosevelt spoke there. When Landon's campaign failed to gain traction, he shifted to embracing the anti–New Deal critique of the right wing. He demanded that Roosevelt answer a set of questions about what he would do in a second term, charged that the president was planning to undermine the Constitution, and joined in an attack on Social Security launched days earlier by employers who inserted a misleading message about the program in workers' pay envelopes. Roosevelt, angry about the distortions, decided to use his October 31 address to respond to the Republican misinformation and reaffirm his campaign themes.

About the Author

Franklin Delano Roosevelt was born on January 30, 1882, in Hyde Park, New York. His was an "old-money" landed family, not nearly as wealthy as the new millionaires of the Gilded Age but prosperous enough for Roosevelt to be educated by tutors at home, then at the elite Groton Academy, and later at Harvard. The only child of his mother, Sara Delano Roosevelt, and distant in years from his older half-brother, James, Roosevelt developed an optimistic and confident personality. His easy way with people became one of his important political assets. Roosevelt attended Columbia Law School, passed the bar, and joined a Wall Street law firm but eventually chose politics as his career. Having learned from his parents the idea of service to others and being a good steward of the land, Roosevelt developed a liberal philosophy. He was influenced by the climate of opinion in the Progressive Era; by the Reverend George H. Peabody, headmaster of Groton; and by his distant cousin, President Theodore Roosevelt, whose advocacy of an active strenuous life of service inspired him. Another important influence was his wife, the social reformer Eleanor Roosevelt. The niece of Theodore Roosevelt, Eleanor was Roosevelt's distant cousin. The Roosevelts were married in 1905 and had six children. Roosevelt's unfaithfulness led to the deterioration of their intimate bond and nearly ended their marriage in 1918, but the couple remained political partners.

Roosevelt was elected to the New York state senate in 1910 and served as assistant secretary of the navy during the administration of Woodrow Wilson, whom Roosevelt greatly admired. A year after an unsuccessful campaign for the vice presidency in 1920, Roosevelt was struck by poliomyelitis, an event that contributed to his identification with those in need. Roosevelt worked hard to regain strength in his arms and back, was able to present the illusion that he was walking with the use of leg braces, and resumed his political career. He was elected governor of New York in 1928, was reelected to the post in 1930, and was elected president in 1932. Facing the challenge of the depression, Roosevelt brought in an array of diverse figures to help chart New Deal programs and provide jobs, relief, and assistance to farmers and those faced with losing their homes. Roosevelt also sought to produce economic recovery and, especially during the Second New Deal, to introduce fundamental reforms, such as the Social Security Act and the National Labor Relations Act. He was reelected to the presidency in 1936, 1940, and 1944. During his second term World War II began, and Roosevelt led the country to a policy of building up its defenses and aiding Great Britain. During his third term, the United States aided the Soviet Union when it was attacked by Nazi Germany and then entered the war directly after it was attacked by Japan. Although Roosevelt's focus during World War II was national unity to win the war, in January 1944 he called for an expansion of the New Deal by establishing an economic bill of rights. Roosevelt died on April 12, 1945, less than one month before victory was achieved in Europe.

Explanation and Analysis of the Document

In the opening paragraphs of his address, President Roosevelt promises to offer a reasoned discussion of "the effect on our Nation" of victory by either party in the upcoming election and then immediately raises the emotional tone by saying that the election was about the fate of "humanity." More is at stake than "the continuance in the Presidency of any single individual."

In paragraph 3, the president argues that what was at stake in the last presidential election, in 1932, was "the restoration of American democracy" and makes clear that his concept of democracy is about majority rule, or people's power. He maintains that in 1932 "the American people were in a mood to win" and "did win." The issue in 1936 is "the preservation of their victory," not going back to rule by the economic royalists. In paragraphs 4 and 5, he characterizes the 1932 campaign as a "crusade to restore America to its own people" and asserts that the crusade is still ongoing.

In paragraph 6, Roosevelt confidently asserts that Americans know what his administration has accomplished, so they will not be misled by the "misrepresentation or statistical contortion" of "unscrupulous enemies" or the "exaggerations of over-zealous friends." Roosevelt is furious at Republican attacks and focuses on them in detail later in the address. Mentioning negatively "over-zealous friends" appears to be an attempt by Roosevelt to appeal to moderate Democrats. Roosevelt indicates that his approach is pragmatic: The "Administration has been hammering [it] out on the anvils of experience." He draws on the thinking of individuals with diverse perspectives, trying out different plans and keeping those that worked.

Time Line

1936

■ **October 29**
Republican nominee Alf Landon speaks to twenty thousand people at Madison Square Garden in New York City.

■ **October 31**
Roosevelt speaks to twenty thousand people at Madison Square Garden in New York City.

■ **November 3**
Roosevelt is reelected with 60.8 percent of the popular vote and 98.5 percent of the electoral vote.

1937

■ **February 11**
General Motors agrees to recognize the United Auto Workers, ending a sixty-six-day sit-down strike and sparking a wave of strikes throughout the country.

■ **March 29**
In *West Coast Hotel Company v. Parrish* the Supreme Court reverses itself and affirms Washington's state minimum wage law for women workers by a 5-to-4 vote.

1938

■ **June 25**
Roosevelt signs the Fair Labor Standards Act establishing a forty-hour week and twenty-five cent minimum wage.

In paragraphs 7 through 11, Roosevelt describes the goals that he and the people had in 1932. In paragraph 7, Roosevelt asserts that their primary goal had been "peace of mind instead of gnawing fear." The threat of war and foreign policy developments were very much on Roosevelt's mind in 1935 and 1936 as the international situation deteriorated. The events leading to Italy's invasion of Ethiopia in 1935 had led the United States to adopt neutrality legislation, and Germany's rearmament caused anxiety about a new general war. In January 1936 Roosevelt had delivered his annual message to Congress in a special evening session. The only other such occasion was when President Woodrow Wilson had appeared to ask for a declaration of war against Germany in 1917. Roosevelt highlights the danger of war and pledges to maintain neutrality, sufficient defenses, and support peace. Shortly after the Spanish Civil War had erupted in July 1936, Roosevelt had spoken out against entangling alliances and made an emotional pledge to keep the nation out of war, affirming in a speech at Chautauqua, New York: "I have seen war … I have seen blood running from the wounded … I hate war" (http://www.ibiblio.org/hyperwar/Dip/PaW/074.html). He reiterates this stance in the Madison Square Garden speech.

In paragraphs 9 and 10, Roosevelt lists the many things in 1932 that had caused people to worry about themselves and the ability of community institutions such as schools, parks, and a "solvent local government" to function. He also lists such goals as "fairer wages, the ending of long hours of toil, the abolition of child labor," and "the safety of their children from kidnappers." Establishing minimum wages and maximum hours and limiting child labor were addressed in the Fair Labor Standards Act enacted in 1938. The allusion to fears of kidnapping stemmed from the widespread attention in 1932 to the tragic case of the kidnapping and murder of the toddler son of the aviator Charles Lindbergh.

In paragraph 12, Roosevelt sums up the section of the address on peace by stating his administration's record. He also connects the internal and external dimensions of the concept by pledging that in the future one could expect peace for the individual, community, and nation and "peace with the world."

In paragraphs 13 to 18, Roosevelt as leader of a people's army for social change calls the "roll of honor" of those "who stood with us in 1932 and still stand with us today." The roll of honor includes the suffering of millions of all classes, "men at starvation wages, women in sweatshops, children at looms … farmers whose acres yield only bitterness," needy youth, business people, home owners, and "frugal citizens" worried about losing their savings. Roosevelt includes on the honor roll better-off liberal-minded people "Americans of all parties and all faiths," and those "who had eyes to see and hearts to understand." New Deal measures offered help to people of all classes and drew support from a number of progressive Republicans and members of left-of-center state-level third parties.

In paragraph 19, Roosevelt pays tribute to the strong faith his supporters had in him ("They stood with us then because in 1932 they believed"), which was reinforced in 1936 by the knowledge they have that the New Deal had delivered improvements ("They stand with us today because in 1936 they know.") Roosevelt also notes that there are "millions of new recruits who have come to know," an assertion that was borne out on election day when the number of new Democratic voters shot up by nearly five million.

In paragraphs 21 and 22, Roosevelt emphasizes the necessity of "struggle" and attacks his Republican predecessors in a striking reference to a proverb about three monkeys who hear no evil, speak no evil, and see no evil: He calls the twelve Republican years before the New Deal a period of "hear-nothing, see-nothing, do-nothing Government." The president's language grows even more colorful as he contrasts the excesses of the 1920s with the disaster of the Herbert Hoover depression years: "Nine mad years of mirage and three long years of despair!" Roosevelt attacks the conservative objective in the election, "to restore that kind of government with its doctrine that that Government is best which is most indifferent." Here Roosevelt engages in a play on words. The Democratic Party in the nineteenth century had emphasized limited government. The New Deal creation of numerous new government agencies and the establishment of the principle that the federal government is responsible for the economic well-being of the people were far removed from the old philosophy. Charging in the campaign that the New Deal had fundamentally altered the nature of American government and was a threat to liberty and the Constitution, the Republicans shifted from their earlier emphasis on a strong national government. Roosevelt parries the Republicans' charge by contrasting his caring philosophy with their indifference.

Paragraphs 24 to 30 are the most radical passages in the address. Roosevelt denounces the right-wing big businesses that oppose his program and his reelection. In paragraph 24 he notes his administration's "struggle with the old enemies of peace," reiterating the peace emphasis of the opening of the address, and lists these enemies as "business and financial monopoly, speculation, reckless banking, class antagonism, sectionalism, war profiteering." Roosevelt alludes here to the recent Senate investigation of war profiteering in World War I led by Senator Gerald Nye. In attacking monopoly, moreover, Roosevelt draws on the pre–Civil War campaign of the Democratic president Andrew Jackson and an ongoing antimonopoly tradition. The president's reference to class antagonism here serves to open the theme that it is not he but his opponents who initiated a class war. The sectionalism reference may be an allusion to racism. During the election campaign, despite the Democratic orientation of white southern voters, Eleanor Roosevelt was vehemently attacked for violating racial norms for actions, such as being photographed treating African Americans as equals.

The monopolists, Roosevelt argues in paragraph 25, had started to view government "as a mere appendage to their own affairs." The control of government by "organized money," Roosevelt proclaims, is "as dangerous" as mob rule.

In the most famous sentences of the address, in paragraphs 26 and 27, Roosevelt personalizes the struggle. He says that the monopoly forces were "united against one candidate" as never before. "They are unanimous in their hate for me—and I welcome their hatred." Roosevelt is moving left to keep in step with and remain the leader of his leftward-moving followers. In the heat of the campaign, Roosevelt expresses his emotional identification with the masses and demonstrates an activist's sensibility that one is accomplishing something significant when one arouses the anger of privileged elites. He indicates both pride in what he has accomplished ("I should like to have it said of my first Administration that in it the forces of selfishness and of lust for power met their match") and hope for future victories ("I should like to have it said of my second Administration that in it these forces met their master"). The latter sentence thrilled the Madison Square Garden crowd, but it was the most controversial of the speech. Republicans attacked it vehemently, charging that it was proof of Roosevelt's dictatorial proclivities, and some of his moderate supporters and advisers were also troubled by it. The phrase was Roosevelt's own; in the initial draft of the speech, the words were "these forces found their oblivion."

The crowd at Madison Square Garden reacts to Franklin Roosevelt's speech on October 31, 1936. (AP Photo)

In paragraph 28, Roosevelt continues the personal theme, asserting that under his administration there is no back door to influence at the White House. The only entry is through the front door; he says that he holds the "pass-key" and will carry it "in my pocket" as "long as I am President." The theme of equality of all and special privileges to none was a long-standing Democratic Party principle. If in actual practice Democrats had failed to apply the concept to women and minorities, belief in the abstract principle remained a key value.

In paragraphs 29 to 37, the president delivers a scathing attack on recent efforts by the Republican presidential nominee, Alf Landon, and his supporters to assail the Social Security program. Roosevelt was outraged at both the form and the substance of the Republican charges. Employers had distributed in workers' pay envelopes a note advising workers that on January 1, 1937, the federal government would take 1 percent of their pay with no certainty that Congress would use the funds for the purposes intended and no certainty that workers would ever get anything back. In paragraph 29, Roosevelt characterizes the "pay-envelope campaign against America's working people" as an act by "desperate" and

"reckless" people and a return to the "tactics of the labor spy." He answers at length the substantive charges after first noting the irony in paragraph 30 that those who "talk most loudly of class antagonism and the destruction of the American system now undermine that system" by attempting to coerce workers' votes. Roosevelt argues that it was "the 1936 version of the old threat to close down the factory" if workers voted the wrong way, a tactic used especially against the Democrat William Jennings Bryan in 1896.

The pay envelope campaign was not only wrong in principle because it was coercive, Roosevelt charges in paragraph 31, it was also dishonest because it failed to mention that employers matched the money contributed by the employee to the old-age pension fund. The employer alone contributed to the unemployment insurance fund also established by the Social Security Act. Having employees pay half the cost of the old-age pension system was regressive, but Roosevelt had insisted on it to make it politically impossible to repeal the system. Roosevelt also points out in paragraph 36 that while the Republican leadership campaigned against Social Security, more than three-quarters of the Republicans in Congress had voted for the measure.

In paragraph 35, Roosevelt accuses the Republicans of attacking the "integrity and honor of American Government itself" when they intimate that a future Congress would divert funds to other purposes. Roosevelt suggests these critics "are already aliens to the spirit of American democracy" and should "emigrate and try their lot under some foreign flag in which they have more confidence," alluding to sympathy on the political right for the fascist regimes of Hitler and Mussolini.

In paragraphs 37 through 40, Roosevelt sounds a conciliatory note, expressing confidence that "law-abiding businessmen" and "the overwhelming majority of employers, workers and the general public" would reject the anti–Social Security campaign on Election Day.

Roosevelt affirms that his thoughts are for the well-being of the "whole Nation," since he, like his predecessors, "is President of all the people." Even in the context of a speech—and a campaign—designed to mobilize constituencies that supported him with class-oriented language, Roosevelt frames part of his argument in terms of the good of the nation as a whole. After all, even the most radical class legislation, the National Labor Relations Act, was based on the idea, as the president put it earlier in his address, of "a new peace between worker and employer."

In paragraphs 41 to 51, Roosevelt defiantly answers, in his own way, questions posed two nights earlier by Landon in the very same venue. Landon had challenged the president to say what he would do in a second term about balancing the budget, restoring business confidence, reducing unemployment, and reviving New Deal measures declared unconstitutional by the Supreme Court. Would he seek to amend the Constitution or "get around the Constitution by tampering with the Supreme Court? ... Does he favor concentrating more and more power in the hands of the chief executive? Or does he favor a return to the American form of government?" ("The Text of Governor Landon's Addresses at Madison Square Garden and over the Radio," p. 16). The president replies, "Our vision for the future contains more than promises. This is our answer to those who, silent about their own plans, ask us to state our objectives." Landon had made a number of promises but had offered few specifics about how to implement those pledges.

Roosevelt lists his accomplishments in meeting people's needs and states "Of course we will continue" to do those things. He pledges to go on providing help to workers by supporting collective bargaining and striving to improve working conditions, increase wages, "end the labor of children" and "wipe out sweatshops." He pledges also to continue to work to end monopoly, and, paraphrasing the words of the Revolutionary naval officer, John Paul Jones, he declares, "We have only just begun to fight." In subsequent paragraphs, the president pledges "of course" to continue to aid farmers and to work for education and opportunity for youth, conservation, and reforestation. At the end of each series of pledges, he repeats the refrain "We have only just begun to fight."

In paragraph 46, Roosevelt pledges "of course" to continue to "provide useful work for the needy unemployed," while in the next paragraph he attacks those "who disparage their fellow citizens on the relief rolls" as "worthless." In paragraph 48, he declares that "you and I will continue to refuse to accept that estimate of our unemployed fellow Americans." The president here introduces a religious theme, which he returns to in closing: "Your Government is still on the same side of the street with the Good Samaritan and not with those who pass by on the other side." The parable of the Good Samaritan is about the duty of service one owes to one's neighbor, in particular, to a neighbor who is of another people or nation. Roosevelt had early in his presidency initiated a new foreign policy toward Latin America, the "Good Neighbor" policy, and during the 1936 campaign, the Democratic National Committee initiated the formation of the Good Neighbor League to win support for Roosevelt's reelection by appealing on moral grounds to liberal middle-class people, especially Protestants.

In paragraph 50, Roosevelt lists all the groups targeted for assistance by the Social Security Act. The act provided aid to those with disabilities and to dependent children and funding for maternity and infant-care programs. The latter provisions were based on need, and funding was limited. Even the programs that were universal in concept, unemployment insurance and old-age pensions, initially excluded large sectors of the workforce. Nevertheless, creating a Social Security system for the first time was popular, the rhetorical promise that all would be protected was reassuring, and coverage and benefits expanded over time.

In the closing paragraphs of the address, Roosevelt returns to the theme of peace at home and abroad. He notes that there was "war and rumor of war" but pledges to work "to remove the causes" of conflict at home that might make it easier for profiteers (who were "not on our side in this campaign") to get the country into a war.

In paragraphs 54 and 55, Roosevelt combines the peace and religion themes. He includes two religious references ("Peace on earth, good will toward men" and "What doth the Lord require of thee—but to do justly, to love mercy and to walk humbly with thy God.") and argues that "true religion ... gives a nation a sense of justice and of moral purpose." He maintains that devotion and faith enable government to persuade people "to work for and to sacrifice for each other" rather than "fight each other." Roosevelt says the "recovery we seek" is "more than economic," it also includes "justice and love and humility." He closes with the observation, "That is the road to peace." A modernist and rationalist, Roosevelt was tolerant of all faiths and of those who were not religious but personally had a strong religious faith that emphasized ethics, service, and social justice.

Audience

Franklin Roosevelt's principal audiences on October 31, 1936, included the enthusiastic crowd in Madison Square Garden and millions of supporters listening on the radio. During the course of the election campaign, Roosevelt was greeted by large and enthusiastic crowds. New Deal policies generated a strong positive response from working peo-

"In 1932 the issue was the restoration of American democracy; and the American people were in a mood to win. They did win. In 1936 the issue is the preservation of their victory. Again they are in a mood to win. Again they will win."

(Paragraph 3)

"We have not come this far without a struggle and I assure you we cannot go further without a struggle. For twelve years this Nation was afflicted with hear-nothing, see-nothing, do-nothing Government.... Powerful influences strive today to restore that kind of government with its doctrine that that Government is best which is most indifferent."

(Paragraphs 21–22)

"We had to struggle with the old enemies of peace—business and financial monopoly, speculation, reckless banking, class antagonism, sectionalism, war profiteering. They had begun to consider the Government of the United States as a mere appendage to their own affairs. We know now that Government by organized money is just as dangerous as Government by organized mob."

(Paragraph 24–25)

"Never before in all our history have these forces been so united against one candidate as they stand today. They are unanimous in their hate for me—and I welcome their hatred. I should like to have it said of my first Administration that in it the forces of selfishness and of lust for power met their match. I should like to have it said of my second Administration that in it these forces met their master."

(Paragraphs 26–27)

"Of course we will continue to seek to improve working conditions for the workers of America—to reduce hours over-long, to increase wages that spell starvation, to end the labor of children, to wipe out sweatshops. Of course we will continue every effort to end monopoly in business, to support collective bargaining.... For all these we have only just begun to fight."

(Paragraph 43)

ple and Roosevelt and First Lady Eleanor Roosevelt were both personally popular. Roosevelt's speech was part of the successful effort to mobilize the largest Democratic vote in U.S. history. Through the repetition of such phrases as "of course we will continue" and "we have only just begun to fight," Roosevelt appeals especially to his more radical working-class supporters. By including references to religious and moral motives for caring policies, Roosevelt appeals to his moderate supporters. The president includes remarks addressed to all people, such as his discussion on peace and references to the needs of the nation as a whole.

Impact

Roosevelt's Madison Square Garden speech culminating the campaign highlights the aggressive and class-oriented approach of his entire reelection struggle. The approach of the speech and of the campaign as a whole was Roosevelt's response to a grassroots upsurge among his supporters, especially among working people. Roosevelt stakes out a pro-working-class position because of the evidence he and his advisers saw that working people were engaged in political and economic life in a new way, supported him and the radical measures of the Second New Deal, and wanted action against conservative forces.

Although early polls had indicated the election would be close, an upswing of the economy in 1936 and the effective Democratic campaign caused Republican nominee Alf Landon to shift away from the moderate positions he espoused early in the campaign. The challenger's attacks on Social Security and his accusations that Roosevelt was seeking to destroy the American governmental system pleased the conservative base of the Republican Party. Roosevelt's effective counterattack in his Madison Square Garden speech may have prevented the Republicans from making inroads with their charges. Roosevelt's October 31 speech contributed to his remarkable landslide on Election Day.

Some scholars have argued that the overwhelming nature of Roosevelt's 1936 victory led him to err in the way he handled his proposal to add more members to the Supreme Court in 1937. Some moderate Democrats had been uncomfortable with the radical character of the 1936 campaign. Conservative Democrats took the lead in attacking Roosevelt's court proposal, and by 1938 an alliance between conservative Democrats and Republicans had developed. On the other hand, the Supreme Court began shifting away from conservatism and toward liberalism with the *West Coast Hotel Company v. Parrish* decision in 1937, reversing its 1936 rejection of a state minimum-wage law for women. Roosevelt's popularity was such that he went on to win two additional presidential elections.

Related Documents

"1935 Law." Social Security Online "In-depth Research: Legislative History" Web site. http://www.ssa.gov/history/law.html. Accessed on February 14, 2008. The site contains the text of the Social Security Act of 1935, the steps leading to the legislation, and the 1937 Supreme Court decision affirming the law along with later amendments.

"Political Party Platforms: Democratic Party Platform 1936." The American Presidency Project Web site. http://www.presidency. ucsb.edu/ws/?pid=29596. Accessed on September 28, 2007. The Democratic Party platform of 1936 outlines the Roosevelt administration's accomplishments and addresses the constitutional issue.

Rosenman, Samuel Irving, ed. *The Public Papers and Addresses of Franklin D. Roosevelt.* 13 vols. New York: Russell & Russell, 1969. In this collection of Roosevelt's papers, volume 5 is subtitled *The People Approve,* 1936. See also volume 1 for Roosevelt's First Inaugural Address and volume 13 for his message to Congress of January 11, 1944, outlining the need for an economic bill of rights.

"The Text of Governor Landon's Addresses at Madison Square Garden and over the Radio," *New York Times,* October 30, 1936. Landon attacks Social Security and demands that Roosevelt answer a series of questions.

Bibliography

■ Articles

Leuchtenburg, William E. "When the People Spoke, What Did They Say? The Election of 1936 and the Ackerman Thesis." *Yale Law Journal* 108, no. 8 (1999): 2077–2114.

■ Books

Burns, James MacGregor. *Roosevelt: The Lion and the Fox.* New York: Harcourt, Brace & World, 1956.

Cook, Blanche Wiesen. *Eleanor Roosevelt,* Vol. 2: *1933–1938.* New York: Viking Press, 1992.

Davis, Kenneth. *FDR: The New Deal Years, 1933–1937.* New York: Random House, 1986.

Freidel, Frank. *Franklin D. Roosevelt: A Rendezvous with Destiny.* Boston: Little, Brown, 1990.

Greer, Thomas, H. *What Roosevelt Thought: The Social and Political Ideas of Franklin D. Roosevelt.* East Lansing: Michigan State University Press, 1958, 2000.

Leuchtenburg, William E. *Franklin D. Roosevelt and the New Deal, 1932–1940: On Roosevelt and His Legacy.* New York: Harper and Row, 1963.

———. *The FDR Years.* New York: Columbia University Press, 1995.

McElvaine, Robert S. *The Encyclopedia of the Great Depression.* New York: Macmillan Reference, 2004.

Ryan, Halford R. *Franklin D. Roosevelt's Rhetorical Presidency.* New York: Greenwood Press, 1988.

Schlesinger, Arthur. *The Politics of Upheaval.* Boston: Houghton Mifflin, 1960.

■ Web Sites

"Address Delivered by President Roosevelt at Chautauqua, New York, August 14, 1936." HyperWar: "Peace and War" Web site.
  http://www.ibiblio.org/hyperwar/Dip/PaW/074.html. Accessed on February 15, 2008.

"Franklin Delano Roosevelt." PBS "American Experience: The Presidents" Web site.
  http://www.pbs.org/wgbh/amex/presidents/32_f_roosevelt/index.html. Accessed on September 25, 2007.

Franklin D. Roosevelt Presidential Library and Museum Web site.
  http://www.fdrlibrary.marist.edu/. Accessed on September 25, 2007.

New Deal Network Web site.
  http://newdeal.feri.org/. Accessed on September 25, 2007.

—By Martin Halpern

1. Compare Roosevelt's speech on October 31, 1936, with his First Inaugural Address (March 4, 1933). Scholars describe two New Deals, a First New Deal that Roosevelt announces in his Inaugural Address and initiates during his first one hundred days in office, and a Second New Deal, involving more radical reforms enacted in 1935. Is there evidence of change in Roosevelt's thinking between the two speeches that is consistent with historians' demarcation? Did the policy shift take place primarily because of the demands of constituencies to which Roosevelt was responsive, because of challenges from opponents, or because of the evolution of thinking within the administration?

2. The Republicans claimed during the 1936 election campaign that New Deal legislation and the creation of numerous new federal agencies had fundamentally changed the character of the government and threatened the Constitution. Roosevelt commented infrequently on Supreme Court decisions declaring New Deal legislation unconstitutional in 1935 and in 1936 and refrained from addressing the issue in the election campaign. In 1937, however, he proposed adding members to the Supreme Court. Examine the debate over Roosevelt's "court-packing" proposal and consider the degree to which Republican charges from 1936 were more politically influential in 1937.

3. Compare the provisions of the Social Security Act with alternative plans for addressing social security in the 1930s, the Townsend plan for pensions for all persons aged sixty years old and older, and the Lundeen bill for unemployment and old-age insurance for all workers and farmers without regard for age, sex, race, or religious or political opinion.

4. While the old-age pensions provision of the Social Security Act became more comprehensive in coverage over time as well as more generous in terms of benefit levels, the provisions to aid dependent children, those with disabilities, and the needy elderly became vulnerable. In 1996 the basic New Deal commitment to the needy was ended by the Personal Responsibility and Work Opportunity Reconciliation Act. Why do different provisions of the Social Security Act have such different trajectories?

Glossary

aliens	foreigners
contortion	distortion
deceit	dishonesty
disparage	belittle
dole	handout
emigrate	move abroad
humility	humbleness
paradox	contradiction
pauperism	poverty
purge	clear
tyrants	oppressive ruler
unscrupulous	unprincipled
van	forefront

FRANKLIN D. ROOSEVELT'S CAMPAIGN ADDRESS AT MADISON SQUARE GARDEN

Senator Wagner, Governor Lehman, ladies and gentlemen:

On the eve of a national election, it is well for us to stop for a moment and analyze calmly and without prejudice the effect on our Nation of a victory by either of the major political parties.

The problem of the electorate is far deeper, far more vital than the continuance in the Presidency of any individual. For the greater issue goes beyond units of humanity—it goes to humanity itself.

In 1932 the issue was the restoration of American democracy; and the American people were in a mood to win. They did win. In 1936 the issue is the preservation of their victory. Again they are in a mood to win. Again they will win.

More than four years ago in accepting the Democratic nomination in Chicago, I said: "Give me your help not to win votes alone, but to win in this crusade to restore America to its own people."

The banners of that crusade still fly in the van of a Nation that is on the march.

It is needless to repeat the details of the program which this Administration has been hammering out on the anvils of experience. No amount of misrepresentation or statistical contortion can conceal or blur or smear that record. Neither the attacks of unscrupulous enemies nor the exaggerations of over-zealous friends will serve to mislead the American people.

What was our hope in 1932? Above all other things the American people wanted peace. They wanted peace of mind instead of gnawing fear.

First, they sought escape from the personal terror which had stalked them for three years. They wanted the peace that comes from security in their homes: safety for their savings, permanence in their jobs, a fair profit from their enterprise.

Next, they wanted peace in the community, the peace that springs from the ability to meet the needs of community life: schools, playgrounds, parks, sanitation, highways—those things which are expected of solvent local government. They sought escape from

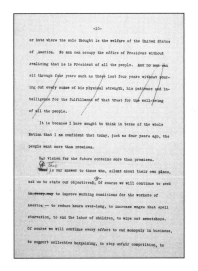

disintegration and bankruptcy in local and state affairs.

They also sought peace within the Nation: protection of their currency, fairer wages, the ending of long hours of toil, the abolition of child labor, the elimination of wild-cat speculation, the safety of their children from kidnappers.

And, finally, they sought peace with other Nations—peace in a world of unrest. The Nation knows that I hate war, and I know that the Nation hates war.

I submit to you a record of peace; and on that record a well-founded expectation for future peace—peace for the individual, peace for the community, peace for the Nation, and peace with the world.

Tonight I call the roll—the roll of honor of those who stood with us in 1932 and still stand with us today.

Written on it are the names of millions who never had a chance—men at starvation wages, women in sweatshops, children at looms.

Written on it are the names of those who despaired, young men and young women for whom opportunity had become a will-o'-the-wisp.

Written on it are the names of farmers whose acres yielded only bitterness, business men whose books were portents of disaster, home owners who were faced with eviction, frugal citizens whose savings were insecure.

Written there in large letters are the names of countless other Americans of all parties and all faiths, Americans who had eyes to see and hearts to understand, whose consciences were burdened because too many of their fellows were burdened, who looked on these things four years ago and said, "This can be changed. We will change it."

We still lead that army in 1936. They stood with us then because in 1932 they believed. They stand with us today because in 1 936 they know. And with them stand millions of new recruits who have come to know.

Their hopes have become our record.

We have not come this far without a struggle and I assure you we cannot go further without a struggle.

For twelve years this Nation was afflicted with hear-nothing, see-nothing, do-nothing Government. The Nation looked to Government but the Government looked away. Nine mocking years with the golden calf and three long years of the scourge! Nine crazy years at the ticker and three long years in the breadlines! Nine mad years of mirage and three long years of despair! Powerful influences strive today to restore that kind of government with its doctrine that that Government is best which is most indifferent.

For nearly four years you have had an Administration which instead of twirling its thumbs has rolled up its sleeves. We will keep our sleeves rolled up.

We had to struggle with the old enemies of peace—business and financial monopoly, speculation, reckless banking, class antagonism, sectionalism, war profiteering.

They had begun to consider the Government of the United States as a mere appendage to their own affairs. We know now that Government by organized money is just as dangerous as Government by organized mob.

Never before in all our history have these forces been so united against one candidate as they stand today. They are unanimous in their hate for me—and I welcome their hatred.

I should like to have it said of my first Administration that in it the forces of selfishness and of lust for power met their match. I should like to have it said of my second Administration that in it these forces met their master.

The American people know from a four-year record that today there is only one entrance to the White House—by the front door. Since March 4, 1933, there has been only one pass-key to the White House. I have carried that key in my pocket. It is there tonight. So long as I am President, it will remain in my pocket.

Those who used to have pass-keys are not happy. Some of them are desperate. Only desperate men with their backs to the wall would descend so far below the level of decent citizenship as to foster the current pay-envelope campaign against America's working people. Only reckless men, heedless of consequences, would risk the disruption of the hope for a new peace between worker and employer by returning to the tactics of the labor spy.

Here is an amazing paradox! The very employers and politicians and publishers who talk most loudly of class antagonism and the destruction of the American system now undermine that system by this attempt to coerce the votes of the wage earners of this country. It is the 1936 version of the old threat to close down the factory or the office if a particular candidate does not win. It is an old strategy of tyrants to delude their victims into fighting their battles for them.

Every message in a pay envelope, even if it is the truth, is a command to vote according to the will of the employer. But this propaganda is worse—it is deceit.

They tell the worker his wage will be reduced by a contribution to some vague form of old-age insurance. They carefully conceal from him the fact that for every dollar of premium he pays for that insurance, the employer pays another dollar. That omission is deceit.

They carefully conceal from him the fact that under the federal law, he receives another insurance policy to help him if he loses his job, and that the premium of that policy is paid 100 percent by the employer and not one cent by the worker. They do not tell him that the insurance policy that is bought for him is far more favorable to him than any policy that any private insurance company could afford to issue. That omission is deceit.

They imply to him that he pays all the cost of both forms of insurance. They carefully conceal from him the fact that for every dollar put up by him his employer puts up three dollars—three for one. And that omission is deceit.

But they are guilty of more than deceit. When they imply that the reserves thus created against both these policies will be stolen by some future Congress, diverted to some wholly foreign purpose, they attack the integrity and honor of American Government itself. Those who suggest that, are already aliens to the spirit of American democracy. Let them emigrate and try their lot under some foreign flag in which they have more confidence.

The fraudulent nature of this attempt is well shown by the record of votes on the passage of the Social Security Act. In addition to an overwhelming majority of Democrats in both Houses, seventy-seven Republican Representatives voted for it and only eighteen against it and fifteen Republican Senators voted for it and only five against it. Where does this last-minute drive of the Republican leadership leave these Republican Representatives and Senators who helped enact this law?

I am sure the vast majority of law-abiding businessmen who are not parties to this propaganda fully appreciate the extent of the threat to honest business contained in this coercion.

I have expressed indignation at this form of campaigning and I am confident that the overwhelming majority of employers, workers and the general public share that indignation and will show it at the polls on Tuesday next.

Aside from this phase of it, I prefer to remember this campaign not as bitter but only as hard-fought. There should be no bitterness or hate where the sole thought is the welfare of the United States of America. No man can occupy the office of President without realizing that he is President of all the people.

It is because I have sought to think in terms of the whole Nation that I am confident that today, just as four years ago, the people want more than promises.

Our vision for the future contains more than promises.

This is our answer to those who, silent about their own plans, ask us to state our objectives.

Of course we will continue to seek to improve working conditions for the workers of America—to reduce hours over-long, to increase wages that spell starvation, to end the labor of children, to wipe out sweatshops. Of course we will continue every effort to end monopoly in business, to support collective bargaining, to stop unfair competition, to abolish dishonorable trade practices. For all these we have only just begun to fight.

Of course we will continue to work for cheaper electricity in the homes and on the farms of America, for better and cheaper transportation, for low interest rates, for sounder home financing, for better banking, for the regulation of security issues, for reciprocal trade among nations, for the wiping out of slums. For all these we have only just begun to fight.

Of course we will continue our efforts in behalf of the farmers of America. With their continued cooperation we will do all in our power to end the piling up of huge surpluses which spelled ruinous prices for their crops. We will persist in successful action for better land use, for reforestation, for the conservation of water all the way from its source to the sea, for drought and flood control, for better marketing facilities for farm commodities, for a definite reduction of farm tenancy, for encouragement of farmer cooperatives, for crop insurance and a stable food supply. For all these we have only just begun to fight.

Of course we will provide useful work for the needy unemployed; we prefer useful work to the pauperism of a dole.

Here and now I want to make myself clear about those who disparage their fellow citizens on the relief rolls. They say that those on relief are not merely jobless—that they are worthless. Their solution for the relief problem is to end relief—to purge the rolls by starvation. To use the language of the stock broker, our needy unemployed would be cared for when, as, and if some fairy godmother should happen on the scene.

You and I will continue to refuse to accept that estimate of our unemployed fellow Americans. Your Government is still on the same side of the street with the Good Samaritan and not with those who pass by on the other side.

Again—what of our objectives?

Of course we will continue our efforts for young men and women so that they may obtain an education and an opportunity to put it to use. Of course we will continue our help for the crippled, for the blind, for the mothers, our insurance for the unemployed, our security for the aged. Of course we will continue to protect the consumer against unnecessary price spreads, against the costs that are added by monopoly and speculation. We will continue our successful efforts to increase his purchasing power and to keep it constant.

For these things, too, and for a multitude of others like them, we have only just begun to fight.

All this—all these objectives—spell peace at home. All our actions, all our ideals, spell also peace with other nations.

Today there is war and rumor of war. We want none of it. But while we guard our shores against threats of war, we will continue to remove the causes of unrest and antagonism at home which might make our people easier victims to those for whom foreign war is profitable. You know well that those who stand to profit by war are not on our side in this campaign.

"Peace on earth, good will toward men"—democracy must cling to that message. For it is my deep conviction that democracy cannot live without that true religion which gives a nation a sense of justice and of moral purpose. Above our political forums, above our market places stand the altars of our faith—altars on which burn the fires of devotion that maintain all that is best in us and all that is best in our Nation.

We have need of that devotion today. It is that which makes it possible for government to persuade those who are mentally prepared to fight each other to go on instead, to work for and to sacrifice for each other. That is why we need to say with the Prophet: "What doth the Lord require of thee—but to do justly, to love mercy and to walk humbly with thy God." That is why the recovery we seek, the recovery we are winning, is more than economic. In it are included justice and love and humility, not for ourselves as individuals alone, but for our Nation.

That is the road to peace.

"We are [dealing with] ... the exclusive power of the President as the sole organ of the federal government in the field of international relations."

Overview

The U.S. Supreme Court's pathbreaking opinion in *United States v. Curtiss-Wright Export Corporation* in 1936 remains the most frequently cited case in the annals of the nation's foreign-affairs jurisprudence and is one of the principal pillars of presidential domination of American foreign policy. The issue in the case was whether Congress, in passing a joint resolution in May of 1934 to grant the president power to place an embargo on the export of munitions or arms under certain conditions, had delegated, or transferred, too much of its legislative authority to the president. The Court upheld the statute against the claim that it was an unconstitutional delegation of legislative power. But in his opinion for the Court, Justice George Sutherland soared beyond the narrow issue and unleashed an expansive interpretation of executive power.

Sutherland articulated a theory of broad and inherent executive power derived not from the Constitution but from other sources. Sutherland characterized the president as the "sole organ" of American foreign policy, a phrase that is frequently used in discussions and debates about the scope of presidential power. Presidents, Justice Department lawyers, and administration officials have so frequently invoked the sole organ doctrine to justify foreign-relations actions and policies that it has become known as the "Curtiss-Wright, so I'm right cite."

The *Curtiss-Wright* opinion represented a dramatic departure from the Court's previous foreign-affairs rulings, which had cast Congress and the president as partners in the formulation of the nation's foreign policy and, on numerous occasions, had viewed Congress as the senior partner. But *Curtiss-Wright* abandoned that prescription and championed executive unilateralism. Its influence may be glimpsed in presidential claims of authority to initiate war, order covert military activities, terminate and suspend treaties, negotiate executive agreements, establish military tribunals, order domestic surveillance and extraordinary rendition (the transfer of a person to a foreign nation outside the legal process and often by the use of force), and, generally, to formulate and manage American foreign relations.

Context

The immediate context of the *Curtiss-Wright* case involved a joint resolution that authorized the president, Franklin D. Roosevelt, to halt the sale of arms to Bolivia and Paraguay, then engaged in armed conflict in the Chaco region of Paraguay, if it would help restore peace between the countries. The resolution, an exercise in contingent delegation—a congressional grant of authority to the president that could be implemented upon presidential findings of fact, as required by the statute—reflected a worldwide effort, first undertaken by the League of Nations, to curb violence and war. It was relatively easy for Roosevelt to determine that invoking the statute would help to restore peace, because the Curtiss-Wright Export Corporation was the principal arms supplier for both nations.

The issue was viewed within the context of delegation cases that had established standards and guidelines to govern the exercise of delegated authority. Sutherland's opinion for the Supreme Court reflected his long-standing interest in the constitutional governance of foreign policy. As a U.S. senator, Sutherland had delivered speeches and written articles on the subject. After he left the Senate, he gave a series of lectures on the scope and exercise of presidential power in foreign relations, and they were subsequently published as a book. Sutherland thus wrote about a subject in which he had been deeply immersed. Sutherland's reference to the president as the sole organ of foreign affairs drew upon a speech delivered in 1800 to the House of Representatives by then congressman (and later chief justice) John Marshall, in which he referred to the president as the sole organ of the nation in its foreign relations.

Finally, the question of congressional authority to delegate to the president its power to regulate interstate commerce stood at the center of the lawsuit brought by the Curtiss-Wright Corporation, which was angered by President Roosevelt's order to impose an embargo on its sales of war weapons to Paraguay and Bolivia. Sutherland's opinion, upholding Roosevelt's order based on the statutory authority delegated to him, would have excited little interest. But his opinion, a broad dissertation on the president's power over foreign affairs, has become a focal point of interest since then, as Americans have

Time Line

1910

■ **March**
Sutherland writes an article for *North American Review*, "The Internal and External Powers of the National Government," presaging his views in *Curtiss-Wright*.

1918

■ **December**
Sutherland delivers a set of lectures at Columbia University, which track his previous article. The lectures are published in 1919 under the title *Constitutional Power and World Affairs*.

1922

■ **September 5**
Sutherland is appointed to the U.S. Supreme Court by President Warren G. Harding.

1934

■ **May 28**
Congress passes a joint resolution delegating to the president authority to halt arms sales to the belligerents in the Chaco War.

■ **May 28**
President Franklin D. Roosevelt invokes the resolution and imposes an embargo on weapons sales to Bolivia and Paraguay as a means of restoring peace.

1935

■ **November 14**
Roosevelt revokes the order, having determined that peace has been restored. However, violations of the order before the revocation will be prosecuted.

1936

■ A federal district court in New York upholds the argument of the Curtiss-Wright Export Corporation that the joint resolution represents an unconstitutional delegation of legislative power.

■ **November 19 and 20**
The Supreme Court hears the appeal by the United States in *United States v. Curtiss-Wright Export Corporation*.

debated the relative powers of the legislative and executive branches.

About the Author

George Sutherland, one of only four justices of the Supreme Court of foreign birth, was born to British parents in 1862 in Buckinghamshire, England. The Sutherlands, who embraced the faith of the Church of Jesus Christ of Latter-day Saints, immigrated to Springville, Utah, in 1863. Within a few years, the elder Sutherland renounced his faith in the Mormon Church and moved his family to Montana. By 1869, however, they had returned to Utah, where young George Sutherland was educated.

In 1879 Sutherland was enrolled in the newly established Brigham Young Academy in Provo. That school, later renamed Brigham Young University, was sponsored by the Mormon Church and exerted considerable influence on Sutherland. Among other lessons, he took to heart the teaching of Section 101 of the *Doctrine and Covenants*, the official doctrine of the church, that the Constitution was a divinely inspired instrument. Church doctrine, moreover, provided that at some distant point, the Constitution would be hanging by a thread and that church faithful would save it.

Following his education in Utah, Sutherland in 1882 enrolled in law school at the University of Michigan. While at Michigan, he studied under the celebrated chief justice of the Michigan Supreme Court, James Valentine Campbell, from whom he learned the basic outline of his opinion in the *Curtiss-Wright* case. He also was a student of the renowned judge and legal scholar Thomas M. Cooley, a disciple of the philosopher Herbert Spencer, whose advocacy of laissez-faire capitalism, liberty, and individual responsibility greatly influenced Sutherland's conservative philosophy, which emphasized a sharply limited government and discouraged governmental roles in social programs.

Sutherland did not earn a degree at Michigan. He stayed there for a year, married a woman from Utah in 1883, and returned to Provo to practice law with his father. In 1893 he moved to Salt Lake City and joined a leading law firm, which brought greater opportunities and wealth. In 1894, he was one of the principal organizers of the Utah State Bar Association, and the next year he delivered at its annual meeting an address that outlined the role of the judiciary in protecting individuals against society, including its duty to ignore views and sentiments of the majority, a widely held view in America at that time.

Sutherland's prominence in legal and political circles earned for him in 1896 election to Utah's first state legislature. As chair of the Senate Judiciary Committee, he played a key role in advancing legislation that imposed an eight-hour workday limit for miners. The surprisingly progressive stance reflected an independent political streak that enabled him to support the presidential campaign of Democrat William Jennings Bryan. His support of Bryan, he explained, lay in Bryan's advocacy of the free coinage of silver, a mining interest of great importance to Utah.

In 1900, at the age of thirty-eight, Sutherland was elected to the U.S. House of Representatives. He served a single term in Congress before repairing to Utah to broaden his political base in the Utah legislature, which, before the passage of the Seventeenth Amendment (calling for two senators to be elected from each state), would select one U.S. senator. In 1905, Sutherland was elected to the Senate for the first of two terms. His bid for a third term in the 1916 election, the first held under the Seventeenth Amendment, was rejected by Utah voters.

While he was in the Senate, Sutherland became a national figure. He exhibited an abiding interest in the nation's foreign policy. As a member of the Senate Foreign Relations Committee, he became an outspoken critic of President Woodrow Wilson's cautious and, occasionally, pacifistic approach. Nevertheless, he advocated broad, unilateral presidential power in foreign affairs, an approach for which he became well known when he authored the Court's opinion in *United States v. Curtiss-Wright*.

After Sutherland left the Senate, he practiced law in Washington, D.C., and served a term as president of the American Bar Association. In 1922, President Warren G. Harding appointed him to the Court. He was regarded as the leader of the so-called Four Horsemen, a bloc of conservative justices who, for a period of fifteen years, prevailed on many issues before the Court and defeated important New Deal programs. He advanced a robust view of judicial power, which, he believed, was necessary to check governmental encroachments and majoritarian impulses. Much of Sutherland's judicial record has been relegated to the realm of obsolescence, since more of his opinions have been overturned than any other member of the Supreme Court in American history.

Still, some of Sutherland's work enjoys lasting status. His opinion in 1932 in *Powell v. Alabama* was the first to recognize the right to counsel as an attribute of due process of law. His most significant contribution to American constitutional law, however, is to be found in his opinions reflecting an expansive view of presidential power in foreign relations. Sutherland retired from the Court in 1938 and died in 1942.

Explanation and Analysis of the Document

Curtiss-Wright brought a lawsuit in which it asserted that Congress had violated the Constitution by delegating its legislative power to the president in the joint resolution granting the president power to stop the sale of arms and munitions. The previous year, the Supreme Court had struck down the delegation of legislative power to the president, and Curtiss-Wright claimed that those precedents should be used to hold unconstitutional the delegation of power in this case.

A federal district court agreed with Curtiss-Wright that the measure represented an unconstitutional delegation of legislative power. It did acknowledge the "traditional practice of Congress in reposing the widest discretion in the

Time Line

1936
■ December 21
The Supreme Court overturns the federal district court ruling and upholds the constitutionality of the joint resolution.

1938
■ January 6
Sutherland informs Roosevelt of his decision to retire on January 18, 1938.

1942
■ July 18
Sutherland dies while on vacation in Stockbridge, Massachusetts.

Executive Department of the government in the conduct of the delicate and nicely posed issues of international relations" (14 F. Supp. 230 [S.D.N.Y. 1936]), but that recognition did not save the statute.

The district court decision was appealed directly to the Supreme Court, where both parties addressed the issue of delegation. The Justice Department defended the delegation by asserting that Congress may delegate to the president authority to investigate, make findings of fact, and implement the legislation in accordance with congressional purpose. In short, the delegation was a valid exercise in contingent delegation; the president had implemented the embargo, since he had determined that it would help restore peace in South America. Government attorneys maintained that previous delegation rulings provided more than adequate support to uphold this act of delegation. Curtiss-Wright argued that the delegation was invalid since it did not provide adequate standards to guide the president. Thus the president was exercising the lawmaking power of Congress in violation of the Constitution's separation of powers.

◆ Sutherland's Opinion

In his opinion for the Supreme Court, Justice Sutherland reversed the district court and upheld the delegation of legislative power to the president to impose an embargo on the sale of arms and munitions to the Chaco region. Sutherland observed that though "we find it unnecessary to determine" whether or not the resolution "had related solely to internal affairs," it would be open to the charge of unlawful delegation. The "whole aim of the resolution is to affect a situation entirely external to the United States, and falling within the category of foreign affairs." Sutherland declared that the two categories of external and internal affairs are different "both in respect of their origin and nature." The principle that the federal government is limited to either enumerated or implied powers "is categorically true only in respect of our internal affairs." The purpose, he wrote, was "to carve from the general mass of legislative powers then possessed by the states such portions as it was thought desirable to vest in the federal government, leaving those not included in the enumeration still in the states." However, that doctrine "applies only to powers which the states had ... since the states severally never possessed international powers."

The transfer of foreign-affairs powers, Sutherland explained, occurred as a result of the colonies' separation from Great Britain. After the Declaration of Independence, "the powers of external sovereignty passed from the Crown not to the colonies severally, but to the colonies in their collective and corporate capacity as the United States of America." Accordingly, the "external sovereignty of Great Britain ... passed to the Union." The foreign-affairs powers of the nation were extraconstitutional, that is, independent of the Constitution. "The powers to declare and wage war, to conclude peace, to make treaties, to maintain diplomatic relations with other sovereignties, if they had never been mentioned in the Constitution," Sutherland noted, "would have vested in the federal government as necessary concomitants of nationality."

Sutherland's theory of extraconstitutional power in the realm of external sovereignty creates a virtually unlimited foreign-affairs power for the president:

In this vast external realm, with its important, complicated, delicate and manifold problems, the President alone has the power to speak or listen as a representative of the nation. He makes treaties with the advice and consent of the Senate; but he alone negotiates. Into the field of negotiation the Senate cannot intrude; and Congress itself is powerless to invade it.

The president's power, Sutherland explains, is not dependent on authority from Congress:

It is important to bear in mind that we are here dealing not alone with an authority vested in the President by an exertion of legislative power, but with such an authority plus the very delicate, plenary and exclusive power of the President as the sole organ of the federal government in the field of international relations—a power which does not require as a basis for its exercise an act of Congress, but which, of course, like every other governmental power, must be exercised in subordination to the applicable provisions of the Constitution. It is quite apparent that if, in the maintenance of our international relations, embarrassment—perhaps serious embarrassment—is to be avoided and success for our aims achieved, congressional legislation which is to be made effective through negotiation and inquiry within the international field must often accord to the President a degree of discretion and freedom from statutory restriction which would not be admissible were domestic affairs alone involved.

Sutherland's assertion of vast and sweeping inherent presidential power in foreign affairs, essentially the exercise of the nation's external sovereignty, is vulnerable to historical scrutiny. First, external sovereignty did not circumvent the colonies and the independent states and pass directly to the national government. When Great Britain entered into a peace treaty with America, the so-called preliminary articles of peace of November 30, 1782, these articles were not with a national government. Rather, "His Brittanic Majesty acknowledges the said United States, viz. New Hampshire, Massachusetts-Bay, Rhode-Island and Providence Plantations, Connecticut, New-York, New-Jersey, Pennsylvania, Delaware, Maryland, Virginia, North-Carolina, South Carolina, and Georgia," and referred to them as "free, sovereign and independent States" (http://www.yale.edu/lawweb/avalon/diplomacy/britain/prel1782.htm). The colonies formed a Continental Congress in 1774, and it provided a form of national government until the passage of the Articles of Confederation, ratified in 1781, and the drafting of the U.S. Constitution. In 1776 states were acting as sovereign entities. Proof may be found in the Articles of Confederation. Article II of that document stated: "Each State retains its Sovereignty, freedom and independence, and every power ... which is not ... expressly delegated to the United States, in Congress assembled." Further, in Article III, it was provided that "the said states hereby severally enter into a firm league of friendship with each other, for their common defense." Finally, Article IX stated: "The United States in Congress assembled, shall have the sole and exclusive right and power of determining on peace and war ... [and of] entering into treaties and alliances." The decision by the states to delegate to the Continental Congress power over war and treaties demonstrates the error in Sutherland's premise that these powers were derived from "some other source" than the several states (http://www.yale.edu/lawweb/avalon/ artconf.htm).

Even if it were to be assumed that the power of external sovereignty had been by some method transferred directly from the British Crown to the Union, it remains to be explained why that power would be vested in the president. As Justice Felix Frankfurter stated in *Youngstown Sheet and Tube Co. v. Sawyer*, "The fact that power exists in the Government does not vest it in the President" (343 U.S. 579, 604 [1952]). Indeed, the Supreme Court has ruled on several occasions that sovereign power in foreign affairs is held by Congress. At any rate, there is nothing in Sutherland's theory that would explain the location of this power in the presidency. It may be added that Sutherland's assertion of extraconstitutional foreign-affairs powers is undermined by James Madison's statement in Federalist Paper number 45 that "the powers delegated by the proposed Constitution are few and defined.... [They] will be exercised principally on external objects, as war, peace, negotiation, and foreign commerce" (http://www.foundingfathers.info/federalistpapers/fed45.htm). Finally, the Court, since *Curtiss-Wright*, has consistently taken the position that powers are tethered to the Constitution. In 1957, in *Reid v. Covert*, Justice Hugo Black, writing the opinion for the Court, stated: "The United States is entirely a creature of the Constitution. Its powers and authority have no other source. It can act only in accordance with all the limitations imposed by the Constitution" (354 U.S. 1, 16–17 [1957]).

◆ The Sole Organ Doctrine

Sutherland's treatment of foreign-relations powers as essentially executive in nature found clear expression in his reference to the president "as the sole organ of the federal government in the field of international relations—a power which does not require as a basis for its exercise an act of Congress." In that capacity, the president's powers are "plenary and exclusive." Sutherland's depiction of the president as "sole organ" drew upon a speech delivered in 1800 in the House of Representatives by then Congressman (and later chief justice) John Marshall, who stated: "The President is the sole organ of the nation in its external relations.... Of consequence, the demand of a foreign nation can only be made on him" (U.S. Congress, vol. 10, pp. 613–614).

Marshall was defending the decision of President John Adams to surrender a British deserter, Jonathan Robbins, in accordance with the Jay Treaty. According to Marshall, the Robbins affair involved a demand upon the United States, and it required a response from the president on behalf of the American people. In the course of his speech, Marshall never asserted that the president's well-established role as sole organ of communication implies authority to make policy. The president, moreover, was fulfilling his duty to implement the extradition provisions of the treaty. Article II of the Constitution provides that it is the president's duty to "take Care that the Laws be faithfully executed." Article VI states that all treaties made "shall be the supreme law of the land." The president, in the performance of his constitutional role, was implementing, not making, a treaty. It is worth noting that Marshall, in his thirty-four years on the Supreme Court, never wrote an opinion in which he embraced Sutherland's characterization of the president as the sole organ of American foreign policy. On the contrary, he wrote numerous opinions in which he asserted the primacy of Congress in matters of war and peace and of national security and foreign affairs.

In drawing upon Marshall's speech, Sutherland infused a purely communicative role with a substantive policy-making role. As a consequence, Sutherland transformed Marshall's depiction of that narrow duty into a vast and sweeping power that exalted presidential domination of American foreign policy. In fact, seeing of the president as the "sole" organ of the nation's foreign policy is at odds with the textual assignment of foreign-relations powers to both the president and Congress. Article I grants to Congress broad powers, including the authority to regulate foreign commerce; raise armies; declare war; grant letters of marque and reprisal (the authority to order military hostilities short of war); make rules governing immigration and naturalization; make regulations governing land and naval forces; define and punish acts of piracy; define offenses against the law of nations; organize, arm, and discipline the militia; and make rules for calling for the militia, among others. The president is vested with only two exclusive foreign-

affairs powers. He is commander in chief, but he acts in this capacity by and under the authority of Congress. He also has the power to receive ambassadors. Hamilton, Madison, and Jefferson, among others, agreed that this clerklike function was ceremonial in character. Of course, the president shares with the Senate the authority to make treaties and to appoint ambassadors. The textual grant of authority to the president pales in comparison to that allocated to Congress. The framers of the Constitution did not make the president the sole organ of American foreign policy either by definition or substance. Indeed, most foreign-relations powers are vested in Congress.

Audience

The Court's opinion in *United States v. Curtiss-Wright* might have expected to enjoy a large audience, given Justice Sutherland's assertions of presidential power, but in truth only a relatively small number of people knew of the case, and few perceived it to possess much in the way of importance. In principle, every Supreme Court opinion is of interest to the citizenry. In theory, of course, every citizen has an interest, and perhaps an immediate stake, in judicial interpretations of the Constitution, since it is the law of the land to which the government and governed alike are subject. Moreover, a separation-of-powers case, such as *United States v. Curtiss-Wright*, is likely to generate immediate concerns for the three branches of government—legislative, executive, and judicial—because the ruling will have significant implications for the scope and exercise of their respective powers.

United States v. Curtiss-Wright had a small if intensely interested audience, since the Court's ruling would have immediate consequences not only for Congress and the president but also for the corporation itself. The Curtiss-Wright Export Corporation lost its legal bid to continue its lucrative sales of war weapons and munitions to two nations at war with one another. Few companies find themselves in such an enviable business arrangement. Congress was immediately concerned to know whether, through the joint resolution of Congress, it might delegate authority to the president to impose an embargo as a means of restoring peace in the Chaco region. At that juncture, Congress was fairly uncertain as to the scope of authority that it might delegate. The president, Franklin D. Roosevelt, was anxious to learn whether his ban on sales would be upheld, for he believed that the authority granted to him by Congress was an important tool in reducing military hostilities and violence. Roosevelt could not have anticipated Sutherland's broad dicta asserting extraconstitutional foreign-affairs powers for the president. The Justice Department certainly was part of an engaged and interested audience, since the Court's opinion would have a major affect on future litigation and its approach to briefing cases involving presidential power.

Upon its release, the opinion received scant attention from the press and only passing attention from the scholar-

> "As a result of the separation from Great Britain by the colonies, acting as a unit, the powers of external sovereignty passed from the Crown not to the colonies severally, but to the colonies in their collective and corporate capacity as the United States of America."
>
> (Justice George Sutherland, Opinion of the Court)

> "It results that the investment of the federal government with the powers of external sovereignty did not depend upon the affirmative grants of the Constitution."
>
> (Justice George Sutherland, Opinion of the Court)

> "It is important to bear in mind that we are here dealing not alone with an authority vested in the President by an exertion of legislative power, but with such an authority plus the very delicate, plenary and exclusive power of the President as the sole organ of the federal government in the field of international relations."
>
> (Justice George Sutherland, Opinion of the Court)

ly community, although a handful of scholars would, within a few years, note its groundbreaking assertions. The opinion's audience has grown tremendously over the years, as citizens, scholars, and governmental actors have focused on the powers, roles, and duties of Congress and the president in the formulation, management, and conduct of the nation's foreign relations.

Impact

It is difficult to overestimate the impact of the *Curtiss-Wright* opinion on the scope of executive power. It has been invoked and embraced by presidents and judges, and, as a consequence, it has become a principal pillar of presidential domination of American foreign affairs. For their part, presidents have cited the sole organ doctrine to justify unilateral executive war making, domestic surveillance, the termination and suspension of treaties, extraordinary rendition, the creation of military tribunals, covert acts, the detention of enemy combatants, and executive agreements, as well as a general authority to formulate, manage, and conduct the nation's foreign relations. Courts, moreover, have endorsed the sole organ doctrine, principally as a means of justifying deference to the executive in the conduct of foreign policy.

The sole organ doctrine was invoked by President Roosevelt and embraced by the Supreme Court shortly after it was announced. In 1937, in *United States v. Belmont*, and in 1942, in *United States v. Pink*, the Court cited the doctrine to uphold executive agreements with the Soviet Union. Sutherland himself wrote the opinion in *Belmont*. In recent years, the courts have cited the Sutherland opinion for the proposition that Congress might delegate its power more freely in the area of foreign affairs than in domestic affairs. In other cases, the courts have invoked *Curtiss-Wright* to justify traditional deference to executive judgment in the realm of foreign relations. The Bush administration has drawn upon the opinion to advance broad presidential powers in the conduct of the war in Iraq and in the war on terror.

The opinion has its critics. Scholars have denounced Sutherland's claims of extraconstitutional and inherent powers, his historical theory about the flow of external sovereignty, and the sole organ doctrine itself. To critics, the sole organ doctrine is irreconcilable with the text of the Constitution. The assertion of inherent executive power, moreover, is difficult to square with the framers' conception of executive power and their design of the presidency. In the landmark case *Youngstown Sheet and Tube Co. v. Sawyer* (1952), Justice Robert H. Jackson dismissed much of Sutherland's opinion as "dictum." The issue in the case, it should be recalled, involved the authority of Congress to delegate its legislative power to the president to impose an arms embargo. The issue, then, involved legislative and not executive power. Sutherland's long discourse on executive power was irrelevant to the issue at hand and thus viewed as dictum.

Related Documents

Elliot, Jonathan, ed. *The Debates in the Several State Conventions on the Adoption of the Federal Constitution.* 5 vols. Philadelphia: J. P. Lippincott, 1861. Reprint. New York: Burt Franklin, 1974. This important collection provides a record of the discussions and debates in the various state ratifying conventions on the issue of the ratification of the proposed Constitution. The discussions on presidential power offer a basis for evaluating Sutherland's opinion.

Farrand, Max, ed. *The Records of the Federal Convention of 1787.* 4 vols. New Haven, Conn.: Yale University Press, 1966. Derived principally from the notes of the proceedings of the Constitutional Convention kept by James Madison but including notes from other delegates to the convention, these records of the discussions and debates among the framers of the Constitution illuminate their work. The discussions of presidential power provide a context within which to view the opinion of Justice Sutherland.

Pole, J. R., ed. *The Federalist.* Indianapolis, Ind.: Hackett, 2005. The Federalist Papers were viewed by Thomas Jefferson, among others, as the authoritative explanation of the meaning of the Constitution. They represent an argument urging the American people to ratify the proposed Constitution. These eighty-five essays are indispensable to an understanding of the values, concerns, and goals of the framers of the Constitution. The papers on presidential power provide a measuring stick by which to assess Sutherland's opinion.

"Youngstown Sheet and Tube Co. v. Sawyer 343 U.S. 579 (1952)." FindLaw Web site. http://caselaw.lp.findlaw.com/scripts/getcase. pl?court=US&vol=343&invol=579. Accessed on February 8, 2008. The Supreme Court opinions in this landmark case on presidential power afford an opportunity to compare and contrast Sutherland's views with those of the justices in this case, prominently known as the Steel Seizure Case. *Youngstown* is widely regarded as the most penetrating judicial examination of presidential power in the nation's history.

Bibliography

■ Articles

Garner, James W. "Executive Discretion in the Conduct of Foreign Relations." *American Journal of International Law* 31, no. 2 (1937): 289–293.

Gobel, Jr., Julius. "Constitutional History and Constitutional Law." *Columbia Law Review* 38, no. 4 (1938): 555–577.

Levitan, David M. "The Foreign Relations Power: An Analysis of Mr. Justice Sutherland's Theory." *Yale Law Journal* 55, no. 3 (1946): 467–497.

Lofgren, Charles. "*United States v. Curtiss-Wright Export Corporation:* An Historical Reassessment." *Yale Law Journal* 83, no. 1 (1973): 1–32.

Patterson, C. Perry. "In Re *The United States v. The Curtiss-Wright Corporation.*" *Texas Law Review* 22 (1944): 286–308.

Quarles, James. "The Federal Government: As to Foreign Affairs, Are Its Powers Inherent as Distinguished from Delegated?" *Georgetown Law Journal* 32 (1944): 375–383.

■ Books

Arkes, Hadley. *The Return of George Sutherland: Restoring a Jurisprudence of Natural Rights.* Princeton, N.J.: Princeton University Press, 1994.

Paschal, Joel Francis. *Mr. Justice Sutherland: A Man against the State.* Princeton, N.J.: Princeton University Press, 1951.

Sutherland, George. *Constitutional Power and World Affairs.* New York: Columbia University Press, 1919.

U.S. Congress. *Annals of the Congress of the United States, 1789–1824.* 42 vols. Washington, D.C., 1834–1856.

■ Web Sites

"Articles of Confederation." The Avalon Project at Yale Law School Web site.
> http://www.yale.edu/lawweb/avalon/artconf.htm. Accessed on February 8, 2008.

"Federalist No. 45." Founding Fathers Web site.
> http://www.foundingfathers.info/federalistpapers/fed45.htm. Accessed on February 8, 2008.

"Preliminary Articles of Peace: November 30, 1782." The Avalon Project at Yale Law School Web site.
> http://www.yale.edu/lawweb/avalon/diplomacy/britain/prel1782. htm. Accessed on February 12, 2008.

"United States v. Curtiss-Wright Export Corporation, 299 U.S. 304 (1936)." FindLaw Web site.
> http://caselaw.lp.findlaw.com/cgi-bin/getcase.pl?court=us &vol=299&invol=304. Accessed on February 8, 2008.

"United States v. Curtiss-Wright Export Corp. (No. 98) 14 F.Supp. 230, reversed." Cornell University Law School Supreme Court Collection Web site.
> http://www.law.cornell.edu/supct/html/historics/USSC_CR_02 99_0304_ZO.html. Accessed on February 8, 2008.

—By David Gray Adler

1. The Court's opinion in *United States v. Curtiss-Wright* has become a principal pillar of presidential domination of American foreign policy. How do Justice Sutherland's assertions of "extraconstitutional" power square with the Founders' conception of the Constitution and presidential power?

2. Justice Sutherland described the president as the "sole organ" of American foreign policy. Does that description reflect the constitutional allocation of foreign-affairs powers? Does that characterization of presidential power find support in the discussions and debates of the Constitutional Convention? What, if anything, do the Federalist Papers have to say about presidential power in foreign affairs?

3. In the *Curtiss-Wright* case, Justice Sutherland characterized the president as the "sole organ" of American foreign policy. In drawing this conclusion he relied on John Marshall's speech in 1800 in which he referred to the president as the "sole organ" of the nation's foreign relations. In your view, was Sutherland's understanding of the president as "sole organ" consistent with Marshall's? If not, what were the substantive differences between the two? Compare and contrast the two views.

4. How has Justice Sutherland's opinion been understood and utilized by presidents and courts over the years? Provide a critique of judicial citations to the *Curtiss-Wright* opinion and presidential invocation of Sutherland's reasoning.

5. Describe and discuss critical evaluations of Justice Sutherland's opinion. Do you agree with criticisms? Why or why not? Explain your position.

6. Compare and contrast Justice Sutherland's description of presidential power with the opinions of the justices in *Youngstown Sheet and Tube. Co. v. Sawyer* (1952).

Glossary

delegation	congressional grant or transfer of power to the president
manifold	of many and varied kinds; having many forms
plenary	complete, unlimited
seriatim	separately, or severally
sovereignty	supreme power over a subject, a government or a nation; ultimate authority or dominion
unfettered	unlimited or unrestricted

UNITED STATES V. CURTISS-WRIGHT

◆ Mr. Justice Sutherland Delivered the Opinion of the Court

On January 27, 1936, an indictment was returned in the court below, the first count of which charges that appellees, beginning with the 29th day of May, 1934, conspired to sell in the United States certain arms of war, namely, fifteen machine guns, to Bolivia, a country then engaged in armed conflict in the Chaco, in violation of the Joint Resolution of Congress approved May 28, 1934, and the provisions of a proclamation issued on the same day by the President of the United States pursuant to authority conferred by section 1 of the resolution. In pursuance of the conspiracy, the commission of certain overt acts was alleged, details of which need not be stated. The Joint Resolution (chapter 365, 48 Stat. 811) follows: "Resolved by the Senate and House of Representatives of the United States of America in Congress assembled, That if the President finds that the prohibition of the sale of arms and munitions of war in the United States to those countries now engaged in armed conflict in the Chaco may contribute to the reestablishment of peace between those countries, and if after consultation with the governments of other American Republics and with their cooperation, as well as that of such other governments as he may deem necessary, he makes proclamation to that effect, it shall be unlawful to sell, except under such limitations and exceptions as the President prescribes, any arms or munitions of war in any place in the United States to the countries now engaged in that armed conflict, or to any person, company, or association acting in the interest of either country, until otherwise ordered by the President or by Congress. Sec. 2. Whoever sells any arms or munitions of war in violation of section 1 shall, on conviction, be punished by a fine not exceeding $10,000 or by imprisonment not exceeding two years, or both."

The President's proclamation (48 Stat. 1744, No. 2087), after reciting the terms of the Joint Resolution, declares:

"Now, Therefore, I, Franklin D. Roosevelt, President of the United States of America, acting under and by virtue of the authority con-ferred in me by the said joint resolution of Congress, do hereby declare and proclaim that I have found that the prohibition of the sale of arms and munitions of war in the United States to those countries now engaged in armed conflict in the Chaco may contribute to the reestablishment of peace between those countries, and that I have consulted with the governments of other American Republics and have been assured of the cooperation of such governments as I have deemed necessary as contemplated by the said joint resolution; and I do hereby admonish all citizens of the United States and every person to abstain from every violation of the provisions of the joint resolution above set forth, hereby made applicable to Bolivia and Paraguay, and I do hereby warn them that all violations of such provisions will be rigorously prosecuted.

And I do hereby enjoin upon all officers of the United States charged with the execution of the laws thereof, the utmost diligence in preventing violations of the said joint resolution and this my proclamation issued thereunder, and in bringing to trial and punishment any offenders against the same.

And I do hereby delegate to the Secretary of State the power of prescribing exceptions and limitations to the application of the said joint resolution of May 28, 1934, as made effective by this my proclamation issued thereunder."

On November 14, 1935, this proclamation was revoked (49 Stat. 3480), in the following terms:

"Now, therefore, I, Franklin D. Roosevelt, President of the United States of America, do hereby declare and proclaim that I have found that the prohibition of the sale of arms and munitions of war in the United States to Bolivia or Paraguay will no longer be necessary as a contribution to the reestablishment of peace between those countries, and the above-mentioned Proclamation of May 28, 1934, is hereby revoked as to the sale of arms and munitions of war to Bolivia or Paraguay from and after November 29, 1935, provided, however, that this action shall not have the effect of releasing or extinguishing any penalty, forfeiture or liability incurred under the aforesaid Proclamation of May 28, 1934, or the Joint Resolution of Congress approved by the President on the same date; and that the said Proclamation and Joint Resolution shall be treated as remaining in force for the purpose of sustaining any proper action or prosecution for the enforcement of such penalty, forfeiture or liability."

Appellees severally demurred to the first count of the indictment on the grounds (1) that it did not charge facts sufficient to show the commission by appellees of any offense against any law of the United States; (2) that this court of the indictment charges a conspiracy to violate the Joint Resolution and the Presidential proclamation, both of which had expired according to the terms of the Joint Resolution by reason of the revocation contained in the Presidential proclamation of November 14, 1935, and were not in force at the time when the indictment was found. The points urged in support of the demurrers were, first, that the Joint Resolution effects an invalid delegation of legislative power to the executive; second, that the Joint Resolution never became effective because of the failure of the President to find essential jurisdictional facts; and, third, that the second proclamation operated to put an end to the alleged liability under the Joint Resolution.

The court below sustained the demurrers upon the first point, but overruled them on the second and third points. (D.C.) 14 F.Supp. 230. The government appealed to this court under the provisions of the Criminal Appeals Act of March 2, 1907, 34 Stat. 1246, as amended, U.S.C., title 18, 682 (18 U.S.C.A. 682). That act authorizes the United States to appeal from a district court direct to this court in criminal cases where, among other things, the decision sustaining a demurrer to the indictment or any count thereof is based upon the invalidity or construction of the statute upon which the indictment is founded.

First. It is contended that by the Joint Resolution the going into effect and continued operation of the resolution was conditioned (a) upon the President's judgment as to its beneficial effect upon the re-establishment of peace between the countries engaged in armed conflict in the Chaco; (b) upon the making of a proclamation, which was left to his unfettered discretion, thus constituting an attempted substitution of the President's will for that of Congress; (c) upon the making of a proclamation putting an end to the operation of the resolution, which again was left to the President's unfettered discretion; and (d) further, that the extent of its operation in particular cases was subject to limitation and exception by the President, controlled by no standard. In each of these particulars, appellees urge that Congress abdicated its essential functions and delegated them to the Executive.

Whether, if the Joint Resolution had related solely to internal affairs, it would be open to the challenge that it constituted an unlawful delegation of legislative power to the Executive, we find it unnecessary to determine. The whole aim of the resolution is to affect a situation entirely external to the United States, and falling within the category of foreign affairs. The determination which we are called to make, therefore, is whether the Joint Resolution, as applied to that situation, is vulnerable to attack under the rule that forbids a delegation of the law-making power. In other words, assuming (but not deciding) that the challenged delegation, if it were confined to internal affairs, would be invalid, may it nevertheless be sustained on the ground that its exclusive aim is to afford a remedy for a hurtful condition within foreign territory?

It will contribute to the elucidation of the question if we first consider the differences between the powers of the federal government in respect of foreign or external affairs and those in respect of domestic or internal affairs. That there are differences between them, and that these differences are fundamental, may not be doubted.

The two classes of powers are different, both in respect of their origin and their nature. The broad statement that the federal government can exercise no powers except those specifically enumerated in the Constitution, and such implied powers as are necessary and proper to carry into effect the enumerated powers, is categorically true only in respect of our internal affairs. In that field, the primary purpose of the Constitution was to carve from the general mass of legislative powers then possessed by the states such portions as it was thought desirable to vest in the federal government, leaving those not included in the enumeration still in the states. *Carter v. Carter Coal Co.*, 298 U.S. 238, 294, 56 S.Ct. 855, 865. That this doctrine applies only to powers which the states had is self-evident. And since the states severally never possessed international powers, such powers could not have been carved from the mass of state powers but obviously were transmitted to the United States from some other source. During the Colonial period, those powers were possessed exclusively by and were entirely under the control of the Crown. By the Declaration of Independence, "the Representatives of the United States of America" declared the United (not the several) Colonies to be free and independent states, and as such to have "full Power to levy War, conclude Peace, contract Alliances, establish Commerce and to do all other Acts and Things which Independent States may of right do."

As a result of the separation from Great Britain by the colonies, acting as a unit, the powers of external sovereignty passed from the Crown not to the colonies severally, but to the colonies in their collective and corporate capacity as the United States of America. Even before the Declaration, the colonies were a unit in foreign affairs, acting through a common agency—namely, the Continental Congress, composed of delegates from the thirteen colonies. That agency exercised the powers of war and peace, raised an army, created a navy, and finally adopted the Declaration of Independence. Rulers come and go; governments end and forms of government change; but sovereignty survives. A political society cannot endure without a supreme will somewhere. Sovereignty is never held in suspense. When, therefore, the external sovereignty of Great Britain in respect of the colonies ceased, it immediately passed to the Union. See *Penhallow v. Doane*, 3 Dall. 54, 80, 81, Fed.Cas. No. 10925. That fact was given practical application almost at once. The treaty of peace, made on September 3, 1783, was concluded between his Brittanic Majesty and the "United States of America."

The Union existed before the Constitution, which was ordained and established among other things to form "a more perfect Union." Prior to that event, it is clear that the Union, declared by the Articles of Confederation to be "perpetual," was the sole possessor of external sovereignty, and in the Union it remained without change save in so far as the Constitution in express terms qualified its exercise. The Framers' Convention was called and exerted its powers upon the irrefutable postulate that though the states were several their people in respect of foreign affairs were one. Compare The Chinese Exclusion Case, 130 U.S. 581, 604, 606 S., 9 S.Ct. 623. In that convention, the entire absence of state power to deal with those affairs was thus forcefully stated by Rufus King:

"The states were not 'sovereigns' in the sense contended for by some. They did not possess the peculiar features of sovereignty,—they could not make war, nor peace, nor alliances, nor treaties. Considering them as political beings, they were dumb, for they could not speak to any foreign sovereign whatever. They were deaf, for they could not hear any propositions from such sovereign. They had not even the organs or faculties of defence or offence, for they could not of themselves raise troops, or equip vessels, for war." 5 Elliot's Debates, 212.1.

It results that the investment of the federal government with the powers of external sovereignty did not depend upon the affirmative grants of the Constitution. The powers to declare and wage war, to conclude peace, to make treaties, to maintain diplomatic relations with other sovereignties, if they had never been mentioned in the Constitution, would have vested in the federal government as necessary concomitants of nationality. Neither the Constitution nor the laws passed in pursuance of it have any force in foreign territory unless in respect of our own citizens (see *American Banana Co. v. United Fruit Co.*, 213 U.S. 347, 356, 29 S.Ct. 511, 16 Ann.Cas. 1047); and operations of the nation in such territory must be governed by treaties, international understandings and compacts, and the principles of international law. As a member of the family of nations, the right and power of the United States in that field are equal to the right and power of the other members of the international family. Otherwise, the United States is not completely sovereign. The power to acquire territory by discovery and occupation (*Jones v. United States*, 137 U.S. 202, 212, 11 S.Ct. 80), the power to expel undesirable aliens (*Fong Yue Ting v. United States*, 149 U.S. 698, 705 et seq., 13 S.Ct. 1016), the power to make such international agreements as do not constitute treaties in the constitutional sense (*Altman & Co. v. United States*, 224 U.S. 583, 600, 601 S., 32 S.Ct. 593; Crandall, Treaties, Their Making and Enforcement (2d Ed.) p. 102 and note 1), none of which is expressly affirmed by the Constitution, nevertheless exist as inherently inseparable from the conception of nationality. This the court recognized, and in each of the cases cited found the warrant for its conclusions not in the provisions of the Constitution, but in the law of nations.

In *Burnet v. Brooks*, 288 U.S. 378, 396, 53 S.Ct. 457, 461, 86 A.L.R. 747, we said, "As a nation with all the attributes of sovereignty, the United States is vested with all the powers of government necessary to maintain an effective control of international relations." Cf. *Carter v. Carter Coal Co.*, supra, 298 U.S. 238, at page 295, 56 S.Ct. 855, 865. Not only, as we have shown, is the federal power over external affairs in origin and essential character different from that over internal affairs, but participation in the exercise of the power is significantly limited. In this vast external realm, with its important, complicated, delicate and manifold problems, the President alone has the power to speak or listen as a representative of the nation. He makes treaties with the advice and consent of the Senate; but he alone negotiates. Into the field of negotiation the Senate cannot intrude; and Congress itself is powerless to invade it. As Marshall said in his great argument of March 7, 1800, in the House of Representatives, "The President is the sole organ of the nation in its external relations, and its sole representative with foreign nations." Annals, 6th Cong., col. 613. The Senate Committee on Foreign Relations at a very early day in our history (February 15, 1816), reported to the Senate, among other things, as follows:

> "The President is the constitutional representative of the United States with regard to foreign nations. He manages our concerns with foreign nations and must necessarily be most competent to determine when, how, and upon what subjects negotiation may be urged with the greatest prospect of success. For his conduct he is responsible to the Constitution. The committee considers this responsibility the surest pledge for the faithful discharge of his duty. They think the interference of the Senate in the direction of foreign negotiations calculated to diminish that responsibility and thereby to impair the best security for the national safety. The nature of transactions with foreign nations, moreover, requires caution and unity of design, and their success frequently depends on secrecy and dispatch."

It is important to bear in mind that we are here dealing not alone with an authority vested in the President by an exertion of legislative power, but with such an authority plus the very delicate, plenary and exclusive power of the President as the sole organ of the federal government in the field of international relations—a power which does not require as a basis for its exercise an act of Congress, but which, of course, like every other governmental power, must be exercised in subordination to the applicable provisions of the Constitution. It is quite apparent that if, in the maintenance of our international relations, embarrassment—perhaps serious embarrassment—is to be avoided and success for our aims achieved, congressional legislation which is to be made effective through negotiation and inquiry within the international field must often accord to the President a degree of discretion and freedom from statutory restriction which would not be admissible were domestic affairs alone involved. Moreover, he, not Congress, has the better opportunity of knowing the conditions which prevail in foreign countries, and especially is this true in time of war. He has his confidential sources of information. He has his agents in the form of diplomatic, consular and other officials. Secrecy in respect of information gathered by them may be highly necessary, and the premature disclosure of it productive of harmful results. Indeed, so clearly is this true that the first President refused to accede to a request to lay before the House of Representatives the instructions, correspondence and documents relating to the negotiation of the Jay Treaty—a refusal the wisdom of which was recognized by the House itself and has never since been doubted. In his reply to the request, President Washington said:

> "The nature of foreign negotiations requires caution, and their success must often depend on secrecy; and even when brought to a conclusion a full disclosure of all the measures, demands, or eventual concessions which may have been proposed or contemplated would be extremely impolitic; for this might have a pernicious influence on future negotiations, or produce immediate inconveniences, perhaps danger and mischief, in relation to other powers. The necessity of such caution and secrecy was one cogent reason for vesting the power of making treaties in the President, with the advice and consent of the Senate, the principle on which that body was formed confining it to a small number of members. To admit, then, a right in the House of Representatives to demand and to have as a matter of course all the papers respecting a negotiation with a foreign power would be to establish a dangerous precedent."

The marked difference between foreign affairs and domestic affairs in this respect is recognized by both houses of Congress in the very form of their requisitions for information from the executive departments. In the case of every department except the Department of State, the resolution directs the official to furnish the information. In the case of the State Department, dealing with foreign affairs, the President is requested to furnish the information "if not incompatible with the public interest." A statement that to furnish the information is not compatible with the public interest rarely, if ever, is questioned.

When the President is to be authorized by legislation to act in respect of a matter intended to affect a situation in foreign territory, the legislator properly bears in mind the important consideration that the form of the President's action—or, indeed, whether he shall act at all—may well depend, among other things, upon the nature of the confidential information which he has or may thereafter receive, or upon the effect which his action may have upon our foreign relations. This consideration, in connection with what we have already said on the subject discloses the unwisdom of requiring Congress in this field of governmental power to lay down narrowly definite standards by which the President is to be governed. As this court said in *Mackenzie v. Hare*, 239 U.S. 299, 311, 36 S.Ct. 106, 108, Ann.Cas. 1916E, 645, "As a government, the United States is invested with all the attributes of sovereignty. As it has the character of nationality it has the powers of nationality, especially those which concern its relations and intercourse with other countries. We should hesitate long before limiting or embarrassing such powers."

In the light of the foregoing observations, it is evident that this court should not be in haste to apply a general rule which will have the effect of condemning legislation like that under review as constituting an unlawful delegation of legislative power. The principles which justify such legislation find overwhelming support in the unbroken legislative practice which has prevailed almost from the inception of the national government to the present day.

Let us examine, in chronological order, the acts of legislation which warrant this conclusion:

The Act of June 4, 1794, authorized the President to lay, regulate and revoke embargoes. He was "authorized" "whenever, in his opinion, the public safety shall so require," to lay the embargo upon all ships and vessels in the ports of the United States, including those of foreign nations, "under such regulations as the circumstances of the case may require, and to continue or revoke the same, when-

ever he shall think proper." C. 41, 1 Stat. 372. A prior joint resolution of May 7, 1794, (1 Stat. 401), had conferred unqualified power on the President to grant clearances, notwithstanding an existing embargo, to ships or vessels belonging to citizens of the United States bound to any port beyond the Cape of Good Hope.

The Act of March 3, 1795 (c. 53, 1 Stat. 444), gave the President authority to permit the exportation of arms, cannon and military stores, the law prohibiting such exports to the contrary notwithstanding, the only prescribed guide for his action being that such exports should be in "cases connected with the security of the commercial interest of the United States, and for public purposes only."

By the Act of June 13, 1798 (c. 53, 5, 1 Stat. 566), it was provided that if the government of France "shall clearly disavow, and shall be found to refrain from the aggressions, depredations and hostilities" theretofore maintained against vessels and property of the citizens of the United States, "in violation of the faith of treaties, and the laws of nations, and shall thereby acknowledge the just claims of the United States to be considered as in all respects neutral, ... it shall be lawful for the President of the United States, being well ascertained of the premises, to remit and discontinue the prohibitions and restraints hereby enacted and declared; and he shall be, and is hereby authorized to make proclamation thereof accordingly."

By section 4 of the Act of February 9, 1799 (c. 2, 1 Stat. 615), it was made "lawful" for the President, "if he shall deem it expedient and consistent with the interest of the United States," by order to remit certain restraints and prohibitions imposed by the act with respect to the French Republic, and also to revoke any such order "whenever, in his opinion, the interest of the United States shall require."

Similar authority, qualified in the same way was conferred by section 6 of the Act of February 7, 1800, c. 10, 2 Stat. 9.

Section 5 of the Act of March 3, 1805 (c. 41, 2 Stat. 341), made it lawful for the President, whenever an armed vessel entering the harbors or waters within the jurisdiction of the United States and required to depart therefrom should fail to do so, not only to employ the land and naval forces to compel obedience, but, "if he shall think it proper, it shall be lawful for him to forbid, by proclamation, all intercourse with such vessel, and with every armed vessel of the same nation, and the officers and crew thereof; to prohibit all supplies and aid from being furnished them" and to do various other things connected therewith. Violation of the President's proclamation was penalized.

On February 28, 1806, an act was passed (c. 9, 2 Stat. 351) to suspend commercial intercourse between the United States and certain parts of the Island of St. Domingo. A penalty was prescribed for its violation. Notwithstanding the positive provisions of the act, it was by section 5 (2 Stat. 352) made "lawful" for the President to remit and discontinue the restraints and prohibitions imposed by the act at any time "if he shall deem it expedient and consistent with the interests of the United States" to do so. Likewise in respect of the Non-intercourse Act of March 1, 1809 (c. 24, 2 Stat. 528); the President was "authorized" (section 11, p. 530), in case either of the countries affected should so revoke or modify her edicts "as that they shall cease to violate the neutral commerce of the United States," to proclaim the fact, after which the suspended trade might be renewed with the nation so doing.

Practically every volume of the United States Statutes contains one or more acts or joint resolutions of Congress authorizing action by the President in respect of subjects affecting foreign relations, which either leave the exercise of the power to his unrestricted judgment, or provide a standard far more general than that which has always been considered requisite with regard to domestic affairs. Many, though not all, of these acts are designated in the footnote. It well may be assumed that these legislative precedents were in mind when Congress passed the joint resolutions of April 22, 1898, 30 Stat. 739; March 14, 1912, 37 Stat. 630 (22 U.S.C.A. 236 and note); and January 31, 1922, 42 Stat. 361 (22 U.S.C.A. 236), to prohibit the export of coal or other war material. The resolution of 1898 authorized the President "in his discretion, and with such limitation and exceptions as shall seem to him expedient" to prohibit such exportations. The striking identity of language found in the second resolution mentioned above and in the one now under review will be seen upon comparison. The resolution of March 14, 1912 (see 22 U.S.C.A. 236 and note) provides:

"That whenever the President shall find that in any American country conditions of domestic violence exist which are promoted by the use of arms or munitions of war procured from the United States, and shall make proclamation thereof, it shall be unlawful to export except

under such limitations and exceptions as the President shall prescribe any arms or munitions of war from any place in the United States to such country until otherwise ordered by the President or by Congress.

Sec. 2. That any shipment of material hereby declared unlawful after such a proclamation shall be punishable by fine not exceeding ten thousand dollars, or imprisonment not exceeding two years, or both."

The third resolution is in substantially the same terms, but extends to any country in which the United States exercises extraterritorial jurisdiction, and provides for the President's action not only when conditions of domestic violence exist which are promoted, but also when such conditions may be promoted, by the use of such arms or munitions of war.

We had occasion to review these embargo and kindred acts in connection with an exhaustive discussion of the general subject of delegation of legislative power in a recent case, *Panama Refining Co. v. Ryan*, 293 U.S. 388, 421, 422 S., 55 S.Ct. 241, 249, and, in justifying such acts, pointed out that they confided to the President "an authority which was cognate to the conduct by him of the foreign relations of the government."

The result of holding that the joint resolution here under attack is void and unenforceable as constituting an unlawful delegation of legislative power would be to stamp this multitude of comparable acts and resolutions as likewise invalid. And while this court may not, and should not, hesitate to declare acts of Congress, however many times repeated, to be unconstitutional if beyond all rational doubt it finds them to be so, an impressive array of legislation such as we have just set forth, enacted by nearly every Congress from the beginning of our national existence to the present day, must be given unusual weight in the process of reaching a correct determination of the problem. A legislative practice such as we have here, evidenced not by only occasional instances, but marked by the movement of a steady stream for a century and a half of time, goes a long way in the direction of proving the presence of unassailable ground for the constitutionality of the practice, to be found in the origin and history of the power involved, or in its nature, or in both combined.

In *The Laura*, 114 U.S. 411, 416, 5 S.Ct. 881, 883, this court answered a challenge to the constitutionality of a statute authorizing the Secretary of the

Treasury to remit or mitigate fines and penalties in certain cases, by repeating the language of a very early case (*Stuart v. Laird*, 1 Cranch 299, 309) that the long practice and acquiescence under the statute was a "practical exposition ... too strong and obstinate to be shaken or controlled. Of course, the question is at rest, and ought not now to be disturbed." In *Burrow-Giles Lithographic Co. v. Sarony*, 111 U.S. 53, 57, 4 S.Ct. 279, 281, the constitutionality of R.S. 4952, conferring upon the author, inventor, designer or proprietor of a photograph certain rights, was involved. Mr. Justice Miller, speaking for the court, disposed of the point by saying: "The construction placed upon the constitution by the first act of 1790 and the act of 1802, by the men who were contemporary with its formation, many of whom were members of the convention which framed it, is of itself entitled to very great weight, and when it is remembered that the rights thus established have not been disputed during a period of nearly a century, it is almost conclusive."

In *Field v. Clark*, 143 U.S. 649, 691, 12 S.Ct. 495, 504, this court declared that "the practical construction of the constitution, as given by so many acts of congress, and embracing almost the entire period of our national existence, should not be overruled, unless upon a conviction that such legislation was clearly incompatible with the supreme law of the land." The rule is one which has been stated and applied many times by this court. As examples, see *Ames v. Kansas*, 111 U.S. 449, 469, 4 S.Ct. 437; *McCulloch v. Maryland*, 4 Wheat. 316, 401; *Downes v. Bidwell*, 182 U.S. 244, 286, 21 S.Ct. 770.

The uniform, long-continued and undisputed legislative practice just disclosed rests upon an admissible view of the Constitution which, even if the practice found far less support in principle than we think it does, we should not feel at liberty at this late day to disturb.

We deem it unnecessary to consider, seriatim, the several clauses which are said to evidence the unconstitutionality of the Joint Resolution as involving an unlawful delegation of legislative power. It is enough to summarize by saying that, both upon principle and in accordance with precedent, we conclude there is sufficient warrant for the broad discretion vested in the President to determine whether the enforcement of the statute will have a beneficial effect upon the re-establishment of peace in the affected countries; whether he shall make proclamation to bring the resolution into operation; whether and when the resolution shall cease to operate and to make proclamation accordingly; and

to prescribe limitations and exceptions to which the enforcement of the resolution shall be subject.

Second. The second point raised by the demurrer was that the Joint Resolution never became effective because the President failed to find essential jurisdictional facts; and the third point was that the second proclamation of the President operated to put an end to the alleged liability of appellees under the Joint Resolution. In respect of both points, the court below overruled the demurrer, and thus far sustained the government.

The government contends that, upon an appeal by the United States under the Criminal Appeals Act from a decision holding an indictment bad, the jurisdiction of the court does not extend to questions decided in favor of the United States, but that such questions may only be reviewed in the usual way after conviction. We find nothing in the words of the statute or in its purposes which justify this conclusion. The demurrer in the present case challenges the validity of the statute upon three separate and distinct grounds. If the court below had sustained the demurrer without more, an appeal by the government necessarily would have brought here for our determination all of these grounds, since in that case the record would not have disclosed whether the court considered the statute invalid upon one particular ground or upon all of the grounds alleged. The judgment of the lower court is that the statute is invalid. Having held that this judgment cannot be sustained upon the particular ground which that court assigned, it is now open to this court to inquire whether or not the judgment can be sustained upon the rejected grounds which also challenge the validity of the statute and, therefore, constitute a proper subject of review by this court under the Criminal Appeals Act (18 U.S.C.A. 682). *United States v. Hastings*, 296 U.S. 188, 192, 56 S.Ct. 218, 219.

In *Langnes v. Green*, 282 U.S. 531, 51 S.Ct. 243, where the decree of a District Court (32 F.(2d) 284) had been assailed upon two grounds and the Circuit Court of Appeals (35 F(2d) 447) had sustained the attack upon one of such grounds only, we held that a respondent in certiorari might nevertheless urge in this court in support of the decree the ground which the intermediate appellate court had rejected. That principle is applicable here.

We proceed, then, to a consideration of the second and third grounds of the demurrers which, as we have said, the court below rejected.

1. The Executive proclamation recites, "I have found that the prohibition of the sale of arms and

munitions of war in the United States to those countries now engaged in armed conflict in the Chaco may contribute to the reestablishment of peace between those countries, and that I have consulted with the governments of other American Republics and have been assured of the cooperation of such governments as I have deemed necessary as contemplated by the said joint resolution." This finding satisfies every requirement of the Joint Resolution. There is no suggestion that the resolution is fatally uncertain or indefinite; and a finding which follows its language, as this finding does, cannot well be challenged as insufficient.

But appellees, referring to the words which we have italicized above, contend that the finding is insufficient because the President does not declare that the cooperation of such governments as he deemed necessary included any American republic, and, therefore, the recital contains no affirmative showing of compliance in this respect with the Joint Resolution. The criticism seems to us wholly wanting in substance. The President recites that he has consulted with the governments of other American republics, and that he has been assured of the cooperation of such governments as he deemed necessary as contemplated by the joint resolution. These recitals, construed together, fairly include within their meaning American republics.

2. The second proclamation of the President, revoking the first proclamation, it is urged, had the effect of putting an end to the Joint Resolution, and in accordance with a well-settled rule no penalty could be enforced or punishment inflicted thereafter for an offense committed during the life of the Joint Resolution in the absence of a provision in the resolution to that effect. There is no doubt as to the general rule or as to the absence of a saving clause in the Joint Resolution. But is the case presented one which makes the rule applicable?

It was not within the power of the President to repeal the Joint Resolution; and his second proclamation did not purport to do so. It "revoked" the first proclamation; and the question is, did the revocation of the proclamation have the effect of abrogating the resolution or of precluding its enforcement in so far as that involved the prosecution and punishment of offenses committed during the life of the first proclamation? We are of opinion that it did not.

Prior to the first proclamation, the Joint Resolution was an existing law, but dormant, awaiting the creation of a particular situation to render it active. No action or lack of action on the part of the Presi-dent could destroy its potentiality. Congress alone could do that. The happening of the designated events—namely, the finding of certain conditions and the proclamation by the President—did not call the law into being. It created the occasion for it to function. The second proclamation did not put an end to the law or affect what had been done in violation of the law. The effect of the proclamation was simply to remove for the future a condition of affairs which admitted of its exercise.

We should have had a different case if the Joint Resolution had expired by its own terms upon the issue of the second proclamation. Its operative force, it is true, was limited to the period of time covered by the first proclamation. And when the second proclamation was issued. the resolution ceased to be a rule for the future. It did not cease to be the law for the antecedent period of time. The distinction is clearly pointed out by the Superior Court of Judicature of New Hampshire in *Stevens v. Dimond*, 6 N.H. 330, 332, 333. There, a town by-law provided that, if certain animals should be found going at large between the first day of April and the last day of October, etc., the owner would incur a prescribed penalty. The trial court directed the jury that the by-law, being in force for a year only, had expired so that the defendant could not be called upon to answer for a violation which occurred during the designated period. The state appellate court reversed, saying that when laws "expire by their own limitation, or are repealed, they cease to be the law in relation to past, as well as the future, and can no longer be enforced in any case. No case is, however, to be found in which it was ever held before that they thus ceased to be law, unless they expired by express limitation in themselves, or were repealed. It has never been decided that they cease to be law, merely because the time they were intended to regulate had expired.... A very little consideration of the subject will convince any one that a limitation of the time to which a statute is to apply, is a very different thing from the limitation of the time a statute is to continue in force."

The first proclamation of the President was in force from the 28th day of May, 1934, to the 14th day of November, 1935. If the Joint Resolution had in no way depended upon Presidential action, but had provided explicitly that, at any time between May 28, 1934, and November 14, 1935, it should be unlawful to sell arms or munitions of war to the countries engaged in armed conflict in the Chaco, it certainly could not be successfully contended that the law would expire with the passing of the

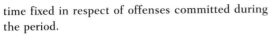

time fixed in respect of offenses committed during the period.

The judgment of the court below must be reversed and the cause remanded for further proceedings in accordance with the foregoing opinion.

It is so ordered.

TO THE CONGRESS OF THE UNITED STATES:

I address you, the Members of the Seventy-Seventh Congress, at a moment unprecedented in the history of the Union. I use the word "unprecedented", because at no previous time has American security been as seriously threatened from without as it is today.

Since the permanent formation of our government under the Constitution, in 1789, most of the periods of crisis in our history have related to our domestic affairs. Fortunately, only one of these -- the four year War Between the States -- ever threatened our national unity. Today, thank God, one hundred and thirty million Americans, in forty-eight States, have forgotten points of the compass in our national unity.

It is true that prior to 1914 the United States often had been disturbed by events in other Continents. We had even engaged in two wars with European nations and in a number of undeclared wars in the West Indies, in the Mediterranean and in the Pacific for the maintenance of American rights and for the principles of peaceful commerce. In no case, however, had a serious threat been raised against our national safety or our independence.

What I seek to convey is the historic truth that the United States as a nation has at all times maintained opposition to any attempt to lock us in behind an ancient Chinese wall while the procession of civilization went past.

Franklin D. Roosevelt's Four Freedoms Message to Congress (National Archives and Records Administration)

Franklin D. Roosevelt's Four Freedoms Message to Congress

"Freedom means the supremacy of human rights everywhere."

Overview

In the spring of 1940, the war raging in Europe showed no signs of lessening. The German blitzkrieg ("lightening war") had torn through Norway, Denmark, the Low Countries, and, finally, France. Mussolini declared war against France and Britain in June, while Japan negotiated a formal alliance with Germany and Italy. In the face of a truly world war, the United States, convinced of its safety (guaranteed by an ocean's separation from the fighting to the east and west) and terrified at the prospect of a repeat of World War I, maintained a precarious position of neutrality. Fresh from a remarkable reelection to a third term as president, Franklin Delano Roosevelt faced a daunting challenge: responding to British Prime Minister Winston Churchill's requests for aid without involving America in the conflict. His solution was the Lend-Lease Act, which would allow Britain to borrow war materials from the United States with the understanding that they would be returned (or replaced with other goods) after the war. In his Four Freedoms Message to Congress on January 6, 1941, Roosevelt not only made the case for American aid to Britain but also equated Lend-Lease with preserving "four essential human freedoms" that were universal to humankind.

Roosevelt's speech—delivered as his annual address to Congress—marked an important shift in America's attitude toward the war in Europe, moving the nation dramatically closer to direct involvement in the conflict. His Four Freedoms also became symbols of America's purpose and goals once Japan's attack on Pearl Harbor drew the nation into combat. Roosevelt presented the war as a moral battle between supporters of universal human rights and the powers of despotism and slavery. The Four Freedoms he highlighted—freedom of speech, freedom of religion, freedom from want, and freedom from fear—forced Americans to reevaluate the very concept of freedom in a democratic society. Captured in Norman Rockwell's paintings, which spoke to millions during the 1940s, the Four Freedoms had far-reaching, international influence; they are enshrined in the United Nations' Universal Declaration of Human Rights.

Context

By the time of Roosevelt's reelection in 1936, conditions in Europe under the dictatorships of Hitler and Mussolini were deteriorating rapidly. In Germany, Hitler promised to restore the nation to its rightful place. The Treaty of Versailles, which ended World War I, required Germany to pay war reparations to England and France, imposed limitations on German military size and power, and redistributed German territory—all in an effort to weaken the nation's potential to wage war on such a scale again. The terms of the treaty rankled Germany to no end. Its pride wounded and its economy drastically eroded by rampant inflation and the effects of the worldwide depression of the 1930s, Germany was ripe for a leader with promises of newfound glory and military prowess. Not long after Hitler rose to chancellor in 1933, he embarked on a campaign of aggression that increasingly recognized no boundaries.

As Hitler's armies marched through Austria, Czechoslovakia, and Poland in the late 1930s, the United States was deeply divided as to how it should respond. Americans were haunted by memories of World War I, including disgust with the new technology of war and the failure of Woodrow Wilson's vision for the League of Nations. Critics at home dissected America's participation in World War I. Senator Nye's committee to investigate the munitions industry's activities during wartime issued a report describing the manufacturers as "merchants of death" who profited handsomely from the war (Kennedy, pp. 385–386). These ghosts of World War I as well as a deepening economic crisis at home made many Americans, including Republican senators, favor a policy of neutrality. Seeking to avoid the very pitfalls that had drawn America into World War I in 1936, Congress renewed the year-old Neutrality Act, which prevented arms sales to either side and prohibited American ships from carrying arms to belligerent nations. The 1936 act included a new clause banning loans to governments at war.

After Germany invaded Poland on September 1, 1939, Hitler's militaristic motives were clear to all. Roosevelt faced a dilemma: how to respond to a deteriorating international situation while maintaining political viability at home. On September 5, 1939, Roosevelt proclaimed America's neutrality, just two days after Britain and France

1932

■ **November 8**
Franklin D. Roosevelt is elected to his first term as president.

1933

■ **January 30**
Adolf Hitler is named chancellor of Germany.

1935

■ **August 31**
Congress passes Neutrality Act of 1935, preventing arms sales to either side in a state of war and prohibiting U.S. ships from carrying arms to fighting nations.

■ **September 15**
German Reichstag publishes Nuremberg Laws denying civil rights to Jews in Germany.

1936

■ **March 7**
Hitler occupies Rhineland.

■ **November 3**
Franklin D. Roosevelt is elected to second term.

1938

■ **November 9–10**
Kristallnacht ("Night of Broken Glass"): Nazi storm troopers target Jews in Germany, destroying synagogues, businesses, and other establishments.

1939

■ **March 15**
Hitler occupies Czechoslovakia.

■ **September 1**
Hitler invades Poland.

■ **September 3**
Great Britain and France declare war against Germany.

■ **September 5**
United States declares neutrality.

■ **November 4**
Congress passes Neutrality Act of 1939, allowing the United States to sell military supplies to Britain and France for cash, but prohibiting its ships from sailing into combat areas.

declared war against Germany. Roosevelt knew, however, that most Americans sided with Britain even if they opposed any direct involvement in the hostilities. He proposed what became the Neutrality Act of 1939, which allowed belligerents to pay cash for American supplies and transport these supplies using non-American ships. Congress passed the act by a large margin, representing a subtle but important shift in America's stance in the European conflict.

As Hitler's offensive spread through Western Europe and as the Germans began their aerial assault on Britain, the new British Prime Minister, Winston Churchill, pleaded desperately with Roosevelt for help. Britain had virtually no cash to pay for supplies, but was defenseless in the face of Hitler's attack. Roosevelt initially provided fifty aged U.S. naval destroyers to Britain in exchange for ninety-nine-year leases on several British military bases. After his reelection in November 1940, Roosevelt devised a plan to expand aid to Britain—this became the Lend-Lease Act. Using the image of a neighbor borrowing a garden hose to fight a fire, Roosevelt proposed that America would lend supplies to Britain with no expectation of payment but would expect to receive the materials back after the war.

Roosevelt also feared America's lack of preparedness for war. The nation was poorly equipped to defend itself, much less provide aid to Europe. Given the rapid expansion of German, Italian, and Japanese military aggression, Roosevelt saw no reason why the Americas might not be likely targets. His reelection campaign successfully completed, Roosevelt had political breathing room to publicly float his plan for increased involvement. The response to his December 29, 1940, address to the nation, in which he called for America to serve as "the great arsenal of democracy" (http://www.millercenter.virginia.edu/scripps/ digitalarchive/speeches/spe_1940_1229_roosevelt), was overwhelmingly favorable. In his Four Freedoms Message of January 6, 1941, the president presented the Lend-Lease program to Congress, along with a plan for American preparedness, arguing that this action was necessary to protect and preserve democratic freedoms throughout the world. Roosevelt not only sealed the passage of the Lend-Lease Act but also established an ideological view of America's role in World War II that remains with us today.

About the Author

Franklin Delano Roosevelt was born on January 30, 1882, and spent a privileged childhood in his Hyde Park home along the Hudson River. His adult cousin, Theodore, hero of the Spanish-American War and twenty-sixth president of the United States, exerted an enormous influence on Franklin. Both Theodore and Franklin attended Harvard, but, in contrast to his cousin, Franklin allied himself with the Democratic Party. Franklin married Eleanor, his fifth cousin and daughter of Theodore's younger brother, in New York on March 17, 1905; President Theodore Roosevelt was there to give the bride away.

Roosevelt studied law at Columbia University but aspired to a political career like his cousin. In 1910, he ran a successful campaign for a seat in the New York state senate, where he became a champion of political and labor reforms. In 1913, President Woodrow Wilson offered Roosevelt a position in his cabinet as assistant secretary of the navy, the very same position that Theodore had once held. Roosevelt made an unsuccessful bid for the vice presidency in 1920 and returned to life as a private citizen. In 1921, he was struck with polio and spent several years trying to gain partial mobility of his limbs. Roosevelt reentered the political arena in 1928, successfully running for governor of New York, where he continued his advocacy of Progressive politics.

By 1932, with the country in the throes of the Great Depression, Roosevelt was a viable candidate to replace the beleaguered Herbert Hoover, the troubled Republican president who seemed incapable of solving the nation's woes. Although he never had a specific plan of action, Roosevelt gained the presidency on his broad promise of change, winning by an electoral margin of 472 to 59 votes. During the early days of his first term (often referred to as the "First Hundred Days"), Roosevelt instituted a flurry of programs to combat the depression, including the Public Works Administration, which established a massive infrastructure-improvement program that also provided Americans with new jobs. After his reelection in 1936, Roosevelt expanded these programs (known collectively as the New Deal) to include modern reforms we take for granted today, such as Social Security. Not everyone supported Roosevelt's New Deal programs, however; many businesses opposed government intrusion in the private sector, and Roosevelt's plan to appoint sympathetic judges on the Supreme Court nearly undid his presidency. In many ways, Roosevelt embraced a new definition of freedom, one that included protection from both government and private-sector intrusion on civil liberties. As the historian Robert S. McElvaine notes, "Where his detractors saw a lack of principle, his supporters saw an admirable flexibility" (pp. 306–307).

By 1940, hostilities had increased in Europe, and Roosevelt felt responsible for guiding the United States through this next challenge. He won an unprecedented third term and shortly after described the "unprecedented" threat to American security in his annual message to Congress (the Four Freedoms speech). Facing a public hesitant to commit to direct involvement in the European conflict and an even more divided Congress, Roosevelt managed to persuade the legislature to provide military assistance to belligerents in the conflict. The Japanese attack on Pearl Harbor ended any pretence of U.S. neutrality, and Roosevelt became a war president, guiding the nation through radio addresses, called "fireside chats," that simultaneously reassured Americans and called for sacrifice. America's entry had a significant impact on the Allied war effort, but not all the nation's efforts were heroic. Perhaps one of the most ignominious decisions of Roosevelt's presidency was Executive Order 9066, which paved the way for the internment of Japanese Americans.

Time Line

1940

■ April 9
Germany invades Denmark and Norway, beginning a campaign against Western Europe that eventually extends to Holland, Belgium, and Luxembourg.

■ May 14
Germany invades France.

■ July 10
The Battle of Britain begins.

1941

■ January 6
Franklin D. Roosevelt delivers his annual message (Four Freedoms) to Congress.

■ March 11
Congress passes the Lend-Lease Act, giving the president the power to sell, transfer, or lease war supplies to any nation "vital to the defense of the United States" (http://www.ourdocuments. gov/doc.php?doc=71&page= transcript).

■ August 14
Roosevelt and Winston Churchill draw up the Atlantic Charter, which frames goals for British and American military strategy and vision of the postwar world (which cites two of the Four Freedoms).

■ December 7
Japan attacks Pearl Harbor.

■ December 8
The United States declares war against Japan.

In poor health in the midst of war, Roosevelt nevertheless ran successfully for a fourth term—the only president in history to do so. He delivered his fourth inaugural address in January of 1945 and died on April 12 of the same year—a few weeks before the Germans surrendered on May 8.

Explanation and Analysis of the Document

Roosevelt establishes his tone of urgency from the very beginning. He describes the current threat to American security as "unprecedented," setting the stage for his call for a change in the United States' position in the European conflict.

In the following eight paragraphs, Roosevelt analyzes past conflicts faced by the United States, both national and international, and builds a case for why the threat posed by

President Franklin D. Roosevelt is shown at the rostrum during his address to Congress on January 6, 1941. (AP Photo)

the Axis powers is indeed unprecedented. In the second paragraph, he notes that most Americans have forgotten the importance of north and south, compass points that meant so much during the Civil War. The "two wars with European nations" to which Roosevelt refers in paragraph 3 are the War of 1812 and the Spanish-American War; he indicates in paragraph 6 that these struggles were over trade disputes, not world domination. Similarly, conflicts in the West Indies (including those during George Washington's second term and the Napoleonic Wars), the Mediterranean (including battles against piracy during the presidency of John Adams), and the Pacific (particularly the occupation of the Philippines) were stimulated by economic concerns.

Although Europe had experienced a wave of revolutions during the mid-nineteenth century, they did not pose a threat to the Americas, as Roosevelt notes in paragraph 7. The "Maximilian interlude in Mexico," to which he refers in paragraph 8, was an episode involving the Austrian archduke Ferdinand Maximilian. Seeking an empire of his own apart from the Austro-Hungarian Empire headed by his brother, the emperor Francis Joseph, Maximilian had a brief and disastrous reign as emperor of Mexico from 1864 to 1867.

Roosevelt's tone changes in paragraph 9, as he turns to the aftermath of World War I. Here he links the threat in Europe directly to the United States: If democracy is

undermined there, it might have an impact on us here. This is a crucial moment in the address; Roosevelt faced a Congress (and American public) hesitant to become involved in the European conflict. By showing that the "downfall of democratic nations" anywhere served as a potential threat to the United States, he makes a case that involvement would be in the nation's best interest. Many isolationists in America argued that since the nation was sheltered by the Pacific and Atlantic Oceans, it was immune from attack. Roosevelt directly addresses this position, elevating the war to a battle between democratic interests and their enemies. Tying the conflict to democracy also defused the concern of many Americans that the interests of Great Britain, a monarchy, were vastly different from those of the United States.

Paragraph 10 addresses the Treaty of Versailles (the "Peace of 1919"), which ended World War I and was the subject of much controversy. The Germans felt that the terms of the treaty were much too harsh and subjected their nation to undue economic and social hardships as well as loss of territory. Even before Hitler's dictatorship, there was growing concern regarding the reparations and other requirements of the Versailles Treaty. Some European leaders called for modifications to the treaty's terms as a means of appeasing the Germans and preventing another war. Neville Chamberlain, prime minister of Great Britain before Winston Churchill, repeatedly acquiesced to Hitler's violations of the Versailles Treaty in a vain attempt to fend off another European conflict. Roosevelt warns against "pacification" of the Germans, which he states began "even before Munich." This is a reference to the Munich Conference, during which Britain and France agreed to Hitler's demand for a portion of Czechoslovakia, the Sudetenland. Hoping to avoid war, Chamberlain was firmly committed to a policy of appeasement (which had been going on long before the Munich conference, as Roosevelt notes) and was convinced that he had negotiated a lasting peace at Munich. When Hitler laid claim to all of the newly divided Czech territory, his duplicity was clear.

In paragraphs 11 and 12, Roosevelt describes the nature of the threat of the Axis powers, reinforcing the point that this threat is unprecedented. As he began in paragraph 9, he characterizes this conflict as a threat to democracy itself; he uses the phrases "democratic life" and "democratic way of life" in these two paragraphs. In paragraph 13, Roosevelt summarizes the introduction of his speech: The safety of America and democracy is intertwined with the conflict overseas.

In the next section of his speech, Roosevelt discusses the concerns of isolationists in America. Point by point, he addresses the objections raised by the public and senators to U.S. involvement in the growing conflict, while also responding to those who supported an immediate entry into the war. In answer to the latter, Roosevelt notes America's lack of military preparedness (paragraph 15) and, to the former, points out that peace in this conflict comes at a very dear price (paragraphs 16 and 17). He is particularly biting in his criticism of the pacifists, using a famous quotation from Benjamin Franklin: "Those who would give up essential liberty to purchase a little temporary safety, deserve neither liberty nor safety." In paragraphs 19 and 20, Roosevelt again warns of the danger of appeasement and directly addresses the question of war profiteering, a subject that received much public scrutiny following Senator Nye's congressional hearings into the munitions industry's practices during World War I. Finally, Roosevelt makes clear that America is not immune because of its geography. He notes that the use of espionage and surprise attacks are very real threats to both the United States and Latin America (paragraphs 21 through 25).

Having described the imminent danger to the nation, Roosevelt then outlines his planned response, presenting his Lend-Lease bill. He first calls for increased military production and associated spending, making it clear that these armaments are for defending America and supporting "those nations which are now in actual war with aggressor nations" (paragraph 45). Roosevelt spells out the terms of this aid. He clearly distinguishes between "the democracies" and "the dictators," returning to the idea that Britain and the United States are joined by their mutual ideals.

The nation was still suffering from the Great Depression, and Roosevelt acknowledges the "social and economic problems" facing America. He makes clear reference to

the New Deal programs of his first two terms, including Social Security, unemployment insurance, and government jobs programs, as fundamental elements of democracy (paragraphs 62 through 67). Roosevelt recognized that one of the protests against increased defense spending, especially during a period of economic turmoil, would be an increase in taxes.

The final paragraphs delineate the Four Freedoms for which this speech is best known. In these closing statements, Roosevelt paints his defense buildup and Lend-Lease plan as means to secure a world of freedom, making it clear that America's sacrifice is not just for one nation. The Four Freedoms selected by Roosevelt are important. The first two, freedom of speech and expression and freedom of worship, echo the First Amendment of the Constitution. The third, freedom from want, would resonate with a nation in the midst of the Great Depression, and reflects Roosevelt's New Deal programs. The final freedom, freedom from fear, brings the speech full circle as Roosevelt portrays a world devoid of unprecedented threats—but only if America takes action. Roosevelt punctuates each freedom with the phrase "everywhere in the world" to emphasize the universality of these ideals. These are not simply American goals, but "human freedoms." The addition of the Four Freedoms to this speech elevates it from simply a request for congressional action (appropriations for military spending and approval of the Lend-Lease bill) to a case for American aid to Britain as a matter of moral imperative to humanity.

Audience

The annual message to Congress, mandated by the U.S. Constitution, conveys the president's agenda and concerns for the United States in the coming year. Roosevelt dubbed this speech the "State of the Union address," which became the official title of the speech under his successor, President Harry Truman. Since 1923, the public could hear the message live via radio broadcast. Therefore, although Roosevelt addressed his remarks to the members of the House and Senate, he also geared his statement toward the general public.

In many ways, Roosevelt's Four Freedoms Message mirrors his December 29, 1940, fireside chat, otherwise known as the "Arsenal of Democracy" speech. In essence, Roosevelt had made his case for increased American involvement directly to the public in his earlier radio address, structuring his argument in much the same way as his annual message to Congress. A master at using the media to reach the American public, Roosevelt broadcast his fireside chats, speeches in which he used a casual and down-to-earth style, over the radio on Sunday evenings. The December 29 speech was one of his most successful; 80 percent of Americans who heard it expressed approval of his plan to aid Britain.

Despite the positive public reaction, the congressional audience for Roosevelt's 1941 Four Freedoms Message was far from sympathetic to his cause. Roosevelt was well aware

"We must always be wary of those who with sounding brass and a tinkling cymbal preach the 'ism' of appeasement."

(Paragraph 19)

"We must especially beware of that small group of selfish men who would clip the wings of the American eagle in order to feather their own nests."

(Paragraph 20)

"In the future days, which we seek to make secure, we look forward to a world founded upon four essential human freedoms. The first is freedom of speech and expression.... The second is freedom of every person to worship God in his own way.... The third is freedom from want.... The fourth is freedom from fear."

(Paragraphs 72–78)

"Freedom means the supremacy of human rights everywhere. Our support goes to those who struggle to gain those rights or keep them."

(Paragraph 82)

that ardent isolationists in both houses might undermine his plan. He did not consult with Congress regarding his decision to transfer World War I era destroyers to Britain in exchange for long-term leases on British military bases, for fear that isolationists would block the transfer. The America First Committee, an active isolationist organization, campaigned against any American assistance to Britain. Senators Gerald Nye of North Dakota and Burton Wheeler of Montana, as well as the renowned aviator Charles Lindbergh, were involved in this organization. During the debate over Lend-Lease, Senator Wheeler commented that the bill would "plow under every fourth American boy" (qtd. in Kennedy, pp. 472–473). Given this degree of dissent within Congress, it is clear why Roosevelt structured his address to counter the various objections raised by isolationists.

Roosevelt did not just face opposition from those who favored no involvement in the European conflict. He also faced criticism from those who felt he was power hungry and acting like a dictator. The Republican opposition was particularly displeased with his decision to run for an unprecedented third term, and Roosevelt's victory over Wendell Willkie in 1940 was decisive. Thus, although he was a popular president, Roosevelt had his critics, both in

the legislature and among the American public. By framing U.S. aid to Britain in terms of preserving democratic freedoms for humanity rather than in terms of advancing America's particular agenda, Roosevelt removed himself personally from the fray. The Four Freedoms Message masterfully addressed the concerns of Roosevelt's critics by phrasing political matters in terms of universal morality.

Impact

Roosevelt's Four Freedoms Message had an immediate political impact and a much longer-term effect on the way Americans viewed both their nation's role in World War II and the concept of democratic freedom. In spite of isolationist opposition, Congress passed an amended the Lend-Lease bill in March of 1941 by substantial majorities on both the House and Senate. In winning over the legislature—and the American public—to his plan, Roosevelt moved the nation a significant step away from isolationism and toward the very real possibility of being drawn into the conflict. Lend-Lease opened a virtual can of worms in terms of U.S. policy: Could the nation, in fact, produce enough materials to both defend itself in case of attack and meet Britain's demands? How could America safeguard its investment and ensure the safety of British ships transporting American munitions, given that U.S. neutrality laws forbade American ships from escorting the British navy in hostile waters? As German U-boats increased their attacks on British ships, America walked an ever-thinning tightrope of neutrality. Politically, Roosevelt's Four Freedoms Message was a major step in allying the United States with Great Britain.

Once America had declared war against Japan and officially entered the conflict Roosevelt's address took on a new life apart from its immediate political one. Whereas he enunciated the Four Freedoms while America still claimed neutrality, after the Japanese attack on Pearl Harbor, the speech's ending became a rallying point for a nation at war. In 1942 the Office of War Information published a pamphlet titled "The United Nations Fight for the Four Freedoms," which defined each of Roosevelt's freedoms in detail as a means of differentiating America and its Allies from their enemies. The pamphlet opens with a quotation from Roosevelt, that the Allied powers' "belief in the four freedoms of common humanity … is the crucial difference between ourselves and the enemies we face today" ("The United Nations Fight for the Four Freedoms," http://www.udhr.org/history/default.htm). The Office of War Information also called for a group of artists, termed Artists for Victory, to sponsor a competition of visual depictions of the Four Freedoms. One of the most enduring manifestations of Roosevelt's Four Freedoms Message is a series of four paintings by Norman Rockwell, which he completed for the *Saturday Evening Post* in 1943. The images were enormously successful; the Office of War Information distributed four million copies worldwide, and Rockwell received some sixty thousand letters from both fans and critics of his work.

Forged in the fires of a nation bent on avoiding war, the Four Freedoms Message was transformed into the justification for a nation entering into a war. Tying First Amendment rights into his New Deal economic programs, Roosevelt initially linked aid to Britain with the goals of his previous terms in office. As all pretenses of neutrality faded and Americans faced the reality of war, Roosevelt's freedoms took on new life. As the historian David Hackett Fischer notes, "The meaning of liberty and freedom changed profoundly during the Second World War" (p. 558). The Four Freedoms Message continued to resonate with Americans even after the war. At the 1945 San Francisco United Nations conference, four white columns were erected on the main podium, symbolizing Roosevelt's Four Freedoms. In 1948 the United Nations included the Four Freedoms in its Universal Declaration of Human Rights.

Related Documents

Beard, Charles A., *American Foreign Policy in the Making, 1932–1940*. New Haven, Conn.: Yale University Press, 1946; *President Roosevelt and the Coming of the War, 1941*. New Haven, Conn.: Yale University Press, 1948. Several of Roosevelt's contemporaries published critiques of his policies, including his foreign policy decisions. These two works by the historian Charles Beard, a vocal opponent of American involvement in the war, are excellent examples of the isolationists' position.

Kimball, Warren F., ed. *Churchill and Roosevelt: The Complete Correspondence*. 13 vols. Princeton, N.J.: Princeton University Press, 1984. The letters in this volume put a human face on American and British diplomacy during this period.

Polenberg, Richard D. *The Era of Franklin D. Roosevelt, 1933–1945: A Brief History with Documents*. New York: Bedford/St. Martin's, 2000. This volume contains a variety of primary sources from Roosevelt's presidency, including several criticisms of Roosevelt's Supreme Court "packing" plan and his New Deal programs.

Roosevelt, Eleanor. *The Autobiography of Eleanor Roosevelt*. New York: Harper & Brothers Publishers, 1958. No ordinary first lady, Eleanor Roosevelt was actively involved in Roosevelt's administration, primarily with his social programs. Her perspective on their relationship and his presidency sheds light on Roosevelt's commitment to human rights.

Rosenman, Samuel I., ed. *The Public Papers and Addresses of Franklin D. Roosevelt*. 1950. Reprint. New York: Russell and Russell, 1969. Roosevelt's published papers, including the texts of his speeches, are collected in thirteen volumes and are also available on the Internet at the American Presidency Project (http://www.presidency.ucsb.edu/).

Bibliography

■ Books

Borgwardt, Elizabeth. *A New Deal for the World*. Cambridge, Mass.: Belknap Press of Harvard University Press, 2005.

Cashman, Sean Dennis. *America, Roosevelt, and World War II*. New York: New York University Press, 1989.

Dallek, Robert. *Franklin D. Roosevelt and American Foreign Policy, 1932–1945*. New York: Oxford University Press, 1979.

Davis, Kenneth S. *FDR: The War President, 1940–1945*. New York: Random House, 2000.

Divine, Robert A. *The Reluctant Belligerent: American Entry into World War II*. New York: John Wiley & Sons, 1965.

Fischer, David Hackett. *Liberty and Freedom: A Visual History of America's Founding Ideas*. New York: Oxford University Press, 2005.

Jenkins, Roy. *Franklin Delano Roosevelt*. New York: Times Books, 2003.

Kennedy, David M. *Freedom from Fear: The American People in Depression and War, 1929–1945*. New York: Oxford University Press, 2005.

McElvaine, Robert S. *Franklin Delano Roosevelt*. Washington, D.C.: CQ Press, 2002.

Wilz, John E. *From Isolation to War, 1931–1941*. New York: Thomas Y. Crowell Company, 1968.

Winkler, Allan M. *Franklin D. Roosevelt and the Making of Modern America*. New York: Pearson Longman, 2006.

■ **Web Sites**

Franklin D. Roosevelt Presidential Library and Museum Web site.
   http://www.fdrlibrary.marist.edu/index.html. Accessed on July 6, 2007.

"Franklin D. Roosevelt Speeches: Fireside Chat 16 (December 29, 1940)." Miller Center of Public Affairs "American President Online Reference Resource" Web site.
   http://www.millercenter.virginia.edu/scripps/digitalarchive/ speeches/spe_1940_1229_roosevelt. Accessed on February 14, 2008.

"Transcript of Lend-Lease Act (1941)." National Archives "Our Documents" Web site.
   http://www.ourdocuments.gov/doc.php?doc=71&page=tran script. Accessed on February 14, 2008.

"The United Nations Fight for the Four Freedoms." Franklin and Eleanor Roosevelt Institute "Universal Declaration of Human Rights" Web site.
   http://www.udhr.org/history/default.htm. Accessed on July 6, 2007.

—By Karen Linkletter

Questions for Further Study

1. Roosevelt crafted his Four Freedoms Message to persuade a deeply divided Congress to support Lend-Lease. Do you believe that Roosevelt was more or less effective than recent administrations in working with divided legislatures?

2. At the time of Roosevelt's Four Freedoms Message, Americans were extremely anxious about being drawn into war. What are Americans' attitudes about war today? Are we as reluctant to go to war? Are we hesitant for the same reasons as Americans were in 1940?

3. Compare and contrast Roosevelt's "Arsenal of Democracy" fireside chat with his Four Freedoms Message. How did he change the message to serve his different audiences? How are the speeches similar?

4. If the president were to pick four freedoms today to illustrate universal human concerns, which four would be chosen and why?

5. Compare Roosevelt's Four Freedoms Message with another president's State of the Union address preparing Americans for war (George W. Bush's State of the Union address of January 29, 2002, and Woodrow Wilson's State of the Union address of December 8, 1914, are two good examples).

6. Look at Norman Rockwell's paintings of the Four Freedoms (available at the National Archives Web site at http://www.archives.gov/exhibits/powers_of_persuasion/four_freedoms/four_freedoms.html). Do you think Rockwell's depictions accurately reflect Roosevelt's descriptions of the four freedoms? How might a popular artist today depict Roosevelt's concepts?

acquiesce	to agree or comply with something passively
antithesis	the complete opposite
appeasement	the political strategy of pacifying a potentially hostile nation in order to avoid conflict
assailed	attacked
begetting	causing
discord	lack of agreement, strife
dupes	people tricked or deceived
foothold	starting place for progress
gallantly	bravely, honorably
harp	to stress something repeatedly in a way that becomes tiresome
innumerable	too many to be counted
pacification	the process of bringing about peace by calming someone or ending conflict
peril	danger, harm
resolute	determined, purposeful
sovereignty	right to self-government; supreme authority
tempo	pace, speed
tyranny	cruel and unjust use of power or authority over others
vindicate	to clear of blame, guilt, suspicion, or doubt

www.milestonedocuments.com

FRANKLIN D. ROOSEVELT'S
FOUR FREEDOMS MESSAGE TO CONGRESS

Mr. President, Mr. Speaker, Members of the Seventy-seventh Congress:

I address you, the Members of the Seventy-seventh Congress, at a moment unprecedented in the history of the Union. I use the word "unprecedented," because at no previous time has American security been as seriously threatened from without as it is today.

Since the permanent formation of our Government under the Constitution, in 1789, most of the periods of crisis in our history have related to our domestic affairs. Fortunately, only one of these—the four-year War Between the States—ever threatened our national unity. Today, thank God, one hundred and thirty million Americans, in forty-eight States, have forgotten points of the compass in our national unity.

It is true that prior to 1914 the United States often had been disturbed by events in other Continents. We had even engaged in two wars with European nations and in a number of undeclared wars in the West Indies, in the Mediterranean and in the Pacific for the maintenance of American rights and for the principles of peaceful commerce. But in no case had a serious threat been raised against our national safety or our continued independence.

What I seek to convey is the historic truth that the United States as a nation has at all times maintained clear, definite opposition, to any attempt to lock us in behind an ancient Chinese wall while the procession of civilization went past. Today, thinking of our children and of their children, we oppose enforced isolation for ourselves or for any other part of the Americas.

That determination of ours, extending over all these years, was proved, for example, during the quarter century of wars following the French Revolution.

While the Napoleonic struggles did threaten interests of the United States because of the French foothold in the West Indies and in Louisiana, and while we engaged in the War of 1812 to vindicate our right to peaceful trade, it is nevertheless clear that neither France nor Great Britain, nor any other nation, was aiming at domination of the whole world.

In like fashion from 1815 to 1914—ninety-nine years—no single war in Europe or in Asia constituted a real threat against our future or against the future of any other American nation.

Except in the Maximilian interlude in Mexico, no foreign power sought to establish itself in this Hemisphere; and the strength of the British fleet in the Atlantic has been a friendly strength. It is still a friendly strength.

Even when the World War broke out in 1914, it seemed to contain only small threat of danger to our own American future. But, as time went on, the American people began to visualize what the downfall of democratic nations might mean to our own democracy.

We need not overemphasize imperfections in the Peace of Versailles. We need not harp on failure of the democracies to deal with problems of world reconstruction. We should remember that the Peace of 1919 was far less unjust than the kind of "pacification" which began even before Munich, and which is being carried on under the new order of tyranny that seeks to spread over every continent today. The American people have unalterably set their faces against that tyranny.

Every realist knows that the democratic way of life is at this moment being directly assailed in every part of the world—assailed either by arms, or by secret spreading of poisonous propaganda by those who seek to destroy unity and promote discord in nations that are still at peace.

During sixteen long months this assault has blotted out the whole pattern of democratic life in an appalling number of independent nations, great and small. The assailants are still on the march, threatening other nations, great and small.

Therefore, as your President, performing my constitutional duty to "give to the Congress information of the state of the Union," I find it, unhappily, necessary to report that the future and the safety of our country and of our democracy are overwhelmingly involved in events far beyond our borders.

Armed defense of democratic existence is now being gallantly waged in four continents. If that defense fails, all the population and all the resources of Europe, Asia, Africa and Australasia will be dominated by the conquerors. Let us remember that the total of those populations and their resources in those four continents greatly exceeds the sum total of the population and the resources of the whole of the Western Hemisphere—many times over.

In times like these it is immature—and incidentally, untrue—for anybody to brag that an unprepared America, single-handed, and with one hand tied behind its back, can hold off the whole world.

No realistic American can expect from a dictator's peace international generosity, or return of true independence, or world disarmament, or freedom of expression, or freedom of religion—or even good business.

Such a peace would bring no security for us or for our neighbors. "Those, who would give up essential liberty to purchase a little temporary safety, deserve neither liberty nor safety."

As a nation, we may take pride in the fact that we are softhearted; but we cannot afford to be soft-headed.

We must always be wary of those who with sounding brass and a tinkling cymbal preach the "ism" of appeasement.

We must especially beware of that small group of selfish men who would clip the wings of the American eagle in order to feather their own nests.

I have recently pointed out how quickly the tempo of modern warfare could bring into our very midst the physical attack which we must eventually expect if the dictator nations win this war.

There is much loose talk of our immunity from immediate and direct invasion from across the seas. Obviously, as long as the British Navy retains its power, no such danger exists. Even if there were no British Navy, it is not probable that any enemy would be stupid enough to attack us by landing troops in the United States from across thousands of miles of ocean, until it had acquired strategic bases from which to operate.

But we learn much from the lessons of the past years in Europe—particularly the lesson of Norway, whose essential seaports were captured by treachery and surprise built up over a series of years.

The first phase of the invasion of this Hemisphere would not be the landing of regular troops. The necessary strategic points would be occupied by secret agents and their dupes—and great numbers of them are already here, and in Latin America.

As long as the aggressor nations maintain the offensive, they—not we—will choose the time and the place and the method of their attack.

That is why the future of all the American Republics is today in serious danger.

That is why this Annual Message to the Congress is unique in our history.

That is why every member of the Executive Branch of the Government and every member of the Congress faces great responsibility and great accountability.

The need of the moment is that our actions and our policy should be devoted primarily—almost exclusively—to meeting this foreign peril. For all our domestic problems are now a part of the great emergency.

Just as our national policy in internal affairs has been based upon a decent respect for the rights and the dignity of all our fellow men within our gates, so our national policy in foreign affairs has been based on a decent respect for the rights and dignity of all nations, large and small. And the justice of morality must and will win in the end.

Our national policy is this:

First, by an impressive expression of the public will and without regard to partisanship, we are committed to all-inclusive national defense.

Second, by an impressive expression of the public will and without regard to partisanship, we are committed to full support of all those resolute peoples, everywhere, who are resisting aggression and are thereby keeping war away from our Hemisphere. By this support, we express our determination that the democratic cause shall prevail; and we strengthen the defense and the security of our own nation.

Third, by an impressive expression of the public will and without regard to partisanship, we are committed to the proposition that principles of morality and considerations for our own security will never permit us to acquiesce in a peace dictated by aggressors and sponsored by appeasers. We know that enduring peace cannot be bought at the cost of other people's freedom.

In the recent national election there was no substantial difference between the two great parties in respect to that national policy. No issue was fought out on this line before the American electorate. Today it is abundantly evident that American citizens everywhere are demanding and supporting speedy and complete action in recognition of obvious danger.

Therefore, the immediate need is a swift and driving increase in our armament production.

Leaders of industry and labor have responded to our summons. Goals of speed have been set. In some cases these goals are being reached ahead of time; in some cases we are on schedule; in other cases there are slight but not serious delays; and in some cases—and I am sorry to say very important cases—we are all concerned by the slowness of the accomplishment of our plans.

The Army and Navy, however, have made substantial progress during the past year. Actual experience is improving and speeding up our methods of production with every passing day. And today's best is not good enough for tomorrow.

I am not satisfied with the progress thus far made. The men in charge of the program represent the best in training, in ability, and in patriotism. They are not satisfied with the progress thus far made. None of us will be satisfied until the job is done.

No matter whether the original goal was set too high or too low, our objective is quicker and better results. To give you two illustrations:

We are behind schedule in turning out finished airplanes; we are working day and night to solve the innumerable problems and to catch up.

We are ahead of schedule in building warships but we are working to get even further ahead of that schedule.

To change a whole nation from a basis of peacetime production of implements of peace to a basis of wartime production of implements of war is no small task. And the greatest difficulty comes at the beginning of the program, when new tools, new plant facilities, new assembly lines, and new ship ways must first be constructed before the actual materiel begins to flow steadily and speedily from them.

The Congress, of course, must rightly keep itself informed at all times of the progress of the program. However, there is certain information, as the Congress itself will readily recognize, which, in the interests of our own security and those of the nations that we are supporting, must of needs be kept in confidence.

New circumstances are constantly begetting new needs for our safety. I shall ask this Congress for greatly increased new appropriations and authorizations to carry on what we have begun.

I also ask this Congress for authority and for funds sufficient to manufacture additional munitions and war supplies of many kinds, to be turned over to those nations which are now in actual war with aggressor nations.

Our most useful and immediate role is to act as an arsenal for them as well as for ourselves. They do not need man power, but they do need billions of dollars worth of the weapons of defense.

The time is near when they will not be able to pay for them all in ready cash. We cannot, and we will not, tell them that they must surrender, merely because of present inability to pay for the weapons which we know they must have.

I do not recommend that we make them a loan of dollars with which to pay for these weapons—a loan to be repaid in dollars.

I recommend that we make it possible for those nations to continue to obtain war materials in the United States, fitting their orders into our own program. Nearly all their materiel would, if the time ever came, be useful for our own defense.

Taking counsel of expert military and naval authorities, considering what is best for our own security, we are free to decide how much should be kept here and how much should be sent abroad to our friends who by their determined and heroic resistance are giving us time in which to make ready our own defense.

For what we send abroad, we shall be repaid within a reasonable time following the close of hostilities, in similar materials, or, at our option, in other goods of many kinds, which they can produce and which we need.

Let us say to the democracies: "We Americans are vitally concerned in your defense of freedom. We are putting forth our energies, our resources and our organizing powers to give you the strength to regain and maintain a free world. We shall send you, in ever-increasing numbers, ships, planes, tanks, guns. This is our purpose and our pledge."

In fulfillment of this purpose we will not be intimidated by the threats of dictators that they will regard as a breach of international law or as an act of war our aid to the democracies which dare to resist their aggression. Such aid is not an act of war, even if a dictator should unilaterally proclaim it so to be.

When the dictators, if the dictators, are ready to make war upon us, they will not wait for an act of war on our part. They did not wait for Norway or Belgium or the Netherlands to commit an act of war.

Their only interest is in a new one-way international law, which lacks mutuality in its observance, and, therefore, becomes an instrument of oppression.

The happiness of future generations of Americans may well depend upon how effective and how immediate we can make our aid felt. No one can tell the exact character of the emergency situations that we may be called upon to meet. The Nation's hands must not be tied when the Nation's life is in danger.

We must all prepare to make the sacrifices that the emergency—almost as serious as war itself—demands. Whatever stands in the way of speed and efficiency in defense preparations must give way to the national need.

A free nation has the right to expect full cooperation from all groups. A free nation has the right to look to the leaders of business, of labor, and of agriculture to take the lead in stimulating effort, not among other groups but within their own groups.

The best way of dealing with the few slackers or trouble makers in our midst is, first, to shame them by patriotic example, and, if that fails, to use the sovereignty of Government to save Government.

As men do not live by bread alone, they do not fight by armaments alone. Those who man our defenses, and those behind them who build our defenses, must have the stamina and the courage which come from unshakable belief in the manner of life which they are defending. The mighty action that we are calling for cannot be based on a disregard of all things worth fighting for.

The Nation takes great satisfaction and much strength from the things which have been done to make its people conscious of their individual stake in the preservation of democratic life in America. Those things have toughened the fibre of our people, have renewed their faith and strengthened their devotion to the institutions we make ready to protect.

Certainly this is no time for any of us to stop thinking about the social and economic problems which are the root cause of the social revolution which is today a supreme factor in the world.

For there is nothing mysterious about the foundations of a healthy and strong democracy. The basic things expected by our people of their political and economic systems are simple. They are:

Equality of opportunity for youth and for others.

Jobs for those who can work.

Security for those who need it.

The ending of special privilege for the few.

The preservation of civil liberties for all.

The enjoyment of the fruits of scientific progress in a wider and constantly rising standard of living.

These are the simple, basic things that must never be lost sight of in the turmoil and unbelievable complexity of our modern world. The inner and abiding strength of our economic and political systems is dependent upon the degree to which they fulfill these expectations.

Many subjects connected with our social economy call for immediate improvement.

As examples:

We should bring more citizens under the coverage of old-age pensions and unemployment insurance.

We should widen the opportunities for adequate medical care.

We should plan a better system by which persons deserving or needing gainful employment may obtain it.

I have called for personal sacrifice. I am assured of the willingness of almost all Americans to respond to that call.

A part of the sacrifice means the payment of more money in taxes. In my Budget Message I shall recommend that a greater portion of this great defense program be paid for from taxation than we are paying today. No person should try, or be allowed, to get rich out of this program; and the principle of tax payments in accordance with ability to pay should be constantly before our eyes to guide our legislation.

If the Congress maintains these principles, the voters, putting patriotism ahead of pocketbooks, will give you their applause.

In the future days, which we seek to make secure, we look forward to a world founded upon four essential human freedoms.

The first is freedom of speech and expression—everywhere in the world.

The second is freedom of every person to worship God in his own way—everywhere in the world.

The third is freedom from want—which, translated into world terms, means economic understandings which will secure to every nation a healthy peacetime life for its inhabitants—everywhere in the world.

The fourth is freedom from fear—which, translated into world terms, means a world-wide reduction of armaments to such a point and in such a thorough fashion that no nation will be in a position to commit an act of physical aggression against any neighbor—anywhere in the world.

That is no vision of a distant millennium. It is a definite basis for a kind of world attainable in our own time and generation. That kind of world is the very antithesis of the so-called new order of tyranny which the dictators seek to create with the crash of a bomb.

To that new order we oppose the greater conception—the moral order. A good society is able to face schemes of world domination and foreign revolutions alike without fear.

Since the beginning of our American history, we have been engaged in change—in a perpetual peaceful revolution—a revolution which goes on steadily, quietly adjusting itself to changing conditions—without the concentration camp or the quick-lime in the ditch. The world order which we seek is the cooperation of free countries, working together in a friendly, civilized society.

This nation has placed its destiny in the hands and heads and hearts of its millions of free men and women; and its faith in freedom under the guidance of God. Freedom means the supremacy of human rights everywhere. Our support goes to those who struggle to gain those rights or keep them. Our strength is our unity of purpose. To that high concept there can be no end save victory.

H. R. 1776

IN THE HOUSE OF REPRESENTATIVES

JANUARY 10, 1941

Mr. McCORMACK introduced the following bill; which was referred to the Committee on Foreign Affairs

A BILL

Further to promote the defense of the United States, and for other purposes.

1   *Be it enacted by the Senate and House of Representa-*

2   *tives of the United States of America in Congress assembled,*

3   That this Act may be cited as "An Act to Promote the

4   Defense of the United States".

5   SEC. 2. As used in this Act—

6   (a) The term "defense article" means—

7   (1) Any weapon, munition, aircraft, vessel, or

8   boat;

9   (2) Any machinery, facility, tool, material, or

10   supply necessary for the manufacture, production, proc-

The Lend-Lease Act (National Archives and Records Administration)

LEND-LEASE ACT

"The benefit to the United States may be payment or repayment in kind or property, or any other direct or indirect benefit which the President deems satisfactory."

Overview

The Lend-Lease Act, passed in March 1941 after two months of vigorous public debate, provided new legal authority for the president to offer war supplies to the country's allies, thereby pushing the United States closer to full participation in World War II. Its enactment marked a victory for the administration of President Franklin D. Roosevelt and a defeat for his opponents. These included isolationists and pacifists, who had succeeded during the 1930s in passing neutrality laws designed to keep America out of foreign wars. Between the beginnings of World War II in Asia and Europe in the late 1930s and the attack on Pearl Harbor in December 1941, the Lend-Lease Act was the biggest step taken by the United States toward entry into the global conflict.

Lend-Lease, dubbed "the most unsordid act in the history of any nation" by the British prime minister Winston Churchill (Kimball, 1969, p. 236), was the mechanism by which the output of the vast American economy was channeled to the nation's allies. Nine months before Pearl Harbor, the new statute launched a massive program of exports designed to help Britain, China, and other nations hold off attacks from Germany, Italy, and Japan. By the end of the war, it had supplied thirty-eight foreign nations with $50 billion worth of war goods. While its effects on particular military outcomes are difficult to determine, Lend-Lease was certainly an important part of the Allies' successful effort to win World War II.

Context

In the months and years after the Great War of 1914 to 1918, now called World War I, many Americans were wary of commitments that might involve them in another expensive and bloody conflict. Immediately after the war, Congress rejected President Woodrow Wilson's efforts to have the United States join the new League of Nations. By the 1930s, during the Great Depression, isolationist and pacifist sentiment was stronger than ever. In 1935 Congress passed the first in a series of neutrality acts, which prohib-

ited the country from supplying foreign nations at war. Meanwhile, a prominent Senate committee held hearings to determine whether arms contractors had collected excessive profits or improperly influenced the country's entry into World War I. In late 1939, after the beginning of World War II in Asia and Europe, public opinion polls found that a significant majority of Americans believed it had been a mistake to enter World War I. At this point only a tiny minority of Americans said they wanted to join France and Britain in going to war against Adolf Hitler's Germany.

As authoritarian regimes in Germany and Japan began to conquer their neighbors, however, Americans and their leaders became less comfortable with neutrality. In November 1939 Congress revised the Neutrality Act to allow "cash and carry" arms sales. This meant that foreign nations at war could now buy weapons in the United States, but only if they paid for them in cash and transported them in their own ships. Although it technically preserved American neutrality, this policy promised to benefit Britain and France, which had more shipping capacity and cash than their enemies. Then, in the spring and summer of 1940, there were stunning new developments in Europe. In April, Germany invaded Denmark. France fell in June. In the late summer and fall British cities were bombed by German planes. Thanks to a nonaggression pact signed in August 1939 between Hitler and the Soviet leader Joseph Stalin, Germany seemed free to concentrate its energies on defeating Britain. Americans were now faced with the possibility that they might soon be left alone to deal with a powerful military alliance consisting of Germany, Italy, and Japan.

By the autumn of 1940 President Roosevelt was leading the country closer to fighting an indirect war against Germany by aiding its enemies. As Britain prepared for a possible invasion by German forces, the new prime minister Winston Churchill appealed to a sympathetic Roosevelt for more help. In his first letter to Roosevelt as prime minister, dated May 15, 1940, Churchill asked for forty or fifty American destroyers from World War I as well as aircraft and other munitions. In the same letter, Churchill suggested that the Americans should prepare for a day when Britain would not be able to pay for such supplies. The prime minister audaciously wrote, "We shall go on paying dollars as long as we can but I should like to feel reason-

1935

■ **August 31**
The Neutrality Act bans arms shipments to foreign nations at war.

1939

■ **September 1**
Germany invades Poland; an open war begins in Europe.

■ **November 4**
The revised Neutrality Act allows "cash and carry" arms sales.

1940

■ **September 2**
Roosevelt signs a destroyers-bases deal with Britain.

■ **December 7**
A long letter from Churchill to Roosevelt says that Britain cannot pay for supplies.

■ **December 17**
Roosevelt uses the fire-hose analogy at a press conference.

■ **December 29**
Roosevelt gives his "Arsenal of Democracy" fireside chat.

1941

■ **January 2**
Treasury Department lawyers begin drafting a lend-lease bill.

■ **January 10**
Congressional hearings on the bill begin.

■ **March 11**
Roosevelt signs the Lend-Lease Act.

■ **March 24**
Congress provides $7 billion in its first Lend-Lease appropriation.

■ **November 7**
Roosevelt declares that the Soviet Union is eligible for Lend-Lease funds.

■ **December 7**
Japanese planes attack the U.S. naval base at Pearl Harbor, prompting the United States to enter the war.

---

ably sure that when we can pay no more, you will give us the stuff all the same" (Kimball, 1969, p. 43). Churchill soon got his fifty destroyers. In an agreement signed on September 2, 1940, the old American ships were exchanged for ninety-nine-year leases of land in the Caribbean, suitable for the construction of new U.S. military bases. On September 14 Congress passed the Selective Service Act, the first peacetime draft law in American history. On September 27 Japan signed the Tripartite Pact with Germany and Italy, solidifying a military alliance between the so-called Axis forces. As Japan made preparations to attack the United States, American ships were already participating, without public knowledge, in the naval war in the Atlantic.

In December 1940, just after he was elected to an unprecedented third term as president, Roosevelt introduced the concept of lend-lease to the American public. As usual, Roosevelt's actions were influenced by Churchill, who in a long letter of December 7 had warned, "The moment approaches when we shall no longer be able to pay cash for shipping and other supplies" (Kennedy, p. 468). In a press conference on December 17, Roosevelt likened the country's situation to that of a homeowner whose neighbor's house was on fire. The president explained that in such a situation, simple self-interest dictated that one would quickly lend the neighbor a hose without demanding cash on the spot. Twelve days later, in one of his so-called fireside chats (nationally broadcast radio addresses to the American people), Roosevelt made clear that he intended to support Britain by allowing it to tap the vast industrial capacity of the United States. Roosevelt declared, "We must be the great arsenal of democracy" (http://www.miller center.virginia.edu/scripps/digitalarchive/speeches/spe_194 0_1229_roosevelt).

Less than a week after Roosevelt's "Arsenal of Democracy" fireside chat of December 29, 1940, Treasury Department lawyers started to draft the bill that would become the Lend-Lease Act. Congressional hearings on the bill began on January 10, 1941. Over the next two months, the spirited debates over the lend-lease idea in Congress were followed closely by the press, the American public, and many interested parties abroad. In the hearings, several members of Roosevelt's cabinet defended the bill; lend-lease was attacked by such well-known public figures as the aviator Charles A. Lindbergh and the socialist and pacifist Norman Thomas. Congressional opponents of the bill criticized it as a dangerous step toward full participation in a costly war and an unwise grant of power to President Roosevelt. But these critics failed to win over the public, a majority of which—according to public opinion polls—supported the bill. As Congress debated the bill, Churchill used a radio address to imply that lend-lease would allow the United States to avoid war. On February 9, the prime minister promised, "Give us the tools and we will finish the job" (Kimball, 1969, p. 179). In early March the bill easily passed Congress; the vote was 62 to 33 in the Senate and 317 to 71 in the House. On March 11, the same day as the House vote, a pleased President Roosevelt signed the Lend-Lease Act.

There are good reasons to conclude that the main author of the Lend-Lease Act—or at least the lend-lease idea—was President Roosevelt himself. By the late summer of 1940, Roosevelt was indicating to his advisers that he was interested in lending war goods to Britain. Certainly, by December 1940, when he gave his "garden hose" press conference and "Arsenal of Democracy" fireside chat, Roosevelt had taken the lead in presenting the lend-lease idea to the public.

Like many modern laws, however, the Lend-Lease Act itself had several authors, many of them rather obscure. At the end of December, President Roosevelt described the outlines of what he wanted to Henry Morgenthau, the secretary of the treasury. The first draft of the bill was written on January 2, 1941, by a small group of Treasury Department lawyers, including Edward Foley, Oscar Cox, Stephen Spingarn, and Ernest Feidler. Over the next several days, the document was revised after consultations with a number of influential men in Washington, including the Roosevelt adviser Ben Cohen, Supreme Court Justice Felix Frankfurter, and Speaker of the House Sam Rayburn as well as several cabinet members and British purchasing officials. Because there were few significant changes to the bill after it was introduced in Congress, it is fair to say that its lead authors were the treasury lawyers, none of whom were especially well known to the American public at the time or especially well remembered today.

Explanation and Analysis of the Document

◆ Section 1: "To Promote the Defense of the United States"

The first section of the act provides its title. At first glance this may seem unimportant, but the language of the title was significant. It emphasizes the national security of the United States without referring to the welfare of other nations and peoples who stood to benefit from the legislation, as an earlier version of the act had done. This language, which appears to have been suggested by Justice Frankfurter, was designed to deflect the charges of those critics who would claim that Lend-Lease would undermine national security.

◆ Section 2: Defining the Terms *Defense Article* and *Defense Information*

This section provides broad definitions of the goods and intelligence that could be supplied under Lend-Lease. In practice, it served to authorize shipments of food, steel, petroleum products, machinery, and trucks as well as weapons. Huge quantities of all these products would be shipped to America's allies under Lend-Lease.

◆ Section 3: Authority Given to the President

The longest and most complex part of the document, Section 3 explains what the act allows the president to do. Subsection (a) authorizes the president to direct members of his cabinet to provide goods, services, and information to any country designated by the president as "vital" to American defense. As critics of the act pointed out, this gave the president considerable new powers over the shape of American foreign policy. Significantly, it does not limit Lend-Lease to specific countries, nor does it exclude any countries. This flexibility would make it easier, later in the year, for Roosevelt to declare the Soviet Union eligible for Lend-Lease. Even this part of the act establishes important limits to presidential power, however. The most important of these limits was Congress's retention of the power of the purse: Lend-Lease orders could be placed only "to the extent to which funds are made available" by Congress. This subsection also imposes a limit of $1.3 billion on the total value of goods ordered before the act's passage that could be treated as Lend-Lease items. This clause, which was added to the bill in the House in February, disappointed the British, who had wanted the act to cover all orders placed since the beginning of the year.

Although it is only one sentence long, subsection (b) of Section 3 of the act is an important one: It explains how, if at all, the United States would arrange to be reimbursed for Lend-Lease aid. Here again the act granted the chief executive broad discretion. It would be up to the president to determine conditions attached to the aid. The president was free to decide what the United States would ask in return for Lend-Lease shipments. This repayment might be "in kind or property"; it might be "direct or indirect." Especially after Pearl Harbor, Roosevelt and many other Americans understood that much of the repayment took the form of costly fighting against enemies of the United States. Other considerations were also expected, however. In the case of Britain, the most important of these were agreements to lower trade barriers.

Section 3(c) of the act sets time limits for its operation. It allows the act to run through the end of the 1943 fiscal year while giving Congress the right to cancel it early with a concurrent resolution. This subsection also sets up a three-year window in the postwar period for the completion of Lend-Lease contracts or agreements made during the war. In early 1943 Congress passed the first of what would be three one-year extensions of the act. The only significant revision of the original act came in the 1945 renewal, when Congress altered Section 3(c) to order that Lend-Lease could not be used for postwar relief or reconstruc-

Time Line

1945

■ **May 11–12**
President Truman orders cuts in Lend-Lease aid.

■ **September 2**
Lend-Lease shipments are terminated with the formal surrender of Japan.

tion regardless of any agreements that might be signed during wartime. This revision disappointed Britain and other allies, which had been expecting to use Lend-Lease for postwar rebuilding.

The last two parts of Section 3, which were added to the bill as it went through Congress, state that the act does not provide any new authority that would permit the sending of any American ships into combat areas or the use of U.S. Navy ships to protect convoys of merchant ships. These subsections lessened the concerns of the many members of Congress who believed that the United States should keep trying to avoid joining the war. The language was not of great concern to President Roosevelt and his advisers, because they believed the president already had ample powers over the deployment of American vessels.

◆ Section 4: Nontransferability Clause

This brief section prohibits recipients of Lend-Lease goods from transferring them without the president's approval. This helped protect the United States by keeping Lend-Lease goods out of the hands of its enemies.

◆ Section 5: Reporting Requirements

This section demands that Lend-Lease operations be carefully tracked and reported. Subsection (a) calls upon any agency involved in exporting Lend-Lease goods to report the details of the shipment to the department or agency charged with tracking such goods under the Export Control Act of 1940. Subsection (b) requires the president to submit regular reports to Congress on the operations of the Lend-Lease program.

◆ Section 6: Appropriations

This section charges Congress with appropriating funds for the Lend-Lease program. Congress would do so for the first time on March 24, 1941, when it provided $7 billion. This section also establishes a budgetary mechanism for receiving any funds or goods received from other nations in return for Lend-Lease aid.

◆ Section 7: Patent Rights and Royalties

The act demands that the patent rights of American citizens be respected and that Americans be paid royalties for use of their patents in Lend-Lease orders. This is an example of how Americans' private property and profits were protected even as Lend-Lease and the growing demands of war called for great altruism and sacrifice.

◆ Section 8: Acquisitions Abroad

This section allows the army and navy to buy arms from countries designated by the president as eligible for Lend-Lease.

◆ Section 9: Any Necessary Regulations Allowed

Here the act makes it clear that the president is allowed to take those actions necessary to carry out the work authorized by the legislation.

◆ Section 10: No Implied Change in President's Authority to Use the Army and Navy

Like the end of Section 3, this part of the act emphasizes that it does not give the president additional authority to send the army and navy to war. During the second week of December 1941, after Pearl Harbor, Congress would overwhelmingly approve the declarations of war that removed existing constraints on the president's ability to direct the armed forces.

◆ Section 11: Whole Not Invalidated by Striking Down of a Part

The act's final section attempts to protect it from unforeseen problems in the courts. If the Supreme Court were to rule that one part of the act violated the Constitution by improperly limiting Congress's powers over foreign commerce or treaty making, for example, the rest of the act might be preserved. Ironically, given the wide powers that the act granted to the chief executive, some observers—including President Roosevelt himself—believed that its only unconstitutional provision was the clause in Section 3(c) that provided for a kind of congressional veto by concurrent resolution.

Audience

While the text itself was addressed to a rather narrow audience of government officials in Washington, the actions it authorized were of great interest to millions of people in America and around the globe. Most of those who read the document will conclude that because of its dense, formal, technical language, the act was not written for the general public. In a narrow sense, the act as a law spoke mainly to officials in the executive branch. These included not only the president, whose powers and responsibilities under the law were described in some detail, but also the offices of the secretary of the navy, the secretary of war, the chief of staff of the army, and the chief of naval operations. Before it became law, however, the text was aimed mainly at members of Congress whose support was required for its passage.

There was also a much wider group of "readers" of the document, many of whom never read the full text but understood its essentials from newspaper headlines and word of mouth. This audience included the American public, which had closely followed the progress of the bill and understood its significance, and the leaders and populations of foreign countries, who knew that the act dramatically changed the dynamics of the global conflict even if it did not include a formal declaration of war.

Impact

Although it represented a major victory for President Roosevelt's pro-British foreign policy, the passage of the Lend-Lease Act did not lead the United States immediately into World War II. Such a development had been expected by many of Roosevelt's opponents in America, who feared

> "The President may … authorize the Secretary of War, the Secretary of the Navy, or the head of any other department or agency of the Government … to manufacture in arsenals, factories, and shipyards under their jurisdiction, or otherwise procure, to the extent to which funds are made available therefor, or contracts are authorized from time to time by the Congress, or both, any defense article for the government of any country whose defense the President deems vital to the defense of the United States."
>
> (Section 3[a])

> "The terms and conditions upon which any such foreign government receives any aid under subsection (a) shall be those which the President deems satisfactory, and the benefit to the United States may be payment or repayment in kind or property, or any other direct or indirect benefit which the President deems satisfactory."
>
> (Section 3[b])

> "Nothing in this Act shall be construed to authorize or to permit the authorization of the entry of any American vessel into a combat area in violation of section 3 of the neutrality Act of 1939."
>
> (Section 3[e])

the possibility, and officials in Britain, who welcomed it. The evidence suggests, however, that Roosevelt sincerely believed in Lend-Lease in the sense that he still hoped, in the weeks after the act was passed, to be able to defeat Germany by serving as a giant arsenal for Britain without sending large numbers of American soldiers and sailors to war. In Roosevelt's mind, at least, the act did not automatically commit the United States to all-out participation in the global war.

By putting into place a mechanism for placing huge quantities of American-made goods in the hands of its Allies, the Lend-Lease Act had tremendous effects on the progress of World War II. Among the most important was the stimulus that Lend-Lease provided to convert American industry to war production, a conversion that began nine months before the attacks on Pearl Harbor. Although the pre-Lend-Lease cash purchases of Britain and France had already begun to do this, the initial $7 billion appropriation for Lend-Lease, supplemented in October 1941 by an additional appropriation of nearly $6 billion, helped prepare the American economy for the even greater demands for munitions after Pearl Harbor. This early Lend-Lease spending was an important component of the rising volume of gov-

ernment orders that evidently pulled the country out of a decade-long economic depression.

The significance of Lend-Lease for the military performance of America's allies is much debated. Few would dispute that the Lend-Lease shipments of food, machinery, and munitions were welcomed by soldiers and civilians in Britain, the Soviet Union, and China, but it is not clear exactly how much of a difference the American-made goods made in their struggles against the Axis forces. In 1941, when many orders were placed but the volume of Lend-Lease shipments remained low, the act's most important effects were probably more psychological than material. While the effects of Lend-Lease on the morale of Allied soldiers and civilians are impossible to measure, it was surely comforting to know that important supplies were forthcoming from the world's largest national economy; conversely, the passage of the act was surely damaging to Axis morale.

In any case, the material assistance provided by Lend-Lease in 1941, when Britain and the Soviet Union both avoided defeat, was relatively tiny. Only about 1 percent of Britain's available munitions in 1941 were provided via Lend-Lease. On the other hand, over the course of the entire war, the economic and military value of Lend-Lease was considerable. Over half of Allied munitions were made in the United States. Although over four-fifths of the tanks and aircraft used by Soviet forces were manufactured by the Soviets themselves, the United States provided four hundred thousand trucks and jeeps, nearly two thousand railroad locomotives, large quantities of petroleum products, and $1.6 billion worth of agricultural goods, which evidently made important contributions to the quality of the Soviets' logistics and food supply. The largest recipient of Lend-Lease aid was the United Kingdom, which received $21 billion worth of goods, double the amount provided to the Soviets. The British Empire (including the United Kingdom) was provided a total of $30 billion worth of goods, or 60 percent of the value of all Lend-Lease shipments. So-called reverse Lend-Lease supplies provided to American forces by the British Empire were valued at about $6 billion.

The termination of Lend-Lease in 1945, which historians often describe as having been poorly handled and excessively abrupt, caused America's Allies to lower their opinions of the extent of America's generosity in what Churchill had called in 1941 the "most unsordid act." In early 1945 Congress amended Section 3(c) of the original act to prohibit any aid for postwar relief or reconstruction. President Roosevelt's death in April 1945 elevated Harry S. Truman to the presidency. Truman was less able and willing to resist the many members of Congress and military leaders who called for a swift end to Lend-Lease shipments after the Allied victory in Europe. In May and July, Truman issued orders to limit Lend-Lease that alienated both British and Soviet officials who felt that they had paid amply for Lend-Lease in the blood, sweat, and tears expended in a victory that benefited the United States. They were also disappointed by America's unwillingness to use Lend-Lease to provide substantial postwar assistance.

Immediately after the defeat of Japan in August and that country's surrender in September, Lend-Lease ended. (An exception was made for China, which continued to receive large shipments through the end of the year.) Although the British were never asked to repay more than a small fraction of the total value of the goods they had received, they did submit to American demands that they lower trade barriers. Many in Britain felt that Americans were taking advantage of the situation to extend their new global dominance; Anglo-American relations now cooled. Meanwhile, the wartime alliance with the Soviets was quickly replaced with the beginnings of a potentially disastrous rivalry. By the time the United States created a kind of postwar equivalent of Lend-Lease in the form of the Marshall Plan approved by Congress in early 1948, the cold war was well under way.

Related Documents

Blum, John Morton, ed. *From the Morgenthau Diaries*. 3 vols. Boston: Houghton Mifflin, 1959–1967. These volumes provide selections from the diaries of Henry Morgenthau, Jr., who served

as Roosevelt's treasury secretary and who was involved in the drafting of the Lend-Lease Act.

Gallup, George H. *The Gallup Poll: Public Opinion, 1935–1971*. Vol. 1: *1935–1948*. New York: Random House, 1972. This compilation of poll questions and results provides one measure of the American public's changing views of foreign policy during the World War II era.

Kimball, Warren F., ed. *Churchill and Roosevelt: The Complete Correspondence*. 3 vols. Princeton, N.J.: Princeton University Press, 1984. This is a collection of the correspondence of the British and American leaders edited by a leading authority on Lend-Lease.

Stettinius, Edward R., Jr. *Lend-Lease: Weapon for Victory*. New York: Macmillan, 1944. This is a firsthand account of Lend-Lease and its early operations by the first chief of the Office of Lend-Lease Administration.

Bibliography

■ Books

Davis, Kenneth S. *FDR: The War President, 1940–1943*. New York: Random House, 2000.

Dobson, Alan P. *U.S. Wartime Aid to Britain, 1940–1946*. New York: St. Martin's Press, 1986.

Doenecke, Justus D. *Storm on the Horizon: The Challenge to American Intervention, 1939–1941*. Lanham, Md.: Rowman and Littlefield, 2000.

Dougherty, James J. *The Politics of Wartime Aid: American Economic Assistance to France and French Northwest Africa, 1940–1946*. Westport, Conn.: Greenwood Press, 1978.

Herring, George C., Jr. *Aid to Russia, 1941–1946: Strategy, Diplomacy, the Origins of the Cold War*. New York: Columbia University Press, 1973.

Kennedy, David M. *Freedom from Fear: The American People in Depression and War, 1929–1945*. New York: Oxford University Press, 1999.

Kimball, Warren F. *The Most Unsordid Act: Lend-Lease, 1939–1941*. Baltimore, Md.: Johns Hopkins University Press, 1969.

Martel, Leon. *Lend-Lease, Loans, and the Coming of the Cold War: A Study in the Implementation of Foreign Policy*. Boulder, Colo.: Westview Press, 1979.

Reynolds, David. *The Creation of the Anglo-American Alliance, 1937–41: A Study in Competitive Co-operation*. Chapel Hill: University of North Carolina Press, 1982.

Van Tuyll, Hubert P. *Feeding the Bear: American Aid to the Soviet Union, 1941–1945*. New York: Greenwood Press, 1989.

Woods, Randall B. *A Changing of the Guard: Anglo-American Relations, 1941–1946.* Chapel Hill: University of North Carolina Press, 1990.

■ Web Sites

Franklin D. Roosevelt Presidential Library and Museum Web site. http://www.fdrlibrary.marist.edu. Accessed on October 8, 2007.

"Franklin D. Roosevelt Speeches: Fireside Chat 16 (December 29, 1940)." Miller Center of Public Affairs "American President Online Reference Resource" Web site.
  http://www.millercenter.virginia.edu/scripps/digitalarchive/speeches/spe_1940_1229_roosevelt. Accessed on February 14, 2008.

—By Mark R. Wilson

Questions for Further Study

1. When the lend-lease bill was being debated in early 1941, opponents of the bill criticized it for granting vast, excessive powers to the president. To what extent were these criticisms reasonable? As you carefully read the text of the final act, consider any limits or counterbalances to presidential authority it may offer as well as the powers it gives the chief executive.

2. On December 7, 1941, nearly nine months after the passage of the Lend-Lease Act, the attack by Japanese forces at Pearl Harbor led the United States to declare war and fully enter the conflict. How does our knowledge of Pearl Harbor and other important subsequent developments make our understanding of the text different from the understanding of those who read it in March 1941?

3. The act left it up to the president to decide what kind of repayment to ask of Lend-Lease recipients. We know that the United States received $6 billion in reverse Lend-Lease from the British Empire, including several hundreds of millions of dollars in monetary payments and significant postwar trade concessions, among other things. The United States also enjoyed a variety of benefits from the winning of a war in which much of the fighting was done by Soviet and British forces. What, if anything, should the United States have asked for in return for the $50 billion worth of shipments it made under the act?

Glossary

concurrent resolution	legislative resolution adopted by both houses not requiring the signature of the chief executive
construed	interpreted, inferred
convoying vessels	warships escorting merchant ships to protect them from attack
fiscal year	any twelve-month period used for financial purposes; during the World War II era the U.S. government used a fiscal year running from July 1 to June 30
munition	material used in war
procure	obtain

Lend-Lease Act

A BILL

Further to promote the defense of the United States, and for other purposes.

Be it enacted by the Senate and House of Representatives of the United States of America in Congress assembled, That this Act may be cited as "An Act to Promote the Defense of the United States."

SEC. 2. As used in this Act—

(a) The term "defense article" means—

(1) Any weapon, munition, aircraft, vessel, or boat;

(2) Any machinery, facility, tool, material, or supply necessary for the manufacture, production, processing, repair, servicing, or operation of any article described in this subsection;

(3) Any component material or part of or equipment for any article described in this subsection;

(4) Any agricultural, industrial or other commodity or article for defense.

Such term "defense article" includes any article described in this subsection: Manufactured or procured pursuant to section 3, or to which the United States or any foreign government has or hereafter acquires title, possession, or control.

(b) The term "defense information" means any plan, specification, design, prototype, or information pertaining to any defense article.

SEC. 3. (a) Notwithstanding the provisions of any other law, the President may, from time to time. when he deems it in the interest of national defense, authorize the Secretary of War, the Secretary of the Navy, or the head of any other department or agency of the Government—

(1) To manufacture in arsenals, factories, and shipyards under their jurisdiction, or otherwise procure, to the extent to which funds are made available therefore, or contracts are authorized from time to time by the Congress, or both, any defense article for the government of any country whose defense the President deems vital to the defense of the United States

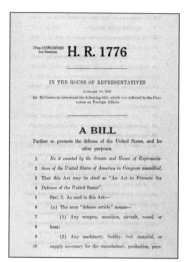

(2) To sell, transfer title to, exchange, lease, lend, or otherwise dispose of, to any such government any defense article, but no defense article not manufactured or procured under paragraph (1) shall in any way be disposed of under this paragraph, except after consultation with the Chief of Staff of the Army or the Chief of Naval Operations of the Navy, or both. The value of defense articles disposed of in any way under authority of this paragraph, and procured from funds heretofore appropriated, shall not exceed $1,300,000,000. The value of such defense articles shall be determined by the head of the department or agency concerned or such other department, agency or officer as shall be designated in the manner provided in the rules and regulations issued hereunder. Defense articles procured from funds hereafter appropriated to any department or agency of the Government, other than from funds authorized to he appropriated under this Act, shall not be disposed of in any way under authority of this paragraph except to the extent hereafter authorized by the Congress in the Acts appropriating such funds or otherwise.

(3) To test, inspect, prove, repair, outfit, recondition, or otherwise to place in good working order, to the extent to which funds are made available therefore, or contracts are authorized from time to time by the Congress, or both, any defense article for any such government, or to procure any or all such services by private contract.

(4) To communicate to any such government any defense information pertaining to any defense article furnished to such government under paragraph (2) of this subsection.

(5) To release for export any defense article disposed of in any way under this subsection to any such government.

(b) The terms and conditions upon which any such foreign government receives any aid authorized under subsection (a) shall be those which the President deems satisfactory, and the benefit to the United States may be payment or repayment in kind or property, or any other direct or indirect benefit which the President deems satisfactory.

(c) After June 30, 1943, or after the passage of a concurrent resolution by the two Houses before June 30, 1943, which declares that the powers conferred by or pursuant to subsection (a) are no longer necessary to promote the defense of the United States, neither the President nor the head of any department or agency shall exercise any of the powers conferred by or pursuant to subsection (a) except that until July 1, 1946, any of such powers may be exercised to the extent necessary to carry out a contract or agreement with such a foreign government made before July 1,1943, or before the passage of such concurrent resolution, whichever is the earlier.

(d) Nothing in this Act shall be construed to authorize or to permit the authorization of convoying vessels by naval vessels of the United States.

(e) Nothing in this Act shall be construed to authorize or to permit the authorization of the entry of any American vessel into a combat area in violation of section 3 of the neutrality Act of 1939.

SEC. 4. All contracts or agreements made for the disposition of any defense article or defense information pursuant to section 3 shall contain a clause by which the foreign government undertakes that it will not, without the consent of the President, transfer title to or possession of such defense article or defense information by gift, sale, or otherwise, or permit its use by anyone not an officer, employee, or agent of such foreign government.

SEC. 5. (a) The Secretary of War, the Secretary of the Navy, or the head of any other department or agency of the Government involved shall when any such defense article or defense information is exported, immediately inform the department or agency designated by the President to administer section 6 of the Act of July 2, 1940 (54 Stat. 714) of the quantities, character, value, terms of disposition and destination of the article and information so exported.

(b) The President from time to time, but not less frequently than once every ninety days, shall transmit to the Congress a report of operations under this Act except such information as he deems incompatible with the public interest to disclose. Reports provided for under this subsection shall be transmitted to the Secretary of the Senate or the Clerk of the House of representatives, as the case may be, if the Senate or the House of Representatives, as the case may be, is not in session.

SEC. 6. (a) There is hereby authorized to be appropriated from time to time, out of any money in the Treasury not otherwise appropriated, such amounts as may be necessary to carry out the provisions and accomplish the purposes of this Act.

(b) All money and all property which is converted into money received under section 3 from any government shall, with the approval of the Director of the Budget. revert to the respective appropriation or appropriations out of which funds were expended with respect to the defense article or defense information for which such consideration is received, and shall be available for expenditure for the purpose for which such expended funds were appropriated by law, during the fiscal year in which such funds are received and the ensuing fiscal year; but in no event shall any funds so received be available for expenditure after June 30, 1946.

SEC. 7. The Secretary of War, the Secretary of the Navy, and the head of the department or agency shall in all contracts or agreements for the disposition of any defense article or defense information fully protect the rights of all citizens of the United States who have patent rights in and to any such article or information which is hereby authorized to he disposed of and the payments collected for royalties on such patents shall be paid to the owners and holders of such patents.

SEC. 8. The Secretaries of War and of the Navy are hereby authorized to purchase or otherwise acquire arms, ammunition, and implements of war produced within the jurisdiction of any country to which section 3 is applicable, whenever the President deems such purchase or acquisition to be necessary in the interests of the defense of the United States.

SEC. 9. The President may, from time to time, promulgate such rules and regulations as may be necessary and proper to carry out any of the provisions of this Act; and he may exercise any power or authority conferred on him by this Act through such department, agency, or officer as be shall direct.

SEC. 10. Nothing in this Act shall be construed to change existing law relating to the use of the land and naval forces of the United States, except insofar as such use relates to the manufacture, procurement, and repair of defense articles, the communication of information and other noncombatant purposes enumerated in this Act.

SEC 11. If any provision of this Act or the application of such provision to any circumstance shall be held invalid, the validity of the remainder of the Act and the applicability of such provision to other circumstances shall not be affected thereby.

Approved, March 11, 1941.

EXECUTIVE ORDER

—

REAFFIRMING POLICY OF FULL PARTICIPATION IN
THE DEFENSE PROGRAM BY ALL PERSONS, REGARDLESS
OF RACE, CREED, COLOR, OR NATIONAL ORIGIN, AND
DIRECTING CERTAIN ACTION IN FURTHERANCE OF
SAID POLICY.

WHEREAS it is the policy of the United States to encourage
full participation in the national defense program by all
citizens of the United States, regardless of race, creed, color,
or national origin, in the firm belief that the democratic way
of life within the Nation can be defended successfully only with
the help and support of all groups within its borders; and

WHEREAS there is evidence that available and needed workers
have been barred from employment in industries engaged in defense
production solely because of considerations of race, creed, color,
or national origin, to the detriment of workers' morale and of
national unity:

NOW, THEREFORE, by virtue of the authority vested in me by
the Constitution and the statutes, and as a prerequisite to the
successful conduct of our national defense production effort, I
do hereby reaffirm the policy of the United States that there shall
be no discrimination in the employment of workers in defense
industries *or government* because of race, creed, color, or national origin, and
I do hereby declare that it is the duty of employers and of labor
organizations, in furtherance of said policy and of this order, to
provide for the full and equitable participation of all workers
in defense industries, without discrimination because of race, creed,
color, or national origin;

And it is hereby ordered as follows:

1. All departments and agencies of the Government of the

Executive Order 8802 (National Archives and Records Administration)

"There shall be no discrimination in the employment of workers in defense industries or government because of race."

Overview

In 1941 the African American labor leader A. Philip Randolph announced plans for a mass demonstration in the nation's capital to demand fair employment opportunities in defense industries and the desegregation of the armed forces. President Franklin D. Roosevelt was the target of this protest. Although he had won overwhelming black support, Roosevelt was reluctant to take action against racial discrimination because he feared antagonizing southern Democrats who controlled key congressional committees.

March on Washington Movement committees sprang up in major cities across the United States and began recruiting delegations to send to the capital. The prospect of thousands of militant blacks marching on Washington, D.C., troubled the White House, but Randolph did not back down. He told the president that only an executive order banning discrimination in the government and defense industries would satisfy his demands. Roosevelt capitulated and issued Executive Order 8802 on June 25, 1941, six days before the scheduled date for the march.

Roosevelt's order was the first significant presidential action on behalf of African American civil rights since Reconstruction. Although the Fair Employment Practices Committee (FEPC) it created did not fully live up to its promise, it was an opening wedge in the battle against Jim Crow laws. Roosevelt's action established a precedent that other chief executives would follow. African American leaders learned that organized mass action was a powerful weapon in their quest for full civil rights.

Context

Lack of adequate employment was the most serious problem facing African Americans at the end of the Great Depression. Unemployment rates were high, and black workers were concentrated in menial occupations, working as laborers, porters, cooks, and maids. Even well-educated African Americans found that many positions were closed to them because of their race. Limited job opportunities

had far-reaching consequences, keeping black families mired in poverty.

By 1941 American involvement in the European war appeared imminent. Germany had annexed Austria in 1938, invaded Poland in 1939, and conquered Denmark, Norway, Belgium, the Netherlands, and France in 1940. The United States was expanding its armed forces and had instituted its first peacetime draft. Early in 1941 President Roosevelt secured passage of the Lend-Lease program to send military supplies to England. Industry was increasing production of military equipment and supplies at a rapid pace, but black workers were largely excluded from the newly created jobs. African American leaders, most notably the veteran union organizer A. Philip Randolph, sensed that the time was right to demand federal action against employment discrimination. Because there was little chance that Congress would pass fair employment legislation, a presidential order was their best hope.

Roosevelt's New Deal programs had received enthusiastic support from large numbers of black voters, who switched their allegiance to the Democratic Party. Eleanor Roosevelt, the president's wife, was a prominent advocate of racial equality, but her husband was a pragmatic politician. He needed the votes of southern senators and representatives and was unwilling to lose their backing by supporting measures that threatened Jim Crow laws.

On January 15, 1941, Randolph issued a press release calling on African Americans to join a mass protest at the capital to demand equal treatment in defense industries and the armed forces. He formed a March on Washington Movement committee with branches in major northern cities, which began seeking volunteers for a midsummer demonstration. As the scheduled date approached, officials in the Roosevelt administration, including the president's wife, grew alarmed at the prospect of thousands of African Americans descending on the capital. They tried to talk black leaders out of their demonstration, but Randolph refused to call off the march; it would take place as planned.

Finally, Roosevelt met with Randolph on June 18. Randolph told the president that one hundred thousand black protestors were coming to Washington on July 1; only an executive order would persuade them to stay home. Roosevelt realized that not even his legendary powers of per-

1940

■ **September 27**
Black leaders meet with
President Roosevelt to discuss
African American participation
in defense industries and the
armed forces; they come away
with no tangible gains.

1941

■ **January 15**
A. Philip Randolph issues a
press release announcing a
march on Washington to
demand government action
against discrimination in
defense industries and the
armed forces.

■ **June 13**
New York's mayor, Fiorello
LaGuardia, and Eleanor
Roosevelt meet with Randolph
in an attempt to persuade him
to cancel the march.

■ **June 18**
President Roosevelt meets
with Randolph and urges him
to call off the march;
Randolph insists that only an
executive order banning
discrimination in defense
industries will persuade him to
do this.

■ **June 24**
LaGuardia meets with
Randolph to review a draft of
the presidential order.

■ **June 25**
Roosevelt issues Executive
Order 8802; Randolph
announces that the march will
not be held.

■ **July 19**
Roosevelt names the first
members of the Fair
Employment Practices
Committee.

1942

■ **June 30**
Roosevelt transfers control of
the FEPC to the War
Manpower Commission.

1943

■ **May 27**
Roosevelt issues Executive
Order 9346 creating a new
FEPC and expanding its
powers.

suasion would prevent the demonstration and instructed aides to prepare a document acceptable to black leaders. On June 25, 1941, Roosevelt issued Executive Order 8802, which articulated a policy of nondiscriminatory hiring in both the federal government and the defense industries. He refused to command the desegregation of the armed forces, but he did create a committee on fair employment practices to investigate and act on claims of discrimination. Randolph was satisfied with the compromise and abandoned the march.

About the Author

Executive Order 8802 was issued by President Franklin Delano Roosevelt, but the text was written and revised by Joseph L. Rauh, Jr., a White House aide. Roosevelt, the thirty-second president of the United States, was born at Hyde Park, New York, on January 30, 1882. He graduated from Harvard University and studied law at Columbia University. He married Eleanor Roosevelt, a niece of President Theodore Roosevelt, in 1905. They had six children.

In 1910 Roosevelt entered politics as a Democrat, winning election to the New York state senate from a heavily Republican district. From 1913 to 1920 he served as assistant secretary of the navy in President Woodrow Wilson's administration. At the 1920 Democratic Convention, Roosevelt was nominated for vice president on a ticket headed by James M. Cox. They were defeated by Warren G. Harding in the general election. While vacationing in 1921 at the family summer home on Campobello Island, Canada, Roosevelt was stricken with polio. Despite extensive physical therapy at Warm Springs, Georgia, he never regained the use of his legs.

Roosevelt reentered politics in 1924 when he nominated Al Smith for president at the Democratic National Convention. In 1928 he won election as governor of New York and was reelected in 1930. Two years later, he was nominated as the Democratic candidate for president. He campaigned on a platform advocating government intervention in the economy to combat the depression. He defeated Herbert Hoover by seven million votes.

As president, Roosevelt initiated a series of government programs to aid the unemployed and restore faith in the economy. These measures became known as the New Deal. One of the most enduring of Roosevelt's creations was the Social Security Administration, which provided benefits for widows, orphans, and the elderly. The popularity of his programs enabled Roosevelt to win reelection in 1936, 1940, and 1944. He is the only American president to serve more than two terms.

As war in Europe loomed, Roosevelt turned his attention to foreign affairs. He overcame isolationist opposition to strengthen American armed forces and provide military assistance to allies overseas. When the Japanese attacked Pearl Harbor in December of 1941, Roosevelt asked Congress for a declaration of war against Japan, Germany, and Italy. As commander in chief, he was actively involved in planning the military strategy that led to the defeat of the Axis powers. On the diplomatic front, Roosevelt built the alliance of nations that won the war and laid the foundation for the United Nations. Roosevelt's health declined rapidly during the war years. He died of a stroke in Warm Springs on April 12, 1945, only days before the Allied victory in Europe and months before the defeat of Japan.

Joseph L. Rauh, Jr., was a thirty-year-old White House aide when he was assigned the task of preparing Executive Order 8802. A graduate of Harvard Law School, he had served as law clerk to the Supreme Court justices Benjamin Cardozo and Felix Frankfurter. His first draft of the order was rejected as too weak by A. Philip Randolph, but a second, stronger version was acceptable. Rauh was a lifelong Democratic political activist. In 1947 he helped found the liberal organization Americans for Democratic Action. He was active in both the civil rights and labor movements, serving as legal counsel to the United Auto Workers, the Brotherhood of Sleeping Car Porters, the National Association for the Advancement of Colored People's Legal Defense and Education Fund, and the Mississippi Freedom Democratic Party.

Explanation and Analysis of the Document

The first two paragraphs of the order constitute a preamble, which establishes the need and basis for presidential action. The preamble cites national defense as the primary justification for government intervention in employment practices. Although the United States would not enter World War II for another five months, the conflicts then raging in Europe and Asia made military preparedness Roosevelt's top priority. He overcame widespread isolationist sentiment to place the United States on a wartime footing. In his famous fireside chat of December 29, 1940, Roosevelt rallied support for this buildup. He said, "We must be the great arsenal of democracy. For us this is an emergency as serious as war itself" (http://www.miller-center.virginia.edu/scripps/digitalarchive/speeches/spe_1940_1229_roosevelt).

The order goes on to state that the nation's defense requires "full participation" by all citizens. The exclusion of black workers from industrial and white-collar employment was a common practice before World War II. Roosevelt's order declares that this is no longer acceptable. Although pressure for executive action came from African American organizations, all racial and ethnic groups were covered by its provisions. In six separate places, the order specifies that it applies to all persons regardless of "race, creed, color, or national origin." In the southwestern United States, Mexican Americans would benefit from the lowering of discriminatory barriers. Jewish workers also realized gains when employers removed "Gentiles only" wording from their job notices. The order did not prohibit gender-based discrimination, however. Thousands of women entered nontraditional industrial jobs as labor shortages became more severe in 1943 and 1944, but this was not a

result of Executive Order 8802. Employers were still free to exclude female workers. It would be more than twenty years before bias against women would be banned.

The order's second paragraph acknowledges that discrimination against "available and needed workers" had occurred. Examples of blatant job bias were not hard to find. Richard Polenberg, author of *War and Society*, reports that only 240 of 100,000 workers in the aircraft industry in late 1940 were African American and most of these were janitors. The exclusion of black workers from defense industries prompted the National Defense Advisory Commission to issue a letter to employers in September 1940 stating that workers should not be discriminated against because of age, sex, race, or color. Although many employers and unions pledged to abide by this policy, it had little impact, since this presidential commission had no enforcement power. While the commission's statement was a welcome proclamation of federal policy, it lacked the force of law. An executive order would provide a much stronger declaration.

The third paragraph of the document boldly sets forth federal policy by stating that "there shall be no discrimination in the employment of workers in defense industries or government." Although the order was a welcome step against racial bias, it was limited both in duration and scope. Because it relied on the president's constitutional powers as commander in chief and was justified by military necessity, the order did not extend beyond the wartime emergency. It applied to defense industries and the federal government but did not cover companies with no government contracts or not doing work essential to the war effort. The defense industry, however, was the most dynamic sector of the economy; tens of thousands of new jobs were created between 1941 and 1945. In the next four years, nearly all large employers became engaged in some war-related work.

The order also specifies that labor unions as well as employers fall within its scope. This was a significant addition. In 1941 most unions, especially those affiliated with the American Federation of Labor, either excluded black workers or confined them to segregated locals. Employers with unionized workforces sometimes justified discriminatory hiring practices by citing "whites only" clauses in their collective bargaining agreements. These employers argued that white workers would walk out if forced to work beside

Time Line

1945

■ **December 18**
President Truman issues Executive Order 9664 removing enforcement powers from the FEPC, limiting it to a fact-finding role.

1946

■ **May 3**
FEPC staff are placed on leave; the agency ceases to operate.

A. Philip Randolph, shown in a photograph from 1963. (AP Photo)

blacks. The order clearly states that such practices are no longer acceptable.

The executive order contains three key provisions. The first is directed toward government agencies responsible for job-training programs in defense industries. It instructs them to "take special measures to assure" that these programs would be administered without discrimination. For example, the United States Employment Service, in referring applicants for defense jobs, could no longer honor employers' requests to send only white workers.

The second provision of Roosevelt's order requires that nondiscrimination clauses be included in all defense contracts. This was the first time the federal government required such action, and it was a controversial measure. Some southern politicians complained that this would destroy the Jim Crow system and lead to racial conflict. According to Andrew Edmund Kersten in *Race, Jobs, and the War*, Mississippi's Senator Theodore Bilbo angrily proclaimed that mixing black and white workers on the job ultimately would lead to "miscegenation and mongrelization of both the white race and the black race" (p. 132). Bilbo's fears were exaggerated because the order did not require workplace integration. In many instances, especially in the South, separate training programs and work sites were instituted for African Americans. Under the prevailing legal doctrine of "separate but equal" established in 1896 by *Plessy v. Ferguson*, segregation itself was not considered discriminatory. This would remain the law of the land until the *Brown v. Board of Education* decision thirteen years after Executive Order 8802.

Including a nondiscrimination clause in a contract, though an important first step, did not guarantee an end to unfair hiring practices. Without an adequate enforcement mechanism, the order was meaningless. That is why the

order's third provision ultimately is the most important. It creates a five-member Fair Employment Practices Committee "to receive and investigate complaints of discrimination" in defense industries. Such an agency had long been sought by civil rights advocates, who considered it an important tool to open employment opportunities for African Americans and other minorities. The FEPC legislation had been introduced in Congress earlier in 1941, but since conservative southern Democrats controlled many important congressional committees, it had little chance of passage. The only way such an agency could become a reality was through executive action.

Authority to investigate discrimination meant little without the power to act against offending employers. Roosevelt's order authorized the committee to "take appropriate steps to redress grievances." These deliberately vague words were the subject of considerable debate. Because the order did not specify what measures were considered "appropriate," some critics grumbled that the FEPC would be a toothless tiger. The order contains an implied threat to deny or invalidate federal contracts for defense contractors found guilty of discrimination. If this threat materialized, the FEPC would be a force to be reckoned with. If its powers were limited to mediation and negotiation, however, its clout would be considerably less. This would become a source of contention as the committee began its work.

Roosevelt's 1942 decision to locate the FEPC within the Office of Production Management placed the committee in a difficult position. Since the main responsibility of the Office of Production Management was to facilitate the production of essential war materials, it was cautious about taking any action that would interfere with or curtail the production of key military supplies. Therefore, the FEPC was forced to rely mainly on persuasion, education, and negotiation to carry out its mission. From its creation in 1941 until the end of the war in 1945, not a single federal contract was voided for discriminatory practices.

The FEPC was also authorized to recommend to government departments and the president "all measures ... deemed by it necessary or proper to effectuate" the order. Because it lacked the power to compel government agencies to change their practices, the committee's role was largely advisory rather than regulatory. Civil rights leaders were well aware of the limitations of Executive Order 8802. Still, they greeted its proclamation as a significant first step in the battle for better employment opportunities. Randolph hailed it as a "second Emancipation Proclamation" (Kersten, p. 18). Such an assessment would prove excessively optimistic, but the order does make an important difference. At a time when racial discrimination was widespread, it signals that the federal government had enlisted as an ally in the struggle for civil rights.

Audience

President Franklin Delano Roosevelt's order was intended to pacify black critics such as A. Philip Randolph, and in

> "*It is the policy of the United States to encourage full participation in the national defense program by all citizens of the United States, regardless of race, creed, color, or national origin.*"
>
> (Paragraph 1)

> "*There shall be no discrimination in the employment of workers in defense industries or government because of race, creed, color, or national origin.*"
>
> (Paragraph 3)

> "*The Committee [on Fair Employment Practice] shall receive and investigate complaints of discrimination in violation of the provisions of this order and shall take appropriate steps to redress grievances which it finds to be valid.*"
>
> (Paragraph 6)

that respect it was successful. It sent a message to African Americans that their contributions to the national war effort were valued and the federal government was willing to intervene on their behalf to win improved job opportunities. Mary McLeod Bethune, an influential black educator, praised Roosevelt's action. Andrew Edmund Kersten quotes her letter to the president: Executive Order 8802, she writes, had "come to us as a refreshing shower in a thirsty land" (p. 18).

Initially, Executive Order 8802 was largely overlooked by the white press; the unsettled world situation made for more compelling news. As the FEPC began to pressure employers and unions to change discriminatory hiring practices, however, white politicians, businessmen, and labor leaders realized that racial discrimination in employment was no longer acceptable, and they objected strongly. Although the Jim Crow laws would remain in place for two more decades, the tide was beginning to turn against racist practices.

Impact

Executive Order 8802 was an important symbolic victory for African Americans in their quest for full civil rights. For the first time since Reconstruction, a federal agency was given responsibility for fighting racial discrimination. This precedent of strong presidential action on behalf of equal rights would be followed by the next four chief executives: Harry S. Truman ordered an end to military segregation in 1948, Dwight D. Eisenhower dispatched troops

to Little Rock in 1957 to enforce school desegregation, John F. Kennedy proposed the Civil Rights Act that became law in 1964 after his assassination, and Lyndon B. Johnson secured passage of the 1965 Voting Rights Act.

However, the historian Richard M. Dalfiume has questioned the magnitude of the victory gained by civil rights leaders. In *Desegregation of the U.S. Armed Forces*, he raises the possibility that the creation of the FEPC was "a shrewd victory by a politically wise president over the demands of a militant minority" (p. 117). He emphasizes that Roosevelt's executive order satisfied only one of the six original actions endorsed by the March on Washington Movement. The most important of the unrecognized demands, the desegregation of the armed forces, was strongly opposed by military leaders. African American soldiers, sailors, and airmen would continue to serve in Jim Crow units throughout the war.

The apparent success of the threatened march on Washington strengthened the credibility of militant black leaders such as A. Philip Randolph. In subsequent decades a new generation of civil rights activists would not shy away from confronting the White House and Congress with demands for action against all forms of racism. The 1963 March on Washington, which drew 250,000 demonstrators to the capital to petition for jobs and freedom, can be seen as a culmination of the movement begun in 1941. Indeed, A. Philip Randolph was the catalyst behind both protests.

While African Americans cheered the creation of the FEPC, many whites vehemently opposed its efforts to upgrade black workers. On May 25, 1943, white workers at the Alabama Shipbuilding and Dry Dock Company in Mobile rioted following the promotion of twelve blacks to welders' positions. More than twenty people were injured and all work at the yard was halted until an army detachment stopped the violence. In August 1944 white workers struck against the Philadelphia Transportation Company to protest the promotion of eight African American workers, bringing all public transit in the city to a halt. President Roosevelt had to dispatch army troops to restore order. Rising racial tensions and concerns over possible violence frequently were invoked by those opposed to the FEPC's efforts.

The original FEPC was not a powerful agency. It began work with a part-time staff of eleven persons and an annual budget of only $80,000. Because it was an executive agency, it lacked the power to subpoena, fine, or jail those who ignored its directives. It had to rely on publicity and persuasion to accomplish its objectives. On July 30, 1942, Roosevelt announced that he was placing the FECP under the administration of the War Manpower Commission (WMC). Paul V. McNutt, the former Indiana governor who headed the WMC, was unsympathetic to the work of the FEPC. He promptly cut the committee's budget, denied it access to WMC's field offices, and refused to hire more staff. Then, in January 1943, he indefinitely postponed the scheduled hearings on discrimination in the railroad industry. This action prompted the resignations of three committee members and several key staffers. A. Philip Randolph revived his March on Washington Movement to save the FEPC. Roosevelt eventually bowed to pressure and on May 27, 1943, he issued Executive Order 9346 reorganizing and strengthening the FEPC. He took the committee out from under McNutt's supervision and appointed Monsignor Francis J. Haas, a Catholic priest with strong labor credentials, as its chairman. By September the committee was operating from nine regional offices and three suboffices.

Assessing the effectiveness of the FEPC is a difficult endeavor. Scholars agree that African American workers made substantial gains between 1941 and 1945. A million and a half minority workers were employed in war industries and another three hundred thousand civilians worked for the federal government. The African American share of the defense industry labor force more than tripled, from 2.5 percent in 1942 to 8.3 percent by the end of 1944. But how much was due to the efforts of the FECP, and how much of this increase was the result of the tight wartime job market? Richard Polenberg observes, "As the manpower pinch grew tighter in 1943, many of the obstacles to Negro employment collapsed" (p. 116). Defenders of the FEPC, however, claim significant victories in public transportation, utilities, post offices, shipbuilding, and steel mills. Merl E. Reed, in, *Seedtime for the Modern Civil Rights Movement*, a comprehensive history of the FEPC, concludes that "the FEPC functioned more effectively than anyone in the administrative establishment believed possible" (p. 350).

Judging from the vehemence of congressional opposition, southern segregationists viewed the FEPC as a dangerous threat to the Jim Crow system. Andrew Edmund Kersten documented the reaction of two outspoken opponents. Mississippi's Representative John Rankin described committee members as "a bunch of crackpots" who were "doing everything they possibly can to … force [whites] to accept Negroes on terms of social equality" (p. 126). Virginia's Congressman Howard W. Smith conducted hearings to discredit the agency by alleging that it had exceeded its authority and claiming its members were Communist sympathizers. Testimony before Smith's committee provided ammunition for conservative members of Congress trying to cut off funding for the FEPC. With Roosevelt's backing, liberals were able to secure adequate appropriations for 1945, but they would not be so successful in the following year. With the end of the war and Roosevelt's death, congressional support for fair employment waned. A coalition of southern Democrats and western Republicans slashed funds and blocked the creation of a permanent FEPC. President Harry Truman further weakened the committee in December 1945 by issuing Executive Order 9664, which removed its enforcement powers, limiting it to a fact-finding role. Lacking appropriations to continue its work, the agency ceased operations in May 1946.

The idea of a fair employment agency was not dead, however. By 1948 eight states had established their own antibias bureaus modeled on the federal example. The spirit of Executive Order 8802 was revived in 1963 when President John F. Kennedy introduced his Civil Rights Act. Title VII of the bill called for the creation of an equal employment opportunities commission with power to act against employers engaging in unlawful discrimination. Passage of the act in 1964 and the subsequent creation of the Equal Employment Opportunities Commission was the successful conclusion of the efforts begun by A. Philip Randolph in 1941.

Related Documents

Anderson, Jervis. *A. Philip Randolph: A Biographical Portrait*. New York: Harcourt Brace Jovanovich, 1973. Anderson provides a biography of the man responsible for persuading Franklin Roosevelt to issue Executive Order 8802.

Garfinkel, Herbert. *When Negroes March: The March on Washington Movement in the Organizational Politics for FEPC*. New York: Atheneum, 1969. This is a definitive study of the movement Randolph created.

Ruchames, Louis. *Race, Jobs, and Politics: The Story of FEPC*. New York: Columbia University Press, 1953. This is the first study to document the accomplishments of the FEPC.

Sitkoff, Harvard. *A New Deal for Blacks: The Emergence of Civil Rights as a National Issue*. New York: Oxford University Press, 1978. Sitkoff examines the impact of Roosevelt's New Deal agencies on African Americans.

Wynn, Neil A. *The Afro-American and the Second World War*. New York: Holmes & Meier, 1975. Wynn offers a comprehensive review of African American participation in the war effort in the military and on the home front.

Bibliography

■ Books

Dalfiume, Richard M. *Desegregation of the U.S. Armed Forces: Fighting on Two Fronts, 1939–1953.* Columbia: University of Missouri Press, 1969.

Kersten, Andrew Edmund. *Race, Jobs, and the War: The FEPC in the Midwest, 1941–46.* Urbana: University of Illinois Press, 2000.

Polenberg, Richard. *War and Society: The United States, 1941–1945.* Philadelphia: J. B. Lippincott, 1972.

Reed, Merl E. *Seedtime of the Modern Civil Rights Movement: The President's Committee on Fair Employment Practice, 1941–1946.* Urbana: University of Illinois Press, 2000.

■ Web Sites

"Executive Order 9346 Establishing a Committee on Fair Employment Practice." The American Presidency Project Web site.
  http://www.presidency.ucsb.edu/ws/index.php?pid=16404. Accessed on February 19, 2008.

"Executive Order 9981." Harry S. Truman Library and Museum Web site.
  http://www.trumanlibrary.org/9981a.htm. Accessed on February 19, 2008.

"Fireside Chat 16 (December 29, 1940) 'Arsenal of Democracy'." Miller Center of Public Affairs Web site.
  http://www.millercenter.virginia.edu/scripps/digitalarchive/speeches/spe_1940_1229_roosevelt. Accessed on February 19, 2008.

"Title VII of the Civil Rights Act of 1964." The U.S. Equal Employment Opportunity Commission Web site.
  http://www.eeoc.gov/policy/vii.html. Accessed on February 19, 2008.

—By Paul T. Murray

1. During World War II, African American leaders launched the "Double V" campaign—victory over fascism abroad and victory over racism at home. In addition to Executive Order 8802, what were other specific achievements of this campaign?

2. In the opinion of many historians, Roosevelt's success as president was due in large part to his ability to balance the demands of competing interest groups. In the case of Executive Order 8802, what factors influenced Roosevelt to accede to the demands of African Americans when he had not previously done so?

3. Members of the Roosevelt administration tried to persuade A. Philip Randolph to call off the March on Washington because "the time was not right." What reasons persuaded Randolph that the time was right for militant mass protest by African Americans?

4. On August 28, 1963, Randolph was the prime mover behind the March on Washington. In terms of organization, it was very similar to the aborted 1941 march. How did the objectives of the two protests differ? Compare the responses of Roosevelt and Kennedy to the two protests.

5. During Roosevelt's presidency, his wife, Eleanor, frequently acted as an intermediary for African American leaders, urging her husband to take action on behalf of civil rights. Her actions at the time of the March on Washington Movement, however, did not fit this pattern. Why did Eleanor Roosevelt try to persuade Randolph to cancel the march?

Glossary

effectuate	accomplish
grievances	complaints of unfair treatment
Office of Production Management	a federal agency created by President Franklin Roosevelt in 1941 to oversee and coordinate production of equipment and supplies essential for national defense
prerequisite	a necessary condition
redress	to correct
statutes	laws

EXECUTIVE ORDER 8802

Reaffirming Policy of Full Participation in The Defense Program by All Persons, Regardless of Race, Creed, Color, or National Origin, and Directing Certain Action in Furtherance of Said Policy

June 25, 1941

WHEREAS it is the policy of the United States to encourage full participation in the national defense program by all citizens of the United States, regardless of race, creed, color, or national origin, in the firm belief that the democratic way of life within the Nation can be defended successfully only with the help and support of all groups within its borders; and:

WHEREAS there is evidence that available and needed workers have been barred from employment in industries engaged in defense production solely because of considerations of race, creed, color, or national origin, to the detriment of workers' morale and of national unity:

NOW, THEREFORE, by virtue of the authority vested in me by the Constitution and the statutes, and as a prerequisite to the successful conduct of our national defense production effort, I do hereby reaffirm the policy of the United States that there shall be no discrimination in the employment of workers in defense industries or government because of race, creed, color, or national origin, and I do hereby declare that it is the duty of employers and of labor organizations, in furtherance of said policy and of this order, to provide for the full and equitable participation of all workers in defense industries, without discrimination because of race, creed, color, or national origin;

And it is hereby ordered as follows:

1. All departments and agencies of the Government of the United States concerned with vocational and training programs for defense production shall take special measures appropriate to assure that such programs are administered without discrimination because of race, creed, color, or national origin;

2. All contracting agencies of the Government of the United States shall include in all defense contracts hereafter negotiated by them a provision obligating the contractor not to discriminate against any worker because of race, creed, color, or national origin;

3. There is established in the Office of Production Management a Committee on Fair Employment Practice, which shall consist of a chairman and four other members to be appointed by the President. The Chairman and members of the Committee shall serve as such without compensation but shall be entitled to actual and necessary transportation, subsistence and other expenses incidental to performance of their duties. The Committee shall receive and investigate complaints of discrimination in violation of the provisions of this order and shall take appropriate steps to redress grievances which it finds to be valid. The Committee shall also recommend to the several departments and agencies of the Government of the United States and to the President all measures which may be deemed by it necessary or proper to effectuate the provisions of this order.

Franklin D. Roosevelt

The White House, June 25, 1941.

TO THE CONGRESS OF THE UNITED STATES:

Yesterday, December 7, 1941 — a date which will live in infamy — the United States of America was suddenly and deliberately attacked by naval and air forces of the Empire of Japan.

The United States was at peace with that nation and, at the solicitation of Japan, was still in conversation with its Government and its Emperor looking toward the maintenance of peace in the Pacific. Indeed, one hour after Japanese air squadrons had commenced bombing in Oahu, the Japanese Ambassador to the United States and his colleague delivered to the Secretary of State a formal reply to a recent American message. While this reply stated that it seemed useless to continue the existing diplomatic negotiations, it contained no threat or hint of war or armed attack.

It will be recorded that the distance of Hawaii from Japan makes it obvious that the attack was deliberately planned many days or even weeks ago. During the intervening time the Japanese Government has deliberately sought to deceive the United States by false statements and expressions of hope for continued peace.

The attack yesterday on the Hawaiian Islands has caused severe damage to American naval and military forces. Very many American lives have been lost. In addition American ships have been reported torpedoed on the high seas between San Francisco and Honolulu.

Franklin D. Roosevelt's "Pearl Harbor" Speech (National Archives and Records Administration)

FRANKLIN D. ROOSEVELT'S "PEARL HARBOR" SPEECH

"Always will our whole Nation remember the character of the onslaught against us."

Overview

On December 7, 1941, with World War II well under way but with the United States only indirectly involved, the Japanese air force attacked the U.S. naval base at Pearl Harbor, on the Hawaiian island of Oahu. The attack devastated the U.S. Pacific Fleet in less than two hours. More than 2,500 Americans died, five battleships were sunk, three destroyers were wrecked, and several other ships would have to be put out of commission; of the eight battleships in the harbor, not one was deemed seaworthy after the attack. Only three of the Pacific Fleet's aircraft carriers—those not stationed at Pearl Harbor—escaped the onslaught.

Addressing both houses of Congress on the following day, December 8, 1941, President Franklin D. Roosevelt set out the case for engaging in the war. He pointed out that the United States had been at peace with Japan and had been consulting with that nation about ways to maintain peace in the Pacific. He conceded that diplomatic negotiation had seemed to reach a stalemate, with the Japanese expressing no confidence in continuing the dialogue. And he noted that Japan had nevertheless given no sign of intent to attack the United States.

In asking for a declaration of war, Roosevelt pointed out that the United States had no choice but to respond with military force to an unprovoked and planned attack. A further reason to respond as such was that the nation had been the victim of deception, since the Japanese had signaled that they were seeking diplomatic solutions. Roosevelt also noted that the Japanese had attacked several other sites in Asia and were intent on permanently injuring U.S. property and interests in the Pacific. Therefore, the only just response, in his opinion, was a call for "absolute victory" and for Congress to declare that a state of war existed between the United States and Japan.

Context

Although World War II began in Europe in September 1939, the United States remained officially neutral for over two years. The country's position was basically isolationist, as many Americans conceived that for a second time Europeans had failed to keep the peace and that they were responsible for resolving their own conflicts. Roosevelt respected public opinion, but he was also aware that vital U.S. interests could be damaged should the Axis powers win the war. At the same time, he was keenly aware of the increasing militancy of the recent Japanese governments, beginning in the early 1930s, when military men began dominating Japanese politics and promoted the extension of Japanese rule to other parts of Asia.

Roosevelt pursued policies aimed at strengthening the U.S. military, aiding Great Britain—through a lend-lease program that provided Britain with ships, planes, and other valuable equipment—and checking Japanese expansionism through trade embargoes. Although Roosevelt was warned that Japan might strike directly at the United States, he was unclear as to when or where that attack might come. Washington actually sent warnings to the fleet at Pearl Harbor and at other ports, but postwar congressional investigations would conclude that the warnings were not taken very seriously.

Without question, Roosevelt's efforts to curtail Japanese access to the raw materials required for conducting war was viewed by the Japanese as an assault on their own sphere of influence in Asia. Japan did not underestimate the strength of U.S. forces, which is precisely why the Japanese high command believed that a surprise opening strike at the Pacific Fleet in Pearl Harbor would be an essential part of their effort to preserve and enlarge their empire.

About the Author

Franklin Delano Roosevelt was born on January 30, 1882, in Hyde Park, New York. The Roosevelts were a wealthy family and sent their son to the best private schools—Groton, Harvard, and Columbia. Roosevelt became a member of the New York State Bar and practiced law in New York City for three years.

Early on, Roosevelt developed an interest in politics, as stimulated in part by the career of his fifth cousin, Theodore Roosevelt, who in 1901, at age forty-two, became the youngest man to serve as president of the United

Time Line

1931–1932

■ **September 18, 1931–December 1932**
Japan begins military operations in Manchuria, installing a puppet government there; occupies Shanghai; and invades China's Jehol Province.

1933

■ **February 23–March 12**
Japanese occupy China north of the Great Wall.

1936

■ **July 19–29**
Japanese troops occupy Beijing and Tianjin.

1937

■ **November 20–December 24**
Japanese take Nanjing, killing approximately 350,000 civilians. Japanese forces sink the U.S. Navy gunboat *Panay* and two merchant ships near Nanjing and occupy Hangzhou.

1938

■ **October 21–25**
Japanese enter Guangzhou and Hankow.

1939

■ **September 3**
Britain and France declare war on Germany after the latter invades Poland.

■ **November 24**
Japanese sever China from French Indochina.

1940

■ Japanese control northeastern third of China and all major seaports.

■ **December 10**
U.S companies are no longer allowed to export iron and steel products to Japan.

1941

■ **June 22**
Germany invades Russia.

■ **July 26**
Roosevelt freezes Japanese assets in United States and closes Panama Canal to Japanese vessels.

States. In 1910, Franklin Roosevelt was elected to the New York state senate as a Democrat, proving himself a zealous campaigner and ambitious legislator. His political connections led to his appointment as assistant secretary of the navy in Woodrow Wilson's administration (1913–1921). An able hands-on administrator, Roosevelt modernized the navy and schooled himself in the workings of the federal government—experiences that would serve him especially well as a wartime president.

Roosevelt's rapid rise in politics seemed to be halted when he contracted polio in 1921. Although his legs became paralyzed and he would never walk again, his physical stamina eventually returned, and he courageously reentered public life. In 1929 he was elected governor of New York. Continuing the progressive agenda pursued by his predecessor, Al Smith, Roosevelt captured the Democratic Party's nomination for president in 1932 and won the office, over Herbert Hoover, later that year.

Roosevelt was elected president at a time when forceful action was needed to restore the country to prosperity. The United States had been suffering from mass unemployment and a poorly performing economy—the Great Depression—for three years. In the midst of this depression, Roosevelt used his large Democratic majority in Congress to pass an unprecedented number of legislative acts aimed at economic recovery in both the agricultural and industrial sectors.

Even as he devoted most of his attention to domestic problems, Roosevelt sought to prepare the country for possible involvement in what would become World War II. Although he declared his support for several Neutrality Acts amid a public mood of isolationism, he moved toward open support of the western democracies when Germany invaded Poland in September 1939 and later occupied France and most of western Europe. When Great Britain stood virtually alone as Germany's foe, Roosevelt effected passage of the Lend-Lease Act (1941), which supplied munitions to those countries opposing the Axis powers.

With the attack on Pearl Harbor, public outrage was such that Roosevelt easily secured a declaration of war against Japan, a country now seen as spreading the same kind of totalitarian rule that Great Britain had been fighting in Europe. Roosevelt's vigorous prosecution of the war, his steadfast support of the Allies, and his postwar plans for the United Nations would become part of his enduring legacy as a war leader. Roosevelt broke the tradition of presidents serving no more than two terms, gaining election to a third term in 1940 and to a fourth term in 1944. He died of a cerebral hemorrhage on April 12, 1945.

Explanation and Analysis of the Document

Franklin D. Roosevelt dictated virtually every word of his short address—fewer than 500 words—to his secretary, Grace Tully. The phrasing of the next-to-last sentence alone was suggested by another, his close adviser Harry Hopkins.

Roosevelt begins his address to the joint session of Congress by baldly and solemnly stating that the United States has been attacked "suddenly and deliberately" by the "Empire of Japan." By citing the day, December 7, as "yesterday," the president captures the immediacy and shock of the event. Further, it was not just an attack on the United States but a "day which will live in infamy." In other words, what the Japanese did was far worse than just one country attacking another; Roosevelt's words imply that this was a disgraceful deed that could never be forgotten. Roosevelt also pointedly uses the term "Empire of Japan," wording that was sure to remind Congress and the American people of Japan's occupation of vast areas of China and its militaristic campaigns throughout the 1930s. Implicitly, the "United States," a republic, was by definition different in kind from the expansionist Japanese state, which was ruled not only by a military-dominated government but also by an emperor.

To open the second paragraph, Roosevelt notes that the United States had itself made no attacks and had been conducting talks with the Japanese government and its emperor about how to maintain peace in the Pacific. In fact, the Japanese had themselves asked for such talks, as though their intentions had been honorable and peaceful. Even as Japanese airplanes were bombing the naval base at Pearl Harbor on the Hawaiian island of Oahu, where much of the U.S. fleet was based, their ambassador delivered to the U.S. government a "formal reply to a recent American message." By using the word "conversation," Roosevelt suggests that he had understood the two nations to have a rather relaxed, ongoing relationship far removed from plans for war. No suggestion is made in this paragraph that the United States had perceived a need to be on high alert or that the negotiations had been tense. Indeed, "maintenance of the peace"—the phrase that Roosevelt uses—suggests routine, standard procedures.

The United States was not, in other words, prepared for hostilities. The fact that the Japanese ambassador had delivered a "formal reply" further suggests that he and his associates were acting with the full backing of their government. Moreover, the contact between the two countries was at the highest level—between the U.S. secretary of state and the Japanese ambassador, who not only spoke for his government but also was in contact, Roosevelt implies, with the emperor himself. Roosevelt concedes that the formal reply indicated that further talks "seemed useless," but the American government was given no inkling that the Japanese were about to wage war. This point is important because it establishes that the United States not only was unprepared for the Pearl Harbor attack in particular but also was given no warning that Japan intended to wage war.

Roosevelt's congressional audience surely had in mind the events that had precipitated World War I—the assassination of the Austrian archduke Francis Ferdinand, Germany's declaration of war on Russia, and Britain's and France's coming to the aid of their ally Russia by declaring war on Germany. The United States had not entered World War I until a series of provocative military actions were carried out by the Germans. In other words, an ominous buildup to war

Time Line

1941

■ **December 7**
The U.S. Navy base at Pearl Harbor, Hawaii, is attacked by the Japanese air force.

■ **December 8**
In his "Pearl Harbor" Speech, President Roosevelt requests a declaration of war on Japan that is granted by Congress.

■ **December 11**
Germany and Italy declare war on the United States, and Roosevelt secures from Congress a declaration of war on the Axis powers.

1942

■ **June 4–7**
Battle of Midway; U.S. Navy destroys four irreplaceable Japanese aircraft carriers and overcomes Japan's naval superiority.

1945

■ **August 6 and 9**
United States drops atomic bombs on Hiroshima and Nagasaki, causing the Japanese to surrender and ending World War II.

had occurred, with actions taken that clearly presaged open conflict. The Japanese, on the other hand, had brought about conflict much differently—barely signaling dissatisfaction with the United States while scheming to bomb its Pacific Fleet. The fact that the Japanese might have had valid cause for concern about the U.S. presence in the Pacific—the point of the talks in Washington—no longer mattered, since any sympathy for Japanese apprehensions about U.S. power was obliterated by Japan's sneak attack.

In the third paragraph, Roosevelt wholly dismisses the notion that the Japanese attack should be considered impulsive or irrational. In order to attack Hawaii—a long distance from Japan—deliberate planning would have been conducted for "many days or even weeks," Roosevelt observes. In other words, the Japanese were preparing to attack the United States even as they conducted talks in Washington emphasizing their desire for peace. No other conclusion, then, can be drawn than that Japan had practiced an elaborate deception.

Only after establishing Japanese culpability and exonerating the United States of any hostile intentions does Roosevelt turn to the damage the enemy had wrought. Without providing specifics, Roosevelt indicates that the losses had been devastating. He refers to "severe damage to American naval and military forces" in Hawaii, the loss of many American lives, and yet more damage to American ships torpedoed between Hawaii and San Francisco. Thus, the attack

President Franklin D. Roosevelt signing the declaration of war against Japan, December 8, 1941. (Library of Congress)

had been directed both at the major source of American naval strength and at the nation's command of the Pacific.

Without a word about his personal response to this devastation—other than his comment on the "day which will live in infamy"—Roosevelt enters the fourth paragraph to deliver a series of stark reports of coincidental Japanese attacks on Hong Kong, Guam, the Philippines, Wake Island, and Midway. The mention of all of these attacks of "last night" evokes the enormous scale of the Japanese Empire's advances. Roosevelt seemingly felt that with such obvious evidence of aggression, no further comment was necessary; in presenting the attacks in rapid succession, the president emphasizes how quickly and brutally Japan had moved not only against the United States but also against the British in Hong Kong, for example. In effect, Japan, like Germany, was understood to be attempting to conquer vast stretches of the world; regardless, Roosevelt chose merely to report the dramatic events rather than editorialize about them.

Not until the sixth paragraph does Roosevelt summarize the implications of these attacks: "Japan has, therefore, undertaken a surprise offensive extending throughout the Pacific area." Even here the president's words are measured, as he confines his comment to what Japan had done in the "Pacific area." Rather than indulging in any sort of broad characterization or speculating further on Japan's motives, Roosevelt states that the "facts … speak for themselves" while also noting, "The people of the United States have already formed their opinions and well understand the

implications to the very life and safety of our Nation." In effect, Roosevelt felt no need to explain the causes of the war, since he was confident that Americans understood the threat represented by the attack. Saying more, perhaps, would have only detracted from the stark outrage of the moment. Roosevelt also felt no need to say anything specific about the need to retaliate, other than to state in the seventh paragraph that as commander in chief he would take the appropriate measures for the defense of his country.

Echoing his first paragraph, Roosevelt sums up in a one-sentence paragraph the national anger over this unprecedented attack and the notion that it could never be erased from history: "But always will our whole Nation remember the character of the onslaught against us." December 7, 1941, in other words, was already a historic moment, even a defining event, in the country's history. Roosevelt's use of the future tense—"always will"—reflected a certainty and sense of command that reinforced his role as commander in chief.

Having made the case so powerfully, leaving no doubt about Japanese perfidy, Roosevelt finally resorts to language of morality in the ninth paragraph, speaking of the American people's "righteous might," which would lead to "absolute victory." This conviction he balances against his awareness that it may take considerable time—"no matter how long"—to "overcome this premeditated invasion." Coupled with his assurance that the Japanese attack will never be forgotten is Roosevelt's vow that through the will of Congress and the American people, this "form of treachery shall never again endanger us." Thus, he is calling for a war that perhaps will not end all wars—as Woodrow Wilson once promised in regard to World War I—but will nevertheless result in greater security for the American people and in greater certainty that no power like Japan will ever rise again to threaten Americans so directly.

Roosevelt's call for "absolute victory" presaged the later decision to firebomb Tokyo and other Japanese cities and to wage war until the Japanese surrendered unconditionally. This grand call for total victory also helps to explain why the United States decided to drop the atomic bombs on Japan: The goal of the nation was not merely to deprive Japan of the ability to defeat the United States but furthermore to ensure that Japan—as well as any other country, with the example set—would never even suppose it could vanquish the United States.

In paragraph 10, having situated the Japanese attack in the context of history, viewing it as one of his country's defining moments, Roosevelt returns to the present, cautioning his audience that the people and the property of the United States are in "grave danger." In other words, an attack on Hawaii—which was at the time a territory, not a state—had ramifications for the continental United States; the Japanese had effectively brought war onto American soil. Later, serious concern would be expressed about the Japanese ability to bomb West Coast cities. This atmosphere of dread that for the first time the continental United States itself might be bombed would lead, in part, to the incarceration of Japanese Americans in internment camps. Agents of the government mistakenly thought that this segment of

> "Yesterday, December 7, 1941—a date which will live in infamy—the United States of America was suddenly and deliberately attacked by naval and air forces of the Empire of Japan."
>
> (Paragraph 1)

> "But always will our whole Nation remember the character of the onslaught against us."
>
> (Paragraph 8)

> "With confidence in our armed forces—with the unbounding determination of our people—we will gain the inevitable triumph—so help us God."
>
> (Paragraph 11)

the population—the majority of which were citizens—might have posed a subversive threat to the homeland.

In the next paragraph the president expresses confidence in the U.S. armed forces and in the "unbounding determination of our people," in wording that now submerges his own role into the will of all Americans facing a common threat. His addition of the phrase "so help us God" is reminiscent of his oath of office; the phrase would become a sort of uniting pledge given by any Americans who feel that their might is on the side of right.

In his closing paragraph, Roosevelt asks Congress for a declaration of war, saying that the war between the United States and the Japanese Empire is already in progress, as of December 7. Calling Japan's attack "dastardly," Roosevelt revisits the beginning of his speech, declaring the "infamy" of this day in history. *Dastardly*, a rather old-fashioned word that would now seem melodramatic or even faintly comic, meant something quite different to Roosevelt's audience: that what the Japanese had done, attacking without warning and giving the United States no opportunity to defend itself, was both treacherous and cowardly. The word gave the president and his country the high moral ground and the impetus to fight a war against a despicable, immoral, and devious enemy. To wage war against Japan would be not merely to conquer a foe but furthermore to reassert decency and to destroy evil itself.

Audience

President Roosevelt was greeted with loud cheers when he entered the House chamber to deliver his joint address to Congress. "Twelve times in a speech of only twenty-five sentences the president was interrupted by thunderous applause," notes the historian Jean Edward Smith (p. 539). In less than seven minutes, with loud cheers breaking over his concluding remarks, Roosevelt effectively took command of the U.S. position regarding the war. One of his bitterest critics, the former president Herbert Hoover, announced his unqualified support of Roosevelt's declaration of war. Very few responded as Senator Gerald P. Nye did, alleging that the president had manipulated the nation into war. Even Nye, in fact, voted for the war resolution, which needed only thirty-three minutes to pass both houses of Congress.

Roosevelt's speech to Congress was swiftly followed by one to a radio audience estimated at 60 million. Therein, Roosevelt buttressed his congressional address by denouncing Japan's decade-long aggressive behavior, which he compared to the immoral actions of both the German leader Adolf Hitler and the Italian dictator Benito Mussolini. This linkage, which Roosevelt had not drawn in his speech to Congress, made the case for U.S. involvement in the European theater of war as well. Hitler's declaration of war on the United States relieved Roosevelt of his concern that Americans would support a conflict only with Japan. The sneak attack on Pearl Harbor was analogous to Germany's surprise invasion of Russia, Roosevelt told his radio audience. Telegrams to the White House actually indicated that Americans believed that they were now at war with the Axis powers—Germany and Italy and their client states—and not just Japan. Nevertheless, a number of isolationists were already arguing that the United States should limit its war to the Pacific. Hitler saved Roosevelt considerable trouble by declaring war on the United States first.

Clearly, President Roosevelt's address to Congress and his speech to the American people via radio were meant to galvanize public support for the war. Thus, the president concentrated on Japan's outrageous attack and why it constituted a direct threat to the United States. Above all, Roosevelt wanted to solidify American unity in the face of a formidable enemy.

Impact

Perhaps no other site on U.S. territory—excluding the continental forty-eight states—would have provoked such a resounding and unified response if attacked as did Pearl Harbor. Jean Edward Smith suggests, "If the Japanese had attacked Singapore, Borneo, or even the Philippines, the nation would have been divided over how to respond" (p. 540). President Roosevelt told his radio audience, "We are all in it—all the way. We must share together the bad news and the good news, the defeats and the victories—the changing fortunes of war" (Smith, pp. 540–541). No war since the Civil War had brought such crisis home to Americans.

After Roosevelt's addresses to Congress and to the nation, Americans responded with patriotic fervor and an unshakeable commitment to victory. Even many of those staunchly opposing America's involvement in World War II—like the aviator Charles Lindbergh, who was a leader in the antiwar America First Committee—now announced that the country had no choice but to fight. The declaration of war passed unanimously in the Senate, and in the House of Representatives only one dissenting vote was cast, by Jeannette Rankin, a pacifist who had also voted against American entry into World War I.

The symbolic nature of the Pearl Harbor attack remains a potent force in American history—as attested by references made to that event when the World Trade Center towers were destroyed on September 11, 2001. As the biographer Ted Morgan observes, "Pearl Harbor became embedded in the national psyche as the outstanding example of American vulnerability, as the model of what happened when everything went wrong in a battle" (Morgan, p. 622). The attack on Pearl Harbor led the United States into a global conflict that has often been called "the good war" because it seemed so clear that the Allies were responding to an unappeasable enemy bent on world domination. Roosevelt's joint address to Congress set the tone for the war: It would be a battle against evil incarnate in the form of figures like Hitler and Hirohito, the Japanese emperor.

Related Documents

"Fourth Inaugural Address of Franklin D. Roosevelt." The Avalon Project at Yale Law School Web site. http://www.yale.edu/lawweb/avalon/presiden/inaug/froos4.htm. In this address, given on January 20, 1945, in the final phases of World War II, Roosevelt reminds the public that the nation has been able to preserve itself and the Constitution even in times of war; he looks forward to the challenge of creating a "durable peace."

"On the Declaration of War with Japan." Franklin D. Roosevelt Presidential Library and Museum Web site. http://www.fdrlibrary.marist.edu/120941.html. Accessed on February 7, 2008. This site provides Roosevelt's radio address to the nation of December 9, 1941, in which he elaborates on his war message to Congress, detailing Japan's aggressive behavior and the measures that the United States will take to win the war and establish peace.

"State of the Union Message to Congress." Franklin D. Roosevelt Presidential Library and Museum Web site. http://www.fdrlibrary.marist.edu/011144.html. Accessed on February 7, 2008. In this address, from January 11, 1944, President Roosevelt cautions against overconfidence and the need to plan ahead so as to establish a world in which no such war could be waged again; he declares, "We are united in determination that this war shall not be followed by another interim which leads to new disaster—that we shall not repeat the tragic errors of ostrich isolationism."

Bibliography

■ Books

Black, Conrad. *Franklin Delano Roosevelt: Champion of Freedom.* New York: Public Affairs, 2003.

Burns, James MacGregor. *Roosevelt: The Lion and the Fox.* New York: Harcourt, Brace, 1956.

Dallek, Robert. *Franklin D. Roosevelt and American Foreign Policy, 1932–1945.* New York: Oxford University Press, 1979.

Davis, Kenneth S. *FDR, the War President, 1940–1943: A History.* New York: Random House, 2000.

Fleming, Thomas J. *The New Dealers' War: FDR and the War within World War II.* New York: Basic Books, 2001.

Freidel, Frank. *Franklin D. Roosevelt: A Rendezvous with Destiny.* Boston: Little, Brown, 1990.

Jenkins, Roy. *Franklin Delano Roosevelt.* New York: Times Books, 2003.

McJimsey, George. *The Presidency of Franklin Delano Roosevelt.* Lawrence: University Press of Kansas, 2000.

Morgan, Ted. *FDR: A Biography.* New York: Simon and Schuster, 1985.

Schlesinger, Arthur M. *The Age of Roosevelt.* 3 vols. Boston: Houghton Mifflin, 1957–1960.

Smith, Jean Edward. *FDR.* New York: Random House, 2007.

■ **Web Sites**

"Franklin Delano Roosevelt: Pearl Harbor Address to the Nation."
American Rhetoric Web site.
   http://www.americanrhetoric.com/speeches/fdrpearlharbor.htm.
   Accessed on September 7. 2007.

"The Perilous Fight: Pearl Harbor." PBS Web site.
   http://www.pbs.org/perilousfight/battlefield/pearl_harbor/.
   Accessed on September 7. 2007.

—By Carl Rollyson

Questions for Further Study

1. President Franklin D. Roosevelt's joint address to Congress conveys the impression that the United States was caught completely by surprise. Yet American commanders in the Pacific had been warned of impending hostile action against American bases, especially in the Philippines. By December 1 the president was discussing the imminent threat of war with the British ambassador. Compare the president's address to what historians now know about the events leading up to the Pearl Harbor attack. Why did Roosevelt omit any mention of U.S. suspicion of an impending Japanese attack?

2. The attack on Pearl Harbor signaled the end of any peaceful accommodation with Japan. What measures did the U.S. government take to "check" Japan, and why did these measures fail? Why did President Roosevelt not discuss these measures in his joint address to Congress or with the American people?

3. While President Roosevelt presented the attack on Pearl Harbor as a complete surprise, historians have disagreed about the extent to which he should have anticipated such an attack based on the intelligence he was receiving about Japanese military plans. Ted Morgan, for example, suggests that the "signs pointing to Pearl Harbor were raindrops in a squall of messages. So what if the Japanese were asking about ship movements in Honolulu? They were asking about ship movements in a lot of other ports" (p. 605). Compare and contrast how other historians and biographers have assessed what Roosevelt knew about Japanese intentions at the time of the Pearl Harbor attack.

4. Most historians have rejected the conspiratorial charge that Roosevelt deliberately set up an attack on Pearl Harbor so as to involve the United States in World War II. Compare and contrast how historians and biographers have addressed this accusation.

5. To what extent has Franklin D. Roosevelt's character complicated the task of assessing how he felt about the imminence of war with Japan? Roosevelt's motives on the eve of war are difficult to interpret. What components of the president's personality have made determining his mood on the eve of the Pearl Harbor attack so challenging?

6. Compare and contrast the tone and substance of President Roosevelt's short fourth inaugural address with his terse war message to Congress after the Pearl Harbor attack.

7. Compare and contrast President Roosevelt's stark address to Congress asking for a declaration of war against Japan with his radio address to the nation on December 9, 1941.

8. What themes remain consistent throughout Roosevelt's communications to the public regarding the prosecution of the war—from his war message to Congress, to his radio address to the nation after the Pearl Harbor attack, to his subsequent annual messages to Congress, and to his fourth inaugural address?

Glossary

dastardly   treacherous and devious

infamy   the state of having a disgraced reputation, often due to criminal behavior that deserves the heaviest condemnation

FRANKLIN D. ROOSEVELT'S "PEARL HARBOR" SPEECH

Mr. Vice President, and Mr. Speaker, and Members of the Senate and House of Representatives:

Yesterday, December 7, 1941—a date which will live in infamy—the United States of America was suddenly and deliberately attacked by naval and air forces of the Empire of Japan.

The United States was at peace with that Nation and, at the solicitation of Japan, was still in conversation with its Government and its Emperor looking toward the maintenance of peace in the Pacific. Indeed, one hour after Japanese air squadrons had commenced bombing in the American Island of Oahu, the Japanese Ambassador to the United States and his colleague delivered to our Secretary of State a formal reply to a recent American message. And while this reply stated that it seemed useless to continue the existing diplomatic negotiations, it contained no threat or hint of war or of armed attack.

It will be recorded that the distance of Hawaii from Japan makes it obvious that the attack was deliberately planned many days or even weeks ago. During the intervening time the Japanese Government has deliberately sought to deceive the United States by false statements and expressions of hope for continued peace.

The attack yesterday on the Hawaiian Islands has caused severe damage to American naval and military forces. I regret to tell you that very many American lives have been lost. In addition American ships have been reported torpedoed on the high seas between San Francisco and Honolulu.

Yesterday the Japanese Government also launched an attack against Malaya.

Last night Japanese forces attacked Hong Kong.

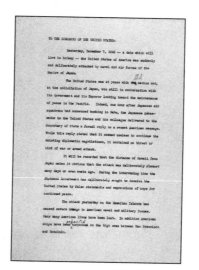

Last night Japanese forces attacked Guam.

Last night Japanese forces attacked the Philippine Islands.

Last night the Japanese attacked Wake Island. And this morning the Japanese attacked Midway Island.

Japan has, therefore, undertaken a surprise offensive extending throughout the Pacific area. The facts of yesterday and today speak for themselves. The people of the United States have already formed their opinions and well understand the implications to the very life and safety of our Nation.

As Commander in Chief of the Army and Navy I have directed that all measures be taken for our defense.

But always will our whole Nation remember the character of the onslaught against us.

No matter how long it may take us to overcome this premeditated invasion, the American people in their righteous might will win through to absolute victory. I believe that I interpret the will of the Congress and of the people when I assert that we will not only defend ourselves to the uttermost but will make it very certain that this form of treachery shall never again endanger us.

Hostilities exist. There is no blinking at the fact that our people, our territory, and our interests are in grave danger.

With confidence in our armed forces—with the unbounding determination of our people—we will gain the inevitable triumph—so help us God.

I ask that the Congress declare that since the unprovoked and dastardly attack by Japan on Sunday, December 7, 1941, a state of war has existed between the United States and the Japanese Empire.

EXECUTIVE ORDER

- - - - - - -

AUTHORIZING THE SECRETARY OF WAR TO PRESCRIBE
MILITARY AREAS

WHEREAS the successful prosecution of the war

requires every possible protection against espionage

and against sabotage to national-defense material,

national-defense premises, and national-defense util-

ities as defined in Section 4, Act of April 20, 1918,

40 Stat. 533, as amended by the Act of November 30,

1940, 54 Stat. 1220, and the Act of August 21, 1941,

55 Stat. 655 (U. S. C., Title 50, Sec. 104):

NOW, THEREFORE, by virtue of the authority

vested in me as President of the United States, and

Commander in Chief of the Army and Navy, I hereby

authorize and direct the Secretary of War, and the

Military Commanders whom he may from time to time

designate, whenever he or any designated Commander

deems such action necessary or desirable, to prescribe

military areas in such places and of such extent as he

or the appropriate Military Commander may determine,

from which any or all persons may be excluded, and with

respect to which, the right of any person to enter, re-

main in, or leave shall be subject to whatever restric-

Executive Order 9066 (National Archives and Records Administration)

"The successful prosecution of the war requires every possible protection against espionage."

Overview

Executive Order 9066, promulgated on February 19, 1942, was the first and most important document in a series of military and government directives in the aftermath of the Japanese attack on the United States Pacific Fleet at Pearl Harbor, Hawaii, on December 7, 1941. That order from President Franklin D. Roosevelt led directly to the incarceration of 120,000 men, women, and children of Japanese ancestry residing in four western states in the spring of 1942. The order authorized the secretary of war to establish military zones on the West Coast from which enemy aliens could be removed as security risks—a label that was soon applied to the entire Japanese population residing on the West Coast. Although two-thirds of them were natural-born citizens of the United States, the initial order and nearly all subsequent directives took no notice of their status and, in effect, suspended their civil rights under the Constitution. With few exceptions, no arrest warrants were issued, and no arraignments took place.

Forced to close their businesses and sell their homes, the evacuees, carrying the few belongings the army permitted them to take, were placed in ten concentration camps in remote and desolate places in seven western or midwestern states, where they remained behind barbed-wire fences and were watched over by military police until shortly before the end of World War II. The forced removal of an entire population based on ethnicity and race, which was hailed at the time as a justified response to the treacherous attack by Imperial Japan on the United States and as a military necessity to protect the American homeland, later came to be seen as a violation of fundamental American values. In 1976 President Gerald Ford rescinded Executive Order 9066. Twelve years later, Congress apologized to the sixty thousand survivors of the camps and paid modest reparations to each of them, thus closing a dark chapter in American history.

Context

In the days following the Japanese attack on Pearl Harbor, rumors circulated on the American West Coast that Japanese aliens (the Issei) and American citizens of Japanese extraction (the Nisei and their children, Sansei) were a threat to the nation's security. Despite assurances from the Federal Bureau of Investigation (FBI) director J. Edgar Hoover that the bureau had already taken suspected subversives into custody and that widely reported acts of espionage and sabotage were false, by late January the rumors had taken on a life of their own. Newspapers across the country, national columnists, radio commentators, a number of congressmen, and state officials in Oregon, California, and Washington, D.C., demanded that all Japanese—aliens and native-born alike—be rounded up and removed from the Pacific Coast.

The resulting hysteria, including isolated attacks on Japanese families, was fueled not only by fear of invasion or coastal shelling but also by a long-standing hostility in California and other western states toward Asian immigrants in general and the Issei in particular. From their first arrival in America as contract laborers at the end of the nineteenth century, the Japanese had been denied citizenship because of their race under the Naturalization Act of 1790 and, in 1924, had been barred from further immigration altogether because they were ineligible for citizenship. The California legislature denied them the right to own land, their children were forced into segregated schools, and several hate groups regularly campaigned for their expulsion from the United States.

Despite these problems, by 1940 the Japanese population had become a prosperous, law-abiding segment of society and a major force in California's agriculture, producing 10 percent of the value of the state's farm output on less than 4 percent of the land. But like many immigrant groups that faced hostility and discrimination, they also had become insular, gathering in ethnic neighborhoods with their own shops, customs, and language. For many Americans, these separate ways were sufficient reason to doubt their loyalty, especially after Japan invaded China in 1937 and expanded into Southeast Asia in 1941. War between Japan and the United States seemed possible. As tensions increased between the two countries, in 1941 the State Department dispatched a special investigator, Curtis B. Munson, to the West Coast and Hawaii to study the likelihood of disloyalty among the Issei and Nisei should there be a war with Japan. His conclusion after a two-month study from October to

November was unequivocal: "There is no Japanese 'problem' on the Coast. There will be no armed uprising of Japanese" (http://www.digitalhistory.uh. edu/learning_history/japanese_internment/munson_report.cfm). Following the surprise attack of December 7, the State Department suppressed the report—President Roosevelt did not see it until late in February of 1942—and it was not made public until the Pearl Harbor hearings in 1946. Whether its publication earlier would have dampened the hysteria and aided the Japanese population in early 1942 is an open question.

The American public clearly received misinformation and fabricated claims of domestic treachery involving Japanese aliens in California and Hawaii. Owen Roberts, an associate justice of the Supreme Court sent by President Roosevelt to investigate the attack on Pearl Harbor, reported without any evidence that there had been numerous instances of sabotage and assistance offered to the Japanese fleet prior to the raid. He confirmed a widely circulated, though false, story that Japanese farmers on the Hawaiian island of Oahu had cut arrows into their fields pointing the way toward Pearl Harbor. Lieutenant General John DeWitt, the aging commander of the Fourth Army at the Presidio in San Francisco and, after March 2, 1942, the officer in charge of the Japanese civilian population, assured the president that enemy submarines off the coast received nightly radio and flashlight signals from disloyal Nisei on shore and that a fifth column—a vast network of saboteurs—lurked in the Japanese communities, waiting for the appropriate time to strike. It mattered very little that the FBI dismissed all such reports as false.

In the weeks after Pearl Harbor, as the Japanese army and navy moved relentlessly across the South Pacific and Southeast Asia, a legion of lobbyists descended on Washington, D.C., demanding that the government remove the Japanese as soon as possible from the West Coast to protect the nation's security. In February, under pressure from Congress, the Roosevelt administration debated what course of action should be taken. When Attorney General Francis Biddle and members of the Justice Department raised constitutional and ethical questions about relocating a population solely on the basis of race, the matter fell into the hands of the War Department, whose two top officials, with the consent of the president, were prepared to do whatever military necessity required.

About the Author

Executive Order 9066 is the work of Franklin D. Roosevelt, who as chief executive set its drafting in motion, approved its provisions, and signed it but played no part in its composition, which was principally the work of Henry Stimson, the secretary of war, and John McCloy, the assistant secretary of war.

Roosevelt was the only person to be elected president of the United States for four consecutive terms. He was born to wealth in Hyde Park, New York, on January 30, 1882. He graduated from Harvard in 1904 and from Columbia Law

School in 1907. He served as assistant secretary of the navy from 1913 to 1920, during Woodrow Wilson's administration, and in 1920 he was the unsuccessful Democratic candidate for vice president. The next year, Roosevelt, at age thirty-nine, was permanently crippled by poliomyelitis. He could walk only short distances wearing heavy leg braces and with considerable difficulty, and he was confined to a wheelchair until his death in 1945. Undaunted, he returned to public life in 1924 and began his first of two terms as governor of New York four years later. In 1932 he became the nation's thirty-second president.

Roosevelt's New Deal greatly increased the power of the federal government to meet the economic and social challenges of the Great Depression. Among the legacies of his domestic program are banking reform, the Federal Deposit Insurance Corporation, the Securities and Exchange Commission, and the Tennessee Valley Authority, which brought electrical power to the rural South. His greatest triumphs came in his wartime leadership during World War II. He died at Warm Springs, Georgia, on April 12, 1945, less than one month before Nazi Germany's surrender.

When the Japanese attacked Pearl Harbor, Roosevelt was nearly eleven months into his third term. In the following weeks, his primary tasks were rallying the nation and preparing to defeat the Axis powers. He took little note of the West Coast's Japanese problem and, as was his custom in matters of secondary importance, turned it over to a member of his cabinet, in this case, the secretary of war, for resolution.

The secretary of war was Stimson, who like Roosevelt came from a wealthy family and spent most of his life in public service. Stimson, born in New York City on September 21, 1867, was a member of Yale's class of 1888 and earned master's and law degrees from Harvard in 1900. After a decade in private practice, he went to Washington, D.C., in 1911 to serve as secretary of war to President William Howard Taft. During World War I, he was a colonel in the field artillery in France. President Calvin Coolidge sent him to resolve political unrest in Nicaragua and then appointed him governor-general for the Philippines, where he served from 1927 to 1929. Stimson returned to the capital as secretary of state to President Herbert Hoover from 1929 to 1933. In his private life, he actively supported Roosevelt's foreign policy initiatives, and despite his Republican ties, in 1940 he became secretary of war, serving ably in that office until 1945. He retired on September 5, three days after the Japanese formal surrender, to write his memoirs. He died on October 20, 1950 in Huntington, New York.

When Roosevelt asked him to prepare Executive Order 9066, Stimson had reservations about the constitutionality of removing the Japanese population from the West Coast, but he was persuaded by his assistant John McCloy to accept the wartime necessity for such a move. McCloy, the assistant secretary of war, was born in Philadelphia, Pennsylvania, on March 31, 1895, into a family of modest means. In 1916 he graduated with honors from Amherst, where he waited on tables to pay his way. He left Harvard Law School in 1917 for the army, rising to captain in the field artillery in France before returning to Harvard to grad-

Time Line

1941

■ July–August
As the Japanese government expands its war with China (begun in 1937) into Southeast Asia, the United States embargoes trade with Japan (including oil and scrap metal) and freezes Japanese assets.

■ December 7
In a surprise attack, Japanese naval aircraft bomb the United States Pacific Fleet at Pearl Harbor, on the island of Oahu, Hawaii, sinking four battleships, severely damaging four others, killing 2,340 servicemen, and wounding 1,143 others. President Roosevelt issues Proclamation 2525, which requires Japanese aliens to register as enemies of the state.

■ December 8
The U.S. Congress declares war on Japan; President Roosevelt issues Proclamation 2526 and Proclamation 2527, which require German and Italian aliens to register as enemies of the state.

1942

■ February 19
President Roosevelt signs Executive Order 9066.

■ March 2
Lieutenant General John DeWitt issues Public Proclamation 1, which declares California, Oregon, Washington, and southern Arizona "military areas" and stipulates that all persons of Japanese ancestry will be evacuated.

■ March 18
President Roosevelt signs Executive Order 9102, which creates the War Relocation Authority.

■ March 21
Congress passes Public Law 503, which adds criminal sanctions, penalties, and other enforcement powers to Executive Order 9066.

■ May 20
The *San Francisco Chronicle* reports that 94,330 evacuees are in assembly or relocation centers, 2,342 are being moved, and 3,035 have received orders to evacuate within the next ten days.

1943

■ June 21
The Supreme Court upholds the curfew and exclusion orders imposed in *Hirabayashi v. United States* (1943) and *Yasui v. United States* (1943).

1945

■ January 2
Public Proclamation 21 rescinds the mass exclusion ordered under Executive Order 9066 and allows the 85,000 evacuees who remain in the camps to return home.

1948

■ July 2
President Harry S. Truman signs the Japanese-American Evacuation Claims Act, providing about $28 million in limited compensation for economic losses because of the evacuation.

1952

■ June 27
The Immigration and Naturalization Act ends the racially based 1790 naturalization ban and the 1924 ban on Asian immigration.

1976

■ February 19
President Gerald Ford issues Proclamation 4417 ("An American Promise"), which rescinds Executive Order 9066.

1982

■ December
The Commission on Wartime Relocation and Internment of Civilians issues its report *Personal Justice Denied*, in which it concludes that no military necessity or security threat justified the exclusions under Executive Order 9066.

1988

■ August 10
President Ronald Reagan signs the Redress Act, providing restitution for the wartime internment of Japanese-American civilians.

uate in 1921. By 1929 he was a partner at a prestigious Wall Street law firm, where he developed a reputation as a high-powered, gifted professional. Stimson invited him to Washington, D.C., in 1940 and, the following year, persuaded Roosevelt to appoint him assistant secretary of war. In 1942 McCloy worked out most of the details of Executive Order 9066 and oversaw its implementation. At the war's end, he and Stimson were two of the few advisers President Harry Truman consulted on using the atomic bomb.

After the war McCloy resumed his law practice and, in 1947, came back to public service as head of the World Bank for two years. He served for three years as high commissioner for Germany, overseeing that country's transition from military to civilian government, after which he became chairman of the Chase National Bank and directed its merger into Chase Manhattan Bank. Following a term as chief disarmament negotiator for President John F. Kennedy, he served on the Warren Commission and continued as chairman of the General Advisory Committee on Arms Control and Disarmament for a dozen years. Moving easily from public service to private business and back throughout his career, McCloy maintained his law practice while advising every president from Roosevelt to Ronald Reagan.

In 1981, eight years before his death on March 11, 1989, in Greenwich, Connecticut, McCloy defended Executive Order 9066 before a congressional commission. He said the internment of the Japanese was a reasonable step that was handled humanely. He refused to apologize for it.

Explanation and Analysis of the Document

The language of Executive Order 9066 does not suggest its historical importance or its life-changing impact on the Japanese communities in America in the late winter and spring of 1942. It is written in bland, uninflected prose, and it reads like dozens of other orders that flowed from the White House in the first months of World War II—all of them are work-a-day directives designed to put the nation on a war footing.

The document is directed toward dampening the hysteria that had marked the public discussion on how to secure the West Coast from enemy attack. The Japanese population on the coast and in Hawaii, the executive order's target, is not mentioned anywhere in the document. Also not mentioned are the civil rights issues the Justice Department had raised in earlier discussions concerning how much authority the military would be granted in securing the nation's defenses. The expansion of authority under Executive Order 9066 is justified by references to statutory precedents or imperatives and by an appeal to the inherent powers of the president as commander in chief.

◆ Introduction

The first paragraph states that to win the war the United States must take every step to guard against espionage and sabotage by its enemies. What will be guarded is found in the act of April 20, 1918, as amended in 1940 and 1941, known collectively in the United States Code as Title 50, "War and National Defense," which describes in specific detail a broad range of war-related industries, farms, transportation and port facilities, and military installations essential to wartime national defense.

◆ Authority

The second paragraph establishes the president's authority to provide for the national defense. Because the president is chief executive, he is responsible for carrying out the laws of the United States as noted in Article II of the Constitution. As commander in chief of the army and navy, his constitutionally established role is to ensure civilian control of the military, a principle that reaches back to the Continental Congress and the American Revolution.

◆ Main Provisions

Later in the second paragraph the president authorizes the secretary of war and such military commanders as the secretary chooses to "prescribe," or designate, areas containing war-related industries, military bases, and the like from which "any or all persons" may be excluded, denied entry, or otherwise restricted at the "discretion" of the secretary or his commanders. This is the key provision that will be used to remove all persons of Japanese ancestry from the West Coast in spring 1942, even though no specific race or ethnic group is identified.

The president requires the War Department to provide food, shelter, and transportation to any persons excluded from the areas to be designated until other arrangements are made. On March 18, 1942, Executive Order 9102 transferred virtually all custodial responsibilities for the evacuees from the War Department to a civilian agency, the War Relocation Authority, which thenceforth would manage the camps.

The second paragraph also gives the military the authority to change the restricted areas designated earlier by the Justice Department under Proclamation 2525, dated December 7, 1941, and Proclamations 2526 and 2527, dated December 8, 1941. In those orders, the president invokes the Alien Enemies Act (Chapter 3 of U.S. Code Title 50); identifies Japanese, German, and Italian aliens as subject to restraint and removal as enemies of the United States; and directs the attorney general to identify areas from which they would be barred. Those proclamations also require the aliens as individuals to register with the FBI and contain a long list of prohibited behaviors, contraband items, and travel restrictions, the violation of which could lead to arrest and internment.

In the third paragraph the military in each designated area is authorized to do whatever is necessary to enforce the provisions of Executive Order 9066, including accepting the assistance of state and local law enforcement agencies. On March 21, 1942, Congress passed Public Law 503, which provided specific criminal sanctions and penalties to enforce Executive Order 9066. In the fourth paragraph the president directs the executive departments, or the cabinet, and the federal agencies under their authority

Henry L. Stimson (Library of Congress)

to give the military any assistance that might be needed in providing custodial care for the evacuees.

The fifth paragraph of the document ends with three disclaimers: (1) Nothing in Executive Order 9066 will limit the authority given to the secretary of war and the secretary of the navy by Executive Order 8972, dated December 12, 1941, to set up guards and patrols to protect national defense industries, installations, or utilities; (2) nothing will it limit in any way the authority of the FBI to investigate alleged acts of sabotage; and (3) the order will not interfere with the Justice Department's control of enemy aliens, as defined in Proclamations 2525, 2526, and 2527.

Audience

Executive Order 9066 is written for a limited audience. It is directed to the secretary of war—and through him—to military commanders across the country and, in particular, to DeWitt, commanding general of the Western Defense Command and Fourth Army on the West Coast, who will later oversee the removal of the Japanese population. A secondary audience consists of the congressional delegations, state governments, and newspaper editors in Washington, Oregon, California, Arizona, and elsewhere, who had been clamoring for the federal government to do something about the "Japan-

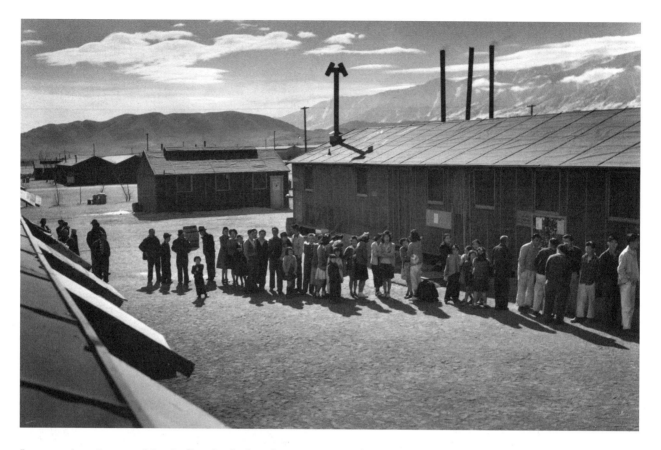

Japanese Americans waiting in line for food at the Manzanar Relocation Center in California, 1943 (Library of Congress)

ese problem." Little suggests that the Japanese themselves, the target of the executive order, are part of the intended audience because they are not mentioned in the document.

Like all presidential proclamations and executive orders since 1936, Executive Order 9066 was first published in the *Federal Register*, which prints all documents from the executive branch that have legal ramifications—for example, the rules and regulations put forward by its agencies, such as the Internal Revenue Service—and provides a daily record of the federal government's business.

Impact

The secretary of war gave the Western Defense Command and Fourth Army under DeWitt responsibility for enforcing Executive Order 9066. On March 2, 1942, the general, in the first of 108 proclamations issued from the command over the next three years, announced the demarcation of military zones from which the Japanese would be removed, encompassing the western half of Washington and Oregon; the lower, southwestern corner of Arizona; and all of California. (The Japanese population of Hawaii, then a U.S. territory, was unaffected by the relocation program because of its important place in the islands' economies.) By June 2 more than 120,000 men, women, and children, with only the personal belongings they could carry, were moved

to widely scattered assembly centers and placed in makeshift quarters at abandoned military facilities. Some were housed in horse stalls at the Santa Anita Race Track.

DeWitt's men had swept up foster children, orphans, infants, the elderly, and children of mixed marriages. One-third of the detainees were Issei, many were over age fifty, and a large number were infirm. Of the approximately seventy thousand Nisei, who were American citizens by birth, roughly one-half were female, and a majority of them were under age twenty-one. No charges were leveled against them, and no one could appeal their incarceration. They lost their civil rights, jobs, businesses, homes, and personal property.

By fall they were moved under armed guard to live behind barbed wire for up to three years in ten remote relocation centers in seven states; the civilian War Relocation Authority built and managed Heart Mountain in Wyoming, Tule Lake and Manzanar in California, Topaz in Utah, Poston and Gila River in Arizona, Granada in Colorado, Minidoka in Idaho, and Jerome and Rowher in Arkansas.

When the Japanese first arrived in the camps, they found them to consist of rows of tar-paper-covered barracks, with communal bathrooms (separated by gender but, at first, without stalls and without doors after stalls were built) and community dining halls. Over time, the camps, designed to be self-sufficient, had hospitals, post offices, and schools. The evacuees produced their own food from

"*The successful prosecution of the war requires every possible protection against espionage and against sabotage to national-defense material, national-defense premises, and national-defense utilities.*"

(Paragraph 1)

"*As President of the United States, and Commander in Chief of the Army and Navy, I hereby authorize and direct the Secretary of War, and the Military Commanders whom he may from time to time designate … to prescribe military areas … from which any or all persons may be excluded.*"

(Paragraph 2)

"*The Secretary of War is hereby authorized to provide for residents of any such area who are excluded therefrom, such transportation, food, shelter, and other accommodations as may be necessary … to accomplish the purpose of this order.*"

(Paragraph 2)

"*Because of the ties of race, the intense feeling of filial piety and the strong bonds of common tradition, culture and customs, this population presented a tightly-knit racial group.… Whether by design or accident, virtually always their communities were adjacent to very vital shore installations, war plants, etc. While it is believed that some were loyal, it was known that many were not. It was impossible to establish the identity of the loyal and the disloyal with any degree of safety.*"

(http://www.sfmuseum.org/war/dewitt1.html)

"*Careful review of the facts by the Commission has not revealed any security or military threat from the West Coast ethnic Japanese in 1942. The record does not support that military necessity justified the exclusion of the ethnic Japanese from the West Coast, with the consequent loss of property and personal liberty.*"

(Commission on Wartime Relocation and Internment of Civilians, pp. 457–458) the hardscrabble soil that lay beyond the barbed wire and guard tower. In time, the evacuees also planted flower gardens and painted the churches and schools white. The heat in summer was unbearable, with temperatures regularly rising above 100 degrees; in winter the buildings were not wind resistant, and the temperatures were often well below freezing. This difficult existence did not end for many until 1946, when the last of the camps (Tule in northern California) was closed.

The effects of Executive Order 9066 lived on to near the end of the century, beginning in 1948 when President Truman signed the Japanese-American Evacuation Claims Act, making $28 million dollars available for token payments to Japanese business owners for their property losses during the evacuation. Twenty-eight years later Gerald Ford rescinded Executive Order 9066, to lay to rest the fears of some former detainees that the document's authority was still available to the government. In December 1982 the Commission on Wartime Relocation and Internment of Civilians, charged by Congress to investigate the events of 1942 to 1946, concluded in its report *Personal Justice Denied* that no military necessity or security threat justified the exclusions under Executive Order 9066. The commission recommended that reparations be made. Six years later, in 1988, Ronald Reagan signed Public Law 100-383, the Redress Act, which offered an apology and compensation of $20,000 to each of the sixty thousand surviving evacuees and officially discredited the document that produced one of the nation's worst offenses against personal freedom.

Related Documents

Daniels, Roger. *American Concentration Camps: A Documentary History of the Relocation and Incarceration of Japanese Americans, 1942–1945*. 9 vols. New York: Garland, 1989. Daniels, the foremost historian of the camps and the Japanese American experience, assembled and annotated this month-by-month compilation of official, personal, and other primary documents.

Grapes, Bryan J., ed. *Japanese American Internment Camps*. San Diego: Greenhaven Press, 2001. This collection, directed toward high school students and undergraduates beginning historical studies, consists of contemporary articles and essays, memoirs, and diary entries by evacuees and others.

Inada, Lawson F., ed. *Only What We Could Carry: The Japanese American Internment Experience*. Berkeley: Heyday Books, 2000. Personal accounts from internees, letters, diary entries, and family photographs supplemented by posters, political cartoons, and other artwork illustrating life in the detention camps.

Irons, Peter H., ed. *Justice Delayed: The Record of the Japanese American Internment Cases*. Middletown, Conn.: Wesleyan University Press, 1989. The documents include the Supreme Court's decisions in *Hirabayashi v. United States* (1943), *Yasui v. United States* (1943), and *Korematsu v. United States* (1944), in which the court upheld arrests and imprisonment under Executive Order 9066, as

well as selected court papers from the judicial hearings from 1982 to 1985 that led the federal courts to vacate those earlier decisions.

Spicer, Edward H., et al. *Impounded People: Japanese-Americans in the Relocation Centers*. Tucson: University of Arizona Press, 1969. The authors were workers in the relocation centers. The book is a reprint of their 1946 report for the War Relocation Authority, describing and analyzing the effects of relocation on the thirty thousand families in the camps from 1942 to 1945.

Tateishi, John. *And Justice for All: An Oral History of the Japanese American Detention Camps*. New York: Random House, 1984. Tateishi presents interviews with former internees, documenting their experiences in the camps and their feelings after their release.

Bibliography

■ Books

Armor, John, and Peter Wright. *Manzanar*. New York: Times Books, 1988.

Benti, Wynne. *Born Free and Equal: The Story of Loyal Japanese Americans*. Bishop, Calif.: Spotted Dog Press, 2002.

Commission on Wartime Relocation and Internment of Civilians. *Personal Justice Denied*. Seattle: University of Washington Press, 1997.

Conrat, Maisie, and Richard Conrat. *Executive Order No. 9066: The Internment of 110,000 Japanese Americans*. San Francisco, Calif.: California Historical Society, 1972.

Daniels, Roger. *Concentration Camps, North America: Japanese in the United States and Canada during World War II*. Melbourne, Fla.: Krieger, 1993.

———. *The Politics of Prejudice: The Anti-Japanese Movement in California and the Struggle for Japanese Exclusion*. Berkeley: University of California Press, 1999.

———. *Prisoners without Trial: Japanese Americans in World War II*. Rev. ed. New York: Hill and Wang, 2004.

Girdner, Audrie, and Anne Loftis. *The Great Betrayal: The Evacuation of the Japanese-Americans during World War II*. New York: Macmillan, 1969.

Gordon, Linda, and Gary Okihiro. *Dorothea Lange and the Censored Images of Japanese Internment*. New York, N.Y.: W.W. Norton, 2006.

Irons, Peter. *Justice at War: The Story of the Japanese American Internment Cases*. New York: Oxford University Press, 1983.

Robinson, Greg. *By Order of the President: FDR and the Internment of Japanese Americans*. Cambridge, Mass.: Harvard University Press, 2001.

Weglyn, Michi. *Years of Infamy: The Untold Story of America's Concentration Camps.* New York: Morrow, 1976.

■ Web Sites

"Asian American Voices—Part 3: World War II and Asian Americans." Digital History Web site.
   http://www.digitalhistory.uh.edu/asianvoices/asian_voices.cfm. Accessed on February 19, 2008.

"Final Report: Japanese Evacuation from the West Coast 1942." The Virtual Museum of the City of San Francisco Web site.
   http://www.sfmuseum.org/war/dewitt1.html. Accessed on February 19, 2008.

"The Munson Report." Digital History Web site.
   http://www.digitalhistory.uh.edu/learning_history/japanese_int ernment/munson_report.cfm. Accessed on February 19, 2008.

"Personal Justice Denied." The National Archives "Japanese Americans during WWII: Relocation and Internment" Web site.
   http://www.archives.gov/research/japanese-americans/justice-denied. Accessed on February 19, 2008.

"Uniting and Strengthening America by Providing Appropriate Tools Required to Intercept and Obstruct Terrorism (US Patriot Act) 2001." FindLaw Web site.
   http://fl1.findlaw.com/news.findlaw.com/cnn/docs/terrorism/hr3162.pdf. Accessed on February 19, 2008.

"The War Relocation Authority and the Incarceration of Japanese-Americans during WW II." Harry S. Truman Library and Museum Web site.
   http://www.trumanlibrary.org/whistlestop/study_collections/japanese_internment/docs.php. Accessed on February 19, 2008.

—By Allan L. Damon

Questions for Further Study

1. Given the hysteria on the West Coast in 1942, the successes of Imperial Japan in the Pacific and Southeast Asia, and uncertainty about the future, what alternatives did the Roosevelt administration have to the relocation and incarceration of the Japanese?

2. Long after the internment camps were closed, the survivors of the relocation authorized by Executive Order 9066 pressured the U.S. government for reparations for their economic and personal losses forty years earlier. Did the government of a later generation of Americans have a moral obligation to meet their demands?

3. Compare Executive Order 9066, which is intended to protect the United States from sabotage and espionage by resident enemy aliens, to the Patriot Act (House Resolution 3162) of October 26, 2001, which is designed "to deter and punish terrorist acts in the United States and around the world, to enhance law enforcement investigatory tools, and for other purposes." Given the circumstances (the attack on Pearl Harbor and the 9/11 terrorist attacks), was the legislation in each case justified or an overreaction?

Glossary

Executive Order   a presidential directive that implements or interprets a policy, a law, or a constitutional provision; it does not require, but often receives, congressional approval

Executive Order 9066

Executive Order Authorizing the Secretary of War to Prescribe Military Areas

Whereas the successful prosecution of the war requires every possible protection against espionage and against sabotage to national-defense material, national-defense premises, and national-defense utilities as defined in Section 4, Act of April 20, 1918, 40 Stat. 533, as amended by the Act of November 30, 1940, 54 Stat. 1220, and the Act of August 21, 1941, 55 Stat. 655 (U.S.C., Title 50, Sec. 104);

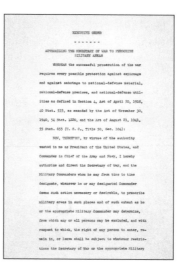

Now, therefore, by virtue of the authority vested in me as President of the United States, and Commander in Chief of the Army and Navy, I hereby authorize and direct the Secretary of War, and the Military Commanders whom he may from time to time designate, whenever he or any designated Commander deems such action necessary or desirable, to prescribe military areas in such places and of such extent as he or the appropriate Military Commander may determine, from which any or all persons may be excluded, and with respect to which, the right of any person to enter, remain in, or leave shall be subject to whatever restrictions the Secretary of War or the appropriate Military Commander may impose in his discretion. The Secretary of War is hereby authorized to provide for residents of any such area who are excluded therefrom, such transportation, food, shelter, and other accommodations as may be necessary, in the judgment of the Secretary of War or the said Military Commander, and until other arrangements are made, to accomplish the purpose of this order. The designation of military areas in any region or locality shall supersede designations of prohibited and restricted areas by the Attorney General under the Proclamations of December 7 and 8, 1941, and shall supersede the responsibility and authority of the Attorney General under the said Proclamations in respect of such prohibited and restricted areas.

I hereby further authorize and direct the Secretary of War and the said Military Commanders to take such other steps as he or the appropriate Military Commander may deem advisable to enforce compliance with the restrictions applicable to each Military area hereinabove authorized to be designated, including the use of Federal troops and other Federal Agencies, with authority to accept assistance of state and local agencies.

I hereby further authorize and direct all Executive Departments, independent establishments and other Federal Agencies, to assist the Secretary of War or the said Military Commanders in carrying out this Executive Order, including the furnishing of medical aid, hospitalization, food, clothing, transportation, use of land, shelter, and other supplies, equipment, utilities, facilities, and services.

This order shall not be construed as modifying or limiting in any way the authority heretofore granted under Executive Order No. 8972, dated December 12, 1941, nor shall it be construed as limiting or modifying the duty and responsibility of the Federal Bureau of Investigation, with respect to the investigation of alleged acts of sabotage or the duty and responsibility of the Attorney General and the Department of Justice under the Proclamations of December 7 and 8, 1941, prescribing regulations for the conduct and control of alien enemies, except as such duty and responsibility is superseded by the designation of military areas hereunder.

Franklin D. Roosevelt

The White House, February 19, 1942.

Soldiers, Sailors and Airmen of the Allied Expeditionary Force!

You are about to embark upon the Great Crusade, toward which we have striven these many months. The eyes of the world are upon you. The hopes and prayers of liberty-loving people everywhere march with you. In company with our brave Allies and brothers-in-arms on other Fronts, you will bring about the destruction of the German war machine, the elimination of Nazi tyranny over the oppressed peoples of Europe, and security for ourselves in a free world.

Your task will not be an easy one. Your enemy is well trained, well equipped and battle-hardened. He will fight savagely.

But this is the year 1944 ! Much has happened since the Nazi triumphs of 1940-41. The United Nations have inflicted upon the Germans great defeats, in open battle, man-to-man. Our air offensive has seriously reduced their strength in the air and their capacity to wage war on the ground. Our Home Fronts have given us an overwhelming superiority in weapons and munitions of war, and placed at our disposal great reserves of trained fighting men. The tide has turned ! The free men of the world are marching together to Victory !

I have full confidence in your courage, devotion to duty and skill in battle. We will accept nothing less than full Victory !

Good Luck ! And let us all beseech the blessing of Almighty God upon this great and noble undertaking.

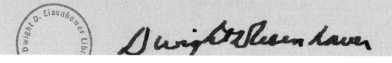

Dwight D. Eisenhower's Order of the Day (National Archives and Records Administration)

*"I have full confidence in your courage,
devotion to duty and skill in battle."*

Overview

On June 6, 1944, General Dwight D. Eisenhower oversaw the launching of the world's largest armada. An extraordinary flotilla of 176,000 men, 20,000 vehicles, and thousands of tons of stores and munitions left the shores of England and headed toward Normandy in France as part of the D-day invasion. Eisenhower's description of this colossal human enterprise drew from a spiritual, not secular, vocabulary. This Texas-born Presbyterian saw the invasion quite simply as "the Great Crusade." He also sought "the blessing of Almighty God upon this great and noble undertaking." Eisenhower's Order of the Day is a remarkably succinct call to arms and rallying cry for battle. Essentially, Eisenhower's appeal to the assembled forces—"Soldiers, Sailors, and Airmen of the Allied Expeditionary Force"—is built around no more than two full paragraphs; five exclamation points; less than three hundred words; and a terse, staccato, intensive series of short sentences. The tone, while calm and collected, is quintessential Eisenhower. His message is that the country was facing a monumental challenge and a daunting task but that the outcome could not be in doubt.

Context

In September 1941 Eisenhower was promoted to brigadier general. Although he would eventually become the conductor of Operation Overlord (the code name for the Allied assault on German-held France), by late 1941 he had never enjoyed command of an active wing of the military. Eisenhower was seen as an able and collegial organizer, not a brilliant strategist who stood out from his peers.

In 1943, however, Eisenhower gained his fourth star and played a key role in overseeing the Allied victory in North Africa. His skill in coexisting with the feisty commander of the British Eighth Army, General Bernard Law Montgomery, proved that Eisenhower was a good soldier who possessed considerable diplomatic skill. In late 1943 he oversaw the assault on Sicily in the Mediterranean Sea and the successful entry into mainland Italy.

In the spring of 1944 Eisenhower was based in southern England, which had been turned into the world's biggest military base as a vast Allied force was being brought together. Eventually some three million people would be involved in Operation Overlord. While German forces stuck to the notion that the invasion would take place at Calais, the Allied thrust was at Normandy with frontal assault forces targeting five beaches: Utah Beach, Omaha Beach, Gold Beach, Juno Beach, and Sword Beach. Additionally, paratrooper landings were carried out behind enemy lines.

With such a massive undertaking, timing was of critical importance. Despite the relative narrowness of the English Channel, the size and scale of the operation meant that adequate weather was a top priority. On June 4, Eisenhower had to make an agonizing decision to postpone the invasion because of rough seas and storm clouds. Twenty-four hours later conditions had worsened. Eisenhower was confronted with a colossal dilemma: hold off yet again and face the possibility of a delay of weeks, or press on in conditions that were far from ideal. The decision was of monumental importance. Winston S. Churchill, in his book *The Second World War*, highlights these moments of historical drama that took place on June 4 at 9:15 PM at Eisenhower's headquarters:

> General Eisenhower, with the advice of his commanders, boldly and as it proved wisely, chose to go ahead with the operations at 4 am. On June 5 the die was irrevocably cast: the invasion would be launched on June 6. In retrospect this decision rightly evokes admiration. It was amply justified by events, and was largely responsible for gaining us the precious advantage of surprise. (Churchill, p. 208)

About the Author

Dwight David "Ike" Eisenhower was born in Texas on October 14, 1890, but he was raised in Abilene, Kansas. The Eisenhower family settled in Kansas when Eisenhower was only two. His father was an engineer, and his mother, Idak Eisenhower, was a member of a religious group called the River Brethren, now known as the Jehovah's Witnesses. It is intriguing to think of the young Eisenhower

1939

- **September 1**
Germany's innovative blitzkrieg strike (a swift concerted air and land assault) demolishes Poland.

- **September 3**
Great Britain and France declare war on Germany, signaling the start of World War II.

1940

- **May 10**
German troops pour into the Benelux countries (Netherlands, Belgium, and Luxembourg); Winston Churchill becomes Great Britain's prime minister following the resignation of Neville Chamberlain.

- **June 22**
France essentially removes itself as an Ally by signing an armistice with Germany.

- **July 10–October 31**
The vital Battle of Britain takes place as the Royal Air Force prevents the German Luftwaffe from dominating the skies over southern England. Had the Royal Air Force been bested, a German invasion of England would very likely have been planned for 1940 to 1941.

1941

- **June 22**
The Germans launch a massive invasion of the Soviet Union.

- **December 7–8**
The U.S. Pacific Fleet is attacked by the Japanese at Pearl Harbor, Hawaii. The United States declares war on Japan.

- **December 11**
The U.S. Congress recognizes a state of war with Germany and Italy.

1942

- **November 8**
Allied troops under General Eisenhower land in North Africa.

- **November 23**
The German Sixth Army is surrounded and blocked in Stalingrad owing to stubborn Soviet resistance.

worshipping in his own home, which served as a meeting hall, with people whose vows and beliefs were antimilitary and who did not think it right to salute the flag.

Although Eisenhower graduated from Abilene High School in Kansas in 1909, his goal was to help financially a brother, Edgar, who was attending college. In 1911, however, with the support of the Kansas senator Joseph L. Bristow, Eisenhower was awarded a place at West Point Military Academy, from which he graduated in 1915.

From 1915 to 1918 Eisenhower's duties were with the infantry; although he saw neither overseas deployment nor armed action, he found tank warfare to be of great interest. Throughout his career, Eisenhower's trademark was his capacity to soak up the expertise of, and be an apt pupil to, a wide range of military leaders. To review Eisenhower's years up to his February 1944 appointment as supreme Allied commander of the Allied Expeditionary Force is to look on a career shaped and molded by a succession of inspirational mentors. In the early 1920s General Fox Conner in the Panama Canal Zone directed Eisenhower to immerse himself in military history and theory. In the 1930s and in the Philippines, General Douglas MacArthur allowed Eisenhower a rare opportunity to be a military adviser in a land and culture focused primarily on peacetime diplomacy. By 1941 Eisenhower was chief of staff to the commander of the Third Army, General Walter Krueger.

The move that catapulted Eisenhower into a senior leadership role was his appointment as assistant chief of staff of the Operations Division. His immediate superior was Chief of Staff General George C. Marshall. Marshall's championing of Eisenhower quickly saw him move from commanding general of the European theater of operations to supreme commander of the Allied (Expeditionary) Force of the North African theater of operations in November 1942. By early 1943 it was Eisenhower who was the senior Allied leader overseeing the defeat of the Axis forces in North Africa.

In December 1943 Eisenhower was appointed supreme Allied commander in Europe. Winston Churchill, however, spells out a conversation from that period in which he and Roosevelt discuss the issue of exactly who should be the leader of Operation Overlord. Churchill thinks it is to be Marshall; Roosevelt says that Marshall cannot be spared. Marshall's "great influence at the head of military affairs and of the war directions under the President, was invaluable, and indispensable to the successful conduct of the war"—and thus he nominates Eisenhower. Churchill replies, "We had also the warmest regard for General Eisenhower, and would trust our fortunes to his direction with hearty goodwill" (Churchill, p. 208).

On December 20, 1944, Eisenhower was made General of the Army. After the war, he became president of Columbia University and then took on a different presidency—two terms in the White House (1954–1962). Congress saw to it that in his retirement years the D-day commander, very fittingly, was reappointed General Eisenhower. He died on March 28, 1969, at age seventy-eight.

Explanation and Analysis of the Document

In his introduction to Order of the Day, Eisenhower addresses his multinational task force as "Soldiers, Sailors, and Airmen of the Allied Expeditionary Force." He then goes on to describe the mission of the force as "the Great Crusade." He may understate the size and scale of the world's greatest invasion. The enormousness of the undertaking is evident in that it took nearly two years to plan and prepare and eventually deployed some 133,000 personnel along with 5,000 Channel vessels, 14,000 land vehicles, 7,000 support aircraft, and 14,500 tons of supplies and munitions to be landed on the Normandy bridgehead on the very first day of the assault (June 6). Prior to the landings, 76,000 tons of bombs were dropped on the German defenses, and 23,000 paratroopers were dropped behind enemy lines.

David Eisenhower, Dwight's grandson and author of *Eisenhower at War 1943–1945*, analyzes in his book the assembly of the armada in the hours leading up to the final go-ahead for the attack. He writes of five lanes of ships in attack formation and describes those five lanes dividing into ten channels of vessels as the flotilla neared the Normandy beaches. In Eisenhower's words, it was a "Piccadilly Circus"—a reference to a road junction in London frequently packed with people and vehicles (Eisenhower, p. 256).

David Eisenhower also gives us a detailed background history on the origins and the eventual writing of Order of the Day. As early as February 1944, General Raymond Barker had indicated the need for a proclamation on D-day. His thesis was that Eisenhower had a bounden duty to remind the invading forces of the nature of their enemy, to ask each soldier to be committed and resolute, and to state unequivocally that victory would be theirs:

The several drafts, and Eisenhower's handwritten corrections, survive. Eisenhower's deletions and militantly phrased substitutions hardened the graceful, complex message aimed at the world to convey the spirit of the great crusade launched on Hitler's Europe. Eisenhower deleted a recital of past victories, for clearly "Overlord" was a beginning. In defining the purpose of the invasion, he struck out "overthrow" and inserted "the elimination of Nazi tyranny" (Eisenhower, p. 256).

The leading paragraph of Order of the Day goes on to underscore the fact that the Allied Expeditionary Force is multinational and made up of representatives from all over the world. On June 6, according to Stephen Ambrose, 57,500 American and 75,215 British and Canadian troops came ashore at Normandy. The paragraph concludes with Eisenhower taking the moral high ground and describing the coming battle as being about the forces of good triumphing over the specter of evil. Eisenhower sees the contest as leading to the destruction of the German war machine and "the elimination of Nazi tyranny over the oppressed peoples of Europe." When one considers the Jewish Holocaust, the Nazi treatment of Romani (some-

times known as Gypsies) and the handicapped and homosexual populations, and the horrific actions taken by German forces against, for example, Russian civilians on the Eastern Front, Eisenhower's trumpet blast about tyranny is neither propaganda nor sermonizing. It is a rational outpouring of his conviction that good must prevail.

Eisenhower was a pragmatist and a realist. He knew well that the Normandy beaches and the French hinterland would be a daunting battleground. The clipped cadences and spare prose of his call to arms remain to this day a stirring account of the challenges that faced the Allied Expeditionary Force. Three short sentences spell out challenge, confrontation, and the recognition of extreme peril. "Your task will not be an easy one. Your enemy is well trained, well equipped and battle-hardened. He will fight savagely."

In hindsight a case can be made that Eisenhower overstates the quality and quantity of the German defenses. The Luftwaffe was in disarray, and of fifty-eight German combat divisions in Western Europe, more than half were not at a high level of fighting efficiency. Many of Germany's premier troops were engaged on the Eastern Front in the Soviet Union. Field Marshal Gerd von Rundstedt was theoretically in control of the German forces, but in terms of overall command Adolf Hitler had assumed the role of

www.milestonedocuments.com

Time Line

1943

■ **January 17–27**
Roosevelt and Churchill agree in principle on an Allied attack on Hitler and the Third Reich.

1944

■ **June 4**
The U.S. Fifth Army takes over the city of Rome.

■ **June 6**
D-day occurs; Eisenhower's Order of the Day is issued.

■ **December, 16**
The Battle of the Bulge begins as a major setback for Allied forces but is, in actuality, the last significant military success by Germany in World War II.

1945

■ **March 7**
The U.S. First Army crosses the Rhine and establishes a foothold in Germany.

■ **April 30**
Adolf Hitler commits suicide in a Berlin command headquarters bunker.

■ **May 7**
Germany announces unconditional surrender, ending the war in Europe.

General Dwight D. Eisenhower gives the Order of the Day to paratroopers in England just before they board their airplanes to participate in the D-Day invasion of June 6, 1944. (AP Photo/U.S. Army Signal Corps Photo)

supreme commander of all German armed forces in 1943. Field Marshal Erwin Rommel, the ablest of the German commanders, arrived at Normandy in the late hours of June 6, after the landings had taken place. Because of the inclement weather, German military leaders were unconvinced that an invasion was imminent.

German resistance to the invasion was committed and sustained, but the result was never in doubt. Ambrose writes of a "striking victory" (1983–1984, vol. 1, p. 310). Several of Eisenhower's advisers were convinced that the airborne sorties might result in operational losses and casualties of up to 70 percent of the force. That did not occur. Nevertheless, the airborne troops did suffer considerable losses and face stiff resistance in establishing the bridgehead at Omaha Beach. In Eisenhower's prescient words, "Your task will not be an easy one.... He [the enemy] will fight savagely." Carlos D'Este graphically recounts the horror and heroism at Omaha Beach. At one point, General Omar Bradley thought of evacuating; according to D'Este, "American leadership and exceptional acts of gallantry by

terrified men of all ranks saved the day" (p. 534). American D-day casualties alone were more than ten thousand killed, wounded, or missing.

In his second and final full paragraph Eisenhower forcefully spells out that the "Nazi triumphs of 1940–41" are over. He notes that "our air offensive has seriously reduced their strength in the air." Geoffrey Perret writes of the general in England, just a few days after D-day, enjoying a visit from his son John. John Eisenhower was confounded by the presence of so much military traffic. He raised with his father the question of the Luftwaffe and air safety. Eisenhower tersely replied, "If I didn't have air supremacy, I wouldn't even be here!" (Perret, p. 291). In light of the ten thousand ground force casualties at D-day, it is enlightening to explore Eisenhower's proactive plan to ensure safe skies over Normandy. Robert F. Burk notes that in the two months leading up to D-day twelve thousand Allied airmen lost their lives.

Eisenhower goes on to address the issue of Allied might. "Our Home Fronts have given us an overwhelming superiority in weapons and munitions of war, and placed at our dis-

"*You are about to embark upon the Great Crusade, toward which we have striven these many months. The eyes of the world are upon you.*"

(Paragraph 1)

"*Your task will not be an easy one. Your enemy is well trained, well equipped and battle-hardened. He will fight savagely.*"

(Sentences following Paragraph 1)

"*The tide has turned! The free men of the world are marching together to Victory!*"

(Paragraph 2)

"*I have full confidence in your courage, devotion to duty and skill in battle. We will accept nothing less than full victory!*"

(Paragraph 4)

posal great reserves of trained fighting men." While Omaha Beach serves as a reminder about setback, trial, and loss, the fact remains that as early as June 11 the five separate Normandy beach landings had merged into one unified front line and by June 17 the bridgehead was consolidated with six hundred thousand men and one hundred thousand vehicles. By July 2 fully one million Allied troops were firmly established on French soil, and a major hole had been driven through Germany's European defenses. The sheer scope of Allied resources needs to be stressed in light of Eisenhower's focus on "overwhelming superiority." According to Eisenhower's narrative, on June 5 and 6, for example, the Allied air forces flew no fewer than 14,674 sorties. It is hardly surprising that D-day was such an unqualified success.

In Eisenhower's second-to-last sentence, the tenor of the piece would be appropriate for a coach eager to do battle and seek success. "I have full confidence in your courage, devotion to duty and skill.... We will accept nothing less than full Victory!" The Order of the Day concludes with these words: "And let us beseech the blessing of Almighty God upon this great and noble undertaking." Spiritual faith and Christian beliefs were Eisenhower's bedrocks. Martin J. Medhurst highlights Eisenhower's rarest gift, an uncanny flair for getting along with people and, more often than not, getting those people to cooperate. Medhurst's words encapsulate Eisenhower's genius as communicator and commander:

To the River Brethren community, cooperation was a virtue. The Bible commanded one to love and serve his neighbor, and the Brethren strove to fulfill the sacred mandate. In the later years, Dwight Eisenhower's ability to submerge the idiosyncrasies of self and national pride would contribute in no small measure to success as supreme allied commander, weaving together British, American, Canadian, Australian, South African and Free French forces in a mighty crusade for freedom." (Medhurst, p. 7)

Audience

General Dwight D. Eisenhower's Order of the Day went out to the vast numbers of soldiers, sailors, and airmen who made up the D-day landing force. Eisenhower did not mince words in his call to arms. While his narrative was robust and tough, the spirit and tone of the prose was a careful blend of a rallying call to be brave and a buoy of optimistic pragmatism. It would be imprudent to claim that the D-day force going into battle on June 5 found Eisenhower's words inspirational. Eisenhower was not a "blood and guts" general who stormed into battle like an avenging angel. Nevertheless, a rereading of his Order of the Day sheds light on the mind of a leader who fully realized the dangers of battle and the steadfast nature of the enemy and yet was buoyed by the certainty that Allied preparations were so thorough and complete that the only possible outcome was triumph.

Eisenhower's Order of the Day was broadcast by the Columbia Broadcasting System so that his words would reach the world. When Eisenhower speaks the words "The eyes of the world are upon you" he is fully cognizant that his "Great Crusade" makes it seem not only possible but indeed probable that Germany would be defeated and that the tide had indeed turned. The Order of the Day was actually a subset of a larger address in which Eisenhower appeals to all sorts of people, including patriots, resistance groups, citizens of France, and the huge audience that was the population of Western Europe.

Impact

In the hours leading up to the invasion, all 175,000 members of the Allied Expeditionary Force were given a small piece of paper containing the order. These papers were small enough to fit into a billfold. Thus Eisenhower's Order of the Day became part of the fighting men's equipment as they moved toward the French coast.

In his opening paragraph Eisenhower notes that "the eyes of the world are upon" the fighting forces. While such a statement seems all too obvious—Overlord was unquestionably the most important single military operation of World War II—one should not forget that Eisenhower was always concerned about his fellow soldiers and ever mindful that he was sending vast numbers of men to fight on a foreign battlefield. On the evening of June 5, he visited the 101st Airborne, which was preparing to fly parachute sorties to Normandy. Stephen E. Ambrose describes the scene: "Eisenhower wandered around among the men, whose blackened faces gave them a grotesque look, stepping over packs, guns, and other equipment. A group recognized him and gathered around. He chatted with them easily. He told them not to worry, that they had the best equipment and leaders" (1983–1984, vol. 1, p. 309). These American soldiers, many of whom were very young men, would have read Eisenhower's Order of the Day, and Eisenhower wanted them to know that what they were about to do was of great importance. His psychological tactic was to reach out to his warriors and make them comprehend the significance of who they were and what they were about to undertake. They were not supporting characters performing in some distant drama. They were key protagonists, and the stage was theirs.

As has been noted, the Allied Expeditionary Force deployment of June 6, 1944, otherwise called the D-day landings and Operation Overlord, was perhaps the biggest invasion that the world has ever seen. Five attack columns struck hard at five Normandy beach sites. The armada was made up of 1,000 assorted ships with 195,000 supporting personnel. No fewer than eight countries supplied naval units. In terms of the combat forces engaged in the actual landings, 133,000 troops were offloaded on June 6, 1944. Landing casualties were on the order of 10,300. By the end of June 1944, nearly a million men and half a million tons of supplies were deposited on French soil. Nonetheless, despite an enormous squeeze being placed on German forces by Allied forces from the West and Russian troops in the East, Germany did not surrender until May 7, 1945.

Related Documents

D'Este, Carlo. *Eisenhower: A Soldier's Life*. New York: Henry Holt, 2002. Written by a retired U.S. Army lieutenant, this 848-page book is a detailed biography of Eisenhower.

Hobbs, Joseph Patrick, ed. *Dear General: Eisenhower's Wartime Letters to Marshall*. Baltimore: Johns Hopkins University Press, 1971. This work provides perspectives on Eisenhower at war and at work.

Lee, R. Alton. *Dwight D. Eisenhower, Soldier and Statesman*. Chicago: Nelson-Hall, 1981. This skillfully written biography reveals the political maneuvering of the leadership in the run-up to D-day.

Bibliography

■ Books

Ambrose, Stephen E. *Ike: Abilene to Berlin*. New York: Harper and Row, 1973.

———. *Eisenhower*. 2 vols. New York: Simon and Schuster, 1983–1984.

Bondi, Victor, ed. *American Decades 1940–1949*. Detroit: Gale Research, 1995.

Boyle, Peter G. *Eisenhower*. New York: Longman/Pearson, 2005.

Burk, Robert F. *Dwight D. Eisenhower, Hero and Politician*. Boston: Twayne Publishers, 1986.

Churchill, Winston. *The Second World War*. London: TAK Books, 2003.

Eisenhower, David. *Eisenhower at War 1943–1945*. New York: Random House, 1986.

Hastings, Max, and Simon Jenkins. *The Battle for the Falklands*. New York: W. W. Norton, 1983.

Kornitzer, Bela. *The Great American Heritage: The Story of the Five Eisenhower Brothers*. New York: Farrar, Straus and Cudahy, 1955.

Medhurst, Martin J. *Dwight D. Eisenhower: Strategic Communicator*. Westport, Conn.: Greenwood Press, 1993.

Perret, Geoffrey. *Eisenhower*. New York: Random House, 1999.

Sixsmith, E. K. G. *Eisenhower as Military Commander*. New York: Stein and Day, 1973.

Wicker, Tom. *Dwight D. Eisenhower*. New York: Times Books, 2002.

■ **Web Sites**

D-day Museum and Overlord Embroidery Web site. http://www.ddaymuseum.co.uk/. Accessed on July 30, 2007.

The Eisenhower Presidential Library and Museum Web site. http://www.eisenhower.utexas.edu/. Accessed on July 30, 2007.

The National World War II Museum Web site. http://www.nationalww2museum.org/. Accessed on July 30, 2007.

The U.S. Military Academy at West Point "Special Collections and Archives" Web site. http://www.library.usma.edu/archives/default.asp. Accessed on July 30, 2007.

—By Scott A. G. M. Crawford

Questions for Further Study

1. Study a synopsis of the Spanish Armada and its 1588 attack on England. The massed Spanish fleet was poised for assault in the English Channel. Explore the important aspect of weather that affected the outcome of this attack in 1588 as well as on June 6, 1944.

2. Eisenhower spells out in his Order of the Day that the Allies' "air offensive has seriously reduced" German strength in the air. The importance of this aspect of the assault cannot be overestimated. Compare this offensive with the U.S. war in Afghanistan and Iraq in the early 2000s. Assess and explain how total air superiority for the United States has limited impact in that sphere of conflict.

3. Some military commanders felt that the invasion of Europe should have taken place earlier. In light of events in 1944 and with hindsight, how correct was Eisenhower's decision of June 6?

4. In many respects Eisenhower's genius was as a diplomat. Account for the manner in which he maintained effective dialogue with such diverse personalities as Prime Minister Winston Churchill, General Charles de Gaulle, Field Marshal Bernard Montgomery, General Omar Bradley, and General George Patton.

5. From February 19 to March 16, 1945, U.S. Marines fought to take Iwo Jima from the Japanese. Nearly seven thousand American soldiers were killed. The number is near to the death toll on June 6, 1944, at Normandy. Speculate on Eisenhower's response if, like the Japanese on Iwo Jima, the Germans had been well protected by deep mines and bunkers and had fought with suicidal tactics.

Glossary

Crusade	a military expedition to right injustice, with reference to those undertaken by Christians in the Middle Ages to recover the Holy Land from Muslims
tyranny	oppressive and unjust government
munitions	weapons and ammunition

DWIGHT D. EISENHOWER'S ORDER OF THE DAY

SUPREME HEADQUARTERS

ALLIED EXPEDITIONARY FORCE

Soldiers, Sailors, and Airmen of the Allied Expeditionary Force!

You are about to embark upon the Great Crusade, toward which we have striven these many months. The eyes of the world are upon you. The hope and prayers of liberty-loving people everywhere march with you. In company with our brave Allies and brothers-in-arms on other Fronts, you will bring about the destruction of the German war machine, the elimination of Nazi tyranny over the oppressed peoples of Europe, and security for ourselves in a free world.

Your task will not be an easy one. Your enemy is will trained, well equipped and battle-hardened. He will fight savagely.

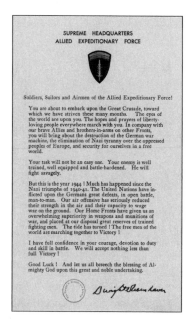

But this is the year 1944! Much has happened since the Nazi triumphs of 1940-41. The United Nations have inflicted upon the Germans great defeats, in open battle, man-to-man. Our air offensive has seriously reduced their strength in the air and their capacity to wage war on the ground. Our Home Fronts have given us an overwhelming superiority in weapons and munitions of war, and placed at our disposal great reserves of trained fighting men. The tide has turned! The free men of the world are marching together to Victory!

I have full confidence in your courage, devotion to duty and skill in battle. We will accept nothing less than full Victory!

Good luck! And let us beseech the blessing of Almighty God upon this great and noble undertaking.

S. 1767

[PUBLIC LAW 346]
[CHAPTER 268]

Seventy-eighth Congress of the United States of America;

At the Second Session

Begun and held at the City of Washington on Monday, the tenth
day of January, one thousand nine hundred and forty-four

AN ACT

To provide Federal Government aid for the readjustment in civilian
life of returning World War II veterans.

*Be it enacted by the Senate and House of Representatives of the
United States of America in Congress assembled,* That this Act may
be cited as the "Servicemen's Readjustment Act of 1944".

TITLE I

CHAPTER I—HOSPITALIZATION, CLAIMS, AND PROCEDURES

SEC. 100. The Veterans' Administration is hereby declared to be
an essential war agency and entitled, second only to the War and
Navy Departments, to priorities in personnel, equipment, supplies,
and material under any laws, Executive orders, and regulations pertaining to priorities, and in appointments of personnel from civil-
service registers the Administrator of Veterans' Affairs is hereby
granted the same authority and discretion as the War and Navy
Departments and the United States Public Health Service: *Provided,*
That the provisions of this section as to priorities for materials shall
apply to any State institution to be built for the care or hospitalization of veterans.

SEC. 101. The Administrator of Veterans' Affairs and the Federal
Board of Hospitalization are hereby authorized and directed to
expedite and complete the construction of additional hospital facilities for war veterans, and to enter into agreements and contracts
for the use by or transfer to the Veterans' Administration of suitable
Army and Navy hospitals after termination of hostilities in the
present war or after such institutions are no longer needed by the
armed services; and the Administrator of Veterans' Affairs is hereby
authorized and directed to establish necessary regional offices, sub-
offices, branch offices, contact units, or other subordinate offices in
centers of population where there is no Veterans' Administration
facility, or where such a facility is not readily available or accessible:
Provided, That there is hereby authorized to be appropriated the sum
of $500,000,000 for the construction of additional hospital facilities.

SEC. 102. The Administrator of Veterans' Affairs and the Secretary
of War and Secretary of the Navy are hereby granted authority to
enter into agreements and contracts for the mutual use or exchange

The Servicemen's Readjustment Act (National Archives and Records Administration)

"Any such eligible person shall be entitled to education or training."

Overview

The Servicemen's Readjustment Act of 1944, commonly called the GI Bill, was one of the most important—and popular—federal programs in American history. This legislation provided generous benefits to help veterans buy homes or farms, attend college or vocational school, pay living expenses while searching for employment, and ensure access to essential medical care or therapy to heal wounds or overcome disabilities. These benefits changed individual lives and—just as important—transformed American society. The economy boomed, suburbs burgeoned, and colleges and universities expanded because of the Servicemen's Readjustment Act. In reality, this legislation created a large federal welfare program, but one without most of the liabilities that critics often associated with government efforts to improve social conditions. Even President Ronald Reagan, an unrelenting opponent of big government, declared, "No investment our government has ever made returned better dividends" (Reagan, vol. 1, p. 588).

Context

During World War II, as Americans planned for peace, grim memories of the past haunted their vision of the future. The Great Depression, the worst in U.S. history, had lasted for eleven years, from the stock market crash of 1929 until the eve of American entry into World War II. Since defense mobilization had finally ended the depression, it seemed likely that demobilization at the end of the fighting would cause the economy to sputter. Polls showed that while Americans yearned for victory, they worried that hard times would accompany a return to peace. More than fifteen million veterans would be looking for work once Germany and Japan surrendered. Where would they find jobs as the factories that had built tanks, planes, and ships scaled back production, laid off workers, and closed down operations?

Many Americans, too, remembered recent problems in dealing with veterans. After World War I, Congress approved payment of $60 in mustering-out pay to each veteran, along with money for train fare home. Some veterans' groups complained that they deserved more for their wartime service. The American Legion, founded in 1919, called for additional compensation in the form of a bonus, which became law in 1924. Most veterans, however, had to wait twenty years for the payment of the full amount of their bonus. As the Great Depression became more severe, veterans pressed Congress to pay the bonuses immediately. In 1932, a Bonus Army of veterans came to Washington, D.C., to make their case but failed to secure the necessary legislation. On July 28, 1932, President Herbert Hoover ordered federal troops to drive the Bonus Army from the nation's capital. Many Americans sympathized with these veterans, who, like them, were trying to find some way to meet their daily expenses during those hard economic times. Others, though, wondered why veterans deserved special treatment when millions of Americans were unemployed or living in poverty. Whatever their views about the Bonus Army, no one wanted a similar incident to occur after World War II.

President Franklin D. Roosevelt took the lead in shaping plans for returning those in uniform to civilian life. In a radio address on July 28, 1943, he declared that "our gallant men and women in the armed services" must not come home to "inflation and unemployment, to a place on a bread line, or on a corner selling apples" (Rosenman, vol. 12, p. 333). Ensuring that prosperity would follow the peace, the president said, would open economic opportunities for all Americans, not just veterans. But because they had made greater sacrifices, veterans deserved special assistance, including compensation to cover expenses while looking for postwar employment, federal aid for education or job-training programs, and adequate medical care and rehabilitation services for those with illnesses or disabilities. Three months later, on October 27, Roosevelt sent Congress a report from an advisory panel of educators recommending that young men and women who had served their country in war have a chance to resume their education or technical training. Congress began to consider the president's proposals, and on February 3, 1944, Roosevelt signed legislation providing a final (or mustering-out) payment of $100, $200, or $300, depending on length

1932

- **July 28**
  President Herbert Hoover orders federal troops to force the Bonus Army from Washington, D.C.

1943

- **July 28**
  In a radio address, President Franklin D. Roosevelt calls for benefits to veterans to help them make the transition to civilian life.

- **October 27**
  Roosevelt asks Congress to pass legislation providing educational benefits to veterans.

1944

- **January 8**
  The American Legion proposes a bill of rights for G.I. Joe and G.I. Jane.

- **February 3**
  Roosevelt signs the Mustering-Out Payment Act, which gives World War II veterans $100, $200, or $300, depending on their length and type of military service.

- **June 22**
  Roosevelt signs into law the Servicemen's Readjustment Act.

1987

- **July 1**
  President Ronald Reagan signs the New GI Bill Continuation Act, which makes permanent educational benefits for veterans of active duty and reserve service in the armed forces.

of time in the armed forces and whether an individual had served overseas.

On January 8, 1944, the American Legion took a dramatic step that hastened action on the other proposals for veterans benefits. Under the leadership of National Commander Warren H. Atherton, the Legion proposed combining all benefits for veterans of World War II in a single piece of legislation, "a bill of rights for G.I. Joe and G.I. Jane" (Ross, p. 99). Within a few days, the proposal became known as the GI Bill of Rights. The title was as important as the substance of the proposal. "GI," standing for "government issue," was a common term for someone in the armed forces; the Bill of Rights—the first ten amendments to the Constitution—guaranteed precious individual free-

doms. Combining the two was a stroke of genius. The Legion also used its influence to mount a powerful public relations campaign in early 1944 in favor of quick approval of this all-American piece of legislation.

In an election year, many members of Congress were eager to enact a program certain to be popular with voters. But one influential representative, John Rankin, slowed consideration of the legislation. Rankin was a strong advocate of veterans benefits. A Democrat from Mississippi, he was also a white supremacist at a time when racial segregation was a sad but pervasive reality of American life. He wanted to restrict eligibility requirements for some benefits in order to limit assistance to African Americans. He was also a strong opponent of organized labor and was determined that striking workers not collect unemployment compensation. Rankin held up the legislation as he tried to amend the legislation—and, in some cases he succeeded. But Congress gave its final approval on June 13, 1944. On June 22, Roosevelt signed what almost everybody called the GI Bill of Rights, even if its official name was the Servicemen's Readjustment Act of 1944.

About the Author

No single individual wrote the Servicemen's Readjustment Act of 1944. Officials of the Roosevelt administration, officers of the American Legion, and members of Congress all helped to formulate the legislation. Three individuals, however, played major roles: President Franklin D. Roosevelt, Warren H. Atherton, and John Rankin.

Born in Hyde Park, New York, on January 30, 1882, Franklin D. Roosevelt grew up in a wealthy, aristocratic family. He graduated from Harvard University in 1904, attended Columbia Law School, and passed the New York bar examination in 1907. Inspired by his cousin, the Republican president Theodore Roosevelt, he entered politics but joined the Democratic Party. After serving in the New York State Senate, he became assistant secretary of the navy in 1913, a position he held during World War I. Roosevelt was the Democratic nominee for vice president in 1920, but he lost the election in a landslide. In 1921, Roosevelt became ill with polio and could never walk again unaided. But he resumed his political career and was elected governor of New York in 1928. In 1932 he defeated Herbert Hoover to win the presidency.

Roosevelt became president during the worst period of the Great Depression, which had begun in 1929. When he entered the White House, unemployment stood at 25 percent, banks were failing in record numbers, and many Americans were losing homes or farms because they could not make mortgage payments. Roosevelt took immediate and swift action during what became known as the Hundred Days, as he persuaded Congress to pass a variety of measures to boost the economy and provide help to workers, farmers, and businesses. This New Deal, which created many new government agencies to regulate the economy, also afforded protections for workers and consumers.

During Roosevelt's first term, the New Deal expanded to include some important social and economic reforms, such as Social Security. But while the New Deal improved the economy and gave people hope for the future, it still did not end the depression. Not until war broke out in Europe and in Asia and the United States began to strengthen its defenses in 1939–1940 did the unemployment rate drop to single digits.

In 1940 Roosevelt won an unprecedented third term as president. During his last four years in the White House, he met the global challenges of World War II and helped organize the United Nations to prevent another major conflict. He was elected president for a fourth time in 1944; as his final term began, victory in World War II had almost been achieved. But only weeks before the end of the fighting in Europe, on April 12, 1945, Roosevelt died of a stroke. Millions of American mourned a leader whose achievements in war and peace made him one of the greatest presidents in U.S. history.

Warren H. Atherton was born in San Francisco on December 28, 1891, and passed the California bar examination in 1913 even though he had no formal training in law. He enlisted in the army in 1917 and served in France during World War I. He became a judge in Stockton, California, and also participated in the activities of the American Legion, a new veterans organization. In 1943 he became the American Legion's national commander and took the lead in pressing Congress to pass a comprehensive package of benefits for men and women who served in World War II. In 1953 he was a member of a commission that advised President Dwight D. Eisenhower on military training. He died on March 7, 1976.

John Rankin was born on March 29, 1882, in Itawamba County, Mississippi, and earned a law degree from the University of Mississippi in 1910. He won election to the U.S. Congress as a Democrat in 1920, the first of sixteen consecutive terms. In Congress, Rankin was a champion of public power projects. In 1933 he cosponsored the legislation that created the Tennessee Valley Authority, which helped bring electricity to his largely rural district. Rankin was also keenly interested in veterans issues and served as chair of the House Committee on Veterans' Legislation for more than two decades. A fierce anti-Communist, he was a member of the House Un-American Activities Committee during the early years of the cold war. A white supremacist and staunch segregationist, Rankin made vicious verbal attacks on African Americans and denounced legislation to make lynching a federal crime. He easily won reelection until the boundaries of his district changed after the census of 1950, and he failed to gain renomination in 1952. He died on November 26, 1960.

Explanation and Analysis of the Document

The Servicemen's Readjustment Act begins with provisions concerning disabled veterans, those most in need of immediate help. American Legion head Warren Atherton thought that disabled veterans had experienced delays when they made claims for medical services or therapy. He believed that new legislation should give high priority to the needs of those men and women in uniform who came home with physical or mental disabilities. Title I, Section 100, gives the Veterans Administration (VA) the status of an "essential war agency" and authority to secure personnel and equipment to meet its obligation to care for disabled veterans. Only the War Department and the Department of the Navy had a higher claim on scarce resources. Section 101 provides the VA with $500 million for the construction of new hospitals, authority to secure supplies and equipment to operate medical facilities, and authorization to use members of the army and navy to carry out its duties.

The remaining sections of Title I, Chapter I, reflect the American Legion's concern that those who served in the armed forces had not been getting prompt payment of the money due them or sufficient information about how to secure any unpaid compensation or necessary medical treatment. The legislation addresses these matters by stating that at the time of discharge, a member of the armed services must receive most or all of the pay he or she is owed and information about how to file "a claim for compensation, pension, or hospitalization." In addition, the legislation stipulates that those who require a prosthesis, such as an artificial limb, are entitled to therapy to help them use such a device properly. The qualifications in this part of the legislation (Sections 103–105) protect veterans against any loss of their rights or benefits. According to Chapter II, representatives of veterans organizations, such as the American Legion or the Disabled Veterans of America, can be stationed on bases or posts where members of the armed forces are discharged to help those men and women take advantage of all the benefits the legislation provides. The final sections of this title ensure that veterans can appeal the terms of their discharge or the decisions of retirement boards.

Title II, which covers educational benefits, is one of the two most important parts of the GI Bill. This title begins by establishing eligibility requirements. To qualify, a man or woman had to be discharged on terms other than dishonorable after serving at least ninety days in the armed forces between September 16, 1940, and the end of World War II. The beginning date was when the Selective Service Act, the first peacetime draft law in U.S. history, took effect. Eligible veterans are those whose education had been "impeded, delayed, interrupted, or interfered with." Congress made it easy for most veterans to meet this last requirement, since it deemed qualified those who were no more than twenty-five years of age at the beginning of their military service. Any veteran who satisfied these requirements could receive $500 to study for one year at a college or university, vocational school, professional school, or another type of educational institution specified at the end of Section 400. Benefits for additional years of study, up to a maximum of four, could go to veterans based on the length of their service in uniform.

The annual allowance of $500 for tuition, books, equipment, and supplies may seem extremely small in view of the enormous increase in higher education costs since the passage of the GI Bill. But at the end of World War II, tuition at even the most expensive American universities was less than $500. In addition, the legislation provides a monthly living allowance of $50 to single veterans and $75 to those with families, amounts that were sufficient to pay for room and board. Former GIs who applied for these educational benefits as well as other types of cash payments under this legislation did not have to prove financial need. A majority of the veterans who got financial help from the GI Bill could have paid their college expenses without government assistance. But these generous subsidies made it possible for many veterans who otherwise could not have afforded the cost of additional education to graduate from a college or learn a new trade.

The other most important provision of the legislation provides loan guarantees for the purchase of homes, farms, or business property. The GI Bill states that an eligible veteran can apply for a guarantee of half of the amount of any such loan up to $2,000. Home, farm, and business prices are much higher today. But at the end of World War II, houses in many towns and cities cost $4,000 or less. Even if the loan guarantee did not cover the entire purchase price, government backing made it possible for many veterans to get loans that financial institutions might not have otherwise granted, and at lower interest rates. The law allows loan guarantees for the purchase of an existing home or the construction of a new one. For veterans interested in agriculture, loan guarantees could make possible the purchase of land, livestock, or farm equipment, provided, as specified in Section 502 (3), that the farming operations are likely to be successful. The same requirement applied to loan guarantees for business property.

The legislation next deals with helping veterans secure postwar employment. Memories of the Great Depression were fresh when the GI Bill became law in 1944; fears of a postwar depression were strong. Maximum job opportunity for veterans was the goal, and a new Veterans' Placement Service Board would have responsibility for providing job counseling and placement services for veterans looking for work. The legislation divides responsibility for helping veterans find jobs between the United States Employment Service, a federal agency, and the public employment services of each state.

Title V deals with veterans who do not immediately find work, and its provisions were controversial. This section states that a veteran who does not have a job can receive a "readjustment allowance," or what amounted to unemployment compensation. The maximum benefit is $20 per week for up to fifty-two weeks, depending on the length of the veteran's military service. Some people thought that veterans who returned home would be eager to join the "52-20 Club." This benefit, they argued, could persuade some former GIs that there was no need to take swift action to find a job. Racist thinking also contributed to opposition to the unemployment benefits. John Rankin, for example, insisted that the "vast majority" of African American veterans from his home state of Mississippi "would remain unem-

ployed for at least a year" if they could count on a weekly payment of $20. Atherton, however, replied, that any suggestion that returning veterans would prefer to collect unemployment benefits rather than find jobs was "an insult to the men in the service" (Ross, pp. 108–109).

Disputes also arose in Congress over the disqualification provisions included in Chapter VIII. Disagreements occurred over depriving veterans of unemployment benefits if they were out of work because of a strike. Some members of Congress, such as Rankin, were strongly antiunion and did not want government funds to support, even indirectly, strikes that unions organized. Other legislators favored organized labor and thought that veterans should not suffer penalties for participating in legitimate union activities. The conditions in Section 800 (b) eliminate or soften some of the antiunion provisions of earlier versions of the bill, but they still prevent a veteran from receiving unemployment compensation if he or she is participating in a strike. Other conditions aim at discouraging veterans from leaving a job without good cause or for rejecting the advice or assistance of an employment service.

The remainder of the GI Bill deals with administrative issues, penalties for violations, and definitions of important terms. Because of congressional concerns about increasing the size of the federal government at a time when the demands of war had made it larger than ever before, the VA administrator is required to use "existing facilities and services of Federal and State departments or agencies" as much as possible to carry out the provisions of the legislation. Penalties for violations of this law include the termination of benefits to anybody who "knowingly accepts an allowance" to which he or she is not entitled. Those who commit fraud or make false statements to obtain benefits could pay a fine of $1,000 or go to jail for as long as one year. Finally, the GI Bill was written at a time when public documents used masculine language—he, him, or his—to describe men and women. Perhaps the authors of the legislation were keenly aware that their gendered language did not acknowledge the vital contribution of the 350,000 women who served in the U.S. armed forces during World War II. Whatever the reason, the legislation explains awkwardly that "the masculine includes the feminine."

Audience

Congress wrote the Servicemen's Readjustment Act for the American people. As the law of the land, it applied to all Americans and, in particular, to the veterans who met the eligibility requirements for the benefits it made available. But very few ordinary citizens read the legislation. The lawmakers did not use simple language that most people could easily understand or inspiring words that could convey the lofty goals they hoped to achieve. Instead, they used legal, technical, and—on occasion—complicated terminology so that government departments that carried out the law or courts that decided disputes about the law's provisions would understand precisely what the law allowed. The main

"*Any such eligible person shall be entitled to education or training, or a refresher or retraining course, at an approved educational or training institution, for a period of one year (or the equivalent thereof in continuous part-time study), or for such lesser time as may be required for the course of instruction chosen by him. Upon satisfactory completion of such course of education or training, according to the regularly prescribed standards and practices of the institutions, except a refresher or retraining course, such person shall be entitled to an additional period or periods of education or training, not to the exceed the time such person was in the active service on or after September 16, 1940, and before the termination of the war, ... but in no event shall the total period of education or training exceed four years.*"

(Title II, Chapter IV, Section 400)

"*Any such veteran may apply within two years after separation from the military or naval forces, or two years after termination of the war, whichever is the later date, but in no event more than five years after the termination of the war, to the Administrator of Veterans' Affairs for the guaranty by the Administrator of not to exceed 50 per centum of a loan or loans for any of the purposes specified in sections 501, 502 and 503: Provided, That the aggregate amount guaranteed shall not exceed $2,000.*"

(Title III, Section 500 [a])

"*Any person who shall have served in the active military or naval service of the United States at any time after September 16, 1940, and prior to the termination of the present war, and who shall have been discharged or released from active service under conditions other than dishonorable, after active service of ninety days or more, or by reason of an injury or disability incurred in service in line of duty, shall be entitled, in accordance with the provisions of this title and regulations issued by the Administrator of Veterans' Affairs pursuant thereto, to receive a readjustment allowance as provided herein for each week of unemployment, not to exceed a total of fifty-two weeks.*"

(Title V, Chapter VII, Section 700 [a])

audiences, then, were the public officials in the Veterans Administration, the state employment services, or other federal or state agencies that had to provide the benefits that the law specified. Most Americans who were interested in the GI Bill probably read summaries of its main provisions in newspapers or magazines, in newsletters from veterans organizations such as the American Legion, or in brochures and pamphlets from the Veterans Administration.

Impact

The GI Bill had a profound effect on postwar American life. Fifteen million men and 335,000 women who wore their country's uniform returned to civilian life after World War II. The GI Bill gave them financial aid they used to help fuel a postwar economic boom. Instead of a new depression that so many Americans dreaded, the economy soared, as it created new jobs, new homes in rapidly expanding suburbs, and new opportunities in higher education.

The loan guarantee provisions of the GI Bill helped alleviate a severe housing shortage during the first years of peace. Residential construction had lagged for many years because of the Great Depression and the economic demands of World War II. A sharp jump in the marriage rate as veterans returned home only added to the shortage of housing. In 1946, 1.5 million former GIs were living with parents, other family members, or friends because they could not find a house to buy or an apartment to rent. The shortage drove up house prices so much that Congress increased the amount of the loan guarantee under the GI Bill first to $4,000 in December 1945 and then to $7,500 in April 1950. The demand for housing encouraged home builders to develop innovative methods. New suburbs appeared in what had been corn or potato fields just months earlier, and mass-production techniques allowed the construction of homes at record rates. World War II veterans flocked to these new communities. Many of them, however, were racially segregated; African Americans did not have the same opportunities as whites to move to the suburbs or live the American dream. Approximately 3.75 million former GIs secured government-backed mortgages under the Servicemen's Readjustment Act. Home ownership became far more common in postwar America than it had been previously, partly because of the GI Bill.

There were also important changes in higher education as World War II veterans started or continued work toward a college diploma. By 1947, 49 percent of those enrolled in institutions of higher education were veterans. Some educators feared such an influx of "nontraditional" students would have an adverse affect on university campuses. For example, James B. Conant, the president of Harvard University, predicted that the GI Bill could lead to "the least capable among the war generation ... flooding the facilities for advanced education" (Olson, p. 33). Such warnings proved wrong. Former GIs were usually serious students who were determined to use their educational opportunities to better their lives. They did create problems on many campuses, but mainly because of their numbers. At the University of Michigan, for example, enrollment quickly tripled to thirty thousand students. Michigan and many other colleges and universities had to scramble to provide sufficient housing and classroom space. The soaring enrollments, however, brought significant and enduring changes in university life. In only a decade, between 1940 and 1950, college and university enrollment in the United States increased by 80 percent, to 2.7 million students. No longer was a college education only for a minority of wealthy, privileged Americans. The GI Bill helped democratize American higher education.

Vocational schools attracted more veterans than college campuses. While 2.2 million former servicemen and women used the GI Bill to attend an institution of higher education, 3.5 million utilized its benefits for vocational training. In addition, the dire predictions about the popularity of the "52-20 Club" were wildly inaccurate. About 57 percent of eligible veterans collected unemployment compensation, but usually for only brief periods. Overall, the expenditures for readjustment compensation were just 20 percent of the expected costs, proof that those who returned home from war in the mid-1940s were eager to seize opportunities and build new lives.

The GI Bill became one of the most celebrated pieces of legislation in American history. The American people and their political leaders praised it for contributing to the prosperity of the late 1940s and early 1950s. Even those who disliked government welfare programs considered the GI Bill a success because it gave millions of people the opportunity to acquire new skills, fulfill their potential, and improve their quality of life with the help of a short-term government investment. Successors to the GI Bill provided educational benefits and employment assistance to veterans of the Korean and Vietnam wars. In June 1987, President Ronald Reagan signed the New GI Bill Continuation Act, which furnished educational benefits to reservists as well as veterans of active duty. The law became known as the Montgomery GI Bill because of the important role of Representative G. V. "Sonny" Montgomery, Democrat of Mississippi, in its passage. The legislation was still in effect in the early twenty-first century.

Related Documents

Rosenman, Samuel I., ed. *The Public Papers and Addresses of Franklin D. Roosevelt*. 13 vols. New York: Harper and Brothers, 1938–1950. These volumes contain the speeches and messages to Congress of President Roosevelt, including those pertaining to the preparation and passage of the GI Bill.

"Transforming Society: The GI Bill Experience at NC State." North Carolina State University Libraries Exhibits Web site. http://www.lib.ncsu.edu/exhibits/gibill/. Accessed on January 5, 2008. This online exhibit includes photographs and oral histories to show how North Carolina State University and some of the students who attended it were affected by the GI Bill.

Bibliography

■ Books

Bennett, Michael J. *When Dreams Came True: The GI Bill and the Making of Modern America*. Washington, D.C.: Brassey's, 1996.

Humes, Edward. *Over Here: How the G.I. Bill Transformed the American Dream*. New York: Harcourt, 2006.

Greenberg, Milton. *The GI Bill: The Law That Changed America*. New York: Lickle Publishing, 1997.

Mettler, Suzanne. *Soldiers to Citizens: The G. I. Bill and the Making of the Greatest Generation*. New York: Oxford University Press, 2005.

Olson, Keith W. *The G.I. Bill, the Veterans, and the Colleges*. Lexington: University Press of Kentucky, 1974.

Reagan, Ronald. *Public Papers of the Presidents of the United States: Ronald Reagan, 1987*. 2 vols. Washington, D.C.: Government Printing Office, 1989.

Ross, David R. B. *Preparing for Ulysses: Politics and Veterans during World War II*. New York: Columbia University Press, 1969.

Rumer, Thomas A. *The American Legion: An Official History, 1919–1989*. New York: M. Evans, 1990.

■ Web Sites

Franklin D. Roosevelt Presidential Library and Museum Web site. http://www.fdrlibrary.marist.edu. Accessed on January 5, 2008.

U.S. Department of Veterans Affairs "GI Bill" Web site. http://www.gibill.va.gov/. Accessed on January 5, 2008.

—By Chester Pach

Questions for Further Study

1. The GI Bill was a popular program at the time of its passage and in the following decades. How do you account for its popularity, especially since many people are often skeptical of or hostile toward federal programs designed to improve social conditions? Do you think that the GI Bill accomplished its main goals?

2. During World War II, some Americans said that veterans deserved special treatment—programs designed expressly for their welfare—when they returned from military service. Others questioned whether the federal government should lavish benefits on soldiers who did not even have to show that they needed the financial aid they were receiving. What do you think are the strongest arguments for each position? Which view do you favor? How does the change from military conscription—a draft—which existed during World War II, to all-volunteer armed forces affect the debate about whether veterans deserve special federal benefits?

3. How did the GI Bill affect life in the late 1940s in the area where you live? What effects did it have on nearby colleges or universities? Visit your public or university library and use local newspapers, magazines, or other records to determine the local effects of the GI Bill. If those records are difficult or impossible to secure, visit the Web site "Transforming Society: The GI Bill Experience at NC State." Use the online documents to trace the major changes at North Carolina State University. Read an oral history transcript and explain how the GI Bill affected the life of one student who used the legislation's economic benefits to attend college.

Glossary

adjudicating	deciding or resolving a dispute, often through a formal procedure
apprenticeship	a period during which one learns a trade or craft by working with someone who already has those skills
court martial	a military or naval court to hear charges under military law; a trial according to those procedures
domiciliary	residential; related to home, lodging, or living accommodations
lien	a right to take possession of a piece of property and, if necessary, sell it to pay off a debt
prosthesis	relating to an artificial device to replace a body part, such as a leg or arm
subsistence	something that helps to maintain life or necessary living conditions

SERVICEMEN'S READJUSTMENT ACT

An Act to Provide Federal Government Aid for the Readjustment in Civilian Life of Returning World War II Veterans

Be it enacted by the Senate and House of Representatives of the United States of America in Congress assembled, That this Act may be cited as the "Servicemen's Readjustment Act of 1944".

Title I

◆ Chapter I—Hospitalization, Claims and Procedures

Sec. 100. The Veterans' Administration is hereby declared to be an essential war agency and entitled, second only to the War and Navy Departments, to priorities in personnel, equipment, supplies, and material under any laws, Executive orders, and regulations pertaining to priorities, and in appointments of personnel from civil-service registers the Administrator of Veterans' Affairs is hereby granted the same authority and discretion as the War and Navy Departments and the United States Public Health Service: *Provided* That the provisions of this section as to priorities for materials shall apply to any State institution to be built for the care or hospitalization of veterans.

Sec. 101. The Administrator of Veterans' Affairs and the Federal Board of Hospitalization are hereby authorized and directed to expedite and complete the construction of additional hospital facilities for war veterans, and to enter into agreements and contracts for the use by or transfer to the Veterans' Administration of suitable Army and Navy hospitals after termination of hostilities in the present war or after such institutions are no longer needed by the armed services; and the Administrator of Veterans Affairs is hereby authorized and directed to establish necessary regional offices, sub-offices, branch offices, contact units, or other subordinate offices in centers of population where there is no Veterans' Administra-

tion facility, or where such a facility is not readily available or accessible: *Provided*, That there is hereby authorized to be appropriated the sum of $500,000,000 for the construction of additional hospital facilities.

Sec. 102. The Administrator of Veterans' Affairs and the Secretary of War and Secretary of the Navy are hereby granted authority to enter into agreements and contracts for the mutual use or exchange of use of hospital and domiciliary facilities, and such supplies, equipment, and material as may be needed to operate properly such facilities, or for the transfer, without reimbursement of appropriations, of facilities, supplies, equipment, or material necessary and proper for authorized care for veterans, except that at no time shall the Administrator of Veterans' Affairs enter into any agreement which will result in a permanent reduction of Veterans' Administration hospital and domiciliary beds below the number now established or approved, plus the estimated number required to meet the load of eligibles under laws administered by the Veterans' Administration, or in any way subordinate or transfer the operation of the Veterans' Administration to any other agency of the Government.

Nothing in the Selective Training and Service Act of 1940, as amended, or any other Act, shall be construed to prevent the transfer or detail of any commissioned, appointed or enlisted personnel from the armed forces to the Veterans' Administration subject to agreements between the Secretary of War or the Secretary of the Navy and the Administrator of Veterans' Affairs: *Provided*, That no such detail shall be made or extend beyond six months alter the termination of the war.

Sec. 103. The Administrator of Veterans' Affairs shall have authority to place officials and employees designated by him in such Army and Navy installations as may be deemed advisable for the purpose of adjudicating disability claims of, and giving aid and advice to, members of the Army and Navy who are about to be discharged or released from active service.

Sec. 104. No person shall be discharged or released from active duty in the armed forces until his certificate of discharge or release from active duty and final pay, or a substantial portion thereof, are ready for delivery to him or to his next of kin or legal representative; and no person shall be discharged or released from active service on account of disability until and unless he has executed a claim for compensation, pension, or hospitalization, to be filed with the Veterans' Administration or has signed a statement that he has had explained to him the right to file such claim: *Provided*, That this section shall not preclude immediate transfer to a veterans' facility for necessary hospital care, nor preclude the discharge of any person who refuses to sign such claim or statement: *And provided further*, That refusal or failure to file a claim shall be without prejudice to any right the veteran may subsequently assert.

Any person entitled to a prosthetic appliance shall be entitled, in addition, to necessary fitting and training, including institutional training, in the use of such appliance, whether in a Service or a Veterans' Administration hospital, or by out-patient treatment, including such service under contract.

Sec. 105. No person in the armed forces shall be required to sign a statement of any nature relating to the origin, incurrence, or aggravation of any disease or injury he may have, and any such statement against his own interest signed at any time, shall be null and void and of no force and effect.

◆ Chapter II—Aid by Veterans' Organizations

Sec. 200. (a) That upon certification to the Secretary of War or Secretary of the Navy by the Administrator of Veterans' Affairs of paid full time accredited representatives of the veterans' organizations specified in section 200 of the Act of June 29, 1936 (Public Law Numbered 844, Seventy-fourth Congress), and other such national organizations recognized by the Administrator of Veterans' Affairs thereunder in the presentation of claims under laws administered by the Veterans' Administration, the Secretary of War and Secretary of the Navy are hereby authorized and directed to permit the functioning, in accordance with regulations prescribed pursuant to subsection (b) of this section, of such accredited representatives in military or naval installations on shore from which persons are discharged or released from the active military or naval service: *Provided*, That nothing in this section shall operate to affect

measures of military security now in effect or which may hereafter be placed in effect, nor to prejudice the right of the American Red Cross to recognition under existing statutes.

(b) The necessary regulations shall be promulgated by the Secretary of War and the Secretary of the Navy jointly with the Administrator of Veterans' Affairs to accomplish the purpose of this section, and in the preparation of such regulations the national officer of each of such veterans' organizations who is responsible for claims and rehabilitation activities shall be consulted. The commanding officer of each such military or naval installation shall cooperate fully with such authorized representatives in the providing of available space and equipment for such representatives.

◆ Chapter III—Reviewing Authority

Sec. 300. The discharge or dismissal by reason of the sentence of a general court martial of any person from the military or naval forces, or the discharge of any such person on the ground that he was a conscientious objector who refused to perform military duty or refused to wear the uniform or otherwise to comply with lawful orders of competent military authority, or as a deserter, or of an officer by the acceptance of his resignation for the good of the service, shall bar all rights of such person, based upon the period of service from which he is so discharged or dismissed, under any laws administered by the Veterans' Administration: *Provided*, That in the case of any such person, if it be established to the satisfaction of the Administrator that at the time of the commission of the offense such person was insane, he shall not be precluded from benefits to which he is otherwise entitled under the laws administered by the Veterans' Administration: *And provided further*, That this section shall not apply to any war risk, Government (converted) or national service life-insurance policy.

Sec. 301. The Secretary of War and the Secretary of the Navy, after conference with the Administrator of Veterans' Affairs, are authorized and directed to establish in the War and Navy Departments, respectively, boards of review composed of five members each, whose duties shall be to review, on their own motion or upon the request of a former officer or enlisted man or woman or, if deceased, by the surviving spouse, next of kin, or legal representative, the type and nature of his discharge or dismissal, except a discharge or dismissal by reason of the sentence of a general court martial. Such review shall be based upon all available records of the service department relating to the person requesting such review, and such other evidence as may be presented by such person. Witnesses shall be permitted to present testimony either in person or by affidavit and the person requesting review shall be allowed to appear before such board in person or by counsel: *Provided*, That the term "counsel" as used in this section shall be construed to include, among others, accredited representatives of veterans' organizations recognized by the Veterans' Administration under section 200 of the Act of June 29, 1936 (Public Law Numbered 844, Seventy-fourth Congress). Such board shall have authority, except in the case of a discharge or dismissal by reason of the sentence of a general court martial, to change, correct, or modify any discharge or dismissal, and to issue a new discharge in accord with the facts presented to the board. The Articles of War and the Articles for the Government of the Navy are hereby amended to authorize the Secretary of War and the Secretary of the Navy to establish such boards of review, the findings thereof to be final subject only to review by the Secretary of War or the Secretary of the Navy, respectively: *Provided*, That no request for review by such board of a discharge or dismissal under the provisions of this section shall be valid unless filed within fifteen years after such discharge or dismissal or within fifteen years after the effective date of this Act whichever be the later.

Sec. 302. (a) The Secretary of War, the Secretary of the Navy, and the Secretary of the Treasury are authorized and directed to establish, from time to time, boards of review composed of five commissioned officers, two of whom shall be selected from the Medical Corps of the Army or Navy, or from the Public Health Service, as the case may be. It shall be the duty of any such board to review, at the request of any officer retired or released to inactive service, without pay, for physical disability pursuant to the decision of a retiring board, the findings and decision of such retiring board. Such review shall be based upon all available service records relating to the officer requesting such review, and such other evidence as may be presented by such officer. Witnesses shall be permitted to present testimony either in person or by affidavit and the officer requesting review shall be allowed to appear before such board of review in person or by counsel. In carrying out its duties under this section such board of review shall have the same powers as exercised by, or vested in, the retiring board whose findings and decision are being reviewed. The proceedings and decision of each such

board of review affirming or reversing the decision of the retiring board shall be transmitted to the Secretary of War, the Secretary of the Navy, or the Secretary of the Treasury, as the case may be, and shall be laid by him before the President for his approval or disapproval and orders in the case.

(b) No request for review under this section shall be valid unless filed within fifteen years after the date of retirement for disability or after the effective date of this Act, whichever is the later.

(c) As used in this section—

(l) the term "officer" means any officer subject to the laws granting retirement for active service in the Army, Navy, Marine Corps, or Coast Guard, or any of their respective components;

(2) the term "counsel" shall have the same meaning as when used in section 301 of this Act.

Title II

◆ Chapter IV—Education of Veterans

Sec. 400. (a) Subsection (f) of section 1, title I, Public Law Numbered 2, Seventy-third Congress, added by the Act of March 24, 1943 (Public Law Numbered 16, Seventy-eighth Congress), is hereby amended to read as follows:

"(f) Any person who served in the active military or naval forces on or after September 16, 1940, and prior to the termination of hostilities in the present war, shall be entitled to vocational rehabilitation subject to the provisions and limitations of Veterans Regulation Numbered 1 (a), as amended, part VII, or to education or training subject to the provisions and limitations of part VIII."

(b) Veterans Regulation Numbered 1 (a), is hereby amended by adding a new part VIII as follows:

"PART VIII

"1. Any person who served in the active military or naval service on or after September 16, 1940, and prior to the termination of the present war, and who shall have been discharged or released there-from under conditions other than dishonorable, and whose education or training was impeded, delayed, interrupted, or interfered with by reason of his entrance into the service, or who desires a refresher or retraining course, and who either shall have served ninety days or more, exclusive of any period he was assigned for a course of education or training under the Army specialized training program or the Navy college training program, which course was a continuation of his civilian course and was pursued to completion, or as a cadet or midshipman at one of the service academies, or shall have been discharged or released from active service by reason of an actual service-incurred injury or disability, shall be eligible for and entitled to receive education or training under this part: *Provided*, That such course shall be initiated not later than two years after either the date of his discharge or the termination of the present war, whichever is the later: *Provided further*, That no such education or training shall be afforded beyond seven years after the termination of the present war: *And provided further*, That any such person who was not over 25 years of age at the tune he entered the service shall be deemed to have had his education or training impeded, delayed, interrupted, or interfered with.

"2. Any such eligible person shall be entitled to education or training, or a refresher or retraining course, at an approved educational or training institution, for a period of one year (or the equivalent thereof in continuous part-time study), or for such lesser time as may be required for the course of instruction chosen by him. Upon satisfactory completion of such course of education or training, according to the regularly prescribed standards and practices of the institutions, except a refresher or retraining course, such person shall be entitled to an additional period or periods of education or training, not to exceed the time such person was in the active service on or after September 16, 1940, and before the termination of the war, exclusive of any period he was assigned for a course of education or training under the Army specialized training program or the Navy college training program, which course was a continuation of his civilian course and was pursued to completion, or as a cadet or midshipman at one of the service academies, but in no event shall the total period of education or training exceed four years: *Provided*, That his work continues to be satisfactory throughout the period, according to the regularly prescribed standards and practices of the institution: *Provided, however*, That wherever the additional period of instruction ends during a quarter or semester and after a major part of such quarter or semester has expired, such period of instruction shall be extended to the termination of such unexpired quarter or semester.

"3. Such person shall be eligible for and entitled to such course of education or training as he may elect, and at any approved educational or training institution at which he chooses to enroll, whether or not located in the State in which he resides, which will accept or retain him as a student or trainee in any field or branch of knowledge which such institution finds him qualified to undertake or pursue: *Provided*, That, for reasons satisfactory to the Administrator, he may change a course of instruction: *And provided further*, That any such course of education or training may be discontinued at any time, if it is found by the Administrator that, according to the regularly prescribed standards and practices of the institution, the conduct or progress of such person is unsatisfactory.

"4. From time to time the Administrator shall secure from the appropriate agency of each State a list of the educational and training institutions (including industrial establishments), within such jurisdiction, which are qualified and equipped to furnish education or training (including apprenticeship and refresher or retraining training), which institutions, together with such additional ones as may be recognized and approved by the Administrator, shall be deemed qualified and approved to furnish education or training to such persons as shall enroll under this part: *Provided*, That wherever there are established State apprenticeship agencies expressly charged by State laws to administer apprentice training, whenever possible, the Administrator shall utilize such existing facilities and services in training on the job when such training is of one year's duration or more.

"5. The Administrator shall pay to the educational or training institution, for each person enrolled in full time or part time course of education or training, the customary cost of tuition, and such laboratory, library, health, infirmary, and other similar fees as are customarily charged, and may pay for books, supplies, equipment, and other necessary expenses, exclusive of board, lodging, other living expenses, and travel, as are generally required for the successful pursuit and completion of the course by other students in the institution: *Provided*, That in no event shall such payments, with respect to any person, exceed $500 for an ordinary school year: *Provided further*, That no payments shall be made to institutions, business or other establishments furnishing apprentice training on the job: *And provided further*, That if any such institution has no established tuition fee, or if its established tuition fee shall be found by the Administrator to be inadequate compensation to such institution for furnishing such education or training, he is authorized to provide for the payment, with respect to any such person, of such fair and reasonable compensation as will not exceed $500 for an ordinary school year.

"6. While enrolled in and pursuing a course under this part, such person, upon application to the Administrator, shall be paid a subsistence allowance of $50 per month, if without a dependent or dependents, or $75 per month, if he has a dependent or dependents, including regular holidays and leave not exceeding thirty days in a calendar year. Such person attending a course on a part-time basis, and such person receiving compensation for productive labor performed as part of their apprentice or other training on the job at institutions, business or other establishments, shall be entitled to receive such lesser sums, if any, as subsistence or dependency allowances, as may be determined by the Administrator: *Provided,* That any such person eligible under this part, and within the limitations thereof, may pursue such full time or part-time course or courses as he may elect, without subsistence allowance.

"7. Any such person eligible for the benefits of this part, who is also eligible for the benefit of part VII, may elect which benefit he desires: *Provided,* That, in the event of such election, subsistence allowance hereunder shall not exceed the amount of additional pension payable for training under said part VII.

"8. No department, agency, or officer of the United States, in carrying out the provisions of this part, shall exercise any supervision or control, whatsoever, over any State educational agency, or State apprenticeship agency, or any educational or training institution: *Provided,* That nothing in this section shall be deemed to prevent any department, agency, or officer of the United States from exercising any supervision or control which such department, agency, or officer is authorized, by existing provisions of law, to exercise over any Federal educational or training institution, or to prevent the furnishing of education or training under this part in any institution over which supervision or control is exercised by such other department, agency, or officer under authority of existing provisions of law.

"9. The Administrator of Veterans' Affairs is authorized and empowered to administer this title, and, insofar as he deems practicable, shall utilize existing facilities and services of Federal and State departments and agencies on the basis of mutual agreements with them. Consistent with and subject to the provisions and limitations set forth in this title, the Administrator shall, from time to time, prescribe and promulgate such rules and regulations as may be necessary to carry out its purposes and provisions.

"10. The Administrator may arrange for educational and vocational guidance to persons eligible for education and training under this part. At such intervals as he deems necessary, he shall make available information respecting the need for general education and for trained personnel in the various crafts, trades, and professions: *Provided,* That facilities of other Federal agencies collecting such information shall be utilized to the extent he deems practicable.

"11. As used in this part, the term 'educational or training institutions' shall include all public or private elementary, secondary, and other schools furnishing education for adults, business schools and colleges, scientific and technical institutions, colleges, vocational schools, junior colleges, teachers colleges, normal schools, professional schools, universities, and other educational institutions, and shall also include business or other establishments providing apprentice or other training on the job, including those under the supervision of an approved college or university or any State department of education, or any State apprenticeship agency or State board of vocational education, or any State apprenticeship council or the Federal Apprentice Training Service established in accordance with Public, Numbered 308, Seventy-fifth Congress, or any agency in the executive branch of the Federal Government authorized under other laws to supervise such training."

Sec. 401. Section 3, Public Law Numbered 16, Seventy-eighth Congress, is hereby amended to read as follows:

"Sec. 3. The appropriation for the Veterans' Administration, 'Salaries and expenses, medical and hospital, and compensation and pensions', shall be available for necessary expenses under part VII, as amended, or part VIII of Veterans Regulation Numbered 1 (a), and there is hereby authorized to be appropriated such additional amount or amounts as may be necessary to accomplish the purposes thereof. Such expenses pay include, subject to regulations issued by the Administrator and in addition to medical care, treatment, hospitalization, and prosthesis, otherwise authorized, such care, treatment, and supplies as may be necessary to accomplish the purposes of part VII, as amended, or part VIII of Veterans Regulation Numbered 1 (a)."

Sec. 402. Public Law Numbered 16, Seventy-eighth Congress, is hereby amended by adding thereto a new section 4 to read as follows:

"Sec. 4. Any books, supplies, or equipment furnished a trainee or student under part VII or part VIII of Veterans Regulation Numbered 1 (a) shall be deemed released to him: *Provided,* That if he fail, because of fault on his part to complete the course of training or education afforded thereunder, he may be required, in the discretion of the Administrator, to return any or all of such books, supplies, or equipment not actually expended or to repay the reasonable value thereof."

Sec. 403. Paragraph 1, part VII, Veterans Regulation Numbered 1 (a) (Public Law Numbered 16, Seventy-eighth Congress), is hereby amended by inserting after the word "time" the words "on or" and deleting the date "December 6, 1941" and substituting therefor the date "September 16,1940".

Title III—Loans For the Purchase Or Construction of Homes Farms, And Business Property

◆ Chapter V—General Provisions for Loans

Sec. 500. (a) Any person who shall have served in the active military or naval service of the United States at any time on or after September 16, 1940, and prior to the termination of the present war and who shall have been discharged or released therefrom under conditions other than dishonorable after active service of ninety days or more, or by reason of an injury or disability incurred in service in line of duty, shall be eligible for the benefits of this title. Any such veteran may apply within two years after separation from the military or naval forces, or two years after termination of the war, whichever is the later date, but in no event more than five years after the termination of the war, to the Administrator of Veterans' Affairs for the guaranty by the Administrator of not to exceed 50 per centum of a loan or loans for any of the purposes specified in sections 501. 502 and 503: *Provided,* That the aggregate amount guaranteed shall not exceed $2,000. If the Administrator finds that the veteran is eligible for the benefits of this title and that the loan applied for appears practicable, the Administrator shall guarantee the payment of the part thereof as set forth in this title.

(b) Interest for the first year on that part of the loan guaranteed by the Administrator shall be paid by the Administrator out of available appropriations. No security for the guaranty of a loan shall be required except the right to be subrogated to the lien rights of the holder of the obligation which is guaranteed: *Provided,* That pursuant to regulations to be issued by the Administrator the mortgagor and mortgagee shall agree that before beginning foreclosure proceedings for default in payment of principal or interest due, the Administrator shall have at least thirty days' notice with the option of bidding in the property on foreclosure or of refinancing the loan with any other agency or by any other means available.

(c) Loans guaranteed by the Administrator under this title shall be payable under such terms and conditions as may be approved by the Administrator: *Provided,* That the liability under the guaranty, within the limitations of this title, shall decrease or increase pro rata with any decrease or increase of the amount of the unpaid portion of the obligation: *Provided further,* That loans guaranteed by the Administrator shall bear interest at a rate not exceeding 4 per centum per annum and shall be payable in full in not more than twenty years. The Administrator is authorized and directed to guarantee loans to veterans subject to the provisions of this title on approved applications made to persons, firms, associations, and corporations and to governmental agencies and corporations, either State or Federal.

PURCHASE OR CONSTRUCTION OF HOMES

Sec 501. (a) Any application made by a veteran under this title for the guaranty of a loan to be used in purchasing residential property or in constructing a dwelling on unimproved property owned by him to be occupied as his home may be approved the Administrator of Veterans' Affairs if he finds —

(1) that the proceeds of such loans will be used for payment for such property to be purchased or constructed by the veteran;

(2) that the contemplated terms of payment required in any mortgage to be given in part payment of the purchase price or the construction cost bear a proper relation to the veteran's present and anticipated income and expenses; and that the nature and condition of the property is such as to be suitable for dwelling purposes; and

(3) that the purchase price paid or to be paid by the veteran for such property or the construction cost, including the value of the unimproved lot, does not exceed the reasonable normal value thereof as determined by proper appraisal.

(b) Any application for the guaranty of a loan under this section for the purpose of making repairs, alterations, or improvements in, or paying delinquent indebtedness, taxes, or special assessments on, residential property owned by the veteran and used by him as his home, may be approved by the Administrator if he finds that the proceeds of such loan will be used for such purpose or purposes.

(c) No first mortgage shall be ineligible for insurance under the National Housing Act, as amended, by reason of any loan guaranteed under this title, or by reason of any secondary lien upon the property involved securing such loan.

PURCHASE OF FARMS AND FARM EQUIPMENT

Sec. 502. Any application made under this title for the guaranty of a loan to be used in purchasing any land, buildings, livestock, equipment, machinery, or implements, or in repairing, altering, or improving any buildings or equipment, to be used in forming operations conducted by the applicant, may be approved by the Administrator of Veterans' Affairs if he finds —

(1) that the proceeds of such loan will be used in payment for or personal property purchased or to be purchased by the veteran, or for repairing, altering, or improving any buildings or equipment to be used in bona fide farming operations conducted by him;

(2) that such property will be useful in and reasonably necessary for efficiently conducting such operations;

(3) that the ability and experience of the veteran, and the nature of the proposed farming operations to be conducted by him, are such that there is a reasonable likelihood that such operations will be successful; and

(4) that the purchase price paid or to be paid by the veteran for such property does not exceed the reasonable normal value thereof as determined by proper appraisal.

PURCHASE OF BUSINESS PROPERTY

Sec. 503. Any application made under this title for the guaranty of a loan to be used in purchasing any business, land, buildings, supplies, equipment, machinery, or tools, to be used by the applicant in pursuing a gainful occupation (other than farming) may be approved by the Administrator of Veterans' Affairs if he finds —

(1) that the proceeds of such loan will be used for payment for real or personal property purchased or to be purchased by the veteran and used by him in the bona fide pursuit of such gainful occupation;

(2) that such property will be useful in and reasonably necessary for the efficient and successful pursuit of such occupation;

(3) that the ability and experience of the veteran, and the conditions under which he proposes to pursue such occupation, are such that there is a reasonable likelihood that he will be successful in the pursuit of such occupation; and

(4) that the purchase price paid or to be paid by the veteran for such property does not exceed the reasonable normal value thereof as determined by proper appraisal.

Sec. 504. The Administrator of Veterans' Affairs is authorized to promulgate such rules and regulations as are deemed necessary and appropriate for carrying out the provisions of this title, and may delegate to a subordinate employee authority to approve loans subject to the provisions of this title and the rules promulgated thereunder.

Sec. 505. (a) The Administrator shall designate such agency or agencies, if any, as he finds equipped to determine whether the guaranty of loan should be approved under this title. In any case wherein a principal loan, for any of the purposes stated in section 501, 502, or 503, is approved by a Federal agency to be made or guaranteed or insured by it pursuant to applicable law and regulations, and the veteran is in need of a second loan to cover the remainder of the purchase price or cost, or a part thereof, the Administrator, subject otherwise to the provisions of this title, including the limitation of $2,000 on the total amount which may be guaranteed, may guarantee the full amount of the second loan: *Provided*, That such second loan shall not exceed 20 per centum of the purchase price or cost and that the rate of interest thereon shall not exceed that on the principal loan by more than 1 per centum: *And provided further*, That regulations to be promulgated jointly, by the Administrator and the head of such agency may provide for servicing of both loans by such agency and for refinancing of the principal loan to include any unpaid portion of the secondary loan with accrued interest, if any, after the curtailment thereon equals twice the amount of the secondary loan.

(b) Any person who is found by the Administrator of Veterans' Affairs to be a veteran eligible for the benefits of this title, as provided in section 500 hereof, and who is found by the Secretary of Agriculture, by reason of his ability and experience, including training as a vocational trainee, to be likely to carry out successfully undertakings required of him under a loan which may be made under the Bankhead-Jones Farm Tenant Act, shall be eligible for the benefits of such Act to the same extent as if he were a farm tenant.

Title IV

◆ Chapter VI—Employment of Veterans

Sec. 600. (a) In the enactment of the provisions of this title Congress declares as its intent and purpose that there shall be an effective job counseling and employment placement service for veterans, and that, to this end, policies shall be promulgated and administered, so as to provide for them the maximum of job opportunity in the field of gainful employment. For the purpose there is hereby created to cooperate with and assist the United States Employment Service, as established by the provisions of the Act of June 6, 1933, a Veterans' Placement Service Board, which shall consist of the Administrator of Veterans' Affairs, as Chairman, the Director of the National Selective Service System, and the Administrator of the Federal Security Agency, or whoever may have the responsibility of administering the functions of the United States Employment Service. The Board shall determine all matters of policy relating to the administration of the Veterans' Employment Service of the United States Employment Service.

(b) The Chairman of the Board shall have direct authority and responsibility for carrying out its policies through the veterans' employment representatives in the several States or through persons engaged in activities authorized by subsection (g) of section 8 of the Selective Service Act of 1940 (Public Law 783, Seventy-sixth Congress, approved September 16, 1940, as amended (U. S.C., title 50, sec. 308)). The Chairman may delegate such authority to an executive secretary who shall be appointed by him and who shall thereupon be the Chief of the Veterans' Employment Service of the United States Employment Service.

(c) The public records of the Veterans' Personnel Division, National Selective Service System, and the Veterans' Employment Service of the United States Employment Service shall be available to the Board.

Sec. 601. The United States Employment Service shall assign to each of the States a veterans' employment representative, who shall be a veteran of the wars of the United States separated from active service under honorable conditions, who at the time of appointment shall have been a bona fide resident of the State for at least two years, and who shall be appointed, subject to the approval of the Board, in accordance with the civil-service laws, and whose compensation shall be fixed in accordance with the Classification Act of 1923, as amended. Each such veterans' employment representative shall be attached to the staff of the public employment service in the State to which he has been assigned. He shall be administratively responsible to the Board, through its executive secretary, for the execution of the Board's veterans' placement policies through the public employment service in the State. In cooperation with the public employment service staff in the State, he shall —

(a) be functionally responsible for the supervision of the registration of veterans in local employment offices for suitable types of employment and for placement of veterans in employment;

(b) assist in securing and maintaining current information as to the various types of available employment in public works and private industry or business;

(c) promote the interest of employers in employing veterans;

(d) maintain regular contact with employers and veterans' organizations with a view of keeping employers advised of veterans available for employment and veterans advised of opportunities for employment; and

(e) assist in every possible way in improving working conditions and the advancement of employment of veterans.

Sec. 602. Where deemed necessary by the Board, there shall be assigned by the administrative head of the employment service in the State one or more employees, preferably veterans, of the staffs of local employment service offices, whose services shall be primarily devoted to discharging the duties prescribed for the veterans' employment representative.

Sec. 603. All Federal agencies shall furnish the Board such records, statistics, or information as may be deemed necessary or appropriate in administering the provisions of this title, and shall otherwise cooperate with the Board in providing continuous employment opportunities for veterans.

Sec. 604. The Federal agency administering the United States Employment Service shall maintain that service as an operating entity and, during the period of its administration, shall effectuate the provisions of this title.

Sec. 605. (a) The Board through its executive secretary shall estimate the funds necessary for the proper and efficient administration of this title; such estimated sums shall include the annual amounts necessary for salaries, rents, printing and binding, travel, and communications. Sums thus estimated shall be included as a special item in the annual budget of the United States Employment Service. Any funds appropriated pursuant to this special item as contained in the budget of the United States Employment Service shall not be available for any purpose other than that for which they were appropriated, except with the approval of the Board.

(b) The War Manpower Commission shall from its current appropriation allocate and make available sufficient funds to carry out the provisions of this title during the current fiscal year.

Sec. 606. The term "United States Employment Service" as used in this title means that Bureau created by the provisions of the Act of June 6, 1933, or such successor agencies as from time to time shall perform its functions and duties, as now performed by the War Manpower Commission.

Sec. 607. The term "veteran" as used in this title shall mean a person who served in the active service of the armed forces during a period of war in which the United States has been, or is, engaged, and who has been discharged or released therefrom under conditions other than dishonorable.

Title V

♦ Chapter VII—Readjustment Allowances for Former Members of the Armed Forces Who Are Unemployed

Sec. 700. (a) Any person who shall have served in the active military or naval service of the United States at any time after September 16, 1940, and prior to the termination of the present war, and who shall have been discharged or released from active service under conditions other than dishonorable, after active service of ninety days or more, or by reason of an injury or disability incurred in service in line of duty, shall be entitled, in accordance with the provisions of this title and regulations issued by the Administrator of Veterans' Affairs pursuant thereto, to receive a readjustment allowance as provided herein for each week of unemployment, not to exceed a total of fifty-two weeks, which (1) begins after the first Sunday of the third calendar month after the date of enactment hereof, and (2) occurs not later than two years after discharge or release or the termination of the war, whichever is the later date: *Provided,* That no such allowance shall be paid for any period for which he receives increased pension under part VII of Veterans Regulation 1 (a) or a subsistence allowance under part VIII of such regulation; *Provided further,* That no readjustment allowance shall be payable for any week commencing more than five years after the termination of hostilities in the present war.

(b) Such person shall be deemed eligible to receive an allowance for any week of unemployment if claim is made for such allowance and the Administrator finds with respect to such week that —

(1) the person is residing in the United States at the time of such claim;

(2) the person is completely unemployed, having performed no service and received no wages, or is partially unemployed in that services have been performed for less than a full workweek and the wages for the week are less than the allowance under this title plus $3;

(3) the person is registered with and continues to report to a public employment office, in accordance with its regulations;

(4) the person is able to work and available for suitable work: *Provided,* That no claimant shall be considered ineligible in any period of continuous unemployment for failure to comply with the provisions of this subparagraph if such failure is due to an illness or disability which occurs after the commencement of such period.

♦ Chapter VIII—Disqualifications

Sec. 800. (a) Notwithstanding the provisions of section 700, a claimant shall be disqualified from receiving an allowance if —

(1) he leaves suitable work voluntarily, without good cause, or is suspended or discharged for misconduct in the course of employment;

(2) he, without good cause, fails to apply for suitable work to which he has been referred by a public employment office, or to accept suitable work when offered him; or

(3) he, without good cause, does not attend an available free training course as required by regulations issued pursuant to the provisions of this title.

(b) Notwithstanding the provisions of section 700, a claimant shall also be disqualified from receiving an allowance for any week with respect to which it is found that his unemployment is due to a stoppage of work which exists because of a labor dispute at the factory, establishment, or other premises at which he is or was last employed: *Provided,* That this subsection shall not apply if it is shown that —

(1) he is not participating in or directly interested in the labor dispute which causes the stoppage of work; and

(2) he does not belong to a grade or class of workers of which, immediately before the commencement of the stoppage there were members employed at the premises at which the stoppage occurs, any of whom are participating in or directly interested in the dispute: *Provided however,* That if in any case separate branches of work, which are commonly conducted as separate business in separate premises, are conducted in separate departments of the same premises, each such department shall, for the pur-

poses of this subsection, be deemed to be a separate factory, establishment, or other premises.

(c) (1) If a claimant is disqualified under the provisions of subsection (a) of this section, he shall be disqualified to receive any readjustment allowance for the week in which the cause of his disqualification occurred and for not more than four immediately following weeks.

(2) In addition to the disqualification prescribed in paragraph (1) above, the Administrator may, in cases of successive disqualifications under the provisions of subsection (a) of this section, extend the period of disqualification for such additional period as the Administrator may prescribe, but not to exceed eight additional weeks in the case of any one disqualification.

(d) (1) In determining under subsection (a) of this section the suitability of work or the existence of good cause with respect to a claimant, the conditions and standards prescribed by the unemployment compensation laws of the State in which he files his claim shall govern: *Provided*, That the Administrator may prescribe conditions and standards for applicants in any State having no applicable statute.

(2) In determining under subsection (a) of this section the suitability of work, no work shall be deemed suitable for an individual if —

(A) the position offered is vacant due directly to a strike, lock-out, or other labor dispute; or

(B) the wages, hours, or other conditions of the work offered are substantially less favorable to him than those prevailing for similar work in the locality.

◆ Chapter IX—Amount of Allowance and Payment

Sec. 900. (a) The allowance for a week shall be $20 less that part of the wages payable to him for such week which is in excess of $3: *Provided*, That where the allowance is not a multiple of $1, it shall be computed to the next highest multiple of $l.

(b) The number of weeks of allowances to which each eligible veteran shall be entitled shall be determined as follows: For each calendar month or major fraction thereof of active service during the period stated in section 700 the veteran shall be entitled to four weeks of allowances, but in no event to exceed the maximum provided in section 700: *Provided*, That the allowance for the qualifying ninety days service shall be eight weeks for each such month.

Sec. 901. (a) Readjustment allowances shall be paid at the intervals prescribed by the unemployment compensation law of the State in which the claim was made: *Provided*, That if none are so prescribed

readjustment allowances shall be paid at such reasonable intervals as may be determined by the Administrator.

(b) Any allowances remaining unpaid upon the death of a claimant shall not be considered a part of the assets of the estate of the claimant, or liable for the payment of his debts, or subject to any administration of his estate, and the Administrator may make payment thereof to such person or persons he finds most equitably entitled thereto.

Sec. 902. (a) Any person qualified under subsection (a) of section 700, and residing in the United States who is self-employed for profit in an independent establishment, trade, business, profession, or other vocation shall be eligible for readjustment allowances under this title within the time periods applicable, and not in excess of the total amount provided in this title.

(b) Upon application by the veteran showing, in accordance with rules prescribed by the Administrator, that he has been fully engaged in such self-employment and that his net earnings in a trade, business, profession, or vocation, have been less than $100 in the previous calendar month, the veteran shall be entitled to receive, subject to the limitations of this title as to time and amount, the difference (adjusted to the next highest multiple of $1), between $100 and his net earnings for such month.

(c) Payment of such allowance shall be made by the Administrator to each eligible veteran at the time and in the manner other payments are made directly to veterans by the Administrator.

(d) Subsection (b) of section 700 and section 800 shall not apply in determining the eligibility for allowances of a claimant under this section.

◆ Chapter X—Adjustment of Duplicate Benefits

Sec. 1000. Where an allowance is payable to a claimant under this title and where, for the same period, either an allowance or benefit is received under any Federal or State unemployment or disability compensation law, the amount received or accrued from such other source shall be subtracted from the allowance payable under this title (except that this section shall not apply to pension, compensation, or retired pay paid by the Veterans' Administration); and the resulting allowances, if not a multiple of $1, shall be readjusted to the next higher multiple of $1.

◆ Chapter XI—Administration

Sec. 1100. (a) The Administrator of Veterans' Affairs is authorized to administer this title and shall, insofar as possible, utilize existing facilities and services of Federal and State departments or agencies on the basis of mutual agreements with such departments or agencies. Such agreements shall provide for the filing of claims for readjustment allowances with the Administrator through established public employment offices and State unemployment-compensation agencies. Such agencies, through agreement, shall also be utilized in the processing, adjustment, and determination of such claims and the payment of such allowances. To facilitate the carrying out of agreements with State departments or agencies and to assist in the discharge of the Administrator's duties under this title, a representative of the Administrator, who shall be a war veteran separated from active service under honorable conditions and who at the time of appointment shall have been a bona fide resident of the State for at least two years, shall be located in each participating State department or agency.

(b) The Administrator, consistent with the provisions of this title, shall prescribe such rules and regulations and require such records and reports as he may find necessary to carry out its purposes: *Provided however*, That cooperative rules and regulations relating to the performance by Federal or State departments, or agencies, of functions under agreements made therewith may be made by the Administrator after consultation and advisement with representatives of such departments or agencies.

(c) The Administrator may delegate to any officer or employee of his own or of any cooperating department or agency of any State such of his powers and duties, except that of prescribing rules and regulations, as the Administrator may consider necessary and proper to carry out the purposes of this title.

(d) Allowances paid by the cooperating State agencies shall be repaid upon certification by the Administrator. The Secretary of the Treasury, through the Division of Disbursement of the Treasury, and without the necessity of audit and settlement by the General Accounting Office, shall pay monthly to the departments, agencies, or individuals designated, the amounts so certified.

(e) The Administrator shall from time to time certify to the Secretary of the Treasury for payment in advance or otherwise such sums as he estimates to be necessary to compensate any Federal department or agency for its administrative expenses under this title. Such sums shall cover periods of no longer than six months.

(f) The Administrator shall also from time to time certify to the the Social Security Board such State

departments or agencies as may be participating in the administration of this title, and the amount of the administrative expense incurred or to be incurred by a State under agreements made pursuant to this section. Upon such certification the Social Security Board shall certify such amount to the Secretary of the Treasury, in addition to the amount, if any, payable by said Board under the provisions of section 302 (a) of the Social Security Act, as amended, and the additional amount so certified shall be paid to each State by the Secretary of the Treasury out of the appropriation for the Veterans' Administration.

(g) Any money paid to any cooperating agency or person, which is not used for the purpose for which it was paid shall, upon termination of the period covered by such payment or the agreement with such agency or person, be returned to the Treasury and credited to the current appropriation for carrying out the purpose of this title, or, if returned after the expiration of period covered by this title, shall be covered into the Treasury as miscellaneous receipts.

Sec. 1101. (a) No person designated by the Administrator as a certifying officer shall, in the absence of gross negligence, or intent to defraud the United States, be liable with respect to the payment of any allowance certified by him under this title.

(b) No disbursing officer shall, in the absence of gross negligence, or intent to defraud the United States, be liable with respect to any payment by him under this title if it was based upon a voucher signed by a certifying officer designated by the Administrator.

Sec. 1102. Any claimant whose claim for an allowance has been denied shall be entitled to a fair hearing before an impartial tribunal of the State agency or such other agency as may be designated by the Administrator. The representative of the Administrator located in each State shall be the final appellate authority in regard to contested claims arising in such State, subject to review by the Administrator.

Sec. 1103. In the case of any veteran eligible under the provisions of this title who either at the time of application for the benefits herein provided is a "qualified employee" as defined in section 3 of the Railroad Unemployment Insurance Act, as amended, or was last employed prior to such application by an employer as defined in section 1 (a) of the said Act, claim may be made through an office operated by or a facility designated as a free employment office by the Railroad Retirement Board pursuant to the provisions of said Act. In such cases, the conditions and standards as to suitability of work or existence of good cause, the intervals for making claim for and payment of benefits, and the administrative and appellate procedures prescribed by or under said Act shall govern, if not in conflict with the provisions of this title, the appellate procedures being subject to final appeal to the Administrator. In such cases, a reference in this title to a cooperating State agency shall be deemed to include the Railroad Retirement Board.

◆ Chapter XII—Decisions and Procedures

Sec. 1200. The authority to issue subpenas and provisions for invoking aid of the courts of the United States in case of disobedience thereto, to make investigations, and to administer oaths, as contained in title III of the Act of June 29, 1936 (49 Stat. 2033-34; U. S. C., title 38, secs. 131-133), shall be applicable in the administration of this title.

◆ Chapter XIII—Penalties

Sec. 1300. Any claimant who knowingly accepts an allowance to which he is not entitled shall be ineligible to receive any further allowance under this title.

Sec. 1301. (a) Whoever, for the purpose of causing an increase in any allowance authorized under this title, or for the purpose of causing any allowance to be paid where none is authorized under this title, shall make or cause to be made any false statement or representation as to any wages paid or received, or whoever makes or causes to be made any false statement of a material fact in any claim for any allowance under this title, or whoever makes or causes to be made any false statement, representation, affidavit, or document in connection with such claim, shall be guilty of a misdemeanor and upon conviction thereof shall be fined not more than $1,000 or imprisoned for not more than one year, or both.

(b) Whoever shall obtain or receive any money, check, or allowance under this title, without being entitled thereto and with intent to defraud the United States, shall be punished by a fine of not more than $1,000 or by imprisonment for not more than one year, or both.

◆ Chapter XIV—Definitions

Sec. 1400. As used in this title —

(a) The term "week" means such period or periods of seven consecutive calendar days as may be prescribed in regulations by the Administrator.

(b) The term "wages" means all remuneration for services from whatever sources, including commissions and bonuses and the cash value of all remuneration in any medium other than cash.

Title VI

◆ Chapter XV General Administrative and Penal Provisions

Sec. 1500. Except as otherwise provided in this Act, the administrative, definitive, and penal provisions under Public, Numbered 2, Seventy-third Congress, as amended, and the provisions of Public, Numbered 262, Seventy-fourth Congress, as amended (38 U. S. C. 450, 451, 454a and 556a), shall be for application under this Act. For the purpose of carrying out any of the provisions of Public, Numbered 2, as amended, and this Act, the Administrator shall have authority to accept uncompensated services, and to enter into contracts or agreements with private or public agencies, or persons, for necessary services, including personal services, as he may deem practicable.

Sec. 1501. Except as otherwise specified, the appropriations for the Veterans' Administration are hereby made available for expenditures necessary to carry out the provisions of this Act and there is hereby authorized to be appropriated such additional amounts as may be necessary to accomplish the purposes of this Act.

Sec. 1502. Wherever used in this Act, unless the context otherwise requires, the singular includes the plural; the masculine includes the feminine; the term "Administrator" means the Administrator of Veterans' Affairs; the term "United States" used geographically means the several States, Territories and possessions, and the District of Columbia; the term "State" means the several States, Territories and possessions, and the District of Columbia; and the phrases "termination of hostilities in the present war", "termination of the present war", and "termination of the war", mean termination of the war as declared by Presidential proclamation or concurrent resolution of the Congress.

Sec. 1503. A discharge or release from active service under conditions other than dishonorable shall be a prerequisite to entitlement to veterans' benefits provided by this Act or Public Law Numbered 2, Seventy-third Congress as amended.

Sec. 1504. The Administrator shall transmit to the Congress annually a report of operations under this Act. If the Senate or the House of Representatives is not in session, such reports shall be transmitted to the Secretary of the Senate or the Clerk of the House of Representatives, as the case may be.

Sec. 1505. In the event there shall hereafter be authorized any allowance in the nature of adjusted compensation, any benefits received by, or paid for, any veteran under this Act shall be charged against and deducted from such adjusted compensation; and in the event a veteran has obtained a loan under the terms of this Act, the agency disbursing such adjusted compensation shall first pay the unpaid balance and accrued interest due on such loan to the holder of the evidence of such indebtedness to the extent that the amount of adjusted compensation which may be payable will permit.

RECOMMENDATION FOR ASSISTANCE TO GREECE AND TURKEY

ADDRESS

OF

THE PRESIDENT OF THE UNITED STATES

DELIVERED

BEFORE A JOINT SESSION OF THE SENATE AND THE HOUSE OF REPRESENTATIVES, RECOMMENDING ASSISTANCE TO GREECE AND TURKEY

MARCH 12, 1947.—Referred to the Committee on Foreign Affairs, and ordered to be printed

---

MR. PRESIDENT, MR. SPEAKER, MEMBERS OF THE CONGRESS OF THE UNITED STATES:

The gravity of the situation which confronts the world today necessitates my appearance before a joint session of the Congress.

The foreign policy and the national security of this country are involved.

One aspect of the present situation, which I wish to present to you at this time for your consideration and decision, concerns Greece and Turkey.

The United States has received from the Greek Government an urgent appeal for financial and economic assistance. Preliminary reports from the American Economic Mission now in Greece and reports from the American Ambassador in Greece corroborate the statement of the Greek Government that assistance is imperative if Greece is to survive as a free nation.

I do not believe that the American people and the Congress wish to turn a deaf ear to the appeal of the Greek Government.

Greece is not a rich country. Lack of sufficient natural resources has always forced the Greek people to work hard to make both ends meet. Since 1940, this industrious and peace-loving country has suffered invasion, 4 years of cruel enemy occupation, and bitter internal strife.

When forces of liberation entered Greece they found that the retreating Germans had destroyed virtually all the railways, roads,

The Truman Doctrine (National Archives and Records Administration)

"The free peoples of the world look to us for support in maintaining their freedoms."

Overview

On March 12, 1947, Democratic President Harry S. Truman addressed a joint session of the Republican-controlled Congress, requesting that $400 million in military and financial aid be appropriated to the struggling governments of Greece and Turkey. The president, seeking bipartisan support for a more interventionist foreign policy aimed at limiting the global influence of the Soviet Union, articulated what would become known as the Truman Doctrine, in which the United States pledged assistance to any democratic government threatened internally or externally by the forces of totalitarianism.

Although Truman did not mention the Soviet Union by name, the totalitarian designation was certainly a commentary on the deteriorating relationship between the United States and Soviet Union after World War II. The immediate crisis leading to the Truman speech was the announcement by the British government in February 1947 that it would no longer be able to support the Greek government in its military engagements with a Communist insurgency. Soviet demands on the Turkish government for greater influence in the Dardanelles encouraged Truman to include Turkey in his address. Congress appropriated the requested funds, and military personnel and supplies were dispatched to Turkey and Greece. American assistance stabilized the governments, and in 1952 both nations joined the North Atlantic Treaty Organization.

The Truman Doctrine became a policy followed throughout the cold war by both Republican and Democratic presidents. Many credit the Truman Doctrine with fostering global democracy while limiting the influence of an expansionist Soviet Union. While the Truman Doctrine is often celebrated for playing a key role in the cold war victory of the United States, critics assert that the Truman Doctrine's anti-Communist obsession led the United States to support anti-democratic authoritarian regimes able to procure American aid by claiming they were fighting Communism. According to this reading, implementation of the Truman Doctrine often encouraged an anti-Americanism manifest in many parts of the Middle East and Asia after the cold war era.

Context

The Truman Doctrine must be understood within the emerging cold war and the impact of this conflict upon American foreign policy as well as domestic politics. The wartime alliance between Americans and Soviets began to unravel during the Yalta Conference in February 1945 and Potsdam Conference in July 1945, with disputes over the postwar reconstruction of Germany and free elections in the Eastern European nations liberated by the Soviet military. Increasing concern about the democratic future of Eastern Europe was expressed by Britain's prime minister Winston Churchill's speech at a college in Fulton, Missouri, on March 5, 1946, which employed the expression *Iron Curtain*, a concept endorsed by President Truman and that characterized the Soviet-controlled areas of the world as existing in isolation behind an invisible barrier to reciprocal communication.

Truman, influenced by the Soviet expert George Kennan's argument that a tough policy was needed to deal with Soviet expansionism, seized on the opportunity presented by the crisis in Greece. On February 21, 1947, the British Embassy informed the U.S. State Department that Great Britain could no longer afford to extend assistance to the Greek government engaged in civil war with Communist forces. While President Truman claimed that the Soviets were funding the insurgency, the political situation in Greece was more ambiguous, and Stalin was evidently adhering to a 1944 understanding with Churchill that the Soviet leader would not extend military aid to the Greek Communists.

Truman, however, was convinced that the Soviets were engaged in a policy of expansionism that had to be checked. In early 1946 the Soviets refused to withdraw from northern Iran, as stipulated in the 1943 Tehran Conference, while pressuring the Iranian government to grant them oil concessions. Truman also was concerned about Soviet efforts to force the Turkish government to grant transit rights through the Turkish Straits as well as Soviet rejection of the United States' Baruch Plan for sharing atomic energy.

Truman was thus not in a mood to compromise when he met with congressional leaders at the White House on Feb-

1945

■ **February 4–11**
During the Yalta Conference, Franklin Roosevelt, Winston Churchill, and the Soviet Union's Joseph Stalin meet and pave over differences with the agreement that the Soviets would supervise free elections in Poland and later enter the war against Japan.

■ **July 17–August 2**
In the Potsdam Conference postwar division continues over German reconstruction and formation of governments in Eastern Europe; the United States and Great Britain issue the Potsdam Declaration, which calls for Japan's immediate, unconditional surrender.

■ **August 6 and 9**
President Truman orders the dropping of atomic bombs on Hiroshima and Nagasaki.

■ **October 24**
The United Nations is formed and ratified by a majority of fifty-one member states.

1945–1946

■ **November 1945–December 1946**
The Eastern European People's Republics of Yugoslavia, Albania, and Bulgaria are created, with close ties to the Soviet Union.

1946

■ **February 22**
George Kennan sends his "long telegram," which outlines a policy for containing the Soviet Union, to the State Department.

■ **March 5**
British Prime Minister Winston Churchill, speaking in Fulton, Missouri, announces that an "Iron Curtain" has descended upon Eastern Europe under Soviet influence.

1947

■ **February 21**
The British Embassy informs the United States that it cannot continue military assistance for the Greek government.

ruary 27, 1947. Republican Senator Arthur Vandenberg of Michigan, chairman of the Foreign Relations Committee, told Truman that Congress would authorize aid for Greece if the president would explain to a joint session of Congress that Soviet expansionism into Greece threatened Turkey and the entire Middle East. The president responded with the Truman Doctrine, followed by the Marshall Plan, which he considered related efforts. The Marshall Plan, announced by Secretary of State George C. Marshall at a Harvard University speech on June 5, 1947, called for spending more than $12 billion for European recovery, checking the popularity of Communism, and providing an outlet for American exports. Congressional approval for the Truman Doctrine and Marshall Plan in 1947 provided the framework for the policy of containing the Soviet Union that the United States pursued throughout the cold war.

The Truman administration, perceiving that American interests were threatened in Europe, Asia, and the Middle East, moved to limit dissent on the home front. On March 22, 1947, Truman issued Executive Order 9835, which instigated a review process to identify "disloyal persons" within the government (http://teachingamericanhistory.org/library/index.asp?document=930). Anti-Communism would be a dominant element in American politics for the next forty years.

About the Author

Harry S. Truman was born on May 8, 1884, in Lamar, Missouri, to a farming family. His family moved to Independence, Missouri, when Truman was six years old. Although he suffered from myopic vision, as a boy Truman enjoyed reading history and pleased his mother by playing the piano. In 1901 he graduated from Independence High School. Although he failed to pursue a college degree, in 1923 and 1924 he enrolled in night classes at the Kansas City School of Law.

After serving as a construction timekeeper and bank clerk, in 1906 he helped his family by working at the Grandview, Missouri, farm owned by his grandmother. Truman continued his farm labors until his military service during World War I. Truman, who had been a member of the Missouri National Guard since 1905, served as a captain with the 129th Artillery Regiment in France.

After the war, Truman married Bess Wallace, and they had a daughter, named Margaret. He also opened a haberdashery in Kansas City with Eddie Johnson, an army friend, but the business went bankrupt during the farm depression of 1920 to 1922. Truman turned to politics, winning an election in 1922 as eastern district judge, the equivalent of a county commissioner, in Jackson County. After being defeated for reelection in 1924, Truman joined the Democratic Kansas City political machine of Tom Pendergast, which was extending its influence into more rural areas of the state. In 1926 and 1930 he was elected presiding judge of the county court, earning a reputation for personal honesty despite his connection with the Pendergast machine.

Truman was the Pendergast candidate for Senate in 1934, and he easily won the general election after a difficult Democratic primary campaign. In the Senate, Truman was a consistent supporter of President Franklin Delano Roosevelt's New Deal, and he served on the Interstate Commerce Committee, sponsored the Civil Aeronautics Act of 1938, and urged national military preparedness.

During his second Senate term, Truman won acclaim for his chairmanship of a committee investigating fraud and corruption in the national defense effort. In 1944 party regulars at the Democratic National Convention dumped liberal Vice President Henry A. Wallace in favor of Truman as Roosevelt's running mate. Truman and Roosevelt were not close, and the vice president was not well informed when Roosevelt died on April 12, 1945. Despite his lack of foreign policy experience and being left out of planning for the Manhattan Project to develop the atomic bomb, Truman's presidency was consumed by the developing cold war with the Soviet Union. He argued with Stalin over postwar developments in Germany and Eastern Europe at the Potsdam Conference in July 1945. Truman also ordered the dropping of atomic bombs on Hiroshima and Nagasaki, insisting in his memoirs that this decision shortened the war and saved lives. Deteriorating relations with the Soviet Union persuaded Truman to institute a policy of containment with the Truman Doctrine, Marshall Plan, National Security Act, and Berlin airlift after the Soviets blocked access to the western sector of Berlin.

On the domestic front Truman called for a Fair Deal, a reform program similar to Roosevelt's New Deal. Truman advocated national health insurance, expanded public housing, civil rights legislation, and repeal of the antilabor Taft-Hartley Act. Most of his legislative efforts, however, were blocked by the Republican Congress. Truman's reelection prospects appeared dim in 1948 when the Democratic Party split, with former Vice President Henry A. Wallace running as a Progressive in protest of Truman's aggressive cold war policies and with the governor of South Carolina, Strom Thurmond, forming the Dixiecrats in opposition to Truman's support for civil rights. Wallace's campaign was beset with accusations of Communist influence, while Thurmond's candidacy was unable to resonate beyond the Deep South. Truman's Republican opponent, New York's Governor Thomas Dewey, was overconfident, and the embattled Truman campaign was able to attain one of the greatest upsets in American political history.

Truman's second term, however, was troubled. The cold war accelerated with the Soviet explosion of an atomic bomb in 1949 and the triumph of Mao Zedong's Communist forces in the Chinese Civil War. On June 25, 1950, North Korean troops invaded South Korea, and under the auspices of the United Nations, the Truman administration came to the defense of South Korea. Under the leadership of General Douglas MacArthur, the American troops pushed the North Koreans toward the Yalu River and border with China. However, when Chinese forces entered the conflict, the war bogged down along the thirty-eighth parallel, dividing the two Koreas. When MacArthur openly dis-

Time Line

1947

■ **March 12**
President Truman addresses Congress and establishes the Truman Doctrine.

■ **March 22**
President Truman issues Executive Order 9835 to search out disloyal persons in the U.S. government.

■ **June 5**
At Harvard, Secretary of State George C. Marshall unveils the Marshall Plan for economic reconstruction of Europe.

■ **July 26**
The National Security Act unifies military services under the secretary of defense and establishes the National Security Council and Central Intelligence Agency.

agreed with the president's strategy in Korea, Truman fired the general despite his widespread popularity.

Although Truman instituted a policy of loyalty review boards, the president was continually hounded by such critics as Wisconsin's Senator Joseph McCarthy, who asserted that the administration needed to take a tougher stance against Communism. Truman, who was personally honest, was censured for corruption within his administration. With his popularity ratings low, Truman did not seek reelection in 1952. He endorsed Democratic Governor Adlai Stevenson of Illinois, who was defeated by the Republican nominee, General Dwight D. Eisenhower. Truman and his wife, Bess, in retirement, moved back to Independence, Missouri, where he wrote his memoirs and organized a presidential library. Truman died from pneumonia in Kansas City on December 26, 1972. Often maligned during his presidency, Truman is usually rated a near-great president in polls of professional historians.

Explanation and Analysis of the Document

President Truman, attempting to follow the reported suggestion of Senator Arthur Vandenberg that he play on the fear of the American people in his address, begins his short congressional address by announcing that the situations in Greece and Turkey are grave and that they directly involve the national security of the United States.

The first half of the speech focuses on the situation in Greece and on the Greek government's request for financial and military assistance. The president bluntly declares that Greece's survival as a democratic nation is dependent on the United States. The dire economic plight of Greece was due to four years of occupation under Nazi Germany, during which crops and fields had been destroyed, inflation had run rampant, and health conditions had deteriorated. Lacking the funds to import goods and services necessary for recovery, the Greek government called on the United States for technological and economic aid so that it might again become a self-sustaining nation. While Truman describes providing this assistance in altruistic terms, fostering economic recovery in Greece would also provide markets for American businesses afraid of another depression.

The president also asserts that political chaos in Greece is hindering economic recovery. Blame for this state of affairs is placed upon a "militant minority, exploiting human want and misery." This militant minority is, of course, the Greek Communists, who were supported by external forces seeking to exploit Greek unrest. While not mentioning the Soviet Union by name, Truman reports allegations of border violations along Greece's northern frontier, which borders Soviet satellite states of Albania, Bulgaria, and Yugoslavia. The small, undermanned Greek army was unable to deal with the insurgency and border violations, which leads Truman to conclude that only the United States is in a position to provide the required military security on which Greek economic recovery is dependent. The president acknowledges that historically Greece has been an area of British influence. Postwar issues of economic reconstruction, however, made it impossible for the British to continue their military support of Greece. In claiming America's unilateral right to replace the British, Truman dismisses the United Nations as a means for providing collective security, simply asserting that the international body is in no position to provide the type of urgent and immediate aid required by the Greek government. Truman apparently believed that a Soviet veto would block Security Council consideration of the Greek situation. Still, the Truman administration, which preferred to go it alone in Greece, did not bring the Greek issue to the United Nations.

Truman provides little detail on the Greek government, although he does concede that the current regime has made mistakes. Observing that the United States condemned violence by both the political Left and Right, he nevertheless argues that it is easier for a democratic government, rather than an authoritarian or Communist government, to correct abuses. The president counters critics of the Greek regime's level of democracy by proclaiming that it represents 85 percent of Greek parliament members chosen in 1946 elections. Military assistance to the Greek government would thus further democracy and limit Communist aggression.

The president includes little concrete information on the Greek political situation, however, which is far more complex than the rhetoric the president employs in his speech might lead one to believe. When the Nazis were driven out of Greece in October 1944, the British had restored to power the exiled monarchist government of Prime Minister George Papandreou. That same month British Prime Minister Churchill journeyed to Moscow, making an agreement with Stalin that recognized Britain's sphere of influence within Greece in exchange for giving the Soviets an upper hand in Romania. Greek Communists, who had played a leading role in resisting the Nazi

occupation and forming the National Liberation Front (EAM) and its military arm, the National Popular Liberation Army (ELAS), upset this understanding. The British encouraged the EAM to join a coalition government, but the ELAS would not disarm unless returning royalist forces reciprocated. In December 1944 fighting broke out between the ELAS and the royalists. Both sides committed atrocities, and British troops attempted to restore order. At British insistence, parliamentary elections were held in March 1946, but EAM-ELAS boycotted voting. The election led to a Rightist regime under Prime Minister Constantine Tsaldaris, who increased military pressure against Leftists and recalled King George II—a symbol of oppression to those on the political Left—to the Greek throne.

At this point, the Communists and other factions of the EAM deserted electoral politics and turned to a military strategy of toppling the Greek government. The Democratic army under the leadership of Communist Markos Vafiades was formed, and support was forthcoming from the neighboring Communist nations of Albania, Bulgaria, and Yugoslavia. Stalin, however, adhered to his agreement with Churchill, refusing to aid the Greek insurrection. In fact, Stalin did not extend assistance to the Greek Communists until June 1947, after the United States authorized the Truman Doctrine and military intervention in support of the Greek government. But Stalin's interest was limited and lukewarm. Fearing Yugoslav independence and dominance in the Balkans, Stalin in October 1948 announced that aid to the Greek rebels was to be terminated. When the Yugoslav leader Josip Broz Tito refused to follow his dictates, Stalin pulled his military advisers from Yugoslavia. The Soviet pressure finally resulted in the July 1949 decision by Tito to close the Greek and Yugoslav border, abandoning support for the Greek insurrection, which ultimately collapsed. A more detailed investigation of the Greek Civil War (1944–1949) fails to buttress the Soviet-inspired rebellion assumed by the Truman Doctrine.

The second part of Truman's speech addresses the needs of the Turkish government, but here the president provides even fewer specifics than in his summary of Greek affairs. Truman acknowledges that Turkey did not suffer from military occupation during the war as Greece had, but the Turks are in desperate need of financial and technical assistance to modernize and maintain their territorial integrity. Truman concludes that bolstering the Turkish government is essential to the "preservation of order in the Middle East." The president observes that the British are no longer able to extend their financial support of Turkey and that this gap could be filled only by the United States undertaking a larger role in the region. By linking the fates of Greece and Turkey, Truman implies that the collapse of the Greek government could lead to Soviet penetration of the entire Middle East.

This early version of what would later be termed the "domino theory" of Communist expansion is formulated by Undersecretary of State Dean Acheson and presidential adviser Clark Clifford. At a February 27, 1944, meeting between the president and congressional leaders, Acheson had vehemently argued that if Greece fell under Soviet influence, the door would be open to Stalin's control of Turkey and Iran. Stalin would not stop with the Middle East—control over Turkey and Greece would provide the opportunity for penetration into Africa and Western Europe. In a rhetorical flourish, Acheson proclaimed that the world faced a choice between American democracy and Soviet dictatorship. The congressional leaders had been impressed with Acheson's arguments, insisting that they be incorporated into a presidential speech. Truman then assigned the drafting of the address to Acheson and Clifford. The grandiose principles that Acheson enunciated were a bit much for Clifford, who suggested that Truman use more practical arguments, such as safeguarding natural resources in places such as the Middle East. This approach would have introduced such economic issues as oil into the conversation. While such considerations were clearly on the minds of policy makers, Truman elected to make the case for American intervention well within the tradition of Wilsonian idealism.

The final section of the Truman Doctrine employs the language of Acheson, calling for Congress and the American people to invest in a crusade against Soviet dictatorship and expansionism. While the Soviet Union and Stalin are not mentioned directly, the focus of Truman's rhetoric remains obvious. The president argues that World War II has taught that efforts to coerce free nations and peoples anywhere are a threat to the United States. Accordingly, the United States must assume a leading role in the formation of the United Nations and collective security, but the president also asserts that he would not hesitate to act unilaterally in an increasingly polarized world.

Truman describes democratic governments as characterized by free elections and individual liberties such as freedom of speech and religion. On the other hand, liberty around the world is threatened by a growing totalitarianism based on terrorism, rigged elections, and control over the press and radio. Truman notes the United States had protested the "coercion and intimidation" used in Poland, Romania, and Bulgaria (all within the Soviet sphere of influence) in violation of the Yalta agreements signed by President Roosevelt and Joseph Stalin.

Truman announces that it is incumbent on the United States to ensure that the democratic principles of the United Nations charter are implemented. Employing Acheson's domino-theory argument, Truman insists that if an armed minority is able to impose its will on Greece, then Turkey would be vulnerable, and chaos might spread throughout the Middle East. Furthermore, he maintains that the defeat of democracy in Greece might have serious repercussions for free nations throughout Western Europe. In making his case, Truman relies primarily on democratic rhetoric and eschews more materialistic explanations, such as securing natural resources and markets.

The speech concludes with a request for congressional authorization of $400 million and the dispatching of American civilian and military personnel to supervise reconstruction in Greece. Conscious of Republican efforts to curtail the budgetary requests of the president, Truman attempts a more practical argument that, in some ways,

Harry S. Truman (Library of Congress)

undermines his sense of urgency. Noting that the nation spent over $341 billion in winning World War II, Truman suggests that the price tag to defend Greece and Turkey is relatively cheap. Yet if the world crisis is as dire as the president claims earlier in the address, then it would seem that money should not be a major consideration in the struggle between freedom and totalitarianism.

In a grand finish, however, President Truman brushes aside this inconsistency, returning to his theme that America must embark upon a world crusade to preserve freedom against the forces of darkness constituted by the Soviet Union. Truman argues that the free peoples of the world are looking to the United States to assume the responsibility of protecting global liberty. With the Truman Doctrine, the United States would announce that the nation would use its military and economic power in a struggle for global supremacy against the Soviet Union. The ensuing Cold War would rage for the next forty years with wars in Korea, Vietnam, and Afghanistan. The United States would emerge triumphant, but the aid for more authoritarian regimes in areas such as the Philippines, Indonesia, Iran, and Nicaragua would also lead some nations to question the legacy of Truman's commitment to free institutions.

Audience

President Truman's speech before Congress on March 12, 1947, extolling what would become known as the Tru-

"No other nation is willing and able to provide the necessary support for a democratic Greek government."

(Paragraph 14)

"But the situation is an urgent one requiring immediate action and the United Nations and its related organizations are not in a position to extend help of the kind that is required."

(Paragraph 16)

"One of the primary objectives of the foreign policy of the United States is the creation of conditions in which we and other nations will be able to work out a way of life free from coercion."

(Paragraph 28)

"I believe that it must be the policy of the United States to support free peoples who are resisting attempted subjugation by armed minorities or by outside pressures."

(Paragraph 34)

"If Greece should fall under the control of an armed minority, the effect upon its neighbor, Turkey, would be immediate and serious. Confusion and disorder might well spread throughout the entire Middle East."

(Paragraph 38)

"The free peoples of the world look to us for support in maintaining their freedoms."

(Paragraph 51)

man Doctrine was intended to convince the American people and their representatives that the Soviet Union and spread of Communism constituted a threat to world freedom, international stability, and the national security of the United States. The speech was generally embraced by the nation's newspapers, and Congress approved the president's authorization of $400 million in financial and military assistance to the nations of Greece and Turkey. The Senate passed the measure by a vote of 69 to 23 on April

22, 1947, and the House followed on May 8 by a margin of 287 to 107. President Truman signed the legislation on May 22.

The Truman Doctrine was not without its domestic critics, however. One of the more vocal opponents was former Vice President Henry A. Wallace, who had been dismissed by Truman as secretary of commerce in September 1946 for his criticism of the president's handling of relations with the Soviet Union. Wallace berated Truman for betraying American's democratic foreign policy traditions. According to Wallace, Truman was placing the United States as the defender of the status quo against the forces of global progress and change. The United States would become the champion of repressive regimes that could secure American support by stressing their anti-Communist credentials. Wallace concluded that Truman was offering the world military hardware instead of economic development, which was needed to restore international peace and stability. Such domestic dissent was increasingly silenced in the early 1950s, when the extreme anti-Communism of Joseph McCarthy dominated American politics.

Internationally, President Truman called upon the world to join a global crusade under American leadership against the Soviet Union. In response, the Soviet representative Andrei Vyshinsky, speaking at the United Nations on September 18, 1947, asserted that the Truman Doctrine and Marshall Plan were examples of how the United States was ignoring the United Nations and attempting to exert economic and political dominion over European nations. The Soviets perceived the Truman Doctrine as a virtual declaration of war, implementing the containment strategy of George Kennan, who believed that the United States must regard the Soviets as rivals and not partners in the international arena. The ensuing cold war dominated international politics for the next forty years.

Impact

The Truman Doctrine crystallized the emerging cold war between the United States and Soviet Union, proclaiming that the United States must play a leading role in shaping international politics. In response to British abandonment of its historical imperial role in the Balkans and Middle East, President Truman outlined an aggressive policy in which the United Sates would fulfill the British power vacuum. The Soviet Union, with its expansion into Eastern Europe, however, posed a challenge to American hegemony. To justify America's expanding world role, President Truman employed the Wilsonian language of America's mission to extend the benefits of democracy throughout the world. Democratic governments would ensure a more stable international community and would foster the national security of the United States. While extolling democratic rhetoric, President Truman was also interested in securing American access to international markets and natural resources.

In the short run, the anti-Communist government in Greece prevailed over a Communist insurgency that did not enjoy the Soviet support Truman had suggested. By 1952 both Turkey and Greece had joined the North Atlantic Treaty Organization. Concern regarding the domino threat posed by Soviet expansion into Greece and Turkey was soon extended to other regions, such as Latin America, Africa, and Asia. While American diplomats enunciated the role of economic reconstruction in combating Communism, the implementation of the Truman Doctrine focused upon military aid. Of the $50 billion in aid awarded to more than ninety countries by 1960, only $5 billion was extended for nonmilitary purposes. And the cost was even higher in human terms, with more than one hundred thousand Americans dying in the Korean and Vietnam conflicts, while a nuclear holocaust was narrowly avoided during the Cuban missile crisis of October 1962.

In the final analysis, however, supporters of the Truman Doctrine believe that American military assistance to democratic governments around the world stemmed Communist expansion, paving the way for Ronald Reagan's cold war victory with the collapse of the Soviet Union. Critics of American foreign policy during the cold war, nevertheless, side with Henry A. Wallace and insist that the Truman Doctrine resulted in American military assistance to repressive anti-Communist regimes and prepared the ground for the anti-Americanism and "blowback" of the world after the cold war. In addition, those who question the wisdom of Truman's foreign policy often point out that the domestic anti-Communism that accompanied the Truman Doctrine limited dissent and domestic reform during the 1950s. The issues of civil liberties and national security, which often collided during the cold war, continue to challenge Americans in the post-9/11 world. The legacy of the Truman Doctrine is a contested one.

Related Documents

Acheson, Dean. *Present at the Creation: My Years in the State Department*. New York: W. W. Norton, 1969. In this memoir, Acheson describes his role in formulating the Truman Doctrine and the policy of containment during the cold war.

Churchill, Winston S. *The Second World War*. Vol. 6: *Triumph and Tragedy*. Boston: Houghton Mifflin Company, 1953. In this final volume of his World War II memoirs, British Prime Minister Winston Churchill maintains that Joseph Stalin and the Soviet Union bear responsibility for initiating the cold war.

Kennan, George F. *Memoirs, 1925–1950*. New York: Pantheon, 1957. In this memoir, the diplomat and scholar George Kennan analyzes the expansionist foreign policy of the Soviet Union and argues for the policy of containment exemplified by the Truman Doctrine and the Marshall Plan.

Truman, Harry S. *Memoirs*. New York: Doubleday, 1955–1956. In these memoirs, Truman argues that the atomic bombs saved both Japanese and American lives. Truman also places blame for the cold war squarely upon Soviet aggression.

Wallace, Henry A. *The Diary of Henry Agard Wallace, January 18, 1935–September 19, 1946*. Iowa City: University of Iowa Libraries, 1977. In his diary accounts of the emerging cold war, the former vice president and secretary of commerce Henry A. Wallace provides a critique of President Harry S. Truman. Wallace believes that the aggressive posturing of Truman with the Soviet Union provoked an unnecessary cold war.

Bibliography

■ Books

Freeland, Richard M. *The Truman Doctrine and the Origins of McCarthyism: Foreign Policy, Domestic Politics, and Internal Security, 1946–1948*. New York: Knopf, 1972.

Gaddis, John L. *We Now Know: Rethinking Cold War History*. New York: Oxford University Press, 1997.

Kofsky, Frank. *Harry S. Truman and the War Scare of 1948: A Successful Campaign to Deceive the Nation*. New York: St. Martin's Press, 1993.

LaFeber, Walter. *America, Russia, and the Cold War, 1945–2005*, 7th ed. New York: McGraw Hill, 2008.

Leffler, Melvyn P. *A Preponderance of Power: National Security, the Truman Administration, and the Cold War*. Stanford, Calif.: Stanford University Press, 1992.

McCullough, David. *Truman*. New York: Simon and Schuster, 1992.

Offner, Arnold A. *Another Such Victory: President Truman and the Cold War, 1945–1953*. Stanford, Calif.: Stanford University Press, 2002.

Spalding, Elizabeth E. *The First Cold Warrior: Harry Truman, Containment, and the Remaking of Liberal Internationalism*. Lexington: University Press of Kentucky, 2006.

Walton, Richard. *Henry Wallace, Harry Truman, and the Cold War*. New York: Viking, 1976.

Yergin, Daniel. *Shattered Peace: The Origins of the Cold War and the National Security State*. Boston: Houghton Mifflin, 1977.

■ Web Sites

"Executive Order 9835." Teaching American History Web site. http://teachingamericanhistory.org/library/index.asp?document=930. Accessed on February 20, 2008.

"Speech on the Truman Doctrine." Teaching American History Web site. http://teachingamericanhistory.org/library/index.asp?document=852 Accessed on February 20, 2008.

"The Truman Doctrine." Harry S. Truman Library and Museum Web site. http://www.trumanlibrary.org/whistlestop/study_collections/doctrine/large/. Accessed on July 15, 2007.

"Truman Doctrine." Spartacus Educational Web site. http://www.spartacus.schoolnet.co.uk/USAtrumanD.htm. Accessed on July 15, 2007.

"The Truman Doctrine, 1947." U.S. Department of State Web site. http://www.state.gov/r/pa/ho/time/cwr/82210.htm Accessed on February 20, 2008.

—By Ron Briley

1. In his speech establishing the Truman Doctrine, President Truman employs the rhetoric of Woodrow Wilson to justify an interventionist foreign policy, eschewing more materialistic economic motives. President George W. Bush has also used Wilsonian language to explain the 2003 invasion of Iraq, insisting that the United States must use its military power to promote democracy in the Middle East. Does democratic rhetoric disguise a more economy-driven foreign policy based on ensuring access to markets and natural resources such as oil? Should American foreign policy be focused on abstract ideas or notions of national security that are more realistic, which include economic considerations?

2. In the Truman Doctrine, President Truman asserts that the United States cannot rely on the United Nations and must bear the burden of combating the Soviet Union. A similar unilateral approach was taken by the Bush administration with the 2003 invasion of Iraq. Is American national security better served by collective security and work through international bodies such as the United Nations or by a more unilateral approach? Does unilateralism encourage a sense of American messianic mission and exceptionalism, and is this a dangerous approach to international relations in the twenty-first century?

3. In his criticism of the Truman Doctrine, former Vice President Henry A. Wallace argued that American military support for anti-Communist regimes could be manipulated to ensure backing for repressive regimes opposed to progressive democratic change. Did Wallace's warning come to fruition in the aid provided for authoritarian anti-Communist regimes in the Philippines, Indonesia, Iran, Nicaragua, Vietnam, and other countries? Did the Truman Doctrine ensure American victory over the totalitarian Soviet state, or did the interventionism justified by Truman's speech provoke a sense of "blowback" and anti-Americanism in the world?

4. The domino theory has dominated foreign policy discussions since World War II and the Munich Conference of 1938. The Munich analogy argues that western democracies followed a policy of appeasement that allowed Hitler to expand when he could have been stopped earlier, short of a global conflict. President Truman applied similar reasoning to Soviet designs toward Greece, Turkey, the Middle East, and Western Europe. The domino theory was also employed to justify the American military presence in Vietnam. Likewise, President George W. Bush insisted that the United States must fight terrorists in Iraq or the struggle would expand to the homeland. Do the domino theory and its corollary, the Munich analogy, misapply history and use generalizations to simplify historical realities that are more complex?

5. Many scholars have found connections between the anti-Communist foreign policy of the Truman Doctrine and the emergence of a national security state in which dissent is limited. Has the post-9/11 environment in the United States produced a similar sense of conformity and restrictions upon civil liberties? How does a society best navigate the balance between security and freedom?

Glossary

beset	to trouble persistently or to harass
coercion	force
condones	approves
corroborate	support with evidence
defects	problems
liquidating	terminating
modernization	acceptance of current ideas; in economic terms, the movement from an agricultural to an industrial economy and the growth of a middle class
national integrity	freedom from outside interference
static	unchanging
status quo	the existing condition or state of affairs
subterfuges	deceptive strategies or approaches
totalitarian regimes	forms of government in which one person or party exercises absolute control over all spheres of human life; often used to refer to Communist or Fascist dictatorships

TRUMAN DOCTRINE

Mr. President, Mr. Speaker, Members of the Congress of the United States:

The gravity of the situation which confronts the world today necessitates my appearance before a joint session of the Congress. The foreign policy and the national security of this country are involved.

One aspect of the present situation, which I wish to present to you at this time for your consideration and decision, concerns Greece and Turkey.

The United States has received from the Greek Government an urgent appeal for financial and economic assistance. Preliminary reports from the American Economic Mission now in Greece and reports from the American Ambassador in Greece corroborate the statement of the Greek Government that assistance is imperative if Greece is to survive as a free nation.

I do not believe that the American people and the Congress wish to turn a deaf ear to the appeal of the Greek Government.

Greece is not a rich country. Lack of sufficient natural resources has always forced the Greek people to work hard to make both ends meet. Since 1940, this industrious and peace loving country has suffered invasion, four years of cruel enemy occupation, and bitter internal strife.

When forces of liberation entered Greece they found that the retreating Germans had destroyed virtually all the railways, roads, port facilities, communications, and merchant marine. More than a thousand villages had been burned. Eighty-five per cent of the children were tubercular. Livestock, poultry, and draft animals had almost disappeared. Inflation had wiped out practically all savings.

As a result of these tragic conditions, a militant minority, exploiting human want and misery, was able to create political chaos which, until now, has made economic recovery impossible.

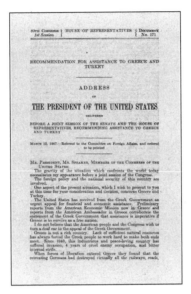

Greece is today without funds to finance the importation of those goods which are essential to bare subsistence. Under these circumstances the people of Greece cannot make progress in solving their problems of reconstruction. Greece is in desperate need of financial and economic assistance to enable it to resume purchases of food, clothing, fuel and seeds. These are indispensable for the subsistence of its people and are obtainable only from abroad. Greece must have help to import the goods necessary to restore internal order and security, so essential for economic and political recovery.

The Greek Government has also asked for the assistance of experienced American administrators, economists and technicians to insure that the financial and other aid given to Greece shall be used effectively in creating a stable and self-sustaining economy and in improving its public administration.

The very existence of the Greek state is today threatened by the terrorist activities of several thousand armed men, led by Communists, who defy the government's authority at a number of points, particularly along the northern boundaries. A Commission appointed by the United Nations Security Council is at present investigating disturbed conditions in northern Greece and alleged border violations along the frontier between Greece on the one hand and Albania, Bulgaria, and Yugoslavia on the other.

Meanwhile, the Greek Government is unable to cope with the situation. The Greek army is small and poorly equipped. It needs supplies and equipment if it is to restore the authority of the government throughout Greek territory. Greece must have assistance if it is to become a self-supporting and self-respecting democracy.

The United States must supply that assistance. We have already extended to Greece certain types of relief and economic aid but these are inadequate.

There is no other country to which democratic Greece can turn.

No other nation is willing and able to provide the necessary support for a democratic Greek government.

The British Government, which has been helping Greece, can give no further financial or economic aid after March 31. Great Britain finds itself under the necessity of reducing or liquidating its commitments in several parts of the world, including Greece.

We have considered how the United Nations might assist in this crisis. But the situation is an urgent one requiring immediate action and the United Nations and its related organizations are not in a position to extend help of the kind that is required.

It is important to note that the Greek Government has asked for our aid in utilizing effectively the financial and other assistance we may give to Greece, and in improving its public administration. It is of the utmost importance that we supervise the use of any funds made available to Greece; in such a manner that each dollar spent will count toward making Greece self-supporting, and will help to build an economy in which a healthy democracy can flourish.

No government is perfect. One of the chief virtues of a democracy, however, is that its defects are always visible and under democratic processes can be pointed out and corrected. The Government of Greece is not perfect. Nevertheless it represents eighty-five per cent of the members of the Greek Parliament who were chosen in an election last year. Foreign observers, including 692 Americans, considered this election to be a fair expression of the views of the Greek people.

The Greek Government has been operating in an atmosphere of chaos and extremism. It has made mistakes. The extension of aid by this country does not mean that the United States condones everything that the Greek Government has done or will do. We have condemned in the past, and we condemn now, extremist measures of the right or the left. We have in the past advised tolerance, and we advise tolerance now.

Greece's neighbor, Turkey, also deserves our attention.

The future of Turkey as an independent and economically sound state is clearly no less important to the freedom-loving peoples of the world than the future of Greece. The circumstances in which Turkey finds itself today are considerably different from those of Greece. Turkey has been spared the disasters that have beset Greece. And during the war, the United States and Great Britain furnished Turkey with material aid.

Nevertheless, Turkey now needs our support.

Since the war Turkey has sought financial assistance from Great Britain and the United States for the purpose of effecting that modernization necessary for the maintenance of its national integrity.

That integrity is essential to the preservation of order in the Middle East.

The British government has informed us that, owing to its own difficulties can no longer extend financial or economic aid to Turkey.

As in the case of Greece, if Turkey is to have the assistance it needs, the United States must supply it. We are the only country able to provide that help.

I am fully aware of the broad implications involved if the United States extends assistance to Greece and Turkey, and I shall discuss these implications with you at this time.

One of the primary objectives of the foreign policy of the United States is the creation of conditions in which we and other nations will be able to work out a way of life free from coercion. This was a fundamental issue in the war with Germany and Japan. Our victory was won over countries which sought to impose their will, and their way of life, upon other nations.

To ensure the peaceful development of nations, free from coercion, the United States has taken a leading part in establishing the United Nations. The United Nations is designed to make possible lasting freedom and independence for all its members. We shall not realize our objectives, however, unless we are willing to help free peoples to maintain their free institutions and their national integrity against aggressive movements that seek to impose upon them totalitarian regimes. This is no more than a frank recognition that totalitarian regimes imposed on free peoples, by direct or indirect aggression, undermine the foundations of international peace and hence the security of the United States.

The peoples of a number of countries of the world have recently had totalitarian regimes forced upon them against their will. The Government of the United States has made frequent protests against coercion and intimidation, in violation of the Yalta agreement, in Poland, Rumania, and Bulgaria. I must also state that in a number of other countries there have been similar developments.

At the present moment in world history nearly every nation must choose between alternative ways of life. The choice is too often not a free one.

One way of life is based upon the will of the majority, and is distinguished by free institutions, representative government, free elections, guarantees of individual liberty, freedom of speech and religion, and freedom from political oppression.

The second way of life is based upon the will of a minority forcibly imposed upon the majority. It relies upon terror and oppression, a controlled press and radio; fixed elections, and the suppression of personal freedoms.

I believe that it must be the policy of the United States to support free peoples who are resisting attempted subjugation by armed minorities or by outside pressures.

I believe that we must assist free peoples to work out their own destinies in their own way.

I believe that our help should be primarily through economic and financial aid which is essential to economic stability and orderly political processes.

The world is not static, and the status quo is not sacred. But we cannot allow changes in the status quo in violation of the Charter of the United Nations by such methods as coercion, or by such subterfuges as political infiltration. In helping free and independent nations to maintain their freedom, the United States will be giving effect to the principles of the Charter of the United Nations.

It is necessary only to glance at a map to realize that the survival and integrity of the Greek nation are of grave importance in a much wider situation. If Greece should fall under the control of an armed minority, the effect upon its neighbor, Turkey, would be immediate and serious. Confusion and disorder might well spread throughout the entire Middle East.

Moreover, the disappearance of Greece as an independent state would have a profound effect upon those countries in Europe whose peoples are struggling against great difficulties to maintain their freedoms and their independence while they repair the damages of war.

It would be an unspeakable tragedy if these countries, which have struggled so long against overwhelming odds, should lose that victory for which they sacrificed so much. Collapse of free institutions and loss of independence would be disastrous not only for them but for the world. Discouragement and possibly failure would quickly be the lot of neighboring peoples striving to maintain their freedom and independence.

Should we fail to aid Greece and Turkey in this fateful hour, the effect will be far reaching to the West as well as to the East.

We must take immediate and resolute action.

I therefore ask the Congress to provide authority for assistance to Greece and Turkey in the amount of $400,000,000 for the period ending June 30, 1948. In requesting these funds, I have taken into consideration the maximum amount of relief assistance which would be furnished to Greece out of the $350,000,000 which I recently requested that the Congress authorize for the prevention of starvation and suffering in countries devastated by the war.

In addition to funds, I ask the Congress to authorize the detail of American civilian and military personnel to Greece and Turkey, at the request of those countries, to assist in the tasks of reconstruction, and for the purpose of supervising the use of such financial and material assistance as may be furnished. I recommend that authority also be provided for the instruction and training of selected Greek and Turkish personnel.

Finally, I ask that the Congress provide authority which will permit the speediest and most effective use, in terms of needed commodities, supplies, and equipment, of such funds as may be authorized.

If further funds, or further authority, should be needed for purposes indicated in this message, I shall not hesitate to bring the situation before the Congress. On this subject the Executive and Legislative branches of the Government must work together.

This is a serious course upon which we embark.

I would not recommend it except that the alternative is much more serious. The United States contributed $341,000,000,000 toward winning World War II. This is an investment in world freedom and world peace.

The assistance that I am recommending for Greece and Turkey amounts to little more than 1 tenth of 1 per cent of this investment. It is only common sense that we should safeguard this investment and make sure that it was not in vain.

The seeds of totalitarian regimes are nurtured by misery and want. They spread and grow in the evil soil of poverty and strife. They reach their full growth when the hope of a people for a better life has died. We must keep that hope alive.

The free peoples of the world look to us for support in maintaining their freedoms.

If we falter in our leadership, we may endanger the peace of the world—and we shall surely endanger the welfare of our own nation.

Great responsibilities have been placed upon us by the swift movement of events.

I am confident that the Congress will face these responsibilities squarely.

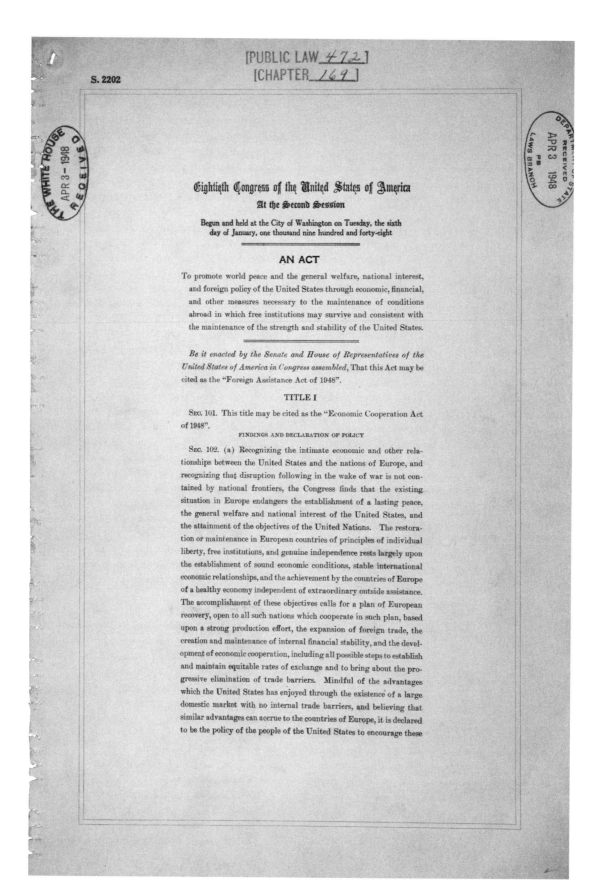

S. 2202

Eightieth Congress of the United States of America

At the Second Session

Begun and held at the City of Washington on Tuesday, the sixth
day of January, one thousand nine hundred and forty-eight

AN ACT

To promote world peace and the general welfare, national interest,
and foreign policy of the United States through economic, financial,
and other measures necessary to the maintenance of conditions
abroad in which free institutions may survive and consistent with
the maintenance of the strength and stability of the United States.

Be it enacted by the Senate and House of Representatives of the
United States of America in Congress assembled, That this Act may be
cited as the "Foreign Assistance Act of 1948".

TITLE I

SEC. 101. This title may be cited as the "Economic Cooperation Act
of 1948".

FINDINGS AND DECLARATION OF POLICY

SEC. 102. (a) Recognizing the intimate economic and other relationships between the United States and the nations of Europe, and
recognizing that disruption following in the wake of war is not contained by national frontiers, the Congress finds that the existing
situation in Europe endangers the establishment of a lasting peace,
the general welfare and national interest of the United States, and
the attainment of the objectives of the United Nations. The restoration or maintenance in European countries of principles of individual
liberty, free institutions, and genuine independence rests largely upon
the establishment of sound economic conditions, stable international
economic relationships, and the achievement by the countries of Europe
of a healthy economy independent of extraordinary outside assistance.
The accomplishment of these objectives calls for a plan of European
recovery, open to all such nations which cooperate in such plan, based
upon a strong production effort, the expansion of foreign trade, the
creation and maintenance of internal financial stability, and the development of economic cooperation, including all possible steps to establish
and maintain equitable rates of exchange and to bring about the progressive elimination of trade barriers. Mindful of the advantages
which the United States has enjoyed through the existence of a large
domestic market with no internal trade barriers, and believing that
similar advantages can accrue to the countries of Europe, it is declared
to be the policy of the people of the United States to encourage these

The Economic Cooperation Act of 1948 was initiated by George Marshall's address of June 5, 1947. (National Archives
and Records Administration)

MARSHALL PLAN

"Our policy is directed not against any country or doctrine but against hunger, poverty, desperation, and chaos."

Overview

On June 5, 1947, in a commencement address at Harvard University, General George C. Marshall announced the Marshall Plan, or the European Recovery Program, designed to aid in the economic rehabilitation of Europe after World War II. Marshall was a career army officer who served as chief of staff during World War II and later as secretary of state and secretary of defense. Fearing the expansion of Soviet Communism into Western Europe and further expansion into Eastern Europe if the European economy was not stabilized, U.S. officials allocated approximately $13 billion to rebuild the economy over four years. This aid hastened economic recovery in Europe and slowed the expansion of Communism on the Continent, prompting a number of hostile actions, such as the Berlin blockade, from the leaders of the Soviet Union. Scholars today generally regard the Marshall Plan as a successful initiative and a triumph of U.S. foreign policy in the post–World War II era. The program demonstrated to U.S. strategists the importance of economic aid in combating the spread of Communism.

Context

When President Harry Truman signed the Marshall Plan into law in April 1948 (under the name "Economic Cooperation Act of 1948"), World War II had been over for nearly three years, but the devastating impact of the fighting remained clearly evident. Approximately sixty million people perished as a result of the war, with twenty-five million under Soviet rule and four million from Germany dying during the fighting. U.S. casualties ran as high as 300,000. The Allied bombing campaign, which resulted in the deaths of 600,000 German civilians, left most of Germany's major cities severely damaged. Nazi efforts to eliminate Europe's Jews claimed the lives of six million Jews, and the war led to the dislocation of thousands more. As the historian Gerhard L. Weinberg points out, during the war years, "the costs in human life and suffering, in destruction and economic dislocation, had been of

absolutely unprecedented magnitude" (p. 898). Furthermore, with communication, transportation, and agricultural systems severely disrupted, the chances of reviving viable social, political, and economic systems seemed remote.

Tensions between Soviet officials and the leaders of the other Allied nations contributed to the difficulty in rebuilding Europe after the war. Poland, Czechoslovakia, Hungary, Romania, Bulgaria, Yugoslavia, and Albania remained under Soviet control at war's end, and the Soviets showed no sign of being willing to relinquish dominance of these countries. Germany had been split into four zones, with the Soviet Union, the United States, France, and Great Britain each controlling a zone. Berlin rested within the Soviet zone, and it, too, had been separated into four areas, each one under the control of one of these four countries. The wartime cooperation between the Soviets and the other Allied powers, however, withered away after the war, as some strategists began to fear the possibility of a third world war between Communist and capitalist nations. For the Allies, stopping Soviet expansion, while avoiding war, became a bedeviling problem.

In the two years following the war, starvation and a shortage of coal combined with harsh winter weather made life a misery for many Europeans. President Truman, a Missourian, compared postwar Europe's desperation with the hardship that had descended on the southern United States after the American Civil War. U.S. officials worried that the suffering and dislocation endured by Europeans after the war would encourage those who were suffering to turn to the Communists for relief, evident by the growing Communist insurgencies in Greece, Turkey, and Italy.

To combat this threat, Truman developed a two-pronged strategy. The first part was the Truman Doctrine, under which the governments of Greece and Turkey received large sums of U.S. money to help in their resistance against Communist insurgencies. This aid proved important in light of the fact that at this time Greek officials lost access to British economic aid, which had been helping to stabilize their government. British officials, lacking money for foreign ventures, were struggling with their own economic ills. The other part of Truman's strategy was the Marshall Plan, designed to help lift Europe out of an economic quagmire and alleviate the desperate conditions in which Communism might thrive. A conference to be held in Paris was called to

1945

■ **April 12**
President Franklin D.
Roosevelt dies at Warm
Springs, Georgia.

■ **May 7**
The Nazis surrender to Allies,
ending the war in the
European theater.

■ **August 6**
Americans drop atomic bomb
on Hiroshima, Japan.

■ **August 9**
Americans drop atomic bomb
on Nagasaki, Japan.

■ **September 2**
Japanese surrender to Allies,
ending the war in the Pacific
theater.

■ **October 24**
UN officials ratify United
Nations charter.

1947

■ **May 22**
President Harry S. Truman
signs bill allocating aid to
Greece and Turkey to combat
Communist influence in those
two countries.

■ **June 5**
Secretary of State George C.
Marshall outlines what would
become the European
Recovery Program, or the
Marshall Plan, in a Harvard
University graduation speech.

■ **July**
"The Sources of Soviet
Conduct," George F. Kennan's
article dealing with his
proposed "containment"
policy, appears in Foreign
Affairs.

1948

■ **April 3**
President Truman signs law
allocating first Marshall Plan
payments for European
recovery.

■ **June 12**
Soviet blockade of Berlin
begins.

■ **June 26**
The Allies, refusing to
surrender their sectors of
Berlin to Soviet control,
respond to the blockade with
an airlift.

discuss Europe's economic needs and the U.S. aid offer. Sixteen nations, including Greece, Great Britain, France, and Italy, sent officials to the meeting, but Soviet leaders refused to attend. From these first steps the Marshall Plan would grow into a massive effort to rebuild Europe.

The Truman Doctrine and the Marshall Plan became significant aspects of the "containment" policy of U.S. officials. First developed by George F. Kennan, the containment policy was based on the view that only Soviet expansionist tendencies posed a long-term threat to the West. The Soviets' Communist ideology and Josef Stalin's dictatorship, Kennan argued, would dissolve in the near future and therefore pose less of a threat. Containment became the pillar of U.S. strategy for the next thirty years, and the collapse of the Soviet Union proved Kennan's analysis trenchant and his strategy effective. During that time, U.S. officials implemented an array of military, ideological, and economic strategies to contain Communism. The European Recovery Program represented their boldest and most extensive effort to halt Communist expansion through economic aid.

About the Author

Born on December 31, 1880, in Uniontown, Pennsylvania, George Catlett Marshall grew up in a prosperous family coal-mining region in western Pennsylvania. As a boy, he was a below-average student, struggling especially with mathematics. History, however, interested him, and he showed promise in that subject. Despite his academic deficiencies, he enrolled in 1897 at Virginia Military Institute (VMI) in Lexington, Virginia. Marshall matured at VMI, showing improvement as a student, playing on the football team, and graduating with a degree in civil engineering in 1901. "What I learned at VMI," he would later say, "was self-control, discipline, so that it was ground in. I learned also the problem of managing men" (http://www.marshall-foundation.org/about/chronology.html). These lessons served him well over a military and civilian career spanning half a century.

Marshall developed a gift for the organizational work related to combat, although throughout his career he rarely fought in battle. For instance, a major offensive launched toward the end of World War I owed its success partly to his expertise at moving and positioning troops. During the war, he worked with General John J. Pershing and gained important military experience, emerging from the war as a trusted military thinker with a bright future.

Marshall served as chief of staff throughout World War II, showing again his brilliant skill for organization and strategy. Prior to U.S. entry into the war, he had urged President Franklin Roosevelt to strengthen and enlarge the relatively small U.S. fighting force, proving effective in procuring funds from Congress for the military. He later traveled widely throughout the European and Pacific theaters while playing a major role in formulating Allied strategy.

Marshall also played a major part in the D-day invasion, code-named Operation Overlord. The successful invasion of the Normandy beaches on the coast of France opened a second front in the European theater, placing Nazi forces in a vice between the American, British, and Canadian forces that, after landing at Normandy, began closing in on them from the west and Russian troops who had been fighting the Nazis since 1941 in the east. High-ranking officers who participated in the invasion had often received Marshall's recommendation to participate in this crucial mission. Marshall also suggested deception plans implemented by the Allies to trick Nazi forces into thinking the invasion force would land somewhere other than Normandy. So crucial was his work to the Allied victory that President Truman declared, "General Marshall, more than any other man, was responsible for winning that war" (qtd. in Miller, p. 234). Marshall became secretary of state in 1945.

Truman clearly admired Marshall and wanted him to receive credit for the European recovery program. He also feared that if his name were attached to the plan, Congress would refuse to pass it into law, so unpopular was he with many members of that body. Truman made the correct decision: Congress passed the Marshall Plan by wide margins in both the House of Representatives and the Senate.

Marshall married twice. His first wife, Elizabeth Coles, whom Marshall had wed in 1902, died suddenly in 1927. Three years later, he and Katherine Tupper Brown wed, their marriage lasting nearly thirty years. Upon his death in 1959, Marshall, having rarely seen combat, ranked as one of the country's most admired military figures, remembered for his contributions to Allied victory and his sterling personal qualities.

Explanation and Analysis of the Document

Marshall offers a vague outline of the U.S. plan to revive Western Europe's economy in a Harvard University commencement address on June 5, 1947. No specific aspects of the Marshall Plan receive attention during his brief talk. In paragraph 1, he describes the mind-boggling decline Europe had experienced as a result of the war. The suffering of Europeans, Marshall laments, was lost on citizens of the United States. It also threatens, he says, the stability of European governments. Marshall's assessment contains no hint of exaggeration. World War II had left Europe's economy in shambles while boosting the U.S. economy. The war improved the financial state of many Americans, who, as Marshall suggests, know little about the hardships of Europeans. His mention of unstable European governments is no doubt an oblique reference to Greece and Turkey, where Communist insurgencies were growing, as well as a reference to the struggling governments of a number of other countries.

Marshall outlines in more detail the economic disarray afflicting Europe in the wake of World War II in paragraph 2. The fighting, he points out, soaked up the resources of the warring nations. Since virtually no sphere of the European economy—banking, currency, insurance, and industrial production—emerged from the war unscathed, only a

www.milestonedocuments.com

Time Line

1948

■ **November**
Truman wins election to a full term as president, defeating Republican Thomas E. Dewey.

1949

■ **April 4**
U.S. joins the North Atlantic Treaty Organization.

■ **May 11**
Berlin blockade ends. French, British, and U.S. sectors of Berlin remain under the control of these countries.

■ **September**
Allies end Berlin airlift.

major long-term effort holds out the hope of reestablishing a sound economy. Marshall makes no estimate concerning the amount of money the United States might be willing to contribute to economic recovery. President Truman suggested privately that the United States would have to contribute approximately $16 billion to make the plan effective.

In paragraph 3, Marshall explains that the breakdown of the economic relationship between rural and urban areas stands out as an especially severe economic crisis. Worthless currencies and a scarcity of consumer goods provide no motivation for farmers to produce crops for transport to cities, causing starvation in urban areas and straining government budgets. A revival of the urban-rural relationship, Marshall declares, is crucial to the resumption of normal economic life.

In paragraphs 4 and 5, Marshall explains that U.S. aid, especially food, is also vital to Europeans, who lack the money to pay for such necessities. If the United States refuses to give this aid, which Marshall estimates would have to be extended for at least three years, it faces the daunting prospect of greater chaos in Europe. To Marshall, reestablishing sound European currencies stands out as a prerequisite for the rebuilding of industry and agriculture.

In paragraph 6, Marshall points out an obvious fact: The economic turmoil in Europe threatens the U.S. economy; therefore, it is in the best interests of the United States to help rebuild war-torn countries. Marshall also links Europe's economic soundness to its political stability. Although the Marshall Plan would be designed specifically to improve the economies of Europe to thwart the advancing tide of Communism, Marshall claims that U.S. officials hope only to restore economic confidence and prosperity to the Continent. Without referring specifically to the Soviet Union, Marshall condemns any effort to interfere with the economic rebuilding of Europe and promises U.S. opposition to any country that does so, subtly casting the United States as Europe's protector and the Soviet Union as its antagonist working against the humanitarian goal of helping to resurrect normal productive life for Europeans out of the chaos that engulfed them.

George Marshall (Library of Congress)

In paragraph 7, Marshall rejects the possibility that the United States will act alone to rebuild Europe in favor of a plan calling for the cooperation of European powers in recovery efforts. Inviting the leaders of every country willing to participate to join in the planning for recovery, he adroitly describes the plan as a humanitarian effort dependent on European leadership. In the eighth and final paragraph, Marshall expresses confidence in this venture to solve Europe's serious economic ills while simultaneously allowing the United States to fulfill its mission as a world leader.

Audience

Marshall's immediate audience was, of course, the crowd that attended Harvard University's graduation exercises in the spring of 1947, but he designed his address for a worldwide audience. More specifically, he aimed to impress members of the U.S. Congress, which would either reject his plan or craft it into legislation. He was also addressing all U.S. citizens, whose taxes would pay for the Marshall Plan; the citizens of Europe's war-torn countries, who stood to benefit from the plan; and the leaders of the Soviet Union, whose expansionist policy the Marshall Plan was designed to counter. Each group found in the speech reason to take seriously Marshall's proposal for U.S. aid.

The Republican Party controlled Congress in 1947; therefore, President Truman, a Democrat, was forced to rely on Republican votes to have his initiatives passed into

legislation. Perhaps because some Republicans, such as Ohio's senator Robert A. Taft, were repelled by the amount of money the Marshall Plan might cost, Marshall avoided mentioning any dollar figure in his speech and stressed the importance of European leadership in economic recovery. The Marshall Plan, however, won the approval of the more liberal wing of the Republican Party, led by Thomas E. Dewey, Truman's opponent in the 1948 presidential contest. A year after congressional passage of the European Recovery Program, Truman never missed an opportunity to ridicule the "do nothing" Congress on the campaign trail. Over the next three years, however, the Republican Congress allocated $13 billion of Marshall Plan money to aid in the restoration of the European economy.

U.S. strategists originally believed that the European Recovery Program would cost the United States $17 billion, a huge sum in the late 1940s. They pointed out, however, that this investment in European economic recovery would reap dividends for the United States because halting the spread of Communism through economic aid lessened the chances of a more expensive war with the Soviet Union, thereby bolstering American security. These arguments impressed the public. Polls revealed strong public support for the Marshall Plan, support that made it easier for Congress to endorse the program.

Along with targeting his message to members of Congress and the American public, Marshall surely hoped to encourage the suffering peoples of Europe to resist the lure of Communism by his offer of U.S. aid. He showed sensitivity to their plight by describing their ordeal to his listeners, making clear that American officials had not forgotten them. Many European leaders would eagerly accept help from the United States.

Soviet leaders, condemning the European Recovery Program as a capitalist scheme, rejected aid through the Marshall Plan and ordered its satellites to do likewise. The Soviet dictator Josef Stalin's hostility toward the Marshall Plan came as no surprise to the Truman administration. The Soviets surely understood the warning not to interfere. They nevertheless prepared to resist the execution of the Marshall Plan in Europe.

Impact

The historian Thomas A. Bailey praised the Marshall Plan as "a spectacular success," benefiting both Western Europe and the United States (p. 801). The collapse of European economic life directly threatened the U.S. economy, which needed Europe, especially Germany, to rebound from the war in order to maintain a stable international economic order and its own economic soundness as well. Reestablishing a stable German economy helped prevent the repeat of the mistakes the Allies made after World War I, when the German economy collapsed partly because of vindictive Allied policies, such as forcing the Germans to pay war reparations to the Allies. U.S. officials blocked the implementation of such vindictive policies

"The truth of the matter is that Europe's requirements for the next 3 or 4 years of foreign food and other essential products—principally from America—are so much greater than her present ability to pay that she must have substantial additional help, or face economic, social, and political deterioration of a very grave character."

(Paragraph 4)

"The remedy lies in breaking the vicious circle and restoring the confidence of the European people in the economic future of their own countries and of Europe as a whole."

(Paragraph 5)

"It is logical that the United States should do whatever it is able to do to assist in the return of normal economic health in the world, without which there can be no political stability and no assured peace. Our policy is directed not against any country or doctrine but against hunger, poverty, desperation, and chaos. Its purpose should be the revival of working economy in the world so as to permit the emergence of political and social conditions in which free institutions can exist."

(Paragraph 6)

"Any government that is willing to assist in the task of recovery will find full cooperation, I am sure, on the part of the United States Government. Any government which maneuvers to block the recovery of other countries cannot expect help from us."

(Paragraph 6)

"It would be neither fitting nor efficacious for this Government to undertake to draw up unilaterally a program designed to place Europe on its feet economically. This is the business of the Europeans. The initiative, I think, must come from Europe."

(Paragraph 7)

toward Germany after World War II, showing that the Marshall Plan allowed U.S. strategists immense influence in shaping postwar Europe.

Although it has been suggested that the revival of the German economy was the main reason for the European Recovery Program, not the halting of Communist expansion, U.S. aid was effective in combating Communist influence in Europe. In Italian elections after the war, Marshall Plan money played a role in the Communist defeat at the polls. Thirty nine billion dollars was added to the gross national product of Western Europe, agricultural output improved slightly, and industrial production made impressive gains while the Marshall Plan was in effect. The Marshall Plan proved a boon to the United States and Western Europe.

Smarting over the U.S. effort, Soviet authorities attempted to force the French, British, and Americans out of the sectors of Berlin each power controlled by ordering all roads leading into these zones closed. Wrote Truman, "The European Recovery Program was beginning to succeed. The blockade of Berlin was international Communism's counterattack" (vol. 2, p. 123). The three Allied powers, instead of evacuating Berlin, sustained the citizens living in their sectors with food and other necessary goods by flying them into the city. Lasting for approximately one year, the Berlin airlift demonstrated Allied resolve to protect the sections of Berlin under its control. The city had become a focal point of the cold war and a symbol of the struggle against Communism. The Allies even decided to risk a remote possibility of war by implementing the airlift. Their efforts reaped benefits, however, for the Soviet blockade ended in the spring of 1949.

The impact of the Marshall Plan on Europe and on the cold war was enormous. In Truman's opinion, "The Marshall Plan will go down in history as one of America's greatest contributions to the peace of the world. I think the world now realizes that without the Marshall Plan it would have been difficult for Western Europe to remain free from the tyranny of Communism" (vol. 2, p. 119). Marshall's career as an officer had already been outstanding before his name was attached to the European Recovery Program, but the plan burnished his reputation even further, and he won the Nobel Peace Prize in December 1953, the only soldier ever to receive the award.

Related Documents

Bland, Larry I., and Sharon Ritenour Stevens, eds. *The Papers of George Catlett Marshall*. 5 vols. Baltimore, Md.: Johns Hopkins University Press, 1981–2003. These papers deal with Marshall's life and career from December 1880 to January 1947, several months prior to Marshall's announcement that the Truman administration planned to revitalize the war-torn economies of Europe.

Ferrell, Robert H., ed. *Off the Record: The Private Papers of Harry S. Truman*. New York: Harper & Row, 1980. In this book, President Truman and Secretary of State Dean Acheson discuss the Marshall Plan and the officer for which it was named in chapter 21, "General Marshall and the Marshall Plan."

Bibliography

■ Articles

Ellwood, David. "'You Too Can Be Like Us'": Selling The Marshall Plan." *History Today* 48 (October 1998): 33–39.

Kennan, George A. "The Sources of Soviet Conduct." *Foreign Affairs* 25 (July 1947): 566–582.

■ Books

Bailey, Thomas A. *A Diplomatic History of the American People*, 10th ed. Englewood Cliffs, N.J.: Prentice-Hall, 1980.

Gaddis, John Lewis. *We Now Know: Rethinking Cold War History*. New York: Oxford University Press, 1997.

———. *The Cold War: A New History*. New York: Penguin, 2005.

Gimbel, John. *The Origins of the Marshall Plan*. Stanford, Calif.: Stanford University Press, 1976.

Judt, Tony. *Postwar: A History of Europe since 1945*. New York: Penguin, 2005.

Kimball, Warren F. *The Juggler: Franklin Roosevelt as Wartime Statesman*. Princeton, N.J.: Princeton University Press, 1991.

McCullough, David L. *Truman*. New York: Simon and Schuster, 1992.

Miller, Merle. *Plain Speaking: An Oral Biography of Harry S Truman*. New York: Putnam, 1973.

Pogue, Forrest C. *George C. Marshall*. 4 vols. New York: Viking, 1963–1987.

Schulzinger, Robert D. *U.S. Diplomacy since 1900*, 5th ed. New York: Oxford University Press, 2002.

Truman, Harry S. *Memoirs of Harry S. Truman: Years of Trial and Hope*. 2 vols. Garden City, N.Y.: Doubleday, 1955–1956.

Weinberg, Gerhard L. *A World at Arms: A Global History of World War II*, 2nd ed. New York: Cambridge University Press, 2005.

■ Web Sites

"Detailed Marshall Chronology." George C. Marshall Foundation Web site.
http://www.marshallfoundation.org/about/chronology.html. Accessed on February 13, 2008.

Harry S. Truman Library and Museum Web site.
http://www.trumanlibrary.org/. Accessed on January 4, 2008.

—By James Humphreys

Questions for Further Study

1. Leaders of the United States faced in 1865 the difficulty of rebuilding the southern states after the Civil War. How does the Marshall Plan compare with efforts implemented by the U.S. government to reconstruct the southern states?

2. The Marshall Plan was designed to aid in the economic rebuilding of Europe, to alleviate human suffering, and to stem Communist advances. What other methods did U.S. strategists employ during the cold war to weaken Communism around the globe?

3. The Soviet Union collapsed in the early 1990s. In the long run, what role did the Marshall Plan play in the Soviet Union's demise?

4. U.S. forces have occupied Iraq since 2003. Should the United States implement a plan similar to the Marshall Plan for Iraq? What lessons does the assistance given Europe to rebuild economically after World War II hold for U.S. strategists dealing with Iraq?

5. Is there a contradiction in a military officer, like Marshall, receiving the Nobel Peace Prize? In your opinion, did he deserve the prize? Why or why not?

Glossary

appraisement	analysis
close of hostilities	end of a war
palliative	anything that lessens suffering
perpetuate	promote
piecemeal	gradually

MARSHALL PLAN

I need not tell you gentlemen that the world situation is very serious. That must be apparent to all intelligent people. I think one difficulty is that the problem is one of such enormous complexity that the very mass of facts presented to the public by press and radio make it exceedingly difficult for the man in the street to reach a clear appraisement of the situation. Furthermore, the people of this country are distant from the troubled areas of the earth and it is hard for them to comprehend the plight and consequent reaction of the long-suffering peoples, and the effect of those reactions on their governments in connection with our efforts to promote peace in the world.

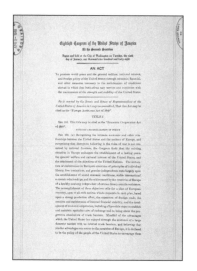

In considering the requirements for the rehabilitation of Europe the physical loss of life, the visible destruction of cities, factories, mines, and railroads was correctly estimated, but it has become obvious during recent months that this visible destruction was probably less serious than the dislocation of the entire fabric of European economy. For the past 10 years conditions have been highly abnormal. The feverish maintenance of the war effort engulfed all aspects of national economics. Machinery has fallen into disrepair or is entirely obsolete. Under the arbitrary and destructive Nazi rule, virtually every possible enterprise was geared into the German war machine. Long-standing commercial ties, private institutions, banks, insurance companies and shipping companies disappeared, through the loss of capital, absorption through nationalization or by simple destruction. In many countries, confidence in the local currency has been severely shaken. The breakdown of the business structure of Europe during the war was complete. Recovery has been seriously retarded by the fact that 2 years after the close of hostilities a peace settlement with Germany and Austria has not been agreed upon. But even given a more prompt solution of these difficult problems, the rehabilitation of the economic structure of Europe quite evidently will require a much longer time and greater effort than had been foreseen.

There is a phase of this matter which is both interesting and serious. The farmer has always produced the foodstuffs to exchange with the city dweller for the other necessities of life. This division of labor is the basis of modern civilization. At the present time it is threatened with breakdown. The town and city industries are not producing adequate goods to exchange with the food-producing farmer. Raw materials and fuel are in short supply. Machinery is lacking or worn out. The farmer or the peasant cannot find the goods for sale which he desires to purchase. So the sale of his farm produce for money which he cannot use seems to him unprofitable transaction. He, therefore, has withdrawn many fields from crop cultivation and is using them for grazing. He feeds more grain to stock and finds for himself and his family an ample supply of food, however short he may be on clothing and the other ordinary gadgets of civilization. Meanwhile people in the cities are short of food and fuel. So the governments are forced to use their foreign money and credits to procure these necessities abroad. This process exhausts funds which are urgently needed for reconstruction. Thus a very serious situation is rapidly developing which bodes no good for the world. The modern system of the division of labor upon which the exchange of products is based is in danger of breaking down.

The truth of the matter is that Europe's requirements for the next 3 or 4 years of foreign food and other essential products—principally from America—are so much greater than her present ability to pay that she must have substantial additional help, or face economic, social, and political deterioration of a very grave character.

The remedy lies in breaking the vicious circle and restoring the confidence of the European people in the economic future of their own countries and of

Europe as a whole. The manufacturer and the farmer throughout wide areas must be able and willing to exchange their products for currencies the continuing value of which is not open to question.

Aside from the demoralizing effect on the world at large and the possibilities of disturbances arising as a result of the desperation of the people concerned, the consequences to the economy of the United States should be apparent to all. It is logical that the United States should do whatever it is able to do to assist in the return of normal economic health in the world, without which there can be no political stability and no assured peace. Our policy is directed not against any country or doctrine but against hunger, poverty, desperation, and chaos. Its purpose should be the revival of working economy in the world so as to permit the emergence of political and social conditions in which free institutions can exist. Such assistance, I am convinced, must not be on a piecemeal basis as various crises develop. Any assistance that this Government may render in the future should provide a cure rather than a mere palliative. Any government that is willing to assist in the task of recovery will find full cooperation, I am sure, on the part of the United States Government. Any government which maneuvers to block the recovery of other countries cannot expect help from us. Furthermore, governments, political parties, or groups which seek to perpetuate human misery in order to profit therefrom politically or otherwise will encounter the opposition of the United States.

It is already evident that, before the United States Government can proceed much further in its efforts to alleviate the situation and help start the European world on its way to recovery, there must be some agreement among the countries of Europe as to the requirements of the situation and the part those countries themselves will take in order to give proper effect to whatever action might be undertaken by this Government. It would be neither fitting nor efficacious for this Government to undertake to draw up unilaterally a program designed to place Europe on its feet economically. This is the business of the Europeans. The initiative, I think, must come from Europe. The role of this country should consist of friendly aid in the drafting of a European program so far as it may be practical for us to do so. The program should be a joint one, agreed to by a number, if not all European nations.

An essential part of any successful action on the part of the United States is an understanding on the part of the people of America of the character of the problem and the remedies to be applied. Political passion and prejudice should have no part. With foresight, and a willingness on the part of our people to face up to the vast responsibilities which history has clearly placed upon our country, the difficulties I have outlined can and will be overcome.

"It shall be unlawful for any individual employed by the United States ... to participate in any strike."

Overview

The passage of the Taft-Hartley Act, also called the Labor-Management Relations Act, over President Harry Truman's veto on June 23, 1947, ended the national policy established with the enactment of the Wagner Act (National Labor Relations Act) in 1935. Under this policy, the federal government had supported workers' self-organization into unions and for collective bargaining. Unions increased their membership more than fourfold between 1933 and 1945 thanks in part to the Wagner Act, the friendliness of the New Deal Democratic administration of Franklin D. Roosevelt, and the expansion of the economy during World War II. The campaign of business organizations to amend the Wagner Act, begun after the Supreme Court declared the law constitutional in 1937, was renewed in earnest after World War II. After a year of numerous strikes, some of which found unions and Truman seriously at odds, the Republicans campaigned on the slogan "Had Enough?" and won decisive control of both houses of Congress in the 1946 election. Passage of the Taft-Hartley Act followed, with the majority of House Democrats and nearly half of Senate Democrats joining their Republican colleagues.

The 1947 law retained National Labor Relations Board (NLRB) responsibility for acting on complaints of unfair labor practices by employers and conducting representation elections for employees to select collective bargaining agents. It added to the NLRB's purview a set of union unfair labor practices. In addition, the act outlawed the closed shop, the secondary boycott, political contributions and expenditures by unions for candidates for federal offices, and strikes by federal employees. It permitted states to outlaw the union shop and private parties to sue unions. The protection of unions against injunctions established by the 1932 Norris-LaGuardia Act was removed, with both the NLRB and the president authorized to seek injunctions, the latter in strikes affecting the nation's health and welfare. The act requires unions to file financial and other reports and union officials to file affidavits declaring they were not Communists for the union to have access to the NLRB. Although Truman secured election in his own right in 1948

by campaigning against the Taft-Hartley Act and the "do-nothing" Republican Congress, the new Democratic-controlled Congress did not repeal the Taft-Hartley Act. Union efforts to secure revisions of the act in subsequent decades failed, and most of its provisions remained in effect six decades later. In part because of the unfavorable legal climate created by Taft-Hartley, union membership as a percentage of the labor force plummeted to the pre–New Deal level by the early twenty-first century.

Context

Business executives and conservatives reacted negatively to the support for labor unions demonstrated by Franklin Roosevelt's New Deal. The business campaign to amend the Wagner Act led to a House of Representatives investigation by a special committee to investigate the NLRB in 1939–1940, named the Smith Committee, for chairperson Howard Smith, a Virginia Democrat. Investigators publicized charges of pro–Congress of Industrial Organizations (CIO) and pro-Communist bias in the administration of the law. Although a restrictive bill was passed by the House of Representatives, Roosevelt was able to fend off the drive to amend the Wagner Act by appointing moderates to replace liberals on the NLRB. This led to resignations by left-wingers who held leading staff positions at the agency.

Business remained dissatisfied with unions' economic and political power, but a climate of cooperation between business and the Roosevelt administration and business and labor prevailed when the country pulled together during World War II. The National War Labor Board gave some assistance to unions but kept wages in check. Unions made a no-strike pledge and, for the most part, restrained their members during the war. Negative public reaction to wartime coal mine strikes, however, led to the passage over Roosevelt's veto of the Smith-Connally Anti-Strike Act (also called the War Labor Disputes Act) in 1943. This act provided for a notification procedure and injunctions against nationally significant strikes during the war emergency.

After World War II, several large corporations, the National Association of Manufacturers, and the U.S. Chamber of Commerce renewed the campaign to amend

Time Line

1932

■ **March 23**
President Herbert Hoover signs Norris-LaGuardia Act outlawing use of anti-union injunctions.

1935

■ **July 5**
President Franklin Roosevelt signs the Wagner Act (National Labor Relations Act).

1937

■ **April 12**
National Labor Relations Board v. Jones & Laughlin Steel Corp.; Supreme Court affirms the constitutionality of the Wagner Act.

1939

■ **July 20**
House of Representatives creates a special committee to investigate the NLRB (Smith Committee), which conducts extensive hearings.

1940

■ **June 7**
House passes Smith Bill to amend the Wagner Act, but it fails in Senate Labor Committee.

■ **November 15**
Roosevelt appoints Harry Millis to replace liberal J. Warren Madden as chair of NLRB.

1943

■ **June 25**
Smith-Connally Anti-Strike Act (War Labor Disputes Act) is enacted over President Roosevelt's veto.

1946

■ **January**
U.S. strike wave begins; by the end of the year 4.6 million workers strike.

■ **May**
President Harry Truman authorizes government seizure of railroads in response to strike threat and of coal mines in response to strike and proposes temporary emergency legislation drafting railroad workers.

---

the Wagner Act. CIO unions sought sizable wage increases to make up for reduced take-home pay after the war. Hoping to avoid reconversion shutdowns, Truman vacillated between supporting and opposing unions. In May 1946 he proposed legislation to draft railroad workers in response to a union strike threat. With few reform achievements and divisions on labor and foreign policy issues, Democrats failed to turn out their vote in the 1946 congressional election. The Republican campaign against shortages, strikes, and Communists in government gave them majorities in both houses of Congress. A massively financed antiunion campaign by business groups created a climate that led Congress to ignore large protests by unions and enact the Taft-Hartley Act, overriding Truman's veto. Truman's veto message contained sharp criticisms of the law, but he did not work to persuade Democrats to sustain his veto. His message was aimed at securing labor's vote in the 1948 election rather than preventing the bill, which he privately favored, from becoming law.

About the Author

The Taft-Hartley Act combined features of the Senate's Taft bill and the House of Representative's Hartley bill. The authors of both bills, which had many elements in common, drew on the 1940 Smith Committee investigation of the NLRB. Representative Howard Smith was involved in the drafting of the Hartley bill, with much of the drafting taking place in his congressional office.

Elected to the Senate in 1938, Robert A. Taft of Ohio was the son of the former president William Howard Taft. He was a leader of Republican conservatives and isolationists, chair of the Republican Policy Committee, and chair of the Senate Labor and Public Welfare Committee in the Eightieth Congress. Taft believed that rank-and-file workers were being misused by union leaders. Representative Fred Hartley, Jr., of New Jersey, chair of the House Committee on Education and Labor, was first elected to the House of Representatives in 1928 and retired at the end of the Eightieth Congress.

Assisting in the drafting of the Hartley bill, in addition to Representative Smith, were several attorneys and representatives of large corporations, who consulted closely with the National Association of Manufacturers. House Majority Leader Charles Halleck, an Indiana Republican and key figure in the attempt to pass the Case bill in 1946, secured the services for the House Committee on Education and Labor of Gerald Morgan, a District of Columbia attorney with corporate clients, as chief drafter of the bill. Others involved in writing the Hartley bill were William Ingles, a lobbyist for Allis-Chalmers, J. I. Case, and Inland Steel; Theodore Iserman, an attorney for Chrysler; and Gerald Reilly, a former NLRB member disliked by unions who became a lobbyist for General Electric and General Motors in 1949. The Hartley bill was reviewed by the House Republican Steering Committee and submitted on the House floor on April 10, 1947. Members of the House

Committee on Education and Labor had the bill read to them on April 10 and April 11. The minority had two days to draft its report, and the committee voted to approve the majority Hartley bill on April 12, 1947.

In drafting the Taft bill, individuals with NLRB experience played important roles, including Reilly, special counsel to the committee and the key author; Thomas Shroyer, counsel to the committee; and Robert Denham, an NLRB trial examiner known as an opponent of the Wagner Act. The Democratic minority had a chance to voice its ideas, and Senator James Murray, a Montana Democrat, presented a substitute bill that was defeated by a wide margin. In the conference committee reconciling the two bills, Morgan, Reilly, and Shroyer were key advisers. Although the press painted the Taft bill as mild, Taft himself stated that the Senate bill included "three-fourths of the objectives 'pressed on us very strenuously by employers'" (Lee, p. 73). The final legislation was closer to the House version.

Explanation and Analysis of the Document

◆ Statements of Purpose in Section 1 and Title I, Section 101, Section 1

Section 1 gives a short title, the "Labor Management Relations Act, 1947," to this first revision of the Wagner Act and specifies the purposes of the legislation. One purpose is to minimize "industrial strife." This can be done, the paragraph asserts, if "employers, employees, and labor organization" recognize one another's "legitimate rights" but, more important, recognize that no one has the right to threaten "the public health, safety, or interest." The second paragraph indicates that the act will "prescribe the legitimate rights of both employees and employers" and provide procedures to prevent either party from interfering with the rights of the other and, most important, to forbid "practices" by either party that harm "the general welfare" and protect the "rights of the public" in labor disputes.

Title 1, Section 101, Section 1 amends the Wagner Act's Findings and Declaration of Policy. According to the 1935 law, the causes of industrial strife were the denial by employers of workers' right to organize and their failure to accept collective bargaining. The purposes of the law were to correct an imbalance of bargaining power between labor and management, protect workers' right to organize, and encourage the practice of collective bargaining. Whereas the Wagner Act stated that employers deny rights and refuse to bargain, the 1947 act makes the far less sweeping critical judgment that "some employers" commit such acts. The Taft-Hartley Act also adds an antilabor paragraph that states that the rights guaranteed by the act are contingent on the elimination of some union practices such as "strikes and other forms of industrial strife or unrest" or other "concerted activities" that hurt the interests of the public and "the free flow of ... commerce."

The conflicting statements of purpose in the 1947 legislation stem from the differing visions of the Hartley bill passed by the House of Representatives and the Taft bill

www.milestonedocuments.com

Time Line

1946

■ **June 11**
Truman vetoes the Case bill, major permanent revision of Wagner Act.

■ **November 5**
Republicans win control of both the House of Representatives and the Senate, the first time in sixteen years it has had control of either house.

1947

■ **June 23**
Taft-Hartley Act (Labor-Management Relations Act of 1947) becomes law as Senate joins House in overriding Truman's veto.

■ **August 22**
Taft-Hartley amendments to Wagner Act take effect.

1959

■ **September 14**
Landrum-Griffin Act (Labor Management Reporting and Disclosure Act) becomes law, dropping some Taft-Hartley Act provisions but adding new measures to review internal union procedures.

1978

■ **June**
Senate with fifty-eight affirmative votes falls two votes short of ending filibuster and passing a labor law reform bill.

passed by the Senate. The Taft bill, a bit less harsh toward unions, kept the Wagner Act wording with its pro–collective bargaining statement but added changes that made it less pro-labor. The new declaration of policy, which originated in the Hartley bill, focuses on ending industrial strife. The Hartley bill would have eliminated the pro–collective bargaining statement. The Conference Committee compromised by including the new statement of policy and the Senate's amended version of the Wagner Act wording.

◆ Section 2: Definitions

The definition of "person" in paragraph (1) is modified in the 1947 act to include labor organizations, consistent with the addition to the act of a list of unfair labor practices by unions, a concept foreign to the Wagner Act. In defining employers in paragraph (2), the Wagner Act had included any person acting in the interest of an employer. The 1947 act revises this to those acting "as an agent" of an employer. Labor-relations professionals worried that some

Representative Howard Smith, 1957 (AP Photo/Henry Griffin)

persons committing unfair labor practices for the employer would not be held accountable for their acts with the new wording. The 1947 law also expands the list of excluded employers by adding government corporations, Federal Reserve banks, and nonprofit hospitals. The latter exclusion nullified a 1944 Supreme Court decision supporting workers' collective bargaining rights at a Washington, D.C., nonprofit hospital. The nonprofit hospital exclusion ended in 1974 when workers won a qualified right to bargain collectively and strike.

In defining who was considered a covered employee in paragraph 3, the act for the first time excludes independent contractors and supervisors. Paragraph 11 provides a definition of "supervisors" that includes individuals who merely recommend actions such as hiring, recalling, or disciplining other employees. The exclusion of independent contractors reversed a victory by the Los Angeles Newsboys Local Industrial Union No. 75 against the Hearst Corporation. The supervisor exclusion meant the loss of coverage under collective bargaining agreements for unionized supervisors in printing, mining, and other industries. It also voided NLRB election victories won by the Foreman's Association of America in its campaign to unionize supervisors in the automobile industry.

◆ Sections 3–6: National Labor Relations Board

In Section 3, the 1947 act increases the number of members of the National Labor Relations Board from three to five. A quorum of three members is sufficient to issue

rulings. Much of the power of the NLRB is shifted to a new position of general counsel. Appointed to a four-year term by the president, the general counsel supervises the regional offices and all attorneys except administrative law judges and board members' legal assistants. The general counsel has "final authority" with respect to investigations of charges and issuing unfair labor practices complaints.

The theory behind dividing the investigative and decision-making functions was that the NLRB had an interest in upholding complaints against employers it had investigated and was being unfair to them. In fact, the two activities had been functionally separate and were required to be so by the Administrative Procedure Act of 1946. The Attorney General's Committee on Administrative Procedure had recommended against creating independent counsels in federal agencies because doing so was likely to lead to excessive litigation. The separation the act imposes on the NLRB was greater than that for any other federal agency. A significant increase in litigation did occur during the term of the first general counsel, Robert N. Denham (1947–1950), but the board was able to reassert its leadership role in policy making.

◆ Section 7: Rights of Employees

The Wagner Act emphasized workers' rights to organize unions and "to engage in concerted activities for the purpose of collective bargaining" (http://www.ourdocuments. gov/doc.php?doc=67&page=transcript). The 1947 law keeps this statement intact, merely adding the word "other" before "concerted activities." It adds, however, a "right to refrain from any or all such activities" unless an authorized union shop agreement between union and employer makes union membership a condition of employment. By declaring a "right to refrain" from collective action and equating it with a right to join in collective action, the new paragraph emphasizes the importance of the individual. It also weakens the Section 1 declaration that it is government policy to protect workers' self-organization and to encourage collective bargaining.

◆ Section 8: Unfair Labor Practices

Wagner Act language permitting closed and union shop agreements is changed by Section 8 (a) (3). The act prohibits the closed shop and qualifies the sanction given to union shop agreements. In a closed shop, only union members are hired, while in a union shop one must join the union after a probationary period. At the time of the enactment of the Taft-Hartley Act, many unions had closed-shop agreements. These agreements remained in effect, but the parties were unable to renew them. Union attempts to formally challenge what they saw as a loss of their traditional rights were unsuccessful, but de facto closed-shop agreements persisted in some areas of the economy. The Taft-Hartley Act specifies that union shop agreements can take effect "on or after the thirtieth day" a worker is employed or on the effective date of the agreement, whichever is later.

One additional qualification is that 30 percent of the workers have to petition for an election in which a majority of workers voting favor authorizing a union shop agreement. Another is that employers can refuse to discriminate against workers for nonmembership in unions if they think the union is discriminating on any other ground than nonpayment of dues and initiation fees. These qualifications abridge the Wagner Act's emphasis on noninterference of employers in workers' self-organization activities, since they provided for government and employer review of union internal procedures. Overwhelming worker votes in favor of union shop agreements dashed conservative expectations. A bipartisan coalition in Congress in October 1951 eliminated the requirement that such elections be conducted, since they were wasting the NLRB's time and resources.

The addition of unfair labor practices by labor organizations in paragraph (b) is new in the 1947 act. The NLRB is hereby given responsibility for issuing cease-and-desist orders against a number of union activities now deemed improper. The act prohibits unions from coercing employees in the exercise of their right of self-organization or employers in selecting their representatives. The implication of these prohibitions is that unions are, at least in some instances, an outside gangsterlike entity in labor-management relations rather than, in the Wagner Act theory, an instrument for securing more peaceful labor relations by providing employees with representation and a say over their wages and working conditions.

In Section (b) (4) (A), unions or their agents are prohibited from organizing or encouraging secondary boycotts—acts of solidarity by workers not directly engaged in a dispute. such as refusing to handle products of a struck company. Section (b) (4) (B) prohibits unions from forcing "any other employer" to recognize a union unless it is certified by the NRLB. Sections (b) (4) (C) and (D) prohibit actions to gain recognition when another union is certified or to get work reassigned from one union or craft to another union or craft; these two provision target jurisdictional disputes common in the construction trades. A qualification to these numerous antistrike provisions is that an employee may lawfully refuse to enter the premises of a struck employer if a certified union sanctions the strike.

In paragraph (c), the 1947 law grants a free speech right to employers that, as former NRLB chair Harry Millis put it, "went far beyond the constitutional protection of free speech" (Millis and Brown, p. 422). No longer would the NLRB be able to cite expressions of views "whether in written, printed, graphic, or visual form" as "evidence of an unfair labor practice … if such expression contains no threat of reprisal or force or promise of benefit." Under this provision, employers are given the right to be a party to the debate among workers on whether unionization is a good idea, thereby reversing the Wagner Act approach that decisions about self-organization were to be made by the workers alone. During the first five years of its existence under chair J. Warren Madden, the NLRB had held that the law required employers to maintain strict neutrality and not communicate antiunion views, because such communications were inherently intimidating. Employers had won court decisions in 1940 and 1941 that caused the NLRB to

drop that approach. The NLRB had Supreme Court support, however, for using evidence of employer antiunion statements in the context of a pattern of antiunion conduct, but it had stopped using such evidence six months before passage of Taft-Hartley. Employers are now permitted to campaign against a union vote in compulsory employee meetings. Employers may not, however, make a direct threat to close a plant if workers vote for a union.

Paragraph (d) states that the employer and the representative of the employees are required to engage in good-faith collective bargaining over contract terms and over issues arising under terms of agreements. Neither party, however, is required to "agree to a proposal" or make a "concession." The latter admonition had little consequence, but the remainder of the section includes several specific limitations on collective bargaining. A party desiring to modify or terminate an existing contract has four obligations: to provide the other party with sixty days' notice; to offer to meet and confer on contract terms; to provide thirty days' notice to the Federal Mediation and Conciliation Service and appropriate state and territorial mediation agencies of the existence of a dispute; and to continue "in full force and effect, without resorting to strike or lock-out, all the terms of the existing contract" for sixty days after notification or until the end of the contract, whichever was later. Paragraph (d) also gives management a new weapon. Any worker who engages in a strike during the sixty-day period loses his or her "status as an employee" and thus the right to use the services of the NLRB to complain about an unfair labor practice or to vote in an NLRB election. In the event that workers are rehired by the employer, they regain their status.

◆ Section 9: Representatives and Elections

In keeping with the emphasis on individual employees rather than on employees organized in unions, paragraph (a) states that an individual employee or group of employees can present grievances to the employer. They could also have the grievances "adjusted, without the intervention of the bargaining representative" as long as the adjustment does not contradict a collective bargaining agreement provision. A bargaining representative has a right to be present, but the paragraph forbids his or her "intervention" in the handling of the grievance.

Paragraph (b) gives special rights to professionals and craft workers. The NLRB is required to give those groups of employees separate elections unless the majority of them opt to be part of a larger bargaining unit. The craft-unit provision met a long-standing goal of the American Federation of Labor (AFL). The NLRB was prohibited, on the other hand, from including plant guards in the same bargaining unit with other employees and from certifying a union that included plant guards and other employees alike as members. Although they are not excluded from coverage under the law, plant guard unions are segregated from the rest of the labor movement.

In eliminating the option of a prehearing election, which the NLRB had been using effectively, paragraph (c) continues the emphasis on litigation rather than quick resolution of representation issues. This paragraph also establishes a one-year minimum period between representation elections. The NLRB had established a one-year rule for a new election when a union was certified or a contract was in place. Under the new law, it loses the discretion of ordering a second election when there is clear evidence that employee opinion has changed. Millis commented that the drafters of the new law thought "the right of collective bargaining ... was of less importance than the right not to bargain and the desirability of avoiding agitation" (Millis and Brown, pp. 517–518). The most startling changes introduced by paragraph (c) give employers the right to request a representation election and giving employees the right to seek an election to decertify a union. These procedures reverse the Wagner Act principles of support for the self-organization of employees and encouragement of collective bargaining.

In a major intrusion into internal union affairs, paragraphs (f) and (g) require local, national, and international unions wishing access to the NLRB to file their constitution, bylaws, membership requirements, and financial reports with the secretary of labor. A union failing to file the specified documents cannot be certified. Under paragraph (h), unions lose access to the NLRB unless local, national, and international union officers file affidavits with the NLRB stating that they are not members of the "Communist Party or affiliated with such party" and do not "believe in" or support any organization that "believes in or teaches, the overthrow of the United States Government by force or by any illegal or unconstitutional methods." The paragraph further states that criminal sanctions apply for filing a false affidavit: a fine of $10,000 or ten years in prison or both.

The non-Communist affidavit provision, adopted in the context of the developing cold war, proved especially important. Along with Truman's Loyalty Program for federal employees, the House Un-American Activities Committee investigations of Communism, the Justice Department's prosecution of the leaders of the Communist Party, and blacklisting by many industries, the non-Communist affidavits were one of the central pillars of the architecture of the domestic side of U.S. policy in the cold war, the red scare. Initially, however, labor leaders of various political persuasions opposed the non-Communist affidavit requirement as a violation of civil liberties that impugned their loyalty and was discriminatory, since there was no such requirement imposed on management. Unions condemned the Taft-Hartley Act as a whole, and many initially boycotted the filing requirements. Once some unions began to comply, noncomplying unions were in a vulnerable position, since they could not appear on election ballots. Even Communist-led unions eventually felt the need to comply. Communists who were union officers sometimes resigned from union leadership, occasionally resigned from the Communist Party, and at times were prosecuted for filing false affidavits.

Paragraphs 9 (f), (g), and (h) were replaced by new provisions regulating internal union conduct in the Landrum-Griffin Act of 1959. Section 504 of the latter act made it a crime for members of the Communist Party and those who had been members in the previous five years from serving as union officers. The initial legal protest of the non-Communist affidavit requirement of Taft-Hartley failed in 1950 when the Supreme Court, in a 4-to-1 decision (with one abstention), sanctioned them in *American Communications Association v. Douds*, 339 U.S. 382 (1950). The Supreme Court struck down the Landrum-Griffin regulation as an unconstitutional bill of attainder—a legislative punishment of an individual or group—in *United States v. Brown* 381 U.S. 437 (1965).

◆ **Section 10: Prevention of Unfair Labor Practices**

Section 10 (b) was amended to disallow filing of complaints when more than six months had elapsed from the date of the unfair labor practice and to provide that NLRB proceedings use the "rules of evidence" applicable in federal district courts. Note, however, that the free speech provision in Section 8 (c) prevents the board from considering employer statements as evidence.

While the Wagner Act granted the NLRB authority to seek injunctions to enforce its orders, Section 10 (j) expands that power by permitting the agency to seek an injunction when it issues a complaint. An even more important change provided for by Section 10 (l) is a mandatory injunction provision in cases of alleged violations of Section 8 (b) (4) (A) (B) and (C) (secondary boycotts, jurisdictional strikes, and strikes to force recognition by another employer of an uncertified union). The "preliminary investigation of such charge" must be immediate and "given priority over all other cases except cases of like character." Once the NLRB general counsel decides that a complaint is warranted, he or she is required to seek an injunction to stop the violation. Courts may issue injunctions without regard to "other provisions of law," thereby ending the protection against injunctions established by the Norris-LaGuardia Act. Two qualifications are added: The petition must allege that there will be "substantial or irreparable injury to the charging party," and the temporary restraining order shall be for a period of no more than five days.

◆ **Sections 11 and 12: Investigatory Powers**

The Wagner Act had granted any NLRB member the power to issue subpoenas relevant to "any matter under investigation or in question before the Board" (http://www. ourdocuments.gov/doc.php?doc=67&page=transcript). This provision was deleted. The NLRB is now required to issue subpoenas "upon application of any party" rather than by its own initiative and at its own discretion.

◆ **Sections 13–14: Limitations**

Section 13 qualifies the Wagner Act affirmation of the right to strike: "Nothing in this Act, **except as specifically provided for herein**, shall be construed so as **either** to interfere with or impede or diminish in any way the right to strike, **or to affect the limitations or qualification on that right**." (Taft-Hartley additions are in bold.) The act contains several restrictions on the right to strike. The pur-

Senator Robert A. Taft, 1945 (AP Photo/John Lindsay)

pose of the latter phrase in the sentence is to ensure that limitations that other legislation, such as the Railway Labor Act, placed on the right to strike are not challenged.

New to the 1947 act is a statement in Section 14 (a) that supervisors have a right to belong to unions. This affirmation is coupled, though, with the statement that employers covered by the act do not have to recognize supervisors as employees for the purpose of collective bargaining under any local, state, or national laws. The exclusion of supervisors from coverage under the act in Section 2 (3) is extended to prevent local and state laws from granting them collective bargaining rights.

One of the most important and controversial provisions of the Taft-Hartley Act is Section 14 (b), the so-called "right to work" provision: "Nothing in this Act shall be construed as authorizing the execution or application of agreements requiring membership in a labor organization as a condition of employment in any State or Territory in which such execution or application is prohibited by State or Territorial law." A few states had passed laws against union and closed-shop agreements, and many more would do so with the green light given by this section. Allowing a significant diminution of union rights in antilabor states subverted the existing uniform national labor policy. It also encouraged

campaigns to enact such restrictive laws in conservative states and efforts by those states to attract runaway shops from states where unions were not so restricted. In 2007 laws or constitutional amendments barred union shop contract provisions in twenty-three states.

◆ **Title II: Conciliation of Labor Disputes and National Emergencies**

Section 202 creates the independent Federal Mediation and Conciliation Service (FMCS) to replace the Conciliation Service in the Department of Labor. The drafters of the Taft-Hartley Act felt that as long as the service remained in the Department of Labor, it would tilt in a prolabor direction, limiting its effectiveness as a mediator. Critics thought the decision failed to recognize the effective mediating role played by the old agency and saw the move as weakening the Department of Labor. The new agency is to take over the staff and records of the old agency. The president appoints the director with the advice and consent of the Senate; a National Labor-Management Panel advises the director.

Section 203 directs the FMCS to avoid mediating disputes having a minor impact on commerce. If the FMCS is unable to "bring the parties to agreement ... within a reasonable time," it "shall seek to induce the parties" to find other means of resolving their dispute without resorting to a strike or lockout, "including submission to the employees in the bargaining unit of the employer's last offer of settlement for approval or rejection in a secret ballot." There is no recommendation for a vote by a corporation board of directors on the union's last best offer. Based on the theory that union leaders are sometimes unrepresentative, the recommendation is another example of interference in union internal affairs.

Sections 206 to 210 govern disputes deemed national emergencies. Government operation of the coal mines, authorized by Truman under terms of the War Labor Disputes Act in response to a coal strike in May 1946, was scheduled to end on June 30, 1947, with the expiration of the wartime legislation. The authors of Taft-Hartley sought to establish a permanent mechanism for preventing stoppages in critical industries. If the president believes a strike or lockout would "imperil the national health or safety," he or she "may appoint a board of inquiry" to look into the facts and make a report, without recommendations, to the president, who "shall" file it with the FMCS and "make its contents available to the public" (Section 206). This provision is similar to a proposal Truman made for a fact-finding procedure in nationally important disputes on December 3, 1945.

Section 208 gives the president the power to direct the attorney general to seek court injunctions to "enjoin" a strike or lockout in such disputes. When such an order has been issued, the parties have a "duty … to make every effort to adjust and settle their differences" with the aid of the FMCS, but they are not obligated to accept any FMCS proposal, according to Section 209 (a). If the enjoined dispute is not settled at the end of sixty days, the board of inquiry reports to the president on the current state of negotiations and includes in the report a statement of the current position of each party and the employer's "last offer of settlement." The NLRB then conducts an election within fifteen days "of the employees of each employer involved in the dispute" on their employer's final offer and certifies the results to the attorney general, according to Section 209 (b).

Section 210 provides for the termination of the injunction upon settlement of the dispute or certification of the election and for a presidential report to Congress on the dispute "together with such recommendations as he may see fit to make for consideration and appropriate action." Section 208 (b) states that the Norris-LaGuardia restrictions on injunctions are not applicable, but, according to Section 208 (c), the writs may be appealed to circuit courts of appeal and the Supreme Court.

◆ Title III: Suits by and against Labor Organizations

Section 301 provides for lawsuits against unions for contract breaches. Paragraph (b) provides for suits "in behalf of the employees whom it represents" but states that judgments are not enforceable against individual members. Some state laws had allowed for judgments against individuals, as had occurred in the Danbury Hatters' case of 1908 (*Loewe v. Lawlor*). Paragraph (e) makes the union liable for the act of

its agents even if it does not know in advance about the acts and does not approve of them after they occur.

Section 302 (a) and (b) prohibits and provides criminal penalties for payments or acceptance of payments of "any money or other thing of value" by employers to employees. Exceptions are provided for compensation for services, arbitration awards, satisfying court judgments, and sales of commodities.

Section 302 (c) (4) provides that employers may send dues payments to unions under checkoff provisions, provided that each individual has authorized the payment and the authorizations are annually renewed. Automatic dues checkoff provisions in contracts covering more than three million workers would no longer be permitted after July 1, 1948. Section 302 also regulates health and welfare funds that were becoming an important feature of collective bargaining contracts. In place of the diverse forms of administration agreed upon by the parties, the act requires that funds be jointly administered by employer and union, with provisions included for breaking deadlocks by resort to a third party. Pension funds are to be kept separate from other funds.

Section 302 (d) provides for criminal penalties for anyone "willfully" violating this section of the law. Paragraph 302 (e) provides for court enforcement of the provisions of this section "without regard to" the exemptions from injunctions against unions in the Clayton and Norris-LaGuardia acts.

Section 303 provides the right of any private party injured "in his business or property" by a secondary boycott, pressure to recognize a noncertified union, or jurisdictional disputes to sue to recover damages.

Section 304 amends the Corrupt Practices Act to prohibit political contributions and expenditures by unions in federal elections and in primaries, caucuses, and conventions to select federal candidates. In the Senate debate over the bill, Taft stated that unions would be forbidden from commenting on candidates in their newspapers, in a pamphlet, or in a radio broadcast. The CIO was able to win a Supreme Court decision—*United States v. Congress of Industrial Organizations,* 335 U.S. 106 (1948)—allowing its newspaper to report the endorsement of a federal candidate by CIO President Murray but was unable to overturn the general restriction on the political expenditure of union funds. As a result, union engagement in political activity has been based on collecting contributions from members rather than expending general union funds.

Although Section 2 of the act continues the Wagner Act exclusion of federal and state governments from the law's provisions, Section 305 forbids individuals employed by the federal government or by "wholly owned Government corporations" from taking strike action. Strikers "shall be discharged immediately," lose their civil service status, and become ineligible for reemployment for three years. Section 305 was repealed in 1955 and replaced with Public Law 330 which "made it a felony for federal workers to strike, assert the right to strike, or belong to an organization that asserts such rights" (Halpern, p. 82).

"Employees shall have the right to self-organization, to form, join, or assist labor organizations, to bargain collectively through representatives of their own choosing, and to engage in other concerted activities for the purpose of collective bargaining or other mutual aid or protection, and shall also have the right to refrain from any or all of such activities except to the extent that such right may be affected by an agreement requiring membership in a labor organization as a condition of employment as authorized in section 8 (a) (3) of this title."

(Section 7)

"Upon the filing of any such petition the district court shall have jurisdiction to grant such injunctive relief or temporary restraining order as it deems just and proper, notwithstanding any other provision of law."

(Section 10)

"Nothing in this Act shall be construed as authorizing the execution or application of agreements requiring membership in a labor organization as a condition of employment in any State or Territory in which such execution or application is prohibited by State or Territorial law."

(Section 14)

"Upon receiving a report from a board of inquiry the President may direct the Attorney General to petition any district court of the United States having jurisdiction ... to enjoin such strike or lock-out or the continuing thereof."

(Section 208)

"It is unlawful for ... any labor organization to make a contribution or expenditure in connection with any election ... [for federal offices] or in connection with any primary election or political convention or caucus held to select candidates [for federal offices]."

(Section 304)

"It shall be unlawful for any individual employed by the United States or any agency thereof including wholly owned Government corporations to participate in any strike."

(Section 305)

Audience

The audience for the Taft-Hartley Act included the entire adult population of the United States, but it was especially designed to appeal to critics of the labor movement and, more specifically, to the National Association of Manufacturers, the U.S. Chamber of Commerce, the newspapers and magazines that advocated modifications in the nation's labor law, and the law firms and corporations that had lobbied for the legislation. The audience also included core constituencies of the Republican Party antagonistic to unions and a public opinion aroused against unions by the business organizations' publicity campaign and hostile press coverage of strike actions. Liberal Republican senator George Aiken of Vermont estimated in May 1947 that the National Association of Manufacturers had spent at least $100,000,000 on antilabor publicity. Public opinion polls showed manual workers as the only group supporting a presidential veto of the act in June 1947.

Antilabor sentiment among the general public had developed owing to a variety of factors. With reconversion to a civilian economy, there were hopes that consumer goods would soon be more available, but there were also layoffs, a short-term decline in total production, and anxieties about the future strength of the economy. With the public's experience of postwar shortages of consumer goods, occasional interruptions of normal routines as the result of strikes, and negative media coverage of alleged labor abuses, antilabor sentiment grew. Truman's shift from proposing fact-finding legislation to supporting the steelworkers' strike to seizing the coal mines and proposing the drafting of railroad strikers contributed to a low Democratic turnout in November 1946, while Republicans turned out their vote and won control of Congress. The fact that much of the remaining strength of the Democrats in Congress was concentrated in southern states, where unions were weak and not influential within the Democratic Party, led the majority of Democrats to join in responding to the antiunion climate by voting for the Taft-Hartley Act.

Impact

Labor unions reacted strongly against the Taft-Hartley Act. Many labor leaders characterized the law as a slave labor law. Within one hour of the law's passage, thousands of bituminous coal miners went on a protest strike, with 250,000 on strike within four days. The mine workers stayed out as government control of the mines came to an end on June 30, 1947, and returned to work only after ratifying a new contract with significant gains in wages and benefits. Representative Hartley condemned the agreement as inflationary and specified provisions he viewed as in violation of the letter and spirit of the Taft-Hartley Act. The miners' actions were atypical, however. Although there were calls from left-wing union leaders for strikes to protest the legislation, both the AFL and the CIO decided to rely on legal action and future political activity rather than immediate mass protests or strikes. Moreover, political differences within the union movement undermined concerted action.

In the wake of the passage of the Taft-Hartley Act, there was shift in the battle for power then under way in the United Auto Workers. The anti-Communist faction, led by President Walter Reuther, gained new support from the union's secondary leaders. It was able to defeat a proposal to merge the United Auto Workers with the left-wing Farm Equipment Workers union and then win a majority of delegates to displace a left-center coalition as the dominant force at the union's fall convention and on the union's executive board. The CIO convention in October 1947 adopted a resolution condemning Taft-Hartley and pledging not to acquiesce to it. But the influence of Reuther and other anti-Communist leaders was such that the resolution allowed individual unions the autonomy to make their own decisions on compliance. The AFL at the same time rejected the proposal of United Mine Workers president John L. Lewis to boycott the law.

The division within the labor movement over whether to file non-Communist affidavits and otherwise comply with the law led to raids by complying unions against noncomplying unions. Left-wing unions were particularly vulnerable. Although Truman's attacks on the Taft-Hartley Act and the "do-nothing" Eightieth Congress led to his surprise victory and the recapturing of Congress by the Democrats in 1948, there was neither repeal nor revision of the act, owing to the continuing clout of a coalition of Republicans and conservative Democrats. In the context of the intensifying cold war and red scare, the CIO in 1949 expelled its left-wing unions, and raiding intensified. The Taft-Hartley Act's limitations on unions' solidarity actions and its role in uprooting leftists from a significant role in the unions eventually led to a decline in both grassroots activism and visionary impulses. Under Republican presidents, moreover, the NLRB titled toward a pro-employer perspective in administering the law. Workers seeking to unionize found themselves increasingly enmeshed in bureaucratic delays and litigation, while sanctions against employer violations of the law became ineffective. Union density, the percentage of the nonagricultural labor force that is unionized, declined from about one-third of the labor force in the fifteen years after World War II to 12 percent of the labor force in 2006. The only significant revision in the Taft-Hartley framework came in 1959 with the passage of the Landrum-Griffin Act, which added new federal government regulations of internal union affairs.

Related Documents

"American Communications Association v. Douds (1950)." First Amendment Center Web site. http://www.firstamendmentcenter.org/faclibrary/case.aspx?case=ACA_v_Douds. Accessed on January 9, 2008. The site contains links to the briefs, decision, and dissent in the case in which the Supreme Court affirmed the Taft-Hartley non-

Communist affidavits and a link to the *United States v. Brown* decision (1965) overturning a similar requirement in later legislation.

Harper, Michael C., Samuel Estreicher, and Joan Flynn. *Labor Law: Selected Statutes, Forms, and Agreements.* New York: Aspen Publishers, 2007. Contains the texts of key labor-related statutes.

National Labor Relations Board. *Legislative History of the Labor Management Relations Act, 1947.* 2 vols. Washington, D.C.: Government Printing Office, 1948. Contains the congressional debate and various drafts of the legislation.

The New Labor Law. Washington, D.C.: Bureau of National Affairs, 1947. Summarizes the Taft-Hartley Act, provides the text, and includes excerpts from the congressional debate.

"Transcript of National Labor Relations Act (1935)." National Archives "Our Documents" Web site. http://www.ourdocuments.gov/doc.php?doc=67&page=transcript. Under this act, also known as the Wagner Act, the federal government had supported workers' self-organization into unions and for collective bargaining. Much of the act was amended and undermined by the Taft-Hartley Act.

"Veto of the Taft-Hartley Labor Bill, June 20, 1947." The American Presidency Project Web site. http://www.presidency.ucsb.edu/ws/?pid=12675. Accessed on January 9, 2008. President Truman's veto messages incorporate many union criticisms of the act.

Bibliography

■ Articles
Halpern, Martin. "TaftHartley and the Defeat of the Progressive Alternative in the UAW." *Labor History* 27, no. 2 (Spring 1986): 204–226.

■ Books
Dubofsky, Melvyn. *The State and Labor in Modern America.* Chapel Hill: University of North Carolina Press, 1994.

Ginger, Ann Fagan, and David Christiano, eds. *The Cold War against Labor: An Anthology.* 2 vols. Berkeley, Calif.: Meiklejohn Civil Liberties Institute, 1987.

Gross, James A. *The Reshaping of the National Labor Relations Board: National Labor Policy in Transition, 1937–1947.* Albany: State University of New York Press, 1981.

———. *Broken Promise: The Subversion of U.S. Labor Relations Policy, 1947–1994.* Philadelphia: Temple University Press, 1995.

Halpern, Martin. *UAW Politics in the Cold War Era.* Albany: State University of New York Press, 1988.

———. *Unions, Radicals, and Democratic Presidents: Seeking Social Change in the Twentieth Century.* Westport, Conn.: Praeger, 2003.

Higgins, John E., ed. *The Developing Labor Law: The Board, the Courts, and the National Labor Relations Act.* Washington, D.C.: Bureau of National Affairs, 2006.

Lee, R. Alton, *Truman and Taft-Hartley: A Question of Mandate.* Lexington: University of Kentucky Press, 1966.

Millis, Harry A, and Emily Clark Brown. *From the Wagner Act to Taft-Hartley: A Study of National Labor Policy and Labor Relations.* Chicago: University of Chicago Press, 1950.

Schrecker, Ellen W. "McCarthyism and the Labor Movement: The Role of the State." In *The CIO's Left-Led Unions*, ed. Steve Rosswurm. New Brunswick, N.J.: Rutgers University Press, 1992.

Tomlins, Christopher L. *The State and the Unions: Labor Relations, Law, and the Organized Labor Movement in America, 1880–1960.* New York: Cambridge University Press, 1985.

■ Web Sites
"U.S. Code Collection: Chapter 7—Labor-Management Relations." Cornell University Law School.
    http://www.law.cornell.edu/uscode/html/uscode29/usc_sup_01_29_10_7.html. Accessed on January 9, 2008.

—By Martin Halpern

1. Most labor unions strenuously opposed the passage of the Taft-Hartley Act in 1947. Unions have sought on several occasions either to repeal the 1947 law or to significantly alter its provisions to make it less burdensome to workers' efforts to unionize. Examine one of the following episodes and explain the reasons for unions' lack of success in improving the labor law environment: passage of Landrum-Griffin Act in 1959; failure to enact a labor law reform bill in 1978; failure to enact a workplace fairness bill in 1991–1994; failure to enact the Employee Free Choice Act in 2006–2007.

2. Examine presidential use of the Taft-Hartley-sanctioned injunction to stop strikes deemed to be national emergencies and evaluate whether the use of the injunction produced long-term positive or negative results for labor-management relations in the industry in question.

3. Union density—the proportion of the labor force in unions—has declined dramatically from its peak in the 1945–1960 period. Beginning in the early 1960s, however, union density increased significantly in the public sector and has remained at a high level. Examine the character of the workforces and the distinctive economic, political, and legal environments in the private and public sectors to identify reasons why public employees today are four times as likely to be union members as private-sector employees.

4. Public opinion polls regularly show that a majority of workers would like to be represented by unions but only about one in eight workers are union members. What factors in today's social, economic, and political environment make workers interested in joining unions? What factors, on the other hand, keeps the rate of unionization low?

Glossary

conciliation	production of compromise
contemporaneously	at the same time
disbursement	payment
discretion	the power to decide based on one's own judgment
enjoin	to prohibit or restrain by an injunction
injunction	a writ issued by a court requiring or preventing a specified act
irreparable	not repairable; not able to be made good
levying	imposition of an assessment
mediation	intervention to promote a settlement between conflicting parties
mitigate	lessen
preponderance	superior in influence
pro tempore	temporarily
quorum	number required to be present

Taft-Hartley Act

An Act to Amend the National Labor Relations Act, to Provide Additional Facilities for the Mediation of Labor Disputes Affecting Commerce, to Equalize Legal Responsibilities of Labor Organizations and Employers, and for Other Purposes.

Be it enacted by the Senate and House of Representatives of the United States of America in Congress assembled,

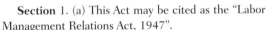

SHORT TITLE AND DECLARATION OF POLICY

Section 1. (a) This Act may be cited as the "Labor Management Relations Act, 1947".

(b) Industrial strife which interferes with the normal flow of commerce and with the full production of articles and commodities for commerce, can be avoided or substantially minimized if employers, employees, and labor organizations each recognize under law one another's legitimate rights in their relations with each other, and above all recognize under law that neither party has any right in its relations with any other to engage in acts or practices which jeopardize the public health, safety, or interest.

It is the purpose and policy of this Act, in order to promote the full flow of commerce, to prescribe the legitimate rights of both employees and employers in their relations affecting commerce, to provide orderly and peaceful procedures for preventing the interference by either with the legitimate rights of the other, to protect the rights of individual employees in their relations with labor organizations whose activities affect commerce, to define and proscribe practices on the part of labor and management which affect commerce and are inimical to the general welfare, and to protect the rights of the public in connection with labor disputes affecting commerce.

Title I—Amendment of National Labor Relations Act

Sec. 101. The National Labor Relations Act is hereby amended to read as follows:

"FINDINGS AND POLICIES

"Section 1. The denial by some employers of the right of employees to organize and the refusal by some employers to accept the procedure of collective bargaining lead to strikes and other forms of industrial strife or unrest, which have the intent or the necessary effect of burdening or obstructing commerce by (a) impairing the efficiency, safety, or operation of the instrumentalities of commerce; (b) occurring in the current of commerce; (c) materially affecting, restraining, or controlling the flow of raw materials or manufactured or processed goods from or into the channels of commerce, or the prices of such materials or goods in commerce; or (d) causing diminution of employment and wages in such volume as substantially to impair or disrupt the market for goods flowing from or into the channels of commerce.

"The inequality of bargaining power between employees who do not possess full freedom of association or actual liberty of contract, and employers who are organized in the corporate or other forms of ownership association substantially burdens and affects the flow of commerce, and tends to aggravate recurrent business depressions, by depressing wage rates and the purchasing power of wage earners in industry and by preventing the stabilization of competitive wage rates and working conditions within and between industries.

"Experience has proved that protection by law of the right of employees to organize and bargain collectively safeguards commerce from injury, impairment, or interruption, and promotes the flow of commerce by removing certain recognized sources of industrial strife and unrest, by encouraging practices fundamental to the friendly adjustment of industrial disputes arising out of differences as to wages, hours, or other working conditions, and by restoring equality of bargaining power between employers and employees.

"Experience has further demonstrated that certain practices by some labor organizations, their officers, and members have the intent or the necessary effect of burdening or obstructing commerce by preventing the free flow of goods in such commerce through strikes and other forms of industrial unrest or through concerted activities which impair the interest of the public in the free flow of such commerce. The elimination of such practices is a necessary condition to the assurance of the rights herein guaranteed.

"It is hereby declared to be the policy of the United States to eliminate the causes of certain substantial obstructions to the free flow of commerce and to mitigate and eliminate these obstructions when they have occurred by encouraging the practice and procedure of collective bargaining and by protecting the exercise by workers of full freedom of association, self-organization, and designation of representatives of their own choosing, for the purpose of negotiating the terms and conditions of their employment or other mutual aid or protection.

"DEFINITIONS

"Sec. 2. When used in this Act —

"(1) The term 'person' includes one or more individuals, labor organizations, partnerships, associations, corporations, legal representatives, trustees, trustees in bankruptcy, or receivers.

"(2) The term 'employer' includes any person acting as an agent of an employer, directly or indirectly, but shall not include the United States or any wholly owned Government corporation, or any Federal Reserve Bank, or any State or political subdivision thereof, or any corporation or association operating a hospital, if no part of the net earnings inures to the benefit of any private shareholder or individual, or any person subject to the Railway Labor Act, as amended from time to time, or any labor organization (other than when acting as an employer), or anyone acting in the capacity of officer or agent of such labor organization.

"(3) The term 'employee' shall include any employee, and shall not be limited to the employees of a particular employer, unless the Act explicitly states otherwise, and shall include any individual whose work has ceased as a consequence of, or in connection with, any current labor dispute or because of any unfair labor practice, and who has not obtained any other regular and substantially equivalent employment, but shall not include any individual employed as an agricultural laborer, or in the domestic service of any family or person at his home, or any individual employed by his parent or spouse, or any individual having the status of an independent contractor, or any individual employed as a supervisor, or any individual employed by an employer subject to the Railway Labor Act, as amended from time to time, or by any other person who is not an employer as herein defined.

"(4) The term 'representatives' includes any individual or labor organization.

"(5) The term 'labor organization' means any organization of any kind, or any agency or employee representation committee or plan, in which employees participate and which exists for the purpose, in whole or in part, of dealing with employers concerning grievances, labor disputes, wages, rates of pay, hours of employment, or conditions of work.

"(6) The term 'commerce' means trade, traffic, commerce, transportation, or communication among the several States, or between the District of Columbia or any Territory of the United States and any State or other Territory, or between any foreign country and any State, Territory, or the District of Columbia, or within the District of Columbia or any Territory, or between points in the same State but through any other State or any Territory or the District of Columbia or any foreign country.

"(7) The term 'affecting commerce' means in commerce, or burdening or obstructing commerce or the free flow of commerce, or having led or tending to lead to a labor dispute burdening or obstructing commerce or the free flow of commerce.

"(8) The term 'unfair labor practice' means any unfair labor practice listed in section 8.

"(9) The term 'labor dispute' includes any controversy concerning terms, tenure or conditions of employment, or concerning the association or representation of persons in negotiating, fixing, maintaining, changing, or seeking to arrange terms or conditions of employment, regardless of whether the disputants stand in the proximate relation of employer and employee.

"(10) The term 'National Labor Relations Board' means the National Labor Relations Board Provided for in section 3 of this Act.

"(11) The term 'supervisor' means any individual having authority, in the interest of the employer, to hire, transfer, suspend, lay off, recall, promote, discharge, assign, reward, or discipline other employees, or responsibly to direct them, or to adjust their grievances, or effectively to recommend such action, if in connection with the foregoing the exercise of such authority is not of a merely routine or clerical nature, but requires the use of independent judgment.

"(12) The term 'professional employee' means —

"(a) any employee engaged in work (i) predominantly intellectual and varied in character as opposed to routine mental, manual, mechanical, or physical work; (ii) involving the consistent exercise of discretion and judgment in its performance; (iii) of such a character that the output produced or the result accomplished cannot be standardized in relation to a given period of time; (iv) requiring knowledge of an advanced type in a field of science or learning customarily acquired by a prolonged course of specialized intellectual instruction and study in an institution of higher learning or a hospital, as distinguished from a general academic education or from an apprenticeship or from training in the performance of routine mental, manual, or physical processes; or

"(b) any employee, who (i) has completed the courses of specialized intellectual instruction and study described in clause (iv) of paragraph (a), and (ii) is performing related work under the supervision of a professional person to qualify himself to become a professional employee as defined in paragraph (a).

"(13) In determining whether any person is acting as an 'agent' of another person so as to make such other person responsible for his acts, the question of whether the specific acts performed were actually authorized or subsequently ratified shall not be controlling.

"NATIONAL LABOR RELATIONS BOARD

"Sec. 3. (a) The National Labor Relations Board (hereinafter called the 'Board') created by this Act prior to its amendment by the Labor Management Relations Act, 1947, is hereby continued as an agency of the United States, except that the Board shall consist of five instead of three members, appointed by the President by and with the advice and consent of the Senate. Of the two additional members so provided for, one shall be appointed for a term of five years and the other for a term of two years. Their successors, and the successors of the other members, shall be appointed for terms of five years each, excepting that any individual chosen to fill a vacancy shall be appointed only for the unexpired term of the member whom he shall succeed. The President shall designate one member to serve as Chairman of the Board. Any member of the Board may be removed by the President, upon notice and hearing, for neglect of duty or malfeasance in office, but for no other cause.

"(b) The Board is authorized to delegate to any group of three or more members any or al of the powers which it may itself exercise. A Vacancy in the Board shall not impair the right of the remaining members to exercise all of the powers of the Board, and three members of the Board shall, at all times, constitute a quorum of the Board, except that two members shall constitute a quorum of any group designated pursuant to the first sentence hereof. The Board shall have an official seal which shall be judicially noticed.

"(c) The Board shall at the close of each fiscal year make a report in writing to Congress and to the President stating in detail the cases it has heard, the decisions it has rendered, the names, salaries, and duties of all employees and officers in the employ or under the supervision of the Board, and an account of all moneys it has disbursed.

"(d) There shall be a General Counsel of the Board who shall be appointed by the President, by and with the advice and consent of the Senate, for a term of four years. The General Counsel of the Board shall exercise general supervision over all attorneys employed by the Board (other than trial examiners and legal assistants to Board members) and over the officers and employees in the regional offices. He shall have final authority, on behalf of the Board, in respect of the investigation of charges and issuance of complaints under section 10, and in respect of the prosecution of such complaints before the Board, and shall have such other duties as the Board may prescribe or as may be provided by law.

"Sec. 4. (a) Each member of the Board and the General Counsel of the Board shall receive a salary of $12,000 a year, shall be eligible for reappointment, and shall not engage in any other business, vocation, or employment. The Board shall appoint an executive secretary, and such attorneys, examiners, and regional directors, and such other employees as it may from time to time find necessary for the proper performance of its duties. The Board may not employ any attorneys for the purpose of reviewing transcripts of hearings or preparing drafts of opinions except that any attorney employed for assignment as a legal assistant to any Board member may for such Board member review such transcripts and prepare such drafts. No trial examiner's report shall be reviewed, either before or after its publication, by any person other than a member of the Board or his legal assistant, and no trial examiner shall advise or consult with the Board with respect to exceptions taken to his findings, rulings, or recommendations.

The Board may establish or utilize such regional, local, or other agencies, and utilize such voluntary and uncompensated services, as may from time to time be needed. Attorneys appointed under this section may, at the direction of the Board, appear for and represent the Board in any case in court. Nothing in this Act shall be construed to authorize the Board to appoint individuals for the purpose of conciliation or mediation, or for economic analysis.

"(b) All of the expenses of the Board, including all necessary traveling and subsistence expenses outside the District of Columbia incurred by the members or employees of the Board under its orders, shall be allowed and paid on the presentation of itemized vouchers therefor approved by the Board or by any individual it designates for that purpose.

"Sec. 5. The principal office of the Board shall be in the District of Columbia, but it may meet and exercise any or all of its powers at any other place. The Board may, by one or more of its members or by such agents or agencies as it may designate, prosecute any inquiry necessary to its functions in any part of the United States. A member who participates in such an inquiry shall not be disqualified from subsequently participating in a decision of the Board in the same case.

"Sec. 6. The Board shall have authority from time to time to make, amend, and rescind, in the manner prescribed by the Administrative Procedure Act, such rules and regulations as may be necessary to carry out the provisions of this Act.

"RIGHTS OF EMPLOYEES

"Sec. 7. Employees shall have the right to self-organization, to form, join, or assist labor organizations, to bargain collectively through representatives of their own choosing, and to engage in other concerted activities for the purpose of collective bargaining or other mutual aid or protection, and shall also have the right to refrain from any or all of such activities except to the extent that such right may be affected by an agreement requiring membership in a labor organization as a condition of employment as authorized in section 8 (a) (3).

"UNFAIR LABOR PRACTICES

"Sec. 8. (a) It shall be an unfair labor practice for an employer —

"(1) to interfere with, restrain, or coerce employees in the exercise of the rights guaranteed in section 7;

"(2) to dominate or interfere with the formation or administration of any labor organization or contribute financial or other support to it: *Provided*,

That subject to rules and regulations made and published by the Board pursuant to section 6, an employer shall not be prohibited from permitting employees to confer with him during working hours without loss of time or pay;

"(3) by discrimination in regard to hire or tenure of employment or any term or condition of employment to encourage or discourage membership in any labor organization: *Provided*, That nothing in this Act, or in any other statute of the United States, shall preclude an employer from making an agreement with a labor organization (not established, maintained, or assisted by any action defined in section 8 (a) of this Act as an unfair labor practice) to require as a condition of employment membership therein on or after the thirtieth day following the beginning of such employment or the effective date of such agreement, whichever is the later, (i) if such labor organization is the representative of the employees as provided in section 9 (a), in the appropriate collective-bargaining unit covered by such agreement when made; and (ii) if, following the most recent election held as provided in section 9 (e) the Board shall have certified that at least a majority of the employees eligible to vote in such election have voted to authorize such labor organization to make such an agreement: *Provided further*, That no employer shall justify any discrimination against an employee for nonmembership in a labor organization (A) if he has reasonable grounds for believing that such membership was not available to the employee on the same terms and conditions generally applicable to other members, or (B) if he has reasonable grounds for believing that membership was denied or terminated for reasons other than the failure of the employee to tender the periodic dues and the initiation fees uniformly required as a condition of acquiring or retaining membership;

"(4) to discharge or otherwise discriminate against an employee because he has filed charges or given testimony under this Act;

"(5) to refuse to bargain collectively with the representatives of his employees, subject to the provisions of section 9 (a).

"(b) It shall be an unfair labor practice for a labor organization or its agents —

"(1) to restrain or coerce (A) employees in the exercise of the rights guaranteed in section 7: *Provided*, That this paragraph shall not impair the right of a labor organization to prescribe its own rules with respect to the acquisition or retention of membership therein; or (B) an employer in the selection of his representatives for the purposes of collective bargaining or the adjustment of grievances;

"(2) to cause or attempt to cause an employer to discriminate against an employee in violation of subsection (a) (3) or to discriminate against an employee with respect to whom membership in such organization has been denied or terminated on some ground other than his failure to tender the periodic dues and the initiation fees uniformly required as a condition of acquiring or retaining membership;

"(3) to refuse to bargain collectively with an employer, provided it is the representative of his employees subject to the provisions of section 9 (a);

"(4) to engage in, or to induce or encourage the employees of any employer to engage in, a strike or a concerted refusal in the curse of their employment to use, manufacture, process, transport, or otherwise handle or work on any goods, articles, materials, or commodities or to perform any services, where an object thereof is:

(A) forcing or requiring any employer or self-employed person to join any labor or employer organization or any employer or other person to cease using, selling, handling, transporting, or otherwise dealing in the products of any other producer, processor, or manufacturer, or to cease doing business with any other person;

(B) forcing or requiring any other employer to recognize or bargain with a labor organization as the representative of his employees unless such labor organization has been certified as the representative of such employees under the provisions of section 9;

(C) forcing or requiring any employer to recognize or bargain with a particular labor organization as the representative of his employees if another labor organization has been certified as the representative of such employees under the provisions of section 9;

(D) forcing or requiring any employer to assign particular work to employees in a particular labor organization or in a particular trade, craft, or class rather than to employees in another labor organization or in another trade, craft, or class, unless such employer is failing to conform to an order or certification of the Board determining the bargaining representative for employees performing such work: *Provided*, That nothing contained in this subsection (b) shall be construed to make unlawful a refusal by any person to enter upon the premises of any employer (other than his own employer), if the employees of such employer are engaged in a strike ratified or approved by a representative of such employees whom such employer is required to recognize under this Act;

"(5) to require of employees covered by an agreement authorized under subsection (a) (3) the payment, as a condition precedent to becoming a member of such organization, of a fee in an amount which the Board finds excessive or discriminatory under all the circumstances. In making such a finding, the Board shall consider, among other relevant factors, the practices and customs of labor organizations in the particular industry, and the wages currently paid to the employees affected; and

"(6) to cause or attempt to cause an employer to pay or deliver or agree to pay or deliver any money or other thing of value, in the nature of an exaction, for services which are not performed or not to be performed.

"(c) The expressing of any views, argument, or opinion, or the dissemination thereof, whether in written, printed, graphic, or visual form, shall not constitute or be evidence of an unfair labor practice under any of the provisions of this Act, if such expression contains no threat of reprisal or force or promise of benefit.

"(d) For the purposes of this section, to bargain collectively is the performance of the mutual obligation of the employer and the representative of the employees to meet at reasonable times and confer in good faith with respect to wages, hours, and other terms and conditions of employment, or the negotiation of an agreement, or any question arising thereunder, and the execution of a written contract incorporating any agreement reached if requested by either party, but such obligation does not compel either party to agree to a proposal or require the making of a concession: *Provided*, That where there is in effect a collective-bargaining contract covering employees in an industry affecting commerce, the duty to bargain collectively shall also mean that no party to such contract shall terminate or modify such contract, unless the party desiring such termination or modification —

"(1) serves a written notice upon the other party to the contract of the proposed termination or modification sixty days prior to the expiration date thereof, or in the event such contract contains no expiration date, sixty days prior to the time it is proposed to make such termination or modification;

"(2) offers to meet and confer with the other party for the purpose of negotiating a new contract or a contract containing the proposed modifications;

"(3) notifies the Federal Mediation and Conciliation Service within thirty days after such notice of the existence of a dispute, and simultaneously therewith notifies any State or Territorial agency established to mediate and conciliate disputes within the State or Territory where the dispute occurred, provided no agreement has been reached by that time; and

"(4) continues in full force and effect, without resorting to strike or lock-out, all the terms and conditions of the existing contract for a period of sixty days after such notice is given or until the expiration date of such contract, whichever occurs later:

The duties imposed upon employers, employees, and labor organizations by paragraphs (2), (3), and (4) shall become inapplicable upon an intervening certification of the Board, under which the labor organization or individual, which is a party ot the contract, has been superseded as or ceased to be the representative of the employees subject to the provisions of section 9 (a), and the duties so imposed shall not be construed as requiring either party to discuss or agree to any modification of the terms and conditions contained in a contract for a fixed period, if such modification is to become effective before such terms and conditions can be reopened under the provisions of the contract. Any employee who engages in a strike within the sixty-day period specified in this subsection shall lose his status as an employee of the employer engaged in the particular labor dispute, for the purposes of sections 8, 9, and 10 of this Act, as amended, but such loss of status for such employee shall terminate if and when he is reemployed by such employer.

"REPRESENTATIVES AND ELECTIONS

"Sec. 9. (a) Representatives designated or selected for the purposes of collective bargaining by the majority of the employees in a unit appropriate for such purposes, shall be the exclusive representatives of all the employees in such unit for the purposes of collective bargaining in respect to rates of pay, wages, hours of employment, or other conditions of employment: *Provided*, That any individual employee or a group of employees shall have the right at any time to present grievances to their employer and to have such grievances adjusted, without the intervention of the bargaining representative, as long as the adjustment is not inconsistent with the terms of a collective-bargaining contract or agreement then in effect: *Provided further*, That the bargaining representative has been given opportunity to be present at such adjustment.

"(b) The Board shall decide in each case whether, in order to assure to employees the fullest freedom in exercising the rights guaranteed by this Act, the unit appropriate for the purposes of collective bargaining shall be the employer unit, craft unit, plant unit, or subdivision thereof: *Provided*, That the Board shall not (1) decide that any unit is appropriate for such purposes if such unit includes both professional employees and employees who are not professional employees unless a majority of such professional employees vote for inclusion in such unit; or (2) decide that any craft unit is inappropriate for such purposes on the ground that a different unit has been established by a prior Board determination, unless a majority of the employees in the proposed craft unit vote against separate representation or (3) decide that any unit is appropriate for such purposes if it includes, together with other employees, any individual employed as a guard to enforce against employees and other persons rules to protect property of the employer or to protect the safety of persons on the employer's premises; but no labor organization shall be certified as the representative of employees in a bargaining unit of guards if such organization admits to membership, or is affiliated directly or indirectly with an organization which admits to membership, employees other than guards.

"(c) (1) Whenever a petition shall have been filed, in accordance with such regulations as may be prescribed by the Board —

"(A) by an employee or group of employees or any individual or labor organization acting in their behalf alleging that a substantial number of employees (i) wish to be represented for collective bargaining and that their employer declines to recognize their representative as the representative defined in section 9 (a), or (ii) assert that the individual or labor organization, which has been certified or is being currently recognized by their employer as the bargaining representative, is no longer a representative as defined in section 9 (a); or

"(B) by an employer, alleging that one or more individuals or labor organizations have presented to him a claim to be recognized as the representative defined in section 9 (a);

the Board shall investigate such petition and if it has reasonable cause to believe that a question of representation affecting commerce exists shall provide for an appropriate hearing upon due notice. Such hearing may be conducted by an officer or employee of the regional office, who shall not make any recommendations with respect thereto. If the Board finds upon the record of such hearing that such a question of representation exists, it shall direct an election by secret ballot and shall certify the results thereof.

"(2) In determining whether or not a question of representation affecting commerce exists, the same regulations and rules of decision shall apply irrespective of the identity of the persons filing the petition or the kind of relief sought and in no case shall the Board deny a labor organization a place on the ballot by reason of an order with respect to such labor organization or its predecessor not issued in conformity with section 10 (c).

"(3) No election shall be directed in any bargaining unit or any subdivision within which, in the preceding twelve-month period, a valid election shall have been held. Employees on strike who are not entitled to reinstatement shall not be eligible to vote. In any election where none of the choices on the ballot receives a majority, a run-off shall be conducted, the ballot providing for a selection between the two choices receiving the largest and second largest number of valid votes cast in the election.

"(4) Nothing in this section shall be construed to prohibit the waiving of hearings by stipulation for the purpose of a consent election in conformity with regulations and rules of decision of the Board.

"(5) In determining whether a unit is appropriate for the purposes specified in subsection (b) the extent to which the employees have organized shall not be controlling.

"(d) Whenever an order of the Board made pursuant to section 10 (c) is based in whole or in part upon facts certified following an investigation pursuant to subsection (c) of this section and there is a petition for the enforcement or review of such order, such certification and the record of such investigation shall be included in the transcript of the entire record required to be filed under section 10 (e) or 10 (f), and thereupon the decree of the court enforcing, modifying, or setting aside in whole or in part the order of the Board shall be made and entered upon the pleadings, testimony, and proceedings set forth in such transcript.

"(e) (1) Upon the filing with the Board by a labor organization, which is the representative of employees as provided in section 9 (a), of a petition alleging that 30 per centum or more of the employees within a unit claimed to be appropriate for such purposes desire to authorize such labor organization to make an agreement with the employer of such employees requiring membership in such labor organization as a condition of employment in such unit, upon an appropriate showing thereof the Board shall, if no question of representation exists, take a secret ballot of such employees, and shall certify the results thereof to such labor organization and to the employer.

"(2) Upon the filing with the Board, by 30 per centum or more of the employees in a bargaining unit covered by an agreement between their employer and a labor organization made pursuant to section 8 (a) (3) (ii), of a petition alleging they desire that such authority be rescinded, the Board shall take a secret ballot of the employees in such unit, and shall certify the results thereof to such labor organization and to the employer.

"(3) No election shall be conducted pursuant to this subsection in any bargaining unit or any subdivision within which, in the preceding twelve-month period, a valid election shall have been held.

"(f) No investigation shall be made by the Board of any question affecting commerce concerning the representation of employees, raised by a labor organization under subsection (c) of this section, no petition under section 9 (e) (1) shall be entertained, and no complaint shall be issued pursuant to a charge made by a labor organization under sub-section (b) of section 10, unless such labor organization and any national or international labor organization of which such labor organization is an affiliate or constituent unit (A.) shall have prior thereto filed with the Secretary of Labor copies of its constitution and bylaws and a report, in such form as the Secretary may prescribe, showing —

"(1) the name of such labor organization and the address of its principal place of business;

"(2) the names, titles, and compensation and allowances of its three principal officers and of any of its other officers or agents whose aggregate compensation and allowances for the preceding year exceeded $5,000, and the amount of the compensation and allowances paid to each such officer or agent during such year;

"(3) the manner in which the officers and agents referred to in clause (2) were elected, appointed, or otherwise selected;

"(4) the initiation fee or fees which new members are required to pay on becoming members of such labor organization;

"(5) the regular dues or fees which members are required to pay in order to remain members in good standing of such labor organization;

"(6) a detailed statement of, or reference to provisions of its constitution and bylaws showing the procedure followed with respect to, (a) qualification for or restrictions on membership, (b) election of officers and stewards, (c) calling of regular and special meetings, (d) levying of assessments, (e) imposition of fines, (f) authorization for bargaining demands,

(g) ratification of contract terms, (h) authorization for strikes, (i) authorization for disbursement of union funds, (j) audit of union financial transactions, (k) participation in insurance or other benefit plans, and (1) expulsion of members and the grounds therefor;

and (B) can show that prior thereto it has —

"(l) filed with the Secretary of Labor, in such form as the Secretary may prescribe, a report showing all of (a,) its receipts of any kind and the sources of such receipts, (b) its total assets and liabilities as of the end of its last fiscal year, (c) the disbursements made by it during such fiscal year, including the purposes for which made; and

"(2) furnished to all of the members of such labor organization copies of the financial report required by paragraph (1) hereof to be filed with the Secretary of Labor.

"(g) It shall be the obligation of all labor organizations to file annually with the Secretary of Labor, in such form as the Secretary of Labor may prescribe, reports bringing up to date the information required to be supplied in the initial filing by subsection (f) (A) of this section, and to file with the Secretary of Labor and furnish to its members annually financial reports in the form and manner prescribed in subsection (f) (B). No labor organization shall be eligible for certification under this section as the representative of any employees, no petition under section 9 (e) (1} shall be entertained, and no complaint shall issue under section 10 with respect to a charge filed by a labor organization unless it can show that it and any national or international labor organization of which it is an affiliate or constituent unit his complied with its obligation under this subsection.

"(h) No investigation shall be made by the Board of any question affecting commerce concerning the representation of employees, raised by a labor organization under subsection (c) of this section, no petition under section 9-(e) (1) shall be entertained, and no complaint shall be issued pursuant to a charge made by a labor organization under subsection (b) of section 10, unless there is on file with the Board an affidavit executed contemporaneously or within the preceding twelve-month period by each officer of such labor organization and the officers of any national or international labor organization of which it is an affiliate or constituent unit that he is not a member of the Communist Party or affiliated with such party, and that he does not believe in, and is not a member of or supports any organization that believes in or teaches, the overthrow of the United States Government by force or by any illegal or unconstitutional methods. The provisions of section 35 A of the Criminal Code shall be applicable in respect to such affidavits.

"PREVENTION OF UNFAIR LABOR PRACTICES

"Sec. 10. (a) The Board is empowered, as hereinafter provided, to prevent any person from engaging in any unfair labor practice (listed in section 8) affecting commerce. This power shall not be affected by any other means of adjustment or prevention that has been or may be established by agreement, law, or otherwise: *Provided*, That the Board is empowered by agreement with any agency of any State or Territory to cede to such agency jurisdiction over any cases in any industry (other than mining, manufacturing, communications, and transportation except where predominantly local in character) even though such cases may involve labor disputes affecting commerce, unless the provision of the State or Territorial statute applicable to the determination of such cases by such agency is inconsistent with the corresponding provision of this Act or has received a construction inconsistent therewith.

"(b) Whenever it is charged that any person has engaged in or is engaging in any such unfair labor practice, the Board, or any agent or agency designated by the Board for such purposes, shall have power to issue and cause to be served upon such person a complaint stating the charges in that respect, and containing a notice of hearing before the Board or a member thereof, or before a designated agent or agency, at a place therein fixed, not less than five days after the serving of said complaint: *Provided*, That no complaint shall issue based upon any unfair labor practice occurring more than six months prior to the filing of the charge with the Board and the service of a copy thereof upon the person against whom such charge is made, unless the person aggrieved thereby was prevented from filing such charge by reason of service in the armed forces, in which event the six-month period shall be computed from the day of his discharge. Any such complaint may be amended by the member, agent, or agency conducting the hearing or the Board, in its discretion at any time prior to the issuance of an order based thereon. The person so complained of shall have the right to file an answer to the original or amended complaint and to appear in person or otherwise and give testimony at the place, and time fixed in the complaint. In the discretion .of the member, agent, or agency conducting the hearing or the Board, any other person may be allowed to intervene in the said proceeding and to present testimony. Any such proceeding shall, so far as practicable, be conducted in accordance with the rules of evidence applicable in the district courts of the United States under the rules of civil procedure for the district courts of the United States, adopted by the Supreme Court of the United States pursuant to the Act-of June 19, 1934 (U. S. C, title 28, secs. 723-B, 723-C).

"(c) The testimony taken by such member, agent, or agency or the Board shall be reduced to writing and filed with the Board. Thereafter, in its discretion, the Board upon notice may take further testimony or hear argument. If upon the preponderance of the testimony taken the Board shall be of the opinion that any person named in the complaint has engaged in or is engaging in any such unfair labor practice, then the Board shall state its findings of fact and shall issue and cause to be served ion such person an order requiring such person to cease and desist from such unfair labor practice, and to take such affirmative action including reinstatement of employees with or without back pay, as will effectuate the policies of this Act: *Provided*, That where an order directs reinstatement of an employee, back pay may be required of the employer or labor organization, as the case may be, responsible for the discrimination suffered by him: *And provided further*, That in determining whether a complaint shall issue alleging a violation of section 8 (a) (1) or section 8 (a) (2), and in deciding such cases, the same regulations and rules of decision shall apply irrespective of whether or not the labor organization affected is affiliated with a labor organization national or international in scope. Such order may further require such person to make reports from time to time showing the-extent to which it has complied with the order. If upon the preponderance of the testimony taken the Board shall not be of the opinion that the person named in the complaint has engaged in or is engaging in any such unfair labor practice, then the Board shall state its findings of fact and shall issue an order dismissing the said complaint. No order of the Board shall require the reinstatement of any individual as an employee, who has been suspended or discharged, or the payment to him of any back pay, if such individual was suspended or discharged, for cause. In case the evidence is presented before a member of the Board, or before an examiner or examiners thereof, such member or such examiner or examiners, as the case may be, shall issue and cause to be served on the parties to the proceeding a proposed report, together with a recommended order,

which shall be filed with the Board, and if no exceptions are filed within twenty days after service thereof upon such parties, or within such further period as the Board may authorize, such recommended order shall become the order of the Board and become effective as therein prescribed.

"(d) Until a transcript of the record in a case shall have been filed in a court, as hereinafter provided, the Board may at any time, upon reasonable notice and in such manner as it shall deem, proper, modify or set aside, in whole or in part, any finding or order made or issued by it.

"(e) The Board shall have power to petition any circuit court of appeals of the United States (including the United States Court of Appeals for the District of Columbia), or if all the circuit courts of appeals to which application may be made are in vacation, any district court of the United States (including the District Court of the United States for the District of Columbia), within any circuit or district, respectively, wherein the unfair labor practice in question occurred or wherein such person resides or transacts business, for the enforcement of such order and for appropriate temporary relief or restraining order, and shall certify and file in the court a transcript of the entire record in the proceedings, including the pleadings and testimony upon which such order was entered and the findings and order of the Board. Upon such filing, the court shall cause notice thereof to be served upon such person, and thereupon shall have jurisdiction of the proceeding and of the question determined therein, and shall have power to grant such temporary relief or restraining order as it deems just and proper, and to make and enter upon the pleadings, testimony, and proceedings set forth in such transcript a decree enforcing, modifying, and enforcing as so modified, or setting aside in whole or in part the order of the Board. No objection that has not been urged before the Board, its member, agent, or agency, shall be considered by the court, unless the failure or neglect to urge such objection shall be excused because of extraordinary circumstances. The findings of the Board with respect to questions of fact if supported by substantial evidence on the record considered as a whole shall be conclusive. If either party shall apply to the court for leave to adduce additional evidence and shall show to the satisfaction of the court that such additional evidence is material and that there were reasonable grounds for the failure to adduce such evidence in the hearing before the Board, its member, agent, or agency, the court may order such additional evidence to be taken before the Board, its members, agent, or agency, and to be made a part of the transcript. The Board may modify its findings as to the facts, or make new findings, by reason of additional evidence so taken and filed, and it shall file such modified or new findings, which findings with respect to questions of fact if supported by substantial evidence on the record considered as a whole shall be conclusive, and shall file its recommendations, if any, for the modification or setting aside of its original order. The jurisdiction of the court shall be exclusive and its judgment and decree shall be final, except that the same shall be subject to review by the appropriate circuit court of appeals if application was made to the district court as hereinabove provided, and by the Supreme Court of the United States upon writ of certiorari or certification as provided in sections 239 and 240 of the Judicial Code, as amended (U. S. C, title 28, secs. 346 and 347).

"(f) Any person aggrieved by a final order of the Board granting or denying in whole or in part the relief sought may obtain a review of such order in any circuit court of appeals of the United States in the circuit wherein the unfair labor practice in question was alleged to have been engaged in or wherein such person resides or transacts business, or in the United States Court of Appeals for the District of Columbia, by filing in such court a written petition praying that the order of the Board be modified or set aside. A copy of such petition shall be forthwith served upon the Board, and thereupon the aggrieved party shall file in the court a transcript of the entire record in the proceeding, certified by the Board, including the pleading and testimony upon which the order complained of was entered, and the findings and order of the Board. Upon such filing, the court shall proceed in the same manner as in the case of an application by the Board under subsection (e), and shall have the same exclusive jurisdiction to grant to the Board such temporary relief or restraining order as it deems just and proper, and in like manner to make and enter a decree enforcing, modifying, and enforcing as so modified, or setting aside in whole or in part the order of the Board; the findings of the Board with respect to questions of fact if supported by substantial evidence on the record considered as a whole shall in like manner be conclusive.

"(g) The commencement of proceedings under subsection (e) or (f) of this section shall not, unless specifically ordered by the court, operate as a stay of the Board's order.

"(h) When granting appropriate temporary relief or a restraining order, or making and entering a decree enforcing, modifying, and enforcing as so modified, or setting aside in whole or in part an order on the Boards as provided in this section, the jurisdiction of courts sitting in equity shall not be limited by the Act entitled 'An Act to amend the Judicial Code and to define and limit the jurisdiction of courts sitting in equity, and for other purposes', approved March 23, 1932 (U. S. C., Supp. VII, title29,secs. 101-115).

"(i) Petitions filed under this Act shall be heard expeditiously, and if possible within ten days after they have been docketed.

"(j) The Board shall have power, upon issuance of a complaint as provided in subsection (b) charging that any person has engaged in or is engaging in an unfair labor practice, to petition any district court of the United States (including the District Court of the United States for the District of Columbia), within any district wherein the unfair labor practice in question is alleged to have occurred or wherein such person resides or transacts business, for appropriate temporary relief or restraining order. Upon the filing of any such petition the court shall cause notice thereof to be served upon such person, and thereupon shall have jurisdiction to grant to the Board such temporary relief or restraining order as it deems just and proper.

"(k) Whenever it is charged that any person has engaged in an unfair labor practice within the meaning of paragraph (4) (D) of section 8 (b), the Board is empowered and directed to hear and determine the dispute out of which such unfair labor practice shall have arisen, unless, within ten days after notice that such charge has been filed, the parties to such dispute submit to the Board satisfactory evidence that they have adjusted, or agreed upon methods for the voluntary adjustment of, the dispute. Upon compliance by the parties to the dispute with the decision of the Board or upon such voluntary adjustment of the dispute, such charge shall be dismissed.

"(1) Whenever it is charged that any person has engaged in an unfair labor practice within the meaning of paragraph (4) (A), (B), or (C) of section 8 (b), the preliminary investigation of such charge shall be made forthwith and given priority over all other cases except cases of like character in the office where it is filed or to which it is referred. If, after such investigation, the officer or regional attorney to whom the matter may be deferred has reasonable cause to believe such charge is true and that a complaint should issue, he shall, on behalf of the Board, petition any district court of the United States (including the District Court of the United States for the District of Columbia) within any district where the unfair labor practice in question has occurred, is alleged to have occurred, or wherein such person resides or transacts business, for appropriate injunctive relief pending the final adjudication of the Board with respect to such matter. Upon the filing of any such petition the district court shall have jurisdiction to grant such injunctive relief or temporary restraining order as it deems just and proper, notwithstanding any other provision of law: *Provided further*, That no temporary restraining order shall be issued without notice unless a petition alleges that substantial and irreparable injury to the charging party will be unavoidable and such temporary restraining order shall be effective for no longer then five days and will become void at the expiration of such period. Upon filing of any such petition the courts shall cause notice thereof to be served upon any person involved in the charge and such person, including the charging party, shall be given an opportunity to appear by counsel and present any relevant testimony: *Provided further*, That for the purposes of this subsection district courts shall be deemed to have jurisdiction of a labor organization (1) in the district in which such organization maintains its principal office, or (2) in any district in which its duly authorized officers or agents are engaged in promoting or protecting the interests of employee members. The service of legal process upon such officer or agent shall constitute service upon the labor organization and make such organization a party to the suit. In situations where such relief is appropriate the procedure specified herein shall apply to charges with respect to section 8 (b) (4) (D).

"INVESTIGATORY POWERS

"Sec. 11. For the purpose of all hearings and investigations, which, in the opinion of the Board, are necessary and proper for the exercise of the powers vested in it by section 9 and section 10 —

"(1) The Board, or its duly authorized agents or agencies, shall at all reasonable times have access to, for the purpose of examination, and the right to copy any evidence of any person being investigated or proceeded against that relates to any matter under investigation or in question. The Board, or any member thereof shall upon application of any party to such proceedings, forthwith issue to such party subpenas requiring the attendance and testimony of witnesses or the production of any evidence in such proceeding or investigation requested in such application. Within five days after the service of a subpena

on any person requiring the production of any evidence in his possession or under his control, such person may petition the Board to revoke, and the Board shall revoke, such subpena if in its opinion the evidence whose production is required does not relate to any matter under investigation, or any matter in question in such proceedings, or if in its opinion such subpena does not describe with sufficient particularity the evidence whose production is required. Any member of the Board, or any agent or agency designated by the Board for such purposes, may administer oaths and affirmations, examine witnesses, and receive evidence. Such attendance of witnesses and the production of such evidence may be required from any place in the United States or any Territory or possession thereof, at any designated place of hearing.

"(2) In case of contumacy or refusal to obey a subpena issued to any person, any district court of the United States or the United States courts of any Territory or possession, or the District Court of the United States for the District of Columbia, within the jurisdiction of which the inquiry is carried on or within the jurisdiction of which said person guilty of contumacy or refusal to obey is found or resides or transacts business, upon application by the Board shall have jurisdiction to issue to such person an order requiring such person to appear before the Board, its member, agent, or agency, there to produce evidence if so ordered, or there to give testimony touching the matter under investigation or in question; and any failure to obey such order of the court may be punished by said court as a contempt thereof.

"(3) No person shall be excused from attending and testifying or from producing books, records, correspondence, documents, or other evidence in obedience to the subpena of the Board, on the ground that the testimony or evidence required of him may tend to incriminate him or subject him to a penalty or forfeiture; but no individual shall be prosecuted or subjected to any penalty or forfeiture for or on account of any transaction, matter, or thing concerning which he is compelled, after having claimed his privilege against self-incrimination, to testify or produce evidence, except that such individual so testifying shall not be exempt from prosecution and punishment for perjury committed in so testifying.

"(4) Complaints, orders, and other process and papers of the Board its member, agent, or agency, may be served either personally or by registered mail or by telegraph or by leaving a copy thereof at the principal office or place of business of the person required to be served. The verified return by the individual so serving the same setting forth the manner of such service shall be proof of the same, and the return post office receipt or telegraph receipt therefor when registered and mailed or telegraphed as aforesaid shall be proof of service of the same. Witnesses summoned before the Board, its member, agent, or agency, shall be paid the same fees and mileage that are paid witnesses in the courts of the United States, and witnesses whose depositions are taken and the persons taking the same shall severally be entitled to the same fees as are paid for like services in the courts of the United States.

"(5) All process of any court to which application may be made under this Act may be served in the judicial district wherein the defendant or other person required to be served resides or may be found.

"(6) The several departments and agencies of the Government, when directed by the President, shall furnish the Board, upon its request, all records, papers, and information in their possession relating to any matter before the Board.

"Sec. 12. Any person who shall willfully resist, prevent, impede, or interfere with any member of the Board or any of its agents or agencies in the performance of duties pursuant to this Act shall be punished by a fine of not more than $5,000 or by imprisonment for not more than one year, or both.

"LIMITATIONS

"Sec. 13. Nothing in this Act, except as specifically provided for herein, shall be construed so as either to interfere with or impede or diminish in any way the right to strike, or to affect the limitations or qualifications on that right.

"Sec. 14. (a) Nothing herein shall prohibit any individual employed as a supervisor from becoming or remaining a member of a labor organization, but no employer subject to this Act shall be compelled to deem individuals defined herein as supervisors as employees for the purpose of any law, either national or local, relating to collective bargaining.

"(b) Nothing in this Act shall be construed as authorizing the execution or application of agreements requiring membership in a labor organization as a condition of employment in any State or Territory in which such execution or application is prohibited by State or Territorial law.

"Sec. 15. Wherever the application of the provisions of section 272 of chapter 10 of the Act entitled 'An Act to establish a uniform system of bankruptcy throughout the United States', approved July 1, 1898, and Acts amendatory thereof and supplementary thereto (U. S. C., title 11, sec. 672), conflicts with the application of the provisions of this Act, this Act shall prevail: *Provided*, That in any situation where the provisions of this Act cannot be validly enforced, the provisions of such other Acts shall remain in full force and effect.

"Sec. 16. If any provision of this Act, or the application of such provision to any person or circumstances, shall be held invalid, the remainder of this Act, or the application of such provision to persons or circumstances other than those as to which it is held invalid, shall not be affected thereby.

"Sec. 17. This Act may be cited as the 'National Labor Relations Act'."

EFFECTIVE DATE OF CERTAIN CHANGES

Sec. 102. No provision of this title shall be deemed to make an unfair labor practice any act which was performed prior to the date of the enactment of this Act which did not constitute an unfair labor practice prior thereto, and the provisions of section 8 (a) (3) and section 8 (b) (2) of the National Labor Relations Act as amended by this title shall not make an unfair labor practice the performance of any obligation under a collective-bargaining agreement entered into prior to the date of the enactment of this Act, or (in the case of an agreement for a period of not more than one year) entered into on or after such date of enactment, but prior to the effective date of this title, if the performance of such obligation would not have constituted an unfair labor practice under section 8 (3) of the National Labor Relations Act prior to the effective date of this title, unless such agreement was renewed or extended subsequent thereto.

Sec. 103. No provisions of this title shall affect any certification of representatives or any determination as to the appropriate collective-bargaining unit, which was made under section 9 of the National Labor Relations Act prior to the effective date of this title until one year after the date of such certification or if, in respect of any such certification, a collective-bargaining contract was entered into prior to the effective date of this title, until the end of the contract period or until one year after such date, whichever first occurs.

Sec. 104. The amendments made by this title shall take effect sixty days after the date of the enactment of this Act, except that the authority of the President to appoint certain officers conferred upon him by section 3 of the National Labor Relations Act as amended by this title may be exercised forthwith.

Title II—Conciliation of Labor Disputes in Industries Affecting Commerce; National Emergencies

Sec. 201. That it is the policy of the United States that —

(a) sound and stable industrial peace and the advancement of the general welfare, health, and safety of the Nation and of the best interests of employers and employees can most satisfactorily be secured by the settlement of issues between employers and employees through the processes of conference and collective bargaining between employers and the representatives of their employees;

(b) the settlement of issues between employers and employees through collective bargaining may be advanced by making available full and adequate governmental facilities for conciliation, mediation, and voluntary arbitration to aid and encourage employers and the representatives of their employees to reach and maintain agreements concerning rates of pay, hours and working conditions, and to make all reasonable efforts to settle their differences by mutual agreement reached through conferences and collective bargaining or by such methods as may be provided for in any applicable agreement for the settlement of disputes; and

(c) certain controversies which arise between parties to collective-bargaining agreements may be avoided or minimized by making available full and adequate governmental facilities for furnishing assistance to employers and the representatives of their employees in formulating for inclusion within such agreements provision for adequate notice of any proposed changes in the terms of such agreements, for the final adjustment of grievances or questions regarding the application or interpretation of such agreements, and other provisions designed to prevent the subsequent arising of such controversies.

Sec. 202. (a) There is hereby created an independent agency to be known as the Federal Mediation and Conciliation Service (herein referred to as the "Service", except that for sixty days after the date of the enactment of this Act such term shall refer to the Conciliation Service of the Department of Labor). The Service shall be under the direction of a Federal Mediation and Conciliation Director (hereinafter referred to as the "Director"), who shall be appointed by the President by and with the advice and consent of the Senate. The Director shall receive compensation at the rate of $12,000 per annum. The Director shall not engage in any other business, vocation, or employment.

(b) The Director is authorized, subject to the civil-service laws, to appoint such clerical and other personnel as may be necessary for the execution of the functions of the Service, and shall fix their compensation in accordance with the Classification Act of 1923, as amended, and may, without regard to the provisions of the civil-service laws and the Classification Act of 1923, as amended, appoint and fix the compensation of such conciliators and mediators as may be necessary to carry out the functions of the Service. The Director is authorized to make such expenditures for supplies, facilities, and services as he deems necessary. Such expenditures shall be allowed and paid upon presentation of itemized vouchers therefor approved by the Director or by any employee designated by him for that purpose.

(c) The principal office of the Service shall be in the District of Columbia, but the Director may establish regional offices convenient to localities in which labor controversies are likely to arise. The Director may by order, subject to revocation at any time, delegate any authority and discretion conferred upon him by this Act to any regional director, or other officer or employee of the Service. The Director may establish suitable procedures for cooperation with State and local mediation agencies. The Director shall make an annual report in writing to Congress at the end of the fiscal year.

(d) All mediation and conciliation functions of the Secretary of Labor or the United States Conciliation Service under section 8 of the Act entitled "An Act to create a Department of Labor", approved March 4, 1913 (U. S. C., title 29, sec. 51), and all functions of the United States Conciliation Service under any other law are hereby transferred to the Federal Mediation and Conciliation Service, together with the personnel and records of the United States Conciliation Service. Such transfer shall take effect upon the sixtieth day after the date of enactment of this Act. Such transfer shall not affect any proceedings pending before the United States Conciliation Service or any certification, order, rule, or regulation theretofore made by it or by the Secretary of Labor. The Director and the Service shall not be subject in any way to the jurisdiction or authority of the Secretary of Labor or any official or division of the Department of Labor.

FUNCTIONS OF THE SERVICE

Sec. 203. (a) It shall be the duty of the Service, in order to prevent or minimize interruptions of the free flow of commerce growing out of labor disputes, to assist parties to labor disputes in industries affecting commerce to settle such disputes through conciliation and mediation.

(b) The Service may proffer its services in any labor dispute in any industry affecting commerce, either upon its own motion or upon the request of one or more of the parties to the dispute, whenever in its judgment such dispute threatens to cause a substantial interruption of commerce. The Director and the Service are directed to avoid attempting to mediate disputes which would have only a minor effect on interstate commerce if State or other conciliation services are available to the parties. Whenever the Service does proffer its services in any dispute, it shall be the duty of the Service promptly to put itself in communication with the parties and to use its best efforts, by mediation and conciliation, to bring them to agreement.

(c) If the Director is not able to bring the parties to agreement by conciliation within a reasonable time, he shall seek to induce the parties voluntarily to seek other means of settling the dispute without resort to strike, lock-out, or other coercion, including submission to the employees in the bargaining unit of the employer's last offer of settlement for approval or rejection in a secret ballot. The failure or refusal of either party to agree to any procedure suggested by the Director shall not be deemed a violation of any duty or obligation imposed by this Act.

(d) Final adjustment by a method agreed upon, by the parties is hereby declared to be the desirable method for settlement of grievance disputes arising over the application or interpretation of an existing collective-bargaining agreement. The Service is directed to make its conciliation and mediation services available in the settlement of such grievance disputes only as a last resort and in exceptional cases.

"**Sec. 204**. (a) In order to prevent or minimize interruptions of the free flow of commerce growing out of labor disputes, employers and employees and their representatives, in any industry affecting commerce, shall —

(1) exert every reasonable effort to make and maintain agreements concerning rates of pay, hours, and working conditions, including provision for adequate notice of any proposed change in the terms of such agreements;

(2) whenever a dispute arises over the terms or application of a collective-bargaining agreement and a conference is requested by a party or prospective party thereto, arrange promptly for such a conference to be held and endeavor in such conference to settle such dispute expeditiously; and

(3) in case such dispute is not settled by conference, participate fully and promptly in such meetings as may be undertaken by the Service under this Act for the purpose of aiding in d settlement of the dispute.

Sec. 205. (a) There is hereby created a National Labor-Management Panel which shall be composed of twelve members appointed by the President, six of whom shall be selected from, among persons outstanding in the field of management and six of whom shall be selected from among persons outstanding in the field of labor. Each member shall hold office for a term of three years, except that any member appointed to fill a vacancy occurring prior to the expiration of the term for which his predecessor was appointed shall be appointed for the remainder of such term, and the terms of office of the members first taking office shall expire, as designated by the President at the time of appointment, four at the end of the first year, four at the end of the second year, and four at the end of the third year after the date bf appointment. Members of the panel, when serving on business of the panel, shall be paid compensation at the rate of $25 per day, and shall also be entitled to receive an allowance for actual and necessary travel and subsistence expenses while so serving away from their places of residence.

(b) It shall be the duty of the panel, at the request of the Director, to advise in the avoidance of industrial controversies and the manner in which mediation and voluntary adjustment shall be administered, particularly with reference to controversies affecting the general welfare of the country.

NATIONAL EMERGENCIES

Sec. 206. Whenever in the opinion of the President of the United States, a threatened or actual strike or lock-out affecting an entire industry or a substantial part thereof engaged in trade, commerce, transportation, transmission, or communication among the several States or with foreign nations, or engaged in the production of goods for commerce, will, if permitted to occur or to continue, imperil the national health or safety, he may appoint a board of inquiry to inquire into the issues involved in the dispute and to make a written report to him within such time as he shall prescribe. Such report shall include a statement of the facts with respect to the dispute, including each party's statement of its position but shall not contain any recommendations. The President shall file a copy of such report with the Service .and shall make its contents available to the public.

Sec. 207. (a) A board of inquiry shall be composed of a chairman and such other members as the

President shall determine, and shall have power to sit and act in any place within the United States and: to conduct such hearings either in public or in private, as it may deem necessary or proper, to ascertain the facts with respect to the causes and circumstances of the dispute.

(b) Members of a board of inquiry shall receive compensation at the rate of $50 for each day actually spent by them in the work of the board, together with necessary travel and subsistence expenses.

(c) For the purpose of any hearing or inquiry conducted by any board appointed under this title, the provisions of sections 9 and 10 (relating to the attendance of witnesses and the production of books, papers, and documents) of the Federal Trade Commission Act of September 16, 1914, as amended (U. S. C. 19, title 16, secs. 49 and 50, as amended), are hereby made applicable to the powers and duties of such board.

Sec. 208. (a) Upon receiving a report from a board of inquiry the President may direct the Attorney General to petition any district court of the United States having jurisdiction of the parties to enjoin such strike or lock-out or the continuing thereof, and if the court finds that such threatened or actual strike or lock-out —

(i) affects an entire industry or a substantial part thereof engaged in trade, commerce, transportation, transmission, or communication among the several States or with foreign nations, or engaged in the production of goods for commerce: and

(ii) if permitted to occur or to continue, will imperil the national health or safety, it shall have jurisdiction to enjoin any such strike or lock-out, or the continuing thereof, and to make such other orders as may be appropriate.

(b) In any case, the provisions of the Act of March 23, 1932, entitled "An Act to amend the Judicial Code and to define and limit the jurisdiction of courts sitting in equity, and for other purposes", shall not be applicable.

(c) The order or orders of the court shall be subject to review by the appropriate circuit court of appeals and by the Supreme Court upon writ of certiorari or certification as provided in sections 239 and 240 of the Judicial Code, as amended (U. S. C., title 29, secs. 346 and 347).

Sec. 209. (a) Whenever a district court has issued an order under section 208 enjoining acts or practices which imperil or threaten to imperil the national health or safety, it shall be the duty of the parties to the labor dispute giving rise to such order

to make every effort to adjust and settle their differences, with the assistance of the Service created by this Act. Neither party shall be under any duty to accept, in whole or in part, any proposal of settlement made by the Service.

(b) Upon the issuance of such order, the President shall reconvene the board of inquiry which has previously reported with respect to the dispute. At the end of a sixty-day period (unless the dispute has bee settled by that time), the board of inquiry shall report to the President the current position of the parties and the efforts which have been made for settlement, and shall include a statement by each party of its position and a statement of the employer's last offer of settlement. The President shall make such report available to the public. The National Labor Relations Board, within the succeeding fifteen days, shall take a secret ballot of the employees of each employer involved in the dispute on the question of whether they wish to accept the final offer of settlement made by their employer as stated by him and shall certify the results thereof to the Attorney General within five days thereafter.

Sec. 210. Upon the certification of the results of such ballot or upon a settlement being reached, whichever happens sooner, the Attorney General shall move the court to discharge tie injunction, which motion shall then be granted and the injunction-discharged. When such motion is granted, the President shall submit to the Congress a full and comprehensive report of the proceeding including the findings of the board of inquiry and the ballot take by the National Labor Relations Board, together with such recommendations as he may see fit to make for consideration and appropriate action.

COMPILATION OF COLLECTIVE BARGAINING AGREEMENTS, ETC.

Sec. 211. (a) For the guidance and information of interested representatives of employers, employees, and the general public, the Bureau of Labor Statistics of the Department of Labor shall maintain a file of copies of all available collective bargaining agreements and other available agreements and actions thereunder settling or adjusting labor disputes. Such file shall be open to inspection under appropriate conditions prescribed by the Secretary of Labor, except that no specific information submitted in confidence shall be disclosed.

(b) The Bureau of Labor Statistics in the Department of Labor is authorized to furnish upon request of the Service, or employers, employees, or their representatives, all available data and factual information which may aid in the settlement of any labor dispute, except that no specific information submitted in confidence shall be disclosed.

EXEMPTION OF RAILWAY LABOR ACT

Sec. 212. The provisions of this title shall not be applicable with respect to any matter which is subject to the provisions of the Railway Labor Act, as amended from time to time.

Title III

SUITS BY AND AGAINST LABOR ORGANIZATIONS

Sec. 301. (a) Suits for violation of contracts between an employer and a labor organization representing employees in an industry affecting commerce as defined in this Act, or between any such labor organizations, may be brought in any district court of the United States having jurisdiction of the parties, without respect to the amount in controversy or without regard to the citizenship of the parties.

(b) Any labor organization which represents employees in an industry affecting commerce as defined in this Act and any employer whose activities affect commerce as defined in this Act shall be bound by the acts of its agents. Any such labor organization may sue or be sued as an entity and in behalf of the employees whom it represents in the courts of the United States. Any money judgment against a labor organization in a district court or the United States shall be enforceable only against the organization as an entity and against its assets, and shall not be enforceable against any individual member or his assets.

(c) For the purposes of actions and proceedings by or against labor organizations in the district courts of the United States, district courts shall be deemed to have jurisdiction of a labor organization (1) in the district in which such organization maintains its principal office, or (2) in any district in which its duly authorized officers or agents are engaged in representing or acting for employee members.

(d) The service of summons, subpena, or other legal process of any court of the United States upon an officer or agent of a labor organization, in his capacity as such, shall constitute service upon the labor organization.

(e) For the purposes of this section, in determining whether any person is acting as an "agent" of another person so as to make such other person responsible for his acts, the question of whether the specific acts performed were actually authorized or subsequently ratified shall not be controlling.

RESTRICTIONS ON PAYMENTS TO EMPLOYEE REPRESENTATIVES

Sec. 302. (a) It shall be unlawful for any employer to pay or deliver, or to agree to pay or deliver, any money or other thing of value to any representative of any of his employees who are employed in an industry affecting commerce.

(b) It shall be unlawful for any representative of any employees who are employed in an industry affecting commerce to receive or accept, or to agree to receive or accept, from the employer of such employees any money or other thing of value.

(c) The provisions of this section shall not be applicable (1) with respect to any money or other thing of value payable by an employer to any, representative who is an employee or former employee of such employer, as compensation for, or by reason of, his services as an employee of such employer; (2) with respect to the payment or delivery of any money or other thing of value in satisfaction of a judgment of any court or a decision or award of an arbitrator or impartial chairman or in compromise, adjustment, settlement or release of any claim, complaint, grievance, or dispute in the absence of fraud or duress; (3) with respect to the sale or purchase of an article or commodity at the prevailing market price in the regular course of business; (4) with respect to money deducted from the wages of employees in payment of membership dues in a labor organization: *Provided*, That the employer, has received from each employee, on whose account such deductions are made, a written assignment which shall not be irrevocable for a period of more than one year, or beyond the termination date of the applicable collective agreement, whichever occurs sooner; or (5) with respect to money or other thing of value paid to a trust fund established by such representative, for the sole and exclusive benefit of the employees of such employer, and their families and dependents (or of such employees, families, and dependents jointly with the employees of other employers making similar payments, and their families and dependents): *Provided*, That (A) such payments are held in trust for the purpose of paying, either from principal or income or both, for the benefit of employees, their families and dependents, for medical or hospital care, pensions on retirement or death of employees, compensation for injuries or illness resulting from occupational activity or insurance to provide any of the foregoing, or unemployment benefits or life insurance, disability and sickness insurance, or accident insurance; (B) the detailed basis on which such payments are to be made is specified in a written agreement with the employer, and employees and employers are equally represented in the administration of such fund, together with such neutral persons as the representatives of the employers and the representatives of the employees may agree upon and in the event the employer and employee groups deadlock on the administration of such fund and there are no neutral persons empowered to break such deadlock, such agreement provides that the two groups shall agree on an impartial umpire to decide such dispute, or in event of their failure to agree within a reasonable length of time, an impartial umpire to decide such dispute shall, on petition of either group, be appointed by the district court of the United States for the district where the trust fund has its principal office, and shall also contain provisions for an annual audit of the trust fund, a statement of the results of which shall be available for inspection by interested persons at the principal office of the trust fund and at such other places as may be designated in such written agreement; and (C) such payments as are intended to be used for the purpose of providing pensions or annuities for employees are made to a separate trust which provides that the funds held therein cannot be used for any purpose other than paying such pensions or annuities.

(d) Any person who willfully violates any of the provisions of this section shall, upon conviction thereof, be guilty of a misdemeanor and be subject to a fine of not more than $10,000 or to imprisonment for not more than one year, or both.

(e) The district courts of the United States and the United States courts of the Territories and possessions shall have jurisdiction, for cause shown, and subject to the provisions of section 17 (relating to notice to opposite party) of the Act entitled "An Act to supplement existing laws against unlawful restraints and monopolies, and for other purposes", approved October 15, 1914, as amended (U. S. C., title 28, sec. 381), to restrain violations of this section, without regard to the provisions of sections 6 and 20 of such Act of October 15, 1914, as amended (U. S. C., title 15, sec. 17, and title 29, sec. 52), and the provisions of the Act entitled "An Act to amend the Judicial Code and to define and limit the jurisdiction of courts sitting in equity, and for other purposes", approved March 23, 1932 (U. S. C., title 29, secs. 101-115).

(f) This section shall not apply to any contract in force on the date of enactment of this Act, until the expiration of such contract, or until July 1, 1948, whichever first occurs.

(g) Compliance with the restrictions contained in subsection (c) (5) (B) upon contributions to trust funds, otherwise lawful, shall not be applicable to contributions to such trust funds established by collective agreement prior to January 1, 1946, nor shall subsection (c) (5) (A) be construed as prohibiting contributions to such trust funds if prior to January 1, 1947, such funds contained provisions for pooled vacation benefits.

BOYCOTTS AND OTHER UNLAWFUL COMBINATIONS

Sec. 303. (a) It shall be unlawful, for the purposes of this section only, in an industry or activity affecting commerce, for any labor organization to engage in, or to induce or encourage the employees of any employer to engage in, a strike or a concerted refusal in the course of their employment to use, manufacture, process, transport, or otherwise handle or work on any goods, articles, materials, or commodities or to perform any services, where an object thereof is —

(1) forcing or requiring any employer or self-employed person to join any labor or employer organization or any employer or other person to cease using, selling, handling, transporting, or otherwise dealing in the products of any other producer, processor, or manufacturer, or to cease doing business with any other person;

(2) forcing or requiring any other employer to recognize or bargain with a labor organization as the representative of his employees unless such labor organization has been certified as the representative of such employees under the provisions of section 9 of the National Labor Relations Act;

(3) forcing or requiring any employer to recognize or bargain with a particular labor organization as the representative of his employees if another labor organization has been certified as the representative of such employees under the provisions of section 9 of the National Labor Relations Act;

(4) forcing or requiring any employer to assign particular work to employees in a particular labor organization or in a particular trade, craft, or class rather than to employees in another labor organization or in another trade, craft, or class unless such employer is failing to conform to an order or certification of the National Labor Relations Board determining the bargaining representative for employees performing such work. Nothing contained in this subsection shall be construed to make unlawful a refusal by any person to enter upon the premises of any employer (other than his own employer), if the employees of such employer are engaged in a strike ratified or approved by a representative of such employees whom such employer is required to recognize under the National Labor Relations Act.

(b) Whoever shall be injured in his business or property by reason or any violation of subsection (a) may sue therefor in any district court of the United States subject to the limitations and provisions of section 301 hereof without respect to the amount in controversy, or in any other court having jurisdiction of the parties, and shall recover the damages by him sustained and the cost of the suit.

RESTRICTION ON POLITICAL CONTRIBUTIONS

Sec. 304. Section 313 of the Federal Corrupt Practices Act, 1925 (U. S. C., 1940 edition, title 2, sec. 251; Supp. V, title 50, App., sec. 1509), as amended, is amended to read as follows:

"Sec. 313. It is unlawful for any national bank, or any corporation organized by authority of any law of Congress, to make a contribution or expenditure in connection with any election to any political office or in connection with any primary election or political convention or caucus held to select candidates for any political office, or for any corporation whatever, or any labor organization to make a contribution or expenditure in connection with any election at which Presidential and Vice Presidential electors or a Senator or Representative in, or a Delegate or Resident Commissioner to Congress are to be voted for, or in connection with any primary election or political convention or caucus held to select candidates for any of the foregoing offices, or for any candidate, political committee, or other person to accept or receive any contribution prohibited by this section. Every corporation or labor organization which makes any contribution or expenditure in violation of this section shall be fined not more than $5,000; and every officer or director of any corporation, or officer of any labor organization, who consents to any contribution or expenditure by the corporation or labor organization, as the case may be, in violation of this section shall be fined not more than $1,000 or imprisoned for not more than one year, or both. For the purposes of this section 'labor organization' means any organization of any kind, or any agency or Employee representation committee or plan, in which employees participate and which exists for the purpose, in whole or in part, of dealing with employers concerning grievances, labor disputes, wages, rates of pay, hours of employment, or conditions of work."

STRIKES BY GOVERNMENT EMPLOYEES

Sec. 305. It shall be unlawful for any individual employed by the United States or any agency thereof including wholly owned Government corporations to participate in any strike. Any individual employed by the United States or by any such agency who strikes shall be discharged immediately from his employment, and shall forfeit his civil service status, if any, and shall not be eligible for reemployment for three years by the United States or any such agency.

Title IV

CREATION OF JOINT COMMITTEE TO STUDY AND REPORT ON BASIC PROBLEMS AFFECTING FRIENDLY LABOR RELATIONS AND PRODUCTIVITY

Sec. 401. There is hereby established a joint congressional committee to be known as the Joint Committee on Labor-Management Relations (hereafter referred to as the committee), and to be composed of seven Members of the Senate Committee on Labor and Public Welfare, to be appointed by the President pro tempore of the Senate, and seven Members of the House of Representatives Committee on Education and Labor, to be appointed by the Speaker of the House of Representatives. A vacancy in membership of the committee shall not affect the powers of the remaining members to execute the functions of the committee, and shall be filled in the same manner as the original selection. The committee shall select a chairman and a vice chairman from among its members.

Sec. 402. The committee, acting as a whole or by subcommittee, shall conduct a thorough study and investigation of the entire field of labor-management relations, including but not limited to —

(1) the means by which permanent friendly cooperation between employers and employees and stability of labor relations may be secured throughout the United States;

(2) the means by which the individual employee may achieve a greater productivity and higher wages, including plans for guaranteed annual wages, incentive profit-sharing and bonus systems;

(3) the internal organization and administration of labor unions, with special attention of the impact on individuals of collective agreements requiring membership in unions as a condition of employment;

(4) the labor relations policies and practices of employers and associations of employers;

(5) the desirability of welfare funds for the benefit of employees and their relation to the social-security system;

(6) the methods and procedures for best carrying out the collective-bargaining processes, with special attention to the effects of industry-wide or regional bargaining upon the national economy;

(7) the administration and operation of existing Federal laws relating to labor relations; and

(8) such other problems and subjects in the field of labor-management relations as the committee deems appropriate.

Sec. 403. The committee shall report to the Senate and the House of Representatives not later than March 15, 1948, the results of its study and investigation, together with such recommendations as to necessary legislation and such other recommendations as it may deem advisable, and shall make its final report not later than January 2, 1949.

Sec. 404. The committee shall have the power, without regard to the civil-service laws and the Classification Act of 1923, as amended, to employ and fix the compensation of such officers, experts, and employees as it deems necessary for the performance of its duties, including consultants who shall receive compensation at a rate not to exceed $35 for each day actually spent by them in the work of the committee, together with their necessary travel and subsistence expenses. The committee is further authorized, with the consent of the head of the department or agency concerned, to utilize the services, information, facilities, and personnel of all agencies in the executive branch of the Government and may request the governments of the several States, representatives of business, industry, finance, and labor, and such other persons, agencies, organizations, and instrumentalities as it deems appropriate to attend its hearings and to give and present information, advice, and recommendations.

Sec. 405. The committee, or any subcommittee thereof, is authorized to hold such hearings; to sit and act at such times and places during the sessions, recesses, and adjourned periods of the Eightieth Congress; to require by subpena or otherwise the attendance of such witnesses and the production of such books, papers, and documents; to administer oaths; to take such testimony; to have such printing and binding done; and to make such expenditures within the amount appropriated therefore; as it deems advisable. The cost of stenographic services in reporting such hearings shall not be in excess of 25 cents per one hundred words. Subpenas shall be issued under the signature of the chairman or vice chairman of the committee and shall be served by any person designated by them.

Sec. 406. The members of the committee shall be reimbursed for travel, subsistence, and other necessary expenses incurred by them in the performance of the duties vested in the committee, other than expenses in connection with meetings of the committee held in the District of Columbia during such times as the Congress is in session.

Sec. 407. There is hereby authorized to be appropriated the sum of $150,000, or so much thereof as may be necessary, to carry out the provisions of this title, to be disbursed by the Secretary of the Senate on vouchers signed by the chairman.

Title V

DEFINITIONS

Sec. 501. When used in this Act —

(1) The term "industry affecting commerce" means any industry or activity in commerce or in which a labor dispute would burden or obstruct commerce or tend to burden or obstruct commerce or the free flow of commerce.

(2) The term "strike" includes any strike or other concerted stoppage of work by employees (including a stoppage by reason of the expiration of a collective-bargaining agreement) and any concerted slow-down or other concerted interruption of operations by employees.

(3) The terms "commerce", "labor disputes", "employer", "employee", "labor organization", "representative", "person", and "supervisor" shall have the same meaning as when used in the National Labor Relations Act as amended by this Act.

SAVINGS PROVISION

Sec. 502. Nothing in this Act shall be construed to require an individual employee to render labor or service without his consent, nor shall anything in. this Act be construed to make the quitting of his labor by an individual employee an illegal act; nor shall any court issue any process to compel the performance by an individual employee of such labor or service, without his consent; nor shall the quitting of labor by an employee or employees in good faith because of abnormally dangerous conditions for work at the place of employment of such employee or employees be deemed a strike under this Act.

SEPARABILITY

Sec. 503. If any provision of this Act, or the application of such provision to any person or circumstance, shall be held invalid, the remainder of this Act, or the application of such provision to persons or circumstances other than those as to which it is held invalid, shall not be affected thereby.

This Government has been informed that a Jewish state has been proclaimed in Palestine, and recognition has been requested by the *provisional* Government thereof.

The United States recognizes the provisional government as the de facto authority of the new ~~Jewish~~ *State of* ~~state.~~ *Israel.*

Harry Truman

*Approved.
May 14, 1948.*

6.11

The Press Release Announcing U.S. Recognition of Israel (National Archives and Records Administration)

"The United States recognizes the provisional government as the de facto authority of the new State of Israel."

Overview

On May 14, 1948, just eleven minutes after David Ben-Gurion began reading Israel's Declaration of Independence in Tel Aviv, President Harry S. Truman signed a brief, tersely worded statement recognizing Ben-Gurion's "provisional government as the de facto authority of the new State of Israel." The United States thus became the first country in the world to recognize the newly founded state of Israel. Eight months later, on January 31, 1949, following the election of a permanent government in Israel and his own reelection and inauguration, Truman extended "de jure recognition to the Government of Israel" (http://www.jewishvirtuallibrary.org/jsource/US-Israel/truman_Israel1), meaning now that the recognition was in law as well as in fact.

Truman's intense personal involvement in the recognition of Israel, the immediacy of his action, and his bifurcation of the recognition process were all expressions of the intense debate over the U.S. role in the Middle East and beyond. This debate over the redefinition of Palestine following the end of the British Mandate in May 1948 had raged inside the White House, throughout the American government, and in the public sector since the end of World War II. The cold war, petro-politics, American domestic politics, and the president's own deep personal beliefs all figured in shaping the complex, often emotionally charged issue. Following two decades of subsequent qualified American support of Israel, the same pro-Israel factors that had led to Truman's initial recognition of the Jewish state in 1948 ultimately contributed to the forging of a unique relationship between the two states and massive American economic, diplomatic, and military support of Israel.

Context

U.S. recognition of Israel took place amidst complex historical circumstances. Global, regional, domestic political, religious, and perhaps even personal factors figured into Truman's decision to recognize the Jewish state without fully consulting or informing numerous key individuals in the State Department or at the United Nations. To fully appreciate the context of Truman's decision, each of these areas needs to be considered individually and collectively.

The end of World War II was accompanied by massive changes on the global political landscape. Nazi Germany and Imperial Japan had been compelled to accept unconditional terms of surrender. Germany was divided up among the victorious Allies in the West and fell under Communist control in the East. Japan was occupied and stripped of all military capacity. On the Allied side, France and the United Kingdom, though victorious in war, began to lose their colonial empires and were rapidly replaced by two new superpowers, the United States and the Soviet Union, and by conflicting Arab and Jewish nationalisms at the regional level in the Middle East.

For the United States, the major concern in its general conduct of foreign policy in the postwar era was the need to contain the Soviet Union from expanding its influence around the world, including the Mediterranean basin. The State Department and, to a somewhat lesser extent, the U.S. military did not see a future Jewish state as an asset in America's effort to counter the Soviets. In their view, a Jewish state was probably not defensible against the Arabs and would require significant, on-the-ground American military protection. Moreover, the Arabs, who all but universally opposed the establishment of Israel, sat on the world's largest-known oil reserves, which were vital to American interests. The predominance of Jews of Russian origin who embraced socialism as an economic, if not a political ideology was also of some concern.

Reasons not to recognize Israel, on the other hand, were counterbalanced by other factors and arguments. The Nazi annihilation of six million Jews as well as the survival of several hundred thousand European Jews, including a significant population of stateless refugees, had created a morally charged political environment inside the United States, despite Jewish terrorism against the British in Palestine. Grassroots American sympathy for the Jewish people had resulted in a broad transformation of grassroots and elite anti-Semitism into an increasingly pro-Israel viewpoint, amplified by an emerging Christian Zionism in the United States. Truman himself had been moved by a special report "on the Treatment of Displaced Jews"

Time Line

1917

■ **November 2**
British government issues the Balfour Declaration.

1923

■ **September 29**
British Mandate in Palestine is finalized.

1933

■ **January 30**
Adolf Hitler is sworn in as chancellor of Germany.

1939

■ **May 17**
British White Paper severely limits Jewish immigration to Palestine as part of the United Kingdom's general appeasement policy toward Hitler and Nazism.

1945

■ **May 8**
Nazi Germany surrenders unconditionally to the Allies.

1946

■ **April**
The Anglo-American Committee of Inquiry, a joint British-American group formed to resolve the escalating conflict between Arabs and Jews in Palestine, submits its report.

■ **October 4**
Truman petitions U.S. Congress to liberalize immigration laws to allow Jewish survivors of the Holocaust to settle in the United States.

1947

■ **February 7**
British government announces its intention to terminate its Mandate in Palestine.

■ **August**
An eleven-country United Nations Special Committee on Palestine recommends the partition of the British Mandate.

■ **November 29**
United Nations votes to partition Palestine into Arab and Jewish sectors and internationalizes Jerusalem.

authored by a special American envoy, Earl G. Harrison, in September 1945. This report was sharply critical of America's handling of the thousands of stateless Jews under Allied protection in postwar Europe. At different times in 1945 and 1946, Truman publicly advocated settling 100,000 displaced Jews in Palestine and 200,000 in the United States.

In the American Jewish community, Zionism, the global Jewish nationalist movement organized by Theodor Herzl at the end of the nineteenth century, had already emerged as a predominant ideology by 1942. Demands for Jewish statehood in Palestine overwhelmingly outweighed a counterthrust of anti-Zionism among some elite American Jews. The heavy concentration of Jews in New York as well as in Pennsylvania, Illinois, and other key states possibly had a bearing on Truman's reelection in November 1948. The matter left the president, who had been sworn into office because of the death of Franklin Delano Roosevelt just before World War II ended, open to charges by his Republican opponents that he was playing politics with American foreign policy. By contrast, neither the Arab states nor Muslims in general had a strong political base in the United States.

By contrast, during the 1930s the Arab countries and the Arabs of Palestine slowly gained a tactical advantage in the Middle East over the Jews of the British Mandate for Palestine. In 1917, the United Kingdom issued the Balfour Declaration, stating that the British government favored "the establishment in Palestine of a national home for the Jewish people" (http://www.yale.edu/lawweb/avalon/mideast/balfour.htm). During World War I, British armies defeated the Ottomans in Palestine. In 1922, the British established its Mandate in Palestine west of the Jordan River. To the east, the larger territory under British control was named the Transjordan, which became the independent Hashemite Kingdom of Jordan. Despite local anti-Jewish Arab violence in the 1920s and 1930s, the Jewish presence in Palestine grew steadily both in outlying areas and in the major cities. But with the rise of Nazism in Germany and the further intensification of Arab resistance to Zionism, London began to change course until it finally issued the White Paper of 1939. This statement essentially choked off Jewish immigration and assured the preservation of an Arab majority in the Mandate. However, British appeasement of the Arabs not only failed to weaken the resolve of the Jews in Palestine but actually intensified their desire to create a state of their own. Following the war, a joint Anglo-American Committee of Inquiry was formed to address the need to find a home for the Jewish displaced persons trapped in Europe after the war. It also addressed the deteriorating situation in Palestine. Its recommendations were largely rejected by the British government under Prime Minister Clement Attlee, the Arabs, and the Jews.

The United Kingdom was fatigued by the failure of all diplomatic efforts and the escalating fighting in Palestine. It was further frustrated by other postwar colonial problems, particularly in India-Pakistan. Thus, the British were determined to leave Palestine and turn over the administration of the Mandate to the United Nations. In May 1947, an eleven-country United Nations Special Committee on Palestine was formed to develop a plan for post-British Palestine. Six months later, in November 1947, the United Nations General Assembly adopted Resolution 181, which called for the partition of British Palestine into three zones: Jewish, Arab, and an international zone with Jerusalem functioning as what the United Nations called a "corpus separatum," or "separate body" (http://www.yale.edu/law web/avalon/un/res181.htm).

The Jews quickly accepted the plan, despite their unhappiness with the international status of Jerusalem and with other border issues, particularly in the Mandate's southern desert. On the other hand, the Arabs rejected the entire plan and from November 1947 to the following May intensified the use of irregular troops in their attempt to destroy the Jewish state. This was followed by a massive invasion of the area by Arab armies from a number of neighboring states. As the eleventh hour drew near, Truman, weary of the constant lobbying by different groups both within and outside his government to influence his thinking, made the historic decision to grant Israel tentative recognition. For the Jews, it was a spectacular victory. For the Arabs, it was a bitter moment resulting in hard feelings against the United States despite continued American oil interests in the Middle East.

In the last analysis, Truman made his decision to recognize Israel because he believed it was in the best interest of the United States to do so. As the American commander in chief who had already made the controversial decision to drop the atomic bomb on Hiroshima and Nagasaki, Truman was capable of making the toughest decision any leader might ever be compelled to do. While his closest advisers were deeply split over what position the president should take on Palestine, he alone determined his course of action. Unwilling both to give the Soviet Union an edge in the Middle East and to leave the 600,000 Jews of Palestine to a sure destiny of destruction at the hands of the Arab armies perched on the borders, he took decisive action.

Truman continued to harbor deep sympathy for the survivors of the Holocaust and apparently had a sense that, like Cyrus the Great, the great Persian emperor of the sixth century B.C.E., he would be able to play a personal role in the restoration of the Jewish people to Zion. His friendship with his Jewish business partner and war friend, Edward Jacobson, also probably figured in his decision, though he often resented the constant high-powered lobbying by American Jews and Jewish organizations. On occasion, he was not beyond using anti-Semitic epithets or vulgar language to express his displeasure.

With an American endorsement in hand and a Soviet statement of recognition just a few days away, the new state of Israel successfully defended itself against an array of Arab armies. At the same time, Israel immediately began gathering Jewish exiles around the world to its now open harbors. Truman, however, did not give Israel carte blanche, and an unpredictable relationship between Israel

Time Line

1948

■ **March 19**
United Nation Delegation endorses its trusteeship in Palestine without authorization from the White House.

■ **May 14**
David Ben-Gurion declares the establishment of the independent state of Israel at 6:00 PM. EST. Truman gives Israel de facto American recognition at 6:11 PM. EST.

■ **May 15**
Arab states attack Israel.

1949

■ **January 25**
Following popular elections, a permanent government takes office in Israel.

■ **January 31**
The United States upgrades its recognition of Israel to full de jure status.

■ **February 24**
First armistice agreement signed between Israel and an Arab state (Egypt).

■ **July 20**
Final armistice signed between Israel and its neighbors (Syria).

and the United States began to emerge until years later, when America began to see Israel both as a strategic partner and a democratic ally. For the time being, a tiny document containing only forty-two typed words linked the fate of the new Jewish state to a great but sometimes ambivalent American superpower, thereby launching a new era in the history of the United States, the Jewish people, and the Middle East.

About the Author

Harry S. Truman, thirty-third president of the United States, was born on May 8, 1884, in Lamar, Missouri, but settled with his family in nearby Independence, Missouri. He learned to farm from his father and remained very close to his mother throughout her life. Truman attended public school and received religious instruction at a Presbyterian Church Sunday school. He was the only twentieth-century president not to have a college degree, but as a young man he was drawn to the study of history, learned to play the piano, and was already attracted to politics, aligning himself with the Democratic Party. He also worked as a timekeeper for the Santa Fe Railroad.

In 1905 Truman enlisted in the Missouri National Guard and served for six years despite poor eyesight, which prevented him from going to West Point to pursue a military career. While he was in the National Guard, he met both Edward Jacobson, a Jewish man with whom he later entered into a business partnership, and James M. Pendergast, a scion of the leading political family in Kansas City at that time. When the United States entered World War I, Truman reenlisted and served as an artillery officer in France. He proved to be a natural leader and exhibited great courage in active combat. Later, he was promoted to the rank of colonel in the Missouri Guard.

Following the war, Truman returned to Independence and married Bess Wallace. The couple had one child, Margaret. He also went into the men's clothing business with Jacobson, but the business failed, so he turned his attention full-time to politics. Truman's friendship with Jacobson, however, remained intact, and Jacobson later played a role as an unofficial adviser to Truman, urging him to recognize the Israel many years later.

Truman was elected as a family court judge in Jackson County in 1922. During the Great Depression he received a position with the assistance of Pendergast family, which supported his successful run for the U.S. Senate in 1934. Despite corruption charges against the Pendergasts, Truman emerged as a viable candidate and remained in the Senate until he was chosen as Franklin Delano Roosevelt's vice presidential running mate in 1944, notwithstanding his professed lack of interest in the job. The Roosevelt-Truman ticket won handily in the Electoral College by a 432-to-99 vote.

On April 12, 1945, after Truman had served less than three months as vice president, Roosevelt died, and Truman was sworn in as president of the United States. Thrust onto the stage of world politics, Truman was called upon to authorize the dropping of the atomic bomb on Japan and help plan for transitioning the United States and much of the world to a peacetime economy. Following in the footsteps of his fellow Democrat Woodrow Wilson, he supported the creation of the United Nations and later enunciated the Truman Doctrine to contain the spread of Communism. He also oversaw the founding of the U.S. Air Force, the Central Intelligence Agency, and the National Security Council. At home, much of his domestic agenda, including his "Fair Deal" and civil rights advocacy work, was generally frustrated by a Republican Congress that had gained power in 1946.

Moreover, Truman's decision to recognize Israel in 1948 took place not only in the context of a busy White House but during a heated primary and presidential campaign, which featured his famed "whistle stop" tour. Against the odds, Truman won the top spot on the Democratic ticket and then, in a classic upset victory, retained the White House. Among his first acts was to give Israel full de jure recognition, although his support for the new Jewish state was far from unequivocal. Truman's second term included the founding of the North Atlantic Treaty Organization, the establishment of Communist China, McCarthyism, and the Korean War.

Truman left public office in 1953 and returned to his wife's family home in Independence, Missouri. He lived a modest life, helped establish the Truman Library, and wrote his immensely popular memoirs. Harry Truman died on December 26, 1972. His wife, Bess, died ten years later. Both were buried in the courtyard of his presidential library.

Explanation and Analysis of the Document

The actual writing and editing of Truman's statement recognizing Israel on May 15, 1948, took place within a specific context inside the American government at that time. The issue of the future of Palestine had been the subject of vigorous debate in the Truman administration, particularly in the periods prior to the United Nations vote in November 1947 to partition Palestine and in May 1948, when the question of the United States' official view of the proposed Jewish state became a matter of intense discussion. It is most likely true that Truman was inclined to recognize Israel all along but was seriously challenged by leading members of his own administration not to do so. The heated politics of the debate also gave him pause as he weighed his decision.

Three groups of people were involved in the debate over U.S. recognition. First, a team of political advisers to Truman, especially Clark Clifford, counsel to the White House and an architect of the president's election campaign effort, and David Niles, a political adviser to Truman and the only American Jew involved in the discussion, argued in favor of American recognition. They were supported by Truman's longtime friend Edward Jacobson; Reform Rabbi Abba Hillel Silver, a staunch Republican and leading American Zionist, whom Truman generally did not favor; and Chaim Weizmann, the "old man" of the world Zionist movement and Israel's unofficial ambassador at large to Washington.

On the other side of the table were some of the most powerful voices in the Truman administration. Secretary of Defense James Forrestal argued that American oil interests in the Middle East precluded U.S. recognition of Israel and that the United States was not in a position to place a large number of troops on the ground in Palestine. Forrestal was supported by Secretary of State George Marshall and all of Marshall's top staff, including Loy W. Henderson, head of the Office for Near Eastern and African Affairs, and George Kennan, director of policy planning at the State Department. The State Department group repeatedly attempted to frame the question of Palestine in terms of the unfolding dynamics of the cold war. They argued that the United Nations trusteeship over Palestine, not partition, best met America's regional and global interests.

On March 18, 1948, with the help of Jacobson, Weizmann was invited to the White House to make the case for an independent Jewish state in Palestine. Weizmann's apparent success was contradicted by the startling announcement by the American ambassador to the United Nations, former Vermont Senator Warren Austin, that the United States favored trusteeship, not partition. An embar-

> *"This Government has been informed that a Jewish state has been proclaimed in Palestine, and recognition has been requested by the provisional Government thereof."*
>
> (Paragraph 1)

> *"The United States recognizes the provisional government as the de facto authority of the new State of Israel."*
>
> (Paragraph 2)

rassed White House tried to make the case that the ambassador was talking only about a phase in a long-term U.S. policy. The explanation, however, did little to calm the storm that erupted among American Zionists.

The final meeting on the issue of Palestine prior to Truman's recognition of the new Jewish state took place at the White House on May 12, 1948. Undersecretary of State Robert Lovett argued on behalf of trusteeship. Clark Clifford not only presented a case for partition but also suggested, to the great displeasure of Marshall, that the United States should recognize Israel before the proclamation of the state of Israel. For his part, Marshall threatened to vote against Truman in the coming elections if the president following the counsel's advice.

By the morning of May 14, 1948, it was increasingly clear that Truman had decided in favor of partition and would recognize Israel. Marshall called the White House and assured Truman that he would not publicly oppose his commander in chief. Clifford and Lovett met privately to work out a brief statement, which was then transmitted to the President. At 5:51 PM the same day, nine minutes before the "State of Israel" was proclaimed in Tel Aviv, Loy Henderson sent a top-secret memo to American embassies and consulates throughout the Middle East anticipating de facto recognition of Israel. For his part, Clifford sent word to the Jewish Agency for Israel, the prestate Israeli government, that recognition was also in the works. However, the United Nations delegation was not informed of the signing, which was about to take place.

At 6:11 PM on May 14, 1948, after hand-editing the document Clifford and Lovett had prepared for him, Truman signed and dated the statement of recognition. To make sure that the most current information was included and that his statement was historically accurate, Truman noted that the new government of Israel was still only "provisional" and that the new Jewish state would be called Israel, reflecting the late agreement reached in Tel Aviv. Thus, the United States became the first country in the world to rec-

ognize Israel and created the basis for a special relationship between those two sovereign states.

For the Zionist movement, Truman's recognition of Israel was a tremendous validation of its tireless efforts to create a Jewish state in Palestine. For the Arabs, it was part of a series of catastrophes called *al-Nakba*. This expression refers not only to the loss of land and sovereignty but also to the beginning of a massive refugee problem as large numbers of Palestinians fled from their homes for a variety of reasons when fighting intensified in the spring of 1948 and beyond. A year later, George Marshall resigned from the State Department. He never spoke to Clark Clifford again. Loy Henderson was reassigned to India.

Audience

As an official act of the United States, Truman's recognition of Israel served as notice to its provisional government that the United States was, indeed, its ally. Further, it was a statement made to the larger community of nations, particularly the United Nations, that, consistent with the American vote in November 1947, the United States continued to support the idea of the partition of Palestine. However, since no Arab State of Palestine was formed at the time, no parallel document recognizing a Palestinian state was prepared by the American government. Finally, with respect to the international community, Truman was sending a clear signal to the Soviet Union that he had no intention of allowing it to use the newly formed Jewish state as a wedge between the Straits of Bosporus and the Suez Canal. Truman was keenly aware that the head of the Soviet delegation to the United Nations, deputy foreign minister Andrey Gromyko, had spoken at the First Special Session of the General Assembly, signaling Moscow's willingness to consider a two-state solution in Palestine. On the other hand, Truman was content to allow the British to maintain their general control in the region.

Truman's decision to recognize Israel quickly and dramatically also was intended to send a message to various groups in the United States. Already during World War II, Truman had strongly assured the American Jewish community that he would aid the survivors of the Holocaust and support a Zionist agenda in the Middle East. The quickness of his action in recognizing Israel made good on those promises, an act that was both principled and political. In so doing, he may have effectively curbed support for his Democratic rival, Henry Wallace, in the Jewish community. Christian Zionism, although still largely nascent, also shaped an audience for Truman. A certain sense of destiny with biblical resonance accompanied Truman's action. Finally, Truman was making a statement to the American people that he was a strong leader capable of making important, historic decisions with confidence based on his own view of America's best interests and more abstract ideas of truth and justice. Later in life, Truman viewed his nearly instant recognition of Israel as one of his most significant acts as president.

Impact

The immediate impact of Truman's recognition of Israel was profound, particularly for the Israelis. Truman received Israel's first president, Chaim Weizmann, in the White House in May 1948 within a few days of Israel's declaring its independence. Weizmann's presidential status was fully honored, and Truman promised him a loan of $100 million for the economic development of the new Jewish state. Two years later, Israel and the United States agreed on a Mutual Security Act, which included a second grant of $65 million.

But beyond the symbolism and much-needed financial support, the U.S. position on Israel was often ambivalent and sometimes even contradictory for several years. Truman was satisfied to leave an arms embargo in place against Israel after its establishment and similarly supported United Nations mediation efforts in the 1948 Arab-Israel War (also known as the War of Independence) at the very moment that Israel was pressing a military advantage on the battlefield. The lack of a general alignment in America-Israeli interests persisted throughout the 1950s and much of the 1960s. Like the vast majority of countries in the world, the United States steadfastly refused to recognize Jerusalem as the legitimate capital of the state of Israel and continues to maintain its embassy in Tel Aviv.

Remarkably, Israel also enjoyed the initial support of the Soviet Union in May 1948. Seeking to counter British imperialism in the Arab world, Moscow expressed its support for Jewish armed resistance in the War of Independence and transmitted arms to Israel through Czechoslovakia and economic assistance through Polish channels. Limited Jewish immigration was allowed from Eastern Europe, and Golda Meir was welcomed as Israel's first ambassador to the Soviet Union. Relations with the Soviets, however, quickly deteriorated after 1949, and by 1953, with state-sponsored anti-Semitism rising at home, the Soviet Union broke off diplomatic relations with Israel.

At first, Israel attempted to steer a neutral course between the Soviet Union and the United States as it needed to defend itself against invading Arab armies and continued British support of the Arabs. Indeed, more than three dozen British officers resigned their commissions and led Arab troops in fighting in the Jerusalem region. The United Kingdom actually delayed until 1950 before it fully recognized the Jewish state. The failure of Britain's pro-Arab policy, the Soviet Union's attempt to exploit that failure along with its domestic sponsorship of state anti-Semitism, and the U.S. commitment to thwart Soviet influence rapidly reshaped the role of the outside powers in the Middle East by 1950. In May of that year the United States, France, and the United Kingdom agreed to a Tripartite Declaration to maintain a balance of arms between Israel and its Arab neighbors. With the outbreak of the Korean War in December 1950, Israel moved closer to the West, and Egypt, led by Gamal Abdel Nasser, embraced the Soviets, Nasser's principal military and economic backer in his unsuccessful 1956 and 1967 wars against Israel.

At the same time, Israel became increasingly isolated at the United Nations, which, ironically, Israelis had at first viewed as the international guarantor of the moral legitimacy of the Jewish state. United Nations–sponsored negotiations led to a series of armistice agreements early in 1949 but not to the demarcation of political borders. Also, in 1949, at the fourth session of the General Assembly, the United Nations Relief and Works Agency was established to deal with the complex issue of the Palestinian refugees, many of whom settled in Jordan, which annexed the West Bank in 1950, and the Gaza Strip, which was occupied by Egypt.

American recognition of Israel, the eventual alignment of American and Israeli strategic interests, the vast increase in American economic and military aid to Israel, the continued political support for Israel in the United States, and the collapse of the Soviet Union all combined to compound the historical significance of Truman's quick recognition of Israel in 1948. Despite several significant, unresolved differences between Israel and the United States, the two countries enjoy a special relationship to the delight and consternation of millions of people around the world to this day. In the last analysis, as the Norwegian diplomat Trygve Lie, the first elected secretary-general of the United Nations, maintained, "If there had been no Harry S. Truman, there would be no Israel today" (http://www.truman-library.org/news/trumanisrael.htm).

Related Documents

"Anglo-American Committee of Inquiry." The Avalon Project at Yale Law School Web site. http://www.yale.edu/lawweb/avalon/anglo/angtoc.htm. Accessed on January 7, 2008. Formed after World War II to address the need to find a home for the Jewish displaced persons trapped in Europe after the war, this committee made recommendations that were largely rejected by the British government under Prime Minister Clement Attlee, the Arabs, and the Jews.

"Statement by Truman on Israel (October 24, 1948)." Jewish Virtual Library Web site. http://jewishvirtuallibrary.org/jsource/US-Israel/truman_Israel1. Accessed on January 7, 2008. In this letter issued prior to the presidential election in 1948, Truman reasserted his support for the recognition and support of Israel.

Bibliography

■ Articles
Bickerton, Ian J. "President Truman's Recognition of Israel." *American Jewish Historical Quarterly* 58 (1968): 173–239.

———. "President Truman's Recognition of Israel: Two Views." *American Jewish Archives* 33, no. 1 (1981): 141–152.

Evensen, Bruce J. "Truman, Palestine and the Cold War." *Middle Eastern Studies* 28, no. 1 (1992): 120–156.

Cohen, Michael J. "Truman and the State Department: The Palestine Trusteeship Proposal, March, 1948." *Jewish Social Studies* 43, no. 2 (1981): 165–178.

———. "Truman, the Holocaust and the Establishment of the State of Israel." *Jerusalem Quarterly* 23 (1982): 79–94.

———. "Truman and Palestine, 1945–1948: Revisionism, Politics and Diplomacy." *Modern Judaism* 2, no. 1 (1982): 1–22.

Parzen, Herbert. "President Truman and the Palestine Quandary: His Initial Experience, April–December, 1945." *Jewish Social Studies* 35 (1973): 42–72.

■ Books
Benson, Michael T. *Harry S. Truman and the Founding of Israel.* Westport, Conn.: Praeger, 1997.

Klieman, Aaron S. *Recognition of Israel: An End and a New Beginning.* New York: Garland, 1991.

Laqueur, Walter. *A History of Zionism.* New York: Holt, Rinehart and Winston, 1972.

McCullough, David. *Truman.* New York: Simon & Schuster, 1992.

Sachar, Howard M. *A History of Israel from the Rise of Zionism to Our Time.* New York: Knopf, 1979.

Safran, Nadav. *The United States and Israel.* Cambridge, Mass.: Harvard University Press, 1963.

Sykes, Christopher. *Crossroads to Israel.* Bloomington: Indiana University Press, 1973.

Urofsky, Melvin I. *American Zionism from Herzl to the Holocaust.* Garden City, N.Y.: Anchor, 1975.

———. *We Are One! American Jewry and Israel.* Garden City, N.Y.: Anchor, 1978.

■ Web Sites
"Balfour Declaration 1917." The Avalon Project at Yale Law School. http://www.yale.edu/lawweb/avalon/mideast/balfour.htm. Accessed on February 22, 2008.

"Report of Earl G. Harrison." United States Holocaust Memorial Musem. http://www.ushmm.org/museum/exhibit/online/dp/resourc1.htm. Accessed on February 22, 2008.

"The Recognition of the State of Israel: Background." Harry S. Truman Library and Museum. http://www.trumanlibrary.org/whistlestop/study_collections/israel/large/israel.htm. Accessed on January 7, 2008.

"60 Years On, New Exhibition Examines President Truman's 1948 Decision to Recognize the State of Israel." Harry S. Truman Library and Museum. http://www.trumanlibrary.org/news/trumanisrael.htm. Accessed on February 22, 2008.

"Truman's Letter Regarding the Harrison Report on the Treatment of Displaced Jews." Jewish Virtual Library Web site. http://jewishvirtuallibrary.org/jsource/Holocaust/truman_on_harrison.html. Accessed on January 7, 2008.

"United Nations General Assembly Resolution 181." The Avalon Project at Yale Law School. http://www.yale.edu/lawweb/avalon/un/res181.htm. Accessed on February 22, 2008.

—By Lance J. Sussman

1. Scholars often view Truman's recognition of Israel as outside or even contrary to his administration's grand strategy of containing Communism and, in a way, as an early example of the special relationship between the United States and Israel. Is this the case, or was Truman's recognition of Israel consistent with broader trends in American foreign policy and, in particular, the post–World War II doctrine of containing Communism?

2. The U.S. Constitution divides the responsibility of conducting foreign policy between the executive and legislative branches of government. Did Truman's recognition of Israel constitute an expansion of presidential powers, and to what extent did it serve or not serve as a precedent for the further strengthening of the executive branch?

3. American foreign policy is conducted with the best interests of the United States in mind. In general, how should American foreign policy be determined, and beyond military and economic factors, to what extent should political ideology (e.g., the promotion of democracy) and domestic considerations (e.g., a well-organized ethnic lobby as in pro-Irish or pro-Israeli activism) be considered in the grand scheme of things?

4. Since 1898, the United States has increasingly viewed itself as a global and not a regional or hemispheric power. Viewed in this light, was Truman's recognition of Israel essentially consistent with America's increased global role?

5. Given the recent history of the Holocaust and the political goals of the Jewish survivors of the Nazi death camps, what other courses of action might Truman have taken in 1947 and 1948 to aid them? To what extent, if any, did domestic anti-Semitism in the United States also shape Truman's decision to recognize Israel?

6. Did the U.S. State Department seriously misunderstand the military capacity of the Jews in Palestine in 1948 and when it raised the possibility of sending 100,000 American troops to Palestine for political purposes?

Glossary

de facto	that which is recognized as "in fact" but not necessarily legal
provisional	temporary

PRESS RELEASE ANNOUNCING U.S. RECOGNITION OF ISRAEL

This Government has been informed that a Jewish state has been proclaimed in Palestine, and recognition has been requested by the provisional Government thereof.

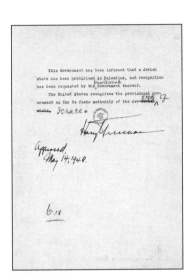

The United States recognizes the provisional government as the de facto authority of the new State of Israel.

Approved, May 14, 1948.

EXECUTIVE ORDER

ESTABLISHING THE PRESIDENT'S COMMITTEE ON EQUALITY OF TREATMENT AND OPPORTUNITY IN THE ARMED SERVICES

WHEREAS it is essential that there be maintained in the armed services of the United States the highest standards of democracy, with equality of treatment and opportunity for all those who serve in our country's defense:

NOW, THEREFORE, by virtue of the authority vested in me as President of the United States, by the Constitution and the statutes of the United States, and as Commander in Chief of the armed services, it is hereby ordered as follows:

1. It is hereby declared to be the policy of the President that there shall be equality of treatment and opportunity for all persons in the armed services without regard to race, color, religion or national origin. This policy shall be put into effect as rapidly as possible, having due regard to the time required to effectuate any necessary changes without impairing efficiency or morale.

2. There shall be created in the National Military Establishment an advisory committee to be known as the President's Committee on Equality of Treatment and Opportunity in the Armed Services, which shall be composed of seven members to be designated by the President.

3. The Committee is authorized on behalf of the President to examine into the rules, procedures and practices of the armed services in order to determine in what respect such rules, procedures and practices may be altered or improved with a view to carrying out the policy of this order. The Committee shall

Executive Order 9981 (National Archives and Records Administration)

"There shall be equality of treatment and opportunity for all persons in the armed services without regard to race."

Overview

In 1948 racial divisions in the United States continued to run deep, but major changes in the social and legal climate were about to occur. During World War II, which the United States entered in 1941 and fought until the war's end in 1945, African Americans and other minorities, including Native Americans and Japanese Americans, fought with great distinction. On the home front, minority-group women made major contributions to the war effort. Nevertheless, segregation in nearly every facet of American life remained entrenched—nowhere more so than in the U.S. armed forces.

In response to growing pressure to remedy this state of affairs, President Harry S. Truman issued Executive Order 9981. Specifically, the executive order was written with the intent of "Establishing the President's Committee on Equality of Treatment and Opportunity in the Armed Forces." The purpose of the order then was twofold. One purpose was to declare that it would be the policy of the United States to provide equality of opportunity for members of the armed forces without regard to race, color, religion, or national origin. In this sense, armed forces desegregation could be said to have launched the civil rights movement that dominated the 1950s and 1960s. The second, more specific, purpose was to establish a seven-member advisory committee to study and recommend specific steps that the armed forces could take to implement the desegregation policy. The order granted the committee investigative authority and ordered the armed forces and other federal executive agencies to provide testimony and documents that the committee needed to carry out its mandate.

Context

Throughout American history, African Americans and members of other minority groups fought in the nation's wars with distinction. However, they did so generally in separate units that were segregated from all-white units. During the Civil War (1861–1865), for example, "colored" brigades were formed in the North, and even the Confederate States of America, starved for troops late in the war, formed brigades of black soldiers (although none ever fought).

In the decades following the Civil War, large numbers of African Americans, many of them former slaves, served in the U.S. Navy, but through the early decades of the twentieth century, they served primarily in menial and service jobs. In the navy and the Marine Corps, for example, many African Americans were pushed into the Steward's Branch, where they worked as cooks and served as waiters in the officers' mess halls. This state of affairs continued through World War II. During the war and its aftermath, minority groups fought in segregated units. There were few African American officers, and those who served commanded African American units. The Marine Corps included few African Americans in its ranks, and the navy continued to limit the service of African Americans to such positions as cooks and stewards. Most military leaders believed that integrated units, where blacks and whites served side by side, would produce conflict and lower the morale of the troops.

President Franklin D. Roosevelt took an early step to remedy this situation in June 1941 when he issued Executive Order 8802. Arguing that the defense of the nation required the participation of all groups, he ordered that all defense contractors eliminate discrimination in employment. More specifically, he ordered that blacks be included in job-training programs at defense plants. He also ordered the formation of a Fair Employment Practices Committee. In 1942 Roosevelt took another step when he ordered the navy to review its racial policies. The navy responded by allowing blacks to fill more positions in technical specialties, such as construction, supply, aviation, metalworking, and shore patrol. Later that year, as the military was rapidly increasing its manpower levels, Roosevelt issued a further executive order requiring that 10 percent of new draftees be black.

Roosevelt's executive orders had no impact on segregation in the military, but they did increase the number of African American troops. Although African Americans made up about 10 percent of the population, and although about 1 million African Americans served during World War II, blacks continued to serve in segregated units.

1945

■ **October 1**
After its appointment in September by U.S. Secretary of War Robert Patterson, the "Gillem Board," a three-member commission directed by Admiral Alvan Gillem, Jr., holds its first meeting to review army racial policies.

1946

■ **February 27**
U.S. Navy, in Circular Letter 48-46, makes African American sailors eligible for all types of naval assignments.

■ **April 10**
U.S. War Department issues Circular 105, explicitly excluding "Negroes" from assignment to critically needed areas, though the circular was later revised to include all enlisted men.

■ **April 27**
War Department Circular 124 maintains racial segregation but makes integration the army's ultimate goal.

■ **July 17**
The U.S. secretary of war puts on hold black enlistments in the regular army.

■ **September 19**
President Truman meets with a delegation from the National Emergency Committee against Mob Violence.

■ **December 5**
President Truman establishes the President's Committee on Civil Rights.

1947

■ Army Air Forces close the flight training school at Alabama's Tuskegee Airfield, the last segregated officer training program.

The civil rights leader A. Philip Randolph, with other black leaders, establishes the Committee against Jim Crow in Military Service.

■ **October 29**
President's Committee on Civil Rights issues its final report.

Opportunities for promotion were limited, sailors were rarely allowed to serve at sea, and most blacks—even those trained for more specialized and technical positions—continued to fill service positions. Throughout this period, the navy took steps to integrate its officer corps by training twelve line officers and one warrant officer at a special training school in 1943. These officers, called the "Golden Thirteen," were the first black officers in the navy's history. Nevertheless, they were trained at a segregated school, and while some 160,000 African Americans served in the navy during World War II, just fifty-eight were officers. All of these were lower-ranking officers who served under the supervision of a white officer.

In the years immediately following the war, the U.S. Department of Defense faced a severe manpower shortage as those who had served in the war left for civilian employment. Nevertheless, the armed services continued to deter African Americans from serving. They tried to ensure that the proportion of African Americans remained no higher than 10 percent primarily by demanding that African Americans achieve higher scores on enlistment tests than their white counterparts. However, as the cold war with the Soviet Union was deepening, it became apparent to President Truman and others that cutting off a valuable population of potential military recruits could hamper the nation's defense.

During these years, African American leaders were clamoring for changes in the nation's attitudes toward civil rights. One of the most outspoken leaders, A. Philip Randolph, formed the Committee against Jim Crow in Military Service; "Jim Crow" refers to the legal and social systems that segregated African Americans and kept them in inferior positions. Randolph and other African American leaders raised the possibility of black workers going on strike, a situation that would have added to the economic turmoil caused by the nation's shift from a wartime to a peacetime economy. Additionally, the horrors of World War II, with the wholesale denial of human rights on the part of the German Nazi Party and the expansionist Japanese Empire, focused attention on human rights throughout the world. In 1948 the United Nations would issue its Universal Declaration of Human Rights, further drawing attention to the pressing issues of discrimination and civil rights. African American soldiers who served in Europe in the postwar years found greater acceptance and tolerance there, and they demanded this same level of acceptance from white American society.

Helping to improve the status of black military personnel was the appointment of James Forrestal as secretary of the navy. His predecessor, Frank Knox, had opposed integration, but Forrestal believed that integration might be a way to reduce racial tensions in the military. To that end, in 1944–1945 he ordered an experiment in which black personnel were placed on twenty-five ships at sea. The experiment proved successful, with few racial incidents reported.

It was in this climate that President Truman took on the issue of civil rights and desegregation in the years following World War II. In 1946 he created the President's Committee on Civil Rights. The committee recommended "more adequate and effective means and procedures for the protection of the civil rights of the people of the United States" (http://www.trumanlibrary.org/civilrights/srights1.htm). In 1947 the committee issued its final report, *To Secure These Rights*, making specific recommendations for ways to ensure the civil rights of African Americans and other minority groups.

Truman urged Congress to enact the recommendations of the committee. However, he faced opposition from members of Congress, including southern senators who threatened to filibuster civil rights legislation. (The word *filibuster* refers to any delaying tactics, such as long, continuous speeches, to block action on proposed legislation.) Frustrated with Congress, Truman took matters into his own hands. He appointed an African American to a federal judgeship, he strengthened the civil rights division of the Department of Justice, and he appointed several African Americans to high-level administrative positions. Most important, he issued Executive Order 9981, calling for desegregation of the armed forces. Although the services resisted, they eventually implemented the president's order. By the end of the Korean War, segregation as a matter of military policy had largely ended.

About the Author

Harry S. Truman, the thirty-third president of the United States (1945–1953), was born in Lamar, Missouri, on May 8, 1884. While it has become conventional to regard "S" as a middle initial, with a period, in fact the S does not stand for anything. It was his middle name, given to him by his parents to honor both of his grandfathers, whose names began with the letter S—a practice not uncommon among people of Scots-Irish descent.

Early in his life, Truman worked as a drugstore clerk before turning to farming. In the 1920s he was co-owner of a men's clothing store, leading to his reputation as the "haberdasher" who became president. He was the nation's last president to serve without benefit of a college degree. In 1905 he joined the Missouri National Guard, remaining a member until 1911. An early goal was to attend the United States Military Academy at West Point, but extremely poor eyesight rendered this goal impossible. After the outbreak of World War I, he rejoined the National Guard; it is believed that he passed the eye examination by memorizing the eye chart. He served as a captain of an infantry battery in France, often organizing and disciplining his men with firmness. His experience as a military officer brought out leadership qualities that enabled him to succeed in politics.

Truman began his political career in 1922, when he was elected to the position of judge of the county court, though the position was not judicial but administrative. In 1933 he was appointed head of Federal Reemployment for Missouri, part of President Franklin Roosevelt's New Deal to overcome the effects of the Great Depression. In 1934 he was elected to the U.S. Senate, and in 1940 he was reelected, despite numerous allegations of irregularities and favoritism in the federal reemployment program. In 1944 Roosevelt, running for a fourth term as president, selected Truman as his running mate. The two were elected, but after just eighty-two days as vice president, Truman ascended to the presidency on April 12, 1945, upon Roosevelt's death.

The nearly eight years of Truman's presidency were eventful. He authorized the atomic bombing of Japan to

Time Line

1948

■ **May 28**
Lieutenant John E. Rudder is the first African American to receive a regular Marine Corps commission as an officer.

■ **July 26**
President Truman issues Executive Order 9981.

1949

■ **February 28**
The Department of Defense's newly formed personnel policy board establishes uniform standards for the military draft and abolishes racial quotas.

■ **May 11**
Air Force Letter 35-3 ends segregation in the workplace and living quarters in the U.S. Air Force.

1950

■ **January 16**
U.S. Army publishes Special Regulation 600-629-1, "Utilization of Negro Manpower in the Army." The new policy creates list of vacancies to be filled without consideration of race.

■ **August**
During the Korean War, in the First Provisional Marine Brigade, African Americans are integrated in combat service for the first time in the nation's history.

1951

■ **March**
By this time the U.S. Army has integrated its nine training divisions.

1954

■ **October 30**
U.S. secretary of defense announces the abolishment of the last racially segregated armed forces unit.

end World War II. He then dealt with the labor turmoil and economic upheavals of the postwar years. He presided over the formation of the United Nations and the Marshall Plan for the reconstruction of Europe, the formation of the state of Israel, the Communist takeover of China, and increasing U.S. involvement in Indochina. The cold war with the Soviet Union deepened during the Berlin airlift of 1948–1949, the formation of the North Atlantic Treaty Organization in 1949, and the Korean War (1950–1952); during the war Truman seized control of the striking steel industry in the interest of national security. One of the most noteworthy incidents of his administration was his reelection in 1948. Until the end of the campaign he badly trailed his opponent, Thomas Dewey. A famous photograph shows Truman holding a newspaper with the headline "Dewey Defeats Truman," run because few people had given Truman any chance to win. Truman died on December 26, 1972. He remains one of the nation's most popular presidents, highly regarded for his pragmatism and blunt outspokenness.

Explanation and Analysis of the Document

Executive Order 9981, similar to most executive orders, is relatively brief and to the point. The purpose of such an order is not to deal with details and procedures but to outline a broad policy or directive that the president wants to give the force of law.

The first two paragraphs of the order contain a broad justification of the new policy. The president states that it is "essential" for the armed forces to maintain "standards of democracy" and for military personnel to have equality of opportunity. In the second paragraph, the president reiterates his authority as president and commander in chief to issue such an order.

Following the two introductory paragraphs are six specific goals. In the first, the president states that U.S. policy will be that all military personnel will be treated equally without regard to their race, color, religion, or national origin. Although the status of African Americans in the military is of primary concern, the new policy applies to all ethnic, racial, and religious groups. While the president calls for the new policy to be implemented as soon as possible, he recognizes that it will not happen overnight—that it has to happen in a way that maintains the efficiency and morale of the troops.

The second item creates a seven-member advisory committee called the President's Committee on Equality of Treatment and Opportunity in the Armed Forces. The president will appoint the members.

The third item outlines the duties of the committee. These duties are to examine the policies and procedures of each of the armed forces with regard to racial segregation. The committee is to confer with and advise the secretaries of each of the military branches, as well as the Department of Defense, and to make recommendations to those branches and to the president.

The fourth item orders other agencies of the government's executive branch to cooperate with the committee as it gathers information, primarily by providing documents and the services of anyone who can help the committee. While the order does not say so, it was understood by all that the president, as the nation's chief executive officer, had the authority to compel cooperation only from the executive branch. The U.S. Constitution's separation of powers gives the president no authority over the legislative branch (Congress) or the judicial branch (the courts). Such agencies as the Department of Defense are part of the executive branch.

The fifth item gives the committee the authority to compel testimony and to obtain documents from all federal executive departments in carrying out its work.

The final item grants to the committee an indefinite life, noting that it will continue to exist until the president, through another executive order, terminates its existence.

Audience

The immediate audience for Executive Order 9981 was the Department of Defense and the commanders of the U.S. armed services, including the army, the army air forces (the precursor to today's air force, which is now a separate branch of the military), the coast guard, and the navy (including the Marine Corps). The U.S. Constitution identifies the president as the commander in chief of the nation's military, giving him the authority to order such a change in personnel policies. Through this executive order, the president instructed the various branches of the military to begin a program of desegregation.

A second, larger audience was the nation's population of African Americans and other groups defined in part by national origin, religion, and race. Although the executive order encompassed all such groups—including, for example, Asian Americans, Hispanics, and Native Americans—the reality was that the focus of the order was African Americans, who made up nearly 10 percent of the total U.S. population in the 1940s. By issuing this executive order, President Truman sought to assure African Americans that the federal government was making efforts to ensure racial equality. In this sense, the audience for Executive Order 9981 was the American population as a whole. The order was one of the first major steps on the part of the federal government to protect the rights of minorities. By issuing the order, Truman sent a message to the American people that segregation was no longer to be tolerated.

A third audience was the U.S. Congress. In February 1948 the president spoke to Congress and urged the nation's senators and congressional representatives to address the problem of racial inequality. He pressed for the strengthening of civil rights laws, the establishment of a permanent commission on civil rights, protection against lynching, protection of the right to vote, the establishment of a fair employment commission, and other steps to promote civil rights. He believed, however, that Congress was not acting on these proposals as quick-

"*It is essential that there be maintained in the armed services of the United States the highest standards of democracy, with equality of treatment and opportunity for all those who serve in our country's defense.*"

(Introductory Paragraph)

"*It is hereby declared to be the policy of the President that there shall be equality of treatment and opportunity for all persons in the armed services without regard to race, color, religion, or national origin.*"

(Item 1)

ly and as forcefully as it should. In particular, he faced a filibuster (delaying tactics) by southern senators on civil rights legislation. By issuing Executive Order 9981, he was able to institute a major change without having to rely on Congress.

Impact

One of the essential problems that arose in connection with Executive Order 9981 and other documents bearing on racial matters in the military had to do with the definition of terms. Another problem concerned precisely how the president's policy might be implemented. Ultimately, the goal of the order was to have a completely integrated military, one in which no regard was given to race in the assignment of personnel to units, in their appointment to fill particular military jobs, and in the selection of officers.

Many military commanders, however, believed that the forces under their command were "integrated" if there were units composed of African Americans attached to "parent" white units. Some military commanders, as well as legislators, believed that both blacks and whites should be allowed to serve in all-white or all-black units if they preferred to do so. Thus, for example, a battalion might have consisted of a number of all-white companies of soldiers and one all-black company, with the all-black company performing essentially the same job as the all-white companies. At bottom, the difficulty was distinguishing "segregation" from "discrimination." Some military commanders and legislators did not believe that a segregated military was discriminatory.

The result is that Truman's order did not have any immediate impact. Neither the army nor the navy altered its policies. The decision of these branches to maintain the status quo was based on their commanders' belief that they were already in compliance with the president's order because they were in compliance with such directives as Circular 124 and Circular Letter 48-46.

Through most of 1949, in the estimation of many historians, the armed services were slow in taking steps to implement the president's policy. Change, however, began to occur in late 1949. Both the navy and the air force significantly changed their racial policies, concluding that they needed to expand the pool of available sailors and airmen in a period when the size of the military was shrinking. The army was slower to respond, but finally, in 1950, the army issued Special Regulation 600-629-1, "Utilization of Negro Manpower in the Army," ordering that opening in critical specialties were to be filled without regard to race. The Marine Corps was slower still, but in 1951, during the Korean War, the corps ended its policy of segregation.

Other changes took place. Military recruiters no longer regarded the race of candidates for service. Training units were fully integrated. All-black units were gradually taken out of commission and replaced with fully integrated units. Additional training was provided to ensure that African American enlistees could overcome the effects of poverty and poor schooling to succeed in the military. Finally, on October 30, 1954, the U.S. secretary of defense announced the abolishment of the last racially segregated unit in the military. In the decades that followed, the U.S. armed forces became a model for complete integration and for a culture in which race plays no role in determining a soldier's or a sailor's opportunities for advancement.

Related Documents

"Circular No. 124—'Utilization of Negro Manpower in the Postwar Army Policy,' April 27, 1946. Army, Record Group 220: Records of the President's Committee on Equality of Treatment and Opportunity in the Armed Services." Harry S. Truman Library and Museum Web site. http://www.trumanlibrary.org/whistlestop/study_collections/desegregation/large/documents/index.php?pagenumber=1&documentdate=1946-04-27&documentid=10-4&studycollectionid=coldwar. Accessed on February 15, 2008. This document called for broader use of "Negro manpower" in the postwar army and recommended that the proportion of African Americans in the army match that of the general population.

"'Digest of War Department Policy Pertaining to Negro Military Personnel' by J.S. Leonard, January 1, 1944. Security Classified Records, Record Group 220: Records of the President's Committee on Equality of Treatment and Opportunity in the Armed Services." Harry S. Truman Library and Museum Web site. http://www.trumanlibrary.org/whistlestop/study_collections/desegregation/large/documents/index.php?documentdate=1944-01-01&documentid=12-7&studycollectionid=&pagenumber=1&sortorder=. Accessed on February 15, 2008. This document called for the "fair and equitable treatment" of African Americans but rejected the "intermingling" of white and black personnel in military units.

"Draft of the Gillem Board Report." Harry S. Truman Library and Museum Web site. http://www.trumanlibrary.org/whistlestop/study_collections/desegregation/large/documents/index.php?documentdate=1946-00-00&documentid=13-1&studycollectionid=&pagenumber=1&sortorder=. Accessed on January 23, 2008. The Gillem Board Report stated that African Americans had "a constitutional right to fight" and advised the U.S. Army "to make the most effective use of every soldier."

Freedom to Serve: Equality of Treatment and Opportunity in the Armed Services. A Report by the President's Committee on Civil Rights. Washington, D.C.: Government Printing Office, 1950. The final report of the president's committee examined the issues of whether African Americans were qualified for all occupational specialties in the military and whether mixing of whites and blacks would have a negative effect on morale.

"Harry S Truman Special Message to the Congress on Civil Rights. February 2, 1948." The Gilder Lerhman Center for the Study of Slavery, Resistance, and Abolition. http://www.yale.edu/glc/archive/972.htm. Accessed on February 15, 2008. In a message to Congress, the president laid out a civil rights program for the nation.

"Interim Report, July 27, 1949. Reports to the White House, Record Group 220: Records of the President's Committee on Equality of Treatment and Opportunity in the Armed Services." Harry S. Truman Library and Museum Web site. http://www.trumanlibrary.org/whistlestop/study_collections/desegregation/large/documents/index.php?documentdate=1949-07-27&documentid=5-27&studycollectionid=&pagenumber=1&sortorder=. Accessed on February 15, 2008. The interim report of the president's committee called for all military occupational specialties to be open to qualified personnel regardless of race.

To Secure These Rights: The Report of the President's Committee on Civil Rights. New York: Simon and Shuster, 1947. This document is the final report of the President's Committee on Civil Rights.

"Universal Declaration of Human Rights." United Nations Web site. www.un.org/Overivew/rights.html. Accessed on January 23, 2008. The United Nations issued this declaration, outlining the basic rights of persons throughout the world.

Bibliography

■ Articles

Barnhill, J. Herschel. "Civil Rights in the 1940's." *Negro History Bulletin* 45, no. 1 (January–March 1982): 21–22.

Chenoweth, Karin. "Taking Jim Crow out of Uniform: A. Philip Randolph and the Desegregation of the U.S. Military: Special Report: The Integrated Military—50 Years." *Black Issues in Higher Education*, August 21, 1997.

■ Books

Bernstein, Barton J., ed. *Politics and Policies of the Truman Administration.* Chicago: Quadrangle Books, 1970.

Bogart, Leo, ed. *Social Research and the Desegregation of the U.S. Army.* Chicago: Markham Publishing, 1969.

Dalfiume, Richard M. *Desegregation of the U. S. Armed Forces: Fighting on Two Fronts, 1939–1953.* Columbia: University of Missouri Press, 1969.

Davis, Lenwood G., and George Hill, comps. *Blacks in the American Armed Forces 1776–1983: A Bibliography.* Westport, Conn.: Greenwood Press, 1985.

Donaldson, Gary A. *The History of African-Americans in the Military: Double V.* Malabar, Fla.: Krieger Publishing, 1991.

Donovan, Robert J. *Conflict and Crisis: The Presidency of Harry Truman, 1945–1948.* New York: W. W. Norton, 1977.

Dornfeld, Margaret. *The Turning Tide, 1946–1958: From the Desegregation of the Armed Forces to the Montgomery Bus Boycott.* New York: Chelsea House 1995.

Foner, Jack. *Blacks and the Military in American History: A New Perspective.* New York: F. A. Praeger, 1974.

Hamby, Alonzo L. *Man of the People: A Life of Harry S. Truman.* New York: Oxford University Press, 1995.

Hope, Richard O. *Racial Strife in the U.S. Military: Toward the Elimination of Discrimination.* New York: Praeger, 1979.

MacGregor, Morris J., Jr. *Integration of the Armed Forces, 1940–1965.* Washington, D.C.: Center for Military History, U.S. Army, 1981.

McGuire, Phillip, ed. *Taps for a Jim Crow Army: Letters from Black Soldiers in World War II.* Santa Barbara, Calif.: ABC-CLIO, 1983.

Mershon, Sherie, and Steven Schlossman. *Foxholes and Color Lines: Desegregating the U.S. Armed Forces.* Baltimore, Md.: Johns Hopkins University Press, 2002.

Motley, Mary P., ed. *The Invisible Soldier: The Experience of the Black Soldier, World War II.* Detroit: Wayne State University Press, 1975.

Nalty, Bernard C. *Strength for the Fight: A History of Black Americans in the Military.* New York: Free Press, 1986.

Nelson, Dennis D. *The Integration of the Negro into the U.S. Navy.* New York: Farrar, Straus, and Young, 1951.

■ **Web Sites**

"Desegregation of the Armed Forces: Chronology." Harry S. Truman Library and Museum Web site.
   http://www.trumanlibrary.org/whistlestop/study_collections/ desegregation/large/. Accessed on February 15, 2008.

"Harry S. Truman (1884–1972). University of Virginia Miller Center of Public Affairs "American President: Online Reference Resource" Web site.
   http://millercenter.org/academic/americanpresident/truman. Accessed on February 15, 2008.

To Secure These Rights: The Report of the President's Committee on Civil Rights. Harry S. Truman Library and Museum Web site.
   http://www.trumanlibrary.org/civilrights/srights1.htm. Accessed on December 10, 2007.

—By Michael J. O'Neal

Questions for Further Study

1. President Truman ordered the desegregation of the armed forces three years after the end of World War II. Discuss the impact of the war on his decision. What effect did the events of the war have on the position of African Americans and other minorities in the military?

2. The U.S. armed forces remained segregated until roughly 1950. However, the United States had participated in a number of wars throughout its history, including the Revolutionary War, the War of 1812, the Civil War, the Spanish American War, World War I, and World War II. To what extent did African Americans and other minorities, including Native Americans, take part in those wars? How did their participation change over time, if at all?

3. By 1948 the United States was entering the cold war with the Soviet Union. One of the battlegrounds on which this war would be fought was Korea. What impact did the cold war have on Truman's goal of desegregating the armed forces?

4. Some historians believe that in ordering desegregation of the armed forces, President Truman was motivated less by a desire for fairness and equality than by a desire to avoid labor strikes and other forms of public protest by African Americans. Further, they argue that the timing of the order suggests that Truman was trying to appeal to black voters in the upcoming 1948 presidential election. What evidence supports the view that Truman may have been motivated by politics rather than by a sense of what was right? What evidence suggests that this view is incorrect?

5. In 1954 the U.S. Supreme Court ordered the desegregation of the nation's public schools. To what extent did the desegregation of the armed forces contribute to the climate of public opinion that led to this decision?

6. In the 1990s President Bill Clinton dealt with the issue of gays and lesbians serving in the armed forces. To what extent was that issue similar to the issues Truman faced in the 1940s? What arguments that applied to African Americans in the 1940s were also applied to gays fifty years later? What arguments against allowing gays to serve in the military were also used in the 1940s in opposition to armed forces desegregation?

www.milestonedocuments.com

Armed Forces	in the 1940s the army, the army air forces, the coast guard, and the navy (which included the Marine Corps)
designated	appointed
effectuate	to bring about; to cause to happen
Executive Order	a rule issued by the executive branch of government (the president) that has the force of law
hereof	of this
impairing	hindering
terminate	to end

EXECUTIVE ORDER 9981

Establishing the President's Committee on Equality of Treatment and Opportunity in the Armed Forces.

WHEREAS it is essential that there be maintained in the armed services of the United States the highest standards of democracy, with equality of treatment and opportunity for all those who serve in our country's defense:

NOW THEREFORE, by virtue of the authority vested in me as President of the United States, by the Constitution and the statutes of the United States, and as Commander in Chief of the armed services, it is hereby ordered as follows:

1. It is hereby declared to be the policy of the President that there shall be equality of treatment and opportunity for all persons in the armed services without regard to race, color, religion or national origin. This policy shall be put into effect as rapidly as possible, having due regard to the time required to effectuate any necessary changes without impairing efficiency or morale.

2. There shall be created in the National Military Establishment an advisory committee to be known as the President's Committee on Equality of Treatment and Opportunity in the Armed Services, which shall be composed of seven members to be designated by the President.

3. The Committee is authorized on behalf of the President to examine into the rules, procedures and practices of the Armed Services in order to determine in what respect such rules, procedures and practices may be altered or improved with a view to carrying out the policy of this order. The Committee shall confer and advise the Secretary of Defense, the Secretary of the Army, the Secretary of the Navy, and the Secretary of the Air Force, and shall make such recommendations to the President and to said Secretaries as in the judgment of the Committee will effectuate the policy hereof.

4. All executive departments and agencies of the Federal Government are authorized and directed to cooperate with the Committee in its work, and to furnish the Committee such information or the services of such persons as the Committee may require in the performance of its duties.

5. When requested by the Committee to do so, persons in the armed services or in any of the executive departments and agencies of the Federal Government shall testify before the Committee and shall make available for use of the Committee such documents and other information as the Committee may require.

6. The Committee shall continue to exist until such time as the President shall terminate its existence by Executive order.

Harry Truman

The White House, July 26, 1948

"The Founders of this Nation entrusted the lawmaking power to Congress alone in both good and bad times."

Overview

Youngstown Sheet and Tube Co. v. Sawyer, famously known as the Steel Seizure Case, is a landmark decision that belongs in the pantheon of great constitutional law cases. The case generated high political drama, sharp legal conflict, and tides of public opinion, with the U.S. Supreme Court facing issues of surpassing importance for a nation committed to the rule of law. The defining issue in the case—whether the president possesses an inherent or emergency power to seize control of an industry, such as the steel mills, in the midst of a crisis—compelled the Supreme Court to engage in the most penetrating examination of executive power in the country's history.

The case originated in a threatened strike by steelworkers. President Harry S Truman announced on April 8, 1952, the issue of Executive Order No. 10340, which directed Secretary of Commerce Charles Sawyer to seize the steel industry to avert a nationwide strike that the president feared would jeopardize America's war effort in Korea as well as other foreign policy and national security objectives. In the executive order, President Truman grounded the seizure order in the authority vested in him by "the Constitution and laws of the United States, and as President of the United States and Commander in Chief of the armed forces" (http://steelseizure.stanford.edu/exec.order 10340.html). The steel companies immediately brought suit to seek a temporary restraining order. In federal court the next day, the assistant attorney general, Holmes Baldridge, asserted that the seizure was based upon the inherent executive powers of the president and not on any statute. The federal judge David A. Pine shocked the nation when he rejected President Truman's assertions and ruled that the action was unconstitutional.

Judge Pine's ruling that nothing in the Constitution supports the assertion of an undefined, unlimited inherent power in the presidency was affirmed by the Supreme Court, by a 6–3 vote. In the majority opinion written by Justice Hugo Black, the Court rejected the claim of such an inherent presidential power. Of the five concurring opinions accompanying Black's opinion, Justice Robert H.

Jackson's became the most influential and, like the decision itself, came to cast a lengthy shadow over the development of American constitutional law.

Context

President Truman was surrounded by controversies and difficulties when he issued the order to seize the steel mills. His approval ratings had plummeted to all-time lows, which deprived him of deference and political stock; indeed, he had little cachet on the eve of the directive. The public's low regard for Truman stemmed from several factors, including anxiety about the Korean War, the considerable economic problems convulsing the nation, the accusations and charges of corruption and incompetence that were hurled at the Truman administration, and the assertions that the administration was soft on communism. In some ways, Truman could not have been more vulnerable to the ill effects of a nationwide strike by steelworkers.

The pressures arising from the Korean War engulfed Truman. The war was one of his own making; on June 27, 1950, Truman ordered land and sea forces to Korea, where they quickly became embroiled in what was increasingly viewed as an unwinnable war. By the time Truman issued the seizure order, the United States had already sustained 128,000 casualties. In addition, there appeared to be no progress in the conflict and no prospect for progress. Negotiations with North Korea were stalled, and Americans were becoming increasingly embittered by the war.

The characterization of the conflict as "Mr. Truman's War" reflected the fact that he had taken the nation to war without any official declaration of war or authorization from Congress. Critics rightly pointed out that Truman was the first president in U.S. history to claim the unilateral constitutional authority to initiate war. Senator Robert Taft (R-Ohio), for one, furthermore justly asserted that Truman's action was unconstitutional, since the Constitution granted to Congress the sole and exclusive authority to initiate or commence war. The Korean War was also unpopular because Americans had made so many sacrifices during World War II (which had ended only five years earlier) that they were exhausted and not equipped for another conflict.

1945

■ **April 12**
Harry Truman becomes president upon the death of President Franklin D. Roosevelt.

1950

■ **June 27**
The United States enters the Korean War when Truman orders land and sea forces to South Korea.

1952

■ **April 3**
Philip Murray, president of the United Steelworkers, announces that a nationwide strike will commence on April 9.

■ **April 8**
In a national radio and television address, Truman announces that he is ordering the federal seizure of the steel industry.

■ **April 9**
Steel companies file suit in federal district court in Washington, D.C.

■ **April 29**
The federal judge David A. Pine holds Truman's seizure to be unconstitutional.

■ **May 2**
The U.S. Circuit Court of Appeals for Washington, D.C., rules that Judge Pine's decision must be stayed.

■ **May 3**
Lawyers for the government and the steel companies appeal to the U.S. Supreme Court.

■ **May 12–13**
The Supreme Court hears oral arguments in *Youngstown Sheet and Tube Co. v. Sawyer*.

■ **June 2**
The Supreme Court rules in *Youngstown Sheet and Tube Co. v. Sawyer* that President Truman's seizure of the steel industry is unconstitutional, by a 6–3 vote. The steel strike begins.

■ **July 24**
The steel strike ends.

The nation's citizens had willingly shouldered the burdens of World War II because the causes, threats, and goals were so clear. Truman recognized this, and he in fact sought to downplay the range and significance of the Korean War by labeling it a police action. The public relations effort was undercut, however, by the high casualties and the seemingly indefinite nature of the war.

Moreover, the great economic sacrifices that Americans had borne in World War II were starting to seem fruitless, since the nation's economy was in distress at the time of the seizure order. Citizens were chafing under the many controls that had been imposed on the economy—the country was fettered with wage controls, price controls, production controls, and rent controls—and they blamed Truman. Inflationary pressures further rocked the economy, and the toll exacted exacerbated political difficulties for the president.

Truman's political problems stemmed from other sources as well. His administration was racked with charges of corruption, and while Truman himself was never accused of dishonesty, it was said that he was aware of the corruption but chose to ignore it. In addition, he was charged with being soft on Communism, a politically deadly assertion at a time when McCarthyism dominated the political landscape. With low public standing, he had little ammunition to defend himself when Americans decried his seizure of the steel industry. Newspaper editorials accused him of dictatorship, and members of Congress called for his impeachment. President Truman thus found himself being politically bashed from all directions.

About the Author

Hugo Black was born on February 27, 1886, in Clay County, Alabama. He attended public schools and Ashland College in Ashland, Alabama. In 1906 he was graduated from the law department at the University of Alabama, in Tuscaloosa. In that same year he embarked on a law practice, and in 1907 he moved to Birmingham, where he renewed his practice. As a lawyer, Black focused on personal injury suits. Black served in World War I, holding the rank of captain in the Eighty-first Field Artillery and serving as regimental adjutant in the Nineteenth Artillery Brigade from 1917 to 1918. After the war, he returned to Birmingham, where he became a judge on the local police court. He subsequently served as prosecuting attorney for Jefferson County, Alabama.

Black's political career assumed a high trajectory when, in 1926, he was elected as a Democrat to the U.S. Senate. He was reelected in 1932 and served until he resigned his seat on August 19, 1937, after his appointment to the U.S. Supreme Court. While he was in the Senate, Black served as chairman of the Committee on Education and Labor, became known as a skillful investigator, and defended governmental investigations into corporate and business practices. He was an ardent proponent of President Franklin D. Roosevelt's New Deal and an advocate of Roosevelt's ill-fated court-packing plan in

1937, in which Roosevelt sought to increase the size of the Supreme Court so as to neutralize the influence of anti–New Deal justices then sitting on the Court.

Black was rewarded for his hard work and loyalty to the New Deal programs on August 17, 1937, when President Roosevelt nominated him to the Supreme Court. After being confirmed by the Senate, Black took his seat on the Court on October 4, 1937. Following his confirmation, news broke that Black had been a member of the Ku Klux Klan while practicing law in Alabama. Black effectively laid concerns to rest when he explained that many young lawyers in the South had joined the Klan during that time period if they wanted any clients.

By virtually all accounts, Black is regarded as one of the great Supreme Court justices. He was a staunch defender of civil liberties and remained an advocate of an absolutist approach to freedom of speech throughout his career on the high bench. However, he did admit in *Korematsu v. United States* (1944) that in certain circumstances civil rights needed to take a backseat to national security concerns, as he authored the Court's opinion upholding the evacuation order of Japanese Americans from their homes on the West Coast.

Justice Black's jurisprudence was characterized by a high regard for the original design. He believed that it was the duty of the Court to apply the intentions of the framers when discernible. He was renowned, moreover, for his advocacy of the concept of the incorporation of the Bill of Rights. In fact, Black was one of the most forceful proponents of the position that the framers of the Fourteenth Amendment had effectively nationalized the Bill of Rights, making it applicable to the states.

He was widely viewed as a champion of First Amendment freedoms. In the area of free speech, for example, he wrote powerful dissents, as in *Dennis v. United States* (1951), in which he condemned the governmental prosecution and persecution of those who espoused communism. However, he was not willing to extend the protection of free speech as broadly where symbolic speech was concerned, because he drew a distinction between pure speech and its representation in symbols.

Black wrote his last opinion in the landmark case of *New York Times Co. v. United States* (1971), also known as the Pentagon Papers Case. In that acclaimed opinion, he defended the right of the *New York Times* and other newspapers to publish the Pentagon Papers—a voluminous study on American involvement in Vietnam—on the ground that the First Amendment prohibited prior restraint and that the American people had a right to know when they had been deceived by their government. Justice Black served on the Court until his resignation on September 17, 1971, just days before his death on September 25, in Bethesda, Maryland.

Explanation and Analysis of the Document

While President Truman grounded his seizure order on the authority under "the Constitution and laws of the Unit-

ed States, and as President of the United States and Commander in Chief of the armed forces of the United States," the Justice Department later argued in federal district court that the president had acted solely on the basis of inherent executive power, without any statutory authority. The assistant attorney general Holmes Baldridge told Judge Pine that the courts were powerless to control the exercise of presidential power under emergency conditions. Baldridge maintained that the president's emergency power was broad enough to meet any emergency. The only limitations on that power, he explained, were at the ballot box and in Congress's power of impeachment. At a news conference shortly after Baldridge's argument in federal court, President Truman was asked whether, if he could seize the steel mills under his inherent powers, he could "also seize the newspapers and/or radio stations?" Truman answered: "Under similar circumstances the President of the United States has to act for whatever is for the best of the country" (Truman, p. 273).

The Truman administration's assertion of an inherent emergency power was rejected by the federal district judge David Pine in a blistering opinion. In holding Truman's seizure of the steel industry to be unconstitutional, he acknowledged that a nationwide strike could cause extensive damage to the country, but he declared that a strike "would be less injurious to the public than the injury which would flow from a timorous judicial recognition that there is some basis for this claim to unlimited and unrestrained Executive power, which would be implicit in a failure to grant the injunction [to prohibit the seizure]" (103 F. Supp. 569, 577 [D.D.C. 1952]).

The case was framed for the Supreme Court by the Truman administration's claim of an inherent presidential power. On June 2, 1952, the Court, by a divided 6–3 vote, sustained Judge Pine's decision. The majority opinion sharply rejected the president's contention. In addition, five members of the Court—William Douglas, Felix Frankfurter, Robert Jackson, Harold Burton, and Tom Clark—wrote concurring opinions exploring presidential power in an emergency; while they expressed different views, they were united in their denial of an inherent executive power to seize private property when Congress has by statute prohibited it. Of the various opinions, Black's and Jackson's are the most significant.

◆ Justice Hugo Black's Majority Opinion

In the first paragraph of his opinion for the Court, Justice Black lays bare the distinctions between the arguments of the two sides. The owners of the steel mills contend that President Truman's order constitutes lawmaking, a power vested by the Constitution in Congress and not in the president. As such, the president has acted unconstitutionally. The administration, on the other hand, argues that the president acted to prevent a nationwide strike that would have inflicted great injury upon the country. In meeting the emergency, it is argued, the president is drawing upon the aggregate of his powers, including his inherent power, his authority as commander in chief, and his power as chief executive of the nation.

In paragraphs 2–4, Justice Black reviews the facts of the case, beginning with the dispute between the steel companies and the steelworkers that precipitated the call for a strike. After reviewing the lower court action, Black states in paragraph 5 that two particular issues have come before the Supreme Court. The first issue involves the question of whether the constitutional validity of the president's order should be determined. The second regards whether the president has the power to issue the order.

In paragraph 6 of his opinion, Justice Black assesses the administration's argument that Judge Pine never should have considered the merits of the case. Lawyers for the government contended that injunctive relief should have been denied to the steel companies, since the seizure of their property did not inflict irreparable damages and since even if damages had been suffered, the companies should have sought compensation in the Court of Claims. Black rejects those arguments by explaining that previous cases have cast doubt on the right to recover compensation in the Court of Claims when property has been unlawfully taken by the government for public use, the alleged purpose behind the seizure. In addition, Black believed that incalculable damages would indeed be sustained by the steel industry. As a result, he ruled that the case was ripe for review and that the Court should consider the merits of the issues.

In paragraph 7, Black states, famously, "The President's power, if any, to issue the order must stem either from an act of Congress or from the Constitution itself." Here, Black is expounding a fundamental principle of American constitutionalism. He notes that the Truman administration has not advanced any statutory authority for the seizure order. Black points out in a critical passage that Congress had, in its deliberation over the 1947 Taft-Hartley Act, given consideration to an amendment that would have authorized the presidential seizure of property in an emergency—but Congress refused to vest the president with such authority. As such, as Black and other justices state, Congress effectively prohibited the president from taking property. Given that denial of authority, Black explains, the president's order would be constitutional only if it were grounded in the Constitution.

In paragraph 9, Justice Black makes short shrift of the commander-in-chief argument. While acknowledging that the "theater of war" is an expanding concept, he holds that it is not so expansive as to authorize the presidential seizure of private property within the United States. That power, Black notes, is vested in Congress, since it is a function to be performed by the nation's lawmakers. Black is surely right on this point. If the president possessed the authority to take private property, one would wonder where his authority would stop; the Constitution rejects the concept of unlimited power.

In paragraph 10, moreover, Justice Black rejects the vesting clause as justification for the president's order. In fact, as a matter of definition and enumeration of powers, the president's duty to execute the laws precludes him from making the laws. Here, Black is emphasizing a fundamental principle of the doctrine of separation of powers:

Where a power is granted to one branch, it may not be exercised by another. Black points out that the president's role in the lawmaking process extends to the recommendation of legislation and to the veto of bills that he thinks unwise. In all events, Black justly insists, Article I of the Constitution vests the lawmaking power in Congress, not in the president.

Thus, the principal vice of Truman's order, as Black explains in paragraph 11, is that the president is engaging in lawmaking. His seizure order is not executing a policy enacted by Congress; it reflects, rather, a presidential policy that the president alone directs to be executed. In fact, as Black points out, the order assumes the form of a statute: It includes a preamble explaining why the president has adopted the policy, just as statutes set forth the reasoning behind the policy adopted by Congress. Truman's order, moreover, authorizes a governmental official to create additional rules and regulations, an act also reflecting the properties of a statute. According to Black, the fact that previous presidents have ordered the seizure of property is of no moment; most of the seizures had involved the exercise of statutory authority, as Justice Frankfurter notes in his concurring opinion. In any case, as Black states, Congress has not and may not surrender its constitutional power to seize property.

In the closing paragraph of his opinion, Justice Black provides a powerful summation, reminding readers that the framers of the Constitution made the solemn decision to entrust the lawmaking power to Congress—in "good and bad times." A recounting of the familiar historical reasons that led the framers to that crucial decision is not necessary, Black explains. Rather, it should suffice to say that in a republic, the legislature is appointed as the lawmaking branch of government. At the time of the founding of the United States, the precise distinction between a monarchy and a republic was clearly understood to lie in the fact that the republican legislature made the law and the executive was subordinate to the law. Black's opinion rests on a solid historical foundation.

◆ Justice Robert Jackson's Concurrence

Jackson's opinion rests on the concept of a "fluid" presidential power, one that reflects the relative actions of the executive and Congress. He provides a framework for analysis that is grounded on three tiers. In the first tier, the president's power is at its zenith when he acts on the basis of his constitutional power plus all that Congress has by statute granted to him. In the second tier, some ambiguity can be occasioned by the uncertain constitutional allocation of power to the president and to Congress or by conflicting powers. In this "zone of twilight," the exercise of power hinges on political imponderables: Which branch might act first? The uncertainty occurs when the president acts in the absence of either a grant or a denial of authority by Congress.

In the third tier, the president's power is at its lowest ebb whenever he acts in a manner that is in conflict with the expressed or implied will of Congress. In such instances, he is left to rely upon his own constitutional powers minus any that Congress might possess. President Truman's seizure order fell into this category; the Court thus ruled that he lacked the constitutional power to issue the order and that it was not authorized by Congress but, in fact, violated the implied will of that body, as indicated by its debate on the Taft-Hartley Act.

Audience

The Supreme Court's ruling in the *Youngstown* case enjoyed a nationwide audience. In fact, few cases in American constitutional history have captured the attention of citizens from all walks of life that *Youngstown* garnered. The tremendous media attention paid to President Truman's seizure of the steel mills and the subsequent legal proceedings in the lower courts had a riveting effect on the public. As a result, many in the nation anxiously awaited the Supreme Court's decision.

The immediate audience in the Steel Seizure Case included, of course, the government and the entire steel industry, both management and workers. Thus, the size of the audience that possessed a direct interest in the outcome of the case numbered in the millions, certainly a rare occurrence in America. Beyond the intense interest of the two sides, lawyers, politicians, and scholars evinced a sharp interest in the case as well, given the great legal questions at stake and the enormous implications that they held for the nation. Indeed, *Youngstown* will hold the rapt attention of students and citizens alike for as long as the United States retains its Constitution.

Impact

Youngstown is, without question, one of the great cases in American constitutional law. It has exerted considerable influence on the minds of judges, scholars, elected officials, and the public. The case represents the most penetrating judicial examination of presidential power ever conducted by the Supreme Court and constitutes one of the rare judicial rebukes to the claim of presidential power during wartime; it also demonstrates the capacity of the Court to play a major role in maintaining constitutional balance. Moreover, the case's denial of the assertion of inherent executive power constitutes a landmark rejection of a claim to near limitless power that endangered the principles of constitutionalism and republicanism.

The impact of *Youngstown* may be measured in both its immediate and its long-term effects on the country. When the decision came down, it signaled to Americans a clear, crisp judicial rejection of the broad claims to presidential power asserted by the Truman administration. Newspapers that had condemned Truman's claim to unlimited emergency power embraced and celebrated the Court's courage and constitutional vision. The administration, of course, was dejected. The president had perceived an emergency,

had acted in a manner that he sincerely believed to be in the best interests of the nation, and was thoroughly rejected by a Court that included several close friends and colleagues. In fact, Truman had been led to believe by Chief Justice Fred Vinson that his actions would be upheld by the Court. In response to the ruling, the steelworkers immediately implemented their planned strike, which lasted 53 days, from June 2 to July 24.

In some ways, the very willingness of the Court to review and reject presidential assertions of power represents *Youngstown*'s real legacy. The Court's ruling helped to reestablish some measure of balance between the president and Congress. It also reminded the nation that the executive is subordinate to the law, not above it. Furthermore, the denial of the claim of an inherent executive power was critical to the maintenance of the American constitutional government. After all, the claim amounted to an assertion of a presidential power to make law, since it would have permitted the president to act not only in the absence of legislation but also in violation of it. The concept of a presidential power to defy law contradicts not only the oath of office but also the duty of the president to enforce the laws of the nation, as required by the "take care" clause. The specter of a president flouting the law, acting arbitrarily, and ignoring the constitutional power of Congress to make law and seize property summons the ghosts of tyrants, dictators, and monarchs.

As a matter of constitutional influence, Justice Robert Jackson's concurring opinion, rather than Justice Black's majority opinion, has been more frequently cited and invoked by scholars and judges in discussions of *Youngstown*. Critics of Black's opinion have derided it as being overly simple and formalistic as well as unmindful of the nuances and subtleties of the separation of powers. Those criticisms may not be altogether fair. After all, the five concurring opinions joined Black in his declaration that Congress had, in consideration of the Taft-Hartley Act, precluded presidential seizure of property when members vote against a provision that would have vested such authority in the president. Moreover, the concurring justices agreed on the essential point that the president has no inherent authority to violate the law. Nonetheless, Jackson's concurring opinion has been more widely celebrated as a more sophisticated explanation of presidential power.

While Jackson's opinion has won praise from scholars and judges for its fluid approach to presidential power, the overarching impact of Youngstown has been seen in its encouragement to subsequent courts to check presidential power. In the Pentagon Papers Case (*New York Times Co. v. United States*, 1972), the Court rejected President Richard Nixon's claim of an inherent presidential power for the defense of national security broad enough to permit him to seek an injunction to prevent the New York Times from publishing the Pentagon Papers. In *United States v. Nixon* (1974), the Court drew upon *Youngstown* to reject Nixon's claim of an absolute executive privilege. In the annals of American constitutional law, *Youngstown* will forever be regarded as a decision that reinforced constitutionalism and the rule of law.

"The President's power, if any, to issue the order must stem either from an act of Congress or from the Constitution itself. There is no statute that expressly authorizes the President to take possession of property as he did here. Nor is there any act of Congress to which our attention has been directed from which such a power can fairly be implied."

(Justice Hugo Black, Majority Opinion)

"It is clear that, if the President had authority to issue the order he did, it must be found in some provision of the Constitution."

(Justice Hugo Black, Majority Opinion)

"The order cannot properly be sustained as an exercise of the President's military power as Commander in Chief of the Armed Forces.... Even though 'theater of war' be an expanding concept, we cannot with faithfulness to our constitutional system hold that the Commander in Chief of the Armed Forces has the ultimate power as such to take possession of private property in order to keep labor disputes from stopping production. This is a job for the Nation's lawmakers, not for its military authorities."

(Justice Hugo Black, Majority Opinion)

"Nor can the seizure order be sustained because of the several constitutional provisions that grant executive power to the President. In the framework of our Constitution, the President's power to see that the laws are faithfully executed refutes the idea that he is to be a lawmaker."

(Justice Hugo Black, Majority Opinion)

"The Founders of this Nation entrusted the lawmaking power to Congress alone in both good and bad times."

(Justice Hugo Black, Majority Opinion)

Related Documents

"Clinton v. Jones." U.S. Supreme Court Media "Oyez" Web site. http://www.oyez.org/cases/1990-1999/1996/1996_95_1853/. Accessed on February 11, 2008. This case (520 U.S. 681 [1997]), which provided a path for President Bill Clinton's impeachment, offers another example of the Court's reasoning about presidential power.

Farrand, Max, ed. The Records of the Federal Convention of 1787. 4 vols. New Haven, Conn.: Yale University Press, 1966. This collection draws together the discussions and debates of the Constitutional Convention and includes an examination of the framers' views on presidential power.

Hamilton, Alexander, James Madison, and John Jay. *The Federalist*, ed. Edward Meade Earle. New York: Modern Library, 1937. The Federalist Papers represent a commentary on the proposed Constitution by its advocates. Federalist Papers nos. 67–77 are particularly useful for understanding presidential powers.

"United States v. Curtiss-Wright Export Corporation, 299 U.S. 304 (1936)." FindLaw Web site. http://caselaw.lp.findlaw.com/cgi-bin/getcase.pl?court=us&vol=299&invol=304. Accessed on February 11, 2008. The Court's reasoning in *Youngstown* merits comparison with the Court's discussion of presidential power in the *Curtiss-Wright* case.

United States v. Nixon, 418 U.S. 683 (1974)." FindLaw Web site. http://caselaw.lp.findlaw.com/scripts/getcase.pl?court=us&vol=418&invol=683. Accessed on February 11, 2008. The Court's opinion on the scope of executive power in the famous Watergate tapes case can also be compared with the Court's decision in *Youngstown*.

Bibliography

■ Articles

Adler, David Gray. "The Steel Seizure Case and Inherent Presidential Power." *Constitutional Commentary* 19 (2002): 155–213.

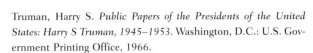

■ Books

Marcus, Maeva. *Truman and the Steel Seizure Case: The Limits of Presidential Power*. Durham, N.C.: Duke University Press, 1994.

Truman, Harry S. *Public Papers of the Presidents of the United States: Harry S Truman, 1945–1953*. Washington, D.C.: U.S. Government Printing Office, 1966.

Westin, Alan F. *The Anatomy of a Constitutional Law Case*. New York: Macmillan, 1958.

■ Web Sites

"Executive Order 10340." Stanford Law School, "Steel Seizure Case Revisited" Web site.
     http://steelseizure.stanford.edu/exec.order10340.html. Accessed on February 11, 2008.

Harry S. Truman Library and Museum.
     http://www.trumanlibrary.org/index.php. Accessed on February 11, 2008.

—By David Gray Adler

1. In his opinion for the Court in *Youngstown*, Justice Black denounces President Truman's assertion of an inherent power to confront emergencies. Do you believe that the president has such power? If so, what are its limits? By what method would you draw limits around such a power?

2. Is it possible to reconcile the concept of a presidency created and defined by the Constitution with the concept of an emergency executive power? Explain.

3. Irrespective of the Court's ruling in *Youngstown*, what did the framers of the Constitution think about the concept of an inherent presidential power? Are their views relevant to the modern era?

4. The Black and Jackson opinions use different approaches in considering the separation of powers. Which approach do you find more useful? If a power, such as the lawmaking power, is granted to one branch, should another branch be permitted to exercise it? Explain.

Glossary

Court of Appeals	a court having jurisdiction, or power, to review and revise lower court rulings
Executive Order	an order or regulation issued by a president pursuant to constitutional or statutory authority
executive power	power to execute laws; in the United States, the enumerated or implied powers vested in the president by Article II of the Constitution
inherent power	power said to originate in the nature of the office, beyond enumerated or implied powers
injunction	a prohibitive remedy issued by a court forbidding the defendant to do or perform some act

YOUNGSTOWN SHEET AND TUBE CO. V. SAWYER

Mr. Justice Black Delivered the Opinion of the Court

We are asked to decide whether the President was acting within his constitutional power when he issued an order directing the Secretary of Commerce to take possession of and operate most of the Nation's steel mills. The mill owners argue that the President's order amounts to lawmaking, a legislative function which the Constitution has expressly confided to the Congress, and not to the President. The Government's position is that the order was made on findings of the President that his action was necessary to avert a national catastrophe which would inevitably result from a stoppage of steel production, and that, in meeting this grave emergency, the President was acting within the aggregate of his constitutional powers as the Nation's Chief Executive and the Commander in Chief of the Armed Forces of the United States. The issue emerges here from the following series of events:

In the latter part of 1951, a dispute arose between the steel companies and their employees over terms and conditions that should be included in new collective bargaining agreements. Long-continued conferences failed to resolve the dispute. On December 18, 1951, the employees' representative, United Steelworkers of America, CIO, gave notice of an intention to strike when the existing bargaining agreements expired on December 31. The Federal Mediation and Conciliation Service then intervened in an effort to get labor and management to agree. This failing, the President on December 22, 1951, referred the dispute to the Federal Wage Stabilization Board to investigate and make recommendations for fair and equitable terms of settlement. This Board's report resulted in no settlement. On April 4, 1952, the Union gave notice of a nationwide strike called to begin at 12:01 a.m. April 9. The indispensability of steel as a component of substantially all weapons and other war materials led the President to believe that the proposed work stoppage would immediately jeopardize our national defense and that governmental seizure of the steel mills was necessary in order to assure the continued availability of steel. Reciting these considerations for his action, the President, a few hours before the strike was to begin, issued Executive Order 10340, a copy of which is attached as an appendix. The order directed the Secretary of Commerce to take possession of most of the steel mills and keep them running. The Secretary immediately issued his own possessory orders, calling upon the presidents of the various seized companies to serve as operating managers for the United States. They were directed to carry on their activities in accordance with regulations and directions of the Secretary. The next morning the President sent a message to Congress reporting his action. Cong.Rec. April 9, 1952, p. 3962. Twelve days later, he sent a second message. Cong.Rec. April 21, 1952, p. 4192. Congress has taken no action.

Obeying the Secretary's orders under protest, the companies brought proceedings against him in the District Court. Their complaints charged that the seizure was not authorized by an act of Congress or by any constitutional provisions. The District Court was asked to declare the orders of the President and the Secretary invalid and to issue preliminary and permanent injunctions restraining their enforcement. Opposing the motion for preliminary injunction, the United States asserted that a strike disrupting steel production for even a brief period would so endanger the wellbeing and safety of the Nation that the President had "inherent power" to do what he had done—power "supported by the Constitution, by historical precedent, and by court decisions." The Government also contended that, in any event, no preliminary injunction should be issued, because the companies had made no showing that their available legal remedies were inadequate or that their injuries from seizure would be irreparable. Holding against the Government on all points, the District Court, on April 30, issued a preliminary injunction restraining the Secretary from "continuing the seizure and possession of the plants … and from acting under the purported authority of Executive Order No. 10340." 103 F.Supp. 569. On the same day, the Court of Appeals stayed the District Court's injunction. 90 U.S.App.D.C., 197 F.2d 582. Deeming it best that the issues raised be promptly decided by this Court, we granted certiorari on May 3 and set the cause for argument on May 12.

Two crucial issues have developed: *First.* Should final determination of the constitutional validity of the President's order be made in this case which has proceeded no further than the preliminary injunction stage? *Second.* If so, is the seizure order within the constitutional power of the President?

It is urged that there were nonconstitutional grounds upon which the District Court could have denied the preliminary injunction, and thus have followed the customary judicial practice of declining to reach and decide constitutional questions until compelled to do so. On this basis, it is argued that equity's extraordinary injunctive relief should have been denied because (a) seizure of the companies' properties did not inflict irreparable damages, and (b) there were available legal remedies adequate to afford compensation for any possible damages which they might suffer. While separately argued by the Government, these two contentions are here closely related, if not identical. Arguments as to both rest in large part on the Government's claim that, should the seizure ultimately be held unlawful, the companies could recover full compensation in the Court of Claims for the unlawful taking. Prior cases in this Court have cast doubt on the right to recover in the Court of Claims on account of properties unlawfully taken by government officials for public use as these properties were alleged to have been. See e.g., *Hooe v. United States*, 218 U.S. 322, 335-336; *United States v. North American Co.*, 253 U.S. 330, 333. But see *Larson v. Domestic & Foreign Corp.*, 337 U.S. 682, 701-702. Moreover, seizure and governmental operation of these going businesses were bound to result in many present and future damages of such nature as to be difficult, if not incapable, of measurement. Viewing the case this way, and in the light of the facts presented, the District Court saw no reason for delaying decision of the constitutional validity of the orders. We agree with the District Court, and can see no reason why that question was not ripe for determination on the record presented. We shall therefore consider and determine that question now.

◆ II

The President's power, if any, to issue the order must stem either from an act of Congress or from the Constitution itself. There is no statute that expressly authorizes the President to take possession of property as he did here. Nor is there any act of Congress to which our attention has been directed from which such a power can fairly be implied. Indeed, we do not understand the Government to rely on statutory

authorization for this seizure. There are two statutes which do authorize the President to take both personal and real property under certain conditions. However, the Government admits that these conditions were not met, and that the President's order was not rooted in either of the statutes. The Government refers to the seizure provisions of one of these statutes (§ 201(b) of the Defense Production Act) as "much too cumbersome, involved, and time-consuming for the crisis which was at hand."

Moreover, the use of the seizure technique to solve labor disputes in order to prevent work stoppages was not only unauthorized by any congressional enactment; prior to this controversy, Congress had refused to adopt that method of settling labor disputes. When the Taft-Hartley Act was under consideration in 1947, Congress rejected an amendment which would have authorized such governmental seizures in cases of emergency. Apparently it was thought that the technique of seizure, like that of compulsory arbitration, would interfere with the process of collective bargaining. Consequently, the plan Congress adopted in that Act did not provide for seizure under any circumstances. Instead, the plan sought to bring about settlements by use of the customary devices of mediation, conciliation, investigation by boards of inquiry, and public reports. In some instances, temporary injunctions were authorized to provide cooling-off periods. All this failing, unions were left free to strike after a secret vote by employees as to whether they wished to accept their employers' final settlement offer.

It is clear that, if the President had authority to issue the order he did, it must be found in some provision of the Constitution. And it is not claimed that express constitutional language grants this power to the President. The contention is that presidential power should be implied from the aggregate of his powers under the Constitution. Particular reliance is placed on provisions in Article II which say that "The executive Power shall be vested in a President ..."; that "he shall take Care that the Laws be faithfully executed," and that he "shall be Commander in Chief of the Army and Navy of the United States."

The order cannot properly be sustained as an exercise of the President's military power as Commander in Chief of the Armed Forces. The Government attempts to do so by citing a number of cases upholding broad powers in military commanders engaged in day-to-day fighting in a theater of war. Such cases need not concern us here. Even though "theater of war" be an expanding concept, we cannot with faithfulness to our constitutional system hold that the Commander in Chief of the Armed Forces has the ultimate power as such to take possession of private property in order to keep labor disputes from stopping production. This is a job for the Nation's lawmakers, not for its military authorities.

Nor can the seizure order be sustained because of the several constitutional provisions that grant executive power to the President. In the framework of our Constitution, the President's power to see that the laws are faithfully executed refutes the idea that he is to be a lawmaker. The Constitution limits his functions in the lawmaking process to the recommending of laws he thinks wise and the vetoing of laws he thinks bad. And the Constitution is neither silent nor equivocal about who shall make laws which the President is to execute. The first section of the first article says that "All legislative Powers herein granted shall be vested in a Congress of the United States...." After granting many powers to the Congress, Article I goes on to provide that Congress may

make all Laws which shall be necessary and proper for carrying into Execution the foregoing Powers, and all other Powers vested by this Constitution in the Government of the United States, or in any Department or Officer thereof.

The President's order does not direct that a congressional policy be executed in a manner prescribed by Congress—it directs that a presidential policy be executed in a manner prescribed by the President. The preamble of the order itself, like that of many statutes, sets out reasons why the President believes certain policies should be adopted, proclaims these policies as rules of conduct to be followed, and again, like a statute, authorizes a government official to promulgate additional rules and regulations consistent with the policy proclaimed and needed to carry that policy into execution. The power of Congress to adopt such public policies as those proclaimed by the order is beyond question. It can authorize the taking of private property for public use. It can make laws regulating the relationships between employers and employees, prescribing rules designed to settle labor disputes, and fixing wages and working conditions in certain fields of our economy. The Constitution does not subject this lawmaking power of Congress to presidential or military supervision or control.

It is said that other Presidents, without congressional authority, have taken possession of private business enterprises in order to settle labor disputes. But even if this be true, Congress has not thereby lost its exclusive constitutional authority to make laws necessary and proper to carry out the powers vested by the Constitution "in the Government of the United States, or any Department or Officer thereof."

The Founders of this Nation entrusted the lawmaking power to the Congress alone in both good and bad times. It would do no good to recall the historical events, the fears of power, and the hopes for freedom that lay behind their choice. Such a review would but confirm our holding that this seizure order cannot stand.

The judgment of the District Court is Affirmed.

SUPREME COURT OF THE UNITED STATES

Nos. 1, 2, 4 AND 10.—OCTOBER TERM, 1953.

Oliver Brown, et al., Appellants, 1 v. Board of Education of Topeka, Shawnee County, Kansas, et al.	On Appeal From the United States District Court for the District of Kansas.
Harry Briggs, Jr., et al., Appellants, 2 v. R. W. Elliott, et al.	On Appeal From the United States District Court for the Eastern District of South Carolina.
Dorothy E. Davis, et al., Appellants, 4 v. County School Board of Prince Edward County, Virginia, et al.	On Appeal From the United States District Court for the Eastern District of Virginia.
Francis B. Gebhart, et al., Petitioners, 10 v. Ethel Louise Belton, et al.	On Writ of Certiorari to the Supreme Court of Delaware.

[May 17, 1954.]

MR. CHIEF JUSTICE WARREN delivered the opinion of the Court.

These cases come to us from the States of Kansas, South Carolina, Virginia, and Delaware. They are premised on different facts and different local conditions,

Brown v. Board of Education (National Archives and Records Administration)

BROWN V. BOARD OF EDUCATION

"Separate educational facilities are inherently unequal."

Overview

Brown v. Board of Education of Topeka was the 1954 Supreme Court decision that declared that legally mandated segregation in public schools was unconstitutional under the Fourteenth Amendment's equal protection clause. The landmark case was actually a combination of five cases that challenged school segregation in Delaware, South Carolina, Virginia, and Topeka, Kansas. In a companion case, Bolling v. Sharpe, segregation in the District of Columbia's public schools was declared unconstitutional under the due process clause of the Fifth Amendment. Brown was a pivotal case in the history of the Supreme Court. Although Brown did not explicitly reverse the Court's earlier ruling in the 1896 case Plessy v. Ferguson, which permitted states to provide "separate but equal" facilities for people of different races, it was clearly the beginning of the end of the Supreme Court's willingness to give constitutional sanction to state-sponsored segregation. Brown was the first decision authored by the recently appointed Chief Justice Earl Warren and was a harbinger of the new, more activist role that the Court would take in protecting civil rights and civil liberties under his leadership.

Brown should be seen against the broader background of segregation in American history. By the end of the nineteenth century, southern states, and indeed quite a few states outside of the South, were developing an American system of apartheid through what were often called Jim Crow laws. This system of segregation mandated the separation of blacks and whites in almost every observable facet of public life. Separate water fountains, park benches, railroad cars, and other facilities were common. All of the southern states and a number of border states also maintained separate school facilities for blacks and whites. Although the Supreme Court's decision in Plessy had declared that blacks could be required to use separate facilities if those facilities were equal to those provided for whites, states that maintained racially separate schools provided schools for African Americans that were usually greatly inferior in resources and programs to those provided for whites. Glaring inequalities in educational facilities prompt-

ed the National Association for the Advancement of Colored People (NAACP) to begin a decades-long litigation campaign to challenge segregation in public education. That campaign would eventually result in the decision in Brown.

Context

The NAACP began to develop its strategy to attack segregation in state schools in the 1930s. The organization began cautiously enough by attacking segregation in professional schools, principally law schools, of state universities. Law schools were selected because state university systems usually had only one law school each, and it would be relatively easy to make the case that providing a state law school for white students while providing none for blacks violated the principle that a state had to provide equal facilities. The NAACP also believed that litigation designed to force states to permit black students to attend state law schools would provoke less adverse political reaction than lawsuits designed to integrate public primary and secondary schools. The architect of the NAACP's litigation strategy, Charles Hamilton Houston, would achieve success before the Second World War with his victory in the 1938 case Missouri ex rel. Gaines v. Canada. In that case the Supreme Court held that Missouri's exclusion of African Americans from the state's law school was unconstitutional even though Missouri was willing to pay tuition for black students to attend law school out of state. The NAACP met with success in similar litigation in other states.

While the NAACP had some success with litigation designed to desegregate professional schools before the Second World War, the changes in racial attitudes brought about by the war played a key role in paving the way for the decision in Brown. In particular, the war brought about a new assertiveness on the part of African Americans, as many blacks left the rural South and traditional patterns of racial domination for the armed forces and the industrial cities of the North and West. With these changes came a new willingness to struggle for equal rights. The fight against Nazi racism also caused many white Americans to question traditional racial attitudes. Furthermore, the social sciences were increasingly calling established racial

1896

■ **May 18**
In *Plessy v. Ferguson*, the Supreme Court declares the "separate but equal" doctrine, permitting segregation in government-run facilities.

1909

■ **February 12**
A group to later be known as the National Association for the Advancement of Colored People is formed to fight segregation.

1929

■ Charles Hamilton Houston is appointed vice-dean of Howard University Law School. Houston would transform the law school into a vehicle for training civil rights lawyers, including Thurgood Marshall, the principal lawyer for the NAACP in *Brown*.

1938

■ **December 12**
In *Missouri ex rel. Gaines v. Canada*, the Supreme Court holds that the state of Missouri must admit black students to the state law school.

1948

■ **May 3**
In *Shelley v. Kraemer*, the Supreme Court bars the judicial enforcement of restrictive covenants used to prevent home owners from selling their homes to members of minority groups.

■ **July 26**
President Harry Truman issues Executive Order 9981, requiring equality of opportunity in and the desegregation of the armed forces.

1950

■ **June 5**
In *Sweatt v. Painter*, the Court orders that black students be admitted to the University of Texas School of Law, declaring that the separate law school established for black students did not provide equal treatment.

1954

■ **May 17**
The Supreme Court issues its decision in *Brown v. Board of Education*, declaring segregation in public schools unconstitutional.

prejudices into question. The publication in 1944 of the Swedish social scientist Gunnar Myrdal's book *An American Dilemma: The Negro Problem and Modern Democracy* also had a significant impact, causing many university-educated people to question the practice of segregation.

The changes in the racial atmosphere in postwar America spurred the NAACP to confront legally mandated segregation. While the organization achieved significant victories in its fight against segregated professional education, other important victories came in the legal struggle against general discrimination. The 1948 case *Shelley v. Kraemer*, in which the Supreme Court declared that courts could not enforce restrictive covenants barring minorities from buying homes in white neighborhoods, was an indication of the Court's willingness to give the Fourteenth Amendment a broader reading than it had in the past. Following this decision, many in the NAACP believed that the time was right for a frontal assault on segregated education.

Between 1950 and 1952 the NAACP, under the leadership of Thurgood Marshall and his associates, began preparing the cases that would come to be known as *Brown v. Board of Education*. The case by which the litigation is known arose in Topeka, Kansas—a state that, unlike those in the South, did not have statewide segregation. Instead, the state gave localities the option to have segregated schools. The elementary schools in Topeka were indeed segregated, and Oliver Brown, a black resident of the city, filed suit so that his daughter might attend a school reserved for whites. That school was nearer to the Brown home and had better facilities.

In 1952 the Supreme Court consolidated the different desegregation cases. The first set of oral arguments were heard by the Court in December of that year; in June 1953, the Court asked for a second set of oral arguments designed to specifically address the issue of whether or not the Fourteenth Amendment was intended to mandate school desegregation. As that issue was being researched, Chief Justice Frederick M. Vinson died, in September 1953. He was replaced by Earl Warren. Most observers agree that the new chief justice made a critical difference to the outcome of the case.

About the Author

Earl Warren was born in Los Angeles, California, in 1891. He was a graduate of the University of California at Berkeley and of that university's law school. Warren served in the U.S. Army during the First World War as an officer in charge of training troops deploying to France.

Warren began his legal career in California in 1920 as a prosecutor with the Alameda County district attorney's office. In 1925 he was appointed district attorney to fill a vacancy. Elected district attorney in his own right the following year, he would remain in that office until his election as California's attorney general in 1938.

Warren was a product of the California Republican politics of the Progressive Era. As district attorney and as attorney general he was generally supportive of reforms in the criminal justice system, such as with his willingness to extend due process rights and legal representation to defendants in criminal cases. These were generally not required at the time by the federal courts, which by and large were not applying most of the criminal defendants' rights provisions of the Fourth, Fifth, and Sixth Amendments to the states. Warren was also somewhat ahead of the times in his attitudes toward African Americans. He considered appointing a black attorney to the attorney general's staff in 1938.

Ironically enough, anti-Asian bias probably helped propel Warren to the national stage. Warren shared the anti-Asian sentiments that were common among whites on the West Coast in the early part of the twentieth century. Near the beginning of his career he was a member of an anti-Asian group, Native Sons of the Golden West. As attorney general in the winter and spring of 1942, Warren was a leading advocate of Japanese internment, at first advocating internment only for Japanese aliens but later supporting the internment of Japanese Americans as well. His support for Japanese internment doubtless aided Warren in his gaining election as governor of California in 1942. Warren would run for vice president on the Republican ticket with Governor Thomas Dewey of New York in 1948.

Warren was appointed chief justice by President Dwight David Eisenhower in 1953 to replace Chief Justice Frederick M. Vinson, who had died in office. Warren's entire tenure as chief justice was marked by controversy, beginning with the decision in *Brown* and continuing until his retirement from the Supreme Court in 1969. Under Warren, the Court dealt with some of the most contentious issues in postwar American life, including school desegregation, reapportionment, the rights of criminal defendants, birth control, and the right to privacy, among others. Warren's critics charged that he extended the reach of the Court into areas unauthorized and unintended by the Constitution's framers and that he and his allies on the Court often employed dubious legal reasoning. Warren's supporters responded by noting that the Court under his direction was a vital force in making equal protection and the Bill of Rights living principles for millions of Americans. Later on as chief justice, at the direction of Lyndon B. Johnson, Warren would head the President's Commission on the Assassination of President Kennedy, often referred to as the Warren Commission. Warren died in 1974.

Explanation and Analysis of Document

Brown v. Board of Education of Topeka is a Supreme Court case and as such begins with a syllabus presenting basic information about the case. This information includes the parties, the lower court whose decision is being appealed, and the dates that the case was argued before the Supreme Court. The case was taken on appeal from a decision by the District Court for the District of Kansas. An asterisked footnote relates that *Brown* is being

Time Line

1955

■ **May 31**
The Court issues its decision in the second *Brown v. Board of Education* case, calling for the implementation of the first decision with "all deliberate speed."

1957

■ **September 24**
President Eisenhower sends federal troops to Little Rock, Arkansas, to enforce a federal district court school desegregation order; the order had produced large-scale mob resistance by opponents of integration.

1960

■ **November 8**
In response to a federal district court order calling for the desegregation of New Orleans schools, the Louisiana State Legislature passes an "interposition statute" declaring that the legislature does not recognize the authority of the ruling in *Brown*.

1962

■ **September**
President John F. Kennedy sends federal marshals and federal troops to Oxford, Mississippi, to assist in the enrollment of the African American student James Meredith in the University of Mississippi; Meredith's enrollment had been ordered by the U.S. Court of Appeals for the Fifth Circuit but was obstructed by state officials, including Governor Ross Barnett.

1971

■ **April 20**
Supreme Court approves of busing as a means of achieving school desegregation.

1974

■ **July 25**
In *Milliken v. Bradley*, the Court declares that the constitutional requirement to desegregate does not require desegregation across municipal lines. The decision means that lower federal courts cannot require the integration of urban and suburban school districts across municipal lines.

Earl Warren (Library of Congress)

consolidated with other school segregation cases from South Carolina, Virginia, and Delaware. The syllabus also gives a summary of the decision and lists the attorneys who made oral arguments before the Court on behalf of the parties in *Brown* and the companion cases. The syllabus also lists briefs filed by amici curiae ("friends of the court," persons or organizations not party to a case who file a brief in support of a party or to inform the court with respect to a legal or policy issue) in *Brown* and the companion cases. Of special interest is the fact that the assistant attorney general J. Lee Rankin argued for the United States in support of desegregation.

♦ Chief Justice Earl Warren's Majority Opinion

Warren begins with a straightforward presentation of the issues. His first paragraph notes that the desegregation cases have come from different states—Kansas, South Carolina, Virginia, and Delaware—and that while each state presents somewhat different issues with respect to local laws and local conditions, the clear principal issue of legal segregation is common to all of the cases.

Stylistically, Warren's opinion makes extensive use of footnotes not only to cite relevant authorities but also to carry the burden of informing the reader of major legal and factual arguments. As had become common in twentieth-century legal writing, footnotes served to supply a judicial decision with a kind of supplemental narrative, augmenting the main points being made in the body of the opinion.

This style of judicial writing was doubtless encouraged, perhaps mandated, by the practice of parties and amici curiae filing extensive briefs in major cases. The increasing use of "Brandeis briefs"—briefs providing wide-ranging amounts of information to the Court from the social and physical sciences, as modeled after that filed by Louis Brandeis in *Muller v. Oregon* (1908)—probably also hastened the development of the lengthy use of footnotes in judicial opinions.

The first footnote here discusses how *Brown* and the companion cases fared in the U.S. district courts. Included in this discussion are the legal and factual findings of these courts. With respect to *Brown*, a three-judge panel of the District Court for the District of Kansas found that segregated public education indeed had a detrimental effect on black students, but that court nonetheless upheld segregated education because the facilities for blacks and whites were held to be equal with respect to buildings, transportation, curricula, and the educational qualifications of the teachers. The district court in South Carolina found that the facilities available to black students were inferior to those of whites, but that court nonetheless upheld segregation on the ground that South Carolina officials were making efforts to equalize facilities. In Virginia, the district court ordered officials to make efforts to equalize the schools. In Delaware, the state courts had ordered desegregation, and state officials were appealing that order.

Warren moves in the second and third paragraphs to presenting the central claims of the NAACP and of the parents that were bringing suit. He zeroes in on the crux of these claims in the third paragraph, noting, "The plaintiffs contend that segregated public schools are not 'equal' and cannot be made 'equal,' and that hence they are deprived of the equal protection of the laws." Warren's opinion spends relatively little time examining the history of this argument, but it is a claim with a long history, one that antedates *Brown* by at least a century. In particular, the NAACP argued that segregation was inherently stigmatizing, an argument that was older than the Fourteenth Amendment (ratified in 1868) and its equal protection clause, under which *Brown* and the other cases were brought. This argument made its first judicial appearance in the antebellum Massachusetts school desegregation case *Roberts v. City of Boston* (1850). In that case, African American parents argued that Boston's system of school segregation essentially stigmatized black children by setting up a caste system dividing black and white. The Massachusetts Supreme Judicial Court rejected the argument, in effect establishing the "separate but equal" doctrine, a point Warren notes in footnote 6. The argument that segregation stigmatized African Americans and hence violated the Fourteenth Amendment's guarantee of equal protection under the law would later be heard and rejected by the Supreme Court in *Plessy v. Ferguson* (1896), with the Supreme Court making the "separate but equal" doctrine a part of federal constitutional law.

Part of the NAACP's aim in *Brown* was to have segregated schools declared unconstitutional on the ground that the system of school segregation forced black children into schools that were vastly inferior to those reserved for white students. The systems of school segregation that prevailed in the southern states usually featured vast inequalities in the levels of education provided to black and white children. Black schools were usually funded at a fraction of the level of white schools. In many districts blacks were confined to one-room schoolhouses in which all grades were to be educated, while whites had separate elementary and secondary schools. Black schools were usually separate and decidedly unequal with respect to the qualifications and pay for black teachers and the physical facilities in which black schools were housed. Correcting all of this was part of the NAACP's aim in litigating against school segregation. In addition, the civil rights organization shared the view held by its nineteenth-century predecessors that the very act of segregating, of signaling out blacks for separate treatment, was inherently stigmatizing and more appropriate to a caste system than to the practices of American democracy. The NAACP advocate Thurgood Marshall, in his oral argument before Earl Warren and other members of the Court on December 8, 1953, presented the issue starkly: "Why of all the multitudinous groups in this country, you have to single out the Negroes and give them this separate treatment?"

This was clearly an issue involving the Fourteenth Amendment's equal protection clause, and in the fourth and fifth paragraphs the new chief justice begins addressing the Fourteenth Amendment and what it mandated in these circumstances. Here, Warren begins moving into territory that would forever make *Brown* an object of controversy among constitutional commentators. He argues that the history of the Fourteenth Amendment is inconclusive regarding what it had to say with respect to school segregation. In fact, Warren frames *Brown* as a case pitting modern realities against inconclusive history. In the fifth paragraph he focuses on the history of public education at the time of the enactment of the Fourteenth Amendment, noting that public education had not yet taken hold in the South and that practically all southern blacks at the time were illiterate. He juxtaposes that situation with modern circumstances: "Today, in contrast, many Negroes have achieved outstanding success in the arts and sciences, as well as in the business and professional world." Warren uses this contrast between the relative lack of importance of public education at the time of the enactment of the Fourteenth Amendment and its much greater importance at the time of the *Brown* decision to set up what will be his principal argument in paragraphs 8 and 9, namely, that the question of segregated education and its constitutionality under the Fourteenth Amendment had to be considered in light of the importance of public education in modern—that is, post–World War II—American society and not in light of its relative unimportance at the beginning of the Reconstruction era.

In the sixth paragraph Warren takes on the "separate but equal" doctrine, seeking to show that it is less than the solid precedent that its champions claimed. Indeed, the argument for the constitutionality of segregated schools rested on the "separate but equal" precedent provided in *Plessy*. The former solicitor general John W. Davis, repre-

Thurgood Marshall argued the NAACP's case before the Supreme Court. (Library of Congress)

senting South Carolina in an oral argument before the Supreme Court, emphasized the importance of *Plessy*, highlighting the fact that the lower federal courts and the Supreme Court had repeatedly reaffirmed the "separate but equal" doctrine and asserting that the Court should follow precedent and apply the doctrine in the case of school segregation. Davis's arguments were echoed by other supporters of school segregation.

Warren notes that the Court's earliest interpretations of the Fourteenth Amendment stressed that the amendment was designed to prohibit state-imposed racial discrimination; the "separate but equal" doctrine did not become part of the Supreme Court's jurisprudence until 1896—more than a generation after the enactment of the amendment. He also notes that *Plessy* involved transportation, not education. Warren further states that since *Plessy*, the Supreme Court had only heard six cases involving the "separate but equal" doctrine, with none reviewing the essential validity of the doctrine. He next cites the decisions involving segregation in graduate and professional schools. Warren's aims in this discussion are clear. While not directly challenging the *Plessy* precedent, he effectively isolates it as a decision that was not consistent with judicial interpretations made close to the enactment of the Fourteenth Amendment. He also gives *Plessy* a narrow reading so that it might be seen as a precedent that at most applies to the field of transportation. That case, according to Warren, was one that had not been thoroughly examined by the Court and in any event was made problematic, particularly in the field of education, by the graduate-school segregation cases.

Paragraphs 7–9 are used to frame the issues before the Court. Warren largely frames these issues in the way that the NAACP and the plaintiffs had presented them. The primary issue is segregation, and it is an issue that goes beyond tangible factors to encompass philosophical ones as well as the subtle reality of stigmatization. In paragraph 7 Warren uses footnote 9 to relate that the district court in Kansas had actually found substantial equality in the black and white schools. Warren indicates that regardless of this finding, segregation itself and its effect on public education remain of paramount concern.

Paragraph 8 is where Warren stakes out a clear claim as a proponent—indeed, one of the earliest explicit proponents—of the notion of a "living constitution," the idea that jurists should go beyond the concerns and assumptions of the framers of constitutional provisions and instead look at and reevaluate the Constitution in light of modern circumstances. He starts the paragraph, "In approaching this problem, we cannot turn the clock back to 1868, when the Amendment was adopted, or even to 1896, when *Plessy v. Ferguson* was written. We must consider public education in the light of its full development and its present place in American life throughout the Nation." In paragraphs 9–11 Warren goes on to outline the importance of education in modern American life and to conclude that segregated schools deprive members of minority groups of equal educational opportunities even when the tangible resources are equal.

Paragraph 12 lays a psychological basis for the opinion—one that would leave the *Brown* decision with a lingering controversy that persists to the present day. Warren cites the works of a number of psychologists—including, most prominently, the black psychologist Kenneth Clark—on the effects of segregation on the self-esteem of black children. These citations would lead many critics to charge that the chief justice was engaging in sociology rather than jurisprudence. Even many critics sympathetic to the outcome in *Brown* later expressed some discomfort with the use of psychological evidence, claiming that it gave the decision less of a firm footing, such that it could potentially be undone by shifts in findings in the social sciences. Clearly, what Warren is doing is examining the plaintiffs' arguments that segregation stigmatized black students by comparing those claims to the findings of the psychological experts of the day.

Paragraph 14 provides the Court's conclusion that "in the field of public education, the doctrine of 'separate but equal' has no place." Paragraph 15 provides a hint about some of the behind-the-scenes negotiations that Warren and the other justices went through in order to secure a unanimous decision in *Brown*. Here, Warren calls for the reargument of the cases to allow the Court to consider remedies for school segregation. Warren recognized the importance of establishing the constitutional principle that segregated public schools violated the equal protection clause of the Fourteenth Amendment. As such, he was greatly concerned with

getting a unanimous Court to agree to that constitutional principle—an achievement that had been very much in doubt during judicial conferences. Thus, as part of the strategy to obtain a unanimous opinion, Warren agreed to have *Brown* initially decide only the principle that segregated schools were unconstitutional, deferring the question of how the decision would be implemented for another day. Paragraph 14, the last paragraph, lays the groundwork for the second case, commonly known as *Brown II*, which would be heard the following year, and the more than two decades of desegregation litigation that would follow.

Audience

Brown v. Board of Education was first and foremost a Supreme Court decision designed to settle the constitutional question of whether or not segregated public schools were prohibited by the Fourteenth Amendment. Warren wrote the opinion to resolve that constitutional controversy and to inform states that they could no longer maintain segregated school systems. It was also written to inform African American parents that they had a legal right to send their children to nonsegregated schools.

Warren clearly also had a broader, national audience in mind while writing the decision. An experienced politician, the chief justice knew that the decision would be controversial and indeed hotly contested. He sought to write the decision in such a way as to present the policy case to the American public at large. His controversial use of psychological evidence to buttress the case against segregated schools was an attempt to appeal to the public by showing that children were being harmed by the policy of segregation. Warren's discussion of Negro accomplishments in education, business, and science can also be seen as an attempt to counter strong prejudices against African Americans, thus fortifying the case for school integration.

Impact

It is probably no exaggeration to say that *Brown* was the most significant case decided by the Supreme Court in its history. While the decision would take decades to implement, *Brown* was critical as a harbinger of the federal government's return to the civil rights arena, an arena from which it had been largely absent since Reconstruction. *Brown* would also provide a tremendous boost to the civil rights movement of the 1950s and 1960s. The knowledge that the Court was now going to interpret the Constitution as prohibiting the kind of caste-like distinctions that had been a feature of black life in the United States from the very beginning helped encourage a greater assertiveness on the part of African Americans, who proceeded to successfully protest the formal segregation of Jim Crow laws in the South and, later, more subtle forms of discrimination throughout the nation.

Brown's impact in the courts was a little more complicated. The case commonly known as *Brown v. Board of*

"*In approaching this problem, we cannot turn the clock back to 1868, when the Amendment was adopted, or even to 1896, when* Plessy v. Ferguson *was written.*"

(Chief Justice Earl Warren, Majority Opinion)

"*Today, education is perhaps the most important function of state and local governments.*"

(Chief Justice Earl Warren, Majority Opinion)

"*Such an opportunity, where the state has undertaken to provide it, is a right which must be made available to all on equal terms.*"

(Chief Justice Earl Warren, Majority Opinion)

"*To separate them from others of similar age and qualifications solely because of their race generates a feeling of inferiority as to their status in the community that may affect their hearts and minds in a way unlikely ever to be undone.*"

(Chief Justice Earl Warren, Majority Opinion)

"*Whatever may have been the extent of psychological knowledge at the time of* Plessy v. Ferguson, *this finding is amply supported by modern authority.*"

(Chief Justice Earl Warren, Majority Opinion)

"*We conclude that, in the field of public education, the doctrine of 'separate but equal' has no place. Separate educational facilities are inherently unequal.*"

(Chief Justice Earl Warren, Majority Opinion)

Education led to a successor case of the same name, known as *Brown II*, in 1955. That case resulted in a ruling that required the desegregation of separate school systems with "all deliberate speed." This order, in turn, led to protracted battles in federal district courts over the precise details and timing of school desegregation plans, which lasted decades. Nonetheless, the decision in *Brown* effectively led to the death of the "separate but equal" doctrine as well as to the negation of the idea that governmental bodies could prac-

tice the kind of formal discrimination against members of minority groups that had been common before *Brown*.

Related Documents

Bolling v. Sharpe, 347 U.S. 497 (1954). *Bolling* was a companion case to *Brown* but was decided on different grounds because it involved school segregation not in a state but in the District of

Columbia; the Fourteenth Amendment's equal protection clause applies to states and not the federal government, which has authority over the district. The Court held in *Bolling*, then, that the due process clause of the Fifth Amendment prohibits racial discrimination and hence segregated schools on the part of the federal government.

Brown v. Board of Education of Topeka (Brown II), 349 U.S. 294 (1955). *Brown II* was the successor case to *Brown I*. Therein, the Court directed district courts to develop plans to implement *Brown II* "with all deliberate speed."

Korematsu v. United States, 323 U.S. 214 (1944). *Korematsu*, a case involving the internment of a Japanese American, helped establish an important principle with respect to racial classification. Although the Supreme Court upheld the power of the government to intern Korematsu and other Japanese Americans, the decision also stated that racial classifications were constitutionally suspect and could survive only if able to withstand strict judicial scrutiny.

Plessy v. Ferguson, 163 U.S. 537 (1896). *Plessy*, with its "separate but equal" doctrine, was the governing law with respect to segregation and the equal protection clause of the Fourteenth Amendment for over fifty years. *Plessy* featured a very vigorous dissent by Justice John Marshall Harlan, ironically the only member of the Court who was a former slaveholder.

Roberts v. City of Boston, 59 Mass (5 Cush.) 198 (1850). This antebellum Boston school desegregation case, antedating *Brown* by a little over a century, is important to the understanding of how the arguments for and against the "separate but equal" doctrine developed. Addressed in *Roberts* are the questions of whether or not segregation stigmatizes, whether segregated facilities are equal if the tangible resources provided are equal, and what a constitutional mandate of equality before the law means.

Sweatt v. Painter, 339 U.S. 629 (1950). In *Sweatt*, the Supreme Court held that the state of Texas had to admit a black man to the law school at the University of Texas because the separate law school established for African Americans was unequal. For the NAACP, *Sweatt* was an important stepping stone on the road to *Brown* because in comparing the qualities of the two law schools, the Court considered intangible as well as tangible differences.

"Thurgood Marshall, on behalf of Harry Briggs, Jr. et al. and John W. Davis on behalf of the School District, No. 22 Clarendon County, South Carolina, et al." http://www.lib.umich.edu/exhibits/brownarchive/oral/Marshall&Davis.pdf. Digital Archive: Brown v. Board of Education Web site. Accessed on February 15, 2008. In his oral argument before the court, Marshall makes the case that

school segregation violated the Fourteenth Amendment and that the only reason to segregate schools was to keep black people as close to enslavement as possible.

Bibliography

■ Books

Cottrol, Robert J., Raymond T. Diamond, and Leland B. Ware. *Brown v. Board of Education: Caste, Culture, and the Constitution*. Lawrence: University Press of Kansas, 2003.

Kluger, Richard. *Simple Justice: The History of* Brown v. Board of Education *and Black America's Struggle for Equality*. New York: Knopf, 2004.

Myrdal, Gunnar. *An American Dilemma: The Negro Problem and Modern Democracy*. New York: Harper & Brothers, 1944.

Patterson, James T. *Brown v. Board of Education: A Civil Rights Milestone and Its Troubled Legacy*. New York: Oxford University Press, 2001.

Tushnet, Mark. *The NAACP's Legal Strategy against Segregated Education, 1925–1950*. Chapel Hill: University of North Carolina Press, 1987.

White, G. Edward. *Earl Warren: A Public Life*. New York: Oxford University Press, 1982.

■ Web Sites

"Brown v. Board of Education: Digital Archive." University of Michigan Library Web site.
    http://www.lib.umich.edu/exhibits/brownarchive/. Accessed on October 19, 2007.

"Civil Rights, Brown v. Board of Education (1954)." Historical Documents in United States History Web site.
    http://www.historicaldocuments.com/BrownvBoardofEducation.htm. Accessed on October 19, 2007.

"Teaching with Documents: Documents Related to *Brown v. Board of Education*." National Archives "Educators and Students" Web site.
    http://www.archives.gov//education/lessons/brown-v-board/. Accessed on October 19, 2007.

—By Robert Cottroll

1. Compare and contrast Chief Justice Earl Warren's opinion in *Brown* with Justice John Marshall Harlan's dissent in *Plessy v. Ferguson*. Although both opinions argue against the "separate but equal" doctrine, they do so in different ways. Which opinion do you believe is stronger and why?

2. Many have criticized Warren's opinion for ignoring the original intent of the Fourteenth Amendment. How important should the intentions of the framers be considered in modern constitutional interpretation?

3. In light of the continued existence of de facto school segregation in many communities, should *Brown* be judged a failure?

4. Some critics fault Warren for writing a weak decision that would take very long to implement. Other students of the case argue that if Warren had not written a cautious decision, he would have had difficulty getting a unanimous Court to agree with the decision, which would have brought about more resistance to *Brown*. Which argument do you find more persuasive?

5. Should Warren have included psychological evidence in his decision or should he have based his decision solely on legal sources?

Glossary

amici curiae	persons or organizations not party to a case who file a brief in support of a party or to inform the court with respect to a legal or policy issue
class actions	suit where representatives of a class of persons may sue on behalf of themselves and similarly situated individuals
common schools	public schools (as used in the nineteenth century)
disposition	settlement; resolution
sanction	approval

BROWN V. BOARD OF EDUCATION

Syllabus

Segregation of white and Negro children in the public schools of a State solely on the basis of race, pursuant to state laws permitting or requiring such segregation, denies to Negro children the equal protection of the laws guaranteed by the Fourteenth Amendment—even though the physical facilities and other "tangible" factors of white and Negro schools may be equal.

(a) The history of the Fourteenth Amendment is inconclusive as to its intended effect on public education.

(b) The question presented in these cases must be determined not on the basis of conditions existing when the Fourteenth Amendment was adopted, but in the light of the full development of public education and its present place in American life throughout the Nation.

(c) Where a State has undertaken to provide an opportunity for an education in its public schools, such an opportunity is a right which must be made available to all on equal terms.

(d) Segregation of children in public schools solely on the basis of race deprives children of the minority group of equal educational opportunities, even though the physical facilities and other "tangible" factors may be equal.

(e) The "separate but equal" doctrine adopted in *Plessy v. Ferguson*, 163 U.S. 537, has no place in the field of public education.

(f) The cases are restored to the docket for further argument on specified questions relating to the forms of the decrees.

Opinion

◆ Mr. Chief Justice Warren Delivered the Opinion of the Court

These cases come to us from the States of Kansas, South Carolina, Virginia, and Delaware. They are premised on different facts and different local conditions, but a common legal question justi-

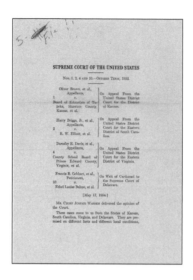

fies their consideration together in this consolidated opinion.

In each of the cases, minors of the Negro race, through their legal representatives, seek the aid of the courts in obtaining admission to the public schools of their community on a nonsegregated basis. In each instance, they had been denied admission to schools attended by white children under laws requiring or permitting segregation according to race. This segregation was alleged to deprive the plaintiffs of the equal protection of the laws under the Fourteenth Amendment. In each of the cases other than the Delaware case, a three-judge federal district court denied relief to the plaintiffs on the so-called "separate but equal" doctrine announced by this Court in *Plessy v. Ferguson*, 163 U.S. 537. Under that doctrine, equality of treatment is accorded when the races are provided substantially equal facilities, even though these facilities be separate. In the Delaware case, the Supreme Court of Delaware adhered to that doctrine, but ordered that the plaintiffs be admitted to the white schools because of their superiority to the Negro schools.

The plaintiffs contend that segregated public schools are not "equal" and cannot be made "equal," and that hence they are deprived of the equal protection of the laws. Because of the obvious importance of the question presented, the Court took jurisdiction. Argument was heard in the 1952 Term, and reargument was heard this Term on certain questions propounded by the Court.

Reargument was largely devoted to the circumstances surrounding the adoption of the Fourteenth Amendment in 1868. It covered exhaustively consideration of the Amendment in Congress, ratification by the states, then-existing practices in racial segregation, and the views of proponents and opponents of the Amendment. This discussion and our own investigation convince us that, although these sources cast some light, it is not enough to resolve the problem with which we are faced. At best, they are inconclusive. The most avid proponents of the post-War Amendments undoubtedly intended them to remove all legal distinctions among "all persons born or naturalized in the United States." Their opponents, just as certainly, were antagonistic to both the letter and the spirit of the Amendments and wished them to have the most limited effect. What others in Congress and the state legislatures had in mind cannot be determined with any degree of certainty.

An additional reason for the inconclusive nature of the Amendment's history with respect to segregated schools is the status of public education at that time. In the South, the movement toward free common schools, supported by general taxation, had not yet taken hold. Education of white children was largely in the hands of private groups. Education of Negroes was almost nonexistent, and practically all of the race were illiterate. In fact, any education of Negroes was forbidden by law in some states. Today, in contrast, many Negroes have achieved outstanding success in the arts and sciences, as well as in the business and professional world. It is true that public school education at the time of the Amendment had advanced further in the North, but the effect of the Amendment on Northern States was generally ignored in the congressional debates. Even in the North, the conditions of public education did not approximate those existing today. The curriculum was usually rudimentary; ungraded schools were common in rural areas; the school term was but three months a year in many states, and compulsory school attendance was virtually unknown. As a consequence, it is not surprising that there should be so little in the history of the Fourteenth Amendment relating to its intended effect on public education.

In the first cases in this Court construing the Fourteenth Amendment, decided shortly after its adoption, the Court interpreted it as proscribing all state-imposed discriminations against the Negro race. The doctrine of "separate but equal" did not make its appearance in this Court until 1896 in the case of *Plessy v. Ferguson*, supra, involving not education but transportation. American courts have since labored with the doctrine for over half a century. In this Court, there have been six cases involving the "separate but equal" doctrine in the field of public education. In *Cumming v. County Board of Education*, 175 U.S. 528, and *Gong Lum v. Rice*, 275 U.S. 78, the validity of the doctrine itself was not challenged. In more recent cases, all on the graduate school level, inequality was found in that specific benefits enjoyed by white students were denied to Negro students of the same

educational qualifications. *Missouri ex rel. Gaines v. Canada*, 305 U.S. 337; *Sipuel v. Oklahoma*, 332 U.S. 631; *Sweatt v. Painter*, 339 U.S. 629; *McLaurin v. Oklahoma State Regents*, 339 U.S. 637. In none of these cases was it necessary to reexamine the doctrine to grant relief to the Negro plaintiff. And in *Sweatt v. Painter*, supra, the Court expressly reserved decision on the question whether *Plessy v. Ferguson* should be held inapplicable to public education.

In the instant cases, that question is directly presented. Here, unlike *Sweatt v. Painter*, there are findings below that the Negro and white schools involved have been equalized, or are being equalized, with respect to buildings, curricula, qualifications and salaries of teachers, and other "tangible" factors. Our decision, therefore, cannot turn on merely a comparison of these tangible factors in the Negro and white schools involved in each of the cases. We must look instead to the effect of segregation itself on public education.

In approaching this problem, we cannot turn the clock back to 1868, when the Amendment was adopted, or even to 1896, when *Plessy v. Ferguson* was written. We must consider public education in the light of its full development and its present place in American life throughout the Nation. Only in this way can it be determined if segregation in public schools deprives these plaintiffs of the equal protection of the laws.

Today, education is perhaps the most important function of state and local governments. Compulsory school attendance laws and the great expenditures for education both demonstrate our recognition of the importance of education to our democratic society. It is required in the performance of our most basic public responsibilities, even service in the armed forces. It is the very foundation of good citizenship. Today it is a principal instrument in awakening the child to cultural values, in preparing him for later professional training, and in helping him to adjust normally to his environment. In these days, it is doubtful that any child may reasonably be expected to succeed in life if he is denied the opportunity of an education. Such an opportunity, where the state has undertaken to provide it, is a right which must be made available to all on equal terms.

We come then to the question presented: Does segregation of children in public schools solely on the basis of race, even though the physical facilities and other "tangible" factors may be equal, deprive the children of the minority group of equal educational opportunities? We believe that it does.

In *Sweatt v. Painter*, supra, in finding that a segregated law school for Negroes could not provide them equal educational opportunities, this Court relied in large part on "those qualities which are incapable of objective measurement but which make for greatness in a law school." In *McLaurin v. Oklahoma State Regents*, supra, the Court, in requiring that a Negro admitted to a white graduate school be treated like all other students, again resorted to intangible considerations: "… his ability to study, to engage in discussions and exchange views with other students, and, in general, to learn his profession." Such considerations apply with added force to children in grade and high schools. To separate them from others of similar age and qualifications solely because of their race generates a feeling of inferiority as to their status in the community that may affect their hearts and minds in a way unlikely ever to be undone. The effect of this separation on their educational opportunities was well stated by a finding in the Kansas case by a court which nevertheless felt compelled to rule against the Negro plaintiffs:

Segregation of white and colored children in public schools has a detrimental effect upon the colored children. The impact is greater when it has the sanction of the law, for the policy of separating the races is usually interpreted as denoting the inferiority of the negro group. A sense of inferiority affects the motivation of a child to learn. Segregation with the sanction of law, therefore, has a tendency to [retard] the educational and mental development of negro children and to deprive them of some of the benefits they would receive in a racial[ly] integrated school system.

Whatever may have been the extent of psychological knowledge at the time of *Plessy v. Ferguson*, this finding is amply supported by modern authority. Any language in *Plessy v. Ferguson* contrary to this finding is rejected.

We conclude that, in the field of public education, the doctrine of "separate but equal" has no place. Separate educational facilities are inherently unequal. Therefore, we hold that the plaintiffs and others similarly situated for whom the actions have been brought are, by reason of the segregation complained of, deprived of the equal protection of the laws guaranteed by the Fourteenth Amendment. This disposition makes unnecessary any discussion whether such segregation also violates the Due Process Clause of the Fourteenth Amendment.

Because these are class actions, because of the wide applicability of this decision, and because of the great variety of local conditions, the formulation of decrees in these cases presents problems of considerable complexity. On reargument, the consideration of appropriate relief was necessarily subordinated to the primary question—the constitutionality of segregation in public education. We have now announced that such segregation is a denial of the equal protection of the laws. In order that we may have the full assistance of the parties in formulating decrees, the cases will be restored to the docket, and the parties are requested to present further argument on Questions 4 and 5 previously propounded by the Court for the reargument this Term. The Attorney General of the United States is again invited to participate. The Attorneys General of the states requiring or permitting segregation in public education will also be permitted to appear as amici curiae upon request to do so by September 15, 1954, and submission of briefs by October 1, 1954.

It is so ordered.

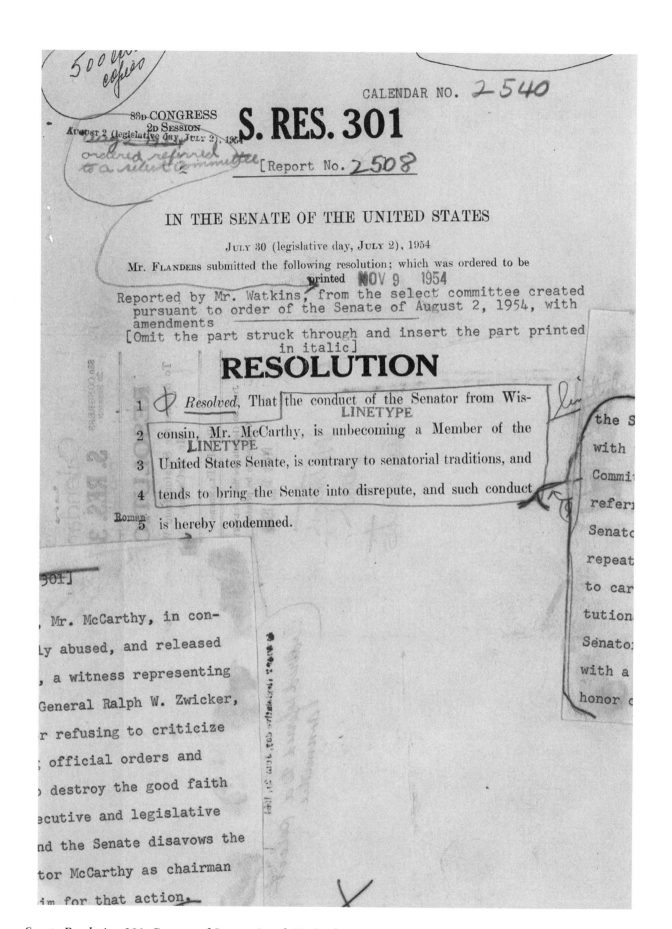

500 [...] copies

CALENDAR NO. 2540

83D CONGRESS
2D SESSION
August 2 (legislative day, July 2), 1954

ordered referred
to a select committee

S. RES. 301

[Report No. 2508]

IN THE SENATE OF THE UNITED STATES

July 30 (legislative day, July 2), 1954

Mr. FLANDERS submitted the following resolution; which was ordered to be printed NOV 9 1954

Reported by Mr. Watkins, from the select committee created pursuant to order of the Senate of August 2, 1954, with amendments

[Omit the part struck through and insert the part printed in italic]

RESOLUTION

1 *Resolved,* That the conduct of the Senator from Wis-
LINETYPE
2 consin, Mr. McCarthy, is unbecoming a Member of the
LINETYPE
3 United States Senate, is contrary to senatorial traditions, and

4 tends to bring the Senate into disrepute, and such conduct

Roman
5 is hereby condemned.

the S
with
Commi
referi
Senato
repeat
to car
tution
Senato
with a
honor

301]

, Mr. McCarthy, in con-
ly abused, and released
, a witness representing
General Ralph W. Zwicker,
r refusing to criticize
official orders and
destroy the good faith
ecutive and legislative
nd the Senate disavows the
tor McCarthy as chairman
im for that action.

Senate Resolution 301: Censure of Senator Joseph McCarthy (National Archives and Records Administration)

"This conduct of the Senator from Wisconsin ... is contrary to senatorial traditions and is hereby condemned."

Overview

On December 2, 1954, the U.S. Senate, by a 67–22 vote, censured the Wisconsin Republican senator Joseph R. McCarthy. Over the preceding four years, McCarthy had been at the center of a firestorm of anti-Communist hysteria in the United States. From his position as chairman of the U.S. Senate's Committee on Government Operations, he formed a subcommittee, the Permanent Subcommittee on Investigations. In this position, he chaired investigations into alleged Communist subversion, espionage, and infiltration of the U.S. government as well as of labor unions, the entertainment industry, and other organizations and industries. According to McCarthy, these organizations were in a position to influence U.S. policies and actions with regard to the Communist Soviet Union.

In the eyes of most observers, the public charges McCarthy leveled at suspected Communists were without foundation; at worst the charges were false, and at best they demonized people who may have sympathized with the ideology of Communism but took no action to subvert the U.S. government or incite revolution. In virtually all cases, the charges McCarthy and others leveled destroyed the careers of actors, politicians, labor leaders, academicians, authors, musicians, intellectuals, and many others, stripping them not only of their livelihoods but also of their dignity and the respect of their colleagues. Fifty years later, the term *McCarthyism*, coined in a *Washington Post* editorial cartoon by Herbert Block in 1950, continues to be used to refer to any perception of indiscriminant attacks on individuals based on unsupported allegations.

The Senate did not censure McCarthy directly on the basis of the substance of his anti-Communist activities. Rather, the censure resolution was based on McCarthy's behavior in conducting his investigations and during the controversies they aroused. In particular, the resolution censured McCarthy for "obstructing the constitutional processes of the Senate" in his failure to cooperate with the Subcommittee on Privileges and Elections of the Senate Committee on Rules and Administration. Further, the resolution censured him for acting "contrary to senatorial ethics" in responding publicly with abusive and inflammatory language to the Senate Select Committee to Study Censure Charges.

Context

Much of the history of the twentieth century was the history of two broad contending political and economic ideologies, capitalism and Communism. According to the capitalist doctrine, prevalent in the United States and in most Western nations, both individual freedom and economic development require that property and the means of production lie in private rather than government hands. Thus, in capitalist countries, individuals own businesses, equipment, and capital; workers sell their labor to employers; and wages, production levels, and the prices of goods are determined by the free market, where goods and labor are exchanged. In contrast, Communism argues that the free market system and private ownership of the means of production lead to poverty, exploitation of the laboring classes, and large and growing gaps between the rich and the poor. The Communist system, therefore, calls for the public ownership of capital and the means of production. Rather than allowing the free market to determine wages, production, and prices, centralized governmental planning does so with a view to eliminating large gaps in wealth and income. Throughout the twentieth century, capitalism came to be associated with free enterprise, liberty, firm religious faith, and social stability; Communism was associated with godlessness, civil unrest, labor agitation, and heavy-handed state intrusion into people's lives. Put simply, Communism was un-American.

Although Communist doctrine was powerfully articulated in the nineteenth century in *Das Kapital*, the seminal book written by Karl Marx and edited by Friedrich Engels, it was not until the end of World War I and the war's aftermath that the spread of Communism became a growing concern in the West. Over the next thirty years Joseph McCarthy was by no means the nation's only ardent Communist hunter. The key event was the 1917 Russian Revolution, when Communists in that nation overthrew the monarchy and established a Communist state. During the "Red scare" ("Reds" being Communists) of 1919–1920, the future director of the Federal Bureau of Investigation (FBI) J. Edgar Hoover, then working for the Department of Justice, helped round up foreign-born radicals during the Palmer raids, so called because, on June 3, 1919, bombs exploded in a number of U.S. cities, including one at the home of the U.S. Attorney General A. Mitchell Palmer.

During the 1920s, the Communist movement provoked fear by spreading to such nations as Germany in the social chaos and economic instability brought about by the war. Many Americans believed that postwar labor unrest in the United States portended a Communist threat. During the 1930s the Great Depression extended its reach throughout much of the world; economic collapse brought with it high rates of unemployment and, for many people, crushing poverty. In the eyes of many, the fault lay with the failures of capitalism, so they turned to Communism as a social and economic program that would correct those failures. Some became active members in the Communist Party; others merely sympathized with the Communist ideology.

In the West, people began to fear that the Communist revolution that had taken root in the Soviet Union would spread, possibly even to the United States. In 1938 the House Un-American Activities Committee (HUAC) was formed in response to this growing fear, and over the next decade HUAC conducted numerous public hearings that "exposed" Communists and their sympathizers—hearings similar to those for which McCarthy became notorious. In many instances, the targets of HUAC were authors and members of the entertainment industry, including such notable figures as Charlie Chaplin, Dashiell Hammett, Leonard Bernstein, Edward G. Robinson, Pete Seeger, and Orson Welles. These and others were "convicted" almost always on the basis of rumor, innuendo, and past statements expressing views that could be construed as sympathetic to Communism. Considerable attention was given to colleges and universities, where leftist and un-American viewpoints were believed to flourish. Attention also focused on the labor movement, long thought to be a breeding ground for subversion and revolutionary sentiments. In 1947, for example, one provision of the Taft-Harley Act (formally, the Labor-Management Relations Act) required union officials, if they wanted access to the services of the National Labor Relations Board, to file affidavits declaring they were not Communists.

During World War II, tensions between the capitalist nations and the Soviet Union abated, at least on the surface, as the Western Allies, in concert with the Soviets, cooperated to defeat fascism in Europe (led primarily by Adolf Hitler) and at the hands of the Japanese empire in the Pacific. But as the war drew to a close, and in the years that followed, numerous events intensified fears of Communism. The Soviets gained control of large areas of Eastern Europe that had been occupied by the Red Army during the war. In 1946 the Soviets tried to gain control of Iran and Turkey. Civil war in Greece in 1947 threatened to turn that nation toward Communism. Communists seized power in Czechoslovakia in 1948, and that year Soviet-backed East Germany blockaded Berlin, cutting off those areas of the city controlled by the victorious Western Allies. In 1949 Communists seized power in China, and that year—the most frightening event—the Soviets detonated their first atomic bomb. The year 1950 was marked by the start of the Korean War, another indication for many that Communism was on the march. During this period and for the ensuing four decades, it was U.S. policy to stop the spread of Communism, based on the belief that only the United States had the power to do so. This tension between the West and the Soviets and their allies was referred to as the cold war.

In the late 1940s and into the 1950s, Communism in general and the Soviet Union in particular were regarded as a menace, a threat to world stability. In the United States, fear grew that American Communists were working as spies and saboteurs for the Soviets, and in this way Communist sentiments were criminalized. Two cases, in particular, attracted widespread public attention. The first was that of Alger Hiss, accused by the *Time* magazine editor and former Communist Whittaker Chambers of having been a member of the Communist Party and of spying for the Soviet Union while working for the U.S. State Department. Hiss was eventually convicted of perjury (the statue of limitations on potential espionage charges having run out) and served nearly four years in prison. The other was the case of Julius and Ethel Rosenberg, American Communists who were convicted and executed for allegedly passing secrets about nuclear technology to the Soviets. Both cases remain highly controversial, especially the Rosenberg case. For the American Left, the Rosenbergs were martyrs, and their trial and execution were indicative of the irrational fear of Communism—of paranoia; for the Right, the Rosenbergs were traitors whose death by electric chair at New York's Sing Sing prison was what they deserved.

It was in this context that Senator Joseph McCarthy rose to influence. His background and upbringing did little to predict his rise to national prominence. He was raised on a farm in Appleton, Wisconsin. He worked in a grocery store, graduated from high school in one year, and attended the Marquette University School of Law. He was elected circuit judge in 1939 and, because of the office, joined the U.S. Marine Corps with automatic standing as a commissioned officer—second lieutenant. He served as a briefing officer for a gunner squadron in the Pacific during World War II, completing military service as a captain. When he returned stateside in 1946, he was elected to the U.S. Senate. In campaign literature, McCarthy portrayed himself as a hero and made claims of combat glory. His detractors ridiculed him, giving him the name "Tail Gunner Joe." He selected, on the advice of friends, an anti-Communism theme for his 1950 U.S. Senate reelection campaign and articulated it in a speech he gave in Wheeling, West Virginia, on February 9, 1950—Lincoln's birthday. Waving sheets of paper for dramatic effect, he proclaimed, "I have here in my hand a list of 205 ... a list of names that were made known to the Secretary of State as being members of the Communist Party and who nevertheless are still working and shaping policy in the State Department" (http://historymatters.gmu.edu/d/6456).

Time Line

1954

■ **September 27**
The committee releases a sixty-eight-page report of its findings; nine public hearings on the charges against Senator McCarthy are held in the Senate Caucus Room, the same location where the Army-McCarthy hearings took place.

■ **December 2**
The U.S. Senate votes 67–22 to "condemn" Senator McCarthy.

1957

■ **May 2**
McCarthy dies after his popularity dwindles in the wake of the hearings and Senate action.

The hysteria about Communist infiltration reached many average Americans. A significant portion of the public, for example, associated public health services with Communism. Fliers and newspaper ads tried to convince readers that such programs as polio vaccination, water fluoridation, and mental health services were the work of Communists. States and even communities had their own "un-American committees" where testimony led to the firing of, for example, state college faculty who were alleged to have Communist sympathies. Many Americans believed that President Franklin D. Roosevelt's New Deal during the Great Depression was a Communist plot. In January 1954, a Gallup poll showed that 50 percent of Americans approved of McCarthy's activities, while only 29 percent disapproved.

What were those activities? Principally, they consisted of public hearings that followed a pattern similar to that of HUAC's hearings. An individual was summoned to a committee hearing and placed under oath. The person was questioned about his or her Communist affiliations, past and present; the question inevitably took the form, "Are you now or have you ever been a member of the Communist Party of the United States?" Persons under investigation were required to give up the names of others they were supposed to have known were members of the party. McCarthy dubbed those who invoked their Fifth Amendment right against self-incrimation "Fifth Amendment Communists." Through the FBI, library card catalogs were inspected for books deemed to be anti-American. This investigation extended to the State Department and its overseas libraries, which actually removed offending books. McCarthy investigated supposed Communist infiltration of the Voice of America, the federal government's radio and television broadcasting service to foreign nations. McCarthy then took on the U.S. Army, alleging that a spy ring was operating out of the Signal Corps at Fort Monmouth, New Jersey.

Senator Joseph McCarthy in a 1954 photograph. (AP Photo/Bob Schutz)

McCarthy's downfall began with the so-called Army-McCarthy hearings, which publicly began on April 22, 1954, and lasted until June 17, 1954. The hearings stemmed from the army's charges that McCarthy sought preferential treatment for one of his staff members, G. David Schine, when Schine was inducted into military service. The army, in confronting McCarthy, was acting at the urging of President Dwight D. Eisenhower, who found McCarthy's tactics reprehensible and wanted him stopped. At one point during the hearings, which were watched by millions of people on television, the army's attorney, Joseph Welch, aggressively demanded that Roy Cohn, Schine's attorney, provide a list of 130 supposed subversives at U.S. defense plants. McCarthy responded to the demand by saying that if Welch was concerned about subversives, he should investigate one Fred Fisher, a member of Welch's law firm who had belonged to the National Lawyers Guild. This organization, according to the U.S. attorney general, Herbert Brownell, Jr., was a Communist front organization. McCarthy's response led to a famous exchange when Welch replied, "Until this moment, Senator, I think I never really gauged your cruelty and your recklessness." McCarthy continued speaking until Welch cut him off: "Let us assassinate this lad [Fisher] no further.... You have done enough. Have you no sense of decency, sir? At long last have you left no sense of decency? (http://www.time.com/time/magazine/article/0,9171,860782,00.html).

In response to a growing sense in Congress—and from journalists such as Edward R. Murrow—that McCarthy was out of control, Senator Ralph Flanders subsequently introduced Senate Resolution 301 on July 30, 1954. After debate, on August 2, 1954, the Select Committee to Study Censure Charges was authorized to consider the charges against McCarthy. When the committee held its first session on August 31, Senator Arthur V. Watkins expressed his objective to ensure a judicial hearing in an atmosphere befitting the issues raised. He clarified that the hearings would be consistent with activities of the Senate and that the opening statement submitted by McCarthy to the committee, including a reference to the peril spread by Communism, was not relevant to issues of the hearing. McCarthy then referred to the political nature of the charges against him.

The Select Committee retained E. Wallace Chadwick as its special counsel. Edward Bennett Williams represented McCarthy. Williams expressed a willingness to accept all documents introduced. The committee chair, however, did not want them to be ignored and wanted them discussed openly, owing to McCarthy's record for having embellished and, in some cases, glossed over some of the aspects of charges presented before his own committee. In exchange for getting strong legal representation, McCarthy promised to minimize any personal efforts to defend himself, uncharacteristically agreeing to defer to his attorney rather than attempting to represent himself.

About the Author

Senator Ralph Flanders, who wrote Senate Resolution 301, was born in Barnet, Vermont, in 1880 and died in Springfield, Vermont, in 1970. He served in the U.S. Senate from 1946 to 1959. He was an ardent critic of McCarthy.

The resolution authored by Flanders was considered by the six members of the Select Committee to Study Censure, a bipartisan committee that was named by Vice President Richard Nixon. The committee was chaired by Arthur V. Watkins, a Republican from Utah. Other members included Frank Carlson, a Republican from Kansas; Francis H. Case, a Republican from South Dakota; Edwin C. Johnson, a Democrat from Colorado; John C. Stennis, a Democrat from Mississippi; and Samuel Ervin, Jr., a Democrat from North Carolina.

Explanation and Analysis of the Document

Flanders's Resolution 301 condemning McCarthy consists of approximately 375 words. It carefully targets McCarthy's failure to cooperate with his senatorial colleagues and to respond to requests by the Subcommittee on Privileges and Elections of the Committee on Rules and Administration. It uses some of McCarthy's statements to the press as ammunition against him. The document specifies that McCarthy's conduct repeatedly abused subcommittee members by failing to respond to their requests in the conduct of their assigned duties. The first section of the document concludes that the senator be condemned as a result of having obstructed the Senate's constitutional processes, contrary to historical traditions of that body.

The second section of the document cites three instances in which McCarthy presented to the press charges of "deliberate deception" and "fraud" on the part of committee members and in which McCarthy characterized

> "*The Senator from Wisconsin, Mr. McCarthy, failed to cooperate with the Subcommittee on Privileges and Elections of the Senate Committee on Rules and Administration in clearing up matters referred to that subcommittee which concerned his conduct as a Senator and affected the honor of the Senate.*"
>
> (Section 1)

> "*This conduct of the Senator from Wisconsin, Mr. McCarthy, is contrary to senatorial traditions and is hereby condemned.*"
>
> (Section 1)

> "*The Senator from Wisconsin … acted contrary to senatorial ethics and tended to bring the Senate into dishonor and disrepute, to obstruct the constitutional processes of the Senate, and to impair its dignity; and such conduct is hereby condemned.*"
>
> (Section 2)

the special Senate session investigating him as a lynch party and a lynch bee. The charges against McCarthy had few precedents; previously, senators had behaved badly, appeared arrogant or rude in public, resorted to name calling, and leveled various discourtesies during committee hearings, particularly during wartime. For instance, Flanders himself went to the extreme of comparing McCarthy to the German dictator Adolf Hitler. The key defining aspect in the case is that the rude behavior was habitual, as opposed to some colleagues' rare, inadvertent, impassioned, or irregular outbursts.

The move to censure McCarthy eventually focused on his failure to cooperate with and to address charges made against him by the Subcommittee on Privileges and Elections of the Senate Committee on Rules and Administration, which affects the Senate's honor. This became a theme of the second set of charges—McCarthy is condemned for attacking Senate committee members, including Senator Watkins, the committee chair.

Senator Watkins and his committee eventually held nine public hearings. Watkins ruled quickly and directly on the relevance of the issues raised—in fact, in some instances he addressed matters before the hearings begin. He also adjourned the committee early on one occasion, calling McCarthy out of order at the start, when the senator attempted to dispute some assertions. Once it was clear that

McCarthy would be ruled out of order in making objections, he skipped much of the remainder of the hearings. McCarthy defiantly stood by his decisions, saying that he and his investigators had requested only evidence of illegal activity, not secret government documents. His failure to appear at the hearings did not help his cause, and the committee noted McCarthy's failure to accept its invitations to appear and to cooperate fully as a lack of fulfilling a duty to himself, his state, and the Senate. Since McCarthy had by this time denounced senators of both parties, Republicans up for reelection that fall refused to come to his defense.

The committee released a sixty-eight-page report of its findings on September 27. In paring down the many charges against McCarthy, the committee's report stresses that it was just targeting areas in which the senator's conduct could have been shown to be illegal. All committee decisions were unanimous, and the speed with which the committee handled McCarthy served as a strong antidote to news accounts that characterized the committee as inept. Before the report was issued, Majority Leader William Knowland remarked that the Senate would not be called back for a vote of censure until six days after the general election. Democrats regained control of the House and the Senate on November 2, with the Senate voting against McCarthy on December 2, 1954. The vote was to "condemn" McCarthy rather than to "censure" him.

Audience

The primary audience for both Flanders's resolution and the subsequent report of the Senate Select Committee was the fully body of the Senate itself. The members of the Senate Select Committee aimed to convince other senators that McCarthy's bad behavior had finally been addressed and dealt with directly with the report's condemnation of him. The fact that McCarthy's abuses had been challenged and studied on prior occasions to no real avail made the mandate for a brief, direct blow to his committee operations necessary. Since McCarthy had found ways to punish senators who had previously attempted to address his behavior, those empowered on this occasion were expected to finalize the verdict against him, even if members of the press were skeptical that this would take place.

Impact

For a time after his condemnation, Senator McCarthy continued to give public speeches and attract small crowds of loyal supporters, but his public support diminished. He maintained a following among members of the conservative press, but the government and liberal press made a consistent effort to ignore his statements. Some speculated that the level of exposure he received during the Army-McCarthy hearings exposed his methods and hurt his image beyond repair.

In the aftermath of Senate Resolution 301 and the Select Committee's vote to condemn McCarthy, he was still a member of the Senate. The irony was that there had been a tradition of tolerance by members of the Senate toward colleagues because of historical instances in which individuals took aberrant stands on issues. On the other hand, McCarthy had attacked elements of his own party's leadership, including colleagues and distinguished military leaders. President Eisenhower congratulated Senator Watkins, chair of the committee that condemned McCarthy for his bad behavior, and proceeded to shun McCarthy socially.

The intense public scrutiny took a toll on a person who had commanded attention for four years and built a reputation as a tough guy. In the wake of hearings and by virtue of Senate action, his popularity plunged. He drank heavily, his health deteriorated, and he died on May 2, 1957. His death was attributed to alcohol-related liver disease and hepatitis.

Related Documents

U.S. Senate Subcommittee on Privileges and Elections of the Committee on Rules and Administration. *Investigation of Senator Joseph R. McCarthy*. Washington, D.C.: Government Printing Office, 1952. The committee studying censure revisited an attempt by Senator William Benton of Connecticut to expel McCarthy by claiming that he had perjured himself when denying under oath that he spec-

ified a number of Communists working in the Department of State in his West Virginia speech. Benton studied the speech and then produced affidavits to validate the number. Benton also investigated whether McCarthy diverted funds for personal use.

U.S. Senate Subcommittee on Privileges and Elections of the Committee on Rules and Administration. *Investigations of Senators Joseph McCarthy and William Benton Pursuant to S. Res. 187 and S. Res. 304 Report of the U. S. Senate*. Washington, D.C.: Government Printing Office, 1952. After McCarthy successfully campaigned against Democratic candidates during the 1950 elections, many eastern politicians tried to avoid ruffling his feathers any further, except for Senator Benton, who was then targeted for defeat by McCarthy for his last investigation of him. Senator Benton was accused of protecting Communists and was subsequently defeated for office in the 1952 elections. The committee investigating censure reviewed what was done by McCarthy in this instance.

U.S. Senate Subcommittee on Privileges and Elections of the Committee on Rules and Administration. *Maryland Senatorial Election of 1950*. Washington, D.C.: Government Printing Office, 1951. The committee revisited this hearing (on Senate Resolution 250) to consider his censure. The hearing focused on McCarthy's methods and determination to successfully drive Maryland Senator Millard Tydings from office during the 1950 campaign.

Bibliography

■ Books

Bayley, Edwin R. *Joe McCarthy and the Press*. Madison: University of Wisconsin Press, 1981.

Buckley, William F., Jr., and L. Brent Bozell. *McCarthy and His Enemies: The Record and Its Meaning*. Chicago: Henry Regnery Company, 1954.

Griffith, Robert. *The Politics of Fear: Joseph R. McCarthy and the Senate*. Amherst: University of Massachusetts Press, 1987.

Murray, Michael D. *The Political Performers*. New York: Praeger, 1994.

Reeves, Thomas C. *The Life and Times of Joe McCarthy*. New York: Stein and Day, 1982.

Rovere, Richard H. *Senator Joe McCarthy*. New York: Harper, 1973.

■ Web Sites

"The Censure of Joe McCarthy." Time Web site.
http://www.time.com/time/magazine/article/0,9171,857533-7,00.html. Accessed on February 21, 2008.

"'Enemies from Within': Senator Joseph R. McCarthy's Accusations of Disloyalty." History Matters Web site.
http://historymatters.gmu.edu/d/6456. Accessed on February 21, 2008.

"The Gauge of Recklessness." Time Web site.
http://www.time.com/time/magazine/article/0,9171,860782,
00.html. Accessed on February 21, 2008.

"Joseph R. McCarthy Career Timeline." Wisconsin Historical
Society Web site.
http://www.wisconsinhistory.org/whi/feature/mccarthy/timeline.
asp. Accessed on February 19, 2008.

"Joseph R. McCarthy Papers, 1930—." Marquette University
Libraries Web site.
http://www.marquette.edu/library/collections/archives/Mss/
JRM/mss-JRM.html. Accessed on February 19, 2008.

"McCarthy, Joseph Raymond, (1908–1957)." Biographical Directory of the U.S. Congress Web site.
http://bioguide.congress.gov/scripts/biodisplay.pl?index=M000
315. Accessed on February 19, 2008.

"Preserving Senatorial Traditions: The Censure of Senator Joseph
R. McCarthy." National Archives "Treasures of Congress" Web site.
http://www.archives.gov/exhibits/treasures_of_congress/text/pa
ge23_text.html. Accessed on February 19, 2008.

—By Michael D. Murray and Michael J. O'Neal

Questions for Further Study

1. To what extent, if any, did McCarthy's anti-Communist focus influence foreign policy? Is it possible to gauge his effect in areas such as the U.S. State Department?

2. Which individuals and institutions were most affected by McCarthy? Among prominent government figures, who spoke out against McCarthy? What was President Dwight Eisenhower's position on McCarthy?

3. Are there any instances in which the senator's charges were verified or possibly justified?

4. The role of the American press in the initial phase of McCarthy's rise to prominence has been the focus of a great deal of speculation. Which periodical publications and which members of the press were supportive of McCarthy? Which were critical?

5. What events have occurred since the 1950s to affect the emergence of a partisan political figure such as McCarthy? What aspects of the new media, including the Internet, may serve to impede or bolster prospects for someone like McCarthy?

Glossary

censure	official disapproval or formal rebuke
lynch-party	a mob formed to administer quick, rough justice without a legal trial to someone thought to be guilty of a crime.

SENATE RESOLUTION 301: CENSURE OF SENATOR JOSEPH MCCARTHY

Resolved, That the Senator from Wisconsin, Mr. McCarthy, failed to cooperate with the Subcommittee on Privileges and Elections of the Senate Committee on Rules and Administration in clearing up matters referred to that subcommittee which concerned his conduct as a Senator and affected the honor of the Senate and, instead, repeatedly abused the subcommittee and its members who were trying to carry out assigned duties, thereby obstructing the constitutional processes of the Senate, and that this conduct of the Senator from Wisconsin, Mr. McCarthy, is contrary to senatorial traditions and is hereby condemned.

Sec 2. The Senator from Wisconsin, Mr. McCarthy, in writing to the chairman of the Select Committee to Study Censure Charges (Mr. Watkins) after the Select Committee had issued its report and before the report was presented to the Senate charging three members of the Select Committee with "deliberate deception" and "fraud" for failure to disqualify themselves; in stating to the press on November 4, 1954, that the special Senate session that was to begin November 8, 1954, was a "lynch-party"; in repeatedly describing this special Senate session as a

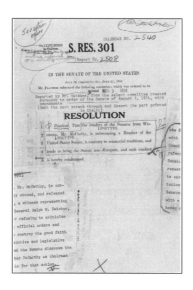

"lynch bee" in a nationwide television and radio show on November 7, 1954; in stating to the public press on November 13, 1954, that the chairman of the Select Committee (Mr. Watkins) was guilty of "the most unusual, most cowardly things I've ever heard of" and stating further: "I expected he would be afraid to answer the questions, but didn't think he'd be stupid enough to make a public statement"; and in characterizing the said committee as the "unwitting handmaiden," "involuntary agent" and "attorneys-infact" of the Communist Party and in charging that the said committee in writing its report "imitated Communist methods — that it distorted, misrepresented, and omitted in its effort to manufacture a plausible rationalization" in support of its recommendations to the Senate, which characterizations and charges were contained in a statement released to the press and inserted in the Congressional Record of November 10, 1954, acted contrary to senatorial ethics and tended to bring the Senate into dishonor and disrepute, to obstruct the constitutional processes of the Senate, and to impair its dignity; and such conduct is hereby condemned.